SECOND EDITION

BUSINESS LAW

TEXT AND CASES

SECOND EDITION

BUSINESS LAW

TEXT AND CASES

Virginia G. Maurer, J.D.
THE UNIVERSITY OF FLORIDA

WITH
Jonathan M. Purver, LL.B.
William D. Farber, J.D., LL.M.
Jimmie E. Tinsley, J.D.
Christian C. Bjorklund, J.D.

HARCOURT BRACE JOVANOVICH, PUBLISHERS
San Diego   New York   Chicago   Austin   Washington, D.C.
London   Sydney   Tokyo   Toronto

BANCROFT-WHITNEY COMPANY
San Francisco

ISBN: 0-15-505648-4
Library of Congress Catalog Card Number: 86-80821
Printed in the United States of America

Preface

The first edition of *Business Law: Text and Cases* was produced as a joint venture of two major publishing houses: Harcourt Brace Jovanovich, Inc., and Bancroft-Whitney Company (a subsidiary of Lawyers Cooperative Publishing Company). The authors, all experienced attorney-editors who are members of Bancroft-Whitney's editorial staff, are

Jonathan M. Purver
William D. Farber
Jimmie E. Tinsley
Christian C. Bjorklund

This Second Edition builds upon their excellent scholarship and craft, and I acknowledge the great debt owed them.

In the Second Edition of *Business Law* the text has been revised extensively to maintain its contemporary approach to the law. The number and variety of cases have been increased; a substantial majority of the cases were decided in the 1980s, many of them involving important recent legal issues. In addition, the Second Edition repeats and includes many classic teaching cases. The salient facts of each case are summarized for the student and presented along with a statement of the legal issue and the result of the case. The reasoning of the court is presented in the original judicial language but is edited carefully to make evident the reasoning process.

The chapter order of *Business Law* has been reorganized and the text expanded in the Second Edition. The 56 chapters are divided into 11 parts: The Legal Environment of Business; Torts and Crimes; Contracts; Sales; Commercial Paper and Money Transfers; The Debtor–Creditor Relationship; Property; Insurance; Business Organizations; Employment; and Government Regulation of Business. The individual parts are self-contained, with cross-referencing to related areas in other chapters, so that the order of coverage can be adjusted to suit the course and the instructor. The book covers the course materials normally included in the first two business law courses, and it is sufficiently rich in legal environment and regulation topics to be useful in a course designed to include legal environment and regulatory aspects of business law.

Present adopters of the book will notice several significant changes in the presentation of the chapters. Three chapters are completely new: "Business and the Federal Constitution" (Chapter 4); "Electronic Funds Transfers" (Chapter 27); and "Environmental Law" (Chapter 56). The first eight chapters reflect a unified approach to the legal environment materials and the area of nonconsensual liability. Part Five approaches commercial paper as a type of payment system to be compared with payment systems in which value is transferred electronically rather than through the use of paper. The agency materials now provide the common-law basis for understanding partnership and corporation law. Attention is drawn to accountants' professional liability in both the employment and securities contexts. Finally, the securities and antitrust materials have been revised and updated to examine contemporary issues in those fields.

A hallmark of the first edition has been retained: the preventive law note, signalled by a small gavel ⊘. These notes help the student see how a businessperson might plan for a particular legal contingency or resolve a legal problem. This approach improves the student's understanding and grasp of law as a tool to resolve conflicts, order human affairs, structure transactions, and plan for the future. In addition, the text continues to highlight clear examples and hypotheticals that illustrate difficult legal concepts.

Each chapter includes a summary of key concepts and terms as a study and review aid for the student. In addition, each chapter ends with case problems or questions. Most of the case problems are drawn from the facts of contemporary appellate cases. Others were chosen because they help identify the implications and limits of legal principles. The book also includes complete statutory appendixes, as well as a table of cases and a table of statutes.

A full set of supporting materials is available with *Business Law*. A Study Guide for students contains, for each chapter, a list of objectives, an outline review, and a self-test comprehension check with answers provided. Each chapter of the Instructor's Manual includes an outline, teaching strategies, case briefs, answers to questions and case problems, and additional case problems with answers for class discussion or tests. The Test Bank contains two sets of fifteen multiple choice questions for each text chapter plus five additional case problems per chapter, all with answers.

The following reviewers offered helpful suggestions for the Second Edition, and I am grateful to them: Dudley Buffa, Oregon State University; Duane Lambert, California State University, Hayward; and Leonard J. Rymsza, California State University, Northridge. In addition, I am grateful to friends, colleagues, and family, and especially my husband and children, for their strong encouragement and support in this endeavor.

I am pleased to offer the Second Edition of *Business Law*. I hope that it enriches students' understanding of and appreciation for the simple beauty of the law, as well as their appreciation for its fascinating complexities.

Virginia G. Maurer

About the Author

Virginia G. Maurer is an associate professor of business law and legal studies in the Graduate School of Business at the University of Florida. She received the B.A. degree from Northwestern University and the M.A. and the J.D. from Stanford University. She is a member of the Iowa bar. She has taught as an adjunct faculty member at the University of Iowa College of Law and the University of Florida College of Law. In addition, Professor Maurer has served as a staff editor of the *American Business Law Journal* and currently serves as senior staff editor on the editorial board. She is vice president of the Southeastern Business Law Association and editor of the proceedings of the annual meeting. She has published widely in law reviews and journals on antitrust, consumer protection, and civil procedure.

Contents

PART THREE
Contracts   153

PART SIX
Creditor–Debtor Relationship 545

PART SEVEN
Property 685

PART EIGHT
Insurance 867

PART NINE
Business Organizations   913

PART TEN
Employment Relationships   1069

SECOND EDITION

BUSINESS LAW

TEXT AND CASES

PART ONE

The Legal Environment of Business

Introductory Comments

Law is a dynamic process. Through law, society establishes values and goals. Supreme Court Justice Felix Frankfurter said American society is a "state" in the sense that almost everything that takes place will sooner or later raise legal questions. The purpose of American business law is to bring reason, fairness, and stability to the marketplace. In understanding business law, the businessperson becomes aware of the means to prevent disputes and, thus, to avoid lawsuits. It is essential for the businessperson to be able to anticipate the legal consequences of his or her actions. The preventive aspect of business law is the polestar that should guide the businessperson through every transaction and management decision.

Part One discusses the historical foundations of law and the sources of American law (Chapter 1). It discusses how the legal process is carried out in the American judicial system and in a lawsuit (Chapter 2). Part One also examines the law that governs administrative agencies—the so-called "invisible fourth branch of government"—which are increasingly active in regulating the marketplace (Chapter 3). Chapter 4, the last chapter in this part, examines the role of the federal Constitution in defining the legal environment of business.

Another important section in this part of the book describes the relationship between the businessperson and the attorney (section 1:7). The section discusses how a businessperson should select and use counsel and what the attorney's role and responsibilities are in the business context.

1 Nature and Sources of Law

The law embodies the story of a nation's development through many centuries, and it cannot be dealt with as if it contained only the axioms and corollaries of a book of mathematics. In order to know what it is, we must know what it has been, and what it tends to become.

Oliver Wendell Holmes, Jr., *The Common Law*

1:1 What Is Law?

Every government is the exact symbol of its people, said the historian Thomas Carlyle. So it is with law: The laws and legal system of a society reflect the values of its people. The fairness of a nation's laws and the extent to which the legal system justly administers the laws is a measure of the enlightenment, humanity, and degree of civilization of its people. What was said by the legal scholar John Dillon nearly a hundred years ago has particular meaning today: Ethical considerations can no more be excluded from the administration of justice, which is the end and purpose of all laws, than one can exclude the vital air from his room and live.[1]

Law consists of the whole body of rules applied and enforced under the authority of established government in determining what conduct is proper and should be permitted and that which should be denied or penalized. In a country such as the United States, most social questions ultimately become *legal* questions, as explained by constitutional scholar Paul Freund:

> More than a century ago Alexis de Tocqueville remarked, with characteristic perception and clairvoyance, that the major issues of American life sooner or later appear as questions for decision by the courts. In the succeeding years this observation has lost none of its validity. Across the forum of the Supreme Court there have passed, like figures in a morality play, most of the great forces whose conflict and resolution have been the themes of American history: the opening of a continent and local rivalries in transportation and trade, the expansion of commerce and business and the pressures for its control, slavery and civil war, organized industry and organized labor, social welfare legislation, taxation, public compulsory military service and internal security, church and state, a free press and public order, efficient law enforcement and the right to a fair trial.[2]

Functions of Law   Law is the means through which society is able to exist by providing protection for the citizenry; by establishing and maintaining

---

[1] J. Dillon, *Laws and Jurisprudence of England and America,* Lecture I (1894).
[2] P. Freund, "The Supreme Court," in *Talks on American Law,* 71 (1961).

order, health, and safety; by providing a peaceful means of dispute resolution; by providing stability and flexibility in economic relations between people; and by prohibiting conduct destructive to society. Rules of law reflect the society and time in which they operate. The growth of American law has been pragmatic, developing from society's need for reasonableness and flexibility in its day-to-day working.

Law as a Dynamic Process   Law is a dynamic process. It is a flow, constantly changing, continually expanding. In a sense, law is similar to language: It consists of rules and has a pattern, but the rules and pattern change as they are used over a period of time. Law is best understood by viewing the legal system as a *process*—a means of pulling together society's needs and goals and translating them into guides for fairness and reasonableness in conduct. Courts, through judicial decisions, reflect the controlling and important social, economic, and political goals and needs of the society in which they function.

Law as an Instrument of Business   Law plays a vital and stabilizing role in business transactions and relationships. Businesspersons can, for example, enter into a valid contract, knowing that the agreement is enforceable in court. Law as an instrument of business may be traced to the law merchant, a body of commercial law embracing the usage of merchants in many countries (see Chapter 19).

Each business transaction, each commercial contact, involves people. The extent to which persons can trust one another and bargain in confidence that the other will act in good faith is the measure of the success of a nation's commerce. The subject of law must never be viewed as a series of isolated technical rules, but should be seen as a system for bringing reason and fairness into the marketplace.

1:2   Common Law and Equity

The English system of law, on which the American legal system is based, developed after the Norman Conquest in the eleventh century. Upon conquering England, the Normans found themselves attempting to govern a land with no uniform nationwide system of law or means for the consistent administration of justice. Such laws as existed were based on the local customs of each township, and in many cases force was the "law." In his goal to unify the legal system of England, William the Conqueror replaced the local, and highly varied, systems of law, with a uniform—or "common"—system of law. This system was administered by royal judges sent out into the land to listen to controversies, disputes, and accusations which arose. This centralized and uniform system for the administration of justice was continued by the Norman kings. By the early thirteenth century, the Norman judicial system had replaced the various local methods of dispute resolution.

When they began the centralization of justice, the Norman kings' royal judges had no body of rules on which to rely. They drew from customs, traditions, business practices, and community standards to create the principles on which to decide cases. Over the years, as the court system grew and became more finely attuned to the needs of society, a system of judge-made rules began to develop. These rules became known as "the common law," because they were common to all the people in the land.

Common law developed at the township level, changing as it developed:

> Common law . . . makes itself up as it goes along; it sets precedents but they are never unalterable, because they are derived ultimately, not from a book of rules, but from a judge's intuitive feeling for equity and fair play—from a man rather than a machine. Code law assumes a pattern laid down once and for all; common law assumes a freely developing pattern which is nevertheless consistent with itself, like the development of a living language.[3]

The Courts of Equity The common law was not always fluid. Because of the extremely rigid, frequently overly technical procedural requirements (such as having to use particular phraseology in a request for relief) of the common-law systems, people were sometimes unable to obtain fair relief in the courts. Furthermore, the common-law judges viewed all relief in terms of money; that is, a royal judge might award money damages, but would not prevent or compel a person's action. In time, persons who felt that the form of relief was inadequate petitioned the King directly. These petitions were turned over to the King's Lord Chancellor. By the late fifteenth and early sixteenth centuries, this practice gave rise to a second court system, called the Court of Chancery. Remedies granted by the Court of Chancery were known as *equity*, from the Latin word *aequitas*, which means fairness or justice.

While a judge under the common-law system would only award money damages for violation of a legal right, an equity chancellor (as the judges of the equity court were called) could fashion a variety of remedies. An equity chancellor, when it was fair to do so, might enjoin (prevent) a person from performing certain activities, or might require a person to perform certain activities. If, for example, a person were obligated under a contract to convey property to the plaintiff, a chancellor in the equity court would order him to make the conveyance. A common-law judge, however, would not be apt to render such an order but would attempt to ascertain an amount of damages for the defendant's failure to convey the property.

Adoption of English Common-law and Equity Systems in the United States The English colonists who settled North America based their legal system on what they had previously experienced, the common-law and equity systems of Europe. Although the *United States Constitution* reflected strong anti-British sentiment and embodied a new, highly untraditional system of laws, the new nation preserved large portions of the British legal heritage.

The colonies, and later the states (with the exception of Louisiana, a former French colony, whose laws are still based on French civil law), established separate court systems to administer law and equity, as had England. Subsequent reform of American court systems in the nineteenth century resulted in

---

[3] A. Watts, *Psychotherapy East and West*, 202 (1969).

simplification of judicial procedures and elimination of equity courts as separate courts in most states. While the two court systems have been joined in most states, the terminology in law and equity cases may remain different. For example, in a "lawsuit," the "plaintiff" initiates an action by bringing a "complaint." In an equity case, the person bringing the suit is a "petitioner," who brings a "bill in equity." The law judge renders a "judgment," while the equity judge renders a "decree."

1:3 Statutory Law

While the common-law and equity systems of jurisprudence in England resulted from judge-made decisions from the period following the Norman Conquest, the primary growth of law in the United States has resulted from *statutes* enacted by state legislatures and by Congress. Under the federal Constitution and the constitutions of all 50 states, it is the function and duty of the legislative branch of government to enact the laws (statutes) under which we live.

There exists, side by side, then, in the American legal system, the common law and statutory law. Through historical development, some areas of law have resulted in less control by statutes than by judicial decisions. The law of contracts, for example, was developed extensively by the common-law judges during the growth of England's legal system. This is not to say that there is no legislation in this area. Legislatures have indeed enacted statutes covering contracts, but the legislation has been phrased broadly and it is the common-law rules which fill out the details of the statutes. Other areas of law, particularly business law, are entirely the result of statutes. For example, corporation and antitrust laws are created by legislation, not court decisions.

Uniform and Model Laws and the Restatement During the latter half of the nineteenth century, considerable variety arose among the various state laws. As commerce between states increased, it became clear that some degree of uniformity of legislation was essential, particularly in the business community. The combined effort of several states resulted in the creation of the National Conference of Commissioners on Uniform State Laws in 1891, which still exists today. The commissioners, a distinguished group of attorneys, propose statutes in various areas of law which might be adopted, in whole or in part, by the state legislatures to secure *uniformity of laws* among the states.

Another way statutes have become more uniform throughout the United States has been through model acts drafted by various committees of the American Bar Association. These model acts, like the various uniform acts, are not statutes until they have been enacted by the states. One example of a model act that has had a significant impact on business law is the Model Business Corporation Act (MBCA), first drafted in 1960. It has gone through several revisions and has been adopted in substance in more than 35 states. Major portions of the act are being followed in many other states.[4]

---

[4] The MBCA is set forth in Appendix C and is discussed in Chapters 45–47.

To promote uniformity in basic principles of law in many fields, the American Law Institute (ALI) was organized in the 1920's by several law professors, judges, and practicing attorneys. In contrast to the National Conference of Commissioners, the ALI is concerned primarily with nonstatutory rules of law. The ALI writes and publishes books containing statements of what it believes to be the proper rules of law in many areas. These books are entitled Restatements of Law, and although the *Restatements* do not constitute actual law, the courts give weight to the principles set forth in them.

How and why a uniform law governing business was created can be seen in the development of the Uniform Commercial Code (UCC).[5] Rapid change and expansion in many areas of commercial life created a demand for broad, flexible, and uniform statutory law. The National Conference of Commissioners on Uniform State Laws and the American Law Institute jointly commenced an intensive research and study program in 1945 with a view toward formulating a uniform law dealing with most aspects of commercial transactions. The outcome of the program was promulgation of the Uniform Commercial Code in 1952. As a result of further studies, refinements, and revisions, the Uniform Commercial Code ultimately was adopted in all states, except Louisiana, which adopted only certain portions.

Ordinances One type of statutory law consists of *ordinances*, which are enactments by the legislative body of a municipal corporation (city). An ordinance is a municipal law of a general and permanent nature. Examples include fire codes, parking regulations, provisions for health and food inspections, provisions for city tax revenues, and city elections. City governments arise only by the power given to them under a state constitution or statute. Therefore, the scope of a city ordinance may not exceed its constitutional or legislative limits.

Treaties A treaty, another form of statutory law, is a written contract between nations executed with the formality customary in dealings between nations, although not necessarily in a particular and prescribed form. In the United States, the power to make treaties with foreign nations is, under the Constitution, given to the President, acting with the advice and consent of the Senate. Treaties require the concurrence of two-thirds of the Senate. Trade treaties have a substantial impact on private business in the United States. The states are prohibited from entering into any treaty without the consent of Congress.

Administrative Rules Administrative rules are the rules laid down by state and federal agencies, such as the Federal Trade Commission, the Environmental Protection Agency, and the Securities and Exchange Commission. These rules are made by the agency pursuant to authority delegated from the legislature or from Congress. An administrative rule has the force of law to

---

[5] The UCC is set forth in Appendix B.

the extent that it is within the authority of the agency to make and enforce the rule. Administrative law as a distinct source of law is considered in Chapter 3.

1:4   The Constitution and the Federal System

A *constitution* is a document that establishes the basic framework of government. In addition, in our political system, the constitution divides power between the federal and the state governments and provides for the supremacy of certain individual rights over the power of government.

From the time of the American Revolution until the adoption of the United States Constitution, the main concern of the colonists was "limited government." They argued that certain inherent rights belonged to the people and could not be divested by government. Thus, the members of the Constitutional Convention resolved to form a central government with broad powers designed to preserve the rights of the individual. Rather than establish a unitary government, the framers of the Constitution formed a system under which governmental powers were divided between the central (or federal) government and other self-governing parts (the states). This system of government is known as *federalism*. The Tenth Amendment of the Constitution states that the powers not delegated to the United States (federal government) by the Constitution, nor prohibited by the Constitution to the states, are reserved to the states or to the people. The power of the federal government is thus expressly limited by the Constitution.[6]

The federal Constitution establishes the basic framework for the legal environment of business. Laws that govern business emanate from grants of law-making authority from the state and federal constitutions. Moreover, the requirements of the federal Constitution that government refrain from making laws in some areas may be equally important. Finally, the particular way the state and federal constitutions allocate power among governments and parts of government also shapes the legal environment. Thus, it is important for the businessperson to understand the major features of the federal Constitution and, to a lesser extent, the constitution of the state in which he or she does business. Chapter 4 discusses the relationship between the federal Constitution and American business.

1:5   Classifications of Law

Substantive Law and Procedural Law   At any level of law-making, there are different basic types of law. For example, the law must be divided into *substantive law* and *procedural law*. Substantive law is the body of common-law principles, statutes, constitutional directives, and administrative rules that define the rights, liabilities, and obligations of the citizenry. Procedural law is the body of law that governs how the judicial or administrative process operates. In a lawsuit for breach of a contract, for example, the substantive law would supply the rule that determined who was liable on the contract.

---

[6] The Constitution is reprinted in Appendix A.

The procedural law would supply the rule that determined what evidence could be admitted at the trial.

Criminal Law and Civil Law   Substantive law may be either *criminal law* or *civil law*. Criminal law protects society's interests in order, safety, and the integrity of social institutions by defining and prohibiting certain behavior. Criminal law is statutory. If a person violates a criminal statute, the criminal justice authorities (usually the police) may prosecute the person through a criminal lawsuit. If the person is found guilty he or she may be deprived of freedom or property or even life. The law of *criminal procedure* governs the process by which a person is apprehended and tried for a crime.

Civil law may be statutory law, common law, constitutional law, or administrative law. Civil law also protects society's interests, but it does so by defining the rights and liabilities of individuals and business entities with respect to one another. If one person injures another—by violating his or her rights—the victim may bring a civil lawsuit. If the court rules in the injured party's favor, he or she may obtain money damages. Sometimes, if the suit is brought in equity, the injured party may obtain an order from the court directing the loser to perform an act, but the usual result is a judgment for money damages. Ultimately, the judgment can be enforced by having the sheriff seize the losing party's assets and sell them to pay the judgment if the losing party does not do so voluntarily. The law that governs the conduct of the civil lawsuit is called *civil procedure*.

Public Law and Private Law   Law may also be classified as *public law* or *private law*. Public law involves the areas of law—such as criminal law, constitutional law, procedural law, and administrative law—that are aimed most distinctly at the interests of society at large. Private law involves areas of law, such as contracts, commercial law, torts, and property, that are aimed most distinctly at individuals and the protection of individual interests. Legislators and judges who make rules in these areas of law are not unmindful of the interests of the larger society in the wisdom and fairness of private law, but the particular law is applied primarily in disputes among private individuals rather than in government actions.

1:6   Preventive Law in Business

To most people, the idea of "the law" is focused primarily on courtroom battles between attorneys representing disputing parties. Courts obviously play an important role in our society and system of government. However, the function of the law should be viewed as being much more than an avenue for the resolution of disputes: *The law should serve as a means for preventing disputes and avoiding court conflicts.*

If persons are aware of the legal consequences of their actions before they act, they may plan their conduct to minimize legal disputes and conflicts. This approach is termed *preventive law*.

Preventive law has the same basis as preventive medicine or preventive dentistry. It seeks to eliminate, or at least minimize, problems before they occur. Obviously, however, a person cannot avoid a problem unless he knows that a problem exists or could exist.

Business law is studied to gain sufficient familiarity with legal principles and the operation of the law so that the legal consequences of planned actions can be anticipated. If business plans can be seen to result in undesirable consequences, they can be modified to effect a desirable result. The focus of this book is on the preventive aspects of business law. Legal principles are set forth in a context enabling the legal consequences of actions to be anticipated and informed business decisions to be made.

Throughout this book we use the symbol ✪ to highlight discussions aimed at cultivating a preventive outlook toward commercial law. Some of these discussions take a very direct approach: "Watch for this"; "Always seek legal counsel if . . . "; other discussions are historical or more reflective. The intent of these discussions, however, is to alert you to areas in which, with a little forethought, you as a businessperson can anticipate a legal problem and prevent it.

1:7   The Attorney–Business Relationship

It is impossible to overestimate the importance of the attorney to modern business. As will be seen throughout this book, the complexity of the laws which regulate, control, and indeed permeate all business and industrial endeavors indicates not only the need, but the absolute necessity, for legal advice and representation in many areas of business. Although courtroom litigation is the most visible, even spectacular, facet of the attorney's work, in business it is usually not legal counsel's most important duty. Quite the contrary. As mentioned in section 1:6, it is the primary function of business law to minimize or prevent legal problems: This is the polestar which must guide any attorney representing a business client.

 An attorney's advice should be sought whenever there is an intimation of possible legal complications. Counsel should be consulted when a businessperson receives any formal legal document, such as a subpoena (a court's demand to appear before it), governmental order or request, demand by another company or private person for a particular legal action, or notification that a lawsuit has been, or will be, filed against the businessperson personally or against the company or organization.

An increasing number of businesses (and their attorneys) have recognized the wisdom of periodic legal checkups. Just as individuals should consult a physician periodically to be certain their medical condition is satisfactory and being taken care of, a business should undergo a periodic check on its legal condition. Laws, as well as individual conditions and circumstances, change from time to time. Unless such changes and their possible legal effects are analyzed on a regular basis, unanticipated legal difficulties could arise.

The business lawyer may be an attorney in a private law firm who is retained to perform legal services on a regular basis. Or, the business attorney may be "inhouse" counsel, a full-time employee of the corporation. Some small companies have legal staffs consisting of one or two attorneys, while large corporations may have dozens of attorneys on their in-house staff.

Whether in-house or privately retained, the attorney performs a variety of functions for the businessperson. The attorney may, for example, advise and represent the client as to labor-management relations, antitrust law, patent or trademark law, or contract law. The attorney will review and prepare documents received and submitted by the business client, examine and evaluate the legal results which may flow from the client's numerous business activities, and, where necessary, represent the client in court or before governmental administrative agencies. Trial work is a complex and specific specialty of law, even for a large corporate client which has in-house counsel. It is frequently farmed out to private law firms specializing in trial litigation.

Selection of Attorney   There are half a million attorneys in the United States. Yet, selecting the right attorney for particular needs may not be an easy task. A businessperson is a consumer and should "comparison shop" to find an attorney who is technically competent and psychologically dedicated to properly represent the client. Some studies indicate, unfortunately, that many persons select an attorney randomly or on the recommendation of someone who has not actually used that attorney.

In selecting an attorney, the businessperson should determine first the type of attorney he or she would need. For example, hiring an attorney whose practice is devoted to domestic relations cases as counsel in an antitrust matter would be equivalent to retaining a physician whose practice is limited to psychiatry to remove an appendix. If questions arise as to antitrust law, an antitrust attorney should be consulted. Questions involving labor law necessitate consultation with a labor attorney. If the questions involve criminal prosecution, consultation should be with a criminal lawyer. Some attorneys specialize in real estate matters, others in corporate law, still others in consumer law. There are many legal areas of concentration.

After determining what kind of lawyer is needed, the businessperson should speak with the attorney in person to find out how much experience and knowledge he or she has in that particular area of law. Besides being competent, the attorney selected should be committed to keeping the client informed at all stages of the case.

The Fee Arrangement   The fee should be discussed with the attorney at the initial meeting. The fee may be a so-called flat fee, a specific sum for performing a particular legal job, or the fee may be charged at an hourly rate. The flat fee or hourly rate will vary with the attorney's experience and degree of competence and the geographical area from which the attorney is selected. Another type of fee arrangement, called the contingency fee, is a percentage of the money, if any, recovered on behalf of the client. Generally, attorneys who represent plaintiffs suing for damages are paid on a contingency fee basis.

Some state and local bar associations publish representative attorney fee schedules which cannot be mandated or suggested but may in some cases guide the consumer.

Attorney–Client Communication   Some attorneys have only cursory contact with their clients. This method of practicing law is not only insensitive, but is a violation of the attorney's duty to the client. Full, accurate, and frequent communication from the attorney to the client is a sign of a careful and competent attorney. It has been said that the primary cause of client dissatisfaction is the lack of communication by busy lawyers.

The businessperson should require from the attorney ongoing communication and status reports as to all work the attorney has undertaken. Furthermore, the attorney's communications should advise the businessperson of all legal rights and duties, recent legal developments affecting the client, and preventive legal measures applicable to the client's business. The attorney should explain these matters in a way which enables the client to understand the law and should not be presented in "legalese." In evaluating litigation, it is particularly important that the client understand the risks and costs involved, and the predictability of a successful outcome. The attorney should be requested to provide a brief written synopsis of the case, containing its strengths and weaknesses, and an estimate of the time, costs, and legal fees probably generated by the case.

If the client is suing another party, the attorney has the duty not only to advise the client as to progress of the case, but also as to all settlement offers made by the other party. While the client is wise to listen to the advice of a seasoned attorney as to reasonableness of any settlement offer, the final decision on making a settlement is the client's alone, not the attorney's.

Privileged Attorney–Client Communications   Under the *attorney–client privilege*, a client (including a corporate client) may be protected from having to disclose confidential communications to an attorney made in seeking legal advice. The client's communications to the attorney are said to be privileged, although the attorney's advice to the client is not always similarly protected. The purpose of attorney–client privilege is to promote a full freedom of communication between counsel and client. In a 1981 decision, the United States Supreme Court held that communications between a corporation's employees and the corporation's general counsel (in-house counsel) were protected by the attorney–client privilege, and that, accordingly, disclosure of such communications could not be compelled by the Internal Revenue Service since such communications were made by the employees to the corporate counsel acting at the direction of corporate superiors.[7]

Key Concepts and Terms

- Law consists of the body of rules applied and enforced under the authority of established government.
- Law is a dynamic process, constantly changing, continually expanding. Law reflects the values which society deems important. Law plays a vital role in modern American business by providing stability in business transactions.
- The English system of common law, on which the American legal system is based, developed over the several hundred years following the Norman

---

[7] *Upjohn Co. v United States*, 449 US 383 (1981).

Conquest in the eleventh century. The common law was the body of rules which resulted from the case-by-case decisions of the Norman kings' judges, who relied on customs and traditions rather than legislation.

- The equity court system parallels the common-law system. In a court of equity, persons who administered relief (chancellors) fashioned a far greater range of remedies than did the common-law judges. The equity and common-law systems were essentially combined in the United States during the nineteenth century.

- The primary growth of law in the United States, particularly in the business area, has resulted from statutes enacted by state legislatures and by Congress, rather than by the courts.

- To obtain greater uniformity of state business laws, many state legislatures have enacted so-called "uniform laws" in certain fields, written and proposed by the National Conference of Commissioners on Uniform State Laws. Many states have also enacted the Model Business Corporation Act, written under the auspices of the American Bar Association.

- The United States Constitution establishes a federalist system, under which governmental powers are divided between the central government and the states.

- The businessperson must learn the approach of preventive law, which is the recognition and elimination of legal problems before they require the aid of legal counsel or court action.

• Administrative Rule	• Preventive Law
• Attorney–Client Privilege	• Procedural Law
• Civil Law	• Public Law
• Common Law	• Restatement
• Criminal Law	• Statutory Law
• Equity	• Substantive Law
• Federalism	• Treaties
• Law	• Uniform Laws
• Ordinance	• United States Constitution
• Private Law	

Questions and Case Problems

1. In what ways is law an instrument of business?

2. Under what types of business circumstances would it be wise to consult an attorney? Conversely, when would it probably be unnecessary to seek legal advice?

3. In what ways is the system of justice that developed from the equity courts different from the system that developed from the common-law courts?

4. What are uniform laws, model laws, and the Restatement? Where do these "laws" come from? What is their significance to the business community?

5. In what ways does the American legal system protect the rights of individuals from arbitrary government action? In this regard, what is "due process of law" and how is it achieved under the United States Constitution?

6. What is the purpose of preventive law in business? Provide some specific examples.

2 The Judicial System

The judge is under a duty, within the limits of his power of innovation, to maintain a relation between law and morals, between the precepts of jurisprudence and those of reason and good conscience.

B. Cardozo, *The Nature of the Judicial Process*

2:1 Judicial Functions

"Laws are a dead letter without courts to expound and define their true meaning and operation," said Alexander Hamilton.[1] The function of the courts has remained essentially the same for centuries. The basic function of the courts is to decide controversies that are brought to them by different parties. To fully appreciate the role of the courts, one must understand that courts must decide cases—they cannot suspend judgment or send the parties elsewhere to resolve their dispute. They must bring rules of law to bear on specific facts. That function is called *adjudication*.

There are two phases in what courts do. First, courts determine what facts are in controversy in a given case. Next, courts identify the principles of law that govern the outcome of the controversy and apply these principles to the facts at hand. Through this process judges arrive at a result, called a *judgment*.

Trial Courts and Appellate Courts   The fact-finding process takes place at a *trial*. During the trial each party provides the fact-finder—which may be the *judge* or may be a jury—with *evidence* supporting what the party believes to be true. If there are no facts in dispute, there is no need for a trial: the judge can apply the rules of law and render a judgment. The power to apply the law to the facts is uniquely a power of the judge, not the jury. The jury, if there is one, decides from the evidence what is true; the judge applies the law. If, after a judgment is rendered, one or the other of the parties believes the judge has applied the wrong law, or has misapplied the law, he or she may *appeal* the judgment to an *appellate court*. That court decides whether the proper law was correctly applied. If the trial judge was mistaken, the appellate court usually *remands* the case, or sends the case back, to the trial court.

Judicial Review   In deciding what law applies in a fact situation, courts sometimes are called on to determine whether a particular law—a common-law principle, a statute, or an administrative rule—is, in fact, law. That is, the

---

[1] A. Hamilton, *The Federalist*, No. 22.

court may be asked to rule that a particular law is inconsistent with and inferior to "higher law." It is inevitable that courts must bring order to conflicting laws by declaring one or the other of them to be inferior and inapplicable.

Courts are sometimes called on to determine whether a statute is constitutionally valid. This is usually referred to as *judicial review* of legislation. The federal Constitution, in Article III, § 2, gives the United States Supreme Court the power to decide all cases and controversies that come from a lower court for final review. The Constitution does not expressly give the Supreme Court power to determine the constitutionality of acts of Congress or state statutes. The Supreme Court has gained these powers through its own decisions. For example, in the famous case *Marbury v Madison,*[2] the Supreme Court held that it has the power to review acts of Congress and declare them void if they are inconsistent with the Constitution. Subsequently, the Supreme Court established its power to review and invalidate state legislation that the Court finds contrary to the Constitution or some treaty or act of Congress.

2:2   The Judicial Structure

The American judicial system consists of two parts: the court system of the federal government and that of each of the 50 states. Figure 2-1 shows the structure and relationship of the American judicial system.

Federal Court System   Article III, § 1, of the United States Constitution states that the judicial power of the United States shall be vested in one Supreme Court and in those inferior courts (inferior to the Supreme Court) that Congress may establish. Congress, in the Judiciary Act of 1789, used this constitutional power to establish the federal judicial system. This system consists of several levels of federal courts. The United States District Courts are the federal trial courts. Every state has at least one United States District Court.

Federal cases tried and lost in the district courts may be appealed to the next level in the federal judicial system, which is the United States Court of Appeals. There are twelve, one for each of the federal circuits, which are judicial districts located throughout the United States. The United States Court of Appeals for a particular federal circuit hears appeals from United States District Courts located in states within that circuit. For example, the United States Court of Appeals for the Ninth Circuit (located in San Francisco) hears appeals from United States District Courts within Guam and the states of Hawaii, Alaska, Idaho, Montana, Nevada, Arizona, Oregon, California, and Washington, because these states are within the Ninth United States Circuit.

The highest level of the federal judicial system is the United States Supreme Court. The Supreme Court's primary function is to review decisions of the lower federal courts or, where federal questions are involved, of state courts. The Supreme Court also conducts trials in a few types of cases, including those

---

[2] 5 US (1 Cranch) 137 (1803).

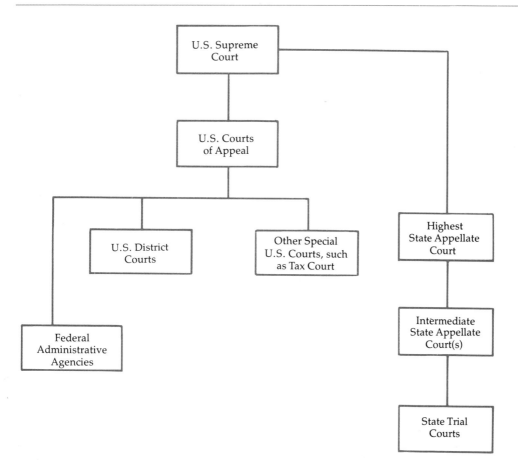

FIGURE 2-1
Diagram of basic appellate structure in federal and state court systems.

affecting ambassadors, consuls and other public ministers, and cases in which a state is a party. Finally, the United States Supreme Court may hear appeals from state courts, usually the state supreme court, if a matter of federal law is in issue. For the most part, the Supreme Court itself decides which cases it will hear. In one year it will hear not more than a few hundred of the thousands of requests for appeal that are made to it.

In addition to the federal courts just discussed, certain courts have been created by Congress to augment its legislative powers. These courts include the Court of Customs and Patent Appeals, the Court of Claims, the Tax Court, and the Court of Military Appeals. These courts have specific functions in dealing with only particular types of cases.

State Court Systems   State courts are generally independent from the federal courts, although in certain cases the United States Supreme Court has the power to review a decision rendered by the highest court of a state. A federal court will not ordinarily interfere with the administration of state law by a state court unless fundamental rights guaranteed by the federal Constitution are invaded or unless the enforcement of state law appears to violate the Constitution, federal laws, or treaties.

Although it may vary from state to state, most state court systems have three levels. On the first level—what might be termed the "battlefield" of the legal process—are the trial courts, in which the litigation actually takes place through presentation of evidence to a judge or jury (see section 2:3). Trial courts are known by different names in different states. They may be called "superior court," "court of common pleas," or "county court."[3]

In addition to trial courts that have power to try most types of criminal or civil cases, most states have specialized courts, frequently called courts of limited jurisdiction. These courts have been given power by the state legislature to hear only particular types of cases. Examples of limited jurisdiction courts are traffic courts (which hear minor traffic violations), domestic relations courts (which hear matrimonial or family disputes), and probate courts (which hear matters pertaining to distribution of estates). Most litigation involving business law occurs in state general trial courts, because a business lawsuit usually does not involve the specialized subject matter of courts of limited jurisdiction.

At the next state court level are the *appellate courts*. The appellate courts review the written trial records, known as transcripts, and make sure that the trial was fair, that procedural safeguards were duly followed, and that proper legal principles were applied by the trial judge. In some states, there are two levels of appellate court: the intermediate appellate court at the first level of appellate review and the state supreme court at the second level. In other states, there are no intermediate appellate courts, but only a state supreme court which serves as the sole appellate judicial body.

Small Claims Courts   Another type of court system found in nearly all states is the small claims court or small debtors' court. The small claims court is usually a separate division of the general trial courts. If a lawsuit involves less than a particular amount of money, typically a few hundred dollars, the person bringing the suit may have the alternative of bringing the action in a small claims court rather than in the general trial court. Depending on the state, the persons involved in the suit may not be allowed to have an attorney, and may not appeal to a higher court.

Small claims litigation is a growing trend and provides a faster and less costly resolution for disputes involving small sums of money. Many procedural technicalities that may encumber an ordinary proceeding are dispensed with in a small claims proceeding.

2:3   Nature of a Lawsuit

A *lawsuit* is an adversary proceeding in which both the person bringing the action and the person defending it each seek to persuade the trier of fact—the jury, if there is one, or the judge—that under the facts of the case, the law

---

[3] It should be noted that in New York the trial court is called the "supreme court" and the highest court of appeals is called the "court of appeals."

entitles him to win. In a civil case, which involves a dispute between private parties, the person bringing the action is called the plaintiff, and the person defending the action is called the defendant. In a criminal case a person is charged with having committed an offense against society (see Chapter 7). That person is called the defendant, as in a civil case, but the "plaintiff" is a representative of the public, called the prosecuting attorney. The basic stages of a lawsuit are set forth below. Although the term "plaintiff" is used, these stages are very similar in a criminal case.

Pleadings and Service of Process   A lawsuit is initiated when counsel (the attorney) files a *complaint* for the plaintiff. The complaint states the *cause of action*, which means the grounds for the lawsuit. The defendant is then notified that a lawsuit has been filed against him. He is given a court-issued *summons* and a copy of the plaintiff's complaint. This procedure is called *service of process* and must occur within a specific period of time after the lawsuit is filed. Typically, process may be served by any person who is at least 18 years old and is not a party to the lawsuit. A marshal or sheriff or any private person may serve the process.

The defendant must file an *answer* or make some other appropriate response within a certain number of days, usually 30, from the date on which he is served the complaint. His failure to answer within this time may result in a *default judgment* against him.

 It is essential that any person, or company, served with notice of a lawsuit immediately determine how many days he has to answer the complaint, and then answer the complaint in time so a default is not taken against him.

In the answer, the defendant may make a *general denial* in which he simply denies the facts stated in the complaint, or he may set forth an *affirmative defense*, which means that he alleges that although what the plaintiff's complaint says is true, there is a defense that will relieve the defendant of legal liability. After the answer is filed, the plaintiff may then file a *reply*, which is a response to the defendant's answer.

Rather than filing an answer, the defendant may file a *demurrer*, which is a formal pleading which, in effect, says "So what?" The defendant argues that even if everything the plaintiff says in the complaint is true, there is no legally recognizable cause of action. The defendant may also file a *cross-complaint*, in which the defendant brings an action against the plaintiff. When a cross-complaint has been filed, both plaintiff and defendant are in fact suing one another simultaneously.

The complaint, answer, reply, demurrer, and cross-complaint are called *pleadings.* After the pleadings are filed, the pleading stage is concluded and it is said that the "issue is joined."

Discovery   After the pleading stage comes the *discovery* stage. Discovery provides each party to a lawsuit with the opportunity to acquire information about the other party's case prior to trial. The theory is that trial may sometimes be avoided when all of the facts are laid out beforehand and that the parties may be more prone to settle the case without costly courtroom litigation. As stated by the United States Supreme Court, discovery rules make a trial less a game of blind man's bluff "and more a fair contest with the basic issues and facts disclosed to the fullest practicable extent."[4]

The primary discovery tools are *depositions*, which are statements taken by an official court reporter on one party's oral examination of the other under oath; *interrogatories*, which are written questions asked by one party of the other party which must be answered under oath; *requests to a party to produce documents*; and *requests to a party for physical or mental examinations*. For example, a person who has been sued for breach of contract may file a motion for discovery to require the plaintiff to submit a copy of the contract allegedly breached.

Pretrial Conference   Closely related to discovery procedures is the *pretrial conference*. In a pretrial conference the judge meets with the attorneys for both sides to encourage *settlement* of the case. If settlement cannot be achieved, then the pretrial conference will at least set the boundaries for the trial and attempt to remove elements of surprise from the trial. The trial judge wants to prevent the trial from becoming a spectacle or a verbal sparring contest between attorneys.

Settlement Negotiation   After extensive discovery procedures, both attorneys know fairly well what evidence will be produced in court. An experienced attorney may even be able to predict what a jury is apt to award in a particular type of case. Thus, counsel frequently will negotiate a settlement prior to trial. Even cases that do proceed to trial are sometimes settled during the actual trial, when both counsel have an even better grasp on what the evidence is revealing.

Trial   If a settlement is not reached, the case will go to trial. While the most common situation is a trial before a judge and jury, sometimes the trial judge acts as both judge and jury.

Before a *jury trial* actually begins, prospective jurors are questioned by counsel (and the judge) about their background and attitudes. This is called *voir dire examination*. If any prospective juror is thought to be prejudiced about the parties in the case or the particular type of case or in any other way seems nonqualified, he or she may be dismissed. After the jurors are selected, they are placed under oath to follow the law as instructed by the judge and not to consider any factors in their determination other than the evidence duly presented at trial.

After the jury is sworn, plaintiff's counsel makes an *opening statement*. The opening statement is a statement of what counsel intends to prove to the jury during trial. Then, defense counsel makes an opening statement. Following the opening statements, plaintiff's counsel presents his client's case to the jury. The case is presented through the introduction of *evidence*. Evidence may take the form of witnesses' *testimony*, documents, and physical items. All evidence

---

[4] *United States v Procter & Gamble Co.*, 356 US 677 (1958).

must be reliable and relevant to the case to be legally admissible. After plaintiff's counsel examines a witness to establish a fact (*direct examination*), defendant's counsel may then *cross-examine* the witness to bring out additional facts or to test the reliability and honesty of the witness. After presentation of plaintiff's case, defense counsel presents the defendant's case.

After each party has presented its case, both counsel, in turn, may make *closing arguments* to the jury. At this point, either party may make a *motion for a directed verdict.* This motion is a request that the judge direct the jury to render a particular verdict. The judge then instructs the jury on the particular laws that can be applied in the case. It is the jury's role to determine the facts from the evidence, and then to apply the laws to those facts. On the basis of its findings, the jury renders a verdict. In a civil case, the jury will find for the plaintiff if there is "a preponderance of evidence," which means that there is more evidence in his favor than against him. In a criminal case, a preponderance of the evidence is not enough. The jury must be convinced of the defendant's guilt "beyond a reasonable doubt."

After presentation of the evidence and a jury verdict, the losing party may make a motion for what is called *judgment notwithstanding the verdict.* In this motion, the losing party argues that he is entitled to judgment under the law even though the verdict was rendered against him by the jury. The motion will be granted only if the trial judge determines that, under the law, the jury's verdict was improper.

Appeal   Sometimes a losing party may appeal the case to a higher court, which means that the party requests the appellate court to review the case. For example, if the trial record indicates that the judge erred in admitting certain evidence that should not have been admitted, or refused to admit evidence that should have been permitted, or gave improper jury instructions, or acted prejudicially to one of the parties, the party harmed may appeal.

When an appellate court accepts a case, a certified record of the trial, which consists of a court reporter's and a clerk's transcript, is sent to the appellate court. The attorneys for both parties then file written briefs with the appellate court, arguing why the case should, or should not, be reversed, and setting forth citations to legal decisions or statutes supporting their positions. Sometimes, an appellate court will permit the attorneys to argue orally and answer questions from the court about their briefs.

The appellate court will only review the record of the lower court; it will not take testimony from witnesses. After analyzing the transcripts of the case, studying the attorneys' written *briefs,* and listening to any *oral arguments,* the appellate court will issue a written opinion that reverses, modifies, or affirms the trial court's judgment. These written opinions may then be published.

2:4   Anatomy of a Judicial Decision

Some published judicial decisions, or portions of them, will be used throughout this book to illustrate principles of law or to show how courts deal with particular types of business cases. The decisions create the "case law" that establishes *precedent* for future cases (see section 2:5).

Usually, the highest court in a jurisdiction will have its opinions published. Decisions of the intermediate appellate courts may or may not be published, depending on the rules of the jurisdiction. Many jurisdictions will publish only those intermediate court opinions that establish a new rule of law, alter or modify an existing rule, or involve legal issues of continuing public interest.

The basic parts of a decision are identified in the following example of a brief but typical decision.

HEADING

Sharon Schwindt

v

Earl Tonglet and Ralph Delrio
d/b/a A-1 Disposal Service *et al.*
389 So2d 883 (1980)
Court of Appeals of Louisiana, Fourth Circuit

Before Redmann, Schott, and Garrison, JJ.
Garrison, Judge.

FACTS

This is an appeal from a judgment of the district court, granting to plaintiff damages in the amount of $3,500.00, plus $332.00 for medicals, and expert fees. The damages awarded were for an injury sustained by plaintiff on November 29, 1976, when the vehicle which she was driving was struck by a dumpster driven by the defendant's employee. The trial court apparently agreed with the plaintiff's evidence which tended to show that the defendant's truck, while in the process of backing up, collided with the driver's side door of plaintiff's stopped vehicle. From that decision, which we now affirm, the defendants appeal.

Defendant–appellant argues on appeal that the trial court erred in finding the defendant negligent, in failing to find the plaintiff negligent or contributorily negligent and abused its discretion by awarding $3,500.00 for personal injury. We disagree.

OPINION

Our independent review of the evidence and testimony presented convinces this court that the trial judge was not manifestly erroneous. This case involves *primarily* a credibility call on the part of the trial judge. Under the rule of *Canter v Koehring*, 283 So.2d 716 (1973) and *Arcenaux v Domingue*, 365 So.2d 1330 (1978), the trial judge's findings of fact will not be disturbed.

Plaintiff–appellee argues on appeal that the damages awarded should be increased. We disagree. Dr. Padua testified that the plaintiff suffered muscle spasms for which she received muscle relaxants, pain medication, and physical therapy. He further testified that she was asymptomatic as of January 11, 1977. Our review of the record coupled with a review of the scale and range of the case law on damages, as applied to this particular plaintiff in this particular case, convinces this court that the trial judge did not abuse his discretion in the damages awarded. *Reck v Stevens*, 373 So.2d 498 (1979).

JUDGMENT   For the reasons discussed, the judgment of the trial court is affirmed.

The *Schwindt* case heading sets forth the name of the parties, name of the court, page and volume number of the book in which the case is published, and date of the decision. In this case, Sharon Schwindt is suing, among others, Earl Tonglet and Ralph Delrio, who are doing business as the A-1 Disposal Service. The court is the Court of Appeals of Louisiana, which is an intermediate appellate court in Louisiana. The case has been appealed to this appellate court from a Louisiana trial court. If the case is further appealed, the appeal would be to the state court at the next highest level, the Louisiana State Supreme Court.

The names of the three judges who rendered the decision appear next. Usually, an intermediate appellate court is composed of three judges. In some states they are called justices. The court then sets forth the facts of the case and the reasons why the party who lost in the trial court appealed the decision. This statement may be very lengthy or very short, depending on the complexity of the case.

Technically, the entire judicial decision is the opinion. However, for purposes of dissecting a decision, the opinion is the portion of the decision in which the court states the rules of law and how it applied the rules to the facts of the case to reach its decision. Length of decisions ranges from one or two paragraphs to as many as several hundred pages. Obviously, very few decisions are as straightforward as the one presented in the example above. Decisions typically involve several legal questions and require a detailed discussion of the facts and law.

The judgment, the court's actual decision, is at the end. In the *Schwindt* case, the court affirms the trial court's judgment, which awarded to Sharon Schwindt a certain sum of money for damages caused by Earl Tonglet and Ralph Delrio's negligence. Had the appellate court agreed with the defendants' arguments, it could have reversed the trial judge's judgment. The appellate court might also have remanded the case, which means that the case would have been returned to the trial court with directions for the trial judge, for example, to retry the case or retry the case in compliance with particular procedures directed by the appellate court.

The cases in this book usually are abbreviated. The authors have summarized the facts and the main issues and the results of the case. Parts of the judge's opinion are reproduced to demonstrate how the judge reasoned to a conclusion. The author of the opinion is named at the end.

Case Citation   The reference to a published judicial decision is called its "citation" or "cite." The citation usually contains the name of the case, the volume and page number in the official (government-issued) case report, the volume and page number in unofficial, regional reports (published by a private publishing company), and the year in which the case was decided.

EXAMPLE (State case):   *Combined Investment Co. v Board of County Commissioners*, 227 Kan 17, 605 P2d 533 (1980). The names at the beginning identify the parties in the lawsuit; the case is published at page 17 of volume 227 of the official Kansas decisions (in this case, the Supreme Court of Kansas). The same case is also located at page 533 of volume 605 of the Pacific Reporter (2d series), published by a private publishing company. The case was decided in 1980.

EXAMPLE (Federal case):   *Sheeran v General Electric Co.*, 593 F2d 93 (United States Court of Appeals, Ninth Circuit, 1979). The names are those of the parties to the suit. The case may be found at page 93 of volume 593 of the Federal Reporter (2d series). The abbreviation "CA9" means that the case was decided by the United States Court of Appeals for the Ninth Circuit. The case was decided in 1979.

2:5   Important Judicial Concepts

To understand how courts operate, it is necessary to be aware of the basic judicial concepts that are set forth below.

Jurisdiction   Jurisdiction is the power of a court to hear a case and render a decision that is enforceable against the parties by that court and by other courts. To hear a case, a court must have two types of jurisdiction. First, it must have the power to render a decision as to the parties to the case, which is called *personal jurisdiction*. In addition, the court must have the power to render a decision in that particular type of case. This type of jurisdiction is called *subject matter jurisdiction*. Moreover, the party must have some "sufficient contact" with the state for the court to be able to determine the party's legal interests. Due process of law, as guaranteed by the Fourteenth Amendment to the federal Constitution, requires that these basic conditions be met before a court has jurisdiction. A court judgment handed down without jurisdiction may be attacked and set aside as violating the due process clause.

Personal Jurisdiction   Personal jurisdiction can be obtained in several ways. A court has personal jurisdiction over a plaintiff, because in bringing the lawsuit the plaintiff voluntarily submits to the court's power. Obtaining personal jurisdiction over a defendant is more complex. If service of process can be completed against the defendant while he or she is physically present in the geographical boundaries of the state, the court may have personal jurisdiction. Or, if the defendant is a resident of the state or employed in the state, or consents to be sued in the state (for example, in a contract), the court may assert jurisdiction. Finally, a state may have "long-arm legislation" that gives the court jurisdiction.

Long-Arm Legislation   A long-arm statute is a state statute that permits a court to acquire jurisdiction over a nonresident without service of process within the state, so long as there are "minimum contacts" between the defendant and the state. The theory is that jurisdiction is acquired if the defendant—whether an individual or a corporation—has enough of a connection with the state that traditional notions of fair play and justice are not jeopardized by the state's jurisdiction over the case. Examples of this kind of contact include doing business within the state when the cause of action arose; forming, within the state, a contract out of which the cause of action arose; and owning, within the state, property that caused injury to the plaintiff. The "minimum contacts" test will vary with the nature of the defendant's activity in the state to which the court belongs.

EXAMPLE: The Acme Trucking Corporation is incorporated and has its home office in New York. Acme Trucking performs a substantial amount of business nationwide, and its trucks travel in California several times a year. During one of its travels in California, an Acme truck collides with a car driven by Paul. Paul sues the Acme Trucking Corporation for negligence. Under the state long-arm statute, the California courts have jurisdiction over the foreign (out-of-state) corporation on at least two tests: (1) It has engaged in a course of conduct or business within the state of California and (2) it has arguably committed a tort (civil wrong) within California. Under either test, Acme has a minimum contact with California that justifies its courts having jurisdiction over Acme. Clearly, this jurisdiction does not offend traditional notions of justice and fair play.

Subject Matter Jurisdiction   In general, state courts have subject matter jurisdiction over any type of lawsuit except for those cases that are within the *exclusive jurisdiction* of the federal courts. That is, most cases can be brought to the state district court, the state *court of general jurisdiction*. Within the state trial court there may be sub-courts, such as family court or small claims court, that hear certain types of cases within the general jurisdiction of the trial court, and the case may be assigned to one of those courts. Note also that appellate courts of the state have only *appellate jurisdiction*; with very few exceptions, they do not have the power to hear cases in the first instance.

The federal courts have *limited* subject matter *jurisdiction*. The federal courts can hear only those types of cases which Congress or the federal Constitution has assigned to the federal courts. Most of these fall into one of three categories. First, the federal courts can hear cases involving federal law, including the Constitution, federal statutes, administrative rules, treaties, and contracts. This is called the *federal question jurisdiction* of the federal courts. Note, however, that, except for cases within the exclusive jurisdiction of the federal courts, federal questions can also be heard by state courts. Such cases are said to fall within the *concurrent jurisdiction* of the state and federal courts. Second, the federal courts can hear cases where the United States is a party to the lawsuit.

Finally, the federal courts can hear cases that involve parties from different states on opposite sides of a lawsuit. This is called the *diversity jurisdiction* of the federal courts. The theory behind diversity jurisdiction is that the federal courts should be available as a neutral forum for cases in which the out-of-state party may feel disadvantaged in state court. There must be at least $10,000 in damages at stake in a diversity case before the federal courts can take jurisdiction.

Standing to Sue   Courts are established to provide relief to persons whose rights have been invaded or are threatened with invasion. These persons have an interest on which to base a lawsuit. This capacity to bring a legal action is called *standing to sue.* A person must have standing to sue in order to maintain a lawsuit. A court will refuse to hear an action at the request of a person whose rights have not been invaded or infringed, such as a person who seeks a remedy on behalf of someone who is not personally seeking redress for grievances.

EXAMPLE: Kramer has breached a contract with Fowler. Kevin, a friend of Fowler, has nothing to do with the contract but wants to protect Fowler's legal rights. Kevin therefore attempts to bring a lawsuit against Kramer for breaching the Kramer–Fowler contract. A court will not permit Kevin to bring such a lawsuit because no legal interests of his have been violated. Fowler may or may not decide to sue Kramer, but that is Fowler's right, not Kevin's. Kevin has no standing to sue.

Class Action   A *class action* is a lawsuit filed by several persons on behalf of so many other persons that their voluntarily and unanimously joining in a suit is impracticable. Under federal law and most state law, one or more members of a class may sue or be sued as representatives of the class if (1) the class is so numerous that joinder of all members is impracticable, (2) there are questions of law or fact common to the class, (3) the claims or defenses of the representative parties are typical of those of the entire class, and (4) the representative parties will fairly and adequately protect the interests of the class. When the suit is filed, a notice that will reach all members of the class must be given.

One example of a class action is a suit by individuals against a city to prevent or limit a particular city appropriation of funds; if each person in the city who contested the distribution of funds brought a separate action, there would be a risk of inconsistent or varying judicial decisions. Defective products frequently are the subject of class actions, because it would be virtually impossible for all injured persons to bring individual lawsuits. For example, a few consumers injured by a defectively designed television set may file a class action on behalf of several thousand people across the country who are injured by the same defect in the same product.

Justiciable Controversy   Courts have the power and duty to hear only an actual controversy; that is, the parties must have actual adverse interests and conflicting claims. Such a controversy is said to be justiciable (capable of being decided by a judicial body). Courts will not hear "friendly" suits, which are suits that have been arranged collusively by persons wanting a judicial decision on a question but not having actual adverse interests.

EXAMPLE: The Clarion Corporation and the Blackmoor Construction Company want a judicial determination as to the precise location of the boundary between their two buildings. Therefore, both companies arrange for Clarion to bring a lawsuit against Blackmoor. If a court learns that this suit is collusive and fabricated, it would refuse to accept the case for decision.

Declaratory Judgments   A declaratory *judgment* is a judicial decision that is made to settle a dispute before there is an actual injury or a violation of legal rights. For example, a court may be asked to determine a question about the interpretation of a contract to prevent circumstances that would lead to a lawsuit. A declaratory judgment has the full effect of any final court judgment.

Res Judicata   The doctrine of *res judicata* is that a final court judgment is conclusive of all issues decided in that case. This judicially created doctrine exists out of fairness as well as practical necessity. It is based on the public policy that a controversy once litigated and decided on its merits should thereafter be "completely decided for all time," that subsequent judicial decisions should not be made on the same set of facts, and that judgments should have stability. If this doctrine did not exist, all litigation could be literally endless.

EXAMPLE: Fieldman Corporation successfully sues Willow Enterprises for breach of a particular contract. Subsequently, Willow Enterprises wants to sue Fieldman Corporation, alleging that the same act that was involved in the first suit was a breach by Fieldman. The court will not permit this lawsuit under the doctrine of res judicata. All questions relating to this particular contract's alleged breach were decided in the prior lawsuit. The doctrine is applicable because the subsequent attempted suit involved the same parties and essentially the same factual setting and was based on the same question.

Stare Decisis   *Stare decisis,* which in Latin means "let the decision stand," is the doctrine that judicial decisions should stand as precedents or guidance for similar future cases. Stemming from the development of the common law by court decisions, this doctrine reflects a strong judicial policy that the determination of legal questions—"points of law"—by a court will generally be followed by future courts, even though different parties are involved in the subsequent cases. This doctrine is intended to promote certainty, stability, and predictability of the law.

A *precedent* is a prior judicial decision that has factual patterns and legal principles similar to those in the case at hand. An attorney may research prior cases and locate precedents for her case. She may present these precedents to the court and argue that they are "controlling precedent" or "on point" for resolving her own case. Since precedents rarely control a given situation completely, it is usually necessary for the attorney to analyze in detail the facts of the cited cases, compare the facts to her own case, and argue that the prior cases are so similar to hers that they should control the outcome of her case.

Deviating from Precedent   Courts are not always bound to follow precedent. They may decide to "create new law" by reaching a decision which they believe will best fit the needs of the parties, or, on a larger scale, the public. In deciding to depart from the doctrine of stare decisis, and not to follow precedent in a particular case, courts may be influenced by the fact that following the rule might result in an injustice in the particular case or that a particular precedent is inconsistent with modern trends in law or is no longer valid public policy.[5]

An illustration of a court's refusal to follow precedent is the 1954 United States Supreme Court decision in *Brown v Board of Education*.[6] The Court in that decision decided that in the field of public education, the doctrine of "separate but equal" has no place; that separate educational facilities are inherently unequal; and that segregation was therefore a violation of the equal protection guaranteed by the Fourteenth Amendment of the Constitution. The court expressly reversed its 1896 decision of *Plessy v Ferguson*, which had held that school segregation did not violate the Constitution. In refusing to follow the *Plessy* decision as precedent, the Supreme Court, by the *Brown* decision, was creating "new precedent":

> In approaching this problem [school segregation], we cannot turn the clock back to 1868 when the [Fourteenth] Amendment was adopted, or even to 1896 when *Plessy v Ferguson* was written. We must consider public education in the light of its full development and its present place in American life throughout the nation. Only in this way can it be determined if segregation in public schools deprives these plaintiffs of the equal protection of the laws.

After examining evidence that racial segregation in public schools has a detrimental effect and fosters a sense of inferiority affecting the child's motivation to learn, the Court explained, "Whatever may have been the extent of

---

[5] In discussing judicial change in precedent, Justice Cardozo explained: "Little by little the old doctrine is undermined. Often the encroachments are so gradual that their significance is at first obscured. Finally we discover that the contour of the landscape has been changed, that the old maps must be cast aside, and the ground charted anew." B. Cardozo, *The Nature of the Judicial Process*, 178 (1921).
[6] 347 US 483 (1954).

psychological knowledge at the time of *Plessy v Ferguson,* this finding [the detrimental effect] is amply supported by modern authority."

2:6   Arbitration: The Growing Trend[7]

Arbitration is a process of dispute resolution between two parties through the efforts of an arbitrator, a person chosen to hear the case and settle the differences. Sometimes the parties agree on a particular arbitrator privately. In other situations, the arbitrator is appointed by the trial court. This is called judicial arbitration. The arbitrator's decision is enforceable under court order. As an alternative to court litigation, arbitration accomplishes much that the formal lawsuit does not, particularly in the commercial field.

In some states, either party may have the arbitrator's award set aside and may obtain a court trial. However, a party who loses at arbitration may not want to set aside the arbitrator's award since the arbitration is sometimes viewed as a "test run" for trial and the loser may have no reason to feel that a judge or jury would make a different award. Moreover, if the loser went into court and lost, he would have to pay attorney's fees and court costs.

Arbitration does have advantages over traditional courtroom litigation. One advantage is the amount of time arbitration takes as compared to litigation. In large cities like New York and Los Angeles, a five-year delay in getting a case to trial is not unusual. Arbitration, on the other hand, may be concluded in a few months or even weeks.

Another advantage of arbitration is that it is a private proceeding. As a general matter, neither the government nor the public is alerted to the evidence presented in the arbitration. This factor may be important to businesspersons who do not want public access to information about particular trade practices or credit standings. A third advantage is that arbitration is less costly than litigation. It is not always essential to retain an attorney for arbitration, since the rules of procedure are simpler than those in court proceedings.

 When negotiating a contract, it is sometimes to the advantage of both parties to include a provision that any disputes will be submitted to an arbitrator rather than to the courts. Even the name of the arbitrator may be set forth in the contract. Therefore, if there is dispute under the contract later, this provision may contribute to a quicker and less expensive resolution than can be obtained from a lawsuit.

Key Concepts and Terms

- Courts determine legal controversies between opposing parties in a lawsuit, create or change rules of law (in the absence of statutory law), and review legislation.
- The American judicial system consists of the courts of the federal government and the court systems of each of the 50 states. The federal judiciary is

---

[7] Labor arbitration is discussed in Chapter 51.

comprised of the United States District Courts, the 12 United States Courts of Appeals, and the United States Supreme Court.

- Court systems are comprised of trial courts and appellate courts.
- A lawsuit is an adversary proceeding in which the person bringing the action—the plaintiff—and the person defending the action—the defendant—each seek to persuade the trier of fact that under the facts of the case the law entitles him to win. The stages of a lawsuit are the filing of pleadings and service of process, discovery, pretrial conference, settlement negotiation, trial, and appeal.
- Judicial jurisdiction is the power of a court to hear and determine a lawsuit. Under long-arm statutes, in certain circumstances a state court is permitted to acquire jurisdiction over a nonresident even though the nonresident is not personally served with process within the state, so long as there are certain "minimum contacts" between the defendant and the state.
- A court will refuse to hear a lawsuit unless the person seeking judicial relief has an actual interest in the case, or "standing to sue."
- Courts have the power and duty to hear only an actual controversy between parties who have adverse interests and conflicting claims. This is called a justiciable controversy.
- The doctrine of res judicata is that a court judgment is final and no issues litigated in that case can be relitigated between the same parties.
- Stare decisis is the doctrine that judicial decisions stand as precedents or guidance for similar future cases.
- Arbitration is a private proceeding for resolving a dispute between two parties. An arbitrator is a person who has been accepted by both parties, hears the case, and makes a decision.

- Adjudication
- Affirmative Defense
- Answer
- Appellate Court
- Arbitration
- Briefs
- Cause of Action
- Case Citation
- Class Action
- Closing Arguments
- Complaint
- Concurrent Jurisdiction
- Cross-Complaint
- Cross-Examination
- Default Judgment

- Demurrer
- Depositions
- Directed Verdict
- Discovery
- Diversity Jurisdiction
- Evidence
- Exclusive Jurisdiction
- Federal Question
- General Denial
- General Jurisdiction
- Interrogatories
- Judgment Notwithstanding the Verdict
- Judicial Review
- Justiciable Controversy
- Lawsuit

- Long-Arm Legislation
- Opening Statements
- Personal Jurisdiction
- Pleadings
- Precedent
- Pretrial Conference
- Remand
- Res Judicata
- Service of Process
- Settlement
- Standing to Sue
- Stare Decisis
- Subject Matter Jurisdiction
- Summons
- Trial
- Voir Dire Examination

Questions and Case Problems

1. What functions do courts perform?
2. What is the difference between the federal and state judicial systems? Explain the structure and function of each.
3. What is an appeal?
4. What is the doctrine of judicial review of legislation and how did it originate in the United States?
5. What does it mean to say that a court must have jurisdiction to hear a case? How does a court obtain jurisdiction?
6. What is long-arm legislation? What is its relevancy to the transaction of modern business?
7. What is the doctrine of standing to sue? Give some examples of the operation of this doctrine.
8. What is a justiciable controversy? Provide some examples of controversies which are justiciable and some which are not.
9. What are the doctrines of res judicata and stare decisis? How do they differ?
10. What is arbitration? How does it relate to the judicial system?

3 Administrative Law

For many Americans, the influence of administrative officials seems far more pervasive than that of judges and legislators. Not only do these officials execute the laws; together they create more legal rules and try more cases than all the legislatures and all the courts.

George Spiro and James L. Houghteling,
The Dynamics of Law, 2nd ed.

3:1 Introduction

In theory, American government consists of three branches: the legislative, to enact law; the executive, to administer and enforce law; and the judicial (the courts), to interpret law. In reality, however, there is a "fourth branch" of government—one consisting of administrative agencies. These agencies carry out certain investigatory, rule-making, or adjudicatory functions which are delegated by the legislative or executive branches of federal, state, or local government.

The quality of the food we eat, the means of transportation and communication available to us, how we heat our homes and conduct our businesses, the houses we build, and the companies we form, even the quality of the air we breathe are controlled and regulated by these sometimes "invisible" administrative agencies. As noted by the United States Supreme Court, "The rise of administrative bodies probably has been the most significant legal trend of the last century and perhaps more values today are affected by their decisions than by those of all the courts."[1]

Reasons for Development *Administrative law* was born of necessity. Its growth as a major force in the legal system began in the mid-nineteenth century as America was transformed from an agricultural to an industrial nation. As industries grew and social problems increased, numerous legal questions concerning the rights and welfare of private persons and businesses arose. Legislative and executive branches of government realized by the turn of the century that they were ill-equipped to gain the practical experience and knowledge required to give day-to-day attention to the complex, ever-changing problems that developed. This realization led to adoption by Congress of the Interstate Commerce Act in 1887. This act established the first federal administrative agency, the Interstate Commerce Commission. This agency was responsible for day-to-day regulation of railroads. (The Interstate Commerce Commission presently regulates virtually all interstate commerce.) As the

---

[1] *Federal Trade Com. v Ruberoid Co.,* 343 US 470 (1952).

Supreme Court, discussing reasons for establishment of the Interstate Commerce Commission, observed: "Congress has delegated the enforcement of transportation policy to a permanent expert body and has charged it with the duty of being responsive to the dynamic character of transportation problems."[2]

Since 1887, Congress has created so many agencies that today they form one of the largest bodies for government regulation in the world. Entire fields of human endeavor are controlled and regulated by specialized, complex agencies whose members have expertise in particular fields. At the federal level, for example, there are the Interstate Commerce Commission, National Labor Relations Board, Federal Communications Commission, Federal Trade Commission, Nuclear Regulatory Commission, Federal Power Commission, Securities and Exchange Commission, Occupational Safety and Health Administration, Bureau of Indian Affairs, Environmental Protection Agency, Civil Rights Commission, Federal Aviation Administration, Civil Aeronautics Board, Bureau of Land Management, and Social Security Administration, to name just a few. In some areas, the states have corresponding or additional administrative agencies to control such matters as workers' compensation, labor relations, civil rights, public utilities, and state unemployment compensation.

Regulatory and Nonregulatory Agencies   Agencies are sometimes classified as regulatory or nonregulatory. Regulatory agencies have authority to regulate economic activities of individuals and businesses. They have licensing power, rate-making power, and power to regulate certain business practices. They also make rules, decide disputes, and impose fines. Examples of regulatory agencies are the Federal Trade Commission, which has power to prevent unfair or deceptive business practices in interstate commerce; Federal Communications Commission, which licenses and delicenses radio and television stations; and Interstate Commerce Commission, which has power to set rates for interstate carriers.

Nonregulatory agencies, on the other hand, are given authority to conduct investigations or administer benefits such as pensions, government insurance, and workers' compensation. Examples of nonregulatory agencies are the Social Security Administration, which administers benefits, and the Federal Bureau of Investigation, which investigates federal crimes.

3:2   State and Federal Regulation of Business

State governments, as well as the federal government, establish administrative agencies to carry out their work. The basis for the states' authority to establish agencies lies in the state constitution. The basis for the states' right to regulate lies in the inherent *police power* of the state. That power may be delegated to political subdivisions of the state, such as cities, counties, or community college districts. The states have power to regulate except as that power is constrained by the federal Constitution or by the state constitution.

---

[2] *Atchison, T. & S. F. R. Co. v Wichita Board of Trade,* 412 US 800 (1973).

The federal government derives its authority to regulate from the federal Constitution, and specifically from Article I, Section 8, which states: "Congress shall have the Power . . . to regulate commerce with foreign Nations, and among the several States, and with the Indian Tribes. . . . " This clause grants regulatory power over commerce to the federal government. It has been interpreted by the courts to limit the federal power to regulate commerce and to restrain the power of the states in the regulation of commerce. At one time the federal power was regarded as narrowly limited to the regulation of purely *interstate commerce*. Since the 1930's, however, the Supreme Court has ruled consistently that the federal government may also regulate wholly *intrastate commerce* that has an effect on interstate commerce.

The second prong of the commerce clause restrains the state's power to regulate commerce if that regulation interferes with interstate commerce or with the federal regulation of commerce. The following classic case explains the reasoning of this interpretation of the commerce clause.

Southern Pacific Co.
v
Arizona
325 US 761 (1945)
United States Supreme Court

FACTS: The Arizona Train Limit Law of 1912 made it unlawful to operate a railroad train of more than 14 passenger cars or 70 freight cars within the state of Arizona. The Southern Pacific Railroad challenged the state's right to impose such a restriction on railroad trains traveling through the state in interstate commerce.

ISSUE: Does the Arizona statute contravene the commerce clause of the federal Constitution?

RESULT: Yes. The state's interest in safety is not significantly advanced by the law, and the burden on interstate commerce is great.

REASONING:

*   *   *

Although the commerce clause conferred on the national government power to regulate commerce, its possession of the power does not exclude all state power of regulation. . . . [I]n the absence of conflicting legislation by Congress, there is a residuum of power in the state to make laws governing matters of local concern or even, to some extent, regulate it. . . . Thus the states may regulate matters which, because of their number and diversity, may never be adequately dealt with by Congress. . . . When the regulation of matters of local concern is local in character and effect, and its impact on the national commerce does not seriously interfere with its operation, and the consequent incentive to deal with them nationally is slight, such regulation has been generally held to be within state authority. . . .

But ever since Gibbons v. Ogden, 9 Wheat 1, the states have not been deemed to have authority to impede substantially the free flow of commerce from state to state, or to regulate those phases of the national commerce which, because of the need of national uniformity, demand that their regulation, if any, be prescribed by a single authority. . . .

In the application of these principles some enactments may be found to be plainly within and others plainly without state power. But between these extremes lies the infinite variety of cases, in which regulation of local matters may also operate as a regulation of commerce, in which reconciliation of the conflicting claims of state and national power is to be attained only by some appraisal and accommodation of the competing demands of the state and national interests involved. . . .

Hence the matters for ultimate determination here are the nature and extent of the burden which the state regulation of interstate trains, adopted as a safety measure, imposes on interstate commerce, and whether the relative weights of the state and national interests involved are such as to make inapplicable the rule, generally observed, that the free flow of interstate commerce and its freedom from local restraints in matters requiring uniformity of regulation are interests safeguarded by the commerce clause from state interference. . . .

Here we conclude that the state does go too far. Its regulation of train lengths, admittedly obstructive to interstate train operation, and having a seriously adverse effect on transportation efficiency and economy, passes beyond what is plainly essential for safety since it does not appear that it will lessen rather than increase the danger of an accident. Its attempted regulation of the operation of interstate trains cannot establish nation-wide control such as is essential to the maintenance of an efficient transportation system, which Congress alone can prescribe. The state interest cannot be preserved at the expense of the national interest by an enactment which regulates interstate train lengths without securing such control, which is a matter of national concern. . . .

Stone, Chief Justice.

3:3 Relationship to the Judicial, Legislative, and Executive Branches of Government

The purpose of all administrative action is to implement policy set by the legislature. The power of the administrative agency is derived from legislation, which is passed by the legislature subject to executive veto. The functions of most administrative agencies can be divided into rule-making and adjudication.

Rule-making   In *rule-making* an agency creates either substantive rules for others to follow or procedural rules for its own operation. The power to make rules is called *quasi-legislative power*, and it is delegated from Congress or the legislature. The agency fills in the rules necessary to effect the legislative purpose; in a sense it is doing something the legislature could have done. The constraint on this delegation of quasi-legislative power is that the legislature cannot delegate away all of its inherent legislative power, and it cannot retain so much control over the agency that agency rule-making is simply a route around the normal statute-making process. That process would include passage by both houses of Congress (called *bicameralism*) and the opportunity for executive veto (called *presentment*). The issue arose recently in the following landmark Supreme Court case involving Congress' retention of veto power over an administrative agency action.

Immigration and Naturalization Service

v

Chadha

462 US 919 (1983)

United States Supreme Court

FACTS: Section 244(c)(2) of the Immigration and Nationality Act authorizes either house of Congress, by resolution, to invalidate a decision of the Immigration and Naturalization Service (INS) to allow a particular deportable alien to remain in the United States.

Chadha, an alien who had been lawfully admitted to the United States on a nonimmigration student visa, remained in the United States after his visa had expired and was ordered by INS to show cause why he should not be deported. He then applied for suspension of the deportation, and the Attorney General exercised his power to suspend deportation proceedings. Thereafter the House of Representatives passed a resolution pursuant to Section 244(c)(2) vetoing the suspension. Chadha challenged the constitutionality of the legislative veto.

ISSUE: Does the legislative veto violate the Constitutional framework of a separation of powers?

RESULT: Yes. The legislative veto violates the federal Constitution's principles of bicameralism and presentment.

REASONING:

*   *   *

The Constitution sought to divide the delegated powers of the new federal government into three defined categories, legislative, executive and judicial, to assure, as nearly as possible, that each Branch of government would confine itself to its assigned responsibility. The hydraulic pressure inherent within each of the separate Branches to exceed the outer limits of its power, even to accomplish desirable objectives, must be resisted.

. . . Not every action taken by either House is subject to the bicameralism and presentment requirements of Art. I. . . . Whether actions taken by either House are, in law and fact, an exercise of legislative power depends not on their form but upon "whether they contain matter which is properly to be regarded as legislative in its character and effect." . . .

Examination of the action taken here by one House pursuant to § 244(c)(2) reveals that it was essentially legislative in purpose and effect. In purporting to exercise power defined in Art. I, § 8, cl. 4 to "establish an uniform Rule of Naturalization," the House took action that had the purpose and effect of altering the legal rights, duties and relations of persons, including the Attorney General, Executive Branch officials and Chadha, all outside the legislative branch. Section 244(c)(2) purports to authorize one House of Congress to require the Attorney General to deport an individual alien whose deportation otherwise would be cancelled under § 244. The one-House veto operated in this case to overrule the Attorney General and mandate Chadha's deportation; absent the House action, Chadha would remain in the United States. Congress has *acted* and its action has altered Chadha's status.

The legislative character of the one-House veto in this case is confirmed by the character of the Congressional action it supplants. Neither the House of Representatives nor the Senate contends that, absent the veto provision in § 244(c)(2), either of them, or both of them acting together, could effectively require the Attorney General to deport an alien once the Attorney General, in the exercise of legislatively delegated authority, had determined the alien should remain in the United States. Without the challenged provision in § 244(c)(2), this could have been achieved, if at all, only by legislation requiring deportation. Similarly, a veto by one House of Congress under § 244(c)(2) cannot be justified as an attempt at amending the standards set out in § 244(a)(1), or as a repeal of § 244 as applied to Chadha. Amendment and repeal of statutes, no less than enactment, must conform with Art. I.

The nature of the decision implemented by the one-House veto in this case further manifests its legislative character. After long experience with the clumsy, time consuming private bill procedure, Congress made a deliberate choice to delegate to the Executive Branch, and specifically to the Attorney General, the authority to allow deportable aliens to remain in this country in certain specified circumstances. It is not disputed that this choice to delegate authority is precisely the kind of decision that can be implemented only in accordance with the procedures set out in Art. I. Disagreement with the Attorney General's decision on Chadha's deportation—that is, Congress' decision to deport Chadha—no less than Congress' original choice to delegate to the Attorney General the authority to make that decision, involves determinations of policy that Congress can implement in only one way; bicameral passage followed by present-ment to the President. Congress must abide by its delegation of authority until that delegation is legislatively altered or revoked. . . .

The veto authorized by § 244(c)(2) doubtless has been in many respects a convenient shortcut; the 'sharing' with the Executive by Congress of its authority over aliens in this manner is, on its face, an appealing com-promise. In purely practical terms, it is obviously easier for action to be taken by one House without submission to the President; but it is crystal clear from the records of the Convention, contemporaneous writings and debates, that the Framers ranked other values higher than efficiency. The records of the Convention and debates in the States preceding ratification underscore the common desire to define and limit the exercise of the newly created federal powers affecting the states and the people. There is unmistakable expression of a determination that legislation by the national Congress be a step-by-step, deliberate and deliberative process.

The choices we discern as having been made in the Constitutional Convention impose burdens on governmental processes that often seem clumsy, inefficient, even unworkable, but those hard choices were con-sciously made by men who had lived under a form of government that permitted arbitrary governmental acts to go unchecked. There is no support in the Constitution or decisions of this Court for the proposition that the cumbersomeness and delays often encountered in complying with explicit Constitutional standards may be avoided, either by the Congress or by the President. . . . With all the obvious flaws of delay, untidiness, and potential for abuse, we have not yet found a better way to preserve freedom than by making the exercise of power subject to the carefully crafted restraints spelled out in the Constitution.

We hold that the Congressional veto provision in § 244(c)(2) . . . is unconstitutional. . . .

Burger, Chief Justice.

Adjudication   When an agency adjudicates, it determines that a particular person has, or has not, violated an agency rule. The power to adjudicate such cases is called the *quasi-judicial power*. This power poses a problem in that the legislature cannot adjudicate, and thus cannot delegate power it does not have. Congress is, in fact, prohibited by Article I, Section 9, of the federal Constitution from issuing a "bill of attainder." A bill of attainder is a legislative act declaring that a particular person is guilty of violating a particular law. Under the *separation of powers doctrine* the power to make such a declaration is allocated to the judiciary. The problem arises because the agency appears, in adjudication, to exercise judicial power that was not delegated from the judiciary. Nevertheless, administrative agency law has not yet been attacked successfully on these grounds. So long as the agency is sufficiently independent of the legislature so that the legislature is not exercising quasi-judicial power, and so long as the agency operates within certain constraints, it has power to adjudicate in order to implement law.

3:4   Limits on Agency Powers

As stated earlier, an administrative agency is created by legislation. The agency's powers are set forth in this legislation. In this sense, the legislature delegates power to the agencies. Consequently, the question whether the *doctrine of delegation* of power by the legislature is appropriate—that is, whether Congress or a state legislature has unconstitutionally "delegated away" its inherent legislative function—has arisen. Prior to 1935, most United States Supreme Court decisions upheld delegations of power to administrative agencies. Essentially, the Supreme Court recognized the impracticality of not permitting delegation of powers since it would clearly have been impossible for Congress to decide every detail of each law it enacted. The court thus used various word formulas to do what was practical and necessary for the administration of government.

During the Depression the Supreme Court for the first time began to disapprove some delegations of congressional power. This disapproval resulted in the striking down of major sections of the National Industrial Recovery Act, which had granted extremely far-reaching powers to the President to control the economy. Theoretically, there may still be some constitutional limitations on the congressional delegation of powers to federal administrative agencies, but from a practical standpoint this issue is probably no longer viable. Recent rulings indicate that the current issue is simply whether, under all the circumstances, the delegation is "reasonable." If Congress has the constitutional power to regulate a field, and is as specific as possible under the circumstances, the delegation will usually be upheld.

The major constraints on federal agency powers lie in the federal Constitution and in federal statutes. As we have seen in the materials on the commerce clause and on the separation of powers doctrine, the Constitution may constrain the nature of an agency's power to act. In addition, the Constitution may constrain the specific actions the agency may take against a person. For example, the Constitution prohibits violations of the freedom of speech by administrative agencies just as surely as it does by statutes and law enforcement officials.

The statutory constraints are (1) the *enabling legislation*, which is the statute that establishes the agency or delegates power to it; and (2) the *Federal Administrative Procedures Act of 1946* (APA) [5 USC §§ 1001 et seq.], which governs generally the operation of all federal agencies. The APA covers nearly every phase of the administrative process in detail. The APA sets forth guidelines for uniform and impartial procedures. It guards against arbitrary official encroachment on private rights. Most states now have laws, patterned after the APA, to govern the procedures of their administrative agencies.

Legislative and Executive Control over Agencies   The legislative and executive branches of government have several means to control agencies. The legislative branch controls and limits agencies through budget appropriations, watchdog committees, investigations, appointment of agency personnel, and intercession in pending agency matters. The legislature can eliminate an agency simply by repealing the statute that created it. The legislature can also override administrative actions by statute. As to executive control over agencies, the President or a governor usually has power to select heads of agencies. With major federal posts, the Senate must approve the President's appointments. Executive control also extends to removing agency personnel and formulating fiscal policy and budgets.

3:5   Rule-making Procedure

In its rule-making capacity, an administrative agency is a "mini-legislature" empowered by the state or federal legislature to promulgate rulings. In light of this, courts have broadly interpreted agency power to make rules that actually have the effect of substantive law. For example, the Supreme Court has held that the Federal Trade Commission could substantively define "unfair methods of competition" by using its rule-making power, on the rationale that rule-making is essential to the regulatory process and in many ways superior to adjudication in making policy.

Thus, an administrative agency may have broad discretion in implementing the statutory scheme for which the legislature has made it responsible. Rule-making is an important area of discretion. The most important limits on rule-making are the doctrine of *ultra vires acts* and the APA.

Ultra Vires Acts   Under the *ultra vires* ("beyond the powers") *doctrine*, actions taken by an administrative agency must not be outside the scope of the power delegated to the agency by the legislature. When an agency acts outside the scope of its purposes and powers, the agency is unconstitutionally exercising legislative power and its actions are void. Most ultra vires acts are those that are in conflict with constitutionally protected civil liberties. In one case, for example, the Supreme Court invalidated agency regulations that permitted withdrawal of security clearances without giving the affected party opportunity for a hearing. The court declared that the regulations were unauthorized by Congress, and therefore were ultra vires and void.

The Administrative Procedure Act   When a federal agency considers proposing a rule, it must first draft it and publish it in the *Federal Register*, a daily official federal publication of executive, legislative, and administrative regulations and actions. Then notice is given and a formal hearing held to give interested parties the opportunity to respond. When the rule is adopted, it is published first in the Federal Register and then in the *Code of Federal Regulations*, a government publication of rules of federal administrative agencies.

 Once the draft of a rule is published in the Federal Register, the public has an opportunity to file comments on the proposal and, sometimes, to testify at hearings with regard to the desirability of the proposal. The public and the business community, at this stage, may also suggest redrafting the proposal. Businesspeople should be alert for proposed administrative regulations that affect their industries, with a view toward submitting comments to the agency before it finalizes its rules.

Investigation   Investigatory, or so-called "inquisitional," powers—such as the power to inspect or require disclosure of information—are conferred on many administrative agencies. Investigatory power is one of the distinctive functions which sets an agency apart from the courts. Some agencies are in fact solely investigatory or advisory bodies; they exist solely to secure and provide information, and in some cases, to make recommendations or to gather public opinion. So pervasive has the investigatory function of agencies become that there is now a considerable body of law relating to methods by which individuals and corporations may seek protection from agency information-gathering functions.

3:6   Adjudication Procedure

When an agency acts as an adjudicative body it is essentially performing court functions. Most adjudicative matters in federal agencies are heard by administrative law judges (formerly known as hearing officers). Administrative law judges preside at the hearing and render an initial decision, which can be appealed to the head of the agency. In some agencies, there is an intermediate review board which hears appeals, with limited right of appeal to the agency head. Policy on the following problems may be properly formulated by an agency on a case-by-case basis: problems that could not reasonably have been foreseen by the agency, problems as to which the agency has only a tentative judgment due to lack of experience in the particular area, and problems so specialized and varied that they cannot be resolved by general rules.

In the administrative system, decisions are made through methods, for reasons, and by persons quite different from those in the judicial system. In the judicial system, the judge or jury makes decisions about the questions presented before it. In the administrative system, it is the members of the agency who set policy or make rules. Unlike judges and juries in the court system, agency members are experts in the particular field in which they are setting policy or making decisions. For example, administrators working for the National Labor Relations Board are experts and are sympathetic to the complex problems of collective bargaining and industrial relations. Members of the Federal Communications Commission have expertise in the electronic communications industry, while members of the Federal Trade Commission have expertise in the field of antitrust and trade practices. Only a few courts, such as the United States Tax Court and the federal Court of Patent Appeals, have specialized knowledge in a field.

Advantages and Disadvantages of the Administrative Process   There are many advantages in having a case heard before an administrative agency rather than a court. Some of these advantages lie in the very functions of an agency. Because courts generally do not have (1) the same power to initiate and control investigations, (2) the power to supervise the parties after a case has been decided, (3) the ability to provide expert knowledge in technical fields, or (4) procedures for easily obtaining decisions in advance of conduct that would lead to lawsuits, an administrative proceeding is more accessible to the parties, gives the parties closer attention, offers expert judgment in a specialized area, and can serve as preventive action against future litigation.

There is one disadvantage, though, to the lack of formality in administrative proceedings: a person's constitutional rights are not as highly guarded as in court proceedings. The United States Supreme Court has repeatedly emphasized that there is more protection of individual rights in a judicial action than in an administrative action.

In regulating certain industries, some statutes have divided the duty of enforcement between courts and administrative agencies. Thus, it is possible for a case to be heard before both an administrative agency and a court. For example, federal antitrust legislation provides remedies against certain business activities detrimental to interstate competition, and these remedies may be sought in both a federal regulatory agency—the Federal Trade Commission—and the federal courts.

Notice and Fair Hearing   Assuming an agency decides to take action against a private person or corporation, the agency must respect certain procedural safeguards imposed by the Constitution. If agency action would deprive a person of interests that are protected by due process, the agency must give the person notice and an opportunity to be heard. Constitutional due process, under the Fifth and Fourteenth Amendments, requires that federal and state governments provide *notice* and *fair hearing* before taking action that deprives an individual of "liberty" or "property." As a basic ingredient of administrative law, the right to notice and fair hearing provides vital protection against arbitrary governmental action. For example, if discharge from a governmental job would involve a stigma or in any other way would foreclose future employment opportunities, a "liberty" interest is involved, requiring an agency to give notice and hold a hearing before taking action. A person receiving welfare benefits under statutory and administrative standards defining eligibility has an interest in the continued receipt of the benefits where the statute provides a claim of entitlement to the benefits ("property") for anyone who qualifies. Hence, the issue of whether a person does qualify must be resolved by a full and fair hearing.

Other situations in which administrative agencies must provide notice and hearing before taking action include the expulsion or suspension of students from public schools, withholding of licenses, exclusion and deportation of aliens, revocation of parole or probation, denial of welfare or housing benefits, and injury to reputation.

Once it is established that the interest involved is protected by due process and that the type of issue requires a hearing, the form of notice and type of hearing must be determined. These vary depending on what is "appropriate to the nature of the case." The specific requirements of due process will be determined in each case by three factors: the nature of the private interest affected, the risk to that interest posed by existing procedures, and the burden on the government if other procedures are imposed.

Administrative hearings must be conducted in a fair, open, and impartial manner to comply with due process of law. This kind of hearing is illustrated in the following decision. An administrative agency (a city's civil service commission) conducted a hearing to suspend a police chief without providing essential due process safeguards.

Adams

v

Marshall

512 P2d 365 (1973)

Kansas Supreme Court

FACTS: A suspended city police chief brought a suit to compel members of the city's civil service commission to follow certain due process procedures during the course of his suspension hearing. The police chief argued that the hearing was not conducted with due process of law because it was not open to the public and because his right to cross-examine was limited to five minutes. Agreeing that due process had been violated by the commission, the trial judge ordered the city civil service commission to open the hearing to the public and not to limit the cross-examination to five minutes. The agency appealed.

ISSUE: Does the due process clause of the federal Constitution require state administrative agencies to provide for cross-examination and a public hearing in quasi-judicial proceedings?

RESULT: Yes. Fundamental due process requires such openness and opportunity for cross-examination in a quasi-judicial administrative hearing.

REASONING:

*   *   *

Where an administrative body acts in a quasi-judicial capacity the requirements of due process will attach to the proceedings held before it. This principle was pointed out in [a Kansas case], where the court said:

" . . . The constitutional guaranty of due process of law applies to administrative as well as judicial proceedings where such proceedings are *quasi* judicial in nature." . . .

Two ground rules laid down by the Commission in this case are said by the plaintiff to violate basic due process demands: (1) the right to examine and cross-examine witnesses and (2) the right to an open or public hearing. We are inclined to agree.

The right to the cross-examination of witnesses in quasi-judicial or adjudicatory proceedings is one of fundamental importance and is generally, if not universally, recognized as an important requirement of due process. . . .

In speaking of due process requirements, the United States Supreme Court [has] said:

> " . . . All parties must be fully apprised of the evidence submitted or to be considered, and must be given opportunity to cross-examine witnesses, to inspect documents, and to offer evidence in explanation or rebuttal. In no other way can a party maintain its rights or make its defense. In no other way can it test the sufficiency of the facts to support the finding. . . . " . . .

It has somewhere been said, if our imperfect recollection can be trusted, that cross-examination is the anvil on which the truth may be forged. We have said many times that the extent of cross-examination lies largely within the sound judicial discretion of the court. . . . However, cross-examination may not be unduly curtailed in testing the soundness of a witness' testimony . . . , nor may it be so limited and circumscribed as to preclude a full disclosure of the facts. . . .

No administrative body, no matter how prescient its members, can foretell in advance of hearing the extent to which the testimony of witnesses may be limited without impinging upon the pursuit of truth. The five-minute limitation which the Commission, before trial, placed on the cross-examination of all witnesses was in our opinion an impermissible restriction on due process.

Passing to the question of public trial, we believe it may generally be said that proceedings of a judicial nature held behind closed doors and shielded from public scrutiny have long been repugnant to our system of justice. The concept that trials and judicatory hearings be open to the public gaze is inherent in our idea of due process. This view was voiced many years ago by the United States Supreme Court . . . in the following words:

> " . . . The vast expansion of this field of administrative regulation in response to the pressure of social needs is made possible under our system by adherence to the basic principles that the legislature shall appropriately determine the standards of administrative action and that in administrative proceedings of a quasi-judicial character the liberty and property of the citizen shall be protected by the rudimentary requirements of fair play. These demand 'a fair and open hearing,' essential alike to the legal validity of the administrative regulation and to the maintenance of public confidence in the value and soundness of this important governmental process. Such a hearing has been described as an 'inexorable safeguard.' . . . " . . .

The requirements of an administrative hearing of a judicial or quasi-judicial character are phrased in this language in 2 Am.Jur.2d, Administrative Law, § 412, p. 222:

" . . . A hearing before an administrative agency exercising judicial, quasi-judicial, or adjudicatory powers must be fair, open, and impartial, and if such a hearing has been denied, the administrative action is void. . . . "

Fontron, Justice.

3:7   Protection from Agency Information Gathering

Although administrative investigations are not criminal proceedings, they sometimes result in imposition of criminal penalties. Therefore, some of the constitutional safeguards which protect a defendant in criminal proceedings have been held applicable to administrative investigations and hearings. While most information sought by agencies is given voluntarily, individuals or corporations sometimes do not desire to provide an agency with requested information. In such cases, many agencies are authorized to use one or more methods to obtain information, including the subpoena power (obtaining testimony and documents under court order), periodic or special reports, and agency inspections of a company's records and business sites.

Agencies are frequently empowered to enforce their requests for information. For example, some agencies can revoke licenses or take other sanctions against a person or company not complying with an order for information.

Fourth Amendment Protection   Administrative officials sometimes desire to inspect homes and businesses in connection with health and fire laws. In these instances, the question may arise as to whether such "searches" violate the Fourth Amendment right to be secure against searches and seizures in the absence of a valid search warrant. The United States Supreme Court has held that a search warrant must be obtained, in the absence of an emergency situation that could be hazardous to a person's welfare, for most administrative inspections of commercial and residential premises pursuant to fire, health, and housing regulations, unless the occupant gives his or her consent to the inspection.

Although evidence seized in an unlawful search is inadmissible in a criminal proceeding, it has sometimes been admitted in administrative proceedings.

Fifth Amendment Protection   Witnesses called to testify in an agency investigation may assert the Fifth Amendment *privilege against self-incrimination* in refusing to answer specific questions if the information requested could supply a link in a chain leading to criminal conviction. The Fifth Amendment privilege is available only to an individual and may not be invoked by a corporation, union, or partnership. Thus, the record custodian of such an organization must produce requested *documents*, but he has a privilege to refuse to answer specific *questions*. The Fifth Amendment privilege against self-incrimination also protects the witness' private papers if they would incriminate the witness. However, the privilege does not extend to records required to be kept by statute.

Right to Counsel   A witness who must appear before an administrative investigatory hearing is entitled to be represented by an attorney.

 Some attorneys, many in the Washington, D.C., area, specialize in representing persons and corporations in dealings with and appearances before federal administrative agencies. Other attorneys specialize in particular agencies, such as the Federal Trade Commission, National Labor Relations Board, and Interstate Commerce Commission. Because of the complexity—and uniqueness—of each agency, a person dealing with or appearing before a particular agency is advised to consult an attorney who has experience with that particular agency.

3:8 Judicial Review

Judicial review is the review of administrative action by a court. A person or corporation suffering harm as a result of agency action may seek judicial review, but unless the case is "ripe" it will be denied judicial review. The ripeness doctrine is designed to avoid litigating in the abstract—that is, before the administrative rule has been definitely applied to the plaintiff. In deciding whether a case is ripe for review, the courts consider the extent of hardship on the parties that would result if the court denied review.

EXAMPLE: A Federal Drug Administration rule requires the brand name of drug labels to be accompanied by the generic name of the chemical. If a manufacturer fails to comply with the regulation, the Attorney General can confiscate its products and seek criminal prosecution. A drug manufacturer argues that this regulation exceeds the agency's powers and seeks to enjoin its enforcement in court. The issues are ripe for review since, if the court withheld review and the drug manufacturer engaged in the prohibited activity, the manufacturer would risk criminal prosecution.

When reviewing agency action, courts are prohibited from second-guessing or changing rulings or findings of agencies. Courts are essentially limited to determining whether the agency ruling was reasonable and whether the agency exceeded its powers under the legislation that created the agency.

Primary Jurisdiction Doctrine   Under the *primary jurisdiction doctrine*, the agency rather than a court is empowered by statute to conduct the initial trial, or "first hearing," of the case. In two areas particularly, the courts have held that the legislative intent was for an administrative agency, not a court, to have primary jurisdiction in deciding a particular type of case. These two areas are antitrust, where the Federal Trade Commission has primary jurisdiction, and labor relations, where the National Labor Relations Board has primary jurisdiction. In these areas, as well as some others, the plaintiff must first seek relief through the agency, even though the agency's action will subsequently be subject to judicial review.

Exhaustion of Administrative Remedies   Generally, judicial review is not available until the party seeking it has exhausted all prescribed administrative remedies. The rationale for this rule is that it permits full development of the facts prior to judicial review. The agency is given the chance to use the discretion or expertise as expected of it by Congress. The rule recognizes the autonomy of the agency and its right to function without undue interruption.

 Of particular importance to the businessperson is the rule that a person who wishes to attack the granting of a license to a competitor must raise any objections at the hearing before the agency empowered to issue the license. If a businessperson fails to do so, he or she will be precluded from seeking judicial review.

Stays   Once a court has determined that an administrative decision is reviewable, it may grant a *stay* to postpone agency action pending outcome of its review. In deciding whether to grant a stay, the court will consider the following factors: whether the plaintiff is likely to prevail on the merits, whether the plaintiff has shown that without such a stay he would be irreparably injured, whether issuance of the stay would not substantially harm other parties in the proceedings, and whether the public interest will be harmed by granting the stay. If it does so, the court in effect is granting a judicial reversal of the agency order until the process of review is complete.

Key Concepts and Terms

- Administrative agencies are legal entities that are delegated certain functions by the legislative or executive branches of government. Administrative law deals with the operation of and limitations on these agencies.
- Administrative agencies usually have broad discretion in exercising their statutory powers. Agencies formulate policy in any of the following ways: adjudication (on a case-by-case basis), rule-making, investigation, or informal action. A federal agency considering a rule must first publish a draft of it in the Federal Register. When the rule is adopted, it is published in the Code of Federal Regulations.
- The federal Administrative Procedure Act sets forth procedures that federal administrative agencies must establish to meet the requirements of uniformity, impartiality, and fairness. The act creates safeguards against arbitrary official encroachment on private rights. Several states have enacted similar legislation patterned after the federal model.
- The "delegation" of power from Congress to the agencies has been the subject of lawsuits. The federal courts usually hold that so long as Congress

has constitutional power to regulate a field and is as specific as possible in such regulation, this delegation of power will be upheld. At the state level, however, courts still hold that legislative delegation of powers to state agencies is sometimes improper.

- Ultra vires, which means "beyond the powers," is the term used to describe acts that an agency performs outside the scope of its powers. Such actions are void.

- Due process, notice, and a fair hearing must be provided to a person or corporation whose liberty or property interests would be affected by an agency's action. The form of notice and type of hearing vary.

- Certain constitutional safeguards that protect a criminal defendant have been held applicable to administrative investigations and hearings. This is because some administrative investigations, while not criminal, may result in imposition of criminal penalties.

- The federal Freedom of Information Act provides that certain records must be disclosed by federal agencies after a person's request reasonably describing the record. The act sets forth exceptions from disclosure of materials relating to national defense, internal personnel rules, trade secrets, interagency memoranda, investigatory files, and some other types of records.

- A person or corporation that has suffered harm as a result of agency action may seek judicial review after all administrative remedies have been exhausted. When a court reviews an administrative agency's decision, it may grant a stay to postpone agency action pending the outcome of the judicial review.

- Adjudication
- Administrative Law
- Bicameralism
- Code of Federal Regulations
- Delegation Doctrine
- Enabling Legislation
- Exhaustion of Remedies
- Federal Administrative Procedure Act
- Federal Register
- Interstate Commerce
- Intrastate Commerce

- Judicial Review
- Notice and Fair Hearing
- Police Power
- Presentment
- Privilege Against Self-Incrimination
- Primary Jurisdiction Doctrine
- Quasi-Legislative
- Quasi-Judicial
- Rule-making
- Separation of Powers Doctrine
- Stays
- Ultra Vires Doctrine

Questions and Case Problems

Explanatory Note about Case Problems   Here, and at the end of all later chapters in this book, you will find both "questions" and "case problems." A question calls for a general type of response, and there is often only one "right" answer. For example, with respect to question 4 below, you either know what the Administrative Procedure Act is or you do not. You can usually prepare the answer to a question by stating in your own words information you learned when you studied the chapter.

A case problem, on the other hand, requires you to apply the general principles you have learned to a specific set of facts. Typically, you are asked to assume the role of a judge who must (1) resolve a particular legal dispute by answering the precise question or questions presented and (2) justify that resolution. Your answer to a question presented might be simply "yes" or "no," but your overall performance on the problem will be rated primarily on the basis of how you justify that answer. Indeed, two students might each prepare an adequate response to a case problem and yet arrive at entirely different answers.

As you can see, case problems require an approach that differs somewhat from the familiar one used in answering questions. To acquaint you with this approach, an analysis of a sample problem is presented below.

Many of the case problems in this book are based on actual cases. The *Adams* case (see page 44) could be the source of the following case problem:

> Pickle, the police chief of Plainsville, Kansas, is dissatisfied with the job performance of patrolman Adams. Pickle suspends Adams for two weeks, without pay, and Adams appeals his suspension to the Plainsville Civil Service Commission. The commission holds a hearing at which Adams is allowed to be heard. However, over Adams' objection, the commission closes the hearing to the public and allows only five minutes for the cross-examination of each witness. After the hearing the commission upholds the suspension and orders it to begin. Adams now seeks judicial review, arguing that his constitutional rights were violated. Should the court review the case? Why or why not? Assuming that the court does review the case, should it find any violation of Adams' constitutional rights? Discuss.

The first step in preparing a response to this problem is to read the problem carefully and, on a worksheet, note the important facts. Here, they are that (1) a public officer was suspended without pay, (2) an administrative agency upheld the suspension after a hearing, and (3) the agency ordered that the hearing be closed to the public and limited the officer's right to question witnesses who testified against him. Ignore any irrelevant facts. For example, Chief Pickle's name may be amusing, but it has nothing to do with how the court should decide the case.

The second step is to identify the legal issues and list them on the worksheet. The questions at the end of the problem can often help in this identification. Here, the first question makes it clear that reviewability of the agency's suspension order is an issue. The second question suggests issues concerning one's constitutional rights; what rights did the officer have with respect to the hearing, and how, if at all, were they violated?

The third step is to apply the appropriate legal principles to the issues. Recalling the discussion in Section 3:8, you conclude (and note on the worksheet) that Adams will suffer harm if the suspension is carried out, thus making the Commission's order both reviewable and ripe for review. Since nothing is said in the problem about the availability of further administrative review, you state as an assumption that Adams has exhausted his administrative remedies. Therefore, you may conclude that the court should review the case.

Your analysis of the issues presented by the second question requires an understanding of what was discussed in Section 3:4. You recall that an individual is guaranteed the right to due process of law by the Fifth and Fourteenth Amendments to the United States Constitution, and that due process requires a fair hearing before an individual can be deprived of a property right. Given those principles, you must decide whether loss of pay for two weeks is a deprivation that requires a hearing, and if so, whether the hearing held by the Commission was "fair" within the meaning of the requirement. The fairness issue requires that you consider the importance of public hearings and the cross-examination of witnesses. In view of the circumstances of the case, you are apt to conclude, as the *Adams* court did, that the commission violated Adams' right to due process both by closing the hearing *and* by limiting the cross-examination.

Having concluded your analysis of the problem, you are prepared to write your response, using your worksheet as a guide. Answer the first question. Then, in a concise and orderly way, proceeding from general principles to their specific application to the facts, defend that answer by explaining how and why you reached it. You can then go on to the second question, which you handle in exactly the same manner.

1. A congressional statute gives the Department of the Interior power to allow or to curtail mining within national forests "as the best interests of all users of the national forest shall dictate." Is this an invalid delegation of legislative power? Discuss.

2. The Interstate Commerce Commission adopts a regulation that railroads that retain boxcars belonging to other railroads for an unreasonable time must pay a penalty of $100 per day. The Nevada Railroad seeks to enjoin the regulation on the theory that it is not authorized by statute. Will the court hear this attack now? Discuss.

3. The Nuclear Regulatory Commission operates a licensing scheme whereby certain laboratories having need for radioactive materials are permitted to use them under strictly limited conditions. The NRC reserves the right to make inspections of the premises where the materials are being used, without a search warrant, at any time. It makes such an inspection, discovers unauthorized uses of the material, and seeks to bar the laboratory from any further access from radioactive materials. Can the laboratory assert that the search was invalid? Discuss.

4. What is the Federal Administrative Procedure Act? What purposes does it serve?

5. Clyde wishes to inspect a report prepared by the Department of Defense concerning Middle East policy. This report has been classified "secret" under the government's classification procedure. Clyde asserts that the material should not be secret since there is nothing in it that would jeopardize foreign policy. If an action is brought to compel disclosure of the document, will Clyde win? Discuss.

6. Why were the framers of the Constitution careful to separate the necessary governmental functions into different parts of the government?

7. What constitutional safeguards, if any, are applicable during an investigation by an administrative agency? Are the same constitutional protections available as in a criminal proceeding? Explain your answer.

8. The rules of the Small Business Administration require that anyone receiving an SBA loan preserve particular financial documents, in order that compliance with the loan restrictions may be ascertained. Henry receives an SBA loan for use in his business. The SBA believes that Henry spent part of the money on a yacht for personal use. This conduct constitutes a violation of the SBA statute and would also be a criminal offense. The SBA orders Henry to produce particular financial records by which it can trace the use of the funds. Can Henry utilize his privilege against self-incrimination to avoid producing the record? Discuss.

9. Alice applies for a pilot's license. The license application remains with the Federal Aviation Administration for two years. The agency refuses to act on it, repeatedly stating that a hearing will be scheduled in the near future. The agency never does schedule a hearing. Can Alice go to court to force the FAA to act? Discuss.

10. Larry, a student at the Air Force Academy, is suspected of cheating. The applicable regulations of the academy provide that he could be given a hearing but that he is not entitled to confront the witnesses against him. Before the hearing begins, Larry goes into federal district court, seeking to enjoin continuation of the hearing. Should the court hear this case? Discuss.

4 Business and the Federal Constitution

4:1 Introduction

Chapter 1 explained that the federal Constitution establishes an important part of the basic framework for the legal environment of business. Chapter 3 examined the relationship between the Constitution and Congress and the states' power to regulate commerce. This chapter examines other significant provisions of the federal Constitution that directly affect business. This material is an important part of the background knowledge a businessperson needs when confronting legal problems.

4:2 The Constitution and the Federal–State System

The United States Supreme Court is the final authority on the meaning of the Constitution. The Constitution does not specifically provide such authority to the Court. In the 1803 case of *Marbury v Madison*,[1] however, Justice Marshall appropriated to the Court the power to pass judgment on the constitutionality of statutes, and the Court has exercised that power of *judicial review* of legislative and executive actions on many occasions. The constitutionality of a statute or executive action is decided only when parties bring a lawsuit and obtain a judgment that is appealed to the Court; the Supreme Court does not give advisory opinions on the acceptability of statutes or answer hypothetical questions for legislators or the President.

"Flexibility of the Constitution" The Constitution is not a lifeless, static instrument whose interpretation is confined to the conditions and outlook which prevailed at the time of its adoption. Nor is it a collection of dry, abstract rules. Rather, the Constitution is a flexible, vital, living document, drafted for the operation and perpetuation of American government and designed for an extended period, in war or in peace.

In determining whether a provision of the Constitution applies to a new area of law, it is of little significance that it is one with which the framers of

---

[1] 5 US (1 Cranch) 137 (1803).

the Constitution were not familiar. As explained by Supreme Court Justice Holmes:

> [W]hen we are dealing with words that also are a constituent act, like the Constitution of the United States, we must realize that they have called into life a being the development of which could not have been foreseen completely by the most gifted of its begetters. It was enough for them to realize or to hope that they had created an organism; it has taken a century and has cost their successors much sweat and blood to prove that they created a nation. The case before us must be considered in the light of our whole experience, and not merely in that of what was said a hundred years ago.[2]

Supremacy Clause The division of power between the states and the federal government under the Constitution creates the possibility of a conflict for supremacy between them. The framers of the Constitution provided for resolution of such a conflict with the *supremacy clause* [Article VI, § 2], which states that the Constitution, laws, and treaties of the United States "shall be the supreme law of the land." Hence, whenever the federal government exercises a power granted by the Constitution, any conflicting exercise of power by the states must yield to the federal power. It follows that the power of judicial review extends to the review of state laws and executive actions.

Structure of the Constitution The body of the Constitution consists of a preamble and seven articles, which are divided into sections. The first three articles provide for the division of governmental power into the Congress, the Presidency, and the judiciary. Article IV allocates power between the federal and state governments. Article V provides for the amendment process. Article VI includes the supremacy clause. Article VII provides for ratification of the Constitution.

In addition, the Constitution has been amended 26 times. The first 10 amendments were ratified in 1791 and are known as the Bill of Rights. The most recent amendment, the 18-year-old vote amendment, was ratified in 1971. Several other amendments have been proposed, but failed. The original articles and the Bill of Rights are summarized in Tables 4-1 and 4-2.

Delegated Powers Doctrine Article I, § 1, of the Constitution lodges all legislative power in Congress. The powers of Congress are specifically enumerated. Since the federal government is one of delegated powers only, every federal statute must have as its basis one of the enumerated powers. Article I, § 8, sets forth many congressional powers, such as the power to lay and collect taxes, to regulate interstate and foreign commerce, and to declare war. The amendments also grant power to Congress. For example, the Fourteenth Amendment, guaranteeing due process and equal protection of the law, has been held to grant Congress the power to legislate the preservation of these guarantees.

Necessary and Proper Clause Chapter 3 introduced the commerce clause of Article I, § 8, as the basis for the federal power to regulate commerce and as a limit on both federal and state power to regulate commerce. Article I, § 8,

---

[2] *Missouri v Holland*, 252 US 416 (1920).

TABLE 4-1

Articles of the Federal Constitution

Article I	Structure and powers of the legislative branch of government
Article II	Structure and powers of the executive branch of government
Article III	Structure and powers of the judicial branch of government
Article IV	Rights and privileges of the states and state citizens
Article V	Constitutional amendment process
Article VI	Supremacy of the Constitution
Article VII	Ratification process

TABLE 4-2

The Bill of Rights

Amendment 1	Freedom of religion; speech; press; peaceable assembly; right to petition government for redress of grievance
Amendment 2	Right to keep and bear arms
Amendment 3	Right against quartering of soldiers in private homes
Amendment 4	Freedom from unreasonable searches and seizures
Amendment 5	Right to grand jury indictment; freedom from double jeopardy; privilege against self-incrimination; right to due process of law; right to just compensation for property taken for public use
Amendment 6	Right to a speedy and public jury trial in criminal prosecutions; right to confront witnesses; compulsory process of witnesses; right to counsel
Amendment 7	Right to trial by jury in civil suits
Amendment 8	Freedom from excessive bail or cruel and unusual punishment
Amendment 9	Rights enumerated in the Constitution are not exclusive; other rights retained by the people
Amendment 10	Powers reserved to the states or to the people

also provides that the specific powers of Congress may be enlarged by the necessary and proper clause, which provides that Congress has the power "to make all laws which shall be necessary and proper for carrying into execution the foregoing powers."

4:3   The Contract Clause

Article I, § 10, of the Constitution provides that "No State shall . . . pass any . . . Law impairing the Obligation of Contracts." This clause has had a fascinating history. Originally it was intended to prevent the states from passing debtor-relief legislation that interfered with private contracts. In the early nineteenth-century cases of *Fletcher v Peck*[3] and *Trustees of Dartmouth College v Woodward*,[4] the Supreme Court applied the clause to land grants and corporate charters granted by the state. Applications of the contract clause to protect the terms of state-granted corporate charters eventually led to the

---

[3] 10 US (6 Cranch) 87 (1810).
[4] 17 US (4 Wheat) 518 (1819).

adoption of general incorporation statutes specifically subjecting new corporations to future changes in state laws. In the twentieth century, the contract
clause gave way in constitutional interpretation to the importance of the state
"police power" to provide and protect the general welfare. The apparent
demise of the contract clause came in the Depression-era case *Home Bldg. &
Loan Assoc. v Blaisdell,*[5] in which the Court upheld a Minnesota mortgage-
moratorium statute—essentially the type of debtor-relief statute the clause
was thought to prohibit.

In recent years the contract clause has been revived as a protection against
state interference with economic interests. In the 1977 case of *United States
Trust Co. v New Jersey,*[6] the Supreme Court struck down a state statute
repealing a covenant, or promise, in a bond issued by the state. In the
following case, decided a year after *United States Trust,* the Court used the
contract clause to strike down a Minnesota statute regulating an existing
private pension plan.

Allied Structural Steel Co.
v
Spannaus
438 US 234 (1978)
United States Supreme Court

FACTS: Allied maintained a pension plan for its employees, the terms of
which permitted the firm to amend or terminate the plan at any time and
for any reason. The pension contract specified that, in the event the plan
was terminated, payment to pensionholders and to those with vested
pension rights would be limited to the assets of the pension plan.
Minnesota enacted the Private Pension Benefits Protection Act under
which Allied's plan would be subject to a "pension funding charge" if
the firm terminated the plan or closed a Minnesota office. The charge
was assessed if pension funds were insufficient to cover full pensions for
all employees who had worked at least 10 years. Shortly after the Act
was passed, Allied closed a Minnesota office; several of its employees
had no vested pension rights under the plan but had worked for Allied
for 10 years or more, thus qualifying for pension rights under the new
Minnesota law. The state notified Allied that it owed a $185,000 "pen-
sion funding charge" for these employees.

ISSUE: Does the statute unconstitutionally impair Allied's contractual obligations to its employees under its pension agreement?

---

[5] 290 US 398 (1934).
[6] 431 US 1 (1977).

RESULT: Yes. The application of the statute to Allied violates the contract clause of the Constitution.

REASONING:

*   *   *

There can be no question of the impact of the Minnesota Private Pension Benefits Protection Act upon the company's contractual relationships with its employees. The Act substantially altered those relationships by superimposing pension obligations upon the company conspicuously beyond those that it had voluntarily agreed to undertake. But it does not inexorably follow that the Act, as applied to the company, violates the Contract Clause of the Constitution.

The language of the Contract Clause appears unambiguously absolute: "No State shall . . . pass any . . . Law impairing the Obligation of Contracts." U.S. Const., Art. I, § 10. The Clause is not, however, the Draconian provision that its words might seem to imply. . . .

The severity of an impairment of contractual obligations can be measured by the factors that reflect the high value the Framers placed on the protection of private contracts. Contracts enable individuals to order their personal and business affairs according to their particular needs and interests. Once arranged, those rights and obligations are binding under the law, and the parties are entitled to rely on them.

Here, the company's contracts of employment with its employees included as a fringe benefit or additional form of compensation, the pension plan. The company's maximum obligation was to set aside each year an amount based on the plan's requirements for vesting. The plan satisfied the current federal income tax code and was subject to no other legislative requirements. And, of course, the company was free to amend or terminate the pension plan at any time. The company thus had no reason to anticipate that its employees' pension rights could become vested except in accordance with the terms of the plan. It relied heavily, and reasonably, on this legitimate contractual expectation in calculating its annual contributions to the pension fund.

The effect of Minnesota's Private Pension Benefits Protection Act on this contractual obligation was severe. The company was required in 1974 to have made its contributions throughout the pre-1974 life of its plan as if employees' pension rights had vested after 10 years, instead of vesting in accord with the terms of the plan. Thus a basic term of the pension contract—one on which the company had relied for 10 years—was substantially modified. The result was that, although the company's past contributions were adequate when made, they were not adequate when computed under the 10-year statutory vesting requirement. The Act thus forced a current recalculation of the past 10 years' contributions based on the new, unanticipated 10-year vesting requirement.

Not only did the state law thus retroactively modify the compensation that the company had agreed to pay its employees from 1963 to 1974, but also it did so by changing the company's obligations in an area where the element of reliance was vital—the funding of a pension plan. . . .

Thus, the statute in question here nullifies express terms of the company's contractual obligations and imposes a completely unexpected liability in potentially disabling amounts. There is not even any provision for gradual applicability or grace periods. . . . Yet there is no showing in the record before us that this severe disruption of contractual expectations was necessary to meet an important general social problem. . . .

. . . This legislation, imposing a sudden, totally unanticipated, and substantial retroactive obligation upon the company to its employees, was not enacted to deal with a situation remotely approaching the broad and desperate emergency economic conditions of the early 1930's— conditions of which the Court in *Blaisdell* took judicial notice.

Entering a field it had never before sought to regulate, the Minnesota Legislature grossly distorted the company's existing contractual relationships with its employees by super-imposing retroactive obligations upon the company substantially beyond the terms of its employment contracts. And that burden was imposed upon the company only because it closed its office in the State.

[We] hold that if the Contract Clause means anything at all, it means that Minnesota could not constitutionally do what it tried to do to the company in this case. . . .

Stewart, Justice.

4:4 Taxes

Article I, § 8, also gives Congress the power to "lay and collect Taxes, Duties, Imposts and Excises." This taxing power has been augmented by the Sixteenth Amendment, which provides for the federal income tax:

> The Congress shall have power to lay and collect taxes on incomes, from whatever source derived, without apportionment among the several States, and without regard to any census or enumeration.

The federal individual and corporate income tax is the primary source of income for the federal government. The federal tax code, plus the regulations of the Treasury Department interpreting the tax code, comprise a vast and complex body of law—perhaps the most complicated law in human history. The impact of federal taxes on business is substantial. In this regard, it is worth noting that taxes are as much a tool of social policy as of revenue generation. Thus, the tax code contains many provisions designed to encourage or discourage particular behavior by businesses and individuals. For example, the tax provisions for political contributions are intended to encourage broad-base funding of political campaigns.

In addition to taxing income, the federal government taxes many imports and the sale of goods such as alcohol, guns, and explosives. Such taxes often are intended as a form of regulation of the sale of these items. The use of taxes in this manner has usually been upheld by the courts.

On the other hand, the states' capacity to tax business is limited by the commerce clause with respect to both interstate commerce and foreign commerce. In recent years state tax schemes that attempt to subject a portion of a multistate firm's income to state taxation have been attacked under the commerce clause. It has been well established that a state cannot tax interstate commerce discriminatorily. In *Moorman Manufacturing Co. v Bair*,[7] Iowa determined that 20 percent of an Illinois firm's gross sales were made in Iowa, and then subjected that portion of the firm's taxable income to Iowa income taxation. The firm demonstrated that a single-factor method of taxation did not produce as fair a measure of income attributable to Iowa sales as the multifactor schemes used by other states. In fact, Iowa's scheme could result in taxation of the same profits by two or more different states. Nevertheless, the Supreme Court upheld the state tax scheme since it did not grossly distort the firm's income.

State business income tax statutes have also been challenged as violative of the foreign commerce part of the commerce clause. In 1979 the Supreme Court invalidated a California personal property tax statute under which Japanese cargo containers, used only in the loading and unloading of ship cargo, were taxed.[8] The court found the taxation of those containers to be a tax on foreign commerce that could be levied only by the federal government. In 1983, however, the Supreme Court upheld a state income taxation scheme that used a formula for allocating the income derived from worldwide activities to California taxation. The plaintiff firm argued that subjecting foreign activities to state taxation constituted a regulation of foreign commerce permissible only under a federal scheme.[9] Under this decision, several states have enacted "unitary" tax laws.

 State and federal taxation is a highly complex area of law that is fraught with expensive consequences. Often it is difficult for any lawyer or accountant to determine with certainty what a firm's tax liability is. In the face of such uncertainty, it is crucial to have legal and accounting advice and tax preparation that are adequate to the task and able to make a credible assertion and defense of a firm's liability.

4:5 The Due Process Clauses of the Fifth and Fourteenth Amendments

Another Constitutional provision particularly significant to business is the Fourteenth Amendment. It was passed after the Civil War to provide for the civil rights of freed slaves, but it has been construed to have much broader application. Section 1 of the Fourteenth Amendment provides:

---

[7] 437 US 267 (1978).
[8] *Japan Line, Ltd. v County of Los Angeles*, 441 US 434 (1979).
[9] *Container Corp. of America v Franchise Tax Board*, 464 US 909 (1983).

All persons born or naturalized in the United States, and subject to the jurisdiction thereof, are citizens of the United States and of the state wherein they reside. No State shall enforce any law which shall abridge the privileges and immunities of citizens of the United States; nor shall any State deprive any person of life, liberty, or property without due process of law; nor deny to any person within its jurisdiction the equal protection of the laws.

The due process clause of the Fourteenth Amendment has its roots in the Fifth Amendment, which declares that no person shall "be deprived of life, liberty, or property without due process of law." The Fifth Amendment is a limitation on the powers of Congress (the federal government); the Fourteenth Amendment is a limitation on the powers of the states. Due process has been defined in many ways and variously described by the Supreme Court as "those principles implicit in the concept of ordered liberty," "the principles of liberty and justice which lie at the base of all our civil and political institutions," and "the principles of justice so rooted in the traditions and conscience of our people as to be ranked fundamental."

The Supreme Court has never attempted to define with precision the words "due process of law," but, through its decisions, has made clear that the term *due process of law* asserts a fundamental principle of justice rather than a specific rule of law. The Supreme Court has said that the concept of due process is not to be frozen within the confines of historical facts or discredited attitudes. Rather, it is to be interpreted in the nature of a free society seeking to advance in its standards of what is deemed reasonable and right. Representing as it does a living principle, due process is not confined within permanent definitions of what may at a given time be deemed the limits or essentials of fundamental rights.

Due process has been used to invalidate statutes that are too vague for a reasonable person to ascertain what conduct is permitted or not permitted or that give a court no fixed standard for determining what conduct violates the law. Also prohibited are state statutes, ordinances, and rules that allocate power to a state agency to terminate a person's rights without an opportunity for a fair hearing.

4:6 The Equal Protection Clause of the Fourteenth Amendment

The portion of the Fourteenth Amendment guaranteeing the equal protection of the laws requires that those who are similarly situated be treated similarly by the state. This does not mean that state law cannot create statutory schemes that classify and treat individuals and firms differently. It does mean that there must be, as a minimum, some rational basis for the classification scheme.

EXAMPLE: A state might create an employment tax reporting scheme that treats firms with fewer than five employees more favorably than firms with five or more employees. Even though the statute subjects firms in the same industry to different treatment, the scheme does not violate the equal protection clause if the state can demonstrate that the cost of the reporting scheme is significantly greater, in relation to the benefit of the report, for small employers. Similarly, a state can impose different safety standards on firms in different industries if it can demonstrate a rational relationship between the safety standards and the dangers posed by firms in the industry.

On the other hand, some classification schemes are so burdensome as to raise the presumption that they are irrational and unrelated to any valid state purpose. For example, segregating schoolchildren solely on the basis of race is regarded as so pernicious and damaging to children that virtually no supposed benefit renders school segregation rational. Similarly, other categories of classification—race, religion, national origin, and, to a lesser degree, sex—are inherently suspect and require a high degree of justification. A statute that permits Catholic-owned businesses, but not Protestant-owned businesses, to bid on state construction projects would be virtually impossible to justify under the equal protection clause. Nevertheless, a New York statute requiring state police officers to be citizens of the United States was upheld as being rationally related to a valid state purpose, in spite of the suspicion with which national origin and citizenship are viewed as classification criteria. While the equal protection clause refers only to *state actions* (including actions of political subdivisions such as cities), the concept of equal protection has been assumed to be inherent in the Fifth Amendment concept of due process and apply as well to actions of the federal government.

4:7   Freedom of Speech and the First Amendment

The First Amendment provides that "Congress shall make no law . . . abridging the freedom of speech." This guarantee of freedom of speech is regarded as the paramount right of the citizen under our form of government, because it provides the means by which the citizen may effectively protect all other rights. Most forms of speech are protected against infringement or regulation by the federal government and, through the Fourteenth Amendment, by the state or local governments.

This freedom is not absolute, but it is highly protected. The Supreme Court has exempted "fighting words," or speech that poses an immediate threat to life or limb or civil order, from First Amendment protection. Thus, the government can punish the proverbial man who falsely shouts "fire" in a crowded theater, or who intentionally incites a frenzied crowd to lawless destruction. On the other hand, the capacity of government to anticipate and prevent speech based on its probable content is highly restricted. In general, it can be limited by reasonable *time, place, and manner restrictions.* Similarly, the government can prohibit and punish public dissemination of pornographic material that offends local standards of decency.

The government also can sanction, through private civil lawsuits, speech that is *defamatory* (see Chapter 5) and injurious to the reputation of an individual. To a great extent, however, defamatory speech that injures the reputation of a *public figure* or concerns matters of *public affairs* is subject to a high degree of protection. The plaintiff in such a defamation case must show that the speaker (or writer) knowingly said false and injurious things about a person—that the speaker acted with *malice*. In effect, there is a privilege to defame public figures where one does so in good-faith comment on public matters. This principle was established in *New York Times Co. v Sullivan*,[10] and its limits have been the subject of many federal cases. A recent case is considered below. In it, a credit reporting agency—which disseminates information about the creditworthiness of individuals—claimed that it had First Amendment protection in the dissemination of credit information.

Dun & Bradstreet, Inc.

v

Greenmoss Builders, Inc.
86 L Ed 2d 593 (1985)
United States Supreme Court

FACTS: Dun & Bradstreet sent a report to five of its subscriber firms, indicating that Greenmoss had filed for bankruptcy. The information was false and resulted in a loss of business and income for Greenmoss. Greenmoss sued for defamation and received a substantial damage award. Dun & Bradstreet sought to have the judgment overturned.

ISSUE: Does the First Amendment give a credit reporting agency the right to speak, even if the content of the speech is false and injurious, so long as the report is not given out with knowledge of its falsity, or maliciously?

RESULT: No. There is no requirement of malice for recovery in defamation if the plaintiff is not a public figure and the speech does not concern a public matter.

REASONING:

*   *   *

In *New York Times Co. v. Sullivan*, . . . the Court . . . held that the First Amendment limits the reach of state defamation laws. That case concerned a public official's recovery of damages for the publication of an advertisement criticizing police conduct in a civil rights demonstration. As the Court noted, the advertisement concerned "one of the major public issues of our time." . . . Noting that "freedom of expression *upon public questions* is secured by the First Amendment," . . . (emphasis added), and that "debate *on public issues* should be uninhibited, robust, and wide-open," . . . (emphasis added), the Court held that a public

---

[10] 376 US 254 (1964).

official cannot recover damages for defamatory falsehood unless he proves that the false statement was made with " 'actual malice'—that is, with knowledge that it was false or with reckless disregard of whether it was false or not,". . . . In later cases, all involving public issues, the Court extended this same constitutional protection to libels of public figures. . . .

In *Gertz* [v. *Robert Welch, Inc.*, 418 U. S. 323 (1974)], we held that the fact that expression concerned a public issue did not by itself entitle the libel defendant to the constitutional protections of *New York Times.* These protections, we found, were not "justified solely by reference to the interest of the press and broadcast media in immunity from liability." . . . Rather, they represented "an accommodation between [First Amendment] concern[s] and the limited state interest present in the context of libel actions brought by public persons." . . . In libel actions brought by private persons we found the competing interests different. Largely because private persons have not voluntarily exposed themselves to increased risk of injury from defamatory statements and because they generally lack effective opportunities for rebutting such statements, . . . we found that the State possessed a "strong and legitimate . . . interest in compensating private individuals for injury to reputation." . . . Balancing this stronger state interest against the same First Amendment interest at stake in *New York Times*, we held that a State could not allow recovery of presumed and punitive damages absent a showing of "actual malice." Nothing in our opinion, however, indicated that this same balance would be struck regardless of the type of speech involved.

We have never considered whether the *Gertz* balance obtains when the defamatory statements involve no issue of public concern. To make this determination, we must . . . balance the State's interest in compensating private individuals for injury to their reputation against the First Amendment interest in protecting this type of expression. This state interest is identical to the one weighed in *Gertz*. There we found that it was "strong and legitimate." . . .

The First Amendment interest, on the other hand, is less important than the one weighed in *Gertz*. We have long recognized that not all speech is of equal First Amendment importance. It is speech on " 'matters of public concern' " that is "at the heart of the First Amendment's protection" . . . :

> "The First Amendment 'was fashioned to assure unfettered interchange of ideas for the bringing about of political and social changes desired by the people.' . . . '[S]peech concerning public affairs is more than self-expression; it is the essence of self-government.' . . . Accordingly, the Court has frequently reaffirmed that speech on public issues occupies the " 'highest rung of the hierarchy of First Amendment values,' " and is entitled to special protection. . . . "

In contrast, speech on matters of purely private concern is of less First Amendment concern. . . . As a number of state courts, including the court below, have recognized, the role of the Constitution in regulating state libel law is far more limited when the concerns that activated *New York Times* and *Gertz* are absent. In such a case,

> "[t]here is no threat to the free and robust debate of public issues; there is no potential interference with a meaningful dialogue of ideas concerning self-government; and there is no threat of liability causing a reaction of self-censorship by the press. The facts of the present case are wholly without the First Amendment concerns with which the Supreme Court of the United States has been struggling." . . .

The only remaining issue is whether petitioner's credit report involved a matter of public concern. In a related context, we have held that "[w]hether . . . speech addresses a matter of public concern must be determined by [the expression's] content, form, and context . . . as revealed by the whole record." . . .

These factors indicate that petitioner's credit report concerns no public issue. It was speech solely in the individual interest of the speaker and its specific business audience. . . . This particular interest warrants no special protection when—as in this case—the speech is wholly false and clearly damaging to the victim's business reputation. . . . Moreover, since the credit report was made available to only five subscribers, who, under the terms of the subscription agreement, could not disseminate it further, it cannot be said that the report involves any "strong interest in the free flow of commercial information." . . . There is simply no credible argument that this type of credit reporting requires special protection to ensure that "debate on public issues [will] be uninhibited, robust, and wide-open." . . .

In addition, the speech here, like advertising, is hardy and unlikely to be deterred by incidental state regulation. . . . It is solely motivated by the desire for profit, which, we have noted, is a force less likely to be deterred than others. . . . Arguably, the reporting here was also more objectively verifiable than speech deserving of greater protection. . . . In any case, the market provides a powerful incentive to a credit reporting agency to be accurate, since false credit reporting is of no use to creditors. Thus, any incremental "chilling" effect of libel suits would be of decreased significance.

We conclude that permitting recovery of presumed and punitive damages in defamation cases absent a showing of "actual malice" does not violate the First Amendment when the defamatory statements do not involve matters of public concern. . . .

Powell, Justice.

Businesses may also seek to exercise the freedom of speech through their attempts to influence government actions or through business activities such as advertising. In *First Nat. Bank v Bellotti*,[11] the Supreme Court held that corporations are accorded the same protection as individual citizens in their efforts to speak on public issues and to influence political thought. Where the content of the speech involves a commercial proposition, however, corporations and businesses are subject to reasonable regulation for the protection of the public interest. Thus, the Federal Trade Commission can punish commercial speech as deceptive advertising, even though it cannot punish political speech as deceptive. Recently the federal Court of Appeals for the Second Circuit upheld the Securities and Exchange Commission's revocation of an investment advisor license to the publisher of an investment newsletter following the investment advisor's conviction of criminal misconduct. The plaintiff argued that his investment advice was speech protected by the First Amendment.

4:8   The Fourth Amendment: Unreasonable Searches and Seizures

The Fourth Amendment provides:

> The right of the people to be secure in their persons, houses, papers, and effects, against unreasonable searches and seizures, shall not be violated, and no Warrants shall issue, but upon probable cause. . . .

This provision of the Constitution has become important to businesses that seek to protect their business records and their operations from unwanted government intrusion or seizure. In general, most business records and most business operations are subject to inspection by a government agency with the appropriate statutory authority. This right is subject to the protection of privileges that may otherwise protect the records. In addition, forceable searches and seizures require that a warrant be obtained prior to the search. To obtain a warrant, the government must prove that it has probable cause to believe a crime has been committed, or, in the case of regulatory searches, such as safety inspections, that the search is made pursuant to a reasonable and fair method of selecting search sites.

The following case represents the Supreme Court's most recent treatment of this problem.

Marshall
v
Barlow's, Inc.
436 US 307 (1978)
United States Supreme Court

FACTS: Section 8(a) of the Occupational Safety and Health Act of 1970 (OSHA) empowered agents of the Secretary of Labor to search the work area of any facility subject to the Act. The purpose of the search was to

---

[11] 435 US 765 (1978).

inspect for safety hazards and violations of OSHA regulations. When an OSHA inspector entered Barlow's business and asked to search the nonpublic work area of the business without a warrant, Barlow refused entry on the ground that the unwarranted search violated his rights under the Fourth Amendment.

ISSUE: Does an unwarranted regulatory safety search of a business like Barlow's violate the warrant provisions of the Fourth Amendment?

RESULT: Yes. Searches of traditionally unregulated businesses such as Barlow's must be made pursuant to a warrant.

REASONING:

*   *   *

The Warrant Clause of the Fourth Amendment protects commercial buildings as well as private homes. To hold otherwise would belie the origin of that Amendment, and the American colonial experience. An important forerunner of the first 10 Amendments to the United States Constitution, the Virginia Bill of Rights, specifically opposed "general warrants, whereby an officer or messenger may be commanded to search suspected places without evidence of a fact committed." The general warrant was a recurring point of contention in the Colonies immediately preceding the Revolution. The particular offensiveness it engendered was acutely felt by the merchants and businessmen whose premises and products were inspected for compliance with the several parliamentary revenue measures that most irritated the colonists. . . . Against this background, it is untenable that the ban on warrantless searches was not intended to shield places of business as well as of residence.

This Court has already held that warrantless searches are generally unreasonable, and that this rule applies to commercial premises as well as homes. . . .

The Secretary urges that an exception from the search warrant requirement has been recognized for "pervasively regulated business[es]," . . . and for "closely regulated" industries "long subject to close supervision and inspection." . . . These cases are indeed exceptions, but they represent responses to relatively unique circumstances. Certain industries have such a history of government oversight that no reasonable expectation of privacy . . . could exist for a proprietor over the stock of such an enterprise. Liquor . . . and firearms . . . are industries of this type; when an enterpreneur embarks upon such a business, he has voluntarily chosen to subject himself to a full arsenal of governmental regulation. . . . The clear import of our cases is that the closely regulated industry of the type involved in [the cases discussed above] is the exception. The Secretary would make it the rule. Invoking the Walsh-Healey Act of 1936, . . . the Secretary attempts to support a conclusion that all businesses involved in interstate commerce have long been subjected to close supervision of employee safety and health conditions.

But the degree of federal involvement in employee working circumstances has never been of the order of specificity and pervasiveness that OSHA mandates. It is quite unconvincing to argue that the imposition of minimum wages and maximum hours on employers who contracted with the Government under the Walsh-Healey Act prepared the entirety of American interstate commerce for regulation of working conditions to the minutest detail. Nor can any but the most fictional sense of voluntary consent to later searches be found in the single fact that one conducts a business affecting interstate commerce; under current practice and law, few businesses can be conducted without having some effect on interstate commerce. . . .

. . . The authority to make warrantless searches devolves almost unbridled discretion upon executive and administrative officers, particularly those in the field, as to when to search and whom to search. A warrant, by contrast, would provide assurances from a neutral officer that the inspection is reasonable under the Constitution, is authorized by statute, and is pursuant to an administrative plan containing specific neutral criteria. Also, a warrant would then and there advise the owner of the scope and objects of the search, beyond which limits the inspector is not expected to proceed. These are important functions for a warrant to perform, functions which underlie the Court's prior decisions that the Warrant Clause applies to inspections for compliance with regulatory statutes. . . . We conclude that the concerns expressed by the Secretary do not suffice to justify warrantless inspections under OSHA or vitiate the general constitutional requirement that for a search to be reasonable a warrant must be obtained. . . .

White, Justice.

Key Concepts and Terms

- The federal Constitution allocates power among the federal government, the states, and the people. The system under which power was divided between the central government and the states is known as *federalism.*

- The United States Supreme Court has appropriated the power to determine the meaning of the Constitution as the occasion arises in the context of judicial decision-making.

- The Constitution is a flexible, vital document rather than a collection of dry, abstract rules.

- The Constitution establishes itself, and the laws made pursuant to it, as the "highest law of the land."

- The Constitution consists of seven articles and 26 amendments.

- Congress has not only the specific powers enumerated under the Constitution but also those "necessary and proper" for the exercise of the enumerated powers.
- Article I, § 8, of the Constitution and the Sixteenth Amendment give Congress substantial power to tax.
- The state taxing power is limited by both the interstate and the foreign commerce aspects of the commerce clause.
- The due process clauses of the Fifth and Fourteenth Amendments embody "those principles implicit in the concept of ordered liberty."
- The equal protection clause of the Fourteenth Amendment requires that states have a rational basis for treating different individuals differently in legislation. If the basis for the classification is "suspect," the state must show that it is protecting a very strong interest in doing so.
- With few exceptions, government can subject speech to reasonable time, place, and manner restrictions, but it cannot prohibit speech altogether based on the content of the speech.
- Under the Constitution, businesses enjoy the same protection that individuals do concerning warrantless searches of their premises.

- Commercial Speech
- Contract Clause
- Delegated Powers Doctrine
- Due Process
- Equal Protection Clause
- Federalism
- Freedom of Speech
- Judicial Review
- Malice

- Necessary and Proper Clause
- Public Affairs
- Public Figure
- Supremacy Clause
- Time, Place, and Manner Restrictions
- Unitary Taxes
- Unreasonable Searches and Seizures

Questions and Case Problems

1. Why do the courts have the power of judicial review of legislative and executive action? Would it be feasible for Congress to have the final say over the constitutionality of legislation, and the President to have the final say over the constitutionality of executive and administrative action?

2. Traditionally, courts do not give "advisory opinions" to parties who seek to test the legality of a proposed action or theory. Rather, courts wait until an actual "case or controversy" between two or more adverse parties with a real conflict is brought to the court. Do you see any reason for courts to take this passive posture?

3. Why would the framers of the Constitution seek to prevent the states from passing debtor-relief statutes that interfered with contracts, such as loan agreements, that created debts? In the *Blaisdell* case mentioned in the text, Minnesota's statute prevented the use of the courts to enforce the terms of mortgages. The state argued, successfully, that the statute did not interfere with the contract between the debtor

and the creditor, only with the creditor's remedy for nonpayment. Would this argument persuade you if you were a judge?

4. Could a state levy a charge against persons entering the state on public highways? Could it levy a *per capita* "landing fee" against persons landing or taking off in airplanes from public airports?

5. If you were accused of serious academic misconduct, such as plagiarism or cheating on an exam, what procedures would you expect to be entitled to at your college or university? To what extent do these procedures derive from the due process clause of the federal Constitution?

6. The due process clause forbids deprivation of property without due process of law. Does this suggest that the framers were interested in the protection of property as well as liberty from intrusion by the state? Are you aware of any other aspects of the Constitution that might support this hypothesis?

7. Why are the due process and equal protection clauses of the Constitution applicable only against the state and federal governments? Why did the drafters of these amendments not make private businesses and institutions subject to these clauses of the Constitution?

8. Review the Supreme Court's opinion in the *Dun & Bradstreet* case (see page 62). What are the major purposes of the First Amendment?

9. A regulated public utility seeks to influence public opinion about the level of utility rates and services in order to improve its public relations position in seeking a rate increase from the public service commission that regulates the utility. It proposes to insert flyers in its bills, explaining its position to its customers. Can the commission pass a rule forbidding the utility from communicating with its rate-payers about this issue through the utility bill? Or would that interfere impermissibly with the firm's First Amendment right to speech?

10. If you were a manager of a company that was inspected frequently for employee health and safety standards, would you insist on seeing a search warrant from the inspector? Should a public health inspector be required to obtain a search warrant before making a surprise inspection of a restaurant kitchen? What is the value of a search warrant to the business or restaurant owner?

PART TWO

Torts and Crimes

Introductory Comments

This part of the book discusses the law of torts and the law of crimes. Torts involve wrongs against others for which the law grants compensation to the injured person. Crimes involve wrongs against society which society seeks to punish. Both branches of law may be properly regarded as "a battleground of social theory"[1] because both involve public policy decisions about what types of social interaction are acceptable. The questions of how reasonable a person's conduct is and when a person can be held liable for acts that injure another person are questions that are confronted in tort law.

The word "tort," a French word introduced into the English language after the Norman Conquest comes from the Latin "tortus," meaning "twisted," and translates to the English word "wrong." Broadly speaking, a tort is any civil (as opposed to criminal) wrong other than a breach of contract.

Individuals and corporations alike may be liable in tort for injuries—in some cases, injuries they did not intend to cause, particularly those that resulted from defective products or services and dangerous premises. Throughout the chapters in this part, potential (yet frequently hidden) areas of a businessperson's tort liability are examined, and ways to reduce or eliminate tort risks in modern business are suggested.

---

[1] William L. Prosser, *The Law of Torts.*

Oliver Wendell Holmes, the American judge who is often characterized as the greatest intellect in the history of the English-speaking judiciary, said that law is a seamless web. This is illustrated often in the relationship between tort and criminal law. Chapters 5 and 6 introduce the law of torts and the major theories of tort liability. Chapter 7 introduces criminal law, while Chapter 8 focuses more narrowly on the types of crimes peculiar to the business environment.

5 The Law of Torts

5:1   Introduction

A *tort* is a civil wrong committed against an individual. When a person is a victim of a tort, he or she may claim and receive a cash award through a court action to compensate for the harm suffered. This award is referred to as civil damages. A tort may be committed by individuals, corporations, or associations. A person or entity who commits a tort is called a tortfeasor. In tort law a person who commits an act, whether it is tortious or not, is called an actor.

Two distinctions must be made at this point. One is that a tort is a civil wrong that does not result from a breach of contract. A breach of contract is a failure of one person to act in a specific manner agreed to by both parties to the contract;[1] it is a breach of the parties' duty to be bound by their agreement. The tortfeasor, in contrast, breaches a more general duty—the duty to act in a manner that would not be harmful to others.

The other distinction is the distinction between a tort and a crime. A criminal act is intentionally harmful and is considered to be committed against society in general. Furthermore, a criminal act is punishable; the actor, if found guilty, is fined, imprisoned, or executed.[2] A tortious act, on the other hand, need not be intentional (although it can be). Also, as mentioned above, a tort is committed against an individual rather than against society, and the tortfeasor is ordered to pay damages to the victim rather than being fined, imprisoned, or executed. It should be noted, however, that a given act, such as striking another person without a legitimate excuse, can be both a crime and a tort.

Joint Tortfeasors   Joint tortfeasors are two or more persons who unite in committing a tort or whose acts injure a third person. A person who joins others in committing a tort cannot escape liability by showing that the others are also liable. Neither is the fact that a third person cooperated in the wrong a justification for the joint tortfeasor's misconduct. Joint tortfeasors are jointly

---

[1] Mutual assent in contract law is discussed in Chapter 10.
[2] Crimes are discussed in Chapter 4. White-collar crime is discussed in Chapter 8.

and severally liable, which means that the recovery may come from one or all joint tortfeasors.

Intent   As used in tort law, the term *intent* means the intent to commit the wrongful act, but not necessarily the intent to do harm or injure anyone. Thus, to prove that an actor is liable for a tort, it need be shown only that his intent affects a legally protected interest in a way not permitted by law. In other words, the actor's intent need not be immoral, malicious, or hostile to constitute an intent to commit a tort. To prove intent it must also be shown that the actor knew or believed that certain results were substantially certain to follow from his conduct. This knowledge or belief is determined on what is called the objective basis—what the reasonable person can be expected to know or believe under the same circumstances. The objective basis must be distinguished from the subjective basis which would be attempting to determine what the actor was actually thinking at the time the tort was committed.

EXAMPLE: As a practical joke, Jack pulls a chair out from under Jill as she begins to sit, causing her to fall and sustain a hip fracture. Although Jack actually meant Jill no harm, a court could reasonably find that he knew with substantial certainty that Jill would attempt to sit down where the chair had been and could fall and be injured. Hence, Jack had the knowledge required to support a finding of intent for tort liability. His intent was to do an act that he could have reasonably foreseen would cause injury to another.

5:2   Invasion of Personal Rights

Some intentional torts take the form of interfering with or invading a person's right to be secure in his or her own body, physically and mentally, and the right simply "to be let alone." Invasion of these rights is not restricted to economic injury, but concerns the integrity of the individual's person, or being.

Battery   A *battery* is the intentional touching of, or harmful or offensive contact with, a person's body or things closely attached to it without the person's consent. To constitute battery, the contact need not cause actual physical harm. It is sufficient that the contact be offensive or insulting, on the theory that a person's right not to be touched without consent is a legally protected interest.

Transferred Intent   If a person intends to commit a battery on a particular person, but through error commits the battery on a third person, he will be considered to be guilty of battery under the doctrine of *transferred intent.* For example, if an employer strikes at an employee and unintentionally hits another employee nearby, the employer will be guilty of battery on the injured employee. Under the doctrine of transferred intent, the employer's intent to commit a battery on *someone* will be "transferred" to the person actually battered.

Assault An *assault* is an act—not mere words—that causes a person fear or apprehension of immediate harmful or offensive contact. The elements of assault are (1) the act, (2) the actor's intent, (3) the target party's fear or apprehension, and (4) the causal relation between the act and the target party's fear or apprehension. The actor's actual present ability to cause the threatened damage need not be shown to establish the tort of assault. Thus, if a person points an unloaded gun at another person, threatening to shoot, there is an assault, because the target party, unaware that the gun is unloaded, will be fearful or apprehensive. It should be noted that apprehension is not the same thing as fear; the target party can be confident of avoiding the actor's threatened force (not be afraid), but the latter will still be liable for assault simply for causing the target party's apprehension of the assault.

Defenses to Assault and Battery The two significant defenses to the tort of assault and battery are *consent* and *privilege*. The plaintiff's consent to participate in certain acts that would otherwise give rise to assault or battery will relieve the defendant of liability. The consent may be expressed or implied, by words or conduct. If two men, for example, engage in a fight, the injured party cannot sue for assault and battery because he consented to the fight. The other defense is privilege. One may be privileged, for example, to use force for self-defense, defense of others, or defense of property. The force must be reasonable under the circumstances and cannot go beyond the necessity of the situation. Force likely to cause death or serious bodily harm may be used in self-defense only if the user of such force *reasonably* believes that the other person's conduct will result in the user's death or serious bodily harm. There is no right to retaliate, and when the danger has passed, the privilege of self-defense expires.

Malicious Prosecution Malicious prosecution is the institution by one person of an unsuccessful, unwarranted legal proceeding against another person, with actual or implied malice, resulting in damage. According to most courts, the same principles govern regardless of whether the malicious prosecution was a criminal prosecution or a civil or administrative proceeding. Some states limit liability for the prosecution of civil suits to those actions in which the present plaintiff—the defendant in the malicious prosecution—was deprived of personal liberty or suffered injury to property or business. To recover for damages, the present plaintiff must show, in a suit against the person who instituted the malicious prosecution, that this person lacked probable cause for filing the original proceeding, whether criminal or civil. The question of probable cause depends on the honest and reasonable belief of the party commencing the prosecution or action.

A defense to a suit for malicious prosecution is the good faith reliance on the advice of counsel. In other words, the defendant in the malicious prosecution suit (who was the plaintiff in the original suit) can claim that his attorney advised him to file the original suit. Of course, the defendant must show that he fully and truthfully disclosed all facts of the case to his attorney. It should be noted that the attorney cannot be held liable for advising or prosecuting a proceeding for the client in good faith, regardless of whether the client may be liable.

Invasion of Privacy   The right to privacy has been defined as the right to be left alone, to be free from unwarranted publicity, and to live without unwarranted interference by the public or third persons in matters in which they are not concerned. The right of privacy is an independent legal right. The *Restatement of Torts* states that a person who unreasonably and seriously interferes with another's interest in not having his affairs known to others, or his likeness exhibited to the public, is liable to the party whose privacy he invaded.[3]

Through judicial decisions, the tort of *invasion of privacy* has come to include four kinds of interference with a person's right to be left alone: (1) intrusion on the plaintiff's solitude or into the plaintiff's private affairs; (2) public disclosure of embarassing private facts about the plaintiff; (3) publicity placing the plaintiff in a false light in the public eye; and (4) appropriation, for the defendant's advantage, of the plaintiff's name or likeness.

Development of the tort of invasion of privacy—as a separate and distinct tort—is a graphic example of how the courts and legislatures created a "new legal right." In the following decision, the court "creates" the tort of invasion of privacy in a state where there was no statute or previous decision. Note that the court discusses how courts in other jurisdictions have dealt with this new tort and explains why it is important, in terms of public policy, that this tort be recognized in its own jurisdiction.

<hr>

Hamberger
v
Eastman
206 A2d 239 (1964)
New Hampshire Supreme Court

FACTS: The plaintiffs, husband and wife, rented a home from the defendant. The defendant, who lived next door, placed an electronic listening device ("bug") in their bedroom "capable of transmitting and recording any sounds and voices originating in said bedroom." The listening device was connected to the defendant's house and was hooked up to a tape recorder. The plaintiffs brought suit for invasion of privacy. The defendant moved to dismiss the case on the ground that the facts stated no recognized cause of action. The trial judge transferred the case to the state supreme court for a ruling.

ISSUE: Can a person recover for breach of privacy in New Hampshire?

---

[3] *Restatement (Second) of Torts* § 867 (1965).

RESULT: Yes. One can recover damages for breach of privacy, depending on the facts of the case.

REASONING:

*   *   *

The question presented is whether the right of privacy is recognized in this state. There is no controlling statute and no previous decision in this jurisdiction which decides the question. Inasmuch as invasion of the right of privacy is not a single tort but consists of four distinct torts, it is probably more concrete and accurate to state the issue in the present case to be whether this state recognizes that intrusion upon one's physical and mental solitude or seclusion is a tort. . . .

In capsule summary the invasion of the right of privacy developed as an independent and distinct tort from the classic and famous article by Warren and Brandeis, The Right to Privacy, 4 Harv.L.Rev. 193 (1890), although Judge Cooley had discussed "the right to be let alone" some years previously. . . . In 1902 the New York Court of Appeals decided that the right of privacy did not have "an abiding place in our jurisprudence." The following year the New York Legislature acted promptly to remedy this deficiency. Shortly thereafter in 1905 *Pavesich v New England Life Ins. Co.*, 122 Ga. 190, 50 S.E. 68 upheld the right of privacy and became the leading case on the subject. Since that time the right of privacy has been given protection in a majority of the jurisdictions in this country, generally without benefit of statute, and only a small minority have rejected the concept and some of these minority decisions are not recent. . . .

The four kinds of invasion comprising the law of privacy include: (1) intrusion upon the plaintiff's physical and mental solitude or seclusion; (2) public disclosure of private facts; (3) publicity which places the plaintiff in a false light in the public eye; (4) appropriation, for the defendant's benefit or advantage, of the plaintiff's name or likeness. In the present case, we are concerned only with the tort of intrusion upon the plaintiffs' solitude or seclusion. . . .

The tort of intrusion upon the plaintiff's solitude or seclusion is not limited to a physical invasion of his home or his room or his quarters. . . .

We have not searched for cases where the bedroom of husband and wife has been "bugged" but it should not be necessary—by way of understatement—to observe that this is the type of intrusion that would be offensive to any person of ordinary sensibilities. What married "people do in the privacy of their bedroom is their own business so long as they are not hurting anyone else." Ernst and Loth, For Better or Worse, 79 (1952). The Restatement, Torts s. 867 provides that "a person who unreasonably and seriously interferes with another's interest in not having his affairs known to others . . . is liable to the other." As is pointed out in *comment* d, "liability exists only if the defendant's conduct was such that he should have realized that it would be offensive to persons of ordinary sensibilities. It is only where the intrusion has gone beyond the limits of decency that liability accrues. These limits are exceeded where intimate details of the life of one who has never manifested a desire to have publicity are exposed to the public. . . . "

The defendant contends that the right of privacy should not be recognized on the facts of the present case as they appear in the pleadings because there are no allegations that anyone listened or overheard any sounds or voices originating from the plaintiffs' bedroom. The tort of intrusion on the plaintiffs' solitude or seclusion does not require publicity and communication to third persons although this would affect the amount of damages. . . . The defendant also contends that the right of privacy is not violated unless something has been published, written or printed and that oral publicity is not sufficient. Recent cases make it clear that this is not a requirement. . . .

If the peeping Tom, the big ear and the electronic eavesdropper (whether ingenious or ingenuous) have a place in the hierarchy of social values, it ought not to be at the expense of a married couple minding their own business in the seclusion of their bedroom who have never asked for or by their conduct deserved a potential projection of their private conversations and actions to their landlord or to others. Whether actual or potential such "publicity with respect to private matters of purely personal concern is an injury to personality. It impairs the mental peace and comfort of the individual and may produce suffering more acute than that produced by a mere bodily injury." III Pound, Jurisprudence 58 (1959). The use of parabolic microphones and sonic wave devices designed to pick up conversations in a room without entering it and at a considerable distance away makes the problem far from fanciful. Dash, Schwartz & Knowlton, The Eavesdroppers pp. 346–358 (1959). . . .

For the purposes of the present case it is sufficient to hold that the invasion of the plaintiffs' solitude or seclusion, as alleged in the pleadings, was a violation of their right of privacy and constituted a tort for which the plaintiffs may recover damages to the extent that they can prove them. "Certainly, no right deserves greater protection, for, as Emerson has well said, 'solitude, the safeguard of mediocrity, is to genius the stern friend.' " Ezer, Intrusion on Solitude: Herein of Civil Rights and Civil Wrongs, 21 Law in Transition 63, 75 (1961). . . .

Kenison, Chief Justice.

5:3   False Imprisonment

False imprisonment is the intentional detention of a person, with that person's knowledge and without his or her consent, within boundaries for any length of time. The detention may be caused by the imposition of either actual or apparent physical boundaries. It is not necessary that there be confinement in a jail or a prison. The tort may be committed by acts or words, or both, or by merely operating on the individual's will, without personal violence. The confinement constituting false imprisonment has particular relevance to a businessperson since the tort may arise from a person's detention in a hospital, mental institution, restaurant, office, store, or even public street.

It is not necessary that the person be *totally* imprisoned to support the tort. False imprisonment will arise if there is no "reasonable avenue of exit" available; an exit is not reasonable if it is unknown to the restrained party, requires taking risks to escape, is dangerous, or is simply discomforting.

Shoplifter Detention   As pointed out by one court, "[t]here are few more horrifying experiences than that of being suddenly snatched from a peaceful and orderly existence and placed in the helpless position of having one's liberty restrained, under the accusation of a crime."[4] The most prevalent occasion of the tort of false imprisonment is the detention of a person who is wrongfully suspected to be a shoplifter. One reason that this tort arises so frequently is reflected in the statistics which show more than five billion dollars' worth of goods is shoplifted annually from the nation's retail stores, and approximately one person in fifteen entering a retail store steals merchandise worth more than five dollars.

Defenses   A defense to an allegation of false imprisonment is the so-called *shopkeeper's privilege.* As the name suggests, this is a storekeeper's privilege to detain a person if he or she has a reasonable belief that the person shoplifted and to conduct an investigation in a reasonable manner. This reasonable belief is known as probable cause. In some states there is legislation that permits detention of customers reasonably suspected of shoplifting. Such legislation constitutes a justification for the merchant's actions. The following decision illustrates how the shopkeeper's privilege does *not* apply. Note the court's detailed discussion of the facts that demonstrate that there was no reasonable cause for believing the plaintiff had shoplifted.

Great Atlantic & Pacific Tea Co.

v

Paul

261 A2d 731 (1970)

Maryland Supreme Court

FACTS: Paul was shopping in an A & P supermarket when he was accosted and detained by Parker, the store's second assistant manager. Paul subsequently sued the store for assault and battery, slander, and false imprisonment.

---

[4] *Halliburton-Abbott Co. v Hodge*, 44 P2d 122 (1935).

ISSUE: Was the shopkeeper legally justified in his detention of the plaintiff?

RESULT: No. The shopkeeper lacked the basis for a reasonable belief that the plaintiff had stolen goods, and thus had no legal justification for detaining him.

REASONING:

*   *   *

This case comes before us on appeal from an action for assault and battery, slander and false imprisonment. It involves as appellant The Great Atlantic and Pacific Tea Co., Inc., the owner of the nationally known chain of A & P food stores, and as appellee John Joseph Paul, a retired police officer suffering from a recent heart condition. On the charge that one of A & P's employees, John Parker, falsely accused the appellee of shoplifting, frisked him, and unlawfully detained him, Paul recovered $10,000 compensatory and $30,000 punitive damages.

Still in a convalescent stage Mr. Paul, in civilian garb, went shopping at his local A & P store in Hillcrest Heights, Maryland, on December 20, 1967. So recent had been his heart attack that this was one of the first times he had ventured out in his automobile. The Hillcrest Heights store was a typical supermarket with checkout counters in the front, many longitudinal rows of self-service aisles in the rear, and of course the usual fleet of shopping carts for the customers' convenience. There was no requirement that a customer must use a cart. On this occasion, due to heavy crowds in the store, Mr. Paul left his cart at the end of one aisle and slowly proceeded to examine carefully the labels of various articles of food to make sure they complied with his strict postcardiac diet. Having examined and selected a particular item he would then return to his cart, deposit the goods and go in search of other merchandise.

Mr. Parker, the second assistant manager, testified that he considered this method of shopping somewhat unusual, and his attention having been attracted, he observed Mr. Paul's shopping techniques for approximately twenty minutes. Although Mr. Paul was a regular shopper at this A & P and known to a number of employees there, Mr. Parker, a relatively new addition to the store, did not know him. Upon completion of his observation Parker came to the conclusion that Paul had taken a can of flea and tick spray and had placed it in his coat pocket with the apparent intention of shoplifting. The policy of A & P on shoplifting as testified to by the manager of the store in question was to let each employee "use his own judgment" as to what steps should be taken. He further testified that Parker was authorized to do what was done in this case.

The testimony conflicts widely at this point. Parker testified he merely questioned Paul about a can of flea and tick spray that had been in his cart earlier. He did not see Paul secrete this item anywhere, but assumed he had because it was no longer in the cart and in his opinion Paul had not had sufficient time to return the spray to its proper place on the shelf. He said appellee became nervous and defensive, demanding to see the manager. Parker said he never touched Paul, there was no commotion and there were few customers in the store. Paul testified that Parker accosted him in the middle of an aisle and demanded in a loud voice to know what he had done with the spray. When Paul said he did not have such an item Parker replied, "Don't tell me, you goddamn thief. You got it in your coat." Paul further testified that when this occurred some twenty-five to thirty customers in the immediate vicinity of the aisle turned and stared, and continued to watch as Parker roughly frisked him, knocking over a display of cans and loudly repeating his accusation of thievery. His testimony continues that Parker then grabbed him by the arm and forced him to march to the manager's office at the front of the store, attracting the attention of shoppers waiting at the check-out counters. No flea spray or any other item belonging to A & P was found on Paul's person. Appellee stated as a result of the experience he was severely upset and reached home in his automobile only with difficulty. . . .

Appellant . . . claims error was committed in the false imprisonment phase of the case. False imprisonment and false arrest are common law torts that apparently differ only in terminology. . . . The necessary elements of a case for false imprisonment are a deprivation of the liberty of another without his consent and without legal justification. . . .

The term legal justification has created some confusion in other courts. . . . This confusion arises because of the frequent statement that probable cause is not a defense to an action for false imprisonment but legal justification is. Probable cause, however, may be shown in mitigation of punitive damages. . . .

Appellant urges that Maryland should adopt the rule expressed in Restatement (Second) of Torts, Sec. 120 A (1965): "One who reasonably believes that another has tortiously taken a chattel [movable personal property] upon his premises, or has failed to make due cash payment for a chattel purchased or services rendered there, is privileged, without arresting the other, to detain him on the premises for the time necessary for a reasonable investigation of the facts." Appellant cites several jurisdictions which have adopted this qualified privilege. It offered an instruction substantially embodying the Restatement language at the trial level, and it is refusal to instruct the jury in accordance with this rule that it assigns as error. It urges strenuously that probable cause should be a defense in this limited situation, detailing the growing problem of shoplifting in this country. It states that the modern self-service style of retail selling makes the shopkeeper powerless to protect his goods unless Section 120 A is adopted in substance. Without being facetious we note that shoplifting may be regarded as the price merchants pay for the success of modern merchandising; goods alluringly displayed to stimulate "impulse buying" inevitably also stimulate "impulse taking." . . .

Whatever technical distinction there may be between an "arrest" and a "detention" the test whether legal justification existed in a particular case has been judged by the principles applicable to the law of arrest. A shopkeeper under these principles has only the rights of a private person. In Maryland a private person has authority to arrest without a warrant only when a) there is a felony being committed in his presence or when a felony has in fact been committed whether or not in his presence, and the arrester has reasonable ground (probable cause) to believe the person he arrests has committed it; or b) a misdemeanor is being committed in the presence or view of the arrester which amounts to a breach of the peace. . . . Breach of the peace signifies disorderly, dangerous conduct disruptive of public peace and it is clear that the usual shoplifting incident does not fit within this category. . . . Since most shoplifters steal inexpensive items, . . . the only crime they are generally guilty of is petit larceny, a misdemeanor. . . . Thus a private person has no power to arrest them, and probable cause to believe they committed the crime is in fact not a defense. . . .

There is a narrow exception to the general rules of arrest stated above. Any property owner, including a storekeeper, has a common law privilege to detain against his will any person he believes has tortiously taken his property. This privilege can be exercised only to prevent theft or to recapture property, and does not extend to detention for the purpose of punishment. This common law right is exercised at the shopkeeper's peril, however, and if the person detained does not unlawfully have any of the arrester's property in his possession, the arrester is liable for false imprisonment. . . .

As it now stands in this state arrest or detention without legal authority, with or without probable cause, will render the arresting person liable for such damages "as the jury may consider actual compensation for the unlawful invasion of his [the plaintiff's] rights and the injury to his person and feelings." In addition, if the act was "inflicted maliciously or wantonly, the jury are not restricted to an award of compensatory damages, but [in its discretion] may award . . . such punitive damages as the circumstances of the case may warrant as a punishment for the wrong done and as an example to others." *Dennis v Baltimore Transit Co.,* 189 Md. 610, 616, 56 A.2d 813, 816 (1948).

There was sufficient evidence for the jury to find that the manner and method of the detention here was not within the privilege "necessary for a reasonable investigation of the facts." See comments to Sec. 120 A, *Restatement (Second) of Torts.* But the reasonableness of the detention does not become an issue unless it is first shown that the person invoking the privilege "reasonably believes that another has tortiously taken a chattel upon his premises." Parker testified he did not see Paul place any merchandise in his coat and did not check the shelf to see if the "missing" item had been returned, although if he had, these activities would not have necessarily constituted probable cause. He further testified he stopped Paul in an aisle before Paul had given any indication of leaving the store, even though customers could not pay for any item until they reached the check-out counters at the front of the store. In a self-service store we think no probable cause . . . for detention exists until the suspected person actually attempts to leave without paying, unless he manifests control over the property in such a way that his intention to steal is unequivocal. Construing all of the evidence in a light most favorable to the defendant, there is no showing of probable cause here. . . .

Digges, Judge.

 Shoplifting is a perpetual problem in most retail businesses. Many states have statutes that provide legal protection for shopowners who briefly detain suspected shoplifters, but often these statutes require conformity with procedures designed to balance the rights of the suspect and the storeowner. It is critical that these procedures be well understood by all employees who may have responsibility in this area.

5:4   Intentional Infliction of Mental Distress

As early as 1899, a court recognized that "[w]ords in themselves may be harmless, while accent and manner may make them deadly."[5] The tort of mental distress is physical injury or severe mental suffering without physical impact, which results from an emotional disturbance caused by intentional highly aggravated or outrageous words or acts. The words or acts must be severe, exceeding all socially acceptable standards and must actually cause serious injury. Since people must occasionally "blow off steam," this tort is difficult to prove. Courts have been reluctant historically to find that an actual tort was committed; their viewpoint is that the tort of mental distress may lead to fictitious claims, and that the damages are of a subtle nature with psychic injuries more difficult to "see" than, for example, a broken arm. In spite of these objections, where the tortfeasor's conduct is sufficiently outrageous and exceeds all standards of propriety, recovery is allowed.

EXAMPLE: Silas is an independent rubbish collector. A local association of rubbish collectors threatens to beat him up, destroy his truck, and put him out of business unless he gives the association proceeds from a territory it has allocated to one of its members. The association may be held liable for causing severe emotional distress as an independent tort, even though there were only threats, no actual assault. The prime factor for recovery here is the association's outrageous behavior.

In the modern business setting, unconscionable debt collection practices sometimes result in this tort.

---

[5] *State v Kerns,* 34 SE 734 (1899).

EXAMPLE: Barry is a debt collector. He comes to the home of Mary, an 11-year-old girl, to repossess a television set, and he knows that Mary is alone at the time. After Mary refuses to admit him, Barry goes to another door and holds up to the glass a note stating that he will get the police and have Mary arrested if she does not admit him. Mary becomes extremely nervous, suffers great anxiety, and is unable to sleep at night. Barry is probably liable for intentional infliction of mental distress because of his deliberate and malicious intent to frighten Mary.

5:5   Defamation

The tort of *defamation* consists of injury to a person's reputation by the making of false statements. When the defamatory material is in the form of printing, writing, or pictures, the defamation is called *libel*. If the defamation is communicated orally or by acts or gestures, it is termed *slander*. Whether transmission of defamatory matter by radio or television is slander or libel is a question on which the courts have not agreed. Even an implication or insinuation against a person may be actionable if it has a clear defamatory meaning. Business partnerships and private corporations can maintain defamation suits respecting their business, integrity, solvency, or credit.

Defenses   There is a constitutional privilege that protects members of the press who publish otherwise defamatory material written about public officials, public figures, or persons of legitimate public interest. This privilege has been extended to cover even false reports of matters of public interest, unless it can be proven that they were published with knowledge of their falsity or in reckless disregard of the truth.

Two other privileges are absolute privilege and conditional privilege. Absolute privilege is a complete defense to defamation. Those who have this privilege are participants in a judicial proceeding, members of federal and state legislatures while in committee or legislative sessions, state and federal government executives at a policy-making level, and a spouse when communicating to the other spouse. A conditional privilege exempts a person from liability only when the defamation was published in good faith and with proper motives. A defendant has a conditional privilege when he or she reasonably believes an important interest in person or property is being threatened or the defamation is necessary to protect a legitimate public interest, or when reporting the happenings in executive, legislative, or judicial proceedings. A conditional privilege is destroyed by publication for an improper purpose, publication not bearing on the interest to be protected, actual malice, or lack of belief in the truth of the statement. Most courts hold truth to be a complete defense to defamation, whatever the motive involved and even if the defendant thought the statement was false at the time he made it.

 A question regarding protected statements sometimes arises when unemployment agencies inquire of employers about an application for unemployment insurance by a former employee discharged for poor conduct.

Statutory provisions in several states provide that the employer's response to an unemployment agency's query is absolutely privileged. Most other states, even in the absence of statute, have reached the same result.

A creditor or credit agency has a privilege to report financial matters to those with a legitimate business interest. This privilege is conditioned on the inquirer's good faith and lack of malice; any conduct showing a reckless disregard for or conscious indifference to the rights of the debtor will destroy the privilege.[6]

Retraction   A retraction is the published withdrawal of defamatory material by the person who made it. At common law, retraction was not a complete defense, but it did remove the elements of malice and bad faith, thereby substantially reducing the damages. Today, several states have retraction statutes that generally relieve the media (television, radio, and newspapers) from some liability if they comply with the injured party's demand for a fair and prompt retraction.

 An employer who discharges an unsatisfactory employee should be alert to a possible defamation suit when responding to others with whom the discharged employee has applied for employment. If defamatory material is communicated to a prospective new employer and the employee can show that the prior employer did not make the communication in good faith or that statements were made with a reckless disregard for the truth, the employee may be able to sue for defamation. To prevent defamation litigation, an employer should consult an attorney as to the precise wording that should be used to communicate information about a prior or present employee.

5:6   Trespass and Conversion

Besides torts that involve invasion of an individual's right to be secure in person or reputation, there are torts that involve injury to the individual's property or property interest. These include trespass to land, trespass to chattels, conversion, and misrepresentation.

Trespass to Land   The tort of *trespass to land* is the unauthorized entry of a person or thing on land belonging to another. The basis of the tort is the right to the exclusive possession of land. Possession sufficient to entitle the land-owner to bring suit for trespass may be actual, as when the owner is actually on the land, or constructive, as when the land is possessed by someone responsible to the owner, such as an agent or employee. A person may sue for trespass even if the entry was made for or resulted in improvement to the land.

Under most decisions, if a person intends to be on another's land, he is liable for trespass even if his presence is based on a good faith mistake, such

---

[6] Credit reporting is discussed further in Chapter 28.

as ignorance as to the land's ownership or boundary lines, or other honest mistake causing him to go on the land.

EXAMPLE: A developer purchases certain land and believes in good faith that her neighbor's land is part of the purchase. She enters the neighbor's unposted, unenclosed land to survey it. The developer has committed the tort of trespass to land even though she did not intend to violate her neighbor's right to exclusive possession of the land. The crucial questions are whether the entry was unauthorized and whether the developer intended to enter the land. Since the answer is yes in both cases, the tort has been committed. However, if the developer were pushed onto the neighbor's land by a third person, and had no intention of entering the land, she would not be liable for trespass. In such a case, it would be the third person who would be liable.

Trespass to Chattels   A *chattel* is movable personal property, as distinguished from real property (land). *Trespass to chattels* is the intentional and harmful interference with possession of personal property without the owner's consent. The gist of the tort is physical interference with the exclusive right of another to use and possess a chattel. As with trespass to land, mistake is no defense to trespass to chattels. This tort is of diminishing importance because the courts are replacing it with the tort of conversion.

Conversion   *Conversion* is the intentional and wrongful acquiring, altering, damaging, transferring, using, or withholding of another person's property. The interest protected is that of possession of, control of, or right to control a chattel. The tort of conversion developed from the merging of several highly technical fifteenth-century English writs, with the result that today conversion has been said by some legal writers to defy a clear definition. The *Restatement (Second) of Torts* § 222A states that a conversion is an intentional exercise of dominion or control over a chattel which so seriously interferes with the right of another to control it that the one interfering is liable for its full value. Several factors are considered in determining whether the interference is serious enough to require full compensation: (1) the extent of dominion, (2) duration of interference, (3) harm to the chattel, and (4) inconvenience and expense to the owner. Neither good faith nor mistake constitute a defense to conversion. Hence, even though a person in good faith purchases converted goods, he or she will be liable to the true owner of the goods.

What May Be Converted   In the context of business, the question arises as to what may be converted. At common law, only property that could be "lost" was considered the subject of conversion; this limited the action to tangible personal property. Because of the need to protect intangible rights evidenced by checks, notes, bonds, stock certificates, and similar documents, the action for conversion was extended so that intangible rights were said to "merge with an instrument." Today, some states now permit recovery for conversion of an intangible right (if the type considered merged with an instrument), even though the instrument itself has not been converted. Recovery may be had, for example, for a corporation's refusal to transfer stock. Generally, intangible rights not considered merged with an instrument such as ideas and goodwill are not recognized as being convertible.

5:7   Misrepresentation

Misrepresentation is an all-embracing term. The human ability to devise fraudulent schemes is so great that courts have not defined misrepresentation, reserving to themselves the liberty to deal with it in whatever form it appears. It may broadly be said, however, that the tort of misrepresentation consists of the false representation of a material fact to a person who justifiably relies on it to his damage.

In the case of failure to disclose information, as opposed to an actual false statement, liability may be an open question. For example, if a person knows that his car's radiator is defective yet says nothing and sells the car to another person, who does not ask about the radiator, there would probably be no recovery for fraudulent concealment. A seller usually does not have to disclose a hidden defect, in the absence of a statutory or other duty to do so. On the other hand, if there has been an *active concealment* on the seller's part, such as attempts to conceal the radiator's defects, then the tort of misrepresentation in the form of fraud would probably be present. In this event, the courts say there is "more than mere failure to speak."

Liability for misrepresentation requires that the injured party's reliance on the misrepresentation be justifiable. To be the basis of liability, the misrepresentation must be of an existing fact, not just an expression of opinion. For example, if a buyer has ample opportunity to examine the goods to be purchased, general statements by the seller as to the performance or value of the goods ("performs well," "runs like a charm," "a great bargain"), which are false, will not usually give rise to a suit for misrepresentation. Courts permit a reasonable amount of "sales talk."

EXAMPLE: A used car salesman tells a potential car buyer "this little beauty is a great buy. It will take you wherever you want to go with no problems at all." After purchasing the car, the buyer discovers it has a leaky radiator and needs transmission work. The salesman probably is not guilty of the tort of misrepresentation because his statements were of a general "selling nature," not specific representations of facts or conditions of the automobile. If, on the other hand, the salesman had been specifically asked the condition of the radiator or transmission and had remained silent or had stated the condition to be good, then the purchaser would have a basis for suit.

5:8   Invasion of Civil Rights[7]

The phrase "civil rights" includes all private legal rights of individuals. The term is also used in a more restricted sense that refers to those rights created by state and federal constitutional and statutory provisions designed to pre-

---

[7] Invasion of civil rights in employment discrimination is discussed in Chapter 51.

vent discrimination relating to race, color, sex, religion, or national origin. Many state and federal constitutional and statutory provisions prohibit discrimination on these grounds in connection with education, voting, transportation, employment, housing, and places of public accommodation or amusement, as well as other activities. Violation of these statutory rights has sometimes resulted in tort suits, as well as criminal prosecution.

Civil rights laws vary considerably in the type of relief permitted. While some give the individual a right to recover a statutory penalty in a specified amount, others give the right to recover both damages and penalties. Some statutes that provide no punishment or remedies at all have nevertheless been held to give an individual the right to recover damages from the violator in a civil action. The same result has been reached under some statutes expressly providing only criminal punishment.

5:9   Interference with Contract and Prospective Advantage

The law recognizes the right that a party to a contract has to the benefits of performance of the contract. Actions by a third party that interfere with the contract may subject the third party to liability for the tort of interference with contract. A related tort doctrine, interference with prospective advantage, protects a person from unreasonable interference with his or her ability to acquire business relationships.

Interference with Contract   Inducing another to breach a contract violates the contract rights of the contracting party. Interfering with the performance of the contract also violates that right. It is important to distinguish between taking advantage of a contracting party's decision to breach a contract and actually inducing the breach. Moreover, it is important to understand that the tort requires intent; thus, the defendant must have reasonably known that his actions would interfere with the contractual relationship. The following case involves intentional interference with a business contract.

Lexington Homes, Inc.

v

W. E. Tyson Builders, Inc.
331 SE2d 318 (1985)
Court of Appeals of North Carolina

FACTS: Tyson, a builder, obtained a construction loan from First Atlantic to build ten houses for resale. The loan was given in the form of a check for $114,210, which Tyson deposited in its checking account at Southern National Bank. Tyson then wrote and mailed checks against that account to several suppliers in payment of bills. One supplier, Lexington, was not paid because Tyson thought Lexington had overcharged the firm. When Lexington was informed that payment would be delayed until verification of the bill, Lexington threatened to call First Atlantic and have that bank stop payment on its $114,210 check. Tyson reassured Lexington that it would be paid, that checks had been written against the $114,210, and that Tyson's business would be severely injured by such an action. Nevertheless, Lexington called First Atlantic and told the bank that Tyson was not using the proceeds of the check to pay suppliers. First Atlantic stopped payment on the $114,210 check, which caused the checks Tyson had written to bounce. Even though First Atlantic later honored the check, suppliers had filed liens against Tyson's properties, and work on the houses was delayed, at about $60,000 in increased expense to Tyson.

ISSUE: Did Lexington's behavior constitute tortious interference with a contract?

RESULT: Yes. Lexington interfered with Tyson's performance of its contract with other suppliers, and it did so without legal justification.

REASONING:

*   *   *

It has long been the law in this State that one who tortiously interferes with the contract rights of another is liable for the damage caused thereby. . . .

While the rule laid down in 86 C.J.S. *Torts* § 44 that an action will lie against one who wrongfully interferes with the contract rights of another had been recognized by our Supreme Court in numerous cases, . . . so far as our research discloses, the proof required for such an action had not been itemized until *Childress v. Abeles,* 240 N.C. 667, 84 S.E.2d 176 (1954). In *Childress* the Court stated that in these cases it is necessary to show: (1) That a valid contract existed between the plaintiff and a third person, conferring upon the plaintiff some contractual right against the third person; (2) that the outsider had knowledge of the plaintiff's contract with the third person; (3) that the outsider intentionally induced the third person not to perform his contract with the plaintiff; (4) that in so doing the outsider acted without justification; (5) that the outsider's act caused the plaintiff actual damages. . . .

The appellees contend here, as they did in obtaining the dismissal in the court below, that the evidence presented was insufficient to establish the following three things defendant was obliged to prove; that First Atlantic *breached* its contract with defendant; that appellees were not justified in having payment on the $114,210 draft stopped; and that defendant was actually damaged as a consequence of the interference. The grounds relied upon for these contentions and the arguments made in support of them are largely irrelevant to the thrust and tenor of defendant's case against them and the recorded evidence in support of it. First of all defendant does not have to prove that appellees caused First Atlantic to *breach* its contract with defendant, because its claim is only that appellees wrongfully *interfered* with defendant's rights under the contract; and clear, direct evidence that appellees did wrongfully interfere with its contract rights was presented. According to the evidence, the appellees caused First Atlantic to stop payment on the draft that defendant lawfully had in its bank account and had written checks against. That defendant had a right to possess the draft and use it free from the wrongful interference of others is clearly inferable from the facts that it had a loan agreement with First Atlantic, a lending rather than an eleemosynary institution, and that First Atlantic issued and delivered the draft to defendant. That defendant did not show, as appellees contend, that the underlying loan agreement required First Atlantic to issue the draft at that time and in that amount, or that the draft might have been issued later or in a different way without recourse on defendant's part, is beside the point. As Justice Barnhill so cogently pointed out . . . , a party to a contract has the right to reap the benefits of it, such as they are, free from the wrongful interference of others; and since First Atlantic as a contracting party issued the draft to defendant at that time and in that manner defendant had a right to use and enjoy that benefit of its contract free from the wrongful interference of the appellees or anyone else.

The appellees' argument as to justification, equally wide of the mark, starts and stops with their legitimate interest in obtaining early payment of the sum owed from the funds received by defendant. The evidence which tends to show that the appellees falsely claimed that defendant was not going to pay it or the other suppliers and contractors with the draft funds, and that their purpose was to obtain several hundred dollars in funds plaintiff was not entitled to, was not even addressed. . . .

Phillips, Judge.

Interference with Prospective Advantage. The very early cases of interference with prospective advantage involved the use of physical violence, or threats of physical violence, to discourage customers of another's business. Later applications include fact situations in which a person, through means such as defamation or intimidation, attempts to prevent a person from deriving economic advantage from a prospective contract. As with interference with contract, the tort must be intentional; often the defendant's bad motive is the central factual issue in the case. Moreover, there must be some provable injury to the plaintiff.

Key Concepts and Terms

- A tort is a civil wrong other than breach of contract. While a crime is a wrong against society and punishable by the state, a tort is a wrong against an individual for which civil damages constitute the remedy. A person who commits a tort is called a tortfeasor. Joint tortfeasors are two or more persons who unite in committing a tort, or whose acts concur in producing an injury to a third person.

- Some intentional torts take the form of interfering with or invading a person's right to be secure in his or her own body and person. They include battery, assault, malicious prosecution, abuse of process, and invasion of privacy.

- False imprisonment is the wrongful obstruction or detention of a person within boundaries for any length of time, without that person's consent. The tort frequently arises in shoplifter detention cases. Under shopkeeper's privilege, followed in some but not all states, a storekeeper, who has a reasonable belief (probable cause) that a theft has been committed, may detain the suspect for a reasonable time and conduct an investigation in a reasonable manner without being liable for false imprisonment, even if the detained person was not a shoplifter.

- The tort of mental distress is characterized by injury to a person resulting from emotional disturbance without physical impact, caused by another's highly aggravated or outrageous words or acts, which exceed all socially acceptable standards. Unconscionable debt collection practices sometimes result in this tort.

- Defamation, which may be libel or slander, is injury to a person's reputation by false statements. Certain defamatory statements, especially those about public persons, are privileged.

- Torts to property or property interests include trespass to land, trespass to chattels, and conversion.

- Misrepresentation is a broad term, referring generally to false representations of a material fact that a person relies on to his or her damage. Simple failure to disclose information, in the absence of a duty to do so, does not usually result in the tort of misrepresentation. However, active concealment of material information gives rise to the tort. In a sales situation, courts permit a reasonable amount of "sales talk."

- Some state and federal constitutional and statutory provisions prohibiting discrimination have been used as the base for tort suits.

- Tort law protects parties to a contract, or a prospective contract, from a third party's intentional interference with the benefit of such contract.

- Assault
- Battery
- Chattel
- Consent
- Conversion
- Defamation
- False Imprisonment
- Intent
- Intentional Infliction of Mental Distress
- Interference with Contract
- Invasion of Privacy
- Joint Tortfeasor
- Libel
- Malicious Prosecution
- Misrepresentation

- Privilege
- Prospective Advantage
- Slander
- Shopkeeper's Privilege
- Shoplifter Detention

- Tort
- Transferred Intent
- Trespass to Chattels
- Trespass to Land

Questions and Case Problems

1. What are the differences between a tort, a crime, and a breach of contract?

2. Katie Valdez, while in a variety store owned by Michelle Whitney, notices a sign on the wall reading "FREE—PLEASE TAKE ONE," below which is a box of transistor radios. She puts one of the radios in her pocket and walks out of the store. Whitney rushes out of the store after Valdez, shouting, "Come back here with that radio, you thief!" The street is crowded, and Valdez, humiliated by the accusation, eludes Whitney and runs home. Later that day, Maria Garcia, a customer who resembles Valdez, enters the restroom of Whitney's store. Whitney, thinking Garcia is Valdez, locks the restroom door and calls the police. There is an open window in the restroom. Garcia decides to climb out the window and gets on a chair to reach the window. As she puts her weight on the back of the chair, it tips. Garcia falls to the floor and breaks her leg. Valdez learns later that the "FREE—PLEASE TAKE ONE" sign referred to advertising bulletins which were usually beneath the sign, and not to the transistor radios. Discuss the rights of Valdez and Whitney against each other and the rights of Garcia against Whitney.

3. As part of a nightclub act, Waldo hypnotizes volunteers from the audience. Horace volunteers and is hypnotized. Waldo directs Horace to pour a glass of water on Sharon, another member of the audience. Horace does so. Has Horace committed a battery on Sharon? Has Waldo committed a battery on Sharon? Discuss.

4. Explain the doctrine of transferred intent.

5. What are the differences between invasion of privacy and defamation?

6. Christopher purchases an expensive house from Dudley. Prior to signing the final papers, Christopher asks Dudley if the house is free of termites. Is there an actionable misrepresentation in any of the following responses by Dudley? (a) Dudley replies that he has recently obtained a termite report showing no visible infestation. In fact, no such report had been obtained, and unbeknown to Dudley, the house is full of termites. (b) Dudley replies that there are no termites, because he has never seen any, but afterwards, just to check, he crawls under the house and finds a large infestation. He decides not to tell Christopher about this, because he did not ask him to crawl under the house and report back to him. (c) Dudley makes no reply to Christopher's inquiry, but knows that there is extensive infestation. (d) Dudley's only reply to Christopher's inquiry is that the house was being sold "as is," while all along Dudley knows there is extensive infestation.

7. As part of the negotiations leading up to the sale of an apartment house, the seller makes the following representations to the buyer, each of which is false. Which of these representations, if any, would subject the seller to liability for misrepresentation if it is relied on by the buyer? (a) This property is worth at least $150,000, but I'll sell it to you for $120,000. (b) I have never previously offered this property for sale. (c) Nothing in the city building code prevents you from splitting the larger apartments into smaller ones, if you want to, thereby increasing the rents.

8. Fastbuck advertises lots for sale in Golden Years Subdivision, which consists of undeveloped desert acreage. Mr. Eager, a retiree, visits the subdivision, and asks what improvements are planned. Fastbuck tells him all about planned swimming pools, shopping areas, and an 18-hole golf course. Relying on Fastbuck's word, Eager buys one of the lots for $5,000. The swimming pools, shopping areas, and golf course are never built. Assume that Fastbuck never had the funds for this development and never had any reasonable prospects of being able to construct the promised amenities. Can Eager recover damages for misrepresentation?

9. Representatives of the Ajax Debt Collection Service come to the front door of Alice's home and in loud voices announce that Alice is four months behind in payments on her new sofa and that the debt collectors want to enter to repossess the sofa. The debt collectors refuse to leave the property and yell through the door that if Alice does not permit them to enter, they will break the door down. Alice then opens the door and the debt collectors enter and remove the sofa. All the while Alice is protesting. She throws a lamp at one of the debt collectors, and he sustains a concussion. Discuss the possible tort liabilities of all parties.

10. Mike's poodle runs away from home and enters Mary's yard. Mary puts a leash on the dog. When Mike comes looking for his dog, Mary refuses to return it and locks the gate to her property. (a) Is Mike privileged to break down Mary's gate to enter her property to reclaim the dog? (b) If Mike is privileged to break Mary's gate, must he pay for any damage to the gate? (c) Is Mike privileged to break and enter Mary's front door if she has taken the dog inside her house?

6 Negligence and Strict Liability

Standards of prudent conduct are declared at times by courts, but they are taken over from the facts of life.

Justice Cardozo, *Pokora v Wabash R. Co.* 292 US 98
(United States Supreme Court, 1934)

6:1 Introduction

Over the course of time the courts have established the elements that constitute the tort of *negligence*. These elements must be shown to exist before an injured person can claim a right to recovery for negligence: (1) that the defendant had a duty to exercise reasonable care, (2) that there was a breach of that duty, (3) that a causal relationship exists between the defendant's conduct and the plaintiff's injury, and (4) that damages resulted. This chapter examines these elements and describes various defenses against the tort of negligence. The final section deals with the area of tort recovery called strict liability.

6:2 Duty to Exercise Reasonable Care

Every person has a duty to exercise the conduct that a reasonable person of ordinary prudence would follow under the same or similar circumstances. This stems from the fact that all persons are deemed to possess certain minimum levels of knowledge and skills, and, as a consequence, they are held to certain minimum standards of care in their activities.

EXAMPLE: Smith fails to replace tread-bare tires on his car. Despite the fact that he may have no actual knowledge of the danger of driving with poor tires, Smith will be liable for negligence in not having replaced them if, because of the poor condition of the tires, his car is in an accident that causes damage to another. Since it is supposed that a reasonable person would know that driving with poor tires is dangerous, Smith has the duty to exercise reasonable care to maintain his tires in a safe condition.

The duty of care that the reasonable person is expected to exercise will vary according to the risk involved; more care must be used, for example, when handling explosives than when handling lumber. The substantive law of tort is largely a problem of defining the duty of care that different people ought to have in different circumstances. In general, the rules of tort liability tend to place liability on the person who was in the best position to avoid the loss or to bear the risk of loss.

Liability of Professionals   A professional, such as a physician, attorney, accountant, or other person whose occupation requires highly specialized knowledge, is obligated to have the same skill and learning as other members of his or her profession and to apply that skill and learning with the same care as generally exercised by other members of that profession.

EXAMPLE: In drafting a document, an attorney fails to take into consideration certain tax consequences. As a result, her client is required to pay more taxes than he would had the attorney prepared the document differently. The attorney will be liable in damages for professional malpractice if the client can show that the attorney failed to have, and to exercise, the same learning and skill as other members of her profession would have exercised.

The courts are slow, however, to impose professional liability where the standards of care are not clearly ascertainable. In the following case, the court refused to permit liability based on educational malpractice in a medical setting.

Swidryk
v
St. Michael's Medical Center
493 A2d 641 (1985)
Superior Court of New Jersey

FACTS: Dr. Swidryk was sued for negligence in the delivery of a child who, allegedly as a result of medical malpractice in the delivery, was born with severe brain damage. Dr. Swidryk had just begun his first year of residency in obstetrics and gynecology when the incident occurred. Dr. Swidryk sued both the hospital and Dr. Smith, medical education director of the hospital, claiming that Smith was negligent in supervising the intern and resident program and that, as a result, Dr. Swidryk had been sued.

ISSUE: Should "educational malpractice" be recognized as a cause of action in tort in New Jersey?

RESULT: No. For reasons of public policy, a cause of action should not be created.

REASONING:

*   *   *

The foundation of Dr. Swidryk's claim is that Dr. Smith's conduct was negligent in that his actions as director of medical education fell below the standard of care essential to protect others from an unreasonable risk of harm. The vast majority of courts to consider this issue have refused to recognize a cause of action for educational malpractice. . . .

In order to find a defendant liable for negligence a legal duty must be found to exist and there must have been a breach of that duty. . . . Whether or not a duty exists is ultimately a question of fairness and the inquiry involves a consideration of the relationship of the parties, the nature of the risk and the public interest in the proposed solution. . . . Public policy considerations must play a major role in the determination of whether a legal duty exists. . . .

As a general rule courts will not interfere with purely academic decisions of a university. . . . The New Jersey courts should not be required to sit in day to day review of the academic decisions of a graduate medical education program. This function is best left to the state board of medical examiners, the board of higher education and the Advisory Graduate Medical Education Council of New Jersey. . . .

The Legislature has vested the board of medical examiners, the board of higher education and the advisory graduate medical education council with the authority to insure that a proper medical education is delivered within New Jersey. It would be against public policy for the court to usurp these functions and inquire into the day to day operation of a graduate medical education program. From the standpoint of court administration, it is also unwise to recognize a claim for educational malpractice where an individual physician is attempting to defend against a malpractice claim. To allow a physician to file suit for educational malpractice against his school and residence program each time he is sued for malpractice would call for a malpractice trial within a malpractice case. Creation of the tort of educational malpractice in this context would substantially increase the amount of time which a medical malpractice case takes to try now as well as have the potential to confuse the jury in its consideration of the underlying issues. The litigation explosion has limits and this is one area in which those limits should be definitely marked. Therefore, for reasons of public policy, there is no legal duty which will support a tort for educational malpractice in this class of case. . . .

Newman, Justice.

Failure to Act Generally, a person has no duty to come to the aid of others. Unless there is some special legal circumstance imposing a duty to rescue, the law does not enforce any moral obligation—one that should be observed out of common decency or humanity. Thus, failure to act, termed *nonfeasance,* does not create liability. However, if a person does render assistance and is thereafter negligent as a result of what he does or does not do, he will be liable. The courts recognize three ways in which a person can be negligent, or make another's situation worse: (1) by increasing the danger, (2) by depriving the person of other aid, and (3) by inducing the person to forego other assistance because of reliance on his aid.

EXAMPLE: Wendy witnesses an automobile accident. She sees that Charles, whom she does not know, is trapped behind the steering wheel of his car and apparently is seriously injured. Wendy tries to extricate Charles from the car, but after a moment she gives up and leaves. She does not notify anyone about the accident. Wendy did not have any initial duty to stop and render aid. Once she did so, however, if it can be established that she acted negligently in rendering the aid (such as by not having tried long enough or by not having contacted other persons), then she may be liable for having left Charles *worse* off than she found him. Other passersby, for example, who may have seen Wendy assisting Charles, might otherwise have stopped to render better aid themselves.

The following case exemplifies the rule that, in the absence of a special relationship, a person does not have responsibility for the actions of another, even where those actions cause injury to a third person.

Martino

v

Leiva

479 NE2d 955 (1985)

Appellate Court of Illinois, First District

FACTS: Juan Leiva was operating his father's car under a learner's permit when the car collided with an automobile driven by plaintiff. Juan's father had given Juan permission to drive the car with the understanding between them that Juan's friend Ulises Castro, who had a driver's license, would accompany Juan. This understanding was never communicated to Castro, who had received his driver's license one month prior to the accident. Castro had never before ridden in an automobile driven by Juan. At the time of the accident, Castro was listening to the radio and looking out the window and talking to Juan.

ISSUE: Was Castro under a duty to control Juan's driving?

RESULT: In the absence of a special undertaking to do so, a passenger is under no obligation to control the driver of an automobile.

REASONING:

*   *   *

A passenger is not liable for the negligent acts of the driver of an automobile unless the passenger is the owner of the automobile or possesses the right to control the driving of it. . . . Unless a special relationship exists between the driver and the passenger, there is no duty imposed upon the passenger to prevent the driver from causing physical harm to another. . . . Persons will not be held to duties beyond those required by the common law unless they have voluntarily assumed such duties. . . .

Here, Castro was just an ordinary passenger in the Leiva automobile. He was not the possessor of the vehicle and he had no right to decide whether Juan would operate the automobile. That decision was made by the Leivas. Castro had no right whatsoever to control the operation of the automobile. He was not instructing or training Juan; he had not been asked to supervise Juan; and he did not undertake to do so.

The line of cases on which plaintiffs rely for the proposition that the passenger has a duty to control the operator's driving is clearly distinguishable. In each case, the passenger was a plaintiff seeking recovery for his own injuries. . . . A plaintiff must exercise ordinary care for his own safety, but the duty to control another's conduct to prevent injury to a third party must be based upon a special relationship.

Plaintiffs contend, however, that pursuant to Illinois statute a special relationship exists between a person driving with a learner's permit and the accompanying passenger with a driver's license. The statute provides in relevant part:

> "[T]he minor shall be restricted to the operation of a motor vehicle only when accompanied by a person who has a license classification to operate such vehicle and at least one year of driving experience and who is occupying a seat beside the driver." . . .

The statute, which is directed at the operator, neither explicitly or implicitly suggests that whenever an operator with a learner's permit operates a motor vehicle on the streets, any ordinary licensed passenger in the front seat is obliged to instruct the operator and thereby have control of the vehicle. Merely riding in an automobile with a person who is not legally entitled to drive will not create a duty to control or even prohibit the driver's operation of the automobile to protect third parties. . . . And even if it could be assumed that the statute in question confers such a duty on a licensed passenger, it could not be imposed here since Castro did not have the required one year's driving experience. The undisputed facts reveal that Castro did not undertake to control the driving nor could he do so. . . .

McNamara, Justice.

Degrees of Negligence   While some cases have talked about "degrees of negligence," most courts hold that there are not different degrees of negligence but rather circumstances that require more or less care. Statutes, however, sometimes speak in terms of "gross negligence" or "recklessness." Such statutory provisions are interpreted to mean a conscious and deliberate disregard of conditions that impose a high probability that someone will be injured.

Modification of Objective Standard of Care   The objective standard of care, or the care exercised by a reasonably prudent person, has been modified in the case of children. Several courts have expressed the view that the standard of a child's care is based on what may be expected of children of similar age, intelligence, and experience. A person with a mental incapacity, however, is held to the same standard of care as a person of ordinary intelligence because of the difficulties involved in determining the degree of disability. Likewise, the courts will not make allowances for voluntary intoxication when determining a defendant's duty to exercise reasonable care.

Clearly, the reasonable person confronted with an emergency may act differently if there were no emergency. This does not mean that a different standard is applied; rather, it means that the emergency conditions become part of all the circumstances taken into consideration in determining how a reasonable person would act in that situation.

6:3   Defendant's Breach of Duty

Perfect conduct is humanly impossible. As such, the law does not exact an unreasonable amount of care from anyone. *Breach of duty* to exercise reasonable care means that a person fails to act as carefully as a reasonable person would have acted under the same or similar circumstances. The greater the danger that is known or that reasonably may be anticipated, the greater the degree of care the law requires one to observe.

The *"reasonable person" standard* is a rule. Yet, what it means in any particular case depends on how the court perceives a reasonable person would have acted. Thus, it is always dependent on proof of the circumstances that existed at the time. From such proof, the court determines what a "reasonable person" would have done and measures the defendant's conduct against this standard.

Res Ipsa Loquitur Doctrine   In certain cases, the very fact that a particular harm has occurred may itself tend to establish a breach of duty on the part of the defendant. Where the circumstances and type of accident strongly suggest that the plaintiff's injuries occurred through the defendant's negligence, the law may permit an inference that the defendant was at fault. This is the *doctrine of res ipsa loquitur,* which means literally "the act speaks for itself." Three factors must be established in order to invoke this doctrine: (1) the accident must be of a type that normally does not occur in the absence of someone's negligence, (2) the source of the negligence must be within the scope of a duty owed by the defendant to the plaintiff, and (3) neither the plaintiff nor any third person must have contributed to or caused the plaintiff's injuries. This doctrine is sometimes applied in airplane crash cases and medical malpractice suits in which the instrumentalities of the accident were completely within the defendant's knowledge and control and where the plaintiff had only limited access to the actual facts of the occurrence. It has also been applied in some cases involving exploding bottles and nonedible substances found in food.

Violation of Statute   If a person violates a criminal statute and in the process injures someone, he or she may be chargeable for negligence in addition to the crime. For the defendant's statutory violation to also constitute negligence, the statute must clearly define the conduct or duty required of the defendant and the types of individuals to whom it applies.

EXAMPLE: A druggist sells a poisonous substance without a "poison label," which is required by statute to be affixed to the container. The purchaser accidentally drinks the poison and dies. The druggist is liable in negligence since the statute created a duty to use reasonable care to protect customers from taking the wrong drug, and the druggist failed to perform this duty in the manner specified in the statute.

Similarly, many states have enacted statutes, commonly known as civil damage acts or *dramshop acts,* giving a right of action to persons injured by an intoxicated person against the individual who sold or furnished the liquor. Although dramshop statutes generally provide for the recovery of damages from "any person" giving or selling intoxicating liquor, it is usually held that such statutes do not create a right of action against one who gives another the beverage as a mere act of hospitality or social courtesy without any connection to the business of selling liquor. Nevertheless, this is not always the case, and in some states a host, who at a social function serves liquor to a guest who subsequently injures another person, may be liable for damages.

6:4 Causation

For a defendant to have "caused" a plaintiff's injury and to be held negligent, the defendant's tortious acts must have been (1) the *cause in fact* and (2) the *proximate cause* of the plaintiff's injury.

Cause in Fact   *Cause in fact* means that the plaintiff's injury would not have happened "but for" the defendant's act or omission; therefore, the defendant's conduct is the cause in fact of the plaintiff's injury. For example, a defendant's failure to supply fire-fighting equipment, which could not have been used anyway because there was no available water, cannot be considered the cause in fact of a plaintiff's loss of property from a fire. The reason is that it could not be shown that "but for" the failure to have the fire-fighting equipment the plaintiff's building could have been saved.

Proximate Cause   Once actual causation (cause in fact) is established, the plaintiff must also establish *proximate cause*. Proximate cause is a concept developed by courts in an attempt to deal with the problem of liability for unforeseeable or unusual consequences following a defendant's act. "Proximate cause" is an unfortunate term, since closeness in time and space has nothing to do with the matter at issue. At issue is how far public policy will extend liability to a defendant for the consequences of an act. Proximate cause is established when there is not an intervening force between a defendant's negligent act and the harm to the plaintiff. For example, if while reaching for his cigarette lighter a driver crashes his car into a telephone pole, which falls onto a house, the driver's negligence is said to be the proximate cause of the damage to the house. Now, it also must be shown that the harm suffered by the plaintiff was a foreseeable consequence of the defendant's negligent act. This does not mean that the precise consequences could or should have been foreseen as they actually occurred; rather, it implies that the events were within the scope of a foreseeable risk.

The following case involves the problem of whether the lack of care of the defendant was the cause of the injury. The decision demonstrates how courts examine the facts and apply the law to those facts to determine whether the defendant (1) owed a duty of care to the plaintiff and (2) breached that duty of care. This decision is a typical negligence case in several respects: namely, it discusses separately (and in order) duty and breach, and it stresses the extent to which public policy requires protection of the public.

Williams
v
Melby
699 P2d 723 (1985)
Supreme Court of Utah

FACTS: Plaintiff tenant was injured when she awoke one night, became disoriented, and fell out of a third story window in defendant landlord's apartment. The building had a mansard roof. As a result of this design, the window in question was placed vertically on a sloping wall and protruded into the room. The glass part of the window was 22 inches off the floor. At the time of the accident, plaintiff had lived in the apartment four months, and she and her husband had placed their bed near the window.

ISSUE: Did the plaintiff's knowledge of the window, and her placement of the bed near the window, constitute a superseding cause of the accident?

RESULT: No. Plaintiff's placement of the bed was foreseeable by the landlord and does not excuse his duty to act with reasonable care.

REASONING:

*   *   *

The essential elements of a negligence action are: (1) a duty of reasonable care owed by the defendant to plaintiff; (2) a breach of that duty; (3) the causation, both actually and proximately, of injury; and (4) the suffering of damages by the plaintiff. . . .

A particularized statement of that duty is found in 2 F. Harper and F. James, *The Law of Torts* § 27.17 at 1516, 1518 (1956) (footnotes omitted):

> The landlord is also under a similar duty [of reasonable care to make conditions reasonably safe] to maintain those parts of the structure which remain in his control but are needed for the safety or protection of the leased premises, such as foundations, outside walls, roofs and the like.

Whether a defendant has breached the required standard of care is generally a question for the jury, . . . to be determined by whether the injury which occurred was of the type that fell within the zone of risk created by the defendant's negligent conduct. "The care to be exercised in any particular case depends upon the circumstances of that case and on the extent of foreseeable danger involved and must be determined as a question of fact." . . .

It appears to be true that the window through which the plaintiff fell was constructed in compliance with the applicable building code, was originally designed by a licensed architect, and was put in the plans by a mechanical engineer. It also appears that the glass in the window complied with building code requirements. Nevertheless, compliance with the building code does not *ipso facto* preclude a finding of a design defect. . . .

If a reasonably prudent person should have known, or could have learned by the exercise of reasonable care, that the design or construction of the window constituted a dangerous condition, the landlord could be held liable for not taking adequate safety precautions. That no one had previously fallen through the window, does not conclude the issue. . . . [T]hat a particular kind of accident has not happened before does not . . . show that such accident is one which might not reasonably have been anticipated. . . .

The instant case is not unlike [a California case in which] the plaintiff was injured when he slipped and fell through an untempered glass shower door in his apartment. The difference between tempered glass and untempered glass was discernible only on close inspection. The court set aside a summary judgment because the case presented a factual issue as to whether the landlord could have learned of the defective condition of the property. Similarly here, a trier of fact might find that the landlord should have known that a defective condition existed and should have taken precautions to avert the risk. Therefore, since we cannot hold as a matter of law that the plaintiff was equally or more negligent than the Melbys, a triable issue of fact exists as to whether the Melbys breached their duty of care.

We are cognizant of the fact that the plaintiff obviously knew of the particular window design. But it does not appear that she knew of the thickness of the glass in the window or that its strength was such that it would not hold if someone inadvertently fell against it. . . .

Finally, we note that defendants place much emphasis upon the fact that it was the plaintiff and her husband who placed their furniture in the position it was in the room, although there was very little choice in the matter because of the size of the room and the size of the furniture. The defendants assert that plaintiff's conduct, being subsequent in time to the design and construction of the window, was an intervening proximate cause that superseded whatever cause may have flowed from their negligence. They rely on . . . the proposition that a subsequent cause to that for which the defendant is responsible is, as a matter of law, a superseding cause. . . .

The law of superseding causation is, as a general proposition, more easily stated than applied. A person's negligence is not superseded by the negligence of another if the subsequent negligence of another is foreseeable. This Court . . . adopted the rule stated in the *Restatement (Second) of Torts* § 447 (1965):

> The fact that an intervening act of a third person is negligent in itself or is done in a negligent manner does not make it a superseding cause of harm to another which the actor's negligent conduct is a substantial factor in bringing about, if
> (a) the actor at the time of his negligent conduct should have realized that a third person might so act, or
> (b) a reasonable man knowing the situation existing when the act of the third person was done would not regard it as highly extraordinary that the third person had so acted, or
> (c) the intervening act is a normal consequence of a situation created by the actor's conduct and the manner in which it is done is not extraordinarily negligent.

The same general rule is stated by Professor Prosser as follows:

> The risk created by the defendant may include the intervention of the foreseeable negligence of others. . . . [T]he standard of reasonable conduct may require the defendant to protect the plaintiff against 'that occasioned negligence which is one of the ordinary incidents of human life and therefore to be anticipated.'

Prosser, *The Law of Torts* § 44 at 274 (4th ed. 1971) (footnotes omitted). . . .

Stewart, Justice.

6:5 Defenses

There are several defenses that a defendant may assert against a plaintiff in a negligence suit. These are described below.

Contributory Negligence *Contributory negligence* refers to conduct on the part of a plaintiff that contributes to his own harm and that falls below the standard of reasonable care to which he must conform. Contributory negligence, which is a defense to a negligence suit, is much like negligence itself—the criteria are the same—but it involves a person's duty to exercise reasonable care for his own safety rather than for the safety of others. The standard of care, as in negligence, is determined by what the reasonable person would have done under the same or similar circumstances. In essence, even though he did not exercise due care, the defendant is not liable if the injury would have been avoided had the plaintiff exercised due care.

Last Clear Chance Doctrine   *The doctrine of last clear chance*—sometimes referred to as the doctrine of discovered peril or the doctrine of supervening negligence or the humanitarian doctrine—states that if the plaintiff is also shown to be negligent, the negligent defendant is held liable for damages only if he was both aware of the plaintiff's peril and had a *later opportunity* than the plaintiff to avoid the accident.

EXAMPLE: Wilson negligently parks her automobile on the right side of a highway. Nichols, although he is able to see Wilson's car from several hundred feet away, collides with it. If Nichols sues Wilson to recover for his injuries, Wilson will probably be able to win by showing that Nichols had the last clear chance to avoid the collision.

Assumption of Risk   The defense of *assumption of risk* may apply when the plaintiff is shown to have voluntarily encountered a known danger (brought about by the defendant's negligence) and, by his own conduct, expressly or impliedly consented to take the risk of that danger. In such cases, the defendant will be relieved of responsibility for his negligence.

The essential elements of the defense of assumption of risk include the plaintiff's knowledge and appreciation of the danger and voluntary exposure to that danger. Thus it is applicable only when the injured person might reasonably have elected to expose himself to the peril. It does not apply when the exposure was due to any inability to escape after the danger became known to him.

Immunities   *Immunity* as a defense to a negligence suit applies when the defendant's status or relationship to the plaintiff exempts him from liability. Applicability of this defense depends on the issue at trial and on the jurisdiction in which the tort occurred. For example, while husband and wife were once considered a single legal entity, some jurisdictions now allow either spouse to sue the other for torts to property but not for personal injuries. Still other states have rejected the doctrine of interspousal immunity entirely. Similarly, several jurisdictions have, by statute or case law, abolished the policy of immunity between parent and child. Under the historical doctrine "the king can do no wrong," some units of government still enjoy governmental immunity from tort suits. Nevertheless, under the Federal Tort Claims Act [26 USC §§ 1346, 2671 et seq.], the federal government, by its consent, has been stripped of some immunities with regard to negligence of government employees. State governments may claim immunity from suit in some jurisdictions.

Most legislation that permits private individuals to sue a state, municipality, or other unit of government contains much shorter deadlines for filing claims than do laws specifying the conditions for initiating a lawsuit against a private party. Whenever suit against a governmental unit is contemplated, the matter should immediately be turned over to an attorney for evaluation and proper filing of the claim in a timely fashion.

Contract Form contracts may be used by the issuer as a defense against negligence in some cases. These often provide *exculpatory clauses* (provisions that tend to relieve a party from liability) that set forth the specific limitations of the area of liability. However, since exculpation clauses are creatures of contract law, there must be agreement between the parties in order for them to be valid. "Fine print" or "boiler plate" contracts, which usually appear on the reverse side of tickets and receipts and typically deny any liability in an all-inclusive fashion, may be ineffective to the extent the attempted limitation was not conspicuous. Even if the limitations do become part of the agreement, they might not be enforced by the courts if they are unconscionable (unreasonably harsh). While some cases hold that persons may agree in advance that one of them shall not be liable to the other for negligence, the modern judicial trend is not to uphold such agreements if one of the parties, such as an employee, was clearly at a bargaining disadvantage.

Releases A defense frequently raised is that the injured person gave a release of his or her rights to claim damages for the defendant's negligence. A *release* is a contract by which the releasor gives up or abandons a claim or right to the person against whom the claim exists. While the law favors and seeks to encourage private settlement of tort disputes and accords great weight to releases as a means of promoting out-of-court settlements, the law also favors just compensation of those who are injured by tortious acts. In many states courts permit the setting aside of a release that was not executed fairly and knowingly by the releasor. The need to protect those who literally sign away their rights of judicial recovery against others is particularly acute in view of the prevalence in modern business of insurance adjusters, who are often experienced business people, or attorneys motivated by a desire to settle claims as quickly and inexpensively as possible.

A release is of no legal effect as a defense to a tort suit if the release was forged, prohibited by law, given by one who was powerless to release the right, executed before any liability arose, or if the releasor was ignorant of the nature of the instrument being signed, or—as in most cases—if the true nature of the plaintiff's injuries was not known at the time he or she signed the release. The last situation may occur when a seriously injured person signs a release in satisfaction "of all present and future claims," not knowing how serious the injuries are.

6:6 Comparative Negligence

At common law, a plaintiff's contributory negligence was a complete bar to recovery against a negligent defendant. The doctrine of *comparative negligence* is an attempt to provide a system in which contributory negligence by the plaintiff is not a complete bar to recovery against a negligent defendant. In the absence of comparative negligence legislation, courts are very reluctant to apportion damages between a negligent plaintiff and a negligent defendant. A comparative negligence statute typically will apportion damages between negligent parties who injure one another in proportion to their fault. For example, if there are $10,000 in damages to the plaintiff, and the plaintiff is found by the court or jury to be 30 percent at fault, the plaintiff would be entitled to recover $7,000 from the defendant.

Under the rule of comparative negligence, even though the plaintiff was guilty of negligence that operated concurrently with the defendant's negligence as the cause of his injury, the plaintiff may recover if the degree of his negligence was less than that of the defendant. Under this doctrine, the plaintiff's negligence does not relieve the defendant entirely from liability, as under the old common-law rule of contributory negligence, but merely diminishes the damages recoverable.

No-fault insurance legislation has been enacted in several jurisdictions. The idea behind no-fault insurance is that regardless of legal fault, an insured motorist who suffers injury from an automobile accident shall receive recompense from his or her own insurer. Under some no-fault statutes tort liability is abolished, although under other no-fault statutes the exemption from tort liability does not apply when injuries of a serious nature are received as the result of an automobile accident. The purpose of no-fault insurance plans is to afford partial reparation for the objectively provable economic losses resulting from automobile accidents.[1]

6:7   Strict Liability

Strict liability is liability without fault. That is, under some circumstances a person can be liable for having caused an injury regardless of whether that person was negligent. Occasionally, a distinction is made between strict liability and so-called "absolute liability," which is liability under all circumstances. Today, however, both phrases are used interchangeably by most courts. Strict liability is based on a policy that an injured person must be given a right of recovery even though the person causing the injury did not act negligently.

Strict liability is applicable in situations in which social policy requires that the defendant make good the harm that results to others from abnormal risks inherent in those activities not considered blameworthy because they are reasonably incident to desirable industries or undertakings. The basis of liability in such cases is the intentional behavior of exposing a community to those abnormal risks. For example, strict liability has been found in cases where the use of chemical sprays, harmful gases, fumes, waste material, or other forms of pollution has resulted in the escape of those substances from one person's land onto the land or into the water supply of another.

Certain activities, which were undoubtedly dangerous when first begun as industries, sometimes over the course of time and through technological

---

[1] No-fault insurance is discussed in Chapter 41.

developments, have become "ordinary" and therefore no longer ultrahazardous. It has been held, for example, that flying is now so common that it is no longer ultrahazardous. Today, an airplane, when properly handled and cared for mechanically, is not inherently dangerous. Experimental planes, however, may still be considered dangerous; therefore, their owners or operators may be held strictly liable for damage. In some jurisdictions, blasting may or may not be subject to strict liability, depending on the location of the activity. If blasting occurs in an urban or highly populated area, it may be considered an ultrahazardous activity for which the defendant is subject to strict liability; if it is done in rural or unpopulated areas, the defendant's conduct may be judged by traditional negligence standards.

In strict liability suits, the defense of assumption of risk may be asserted against a plaintiff who voluntarily encounters a known danger and by his or her conduct expressly or impliedly consents to the risk of the danger. Contributory negligence, on the other hand, is no defense to strict liability.

The theory of strict liability frequently is invoked in product liability law since many products can cause injury if they are defectively designed or manufactured. The rationale for the use of strict liability theory in those cases is that the manufacturer is in a better position than the buyer to bear the risk of loss from a defective product. An additional rationale is that imposing the risk of loss on the manufacturer gives the manufacturer a better basis for deciding whether to produce a particular product. Chapter 21 considers the use of negligence and strict liability in product liability cases.

The following decision is instructive in setting forth the policy considerations behind judicial acceptance of the strict liability doctrine. Tracing the historical development of the doctrine and the present-day policy considerations for its existence, the court expressly holds the strict liability doctrine to be applicable in its jurisdiction.

Cities Service Co.
v
State
312 So2d 799 (1975)
Florida Court of Appeals

FACTS: The state of Florida brought suit against Cities Service, a mining company, seeking, among other things, damages caused by a dam break in one of the defendant's settling ponds, as a result of which one billion gallons of phosphate slime contained in the pond escaped into a state creek, killing countless fish and inflicting other damage. The trial court awarded damages against the defendant, holding it liable without regard to negligence or fault. The defendant appealed.

ISSUE: Is the owner of property on which ultrahazardous products are stored liable for damage caused to downstream landowners by the escape of those products?

RESULT: Yes. Such a landowner is liable for the injury that could foreseeably be caused by the ultrahazardous, nonnatural use of the land.

REASONING:

*   *   *

The determination of this appeal necessarily requires the consideration of the doctrine of strict liability for the hazardous use of one's land which was first announced in *Rylands v Fletcher*, 1868, L.R. 3 H.L. 330. In that case the defendants, who were millowners, had constructed a reservoir upon their land. The water broke through into the shaft of an abandoned coal mine and flooded along connecting passages into the adjoining mine of the plaintiff. When the case reached the Exchequer Chamber, Justice Blackburn said:

> "We think that the true rule of law is that the person who for his own purposes brings on his land and collects and keeps there anything likely to do mischief if it escapes, must keep it at his peril, and if he does not do so he is prima facie answerable for all the damage which is the natural consequences of its escape."

This statement was limited in the House of Lords to the extent that Lord Cairns said that the principle applied only to a "nonnatural" use of the defendant's land as distinguished from "any purpose for which it might in the ordinary course of the enjoyment of land be used."

Since that time there have been countless decisions both in England and America construing the application of this doctrine. Most of the early American decisions rejected the doctrine. However, the pendulum has now decidedly swung toward its acceptance. W. Prosser, *The Law of Torts* § 78 (4th ed. 1971). According to Prosser, by 1971 the doctrine had been approved in principle by thirty jurisdictions with only seven states still rejecting the principle.

While the application of the doctrine has not been specifically passed upon by the appellate courts of Florida, an early Supreme Court case implies its acceptance. In *Pensacola Gas Co. v Pebbly* (1889) 25 Fla. 381, 5 So. 593, the plaintiff claimed damages which resulted when a neighboring landowner constructed a gas works and allowed refuse to spill out onto the land and sink through the sand into the common water thereby polluting the plaintiff's well. The trial court apparently charged the members of the jury that the plaintiff would be entitled to a verdict if they determined that the plaintiff's wells were rendered unfit for use by the defendant without regard to the question of negligence. . . .

In early days it was important to encourage persons to use their land by whatever means were available for the purpose of commercial and industrial development. In a frontier society there was little likelihood that a dangerous use of land could cause damage to one's neighbor. Today our life has become more complex. Many areas are overcrowded, and even the non-negligent use of one's land can cause extensive damages to a neighbor's property. Though there are still many hazardous activities which are socially desirable, it now seems reasonable that they pay their own way. It is too much to ask an innocent neighbor to bear the burden thrust upon him as a consequence of an abnormal use of the land next door. The doctrine of *Rylands v Fletcher* should be applied in Florida.

There remains, however, the serious question of whether the impounding of phosphate slime by Cities Service in connection with its mining operations is a nonnatural use of the land. In opposition to the State's motion, Cities Service filed an affidavit of the manager of the plant where the dam break occurred. The affidavit points out that the property is peculiarly suitable for the mining of phosphate and that the central Florida area of which Polk County is the hub is the largest producer of phosphate rock in Florida. It further appears that Florida produced over 80% of the nation's marketable phosphate rock and one-third of the world production thereof in 1973. The affidavit goes on to explain that the storing of phosphate slimes in diked settling ponds is an essential part of the traditional method of mining phosphate rock. Hence, Cities Service argues that its mining operations were a natural and intended use of this particular land. . . .

The American Law Institute has considered this question in §§ 519 and 520 of the *Restatement of the Law of Torts* (1938). These sections state:

> "§ 519. MISCARRIAGE OF ULTRAHAZARDOUS ACTIVITIES CAREFULLY CARRIED ON.
>
> Except as stated in §§ 521–4, one who carries on an ultrahazardous activity is liable to another whose person, land or chattels the actor should recognize as likely to be harmed by the unpreventable miscarriage of the activity for harm resulting thereto from that which makes the activity ultrahazardous, although the utmost care is exercised to prevent the harm.
>
> § 520. DEFINITION OF ULTRAHAZARDOUS ACTIVITY.
>
> An activity is ultrahazardous if it
>
> (a) necessarily involves a risk of serious harm to the person, land or chattels of others which cannot be eliminated by the exercise of the utmost care, and
>
> (b) is not a matter of common usage."

Recognizing the evolving nature of the law in this area, the American Law Institute published Tentative Draft No. 10 in 1964 in which certain changes were recommended for §§ 519 and 520. Thus, in § 519 and § 520 the substitution of the words "abnormally dangerous" is suggested in place of the word "ultrahazardous." In § 520, the following factors are said to be pertinent in determining whether an activity is abnormally dangerous:

> "(a) Whether the activity involves a high degree of risk of some harm to the person, land or chattels of others;
>
> (b) Whether the harm which may result from it is likely to be great;
>
> (c) Whether the risk cannot be eliminated by the exercise of reasonable care;
>
> (d) Whether the activity is not a matter of common usage;
>
> (e) Whether the activity is inappropriate to the place where it is carried on; and
>
> (f) The value of the activity to the community."

Referring to these factors, F. James, *The Law of Torts*, Supp. to Vol. 2, § 14.4 (1968), states [in part]:

"The justification for strict liability, in other words, is that useful but dangerous activities must pay their own way. . . . There is nothing in this reasoning which would exempt *very* useful activities from the rule, as is shown by the granting of compensation even where the activity is of such paramount importance to society that it justifies the exercise of eminent domain. And if the law were to embrace wholly the principle of strict liability and its underlying rationale, there would be no place for the consideration of this factor. But this is not the present case. Tort law today contains two opposing strains or principles, strict liability and liability based on fault. It is not surprising, therefore, that any attempt to draw a line between them (which is being done in Section 520) should contain factors which would be irrelevant if one principle or the other alone were being consistently pursued. At any rate this factor will probably continue to influence courts in fact for some time to come." . . .

In the final analysis, we are impressed by the magnitude of the activity and the attendant risk of enormous damage. The impounding of billions of gallons of phosphatic slimes behind earthen walls which are subject to breaking even with the exercise of the best of care strikes us as being both "ultrahazardous" and "abnormally dangerous," as the case may be.

This is not clear water which is being impounded. Here, Cities Service introduced water into its mining operation which when combined with phosphatic wastes produced a phosphatic slime which had a high potential for damage to the environment. If a break occurred, it was to be expected that extensive damage would be visited upon property many miles away. In this case, the damage, in fact, extended almost to the mouth of the Peace River, which is far beyond the phosphate mining area described in the Cities Service affidavit. We conclude that the Cities Service slime reservoir constituted a nonnatural use of the land such as to invoke the doctrine of strict liability.

. . . All of the assertions of Cities Service relative to the need to maintain settling ponds in its mining operations, the suitability of the land for this purpose and the importance of phosphate to the community as well as to the world at large may be accepted at face value. Admitting the desirability of phosphate and the necessity of mining in this manner, the rights of adjoining landowners and the interests of the public in our environment require the imposition of a doctrine which places the burden upon the parties whose activity made it possible for the damages to occur. . . .

Grimes, Judge.

Key Concepts and Terms

- All persons have a duty to exercise reasonable care toward others. To recover for negligence, an injured person must show that (1) the defendant had a duty to exercise reasonable care, (2) there was a breach of that duty,

(3) the defendant's conduct caused the plaintiff's injury, and (4) damages resulted.

- A person breaches the duty to exercise reasonable care toward others when he or she fails to exercise the degree of care that a reasonable person would have exercised under the same or similar circumstances. Under the *res ipsa loquitur* doctrine, the very fact that a particular injury has occurred may itself tend to establish a breach of duty on the part of the defendant.

- To recover in a negligence suit, the plaintiff must establish that the defendant's negligent act was both the cause in fact and the proximate cause of the injury. Thus, it must be shown that the injury would not have happened "but for" the defendant's conduct, and that there were no intervening forces between the negligent conduct and the plaintiff's injury. Furthermore, the plaintiff's injury must have been within the scope of a foreseeable risk.

- There are several defenses that a defendant may assert in a negligence suit, including contributory negligence, the last clear chance doctrine, assumption of risk, immunity, contract, and release from liability.

- Comparative negligence legislation, which exists in some states, provides that even though the plaintiff was guilty of negligence that operated concurrently with the defendant's negigence as the cause of his injury, the plaintiff may nevertheless recover if the degree of his negligence was less than that of the defendant. Accordingly, damages are apportioned between the defendant and the plaintiff in proportion to each person's fault.

- Strict liability is liability without fault. It applies under circumstances in which public policy requires the defendant to make good the harm that resulted from an activity that, although socially necessary or desirable, involves an abnormal risk of harm to others.

- Assumption of Risk
- Breach of Duty
- Causation
- Cause in Fact
- Comparative Negligence
- Contributory Negligence
- Dramshop Acts
- Exculpatory Clause
- Immunities from Suit
- Last Clear Chance Doctrine
- Negligence
- Nonfeasance
- Proximate Cause
- "Reasonable Person" Standard
- Release
- Res Ipsa Loquitur Doctrine
- Strict Liability

Questions and Case Problems

1. Under what circumstances, if any, may a failure to act constitute negligence?
2. Discuss the various defenses that may be available to a negligence suit.
3. While operating his lawn mower in a careless manner, Andy strikes and seriously injures Bill's dog. In a frenzy, the dog runs into the house and bites Bill. Is Andy liable to Bill?

4. Amy is a passenger on a bus operated by Bus Company. She is injured when the bus collides with a car driven by Charlie. Both the bus driver and Charlie are negligent. Which, if either, driver's negligence is the "cause in fact" of Amy's injuries?

5. What is the rationale for strict liability? In your explanation indicate whether or not you agree with the rationale.

6. While driving her car in heavy traffic, Joan is distracted by a discussion she is having with her passenger, Peggy. As a result Joan strikes a truck driven by Felix. (a) Assume Felix's truck contained propane fuel and that the collision set off an explosion, injuring Phillip, a pedestrian on the street. Is Joan subject to liability for Phillip's injuries? (b) Assume that the same explosion knocked some bottles off a shelf in a medical laboratory nearby. The bottles shattered and a worker, Wilma, was cut by the flying glass. Is Joan subject to liability for Wilma's injury? (c) Assume that Joan herself was injured and rendered unconscious in the collision and that her car caught on fire. Assume further that a passerby, Sam, saw her predicament and rushed to her aid, but was injured himself in so doing. Is Joan subject to liability for Sam's injuries?

7. What is a release to a negligence claim? Are releases always upheld by the courts? Discuss.

8. A city ordinance prohibits the parking of cars so as to block driveways. In violation of this ordinance, Jones parks his car in front of Dr. Paul's office driveway. Mrs. Smith, a widow who resides in a nearby rural area, telephones Dr. Paul to come out right away to treat her son, Tom, who had just been bitten by a snake. Dr. Paul starts to go but is unable to back his car out of his driveway. Seeing no one around, Dr. Paul releases the brake on Jones's car and attempts to push it away. In so doing, he develops a hernia, suffers excruciating pain, and returns with difficulty to his office, where he makes several phone calls trying to get another doctor to go and see Tom but finds none available. It is agreed that had Dr. Paul been able to respond to Mrs. Smith's call, he would in all probability have been able to save Tom's arm, which had to be amputated because the snake bite was not treated quickly enough. Is Jones liable in negligence to Dr. Paul and/or to Tom? Discuss.

9. What are the elements of a negligence suit? What is the difference between the tort of negligence and an intentional tort?

10. A contractor is blasting rock at a remote desert quarry. Unexpectedly, the vibrations trigger an underground avalanche, which shifts subsurface formations miles away and knocks out a prospector's water well. Assuming no negligence, is the contractor liable for damages to the prospector's well?

7 Criminal Law and Procedure

7:1 Introduction

A crime is an offense, punishable by law, against society. Legislatures identify the interests of society and proscribe behavior that threatens or compromises those interests. Government, through the criminal justice system, punishes criminal offenders by imprisonment, fine, or execution. The harsh reality of criminal law is that, unlike a civil lawsuit, the stakes of a criminal lawsuit may be the loss of personal freedom or life itself. Thus, no field of law more directly affects the core principles of society.

As the interests of society are dynamic, so criminal law is dynamic. Decisions as to what types of conduct should be considered criminal reflect the changing mores and ethical precepts of the community. For example, the laws concerning abortion, prostitution, homosexual behavior, use or possession of marijuana, spousal battery, and rape have changed in recent years, reflecting changing attitudes about what behavior society deems worthy of punishment.

It should be pointed out that there are several theories about the role of punishment in the criminal law. Most people presume that punishing an individual for a particular behavior deters the individual from engaging in that behavior again, although this does not always seem to be the case. Also, it is assumed that that punishment will deter other people from engaging in the punished behavior. Another theory is that the means of punishment may have the effect of rehabilitating the offender. At the very least, punishment fulfills the function of supplying *retribution* against the offender.

Criminal law is statutory; there are no common-law crimes in American society. The rationale behind this is that society ought to specify clearly, and in advance, what behavior will not be tolerated. Thus, criminal statutes are not retroactive. In other ways, particularly in the area of criminal procedure, criminal law exacts greater certainty from the justice system than does the civil law. This reflects the very substantial interest both society and the individual defendant have in certainty and fairness. In both the criminal and the civil justice systems, the parties on each side seek to advance their interests. In the criminal justice system, however, the prosecution (the government) is expected to regard fairness to the defendant and truth in the fact-finding process to be a clear interest of society which the prosecution must protect, even if doing so would cause the government to lose the case.

This chapter explains the major areas of substantive criminal law and criminal procedure. Crimes by and against businesses, often called "white collar crimes," are discussed in Chapter 8.

Classification of Crimes   Traditionally, crimes were divided into two classes: *felonies* and *misdemeanors*. Felonies are more serious crimes than misdemeanors and generally involve harsher punishment. Some states classify felonies as offenses punishable by death or imprisonment for more than one year, while in other states a crime is a felony if it is punishable by death or incarceration in a state prison, as opposed to a county or city jail. Any crime that is not a felony is a misdemeanor.

In some states, certain acts are prohibited but are punishable by only a small fine. These offenses are sometimes referred to as violations or *infractions* and should be distinguished from crimes. Littering and illegal parking are examples of this type of offense.

Role of Defense Counsel   The defense attorney's role in preserving the fundamental constitutional guaranties on which America was founded cannot be overestimated. A lawyer's duty to both his client and the legal system, according to the American Bar Association's Code of Professional Responsibility, is to represent the client zealously within the bounds of the law. Without a dedicated and competent defense lawyer to counterbalance the resources and authority of the prosecution, a criminal defendant's constitutional rights would be jeopardized.

7:2   Elements of a Crime

An act is a crime if (1) the person who committed the act did so voluntarily and intentionally, and (2) the act was overt and unlawful. Under certain circumstances, a failure to act is a crime. If a person allowed something to happen that he could and should have prevented, or failed to do something that the law required him to do, he has committed a crime. This failure to act is called an omission. Examples of omission are a parent's failure to provide medical care to a child, a motorist's failure to stop at the scene of a traffic accident in which he is involved, and a taxpayer's failure to file tax returns.

While not technically considered part of the crime—that is, part of the act and intent—an essential element for criminal liability is causation. The defendant's act or conduct must have been the actual cause of the intended result or at least a material factor in bringing about harm.

EXAMPLE: A mugger observes Harry apparently asleep on a park bench, approaches, and shoots him five times to make sure that he has killed him in order to take his wallet. Unknown to the mugger, Harry had suffered a fatal heart attack an hour before and was already dead when the mugger shot him. Although he may have committed other crimes, the mugger is not guilty of murder since he did not in fact kill anyone, even though he had the intent.

A few criminal statutes dispense entirely with a state-of-mind requirement, giving rise to so-called "strict liability" crimes. A strict liability crime is one for which a person is guilty merely by committing the act. For example, the crime of selling narcotics does not usually require proof that the defendant knew the item sold was a narcotic; and the National Firearms Act, making it a crime to possess unregistered firearms, does not require proof that the defendant knew the firearm was unregistered.

It must be emphasized that the intent to commit a prohibited act, called *mens rea*—and not the *motive*—determines criminality. Thus, a person may have an arguably ethical motive or a "good reason" for committing an act and still be guilty of a crime.

EXAMPLE: A enters the hospital room of B, a terminally ill patient who has only a few days to live. A disconnects B's life-support system to prevent B from experiencing the remaining days of excruciating pain. Under present concepts of criminal law, A, in removing the life-support system, is a criminal because she has committed an unlawful act—killing another human being—with the intent to take the other person's life. The intent is criminal because it is an intent to commit an unlawful act, even though the motive or reason is arguably ethically proper or meritorious.

7:3   Particular Crimes

Crimes are broadly classified as crimes against persons, crimes against property, morals offenses, and crimes against government.

Crimes Against Persons   There are many crimes that are classified as crimes against persons. The following are a few of them:

- Murder: the intentional killing of a person without legal justification or excuse.
- Battery: the unlawful application of force to a person.
- Assault: an unlawful attempt to apply force to a person, also called attempted battery.
- Mayhem: the malicious disfiguring of a person.
- Rape: sexual intercourse with a female without her consent and usually by force.
- False imprisonment: intentional unlawful confinement of a person.

Crimes Against Property   The most common crime against property is the taking of another person's property. The modern trend is to consolidate many of these acquisition offenses into the statutory crime simply called theft. Crimes that constitute theft include

- Larceny: a wrongful taking of personal property with an intent to permanently deprive the owner of it.
- Embezzlement: the fraudulent appropriation of property by a person to whom it has been entrusted.

- False pretenses: the obtaining of title to property by means of a false representation with intent to defraud the victim.
- Robbery: the taking of another's personal property, by means of force or fear, from his person or immediate presence and against his will.
- Extortion: the obtaining of property by means of threats but not necessarily to do violence to the person.
- Receiving stolen property: obtaining unauthorized possession of stolen property with the knowledge that it is stolen.

Most states have enacted bad-check legislation. While the statutes vary, typically the elements of the crime are the making, drawing, or delivering a check at a time when there are not sufficient funds in the account to cover the check, with the knowledge of the insufficiency.

Crimes against property may also involve a structure or dwelling place. They include burglary—the unauthorized entry into a structure with the intent to commit a theft or other felony, and arson—the malicious burning of a structure. Burning property with the intent to defraud an insurer is frequently made a separate crime.

Morals Offenses   In early England, morals offenses were not common-law crimes but were punished by church authorities. Today, such matters are frequently made criminal by statute. There is, however, a trend toward removing some of these offenses from the reach of criminal law. Included in the category of morals offenses are

- Fornication: illicit sexual intercourse between persons not married to each other.
- Adultery: sexual intercourse by a married person with some person other than his or her spouse.
- Illicit cohabitation: living together in adultery or fornication.
- Bigamy: being married to more than one person at the same time.
- Incest: marriage, or sexual relations, between persons who are closely related by blood.

Crimes Against Government   Most criminal statutes set forth particular offenses against the government or against the administration of justice. Such offenses include

- Breach of the peace (or disorderly conduct): to unreasonably disturb the public peace.
- Riot: a tumultuous disturbance of the peace by three or more persons acting together to carry out a common enterprise.
- Treason: levying war against the United States, adhering to its enemies, or giving its enemies aid and comfort.
- Counterfeiting: falsely making, forging, or altering any obligation or other security of the government with intent to defraud.
- Misprision of felony: the failure to report or prosecute a person known to have committed a felony.

- Compounding a crime: agreeing for money not to prosecute another person for a felony.
- Perjury: the willful giving of a false statement under oath in a judicial proceeding.
- Subornation of perjury: the intentional causing of another person to commit perjury.
- Bribery: the giving of something of value to a person holding public office with the intent to influence the discharge of the person's legal duties.

7:4   Criminal Procedure: Pretrial

Underlying criminal procedure is the premise that society can do little to an individual that is worse than imprisoning or executing an innocent person. Criminal procedure assumes that it is worse for an innocent person to be punished than for a guilty person to go free. The strong interest that both society and its individual constituents have in protecting the innocent—both the innocent accused and the innocent victims—is protected by state law on criminal procedure and also by the federal Constitution. Because the two sources of law are so closely intertwined, they are discussed together in the following sections of the chapter.

Arrest and Indictment   When a person is *arrested*, he or she is taken into custody, usually by a police officer. The arrest may be made pursuant to a warrant or, if the police officer has probable cause to believe that the person has committed a felony, without a warrant. A warrant may be obtained through a *grand jury indictment* or may be a *judicial arrest warrant*, according to state or federal law. A grand jury consists of a body of citizens appointed by the court to listen to the sworn evidence against a suspect and determine whether that evidence is sufficient to formally accuse, or indict, the person of a crime. A judicial arrest warrant is issued by a judge on the sworn testimony of a police officer to the effect that there is probable cause to believe the suspect is guilty of a crime. Even if arrest is effected by judicial warrant, a *prosecutor* may take, or may be required to take, the case to a grand jury before the accused is formally charged with a crime. The Fifth Amendment to the federal Constitution requires grand jury indictment in federal felony cases.

Arraignment   After arrest, the accused may be released on bail, which is a kind of bond intended to guarantee that he or she will show up for *arraignment*. Arraignment is the judicial proceeding in which the accused is formally charged with commission of a specific crime. The accused must then plead guilty or not guilty, or else move that the facts stated do not constitute the commission of a crime. If a guilty plea is entered voluntarily and with an understanding of its consequences, the accused need only be *sentenced*. If the accused enters a plea of not guilty, the state is then obliged to prove guilt "beyond a reasonable doubt" in a criminal trial. The high burden of proof for the state reflects the premises discussed above.

Constitutional Safeguards in Pretrial   During the pretrial period law enforcement officers use various methods to obtain evidence against a criminal suspect, including observation, surveillance, searches or seizures of evidence, and interrogations of the victim, witnesses, or the suspect. Inherent in some of these methods is the danger that the evidence obtained may be false and lead to conviction of an innocent person, or that unrestrained police tactics may endanger fundamental individual rights and freedoms.

For federal criminal proceedings, the federal Constitution provides the accused with protection of these rights and freedoms, most significantly through the Bill of Rights. In addition, the Supreme Court has held repeatedly that the concept of due process in the Fourteenth Amendment encompasses most of the Bill of Rights and applies those provisions to state criminal proceedings. The Fourth Amendment protects individuals against unreasonable searches and seizures:

> The right of the people to be secure in their person, houses, papers, and effects, against unreasonable searches and seizures, shall not be violated, and no warrants shall issue, but upon probable cause, supported by oath or affirmation, and particularly describing the place to be searched, and the person or things to be seized.

The Sixth Amendment grants the right to assistance of counsel in criminal prosecutions. This right affects an accused's ability to assert his or her rights. Indeed, the Supreme Court of the United States has held this right to be so fundamental that state and federal courts are required to appoint legal counsel free of charge to persons who cannot otherwise afford a lawyer. Inherent in the concept of the right to counsel is that the representation be competent. Ineffective representation has been held to be worse than no representation at all.

The Fifth Amendment provides additional protection to the accused, including a privilege against compelled testimony against himself, the privilege against self-incrimination:

> No person shall be held to answer for a capital, or otherwise infamous crime, unless on a presentment or indictment of a Grand Jury . . . ; nor shall any person be subject for the same offence to be twice put in jeopardy of life or limb; nor shall be compelled in any criminal case to be a witness against himself, nor be deprived of life, liberty, or property, without due process of law. . . .

Under the landmark case of *Miranda v Arizona*,[1] whenever state or federal law enforcement officers take a person into "custody" or otherwise deprive him of "freedom of action in any significant way," they are required to give the accused, prior to *any* questioning, the following five warnings which are now included under the constitutional privilege against self-incrimination: (1) that he has a right to remain silent; (2) that any statement he does make can and will be used as evidence against him in a court of law; (3) that he has the

---

[1] 384 US 436 (1966).

right to consult with counsel *before* answering any questions; (4) that he has the right to have counsel present with him during the interrogation; (5) that if he cannot afford an attorney, one will be appointed for him without cost, prior to the questioning, if he so desires. The giving of these warnings is an "absolute prerequisite" to any police interrogation and to the admissibility in evidence of any confession or statements made by the accused during in-custody interrogation.

Finally, one of the animating forces of constitutional criminal law is the concept of due process in the Fifth and Fourteenth Amendments. Due process has dynamic meaning: what process is "due" depends on the interest the person has at stake and the seriousness of deprivation. As the following classic case illustrates, due process embodies fundamental beliefs about fairness in the judicial system.

Rochin

v

California
342 US 165 (1952)
United States Supreme Court

FACTS: Police officers had information that Rochin, the defendant, was selling narcotics. They illegally entered his dwelling, whereupon he swallowed two capsules containing morphine. The officers attempted to extract the capsules from his mouth by force. The defendant was handcuffed and taken to a hospital, where, at the direction of one of the officers, a doctor, against the defendant's will, forced an emetic solution through a tube into his stomach. On evidence of the capsules so obtained, the defendant was convicted in a state court of illegal possession of morphine.

ISSUE: Did the state's method of obtaining evidence violate Rochin's right to due process of law?

RESULT: Yes. The force used to extract evidence from Rochin violated fundamental constitutional rules of fairness, and therefore deprived him of his liberty without due process of law.

REASONING:

* * *

. . . Regard for the requirements of the Due Process Clause "inescapably imposes upon this Court an exercise of judgment upon the whole course of the proceedings [resulting in a conviction] in order to ascertain whether they offend those canons of decency and fairness which express the notions of justice of English-speaking peoples even toward those charged with the most heinous offenses." *Malinski v New York*, . . . (324 US at 416, 417, 89 L ed 1039, 65 S Ct 781). These standards of justice are not authoritatively formulated anywhere as though they were specifics. Due process of law is a summarized constitutional guarantee of respect for those personal immunities which, as Mr. Justice Cardozo twice wrote for the Court, are "so rooted in the traditions and conscience of our people as to be ranked as fundamental," . . . or are "implicit in the concept of ordered liberty." . . .

The vague contours of the Due Process Clause do not leave judges at large. We may not draw on our merely personal and private notions and disregard the limits that bind judges in their judicial function. Even though the concept of due process of law is not final and fixed, these limits are derived from considerations that are fused in the whole nature of our judicial process. See Cardozo, The Nature of the Judicial Process; The Growth of the Law; The Paradoxes of Legal Science. These are considerations deeply rooted in reason and in the compelling traditions of the legal profession. The Due Process Clause places upon this Court the duty of exercising a judgment, within the narrow confines of judicial power in reviewing State convictions, upon interests of society pushing in opposite directions.

Due process of law thus conceived is not to be derided as resort to a revival of "natural law." To believe that this judicial exercise of judgment could be avoided by freezing "due process of law" at some fixed stage of time or thought is to suggest that the most important aspect of constitutional adjudication is a function for inanimate machines and not for judges, for whom the independence safeguarded by Article 3 of the Constitution was designed and who are presumably guided by established standards of judicial behavior. Even cybernetics has not yet made that haughty claim. To practice the requisite detachment and to achieve sufficient objectivity no doubt demands of judges the habit of self-discipline and self-criticism, incertitude that one's own views are incontestable and alert tolerance toward views not shared. But these are precisely the presuppositions of our judicial process. They are precisely the qualities society has a right to expect from those entrusted with ultimate judicial power.

Restraints on our jurisdiction are self imposed only in the sense that there is from our decisions no immediate appeal short of impeachment or constitutional amendment. But that does not make due process of law a matter of judicial caprice. The faculties of the Due Process Clause may be indefinite and vague, but the mode of their ascertainment is not selfwilled. In each case "due process of law" requires an evaluation based on a disinterested inquiry pursued in the spirit of science, on a balanced order of facts exactly and fairly stated, on the detached consideration of conflicting claims. . . .

Applying these general considerations to the circumstances of the present case, we are compelled to conclude that the proceedings by which this conviction was obtained do more than offend some fastidious squeamishness or private sentimentalism about combatting crime too energetically. This is conduct that shocks the conscience. Illegally breaking into the privacy of the petitioner, the struggle to open his mouth and remove what was there, the forcible extraction of his stomach's contents—this course of proceeding by agents of government to obtain evidence is bound to offend even hardened sensibilities. They are methods too close to the rack and the screw to permit of constitutional differentiation. . . .

. . . Use of involuntary verbal confessions in State criminal trials is constitutionally obnoxious not only because of their unreliability. They are inadmissible under the Due Process Clause and even though statements contained in them may be independently established as true. Coerced confessions offend the community's sense of fair play and decency. So here, to sanction the brutal conduct which naturally enough was condemned by the court whose judgment is before us, would be to afford brutality the cloak of law. Nothing would be more calculated to discredit law and thereby to brutalize the temper of a society. . . .

We are not unmindful that hypothetical situations can be conjured up, shading imperceptibly from the circumstances of this case and by gradations producing practical differences despite seemingly logical extensions. But the Constitution is "intended to preserve practical and substantial rights, not to maintain theories." . . .

Frankfurter, Justice.

7:5 Criminal Procedure: Trial and Post-trial

The law varies among states with respect to criminal procedure and the admissibility of evidence in criminal trials. The basic structure of the criminal trial, however, parallels that of the civil trial. After the opening statements, the state establishes its case through testimony and physical evidence. The state must prove its case "beyond a reasonable doubt," a standard much higher than the civil standard, which usually is "a preponderance of the evidence." At the close of the state's case, the defendant has the opportunity to test the sufficiency of the state's case through a motion for summary judgment. If the state survives the judge's decision as to whether a reasonable person could fail to have a reasonable doubt, the defendant has the opportunity to present a defense, which may consist of rebuttal of the state's evidence or an affirmative defense to the charge. The sufficiency of the state's case usually can be tested through motions at the close of the defendant's case as well.

Then, if the trial is by jury, the case is submitted to them; otherwise the facts are decided by the judge. If there is a jury, the judge instructs the jury as to the applicable law. When the jury returns a *verdict* on the facts, the judge applies the law and enters judgment of guilty or not guilty. If the defendant is judged not guilty, the case is dismissed and, in effect, cannot be reopened. If the defendant is judged guilty, the judge pronounces a sentence. In certain types of cases, most notably capital cases (punishable by death), state law separates the sentencing phase of the trial from the adjudication of guilt or innocence.

After conviction the defendant may request a new trial on the ground of failure of due process, or an error in the jury instructions or the application of the law, or on the ground of significant new evidence. A defendant who fails to get a new trial may appeal on the ground of one or more legal errors at trial. Even after all grounds for appeal are exhausted, the convicted person may, through a writ of *habeas corpus*, test the sufficiency of the law or the procedure under which he or she was convicted during the *postconviction appeals*.

Constitutional Safeguards in Trial and Post-trial   The significant constitutional safeguards during and after trial include the right to counsel of the Sixth Amendment, the privilege against self-incrimination of the Fifth Amendment, and the right to due process of the Fifth and Fourteenth Amendments. In addition, the Sixth Amendment provides that in all criminal prosecutions the accused

> . . . shall enjoy the right to a speedy and public trial, by an impartial jury of the State and district wherein the crime shall have been committed, which district shall have been previously ascertained by law, and to be informed of the nature and cause of the accusation; to be confronted with the witnesses against him; to have compulsory process for obtaining witnesses in his favor, and to have the Assistance of Counsel for his defense.

These provisions have been held to mean, first, that the state cannot unreasonably delay bringing a defendant to trial. Further, the defendant has the right to *subpoena* (compel testimony of) witnesses, as well as the basic right to present and cross-examine witnesses, in order to defend the case. Both federal law and the law of many states require that a defendant be brought to trial within 60 days after indictment. A jury trial must be available to a defendant if conviction would result in a sentence of more than six months of incarceration. Finally, trials must be public and must be held in the place where the crime was committed, unless to do so would interfere with the defendant's right to a fair and impartial trial. Under appropriate circumstances, the judge may bar spectators from the trial or the defendant may request a *change of venue* (location).

7:6   Defenses to Criminal Charges

It is a basic tenet of the American judicial system that all individuals are presumed innocent of crime unless they are proven guilty beyond a *reasonable doubt* in a court of law after a fair trial with all constitutional safeguards. In many instances, there is no question that the person charged with a crime did commit the act. However, rather than admit to the crime and accept the punishment, the person may claim to have a legitimate defense that justifies, excuses, or mitigates the acts to take away any criminal liability. The commonly asserted defenses in criminal cases are discussed below.

Infancy   At common law, a child under the age of 7 was presumed to be unable to form a criminal intent and therefore could not be convicted of a crime. A child between 7 and 14 years of age was also presumed to be incapable of forming criminal intent, although the presumption was rebuttable if the prosecution could establish that the child knew what he was doing and that it was wrong. At ages 14 and older, children are treated as adults.

Modern statutes vary in their treatment of the infancy defense. Some have made the common-law rules into statutes and others have modified them. In any case, all American jurisdictions have legislation that confers on juvenile courts jurisdiction over children of certain ages alleged to have committed a crime. In juvenile court proceedings, the child is not convicted but is adjudicated "delinquent." Most states permit juvenile court proceedings, and even criminal convictions of persons under certain ages, to be sealed from the public by court order.

Insanity   There is considerable disagreement as to what constitutes *insanity*. In some states, to be legally insane the defendant must prove that as a result of his mental illness he either did not know the nature of his act, or did not know that the act was wrong. This is the M'Naghten Test. In other states, insanity is found if a defendant's acts resulted from an "irresistible impulse." In still other states, the test is whether the defendant's act was the "product of" a mental illness. Finally, a few states consider whether a defendant "lacked substantial capacity" to appreciate the criminality of his conduct or to conform his conduct to the requirements of law.

Intoxication   Voluntary *intoxication* by alcohol or drugs is not normally a defense to crime. However, with certain crimes that require a specific state of mind, evidence of intoxication may be a defense.

Self-defense   Generally, a person may use that force which reasonably appears necessary to defend himself against an apparent threat of unlawful and immediate violence from another person. "Deadly force" may be used in self-defense only if the defendant reasonably believes that the other person is about to inflict death or great bodily injury on him and that deadly force would be necessary to prevent the harm.

At common law, the defendant was required to retreat before using deadly force. Today most American courts do not impose this requirement. If, for example, a person is being threatened with a gun, he is entitled to use deadly force, if necessary, to defend himself from the attacker. Under certain circumstances, a person is entitled to use force in defense of other persons. A person need not simply stand by and watch as another person is attacked. The bystander has as much right to protect another person from crime as he does to protect himself.

The right to use force to protect property is more limited than the right to use force in protecting persons. For example, a person cannot use deadly force simply to defend his property against unlawful interference. The rationale is that the interest in security of property does not justify jeopardizing the lives of others.

Consent   Some crimes are defined in terms of the victim's lack of *consent*. If there is consent, it is a defense to a criminal charge. For example, rape requires the absence of the female's consent to intercourse, and proof of consent will be a bar to conviction.

Courts are more likely to recognize the defense of consent if the act did not involve serious bodily injury or the risk of such injury, or if there is a widespread acceptance of the risk, as in sporting events. For example, if during an ice hockey game one player grabs another player and breaks his nose with a hockey stick, the first player may not be criminally liable for battery because there is some degree of consent to roughness by the injured player.

Entrapment   A defendant may claim to have been lured into committing an act by a law enforcement officer. This is the defense of *entrapment*. Entrapment exists only if the law enforcement officer's conduct, rather than the predisposition of the defendant, created the intent to commit the act. The test is subjective because a court's finding of entrapment depends on what subjectively stimulated the commission of the crime.

Key Concepts and Terms

- A crime is an offense against the people. As the people's representative, the government may seek redress for the crime by prosecuting the person who committed the crime. A crime is an act or a failure to act (omission) that is (1) unlawful and (2) committed with a criminal intent. Crimes are classified as felonies, misdemeanors, and infractions.

- Punishment for a crime is imposed to prevent and deter the offender from committing future crimes, to deter others from committing similar crimes, to rehabilitate the offender, and for retribution.

- The Constitution protects persons who are accused of crimes by granting them certain rights. These rights include the right to be free from unreasonable searches and seizures; the privilege against self-incrimination; the right to a speedy, public trial; the right to confront prosecution witnesses; the right to cross-examination; the right to compel defense witnesses to appear in court in their behalf; and the right to legal counsel, which includes the right to court-appointed counsel if they cannot afford to hire an attorney.

- Conviction of a crime requires that the person accused of committing the crime be proven guilty beyond a reasonable doubt in a court of law after a fair trial and with all constitutional safeguards.

- Commonly asserted defenses in criminal cases are infancy, insanity, intoxication, self-defense, consent, and entrapment.

- Arraignment
- Arrest
- Bill of Rights
- Burden of Proof
- Consent
- Constitutional Safeguards
- Due Process
- Entrapment
- Felony
- Grand Jury
- Habeas Corpus
- Indictment
- Infancy
- Infractions
- Insanity
- Intoxication
- Mens Rea
- Misdemeanor
- Motive
- Postconviction Appeals
- Prosecutor
- Reasonable Doubt
- Retribution
- Self-Defense
- Sentence
- Subpoena
- Venue
- Verdict
- Warrant (Arrest)

Questions and Case Problems

1. Kramer, a trained professional athlete and black belt in karate, is walking down the street when he hears a person scream. He turns around and sees a child being dragged into a dark alley by a man with a knife in his hand. Kramer decides to do nothing and walks away. Is Kramer guilty of any crime? Discuss. Assume Kramer recognized the child and did not like her, and was glad to witness her peril and intentionally decided not to intervene. If the child is killed, is Kramer guilty of any crime? Discuss. What if the person in the alley was not a child but was Kramer's wife and he chose not to intervene? Would the result be the same? Discuss.

2. Donald intends to kill Vance and buys a rifle for this purpose. While Donald is engaged in target practice in his own backyard, Vance unexpectedly runs by and is killed by a bullet that ricochets from the target. Is Donald guilty of murder? Discuss.

3. What are society's reasons for punishing criminal conduct? Discuss.

4. Why should a person who has "obviously committed a crime and is clearly guilty" be entitled to the time and expense of a trial? Discuss.

5. Frank forces John at gunpoint to drive him away from the scene of a robbery. He then forces John to drive into a roadblock, striking and killing a police officer. For what crimes may Frank be prosecuted? Discuss.

6. Henry is speeding down a highway at night when his car strikes and injures Sam. Because of the darkness, Henry is unaware of the accident and does not stop. Has Henry "acted" so as to be guilty of violating a hit-and-run statute? Discuss.

7. Jane is standing on a street corner. A stranger runs past and thrusts a package into her hand. A police officer immediately approaches and arrests Jane for possession of narcotics. Assuming the package contains heroin, can Jane be convicted of possession? Are any defenses applicable? Discuss.

8. John is arrested for engaging in illicit activities at a pool hall. On the way to the police station, the police tell him that they will "treat him easy" if he admits to the activities. He confesses. Is the confession admissible against him at trial? Discuss.

9. Joe intentionally sets fire to his warehouse to collect insurance money. When he attempts to put out the fire, a firefighter has a heart attack and dies. For what possible crimes may Joe be prosecuted? Discuss.

10. Carolyn is charged with violating a statute that prohibits "any conduct infringing upon the public welfare." Is the statute constitutionally valid? Discuss.

8 White-Collar Crime

8:1 Introduction

White-collar crime has received considerable attention in recent years. Government agencies and officials, corporations and their officers, individual businesspersons, and average citizens have all become increasingly aware of the existence and cost of white-collar crime. White-collar crime affects all levels and types of business activity. The businessperson who knowingly sells a defective product that results in injury to the consumer, the businessperson who pays a bribe to obtain a contract, and the businessperson who issues securities in violation of the securities laws all may find themselves facing criminal as well as civil sanctions. Numerous other examples could be given. The point is that white-collar crime does not relate solely to one or another of the specific subjects discussed in this book; it relates to all of them.

It might be thought appropriate to discuss white-collar crime as a subcategory of crime generally. This has not been done because white-collar crime is different from street crime in many respects. Moreover, while street crime certainly has an effect on businesses and businesspersons, it is not uniquely connected to business in the same way that white-collar crime is.

For the above reasons, it seems preferable to treat white-collar crime as a specific subject. Consideration of white-collar crime serves as a useful tool for stressing the importance of the various precautions that are urged throughout this book. The various preventive measures discussed generally are framed in terms of avoidance of civil liability. It bears emphasizing, however, that adherence to the suggested practices might well save a businessperson the cost, not to mention the damage to business and personal reputation, that a criminal prosecution can entail.

Definitions   A major problem in discussing white-collar crime is defining the subject. Professor Sutherland, who coined the phrase "white-collar crime," defined it as "crime committed by a person of respectability and high social status in the course of his occupation."[1] Over the years the concept of white-

---

[1] E. Sutherland, *White-Collar Crime* 9 (1949).

collar crime has broadened, with emphasis placed more on the nature of the criminal activity than on the social status of the offender. According to the definition now most commonly quoted, white-collar crime is "an illegal act or series of illegal acts committed by nonphysical means and by concealment or guile, to obtain money or property, to avoid the payment or loss of money or property, or to obtain business or personal advantage."[2]

Numerous other attempts have been made to define white-collar crime. Most definitions tend to focus on the behavior involved, and certain common characteristics can be identified. The principal attributes of white-collar crime are that (1) it is nonviolent; (2) it is covert in nature, generally involving deceit and concealment; and (3) it is directed toward the acquisition of money, property, or economic or political power. In discussing white-collar crime, emphasis will therefore be placed on crimes involving these characteristics.

It is impossible to discuss all white-collar crimes or all facets of white-collar criminality in one chapter. This chapter will survey some of the more important aspects of the subject. Attention will be given to the magnitude of the problem; to the liability of both business organizations and individuals; and to various specific types of white-collar crimes, both traditional and non-traditional. In addition, two recent federal statutes that have been used to fight white-collar crime will be discussed in some detail. Finally, attention will be given to an emerging problem—computer crime.

8:2   Magnitude of White-Collar Crime

The United States, as a capitalistic nation, has encouraged business. Many business practices which today are labeled white-collar crimes were generally accepted practice only a few years ago. As a result, few people in the past attempted to assess the scope of white-collar crime, since most people did not consider it a serious problem.

Even today, white-collar crime remains largely invisible and therefore difficult to detect. A white-collar crime can be committed by the stroke of a pen or the manipulation of a computer, and the victim or victims may never know that they have been victimized. Indeed, some law-enforcement officials believe that white-collar crime represents the largest category of unreported crime.

Despite the fact that white-collar crime is largely unreported, it has been stated that it is the most serious crime problem in the United States today. Estimates of the total annual cost to the public of white-collar crime range from $40 billion to $200 billion. It has also been estimated that white-collar crime adds 15 percent to the overall price of goods and services and that 20 percent of all business failures, and 30 percent of small-business failures, are due to white-collar crime. Although white-collar crime generally is considered less serious than street crime, most experts believe that the cost of white-collar crime actually exceeds that of street crime. Moreover, white-collar crime can be just as lethal as street crime. For example, knowingly manufacturing

---

[2] H. Edelhertz, *The Nature, Impact, and Prosecution of White-Collar Crime* 3 (1970).

defective products or dumping toxic wastes could result in death, disease, or injury to literally millions of people.

There is great diversity among both white-collar criminals and their victims. Every business organization, every businessperson, and every government worker is a potential white-collar criminal as well as a potential victim of white-collar crime. The businessperson who wrongfully drives a company car on personal business, the employee who pads an expense account, and the employee who takes office supplies home can all be called white-collar criminals.

8:3   Liability for and Punishment of White-Collar Crime

When individuals commit crimes, they are subject to punishment. When a corporation or other business entity commits a crime, it is not so easy to assign responsibility. Questions arise as to whether the corporation, its responsible officers or employees, or both, are liable to criminal prosecution and punishment.

It is clear that corporate officers and employees can be held criminally liable for violations committed on behalf of their corporation, provided the responsible individuals can be identified. However, it is often difficult to pinpoint responsibility on one or more individuals. Situations arise where a crime clearly has been committed, but no person can be identified as the guilty party.

One solution in such a situation is to hold the corporation criminally responsible. At common law, corporations and associations could not be convicted of crimes. Today, however, a corporation can be held criminally responsible, provided the statute in question applies to corporations. If the legislature intended to limit criminal liability to natural persons, a corporation or other artifical entity cannot be found guilty. The question in each case revolves around the legislative intent. The trend today is toward criminal laws generally applicable to corporations and associations.

A prosecutor faced with a corporate violation of a criminal law need not choose between prosecuting the corporation and prosecuting its officers. The corporation and the responsible officers and employees can be prosecuted together and often are. Moreover, it is not necessary to choose between criminal and civil sanctions. In an appropriate case, a corporation and its officers may be subjected both to civil and to criminal liability based on the same acts.

Once a corporation, its officers, or an individual businessperson has been convicted of a white-collar crime, the question of appropriate punishment arises. In the case of corporations, the punishment normally consists of a fine, since a corporation obviously cannot be imprisoned. Under some circumstances, however, a corporate officer might be required to serve a prison sentence on behalf of a corporation. When an individual has been convicted of a white-collar crime, a fine, imprisonment, or both might be imposed as punishment.

The subject of sentencing for white-collar crimes has provoked considerable controversy. In the case of a corporation, questions have been raised as to whether fines really have any deterrent effect. A small fine may well be treated simply as a cost of doing business. In the case of individuals, sentences tend to be lenient. On the one hand, lenient sentences have been justified on the ground that the average white-collar criminal is a highly educated, successful, well-respected person with no prior record, and therefore deserves a light sentence. On the other hand, it has been argued that lenient sentencing of white-collar criminals creates a double standard and causes cynicism among the general public. For example, it has been argued that it is unfair to sentence a bank robber who steals $1,000 to prison for several years while granting probation to a bank president who embezzles a much larger sum, such as $50,000.

The debate over sentencing is likely to go on for some time. It is unlikely that white-collar criminals will ever be sentenced as severely as street criminals. However, it is quite likely that the sentences for white-collar crimes will become more severe. In addition, it is also probable that the fines imposed on corporations convicted of white-collar crimes will become more substantial.

8:4   Traditional White-Collar Crimes

Traditional white-collar crimes have most often been committed by individuals against their employers rather than by corporations. Any distinction between traditional and nontraditional white-collar crimes is necessarily somewhat artificial, however. As used here, the term "traditional" describes acts that have long been considered wrongful and have in fact resulted in criminal prosecution with some degree of regularity. Acts that only recently have been made criminal or in the past have not resulted in prosecution with any regularity are considered nontraditional. The decision as to which category a given crime falls into has been made by discretion. For example, *mail fraud* has long been a crime, but only in recent years have the mail fraud statutes been used aggressively to combat consumer fraud.

The mail fraud statute [18 USC § 1341] makes it a crime, punishable by a fine of $1,000, imprisonment up to five years, or both, to use the mail for any scheme to defraud. A companion statute imposes similar penalties on the use of wire, radio, or television communication to defraud [18 USC § 1343]. The following case illustrates how a garden-variety fraudulent scheme is punishable under federal mail fraud law.

United States

v

Feldman

711 F2d 758 (1983)

United States Court of Appeals, Seventh Circuit

FACTS: Feldman and Joyner, operating under the name of a partnership, created a series of false bank guarantee letters that permitted them to trade in stock options through Merrill Lynch without providing collateral. Feldman was a branch manager for Merrill Lynch, and Joyner, a certified public accountant, was a controller for Brinks, Inc. The defendants used a blank bank guarantee form and overlaid it with a letterhead from Harris Trust and Savings. They then photocopied it and made it appear to guarantee up to $1 million. Feldman did not disclose to Merrill Lynch his interest in the partnership, in violation of Merrill Lynch's employment rules.

Feldman was careful to see that correspondence regarding the partnership account went to Joyner and not to Harris Trust. Once when Feldman was on vacation, however, a letter containing an expired guarantee went to Harris Trust. Bank officials there recognized the forgery and notified Merrill Lynch.

Feldman was indicted on nineteen counts of mail fraud and nine counts of wire fraud. On appeal from his conviction at a jury trial, Feldman argued that the government had only proved that Feldman violated his employer's rules and had failed to prove that Feldman knew the guarantee letters (which were sent through the mails and wires) were false.

ISSUE: Under the mail fraud statute, what elements of fraud must the government prove?

RESULT: The government must prove the existence of a scheme to defraud and the defendant's knowing and intentional participation in the scheme.

REASONING:

*   *   *

It is well established that a scheme which deprives an employer of the honest and faithful services of an employee or the right to have his business conducted in an honest manner can constitute a scheme to defraud under the mail fraud statute. . . . Yet not every breach of duty by an employee works as a criminal fraud, . . . and receipt of secret profits, standing alone, cannot support a mail fraud conviction. . . . Such activities must be accompanied by a scheme formed with the intent *to defraud.* When an employee breaches a fiduciary duty to disclose information to his employer, that breach of duty can support a mail or wire fraud conviction only if the nondisclosed information was material to the conduct of the employer's business and the nondisclosure could or does result in harm to the employer. . . .

While Merrill Lynch no doubt has a reason for prohibiting account executives from sharing a financial interest in customers' accounts, the government has produced no evidence that breach of this rule could have harmed Merrill Lynch. On the other hand, the active concealment of such an interest does render an employee's services less than totally honest and faithful. If we were convinced that Feldman's nondisclosure of his interest in [the partnership] standing alone, could not support a mail or wire fraud conviction, and if we believed that the jury might have convicted Feldman on this basis alone, the convictions could not stand. When a verdict may have rested on any of several grounds, one of which was improper, the conviction cannot be upheld. . . . However, we are convinced that neither the indictment, the government's argument, nor the jury instructions could have misled the jury into convicting on this basis.

Inclusion in the indictment of Feldman's concealment of his interest in the [partnership] accounts was proper, because this was part of an overall scheme to defraud. Not all aspects of a scheme need be illegal if considered separately; rather, it is sufficient that the scheme as a whole involves fraudulent conduct. . . . While the indictment does detail Feldman's nondisclosure of his interest in the accounts, this is set in the context of describing the particulars of "a scheme of artifice to defraud," the purpose of which was to "induce Merrill Lynch to sell put options for the defendants without the defendants producing the required margin. . . ." This was the sole purpose described by the indictment, so that the conviction under the indictment must have entailed a finding that Feldman was involved with the falsified guarantee letters. Simply concealing his interest in the accounts would not enable him to trade in options without advancing sufficient collateral. We conclude that the indictment charged a single scheme to defraud, which by its terms could not mislead the jury into convicting solely on finding that Feldman concealed his interest in the accounts. . . .

Eschbach, Circuit Judge.

It is impossible to discuss all the various other types of traditional white-collar crimes. Discussion here will be limited to three important types of crime: (1) embezzlement, (2) larceny, and (3) tax evasion and avoidance.

Embezzlement   Embezzlement is the fraudulent appropriation of property, often money, by a person to whom it has been voluntarily entrusted. A central element of the crime of embezzlement is the breach of trust. The stereotypical embezzler is a meek bookkeeper, but anyone who is entrusted with the handling of money is a potential embezzler. Embezzlers can do enormous damage to a business. In numerous cases embezzlement has been discovered only after literally thousands of dollars have been siphoned off over a period of 20 or 30 years.

 An employer can take certain steps to minimize the possibility of embezzlement by employees. The most important step is to adopt internal control procedures that will lead to quick detection of any shortages of funds. This can be accomplished by a division of authority among two or more employees. In other words, do not permit one person to do all bookkeeping work without supervision or auditing. An employee who knows that any embezzlement will be rapidly discovered is much less likely to take the risk involved. If the employee does take the risk, detection is much more likely. Finally, without intruding on an employee's privacy, an employer should be alert to any extravagance by individual employees.

Larceny   Larceny is closely related to embezzlement and, like embezzlement, is a form of theft. The basic distinction between embezzlement and larceny is that in embezzlement the original possession is lawful but the property is wrongfully appropriated, while in larceny the original possession is unlawful. From the businessperson's point of view, this distinction may be more theoretical than real. The embezzler is typically someone who has been entrusted with the handling of funds. The larcenist is typically someone who pilfers supplies or inventory items. In both cases, the offender has rightfully had contact with the property taken.

Many businesses treat inventory shortages as a fact of life and a cost of business. Such an approach may have an element of realism. However, an overly fatalistic attitude toward the problem of employee theft may increase the cost to the business far beyond what it would otherwise be and may in fact result in a business' failure. It has been estimated that 60 percent of the crime-related losses sustained by private businesses are due to employee white-collar crime. An employer should therefore adopt all reasonable measures to deter employee pilferage and other forms of employee theft. An important (but often overlooked) fact is that lower-level employees often take their cues from higher management. If the executives of a business adopt high ethical standards and act honestly, they set an example that the employees are more inclined to follow. Other measures can also be adopted to minimize the loss from employee theft. For example, the adoption of warehousing and shipping procedures designed to detect inventory shortages will help minimize losses in that area.

Tax Evasion and Avoidance   Every businessperson is undoubtedly aware that income tax evasion is a crime. However, the federal laws governing the evasion or avoidance of taxes may well be the most commonly enforced white-collar crime statutes. Both individuals and corporations can be guilty of income tax evasion. It is the principal tax crime and the one that has resulted in the most prosecutions and convictions. Other tax crimes include (1) willful failure by an employer to withhold and pay over taxes from employees' wages, (2) willful failure to pay any estimated tax or to file any required return or supply any required information, and (3) commission of various kinds of fraud relating to taxes. In addition to criminal penalties, which may consist of both fines and imprisonment, violation of the income tax laws may result in imposition of civil penalties.

8:5   Emerging Emphasis on Other Types of White-Collar Crime

Criminal law is a reflection of society's moral views. Therefore, as these views change, so does the law. Criminal laws affecting white-collar crime have been undergoing this kind of change. There is a distinct trend toward demanding greater corporate and individual responsibility for business decisions and practices, and toward punishing improper business acts as crimes. This section and 8:6 through 8:9 deal with selected aspects of that trend. Emerging criminality in the following areas will be discussed: (1) consumer fraud, (2) marketing or use of defective or harmful products, (3) pollution, and (4) public corruption. Before discussing these individual categories, however, two points should be made. First, these are developing areas, and there are differences of opinion as to what acts do or should constitute crimes. Second, the categories are not mutually exclusive. As examples, a corporation's use and marketing of harmful chemicals can also result in pollution of the environment; a particular consumer fraud might be facilitated by bribing public officials entrusted with its prevention.

8:6   Consumer Fraud

Attempts to impose criminal sanctions for consumer fraud have focused on massive frauds involving numerous consumers. Examples of this type of fraud are not difficult to find; the sale of swampland or barren desert land as prime residential property, the hawking of miracle medical cures, and the sale of products that are never delivered all cause severe financial, and sometimes psychological, hardship to the victims. Traditional civil remedies are often ineffective, either because each individual consumer has lost little, or because the person perpetrating the fraud is effectively judgment-proof (has limited or no funds to pay any damage awards). As a result, there have been increasing demands to hold the perpetrators of such frauds criminally liable. Some states have criminal laws that can be invoked against such consumer frauds. Because many do not, the criminal statute most often applied is the federal mail fraud statute. Since most large consumer frauds involve the use of either the mail or another means of communication, these statutes are effective weapons, and the federal government in recent years has made substantial use of them.

State and local governments have also become more involved in consumer fraud in recent years. Using a variety of statutes, they are aggressively prosecuting large consumer frauds. As a result, a particular consumer fraud can be subject to state or local prosecution as well as federal prosecution.

8:7   Marketing or Use of Defective or Harmful Products

Numerous consumer products contain defects that pose dangers to life and health. Employees in manufacturing plants are exposed to chemicals and other products that are potentially hazardous. And it has been shown that customary methods of disposing of certain industrial by-products create health dangers to persons in close proximity to the disposed products.

Examples of these problems abound. Defectively designed automobiles and tires have resulted in numerous injuries and deaths. Poorly designed birth-control devices have caused the death and injury of many women. Use of asbestos and polyvinyl chloride in manufacturing processes has contributed to employees' sterility, cancer, total disability, and even death. Dumping of toxic wastes into waterways has resulted in injuries to nearby residents, and dumping of pesticides has resulted in the pollution of groundwater tables.

The consequences of the above activities are truly tragic. Most people, however, recognize the inevitability that business will inadvertently market or use products that prove to be defective or harmful. The real tragedy may lie in the fact that in some instances of the kind described above the businesses involved in fact knew of the dangerous nature of their product. As a matter of economics, they decided that it was preferable to permit customers, employees, or others exposed to the products to suffer the resulting harm than it was to spend the money necessary to eliminate the defect or danger.

The harmful consequences of decisions of this sort have led to calls for the imposition of criminal sanctions, and attempts have been made at the state and federal levels to hold corporations and their management criminally responsible. On the federal level, various statutes have been introduced in Congress, but not adopted. These statutes propose to place criminal liability on corporations and corporate officials who knowingly suppress the fact that their product has harmful defects or may be hazardous to the health of their employees. On the state level, attempts to impose criminal liability have generally taken the form of prosecutions under existing criminal statutes. At least one state prosecutor has obtained a criminal homicide conviction against the owners and managers of a silver-recovery plant that knowingly exposed workers to dangerous chemicals without warning the workers and without taking measures to prevent harm.

Homicide statutes vary in their definition of homicide, but all have typically involved the concept of one natural person killing another. The question therefore arises as to whether a corporation, being an artificial person, can even be charged with homicide. The following case is an example of how one court dealt with that issue.

People
v
Ebasco Services, Inc.
354 NYS2d 807 (1974)
New York Supreme Court

FACTS: Ebasco Services was retained to perform various services in connection with a construction project. The project entailed construction of a temporary structure called a cofferdam. The cofferdam permitted portions of the East River to be pumped out so that construction work could be performed on the river bottom. On August 17, 1973, a portion of the cofferdam collapsed, killing two workers in the dewatered area. Ebasco, another corporate defendant, and three individual defendants were indicted on charges of criminally negligent homicide, based on the alleged improper construction of the cofferdam. The defendants filed a motion to dismiss the indictment on various grounds, including the ground that a corporation could not be indicted for criminally negligent homicide.

ISSUE: May a corporation be indicted for criminally negligent homicide under New York law?

RESULT: Yes. A corporation may be indicted and held to answer for a homicide.

REASONING:

*   *   *

The motions before the court present . . . the novel issue of whether or not a corporation may be convicted of homicide under the revised [New York] Penal Law. . . .

The killing of a human being by a corporation is an act that can be proscribed by the Legislature. As the [New York] Court of Appeals stated [in a 1909 case]:

> "Within the principles thus and elsewhere declared, we have no doubt that a definition of certain forms of manslaughter might have been formulated which would be applicable to a corporation, and make it criminally liable for various acts of misfeasance and nonfeasance when resulting in death, and amongst which very probably might be included conduct in its substance similar to that here charged against the respondent."

The court stated, however, that it was unable to discover in the statute before it any evidence of an intent by the Legislature to hold a corporation criminally liable for a homicide.

Hence, the issue which this court must decide is: "Does section 125.10 of the Penal Law by its terms encompass corporate defendants?" That section reads as follows:

> "A person is guilty of criminally negligent homicide when, with criminal negligence, he causes the death of another person."

A "person" is defined in the homicide article of the Penal Law (125.05[1]) as follows:

> " 'Person,' *when referring to the victim of a homicide,* means a human being who has been born and is alive." [Court's emphasis.]

Defendants assert that, inasmuch as this definition of "person" speaks in terms of a human being, a corporate defendant cannot by its act commit a homicide. This contention flies in the face of the statute which equates "person" with human being only in regard to the victim of the homicide. This statute does not require that the person committing the act of homicide be a human being and the reference to human being is of limited application. As the revisers make clear, the definition contained in section 125.05(1) of the Penal Law was inserted merely to insure that the death of a "person" would not include the abortional killing of an unborn child. . . .

Since no definition of "person" as applied to the actual committing of the homicide has been included by the Legislature in the homicide article, the court must look to the broader definition of "person" contained in the overall definitional article of the Penal Law. Section 10.00(7) defines "person" as follows:

> " 'Person' means a human being, and where appropriate, a public or private corporation. . . . "

It is apparent from a reading of section 10.00(7) of the Penal Law that whenever the term "person" is used in the Penal Law it includes corporations, except in those instances in which inclusion of a corporation is obviously inappropriate. It would be manifestly inappropriate to apply the definition of "person" to corporation in regard to persons who might be seized and arrested . . . or persons who engage in proscribed sex offenses. . . .

There is, however, no manifest impropriety in applying the broader definition of "person" to a corporation in regard to the commission of a homicide, particularly in view of the statement by the Court of Appeals in [the 1909 case] that the Legislature is empowered to impose criminal liability upon a corporation for a homicide. Accordingly, the court concludes that although a corporation cannot be the victim of a homicide, it may commit that offense and be held to answer therefor. . . .

Louis Wallach, Justice.

 Corporate criminal liability for defective or harmful products is shifting. Therefore, informed business decisions should be made on the basis of what the law might become, not what it is currently. Businesspersons who try to stay barely within the bounds of the law may find that the law has passed them by. The damage to a business from a criminal prosecution cannot be overestimated. It should also be remembered that, even if a criminal prosecution is unsuccessful, civil proceedings seeking damages might be brought against the business. Prudent businesspersons must therefore anticipate developments, rather than merely respond to them.

8:8   Pollution

Federal and state statutes have long declared that certain types of pollution are punishable as crimes. Traditionally, however, these statutes have been laxly enforced. Only over the last few years have demands been made for both stricter laws and greater enforcement of the existing laws. Various statutes and amendments to existing statutes have been enacted in response to these demands. For example, under the *Federal Water Pollution Control Act* (FWPCA) [33 USC §§ 1251–1376], as amended in 1972 and 1977, any person or corporation who willfully or negligently discharges pollutants into water in violation of the act can be criminally prosecuted [33 USC § 1319(c)]. It is noteworthy that the FWPCA provides criminal liability not only for willful pollution but also for negligent pollution of water. Other federal statutes provide that (1) willful violations of laws governing air pollution; (2) disposal of hazardous wastes; (3) manufacture, distribution, and disposal of toxic substances; and (4) production, distribution, and disposal of pesticides are subject to criminal prosecution. Various state statutes also make certain types of pollution criminal. While some state statutes penalize only knowing or willful pollution, others penalize all prohibited pollution, regardless of the offender's knowledge of the pollution.

8:9 Public Corruption

Since Watergate, increased attention has been paid to corruption of and graft by public officials. As the Watergate incident illustrated, such corruption could involve only certain public officials and their political subordinates. In more typical cases, however, public corruption involves someone in addition to the official or officials involved. Not infrequently, that someone is a corporation or an individual businessperson.

Bribery is probably the most commonly encountered crime of public corruption. Bribery consists of the voluntary giving to or receiving by a public official of anything of value, with the intent to influence the officials public actions. Both federal and state statutes prohibit bribery of public officials, and these statutes are now being vigorously enforced, as recent convictions of high public officials attest.

Another crime closely related to bribery of a public official is *extortion* by a public official. Although such extortion usually violates state law, cases often are brought by federal prosecutors using the federal mail fraud and wire fraud statutes and also the federal extortion statute [18 USC § 1951]. The following case explores the legal arguments of a state insurance commissioner who was convicted of extortion and mail fraud.

United States
v
O'Malley
707 F2d 1240 (1983)
United States Court of Appeals, Eleventh Circuit

FACTS: O'Malley was elected insurance commissioner of Florida. Before taking office, he worked out an agreement with his former law partners whereby they purchased his interest in the law practice and, in effect, he guaranteed a minimum income for them.

As insurance commissioner, O'Malley met regularly with insurance company executives prior to considering their applications for licenses to do business in Florida. At these meetings O'Malley occasionally urged them to use his old law firm if they needed legal help. Often he distributed the law firm's business cards.

In addition, O'Malley required money from insurance executives. For example, when O'Malley discovered that Snow, an insurance company president, had contributed $4,000 to his defeated opponent in the election, O'Malley recommended that Snow contribute $4,000 to O'Malley if he and Snow were "going to get along." On another occasion O'Malley told Sawyer, an officer in another insurance company, that that company's application for a merger might have problems because of the company's legal counsel, which had not supported O'Malley in the last election and would not, therefore, be an "effective counsel." O'Malley recommended his former law firm, which Sawyer then hired. O'Malley was convicted of extortion and mail fraud under applicable federal statutes. Among other arguments, he appealed the conviction on the ground that extortion had not been proved.

ISSUE: Does the federal extortion statute (the Hobbs Act) require evidence of "force, violence or fear" on the part of the extorted party?

RESULT: No. Extortion by a public official need not be accompanied by fear, force, or violence under federal law.

REASONING:

* * *

The term extortion, as used in section 1951, means "the obtaining of property from another, with his consent, induced by wrongful use of actual or threatened force, violence, or fear, or under color of official right." 18 U.S.C.A. § 1951(b)(2). O'Malley contends that the testimony of Sawyer and Snow failed to reveal extortion because of a lack of "force, violence, or fear."

O'Malley argues that his extortion convictions must be reversed because the government did not show fear or duress on the part of the individuals testifying at trial. This argument is meritless. Hobbs Act violations based on extortion by a public official need not include proof of threat, fear, or duress. . . . Section 1951(b)(2) defines extortion as "obtaining of property from another . . . induced by wrongful use of actual or threatened force . . . or under color of official right." Extortion is either the obtaining of property from another by the wrongful use of actual or threatened force of violence or the obtaining of property from another induced under color of official right. When committed by a public official, no proof of threat, force, or duress is required. . . . The coercive nature of the official office provides all the inducement necessary. . . . Since no requirement exists that the insurance executives be under duress, or fear of violence from O'Malley, the extortion convictions are proved by sufficient evidence. O'Malley conducted his requests for money under the cloak of his official office.

Even if duress is required before the extortion convictions can be upheld, it was shown. Snow testified that O'Malley's position as insurance commissioner provided a coercive influence, making him contribute money which he did not wish to contribute. We find that the evidence is sufficient to support O'Malley's convictions for extortion. . . .

Per Curiam.

Illegal political contributions represent another form of criminal public corruption. Both federal and state statutes limit the type and amount of contributions that can be made by various persons and entities, and violation of the statutes can be criminally punishable.

Two crimes that are peripherally related to public corruption deserve mention because of their frequent commission in the prosecution of political corruption. These are *obstruction of justice* and *perjury*. Both crimes are typically committed in an attempt to prevent detection or prosecution of other crimes. Obstruction of justice, which is prohibited by both federal and state laws, consists of interference with the orderly administration of law. Obstruction of justice can involve not only actual obstruction of proceedings before a court, but improper influence of jurors or witnesses and improper obstruction of criminal investigations. Obstruction of justice is often accompanied by perjury. Perjury is the willful giving of a false statement under oath. Originally, perjury could be committed only in judicial proceedings, but many statutes now classify *any* willfully false statement given under oath as perjury. In many cases, public officials and businesspersons have been convicted of obstruction of justice or perjury, even though they were never convicted of, and possibly never even prosecuted for, the crime that originally focused attention on them.

8:10   Racketeer Influenced and Corrupt Organizations Act (RICO)

This section and Section 8:11 focus on two specific statutory schemes enacted by Congress to combat crime. The *Racketeer Influenced and Corrupt Organizations Act* (RICO) [18 USC §§ 1961–1968], discussed here, originally was enacted to control organized crime, but has become the federal government's major weapon in the fight against white-collar crime. The *Foreign Corrupt Practices Act* (FCPA) [15 USC §§ 78a, 78m et seq.], which is discussed in 8:11, was enacted by Congress to fight a specific type of white-collar crime, that of bribery of foreign officials by American businesses.

RICO was passed by Congress primarily to combat organized crime's control of legitimate business organizations. It focuses on certain types of racketeering activities. These are criminal acts such as gambling, arson, bribery, extortion, mail fraud, and obstruction of justice. When a person engages in two or more racketeering activities, called *predicate offenses*, the person is engaging in a pattern of racketeering activity. A person engaged in racketeering activity commits a crime under RICO if he or she engages in any of four specified activities: (1) use of income derived from a pattern of racketeering activity to acquire an enterprise or an interest in an enterprise; (2) acquisition of an interest in or control of an enterprise through a pattern of racketeering activity; (3) conduct of an enterprise's affairs through a pattern of racketeering activity; and (4) conspiracy to commit any of the first three acts.

To come within the coverage of RICO, the prohibited activities must concern an enterprise that engages in or affects interstate or foreign commerce. As a practical matter, this includes all significant business enterprises, since they all have some effect on interstate commerce. The term "enterprise" includes not only individuals, partnerships, corporations, and unions, but also any other legal entity or any group of individuals associated in fact. For example, a government agency can be considered an enterprise.

RICO provides for both criminal and civil liability. The criminal punishment can include a fine of up to $25,000; imprisonment for up to 20 years; or both. In addition, an offender can be required to forfeit any interest acquired in the legitimate enterprise, as well as any interest in the enterprise that gave the offender a source of influence over the legitimate enterprise.

An examination of RICO shows that its coverage is very broad. RICO not only prohibits the acquisition of a business enterprise through illegal methods or with money obtained by illegal methods, but it also prohibits the use of legal business enterprises to commit illegal activities. RICO has been vigorously enforced, and its potential applications are numerous. RICO has been widely used not only in organized crime prosecutions, but also in white-collar crime prosecutions, especially political corruption cases.

EXAMPLE: Wilson has a lucrative income from an illegal gambling operation. To channel his illegal gambling receipts, Wilson purchases a legitimate business, Acme Construction Corporation. Wilson proceeds to bribe local government contract officers to obtain favorable consideration of Acme's bids for government construction jobs. To keep construction costs low, Wilson arranges with a local union leader to unionize his employees. In exchange for payments to the labor leader, the union agrees to a contract for wages below the prevailing wage levels. To save on other construction costs, Wilson pays government inspectors to overlook violations of the building laws. Wilson, the government contract officer, the labor union leader, and the government inspectors are all potential targets of RICO prosecutions. Money derived from a pattern of racketeering activity (gambling) has been used to acquire a legitimate enterprise. The affairs of that legitimate enterprise have been conducted through a pattern of racketeering activity. Finally, the various potential defendants might be found guilty of conspiracy to commit the above offenses.

The RICO Act provides a private civil action to recover *treble (triple) damages* for injury "by reason of a violation of" its provisions [18 USC § 1964(c)]. This civil damage provision has been used widely in recent years against individuals and corporations who probably would not be regarded as the "racketeers" or "mobsters" Congress had in mind when it passed the statute in 1970. In 1985 the United States Supreme Court issued the following opinion, addressing the question whether RICO civil damage actions can be brought against businesses and individuals not engaged in "organized crime." In the same opinion, the Court held that it was not necessary for the defendant in the civil case to have been convicted criminally of the predicate offenses.

Sedima, S.P.R.L.

v

Imrex Co.
87 L Ed 2d 346 (1985)
United States Supreme Court

FACTS: Sedima, a Belgian corporation, and Imrex Co. were partners in a venture to provide electronic components to a Belgian firm. The buyer was to order parts through Sedima; Imrex was to obtain the parts in the United States and ship them to Europe. Sedima and Imrex were to split the profits. Imrex filled over $8,000,000 in orders. Sedima, however, became convinced that Imrex was presenting inflated bills and cheating Sedima. Sedima filed a lawsuit against Imrex for various claims, including fraud, and sought treble damages under RICO. The trial court dismissed the claim. The United States Circuit Court of Appeals affirmed the trial court's dismissal. Sedima then appealed to the Supreme Court.

ISSUE: Under the RICO Act's private civil damages provisions, must a plaintiff prove a "racketeering injury," an "injury . . . which RICO was designed to deter"?

RESULT: No. The plaintiff need only prove that the defendant committed the predicate offenses.

REASONING:

*   *   *

. . . [W]e perceive no distinct "racketeering injury" requirement. Given that "racketeering activity" consists of no more and no less than commission of a predicate act, . . . we are initially doubtful about a requirement of a "racketeering injury" separate from the harm from the predicate acts. A reading of the statute belies any such requirement. Section 1964(c) authorizes a private suit by "[a]ny person injured in his business or property by reason of a violation of § 1962." Section 1962 in turn makes it unlawful for "any person"—not just mobsters—to use money derived from a pattern of racketeering activity to invest in an enterprise, to acquire control of an enterprise through a pattern of racketeering activity, or to conduct an enterprise through a pattern of racketeering activity. . . . If the defendant engages in a pattern of racketeering activity in a manner forbidden by these provisions, and the racketeering activities injure the plaintiff in his business or property, the plaintiff has a claim under § 1964(c). There is no room in the statutory language for an additional, amorphous "racketeering injury" requirement.

A violation of § 1962(c), the section on which Sedima relies, requires (1) conduct (2) of an enterprise (3) through a pattern (4) of racketeering activity. The plaintiff must, of course, allege each of these elements. . . . As the Seventh Circuit has stated, "[a] defendant who violates section 1962 is not liable for treble damages to everyone he might have injured by other conduct, nor is the defendant liable to those who have not been injured." . . .

But the statute requires no more than this. Where the plaintiff alleges each element of the violation, the compensable injury necessarily is the harm caused by predicate acts sufficiently related to constitute a pattern, for the essence of the violation is the commission of those acts in connection with the conduct of an enterprise. Those acts are, when committed in the circumstances delineated in § 1962(c), "an activity which RICO was designed to deter." Any recoverable damages occurring by reason of a violation of § 1962(c) will flow from the commission of the predicate acts. . . .

Underlying the Court of Appeals' holding was its distress at the "extraordinary, if not outrageous," uses to which civil RICO has been put. . . . Instead of being used against mobsters and organized criminals, it has become a tool for everyday fraud cases brought against "respected and legitimate 'enterprises.' " . . . Yet Congress wanted to reach both "legitimate" and "illegitimate" enterprises. . . . The former enjoy neither an inherent incapacity for criminal activity nor immunity from its consequences. The fact that § 1964(c) is used against respected businesses allegedly engaged in a pattern of specifically identified criminal conduct is hardly a sufficient reason for assuming that the provision is being misconstrued. Nor does it reveal the "ambiguity" discovered by the court below. "[T]he fact that RICO has been applied in situations not expressly anticipated by Congress does not demonstrate ambiguity. It demonstrates breadth." . . .

It is true that private civil actions under the statute are being brought almost solely against such defendants, rather than against the archetypal, intimidating mobster. Yet this defect—if defect it is—is inherent in the statute as written, and its correction must lie with Congress. It is not for the judiciary to eliminate the private action in situations where Congress has provided it simply because plaintiffs are not taking advantage of it in its more difficult applications.

We nonetheless recognize that, in its private civil version, RICO is evolving into something quite different from the original conception of its enactors. . . . Though sharing the doubts of the Court of Appeals about this increasing divergence, we cannot agree with either its diagnosis or its remedy. The "extraordinary" uses to which civil RICO has been put appear to be primarily the result of the breadth of the predicate offenses, in particular the inclusion of wire, mail, and securities fraud, and the failure of Congress and the courts to develop a meaningful concept of "pattern." We do not believe that the amorphous . . . requirement imposed by the Second Circuit effectively responds to these problems, or that it is a form of statutory amendment appropriately undertaken by the courts. . . .

White, Justice.

8:11   Foreign Corrupt Practices Act (FCPA)

Following closely on the heels of Watergate came revelations that American businesses were routinely bribing foreign officials to obtain favorable treatment. The apparent extent of such bribery led to calls for new legislation. The response was the Foreign Corrupt Practices Act (FCPA).

The purpose of the FCPA is to deter corporate bribery of foreign officials and governments. To this end, the act contains two major provisions: (1) it prohibits American businesses and their employees from making payments or giving gifts to foreign officials for the purpose of influencing the decisions of such officials or their government and (2) it requires corporations that are required to report to the Securities and Exchange Commission (SEC) to keep records and make reports that reveal any such payments. In short, the act prohibits American businesses from obtaining foreign business by bribing foreign officials and requires disclosure of any such bribery. A business firm that violates the act can be fined up to $1,000,000; an officer, director or stockholder of a business firm who violates the act can be fined up to $10,000; imprisoned for five years; or both.

The FCPA, if vigorously enforced, would provide a powerful deterrent to corporate bribery of foreign officials and governments. To date, however, the FCPA has not been strongly enforced and there have even been calls for its amendment. An examination of the reasons for the FCPA's relative lack of effectiveness provides a good case study in the difficulty of dealing with international white-collar crime.

International white-collar crime is difficult to control under even the best circumstances. Transnational corporations by their nature tend to be large and to have branches and subsidiaries in various countries. If one country outlaws a certain type of activity, a transnational corporation can often evade the law by conducting that activity in another country that does not prohibit it. The fact that different activities can be carried out in different countries also makes it difficult to detect violations of one country's laws. Therefore, the FCPA is inherently difficult to enforce.

It has also been argued that the FCPA puts American corporations at a competitive disadvantage. Different countries have different philosophies concerning the conduct of business. What Americans call a bribe may be viewed in another country as a perfectly acceptable way of obtaining business. If an American corporation does not make the appropriate payment to obtain a contract in such a country, other countries' corporations may. Thus, the argument goes, the FCPA does not prevent bribery of foreign officials; it merely removes American firms from the marketplace.

Whether the FCPA will ultimately prove to be effective or whether it will be amended significantly remains to be seen. If business bribery of foreign officials and foreign governments is to be effectively eliminated, international action may be required. At the present time, the possibility of obtaining any significant degree of cooperation appears remote.

8:12   Computer Crime

Businesses are increasing their use of computers at a rapid pace. As the use of computers increases, the opportunity for computer-assisted crime also increases. The computer is a prime target for white-collar criminals because access to much of a business' assets and important information can be gained by use of the computer. Businesses of all sizes routinely use computers to perform important functions, such as printing paychecks, keeping books, and storing trade information. Unfortunately, the increased use of computers has not always been accompanied by adequate security systems. Data-processing personnel are given access to a company's computer systems—and thus to the company's assets and secrets—with inadequate security checks. Often companies have no systematic method of overseeing the use of their computers to detect improper use. The result is a relatively easy target for the computer criminal. Often the financial reward of computer crime is great and the chance of apprehension minimal.

Criminal acts involving computer *hardware* (machinery) pose no unique legal problems, and can be punished under traditional criminal law. Crimes involving *software* (programs and data), however, present greater problems. They are difficult to detect, and the existing criminal laws often are inadequate to deal with the types of misuse that occur. Usually, these misuses include (1) improper programming (giving the computer erroneous instructions as to the functions it is to perform); (2) input of improper or erroneous data (giving the computer incorrect information); (3) alteration or theft of computer output; (4) obliteration of or other damage to the information stored in the computer; and/or (5) copying, use, or sale of software in violation of copyright laws.

Criminal misuse of a computer can take only a few seconds. By punching a key or two, a person can direct a computer to pay large sums of money to persons not authorized to receive them, record outstanding bills as paid, or divulge a company's most important trade secrets to a competitor. Computer crimes also tend to be much more costly from the victims' viewpoint than crimes committed without computer assistance. For example, a single computer theft can involve millions of dollars; in one case, a bank employee was convicted of using the bank's computer to transfer over $10 million to a Swiss bank account. It has been estimated that computer bank thefts average $193,000 per theft; that computer crimes against state and local governments average $329,000 per crime; and that computer crimes against corporations average $621,000 per crime.

Computer criminals are usually highly intelligent, capable persons and frequently are good and trusted employees. Computer crime is intellectually challenging to many people—it involves no violence, detection is difficult, and punishment is lenient.

 Any business that makes substantial use of a computer should adopt a security system to lessen the possibility of misuse. The first step is to consult a qualified computer consultant as to the weaknesses in the system and the various methods of eliminating or minimizing those weaknesses. If the computer handles financial transactions, an auditing system should be adopted that can detect computer frauds or misappropriations. For example, an auditor should not accept computer-produced records as automatically correct. Computer software packages are available for auditing computer records; with the aid of such packages, the accuracy of computer-produced records can be checked. The adoption of security procedures and special auditing techniques cannot ensure that a computer will not be misused, but it can lessen the chance of such an occurrence.

Criminal Sanctions   Most criminal laws were enacted long before the advent of computers. Computer misuse often differs substantially from other types of crimes, and it is sometimes difficult to apply the older criminal laws to this new type of misconduct. For example, most states have various types of laws dealing with destruction to or damage of physical property. A person might, however, obliterate the program stored on a computer tape without physically damaging the tape itself. Laws prohibiting physical damage to property obviously were not enacted with such misconduct in mind. The larceny statutes provide another example of the inadequacy of traditional criminal law. Most larceny and other theft statutes were passed to prohibit theft of tangible objects. Computer misuse often involves theft of time or information from the computer. In such cases, the question arises as to whether theft of such intangible objects is prohibited by larceny or other theft statutes. Some courts have held that general theft statutes do apply to theft of intangibles, but a contrary conclusion may be just as logical.

Several states have designed and enacted statutes dealing specifically with computer crimes. For example, Florida enacted a Computer Crimes Act [Florida Statutes §§ 815.01–815.07] in 1978, and California passed an act relating to computer crimes [California Penal Code § 502] in 1979. These acts outlaw and punish various types of unauthorized and fraudulent use of computers, as well as damage to or destruction of computer systems and programs.

Key Concepts and Terms

- White-collar crime is crime that is (1) nonviolent; (2) covert, usually involving deceit and concealment; and (3) directed toward acquisition of money, property, or economic or political power. White-collar crime can be committed by and against businesses. Individuals and corporations alike can be found liable for white-collar criminal acts. Punishment of these acts tends to be lenient.

- White-collar crimes that traditionally have resulted in prosecution with some degree of regularity include embezzlement, larceny, and tax evasion and avoidance. In recent years there has been an increased emphasis on other types of white-collar crime, such as consumer fraud, pollution, and public corruption.

- Perpetrators of consumer frauds now are frequently prosecuted criminally, either under the federal mail or wire fraud statutes or under state or local laws.

- Public demands for legislation imposing sanctions on white-collar criminals have resulted in enactment of (1) statutes prohibiting individuals and corporations from knowingly or negligently making or using defective or harmful products; (2) the Federal Water Pollution Control Act (FWPCA), imposing criminal liability both for willful and for negligent acts of pollution; and (3) laws prohibiting bribery, exercise of improper influence, illegal political contributions, obstruction of justice, and perjury.

- The Racketeer Influenced and Corrupt Organizations Act (RICO) prohibits (1) use of income derived from racketeering activities to acquire an enterprise, (2) acquisition of an enterprise through racketeering activities, (3) conduct of an enterprise through racketeering activities, and (4) a conspiracy to commit any of the first three acts. RICO was passed to combat organized crime, but the act has been used extensively against white-collar crime, including political corruption.

- The Foreign Corrupt Practices Act (FCPA) prohibits American businesses from bribing foreign officials to obtain business and also requires American businesses to disclose these bribes. The FCPA has not been vigorously enforced to date, partly because of problems perceived in fighting international white-collar crime.

- Computer crime is a growing problem. Existing criminal laws are inadequate to combat computer crime, and proposals have been made for new laws directed specifically against computer crimes. Most computer crime is adjudicated under state criminal law. Some states have enacted laws dealing specifically with computer crimes.

- Bribery
- Extortion
- Federal Water Pollution Control Act (FWPCA)
- Foreign Corrupt Practices Act (FCPA)
- Hardware (computer)
- Mail Fraud

- Obstruction of Justice
- Perjury
- Predicate Offense
- Racketeer Influenced and Corrupt Organizations Act (RICO)

- Software (computer)
- Tax Evasion and Avoidance
- Treble Damages
- Wire Fraud

Questions and Case Problems

1. It has been said that there will be continued emphasis on "crime in the suites" during the 1980s. What does that statement mean? What are the ramifications of such increased emphasis for businesspersons?

2. Sullivan placed an advertisement for an elixir capable of "curing all your aches and pains" in a small-town newspaper. The newspaper had a total circulation of 5,000 copies, of which 300 copies were delivered to subscribers by mail. In response to the advertisement 50 people purchased the elixir at the price of $25 per bottle. The elixir in fact had no effect on aches and pains, and Sullivan was promptly charged with mail fraud. Should he be convicted? Does it make any difference whether the people who purchased the elixir received their newspapers by mail?

3. Kemp, president of State Bank, wants to attract deposits of county funds to her bank. To this end she pays for a lunch at which she and the County Treasurer discuss business. A month later Kemp pays the County Treasurer's bill for a hotel convention. At Christmas Kemp gives the County Treasurer a gift of a book costing $20. Kemp and the County Treasurer are then charged with three counts of violating a statute that makes it unlawful for any person to offer, promise, or give, and for any public official to receive, any "gift, commission, discount, bonus, or gratuity." Each of the incidents described is the basis of one count. Should Kemp and the County Treasurer be convicted on any of the counts? Does it matter whether county funds were ever deposited in State Bank? Does it matter whether Kemp and the County Treasurer are personal friends?

4. Cohen is convicted of stealing an automobile worth $2,000. Helms is convicted of tax evasion in the amount of $2,000, based on his fraudulent deduction of the cost of operating his personal automobile as a business expense. What is an appropriate sentence for each? Discuss.

5. Peters is president of a toy-manufacturing company. Walsh, a company employee, discovers that a particular toy may have a defect that could injure a child. Walsh tells Peters that one of the company's toys may be dangerous. Peters responds, "I don't want to hear about it." A child is killed by the toy. The local prosecutor charges Peters, Walsh, and the toy company with negligent homicide. Should they be convicted? Discuss the policy reasons underlying your answer.

6. Lodge was mayor of a city and owner of Exotic Imports, a local business. As mayor, Lodge accepted numerous bribes from contractors dealing with the city. Lodge deposited all the bribes directly into Exotic Imports' bank account. Shortly after her term as mayor ended, Lodge sold Exotic Imports and used the proceeds to purchase International Exports, another local business. Shortly thereafter, Lodge was indicted for violation of the Racketeer Influenced and Corrupt Organizations Act (RICO). The indictment alleged that Lodge had used income derived from a pattern of racketeering activity (the bribes) to acquire an enterprise (International

Exports). In addition to the other penalties, the prosecutor sought an order forfeiting Lodge's interest in International Exports. Lodge defended on the ground that the income from the bribes had been invested in Exotic Imports, not in International Exports. Should Lodge be convicted? Should she be required to forfeit her interest in International Exports?

7. Should the Foreign Corrupt Practices Act be changed? Explain the reasons for your answer.

8. Optimum Systems, Inc. (OSI) operated a computer at Rockville, Maryland. Seidlitz, an employee of OSI, resigned his job and went to work at his own computer firm in Alexandria, Virginia. Seidlitz began obtaining information from the OSI computer surreptitiously. He did this by means of a remote terminal, which he tied into the OSI computer with a telephone. When Seidlitz's activities were discovered, he was indicted for wire fraud, based on the claim that he had transmitted telephone calls in interstate commerce as part of a scheme to defraud OSI of property. The property involved was the information obtained from the computer. Seidlitz defended on the ground that the information did not constitute property within the meaning of the wire statute. Should Seidlitz's contention be upheld?

9. You want your house repainted. Ford tells you that she will paint it for $1,500, provided that you pay her in cash so that she does not have to report it on her income tax return; otherwise, the price is $2,000. What should you do? Why?

10. Should the average businessperson be concerned about computer crime? Discuss.

PART THREE

Contracts

Introductory Comments

Contract law is an important institution of our society. A contract is the means by which people establish rules that will govern a transaction. It permits them to strike the deal that best meets their needs. Thus, contracts are very important to a market economy, and the relative freedom of contract is regarded by many as an important feature of our society. Contract law guides courts in determining how and when the state should force people to follow the rules they make for themselves.

Contracts are a basic tool of business. Yet businesspeople far too often enter contractual relationships in a casual way. Oral agreements are used in situations calling for written ones, and written contracts frequently lack specificity on essential matters. At the outset of a business relationship the parties are optimistic and do not wish to slow performance or destroy a working relationship by writing a contract that accounts for everything that could go wrong. The result is predictable: disagreements and lawsuits often ensue, and good business relationships are destroyed in the process. The lesson is that a businessperson should not enter a contract without considering thoroughly all the ramifications of the contract, even if it is not possible to negotiate every term of it.

The material in Chapters 9 through 18 provides the information necessary to make an appraisal of a contract. These chapters discuss the basic elements needed to create a contract, the various problems that may arise concerning the validity of a contract, and the performance or breach of contracts.

These chapters cover legal rules and include cases illustrating and applying various legal principles. It must be emphasized that the major reason for studying contract law is not to learn how to win court cases; judicial resolution of a contract dispute may take many years, and even the "winner" may in reality lose. The purpose of studying contract law is to learn how to *avoid* disputes and litigation. The contract should be negotiated, planned, and drafted with an eye to avoiding disputes.

While the subject of sales is covered in detail in Chapters 19 to 22, it should be noted that contract law is generally applicable to sales contracts. Contract law is also generally relevant to many of the more specific subjects covered later in this book. The study of contract law is the foundation for the study of all aspects of business law.

9 Nature and Classification of Contracts

9:1 Introduction; Definitions of Contract

Through contracts people agree on the terms that legally obligate them to one another, and sometimes to other persons, in a given transaction. Although contracts often are thought of as long and complex written documents, they may be oral as well as written, and they may relate to relatively trivial matters. Examples of contracts abound; subscription to a magazine, purchase of an automobile, use of a credit card, and many other routine and not-so-routine activities all involve contracts. It is valuable to understand the basic form and structure of the contract and, more importantly, to understand how contracts may be used in everyday business to structure transactions and avoid unnecessary conflict.

There is no uniformly accepted definition of a contract. A contract has been simply defined as a legally enforceable agreement. Another frequently quoted definition is "a promise or a set of promises for the breach of which the law gives a remedy, or the performance of which the law in some way recognizes as a duty."[1] The *Uniform Commercial Code* defines a contract as "the total legal obligation which results from the parties' agreement as affected by this Act and any other applicable rules of law" [UCC § 1-201(11)]. Thus, a contract creates duties of performance and rights to another's performance. The hallmark of a contract is that the state will bring to bear its power to protect the duties and rights that the parties to the contract have created.

---

[1] *Restatement (Second) of Contracts* § 1 (1981).

Curtis Elevator Co., Inc.
v
Hampshire House, Inc.
362 A2d 73 (1976)
New Jersey Superior Court

FACTS: Plaintiff, an elevator company, contracted to install three elevators in an apartment building that was under construction. The contract included a "strike" clause excusing plaintiff from liability for any delays caused by "strikes, lockouts, fire, explosion, theft, floods, riot, civil commotion, war" and similar problems. In fact, a strike caused delay in completion of the elevator installation. Defendant then sought to offset the amount it owed plaintiff by the costs it sustained from the delay in completion.

ISSUE: Did the presence of the "strike clause" render the contract so unfair as to be unenforceable?

RESULT: The strike clause was valid and enforceable in the absence of bad faith by either party.

REASONING:

*   *   *

This court rejects defendant's contentions out of hand. Luppino testified he built for himself or others approximately 10 to 15 buildings. Both plaintiff's principal, Papadia, and defendant's principal, Luppino, are men of long experience and are highly skilled in the construction area. This contract was thoroughly negotiated at arms' length as to both terms and price. Both men had done business together several times previously without incident, involving a contract identical to the one in issue. Each knew that the elevator installers' union had a history of labor problems with strikes occurring at the termination of their contracts every three years since 1966.

There are no reported decisions in this jurisdiction concerning the legality of such a strike clause. Generally, delays occasioned by strikes do not excuse the nonperformance of contracts. . . . However it is the law of this State that competent parties bargaining at arms' length may make their own binding stipulations with regard to the subject matter of their negotiations, unless some strong public policy operates as a bar. . . .

Corbin, in his treatise on contracts, states:

> A promise is not made insufficient as a consideration for a return promise by the fact that it is conditional, even though the condition is one that is purely

fortuitous and may never happen at all. . . .A contract is not invalidated by the fact that a promisor makes his duty to render performance on the nonoccurrence of 'strikes, fires, and other circumstances over which we have no control.' . . .

It may be helpful to analogize the "strike clause" to the cases construing the "no damage" clause in this jurisdiction.

In *A. Kaplen & Son v. Passaic,* . . . the "no damage" clause was held to be enforceable since the court could find "no reason in logic or sound policy why such a contract stipulation as was here voluntarily entered into between the parties should not be held binding." . . .

In the present case it is agreed by both plaintiff and defendant that that strike was the immediate and only cause of the delay. Defendant read and understood the terms of the contract before entering into it. This court will not endeavor to write a better contract than these two highly skilled, intelligent parties bargaining at arms' length wrote for themselves. For the aforegoing reasons it is the opinion of this court that the strike clause in the contract is valid and enforceable. No evidence of bad faith is chargeable to either party.

Therefore plaintiff is entitled to recover on the contract price as adjusted for extras supplied at defendant's request. . . .

Morrison, Judge.

9:2 Nature of a Contract

A contract is a legally enforceable agreement. Agreement has been defined as "a manifestation of mutual assent on the part of two or more persons."[2] It is also "the bargain of the parties in fact as found in their language or by implication from other circumstances" [UCC § 1-201(3)]. Since some agreements are not legally enforceable, not all agreements are contracts. Agreement is, however, normally necessary to form a contract, and an agreement that includes the attributes making it legally enforceable is a contract. It is not surprising, therefore, that the terms "agreement" and "contract" are sometimes used interchangeably.

While various terms may be used to describe the parties to a contract, the words "offeror and offeree" and "promisor and promisee" are often used in discussing the formation of contracts and will be defined briefly at this point. An *offeror* is a party who makes an offer to another party to enter into an agreement; the party to whom the offer is made is the *offeree*. When a contract is entered into, there are usually promises of performance made by both parties. A person making a promise is a *promisor*; the person to whom a

---

[2] *Restatement (Second) of Contracts* § 3 (1981).

promise is made is a *promisee*. As will be shown, a party to a contract typically occupies a position as both a promisor and a promisee.

The law of contracts consists of state common law and statutes. Contracts involving the sale of goods and special types of commercial contracts are covered by the Uniform Commercial Code, which is introduced in this chapter and treated in depth in subsequent chapters of the book. Contracts involving the sale of land or the provision of services are governed by common-law contract principles and state statutes that often codify specific common-law principles. In addition, other law, such as consumer protection law or antitrust law, may also govern a given transaction. Contract law simply establishes contract rights and obligations.

9:3 Elements and Classifications of Contracts

The essential elements of a legally enforceable contract are (1) two or more parties with the legal capacity to contract, (2) a manifestation of mutual assent by the parties to the contract and to its terms, (3) sufficient consideration, and (4) a purpose that is legal and not contrary to public policy. Each of these elements is discussed in detail in later chapters in this part of the text.

It is a useful shorthand to classify contracts by certain important characteristics. The discussion that follows uses some commonly accepted classifications. It should be borne in mind, however, that the classifications are not mutually exclusive. Rather, they are descriptive of certain characteristics of contracts. For example, a bilateral contract may also be an express, valid, executory, and informal contract.

Bilateral and Unilateral Contracts Most contracts involve an exchange of promises by the parties. One party promises to perform some act in exchange for the other party's promise to perform some other act in the future. Such a contract is known as a *bilateral contract* (see Figure 9-1).

EXAMPLE: A university extends an offer in April to provide a student with a dormitory room in September, provided the student agrees to make specified payments beginning in August. Such a proposal is an offer of a bilateral contract. If the student accepts the offer and promises to make the payments specified, a bilateral contract is formed. Under this contract

UNILATERAL CONTRACT

A		B
No right to B's performance		No duty to perform
Duty to perform if B performs	⟶	Right to benefit if performs

BILATERAL CONTRACT

A		B
Duty to perform	⟷	Right to A's performance
Right to B's performance	⟷	Duty to perform

FIGURE 9-1

each party has an obligation to perform and an expectation that the other party will perform.

Notice that in a bilateral contract each party is both a promisor and promisee. In the example, the university as promisor is obligated to provide a dormitory room, and as promisee it has the right to payment from the student. The student as promisor has a duty to make the payments, and as promisee she has the right to a dormitory room.

In some contracts, known as *unilateral contracts*, only one party makes a promise, and that promisor's obligation to perform arises only when the promisee takes some specified action, or perhaps refrains from acting (see Figure 9-1). The promisee make no promise to act. The act may be simultaneous with the promise, or the parties may anticipate that the act will occur at some future time. A simple promissory note is a good example of a unilateral contract; the act of lending money occurs simultaneously with the promise to repay. If the lender has not promised in advance to lend the money, it is not obligated to do so. Unless the lender extends the loan, the borrower is not obligated to repay.

The other type of unilateral contract is exemplified in the reward situation. If one person offers a reward for information leading to the apprehension of a named criminal, no one is obligated to provide the information. If someone does provide the information, a unilateral contract is created. Moreover, the only way to accept the promise is by providing the requested information. A mere promise to provide the information does not result in a contract.

A point that should be made about this second type of unilateral contract is that the offeror is ordinarily not obligated until the act is performed. A unilateral offer may be withdrawn at any time prior to performance. Thus, strictly speaking, the offer of a reward is not a contract at all, but merely an offer to make a contract that becomes a contract once the requested act is performed.

Express and Implied Contracts   A contract is *express* when the parties indicate through words, written or oral, that there is a contractual agreement. The terms and conditions of the contract depend on the parties' words. Even though some terms of the contract are not stated, assent to a contractual relationship is indicated through words. A contract is *implied* when the parties indicate their intent and assent through acts rather than words. The parties' conduct and the surrounding circumstances determine the terms and conditions of the contract. For example, you make an appointment at a dentist's office. You go to the office and permit the dentist to examine your teeth and repair a filling. You have promised, through these acts, to pay the dentist. Even though you have not made an express promise to pay, a court will infer from the circumstances that a duty to pay was understood. Even though you have not agreed on an amount, a court will award the dentist a reasonable fee.

Quasi-Contracts   Classification of contracts as express or implied is not based on any difference in the legal consequences of such contracts. Rather, the classification relates solely to the method by which the parties arrive at an agreement and the type of evidence which proves the contract's existence and its terms. *Quasi-contracts*, which are contracts implied in law, do have different legal consequences because quasi-contracts are not true contracts at all. Quasi-contracts are not based on the parties' intentions, real or presumed. Rather, they are creatures of law.

Quasi-contractual obligations are imposed when justice requires that one person pay for some benefit bestowed on him by another, even though the person receiving the benefit never agreed, either expressly or impliedly, to pay for the benefit. In fact, quasi-contractual obligations are frequently contrary to a party's intentions. The underlying principle is that a person should not be allowed to unjustly enrich himself at the expense of another. A classic example of a quasi-contract is the situation in which one person benefits another by mistake. If the person conferring the benefit reasonably believed that the recipient intended to pay for it, and the latter accepted the benefit knowing payment was expected, then fairness demands that payment be made.

EXAMPLE: Bentley's son, without Bentley's authorization, requests Neilsen to build a fence on Bentley's land. Neilsen proceeds to do so over a period of several days. Bentley knows that the fence is being built and that Neilsen expects payment, but he says nothing. When the fence is completed Bentley refuses to pay Neilsen, saying that there was no contract between them. A court may impose a quasi-contract obligation on Bentley to pay the reasonable value of the benefit he received, since otherwise he would be unjustly enriched at Neilsen's expense.

One point should be made about the above example. Bentley knowingly accepted the benefit from Neilsen. Assume, however, that Neilsen built the fence while Bentley was away on vacation, and that Bentley did not find out about it until his return. Because Bentley had no knowledge that Neilsen was building the fence and expected payment, and perhaps had no desire for a fence, Bentley could not be held liable for payment, and quasi-contractual liability would not be imposed. In fact, Neilsen may be liable to Bentley.

It should be noted that neither a quasi-contract nor an implied contract will be found when circumstances indicate that a service or other benefit was given gratuitously (free of charge).

Valid, Voidable, Void, and Unenforceable Contracts   A valid contract is one which is legally binding on both parties and enforceable in court. A voidable contract is one from which one or both parties have the power to withdraw, but which is otherwise valid and enforceable. A common example of a voidable contract is one between a minor and an adult. The minor may withdraw from (avoid) the contract, or he may affirm it and hold the adult to the contract.[3] Similarly, a contract procured through the fraud of one of the parties is voidable at the option of the defrauded party. A voidable contract is enforceable unless it is voided through a timely act or declaration of the defrauded party.

---

[3] The capacity of parties to enter a contract is discussed in Chapter 13.

Void contracts are different from voidable contracts in that they are legal nullities. A void contract is not binding, and it cannot be ratified and made enforceable by the parties. In legal effect a void contract is not a contract at all. For example, a contract requiring the commission of a crime is void and unenforceable, since it violates express statutory law.

The distinction between a void contract and one which is merely voidable becomes important, for example, when goods that are the subject of the contract are sold to a third party and the question arises whether the third party has ownership rights in the goods. This problem will be addressed in Chapter 20.

An unenforceable contract is one that gives rise to contractual obligations, but for the breach of which there is no remedy available. Unenforceability usually results because the parties fail to comply with some rule of law. For example, some contracts are required by the statute of frauds[4] to be in writing, and noncompliance with the statute renders the contract unenforceable. As with a voidable contract, an unenforceable contract may become enforceable if the defect preventing its enforcement is corrected, or "cured," or if the parties do not object to the enforcement of the contract.

Executory and Executed Contracts Another classification of contracts depends on performance. An executory contract is one in which the parties have not yet performed all the terms and conditions. An executed contract is one that has been fully performed by all parties. A contract may be partly executory and partly executed, as when one party has performed completely but the other party has not.

Formal and Informal Contracts The binding effect of certain contracts depends on their form. These are known as formal contracts. Formal contracts include (1) contracts under seal (sealed contracts), (2) recognizances (obligations entered into before a court of record), (3) negotiable instruments and documents (including commercial instruments such as bills of exchange and warehouse receipts), and (4) letters of credit (under the UCC).

All other contracts are known as informal or simple contracts. It should be noted that even informal contracts may be subject to formal requirements. The word "informal" merely indicates that a contract is not in one of the categories described above as formal.

9:4 Uniform Commercial Code

The Uniform Commercial Code (UCC), formulated through the joint efforts of the National Conference of Commissioners on Uniform State Laws and the American Law Institute, deals with most aspects of modern commercial transactions, although sometimes with amendments to the official text.[5]

The UCC was designed to bring the field of commercial law into line with contemporary business practices, to meet the needs of modern commercial

---

[4] The statute of frauds is discussed in Chapter 15.
[5] The official text of the UCC is set forth in Appendix B.

society, and to promote fair dealing between parties to business transactions. The UCC is liberally interpreted by the courts and applied to promote uniformity and modernization of the laws relating to commercial transactions. The basic philosophy of the UCC is that practical businesspersons cannot govern all their actions by legal formalities.

The UCC is of great importance in those commercial transactions, such as sales,[6] that it specifically covers. Moreover, the UCC is often applied by analogy even to transactions it does not regulate. The UCC is thus of great importance to the law of contracts. Its provisions will be discussed throughout this book, both generally and specifically with respect to certain types of transactions.

9:5   Realities of Standardized Contracts

The law of contracts developed on the assumption that a contract is the result of individual negotiations between the parties, and many principles of contract law are based on that assumption. In reality, however, many contracts today are standardized forms prepared by one of the parties, which require only the filling in of blanks to make them enforceable contracts. Sometimes only the signature of the parties is necessary.

There is nothing improper about using standardized forms. Indeed, use of such forms is often the most economical and efficient method of doing business. It must be recognized, however, that there are potential pitfalls. Failure to read a form contract carefully may result in a person's unwittingly agreeing to undesirable terms. Failure to make certain that the individualized portions of a form conform with the printed ones may also cause unnecessary problems and lead to litigation. It is unrealistic to suggest that such forms not be used, but it is important to stress that they be used with care. If a standardized contract does not accurately reflect the parties' intentions and desires, it either should not be used, or it should be used only after the necessary changes have been made to the form.

 A business that uses standardized forms should review them regularly. Changes in the law, whether by new statutes or court decisions, may make a standardized form obsolete or even legally ineffective. Periodic review and redrafting of forms by an attorney will enable a business to keep its forms current with the law.

As the use of standardized form contracts has increased, the courts and legislative bodies have begun to develop rules of law designed to minimize or prevent some of the abuses resulting from their use. The law's response to oppressive, onesided forms, discussed in Chapter 12 (see 12:13), is an example of the way the law changes to meet new needs and situations.

---

[6] Sales are discussed in Chapters 19–22.

9:6 Government Contracts

Federal, state, and local governmental entities often enter into contracts with individuals or companies. These contracts relate to the entire range of governmental activities, including procurement of services and supplies, construction, and research and development. Although the basic common-law rules of contract generally apply to contracts with governmental entities, a myriad of state and federal statutes and regulations also apply, making government contracting a distinct and special category of contract activity. A businessperson who contracts with a governmental agency must comply with the appropriate rules and regulations. For example, bidding specifications must be met precisely, profits may be expressly limited, records of the supplier may be subject to inspection, or disputes under the contract may be subject to administrative settlement.

In addition to the laws and regulations relating to the actual business relationship between the government and a private contractor, there are others designed to achieve public social goals. For example, statutes and regulations prohibit certain types of discrimination by government contractors and subcontractors. Others give preference to small business entities or domestically produced articles or materials.

Key Concepts and Terms

- A contract is a legally enforceable agreement between two or more parties. Contracts may be oral or written, simple or complex.
- The essential elements of a contract are parties who have the legal capacity to contract, mutual assent, consideration, and legality of purpose.
- Contracts may be classified as bilateral or unilateral; express or implied (implied in fact); valid, voidable, void, or unenforceable; executory or executed; and formal or informal. If no real contract exists, quasi-contractual obligations are sometimes imposed to prevent unjust enrichment.
- The Uniform Commercial Code (UCC), which has been adopted by most states, deals with most aspects of modern commercial transactions.
- Many contracts today actually consist of standardized forms, with or without blank spaces filled in. Use of such forms is legal and often desirable from a business standpoint, but care must be taken to avoid potential pitfalls.
- Persons or entities contracting with government agencies must comply with a wide variety of government statutes and regulations.

- Bilateral Contract
- Express Contract
- Government Contracts
- Implied Contract
- Model Procurement Code
- Offeree
- Offeror
- Promisee
- Promisor
- Quasi-Contract

- Standardized Contracts
- Uniform Commercial Code (UCC)
- Unilateral Contract

Questions and Case Problems

1. What is a contract? What are the essential elements of a contract?
2. What is the difference between a bilateral and unilateral contract?
3. What is a quasi-contract, and how does it differ from a true contract?
4. Discuss the advantages and disadvantages of standardized contracts.
5. Lucas, a minor, told Sharon that if she would steal a set of stereo speakers, he would pay her $50 for them. Sharon stole the speakers and gave them to Lucas, who said he would pay her the following week. Classify the agreement between Lucas and Sharon in as many ways as you can.
6. What is the difference between an express and an implied contract?
7. Jacob asks Eva if she will pay him $5 if he washes her car. Eva says that she will. Jacob washes the car, but Eva refuses to pay, claiming that there is no contract because nothing was put in writing. Is she correct? If there is a contract, is it bilateral or unilateral?
8. What is the difference between voidable, void, and unenforceable contracts?
9. Miller drives into a service station and, with no intention of paying, has the attendant fill his car with gasoline. Does a contract exist? If so, how would you classify it?
10. Discuss the philosophy and the importance of the UCC.

10 Offer and Acceptance

10:1 Introduction

The consequences of entering into a contract may be great. Failure to perform a contract may create very significant liability. Before imposing such liability, a court seeks certainty that an agreement existed, that the parties assented to the terms of the contract, and that the terms of the agreement are sufficiently clear that liability can be established. Courts look to evidence of communication between the parties to be satisfied that a valid contract exists. Usually, an identifiable set of terms and conditions are offered by one party (the *offeror*) and, ultimately, are accepted by the other party (the *offeree*). Looking back over the course of communication, one can discern an *offer* of certain terms and conditions and an *acceptance* of those terms. The communication may take different forms; all terms and conditions may not be contained in a single document. But at some point in the formation of a contract each party expresses intent to enter into a legally binding and enforceable agreement. There is a meeting of the minds.

An objective standard is used in determining whether there is mutual assent. Thus, in determining whether a particular communication is either an offer or an acceptance, the courts look to how a reasonable person would objectively view the language used. If it is reasonable to believe that one party intended to make a legally binding offer, and that the other party intended to make a legally binding acceptance, then a contract exists.

EXAMPLE: Mark tells Natasha, "I will sell you this vintage MG for $5,000." Natasha responds, "It's a deal. I accept your offer." Later that day, Mark refuses to complete the sale, claiming that he really intended to sell the car only if he could not get a better price for it. Mark's argument will be to no avail. His statement, viewed objectively, expressed a present intention to sell the MG, and Natasha's response, viewed objectively, accepted the offer. Thus a contract was created, and Mark's subjective intent is irrelevant. The same would be true if it were Natasha who later attempted to get out of the deal.

The following case is a graphic illustration of the rule that a party's statements will be interpreted by comparison with an objective standard. The result in this particular case may appear harsh. Consider, however, the effect of a contrary ruling. Specifically, if one party can withdraw from a contract on the ground that he entered it in jest, of what value is a contract in the first place? When, if ever, should a party be permitted to avoid contractual obligations on the ground that the contract was entered as a mere joke?

Lucy
v
Zehmer
84 SE2d 516 (1954)
Virginia Supreme Court of Appeals

FACTS: Mr. and Mrs. Zehmer owned the Ferguson Farm. On December 20, 1952, Lucy offered Mr. Zehmer $50,000 for the farm. Mr. Zehmer accepted and wrote an agreement stating: "We hereby agree to sell to W. O. Lucy the Ferguson Farm complete for $50,000.00, title satisfactory to buyer." Mr. and Mrs. Zehmer signed the agreement. Lucy took the agreement and offered $5 to bind the deal, but Mr. Zehmer refused the money. When the Zehmers refused to go through with the deal, Lucy sued to enforce the contract. The Zehmers defended on the ground that both men had been drinking and that the agreement had been written and signed as a joke. The trial court ruled in favor of the Zehmers, and Lucy appealed.

ISSUE: Did evidence of Zehmer's lack of intent to sell the farm prevent a court from finding his express agreement to do so binding on him?

RESULT: Zehmer's manifest expression of intent to agree should be judged by standards of reasonableness without regard to his real but unexpressed state of mind.

REASONING:

*   *   *

The defendants insist that the evidence was ample to support their contention that the writing sought to be enforced was prepared as a bluff or dare to force Lucy to admit that he did not have $50,000; that the whole matter was a joke; [and] that . . . no binding contract was ever made between the parties. . . .

In his testimony Zehmer claimed that he "was high as a Georgia pine," and that the transaction "was just a bunch of two doggoned drunks bluffing to see who could talk the biggest and say the most." That claim is inconsistent with his attempt to testify in great detail as to what was said and what was done. It is contradicted by other evidence as to the condition of both parties, and rendered of no weight by the testimony of his wife that when Lucy left the restaurant she suggested that Zehmer drive him home. The record is convincing that Zehmer was not intoxicated to the extent of being unable to comprehend the nature and consequences of the instrument he executed, and hence that instrument is not to be invalidated on that ground. . . .

The appearance of the contract, the fact that it was under discussion for forty minutes or more before it was signed; Lucy's objection to the first draft because it was written in the singular, and he wanted Mrs. Zehmer to sign it also; the rewriting to meet that objection and the signing by Mrs. Zehmer; the discussion of what was to be included in the sale, the provision for the examination of the title, the completeness of the instrument that was executed, the taking possession of it by Lucy with no request or suggestion by either of the defendants that he give it back, are facts which furnish persuasive evidence that the execution of the contract was a serious business transaction rather than a casual, jesting matter as defendants now contend. . . .

If it be assumed, contrary to what we think the evidence shows, that Zehmer was jesting about selling his farm to Lucy and that the transaction was intended by him to be a joke, nevertheless the evidence shows that Lucy did not so understand it but considered it to be a serious business transaction and the contract to be binding on the Zehmers as well as on himself. . . .

Not only did Lucy actually believe, but the evidence shows he was warranted in believing, that the contract represented a serious business transaction and a good faith sale and purchase of the farm.

In the field of contracts, as generally elsewhere, "We must look to the outward expression of a person as manifesting his intention rather than to his secret and unexpressed intention. 'The law imputes to a person an intention corresponding to the reasonable meaning of his words and acts.'" *First Nat. Exchange Bank of Roanoke v Roanoke Oil Co.* . . .

An agreement or mutual assent is of course essential to a valid contract but the law imputes to a person an intention corresponding to the reasonable meaning of his words and acts. If his words and acts, judged by a reasonable standard, manifest an intention to agree, it is immaterial what may be the real but unexpressed state of his mind. . . .

Whether the writing signed by the defendants and now sought to be enforced by the complainants was the result of a serious offer by Lucy and a serious acceptance by the defendants, or was a serious offer by

Lucy and an acceptance in secret jest by the defendants, in either event it constituted a binding contract of sale between the parties. . . .

Buchanan, Justice.

10:2   Intent to Make an Offer; Preliminary Negotiations

An offer must indicate an intent to be legally bound if the offeree accepts all of the terms and conditions of the offer. An expressed intent merely to do an act is not an offer. For example, Rubio writes to Kelly, "Are you interested in my property on Elm Street? I'm asking $100,000." This language would not indicate an offer; it does not suggest that Rubio would expect to be bound to take $100,000 for the property, and it does not contain a promise to be bound if Kelly tenders $100,000. The first part is mere inquiry, and the second part is mere information. If Kelly replies, making a commitment to purchase the property at the stated price, then his communication would be the offer. Acceptance of that offer by Rubio would form a contract.

Frequently, one person will initiate preliminary or exploratory discussions concerning a possible contract with another person. The first person may suggest the general nature of the contract he would like to enter, and then wait for the second person to come forward with either a specific offer or some specific ideas. Such an invitation to negotiate does not constitute an offer, only the opening of discussions. For example, "Would you be interested in," "I might be willing to," "I hear you're looking for a," or similar words pave the way for an offer but do not constitute one.

Depending on the complexity of the contemplated contract, the negotiating process might continue for some time, with each party making suggestions or comments. For *mutual assent*, and thus a contract, to come into existence, the negotiations must come to an end with an actual offer and acceptance. A series of continuing negotiations does not constitute an offer.

 The complex language of modern commercial transactions sometimes makes it extremely difficult to determine whether particular words or acts were intended as a legally binding offer, as preliminary negotiations, or as an invitation to the other party to make an offer. Whenever a question exists as to whether a person is making an offer or just commencing negotiations, the person should clearly state his or her intent. If no offer is intended, that fact should be clearly and prominently stated. Such a statement may help to eliminate costly litigation. Equally important, such a statement may, by minimizing the possibility of any misunderstanding, help to preserve a valuable business relationship.

Advertisements; Catalogs   Advertising is a major facet of modern commercial life. While the average person may interpret an advertisement as an offer or promise to sell the goods advertised, the courts have generally held otherwise. Most courts have held that advertisements are only invitations to enter into a bargain or to patronize a store, and not actual offers, even if the advertisement specifies the article and the price.

Courts reason that merchants do not intend to be contractually obligated— and therefore liable for damages—to every person who may accept the offer by tendering payment. It is, of course, possible to write an ad so as to indicate an offer; in that event, the merchant probably would limit the offer to the specific number of units to be sold. Similarly, catalogs and company price lists are not considered offers, even though they specify the items, terms, and prices of merchandise. When a prospective customer orders a catalog item or writes a letter of purchase based on the price quotation, such conduct is generally considered the offer. This offer must be accepted by the sender of the catalog or price list before a contract exists.

In addition, some states have statutes dealing with false and misleading advertising. These statutes impose liability on a merchant who refuses to accept offers for the advertised goods. Moreover, the Federal Trade Commission regulates many aspects of business advertising; its rules prohibit deceptive trade practices in advertising. Finally, as a practical matter, a merchant who persistently refuses to sell goods at the prices advertised will suffer adverse business consequences.

 On occasion, goods are advertised for sale at a mistaken price, sometimes through an error by the advertising media. A merchant usually is not obliged to sell the goods for the erroneously stated price. If the difference between the two prices is not great, a merchant may either decide to sell at the advertised price to maintain customer goodwill, or post a prominent notice explaining the erroneous advertisement. As a precautionary step, businesspersons should always check advertising copy before submitting it. If the advertisement is to be repeated, they should also make certain the first advertisement was accurate.

Advertisements for rewards for information leading to the arrest or conviction of a criminal suspect are usually held to constitute offers rather than invitations to make offers. This rule is based on the public policy ground that it is to society's benefit that persons who have committed crimes be apprehended and brought to justice.

Auctions   An announcement of an *auction*, or an auction itself, is not an offer to sell which becomes binding on the owner when a bid is made. Rather, a notice to the public to sell property to the highest bidder is merely an invitation to make bids and a declaration of an intention to receive bids. Unless a sale is "without reserve," the seller of property at an auction, or the auctioneer, may withdraw the property from sale at any time before accepting a bid. When a bid is accepted, a contract is formed. If an auction is held "without reserve," the goods must be sold to the person making the highest bid [UCC § 2-328].

10:3   Reasonable Certainty of Terms

Generally, to be a legally binding contract, an agreement must be reasonably definite as to all material terms and must clearly set out all rights and duties. An offer must be reasonably definite since, for a court to enforce a contractual obligation or to award damages for a breach, it must be able to determine what the parties' obligations were. The time of performance, price to be paid, work to be performed, quantity of items involved, or other material terms must be definite.

Although the terms need to be definite, absolute certainty is not required; reasonable certainty is sufficient. A contract is not indefinite if the parties can reasonably determine their basic rights and duties. While the offer must be definite and certain in its terms, the offeror, for example, may make an offer which gives the other person a reasonable degree of discretion in performance. To illustrate, if a produce wholesaler offers to sell a grocery store as many apples as it needs at 25 cents per pound, such an offer is legally effective. If the store accepts the offer and names the number of apples it will take at the quoted price, a contract is formed and the parties are bound by its terms.

As the following case indicates, the requirement of certainty is to be applied in a practical way. Consider whether, if the defendant's position had prevailed, it would be possible to draft a sufficiently certain contract.

McMurray

v

Bateman
144 SE2d 345 (1965)
Georgia Supreme Court

FACTS: In 1962 Dr. Bateman, who had a medical practice in Atlanta and in nearby Forest Park, Georgia, employed Dr. McMurray as an associate. The employment contract was a three-page letter written by Bateman and signed by him and McMurray. In 1965 the association was terminated, and McMurray set up medical practice in Atlanta. Bateman sued to enforce a provision of the contract that prohibited McMurray, for a period of three years after termination of the association, from engaging in practice within a 50-mile radius of Forest Park. Among the defenses raised by McMurray was the claim that the contract was so indefinite and uncertain as to be invalid. The trial court, rejecting that defense, ruled in favor of Bateman. McMurray appealed.

ISSUE: Was the written agreement insufficiently complete and definite so as to render it unenforceable?

RESULT: The terms of the contract were reasonably certain and sufficiently definite, given the nature of an employment contract.

REASONING:

*   *   *

The defendant insists . . . the contract between the parties . . . is too incomplete and indefinite to be enforceable. The document was primarily an employment contract and possessed all of the requisites of a contract of that nature expressed in reasonably certain terms. It designated, as we construe it, the defendant's place of employment, the period for which he was employed, the nature of the services he was to render and the compensation he was to receive.

While the contract contains no express promise that the defendant's place of employment would be the Forest Park Clinic and the Georgia Professional Building, the contract is explicit that he was to come and practice with the plaintiff and that the latter's practice was conducted at the places mentioned. The contract stipulates services, those incident to the practice of medicine and surgery, and that his compensation is to be arrived at according to an understandable formula. . . .

In reaching this conclusion we have considered the epitome of reasons the defendant contends the terms of the contract were incomplete and indefinite. He points out two provisions of the contract as indicative of its incompleteness: (1) "In the event anything arises not covered in this agreement nor already covered by precedent it shall be decided on the basis of the spirit herein contained and the Golden Rule, plus accepted Christian principles." (2) "Trips, vacations, outside study, time off, etc. to be arranged by mutual consent."

The former really has no legal significance. It is merely a statement that the contract may be altered by subsequent agreement of the parties. This is, as a matter of law, generally true of contracts, where the interest of a third party is not involved. The latter provision does not concern the essential elements of the contract, but simply provides that customary details concerning its performance will, from time to time, be determined by mutual consent of the parties. A contract is not usually incomplete because minor details incident to the performance of its terms are left to be agreed upon. . . .

The defendant further contends that the contract is incomplete because it does not stipulate whether the plaintiff is to provide office space, secretarial services or other facilities for the practice of medicine, and did not define what was meant by "overhead" expenses. We think the letter embodying the contract and the terms of the contract made it clear that the defendant was to practice as the plaintiff's employee and associate at the Forest Park Clinic and this carries with it the inescapable conclusion that he was to have office space, and the use of the clinic's facilities. The term "overhead" is not defined. It was not necessary that the contract define words that are commonly used in the connection of the conduct of business or the practice of professions. "Overhead" has a connotation generally understood. It means those expenses incidental or incident to the practice of a profession. . . . It is impossible to accurately stipulate in advance what will constitute such overhead expenses because from their very nature they depend upon contingencies occurring in the course of practice generally not predictable or certain. . . .

Quillian, Justice.

The fact that an offer contains a choice of terms from which the accepting party may make a selection does not make the offer too indefinite. Acceptance of one of the alternatives will form a binding contract. For example, if a manufacturer offers to sell a customer a particular machine for $3,500 *or* a more complex machine for $7,500, and the customer notifies the manufacturer that he will buy the $3,500 machine, a contract is formed. If, on the other hand, the manufacturer offers to sell a machine for $7,500 *and* a service contract for the repair of that machinery, as a package deal, the customer would have to accept both items of the offer or neither. The precise wording used, and the conjunctions, such as "and" and "or," are of considerable importance.

Under the UCC, a contract for the sale of goods is not too indefinite even though one or more terms are left open, if the parties intended to make a contract and if there is a reasonably certain basis for giving an appropriate remedy [UCC § 2-204]. The UCC provisions concerning open terms is considered in greater detail in Chapter 19.

10:4 Communication of Offer

An offer, to be legally effective, must be communicated by the offeror and received by the offeree. Unless an offer is communicated, no meeting of the minds—or mutual assent—can occur. If two parties make identical offers to each other which cross in the mail, no contract is created. For a contract to exist, one party must make and communicate an offer to the other party, who must accept the offer.

A question sometimes arises, in connection with so-called "fine-print contracts," whether all of an offer was effectively communicated to another party. In general, the law is not generous to the offeree who agrees to the terms of a contract without reading it. While the terms literally were not communicated, the offeree is assumed to have waived, in effect, the necessity of communication. The limit of this reasoning is approached, however, with form contracts that are printed so as to discourage the other party—typically a consumer—from reading the contract. Some courts have held that if particular provisions in a contract are not sufficiently conspicuous, they do not give the other party notice of their existence and the contract or the provisions are held void. In addition, specific legislation, such as the federal Truth in Lending Act (discussed in Chapter 28), requires that important contract terms be printed conspicuously in contracts that bind consumers.

10:5   Termination of Offer

An offer does not remain outstanding forever. If it is accepted, of course, the offer and the acceptance merge into the contract. If the offer is not accepted, there are various ways in which the offer may terminate. These ways include: (1) revocation by the offeror, (2) lapse of time, (3) rejection or counteroffer by the offeree, (4) termination by operation of law, and (5) termination in accordance with the terms of the offer. After the offer is terminated, of course, it can no longer be accepted; the offeree loses the power to bind the offeror in contract.

Withdrawal or Revocation of Offer   Generally, an offer may be withdrawn or revoked at any time before it has been accepted by the offeree. To be effective, the withdrawal or revocation must be communicated to the offeree before the offer is accepted. Thus, the revocation is effective when it is received by the offeree.

A complication arises when the offer states that it will not be revoked before a certain time, thus giving the offeree some "breathing room" to consider the offer. This offer not to revoke can itself be revoked. The rationale is that the right to hold the offeror to a promise is not conferred by a mere offer; the offer must be met with some reciprocal promise or performance of the offeree, consistent with the theory of consideration, or mutuality, developed fully in Chapter 11.

This general common-law rule covering revocation of offers has been modified by the UCC provision on "firm offers" [UCC § 2-205]. Under the UCC, if a merchant, in a signed writing, offers to buy or sell goods and gives his assurance that the offer will be held open, he must abide by that assurance. Thus, a firm offer is not revocable during the time stated in the writing. If no time is stated, the offer must be held open for a reasonable time, not to exceed three months.

An *option contract* represents a second type of irrevocable offer. If the offeree gives something of value, called consideration, to the offeror to keep the offer open for a specified period of time, the offer is called an option, and the offeror (optionor) must hold the offer open for the specified time period. It should be understood that an option is a contract in itself. Thus, with an option there exists: (1) an offer, which does not become a contract unless and until accepted and (2) a completed contract to leave the offer open for the specified time. Option contracts are frequently used in connection with the sale of property. The owner grants a prospective purchaser the option to buy the property under certain terms within a specified time period. During that time the prospective purchaser may either exercise his option and contract to purchase the property, or he may let the option expire.

Lapse of Time   An offer may also expire as the result of a lapse of time. If the offer itself specifies the length of time that it will be held open, it will terminate after that time passes. When the offer does not specify how long it is to remain open, the courts have held that it will continue for a reasonable length of time. What is considered to be a reasonable time depends on the facts and circumstances of each situation. Among the factors that may be considered are the past business practices between the parties and the customs of the particular trade or industry. Such business practices or customs may even be relied on to interpret an expressly stated limitation on the length of time that the offer will remain open.

EXAMPLE: Gillian, an apple grower, has sold apples to Max's Market for many years. In each of the prior 20 contracts with Max, Gillian has given Max "two weeks" to accept the offer and has allowed Max 14 working days. Gillian again offers to sell Max apples and allows him two weeks to accept the offer. Max accepts the offer on the fourteenth working day (the eighteenth calendar day) after it was made. Max's acceptance is timely and effective, because the past practices between Gillian and Max have equated "two weeks" with 14 working days.

Rejection or Counteroffer   An offer will terminate if the offeree either rejects it or makes a counteroffer. If the offeree says or does anything to indicate that he declines the offer or to justify the offeror's belief that the offeree does not intend to accept it, the offer is rejected. Once the offeree has rejected an offer, he cannot later accept it. The rejection has the effect of terminating the offer.

If an intended acceptance is conditional, introduces new terms, or in any way varies from the terms of the offer, it is not an effective acceptance. The courts treat such conditional acceptances as *counteroffers*. A counteroffer is a rejection of the original offer, coupled with the offeree's submission of a new offer. As such, it terminates the original offer.

The offeree may ask the offeror questions about the offer and even ask whether he will alter its terms. Such questions do not necessarily constitute a rejection of the offer. Whether a rejection has occurred may depend on the specific words used. To illustrate, assume that A offers to sell B a car for $3,000. B responds that she will pay A $2,000 for the car. B has made a counteroffer that amounts to a rejection of A's initial offer. If, however, B says, "I'd like to buy the car, but can you lower the price a bit?" B has neither accepted nor rejected the offer. The offer remains open, unless it is revoked by A.

Termination by Operation of Law   Certain events terminate an offer as a matter of law. These events include (1) the death or insanity of either the offeror or the offeree, (2) destruction of the subject matter of the offer, and (3) the subject matter becoming illegal after the offer is made. Any of these events will automatically terminate the offer.

Termination in Accordance with Terms of Offer   An offer may terminate automatically when conditions specifed in the offer occur. For example, Wanda may offer to sell John her car for $2,000 with the provision that the offer expires if she receives a superior offer. Thus, the offer would terminate automatically when Wanda is offered $2,200 for the car. Note that John's acceptance is not binding on Wanda unless it is effectively made before Wanda receives the superior offer.

10:6   Acceptance of Offer

Acceptance of an offer converts it into a binding contract. To be effective, an acceptance must correspond with the terms of the offer. An acceptance must be unequivocal and unconditional, and it must not introduce additional terms or conditions. This does not mean, however, that the acceptance must be phrased in the identical language of the offer. Any form of expression that shows the offeree's intention to accept the offer is an effective acceptance.

The statement that an acceptance may not introduce new or additional terms must be qualified somewhat. For example, if an acceptance includes terms that would be implied as a matter of law anyway, it is a valid acceptance. Also, if an acceptance includes minor or immaterial matters not mentioned in the offer, the courts will generally consider it to be unconditional and effective acceptance. Likewise, an unconditional acceptance coupled with the offeree's requests to the offeror to modify the contract is effective to create a contract. That contract, however, would not include the requested modification.

The UCC sets forth an additional exception to the requirement that an acceptance cannot contain new and additional terms. Under the UCC, an acceptance containing new or additional terms is generally effective to create a contract for the sale of goods, and additional terms not materially altering the contract become a part of it [UCC § 2-207]. This provision, and the reasons for it are covered in greater detail in Chapter 19.

10:7   Communication of Acceptance

Just as an offer must be communicated, so must an acceptance. Depending on the terms of the offer, the offeree's acceptance may be communicated to the offeror by words, acts, or a combination of words and acts, so long as the communication is such that a reasonable person would understand that an acceptance has been made.

If the offer requires the acceptance to be communicated in a particular manner, such as in writing, then the acceptance must be communicated in the way specified or it will not be legally effective to create a contract. Compliance with the term of the offer may, however, be waived by the offeror. So, for example, if the offer requires that acceptance be communicated by "return" mail and the offeree, in fact, telephones immediately and accepts, the offeror may either refuse that mode of acceptance or acknowledge the acceptance as satisfactory and create a contract relationship. If the offer does not indicate any particular means of acceptance, then any reasonable means of acceptance communicated to the offeror will create the contract.

If the offer specifies a time for acceptance, the acceptance must be communicated within that time. The language of the offer must, however, be reasonably interpreted. A requirement in an offer, for example, that it must be accepted "at once" or "immediately" will not be read to mean instantaneously, but will be read to require that an acceptance be communicated within a reasonably short time.

Means of Communication   If an offer is accepted in person or by telephone, the offeror learns of the acceptance at the same time it is made. When the acceptance is indicated by other means, by mail or wire, for example, a lapse of time is involved. Moreover, the acceptance may be lost and never delivered. The question then arises whether acceptance was ever communicated and, if so, when.

Unless the offer provides otherwise, an acceptance may be made by the same medium through which the offer was made. Moreover, the acceptance is effective when it is properly dispatched. If the offer was made by mail, the acceptance can be too. In such a situation, the acceptance is effective when the offeree deposits it with the Postal Service. This is so even if the acceptance never reaches the offeror, provided that the letter was properly addressed and had proper postage. Once a letter of acceptance has been properly mailed, the offer cannot be revoked, even if a letter of revocation was mailed, but not received, prior to the mailing of the letter of acceptance. This principle is known as the "Mailbox Rule" and it applies as well to forms of communication analogous to the Postal Service.

Sometimes, an offer made in person or by telephone is accepted by mail or by telegraph. In such cases, the courts have generally agreed that such acceptance is proper, unless the circumstances indicate otherwise. The courts are not agreed as to when such an acceptance takes effect. Some courts, on the rationale that the offeror has not authorized the use of the mails or the telegraph, have held such an acceptance effective only when it is received by the offeror. Other courts, apparently reflecting a growing trend, make no distinction between cases in which the offer was communicated by mail or telegram and those in which it was not. In other words, if acceptance by mail is proper, the acceptance takes place on its deposit with the Postal Service, regardless of whether the offer was made by mail. Acceptance by telegram is treated similarly.

The offeror can, of course, specify the means of acceptance to be used. The offeror may also provide that any acceptance will not be effective until the offeror receives it. Moreover, past business practices or customs in an industry may indicate that acceptance by mail or by telegram is not permissible. For example, if personal acceptance is normal in a given industry, an acceptance by mail may be considered unauthorized. In such a situation, a letter of acceptance would be effective only when actually received, and not when mailed.

 To avoid problems regarding whether, and when, an acceptance was effectively communicated, the offeror should specify: (1) the manner of acceptance, (2) the time allowed for acceptance, and (3) the time when the acceptance will be effective. The offeree should read an offer with care. If he or she decides to accept the offer, the offeree should be sure to (1) comply with all terms and conditions of the offer, including any expressed manner and time of acceptance; (2) communicate acceptance to the offeror in clear language; and (3) introduce no new or additional material terms or conditions.

Silence as Acceptance   Ordinarily, the offeree's silence cannot be interpreted as an acceptance of the offer. Under some circumstances, however, silence may be equivalent to acceptance. For example, if a seller on previous occasions has sent similar goods to the buyer and the buyer has always accepted and paid for them, the buyer's silence and retention of shipped goods on subsequent occasions will generally be considered an acceptance.

Acceptance of Offer to Enter Sales Contract [UCC § 2-206]   Under the UCC, an offer to enter a sales contract may be accepted in any manner and by any medium reasonable under the circumstances. This is true unless a specific manner or medium is clearly indicated by the language of the offer or the surrounding circumstances. The propriety of the manner of acceptance depends on whether it will be effective to reach the offeror in time to enable him to take the action contemplated by the parties.

10:8   Acceptance of Unilateral Offers

As noted in Chapter 9, an offer for a unilateral contract is accepted by performance of the requested act, not by a promise to perform. The performance of the contract constitutes the acceptance. When performance can be completed quickly, no problems are likely to arise. Sometimes, however, performance may require a long time. The offeree may begin performance, only to have the offeror attempt to withdraw the offer prior to completion. The offeree has not accepted the offer, since he has not completed performance. At common law, the courts generally held that an offer of a unilateral contract could be revoked at any time until the requested act was completed. Thus, an offeree who had started performance could recover only the value of his services under a quasi-contract theory (see 9:3). The modern trend, however, grants more protection to the offeree. Courts now generally hold that, once the offeree has begun performance, the offeror's right to revoke the offer is suspended until the offeree has had a reasonable opportunity to complete performance. Once performance is completed, the offer is then said to have been accepted.

Under the UCC, the offeree's commencement of performance of a contract is an effective acceptance only if, within a reasonable time after commencement, he notifies the offeror of his acceptance. For example, if Baker offers to purchase ball bearings manufactured to order by Carter, Carter may accept by beginning to manufacture the ball bearings. To avoid the possibility that Baker may later decide to revoke the offer, Carter must also notify Baker, within a reasonable time after he begins manufacturing, that he has accepted the offer. If Carter fails to do so, Baker may, after a reasonable time, treat the offer as having lapsed.

Under the UCC, an order or other offer to buy goods for current shipment invites acceptance either by a promise to ship or by actual shipment of the goods. Sometimes a seller may not have the exact goods ordered, but may have similar goods that he believes will be acceptable to the buyer. Shipment of such nonconforming goods also indicates acceptance, unless the seller notifies the buyer that the shipment is offered only as an accommodation to the buyer. (Such notification will protect the seller from a later claim that he breached the contract by sending the alternate goods.)

Key Concepts and Terms

- A contract requires that both parties intend to be bound to the terms and conditions of the agreement. Assent, often referred to as "the meeting of the minds," arises when one party (the offeror) makes an offer and the other party (the offeree) accepts it.

- The objective intention of the parties, expressed by their words or acts, determines whether an offer or an acceptance, and thus a contract, has been made.

- A valid offer must be reasonably definite and certain as to all material terms, and it must be communicated by the offeror and received by the offeree. A communication which merely initiates negotiations or solicits offers is not an offer. Advertisements, catalogs, and auctions are generally considered as only solicitations of offers. To create a contract, the person solicited must make an offer which must then be accepted.

- An offer may terminate by (1) revocation, (2) lapse of time, (3) rejection, (4) counteroffer, or (5) operation of law.

- Generally, an offer may be revoked at any time prior to acceptance. Exceptions to this general rule are (1) firm offers under the UCC, which must be kept open for the time stated or a reasonable time (not to exceed three months) and (2) options, which must be kept open for the time stated in the option contract.

- An acceptance, to be effective, must be unequivocal and unconditional. If an attempted acceptance contains material new terms or conditions, it is generally treated as a counteroffer.

- To be effective, acceptance of an offer must be communicated to the offeror. If the offer specifies a particular means or time for its acceptance, such requirements must be met. Otherwise, any reasonable means and time of acceptance is sufficient. The UCC generally permits acceptance in any manner and by any medium reasonable in the circumstances. Acceptance by an unauthorized means is effective, if at all, only on its actual receipt by the offeror.

- An offer for a unilateral contract is accepted by performance of the requested act. When the requested act requires a period of time for performance, commencement of performance generally suspends the offeror's right of revocation, and the offeree is given a reasonable opportunity to complete performance.

- Acceptance
- Auction
- Counteroffer

- Firm Offer
- Mailbox Rule
- Meeting of the Minds

- Mutual Assent
- Offer
- Offeree
- Offeror

- Option Contract
- Termination by Operation of Law
- Without Reserve

Questions and Case Problems

1. Is there an offer in each of the following situations? Why or why not? (a) A farmer says to the owner of a market chain, "I'll let you have as much corn as you need next season. We'll hammer out the price next month." (b) A farmer says to the owner of a market chain, "I'll sell you all the corn I produce next season." (c) The farmer says, "I'll sell you all the corn I produce next season at $5 a bushel." (d) The farmer says, "I'll sell you 200 bushels of apples next season at $5 a bushel—as long as I'm able to produce that many." (e) The farmer says, "I'll sell you as many apples as you need next season as long as my kids don't get sick."

2. Sands says to Fraser, "I'll sell you my property over on Main Street for $25,000 cash." Fraser responds, "Sounds like a good deal. Will you give me a couple of weeks to see if I can come up with the money?" "Sure," says Sands. Five days later, Fraser comes to Sands with $25,000, and says, "I got the money, I want to buy your property." Sands responds, "I didn't think you would be able to get the money, so I sold the property to Wilson yesterday." What rights does Fraser have in this situation? Should Fraser have done anything differently? If so, what?

3. A written offer is made to Levin. At 10 a.m., Levin mails a letter of rejection, then changes her mind, and mails a letter of acceptance at 1 p.m. the same day. Is Levin's acceptance effective? Does it make any difference which of Levin's letters is received first by the offeror? What if the two letters are received at the same time, but one is opened and read before the other?

4. Jessee and Smith entered into an oral contract whereby Jessee agreed to do the finish carpentry work on the interior of Smith's store. Jessee offered to do the work for "cost plus twenty-five percent." Smith told him "to go ahead and start on Monday." When Jessee completed the work he presented a labor bill of $2,673.26, representing 125% of the cost of the materials. Smith refused to pay, claiming there had never been a meeting of the minds concerning the price for the labor involved. When Jessee sues, Smith presents evidence that the labor was worth about $840.00. Jessee presents evidence that in the customs of the trade "cost plus 25%" contemplated a labor charge of 125% of materials and was reasonable. Could a jury find that there was a "meeting of the minds"?

5. Martin, offering in writing to pay Fong $2,000 to paint Martin's house, states, "This offer must be accepted in writing within 15 days from January 1." Fong does not respond in writing, but on January 2 he comes to Martin's house and begins painting it. He completes the job on January 8. Was there a contract? If there was not a contract, must Martin still pay Fong? Does it make any difference whether Martin was aware that Fong was painting the house?

6. Uhlman writes and signs a letter offering to sell Knapp 200 shares of Ace Corporation stock at $30 per share. The letter gives Knapp ten days in which to accept the offer. Through inadvertence, the letter is never mailed, but Knapp learns of its existence from Uhlman's secretary. Five days after the letter was written, Ace's stock doubles in value. Uhlman writes and mails a second letter revoking

the previous offer. Before Knapp receives Uhlman;s second letter he writes and mails a letter of acceptance to Uhlman. Is there a contract?

7. On May 1, State Bank offers a reward of $250 for information leading to the arrest and conviction of the person who had robbed the bank on the preceding day. On May 2, Lucas, unaware of the reward offer, informs the police that her sister is the robber. On May 3, Lucas learns of the reward offer and asks State Bank for the reward. The bank refuses, and Lucas sues. What is the result?

8. Feder received a credit card from City Bank. He used the credit card on many occasions over a fifteen-year period. One day he presented the card for use at a retail store and, on City Bank's direction, the clerk confiscated the card. Feder sued City Bank for conversion of the credit card. City Bank argues that Feder received written notice from it that City Bank reserved the right to cancel or suspend the card "at any time without prior notice." Feder claims the notice, if he received it, did not constitute a term of a contract because he did not agree to it. What is the result?

9. Watts sued Dickerson in an action for personal injuries arising out of an accident. On October 20, 1987, Dickerson made an offer to compromise the claim by paying Watts $25,000. On November 8, 1987, Watts died of causes unrelated to the accident, without having accepted the settlement offer. Four days later, Watts' adminsitrators accepted the settlement offer. Is Dickerson bound to the offer?

10. In the *McMurray v Bateman* case (see page 170), how should McMurray have handled the contract relationship with Bateman? Would he have been better off with no written contract at all? Should he have negotiated at arms' length with legal representation?

11 Consideration

11:1   Introduction to the Concept of Consideration

One of the basic elements of a contract is that there be *consideration,* or one of the legally accepted substitutes for consideration. Consideration consists of the promises or acts that the parties to a contract exchange with each other. It is the *quid pro quo,* the "price," that one party pays for the promise or performance of the other party. If a promise is not supported by consideration, it is not enforceable.

Courts rarely impose liability for a promise where the promisor has received nothing for the promise. The rationale is that in ordinary human experience it is rare for a person to intend to be held to the terms of a promise where there is no exchange of benefits. For example, A may say to B, "I promise to pay you $100,000," and B may reply, "I accept your offer to pay me $100,000." In the absence of some other communication that puts this exchange in a different context, a court will not enforce the promise, even though there appears to be an offer and an acceptance. For a promise to constitute part of an enforceable contract, something must have been bargained for and given in exchange for that promise. The "something" is the element known as consideration.

In their everyday business dealings, people frequently honor the requirement of consideration without giving any thought to it as such. For example, if A offers to pay B $20 for a book, and B accepts the offer, each party has agreed, as part of the bargain, to provide consideration to the other party. A has promised to give B $20 as consideration for B's promise to give A the book, and B has promised to give A the book as consideration for A's promise to give B $20. On the other hand, if B merely offered to give A the book free of charge, and A immediately accepted the offer, there would be no enforceable contract, since A did not promise B any consideration in exchange for B's offer of the book.

The requirement of consideration may be satisfied by a party giving up something of value—including the right to do something or not do something—or conferring some benefit on the other party. This may consist of an act, a forbearance from acting, or a promise of either. Moreover, the benefit may go to a third party if that is what the promisor sought in the bargain.

Lawyers often speak of consideration as a party suffering a *legal detriment* or conferring a *legal benefit*. A *legal detriment* is suffered by the promisee when the promisee does or promises to do something that he is not legally obligated to do, or when he refrains or promises to refrain from doing something that he otherwise legally could do. A *legal benefit* is conferred on the promisor when the promisor acquires some legal right to which he would not otherwise be entitled. Thus, consideration consists of some benefit to the promisor or some detriment to the promisee bargained for in exchange for the promisor's promise. These terms are used in a legal sense and not necessarily to refer to actual financial or other material advantage or disadvantage to the parties.

Consideration may consist not only of a promise to take some action, but also of a promise to refrain from taking some specific action *(forbearance)*. For example, assume that as a result of prior business dealings A owes B $1,000, that the date specified for payment of the debt has arrived, and that A has insufficient funds to make the payment. B intends to institute legal proceedings to collect the debt, and B so informs A. A requests B to refrain from taking legal action and to give A an additional six months in which to pay the debt. B agrees, on the condition that A agrees to pay an additional amount of money as interest on the original debt. A agrees. A's agreement to pay the additional sum is enforceable, since B's forbearance from filing a lawsuit during the specified period was consideration for A's promise.

11:2 Sufficiency and Adequacy of Consideration

In order for a binding contract to exist, the consideration bargained for must be legally sufficient. The courts tend to treat the terms "sufficient consideration" and "consideration" as synonymous, so that a promise or action that is legally insufficient is no consideration at all. It is nonetheless important to have some familiarity with the concept of sufficiency of consideration, particularly to avoid confusing *sufficiency* of consideration with *adequacy* of consideration.

To put the matter simply, if the consideration received by the promisor from the promisee is legally sufficient—that is, sufficient under contract law—the adequacy of the consideration is, under most circumstances, totally irrelevant. The courts have repeatedly emphasized that they will not inquire into the equality of the considerations exchanged between the parties to a contract, provided that each party in fact bargained for and accepted the consideration provided by the other party. For example, if A and B enter into a contract under which A agrees to sell to B a painting valued at $20,000 in exchange for B's promise to pay to A the sum of $1,000, the contract is supported by sufficient consideration from both parties, and a court asked to enforce the contract will not concern itself with the gross disparity between the value of the consideration being provided by each party.

 Although in theory the adequacy of consideration is irrelevant, in fact a court may be reluctant to find that a contract was intended, or may be reluctant to enforce a contract, when the consideration is clearly inadequate. This is particularly so when the party receiving the more valuable consideration is also the party who occupies the more powerful position in the negotiations leading to the contract. It is certainly permissible to drive a hard bargain, but one should always be wary of a bargain that is "too good," because a contract embodying such a bargain might be held invalid on a variety of grounds, such as fraud, mistake, or unconscionability.[1] Such a contract may also fail to meet specific statutory requirements designed to protect consumers or other unsuspecting persons. Thus, a prudent businessperson should not rely too heavily on the maxim that adequacy of consideration is irrelevant.

The discussion in the following sections focuses on the legal sufficiency or insufficiency of various types of consideration.

11:3 Illusory Promises; Requirements and Output Contracts

A bilateral contract typically involves the exchange of promises by the parties to the contract, with each party's promise serving as consideration for that of the other party. To constitute consideration a promise must impose a binding obligation. The requirement that each party undertake some obligation has been expressed by the statement that there must be mutuality of obligation to have a valid contract. Sometimes, however, the promise of one party is only illusory in nature, in that the promise does not impose definite obligations on the party. For example, if A promises to sell B a used automobile for $2,000, and B promises to pay that price "If I decide I want the car," there is no mutuality of obligation, since B's promise to pay the money is not binding. Consequently, if B later decides that he wants the car and tenders the $2,000 to A, A is not obliged to sell the automobile for that amount, since B's illusory promise did not constitute consideration for A's promise.

Mutuality of obligation is necessary to what are known as *requirements* and *output contracts*. A requirements contract is one in which the seller agrees to supply all of a certain material required for the buyer's business over a specified time, in exchange for the buyer's promise to purchase all of such material from the seller. An output contract is one in which the buyer promises to purchase the seller's entire production, in exchange for the seller's promise to sell the entire production to the buyer. The main advantage of such contracts is that they provide a buyer with an assured source of supply and a seller with an assured market. Provided there is mutuality of obligation, such contracts are valid and enforceable.

Problems of *mutuality of obligation* arise, however, when one party, usually the buyer, inserts a "loophole" provision into the contract that has the effect of relieving the buyer from any obligation to purchase anything. Under this provision, if a seller agrees to supply all of a commodity that a buyer wants

---

[1] The concepts of fraud, mistake, and unconscionability are discussed in Chapter 12.

during a specified period, the buyer may, without violating the agreement, decide that he wants none of that commodity. Since the buyer under such an agreement has no obligation to purchase anything from the seller, the seller likewise is not obligated to sell anything to the buyer. On the other hand, if the seller agrees to supply and the buyer agrees to purchase all of a given commodity required in the buyer's business during a specified period, then there probably is a valid contract, since the buyer is obligated to purchase from the seller whatever he actually needs, not merely what he wants to purchase.

The UCC contains the following provision with respect to output and requirements contracts:

> A term which measures the quantity by the output of the seller or the requirements of the buyer means such actual output or requirements as may occur in good faith, except that no quantity unreasonably disproportionate to any stated estimate or in the absence of a stated estimate to any normal or otherwise comparable prior output or requirements may be tendered or demanded [UCC § 2–306(1)].

 As noted, requirements and output contracts can be extremely advantageous to both buyer and seller. When negotiating such a contract, therefore, a person should strive to ensure that there is true mutuality of obligation, so that the contract can be enforced.

If a buyer draws up the contract with such a loophole provision, the resulting one-sided contract may boomerang against him. For example, if a shortage of the particular commodity develops and the seller finds he can obtain a higher price elsewhere, the buyer will find that the assured supply has disappeared just at the time it is needed. The buyer should therefore be committed to buy all requirements in accordance with the provisions of the UCC, or at least to buy the minimum amount that will ensure that the contract is a meaningful one. Similarly, attempts by one party to write an "escape clause" into the contract may threaten the enforceability of the contract. In the following case, notice the test the court poses for determining whether an option to cancel the contract renders the contract unenforceable.

Omni Group, Inc.

v

Seattle-First Nat. Bank
645 P2d 727 (1982)
Washington Court of Appeals

FACTS: Omni Group, Inc., a real estate development firm, agreed to purchase property from Clark. The "earnest money agreement" provided:

> This transaction is subject to purchaser receiving an engineer's and architect's feasibility report prepared by an engineer and architect of the purchaser's choice. . . . If said report is satisfactory to purchaser, purchaser shall so notify seller in writing within fifteen (15) days of seller's acceptance of this offer. If no such notice is sent to seller, this transaction shall be considered null and void.

Within the fifteen-day period Omni advised Clark that a feasibility study would not be required. When a dispute arose concerning the size of the property, Clark refused to proceed with the sale.

ISSUE: Did the contract provision making Omni's obligation to purchase contingent on a satisfactory engineer's and architect's report render its promise to buy the property illusory?

RESULT: The provision does not render the contract illusory if it can be exercised only under specified conditions.

REASONING:

*   *   *

A promise for a promise is sufficient consideration to support a contract. . . . If, however, a promise is illusory, there is no consideration and therefore no enforceable contract between the parties. . . . Consequently, a party cannot create an enforceable contract by waiving the condition which renders his promise illusory. But that a promise given for a promise is dependent upon a condition does not necessarily render it illusory or affect its validity as consideration. . . . Furthermore,

> a contractor can, by the use of clear and appropriate words, make his own duty expressly conditional upon his own personal satisfaction with the quality of the performance for which he has bargained and in return for which his promise is given. Such a limitation on his own duty does not invalidate the contract as long as the limitation is not so great as to make his own promise illusory.

3A A. Corbin, *Contracts* § 644 at 78–79 (1960).

Paragraph 6 may be analyzed as creating two conditions precedent to Omni's duty to buy the Clarks' property. First, Omni must receive an "engineer's and architect's feasibility report." Undisputed evidence was presented to show that such "feasibility reports" are common in the real estate development field and pertain to the physical suitability of the property for development purposes. Such a condition is analogous to a requirement that a purchaser of real property obtain financing, which imposes upon the purchaser a duty to make a good faith effort to secure financing. . . . In essence, this initial language requires Omni to attempt, in good faith, to obtain an "engineer's and architect's feasibility report" of a type recognized in the real estate trade.

The second condition precedent to Omni's duty to buy the Clarks' property is that the feasibility report must be "satisfactory" to Omni. A condition precedent to the promisor's duty that the promisor be "satisfied" may require performance personally satisfactory to the promisor or it may require performance acceptable to a reasonable person. Whether the promisor was actually satisfied or should reasonably have been satisfied is a question of fact. In neither case is the promisor's promise rendered illusory. . . .

Omni has, by the quoted language, reserved to itself a power to cancel or terminate the contract. . . . Such provisions are valid and do not render the promisor's promise illusory, where the option can be exercised upon the occurrence of specified conditions. . . . Here, Omni can cancel by failing to give notice only if the feasibility report is not "satisfactory." Otherwise, Omni is bound to give notice and purchase the property. Accordingly, we conclude paragraph 6 does not render Omni's promise illusory. The earnest money agreement was supported by consideration. . . .

James, Judge.

11:4 Performance or Promise to Perform Existing Obligation

Ordinarily, the performance of or a promise to perform an existing legal obligation does not constitute consideration for a contract, since a person suffers no legal detriment by doing or promising to do what he was already obligated to do. This principle has various applications. For example, a police officer has a legal duty to enforce the law and to apprehend violators. Thus, a law enforcement officer's apprehension of a suspected criminal cannot serve as consideration for a third party's offer of a reward for such apprehension; the officer was legally obligated to take such action before the reward was ever offered.

This principle also may be applied when a party attempts to modify a contract. Clearly, the parties to a contract can agree to modify its terms if each party provides consideration for the other's agreement to modify the contract. Sometimes, however, the modification is entirely one-sided. For example, assume A and B have entered into a contract whereby A has agreed to install a patio for B in exchange for B's promise to pay $2,000. Thereafter, A decides that the price is not sufficient, and informs B that she wants $2,500 instead. B agrees to pay the increased price. After completion of the patio, B refuses to pay A more than $2,000, claiming that the promise to pay the additional $500 was unsupported by any consideration. B's position would ordinarily prevail. Because A was already obligated to construct the patio at the time she sought the increased price and did not undertake any other obligations as consideration for B's additional promise to pay $500, the modified contract would not be valid.

Under some circumstances, a court might conclude that A was entitled to the additional $500, regardless of the existence of the previous obligation. The parties to a contract are free to cancel the contract if they so desire. If the court concluded that A and B had actually canceled their first contract, thereby releasing both parties from their obligations under that contract, and that they entered a new contract, then A's promise to construct the patio could constitute consideration for B's promise to pay $2,500. However, a court is likely to insist on very clear proof that there was actually a cancellation of the original contract, rather than an unsuccessful attempt by A to modify it and obtain a higher price. Thus, it is important to structure a change in a contract to provide for consideration or a new contract.

It should be noted that under UCC § 2-209(1) a contract for the sale of goods may be modified without consideration. There is a requirement of good faith, however, to prevent the extortion of modifications of sales contracts without legitimate commercial reasons.[2]

11:5 Past Consideration

Often, in attempting to show consideration for a promise, a party can identify some service performed or benefit conferred in the past. If the service or benefit was rendered under circumstances in which no contract was implied, the past service or benefit cannot stand as consideration for the promise. Thus, past consideration is no consideration at all, in the legal sense. This rule is simply a variation of the principle that consideration represents a bargained-for exchange of promises or performance. If the performance took place in the past, it cannot be the bargained-for exchange for a promise made at a later time.

Cases in which an attempt is made to enforce a promise on the basis of past consideration must be distinguished from cases in which the past services were rendered in exchange for an implied promise to pay for them. For example, if one person requests another to perform some act but makes no express promise to pay for that act, the courts often will first imply such a promise and find that an implied contract exists, and then view the subsequent promise to pay as evidence of the reasonable value of such services.

11:6 Moral Obligation

The problem of promises based on a moral obligation of the promisor to benefit the promisee is vexing. In general, a court will not enforce a promise that is, in effect, a promise to make a gift. Often a donor couches the words of a gift in terms of obligation. So, for example, a grandparent may promise to finance a favorite grandchild's college education "in consideration of the love and affection" between the child and grandparent. Because "love and affection"

---

[2] UCC § 2-209, Comment 2; UCC § 1-203. UCC § 2-302, relating to unconscionability, might also be relied on to prevent extortionate modifications. Unconscionability is discussed in Chapter 12. Sales contracts are discussed in Chapter 19.

constitutes neither a detriment to the child nor a bargained-for benefit to the grandparent, it is not legal consideration. Therefore, the child cannot sue to enforce the promise. It should be noted, however, that if the grandparent does pay for the grandchild's college education, then later sues for reimbursement on the ground that there was no legal obligation to make such payments, the claim will be rejected because the payments will be considered a completed gift.

Application of the principle that past consideration or moral obligations do not constitute sufficient consideration could produce harsh results. The following case demonstrates how one court avoided a solution that, while in accord with the principle, would have been harsh.

Griffin

v

Louisville Trust Co.
226 SW2d 786 (1950)
Kentucky Court of Appeals

FACTS: Prior to his death William Mann had given Carrie Griffin, his housekeeper, a check for $6,000, but she was unable to cash the check due to insufficient funds in Mr. Mann's account. After his death she sought to recover the money from his estate, which was worth $130,000. To do so, it was necessary to prove that the check was given by Mr. Mann in exchange for consideration from Mrs. Griffin.

ISSUE: Was Mann's promise of $6,000 supported by consideration?

RESULT: Mann's expectation of Griffin's future services constituted sufficient consideration for the promise.

REASONING:

* * *

. . . [I]t is admitted that if this check was given in payment for past services which Mrs. Griffin rendered deceased, she cannot recover. He had paid her in full by the week for the services as they were rendered, and even though her services were worth more than the wages she received under her contract with deceased, there would be no consideration for this check since a moral obligation does not furnish a consideration for a new contract where there is no legal obligation. . . .

If there was any consideration to support this check, it was for services to be performed in the future for Mr. Mann by Mrs. Griffin. It will be necessary to give a brief picture of the Mann household, the services Mrs. Griffin rendered and then to turn to the evidence for a solution of this controversy.

Mrs. Griffin started working for Mr. Mann in 1938 as a housekeeper when she was 58 years of age. He had been totally blind for some fifteen years and lived in a large house in Louisville with two sisters, one of whom was deaf and dumb. The afflicted sister died soon after Mrs. Griffin entered Mr. Mann's service and the other sister lived only about a year. Mrs. Griffin's wages were $8 a week which were raised to $10 in about 1940. In December 1945 her wages were increased to $25 per week at the suggestion of a nephew of Mr. Mann, and [he] gave her a $50 Christmas present that year.

Mr. Mann was a retired traveling salesman, whose chief interest was in flowers and he maintained a greenhouse on his premises. Although totally blind and a man advanced in years, Mr. Mann was quite active about his place and in caring for his flowers. Mrs. Griffin did everything for him: the housekeeping, the marketing, the cooking, the laundry, and the firing of the furnace. In addition to all this, she read to Mr. Mann and went about town with him and would go into his lockbox. She wrote all of his checks, which he signed. She was Mr. Mann's eyes and hands and cared for him 24 hours a day. Being unable to distinguish night from day, Mr. Mann would at times water and work his flowers in the middle of the night, and sometimes got lost in his garden and would have to call Mrs. Griffin to come and get him. She seems never to have lost patience with, nor tired from serving him.

. . . Oscar Nettleton, an employee of the Yellow Cab Company for 15 years and who often drove Mr. Mann, testified that Mrs. Griffin's health had failed under her strenuous duties. He stated Mr. Mann said, "Mrs. Griffin [was] a godsend to him"; and that he did not want her to die before him because, "I don't know what I would do without her." Deceased mentioned to him several times that he had drawn this $6,000 check and had given it to Mrs. Griffin. . . .

Mrs. Marie L. Haury, a life-long friend of deceased and his family, testified that Mr. Mann told her of his great appreciation of Mrs. Griffin when witness visited his home. She expressed herself in these words: "He said he didn't know what he would do without her. In his later years, when his health became worse, he expressed to me that he was afraid she might die before him, or would have to leave him, and he said he did not know what he would do without her."

Here, we have an old, blind man with no relatives nearer than nephews, living alone in a large house with an old lady who had served him for more than seven years and to such an extent that she had become broken in health, which fact he knew. Mr. Mann appears to have been a gentleman of refinement and appreciation. He was worth something over $130,000 and was paying Mrs. Griffin but a meager wage for the service she was performing, and his great concern was that she might leave him before he died. It is clear to our minds from the competent testimony of the four witnesses to whom we have just referred that Mr. Mann executed this $6,000 check to Mrs. Griffin in consideration of her remaining with and caring for him until the end of his days, which she did, and not for services theretofore performed for which he had paid her in full.

Sims, Chief Justice.

11:7   Compromise or Settlement of Claim; Composition with Creditors

Another common issue involving consideration arises when the parties to a contract attempt to settle disputes or claims arising out of the contract. Typically, one or more of the parties agrees to receive less than the contract provides. If the promisee does not incur a legal detriment or confer a legal benefit, the promisor's promise lacks consideration and is not enforceable. For example, suppose you visit your dentist for a painful toothache. The dentist agrees to perform needed dental work for $300. After the dental work is complete and your mouth is no longer uppermost in your thoughts, you receive the dentist's bill for $300. You call the dentist and ask to pay less. The dentist agrees to take $200 for the work. You pay the $200 and then receive a bill for the remaining $100. The dentist's promise to accept $200 in full payment for the work is not an enforceable promise because of the lack of consideration. You have incurred no legal detriment and have conferred no legal benefit on the dentist by promising to pay less than you owed.

If, on the other hand, there had been no specific agreement on the amount owed, the law would find an implied agreement to pay reasonable fee for service. You and the dentist could reasonably disagree on what constitutes a reasonable fee. Your promise to pay $200 and the dentist's promise to accept $200 would be supported by consideration because both of you would have forborne from claiming a specific amount, which might have been more or less than $200.

In the first hypothetical, the debt is said to have been *liquidated*, which means there was no dispute as to the legal obligation. To create an enforceable obligation to accept less in settlement of a liquidated debt, it is necessary to raise some consideration other than the promise to pay the less-than-liquidated amount. An agreement to pay sooner than would otherwise be required, or on different terms, ordinarily would constitute sufficent consideration. In the second hypothetical, the debt was *unliquidated*, which means there was reasonable disagreement as to the legal obligation. A debt may be partly liquidated and partly unliquidated; some amount of the debt may be undisputed and some part disputed. In that event, an agreement to pay less than the liquidated part in full payment of the total debt would require consideration other than the promise to pay.

The issue of settlement often arises in the context of a check offered in full payment of a debt. Where there is a dispute as to the amount of a debt, and the debtor sends the creditor a check with words to the effect that the check is presented as payment in full of the indebtedness, the creditor's act of cashing the check will ordinarily be considered as acceptance of the debtor's compromise offer, and the debt will be considered discharged. In the case of liquidated claims, the effect of accepting such a check is less certain. Most courts have decided that acceptance of a check under such circumstances does not prevent the creditor from seeking the additional amount due. Under the UCC, however, accepting the check operates to discharge the debt [UCC § 3-408]. However, most courts have held that a creditor under the UCC, by writing the words "without prejudice" or "under protest" on the check, may cash a full-payment check and later seek payment of the balance the creditor believes is still owed. This may also be done with unliquidated debts [UCC § 1-207].

Often, a debtor is unable to pay the liquidated claims of several creditors. Under such circumstances, an agreement called a *composition with creditors* is sometimes reached. Under a composition agreement, two or more creditors of the same debtor agree to accept payment of a specified percentage of their respective claims as full satisfaction of the debts. The significant factor in a composition agreement is that it involves an agreement not only between the debtor and his various creditors, but also among the creditors themselves.[3] Composition agreements are generally enforceable, and a creditor may not later seek payment of the balance of the claim. The rationale for sustaining such agreements varies. Some courts classify composition agreements as an exception to the consideration requirement, while other courts stress that the consideration received by the creditors consists of the promises of their fellow creditors to forgo the opportunity to obtain full payment of their claims.

11:8   Exceptions to Requirement of Consideration

There are various exceptions to the rule that consideration is an essential part of a contract. The following exceptions are among the more important ones.

Promissory Estoppel   Under the doctrine of *promissory estoppel*, a court prevents a promisor from asserting that his promise is unenforceable for lack of consideration. The doctrine requires that the promisor have made a promise under circumstances in which the promisor intends or should reasonably expect the promise to induce action or forbearance by the promisee in reliance on the promise, and the promisee does, in fact, rely on it in some definite and substantial manner. The doctrine is invoked only when enforcement of the promise is necessary to avoid injustice under the circumstances.

Promissory estoppel often is invoked in the family context, where promisees may reasonably rely to their detriment on promises made without the formality of consideration. While these promises ordinarily are merely promises of a gift, and therefore not enforceable, in egregiously unfair situations estoppel may be used to enforce the promise to avoid the injustice. The damages awarded in promissory estoppel cases are those necessary to avoid injustice; they are not necessarily a full measure of damages for breach of contract.

---

[3] Composition agreements are discussed more fully in Chapter 32.

The following classic case illustrates a business situation in which a court concluded that the doctrine was applied properly.

<hr>

Hoffman
v
Red Owl Stores, Inc.
133 NW2d 267 (1965)
Wisconsin Supreme Court

FACTS: Hoffman, the owner of a bakery in Wautoma, Wisconsin, entered into discussions with representatives of Red Owl Stores, a supermarket chain, about operating a Red Owl franchise store. Hoffman had $18,000 to invest, and Red Owl representatives assured him that amount would be sufficient to establish him in a store. Negotiations continued for about two years, during which time Hoffman, at Red Owl's suggestion, bought and operated a small grocery for three months, then sold it; paid $1,000 down on a store lot in Chilton, Wisconsin, where his Red Owl franchise was to be located; sold his bakery in Wautoma; and rented a house in anticipation of a move to Chilton. Red Owl representatives consistently assured Hoffman that he would obtain a Red Owl franchise. However, as time passed, Red Owl first told Hoffman that $24,000 would be necessary, then that $26,000 would be required, and finally that $34,000 would have to be invested. Hoffman refused to invest $34,000, negotiations were terminated, and Hoffman sued Red Owl for breach of agreement. The trial court entered judgment for Hoffman, and Red Owl appealed.

ISSUE: Was the doctrine of promissory estoppel properly invoked against Red Owl in the trial court?

RESULT: The doctrine of promissory estoppel was properly invoked to enforce Red Owl's promise, despite the lack of consideration and the indefiniteness of the promise.

REASONING:

*   *   *

. . . Many courts of other jurisdictions have seen fit over the years to adopt the principle of promissory estoppel, and the tendency in that direction continues. As Mr. Justice McFaddin, speaking in behalf of the Arkansas court, well stated, that the development of the law of promissory estoppel "is an attempt by the courts to keep remedies abreast of increased moral consciousness of honesty and fair representations in all business dealings." . . .

Because we deem the doctrine of promissory estoppel, as stated in sec. 90 of *Restatement, 1 Contracts*, is one which supplies a needed tool which courts may employ in a proper case to prevent injustice, we endorse and adopt it.

Applicability of Doctrine to Facts of This Case

The record here discloses a number of promises and assurances given to Hoffman by Lukowitz in behalf of Red Owl upon which plaintiffs relied and acted upon to their detriment. . . .

. . . There remains for consideration the question of law raised by defendants that agreement was never reached on essential factors necessary to establish a contract between Hoffman and Red Owl. . . . This poses the question of whether the promise necessary to sustain a cause of action for promissory estoppel must embrace all essential details of a proposed transaction between promisor and promisee so as to be the equivalent of an offer that would result in a binding contract between the parties if the promisee were to accept the same.

Originally the doctrine of promissory estoppel was invoked as a substitute for consideration rendering a gratuitous promise enforceable as a contract. See Williston, *Contracts* (1st ed.), p. 307, sec. 139. In other words, the acts of reliance by the promisee to his detriment provided a substitute for consideration. If promissory estoppel were to be limited to only those situations where the promise giving rise to the cause of action must be so definite with respect to all details that a contract would result were the promise supported by consideration, then the defendants' instant promises to Hoffman would not meet this test. However, sec. 90 of *Restatement, 1 Contracts*, does not impose the requirement that the promise giving rise to the cause of action must be so comprehensive in scope as to meet the requirements of an offer that would ripen into a contract if accepted by the promisee. Rather the conditions imposed are:

(1) Was the promise one which the promisor should reasonably expect to induce action or forbearance of a definite and substantial character on the part of the promisee?
(2) Did the promise induce such action or forbearance?
(3) Can injustice be avoided only by enforcement of the promise?

We deem it would be a mistake to regard an action grounded on promissory estoppel as the equivalent of a breach of contract action. As Dean Boyer points out, it is desireable that fluidity in the application of the concept be maintained. . . .

We conclude that injustice would result here if plaintiffs were not granted some relief because of the failure of defendants to keep their promises which induced plaintiffs to act to their detriment. . . .

Currie, Chief Justice.

Charitable Subscriptions   When a person pledges to donate money to a college, church, or similar charitable organization, consideration for the pledge—called a charitable subscription—ordinarily is lacking. Regardless of that fact, the courts tend to enforce charitable subscriptions. Various rationales have been offered in support of their enforceability. Some courts have held that the mutual promises of all the subscribers operate as consideration for the specific promises of each subscriber, while others have relied on a theory of promissory estoppel. The strong public policy of supporting charitable institutions has been the paramount factor in determining that charitable subscriptions may be enforced.

Promise to Pay Debt Rendered Unenforceable by Statute of Limitations or Discharge in Bankruptcy If a debtor makes a promise to pay a debt rendered unenforceable by the *statute of limitations*, most courts will hold the new promise enforceable, even though consideration is lacking for the promise. Each state has laws commonly known as statutes of limitations, which provide that various types of actions must be brought within specified time periods. The effect of failure to file an action within the appropriate time period is that the claim becomes unenforceable.

If a debtor makes a new promise to pay a debt rendered unenforceable by the statute of limitations, most courts will hold the new promise enforceable, even though consideration is lacking for the promise. Moreover, if the debtor in some way acknowledges the existence of the debt after passage of the period of limitations, most courts will hold such acknowledgment to be the equivalent of a new promise to pay and will enforce payment of the debt.

Under the common law this principle was also applied to the reaffirmation of debts discharged in bankruptcy. When a debtor receives a discharge of debts as a result of a federal bankruptcy proceeding, the debts are unenforceable, even though the creditors have received only partial payment of the debts. Traditionally, courts have enforced promises made by a debtor after bankruptcy to pay debts otherwise discharged, even though such promises are made without consideration. Today, however, federal bankruptcy law severely restricts the circumstances under which such reaffirmation may be made. This problem is treated more specifically in Chapter 31.

Contracts under Seal At common law no consideration was necessary to support promises made in a contract under seal. Most states have, however, changed the common-law rule. The UCC provides that the law relating to sealed instruments does not apply to sealed writings with respect to the sale of goods [UCC § 2-203].

Key Concepts and Terms

- Consideration consists of the promises or acts that the parties to a contract, as part of their bargain, exchange with each other. Consideration may consist of legal benefit to the promisor or legal detriment to the promisee. An illusory promise cannot serve as consideration for the other party's promise.
- The consideration exchanged by the parties to a contract must be legally sufficient, but a court generally will not concern itself with the adequacy of the consideration.

- A promise to perform an already existing legal obligation does not, under most circumstances, constitute consideration. Thus, when an existing contract is modified, each party ordinarily must provide consideration. However, when a sales contract is modified, consideration is not necessary under the UCC.
- Past consideration is insufficient to support a promise.
- A moral obligation does not constitute consideration.
- A compromise and settlement agreement requires consideration from both parties. A compromise agreement is valid when a debt is unliquidated. Where a debt is liquidated a compromise agreement is invalid.
- A composition with creditors agreement is an agreement among the debtor and his creditors that each creditor will be paid only a percentage of the debt.
- The courts will enforce certain promises even in the absence of consideration. Such promises include (1) promises held enforceable under the doctrine of promissory estoppel, (2) charitable subscriptions, and (3) promises to pay debts rendered unenforceable by a statute of limitations or a discharge in bankruptcy.

- Bargained-for Exchange
- Composition with Creditors
- Compromise or Settlement of Claim
- Consideration
- Forbearance
- Legal Benefit
- Legal Detriment
- Liquidated Debt
- Mutuality of Obligation
- Output Contract
- Promissory Estoppel
- Requirements Contract
- Statute of Limitations
- Unliquidated Debt

Questions and Case Problems

1. A, having fallen off a cliff, is clinging by her fingers to the edge. Unable to pull herself up, she asks B, who is standing nearby, to rescue her. B says, "I will save you if you promise to pay me $5,000." A promises to do so, and B then rescues A. Do A and B have an enforceable contract (Is A's promise supported by consideration?)?

2. "Plaintiff [Clausen] alleges that it had been a wholesale distributor of defendant's [Hamm Brewing Co.] products since 1911. Clausen states that in 1950 an oral contract was made with Hamm to become an exclusive Hamm's beer distributor for an area defined as Southern Minneapolis and contiguous suburbs. In reliance upon said contract Clausen alleges (1) they discontinued all competitors' products and (2) purchased and maintained inventories, sales, advertising, warehouse space, personnel, and facilities as a Hamm's exclusive distributor. . . . It is alleged that in April 1963 Hamm [illegally] terminated its oral agreement." Do the facts alleged show the existence of a contract supported by consideration? If not, might the plaintiff recover under some other theory?

3. Hunter was insolvent when he died; there was not enough money in his estate to pay his funeral expenses. Plaintiff bank holds Hunter's promissory note for $3,700, which represents a claim against Hunter's estate. Thereafter, Hunter's widow gives the bank her promissory note, "in consideration" of the bank's surrender to her of

Hunter's note. Plaintiff bank brings an action against Mrs. Hunter to recover on her promissory note. How should the case be decided?

4. Russ Financial Co. obtained a judgment for $3,101.03 against Hoberman's, a retail clothing store. Hoberman claims that Russ promised in writing that it would delay a sheriff's sale of Hoberman's property for 45 days if Hoberman tendered $1,000 payment toward the judgment. Hoberman paid the $1,000 and Russ proceeded with the sale nonetheless. Hoberman claims breach of contract or, alternatively, promissory estoppel against Russ. Is Russ' promise enforceable under either theory?

5. In the *Red Owl* case (see page 192) the defendants argued that its promises were not sufficiently definite to constitute an offer. The court said this was not a necessary element of promissory estoppel. How, then, could the court enforce the promise?

6. Schwartzreich contracts in writing to work for Bauman-Basch for $90 per week for a period of one year. Prior to beginning work under the contract, Schwartzreich is offered $115 per week to work for a competitor of Bauman-Basch. Learning of this offer, Bauman-Basch offers to pay Schwartzreich $100 per week if Schwartzreich will stay. Schwartzreich accepts and a new contract, identical to the first one except for the weekly salary, is drafted. The signatures are torn off the original contract. Schwartzreich is subsequently discharged before expiration of the one-year employment period, and he brings a lawsuit for breach of the second contract. Can Schwartzreich recover on the second contract?

7. Levine leases a store to Blumenthal for two years, the rental to be $175 per month the first year and $200 per month the second year. Before the end of the first year, Blumenthal advises Levine that due to business difficulties it will be impossible to pay the increased rental during the second year. Levine thereupon agrees to continue accepting $175 per month. After the end of the lease, Levine sues Blumenthal to collect the additional $25 per month for the second year. Can Levine recover?

8. A requests his friend, B, an automobile mechanic, to repair A's automobile during B's spare time. B does so, and A, after driving the automobile, tells B that she did a fine job and promises to pay her $300. Is A's promise to pay B enforceable? Would your answer be any different if A had never requested B to repair the automobile?

9. Ebling was employed as a manager of Gove's used sailboat office. In return for Ebling's agreement to manage the office, Ebling was promised 35% of all commissions generated by the office. On October 23 Gove informed Ebling that effective November 1 his commission rate would be reduced to 15% plus a salary of $500 per month. Ebling refused to agree to the new arrangement, and on November 3 Ebling terminated his employment, effective November 15. Subsequently, he received commission checks based on sales between November 1 and November 15. The checks reflected a 15% commission rate. Ebling cashed the checks and sued for the difference between the 15% and 35% commissions. What result?

10. Boehm is pregnant and believes that Fiege is the father. Fiege, thinking that he probably is the father, promises to pay child support if Boehm does not institute a paternity proceeding against him. Some time after the child's birth, Fiege learns that blood tests indicated that he could not possibly be the child's father, and he discontinues the support payments. Boehm commences paternity proceedings, and Fiege is found not to be the father. Boehm then files an action to enforce Fiege's promise of support. Is she entitled to recover?

12 Reality of Consent

12:1 Introduction

Consent of the parties is an essential element of a contract. Under some circumstances a contract that appears to be valid is not enforceable because the consent is not a "real" consent, but a consent acquired through fraud, honest misrepresentation, mistake, duress, or undue influence. Contracts that are entered into in any of these ways, and other contracts that are totally or partially unenforceable for lack of consent—adhesion contracts and unconscionable contract—are examined and discussed in this chapter.

12:2 Fraud

Fraud is the intentional misrepresentation of a material fact with the intent of inducing reliance of the other party to the contract. Contracts procured through fraud may be void or voidable, depending on the nature of the fraud. There are two distinct types of fraud: *fraud in the execution* and *fraud in the inducement.*

Fraud in the execution exists when one party surreptitiously obtains the signature of the other party by some fraudulent representation that relates to the signing of the contract. For example, substituting one document for another at the time of signing would be fraud in the execution and would render a contract void. Note, however, the court's reluctance to find fraud in the following case.

Waldrep

v

Nosrat

426 So2d 822 (1983)

Supreme Court of Alabama

FACTS: Nosrat, an Iranian citizen, signed a promissory note for $11,400 payable to Shirley Waldrep. The note was proffered to him by his brother-in-law, Edwin, with whom Nosrat owned a hardware store. Edwin told Nosrat that the document was an application for credit for the hardware store. Relying on this statement, Nosrat signed the note without reading it. The proceeds of the note were used by Edwin and other family members. When Shirley Waldrep sued for payment, Nosrat sought to void the note. The parties agreed that Nosrat could read and write English.

ISSUE: Was Nosrat defrauded by the actions of his brother-in-law, and therefore not liable on the note?

RESULT: Nosrat is liable on the note because, as between two innocent parties, he was in a superior position to avoid the fraud.

REASONING:

*   *   *

Nosrat gave no excuse for not having read the note before signing it. He testified he signed because Edwin told him it was one of the credit applications. That document was clearly entitled:

"PROMISSORY NOTE (SECURED) and Security Agreement"

The note is not vague or ambiguous. The general rule in Alabama is that one who has executed a written contract in ignorance of its contents cannot set up that ignorance to avoid the obligation absent fraud or misrepresentation. . . .

Nosrat attempts to come within the fraud or misrepresentation exception set out in *Gunnels* by arguing that he was defrauded by the actions of Edwin and, thus, he is not liable on the note. The exception is stated thus:

> " . . . [A] party who puts his signature thereto cannot avoid the obligations therein assumed by pleading his ignorance of its contents, unless his signature has been procured thereto by fraudulent representations of the other party or his agent as to its contents. . . . "

. . . Shirley Waldrep was also defrauded in the same transaction. No evidence was offered to prove the "defrauder" was an agent for Shirley or that she had any knowledge of his actions.

When one of two innocent parties must suffer, even by a fraud perpetrated by another, the law imposes the loss upon the party who, by his misplaced confidence, has enabled the fraud to be committed. . . . It is apparent to this court that a closer examination of the document by Nosrat would have revealed the true nature of the document he signed. Nosrat submitted no evidence that he was unable to read the promissory note before he signed it. While we sympathize with Nosrat, we are bound by the principle that imposes the loss upon the party who, by his misplaced confidence, has enabled another to commit the fraud. . . .

Embry, Justice.

Fraud in the inducement exists when one party obtains the agreement of the other party by some fraudulent representation. The defrauded party has the options of seeking money damages for the fraud or voiding the contract. Under the UCC, however, the remedies available to a defrauded party to a sales contract include all remedies available for nonfraudulent breach of such a contract [UCC § 2-721].

To prove fraud, a person claiming to have been defrauded into entering a contract must establish the following elements: (1) that the other party misrepresented (or, under some circumstances, concealed or failed to disclose) a material fact, with knowledge of the falsity of the representation or with reckless disregard of its truth; (2) that the other party had the intent to deceive and to induce the person to act in reliance on such misrepresentation; (3) that he in fact reasonably relied on the misrepresentation; and (4) that he sustained some damage or injury. These elements are discussed individually in the sections that follow.

12:3   Misrepresentation of Fact

One critical element of fraud is false representation of a fact through the words or the conduct of the defrauding party. The representation must relate to a fact that is ascertainable at the time of the representation, not simply to an opinion or prediction about future events. Nondisclosure or concealment may be fraudulent under some circumstances.

EXAMPLE: While looking under the hood of a customer's car, a service station attendant squirts gasoline on the fuel pump. He then tells the customer to take a look at the fuel pump. The customer, seeing that the fuel pump appears to be defective, asks the attendant to replace it. Although the attendant never told the customer that the fuel pump was defective, the attendant, by his conduct and his request to look at the fuel pump, did represent that the fuel pump was defective.

Misrepresentation of Fact or Opinion   Representation about nonfactual matters generally cannot form the basis of a charge of fraud, even though they be false. This is so because a matter of opinion is not capable of exact knowledge; reasonable people may have opinions that differ. The rule that fraud may not be based on a misrepresentation of opinion is frequently applied to situations in which one party to a transaction makes statements concerning the value, quality, or condition of property.

Value is considered largely a matter of judgment. When a person makes a statement concerning the value of some particular property, the statement is treated as only that person's opinion, not as a statement of fact. Even if the statement of value was erroneous, there is no fraud. For example, assume that the owner of a horse tells a prospective buyer that the horse is worth $1,000, and the buyer purchases the horse for that amount. Several other people subsequently tell the purchaser that the horse is not worth more than $800. The buyer cannot claim fraud, since the original owner's statement as to the horse's value was merely her personal estimate or opinion, not a statement of fact.

Statements of value should be distinguished from statements of cost. While a claim that some item has a certain value is only an opinion, a claim that the seller actually paid a certain amount for the item is in the realm of fact since it is capable of knowledge. If a seller says, "This car is easily worth $1,000," it is only an opinion. However, if he says, "I paid $1,000 for this car," he has made an assertion of fact.

Representations as to the quality of products or other property are also considered statements of opinion rather than fact. Statements that a television set is well made and that a particular company produces high quality products, for example, generally are treated merely as expressions of the opinions of the persons making these statements.

The rule that fraud cannot be based on mere expressions of opinion is commonly applied in the area of so-called "trade talk" or dealer's puffing. It often occurs in sales situations and consists of the seller's describing the article to be sold in expansive or glowing terms. The courts generally have held that such "trade talk" does not constitute fraud because it is only an expression of the seller's opinion. Moreover, the courts have often expressed the view that no reasonable person would act in reliance on trade talk.

Misrepresentation Concerning Future Events or Intentions   Misrepresentations concerning future events do not constitute fraud since they do not relate to some past or present fact. Statements as to probabilities, predictions of future business results, and expressions as to what a person intends to do in the future, even if ultimately false, are not classified as fraud. Note, however, that a seller may promise certain results in the future; failure to achieve those results may constitute a nonfraudulent breach of contract. For example, assume that a furnace salesperson informs a potential customer that the customer's usage of natural gas should decrease 20 percent if an old furnace is replaced with a new one that the salesperson has to offer. The customer agrees, the new furnace is installed, and natural gas usage decreases only 5 percent. Because the salesperson's statements were only predictions of a future event, there is no fraud. There may, however, be a breach of contract if the representations are found to be promises that are a part of the contract.

Misrepresentation of Law   Everyone is presumed to know the law and to have equal means of obtaining knowledge of the law. Therefore, a person is generally not considered to be deceived by misrepresentations of law. For example, a statement as to the legal effect of a particular written instrument, even if it is a false statement, does not constitute fraud.

Distinguishing Factual from Nonfactual Representations   It is frequently difficult to distinguish between expressions of opinion and ones of fact, and the circumstances under which a statement was made often must be considered in determining whether it was intended as a factual statement or merely a statement of opinion. For example, assume that a contractor tells a homeowner that it will take one eight-hour day and ten sacks of cement to make a patio. On the basis of that representation the contractor charges, and the homeowner pays, a specified price for performance of the job. In fact, it takes only four hours and five sacks of cement to perform the job. Should the contractor's representations be viewed as statements of fact, based on his superior knowledge gained from past jobs, or merely as estimates (opinions) of the amount of labor and materials necessary?

A representation sometimes constitutes a mixture of fact and opinion. In such a situation, the representation may be fraudulent if it is false. For example, it is one thing to say that particular property is "good agricultural land." Such a statement merely expresses an opinion, because there may be differences of opinion as to what type of land is good agricultural land. It is quite another thing to say that property is "good agricultural land because it has low alkali soil"; the alkalinity of the soil may be measured, placing such a statement in the realm of fact. Thus, it is easy to move from statements of opinion to statements of fact, and the line between fact and opinion is neither clear nor distinct.

12:4   Exceptions to Misrepresentation of Fact Requirement

There are various exceptions to the rule that fraud may be based only on a misrepresentation of past or present fact. The major exceptions typically involve one or both of two types of misrepresentations: (1) a misrepresentation made in the context of a confidential relationship and (2) a misrepresentation made by a party who had or claimed to have superior knowledge about the subject under discussion. In these situations, misrepresentations of opinion or of law may be considered fraudulent. For example, as noted above, the courts traditionally have held puffing to be an expression of opinion and, as such, not fraudulent. However, if a seller who has superior knowledge or means of knowledge about the value or quality of a product misrepresents the value or quality to an ignorant buyer, the misrepresentation can be the basis of fraud. An antique dealer's representations of the value of an antique would be a good example. Similarly, if a party who has superior knowledge of the law misrepresents the law to another party, as an attorney might do to a client, the misrepresentation will constitute fraud. The modern tendency is to view misrepresentations of opinion as fraud if they are made intentionally and with the purpose of inducing another person to rely on them. In addition, various statutes now protect the rights of purchasers and other consumers.

When expressing an opinion, a businessperson should be sure that there is some factual basis that justifies the opinion. The businessperson should not unreasonably exaggerate the qualities or value of a product or service, especially when he or she has superior knowledge about that product or service. When purchasing goods and services, seek and pay attention to factual representations. Honest, straightforward dealing reduces misunderstanding, maintains goodwill, and helps avoid costly and time-consuming legal problems.

12:5 Concealment or Nondisclosure of Fact

There is no general obligation in contract law to disclose any fact to another party. Silence does not constitute fraud, even though it may result in the other person's acting on the basis of erroneous assumptions. In other words, one party may take advantage of the other party's ignorance. This is particularly so when both parties have equal access to the facts. However, where one person, by words or conduct, actively and intentionally attempts to suppress material facts and to conceal them from another, fraud may be found. This is called active concealment and can be fraudulent because it can create in the other party a false impression of a fact.

In certain circumstances, however, there is a duty to disclose information. This duty typically is found (1) when a relationship of confidence and trust exists between the parties to the contract, (2) when one party to a contract has superior knowledge or means of knowledge of the undisclosed facts, or (3) when one party makes a voluntary partial disclosure to the other party that is likely to result in creating a mistaken impression about some material fact. In this last situation, the duty is greater if the partial disclosure is accompanied by intentional concealment of other facts to mislead the other party.

The line between misrepresentation of fact and concealment of fact is not always a distinct one, and fraud may be based on a combination of misrepresentation of some facts and concealment of others. Notice in the following case the court's reasoning to impose a duty to disclose even where the factual information was available to the plaintiff as a matter of public record.

Osterberger

v

Hites Construction Co.
599 SW2d 221 (1980)
Missouri Court of Appeals

FACTS: Plaintiffs bought a house from defendants and gave a deed of trust without knowing there was already an outstanding deed of trust on the property. The trial court found that the sales contract, the promissory note, the deed of trust, and the deed to the property all were executed on the same day, a Sunday. Defendants were aware of the outstanding deed of trust, but although one defendant had explained the contents of the contract documents to plaintiffs, she had made no mention of the outstanding deed to plaintiffs orally or in writing. Defendants had transferred other property to other buyers in this manner, without mentioning the outstanding deeds of trust. When plaintiffs failed to make payments, defendants foreclosed on the property, and plaintiff sued to void the sales contract on the grounds of fraudulent concealment. Defendants claimed that the deed of trust was a matter of public record and there was no duty to disclose its existence.

ISSUE: Were the defendant's obligated to disclose the deed of trust to the plaintiff's at the time of the sale?

RESULT: The defendants' superior knowledge and partial disclosure of the contents of the sales instruments obligated them to disclose this material fact.

REASONING:

*   *   *

To support their general complaints, defendants specifically contend the transaction in question was an arms-length transaction and, thus, they had no duty to disclose to plaintiffs the existence of Ozark's deed of trust. We disagree. Admittedly, business is still business, and normally, where parties are dealing at arm's length, neither can legally complain about the mere silence of the other. . . . However, in factual situations similar to the present case, our courts have carved out a number of important exceptions to the rule of nonliability for failure to disclose material facts. No single factor is necessarily determinative. However, we have imposed a duty to disclose on defendants who concealed facts which induced plaintiffs to refrain from an examination of the public records. . . . Moreover, if a plaintiff is so inexperienced that he would not be able to ascertain the true state of the title to property without employing a third person to examine the records, we have imposed a duty on the defendant to disclose all encumbrances on that title. . . . Furthermore, we have found that partial information may be as misleading and deceptive as active misrepresentation, and we have imposed a duty to disclose material facts where the defendant has invited plaintiff's confidence by making only a partial disclosure. . . .

On the present record, defendants had a duty to disclose to plaintiffs the existence of Ozark's outstanding deed of trust. There was a great disparity between the parties with regard to their knowledge of real estate matters. Neither plaintiff had training or extensive experience in real estate transactions. This was the first house purchased by plaintiff Thomas Osterberger, and plaintiff Janet Osterberger had purchased a house only on one previous occasion with a former husband. In contrast, both defendant Patricia Hites, as secretary-treasurer of defendant Hites

Construction Company, and defendant Eugene F. Hites, as president of the company, had extensive experience not only in building but also in selling homes. Using her superior knowledge, Patricia Hites prepared all the instruments involved in the transfer, and she was well aware that plaintiffs' lack of training and experience caused them to look to her for information, advice and guidance. Moreover, she willingly took it upon herself to explain the contents of the instruments to plaintiffs. However, she made only a partial disclosure. In her explanation, she omitted any reference to the outstanding deed of trust and she failed to insert the description of this encumbrance in any of the instruments in question. Plaintiffs' inexperience coupled with Patricia Hites' partial disclosure was a rational basis for the trial court to conclude that plaintiffs were induced to complete the entire transaction on a Sunday without waiting to hire a third person to examine the records so as to ascertain the true status of the title to the property being transferred. Under these circumstances, the court properly found these defendants concealed a fact they had a duty to disclose. . . .

Satz, Judge.

12:6 Intent to Deceive

The essence of fraud is that one party has intentionally deceived and thereby taken unfair advantage of another. Proof of intent to deceive is, therefore, an essential element of a fraud action. Usually this intent is established by circumstantial evidence—that is, by reference to the other circumstances of the transaction. A showing that a representation was made either with knowledge of its falsity or with reckless disregard of its truth or falsity generally leads to the conclusion that the representation was made with intent to deceive and to induce the other party to rely on it.

12:7 Materiality and Reliance

To establish fraud, it must be shown that a misrepresentation was of a material fact and that the innocent party reasonably relied, to his detriment, on the misrepresentation. The test of materiality is whether the fact was of sufficient importance that it influenced the other party to enter into the contract. The test of reliance is whether the person would have entered into the contract but for the particular misrepresentation. These tests are tantamount to proof of fraud. If one party misrepresented a material fact, but the other party was not misled and did not rely on the misrepresentation, there would be no fraud. For example, assume that the owner of an apartment building tells a potential buyer that the building was constructed 10 years ago. The potential buyer, although she knows that the building was actually constructed 15 years ago, proceeds to enter a contract to purchase the apartment building. If the buyer should later bring suit against the original owner claiming fraud on the basis of the misrepresentation as to the building's age, no fraud should be found, since the buyer was not misled by and did not rely on the misrepresentation.

Under some circumstances, the reasonableness of a party's reliance on a particular misrepresentation is considered in determining fraud. The reasonableness is measured by the rule that one party to a contract cannot rely on a representation by the other party if no reasonable person under similar circumstances would do so. Thus, in some situations a party may have a duty to investigate whether certain representations are true or not.

12:8   Damage or Injury

To secure relief on the basis of fraud, the injured party must have suffered some damage or injury as a consequence of his reliance on the misrepresentation. He may ask for monetary damages or for termination, known as *rescission,* of the contract. Where monetary damages are sought, there must of course be a showing of a pecuniary loss. Where rescission of the contract is sought, a showing of monetary loss usually is not required; a showing that the party was induced by the misrepresentation to enter a contract that he would not otherwise have entered is sufficient. Remedies and damages for breach of contract are discussed more fully in Chapter 18.

12:9   Honest Misrepresentation

Honest misrepresentation may be defined by contrasting it with fraudulent misrepresentation. There are two primary differences: An honest or innocent misrepresentation is one that is made with the belief, although mistaken, that it is true. Recall that a fraudulent misrepresentation is one made with knowledge that it is false or with reckless disregard of truth or falsity. The second difference lies in the remedies available to the injured party. While either monetary damages or rescission of the contract may be sought as a remedy for fraud, rescission is the only remedy available for honest misrepresentation.

12:10   Mistake

The consent of one or both parties to a contract may in some cases be made on the basis of a mistaken assumption or impression. Usually, these mistakes have no bearing on the validity of the contract. Under some circumstances, however, a mistake could lead to a contract's being set aside on the ground that there was no genuine consent to the contract. Several kinds of mistakes may affect the genuineness of a party's consent.

Mutual or Bilateral Mistake   A *mutual mistake,* as the name implies, is a mistake made by both parties. It is also known as a *bilateral mistake.* If both parties to a contract acted on the basis of a mistaken assumption about a material fact, the contract can be rescinded at the request of either party. The mistake must usually (1) relate to the essence of the bargain and (2) involve a fundamental assumption that caused the parties to act as they did. Mutual mistakes typically involve the existence, the identity, or the character of the subject matter of the contract or of some other person or thing essential to the contract.

Many cases have dealt with situations in which the contracting parties assumed the existence of the subject matter of the contract, only to discover later that it either had been destroyed or had never existed at all. Such a mistake usually justifies rescission of the contract. Examples of this kind of mistake are plentiful: a contract for the sale of a house, which unknown to either party had burned down prior to the contract; a contract to paint a portrait of a third person who, unknown to the parties, had died.

Two parties sometimes reach an apparent agreement, only to discover that each was operating under a different assumption as to the identity of the subject matter of the agreement. For example, assume that A, who has a brown horse and a black horse for sale, agrees to sell B a horse for $300. A believes that she has just sold the brown horse, while B believes she has just bought the black one. Under such circumstances there is no contract, because the parties never reached any true agreement.

Even if the subject matter of the contract exists, and the parties agree as to its identity, a mutual mistake that voids the contract could be made about some essential quality or characteristic of the subject matter. For example, assume that A sells B a bar believed by both of them to contain a substantial amount of silver, but the bar turns out to contain only base metal. The contract may be rescinded on the basis of mutual mistake, because the parties acted under an erroneous assumption concerning a basic fact that was fundamental to the agreement.

It is important to distinguish between the situation in which both parties are actually mistaken as to a specific fact and the situation in which there is uncertainty as to a specific fact. In the latter situation the uncertainty is presumed to be taken into consideration in the bargaining process, and one party or the other bears the risk of uncertainty. There is no ground for voiding the contract. The doctrine of mutual mistake assumes mistaken certainty rather than known uncertainty.

The following classic case illustrates the concept of mutual mistake.

Sherwood

v

Walker

33 NW 919 (1887)

Supreme Court of Michigan

FACTS: Plaintiff, a banker, contracted to purchase a cow from defendant farmer for $80. The cow, "Rose 2d of Aberlone," was described by the farmer as "probably barren." About two weeks later, plaintiff tendered payment of $80, but was refused possession of the cow on the ground that the cow was, in fact, with calf and worth $750 to $1,000 as a breeder. Plaintiff sued for possession of Rose.

ISSUE: Is the doctrine of mutual mistake available to excuse defendant from performance of an otherwise valid contract?

RESULT: The mutual mistake of the parties as to the nature of the subject matter of the contract excuses defendant's performance.

REASONING:

* * *

. . . I know that this is a close question, and the dividing line between the adjudicated cases is not easily discerned. But it must be considered as well settled that a party who has given an apparent consent to a contract of sale may refuse to execute it, or he may avoid it after it has been completed, if the assent was founded, or the contract made, upon the mistake of a material fact,—such as the subject–matter of the sale, the price, or some collateral fact materially inducing the agreement; and this can be done when the mistake is mutual. . . .

If there is a difference or misapprehension as to the substance of the thing bargained for, if the thing actually delivered or received is different in substance from the thing bargained for and intended to be sold, then there is no contract; but if it be only a difference in some quality or accident, even though the mistake may have been the actuating motive to the purchaser or seller, or both of them, yet the contract remains binding. . . . It has been held . . . that where a horse is bought under the belief that he is sound, and both vendor and vendee honestly believe him to be sound, the purchaser must stand by his bargain, and pay the full price, unless there was a warranty.

It seems to me, however, in the case made by this record, that the mistake or misapprehension of the parties went to the whole substance of the agreement. If the cow was a breeder, she was worth at least $750; if barren, she was worth not over $80. The parties would not have made the contract of sale except upon the understanding and belief that she was incapable of breeding, and of no use as a cow. It is true she is now the identical animal that they thought her to be when the contract was made; there is no mistake as to the identity of the creature. Yet the mistake was not of the mere quality of the animal, but went to the very nature of the thing. A barren cow is substantially a different creature than a breeding one. There is as much difference between them for all purposes of use as there is between an ox and a cow that is capable of breeding and giving milk. If the mutual mistake had simply related to the fact whether she was with calf or not for one season, then it might have been a good sale; but the mistake affected the character of the animal for all time, and for her present and ultimate use. She was not in fact the animal, or the kind of animal, the defendants intended to sell or the plaintiff to buy. She was not a barren cow, and, if this fact had been known, there would have been no contract. The mistake affected the substance of the whole consideration, and it must be considered that there was no contract to sell or sale of the cow as she actually was. The thing sold and bought had in fact no existence. She was sold as a beef creature would be sold; she is in fact a breeding cow, and a valuable one. . . .

Morse, Justice.

Under the UCC, certain contracts can be avoided under conditions similar to those recognized under the concept of mutual mistake. These conditions apply to avoiding contracts for the sale of identified goods before the risk of loss (see 20:5) has passed to the buyer. If the goods are totally destroyed, the contract *is* avoided. If the goods deteriorate to the extent that they fail to conform to contract conditions, the contract *can be* avoided; that is, the buyer has the option of avoiding it.

Unilateral Mistake   If only one party to a contract acts on the basis of a mistaken assumption, it is a *unilateral mistake*. A unilateral mistake generally does not affect the validity of the contract, and the mistaken party must live with the bargain. However, under certain circumstances a unilateral mistake may justify rescission. These circumstances include the following: (1) if the other party either knew, or in the exercise of reasonable care should have known, of the mistake, such as a mistake that is so obvious that a reasonable person must know or suspect that a mistake was made; (2) if enforcement of the contract would result in such extreme hardship to the mistaken party that an injustice would occur, provided the parties can be returned to the position they held prior to the contract; and (3) if a mistake is made with respect to price bids by contractors for the performance of jobs, such as erroneous mathematical computations or omissions of certain items in computing the cost of the contract, the courts often grant rescission under such circumstances if the mistaken party notifies the other party of the mistake prior to any action by the other party to its detriment.

Mistake of Law   It is often broadly stated that a mistake of law—such as not knowing the legal effect of a particular document or language used in it— does not provide a basis for rescinding a contract. This statement is, however, subject to many qualifications and exceptions, and many courts now treat mistakes of law no differently than mistakes of fact. Therefore, it is probably more accurate to say that whether a mistake of law may affect the genuineness of consent to entering a contract, and thus provide a ground for rescission of the contract, depends on the nature of the mistake and the particular state in which it occurs.

12:11 Duress

A consent to a contract will be held invalid if it was obtained by means of *duress.* A contract is a result of duress if one party, by means of threats or actions, has instilled such fear and apprehension in the other party as to deny that party's exercise of free will, resulting in that party's consent not being truly voluntary.

The *Restatement (Second) of Contracts* defines two forms of duress. First, "if conduct that appears to be a manifestation of assent by a party who does not intend to engage in that conduct is physically compelled by duress, the conduct is not effective as a manifestation of assent" [§ 174]. Thus, the threat of physical injury renders the contract void for duress. Second, "if a party's manifestation of assent is induced by an improper threat by the other party that leaves the victim no reasonable alternative, the contract is voidable by the victim" [§ 175(1)]. Such duress may take the form of threats by one party against the other party's person, family, friends, or property. The threatening behavior may be wrongful and illegal. Usually, threatening to do what one has a right to do is not the basis for a claim of duress unless the threat is morally abhorrent or violates public policy.

In negotiating a contract a party may generally take advantage of the precarious financial situation of another party to secure more favorable terms. Duress would exist only if the party with the advantage exerts extreme economic pressure through some wrongful action and leaves the threatened party with no real alternative but to comply with the threatening party's demands. This is known as the *business compulsion* or *economic duress* doctrine.

12:12 Undue Influence

If one party to a contract so dominates the other party as to deprive the latter of free will, the contract is said to be the result of *undue influence* and may be set aside at the option of the weaker party. Some courts consider undue influence to be a type of constructive fraud, while others have classified it as a type of duress. In any case, to establish undue influence it generally must be shown (1) that, under the circumstances, one party to a contract was particularly susceptible to the influence of the other party; (2) that because of this influence the weaker party lacked free will and was unable to act independent of the dominant party's desires; and (3) that as a result the parties entered a contract that was against the best interests of the weaker party.

In assessing a claim of undue influence, all the factors bearing on the weaker party's susceptibility to influence and the stronger party's position to exert such influence must be considered. The relationship of the parties is one of the most important of these factors. The relationship that is most often subject to such a claim is a confidential relationship, such as a professional relationship or a family relationship. When a contract is entered into between persons in a confidential relationship, and the dominant party in the relationship is the beneficiary of the contract, it is presumed that the contract was the result of the dominant party's influence, and he or she has the burden of proving otherwise.

Other factors include the weaker party's advanced age, impaired physical or mental condition, lack of education, lack of access to independent and disinterested advice, or dependence for necessities on the dominant person, and the adequacy of consideration received by the weaker party. A fairly typical case might involve a contract between a very old person in poor physical health, with no access to outside advisers, and a private housekeeper. Because the housekeeper would be in a position to exert extraordinary influence, it is not unreasonable for the law to scrutinize carefully any contract and presume that a contract extremely favorable to the housekeeper and unfavorable to the other person would be the result of undue influence.

12:13   Contracts of Adhesion; Unconscionable Contracts

Standardized form contracts are often imposed by financially powerful businesses on smaller businesses or on consumers. These contracts frequently contain extremely one-sided provisions. Among the primary responses to the increased use of such contracts is the recognition of two types of standardized contracts for which relief can be given to the weaker party.

Adhesion Contracts   A *contract of adhesion* is a standardized contract that has been drafted by one party and is offered on a take-it-or-leave-it basis. The other party or parties to the contract are not permitted to bargain for its terms. Moreover, they may not be able to obtain better terms elsewhere because the dominant party has a monopoly on the particular goods or services desired, or because all other businesses offering the same goods or services also use the same or similar types of contracts and there appears to be no competition that would produce better terms. Thus, the weaker party may be forced to choose between acceptance of basically unfair contract provisions or forbearance of the desired goods and services. While courts do not regard standard form contracts as necessarily bad, many courts recognize the imbalance of power in the relationship. Such courts carefully scrutinize adhesion contracts and construe any ambiguities against the dominant party.

Modern insurance contracts are typical adhesion contracts. Virtually all insurance contracts contain standard provisions drafted by the insurance companies to restrict their liability and the coverage afforded by their policies. An applicant must fill out a standardized application form and accept a standardized policy, with no opportunity to negotiate particular terms and conditions. For this reason, the courts have construed insurance policies strictly against the insurers.

 Firms that use standardized contracts should keep abreast of court cases that construe standard provisions. In addition, such firms should scrutinize their own clerical process to identify standard form contracts that have, in fact, been altered by the other party and the alteration apparently accepted. Such firms are in a very poor position to argue that an adhesion contract has been altered.

Unconscionable Contracts   "Unconscionable" cannot be precisely defined. Basically, it is the quality of being excessively unfair or unscrupulous. A court's statement that a contract is unconscionable reflects its conclusion that the contract or provision is so oppressive or unfair that the court should refuse to enforce it. Under the UCC the basic test of unconscionability is whether, in light of the general commercial background and the commercial needs of the particular trade or case, the clause or clauses involved are so one-sided as to be unconscionable under the circumstances that existed when the contract was made [UCC § 2-302, Comment 1].

The doctrine of unconscionability, under which a court grants relief from an unconscionable contract, is closely related to but broader than the doctrine of adhesion contracts. The doctrine of unconscionability may be applied to situations where the weaker party was oppressed or unfairly surprised, even though the weaker party might have obtained more favorable contract terms elsewhere. For example, a contract that contains many fine-print, one-sided provisions favorable to the drafter or a contract charging an excessive price might be considered unconscionable. Public policy considerations have led to reliance on the unconscionability doctrine as a means of protecting weak or ignorant parties from consenting to enter contracts with unscrupulous businesses. Cases in which contracts have been found unconscionable generally involve claims by consumers that they were unfairly taken advantage of; the consumers have often been poor, ignorant, or both.

The following is one of the earliest and best-known cases invoking the theory of unconscionability.

Williams

v

Walker-Thomas Furniture Co.
350 F2d 445 (1965)
United States Court of Appeals, District of Columbia Circuit

FACTS: Walker-Thomas, a retail furniture store operator in the District of Columbia, sold household items on an installment basis. At the time of purchase, each customer signed a printed form contract, which provided that title would remain in Walker-Thomas until the item was fully paid off, and that Walker-Thomas could repossess the item in the event the customer failed to make any monthly payment. The contract also contained an obscure and complex provision that provided, in essence, that each new installment purchase was consolidated with all other outstanding accounts. The effect of the provision was that a customer always owed a balance on every item purchased, until all items were fully paid off. From 1957 to 1962 Williams, the appellant, made purchases totaling

$1,800 from Walker-Thomas. Her last purchase, made when her balance was $164, was a $514 stereo set. At the time of that purchase, Walker-Thomas knew that Williams had seven children to support and that her monthly income consisted of a $218 government check. Williams defaulted soon thereafter, and, although she had made payments totaling $1,400 over the years, Walker-Thomas sued to repossess all the items purchased since 1957. The trial court entered judgment for Walker-Thomas, and Williams appealed.

ISSUE: Is the doctrine of unconscionability available to avoid a contract involving gross inequality of bargaining power and commercially unreasonable terms?

RESULT: Where the elements of unconscionability are present at the time a contract is made, the contract should not be enforced.

REASONING:

* * *

[Appellant's] principal contention, rejected . . . below, is that these contracts, or at least some of them, are unconscionable and, hence, not enforceable. . . .

Unconscionability has generally been recognized to include an absence of meaningful choice on the part of one of the parties together with contract terms which are unreasonably favorable to the other party. Whether a meaningful choice is present in a particular case can only be determined by consideration of all the circumstances surrounding the transaction. In many cases the meaningfulness of the choice is negated by a gross inequality of bargaining power. The manner in which the contract was entered is also relevant to this consideration. Did each party to the contract, considering his obvious education or lack of it, have a reasonable opportunity to understand the terms of the contract, or were the important terms hidden in a maze of fine print and minimized by deceptive sales practices? Ordinarily, one who signs an agreement without full knowledge of its terms might be held to assume the risk that he has entered a one-sided bargain. But when a party of little bargaining power, and hence little real choice, signs a commercially unreasonable contract with little or no knowledge of its terms, it is hardly likely that his consent, or even an objective manifestation of his consent, was ever given to all the terms. In such a case the usual rule that the terms of the agreement are not to be questioned should be abandoned and the court should consider whether the terms of the contract are so unfair that enforcement should be withheld. . . .

Because the trial court and the appellate court did not feel that enforcement could be refused, no findings were made on the possible unconscionability of the contracts in these cases. Since the record is not sufficient for our deciding the issue as a matter of law, the cases must be remanded to the trial court for further proceedings. . . .

Wright, Circuit Judge.

The UCC allows a court to refuse to enforce a contract containing one or more unconscionable clauses. The UCC also allows a court to enforce the remainder of the contract without the unconscionable clause, or to so limit the clause as to avoid any unconscionable result. The courts thus are given considerable leeway in dealing with unconscionable contracts.

Key Concepts and Terms

- Consent of the parties to a contract is not a genuine consent if it is acquired through fraud, honest misrepresentation, mistake, or undue influence.
- To establish fraud, the injured party must show (1) that the other party made a knowing or reckless misrepresentation of a material fact, (2) that the other party had an intent to deceive and to induce reliance, (3) that the injured party reasonably relied on the misrepresentation, and (4) that damage or injury resulted. The remedies for fraud are monetary damages or rescission of the contract.
- Fraud requires a misrepresentation, by words, acts, or both, of some present or past fact. A misrepresentation concerning opinion, value, quality, future events or intentions, or law does not usually constitute fraud. A misrepresentation that relates to both factual and nonfactual matters may be fraudulent.
- Nonfactual assertions can be fraudulent where (1) a confidential relationship exists or (2) one party has superior knowledge.
- Nondisclosure ordinarily does not constitute fraud, but concealment of material facts does. Moreover, one party may have a duty of disclosure where a confidential relationship exists between the parties, where that party has superior knowledge, or where partial disclosure may result in a mistaken impression.
- Honest misrepresentation differs from fraud in that (1) the misrepresentation is based on the belief that it is true and (2) rescission is the only remedy.
- A mutual mistake is an erroneous assumption of both parties to the contract as to a material fact, such as the existence, the identity, or the character of some person or thing essential to the contract. Such a mistake is a ground for rescission of the contract.
- A unilateral mistake is a mistake made by one of the parties. It affords no grounds for relief, except when (1) the other party knew or should have known of the mistake, and the mistaken party would otherwise suffer

extreme hardship; or (2) a contractor has made a mistake in computing a bid and has notified the other party before that party has taken any action.

- Duress exists where one party, by wrongful threats or actions, has instilled such fear in the other party that the other party involuntarily consents to enter a contract. Under the doctrine of "business compulsion" or "economic duress," a party is a victim of duress if forced to enter a contract as a result of business necessity and extreme economic pressure exerted by the other party. A contract may be rescinded by the threatened party on the ground of duress.

- Undue influence is the influence exerted by a dominant party on a weaker, more susceptible party to the extent that the weaker party lacked free will in consenting to enter the contract, resulting in a contract that is against the best interests of the weaker party.

- A contract of adhesion is a standardized contract drafted by a stronger party and imposed on a weaker one without allowing the weaker party to bargain and make a meaningful choice. Ambiguities in adhesion contracts are construed against the dominant party. Particular provisions may be held unenforceable as against the public's interests.

- An unconscionable contract is one that is so oppressive or unfair that a court either will refuse to enforce it or will limit its effect. The doctrine of unconscionability is often relied on to protect consumers.

- Adhesion Contract
- Bilateral Mistake
- Business Compulsion (Economic Duress)
- Concealment or Nondisclosure
- Dealer's Puffing
- Duress
- Fraud
- Fraud in the Execution
- Fraud in the Inducement
- Honest Misrepresentation
- Materiality
- Mutual Mistake
- Reliance
- Rescission
- Unconscionability
- Undue Influence
- Unilateral Mistake

Questions and Case Problems

1. A, having fallen off a cliff, is clinging by her fingernails to the edge. Unable to pull herself up, she asks B, who is standing nearby, to rescue her. B says, "I will save you if you promise to pay me $5,000." A promises to do so, and B then rescues A. Do A and B have an enforceable contract? Is A's consent to B's terms a genuine consent?

2. Sunderhaus purchases a diamond ring from a jeweler for $700. At the time of sale the jeweler's agent represents to Sunderhaus that the diamond is worth the amount paid. When Sunderhaus trades the ring in on another, one jeweler appraises its value at $300, and another jeweler values it at $350. Sunderhaus then sues the jeweler who sold her the ring, alleging fraudulent misrepresentation. What is the result?

3. Davis hires Gordon, a real estate broker, to inquire about the possibility of purchasing the Owens Office Building. Gordon knows the building well, since he is its managing agent, and he knows that there have been problems with the heating and cooling system, that the previous owner has spent $10,000 on repairs to the system, and that tenants continue to complain about the system despite the repairs. Before signing the contract for purchase of the building, Davis hears rumors that there are problems with the heating and cooling system. Davis asks Gordon whether there are any problems, and Gordon responds that there were some, but that $10,000 in repairs was made. Davis then buys the building. The tenants' complaints continue, and Davis learns that a complete overhaul of the system, costing $37,000, is required. After the repairs are made, Davis sues Gordon to recover the $37,000. What is the outcome?

4. The Army sets out to obtain bids on the construction of a Pershing missile container. Packages of materials containing specifications, some 1,500 drawings, and parts lists are sent to prospective bidders, including Space Corporation. Space Corporation's chief estimator begins preparing a bid. The estimator realizes that a drawing of a particular monitoring system is missing. He consults his superiors. Based on their experience in building containers for earlier missiles, they tell him the cost of the monitoring system is $35 per unit. Some specifications are unclear, and there are meetings with government representatives to clarify ambiguities, but Space Corporation never mentions the missing drawing or the monitor. After being awarded the contract, Space Corporation receives additional copies of the drawings and realizes that the monitoring system will cost $410 per unit. Space Corporation performs the contract but applies for reimbursement, and the government refuses to pay. Space Corporation sues. How should the case be decided?

5. Loral Corporation is awarded a $6,000,000 Navy contract to produce radar sets. The contract contains a schedule of deliveries, a clause providing damages for late deliveries, and a cancellation clause for unsatisfactory performance. Loral solicits bids for a number of different component gears, and awards Austin Instruments a subcontract to supply most of them. After delivering for a few months, Austin threatens to stop deliveries unless Loral agrees to substantial price increases, both retroactively on parts already delivered and prospectively on those to come. Austin soon stops deliveries as threatened. After contacting its entire list of approved suppliers and finding none who could produce the parts in time for Loral to meet its contract schedules, Loral agrees to Austin's demands for higher prices. After the last delivery is received, Loral sues Austin for the money it has paid over the original price. Who should prevail?

6. Davidson, a musical concert promoter, contracts with Allen, a popular musician, to produce a concert by Allen. The contract calls for submission of any disputes to arbitration before the musicians' union to which Allen belongs. Davidson knows of the arbitration clause, but she also knows that the contract is a standard union form contract, that the union requires its members to use such contracts, and that the union refuses to allow any changes in such standard clauses. Because the union holds a monopoly over the musical service required by promoters, Davidson accepts the arbitration clause. The concert loses money, and a dispute arises as to who should bear the losses. Davidson sues for breach of contract, and Allen moves to compel arbitration by the musicians' union. Davidson objects to arbitration before a partial arbitrator. How should the case be resolved?

7. Cruz, who speaks only Spanish, goes to Al's Appliances to look at refrigerators. He is waited on by Ybarra, who converses with Cruz in Spanish. Cruz ultimately

selects a refrigerator, and he and Ybarra orally negotiate. After they agree on a purchase price of $1,000, Ybarra prepares a retail installment contract written entirely in English and submits it to Cruz for signature. The contract provides for 36 monthly payments of $40, for total payments of $1,440. After making three monthly payments Cruz discovers that comparable refrigerators sell at other stores for no more than $500, and that the actual wholesale cost to Al's Appliances is $350. Cruz then refuses to make further payments on the refrigerator, claiming that the price is excessive. Al's Appliances sues for the balance remaining on the contract. Decide the case.

8. Are you convinced by the judge's reasoning in *Sherwood v Walker* (see page 206)? The dissenting opinion in the case argued that there was no mistake of fact because neither party knew whether Rose was fertile or barren. Said the judge: "There was no difference between the parties, nor misapprehension, as to the substance of the thing bargained for, which was a cow supposed to be barren by one party, and believed not to be by the other. As to the quality of the animal, subsequently developed, both parties were equally ignorant, and as to this each party took his chances. If this were not the law, there would be no safety in purchasing this kind of stock" (Sherwood, Justice, dissenting).

9. Under the City of Miami's civil service rules, an employee can be discharged without cause or explanation at any time during the first six months of service. On the last day of Kory's probation, her supervisor handed her a memorandum telling her she would be terminated as of 2:00 that day. After thinking it over, Kory asked her supervisor whether she could resign in order to avoid being fired. The supervisor said he had no objection to a resignation but that the decision was entirely up to her. Kory then gave the supervisor a handwritten resignation to be effective at 1:55 the same day. Later she learned that the supervisor did not have the authority to fire her; thus his letter firing her would have been ineffective under city regulations. Can Kory have the resignation set aside as a product of duress under contract principles?

13 Legal Capacity of Parties

13:1 Introduction

Contract law assumes that most people are capable of contracting to meet their needs. This assumption is central to the free use of contracts in commerce. At the same time the law protects those who are especially susceptible to sharp business practices or deception. These groups of people include minors and insane, incompetent, or intoxicated persons. To protect such people from their own immaturity, inexperience, or lack of judgment, courts have held that these groups lack the necessary legal capacity to enter binding contracts. Thus, if a member of one of these groups enters into a contract, he or she generally has the right to *repudiate*, or avoid, the contract. As a result, of course, businesses are reluctant to enter into contracts with people in these groups.

This chapter discusses the limited legal capacity of minors and of insane, incompetent, or intoxicated persons.

13:2 Minors

In most states, men and women under the age of 18 are minors and lack the legal capacity to contract. The reason for this public policy of protecting minors—and denying them the full legal capacity to participate in the economy—is that they are likely to be victimized by unfair dealing and to make unwise purchasing decisions. A minor is permitted to repudiate a contract made during his or her minority. To prevent the minor from being thereby left unable to obtain basic necessities of life, the law excepts certain transactions from the general rule of incapacity. To prevent a person from carrying this protection into adulthood, the law permits the minor, when he or she becomes an adult, to *ratify* contracts made during minority; in fact, if the adult fails to repudiate the contract within a reasonable time after attaining adulthood, ratification may be implied.

13:3   Avoidance of Contract by a Minor

A minor's contract is voidable, not void, and it is voidable only by the minor. Thus, while the minor can fully enforce the contract against the other party, the minor (or his or her personal representative) can also avoid the contract at any time during minority without giving any reason other than minority. Any unequivocal act that indicates an intent to repudiate the contract is sufficient. The minor may notify the other party in writing. The minor may return the property received from the other party, or demand from the other party the property given by the minor pursuant to the contract. The minor may even wait until the other party brings a lawsuit to enforce the contract, and then assert minority as a defense.

If a minor repudiates an executory, or unperformed, contract, the minor's avoidance simply terminates the contractual relationship. Where the contract has been partly or wholly executed, so that some material benefit has been passed to the minor or some detriment has been suffered by the other party, the minor must return any consideration received from the other party, if that is possible. If the consideration has been used up, lost, or even destroyed, most courts do not require the minor to pay the other party the reasonable value of the consideration. The risk of such loss is placed squarely on the other party. The minor, on the other hand, is entitled to recover all consideration given to the other party. The potential inequity of these general rules is obvious. For example, assume that A, a minor, buys a car from B for $1,000. The very next day A is in an accident and the car is totally destroyed. A then notifies B that she is exercising her right to avoid the contract and that she wants her $1,000 returned. A is entitled to the return of the consideration ($1,000) she gave to B. Because the consideration she received in return has been destroyed, she has no obligation to return anything to B.

Some states have therefore adopted a contrary view. In these states a minor who avoids a contract must either return the consideration received or account to the other party for the value of the consideration received. Going back to the example above, the minor A would be required to return to B the equivalent of the consideration received from B ($1,000, or whatever lesser amount represented the true value of the car at the time of the sale).

The following case shows one court's resolution of the competing policy interests involved in this area.

Pettit

v

Liston
191 P 660 (1920)
Oregon Supreme Court

FACTS: Pettit, a minor, purchased a motorcycle from Liston, a motorcycle dealer. Pettit made a down payment of $125 on the $325 purchase price and agreed to make monthly payments of $25. After using the motorcycle for one month, Pettit returned it and demanded his money back from Liston. Liston refused, claiming that Pettit had caused damages of $156.65 to the motorcycle. Pettit sued. After a trial court judgment for Liston, Pettit appealed.

ISSUE: Is the minor who disaffirms a contract for the sale of goods, returns the goods, and seeks return of the money paid obligated to account for depreciation and damage to the goods?

RESULT: If the contract was fair and reasonable, the minor is obligated to pay for damage to the goods.

REASONING:

*   *   *

The courts, in an attempt to protect the minor upon the one hand, and to prevent wrong or injustice to persons who have dealt fairly and reasonably with such minor upon the other, have indulged in many fine distinctions and recognized various slight shades of difference. . . .

Many courts have held broadly that a minor may so purchase property and keep it for an indefinite time, if he chooses, until it is worn out and destroyed, and then recover the payments made on the purchase price, without allowing the seller anything whatever for the use and depreciation of the property.

Many other authorities hold that where the transaction is fair and reasonable, and the minor was not overcharged or taken advantage of in any way, and he takes and keeps the property and uses or destroys it, he cannot recover the payments made on the purchase price, without allowing the seller for the wear and tear and depreciation of the article while in his hands. . . .

Our attention has not been called to any Oregon case bearing upon the question, and as far as our investigation has disclosed, there is none. . . .

We think, where the minor has not been overreached in any way, and there has been no undue influence, and the contract is a fair and reasonable one, and the minor has actually paid money on the purchase price, and taken and used the article, that he ought not to be permitted to recover the amount actually paid, without allowing the vendor of the goods the reasonable compensation for the use and depreciation of the article, while in his hands.

Of course, if there has been any fraud or imposition on the part of the seller, or if the contract is unfair, or any unfair advantage has been taken of the minor in inducing him to make the purchase, then a different rule would apply. And whether there had been such an overreaching on the part of the seller would always, in case of a jury trial, be a question for the jury.

We think this rule will fully and fairly protect the minor against injustice or imposition, and at the same time it will be fair to the businessman who has dealt with such minor in good faith. . . .

Again, it will not exert any good moral influence upon boys and young men, and will not tend to encourage honesty and integrity, or lead them to a good and useful business future, if they are taught that they can make purchases with their own money, for their own benefit, and after paying for them in this way, and using them until they are worn out and destroyed, go back and compel the businessman to return to them what they have paid upon the purchase price. Such a doctrine, as it seems to us, can only lead to the corruption of young men's principles and encourage them in habits of trickery and dishonesty.

Bennett, Justice.

Some states impose on the minor the obligation to return any property he or she has subsequently received in exchange for the consideration. For example, if a minor purchases a car from an adult, then trades the car to a third party in exchange for a motorcycle and money, and then seeks to avoid the original contract with the adult, the minor would be obligated to give the adult the motorcycle and the money received from the third party in exchange for the adult's payment of the purchase price to the minor.

At common law, a minor's right to recover the consideration he or she paid ordinarily prevailed even when that consideration had been transferred to a third party. To illustrate, assume that A, a minor, agreed to and did sell a bicycle to B, who resold the bicycle to C. A then decided to avoid the original contract with B and sought to recover the bicycle from C. Under the common law the minor would be entitled to the bicycle. The result would be different, however, if the UCC applied. Under the UCC a good faith purchaser for value who purchases from a person with voidable title prevails [UCC § 2-403(1)]. Thus, C, as a good faith purchaser from B, would be entitled to retain the bicycle.

It should be noted that even if a minor misrepresents his or her age to the adult, the minor nevertheless may avoid the contract. If the misrepresentation is undertaken for the purpose of defrauding the adult, however, the minor could be liable in tort for fraud. Even in the absence of fraud, some courts have imposed tort liability on a minor who knowingly misrepresents his or her age. The minor's misrepresentation of a material fact would be a basis for the other party rescinding the contract.

13:4 Ratification of Minor's Contract

A contract entered into by a minor may be ratified after the minor has achieved the age of majority. The right to ratify such a contract, like the right to repudiate, can only be exercised by the minor. Ratification may be explicit, as in a case where the minor, on attaining majority, specifically promises the other party that he will perform his obligations under the contract. Ratification may also be implied, as when a minor, after attaining majority, commences performance of the contract. If a minor's intent to ratify is not clearly indicated by words or actions, all the circumstances must be considered. One important factor that the courts consider is the amount of time that has passed since the minor attained majority. Many courts have concluded that, if a minor fails to repudiate a contract within a reasonable time after reaching majority, it may be implied that the minor has ratified the contract. This rule has been applied more often to executed contracts than to executory contracts.

Notice in the following case that the plaintiff sought to avoid a contract obligation on the ground of minority and also for lack of meaningful assent to its terms.

Jones

v

Dressel

582 P2d 1057 (1978)

Colorado Court of Appeals

FACTS:　When plaintiff was 17 years old he entered into a contract with Free Flight Aviation, Inc., which provided facilities for parachute jumping. Ten months after plaintiff's eighteenth birthday a Free Flight plane crashed with plaintiff aboard. Plaintiff was injured and sued Free Flight in negligence. Free Flight defended that a "release clause" in plaintiff's contract exonerated it for such injuries. Plaintiff contends that the contract was void on account of plaintiff's minority at the time of the contract.

ISSUE:　Is the contract enforceable against the plaintiff?

RESULT:　Yes. The plaintiff ratified the contract as an adult by accepting the benefits of the contract.

REASONING:

*　　*　　*

In granting the summary judgment the court relied on provisions of the contract, under which plaintiff exempted and released Free Flight, "its owners, officers, agents, servants, employees, and lessors from any and all liability [resulting from negligence and] . . . arising out of any damage, loss or injury to [plaintiff] . . . while upon the . . . aircraft of [Free Flight] or while participating in any of the activities contemplated by this agreement. . . . " The contract also contained a covenant not to sue for such injuries. . . .

It is well settled in Colorado that a contract entered into by a minor is not void but only voidable by the minor. . . . Affirmance is not merely a matter of intent; it may be determined by the actions of a minor who accepts the benefits of a contract after reaching the age of majority, or by his silence or acquiescence in the contract for a considerable length of time. . . . Furthermore, § 13–22–101(1), C.R.S. 1973, states that "every person, otherwise competent, shall be deemed to be of full age at the age of eighteen years or older for the following specific purposes: (a) To enter into any legal contractual obligation and to be legally bound thereby to the full extent as any other adult person; . . . "

Thus, on reaching the age of eighteen plaintiff was required either to disaffirm the contract within a reasonable time, or be bound thereby. . . . And, the undisputed facts establish that, after turning eighteen, plaintiff not only did not disaffirm the contract, but instead ratified it by accepting the benefits thereof. Hence, his being a minor when he entered the contract is without significance as to its present enforceability against him.

Plaintiff also argues that the exculpatory provision of the agreement is void because it is an adhesion contract and lacked consideration. In support of this allegation plaintiff states that he would not have been allowed to participate in the parachute jumping activities if he had not signed the contract, and that there was no contemporaneous passing of consideration. However, plaintiff has alleged no fraud, coercion, or imposition, stated in Sedalia *Land Co. v. Robinson Brick & Tile Co.,* . . . as being necessary to relieve a party to a contract of its consequences. Nor do the facts establish a great disparity of bargaining power, or that the desired services could not be obtained elsewhere, both of which must be present to establish an adhesion contract. . . . Although the terms of the contract may be favorable to the defendants, it was not essential that plaintiff pursue his interest in sky diving or that he pursue it with a particular air service. . . .

Silverstein, Chief Judge.

13:5 Minor's Contracts for Necessaries

The term *necessaries* refers broadly to those items that are reasonably necessary for the proper and suitable maintenance of a person. These items include food, clothing, lodging, and education through high school. The courts have been flexible in determining what items are necessaries. They generally look at the circumstances of a particular case. It has often been noted that one's social position and situation in life are important in determining whether an item is a necessary. A purchase that might constitute a luxury for one person may be a necessary for another person. The courts have also stressed that the minor's actual need is the test. If the minor has a parent or guardian who is capable of or willing to supply certain items, these items will not be considered necessaries.

A minor may be held liable on a contract for the purchase of necessaries, but this liability is quasi-contractual. That is, the minor has a duty to pay only the reasonable value of necessaries actually furnished to him. Since the obligation is quasi-contractual in nature, the emphasis is on the minor's payment for value received; the specific terms are not binding.

While liability for necessaries traditionally has been limited to personal necessaries, some courts have extended the concept to permit liability for business necessaries. For example, under the general rule a car is not a necessary, but if a minor needs a car to conduct business, he will be liable for its purchase price.

The following case (1) demonstrates the manner in which the concept of necessaries may be expanded and (2) discusses, in both the majority and the dissenting opinions, the rationale underlying the rule that minors generally lack legal capacity to contract.

Gastonia Personnel Corp.

v

Rogers
172 SE2d 19 (1970)
North Carolina Supreme Court

FACTS: Rogers, 19 years old, lived with his wife in a rented apartment. He needed one quarter's worth of schooling to complete the requirements for an A.S. degree in civil engineering at Gaston Tech. His wife became pregnant so he had to look for employment. Rogers visited the Gastonia Personnel Corporation office, and, following an interview, signed a contract to pay Gastonia $295 if it found him a job paying at least $4,680 a year to start. Gastonia soon placed him in a position paying $4,784, but Rogers never paid the fee. Gastonia sued, and Rogers defended on the ground that he was a minor at the time of the contract. The age of majority then was 21. Rogers' defense was upheld, and Gastonia appealed.

ISSUE: Is a contract for job placement services enforceable against a minor?

RESULT: Yes. The contract was enforceable because it was a necessity for the minor.

REASONING:

*   *   *

An early commentary on the common law, after the general statement that contracts made by persons (infants) before attaining the age of twenty-one "may be avoided," sets forth "some exceptions out of this generality," to wit: "*An infant may bind himself to pay for his necessary meat, drinke, apparell, necessary physicke, and such other necessaries,* and likewise for his good teaching or instruction, whereby he may profit himself afterwards." [Court's emphasis.] *Coke on Littleton,* 13th ed. (1788), p. 172. . . . If the infant married, "necessaries" included necessary food and clothing for his wife and child. . . .

In accordance with this ancient rule of the common law, this Court has held an infant's contract, unless for "necessaries" or unless authorized by statute, is voidable by the infant, at his election, and may be disaffirmed during infancy or upon attaining the age of twenty-one. . . .

This statement commands respect and approval:

> "Society has a moral obligation to protect the interests of infants from overreaching adults. But this protection must not become a straightjacket, stifling the economic and social advancement of infants who have the need and maturity to contract. Nor should infants be allowed to turn that protective legal shield into a weapon to wield against fair-dealing adults. It is in the interest of society to have its members contribute actively to the general economic and social welfare, if this can be accomplished consistently with the protection of those persons unable to protect themselves in the market place." . . .

The evidence before us tends to show that defendant, when he contracted with plaintiff, was nineteen years of age, emancipated, married, a high school graduate, within "a quarter of 22 hours" of obtaining his degree in applied science, and capable of holding a job at a starting annual salary of $4,784.00. To hold, as a matter of law, that such a person cannot obligate himself to pay for services rendered him in obtaining employment suitable to his ability, education and specialized training, enabling him to provide the necessities of life for himself, his wife and his expected child, would place him and others similarly situated under a serious economic handicap.

In the effort to protect "older minors" from improvident or unfair contracts, the law should not deny to them the opportunity and right to obligate themselves for articles of property or services which are reasonably necessary to enable them to provide for the proper support of themselves and their dependents. The minor should be held liable for the reasonable value of articles of property or services received pursuant to such contract. . . .

To establish liability, plaintiff must satisfy the jury by the greater weight of the evidence that defendant's contract with plaintiff was an appropriate and reasonable means for defendant to obtain suitable employment. If this issue is answered in plaintiff's favor, plaintiff must then establish by the greater weight of the evidence the reasonable value of the services received by defendant pursuant to the contract. Thus, plaintiff's recovery, if any, cannot exceed the reasonable value of its services to defendant. . . .

Bobbitt, Chief Justice.

Lake, Justice (dissenting).

*   *   *

The defendant, a young man nineteen years old, with better than average education, has benefited from his use of the plaintiff's services for which he promised to pay an agreed amount. Now, having received the full benefit he desired, he refuses to pay for it. He does not contend, and there is nothing in the record before us to suggest, that the plaintiff overcharged him, or otherwise took any advantage of him. Nothing in this record arouses sympathy for the defendant. This is one of those hard cases which so frequently have turned out to be "quicksands of the law." In my view, the majority, in its proper desire to avoid an injustice to this plaintiff, has taken a step into quicksand.

As the majority opinion shows clearly, since a time prior to Columbus' discovery of America, it has been the well settled rule of the common law, repeatedly stated by this Court, that an infant's contract may be disaffirmed by him without liability, unless it is a contract for what the law calls "necessaries." If the contract is one for necessaries, the infant is liable for the reasonable value of what he received.

The reason for this rule, in both its aspects, is the desire of the law to protect the infant. His liability to pay for necessaries is not imposed so as to protect an adult supplier against a shrewdly scheming infant. It is imposed solely because otherwise the infant, honest or not, might be unable to acquire that which he must have for the support of himself and his dependents. The rule permits the infant to refuse to carry out other contracts irrespective of the particular infant's intelligence, education or experience in business. It does not depend upon whether the particular contract was fair or unfair. It is immaterial, under this rule, that the application of it results in a loss to an adult who dealt in good faith with an unscrupulous infant. . . .

Stripped of emotional aspects, this case presents but one question, assuming the rule heretofore established is to be followed: Is an infant's contract for the services of an employment agency, under the circumstances disclosed in this record, a contract for necessaries? I do not think it is. . . . It is well settled that a "necessary" is something more urgently needed than a thing or a service which is merely a convenience or an assistance to the infant. This is the established rule both in America and England, apart from statute.

In *Pollock's Principles of Contracts*, pp. 49–50, it is said:

> "It is to be borne in mind . . . that the question is not whether the things are such that a person of the defendant's means may reasonably buy and pay for them, but whether they can reasonably be said to be so necessary for him that, though an infant, he must obtain them on credit rather than go without." [Court's emphasis.] . . .

That the services of the employment agency in giving this defendant names of prospective employers was a convenience and an aid to him in getting a job with a minimum of inquiry and search from door to door is no doubt true. In the present eagerness of industry to find trained engineers, I cannot agree that such services are a "necessary" for an engineering student nearing graduation from Gaston Tech and seeking employment in the Charlotte area. . . . The authority of the people, through their representatives in the State Government, to change the common law when conditions and needs have so changed as to render the law unjust or unwise is clear. They have, however, seen fit to vest this authority in the Legislature and not in us. . . . This power to change established law to meet changes in conditions is the essence of the legislative power. . . .

 The safest approach to dealing with a minor is to contract with the minor's parents. Even if the items sold are necessaries, the minor is liable only for the reasonable value, not for the contract price. Another approach to dealing with a minor is to establish that the minor is acting on behalf of the parent or other adult and is, therefore, an agent of that person.[1] Finally, one must recognize the minority doctrine as a risk of doing business with young people.

13:6   Insane, Incompetent, or Intoxicated Persons

An incompetent person is one who is so lacking in mental capacity that he is unable to understand the nature and consequences of his acts and, in the case of a contract, of the agreement itself. A person may be incompetent by virtue of insanity, severe mental retardation, or mental deterioration accompanying senility. An intoxicated person may be found to lack contractual capacity if he is so intoxicated that he has no knowledge of what he is doing.

The validity of a contract entered into by an incompetent person depends on the time of contract and the status of the person at the time. Contracts entered into by a person who has already been adjudicated insane or otherwise incompetent by a proper court are absolutely void, and such contracts cannot be ratified, even after the person regains sanity. If a person was insane or otherwise incompetent at the time a contract was entered into, but there had been no prior adjudication of such incompetence, the contract is voidable—that is, it may be ratified or repudiated by the person if he recovers, in much the same manner as a minor may repudiate or ratify a contract on attaining majority. Similarly, if a person was so intoxicated when he entered a contract that he was incapable of understanding what he was doing, generally he may, on recovery of sobriety, repudiate or ratify the contract.

Whether a contract is executory or executed also has an effect on repudiation. In the case of executory contracts, the courts generally grant incompetent

---

[1] This principle of agency is developed in Chapter 43.

and intoxicated persons the same right of avoidance as is possessed by minors. For executed contracts, however, the rules are somewhat different. The courts permit avoidance only where the other party may be restored to the position he occupied prior to the contract. Thus, if the incompetent or intoxicated person has dissipated the consideration received and cannot give the other party equally valuable consideration, avoidance will not be permitted. This rule presupposes the good faith of the other party; if the other party in fact knew and intentionally took advantage of the incompetence or intoxication, then fraud is likely to be found and the insane or intoxicated person will be permitted to avoid the contract notwithstanding his inability to return the consideration.

Issues that must be determined when one party to a contract seeks to repudiate it on the ground of his insanity or intoxication include whether the person was in fact either insane or intoxicated, the degree of any such insanity or intoxication, and the effect that such insanity or intoxication had on the person's ability to comprehend what was happening. The mere fact that a person suffers from mental disease, even one that is recognized as a serious impairment, does not necessarily lead to the conclusion that the person does not have the mental capacity to contract.

Incompetent and intoxicated persons generally are liable on their contracts for necessaries in the same manner and to the same extent as are minors.

Uribe

v

Olson

601 P2d 818 (1979)

Court of Appeals of Oregon

FACTS: In September 1976 plaintiff entered into an earnest money contract for 80 acres of land belonging to Mrs. Bonham and 10 acres belonging to Mrs. Bonham's daughter, Mrs. Olson. In December 1976 Mrs. Olson decided that her mother was incompetent at the time the contract was signed; both mother and daughter refused to sign the final contracts on the ground of Mrs. Bonham's incompetence. Plaintiff sued to enforce the contract.

ISSUE: Was Mrs. Bonham sufficiently competent in September 1976 to contract for the sale of the land?

RESULT: Yes. The facts indicate she had sufficient competence to enter into an enforceable contract.

REASONING:

*   *   *

Medical evidence of two doctors who treated Mrs. Bonham beginning in November, 1976, showed that she suffered from a heart blockage which caused seizures and blackouts and involutional psychosis resulting in depression. Both agreed that the condition would have been present prior to September, 1976, and could well have affected her mental processes.

Friends and relatives of Mrs. Bonham all testified to a gradual deterioration of her mental acuity over several years prior to the transaction in question. This deterioration manifested itself in a number of ways, including periods of disorientation and depression, occasional paranoia, an increase in eccentric habits and delusions concerning people long dead and imagined friendships with Barry Goldwater and Frank Sinatra.

On the other hand, plaintiff testified that while Mrs. Bonham appeared eccentric to him, he had no reason to question her capacity. When he visited the property, she showed him around and answered all his questions respecting the features of the property. Mr. Martin testified that she accurately answered all his questions when he prepared the listing agreement and appeared at all times to know that she was engaged in selling her property, apparently intending to move back to Tennessee, where she had grown up.

On September 28, 1976, when Mrs. Bonham signed the earnest money agreement, Mr. Martin testified he explained the details to her carefully, that she read the agreement and appeared to understand. Mrs. Bonham's sister, who was also present, testified that Mrs. Bonham just stared into space while Mr. Martin read the agreement to her and her only comment was, "I don't care what you do with this property. You can give it back to the Indians if you want to."

Mrs. Olson testified that she finally accepted that her mother was incompetent in October, 1976, and first discussed with her attorney the possibility of creating a conservatorship at that time. Based on this decision, she refused to sign the final contracts.

The test of contractual capacity is whether a person is able to understand the nature of his action and apprehend its consequences. . . . This capacity is measured at the time of the execution of the contract, in this case, the earnest money agreement. . . . Even where there are substantial indications of mental incompetence, it is possible that a person may have "lucid intervals" during which he possesses the requisite capacity. . . . Capacity includes the ability to reason and exercise judgment and, in essence, to bargain with the other party. . . . Neither old age, illness nor extreme emotional distress is sufficient of itself to negate such capacity. . . .

In *Gindhart v. Skourtes*, . . . the seller suffered from an arteriosclerotic condition which caused periods of confusion which he claimed reduced his mental competence. He suffered a stroke shortly after the sale. The evidence showed, however, that he had tried to sell the land for two years without success, rejected the buyers' first offer and subsequently reached a compromise price which defendant's experts testified was in line with other prices for land in the area. . . . The court found him competent.

In *Pioneer Trust Co. v. Currin,* . . . plaintiff's ward appeared disoriented and unresponsive and frequently talked to himself. He was committed to a mental hospital four months after selling the land in question. Nevertheless, he had lucid periods and defendant testified he had shown him around the place and answered all his questions in a normal fashion. The ward told defendant he was anxious to sell because he intended to leave the state soon and wanted cash. Defendant purchased the property for cash at a price below what probably could have been obtained. The court held the ward competent to enter into the contract.

While there is ample evidence to establish that Mrs. Bonham's mental state on September 28, 1976, had deteriorated substantially from what it once had been, this does not resolve the matter. We are persuaded, largely by the circumstances of the sale, that Mrs. Bonham was competent to sell her land. Mrs. Bonham had definite ideas about how the property should be listed and accurately supplied all the necessary information. The purchase price was negotiated over several months and the offer that was ultimately accepted was made by Mrs. Bonham and Mrs. Olson. Before obtaining her signature, Mr. Martin read the important features of the earnest money agreement to Mrs. Bonham and had her read the document, a point of considerable significance. . . . Furthermore, Mrs. Olson and her attorney were constantly involved and no one, prior to November, 1976, suggested that Mrs. Bonham did not possess the requisite competence. In fact, defendant's primary dissatisfaction with the deal appears to be the price obtained, not the fact that the property was sold. In sum, the evidence indicates that Mrs. Bonham knew what she was doing and, though her reasons for selling may not have been altogether wise, she intended to sell and was cognizant of the consequences. . . .

Thornton, Judge.

Key Concepts and Terms

- Members of certain classes of people are presumed by the law to lack legal capacity to contract. These classes are minors, insane, incompetent, or intoxicated persons.
- Except as otherwise specified by statute, minors lack legal capacity to contract, and a minor's contract cannot be enforced against him.

- A minor may avoid a contract at any time during minority. When a minor repudiates a contract, he or she must return the consideration received from the other party. If that is impossible, most courts place the loss on the adult party. Other courts require the minor to account to the adult party for the value of the consideration received by the minor.

- A minor may ratify a contract after reaching the age of majority.

- A minor may be liable on a contract for the purchase of necessaries not supplied by a parent or guardian. Such liability is quasi-contractual in nature and is limited to the reasonable value of the necessaries received by the minor.

- A person who is so lacking in mental capacity or so intoxicated as to be incapable of understanding the nature or consequences of his or her acts lacks legal capacity to contract. Contracts entered into by incompetent or intoxicated persons may be either absolutely void or merely voidable, depending on whether there has been a previous judicial declaration of incompetence. Where the contract is voidable, the incompetent or intoxicated person may ratify or repudiate it in much the same manner as a minor.

- Age of Majority
- Insane, Incompetent, or Intoxicated Persons
- Minors (Infants)
- Necessaries
- Ratification
- Repudiation

Questions and Case Problems

1. A, a resident of a state where the age of majority is 18, leaves home and becomes self-supporting at age 16. An avid tennis player, he hopes someday to become a pro. In line with this goal, a year later he purchases tennis equipment worth $200 from B, a store owner, and signs a contract for tennis lessons with C, a tennis professional. A appears older than his years, and neither B nor C inquires about his age. After he completes the tennis lessons, C advises him that he is not good enough to play professionally. When A is 18 years three months old, he voluntarily commits himself to a mental institution, where he is determined to be incompetent. While he is institutionalized, all his tennis equipment is stolen. After two years of treatment A is released from the institution, his competency restored. He immediately notifies B and C that he is repudiating his contracts with them and demands that his money be refunded. Is A's demand justified?

2. Little enters an agreement with Turner, a minor, to assist Turner in financing a college education. Under the agreement Little agrees to loan Turner up to $30 per month, in exchange for Turner's execution of a promissory note when he receives each loan. The promissory notes provide for repayment of the amounts loaned, plus 6 percent interest. Of 23 promissory notes executed by Turner under the agreement, all but four are executed while he is a minor. When Little sues Turner on the 23 promissory notes, Turner pleads infancy as a defense to 19 of the notes. How should the case be decided?

3. What is the rationale behind the conclusion that some persons lack the legal capacity to contract?

4. Are you more persuaded by the majority opinion in *Gastonia Personnel Corp. v Rogers* (see page 223) or by the minority opinion? Why?

5. In 1902 King, a 20-year-old minor, entered into an agreement with Welch, her guardian, which provided that certain property of King's should be held in trust by Welch. The agreement also provided that any income-producing property thereafter acquired by King be transferred to Welch to be included in the trust. Over the years King received and approved annual accounts from Welch and his successor trustees, but never had occasion to transfer any property to the trust. In 1931 King's husband gave her a $1,000 bond. Since the bond constituted income-producing property, the trustees demanded that King turn it over to the trust, but she refused. The trustees sued to recover the value of the bond, and King defended on the ground that she was a minor at the time the contract was entered. How should the case be decided?

6. Bowling, a 16-year-old high school student, goes to Sperry Ford with his grandmother, with whom he lives, and his aunt, and purchases an automobile for $1140. He borrows $900 of the purchase price from his aunt, but the title is placed in his name. Bowling has a summer job at a restaurant some eight or nine miles from his home, and he normally drives to work. Sperry's manager understands that Bowling needs the car for transportation to that job. Within a week of the purchase one of the car's bearings burns out. Bowling returns the car to Sperry Ford. When he is informed that it will cost $100 to $125 to repair the car, he leaves it at Sperry, repudiates the contract, and demands the return of his money. Sperry claims that the bearing has burned out as a result of Bowling's improper operation of the car. When Sperry refuses to refund the money, Bowling sues. How should the case be decided?

7. A fervently believes that she is the Queen of England. On occasion she will don royal regalia and perform her duties as monarch, issuing orders, signing contracts in the name of the Queen, and otherwise behaving as a queen might. On other occasions, however, she appears perfectly normal and owns and operates a small business. She enters a contract with B to have siding placed on her home. A couple of weeks later she has second thoughts and informs B that she wishes to cancel the contract. Is A entitled to repudiate the contract on the ground of lack of competence? Would your answer be any different if the contract had also called for the installation of a moat around her residence?

8. Beginning in 1965 or 1966, Grannen began experiencing memory loss. Other symptoms of organic mental disability later appeared, and by 1968 she was incapable of managing her own checking accounts. Physicians diagnosed her condition as a brain disorder involving gradual physical and mental deterioration, and in April 1972 she was declared incompetent. In 1970, Grannen had transferred certain property to Ey, her brother. After the declaration of incompetency, Grannen's guardian sued for the return of the property. Should he be permitted to recover the property?

9. Abrams purchases a new car for $10,000 from Murphy Motors on Friday. Over the weekend he drives the car 1,000 miles and is involved in an accident that causes $2,000 damage to the car. On Monday he returns the car to Murphy Motors and demands his money back, claiming that he had been on hallucinogenic drugs when he bought the car and had remained under their influence all through the weekend. Must Murphy Motors return Abrams' money? If Murphy does return his money, may it deduct any amount? If so, what amount?

14 Illegal Agreements

14:1 Introduction; Classification of Illegal Agreements

The legality of an agreement is another essential element of contract. If the formation or the performance of the agreement violates law or public policy, the agreement will not be enforced by the courts. When a court refuses to enforce an otherwise valid contract for illegality, the court is asserting the public interest in health, morality, and welfare. The doctrine exemplifies and embodies the idea that the right to contract is subject to the paramount power of the state to protect the public good.

Illegal agreements may be classified as either (1) contrary to law (or statute) or (2) otherwise contrary to public policy. There is no clear-cut distinction between the two. Obviously, contracts that violate a statute also violate public policy. The second category recognizes that some contracts may not violate a statute or the common law, yet enforcement of the contract would produce a result contrary to important public policy. Illegal agreements are void and, with the exceptions noted later, are unenforceable in court.

14:2 Agreements Contrary to Law

An agreement that violates or that cannot be performed without violating some constitutional, statutory, or other rule of law is illegal and void. For the agreement to be declared void for illegality, the agreement itself must contemplate a violation of the law. It may be the nature of the agreement itself that is illegal, or the illegality may lie in the promises or the consideration for the contract. However, the fact that some illegal act is committed during the performance of a contract does not mean the contract is illegal. If the formation of the contract violated no rule of law, and if the contract could have been performed without violating any law, then the contract is not void.

EXAMPLE: A contracts with B for the transportation and delivery of certain goods from one city to another. B loads all the goods into one truck, thereby violating a statutory provision as to the maximum weight that can be carried by the truck. The fact that B has violated the statute in the performance of the contract does not render the contract illegal, because B, by using two trucks, could easily have performed the contract without violating that statute. However, if the contract between A and B had called for the shipment of all the goods in the one truck, then the agreement would have been illegal, because it would have been impossible to perform the agreement without violating the law.

The discussion that follows focuses on several types of statutes that may be violated in the formation or performance of an agreement, thereby causing the agreement to be illegal.

Usury Laws Usury laws have a centuries-long tradition. The underlying purpose of the law is to protect the necessitous borrower from paying exorbitant interest rates. The usury laws of each state specify the maximum rate of interest that may be charged on various types of credit transactions. For various reasons, however, these laws have come to resemble a patchwork quilt.

Typically, state law provides a basic usury rate and then exempts certain types of loans and certain types of lenders and borrowers from the statute. Historically, exemption from the basic usury statute has been the political trade-off for regulation of the small loan business. During times when the market price of money rose above the usury rate, state legislatures often bowed to economic reality and passed further exemptions. For example, some states exempt loans to corporations, thereby inviting businesses to incorporate in order to receive financing; some states exempt banks. In general, federally chartered financial institutions are not subject to state usury laws. The common element of usury laws is that it is illegal for a lender to charge a rate of interest higher than that specified by the applicable statutes, and usurious contracts are not enforceable.

Because the usury laws apply only to loans of money, and not to sales or leases, the parties to a contract may sometimes be tempted to characterize a loan as some other type of transaction. The courts have held that the character of the transaction determines whether it is usurious, and a court will look through a subterfuge to determine whether the transaction is actually a loan of money.

Whether installment sales involve loans of money is a question to which courts have found conflicting answers. The general rule, known as the *time–price doctrine*, is that a seller agreeing to a sale on credit may charge a higher price for a particular item than he or she would charge if the sale were for cash, and that no loan of money is involved in such a transaction. Some courts have held in accordance with this general rule; others have held that installment sales do indeed involve loans of money and are subject to the usury laws. Some states have adopted specific statutes governing the rates of interest permissible on installment sales.

The disposition of a loan contract that is found to be usurious varies from state to state. Under some statutes the contract is absolutely void and the lender can recover neither principal nor interest; other statutes permit the recovery of principal, but not interest; still other statutes permit recovery of principal and interest up to the legally permitted rate, but preclude recovery of any interest in excess of that permitted by law; and others contain variations on these basic approaches.

Gambling Statutes   Most states have adopted statutes that prohibit gambling agreements. The essential element of a gambling agreement is chance—the parties stand to gain or lose on the occurrence or nonoccurrence of some event in which they have no interest other than their gain or loss. Lotteries are also games of chance and are also generally prohibited, although some states now make certain lotteries, notably state lotteries, legal.

Gambling contracts must be distinguished from certain other contracts that also involve an element of speculation. Insurance contracts, for example, condition the right to recover on the occurrence of a contingency, but the insured has some insurable interest.[1] *Futures contracts*, under which the parties contract for the sale of personal property to be delivered at some future date, also involve speculation, but the courts have held such contracts to be valid if an actual delivery of the property is contemplated when the contract is formed. The contract would be an illegal gambling contract only if it involved nothing more than speculation on the future performance of the market, without any intent that the property ever be delivered.

Promotional schemes conducted by retail and other businesses that offer certain prizes as an inducement to customers are valid provided the customer does not pay for the opportunity to participate. If the right to participate is conditioned on the purchase of some product, then the customer is being required to give consideration for a chance at winning the prize. This is considered to be illegal gambling and is prohibited in most states.

Sunday Laws   Many states have statutes that forbid certain types of business transactions on Sundays. These "blue laws" have regulated the sale of certain types of items, the hours of operation of business, and the transaction of business on Sunday. The impact of these laws has diminished greatly in recent years: they are more often breached than observed, and the constitutionality of enforcing them is questioned often. Nevertheless, the legality of a contract entered into on Sunday depends on the particular law that the state has enacted and the interpretations the courts have made. Some statutes expressly declare that particular contracts entered into or performed on Sunday are invalid; in other states, the statutes do not prohibit the making of contracts on Sunday.

 It is better to execute and perform a contract on some day other than Sunday to avoid the possibility of the Sunday law being used to void an otherwise valid contract.

Regulatory and Licensing Statutes   Often federal, state, and local laws require people to have licenses to conduct certain businesses and professions. The question may arise, therefore, whether contracts entered into by illegally

---

[1] Insurable interests are discussed in Chapter 42.

unlicensed businesses or professionals are enforceable. In general, the courts distinguish between those licensing statutes that are regulatory in nature and those that are intended merely to produce revenue. For example, statutes that require physicians to be licensed to practice medicine are regulatory and are intended primarily to protect the public. The use of the courts to enforce a contract for medical care to be provided by an unlicensed professional would undermine the regulatory policy. Thus, a contract for medical care entered into by a physician who is unlicensed is illegal and void. On the other hand, business license taxes that are designed primarily as revenue-raising measures are not as imbued with the public welfare interest. A contract entered into in violation of a business license law usually is considered enforceable, provided the business subsequently obtains the necessary license. Enforcing such a contract conditional on obtaining the license encourages compliance with the law without endangering the public welfare. In determining whether a particular licensing statute is a regulatory or a revenue law, courts attempt to discern the intent of the legislature or other enacting body.

Peniche

v

AeroMexico

580 SW2d 152 (1979)

Court of Civil Appeals of Texas

FACTS: The plaintiff, Peniche, entered into a contract with AeroMexico Airlines whereby plaintiff agreed to provide chauffeur service for AeroMexico airline crews between the airport and a local hotel. AeroMexico agreed to pay $13.00 per trip and to guarantee a minimum number of trips each day for a year. Within the year, AeroMexico ceased using plaintiff's services, and plaintiff sued for breach of contract. The airline defended with the argument that plaintiff did not have a chauffeur's license and, therefore, the contract was unenforceable for illegality.

ISSUE: Is a contract for chauffeur services unenforceable by one who lacks a statutorily imposed chauffeur's license?

RESULT: A chauffeur's license is a condition precedent to the transportation of passengers, and contracts for transportation with a chauffeur who does not have a license are not enforceable.

REASONING:

* * *

Ordinarily the Texas courts will not enforce an illegal contract, particularly where the contract involves the doing of an act prohibited by statutes intended for the protection of the public health and welfare, and it is the duty of the court to at once decline to give it any validity. This question was before the court in *Montgomery Ward & Co. v. Lusk*. . . . There both parties had agreed to pay the plaintiff for 202 hours of overtime work. However, a provision of the Texas Penal Code provided that no female should be employed in a mercantile establishment working more than nine hours per day nor more than fifty-four hours in any calendar week. The court refused to allow a recovery under the contract because the contract was illegal and in violation of Article 1569, Texas Penal Code, 1925. The court further stated, referring to Article 1572 which imposed a penalty on the employer for violation of the act, but did not fix a penalty on the employee, that "[i]t is in the nature of a state police regulation and is intended for the protection of the public health and the perpetuation of the human race, and is therefore for the benefit of the public generally. . . . To permit individuals to enter into contracts to violate the law and then invoke the aid of the court to secure the benefits thereof would be to encourage the doing of the very thing the law prohibits."

The Texas Supreme Court in two cases, *Rogers v. Traders & General Ins. Co.*, . . . and *Service Mutual Ins. Co. of Texas v. Blain et al.*, . . . construes contracts violating Texas State statutes. In *Service Mutual* the court denied recovery of an employee because he had been hired without providing a health certificate to his employer, and the employer did not request one, in violation of the then penal code forbidding persons to be employed in a food company without a health card. The court stated the statute was enacted to safeguard the public health and was not merely regulatory. In *Rogers*, supra, the court again denied recovery where an employee did not get a health certificate to work in a food company, citing the *Montgomery Ward* case. . . . There can be little doubt that Article 6687b requiring a chauffeur's license as a condition precedent to the transportation of passengers was a valid exercise of a state police power for the purpose of protecting the safety of the general public and that any contract in derogation of such article would be illegal. While the general rule is that a contract to do a thing which cannot be performed without a violation of the law is void, where the illegality does not appear on the face of the contract it will not be held void unless the facts showing its illegality are before the court. . . .

The *Tabor* case . . . points out that the court will decide whether a contract is in violation of a statute by looking at the specific facts of the case and deciding the intention of the parties in executing the contract. The court further stated: "It is not every mutual agreement that makes a lawful contract. The law will not enforce an agreement to do that which the same law says shall not be done. . . . A contract to do a thing which cannot be performed without a violation of the law is void, whether the parties knew the law or not, ..." Thus, the trier of fact must determine whether or not a contract, although apparently legal on its face, involves the violation of a statute.

Since the evidence establishes the illegality of the contract, and this is a suit to enforce the contract, our courts will neither aid in the enforcement of such contract, nor grant any relief to a party who has executed it. . . .

Doyle, Justice.

14:3   Agreements Contrary to Public Policy

The underlying premise behind the rule that contracts contrary to public policy are illegal is that no person has a right to do something that is detrimental to the public good or welfare. Hence, the determination as to whether a particular agreement is contrary to public policy necessarily depends on an appraisal of the public good. The meaning of "public policy" is vague and variable, with no fixed definition applicable to all cases. Public policy is not static; it changes in response to the needs and interests of the times. Moreover, each state may have its own public policy, so that a contract illegal in one state as contrary to public policy may be legal and enforceable in another state.

Legislatures declare public policy and enact statutes to further the public good and welfare. The courts, however, also declare public policy. They may declare a contract illegal even though there is no statutory prohibition against such a contract. Often the courts do so when the activity contemplated in the contract is not illegal but the nature of the particular contract offends the court's sense of fair play and good faith in dealing. For example, a court may void a contract of adhesion (as discussed in Chapter 12) where the court perceives such a strong difference in knowledge and bargaining power between the parties that one party effectively had no freedom of choice. Standard form contracts are not illegal; yet a court may decide that, in good conscience, it cannot enforce the contract against the weaker party. It may void the adhesion contract as *unconscionable*. Similarly, a court may strike down a contract that restrains a person's ability to practice a profession or conduct a business, even though the contract does not violate antitrust or trade law, on the ground that enforcement by the court would unconscionably deny a person a right to make a living.

Public policy evolves. For example, in the following case the California Supreme Court was faced with the question of whether it should deny enforcement of a contract that, arguably, promoted sexual immorality. The traditional rule is that any agreement that has the direct effect of promoting sexual immorality is illegal and unenforceable. Hence, an agreement that involves the payment of consideration in exchange for the maintenance of a meretricious (immoral or illegal) sexual relationship has been held contrary to public policy and to the best interests of society. To uphold the contract, the court had to redefine its view of public morality.

Marvin

v

Marvin

557 P2d 106 (1976)

California Supreme Court

FACTS: Plaintiff Michelle Marvin alleged that she and defendant Lee
Marvin had entered an oral agreement in 1964 under which the parties
agreed that, while they lived together, they would share equally all
earnings and property acquired. Plaintiff agreed to give up her career
as a singer and to devote her time exclusively to defendant as a
companion, homemaker, housekeeper, and cook, in exchange for
defendant's promise to support her financially. The parties lived together
seven years, during which time substantial property was acquired, all
in defendant's name. After the parties separated, plaintiff sued to
enforce the alleged contract. After the trial court entered judgment for
defendant, plaintiff appealed.

ISSUE: Is a contract as to the division of property acquired by either of two
unmarried persons living together void as violative of public policy?

RESULT: Such a contract is enforceable unless or except to the extent that it
is expressly based on an illicit consideration for sexual services.

REASONING:

*   *   *

Defendant first and principally relies on the contention that the alleged
contract is so closely related to the supposed "immoral" character of the
relationship between plaintiff and himself that the enforcement of the
contract would violate public policy. He points to cases asserting that a
contract between nonmarital partners is unenforceable if it is "involved
in" an illicit relationship . . . , or made in "contemplation" of such
relationship. . . . A review of the numerous California decisions concerning contracts between nonmarital partners, however, reveals that the
courts have not employed such broad and uncertain standards to strike
down contracts. The decisions instead disclose a narrower and more
precise standard: a contract between nonmarital partners is unenforceable only *to the extent* that it *explicitly* rests upon the immoral and
illicit consideration of meretricious sexual services. [Court's emphasis.] . . .

Although the past decisions hover over the issue in the somewhat
wispy form of the figures of a Chagall painting, we can abstract from
those decisions a clear and simple rule. The fact that a man and a woman
live together without marriage, and engage in a sexual relationship, does

not in itself invalidate agreements between them relating to their earnings, property, or expenses. Neither is such an agreement invalid merely because the parties may have contemplated the creation or continuation of a nonmarital relationship when they entered into it. Agreements between nonmarital partners fail only to the extent that they rest upon a consideration of meretricious sexual services. Thus the rule asserted by defendant, that a contract fails if it is "involved in" or made "in contemplation" of a nonmarital relationship, cannot be reconciled with the decisions. . . .

The principle that a contract between nonmarital partners will be enforced unless expressly and inseparably based upon an illicit consideration of sexual services not only represents the distillation of the decisional law, but also offers a far more precise and workable standard than that advocated by defendant. . . .

[A] standard which inquires whether an agreement is "involved" in or "contemplates" a nonmarital relationship is vague and unworkable. Virtually all agreements between nonmarital partners can be said to be "involved" in some sense in the fact of their sexual relationship, or to "contemplate" the existence of that relationship. Thus defendant's proposed standards, if taken literally, might invalidate all agreements between nonmarital partners, a result no one favors. . . .

In summary, we base our opinion on the principle that adults who voluntarily live together and engage in sexual relations are nonetheless as competent as any other persons to contract respecting their earnings and property rights. Of course, they cannot lawfully contract to pay for the performance of sexual services, for such a contract is, in essence, an agreement for prostitution and unlawful for that reason. But they may agree to pool their earnings and to hold all property acquired during the relationship in accord with the law governing community property; conversely they may agree that each partner's earnings and the property acquired from those earnings remains [sic] the separate property of the earning partner. So long as the agreement does not rest upon illicit meretricious consideration, the parties may order their economic affairs as they choose, and no policy precludes the courts from enforcing such agreements. . . .

In summary, we believe that the prevalence of nonmarital relationships in modern society, and the social acceptance of them, marks this as a time when our courts should by no means apply the doctrine of the unlawfulness of the so-called meretricious relationship to the instant case. As we have explained, the nonenforceability of agreements expressly providing for meretricious conduct rested upon the fact that such conduct, as the word suggests, pertained to and encompassed prostitution. To equate the nonmarital relationship of today to such a subject matter is to do violence to an accepted and wholly different practice. . . .

The mores of the society have indeed changed so radically in regard to cohabitation that we cannot impose a standard based on alleged moral considerations that have apparently been so widely abandoned by so many.

Tobriner, Justice.

The following is a discussion of some of the types of contracts that the courts have frequently held to be illegal on the ground that they are contrary to public policy.

Exculpatory Agreements An *exculpatory agreement* relieves one party of liability for injury or damage caused by his own negligence or other wrong. Some states have adopted statutes that prohibit exculpatory clauses in certain circumstances. Where there is no statutory prohibition, exculpatory clauses are frequently held invalid as a matter of public policy.

Exculpatory clauses typically are included in contracts to enable a party to avoid responsibility that would otherwise be placed on that party by law for the public benefit. For example, a hotel might insert a clause in the registration agreement that it is not liable for any loss sustained by a guest as a result of any cause. The purpose of the clause is to relieve the hotel from any liability, even in the event of a loss caused by the hotel staff's negligence. Thus, exculpatory clauses are frequently objected to on the ground that they tend to induce a lack of care.

Two broad categories of exculpatory agreements have received particular attention in that regard: (1) employment contracts and (2) contracts between business people and members of the general public.

An employer has certain duties toward its employees.[2] Therefore, an employment contract that contains an exculpatory clause absolving an employer from any liability to its employees for injuries caused by the employer's negligence is usually held to be void. Similarly, a contract that contains a clause that exempts a businessperson from liability for injury or damage to customers caused by the businessperson's negligence is usually void.

An important factor in determining the validity of an exculpatory contract is the relative bargaining power of the parties. Where one person has a markedly inferior bargaining position, a contract that relieves the dominant party of liability for negligence will often be held invalid as contrary to public policy. For example, when contracting with an employer, an employee frequently must accept whatever terms the employer offers; similarly, a customer must ordinarily accept the terms proposed by a businessperson. In both these situations, the exculpatory clause would be considered invalid because of the dominant party's ability to take advantage of the weaker party's need for employment or for the particular goods or services offered. Where an exculpatory clause is included in a contract between parties of relatively equal bargaining power, the courts are more inclined to uphold it. For example, if

---

[2] The employer–employee relationship is discussed in Chapter 50.

two businesspersons of equal bargaining position negotiate a contract containing an exculpatory clause, the purpose of which is not the evasion of a legal duty but rather the allocation of the risk of loss, the courts generally will uphold the clause.

As the foregoing discussion suggests, the policy against exculpatory clauses is closely related to the policy against adhesion contracts and unconscionable contracts.[3] In fact, sometimes an invalid exculpatory clause will make the entire contract invalid on the ground that it is an adhesion contract or an unconscionable contract.

The following case illustrates the types of factors that the courts consider in determining whether a particular exculpatory clause should be enforced.

Crowell

v

Housing Authority of Dallas
495 SW2d 887 (1973)
Texas Supreme Court

FACTS: Plaintiff's father was a tenant in a Dallas Housing Authority apartment. The father died as a result of carbon monoxide poisoning caused by a defective gas heater in the apartment. Plaintiff sued, alleging that defendant had exclusive responsibility for maintenance and repair of the heater. Defendant claimed that the following lease provision relieved it of responsibility: "nor shall the Landlord nor any of its representatives or employees be liable for any damage to person or property of the Tenant, his family, or his visitors, which might result from the condition of these or other premises of the Landlord, from theft or from any cause whatsoever. . . . " The lower court dismissed the case on the ground that as a matter of law the lease provision rendered defendant not liable. Plaintiff appealed.

ISSUE: Is the exculpatory clause in the lease void as contrary to public policy?

RESULT: The clause is unenforceable because it was the product of unequal bargaining power between the parties.

REASONING:

*   *   *

Agreements exempting a party from future liability for negligence are generally recognized as valid and effective except where, because of the relationship of the parties, the exculpatory provision is contrary to public

---

[3] Adhesion contracts and unconscionable contracts are discussed in Chapter 12.

policy or the public interest. If the contract is between private persons who bargain from positions of substantially equal strength, the agreement is ordinarily enforced by the courts. The exculpatory agreement will be declared void, however, where one party is at such disadvantage in bargaining power that he is practically compelled to submit to the stipulation. It is generally held, for example, that a contract exempting an employer from all liability for negligent injury of his employees in the course of their employment is void as against public policy. The same rule applies to agreements exempting public utilities from liability for negligence in the performance of their duty of public service. . . .

The rules applicable to public utilities have been applied by some courts to innkeepers and public warehousemen. According to Professor Prosser, there is a definite tendency to extend the same rules to other professional bailees such as garagemen and owners of parking lots and parcel checkrooms. These bailees are under no public duty, but they deal with the public and the indispensable need for their services deprives the customer of any real bargaining power. . . .

The same considerations lead us to the conclusion that the exculpatory agreement in the present case is contrary to public policy. Respondent is a public body organized for the declared public purpose, among others, of providing safe and sanitary dwelling accommodations to persons of low income. It may lease accommodations only to families or persons who lack sufficient income to enable them, without financial assistance, to live in decent, safe and sanitary dwellings without overcrowding. . . . [T]he situation of respondent and its tenants presents a classic example of unequal bargaining power. The terms of the contract are dictated by respondent, and a prospective tenant has no choice but to accept them if he and his family are to enjoy decent housing accommodations not otherwise available to them. We hold that the exculpatory provision quoted above is contrary to public policy and void [insofar] as it purports to affect respondent's liability in the present case. . . .

Walker, Justice.

Agreements in Restraint of Trade   Agreements that tend to restrict competition or otherwise to interfere with the normal flow of goods may be held illegal on public policy grounds. Examples of this kind of agreement are covenants not to compete, price-fixing agreements, and monopoly agreements. Federal and state statutory and common law dealing with contracts in restraint of trade are treated in Chapter 55. It should be noted here, however, that the law has long frowned on various types of anticompetitive agreements and that public policy has often been used as a ground for declaring such agreements illegal.

Agreements Injurious to Public Service   Any agreement that deters a public servant from the proper performance of his duties is obviously contrary to the public interest. The courts have uniformly held such agreements to be invalid. Contracts that call for the use of corrupt or other improper means to secure favorable government service are unenforceable. For example, if A contracts with B to secure a government contract from C, and A authorizes B to offer C future employment in exchange for the award of the contract, the contract between A and B is void; B cannot recover the fee promised by A, even if B in fact secures the contract from C. Similarly, if A and B enter into a lobbying contract under which B is to use his personal influence with various legislators to secure favorable treatment on a particular bill, a court will hold the agreement to be an illegal and unenforceable lobbying contract. On the other hand, if the contract in either of the above situations calls only for the use of proper means to secure favorable governmental action, and proper means are in fact used, B can enforce the contracts against A.

 Procedures for the award of government contracts, as well as the propriety of various lobbying activities, are largely governed by federal and state statutes. Businesspeople desiring to obtain a government contract or to otherwise influence the activities of government officials should always familiarize themselves with the applicable statutes. The use of improper methods may result not only in an unenforceable contract, but in criminal liability as well.[4]

14:4   Effect of Illegality

Generally, illegal agreements are unenforceable; a court will leave the parties to the contract as it finds them. The fact that one party may have parted with consideration, while the other party has not, does not entitle the first party to any relief from a court. For example, assume that A agrees with B to act as a courier for an illegal gambling operation run by B and that A performs the services contracted for, but B refuses to pay A. If A were to sue B for the compensation promised by B, a court would ordinarily refuse to award A any money. The rule that illegal contracts are unenforceable is not based on any desire to punish one party or to reward another. Rather, the rule is based on the premise that it is in the public interest to refuse any assistance to illegal transactions.

Exceptions to the Rule of Unenforceability   In most illegal agreements, both parties are completely aware of the transaction and are considered by the courts to be *in pari delicto* (equally at fault). Under such circumstances, refusal to enforce the agreement does not offend any sense of justice, even though one of the parties may suffer some detriment. Sometimes, however, only one party knows of the facts rendering the contract illegal, and the other party is innocent of any wrong-doing and may even be an innocent victim of

---

[4] Potential criminal liability is discussed in Chapter 7.

the first party. When the facts reveal that the parties were not in pari delicto, a court will ordinarily grant relief to the innocent party and refuse any relief to the guilty party.

The rule that an innocent party may seek relief from a court is especially applicable to situations where the law rendering the agreement illegal was designed for the protection of one party against the other party's acts. Thus, where a law was passed to protect a class of persons from the unscrupulous activities of other persons, and a member of the protected class is victimized in precisely the manner that the law seeks to prevent, the fact that the transaction took the form of an illegal agreement will not deter a court from granting appropriate relief to the victimized party. This principle might be applied, for example, to award relief to a consumer who contracted with a seller in violation of a statute designed to protect consumers.[5]

Partial Illegality; Effect of Divisibility   The discussion thus far has proceeded on the assumption that an agreement is either legal or illegal in its entirety. It is possible, however, for a single agreement to contain both legal and illegal undertakings. Moreover, the same parties may enter into a number of separate and distinct agreements, some legal and some not. The question then arises as to whether any part of the agreement or agreements between parties may be enforced, or whether the illegality of one agreement affects all agreements. In the case of multiple separate agreements, the answer is fairly simple. A contract between two parties entered into for legal purposes is valid and enforceable, even though the same parties may have also entered into an illegal agreement.

However, if an agreement contains both legal and illegal portions, the determination of the enforceability of the legal portions is more complicated. The courts generally look to whether the legal portions of the agreement are divisible or separable from the illegal portions. If the legal part of the agreement can be enforced without the illegal portion and without injustice to the parties, the courts normally will enforce the agreement, provided a statute does not declare the entire agreement void and the agreement itself does not indicate the parties' intent that the contract stand or fall as a whole. The question of *separability* necessarily depends on the circumstances of a given case. Generally, however, an agreement is more likely to be considered separable when the consideration involved is legal and only one of several promises is not legal, than when the consideration itself is illegal. Separability may also depend on whether the illegal portion of the agreement goes to the very essence of the parties' agreement, or whether it is ancillary or incidental to the transaction. If the legal portions cannot be separated from the illegal portions of the agreement, then the entire agreement will be considered void and unenforceable.

The court's inquiry in the *Marvin* case set out earlier demonstrates how a court may determine whether an agreement, or part of an agreement, that is based on legal consideration may be enforced, despite the fact that the

---

[5] Consumer credit protection, which is one type of consumer protection, is discussed in Chapter 28.

agreement also contains illegal undertakings or that the parties contracted for illegal matters in addition to legal ones. Adhesion contracts, unconscionable contracts, and contracts with exculpatory clauses are often held by the courts to be divisible. A court will frequently enforce the legal portions while refusing to enforce those portions that render the contract objectionable. For example, a court might enforce a contract between a health care provider, such as a hospital, and a patient, while refusing to enforce a particular provision of the contract that unfairly limited the health care provider's liability for its employees' negligence.

Key Concepts and Terms

- An agreement that violates or that cannot be performed without violating some rules of law is illegal. Agreements that violate usury laws, gambling laws, Sunday laws, or regulatory laws are illegal.

- An essential element of a gambling contract is chance. Although gambling agreements are illegal, other kinds of agreements involving speculation, such as insurance contracts and futures contracts, are valid and enforceable because they are entered into for legitimate interests. So are promotional schemes, provided the customer does not pay for the opportunity to participate.

- A contract entered into in violation of a regulatory licensing statute is illegal. However, a contract entered into in violation of a revenue-raising licensing measure may be enforced once the license has been obtained.

- Agreements contrary to public policy are invalid. These agreements include agreements in restraint of trade and agreements against the public service. What is considered "public policy" is variable; public policy is not static. It changes with the times.

- An exculpatory clause may be held illegal, particularly if it is used in an employment contract or a contract between a businessperson and a member of the general public. An exculpatory clause that is contained in a contract whose parties have equal bargaining power is likely to be considered legal.

- Agreements in restraint of trade may be held illegal on public policy or statutory grounds.

- Illegal contracts are generally void and unenforceable. However, where the parties are not equally knowledgeable about the contract and are not in pari delicto (equally at fault), the innocent party may be granted relief.

- An illegal portion of a contract does not make the entire contract illegal if it can be enforced without reference to the illegal portion and if the contract is separable. Where the same parties have entered two contracts, one legal and one illegal, the legal contract is enforceable and is not affected by the illegal one.

- Exculpatory Agreements
- Futures Contracts
- Gambling Contracts
- In Pari Delicto

- Public Policy
- Separability (Divisibility)
- Sunday Laws

- Time–Price Doctrine
- Unconscionability
- Usury Laws

Questions and Case Problems

1. As a promotion in connection with a golf tournament sponsored by the Elks, Marcel Motors, an automobile dealer, agrees to give a new car to any golfer who shoots a hole-in-one. Chenard registers for the tournament, pays the entrance fee of $10, and shoots a hole-in-one. Marcel Motors refuses to give Chenard the car. When Chenard sues, Marcel Motors argues that the promotional scheme was an illegal and unenforceable contract. How should the court rule?

2. In March 1962, Lee & Co. contracted to grade and fill land owned by Latipac, for a price of $740,000. Work began promptly. As required by law, Lee held a valid contractor's license. This license expired in June 1963, because Lee inadvertently failed to submit a renewal application and the $30 renewal fee. Lee completed the contracting job in April 1964 and renewed its license in June 1964. A state statute denied unlicensed contractors the right to bring actions in court to recover money owed for contracting work. Latipac still owed $432,000, but refused to pay. Lee sued. Should Lee be permitted to recover?

3. Fidelity is a small corporation that provides business loans and leases business equipment. Dun & Bradstreet is a large commercial credit reporting agency that contracts to supply credit information to subscribers. Fidelity subscribes to Dun & Bradstreet's services under an agreement that contains the following language:

    > Subscriber acknowledges that Dun & Bradstreet does not and cannot guarantee the correctness or completeness of information furnished. . . . It is further understood . . . that every decision to extend credit constitutes, in some degree or another, the assumption of a business risk, and that Dun & Bradstreet, in furnishing information, does not and cannot underwrite the subscriber's risk, in any manner whatsoever. Dun & Bradstreet, therefore, shall not be liable for any loss or injury caused in whole or in part by its negligent acts of omission or commission or that of its officers, agents or employees.

    Fidelity lost money on equipment leases to a fraudulent firm, and then sued Dun & Bradstreet, claiming that Dun & Bradstreet negligently collected and reported information that was relied on by Fidelity in making the lease. Can Fidelity assert a claim for damages based on negligence?

4. When Tunkl entered the University of California, Los Angeles, Medical Center for treatment, he signed a document containing the following:

    > RELEASE: The hospital is a nonprofit, charitable institution. In consideration of the hospital and allied services to be rendered and the rates charged therefor, the patient or his legal representative agrees to and hereby releases The Regents of the University of California, and the hospital from any and all liability for the negligent or wrongful acts or omissions of its employees, if the hospital has used due care in selecting its employees.

    Tunkl subsequently suffered personal injuries, allegedly as a result of the negligence of Medical Center employees, and sued the Medical Center. Should the above release prevent him from recovering for any injuries?

5. Gabl leases commercial space in a multiple-unit residential-business building. A fire damages Gabl's property and Gabl sues the landlord, claiming that the

landlord's negligence caused the fire. As a defense, the landlord claims that Gabl's action is barred by an exculpatory provision in the lease agreement exempting the landlord from liability for any damage to Gabl's property from any cause whatsoever. Should the landlord's position be upheld?

6. Prior to undergoing a tubal ligation, Bowman signed a consent form that absolved the attending physicians "from responsibility for any untoward or unfavorable results arising from this procedure." Due to the operating physician's negligence, the sterilization procedure is unsuccessful. Bowman becomes pregnant and suffers various damages as a result. Bowman sues the physician. Does the consent form protect the physician from liability?

7. Emco, Inc. sued Healy for nonpayment of a note from Healy to Emco, Inc. Healy defends that the note was given in exchange for stock in Emco, Inc. Under Texas law (where the transaction took place) it is illegal for a corporation to sell its own stock on credit. Emco argues that if the transaction was illegal, Healy was an equal participant in the transaction and cannot assert the defense of illegality. Can he?

8. Hendrix was an electrical engineer whose work experience was primarily in the design of gambling devices. He was employed by defendant in Oregon to build a "pull tab" machine, an electro-mechanical or electronic "punchboard." Hendrix testified that he knew the pull tab machine was not an amusement device and that he knew it was illegal in Oregon. When defendant was charged with and pleaded guilty to a charge of promoting gambling, he ceased paying Hendrix. Hendrix sued for breach of the employment contract, claiming he did not actually know of defendant's illegal use of the gambling devices. Should a court entertain such a suit?

9. Karpinski is a dairyman whose economic survival depends on his ability to obtain a grade A milk contract in an area where such contracts are extremely scarce. Collins, the president of a local creamery, offers Karpinski a grade A contract if Karpinski will pay him a specified rebate. Unable to obtain any other grade A contracts, Karpinski accepts the offer. A formal contract is prepared between Karpinski and the creamery, and Karpinski sells his milk to the creamery for approximately two years. He gives Collins approximately $10,000 in rebate payments during that time. After termination of the contract Karpinski sues Collins for refund of the secret rebates. Collins defends on the ground that since such rebates are prohibited by statute, the agreement between him and Karpinski is an illegal contract. Should this defense be sustained?

10. Liebman, living in France in May 1941, wanted to get his family and himself to Portugal to escape the advancing German army. Rosenthal told Liebman that he, Rosenthal, was an intimate friend of the Portuguese Consul and could obtain visas to Portugal for Liebman and his family, but that it would be necessary to give the Consul $30,000. Liebman gave Rosenthal jewelry worth $28,000 to secure the visas, but Rosenthal absconded with the jewelry. Liebman subsequently met Rosenthal in New York and sued to recover the value of the jewelry. Rosenthal moved for a summary judgment on the ground that the agreement between him and Liebman was illegal. Should Rosenthal's motion be granted?

15 Formal Requisites; Statute of Frauds

15:1 Formal Requisites Generally; Oral Contracts

Most oral contracts are enforceable. In the absence of a statute to the contrary, a contract may be oral as well as written, and no particular form is required. A complete contract may be gathered from several different documents. For example, a series of letters, writings, and telegrams may be connected with each other in such a way as to be considered one contract. Also, a contract may be partly oral and partly written. For example, a verbal acceptance of a written offer may result in the creation of an enforceable contract. A contract may even consist of an undated, unsigned, one-page handwritten document, provided all the required elements of a contract are present, and that no statute imposes more specific requirements.

 What one party perceives as preliminary negotiation toward a contract may be perceived by the other party as a contract. It is important in negotiations to expressly state to the other party that there is to be no contract until an appropriate written document is drafted and signed by all parties, if that is intended. Where there is a chance of misunderstanding, the oral communication should be followed up with a clear written statement.

Some contracts, however, must be in writing to be enforceable. First, if the parties indicate a definite intention not to be bound until a written agreement has been made, a writing is necessary to the formation of the contract. Thus, a writing may be required by agreement between the parties. Second, the form of some contracts, such as insurance contracts, is specified by statute, and a contract required to be made in a particular form is not enforceable unless in that form. Thus, statutes may require a particular writing. Third, the *statute of frauds* requires that certain types of contracts be in writing. The statute of frauds has developed peculiar twists and turns with which businesspersons should be familiar. This chapter explains the origins of and the major issues associated with the statute of frauds.

It is sometimes uneconomical or contrary to accepted business practice to insist on a writing. In general, however, written contracts are preferable to oral ones. A written agreement not only provides evidence that a contract does in fact exist, but also provides evidence of the terms and conditions of the contract. Equally important, a writing may be the basis of negotiations leading to amicable resolution of a dispute without litigation.

15:2   Statute of Frauds

In 1677 the English Parliament, concerned about various fraudulent practices, adopted "An Act For the Prevention of Frauds and Perjuries." This act required that certain specified types of contracts be evidenced by a signed writing. The act, commonly called the Statute of Frauds, subsequently became effective in the American colonies, and today each state, either as a matter of common law or by virtue of statutory enactment, now has its own statute of frauds.

The types of contracts that must be in writing, according to § 4 of the English statute, are (1) a promise of an executor or administrator to pay with his own funds a debt of the deceased, (2) a promise to answer for the debt of another, (3) an agreement made on consideration of marriage, (4) a contract for the sale of land or any interest therein, and (5) an agreement that is not to be performed within a year. Most state statutes of frauds have substantially retained the provisions of § 4.

Under § 17 of the English statute, contracts for the sale of goods for a price of 10 pounds or more were required to be in writing. Most states adopted statutes similar to § 17, but those statutes were supplanted first by the Uniform Sales Act, and then by the UCC, which contains its own statute of frauds with respect to the sale of goods [UCC § 2-201]. This provision is discussed in detail in Chapter 19.

Most states, in addition to retaining the basic coverage of § 4 of the English statute, have adopted statutes requiring other particular classes of contracts to be in writing. Moreover, federal laws require that certain contracts be in writing. In determining whether a given contract must be written, therefore, it is essential to consider not only whether the contract falls within the provisions of the classic statute of frauds, but also whether some other statute requires that it be in writing.

Generally, if a contract is required by the statute of frauds to be in writing, any modification of the contract must also be in writing. However, an oral agreement to rescind an executory written contract is usually valid, even if the contract is one required by the statute of frauds to be in writing.

The remainder of this chapter will consider in greater detail some of the more important provisions of § 4 of the English statute and its modern state counterparts.

15:3   Agreements Not to Be Performed Within One Year

The English statute provided that "any agreement that is not to be performed within the space of one year from the making thereof" must be evidenced by a writing. Today, most state statutes have a similar provision. The underlying theory is that contracts intended to be performed over a long period of time should be memorialized by a writing. Although the provision appears simple and straightforward, it has given rise to a good deal of litigation. In most cases, the courts have held that the possibility that a contract may be performed within one year excludes it from the coverage of the statute. A contract that may be performed within one year need not be written, even though performance probably will, and in fact does, take more than a year. In short, to be within the coverage of the statute, it must appear from the terms and conditions of the contract itself that the contract cannot be fully performed within a year. To illustrate, if A enters into a contract to employ B for B's lifetime, the contract is not within the statute, because B may die within a year. On the other hand, if A employs B for a term of two years, the contract must be in writing. The fact that B might still die within a year does not remove the contract from the operation of the statute, because the statute requires full performance. The death of one person will excuse further performance, but that excuse is not the same as full performance.

Note the statute's requirement that performance of the contract be possible within one year from the *making* of the contract, not the commencement of performance. In computing the one-year period, the day the contract is made is excluded, and the period expires at the close of the contract's anniversary date. The following case demonstrates some of the difficulties that may be encountered in determining whether a contract is one that is not to be performed within a year.

Pando

v

Fernandez

485 NYS2d 162 (1984)

Supreme Court, New York County

FACTS: Fernandez won $2.8 million in the New York State lottery. The money was to be paid out over a ten-year period. Pando claimed that Fernandez promised to share her winnings equally with him, if she won, in exchange for Pando's promise that he would select the lottery numbers, buy the tickets with Fernandez' money, and obtain the divine intervention of a saint to make the selected number win. Pando alleged that he performed fully, that the number he selected won, and that Fernandez has a contractual obligation to pay him half the winnings.

Fernandez defended on the ground, among others, that such a contract would be unenforceable under the statute of frauds because it could not be performed within one year.

ISSUE: Could the contract be fully performed within a year?

RESULT: Yes, both parties could perform fully within a year.

REASONING:

* * *

. . . Defendant contends that the alleged agreement cannot be performed within one year. She relies on the line of cases in which an oral agreement to pay commissions over a period of several years has been held to be unenforceable. . . . Similarly treated are contracts for employment for more than one year. . . .

Defendant claims the ten year payout of the total prize here calls for analogous treatment. In this case, however, the contract could be performed well within one year. Defendant was to furnish the funds with which to purchase the ticket. Plaintiff had to purchase the ticket, select the numbers, return it to defendant, and pray. The winning numbers were scheduled to be drawn, and were drawn, within days, and at that time the obligations of the parties became fixed. The defendant would then have to have notified a third party, the state Lottery Division, that all future payments were to be divided equally between herself and the plaintiff, a task which she could perform within days. At that point the obligations of each side would have been performed. . . . The fact that the payout would be extended over several years is of no moment, for the liability, if any, was fixed, the amounts known, and all that remained was the ministerial act of having the annual payouts divided. That is quite different from an agreement by a party to pay out a percentage of sales or earnings over a period of years, which may call for future services, and where the amounts cannot be established until well into the future.

The agreement here more closely resembles that in *Costello Associates Inc. v. Standard Metals Corp.* . . . There the agreement involved was for an executive search agency to provide the name of a prospective employee to be hired the following year, payment being based on a percentage of the first year's compensation. There, despite the contention that payment would necessarily take more than a year from the date of the agreement, it was held that there was full performance of the contract within the year, and the obligation to pay accrued upon performance. The actual computation of the amount due, even if it were to take more than a year, was of no significance, since this was a mere ministerial act. The controlling criterion is the time at which the obligation becomes, or could become fixed. If all the contingencies can occur, and all conditions precedent can be performed within the one year period, with nothing remaining to be done thereafter except the act of payment, there is no violation of the Statute of Frauds.

The ten year payout of the prize in this case is the measure of the obligation of the State Lottery Division. The alleged obligation of the defendant to share that prize with plaintiff was fixed well within the one year period. . . .

Greenfield, Justice.

While the courts agree that the statute contemplates full performance and that partial performance within a year will not take a contract out of the statute, there is disagreement as to whether the possibility of full performance by one party is sufficient. The general rule is that a contract that is capable of full performance within one year by one party need not be in writing. For example, if A agrees to remodel B's store, in exchange for B's promise to make monthly payments to A over a three-year period, most courts would hold that the agreement was not within the statute of frauds, provided the remodeling was capable of being done within a year. Some courts, however, require the possibility of full performance by both parties within a year. A court following that rule would hold that A and B must have a written contract.

15:4   Interests in Land

The English statute required that "any contract for sale of lands . . . or any interest in or concerning them" must be evidenced by a writing. This provision or a variation of it has been carried over into state statutes. The general effect of the provision is to require all contracts concerning real estate to be in writing. Thus, for example, mortgages and grants of easements, which are limited rights to use of another's land, must be in writing to be enforceable. Leases also are required to be in writing, unless the lease term does not exceed one year.

The phrase "interest in land" applies only to agreements that affect the title or right of possession to land; agreements that affect the land in other ways are not within the statute. Determining whether a particular contract affects an interest in land may sometimes be difficult. For example, it is agreed that improvements, such as buildings and other structures, are considered a part of the land and that a sale of the land normally includes the buildings on it. Thus, a contract for the sale or lease of a building ordinarily must be in writing. But the question has been raised as to whether a contract for the sale of a building that is to be removed from the land involves an interest in land. Most courts have held that it does not. Similarly, a contract to construct a building has been held not to involve an interest in land and not to require a writing.

Questions have also arisen as to whether contracts that involve growing crops, timber, minerals, and the like involve personal property and therefore need not be in writing, or involve interests in land and therefore need to be in writing. The courts generally have ruled that items such as growing crops are personal property, whereas items that spontaneously grow on or are an integral part of the land are real property. For example, it has been held that since grass and timber grow spontaneously, they are part of the land, and that contracts relating to grass and standing timber therefore must be in writing. However, once grass or timber has been cut, it is not an integral part of the land and is treated as personal property. A contract to sell downed trees, for example, does not need to be in writing.

A different rule regarding growing crops and timber is provided by the UCC. Under the UCC, a contract for the sale of growing crops or other things capable of severance from the land without material harm to the land, including timber to be cut, is considered a sale of goods, regardless of whether the subject matter is to be severed by the buyer or the seller [UCC § 2-107(2)]. This means, then, that the UCC regards growing crops and timber as personal property. A contract for the sale of minerals or the like (including oil and gas) or a structure to be removed from the land is a contract for the sale of goods if severance is done by the seller, but until severance occurs such a contract is considered a transfer of an interest in land [UCC § 2-107(1)]. This means that a contract for the sale of minerals and like materials must be in writing unless the seller is going to remove them from the land. Once they are removed from the land, they are considered to be personal property that can be transferred by oral contract.

Note, however, that even if a contract for the sale of crops, timber, or minerals is exempt from the "interest in land" provisions of the statute of frauds, the contract may be subject to other provisions of the statute. For example, if a contract is entered into in the spring of one year for the sale of crops to be harvested in the fall of the following year it would need to be in writing even though it is a contract for the sale of personal property. The reason is that the contract would be subject to the statute of frauds provision requiring that contracts not to be performed within a year be in writing. Moreover, if the price of the crops is $500 or more, the contract would also be subject to the UCC statute of frauds provision requiring a written contract for sale of goods worth $500 or more [UCC § 2-201]. Thus, a conclusion that a particular contract affects land but does not involve transfer of an interest in the land does not necessarily mean that the contract is outside the coverage of the statute of frauds.

15:5   Promise to Answer for Debt of Another

Under the English statute, any "promise to answer for the debt, default or miscarriages of another person" was required to be evidenced by a writing. Most American jurisdictions have retained this requirement. The provision has primary application to *guaranty,* or *suretyship, contracts.* These are contracts in which one person (the guarantor or surety) promises a second person (the creditor) to pay the debt of a third person (the debtor) in the event the debtor fails to do so. The debtor is said to have a primary obligation; the guarantor or surety is said to have a secondary, or *collateral,* obligation. The key to the concept of guaranty is that the debtor is primarily liable on the debt; the guarantor becomes liable only after the debtor has failed to pay, and this liability is based on a related but separate promise. Thus, a person who assumes primary responsibility for a debt is not a guarantor—and the promise need not be in writing under this part of the statute of frauds—even though payment of the debt may benefit a third person.

The difficulties that can arise may be illustrated by considering the frequently encountered situation in which one person promises to pay a second person for goods or services delivered to a third person. If the goods or services are delivered on the third person's credit, then that person is liable, and the promisor's promise is an undertaking to pay the third person's debt if he fails to pay. This promise therefore comes under the statute of frauds and must be in writing. If, however, the goods or services were delivered solely on the promisor's credit, there is no promise to pay the debt of another and the promise is not within the statute and may be oral. If the nature of the contract is ambiguous and the promise is oral, there is substantial room for the creditor to argue that the promisor intended to assume primary liability.

The following case illustrates an interesting business circumstance in which the plaintiff creditor, to avoid the statute of frauds, had to prove that a promise was made to the debtor rather than to the creditor.

Brad Ragan, Inc.

v

Callicutt Enterprises, Inc.
326 SE2d 62 (1985)
Court of Appeals of North Carolina

FACTS: Plaintiff sold tires to Callicutt on credit. Callicutt sold trucks on which the tires were mounted to Lewis, the defendant. Plaintiff later claimed that, in return for the sale of the trucks and tires, Lewis orally promised Callicutt that he would pay plaintiff for the tires. Callicutt filed for bankruptcy and plaintiff took no further action against him. However, plaintiff sued Lewis to enforce his promise to pay for the tires. Defendant claimed that the promise was unenforceable under the statute of frauds.

ISSUE: Is plaintiff barred by the statute of frauds from enforcing Lewis' promise to pay Callicutt's debt for the tires?

RESULT: Plaintiff is not so barred if the promise was made to the debtor Callicutt rather than to the creditor plaintiff.

REASONING:

*   *   *

Defendant contends that plaintiff's claim is barred by G.S. 22–1, which states, "[no] action shall be brought . . . to charge any defendant upon a special promise to answer the debt, default or miscarriage of another person, unless the agreement upon which such action shall be brought, or some memorandum or note thereof, shall be in writing. . . . "

The classic instance of a promise within the provisions of this section is the promise made to a creditor to gain credit for another: "If he does not pay you, I will." This is a collateral promise and must be in writing.
. . .

The purpose of G.S. 22–1 is to protect the promisor from the promisee.

> There is a temptation for a promisee, in a case where the real debtor has proved insolvent or unable to pay, to enlarge the scope of the promise. . . . Moreover, . . . it is so obviously just that a promisor receiving none of the benefits for which the debt was incurred should be bound only by the exact terms of his promise.

72 Am.Jur.2d, *Statute of Frauds*, Sec. 179 at 709–10 (1974).

However, "[if] the promise to assume the obligation of the debtor is made to a person other than the one presently entitled to enforce the liability . . . , such promise is not one to answer for the debt of another" and is not within the statute of frauds. *Id.* Sec. 187 at 715. "A promise . . . made to the debtor for an adequate consideration, to discharge the debt, is not regarded as a promise to answer for the debt of another within the meaning of the statute. . . . " *Id.* Sec. 209 at 737.

Thus, for defendant to fall within the protection of the statute, he would have to have promised plaintiff, the creditor, that he would answer for the debt of Callicutt. A promise, as here, to the debtor to pay the debtor's debts—in contrast to a promise to the creditor to pay debts owed by another—is not contemplated by the statute of frauds.

If the facts are as plaintiff alleges, as upon a motion to dismiss we must take them to be, . . . defendant agreed with Callicutt to purchase trucks and tires and to pay for the tires directly to plaintiff. Defendant's promise "is to pay the debt, not of another person, but of the *very person* to whom the promise is made, and it is well settled that such a promise does not fall within the operation of . . . the statute." . . . The sale of trucks and tires here is analogous to the sale of a partnership, a business interest, or a stock of goods upon an agreement to take the goods and pay the debts. For a purchaser who takes the goods under such an agreement the statute of frauds is no defense. . . .

Whichard, Judge.

To illustrate another common situation, if goods are sold on the joint credit of two persons, each person's promise to pay for the goods is an original promise to the creditor even if the goods are to be delivered to and used by only one person. Thus, the promises are not within the statute and need not be in writing.

If the promisor has a personal interest in the transaction and will benefit by paying the other person's debt, the contract may not have to be in writing. This is because under the *main purpose or leading object rule*, no writing is required if the main purpose of the promise is to obtain some substantial benefit for the promisor, rather than to guarantee the third person's debt.

EXAMPLE: A hires B, a contractor, to construct a building. While the building is under construction, B fails to make timely payments to C, a supplier, and C notifies A and B that he will refuse to make further deliveries of supplies unless the outstanding debts are paid. A tells C that, if C will continue to make deliveries, A will pay for the supplies if B fails to do so. A's promise to C constitutes a promise to pay another's debt, but the main purpose of A's promise is not to guarantee B's debt but rather to ensure the uninterrupted construction of the building. A's promise therefore need not be in writing.

A promise made to the debtor, as distinguished from the debtor's creditor, is uniformly held not to be within the statute. This promise may therefore be oral.

15:6   Nature of Writing Required

Section 4 of the English statute provided that a contract within the statute was unenforceable "unless the agreement . . . or some memorandum or note thereof, shall be in writing, and signed by the party to be charged therewith or some other person thereunto by him lawfully authorised." Similar requirements have been incorporated into modern state statutes of frauds. Thus, according to the statute it is not essential that the entire contract be in writing. An oral contract may be enforced as long as there is a *memorandum* or *note* to indicate that the contract exists. Moreover, the writing need not be signed by both parties. Only the party against whom the contract is being enforced ("the party to be charged") need sign.

Generally, a memorandum will be considered to comply with the statute if it contains the names of the parties, the terms and conditions of the contract, a reasonably certain description of the subject matter, and the signature of the party to be charged. Most statutes of frauds expressly allow the memorandum to be signed by an authorized agent. The agent generally need not have written authorization to act; oral authorization is sufficient. The writing, whether signed by the party to be charged or by an agent, need not be made and signed at the time the contract is made. It may be prepared at any time subsequent to the contract, and it may even be made prior to the actual formation of the contract.

EXAMPLE: A writes, signs, and mails a letter to B offering to maintain and repair all of B's office machines for a period of two years, in exchange for a specified monthly payment. After B receives the letter, she informs A by telephone that she accepts his offer. At that time the written offer, coupled with the oral acceptance, creates a contract. If A subsequently refuses to perform, B can rely on the written offer as a memorandum that is sufficient to comply with the statute of frauds. If, however, B refuses to perform, A would be unable to enforce the contract against her; the contract is within the statute of frauds (being incapable of performance within a year), and no writing evidencing a contract was ever signed by B.

No particular form of writing or type of language is necessary to constitute a sufficient memorandum or note. Under appropriate circumstances, a canceled check, receipt, letter, or telegram might be held adequate. Even a request for relief from the obligations of the contract in question might be considered sufficient.

The memorandum may consist of several writings if, taken as a whole, they adequately evidence the agreement and, taken separately, they in some way indicate that they relate to the same transaction. The court must piece together the writings to determine the sufficiency of a writing. The court will consider the policies underlying the statute of frauds in coming to its decision.

Generally, a written communication to a third person constitutes a sufficient memorandum, provided it adequately discloses the terms of and the parties to the contract. However, a minority of states require delivery of the memorandum to the other party.

15:7   Effect of Noncompliance with Statute

The original English statute provided that "no action shall be brought" on an agreement covered by the statute unless the agreement was in writing as required by the statute. Today, the statutes of most states contain similar provisions. Accordingly, the courts in most states have held that an oral contract within the scope of the statute is only voidable, rather than being entirely void. The distinction between a void contract and one that is simply voidable is that a void contract is invalid for all purposes, while a voidable one is valid between the parties unless and until one party sues on the contract. That is, the parties can perform a voidable contract, but neither party can sue either to recover damages for its breach or for a court order requiring the other party to perform. In some states, however, the statute of frauds declares that an agreement covered by the statute is void unless it is in writing.

Complete Performance of Oral Contract   Full performance by both sides to an oral contract clearly removes the contract from the coverage of the statute of frauds. Where only one party has fully performed, the courts are in disagreement. Under the majority view, the lack of written evidence of the agreement does not preclude its enforcement in a court action by the party who fully performed. Under the minority view, that party cannot force the other party to perform, but can recover the reasonable value of the benefit which has been conferred upon the other party. Such a recovery is called recovery in *quasi-contract.* The amount recovered is not necessarily related to the contract agreement.

Part Performance of Oral Contract: Contract for Sale of Land   Under the doctrine of *part performance,* an oral contract for the sale of land may be enforced if certain acts have been taken in reliance on the oral contract. For the doctrine to apply to a contract for the sale of land, the plaintiff must have so changed his position in reliance on the oral agreement that it is impossible to restore him to the status quo that existed prior to the agreement.

EXAMPLE: Norton wants to buy a farm, and he pays for and receives an option to purchase a farm owned by Johnson. Norton then finds a farm he likes better, owned by Williams. He and Williams orally agree to terms for sale of the farm. Relying on the agreement with Williams, Norton allows his option to purchase the Johnson farm to expire, and Johnson then sells it to someone else. Because of Norton's change in position in reliance on the oral agreement with Williams, the agreement is now enforceable by Norton.

The term "part performance" is in a sense a misnomer, since the doctrine may be applied even where certain acts have been performed in reliance on the contract but not in actual execution of it. While various acts may be shown in support of a claim of part performance, the actions most often shown are (1) the taking of possession by the purchaser, (2) the making of valuable permanent improvements on the land by the purchaser, and (3) the payment of money or rendition of services by the purchaser. If part performance is established, a court will grant *specific performance,* which is an order that the defendant deed the land if he is the seller, or pay the money if he is the buyer.

Most courts consider the taking of possession a necessary element of part performance, and a number of courts have even indicated that it is itself sufficient to warrant an order for specific performance. Most cases have involved the taking of possession in conjunction with other acts. The strongest and most unequivocal act of part performance is the making of permanent improvements to the land. Some courts have relied solely on this act in finding sufficient part performance. The payment of money or the performance of services, although almost universally considered insufficient part performance to warrant an order of specific performance, is nonetheless an important factor where there have been other acts as well.

In the following case the court considers the sufficiency of the improvements made by the promisee.

R.W.P. Concessions

v

Rhode Island Zoological Soc.
487 A2d 129 (1985)
Supreme Court of Rhode Island

FACTS: Plaintiff sought the concession rights to sell food, beverages, and novelties in Roger Williams Park. Defendant owned the concession rights and was free to transfer those rights with the consent of the Board of

Park Commissioners. An agreement was reached between plaintiff and defendant, but the agreement was not accepted by the park commissioners. Nevertheless, the chair of defendant's board of directors directed plaintiff to take possession and make the necessary capital improvements to open the concessions, which plaintiff did. Defendant then ordered plaintiff to vacate the premises and ceased negotiations. Plaintiff sued for breach of the oral agreement. Defendant raised the statute of frauds as a bar to enforcement.

ISSUE: Did plaintiff's expenditure of time and money in reliance on the oral agreement constitute sufficient part performance to take the agreement out of the statute of frauds?

RESULT: Plaintiff's capital improvements were not sufficiently permanent to satisfy the statute of frauds.

REASONING:

*   *   *

The plaintiff contends that it made substantial expenditures of time and money in reliance upon the oral agreement, sufficient to constitute part performance and to take an otherwise unenforceable oral agreement out of the statute of frauds.

The sole issue before the court is whether plaintiff had performed part of the agreement sufficient to remove the oral contract from the statute of frauds.

Pursuant to G.L.1956 (1969 Reenactment) § 9–1–4, a contract for the sale of an interest in real estate must be in writing and signed by the party to be charged to be enforceable. We have stated as a general rule, however, that an oral agreement is enforceable under the doctrine of part performance. Nevertheless, the terms of the agreement must be clear and the possession or improvements in reliance thereon must be substantial and clearly shown. . . .

Once these threshold requirements have been met and the party seeking enforcement has performed to such an extent that repudiation of the contract would lead to an unjust or fraudulent result, the court will disregard the requirement of a writing and enforce an oral agreement. . . .

The trial justice, after reviewing and analyzing the evidence, found that plaintiff's performance either arose before the oral agreement or after the August 8 repudiation, and thus performance on the part of plaintiff did not remove the oral contract from the statute of frauds. The trial justice found, however, that an enforceable oral agreement commenced between the parties when defendant informed plaintiff that it could prepare to open the zoo concessions for the season. The term of operation of this concession was to run for less than a year . . . and constituted an extension of an existing agreement between Kelly and defendant rather than an entirely new agreement.

We have repeatedly stated that the findings of fact by a trial justice sitting without a jury are given great weight and will not be overturned unless they are clearly wrong or the trial justice misconceived or overlooked material evidence. The plaintiff in the instant case has failed to show such error by the trial justice. . . .

A reading of the record clearly indicates that there was substantial evidence to support the findings of the trial justice. The evidence demonstrates that no permanent improvements were undertaken by plaintiff to ready the concession for operation. All equipment could be removed at the termination of the operating relationship. The record is also clear that plaintiff failed to meet most of its obligations under the contract. Rent was never paid, the $25,000 payment due June 1, 1980, was not made, nor was appropriate fire insurance procured. Where capital improvements are readily removed and obligations due under the contract have not been satisfied, the reliance necessary to invoke the doctrine of part performance has not been established. . . . Moreover, we are satisfied that the evidence supports a determination that a temporary extension of a prior agreement between the parties was effected. Mr. Meller, defendant president, testified to the temporary arrangement negotiated by Mrs. Danforth. Although defendant's board did not act upon the May 20, 1980, contract proposal for the concession rights within the zoo, it cannot be said that defendant did not countenance Mrs. Danforth's offer for a continuation of the prior concession agreement. . . .

Bevilacqua, Chief Justice.

Part Performance of Oral Contract: Other Contracts Within Scope of Statute The courts have generally held that part performance of an oral contract that is required by the statute to be in writing, other than a contract for the sale of land, does not take the contract out of the scope of the statute. On rare occasions, however, where other remedies are clearly insufficient, specific performance may be ordered. Thus, if a person so changes his position in reliance on a contract that he would be substantially prejudiced by failure to enforce it, the contract may be enforced notwithstanding the lack of a writing.

EXAMPLE: A entered into an oral contract with B. Under this contract A was to be employed as an assistant sales manager in Hawaii for a period of three years. In reliance on the contract, A moved her family 2,200 miles, from Los Angeles to Hawaii. Because such a move was clearly foreseeable by B, and because injustice can be avoided only by enforcement of the contract, specific performance should be granted.

Even if a contract will not be enforced on the ground of part performance, a party who has taken some action in reliance on the contract may be entitled to recover money on a quasi-contract theory. The theory is that if one party, pursuant to a contract that is unenforceable under the statute of frauds, has rendered services to another party, made improvements on the other party's land, or paid money or parted with other consideration, the other party has made an implied promise to pay the reasonable value of such performance. Recovery in such a situation does not rest on the contract, but on the implied obligation to pay for benefits received.

Key Concepts and Terms

- Unless there is a statute to the contrary, a contract may be either oral or written, and no particular form of the contract is required.

- Each state has a statute of frauds, which requires certain specified types of contracts to be evidenced by a signed writing. Other federal and state statutes also regulate the form of other particular classes of contracts.

- An agreement not to be performed within a year from the time it is made must be evidenced by a writing. The possibility of performance by both parties (or, in most states, by one party) within a year removes a contract from the statute's coverage, regardless of whether performance within a year is anticipated or occurs.

- Contracts for the sale of interests in land must be evidenced by a writing. The phrase "interest in land" applies only to agreements that affect title or right of possession. Whether a contract involving improvements, growing crops, timber, or minerals affects an interest in land depends on the particular factual circumstances.

- A promise to answer for another person's debt must be evidenced by a writing. This requirement applies primarily to guaranty contracts. If the main purpose of a contract to answer for another's debt is to benefit the promisor, it is not within the statute's coverage.

- The entire contract need not be written to satisfy the statute. Any memorandum or note is sufficient, provided it adequately identifies the parties, establishes the terms and conditions of the contract, and is signed by the party to be charged.

- A contract that is not in writing as required by the statute ordinarily is unenforceable in court. However, such a contract can be enforceable if there has been (1) complete performance by both parties (or, in most states, by one party); or (2) part performance of a contract for the sale of land. Part performance is most conclusively established by showing that the purchaser made permanent improvements to the land, although other relevant factors are that the purchaser took possession of the land, paid money, or rendered services. If the contract is not for the sale of land and has been partly performed, the performing party may recover on the theory of quasi-contract.

- Specific performance is a judicial remedy by which a court orders performance of a contract. In a suit based on a contract for the sale of land, the court will grant the plaintiff A specific performance if A has established part performance. Therefore, defendant B would have to deed the land if B is the seller, or pay the money for the land if B is the buyer.

- Guarantor
- Guaranty Contract
- Interest in Land
- Leading Object (Main Purpose) Rule
- Memorandum or Note
- Part Performance
- Personal Property
- Specific Performance
- Statute of Frauds
- Surety
- Suretyship Contract
- Quasi-Contract

Questions and Case Problems

1. Acme Company falls behind on premium payments to Jones, its insurance broker, and Jones notifies Acme that she intends to sue. Lopez contacts Jones and explains that his children have just purchased Acme, that they need at least a year to make the company profitable, that he has no financial interest in Acme but has assumed the title of chairman, and that he "will take care of the account" himself if Jones will refrain from suing Acme. Jones agrees. Another 18 months pass without payment. Jones then sues Lopez, seeking recovery of not only the amount due at the time of her meeting with Lopez, but also premium payments that had come due in the succeeding 18 months. Lopez raises the statute of frauds as a defense. How should the case be decided?

2. In May 1970, Fong was negligently injured by an employee of Baker Company. In June 1970, Fong and Baker entered an oral settlement agreement, whereby Fong promised not to bring suit for the injury in exchange for Baker's promise to pay Fong $100 per month for the next 20 years. Baker made payments to Fong for 5 years, then stopped. Fong sued, and Baker raised the statute of frauds as a defense. What is the result? Would the result be the same if the statute of limitations for personal injury actions was one year? If it was two years? If Baker had promised to pay Fong for the rest of Fong's life?

3. Casey holds a good position with ABC Company, but she periodically looks for better job opportunities. One year she receives two attractive job offers. After weighing her options, she accepts an oral offer of a 5-year contract from XYZ Corporation. Although Casey needs only two months to qualify for a pension at ABC, XYZ insists that she start immediately, and Casey reluctantly agrees to do so. Casey resigns from ABC and moves her family across the state to begin work for XYZ. After two years Casey is fired. She sues for breach of contract, and XYZ raises the statute of frauds. What is the decision?

4. Kiyose sued Indiana University and various individual defendants for breach of an oral contract of lifetime employment. He complained that between 1966 and 1973 he was a lecturer and a Ph.D candidate at Indiana University; that during that period he and the defendants orally agreed that, once Kiyose obtained his Ph.D., he would receive perpetual lifetime appointments at the university, commencing with a 3-year appointment as assistant professor; that he received his Ph.D. degree in 1973 and was then appointed assistant professor; and that he was subsequently notified that he would not be reappointed for the 1974–75 year. Is a lawsuit on the oral agreement barred by the statute of frauds?

5. Roberts and Bryan orally agree that Bryan will purchase the entire output of railroad crossties from Roberts' sawmill for as long as Roberts owns the mill. Bryan buys the crossties for over a year, then refuses to make further purchases. Roberts

is forced to close his mill, and he sues Bryan for damages. Bryan raises the statute of frauds as a defense. What is the result?

6. In the case of *Brad Ragan v Callicutt Enterprises* (see page 255), the plaintiff must prove that the oral promise was made to another, not to the plaintiff. How, then, can the plaintiff sue on the basis of a contract to which he was not a party? (Hint: see the materials on third party beneficiary contracts in Chapter 17.)

7. Crabtree orally agrees to become sales manager for Arden Corporation. An unsigned memorandum prepared by Arden indicates that Crabtree is to receive $20,000 to start, $25,000 after six months, and $30,000 after a year, and that he is to have "two years to make good." A payroll card, indicating Crabtree's starting salary and the agreed increases after six months and one year, is prepared and initialed by an Arden officer. Crabtree receives his 6-month increase, and after one year an Arden officer prepares and signs a new payroll card to reflect a salary increase to $30,000. Arden's president refuses to approve the increase. Crabtree quits and sues for breach of contract. What is the outcome?

8. North Coast Cookies, Inc. and Sweet Temptations, Inc. enter into an oral agreement for a lease, trade fixtures, and equipment in a cookie kiosk at a shopping mall. They then sign an agreement stating that

> The undersigned agree that North Coast Cookies, Inc. will purchase the lease agreement, all furniture, trade fixtures and equipment of the store at Beachwood Place Mall in Beachwood, Ohio, known as Sweet Temptations.

> The agreed upon amount is one hundred twenty thousand dollars ($120,000). Terms of physical store transfer and terms of the payment and interest will be further decided and shall be reasonable to both parties.

> This agreement is bound by the consideration of $2500.
>
> Agreed to by
> /s/ Allan Fox pres.
> Sweet Temptations, Inc.
> Agreed to by
> /s/ Kenneth Dery
> /s/ Robert Dery
> North Coast Cookies, Inc.

Sweet Temptations argues that there was no enforceable agreement because (a) the duration of the lease being transferred remained unsettled, and (b) a later prepared document containing miscellaneous additional provisions was never executed. Is Sweet Temptations correct?

9. Brandenburger puts 880 acres of land up for sale at public auction. Klipfel is the successful bidder on 640 acres and Erlinbush on 240 acres. After the sale, the auctioneer prepares, dates, and signs the following memorandum: "Terms not over 20 percent down. Bal. 5 yr., 5 percent Int. Henry Brandenburger Auction. Land sold to Wilbur Erlinbush 240 acres at $44.00 per acre. Alvin Klipfel 640 acres at $39.00 per acre." When Brandenburger refuses to complete the sale to Klipfel, Klipfel sues for specific performance. What is the result?

10. CNS and SWT, both corporations in the waste-treatment industry, negotiated for the purchase of SWT by CNS. The written agreement stated, "This Letter of Intent evidences the mutual understanding and agreement in principle which has been reached between SWT and CNS regarding the proposed merger of SWT with a wholly owned subsidiary of CNS." Furthermore, the written agreement stated that

it was conditioned on the preparation, approval, and execution of a definitive acquisition agreement, the approval of the parties' boards of directors, and agreement on numerous other contract terms. No further agreement was reduced to writing. Assuming the transaction is covered by the statute of frauds, is this writing sufficient to satisfy the statute of frauds so that SWT can enforce the agreement?

16 Construction and Interpretation of Contracts

16:1   Introduction

Language is not a precise tool. It is virtually impossible to write a contract that is not susceptible to varying interpretation. When a dispute arises about the meaning of a contract, and the parties cannot resolve the dispute, the courts may be called upon to interpret, or *construe*, the contract. Over time, principles of interpretation, or *rules of construction*, have evolved; these rules guide courts in choosing between alternative meanings of contract language. The rules of construction should be "taken with a grain of salt," however, because the court's goal in construing contract language is to ascertain and effect the probable intent of the parties. The rules of construction aid the courts; it is more accurate to think of them as guides to interpretation than as legal authority.

16:2   Principles of Interpretation

In seeking the probable intent of the parties, courts examine the language of the contract and, where necessary, the circumstances surrounding its formation. A court seeks to understand what a reasonable person in the same position as the parties would have understood the language to mean. Then the individual provisions of the contract may be interpreted to effect that intent. For example, courts assume that parties intend their entire contract to be enforceable. Thus, if a contract can be interpreted in two ways, one of which would make part of the contract unenforceable, the court will adopt the interpretation that enables the entire contract to be enforceable.

Contract as a Whole   The meaning of a contract is gathered from the entire context; particular words or isolated portions are viewed in light of the whole contract. If a contract consists of two or more instruments, such as a series of letters, all the instruments will be construed together. In trying to give meaning to the entire contract, a court may adopt the role of linguist or logician. Note, for example, the court's reasoning in the following case.

Chapman

v

Orange Rice Milling Co.
747 F2d 981 (1984)
United States Court of Appeals, Fifth Circuit

FACTS: Chapman owned 18,000 acres of wooded land. In June of 1967 he entered into a ten-year lease of the land with defendant Orange Rice Milling Company. Orange Mill agreed that "[d]uring the ten (10) year period of the lease" it would "clear and keep cleared a minimum of 7,000 acres." According to a schedule set in the lease, "a minimum of 700 acres" would be cleared "each year during said term with a minimum of 4,000 acres cleared on or before July 1, 1970." Orange Mill cleared 4,000 acres by July, 1970, as required. In 1978 the lease expired, and at that time both parties believed the contract was completed. In 1980, however, a Department of Agriculture study revealed that Orange Mill had cleared only 5,226 acres. Chapman sued for breach of contract. Orange Mill argued that its obligation to clear 7,000 would have been due in July of 1975, and any breach of contract would have taken place then. Because the statute of limitations bars lawsuits not brought within four years of breach, Orange Mill claimed that Chapman should be barred from pressing his claim. Chapman argued that the contract did not require completion until 1978 and that therefore it was not too late for him to sue Orange Mill.

ISSUE: Did the contract require Orange Mill to clear 4,000 acres by July 1970 and an additional 700 acres per year thereafter, or only to clear an additional 3,000 acres between July 1970 and the end of the lease period?

RESULT: Orange Mill was not obligated to complete the additional 3,000 acres until the end of the lease period.

REASONING:

* * *

. . . Our judicial task is said to be "restricted to the interpretation of the contract as the parties made it for themselves." . . . In so doing, we must abide by tenets of contract construction and seek to ascertain the true intentions of the parties by examining *"the entire writing* in an effort to harmonize and give effect to *all the provisions* of the contract so that none will be rendered meaningless." . . . We must honor the presumption that parties to a contract intend every clause to have some effect, and attempt to reconcile ambiguous provisions unless they are "irreconcilable," . . . or "necessarily repugnant." . . .

We do not read the lease to require that as of July 1, 1970, a minimum of 700 acres would "thereafter" be cleared each year. The lease required Orange Rice Milling to clear at least 7,000 acres "during the ten (10) year period of this lease." It then scheduled such clearing in increments of "a minimum of 700 acres each year *during said term*." (emphasis added). There is no "thereafter" in the contractual language. The trial court's insertion of this implicit deadline added an unintended term to the parties' contract. Construing the lease to require that all clearing be complete by July of 1975, at the end of eight years, does not give meaning to the provision that 7,000 acres be cleared "during the ten (10) year period of [the] lease." Nor can the requirement that a *minimum* of 700 acres be cleared *each* year be read, in harmony with other lease provisions, as a requirement that land be cleared in each year of the lease. Obviously, if 4,000 acres were to be cleared in the first three years of the lease, clearing 700 acres each year thereafter would require that some 8,900 acres be cleared, rather than the contracted for ceiling of 7,000 acres. We must attempt to harmonize "700 acres each year" with 4,000 acres by 1970, and 7,000 acres during ten years. This harmony is found by reading the lease to require a rate of clearing whereby the total acreage to be cleared at any given time was a multiple of the lease year and seven hundred, subject to the requirement that the lessee have created an initial "balance" of 4,000 cleared acres by July 1, 1970. Under this construction, by the eighth year a total of 5,600 acres were to be cleared, regardless of whether 700 acres were actually cleared each year. The lease schedule would thus ensure sufficient spreading of the clearing obligation so that the bulk of the clearing would not be deferred until the end of the lease.

Thus, as we read the lease, Orange Rice Milling had until June 31, 1977, to clear the 7,000 acres. It was not until then that this obligation could have been breached. . . .

Higginbotham, Circuit Judge.

Meaning of Words   The words used in a contract will be given their ordinary meaning, unless the contract shows that they are used in some other sense. Words with an established legal meaning are presumed to have that meaning when used in a contract, unless a contrary intent clearly appears. Words of art or words connected with a particular trade are to be given the meaning attached to them by experts in such art or trade, even though it may differ from the usual meaning. Similarly, technical words are ordinarily to be interpreted as they are usually understood by persons in the profession or business involved.

Conflicting Provisions   If there are conflicting provisions in a contract, the court will first attempt to reconcile them. If the conflict is irreconcilable, the court will normally enforce the provision that ties in more closely with the contract's general purpose. If a contract contains conflicting general and special provisions relating to the same thing, the special provisions will control. Handwritten provisions prevail over contradictory typewritten ones, and typewritten provisions prevail over conflicting printed provisions. For example, when a contract consists of a standardized form with blanks filled in, those portions that have been filled in by the parties will be enforced over conflicting portions of the standardized form.

Interpretation Against Drafting Party   A contract that contains ambiguous language will be interpreted against the party who drafted the contract or who selected the particular language in issue. This rule is especially applicable to adhesion contracts.[1]

Implied Terms or Promises   Every contract carries an implied promise of good faith and fair dealing. Each party has an implied obligation not to do anything intentionally to prevent the other party from carrying out his part of the agreement. The UCC also imposes an obligation of good faith in the performance or enforcement of every contract, requiring that the parties act honestly with each other [UCC §§ 1-201(19), 1-203]. There may be other implied terms or promises that necessarily flow from the provisions of a contract. For example, if a contract specified no time for performance, the allowance of a reasonable time will be implied.

Consideration of Surrounding Circumstances   In determining the meaning of uncertain provisions or clauses, the court may consider the surrounding circumstances at the time the contract was made. In placing itself in the positions occupied by the parties when the agreement was executed, the court will attempt to ascertain the parties' purpose and intention so that it can ascribe meaning to the ambiguous provisions.

Practical Construction by Parties   Often the parties will have performed under a contract for some time before a dispute arises. The court will give great weight to the practical construction placed on the contract as a result of the parties' course of conduct. Under the UCC, a *course of performance* accepted or acquiesced in by the parties without objection is relevant in determining the meaning of a sales contract [UCC § 2-208].

EXAMPLE: A magazine publisher uses a standard form for its contract with the authors from whom it solicits articles. The form provides that the article contracted for will be "about _____ pages in length," and the blank is filled in each time a new contract is prepared. Robinson, an author, has contributed a number of articles to the publisher, each under a separate contract. In the past, the publisher has always accepted articles that varied in length by up to 20 percent from the length stated in the contract. Robinson's most recent submission was supposed to be "about 50 pages in length," but its actual length is 59 pages. The publisher

---

[1] Adhesion contracts are discussed in Chapter 12.

rejects the article, claiming that "about" as used in the contract means plus or minus no more than 5 percent. If Robinson sues the publisher, the court will probably find that "about," as used in this contract, means plus or minus 20 percent.

Course of Dealing and Usage of Trade   Often the parties to a contract have had earlier dealings with one another, and certain understandings have been established between them. Under the UCC, "a course of dealing is a sequence of previous conduct between the parties to a particular transaction which is fairly to be regardéd as establishing a common basis of understanding for interpreting their expressions and other conduct" [UCC § 1-205(1)]. Also, persons in a particular business may engage in certain practices with such repetition that these practices become known as *business or trade customs or usages*. Under the UCC, "a usage of trade is any practice or method of dealing having such regularity of observance in a place, vocation or trade as to justify an expectation that it will be observed with respect to the transaction in question" [UCC § 1-205(2)]. Parties entering into a specific contract often do so with such prior dealings or customs or usages in mind. Under the common law, evidence of prior dealings between the parties, or of trade customs or usages, could be utilized to determine the meaning of terms in the contract in issue. Likewise, under the UCC a *course of dealing* or a usage of trade gives particular meaning to and supplements or qualifies the terms of an agreement, provided there is no conflict between the express terms of the contract and the course of dealing or usage of trade [UCC § 1-205(3), (4)].

Under the UCC, express terms of a contract, course of performance, course of dealing, and usage of trade are to be interpreted as being consistent with each other whenever it is reasonable to do so. When there are irreconcilable conflicts, the order of priority is as follows: (1) express terms, (2) course of performance, (3) course of dealing, and (4) usage of trade [UCC §§ 1-205(4), 2-208(2)].

16:3 Parol Evidence Rule

Contract negotiations are often complex and time consuming. The parties may address certain areas of the transaction and come to tentative agreement, then move on to other negotiation areas. Ultimately, the parties reach final agreement and reduce their contract to writing. The precise form of the written contract is also negotiated. Promises made along the way may not end up in the final contract, either because the parties have changed their minds about the importance of the provision or because they have made strategic trade-offs for other terms in the written contract. The written contract embodies the parties' entire agreement. The agreements entered into in negotiation are assumed to have been either integrated into the final writing or not intended to be a part of it. The written contract, therefore, supersedes all previous verbal or written agreements.

These assumptions about the contract process and the finality of the written contract are embodied in the *parol evidence rule.* The parol evidence rule does not permit the parties to attempt to prove the existence of agreements made prior to the final written contract or of oral agreements made at the same time as the final written contract. The rule also excludes proof of writings other than the final written contract.

The following case illustrates a court's use of the parol evidence rule to exclude proof of an earlier agreement.

International Administrators, Inc.
v
Life Ins. Co.
753 F2d 1373 (1985)
United States Court of Appeals, Seventh Circuit

FACTS: IAI, an insurance broker, asked LINA, a Pennsylvania corporation, to underwrite various insurance policies for the Iowa American Legion. In November 1978 the parties exchanged writings covering the major aspects of the underwriting agreement, including the commission due IAI. In January 1979 the parties entered into a written agreement covering the same subject matter as the November 1978 agreement. When LINA paid a commission lower than what was agreed on in the November 1978 agreement, IAI sued for breach of contract. LINA defended that the parol evidence rule bars IAI from offering proof of the 1978 contract.

ISSUE: Was the January 1979 agreement intended to be an integrated agreement on commissions?

RESULT: The January 1979 agreement was intended to embody all of the terms of the contract, thereby barring proof of terms found in earlier communications.

REASONING:

*   *   *

The January 9, 1979, agreement, signed by both parties, sets out "the commission" payable on a number of policies, including those mentioned in the November 22 letter. In Illinois, the parol evidence rule excludes evidence which would change the meaning of a written document, if the evidence concerns dealings prior to the writing. . . . Where a written agreement shows a complete legal obligation, without uncertainty as to the object and extent of the obligation, evidence of an earlier agreement cannot be introduced to add another term to the agreement, even though the earlier agreement may contain writing on the particular term to which the evidence is directed. . . . It is clear that the January 9, 1979, agreement covers commissions on all of the policies mentioned in the November 22 letter; there is no reason to suppose that only part of the commission is the subject of the agreement. Since the later agreement purports to cover all the commission arrangements, it is not really necessary to consider whether the earlier letter was in fact an agreement. IAI's offer of evidence that the drafter of the November 22 letter from LINA intended it to be the final agreement (evidence which, as we will see, is less than convincing in light of the wording of the document) is therefore irrelevant.

We note, however, that the earlier letter does not purport to be an agreement. The November 22 letter begins: "The following is a synopsis of our continuing discussion on these risks [policies]." The last paragraph but one discusses the merits of various ways of apportioning certain allowances. It would be difficult to support the conclusion that this letter constituted a final agreement rather than a step in an ongoing series of negotiations. The same is true of a letter of November 27, 1978, which IAI introduced on appeal, though not at trial. . . . This second letter amends several parts of the November 22 letter, and the second letter's existence makes clearer the fact that negotiations were ongoing. We conclude that the January 9, 1979, agreement was intended to be an integrated agreement covering the subject matter, though not including all the terms, of the November 22, 1978, letter, and that this intention is evident from the document itself. . . .

Cudahy, Circuit Judge.

 It is not uncommon for people to rely on oral promises as qualifying written contracts, but under the parol evidence rule this reliance is usually misplaced. People may protect themselves from disappointment by asking that oral promises be put in writing at the time the deal is concluded. If the other party does not wish to place these promises in the body of the written contract, they may be attached to the contract and incorporated by reference. This makes them an integral part of the contract. Otherwise, a court will usually find them to have been superseded by the signing of the written contract.

The parol evidence rule applies to all written contracts, whether or not they are required by the statute of frauds to be in writing. It applies, moreover, to all terms of a written contract, whether express or implied. Thus, for example, if a written contract specifies no time for performance, a reasonable time will be implied, and parol evidence will be inadmissible to establish some other specific time for performance, since that would amount to varying the contract.

The UCC has codified the parol evidence rule with respect to sales contracts, but has liberalized the rule somewhat. Unless the court finds the writing to have been intended as a complete and exclusive statement of the terms of the agreement, the UCC permits final written agreements to be explained or supplemented by evidence concerning course of dealing, usage of trade, or course of performance, as well as evidence of consistent additional terms [UCC § 2-202].

Partial Integration   Courts apply the parol evidence rule only when they have determined that the parties' final agreement has been reduced to writing and that the contract before the court constitutes the parties' final and entire agreement. A party may avoid application of the rule by proving that the written instrument is not the complete contract between the parties. A contract may be *partially integrated*. That is, the contract may supersede prior negotiations on only those matters that are integrated into the final written contract and not supersede negotiated agreements in areas that are not integrated into the contract. Both the written and oral portions of a partially integrated contract may be enforced; evidence may be introduced to prove the oral portion and its terms so long as such evidence does not conflict with the written terms.

 The parties to a contract often insert a clause to the effect that the writing contains the entire and final agreement of the parties and that all prior negotiations and agreements are merged in the writing. Such a clause might serve to alert both parties to the fact that they should not rely on any statements or assurances made during negotiations. Courts give great weight to this type of clause in determining whether there has been total or partial integration. It may be particularly important in any situation where there might otherwise be doubt.

The following case illustrates the type of analysis that often is necessary in interpreting a contract and determining the applicability of the parol evidence rule.

Brown

v

Financial Service Corp., International
489 F2d 144 (1974)
United States Court of Appeals, Fifth Circuit

FACTS: In November 1968 Brown was hired by Financial Service Corporation (FSC) as vice-president and director of a subsidiary. The compensation package included an agreement to sell Brown 4,000 shares of FSC's closely (nonpublicly) held stock at $5 per share. In May 1969 Branch, FSC's assistant secretary, wrote Brown a letter concerning the stock purchase. Enclosed was a stock purchase agreement, which contained a stock repurchase option providing that if Brown ceased working for FSC, "the Company shall have one year from the date of such termination to repurchase any shares . . . for their fair market value." In response to the letter, Brown called Branch to discuss the stock purchase.

In June 1969 Brown returned the signed stock purchase agreement, with a cover letter stating: "I wanted also to confirm the discussion you and I had yesterday on the phone on questions that I had raised. Referring to the termination of employment clause in the stock purchase agreement, while it is stated that the company shall have one year to repurchase any shares, we agreed that the company would repurchase almost immediately after termination." When FSC terminated Brown's employment in January 1970, FSC refused to repurchase the stock, despite Brown's desire to sell it. Brown sued, claiming breach of contract. The district court, applying Florida law, held that the parol evidence rule precluded consideration of discussions between Branch and Brown, as well as Brown's cover letter. The court granted judgment to FSC, from which judgment Brown appealed.

ISSUE: Is evidence of the oral conversation and the cover letter barred by the parol evidence rule?

RESULT: The cover letter, which embodied the oral conversation, was part of the contract; therefore, evidence of the letter is not barred by the parol evidence rule.

REASONING:

*   *   *

The flaw in the trial court's analysis is its implicit conclusion that the stock purchase agreement represented the complete agreement of the parties and that therefore Brown's cover letter had no legal significance according to the parol evidence rule. The parol evidence rule is a rule of the substantive law of contract, and its purpose is to preserve the sanctity of a written agreement once it is determined that the writing fully states the agreement of the parties. . . . Of necessity then the first question is whether the writing fulfills this function so as to be an integration of the [parties] understanding. . . . To answer this question a court should consider the writing as well as the circumstances surrounding its execution, . . . and parol and extrinsic evidence may be used in making this determination. . . .

Without doubt a covering letter may constitute a part of the total agreement. . . . Here the cover letter itself clearly establishes that its purpose was to summarize in writing the content of a telephonic conversation concerning the purchase agreement; the cover letter specifically discusses terms of the stock purchase agreement. Moreover, the letter not only accompanied but was a cover to the signed stock purchase agreement when it was returned to Branch's office in Atlanta. And finally, Branch realized that at least to some extent the letter modified the terms of the purchase agreement. In short, the existence of the cover letter and the circumstances surrounding the execution of the stock purchase agreement preclude the conclusion that it was intended by the parties as the final memorial, the integration, of their understanding concerning the terms of the stock sale. Consideration of the cover letter would not, therefore, violate the parol evidence rule because the cover letter was a part of the contract. . . .

The decision that the parties' contract is embodied in both the cover letter and the stock purchase agreement does not, of course, end the matter. For now there are arguably inconsistent contractual provisions dealing with the same subject matter—that is, the rights and duties of the parties on the purchaser's termination of employment. . . . [T]he cover letter says "we agree that the company would repurchase almost immediately after termination." Interpreting these words in the manner urged by Brown would lead to the conclusion that this language means that the company had an obligation to repurchase the stock and that this repurchase must occur immediately after termination. . . . Obviously this interpretation is in direct conflict with the interpretation of the agreement as giving the company an option to repurchase but imposing no affirmative duty.

There is, however, another interpretation which could be accorded to this language from the cover letter. . . . [I]t could be interpreted as imposing only a duty on the company to exercise its option immediately on termination. In the circumstances of this case it is this interpretation which we adopt as representing the intention of the parties at the time this contract was consummated. We reach this conclusion on the basis of the following analysis in which we apply several well established principles for the interpretation and construction of contracts.

The first principle is that in interpreting contractual language to determine the rights and obligations of the parties to the agreement the contract must be considered as a whole in an effort to give meaning to all of its provisions. . . . To interpret the language in Brown's letter as creating a duty in the company to repurchase his stock would render completely nugatory one of the crucial provisions of the document which he signed and returned to FSC. We would have to totally disregard the language in the purchase agreement conferring an option to the company to repurchase. By interpreting the disputed language in Brown's letter as going only to the time of repurchase rather than establishing such a duty, we afford meaning and significance to all parts of the contract. This interpretation also fulfills our duty to reconcile provisions which at first glance appear repugnant to each other. . . .

Another established rule of contract interpretation . . . is that courts may look to subsequent action of the parties to determine the interpretation that they themselves placed on the contractual language. . . . The conduct of both parties subsequent to Brown's termination leaves us convinced that neither FSC nor Brown believed that the company had an affirmative duty to repurchase shares.

The voluminous record . . . is replete with correspondence from Brown to FSC and vice versa. A good portion of these communications deal directly with the disposition of Brown's stock. . . . But none of his many letters exhorting the company to hurry up and repurchase his stock speak in terms of an affirmative obligation on the part of FSC. Likewise, when FSC offered to repurchase and hold the proceeds until the final accounting was completed, the offer spoke in terms of FSC's right to repurchase instead of a duty to do so. . . . The extensive correspondence between Brown and FSC simply does not support the interpretation now sought by Brown. Considering the contract as a whole, the circumstances surrounding its execution, and the conduct of the parties subsequent thereto, our conclusion is that this contract does not impose a duty on FSC to repurchase the 4,000 shares of stock issued to Brown. . . .

Ingraham, Circuit Judge.

16:4   Exceptions to Parol Evidence Rule

The courts have recognized a number of exceptions to the parol evidence rule. A discussion of some of the more important exceptions follows.

Prior or Contemporaneous Collateral Agreements   Parties often enter into several separate contracts. Parol evidence may be used to prove the existence of any prior or contemporaneous oral agreement that is independent of, collateral to, and not inconsistent with the written contract. In determining whether an oral agreement was indeed separate, the primary test is again the parties' intent. If it is reasonable to assume that both the oral and written agreements are intended to be included in the same contract, then it will usually be held that the oral agreement was integrated in the final written contract. However, if it is reasonable to assume that the parties might have executed the oral contract separate from the written contract, then parol evidence is permissible to prove the existence and terms of the oral agreement.

Subsequent Parol Agreements or Modifications   In the absence of a statute providing otherwise, the parties to a written contract may orally agree to modify or cancel that contract and to enter a new one. Parol evidence is admissible to show this modification or cancellation. Parties often insert in the contract a provision that requires any modification to be in writing. Even when this clause is included, however, the courts generally permit parol evidence to be introduced to prove that an oral modification was made.

Fraud and Related Matters   To show that there was no valid written contract, parol evidence is admissible in cases of fraud, misrepresentation, mutual or unilateral mistake, duress, or undue influence.

 Parol evidence is often presented to prove that the failure to include an oral promise or guaranty in the final written contract was fraudulent. These claims are favorably received, particularly with contracts between a consumer and a businessperson. It is always better, however, to read a contract carefully and to insist that it contain all the provisions agreed on prior to signing, than to seek a means of evading the parol evidence rule when a dispute arises after signing. Moreover, when the parties involved are both businesses of relatively equal bargaining power, claims of fraud are likely to be less well received, particularly if there is a clause in the written contract indicating that it is the final and entire agreement of the parties.

Contractual Interpretation   When a contract contains ambiguous or otherwise uncertain terms or provisions, parol evidence may be admitted to assist the court in determining the meaning of the uncertain provisions. However, if the ambiguity can be resolved from the instrument itself in accordance with the established rules of contractual interpretation, parol evidence may be held inadmissible. For example, in a case in which a typewritten provision conflicts with a printed one, reliance on the rule giving priority to the typewritten provision could resolve the conflict without resorting to parol evidence. Parol evidence is admissible to define and explain the meaning of technical words or phrases in a written contract (unless the contract itself defines them). Parol evidence may also be admitted to supply an obvious omission in a written contract.

Conditions Precedent   The existence of a contract may be, and frequently is, premised on the occurrence or performance of some prior act, which is called a condition precedent. Parol evidence may be introduced to prove the existence or nonexistence of the condition, and, therefore, of a valid contract.

Key Concepts and Terms

- In interpreting a contract, a court will seek to ascertain and give effect to the parties' intent. A contract is construed as a whole, and, where possible, conflicting provisions are reconciled. Ambiguous language is interpreted against the drafter. Certain obligations, such as those of good faith and fair dealing, are considered to be implied promises in a contract.
- Words in a contract are given their ordinary meaning, unless the contract shows that they are used in some other sense, or unless they have some established legal or technical meaning.
- Course of performance, course of dealing, and usage of trade may be considered in determining a contract's meaning.
- When an agreement has been reduced to writing, the writing becomes the contract, and all prior negotiations are integrated into the written contract.
- Under the parol evidence rule, oral and other extrinsic evidence cannot be used to prove the existence of prior agreements or contemporaneous oral agreements that vary or contradict the final written contract.
- Parol evidence can, however, be used to prove the existence of (1) prior or contemporaneous collateral agreements, (2) fraud, (3) a condition precedent,

or (4) subsequent parol agreements or modifications. It can also be used to help interpret ambiguous provisions in a written contract.

- A partially integrated agreement is an agreement that is partially in writing and partially oral. Parol evidence is admissible to prove the existence of the nonwritten portion.

- Collateral Agreement
- Contract Construction
- Course of Dealing
- Course of Performance
- Custom or Usage of Trade
- Parol Evidence Rule
- Partial Integration
- Rules of Construction

Questions and Case Problems

1. In 1951 Matula granted the gas company an easement to lay a pipeline through his property. Their agreement contained (1) a printed clause providing that an additional line could be laid in the future, parallel to and not more than 16 feet from the original one; and (2) a handwritten provision that stated: "line to be laid within 50' of the North Property Line." The first line was placed within the 50-foot limitation. In 1968, the gas company decided to lay the second pipeline within 16 feet of the first line, but more than 50 feet from the north boundary. When Matula raised the 50-foot limitation, the gas company replied that the limitation applied only to the first line. Matula sued. Who should prevail?

2. In 1960 Turski became an employee of Park Company and a member of Park's profit-sharing plan. Turski worked for Park until she was discharged in 1973, at which time she had vested rights in the plan worth over $15,000. When Turski went to work for a competing business, Park informed her that she was ineligible for plan benefits under a provision in the written plan disqualifying persons who "enter into a business competitive with the Company." Turski sued to recover the plan benefits. Park sought to prove that when it drafted the plan, it intended the above provision to include employment by a competing business. Should Turski recover?

3. Lane enters into a lease for office space. The lease provides that no rent will be due until the premises are modified to Lane's satisfaction. Lane then asks Specht, the landlord, to make alterations that are structurally impossible. Specht refuses to make the alterations, and Lane refuses to pay rent. Specht then sues Lane. Decide the case.

4. Bay Carpets obtains a job to install carpets in a motel. The carpets have to be ready for installation within 15 days. Bay asks Modern Carpets if it can supply the carpets. Modern replies that it can, but that the carpets will have to be specially dyed. Bay and Modern then execute a purchase order contract for the carpets. In the space for "date required" Bay's president writes "at once." It takes Modern a month to fill the order. By this time Bay has lost its installation contract, and therefore Bay refuses to accept the carpets. A lawsuit follows with Bay and Modern each claiming breach of contract. At trial Modern seeks, over Bay's objection, to present testimony that the phrase "at once" as used in the carpet industry means "as soon as possible," and that one month was a reasonable time for production. Should the testimony be admitted? Under the UCC?

5. In 1970 Lawter and Town & Country Shop entered into a lease that required Lawter to pay a "fixed minimum rent" of $742.88 per month plus additional

charges for taxes and utilities. During the time that lease was in effect Lawter paid additional charges ranging between $881.09 and $1,010.01 per month. In 1972 the parties entered into a new lease that called for a "fixed minimum rent" of $1,566.34, but the word "minimum" was marked through with a solid ink line and the parties' initials appeared in the margin alongside the word. When a conflict arose concerning the amount of money due Town & Country, Lawter sought to introduce evidence of an oral understanding about the charges that were included in the rent in the 1972 lease. Is such evidence barred by the parol evidence rule?

6. Ross orally negotiates with Stinnett to have a house built on Ross's property. After reaching agreement on plans and specifications, the parties execute a written contract by which Stinnett is to build the house for $24,500. After the house is built at a cost to Stinnett of almost $24,000, he demands payment from Ross of cost plus 15 percent, in reliance on an alleged oral agreement entered prior to the written contract. Ross refuses. Stinnett sues, claiming that the recital of consideration in the written contract was a sham executed to enable Ross to obtain a loan and that the oral agreement was the true contract. Decide the case.

7. The Willards owned 27 acres of land which Dean Operations, a real estate developer, sought to acquire in order to construct a dam and create a lake. Dean and the Willards entered into a contract that involved both the Willards' exchange of their acreage for waterfront lots and an option to purchase the property in favor of Dean. The contract provided: "In the event the lake construction is not started by June 17, 1980, or in the event the party of the second part does not exercise its option to purchase by June 17, 1980, this contract shall become null and void." No work was done on the dam or lake. On June 12, 1980, Dean attempted to exercise its option. The Willards refused to sell, arguing that the contract was null and void because lake construction had not started by June 17, 1980. What does "or" mean in this contract?

8. Ayala enters into negotiations with Bauer, a longtime friend of and salesman for Chan, to purchase an airplane with custom features from Chan. During the negotiations Bauer orally assures Ayala that if Ayala changes her mind the order can be canceled and her $500 deposit returned. Bauer also sends Ayala a handwritten note reiterating that assurance. Ayala later signs a formal purchase contract, agreeing to purchase the plane for $40,000, and to be liable for any damages sustained by Chan in the event of a breach of the agreement. Subsequently, Ayala cancels the purchase order, and Chan retains the $500 deposit and sues for $4,000 in damages sustained by Ayala's breach. Can Ayala present evidence of Bauer's promise? If so, is Bauer's promise a part of the contract?

9. Fanning wants a new building for his automobile dealership. In preliminary negotiations with Stevens, an architect, Fanning tells him that the building must contain at least 40,000 square feet and cost no more than $250,000. A written contract is executed. One of its provisions states that Stevens is to design "a multiple-purpose building suitable to the needs of the Owner, at an approximate cost of $250,000." Stevens eventually submits two designs: one based on steel-frame construction at under $250,000, and one based on prestressed-concrete construction at $317,000. Fanning claims that subsequent to the written agreement the parties had orally agreed that the design was to be prestressed-concrete. Fanning terminates the contract for failure to perform, and Stevens sues Fanning for breach of contract. How should the provision as to estimated cost be inter-

preted? Should evidence of the parties' prior oral negotiations be admitted? Evidence of the alleged subsequent agreement?

10. Gans, a contractor, desires to subcontract a job requiring installation of a generator and accessories. She gives Wilson specifications for the equipment and asks if he can provide and install it. Wilson says that he can, and Gans orally places an order with Wilson for the specified equipment. A purchase order is later filled out; this order merely refers to the specified generator "with accessories." Wilson provides the generator specified and the accessories that normally come with it. The specifications, however, called for different accessories. New accessories have to be ordered, resulting in costly delays to Gans, and she sues Wilson for breach of contract. At trial, disputes arise as to the admissibility of the following evidence: (1) the oral order and oral negotiations preceding it and (2) the written specifications. Resolve those disputes.

17 Rights of Third Persons

17:1 Introduction

Ordinarily, only the parties to a contract have enforceable rights in the contract. This is consistent with the theory that contracts are consensual in nature and are binding only on those who consent to be bound by entering into the contract. Under some circumstances, however, a third person may have such an interest in the contract, either as a third-party beneficiary or as an assignee of the contract, that it is proper to permit that person's enforcement of the contract. In addition, a third person may sometimes acquire rights by means of a contract of novation. Third-party beneficiary contracts, assignments of contracts, and contracts of novation will be discussed in this chapter.

17:2 Third-Party Beneficiary Contracts

When two people enter a contract they do so usually to benefit themselves. It is quite possible, however, for one or both parties to execute a contract with the intent of benefitting a third person. Such a contract is known as a *third-party beneficiary contract,* and the third person is known as the *third-party beneficiary.* The basic model of such a contract is quite simple: A promises to perform work for B; B promises to pay money to C. As to the promise to pay C, B is a promisor, A is a promisee, and C is the third-party beneficiary. Whether, and to what extent, C can sue B to enforce the contract depends on the intentions of A and B in entering into the contract.

A may owe money to C and enter into the contract with B to provide the means to repay C. C would be regarded as a *creditor–beneficiary,* a type of third-party beneficiary, and C would be entitled to enforce B's promise to pay. Of course, C would not be able to enforce the contract until A performed and B, therefore, was obligated to pay.

Alternatively, A may enter into a contract with B in order to effect a gift to C. In that circumstance, C would be regarded as a *donee–beneficiary* and would be entitled to enforce the contract against B. For example, A may hire B, a lawyer, to draft A's will to benefit C. If B fails, through negligence, to accomplish this goal in the will drafting, C may sue B for negligent performance of the contract. Life insurance contracts are another good example of a contract for the benefit of a donee: the promisee pays premiums and the promisor agrees to pay the third-party beneficiary at the promisee's death.

The crucial factor in determining whether a third person is entitled to enforce a contract as a third-party beneficiary is whether the parties to the contract intended to benefit the third person. Thus, the third party is entitled to enforcement when the parties clearly intended the contract to be for her benefit. Enforcement by a third person will be denied when that person is only an *incidental beneficiary* of the contract. Contracts often provide unintended benefits to third persons, but the fact that a contract's performance will in some way benefit a third person is not by itself sufficient to confer a right of enforcement on that person. For example, if A promises to lend B money to pay her expenses, performance of the loan contract will obviously benefit the creditors of B. The intent of A and B was, however, to benefit themselves, and the benefit to B's creditors is merely incidental. B's creditors do not have the status of third-party beneficiaries and therefore are not entitled to enforce the contract.

The purpose of permitting the third-party beneficiary to enforce the contract is a practical one. In many instances, only the beneficiary is harmed by the breach of the contract. This is obvious in the life insurance contract situation, with the donee–beneficiary. In the creditor–beneficiary situation, the creation of third-party rights simply facilitates the repayment of the debt; by permitting the beneficiary to sue the promisor directly, the need for two enforcement actions is eliminated.

The careful reader should notice that the beneficiary will have no right to performance from the promisor until the promisor's obligation has arisen under the terms of the contract. Thus, if the promisor has a valid defense for not performing, that defense is as good against the third-party beneficiary as it would be against the promisee.

The following classic case illustrates how public policy considerations influence a court in deciding whether a person is a third-party beneficiary.

H. R. Moch Co.

v

Rensselaer Water Co.
159 NE 896 (1928)
New York Court of Appeals

FACTS: Rensselaer Water Company contracted with the city of Rensselaer to supply water, including water at fire hydrants. Moch's warehouse caught fire and was destroyed, due to the water company's failure to supply adequate water pressure at the hydrants. Moch sued for damages. He claimed that he was a third-party beneficiary and that there was a breach of the contract between the water company and the city.

ISSUE: Can Moch enforce the contract between Rensselaer Water Company and the city as a third-party beneficiary?

RESULT: Moch is only an incidental beneficiary of the contract.

REASONING:

*   *   *

We think the action is not maintainable as one for breach of contract.

No legal duty rests upon a city to supply its inhabitants with protection against fire. . . . That being so, a member of the public may not maintain an action . . . against one contracting with the city to furnish water at the hydrants, unless an intention appears that the promisor is to be answerable to individual members of the public as well as to the city for any loss ensuing from the failure to fulfill the promise. No such intention is discernible here. On the contrary, the contract is significantly divided into two branches: One a promise to the city for the benefit of the city in its corporate capacity, in which branch is included the service at the hydrants; and the other a promise to the city for the benefit of private takers, in which branch is included the service at their homes and factories. In a broad sense it is true that every city contract, not improvident or wasteful, is for the benefit of the public. More than this, however, must be shown to give a right of action to a member of the public not formally a party. The benefit, as it is sometimes said, must be one that is not merely incidental and secondary. . . . It must be primary and immediate in such a sense and to such a degree as to bespeak the assumption of a duty to make reparation directly to the individual members of the public if the benefit is lost. The field of obligation would be expanded beyond reasonable limits if less than this were to be demanded as a condition of liability. A promisor undertakes to supply fuel for heating a public building. He is not liable for breach of contract to a visitor who finds the building without fuel, and thus contracts a cold. The list of illustrations can be indefinitely extended. The carrier of the mails under contract with the government is not answerable to the merchant who has lost the benefit of a bargain through negligent delay. The householder is without a remedy against manufacturers of hose and engines, though prompt performance of their contracts would have stayed the ravages of fire. . . .

So with the case at hand. By the vast preponderance of authority, a contract between a city and a water company to furnish water at the city hydrants has in view a benefit to the public that is incidental rather than immediate, an assumption of duty to the city and not to its inhabitants. . . . An intention to assume an obligation of indefinite extension to every member of the public is seen to be the more improbable when we recall the crushing burden that the obligation would impose. . . . If the plaintiff is to prevail, one who negligently omits to supply sufficient pressure to extinguish a fire started by another assumes an obligation to pay the ensuing damage, though the whole city is laid low. A promisor will not be deemed to have had in mind the assumption of a risk so overwhelming for any trivial reward. . . .

Cardozo, Circuit Judge.

17:3   Assignment of Contract

With few exceptions, a party to a contract may transfer his or her rights under the contract to a third person. The transfer is known as an *assignment*, the party making the assignment is the *assignor*, and the person to whom the assignment is made is the *assignee*. The other party to the contract is referred to as an *obligor* or a debtor or some other designation, depending on the nature of the rights assigned. A party may also transfer obligations under a contract to a third person. This type of transfer is not an assignment but is known as a delegation of duties and is discussed later in this chapter.

Most contractual rights are assignable. A party to a contract may assign all or part of his rights to an assignee, with or without the consent of the other party to the contract. Perhaps the most common type of assignment is the transfer of the right to receive money due or to become due under a contract. For example, in a contract for the sale of goods or services the seller often does not receive immediate payment, but does not wish to wait to receive the money due. The seller may therefore enter into a contract with a third person, under which the seller assigns the right to the payment to the third person in exchange for the third person's payment of some lesser amount to the seller. In this way, the right to receive the money due under the original contract has been transferred by the seller (assignor) to the third person (assignee), to whom the original purchaser (obligor) now owes the duty of payment.

Form of Assignment   In the absence of statutory regulation, an assignment need not be made in any particular form. Any language that sufficiently indicates a party's intent to transfer his rights under a contract will suffice. An assignment may be oral or written, unless it is required by statute to be written.

Nonassignable Contracts   Certain types of contracts or contractual rights are not assignable, unless the obligor consents to the assignment. Among the more important types of nonassignable contracts are the following:

(1) Contracts that involve a close personal relationship. They include contracts for personal services, contracts for professional services, and contracts that involve a relationship of confidence. For example, under an employment contract, the employer cannot ordinarily assign the right to the employee's services to a third person. Likewise, a person who is entitled to a lawyer's or doctor's services cannot assign these services to a third person. It should be noted, however, that a right to the payment that is to be received for services

is assignable. For example, a physician may assign his right to payment from a patient.

 Rights under a personal services contract may be assigned if the contract explicitly so provides or if both parties to the contract consent to the assignment. For example, contracts with professional athletes often contain clauses that permit the team employing the athlete to assign the right to the athlete's services to another team.

(2) Contracts that contain a provision restricting or prohibiting assignment of the contract. The courts generally will enforce anti-assignment provisions but interpret them narrowly and often insist that they be clear and explicit. For example, even though a contract contains a general provision stating that the contract is not assignable, a court will usually permit an assignment of the right to receive money due under the contract. A court may interprete the *nonassignment clause* to prohibit the delegation of duty to perform, but not the right to receive money. The parties to a contract may waive an anti-assignment provision.

(3) Contracts entered into in reliance by one party on the character or credit of the other party. In a contract of this type, the latter may not assign his rights under the contract. For example, if A agrees to loan B money in exchange for B's promise to make specified payments over a period of time, B may not assign his right under the contract to C, since A relied on B's credit in agreeing to the contract.

(4) Contracts whose assignability is limited by law. Many states have statutes that restrict or prohibit the assignment of certain interests, particularly wages. There are also statutes that specify certain formal requisites to the validity of these assignments.

In the following case, the court's reasoning reflects a preference not to enforce a nonassignment clause.

Paperchase Partnership
v
Bruckner
693 P2d 587 (1985)
Supreme Court of New Mexico

FACTS: In 1977 Paperchase sold an apartment complex to the Bruckners. The real estate contract contained a clause prohibiting assignment without Paperchase's consent. The contract provided for monthly payments and, in the event of nonpayment, for forfeiture of the property. In 1979 the Bruckners transferred their interest in the property to A & O Investments, without consent from Paperchase. All payments were made under the contract. However, Paperchase sued to recover the property, claiming that the unauthorized assignment constituted default under its real estate contract with the Bruckners.

ISSUE: Did the contract between the Bruckners and A & O constitute an impermissible assignment under the real estate contract?

RESULT: No. The contract between the Bruckners and A & O was a new contract, not an assignment of rights under the original contract.

REASONING:

* * *

According to the *Restatement (Second) of Contracts*, Section 328 (1979), unless a contrary intention appears from the language or the circumstances, an assignment of the contract is both an assignment of the assignor's rights and a delegation of his duties. But a provision prohibiting assignment of the contract bars only the delegation of duties. . . . Consequently, in most cases, if there is no delegation of duties, there is no violation of the prohibition on assignment.

Promissory restraints by a vendor on the interest of the vendee in land contracts are primarily security devices designed to make more certain the payment of the purchase price and often "it is important to the vendor that the particular individual be kept in contact with the land as an inducement to performance of his obligations." *Restatement of Property*, § 416 (1944), comment a. Even though the vendee has assigned the contract without the vendor's consent, however, if the assignee fully performs the vendee's duties under the contract, the assignee may demand specific performance by the vendor. . . . But until that time, the vendor is not required to recognize the assignee, nor to rely on him for payment of installments toward the purchase price. . . .

Once the meaning of and the reason for the prohibition on assignments is determined, we look to see whether the later transfers in this case violated that prohibition. There is no dispute regarding the performance by the parties under the terms of the various contracts. The question is merely the effect, if any, of those later transfers on the legal rights and duties of Paperchase and the Bruckners under the original contract. . . .

The district court determined that the Bruckner/A & O [contract] had no effect on the rights and duties of the parties to the original contract. That is, the Bruckners are still liable for the installment payments they agreed to undertake, and Paperchase cannot require return of the property or acceleration of the balance due in the absence of default in payments as they become due.

The district court concluded that the later transfers were not assignments of the original contract, but were independent contracts to sell. Since the Bruckner/A & O contract was not designed to relieve the Bruckners of their liabilities to Paperchase, we agree that that contract does not operate as a true assignment, and requires transfer of title to A & O only after the Bruckners have received title from Paperchase.

It is established that a subcontract by a purchaser to sell his interest under a contract of sale is a separate and independent contract between the purchaser and the subpurchaser, and does not meet the definition of an assignment. In *Bishop v. Barndt. . . .* the first purchaser's later contract to sell to a subpurchaser was held not to be an assignment since the subpurchaser, "assumed no obligations under that agreement towards [the original vendor] so as to bring herself into privity with her." [Also] the court ruled that an "entirely new and independent contract for sale" by the vendee under a land sale contract was not a violation of the original contract's prohibition against assignment.

Since neither the Bruckner/A & O or the A & O/Yu contracts attempted to relieve Bruckners of their responsibilities to Paperchase, the clause was not violated. The particular individuals on whom Paperchase chose to rely for payment of the purchase price, Bruckners, have remained in contact with the land and in privity of contract with Paperchase. . . .

Walters, Justice.

17:4   Rights of Assignee

The assignee of a contract acquires all the rights possessed by the assignor, but no more than that. Any defenses that the other party to the contract might have asserted against the assignor can also be asserted against the assignee in the event of an action for enforcement. Some states have adopted statutes to this effect.

17:5   Notice of Assignment

The obligor need not be notified of an assignment. However, if he is not notified, he is free to continue making payment to his original creditor (the assignor). Once the obligor has received notice of the assignment, he must make payments on the contract to the assignee.

An assignor sometimes makes a second or even a third assignment of the same contractual right to successive assignees. When several assignees claim the same right, a court must determine which assignee should receive priority. If the first assignee in time also was the first to give notice to the debtor, then that assignee is clearly entitled to priority. When a later assignee in time is the first assignee to give notice, the courts are not in agreement as to the priority. Some states determine priority on the basis of the time of notice, granting priority to the first assignee to give the debtor notice. Other states base priority on the time of assignment, granting priority to the first assignee in time. If, however, a debtor pays a later assignee before receiving the first assignee's notice, the first assignee will not have priority.

To protect his or her rights under an assignment, an assignee should always give prompt notice of the assignment to the debtor. This protects the assignee against both the possibility of further payments to the assignor and the risk that the assignor might make a second assignment of the same contract rights.

17:6 Delegation of Duties

An assignment of rights does not impose on the assignee any of the assignor's duties or liabilities to the other party to the contract. If the assignor wants to transfer these duties and liabilities, in addition to his rights, he may do so in a separate transaction. This transaction is called a *delegation of duties*, although it is often referred to merely as an assignment.

A party may delegate performance of his duties under a contract to a third person, provided that the third person's performance would be substantially the same as performance by the delegating party himself. For example, if a construction contract of a nonunique nature is involved, and if one contractor is equally as capable as another of performing the job, then the duty of performance can be delegated. However, if a party's personal acts and qualities are material ingredients of the contract, that party's duties may not be delegated to a third person without the other party's consent.

EXAMPLE: An opera association contracts with Mario, a charismatic operatic tenor, to give a recital. Mario can assign to anyone of his choice his right to receive the compensation agreed on for the recital. However, because of Mario's unique personality and skills, he cannot delegate to anyone else his duty to perform the recital, at least without the opera association's consent.

Assignor's Continuing Liability The assignor of a contract remains liable for performance of the contract even though he has delegated duties to the assignee, unless the other party to the contract consents to relieve the assignor of all further responsibility for performance.

17:7 Assignments Under the UCC

The UCC favors the assignability of contracts. Under the UCC, all rights in sales contracts are assignable unless assignment would (1) materially change the duty of the other party, (2) materially increase the burden or risk imposed on the other party, or (3) materially impair the other party's chance of obtaining return performance [UCC § 2-210(2)]. Moreover, unless the circumstances indicate otherwise, a clause that prohibits assignment of "the contract" bars only delegation of duties, not assignment of rights [UCC § 2-210(3)]. The UCC also permits delegation of duties unless the parties agree not to delegate or unless the other party has a substantial interest in having his original promisor perform the contract [UCC § 2-210(1)]. Indeed, under the UCC both an assignment of rights and a delegation of duties have been made if the assignment is made using terms such as "assignment of the contract" or "assignment of all my rights under the contract," unless the circumstances indicate otherwise [UCC § 2-210(4)].

The UCC provides that in a secured transaction,[1] a provision in a contract between an account debtor (the party obligated to pay on an account) and an assignor that prohibits assignment of the account is ineffective [UCC § 9-318(4)]. The UCC also provides that if the assignee must sue the account debtor to obtain payment, the account debtor may raise against the assignee all defenses that he has against the assignor [UCC § 9-318(1)]. The UCC also authorizes an account debtor to continue paying the assignor until he receives notice of the assignment [UCC § 9-318(3)].

17:8   Novation

A contract of *novation*, or simply novation, is an agreement among all parties concerned that (1) cancels an existing contract and (2) simultaneously creates a new one. If the new contract benefits a third party, it may have essentially the same effect as either a third-party beneficiary contract (if the initial parties had used such a contract in the first place) or an assignment. For example, assume that Ellis owes Freed $1,000, and Ellis contracts with Mirza to perform certain services in exchange for Mirza's payment of $1,000. If Ellis wants to use that $1,000 to discharge her obligation to Freed, there are various methods by which she may do so: (1) she may simply wait until she receives the money from Mirza, then pay Freed; (2) Ellis and Mirza may provide in their contract that the $1,000 be paid directly to Freed, thereby making Freed a third-party beneficiary; (3) Ellis may assign her right to the $1,000 to Freed; or (4) after Ellis has performed the services, the three may jointly agree that Mirza will pay the money to Freed and that Mirza' obligation to Ellis will be discharged immediately. The last alternative is a novation. As used in this situation, it creates a new contract between Freed and Mirza while extinguishing the original contract between Ellis and Mirza.

The following case illustrates how a single fact situation may create issues relating to assignments, delegations of duties, and novations.

Sisco

v

Empiregas, Inc. of Belle Mina
237 So2d 463 (1970)
Alabama Supreme Court

FACTS: Sisco was employed as a salesman for Gas and Chemicals, Inc., a liquefied petroleum gas (LP gas) dealer, under a contract executed March 24, 1967. The contract contained a noncompetition provision, prohibiting

---

[1] Secured transactions are discussed in detail in Chapters 29 and 30. Briefly, such a transaction is one in which one party gives to another an interest in personal property or fixtures to secure payment of a debt or performance of some other obligation.

Sisco from engaging in the LP gas business within a 50-mile radius of Jeff, Alabama, for five years after termination of employment. The employment relationship could be terminated by either party on 30 days' notice. Empiregas took over Gas and Chemicals' LP gas business, and Sisco was a salesman for Empiregas from January, 1969, until June 30, 1969, when he voluntarily terminated his employment and began working with another LP gas dealer in the same area. Empiregas sued to enforce the noncompetition clause. It claimed that Gas and Chemicals had assigned Sisco's employment contract to Empiregas. Sisco claimed that the employment contract was a nonassignable personal service contract.

ISSUE: Was Sisco's promise of noncompetition assignable by Gas and Chemicals to Empiregas?

RESULT: No. Sisco's promise was conditioned upon Gas and Chemicals' continued performance as the employer.

REASONING:

*   *   *

. . . Empiregas contends that the rule forbidding the assignment of personal services contracts means only that the "duty" of a party who has contracted to perform personally (the employee) cannot be performed by another (a delegate), that the rule does not prevent the party to whom the personal performance is due (the employer) from assigning his rights and delegating his duties. Under this view, it argues, the fact that Sisco had contracted to perform personally and could not delegate *his duties* did not prevent Gas and Chemicals from assigning *its rights* and delegating *its duties* under the contract. It is our view, hereinafter elaborated, that the performance owed by both Sisco and Gas and Chemicals was personal, and neither could delegate his (its) "duties."

We commence with the general proposition that personal service contracts are not assignable. . . . We think [the complaint] shows on its face that the contract here at issue involved a relationship of personal confidence between the parties. No other conclusion seems logical where the contract by its language permits the employer to discharge the employee on thirty days' notice and then to prevent him for five years from pursuing his livelihood over an area we judicially know to encompass some 7,850 square miles. . . . Surely, one would not be presumed to have intended to commit himself into the hands of a stranger so empowered, and the bill shows on its face that Gas and Chemicals was no stranger to Sisco, having been his employer for some two years and eight months prior to his execution of the contract at issue. These circumstances, we feel, demonstrate that Sisco relied upon the uniqueness of his corporate employer and their relationship of mutual confidence when he entered into this contract. . . .

Thus, it results that the assignee's (Empiregas') right to performance from Sisco (including performance of his covenant not to compete) is conditional upon personal performance of its duties by Gas and Chemicals. . . . The [complaint] does not allege that Gas and Chemicals has acted as Sisco's employer since the alleged assignment. On the contrary, it is clear that the alleged "assignment" of the contract was an attempt by Gas and Chemicals both to assign its "rights" and delegate its "duties." . . . Therefore, the conditions of Sisco's duty to perform having failed, the [complaint] shows that Empiregas, Inc. of Belle Mina has no right to performance from Sisco. . . .

Two additional situations are frequently cited as exceptions to the so-called rule against the assignment of personal services contracts. . . . First, it is said that the employee's "consent" to the assignment permits the attempted assignee to enforce the contract. Second, it is said that the employee's conduct in continuing in the employ of the assignee permits the assignee to enforce the contract, the theory being that the employee has thus "adopted" or "ratified" the contract. We think, however, that these two situations are improperly termed "exceptions." It appears to us that the effect of the employee's "consent" or of his continuing in the employment of the assignor ("adoption" or "ratification") is to create a new contract between employee and assignee rather than merely to permit the assignment of the old contract. . . .

To say that parties have adopted a contract, is . . . merely to say that they have entered into a new contract, referable to the old for its terms. The manifestation of assent required for the creation of this new contract must be as unambiguous and unequivocal as that required to create any other contract. . . .

Contractual obligations partake of a solemn character, and we should be zealous to ensure that no one is fettered who has not manifested his assent to be. The [complaint] did not expressly allege that Sisco and Empiregas entered into a new contract embracing all the terms of the contract between Sisco and Gas and Chemicals, nor did it allege conduct on the part of Sisco and Empiregas sufficiently unambiguous to constitute mutual assent to the terms of the Sisco-Gas and Chemicals contract. . . .

Bloodworth, Justice.

17:9 Combinations of Third-Party Rights

Although the various types of third-party rights have been discussed separately, it must be noted that a given situation may give rise to more than one of these rights. An assignment of rights may involve not only a delegation of duties, but also a third-party beneficiary contract or a novation. If the parties to a contract or potential contract want to benefit or involve a third person in some way, they may choose whatever method or combination of methods is best suited to the specific situation.

EXAMPLE: A, the owner of a catering business, and B enter a contract to sell the business to B. Under the contract, B receives the right to collect all outstanding accounts and agrees to assume all outstanding liabilities of the business. After the sale is completed, A and B conclude an agreement with C, the major supplier of the business.

Under the terms of this agreement, C agrees to release A from all further liability on outstanding debts and to accept B's promise to pay all these debts in the manner specified in the agreement. The three parties have created third-party rights in the following ways: (1) an assignment (B's right to collect the outstanding accounts due A); (2) a delegation of duties (B's assumption of the outstanding liabilities); (3) a third-party beneficiary contract (creditors of the business being third-party beneficiaries of A and B's contract); and (4) a novation (the agreement between A, B, and C).

Key Concepts and Terms

- A third-party beneficiary is a person who is intended by two parties to a contract to benefit from the performance of the contract. As such, the third-party beneficiary is entitled to enforce the contract. An incidental beneficiary is a person who is not specifically intended to, but does, benefit under a contract between two other persons. An incidental beneficiary cannot enforce the contract.

- An assignment is a transfer of rights under a contract. The person making the transfer is the assignor, and the person receiving the rights is the assignee. Most contract rights are assignable. Nonassignable contract rights include (1) those involving a close personal relationship (such as the right to personal services), (2) those containing antiassignment provisions, (3) those based on the character or credit of the party attempting assignment, and (4) those whose assignment is limited by law.

- An assignee acquires all the rights of the assignor, but any defenses available against the assignor are also available against the assignee.

- Notice to the obligor that an assignment has been made is not necessary. However, if the obligor is not notified he may continue to make payments to the assignor. When several assignments of the same rights are made in succession by the same assignor, the order in which the assignments are made may determine which assignment has priority. In some states, the time the notice is given to the obligor is the determining factor.

- A delegation of duties is a party's transfer of his obligations under a contract to a third person. A delegation of duties is permissible if (1) the third person's performance is substantially the same as performance by the party and (2) the party's personal acts or qualifications are not material to the contract. If the acts or qualities are material, the other party to the contract must consent to the transfer. Even though a party has delegated his obligations, he is still liable for performance of the contract.

- The UCC favors assignments and delegations of duties.

- A novation is an agreement among all parties concerned that cancels an existing contract and simultaneously creates a new one. Contracts of novation may be used in lieu of or in conjunction with third-party beneficiary contracts and assignments.

- Assignee
- Assignment
- Assignor
- Creditor–Beneficiary
- Delegation of Duties
- Donee–Beneficiary

- Incidental Beneficiary
- Nonassignment Clause
- Noncompetition Clause
- Novation
- Obligor
- Third-Party Beneficiary

Questions and Case Problems

1. William Lowry and Glenna Hobson divorced in 1966. Their decree of divorce incorporated a stipulation whereby Lowry agreed "that he will keep in force the present insurance policies now existing on his life and will designate as the irrevocable beneficiaries in said policies all of the minor children of the parties." Before his death in 1980, Lowry removed the children as the beneficiaries of the policies and named his second wife as the sole beneficiary. After his death, the second wife received the proceeds of the insurance policy. The children sued the second wife to obtain the proceeds of the insurance policy. Are they donee–beneficiaries of Lowry's promise in the divorce decree? If so, are they entitled to the proceeds now in the hands of the second wife?

2. In 1959 Dooley, a stone quarry operator, contracted to sell stone to Rose at specified prices for a ten-year period. In 1960 Dooley sold his stone quarry to Vulcan. Vulcan wrote to Rose about the acquisition and stated that it "assumes all phases" of the contract between Rose and Dooley. Vulcan continued to sell stone to Rose, but at prices above those specified in the contract. Rose sued for breach of contract. Is Vulcan liable? Is Dooley liable?

3. Tangerman, an Army serviceman, was injured when he was struck by an automobile on a city street. The United States provided or paid for his ambulance and medical care and treatment, the cost of which was about $8,600. The government filed a claim with Allstate, the firm insuring both Tangerman and the driver, claiming to be entitled to payment under Allstate's promise to pay "personal injury protection benefits for medical expense . . . incurred with respect to bodily injury sustained by an eligible insured person." When Allstate refused the claim, the United States sued, claiming it was a third-party beneficiary of the insurance contract. Decision?

4. Chevron contracted with the New York State Thruway Authority to render emergency service to disabled vehicles on the authority's limited-access toll highway. The contract requires Chevron to provide service within 30 minutes after receiving a call. When Kornblut has a flat tire on the thruway, he calls Chevron. Chevron fails to respond. After waiting for two hours Kornblut changes the tire himself and suffers a heart attack. Kornblut dies, and his widow sues for damages on a third-party beneficiary theory. Should she recover?

5. A contracts to sell land to B for $150,000. The contract provides that B is to make a cash down payment of $30,000, with the balance to be paid by means of a

mortgage loan to be secured by B. B assigns her rights under the contract to C. Must A complete the sale to C? If C refuses to purchase the land, may A recover from C for breach of contract?

6. Mr. B was a member of the Augusta Country Club. Mrs. B was not a member of the club but had the privilege to use club facilities as the spouse of a "senior resident member." This use of the club was written in the by-laws and the membership contracts, but spouse use was described as a privilege. When the club suspended her use of its facilities, Mrs. B sued the club, claiming breach of her rights as a third-party beneficiary of the contract between the club and Mr. B. What result?

7. As part of their divorce settlement, Bill and Jane agree that Bill will pay all costs of educating their minor child, Erin. Bill pays for Erin's undergraduate college education. When she enrolls in graduate school he refuses to make further payments. Erin sues, claiming Bill is obligated to pay under the divorce agreement. Result?

8. Roland, a real estate firm, opens a branch office. The branch manager orders furniture on credit from O'Brien for the new office. O'Brien then makes a verbal assignment of the Roland account to Woods, who gives written notice of the assignment to Roland at its main office. O'Brien later makes a written assignment of the Roland account to Brown, who telephones the branch office and informs the person who answers the telephone about the assignment. To whom should Roland make the next payment on the account?

9. Jeans, Incorporated, a clothing manufacturer, contracts with Kane Corporation, a small advertising agency, for promotional advertising of Jeans' products for a one-year period. Shortly afterward, Kane is purchased by and merged into Grimes Company, a larger advertising agency. Grimes assumes all of Kane's rights and liabilities, including Kane's obligations under its contract with Jeans. Jeans refuses to deal with Grimes, claiming that it has no contract with Grimes and prefers to do business with small agencies. Is Jeans' refusal justified?

10. Ross develops and obtains a patent on a new mousetrap. Ross sells the marketing rights to Feiner under a contract that provides for royalty payments to Ross based on sales and requires Feiner to use her best efforts to market the mousetrap over a five-year period. Feiner later sells all her rights under the contract to a third person, Drake. Ross consents to this sale and accepts royalty payments from Drake. Drake eventually abandons efforts to market the mousetrap, and Ross sues Feiner and Drake for breach of contract. Feiner claims that a novation had occurred. Drake claims that the contract between Feiner and him was an assignment of rights, not a delegation of duties. Decide the case.

18 Performance, Discharge, and Remedies

18:1 Introduction

When the parties to a contract no longer have obligations or duties to perform under the contract, the contract is said to be discharged. If the parties fully perform their contract duties, the contract is totally executed and the parties' obligations are discharged *by performance.* If one or the other of the parties does not perform, however, a court may be asked to determine the parties' rights under the contract and the remedies available for the nonperformance. The court must resolve disputes concerning whether the parties have performed or are excused from performance, whether an obligation has been discharged or is breached, and what measure of damages or remedy is appropriate. The material in this chapter addresses the legal issues relating to contract performance, discharge, and remedies.

18:2 Conditions

All but the simplest contracts are structured so that performance by one party gives rise to the other party's obligation to perform. For example, an owner may agree to make partial payments to a building contractor as he completes established percentages of the project. The duty to perform at each stage depends on the other party's performance. Moreover, the parties may *condition* the performance of a duty on the happening, or nonhappening, of some other event. Words such as "if," "when," or "provided that" commonly are used to indicate the existence of an express condition. Moreover, under some circumstances an implied condition may be found.

Conditions may be classified as precedent, subsequent, or concurrent. Sometimes a contract provides that a party's duty to perform some act arises only if or when some fact or event occurs; if that event never occurs, the duty to perform never arises. Such a provision is called *condition precedent;* the occurrence of the event precedes and creates the imposition of the duty. Other times a contract provides that a party is obligated to perform some act, but further provides that the party will be relieved of that obligation if some fact or event occurs. Such a provision is called a *condition subsequent;* the occurrence of the event follows imposition of the duty and extinguishes it. Still other times, the performance of one party is conditioned on performance by the other party, and vice versa, as when the parties are to perform their promises simultaneously. This is a *concurrent condition.*

EXAMPLE: Granucci contracts with Rex Corporation to serve as its president for a period of five years. The contract provides that Granucci is to receive an annual salary of $200,000, with an increase in salary to $300,000 if Rex shows a specified net annual profit within two years. The contract also provides that, in the event Rex should move its corporate headquarters more than 25 miles from its present location, Granucci's obligation to act as president would cease and Rex would give Granucci severance pay of $100,000 if he decides to quit. There are two conditions precedent and one condition subsequent in this contract. The provision regarding a salary increase contains a condition precedent: Rex's obligation to pay the increased salary will arise only if its net profits increase to the level specified within the time specified. The provision regarding possible relocation of the corporate headquarters contains both a condition subsequent and a condition precedent: The relocation is a condition subsequent that will release Granucci from his obligation to serve, and Granucci's quitting is a condition precedent to Rex's obligation to provide the severance pay.

 It is extremely important that at the time a contract is being drafted the parties consider whether there are any possible contingencies that should affect the parties' obligations. If such contingencies can be anticipated, they should be provided for by means of conditions in the contract. As will become clear in the subsequent discussion in this chapter concerning performance and impossibility, failure to provide for contingencies may result in a party's being obligated to render a performance that is virtually, but not legally, impossible, or to pay damages for the failure to perform.

18:3   Sufficiency of Performance

A party to a contract may discharge the contractual duties by fully performing them. Under some conditions it may be sufficient to tender performance; a party tenders performance by offering to perform and being ready, willing, and able to do so. Generally, if performance is tendered and rejected by the other party, the tendering party's duty is discharged and the other party's performance is not discharged. Most problems surrounding performance, however, arise when a party's performance deviates in some way from what is required by the contract. Where there is a deviation, a court may be asked to determine whether the performance is sufficient to entitle the party who deviates to reciprocal performance from the other party.

Substantial Performance   Some contracts contain such numerous and detailed requirements concerning performance that literal compliance is virtually impossible. Construction contracts present the prime example in this area. Construction contracts contain minute specifications, and almost invariably the completed project deviates in some way from the contractual requirements. When a contractor erects a building that is in essential compliance with the general plan, it is obviously unfair to permit the other party to refuse payment on the ground that there were some slight departures from contractual specifications. To prevent such unfairness, the doctrine of *substantial performance* was developed. This doctrine states that a party who substantially performs his obligations under a contract is entitled to performance by the other party, usually in the form of cash payment. To the extent that the other party has suffered some harm from the deviations, he may recover damages, but he may not refuse to perform his own obligations. The doctrine of substantial performance, although most often applied in cases involving building and construction contracts, may be applied to any kind of contract under appropriate circumstances.

The following case illustrates not only the type of situation in which substantial performance might be found, but also the methods used by courts in determining the damages resulting from minor deviations.

Plante

v

Jacobs

103 NW2d 296 (1960)

Wisconsin Supreme Court

FACTS: Eugene Plante contracted to build a house for Frank and Carol Jacobs. Frank and Carol paid $20,000 on the contract price of $26,765, but refused to pay the balance. They claimed that Plante had not substantially performed the contract. Plante sued for the balance due. The trial court held that, although there were some deviations from the contractual specifications, Plante had substantially performed the contract. The trial court entered judgment for Plante, but deducted from his recovery the cost of correcting some of the defects. Note that no deduction was allowed for the misplacement of a wall between the living room and the kitchen. Mr. and Mrs. Jacobs appealed.

ISSUE: Did Plante's misplacement of the wall prevent his substantial performance of the contract?

RESULT: Plante's deviations from the plan entitle the Jacobs to damages based on contract, but they do not discharge the Jacobs' liability for the contract price.

REASONING:

*   *   *

The defendants argue the plaintiff cannot recover any amount because he has failed to substantially perform the contract. . . . The defendants claim some 20 . . . items of incomplete or faulty performance by the plaintiff and no substantial performance because the cost of completing the house in strict compliance with the plans and specifications would amount to 25 or 30 percent of the contract price. The defendants especially stress the misplacing of the wall between the living room and the kitchen, which narrowed the living room in excess of one foot. The cost of tearing down this wall and rebuilding it would be approximately $4,000. . . . Real estate experts testified that the smaller width of the living room would not affect the market price of the house.

. . . [T]here can be no recovery on the contract as distinguished from *quantum meruit* [quasi-contractual recovery] unless there is substantial performance. . . . The question here is whether there has been substantial performance. The test of what amounts to substantial performance seems to be whether the performance meets the essential purpose of the contract. . . .

Substantial performance as applied to construction of a house does not mean that every detail must be in strict compliance with the specifications and the plans. . . . There may be situations in which [there are] features or details of construction of special or of great personal importance, which if not performed, would prevent a finding of substantial performance of the contract. In this case the plan was a stock floor plan. No detailed construction of the house was shown on the plan. There were no blueprints. The specifications were standard printed forms with some modifications and additions written in by the parties. Many of the problems that arose during the construction had to be solved on the basis of practical experience. No mathematical rule relating to the percentage of the price, of cost of completion or of completeness can be laid down to determine substantial performance of a building contract. Although the defendants received a house with which they are dissatisfied in many respects, the trial court was not in error in finding the contract was substantially performed.

The next question is what is the amount of recovery when the plaintiff has substantially, but incompletely, performed. For substantial performance the plaintiff should recover the contract price less the damages caused the defendant by the incomplete performance. . . . [T]he correct rule for damages . . . is the difference between the value of the house as it stands with faulty and incomplete construction and the value of the house if it had been constructed in strict accordance with the plans and specifications. This is the diminished-value rule. The cost of replacement or repair is not the measure of such damage, but is an element to take into consideration in arriving at value under some circumstances. The cost of replacement or the cost to make whole the omissions may equal or be less than the difference in value in some cases and, likewise, the cost to rectify a defect may greatly exceed the added value to the structure as corrected. . . .

Of the defects claimed by the defendants, the court allowed the cost of replacement or repair except as to the misplacement of the living-room wall. Whether a defect should fall under the cost-of-replacement rule or be considered under the diminished-value rule depends upon the nature and magnitude of the defect. . . .

The item of misplacing the living room wall under the facts of this case was clearly under the diminished-value rule. . . . There is no evidence that defendants requested or demanded the replacement of the wall in the place called for by the specifications during the course of construction. To tear down the wall now and rebuild it in its proper place would involve a substantial destruction of the work, if not all of it, which was put into the wall and would cause additional damage to other parts of the house and require replastering and redecorating the walls and ceilings of at least two rooms. Such economic waste is unreasonable and unjustified. The rule of diminished value contemplates the wall is not going to be moved. Expert witnesses . . . agreed that the misplacement of the wall had no effect on the market price. The trial court properly found that the defendants suffered no legal damage, although the defendants' particular desire for specified room size was not satisfied. . . .

Hallows, Justice.

The court in the *Plante* case indicated that whether performance is substantial or not depends on the specificity of the contract and the apparent importance to the owner of exact performance. This test often is formulated as a test of *material, or immaterial, breach.* If the breach is material, the duty to perform is not satisfied, and the other party's duty to perform does not arise. For example, if a contract calls for A to pay $1,000 when B performs, and B's nonperformance constitutes a material breach of the contract, then A is not obligated to pay $1,000. If A must pay at all, she must pay the value of the benefit conferred by B's performance, which may be far less than $1,000 and may even be nothing at all. If the breach is immaterial, A's duty to pay $1,000 is not excused, although she may *offset* (deduct) from $1,000 the damages she has suffered.

To entitle a party to payment on the basis of substantial performance, it is essential that the party have made an honest effort to perform in compliance with the contract. The doctrine cannot be applied where there are intentional omissions or departures from contractual specifications. For example, if a contractor inadvertently installed pipe different from, but of practically equal grade with, that specified in the contract, a court would find that there was substantial performance. But if the contractor intentionally installed a different type of pipe, the court would not find substantial performance.

 The parties to a contract may avoid possible application of the doctrine of substantial performance by specifying that complete performance is required. Courts will uphold such a clause where it is reasonable. In entering such a contract, however, one should be certain that performance is sufficiently well defined.

Partial Performance   Substantial performance is not the same as *partial performance*. Partial performance occurs where a party performs some of the obligations in a contract that contains multiple obligations. Generally, a party rendering partial performance is not entitled to reciprocal performance from the other party and need not be paid. Some courts, however, do permit recovery for the value of the benefit actually conferred by the partial performance.

To illustrate the difference between substantial and partial performance, assume that Jacobs had contracted to build an additional room on and to construct a carport adjacent to Miller's residence. If Jacobs constructs both the additional room and the carport, but deviates in some minor respects from the contract specifications, he has rendered substantial performance and is entitled to payment from Miller on the contract. However, if Jacobs builds only the additional room, and not the carport, he has rendered partial performance, and Miller is relieved of his contractual obligation to pay. Miller might, however, be required to pay for the value of the additional room since he has actually received that benefit.

Satisfaction Clauses   Contracts often contain a requirement that the performance of one party be satisfactory to the other party. This requirement is called a satisfaction clause. Satisfaction clauses typically are inserted in contracts in which one party is to build for or provide some item to the other party. A satisfaction clause operates as a condition precedent to the obligation to pay for the item.

Disputes frequently arise as to whether compliance with a satisfaction clause is to be judged by subjective or objective standards. Generally, if a contract involves matters of personal taste, a party is the sole judge of his own satisfaction. For example, if A contracts to paint a satisfactory portrait of B, then B is the sole judge of whether the portrait is satisfactory. If B is genuinely dissatisfied with the portrait as painted, he has no obligation to pay A, even if everyone else who looks at the portrait considers it very good. This is the subjective standard. If, however, the satisfactory nature of a party's performance can be judged by objective standards, such as mechanical utility or fitness for the purpose intended, then the courts will apply a reasonable-person rule of satisfaction. For example, if A agrees to drill a well on B's land that will produce a satisfactory amount of water, and if the well as drilled produces sufficient water to satisfy a reasonable person, most courts will find that the satisfaction clause has been met and that B is obligated to pay for the drilling.

Obviously, there is a certain element of risk involved when one party agrees to render performance to the satisfaction of another party. Therefore, contracts often provide that performance must be satisfactory to some third person. In building contracts especially, the parties frequently include a contractual provision requiring that the work be done to the satisfaction of some third person, usually an architect or an engineer. The third person's approval constitutes a condition precedent to the contractor's right to payment from the other party.

A contract may also contain a clause providing that performance is to be judged by some specified test or by the ability of the completed item to perform some task. Failure to pass the test would prevent recovery. Such clauses are often inserted in contracts for the construction or supply of items whose physical characteristics or capacity is crucial.

Time of Performance   If a contract does not specify a time or times by which the parties are to complete performance, the contract will be interpreted to require performance within a reasonable time. What constitutes a reasonable time depends on all the facts and circumstances surrounding a given contract.

If a contract states specific times for performance by the parties, then a party's failure to perform by the time specified constitutes a breach of the contract. It does not necessarily follow, however, that the other party is relieved of his own duty to perform. Rather, failure to meet a contractual deadline ordinarily is remedied by permitting the other party to recover any damages caused by the delay.

The parties to a contract can expressly stipulate that performance by the time specified in the contract is essential. This is commonly done by stating in the contract that *time is of the essence.* When time is of the essence, failure to perform within the time specified relieves the other party from his own obligation to perform. Moreover, if the nature of the contract or its subject matter is such as to clearly indicate that time is a critical factor, some courts will find time to be of the essence even when it is not stated in the contract. For example, if a store enters an order with a manufacturer for winter coats to be delivered by September 1, and the coats do not arrive until March 1, the store would probably be permitted to refuse to accept the coats, with or without a time-is-of-the-essence clause in the contract. Some states, however, have statutes providing that time is never considered of the essence unless the contract so provides.

 If time is truly of the essence, the contract should so provide. It is inadvisable, however, to routinely insert such a clause in all contracts. Some courts will ignore a time-is-of-the-essence clause where the nature of the contract clearly reveals that performance by the specified time was not in fact essential. Moreover, a time-is-of-the-essence clause may be waived if a party fails to enforce it. For example, if late payments are accepted on an installment contract that provides that time is of the essence, most courts will hold that the clause has been waived. The best practice, therefore, is (1) to insert time-is-of-the-essence clauses only when performance by the specified time is critical and (2) to enforce the clause promptly when the other party fails to perform by the stated time.

18:4   Impossibility of Performance

A great deal can happen between the time that a contract is formed and the time that performance of it is to occur. Frequently, intervening events make performance extremely difficult or even financially prohibitive. The occurrence of such events does not ordinarily constitute an excuse for nonperformance, unless the contract so provides. The fact that performance has been prevented by events such as a strike, an earthquake, a flood, or a war does not constitute legal justification for nonperformance. The theory of the courts is that such contingencies could have been expressly provided for in the contract.

There are exceptions to this rule of strict liability for performance. Sometimes courts excuse a party's performance under the doctrine of impossibility. In general, this will happen only where the court perceives that circumstances have changed so radically since the contract was undertaken that the parties could not reasonably have contemplated and provided for the change. A variation on this theory is that the parties assumed a set of conditions, or a range of conditions, as a basis for the agreement; if the circumstances vary from what was assumed, the contract was not intended to be performed.

Performance usually will be excused, and the contract terminated, if (1) an essential person has died, (2) some essential item or commodity has been destroyed, or (3) an intervening change of law has rendered performance of the contract illegal. Courts also excuse nonperformance on the ground of *commercial frustration* or impracticability.

Death or Illness   Death of a party will terminate a contract if (1) the contract is one calling for the personal services of the deceased party or (2) the contract in other ways could only be performed by the deceased party. If performance of a contract depends on the continued existence of a particular person who is not a party, that person's death will also excuse performance. If a party is stricken by a disabling illness, the same general principles apply.

 If a party's continued presence is essential, the contract should be written so that the entire agreement is null and void if that party dies or is disabled. Such a clause may be extremely important in a contract in which two or more people undertake joint obligations that neither would undertake if the other were to die. For example, if a husband and wife entered into a contract to purchase a house, the death of one spouse does not excuse nonperformance by the other, because the deceased spouse's personal representative can perform. Often, however, it will be practically impossible to proceed with the purchase because the ability to make monthly mortgage payments may have been based on both spouses' income.

Destruction of Item   Where the contract relates to a specified item or piece of property and that item or property is destroyed prior to the time for performance, nonperformance is excused. If an equivalent item can be substituted, the contract usually must be performed.

Illegality   Nonperformance is excused when, prior to performance, a change in the law makes performance illegal or impossible. Not every change in the law will excuse nonperformance. For example, a law that makes performance more expensive does not create a legal impossibility or an illegal condition that excuses nonperformance.

Commercial Frustration   The doctrine of commercial frustration is invoked to excuse a performance where the contract cannot be performed without extreme and unreasonable difficulty, expense, or loss caused by some anticipated and unforeseen event. Generally, the doctrine can be relied on only when the change is so drastic that it simply could not have been anticipated. In the following case, the court analyzes a claim of impossibility made by a developer who was unable to deliver title to property sold on an installment sales contract because governmental approval of the project could not be obtained. Note that the parties, apparently, did not make performance conditioned on obtaining necessary governmental approval.

Cook
v
Deltona Corp.
753 F2d 1552 (1985)
United States Court of Appeals, Eleventh Circuit

FACTS: In 1971 the Deltona Corporation sold Cook a plot of land in Marco Shores, Florida, on a real estate installment contract. Title was to be delivered in March 1980. The particular plot of land was underwater, but it was part of a project that Deltona had been developing since 1964 through a dredge and fill operation. Between 1964 and 1973 permits to dredge and fill became increasingly difficult to obtain from the Army Corps of Engineers. After failing to obtain permits on nearby developments, Deltona gave up seeking to obtain one for Marco Shores. Cook sued for breach of contract.

ISSUE: Was Deltona's nonperformance rendered impossible, and thereafter legally excused, by the increase in regulatory requirements for the dredge and fill permits?

RESULT: The change in regulatory requirements was sufficiently foreseeable that Deltona could have contracted for the risk of the change in regulations.

REASONING:

*   *   *

At the conclusion of all evidence in the case the district court granted a directed verdict for Cook on the breach of contract claim. Deltona conceded nonperformance but raised the affirmative defense of impossibility, arguing that performance was rendered impossible by the substantial and unforeseeable increase in regulatory requirements for the issuance of the required Army Corps of Engineers dredge and fill permits. In light of this concession and asserted affirmative defense, the propriety of the district court's directed verdict on the breach of contract claim rests upon an issue of law: whether Deltona's performance was rendered impossible by regulatory developments supervening between the formation of the contract in 1971 and the date of its scheduled performance in 1980.

There is a fascinating contradiction inherent in the judicially created impossibility defense which reveals a basic tension in the law. Contracts are born of the need for certainty. They are the merchant's exchange of serendipity for serenity, the deal upon which he can rely, for better or worse, months or years hence. A contract is insurance against change. The early common law enforced the policy by making contractual liability absolute, *see e.g.*, 18 Williston, *The Law of Contracts* § 1939 (3d ed. 1978), on the theory that a contractual duty, unlike a duty imposed by, for example, tort law, is tailored by the party for himself and any eventuality might be provided for in the contract. . . .

But change is what impossibility is about. As Professor Gilmore put it, it arises as a defense when "the real world has in some way failed to correspond with the imaginary world hypothesized by the parties to the contract." G. Gilmore, *The Death of Contract* 81 (1974). By recognizing impossibility as a sort of 'escape hatch' from the self-made chamber of contractual duty, the courts have recognized that absolute contractual liability is economically and socially unworkable. Impossibility accomodates the tension between the changes a party bargains to avoid and the changes, unbargained for and radical, that make enforcement of the bargain unwise.

Thus, it seems to us that the most profitable approach to an impossibility claim is not to pass on the relative difficulty caused by a supervening event, but to ask whether that supervening event so radically altered the world in which the parties were expected to fulfill their promises that it is unwise to hold them to the bargain. Ultimately the issue is whether the change was foreseeable. This is the rule in Florida. . . .

In the case before us it is certainly clear that the regulation of dredge and fill activities on Marco Island including the plaintiff's Marco Shores tract, increased substantially between 1971, the date of contracting, and 1980, the date performance was due. However, it is also clear that this increase in regulation was not beyond the contemplation of Deltona in 1971. As early as 1969 Deltona was informed by the Army Corps of Engineers that the Roberts Bay dredge and fill permit was granted but that subsequent permits would be reviewed independently and a subsequent determination made as to each. Although the Corps advised Deltona it could continue to sell land within an area encompassing the Marco Shores tract, the company was to be on notice that dredge and fill permits were not assured for any additional areas. This advice preceded Deltona's purchase of the Marco Shores tract. While it may be true that the extent of the ensuring regulations could not have been foreseen by the company in 1971, it is equally true that the winds of change were blowing and that Deltona was aware of that fact. This awareness disables Deltona's assertion that the increase in regulation changed basic assumptions upon which the contract was founded. Accordingly, we find no impossibility in this case. . . .

Hill, Circuit Judge.

Commercial impracticability or impossibility is extremely difficult to prove. Businesspersons should ask themselves "What would happen if . . . ?" about every contingency that could render performance of a contract economically prohibitive, and then allocate the risk in the contract. In particular, the possibility of a labor strike should be provided for in the contract.

The Uniform Commercial Code adopts a lenient standard for commercial impracticability. Under the UCC, performance of a sales contract is excused if performance "has been made impracticable by the occurrence of a contingency the nonoccurrence of which was a basic assumption on which the contract was made" [UCC § 2-615].[1]

18:5   Discharge by Agreement

The parties to a contract may agree to modify it or to terminate the contract entirely. They can terminate the contract by either replacing it with a new contract or simply ending their contractual relationship. Discharge by agreement between the parties may take various forms. Among the more important ones are (1) *rescission,* (2) *novation,* and (3) *accord and satisfaction.* The parties may agree to modify a contract by waiver.

---

[1] Performance of sales contracts generally is discussed in Chapter 22.

Rescission   Both parties may agree that their contractual relationship should be terminated without performance. This action is called rescission by agreement. It discharges the contract in its entirety; neither party has any obligation to perform under it. While consideration for the rescission is necessary, the courts will find that each party's agreement to discharge the other party from the performance of his contractual obligations constitutes sufficient consideration.

 Generally, rescission may be done orally, even if the original contract was required to be in writing. Only when the agreement involves a retransfer of land must the rescission be in writing. However, if one party should claim that an oral agreement was made to rescind a written contract, and the other party disputes that, a court will insist on clear proof of the rescission. For that reason, whenever a written contract is to be rescinded by agreement, as a matter of business practice the rescission should also be in writing.

A party's right to rescind a contract on the ground of fraud or for similar reasons has been discussed in Chapter 12. The use of rescission as a remedy for breach of contract will be discussed later in this chapter.

Novation   A contract of novation is an agreement among all the parties concerned that discharges the existing contract and simultaneously creates a new contract. The use of a novation as a means of substituting a third party in the place of one of the original parties was discussed in section 17:8. In the present discussion, the original parties may utilize a novation to discharge their original contract and enter into a new agreement.

Accord and Satisfaction   An accord is an agreement by the parties to give and accept some performance different from that originally promised; a satisfaction is the actual performance of the substituted obligation. In order for an existing contract to be discharged by an accord and satisfaction, therefore, there must not only be a new agreement but also performance of that agreement.

Waiver   Either party to a contract may allow or accept from the other party performance that is not in full compliance with the contract. This allowance or acceptance is called a waiver. A waiver may be express or it may be implied from the acts of the parties. The concept of waiver is frequently applied to excuse a party's nonperformance of some act. For example, if an installment contract calls for payments to be made on the first of each month, and it further provides that time is of the essence, failure to make payments on time would ordinarily constitute a breach of contract. If, however, the creditor consistently accepts late payments, this acceptance may be interpreted as a waiver of the time-is-of-the-essence provision. If the creditor subsequently decides to insist on timely payments, he would probably have to give the debtor notice that in the future the provision is going to be enforced.

18:6   Discharge by Operation of Law

A contract can be discharged as a matter of law by the occurrence of certain events. Among the more important of these events are bankruptcy proceedings, passage of the period prescribed by the statute of limitations, and material alteration of the contract.

Bankruptcy   A bankruptcy proceeding often culminates in an adjudication that a debtor is discharged from his contractual duties to most of his creditors. The subject of bankruptcy is covered in more detail in Chapter 32.

Statute of Limitations   All states have statutes of limitations, which require that legal actions be brought within a specified time. State laws typically specify different limitations periods for different kinds of actions. For example, most states grant a longer period of time within which a party can bring an action on a written contract than they do for an oral contract. The limitations period begins to run when the right to sue arises (in most cases, when the contract was breached). If a party fails to bring suit within the period specified, suit cannot be brought. Although there is no discharge of the contract, the injured party is left without an effective legal remedy.

Alteration   A party's intentional and material alteration of a written contract will discharge the other party's obligations under the contract as a matter of law. To be material, an alteration must change the rights, obligations, or relations of the parties in some way.

18:7   Breach of Contract

A breach of contract is a party's failure to perform some contractual obligation without having a legal excuse for not performing. A material breach of contract has two interrelated consequences: (1) it relieves the other party from his obligation to perform under the contract, and (2) it entitles that party to seek damages or other appropriate relief as a remedy for the breach. A relatively minor or trivial breach of contract may not relieve the other party of his or her obligations, if the performance has been substantial. If the breach may be cured, the breach may only postpone the other party's duty to perform. In either event, the nonbreaching party may be entitled to damages from the breaching party.

Anticipatory Breach of Contract   Prior to the time set for his performance, one party to a contract may inform the other party that he has no intention of performing the contract. This prospective failure to perform is called an *anticipatory breach* of contract. When an anticipatory breach occurs, the other party may treat the contract as broken, cease performance himself, and sue for breach of contract.

The rationale of the doctrine of anticipatory breach is that the innocent party may be able to minimize his losses if he is not forced to wait until an actual breach occurs. For example, assume that in September Yamada and Nance enter a contract under the terms of which Nance agrees to manufacture and provide a line of bathing suits to Yamada, to be delivered by February 28. In December, Nance informs Yamada that he no longer manufactures bathing suits and will be unable to fill Yamada's order. Yamada may treat Nance's statement as an anticipatory breach of contract and place an order elsewhere for the bathing suits without waiting for the actual breach (nondelivery by February 28) to occur. Yamada may also file a lawsuit for breach of contract at this time.

 A party's repudiation of the contract must be absolute and clear before the other party can treat it as an anticipatory breach. The fact that one party complains about his or her obligations under a contract or has a generally negative attitude toward the contract does not constitute an anticipatory breach, and the other party must continue to perform. Moreover, if a repudiation is withdrawn before the other party acts in reliance on it, the repudiation cannot be treated as an anticipatory breach.

The following case illustrates the importance of making certain that there has been an anticipatory breach before acting in reliance on it. In reading the case, consider whether the condition in the lease agreement was truly a condition subsequent, as stated by the parties, or a condition precedent.

STC, Inc.

v

Billings
543 P2d 374 (1975)
Montana Supreme Court

FACTS: In 1972, STC, Inc., a nonprofit corporation, purchased the Old Chamber Building in Billings, Montana, to renovate and preserve it. In June 1972, STC and the city of Billings entered a lease agreement that provided that STC would remodel the premises and the city would rent a portion of the building for ten years at an agreed rental. The agreement was made subject to "the condition subsequent" that STC would obtain financing for remodeling and begin remodeling by the end of March 1973, or the lease would be null and void. STC had difficulty obtaining the necessary financing, but in November 1972 was notified that a lender would consider making a loan, provided, among other things, that STC would show firm ten-year leases for the building. On February 5, 1973, the Billings City Council voted "to not reaffirm the provisions of the original lease." STC made no further attempts to secure financing, and the remodeling was never done.

ISSUE: Did the action of the city council constitute a breach of the lease?

RESULT: The council's action was not sufficiently definite and unequivocal to support an action for anticipatory breach of contract.

REASONING:

*   *   *

The reasons supporting an action for anticipatory breach of contract have been variously stated to be: the uselessness and inequity of requiring the promise to hold himself in readiness to perform his contractual obligation on the date performance is due where the promisor has already repudiated his reciprocal obligations under the contract; the present injury to the implied right of each of the contracting parties to refrain from impairing the ability or willingness of the other to perform when performance is due; the duty of the promisee to mitigate damages by withholding expenditures in preparation for carrying out his contractual obligations where the promisor will not perform in any event; the social and economic waste incident to prolonging a contractual status that is effectively at an end: and the necessity that the law recognize the commercial desirability of fixing legal rights, liabilities and damages as promptly as possible. . . .

The crux of the instant case is whether the action of the city council on February 5, 1973, constituted an anticipatory repudiation of the lease agreement. The city council voted to "not re-affirm provisions of the original lease." Plaintiff treats this as a repudiation or renunciation of the city's obligations under the lease. But was it?

It appears to us that the action of the city council was subject to different interpretations. It might have meant the new mayor and council did not want to go on record as approving the original lease. It might have meant the new mayor and council refused to assist plaintiff corporation in its efforts to secure the necessary financing for remodeling by an affirmative expression of support. It might have meant the new mayor and council were repudiating the lease and refused to perform the city's obligations thereunder.

The language of the proposition on which the council voted is significant in our view. The council voted "not to re-affirm." The council did not vote "not to affirm." The council did not vote to repudiate, renounce, or cancel the lease, nor adopt any language manifesting an intention not to carry out its obligations under the lease. The language of the proposition on which the council voted was equivocal, ambiguous, and subject to conflicting interpretations.

The circumstances support a like conclusion. A city election intervened between the execution of the lease and the vote of the council on February 5, 1973. Some new aldermen and a new mayor had been elected who opposed the lease. STC, Inc. had not secured the necessary financing despite some seven month's effort. Time was running out. Less than two months remained before the lease agreement would expire by its own terms if financing was not secured. No rational basis existed for the city to repudiate the lease at this time and under these circumstances, while a good reason did exist for the new mayor and council to refuse to go on record as approving the lease negotiated by their predecessors, or to refuse to assist STC, Inc. in obtaining financing. At the very least the circumstances are equally consistent with this interpretation of the council's intention. The collective intention of the city council remains ambiguous and equivocal.

A repudiation or renunciation must be entire, absolute and unequivocal to support an action for anticipatory breach. . . .

Anticipatory breach must appear only in the clearest terms of repudiation of the contractual obligation. . . . An expression of intent not to perform, or not to be bound, standing alone, is not enough. . . . [N]or is a mere assertion that a party will be unable, or will refuse, to perform his contract an anticipatory renunciation. . . .

Applying these rules, we hold the action of the city council on February 5, 1973 to "not reaffirm provisions of the original lease" was not a positive, unequivocal, absolute expression of intention by the city not to perform its contractual obligations under the lease. Accordingly, it will not support an action for anticipatory breach and plaintiff's action must fail. . . .

Haswell, Justice.

Most courts have held that the doctrine of anticipatory breach does not apply to promises to pay money. For example, assume that A lends B $1,000, in exchange for B's promise to repay the money two months later. One month later, B tells A that she will not repay the money. A may not treat B's statement as an anticipatory breach. In other words, A must wait until B actually fails to pay the money when due before A can sue B for breach of contract.

18:8   Remedies Generally[2]

When one party breaches a contract, the other party is entitled to a remedy. The goal of the court in awarding a remedy is to protect the nonbreaching party's interest in the contract. Conceptually, this interest may take one or more of three forms. First, the nonbreaching party has an interest in the expected benefit of the bargain, the *expectation interest*. The expectation interest is protected by putting the nonbreaching party in as good a position as he or she would have been in had the contract been performed. The nonbreaching party is given the benefit of the bargain made.

Second, the nonbreaching party may have an interest in the loss suffered by relying on the other party to perform the contract. This is called the *reliance interest*. It is protected by restoring to the nonbreaching party the value of his

---

[2] Remedies in sales cases are discussed in Chapter 22.

loss. The nonbreaching party is put back into the position he or she would have been in had the contract not been entered into. Finally, the nonbreaching party has an interest in recovering the value of the benefit that his or her performance conferred on the other party. This is called the *restitution* interest.

Usually the nonbreaching party's injury can be gauged in monetary terms, so the most common remedy for contract injury is money. There are situations, however, in which money damages are inadequate to redress the injury caused by a breach of contract. In those situations, a court may award an alternate remedy, such as specific performance or restitution. All of these remedies are discussed below.

Where alternative remedies are available, a party often must make what is known as an *election of remedies*. For example, a party cannot seek both an order rescinding a contract and an order requiring specific performance of the same contract. Because the two remedies are inconsistent, the injured party may select only one.

18:9   Damages

Most contract damages awards are designed to compensate the nonbreaching party for the losses caused by the breach of the contract. Such damages are called *compensatory damages*. The issues associated with compensatory damages are discussed below. Courts often speak of *nominal damages* or of *punitive damages*, however, and businesspersons should understand what those terms mean.

Nominal Damages   Nominal damages are awarded when a breach of contract is shown, but the nonbreaching party is unable to prove any actual damages. For example, the breaching party failed to paint the nonbreaching party's house, but another equally competent painter was found who performed the work for less than the price of the original contract. Thus, the nonbreaching party suffered no injury. The usual amount of a nominal damages award is one dollar. Normally, parties do not sue where they contemplate only nominal damages. However, the award of nominal damages may trigger the obligation to pay the nonbreaching party's attorney's fees and costs, if the contract calls for payment of such costs on breach. Attorney's fees are not usually considered an element of damages unless the contract so provides.

Punitive Damages   Punitive damages are damages designed to punish the wrongdoer and to set an example for others. Generally, punitive damages are not recoverable in a breach of contract action because they are inconsistent with the broader theory of contract that permits a breach of contract (with damages) where a breach would be economically better for the breaching party. However, courts increasingly are willing to permit punitive damages under circumstances that would support a tort action. Thus, if the breach is malicious or willful or physically injurious to the nonbreaching party, the court may award punitive damages.

Compensatory Damages   Compensatory damages may be classified as either general (direct) or special (consequential). General damages include those that naturally flow from breach of the kind of contract involved. Such damages are always recoverable. Special damages are those that result from the particular circumstances of the case, rather than from the nature of the contract. To illustrate the distinction, assume that Victor contracted to shoe Elaine's horse. Victor performed the job improperly, and a horseshoe fell off. General damages would certainly include the expense involved in having the horse properly shoed. General damages would also probably include the value of the horse if it broke its leg as a result of the improper shoeing. These types of damages might naturally be expected to result from a breach of the kind of contract involved. Now assume that the horse was Elaine's only means of transportation; that she had intended to ride the horse into town to complete a deal for the sale of cattle; that because of the lost shoe she was unable to reach town in time to complete the deal; and that as a result she lost $50,000. The $50,000 could be considered special, or consequential, damages. Is it fair, however, to award $50,000 as damages for breach of a contract to shoe a horse?

The foregoing example points up the problems posed by special damages. On the one hand, the innocent party has suffered certain damages as a result of the other party's contractual breach. On the other hand, as in many cases, there is no way that the breaching party could have anticipated such a loss. The courts have generally resolved the problem by permitting recovery of special damages only if they could have been reasonably foreseen by the defaulting party. For example, if Victor knew that Elaine needed her horse in order to get to town to complete the deal, then it is reasonable to conclude that he knew or should have known that breach of the horseshoeing contract would probably result in Elaine's being unable to complete the transaction. In such a situation, Elaine could recover her special damages. If, however, Victor was totally unaware of Elaine's intended use of the horse, most courts would not permit recovery of the special damages. The reasoning is that a nonbreaching party should not have damages imposed that represent more than the risk of nonperformance that was undertaken at the time of the contract.

 When one party is likely to suffer special damages if the other party breaches the contract, he or she should communicate this likelihood to the other party. Then, in the event of breach, special damages could probably be recovered. More important, the other party, having knowledge of the special circumstances, might make a special effort to perform. Obviously, the party assuming the risk of substantial special damages will attempt to reflect that risk in the bargain.

Measure of Damages   The usual measure of damages is the amount of money necessary to compensate the nonbreaching party for the loss of the bargain. So, for example, if A contracts with B to paint A's fence and B fails to perform, A is entitled to the difference between the contract price and the amount necessary to obtain *substitute performance* (another painting job) from someone else, together with any *incidental damages* associated with A's attempt to minimize the loss. Running an ad in the paper or making long-distance phone calls to find a new painter would be incidental damages. Similarly, if A has incurred expenses in reliance on B's performance, and B breaches, A is entitled to protection of the *reliance interest*. Note that the amount of damages recoverable takes into consideration the cost of obtaining performance else-where, offset by the obligation to pay the contract price. Thus, A gets what she bargained for. In addition, there may be consequential, or special, dam-ages to A associated with B's nonperformance.

Along the same lines, if B has performed and A refuses to pay, B is entitled to the contract price.

The measure of damages is more complicated if B has tendered performance but A refuses to perform. B is entitled to the contract price, but that amount is offset by the expense B would have incurred in performance. In general, B is entitled to *lost profits*. Thus, for example, if A has failed to manufacture goods that B planned to sell at a profit, B is obligated to prove with some reasonable certainty that a profit would have been made. To sustain this burden it is often necessary to introduce evidence of previous sales of similar products, along with economic and marketing evidence. A court will reject uncertain proof as being too *speculative*.

Liquidated Damages and Penalties   Sometimes it is very difficult, or very expensive, to prove the loss caused by a breach of contract with sufficient certainty. If the parties recognize this potential problem at the time of the contract, they may reach an agreement in advance concerning the amount of damages recoverable under given conditions of a breach. This agreement in a contract is called a *liquidated damages clause*. The purpose of a liquidated damages clause is to ensure that a reasonable estimate of probable damages is available in case of a breach. Such a clause is designed not only to avoid the problem of determining and proving damages but also to avoid the likelihood of conflict over the amount of damages.

Courts will enforce liquidated damages clauses if the amount specified appears to have been a reasonable estimate of probable damages. If the clause appears to be designed to punish a party for default, however, the court will consider it a *penalty for breach* and will not enforce the clause. If the court does not enforce the clause, the nonbreaching party must prove actual damages to recover. Creating a penalty for breach is inconsistent with the contract theory that the parties should be permitted to breach for economic reasons. In addition, the doctrine of unconscionability figures prominently in denying enforcement of penalty provisions. One party is not free to oppress the other party by specifying an exorbitant amount and labeling it liquidated damages. A court must examine the circumstances of each case to determine whether a purported liquidated damages clause is actually a penalty.

Mitigating Damages   When a breach occurs, the nonbreaching party is obligated to take reasonable steps to minimize the damages that result from breach. A party may not recover damages that reasonably could have been avoided. The duty to minimize damages is called the *duty to mitigate*. For example, if A leases an apartment to B for one year, but B leaves after six months, A may not simply leave the apartment vacant and require full payment from B. A must take reasonable steps to rent the apartment to someone else to minimize the damages flowing from B's breach. Similarly, if an employer wrongfully discharges an employee, the employee must ordinarily seek other similar employment. A party's failure to seek to minimize damages will result in a reduction of the amount granted by the court. Actual out-of-pocket costs associated with mitigation may be recovered from the breaching party.

Tort Remedies   The same set of facts may permit a party to sue under either a breach of contract or a tort theory. The damages recoverable in a tort action may be larger. For example, punitive damages may be recovered in a tort action. It may therefore be desirable in some cases to seek recovery on a tort theory, either in addition to or in lieu of a contract theory.

18:10   Other Remedies

A remedy other than damages may be appropriate in some cases. A party might seek specific performance, injunctive relief, rescission, restitution, or arbitration. Each of these possible remedies will be discussed briefly.

Specific Performance   Sometimes an award of damages, no matter how great, is simply inadequate to remedy the injury caused by a breach of contract. In such cases, a decree of *specific performance* may be sought. Specific performance is an equitable remedy, and it will be granted only when the remedy at law is inadequate. To be entitled to specific performance, the plaintiff must show that the subject matter of the contract was unique. Since a unique item cannot be replaced, an award of damages can never have the effect of giving the innocent party the benefit of the bargain. Specific performance is granted primarily in cases involving contracts for the sale of land. Each piece of land is considered unique and therefore irreplaceable. Personal property, in contrast, ordinarily is not considered unique. For example, if a seller breaches a contract for sale of an automobile, the buyer can always purchase a comparable automobile elsewhere. Therefore, if the contract involves personal property, the property must be shown to be truly unique before a court will order specific performance. A court might order specific performance of a contract for the sale of a Gutenberg Bible, for example, since it would probably be impossible for a buyer to purchase another copy.

Specific performance is not a remedy in cases involving personal service contracts. The primary reason for refusing specific performance is that it is impossible to coerce a person to render services.

The following case provides an excellent analysis of the purpose of specific performance in real estate contracts.

Mohrlang

v

Draper

365 NW2d 443 (1985)

Supreme Court of Nebraska

FACTS: In June 1981 Mohrlang contracted with Draper to purchase for $14,875 an unimproved tract of land owned by Draper. As part of the purchase agreement Draper was to obtain the release of a "right-of-way" easement across the lot and to bear the cost of relocating a buried gasline that rendered the lot unusable for the residential construction Mohrlang intended. In early July Draper learned that relocation of the gasline would cost more than $10,000. In the meantime, Mohrlang had hired an architectural firm and embarked on plans for a solar home requiring the southern exposure available on the Draper lot. When Draper refused title, Mohrlang sued for specific performance. Draper claimed that Mohrlang should be limited to money damages. Mohrlang claimed that no other lot had the particular features found in the Draper lot.

ISSUE: Is Mohrlang entitled to specific performance in spite of the hardship that would be imposed on Draper?

RESULT: The hardship on Draper is not so onerous or unpredictable as to defeat Mohrlang's right to specific performance.

REASONING:

*   *   *

When land or any interest therein is the subject matter of a contract, the power of a court of equity to grant specific performance is beyond question. . . . We have held that specific performance should generally be granted as a matter of course or right regarding a contract for the sale of real estate where a valid, binding contract exists which is definite and certain in its terms, mutual in its obligation, free from overreaching fraud and unfairness, and where the remedy at law is inadequate. . . . Real estate is assumed to possess the characteristic of uniqueness, and, therefore, special value, necessary for availability of specific performance. . . . This assumption is based upon the status of land as the favorite and favored subject in England and all countries of Anglo-Saxon origin. . . . In an action for specific performance of a contract to sell real estate, generally, it is no defense that there is other available land as good as or even better than the land which is the subject of the contract to be performed. . . .

Exoneration from specific performance may be available when specific performance would be inequitable or unjust due to hardship on the one from whom performance is sought. Whether a contract is fair, and, therefore, subject to equitable enforcement, is determined by the circumstances existing when the contract is entered rather than by subsequent events intervening before specific performance is sought. . . .

One form of hardship equitably excusing specific performance of a contract may be a circumstance unforeseeable at entry into the contract. Hardship of such nature, however, cannot be self-inflicted or caused through inexcusable neglect on the part of the person seeking to be excused or exonerated from specific performance. . . . Were the rule otherwise, one would derive a benefit from his or her own inexcusable neglect.

Draper entered the contract on June 9 and through the gas company's estimate of July 7 learned about the cost of relocating the gasline. The inescapable inference is that complete information about relocating the gasline was available when Draper entered the contract to sell his lot. The contract expressly required that Draper bear the cost of relocating the gasline. . . .

Although the exact extent of expense for relocating the gasline was apparently unknown to Draper when he entered the agreement, relocating the gasline was a burden undertaken by Draper when the parties made their contract. Draper's belated realization that his financial burden under the contract was greater than initially anticipated at origination of the agreement does not constitute hardship excusing specific performance of his contract with Mohrlang. An imprudent or bad bargain in and of itself is not an excuse for nonperformance of a contract. . . . It was Draper's neglect which increased his burden, not an unforeseeable circumstance. . . .

Shanahan, Justice.

Injunction   The equitable remedy of obtaining an injunction is closely related to, and in many cases has the same effect as, an award of specific performance. An injunction in contract actions is a court order to restrain a breach or a continuing breach of the contract. As with specific performance, injunctive relief is granted when the remedy at law is inadequate. In addition, there normally must be a showing that irreparable injury will result to the other party if the injunctive relief is not granted.

Injunctive relief may be utilized to effectively compel specific performance of a contract for personal services. When an employee possesses truly special, unique, or extraordinary qualifications, so that his services cannot be replaced, and the employee refuses to perform, a court might issue a kind of injunction called a negative injunction. This injunction prohibits the employee from performing services for any other person. For example, if an exceptional professional athlete or entertainer refused to honor his contractual obligation, a court might enjoin him from performing for any other person.

Injunctive relief is also often used to enforce anticompetition contracts. For example, assume that A sells her hamburger stand to B and that the contract prohibits A from operating another hamburger stand within a radius of five miles for a period of three years. If A immediately opens another hamburger stand across the street, B can seek an injunction ordering A to honor the anticompetition clause.

Rescission and Restitution   A contract may be avoided, or *rescinded*, by either the court or the parties. Court rescission may occur when the contract is cancelled for illegality, misrepresentation, incapacity, or any other reason that gives rise to a right to rescind. The parties may at any time decide to cancel the contract. When a contract is rescinded, contract remedies are no longer available. Nevertheless, rescission may injure a party unless the parties can be put back in the position they would have been in had there been no contract. If one party has conferred a benefit on the other, *restitution* may be necessary to restore the benefit.

Where one party has paid another money, restitution may simply consist of the return of the money. If one party's performance was a service, however, a court must determine whether the correct measure of restitution would be the market value of the service or the extent to which the other party was enriched. As a minimum, a court will not permit *unjust enrichment* in the rescission of a contract.

Key Concepts and Terms

- A contract is discharged when the parties no longer have any obligations under it. Performance is the normal method of discharge.

- A party's duty to perform may be contingent on the occurrence or nonoccurrence of certain conditions. A condition precedent involves an event, the occurrence of which precedes and creates imposition of the duty. A condition subsequent involves an event the occurrence of which follows and extinguishes the duty. A concurrent condition involves one party's performance being conditioned on performance by the other party, and vice versa.

- Substantial performance by a party is the performance of a contract with slight departures from contractual specification. Substantial performance entitles the performing party to performance by the other party. Partial performance is performance of some but not all of the contract's provisions. Partial performance does not generally entitle the performing party to performance by the other party.

- If a contract involves matters of personal taste, compliance with a clause requiring one party to render satisfactory performance is determined solely by the other party. In other situations, a reasonable-person rule of satisfaction is applied.

- When a contract specifies no time for performance, a reasonable time is allowed. If time is of the essence, failure to perform by the time specified relieves the other party from the obligation to perform. Otherwise, delay in performance merely entitles the other party to damages.

- The fact that intervening events render performance of a contract extremely difficult does not ordinarily excuse nonperformance. Acceptable excuses for nonperformance include (1) death or illness of an essential person, (2) destruction of an essential item, (3) a change in law rendering performance illegal, and (4) commercial frustration.

- A contract may be discharged by agreement of the parties (rescission, novation, or accord and satisfaction) or by operation of law (discharge in bankruptcy, passage of the period prescribed by the statute of limitations, or material alteration). Performance of an obligation may also be waived.

- A breach of contract is a party's failure to perform a contractual obligation without having a legal excuse for not performing. An anticipatory breach, which also excuses performance by the innocent party, occurs when one party informs the other of his or her intention not to perform the contract, even though the time for performance has not yet arrived.

- The purpose of a remedy is to place an innocent party in the position he or she would have occupied were it not for a breach of contract. The usual remedy in a contract action is an award of compensatory damages, which are classified as either general (direct) or special (consequential).

- Liquidated damages are a kind of compensatory damages that are specified in a contract provision when it would be difficult or impossible to calculate the value of a loss caused by a breach of the contract.

- Specific performance and injunctions are court-ordered remedies granted to the injured party when damages are an insufficient remedy.

- Rescission, restitution, and arbitration are other remedies available for breach of contract.

- Accord and Satisfaction
- Anticipatory Breach
- Commercial Frustration
- Compensatory Damages
- Concurrent Conditions
- Condition Precedent
- Condition Subsequent
- Discharge
- Election of Remedies
- Expectation Interest
- Impossibility
- Incidental Damages
- Injunction
- Lost Profits

- Material or Immaterial Breach
- Mitigation of Damages
- Nominal Damages
- Offset
- Penalty for Breach
- Punitive Damages
- Reliance Interest
- Restitution Interest
- Satisfaction Clause
- Speculative Damages
- Statute of Limitations
- Substitute Performance
- Time-of-the-Essence Clause
- Unjust Enrichment

Questions and Case Problems

1. How does a court sort out *when* the parties are obligated to perform if the parties do not stipulate the order of performance in the contract? Can the court infer conditions when the parties did not create them in the contract?

2. Peters contracts to build a house for Jayo, a wheelchair-bound paraplegic. The house is generally constructed according to specifications. The only deviation from the contract is that the entrances and the bathrooms are not built for access by wheelchairs. This deviation does not affect the value of the house, but the cost of making the entrances and bathrooms accessible to wheelchairs would be $3,000. In making final payment to Peters, Jayo deducts $3,000 from the agreed price. Peters sues. What is the result?

3. In March, Schmidt contracted to supply eggs to the City College cafeteria for a year, beginning in September. During a heat wave in June, many of Schmidt's chickens died, and on July 1 he informed the cafeteria manager that he would be unable to supply the eggs as agreed. On July 10, Schmidt informed the manager that he might be able to replace his hens faster than he thought; that if he did replace them he would be able to perform the contract; and that he would know for certain by July 31. On July 15, the manager, unwilling to wait, contracted with another egg supplier at a substantially higher price. On July 25, Schmidt informed the manager that he would perform the contract, but the manager told him that his eggs were no longer needed. Schmidt sued for damages due to loss of business, and the cafeteria counterclaimed for damages due to the increased price paid the second supplier. What is the result?

4. Mills contracts with Fauna Productions to serve as technical advisor on a movie concerning coyotes and to train a coyote named Alpha to perform in the movie. As partial compensation, Mills is to receive Alpha when the movie is completed. Fauna reneges on the promise to give Alpha to Mills, and Mills sues for specific performance. Although she admits that other coyotes could be trained as well as Alpha, Mills claims that Alpha is unique because her children had become attached to him during the filming. Should Mills be granted specific performance?

5. Johnson contracted with the Wallowa County School District to drive a bus for two years. The contract granted him an option to renew the contract for three additional years if his service proved to be satisfactory. Although there was no evidence of unsatisfactory service, the school board declined to renew the contract when it expired. Johnson sued for damages. Result?

6. In March 1967 Shell International hired ATP Corp. to carry oil by ship from Texas to India. The fee was based on a standard rate schedule, plus 75 percent, plus toll charges for the Suez Canal. The ship left Texas and arrived in the Mediterranean just before the Arab–Israeli war closed the Suez Canal. The ship was forced to turn back and go around the Cape of Good Hope to India at an additional cost of $131,978.44. ATP Corp. sued Shell for the additional cost of going around the cape. ATP's theory is that performance of the original contract was rendered commercially impracticable by the war; ATP sued in quasi-contract for the benefit it rendered to Shell. Shell claimed that travel through the Suez Canal was not a condition of the contract and that the war made the travel route expensive but not impracticable. What result?

7. Mr. and Mrs. Weizenbaum signed a real estate contract to purchase realty from the Links. The closing was set for July 31, 1980. On several occasions before the

closing date Mr. Weizenbaum advised the Links that he could not come up with the money and would not close the contract. On July 29 the Links filed suit against the Weizenbaums for anticipatory breach of the contract. In defense, Weizenbaum argued that Mrs. Weizenbaum, his co-obligor, never repudiated the contract and that the apparent anticipatory breach of the contract, therefore, was not clear and unequivocal and did not cover the entire performance of the contract. How would you analyze this problem?

8. Wafer sells his accounting business and equipment to Mullen. The contract of sale provides that Wafer will remain active in the business for two years to assist Mullen in making a satifactory transition. Less than a month after the sale, Wafer dies. Mullen sues to rescind the contract on the ground that Wafer's services were indispensable to the contract. What is the decision?

9. In December, Adam reserved a room at the Ras Hotel for the three days of the Memorial Day weekend; he made full advance payment of $315. In March, Adam canceled the reservation and asked for return of his advance payment. The Ras refused, and made no attempt to rent the room over the holiday. Adam sued. What amount, if any, should he recover? Would the answer be different if Adam had waited until the day before to cancel his reservation? If the reservation had been for a nonholiday period?

10. Cook contracted to sell his condominium to Dean, with a closing date of November 1. The contract provided that time was of the essence. On October 15, Dean informed Cook that she would not be able to close the sale on November 1, and that an additional month might be required. Cook told Dean not to worry and that the deal could be closed after November 1. On November 3, Cook received a better offer for the condominium. He immediately notified Dean that, unless the sale was closed within 15 days, he would consider the contract rescinded. When Dean was unable to close by November 18, Cook contracted to sell the condominium to the other buyer. On December 1, Dean sued for specific performance. Should specific performance be granted? Should the availability of identical condominium units in the same complex affect the result?

PART FOUR

Sales

Introductory Comments

Virtually every business engages in the sale of goods, often as both buyer and seller. A closhing manufacturer, for example, must buy raw materials to make the clothing he sells. It is therefore imperative that a businessperson have some knowledge of the legal rights and obligations of both buyer and seller.

The material in Chapters 19 through 22 focuses on the law of sales, with emphasis on the provisions of the UCC. These chapters discuss the formation of sales contracts, the actual transfer of goods and title to goods, the determination of which party bears the loss when goods are damaged, warranties relating to the quality and performance of goods, performance of sales contracts, and remedies for breach of these contracts.

Throughout this division, the practical aspects of sales transactions are considered because they are critical in determining the resolution of any sales dispute. The particular characteristics of an industry and the way in which it conducts its business must be taken into account. For example, the diamond industry conducts business differently than the aerospace industry, and it follows that the customary method of making a sale may also differ. As much as possible a buyer or seller should familiarize himself with and follow these customs.

At the heart of a sales transaction is the sales contract. Such a contract is just as binding as any other, and a businessperson should approach it with the same care as he approaches other contracts. Care should also be taken both in drafting and in using standardized forms.

In the same light, the value of cooperation should not be overlooked. Disagreements do arise in sales transactions. Often these disagreements may be settled amicably by the parties involved. A friendly settlement may prevent litigation, preserve a contract, and maintain a valuable business relationship. In other words, legal action is normally the last option to be pursued, not the first.

Finally, it should be noted that the area of sales does not constitute an island unto itself. General contract law, as discussed earlier in this book, is obviously relevant to sales contracts. The law of sales may also interact with the law of torts, the law of commercial paper, the law governing creditor–debtor relationships, and the law of insurance. For example, when a person is injured by a defective product, both tort and sales law may be applicable. When a buyer pays for goods with a check or other commercial paper, the law governing commercial paper must be considered. When a buyer takes out a loan to finance a purchase, sales law and the law governing creditor–debtor relationships interact. And when insurance is taken out on goods, insurance law becomes relevant. Thus, although sales law is considered here as a separate subject, its relationship to other areas of law must always be borne in mind.

19 Introduction to the Law of Sales

19:1 Historical Background

Commerce as it is practiced today had its beginning in the latter part of the Middle Ages. It was virtually nonexistent in the centuries following the collapse of the Roman Empire, but began a gradual revival around the twelfth century. A significant contribution to this revival was the European fair. Held in different areas of the continent, these great fairs generated a tremendous amount of commercial activity as merchants from all parts of Europe gathered to exchange their goods. Out of necessity these merchants eventually developed a set of general rules to govern their commercial dealings. These rules, known as the *law merchant*, became recognized throughout Europe and England as the body of law that governed the resolution of commercial disputes.

In time the law merchant became a part of the English common law. The English common law of sales was codified into the English Sale of Goods Act. This act served as the basis for the Uniform Sales Act, which was adopted by most American states. Finally, the Uniform Commercial Code (UCC) was proposed. It has been enacted by 49 states, the District of Columbia, and the Virgin Islands. (Louisiana has not adopted the UCC as a whole, but has adopted some portions of it.) Article 2 of the UCC deals with sales of goods and has replaced the Uniform Sales Act as the basic law of sales.

As this brief survey indicates, the law of sales has developed over hundreds of years. In deciding controversies concerning sales, the courts therefore have a great body of legal tradition from which to draw. Indeed, the UCC itself recognizes that the law merchant may still be applied in appropriate situations [UCC § 1-103].

Portions of the UCC other than Article 2 also may be applicable to some sales contracts. These are Article 1, which contains general provisions applicable to all the remaining articles; Article 6, which relates to particular kinds of transfers of goods known as bulk transfers and is covered in Chapter 20 of this book; and Article 7, which deals with documents of title and is also covered in Chapter 20.

19:2   Subject Matter of Sales

Article 2 governs "transactions in goods" [UCC § 2-102]. While these trans-actions include more than sales, for practical purposes Article 2 deals with sales of goods. It becomes important, therefore, to determine what constitutes a sale, as well as what constitutes goods.

Sale   The basic feature of a *sale* is the passage of title from the seller to the buyer for a price [UCC § 2-106(1)]. This feature distinguishes a sale from various similar transactions. For example, in a lease of personal property, there is no transfer of title; the lessee is expected to return the property to the lessor at the conclusion of the lease.[1] In the case of a gift, there is passage of title, but no price is paid.

The payment in a sale need not be money. The price may be partially or wholly paid in other goods or services. For example, if Susan trades in her old car as down payment on a new car, the price paid by her for the new car consists in part of goods (her old car) rather than money.

 For various reasons, parties to a contract sometimes wish to disguise its true nature. Installment sales, for example, are sometimes labeled leases. By calling a sale a lease, the parties may hope to avoid appli-cation not only of Article 2, but also of Article 9, which deals with secured transactions. This may lead to unforeseen difficulties because a court will look behind the name given a transaction to ascertain its true nature. In other words, a court might end up applying UCC provisions that the parties were seeking to avoid. Therefore, it is usually preferable to structure the transaction in a straightforward way so that the parties will know what to expect and will be aware of what law applies.

Goods   Under Article 2, *goods* includes all things that are movable at the time of identification to the contract [UCC § 2-105(1)].[2] Basically, this means that Article 2 governs all sales of tangible personal property of every variety. "Goods" includes the unborn young of animals, growing crops, timber to be cut, minerals, oil, gas, and structures that are attached to land if they are capable of being severed without material harm to the land, and are to be severed by the seller [UCC §§ 2-105(1), 2-107].

Land and intangible personal property are not "goods" under Article 2. For example, sales of intangible rights of action (such as one person's right to sue another for damages) or investment securities are not covered by Article 2 [UCC § 2-105(1)].

For a sale of goods to occur, the goods must be both existing and identified. Where the goods are not existing and identified, the parties may enter into a

---

[1] Personal property leases and bailments, and the applicability of UCC principles to bailments, are discussed in Chapter 34.

[2] "Identification to the contract" is discussed in Chapter 20.

contract for the sale of *future goods* [UCC § 2-105(2)]. Both a present sale and a contract for a future sale come within Article 2, and the status of a transaction as a present sale or a contract to sell generally has no bearing on the rights of the parties. The UCC has specifically addressed some areas of previous difficulty. For example, Article 2 provides that "goods" includes specially manufactured items [UCC § 2-105(1)], and that the serving of food and drink is considered a sale [UCC § 2-314(1)].

Mixed Transactions The general principles presented above are easy to apply in most instances to determine whether a transaction is a sale of goods. If a person sells a desk, a suit, or a can of beans, he has sold goods. If a person sells a house, he has not sold goods. Similarly, a contract for legal or other professional services usually does not involve a sale of goods, and is therefore not within the scope of Article 2.

Often, however, a contract involves not only the rendition of services, but also the transfer of goods. A question then arises as to what part, if any, of the transaction should be governed by Article 2. To determine this, courts have generally looked to the primary focus of the contract. If it was essentially a contract for the rendition of services, with the transfer of goods being merely incidental to those services, Article 2 is inapplicable. However, if the transaction was primarily a sale, Article 2 is applicable to the entire transaction.

Under Article 2, certain warranties come into existence when a sale of goods occurs.[3] Service contracts, since they do not come under Article 2, do not carry similar warranties. Therefore, the determination of whether a transaction involves a sale of goods or merely a rendition of services may be extremely important. For example, assume that a water company provides contaminated water to its customers and that several of them become ill as a result. Does the provision of water constitute a sale, or is it merely a rendition of a service? There has been disagreement on the answer, with courts holding both ways.

The above discussion points up two additional important factors. First, while goods must be tangible and movable, they need not be solid. For example, a sale of electricity could constitute a sale of goods. Second, determination of whether a transaction involves a sale of goods or only a rendition of services may be extremely important in a product liability case.[4] For example, assume that a person goes to a physician, the physician gives the person a vaccination, and the person becomes ill because the serum was improperly constituted. May the physician be sued for breach of warranty for selling a defective product, or is he immune from suit on this theory because he was providing professional services?

The following case illustrates how the courts approach the issue of whether a contract should be classified as a sales contract or a services contract.

---

[3] Warranties are discussed in Chapter 21.
[4] Product liability is discussed in Chapter 21.

Mennonite Deaconess Home & Hospital Inc.

v

Gates Engineering Co.
363 NW2d 155 (1985)
Supreme Court of Nebraska

FACTS: The Mennonite Deaconess Hospital agreed to buy a "one-ply roofing system" from Gates, to be installed by an installer approved by Gates. When the work was substantially completed, the hospital paid the installer 90%, withholding the balance until Gates approved the installation. Gates withheld its approval. Moreover, the roof began to leak badly and had to be completely replaced at the hospital's expense. The hospital sought to hold Gates to warranties under the UCC, and Gates defended that the transaction was not covered under the UCC.

ISSUE: Is a contract for a "one-ply roofing system" a contract for a sale of goods?

RESULT: Because the predominant factor in the transaction was the roofing material, the sale is within the UCC and subject to the warranties provisions of Article 2.

REASONING:

*　　*　　*

. . . The cases are uniform in holding that the U.C.C. applies where the principal purpose of the contract is the sale of goods, even though in order for the goods to be utilized, some installation is required. On the other hand, if the contract is principally for services and the goods are merely incidental to the contract, the provisions of the U.C.C. do not apply.

The test for inclusion in or exclusion from the sales provisions is not whether the contracts are mixed but, granting that they are mixed, whether their predominant factor, their thrust, their purpose, reasonably stated, is the rendition of service, with goods incidentally involved, or whether they are transactions of sale, with labor incidentally involved. . . . [In] *Colorado Carpet Installation, Inc. v Palermo* 668 P.2d 1384, 1388 (Colo.1983), the Supreme Court of Colorado said:

> The scope of the contract, however, included not only the sale of goods but also the performance of labor or service. Thus, we must determine whether such a mixed contract qualified as a contract for the sale of goods or, instead, constituted a contract for labor or service outside the scope of [UCC § 2-201].
>
> The performance of some labor or service frequently plays a role in sales transactions. "Goods," however, are not the less "goods" merely because labor

or service may be essential to their ultimate use by the purchaser. The mere furnishing of some labor or service, in our view, should not determine the ultimate character of a contract for purposes of section 4-2-201(1) of the Uniform Commercial Code. Rather, the controlling criterion should be the primary purpose of the contract—that is, whether the circumstances underlying the formation of the agreement and the performance reasonably expected of the parties demonstrates the primary purpose of the contract as the sale of goods or, in contrast, the sale of labor or service. We agree in this respect with the following statement in *Bonebrake v. Cox*, 499 F2d 951, 960 (8th Cir.1974):

"The test for inclusion or exclusion is not whether (goods and services) are mixed, but, granting that they are mixed, whether their predominant factor, their thrust, their purpose, reasonably stated, is the rendition of service, with goods incidentally involved (*e.g.,* contract with artist for painting) or is a transaction of sale, with labor incidentally involved (*e.g.,* insulation of a water heater in a bathroom)." . . .

This "primary purpose" test, we believe, is designed to promote one of the expressed statutory policies of the Uniform Commercial Code—"(t)o simplify, clarify, and modernize the law governing commercial transactions." . . .

We believe that an examination of the contract, the brochures, and the evidence adduced at trial makes it manifestly clear that this contract had as its predominant factor the roofing material manufactured by Gates and only incidentally involved installation by a contractor approved by Gates. The evidence establishes that the hospital was not simply purchasing a new roof of any type or description. Quite to the contrary, as reflected by the evidence, the hospital determined, after careful consideration, to use the one-ply system specifically manufactured and supplied by Gates. The contract specifically identified the type of roof to be installed and further identified it in such a manner that nothing other than the Gates material could be used. It is clear to us that what was being purchased here was a completed roof of the type manufactured by Gates, though installed by others approved by Gates. We believe that the situation here clearly falls into that category in which courts have uniformly held that the contract was for the sale of goods and covered by the Uniform Commercial Code. . . .

Krivosha, Chief Justice.

19:3   General Principles Governing Sales Transactions

In studying the law of sales, it is worth bearing in mind that the UCC stresses the concept of fairness. The UCC specifically imposes an obligation of *good faith* in the performance or enforcement of every contract or duty that comes within the act [UCC § 1-203]. The UCC also prohibits the parties from disclaiming the "obligations of good faith, diligence, reasonableness and care" imposed by the code [UCC § 1-102(3)]. The question of whether a party's actions were taken in good faith or were reasonable may therefore be crucial in resolving a sales dispute.

Merchants   The UCC makes a sharp distinction between transactions that involve a professional in a given field and those that involve amateurs or consumers. In keeping with the underlying premise that fairness should be an element of commercial transactions, several UCC provisions require higher standards of conduct by merchants as opposed to nonmerchants. In particular, merchants are held to a higher standard of good faith than are nonmerchants. The good-faith obligation requires simple honesty from nonmerchants [UCC § 1-201(19)], whereas for merchants good faith also requires the observance of reasonable commercial standards of fair dealing in the trade [UCC § 2-103(1)(b)]. Thus, merchants are held not only to a subjective standard of honesty, but also to an objective, reasonable person standard.

The rationale behind the imposition of higher standards on merchants is that a merchant is more knowledgeable or experienced in sales transactions. It is not surprising, therefore, that the definition of merchant revolves around the concepts of knowledge and experience. Under the UCC, a merchant is a person who (1) deals in goods of the kind involved in the transaction; or (2) otherwise holds himself out as having knowledge or skill peculiar to the practices or goods involved; or (3) employs an agent, broker, or other intermediary who holds himself out as having such knowledge or skill [UCC § 2-104(1)].

It is important to note that a person may be considered a merchant even though he or she is not a dealer in the type of goods involved. Assume, for example, that a university music professor decides to sell his rare violin. Although he had never sold a violin before, the professor would probably be considered a merchant under the UCC definition because he has special knowledge and skill with respect to the goods for sale. It is also worth noting that a person may be a merchant for some purposes but not others. For example, a bank president would be a merchant with respect to banking transactions, but not with respect to a sale of fishing tackle.

Applicability of General Principles of Law   While the UCC, and specifically Article 2, contains the basic law of sales, it by no means contains the only law applicable to sales. General legal and equitable principles, including principles of contract law, may be applied in sales cases, unless they would conflict with the UCC [UCC § 1-103].

19:4   The Sales Contract

A sales contract is in most respects just like any other contract. There must be an offer and acceptance, consideration, competent parties, and legality of purpose. Therefore, general principles of contract law, discussed in detail previously (see Chapters 9–18), are frequently applied in disputes involving sales contracts. The UCC does, however, make significant changes. Many changes, such as the UCC rules on firm offers and method of acceptance, have been covered in Chapter 10. Others will be discussed here.

The changes made by the UCC result largely from recognition of the fact that contracts, particularly sales contracts, often are not the result of careful negotiations. The parties may overlook or choose to ignore certain items, or not make a specific offer or acceptance. The UCC disregards these defects as long as there is a true basis for agreement. Take § 2-204(1), for example. It provides that a sales contract may be made in any manner sufficient to show agreement, including conduct by both parties recognizing the existence of the contract. Moreover, under § 2-204(2), a sales contract may be found even though the time of its making cannot be determined.

Open Terms   The material terms of an ordinary contract must be reasonably definite. In a sales agreement, however, certain terms may be left open without making the contract invalid for indefiniteness, provided the parties intended to make a contract [UCC § 2-204(3)]. The UCC provides generally that missing terms may be filled in by resort to course of performance, course of dealing, or usage of trade [UCC §§ 1-205, 2-208]. The following case illustrates the application of these principles in a sales contract.

KN Energy, Inc.
v
Great Western Sugar Co.
698 P2d 769 (1985)
Supreme Court of Colorado

FACTS: KN is a natural gas pipeline company. Beginning in 1955 KN executed a series of contracts with Great Western (GW) to supply natural gas to GW's sugar processing plants in Colorado and Nebraska. The contracts included a clause describing GW's service as "interruptible." Between 1955 and 1973 KN used this clause to terminate service only when continued service jeopardized the pressure in the gas line and threatened service to higher priority users. In 1973 KN negotiated contracts with new rates, but the interruption clause remained unchanged. In addition, KN instituted a new interruption policy that resulted in more frequent service interruptions. In 1978 GW sued KN for damages, claiming that KN breached its contract by instituting the new policy. KN argued that the contract permitted "absolute discretion" in interruption policy and that prior policy was irrelevant to the meaning of the contract.

ISSUE: Is KN's course of performance of the interruption clause between 1955 and 1973 relevant to KN's intent in agreeing to the interruption clause in the 1973 contract?

RESULT: Yes. The prior course of performance is evidence of KN's intended meaning.

REASONING:

*   *   *

Under the provisions of the Uniform Commercial Code as adopted in Colorado, the parties' course of dealing prior to execution of the contract always may be considered in interpreting the express terms of the contract in order that the true understanding of the parties to the agreement may be determined, whether or not the express terms of the agreement are found to be ambiguous. [UCC § 2–202(a), official comment 1(c)] . . . Prior dealings are relevant and are generally the "best possible guide" to the parties' true intent. . . . Therefore, the intent evidenced by such conduct is presumed to have been incorporated into the written contract unless the intent evidenced by the conduct has been "carefully negated" by the written terms. [UCC § 2–202, official comment 2] In the present case, the district court was justified in considering the intent manifested by the parties' eighteen year course of dealing under the twenty-four to thirty-six hour historical analysis.

The parties' course of performance following execution of the contract is also relevant to the interpretation of the agreement. [UCC § 2–202(a)] Course of performance may be used as an aid to interpretation whenever one party accepts repeated performance by the other party with knowledge of the nature of that performance and an opportunity to object to it. [UCC § 2–208] . . . Even assuming that these conditions were met here, and that the parties' post-1973 course of performance could be considered, the district court's interpretation of the agreements at issue remains proper. Although a court must strive to harmonize the express terms of an agreement with the subsequent course of performance under that agreement, the express terms control where harmony cannot be found. [UCC § 2–208(2)] . . . The court's goal is to give effect to the parties' intention as of the time the contract was made, Williston § 607 at 379; therefore, a course of performance may explain but not contradict the express terms of the writing. The parties' post-1973 course of performance cannot alter the intent expressed in the contract here.

Here, moreover, KN drafted the 1973 contract without materially changing the provisions governing interruption of service, despite the fact that KN was aware at the time both of the meaning with which the contractual provisions had been invested by an eighteen year course of dealing, and of the changed circumstances that purportedly necessitated abandonment of that course of dealing. KN's failure to alter the contract language in 1973 renders doubtful its assertion that it intended to change the meaning of the contractual language. . . . Under these circumstances, KN's post-1973 course of performance is a unilateral breach of contractual terms rather than an expression of the parties' mutual intent at the time the contract was made.

We hold that the district court properly enforced the express terms of the contract in light of the parties' course of dealing and course of performance. . . .

Dubofsky, Justice.

If terms are left open, the UCC has provisions concerning specific ways in which the terms may be set. For example, the UCC permits parties to enter a sales contract with an open price. There are various ways in which the price might ultimately be set. The contract might specify that one party is to fix the price, in which case the UCC requires that the price be fixed in good faith. The contract might provide that the price is to be fixed by some third person or by reference to some set standard, or it might provide that it is to be agreed on later by the parties. Finally, the contract might provide no mechanism at all for setting the price. In this last instance if the price is never set, a court will allow a reasonable price at the time of delivery [UCC § 2-305]. For example, assume that Gaines, a retailer, orders some cloth from Lang, a wholesaler, but neither party mentions price. Lang delivers the cloth, and a dispute then develops as to what the price should be. A court might allow Lang a price based on the going wholesale rate at the time the delivery was made.

Additional Terms in Acceptance—The Battle of the Forms   There is often very little true bargaining involved in a sales transaction. A buyer sends a preprinted form to the seller. This constitutes the offer. The seller, in turn, fills out his or her own preprinted form and returns it to the buyer. This is the acceptance. Since each party's form was drafted with that party's interests in mind, there are almost always discrepancies between the forms. A court applying traditional contract law would conclude that no contract existed under such circumstances. The UCC, in recognition of the reality of this battle of the forms in commercial transactions, deals with the situation in a different manner.

Under the UCC, an acceptance creates a contract, even though it includes additional or different terms, unless the acceptance is expressly conditioned on the offeror's assent to the new terms [UCC § 2-207(1)]. The new terms do not, however, automatically become part of the contract. New terms that are different from those contained in the offer become part of the contract only if the offeror assents. Additional terms are considered proposals for addition to the contract. If both parties are merchants, the additional terms become part of the contract unless (1) the offer expressly limits acceptance to the terms of the offer, (2) the additional terms materially alter the contract, or (3) the offeror gives notice of his or her objection to the additional terms within a reasonable time [UCC § 2-207(2)].

Often parties dispute the legal effectiveness of a contract clause requiring arbitration in the event of conflict. The following case graphically illustrates the dangers of signing a form without reading it. Note how the court concluded that a contract existed despite the presence of open terms. Observe also how the court applied general principles of contract law to resolve the consent issue.

N&D Fashions, Inc.

v

DHJ Industries, Inc.
548 F2d 722 (1976)
United States Court of Appeals, Eighth Circuit

FACTS: N&D Fashions, a wholly owned subsidiary of Nelly Don, Inc., was a purchaser of fabric for apparel manufacturers. DHJ Industries made and sold this fabric. In 1973 Shriber, an agent for N&D, met with DHJ representatives to arrange for the purchase of certain fabric. Shriber emphasized that the fabric had to have colorfast dye. The parties orally agreed on 75,000 yards of fabric and settled type, color, price, and delivery terms. A few days later, Shriber sent a Nelly Don purchase order form to DHJ. The bottom of the form said: "This Purchase Order shall become a binding contract when acknowledged by Seller, or upon whole or partial shipment by Seller. "The purchase order contained no arbitration clause. In response, DHJ sent a confirmation consisting of four documents, one of which was a reply form. Just above the blanks provided for signatures was this statement:

> THIS CONTRACT IS SUBJECT TO ALL THE TERMS AND CONDITIONS PRINTED ON THE REVERSE SIDE.

In fine print on the back were 16 terms and conditions, including a clause providing for arbitration of contract disputes. Shriber signed the reply form and returned it to DHJ. DHJ delivered the fabric, but it was not colorfast. N&D sued for misrepresentation and fraud, and DHJ requested the court to order arbitration. The district court held that the arbitration provision was a material alteration to which N&D had not consented, and thus denied the motion for arbitration. DHJ appealed.

ISSUE: Was the arbitration clause expressly agreed to by N&D?

RESULT: Yes. N&D indicated its agreement by signing DHJ's contract form.

REASONING:

*   *   *

This litigation centers upon the effect to be given to a condition of sale requiring arbitration of disputes that was contained in the seller's acknowledgment of the buyer's written purchase order. It implicates the sometimes murky provisions of Section 2-207 of the Uniform Commercial Code, which was intended to put to rest uncertainty arising from the "battle of the forms." . . .

It is undisputed that the parties reached an agreement with respect to the nature and quantity of the merchandise to be sold and delivered by appellant DHJ, as well as the price to be paid by the buyers. The Uniform Commercial Code does not require that all of the terms of the agreement be decided provided "the parties have intended to make a contract and there is a reasonably certain basis for giving an appropriate remedy." Uniform Commercial Code § 2-204(3). A problem is presented, however, when an acceptance or confirmation contains terms which are "additional to or different from" an offer or prior agreement. Under Uniform Commercial Code § 2-207, if the dealings are between merchants, the additional terms become a part of the agreement provided (1) the original offer did not expressly preclude such additions (the offer here did not), (2) the additions do not materially alter the agreement, and (3) no seasonable notice is given of objections to the additions (none was given here). From this it follows that the provision for arbitration in this case, as a proposed additional term, became a part of the agreement unless, as the District Court found, it was a material alteration of the agreement. . . .

A clause will be held to "materially alter" a contract when it would "result in surprise or hardship if incorporated without express awareness by the other party." Uniform Commercial Code § 2-207, Comment 4. Official Comments 4 and 5 provide examples of terms which would and would not materially alter a contract, and an arbitration clause is listed under neither. While other cases have held that an arbitration clause would materially alter a contract under § 2-207, the better reasoned position is that the question whether an additional term in a written confirmation constitutes a "material alteration" is a question of fact to be resolved by the circumstances of each particular case. . . .

. . . [W]e cannot say on this record that the District Court was clearly erroneous in holding that the arbitration provision in DHJ's acknowledgment form was a "material alteration." . . .

The effect of this holding is that we may not presume acceptance from mere failure to object; the arbitration clause in this case will not be considered a part of the agreement unless it was in fact [expressly] agreed to by N&D. . . .

The only mutually executed documents evidencing the agreement are the acknowledgments which DHJ sent to Nelly Don and which Shriber "accepted" and returned to DHJ. These contracts clearly stated just above the parties' signatures, that they were "subject to all the terms and conditions printed on the reverse side." The arbitration clause was printed on the reverse side and it would thus appear that the clause, although a material alteration to the oral agreement, was "expressly agreed to" by Nelly Don. Appellees contend, however, as the District Court found, that Shriber's failure to read the contracts, coupled with the absence of the word "arbitration" on the front of the document to indicate the presence of an arbitration clause on the reverse, precluded actual consent to the inclusion of this clause in the final agreement. We disagree.

The holding of the District Court ignores the general rule of contract law that, in the absence of fraud, misrepresentation or deceit, one who executes a contract cannot avoid it on the ground that he did not read it or supposed it to be different in its terms. . . .

. . . While a party may not be subjected to a provision which materially alters the contract by failing to object to it, he cannot avoid the effect of his written acceptance of a contract which expressly, above his signature on the face of the contract, incorporates the provisions on the reverse side of the document. There being no evidence of fraud, misrepresentation or deceit in that execution of the acceptance, it follows that the agreement to arbitrate became a part of the agreement and must govern the resolution of the dispute between the parties which produced this litigation. . . .

Webster, Circuit Judge.

 Many sellers and buyers have their own forms drafted and periodically reviewed by their attorneys. However, few sellers and buyers pay close attention to the forms they receive from the other party. Purchase orders and confirmations are often received and filed unread by clerks, and discrepancies go unnoticed until a dispute arises. The final battleground in the battle of the forms is often the courts, where the results are unpredictable. These problems may often be avoided if closer scrutiny is given to the other party's form. The major issue usually revolves around whether the additional terms contained in the seller's confirmation form materially alter the contract. A buyer should therefore read the confirmation form with an eye to detecting any objectionable additional terms. Too often a buyer does not discover objectionable terms until a dispute has arisen, by which time it is too late to object.

Firm Offer Under UCC § 2-205 a merchant may make a *firm offer* to buy or sell goods, promising not to revoke the offer pending the offeree's acceptance. Under the common law such a promise would be unenforceable for lack of consideration. The UCC, however, permits the offeree to enforce the firm offer if the offer is made in a signed writing by a merchant. The firm offer is good for the time stated in the offer or, if no time is stated, for a reasonable period not to exceed three months. If the firm offer is made on a form supplied by the *offeree*, the offeror must sign the provision separately so that the court is assured that the offeror knew of the firm offer.

19:5   Statute of Frauds

Section 17 of the English Statute of Frauds required a contract for the sale of goods costing ten pounds or more to be evidenced by a written note or memorandum signed by the party to be charged. The Uniform Sales Act also contained a statute of frauds, and the UCC has its own statute of frauds in § 2-201. The UCC statute is, however, more liberal than the original English version.

Under the UCC, a contract for the sale of goods costing $500 or more must be evidenced by a writing to be enforceable. Unlike statutes of fraud generally, however, the UCC section provides that the writing need not contain all the essential terms of the contract. All that is required is "some writing sufficient to indicate" that a sales contract has been made. The only term that must be included is the quantity of goods to be sold.

The writing must be signed by the party against whom enforcement is sought or by the party's authorized agent or broker [UCC § 2-201(1)]. The signature need not be handwritten. Rather, any authentication that identifies the party to be charged is considered a signature. For example, a letterhead might suffice if it represented the party's intention to authenticate the writing.

The UCC has a provision under which a writing signed by only one party is sometimes sufficient to be enforced against a nonsigning party. The essence of the provision is that a written confirmation of the contract that is signed by one party and sent to the other party may be used against the receiving party. The provision is applicable only to contracts between merchants, only if the confirmation is received within a reasonable time, and only if the party receiving it has reason to know its contents. If the nonsigning party objects, he must give written notice of such objection within ten days after receipt of the confirmation [UCC § 2-201(2)]. The purpose of this provision is to equalize the parties' position. Under prior law, a person who received a letter confirming a sale could bind the sender while remaining not bound himself. If there were a market with fluctuating prices, the nonsigning party could wait until the time for performance, check the market price, and then decide to perform or not perform without penalty. Under the UCC, such a waiting game is not possible.

 The confirmation or other writing evidencing the contract need not be the contract itself. Rather, it can be any evidence that satisfies the statute of frauds. In other words, the contract may be oral, provided there is a sufficient writing indicating the contract's existence. A written confirmation that specifies terms will, however, be given great weight by a court. A merchant who receives a confirmation of an oral agreement should therefore scrutinize it and object promptly if it departs from his or her understanding of the agreement.

Exceptions to Statute   There are three exceptions to the sales statute of frauds.

(1) A contract for the sale of goods that are to be specially manufactured for the buyer may be enforced without any writing if (a) the goods are not suitable for sale to others in the ordinary course of the seller's business and (b) the seller either has made a substantial beginning of the manufacture of the goods or has made commitments for their procurement before receiving notice of the buyer's repudiation [UCC § 2-201(3)(a)]. This exception might be applied not only to goods that are originally manufactured specially for the buyer, but also to standard products that are extensively modified at the buyer's request. To illustrate, assume that Sam orally agrees to buy a car for $10,000 from Mary, a dealer. A signed writing would be required to make the contract enforceable. However, if Sam requested that Mary make extensive modifications to the car, as a result of which it would no longer be suitable for sale to others in the ordinary course of her business, and if Mary actually made a substantial start on the modifications, then the contract would be enforceable despite the lack of a writing.

(2) The statute does not apply if the party against whom enforcement is sought admits in a legal proceeding the existence of a sales contract. In such a case, the contract is enforceable only for the quantity of goods admitted [UCC § 2-201(3)(b)].

(3) The statute does not apply to the sale of goods for which payment has been made and accepted or which have been received and accepted [UCC § 2-201(3)(c)]. The contract is, however, enforceable *only* to the extent of such payment or receipt of goods. For example, if a buyer orally contracts to purchase 100 typewriters and actually accepts delivery of 50, the seller can enforce the contract with respect to those 50, but not with respect to the rest. Similarly, if the seller accepts payment for 50 of the typewriters, the buyer can enforce the contract with respect to those 50, but not with respect to the remainder. Part payment on a single indivisible item may take the contract out of the statute of frauds, although some courts have held to the contrary.

 The fact that a contract is not required by the sales statute of frauds to be in writing does not mean that an oral contract is necessarily enforceable. Particularly with respect to consumer transactions, various statutes require not only that certain types of contracts be in writing, but also that the writing make certain disclosures or meet other specified requirements. Merchants should keep these statutes in mind when dealing with consumers.

Key Concepts and Terms

- Article 2 of the UCC deals with sales of goods and is the primary source of sales law. General legal and equitable principles, including principles of contract law and the law merchant, are also applicable.
- A sale consists of the passage of title from seller to buyer for a price, which may be payable either in money or in other goods.

- Goods include all things that are movable at the time of identification to the contract. Article 2 therefore is applicable to sales of tangible personal property, but not to rendition of services or sales of realty or intangible personal property. When a contract involves a mixed transaction, such as a transfer of goods and the rendition of services, the applicability of Article 2 depends on the focus of the contract.

- The UCC stresses the concept of fairness and imposes an obligation of good faith in the performance or enforcement of every contract or duty that comes within the act. The UCC often imposes higher standards on merchants than on nonmerchants. A party is classified as a merchant on the basis of his experience, knowledge, or skill with respect to the goods or practices involved.

- In most respects a sales contract must meet the requirements of common law contracts. Changes made by the UCC have tended toward more liberal recognition of the existence of contracts with the results that (1) a sales contract may contain open terms and still be enforceable; (2) an acceptance may create a contract even though it includes terms not contained in the offer, as long as they do not materially alter it and the offeror does not object; and (3) a sales contract is enforceable as long as there is a true basis for agreement.

- The UCC Statute of Frauds requires a contract for the sale of goods costing $500 or more to be evidenced by a signed writing. The writing must include the quantity of goods, but need not contain all essential terms. A writing signed by one party is sometimes sufficient to enforce a sales contract against the other party. A writing is not required if the goods are to be specially manufactured, if the party to be charged admits the contract's existence in a legal proceeding, or if partial payment or receipt of goods has occurred.

- Additional Terms
- Arbitration Clause
- Battle of the Forms
- Course of Performance
- Course of Dealing
- Firm Offer
- Future Goods
- Good Faith
- Goods
- Law Merchant
- Merchant
- Mixed Transactions
- Open Terms
- Sale
- Special Manufacturer
- Title
- Uniform Sales Act
- Usage of Trade

Questions and Case Problems

1. Carroll goes to her dentist, Dr. Grabavoy, to have new dentures made. Grabavoy prepares a set of wax dentures, has Carroll try them on, and then prepares a set of dentures from the wax impressions. The dentures are too large and Carroll develops mouth sores, blisters, bloody gums, and mouth swellings. She returns

the dentures to Grabavoy and demands a refund of the $775 that she had paid for them. Grabavoy refuses to give her a refund. Carroll sues, claiming breach of warranties under Article 2 of the UCC. Grabavoy claims Article 2 is inapplicable, since there has been no sale of goods. What is the result?

2. Commodore purchased electronic weighing and measuring devices from NCI. Over the telephone, Commodore gave NCI the number of its purchase order. NCI entered the Commodore purchase order number on its sales order and sent a copy of the sales order to Commodore. Commodore then mailed a copy of its purchase order to NCI. The Commodore purchase order included a provision limiting the damages for which Commodore would respond in the event of breach. At no time in the negotiations by telephone was the damage limitation mentioned. However, terms such as quantity, price, and delivery schedule were agreed to in the telephone negotiations. Commodore testified that the primary purpose of its purchase order was to confirm what had been discussed by telephone and to provide a written copy of the delivery schedule. Was the damage limitation provision a part of the contract, or was it a proposal for an additional term? Is a damage limitation clause "material"?

3. Ozark Airlines is a commercial air carrier. Ozark sells 40 used planes to Fairchild-Hiller, an aircraft manufacturer, as part of a deal for the purchase of planes from Fairchild-Hiller. Fairchild-Hiller later resells one of the planes to a third party. The plane is involved in a fatal crash, and suit is filed against various defendants, including Ozark. The claim against Ozark is premised on the contention that Ozark is in the business of selling airplanes and is therefore a merchant under the UCC. Should that contention be upheld?

4. The Denim Company orally agrees to purchase a specified amount of cotton from Western Farms. The parties do not discuss either price or arbitration. Denim sends Western a formal purchase order, and Western sends Denim a confirmation form. These forms pass in the mail. Later a dispute over price arises. Denim insists that the dispute be submitted to arbitration in Oregon, as provided in its purchase order form, while Western insists on arbitration in California, as provided in its confirmation form. How should the disputes as to arbitration on the price be resolved?

5. Eason, an attorney, decides to retire. He orally agrees to sell his law books to Duffy, another attorney, for $5,000. Duffy mails Eason a written confirmation of "our agreement for purchase of your books." Eason does not respond to the confirmation but later refuses to complete the sale. When Duffy sues for breach of contract, Eason claims in his answer that the contract was oral and therefore unenforceable. Should Eason's claim be upheld?

6. The Pioneer Company sustains extensive damage from a fire caused by escaping gas. Pioneer sues Northern Illinois Gas Company, the gas supplier, claiming breach of certain Article 2 warranties with respect to the gas company's meters and service lines. Is Article 2 properly applicable?

7. Wade orally agrees to sell Dalton a small plot of land and a new mobile home, which Wade intends to place on a foundation on the plot. The price of the purchase is $5,000 for the land and $25,000 for the mobile home. Dalton pays $2,000 down, and Wade gives him a receipt with the notation, "Down payment on lot and mobile home." Discuss (1) whether the parties contracted for a sale of goods subject to Article 2, (2) what statute of frauds should be applied in the event of a lawsuit, and (3) whether the applicable statute of frauds has been complied with. Would your answers differ if the contract had been for a sale of land and a mobile

home that was already located on the land? If Dalton had bought the mobile home and had it installed on land he already owned?

8. Pennwalt submitted a proposal to sell two rotary vacuum dryers for Daitom's chemical plant, which was designed by Kintech. The proposal included specific conditions of sale, including a provision that suit would not be brought for breach of contract after one year from breach instead of the four years permitted under state statute. Daitom responded by submitting its own preprinted purchase order that contained numerous conditions but did not include a one-year limit on suit. There was a significant delay in the installation of the dryers after Pennwalt delivered them, and when they finally were installed, they were defective. Daitom sued for breach of contract, and Pennwalt sought to bar the suit because it was brought more than a year after the dryers were delivered. Is Daitom bound by the one-year provision?

9. Electro Flo Corporation wants to develop and market a portable electrified floor for carnivals. Alcoa agrees to design, produce, and deliver flooring material to Electro Flo for that purpose. The flooring material proves unsatisfactory, and Electro Flo claims breach of warranty under the UCC. Alcoa responds that the transaction involves the sale of professional engineering and design devices, not goods, and that the UCC is therefore inapplicable. Is Alcoa correct?

10. What is the battle of the forms, and how does the UCC deal with it?

20 Transfer of Title and Risk of Loss

20:1 Introduction

A transfer of title is the essence of a sale of goods. Usually, it is accompanied by a transfer of possession. The transfer of title and possession may occur at the time of the contract, as when goods are purchased at a retail store, or it may be delayed, as when goods are ordered for future delivery. Transfer of the goods can be made directly from the seller to the buyer or through a middleman, such as a public carrier. If all goes well, the buyer eventually receives the goods, the seller receives payment, and the transaction is concluded.

Sometimes, however, all does not go well. Goods may be lost, destroyed, or stolen in transit between seller and buyer. In such a situation, the obvious question is who bears the loss. While courts are commonly called on to resolve that question after a loss has actually occurred, the parties to a sales transaction can and should consider the question when the contract is entered. The method by which the parties structure the transaction may affect the allocation of risk of loss, and if the parties know the point at which the risk of loss passes from seller to buyer, they may take appropriate steps to insure the goods.

Prior to the UCC, the concept of title was all-important in determining the rights and responsibilities of the parties to a sales transaction. The risk of loss was placed on the party who had title. The UCC has drastically de-emphasized the importance of title, although it is still important under some circumstances. The UCC provisions concerning both passage of title and risk of loss will be considered in this chapter. Related subjects, such as documents of title and insurable interest, will also be examined. Finally, attention will be given to the specific provisions that govern (1) contracts permitting the return of goods and (2) the rights of third persons who have received goods from either the buyer or the seller.

20:2   The Concept of Title

The legal concept of title embodies the idea of ownership, of superior rights that the state will protect. Title is a concept of property law, not contract law. Through a contract, one may bargain for the transfer of title to goods or of interests short of title to goods. Through a contract, various people simultaneously may have different interests in goods; yet "title" to the goods remains somewhere, with someone, at any given time. Ultimately, title to goods confers the right to possession of the goods, even if enforcing this right would cause a breach of contract for which the breacher would have to pay damages.

A related idea is that title can be parted with only voluntarily; a thief does not obtain good title. Ordinarily, a person cannot transfer a better title to goods than he himself has. Thus, the rightful owner of stolen goods can recover the goods not only from the thief, but also from any person to whom the thief has sold the goods. The few exceptions to this principle are discussed later in this chapter.

The "title" to most goods is just a legal concept. For example, no document represents the title to the pen in your hand, although you may still have the sales receipt indicating that you purchased the pen from someone. Even if you do not have the receipt, you have title to the pen, if the pen is yours. Your possession is good enough evidence of title unless someone claiming true ownership seeks to prove otherwise. The needs of commerce, however, often require that title be evidenced by some form of paper title. The Uniform Commercial Code accommodates this need through the concept of the *document of title*, discussed below.

In addition, for administrative and safety reasons, the state requires that ownership of some types of goods, such as motor vehicles, be embodied in a paper document, usually called a *certificate of title*. For these types of goods, state statutes require that true ownership be evidenced by a certificate obtained from the state, and transfer of ownership requires compliance with the applicable statute. Note in the following case how and why the court separates the property concept of title from the contract problem of who bears the risk of loss.

Hughes

v

Al Green, Inc.
418 NE2d 1355 (1981)
Supreme Court of Ohio

FACTS: On Saturday morning Hughes contracted with Al Green, Inc., a car dealership, to purchase a new Lincoln Continental. Hughes made a cash down payment, with the balance to be financed by a loan from a local bank. Hughes took immediate possession of the car but agreed to return the car the following Monday for completion of new car preparation and installation of a CB radio. Hughes signed a purchase contract, an application for a certificate of title, and other papers. On the way home Hughes wrecked the car in an accident. After it learned of the accident, the dealership presented the proper papers to the bank and obtained the balance of the purchase price of the car from the bank. The bank arranged for the certificate of title to be issued in Hughes' name.

Ohio's automobile certificate of title statute (R.C. 4505.01 et seq.) states in part that

> No person acquiring a motor vehicle from the owner thereof . . . shall acquire any right, title, claim, or interest in or to said vehicle until such person has had issued to him a certificate of title to said motor vehicle.

ISSUE: As between a merchant with title to an automobile and a buyer who has taken possession without title, who bears the risk of loss?

RESULT: The court determined that the buyer bore the risk of loss even though the buyer did not have title to the automobile.

REASONING:

*   *   *

Simplified, [Hughes'] argument is that [Al Green, Inc.] was in breach of contract because on September 21, 1977, when the certificate of title was issued in [Hughes'] name and ownership of the automobile thereby legally transferred to her, [she] no longer possessed that for which she bargained, *i.e.* an *undamaged* 1977 Lincoln Continental. . . .

Resolution of this cause mandates that we determine whether the buyer or the seller bore the risk of loss or damage to the automobile at the time of the collision. . . .

[UCC § 2-509] provides that in any case where the contract goods are neither delivered by carrier not entrusted to a bailee, " . . . the risk of loss passes to the buyer on his receipt of the goods if the seller is a merchant; otherwise the risk passes to the buyer on tender of delivery."

This provision represents a significant shift away from the prior importance of the concept of title in determining the point at which risk of loss passes from the seller to buyer. Under the common law, not only did title to the contract goods determine risk of loss, but it also determined the issues of the buyer's right to the goods . . . , the seller's right to the purchase price, and the right to proceed against tortfeasors. Under the U.C.C., however, "[e]ach provision [of the UCC] with regard to the rights, obligations, and remedies of the seller, the buyer, purchasers, or other third parties applies irrespective of title to the goods except where the provision refers to such title." [UCC § 2-401]

Thus, as noted in Nordstrom, Sales, Section 130, at page 393:

"[T]here is . . . one principle which applies to all risk of loss problems. This principle is summarized in one sentence from the Comments:

The underlying theory of these sections on risk of loss is the adoption of the contractual approach rather than an arbitrary shifting of the risk with the 'property' in the goods.

"No longer is the question of title of any importance in determining whether a buyer or a seller bears the risk of loss. It is true that the person with title will also (and incidentally) often bear the risk that the goods may be destroyed or lost; *but the seller may have title and the buyer the risk,* or the seller may have the risk and the buyer the title. In short, title is not a relevant consideration in deciding whether the risk has shifted to the buyer." . . .

In the instant cause, the appellant-buyer had received possession of the automobile as partial execution of a merchant-seller's obligations under a purchase contract. Thus, unless other statutory provisions make [UCC § 2-509] inapplicable, the appellant, as a buyer in receipt of goods identified to a contract, must bear the loss of the car's value resulting from the collision.

[UCC § 2-509] does not conflict with [the Ohio Certificate of Title Act]. The purpose of the Certificate of Title Act is to prevent the importation of stolen motor vehicles, to protect Ohio bona fide purchasers against thieves and wrongdoers, and to create an instrument evidencing title to, and ownership of, motor vehicles. . . . The Act was not adopted to clarify contractual rights and duties. . . .

. . . With ownership no longer being determinative, [the Certificate of Title Act] is irrelevant to the issue of risk of loss, and thus does not conflict with a U.C.C. risk of loss analysis. . . .

Sweeney, Justice.

20:3 Documents of Title

Bills of lading and *warehouse receipts,* collectively known as *documents of title,* are the subject of Article 7 of the UCC. When a seller ships goods to the buyer by means of a carrier, the carrier gives the seller a document known as a bill of lading. When the seller stores the goods in a warehouse and the buyer is to pick the goods up there, the warehouser gives the seller a document known as a warehouse receipt.

Typically, a document of title lists the goods received by the carrier or warehouser and contains the terms of the agreement for carriage or storage. It may be in the form of a combined receipt and carriage or storage contract, but it represents much more. A document of title is intended to take the place of and to represent the goods. If the document is a *negotiable* document of title, possession of it amounts to the right of possession of and title to the goods. For example, when goods have been delivered to a carrier for shipment and the carrier has issued a negotiable bill of lading, whoever rightfully has or obtains possession of the bill of lading has both title to the goods and the right to possess them.

A document of title is negotiable if by its terms (1) the goods are to be delivered to the bearer of the document; (2) the goods are to be delivered to the order of a named person; or (3) if negotiability of the document is recognized in overseas trade, the goods are to be delivered to a named person or his assigns. Any other document of title is nonnegotiable [UCC § 7-104]. If, for example, a document provides for delivery "to" a named person instead of "to the order of" a named person, the document is nonnegotiable.

A negotiable document of title is much more easily transferred than a nonnegotiable one. For example, a negotiable document that provides for delivery to the bearer permits the goods to be delivered to any person presenting the document, and possession is tantamount to title to the goods. A negotiable document that provides for delivery to the order of a named person allows delivery to be made to that person or to any other person presenting the document after its proper indorsement by the named person [UCC §§ 7-403, 7-501, 7-502]. In contrast, a nonnegotiable document transfers title only to the person named; the carrier or warehouser must deliver the goods in accordance with the instructions contained in the document. To sell title to the goods, the carrier or warehouser must reissue a document of title to the purchaser.

20:4   Passage of Title

Title to goods is normally irrelevant in determining the rights of the parties to a sales contract under the UCC. There are, however, residual areas where solution of a problem may be influenced by the question of title. Such problems are most likely to arise in areas of law not covered by the UCC. For example, issues as to which party is liable for a property tax may be determined on the basis of which party held title to the goods on a given date. To cover such situations, the UCC has a passage-of-title provision [UCC § 2-401].

Before title can pass under UCC § 2-401, the goods must be identified to the contract. This requirement is satisfied when the specific goods to be sold are in some way designated by the seller. To illustrate, assume that Wilson goes into Brown's retail camera store and places an order for a particular type of camera. Brown goes into the storeroom, where she has ten of these cameras, selects one of them, and sets it aside to give to Wilson when he returns to the store. The camera was identified as the subject matter of the contract when Brown singled it out from all the other cameras of the same type. Prior to that time, it was clear what type of camera Wilson wanted, but the specific camera to be sold to him was unknown.

If the goods have been identified to the contract, title can pass from the seller to the buyer in any manner explicitly agreed on by the parties. If there is no explicit agreement, title passes "at the time and place at which the seller completes his performance with reference to the physical delivery of the goods . . . even though a document of title is to be delivered at a different time or place . . . [UCC § 2-401(2)]. When the seller has completed his or her performance depends on whether the contract is a *shipment contract*, a *destination contract*, or a contract that does not require the goods to be moved.

Shipment Contract   Under a shipment contract the seller must send the goods to the buyer but is not required to actually deliver them at the destination. To fully perform, the seller must put the goods in the possession of a carrier, make a reasonable contract for their transportation, provide the buyer with any document necessary for the buyer to take possession of the goods from the carrier, and notify the buyer of the shipment [UCC § 2-504]. Title passes to the buyer at the time and place of shipment, that is, when the goods are delivered to the carrier.

Destination Contract   A destination contract requires the seller to deliver the goods at a particular destination. Delivery occurs when the seller tenders the goods by making them available for the buyer to possess and gives the buyer any notification reasonably necessary to enable the buyer to take possession. The tender must be at a reasonable hour, and goods must be kept available for a reasonable period to enable the buyer to take possession [UCC § 2-503(1)]. If the seller is required to deliver documents, the documents must also be tendered in the correct form [§§ 2-503(3) and (5)]. Title passes to the buyer only when the goods are delivered at the specified destination.

Other Shipping Terms   Parties to sales contracts commonly use specific shipping terms to indicate whether a contract is a shipment or a destination contract. Probably the most common shipping term is "F.O.B." (free on board). When a contract requires "delivery F.O.B. the place of shipment," it is a shipment contract. A contract that requires "delivery F.O.B. the place of destination" is a destination contract [UCC § 2-319(1)].

Various other shipping terms may be used to denote specific types of shipment contracts. "F.A.S. vessel" (free alongside the vessel) denotes a shipment contract that requires the seller to deliver the goods alongside the vessel [UCC § 2-319(2)]. "C.I.F." (cost-insurance-freight) indicates a shipment contract under which the seller must put the goods in the carrier's possession, load the goods, and pay the cost of freight and insurance to the point of destination. "C.&F." or "C.F." imposes like obligations, except that the seller need not purchase insurance [UCC § 2-320].

A destination contract may be indicated by a term that requires "delivery F.O.B. the place of destination" or by a term that requires delivery of goods "ex-ship." The latter term requires delivery from a ship that has reached the port of destination [UCC § 2-322].

 All these terms are commonly used by businesspersons and should be included in contracts to clearly indicate the parties' obligations. A contract that requires shipment by carrier should therefore ordinarily include the appropriate term. The UCC itself regards the shipment contract as the normal one and the destination contract as the variant type. Unless the contract clearly indicates that it is a destination contract, a court will regard it as a shipment one.

Contracts Not Requiring Moving of Goods Sometimes the seller makes delivery to the buyer without the goods actually being moved. This may occur, for example, in a situation in which a third person, called a bailee, has actual possession of the goods at all times. When delivery is to be made without moving the goods, title passes when the seller delivers the necessary document of title to the buyer. If, however, the goods are already identified, and if the contract does not call for delivery of any documents of title, then title passes at the time of contracting.

 Conditional sales contracts often provide that title shall remain in the seller until the buyer completes payment of all installments. Under the UCC, such a reservation of title is construed as a reservation of a security interest,[1] but it has no effect on the passing of title as provided by UCC § 2-401.

Revesting of the Title in the Seller A buyer may refuse to receive or retain the goods, perhaps claiming that the delivery was improper or the goods nonconforming. When that happens, title to the goods revests in the seller, whether the buyer is right or wrong. If a buyer accepts the goods and then, on inspection of the goods, determines that they are nonconforming and revokes the acceptance, the title to the goods revests in the seller [UCC § 2-401(4)]. These rules simply establish who has the title when there is a dispute and one or both parties claim rights in the goods.

20:5 Insurable Interest[2]

A purchaser of insurance must have some legally recognized interest in the person or item being insured. A person, for example, cannot take out insurance on the life of a total stranger or purchase insurance on property in which he has no legal interest.

Under the UCC, a buyer obtains an *insurable interest* in existing goods once they have been identified to the contract, regardless of (1) whether title has passed or the risk of loss has been placed on the buyer, (2) whether the goods conform to the specifications of the contract, and (3) whether the buyer has an option to return or reject the goods. The seller has an insurable interest in goods so long as the title to or any security interest in the goods remains in the seller. In addition, a buyer or seller may have an insurable interest in goods if an insurable interest is recognized under any other statute or rule of law [UCC § 2-501]. Under the UCC, therefore, the buyer and seller may have insurable interests in the same goods at the same time.

 It may sometimes be prudent for a buyer to insure goods that have been identified to the contract, even though the risk of loss has not yet passed to the buyer, and even if the contract calls for the seller to maintain insurance. For example, if the buyer has already made partial or full

---

[1] The reservation of security interests is discussed in Chapter 29.
[2] For a discussion of insurance law and insurable interest generally, see Chapter 42.

payment, and if the buyer doubts the seller's ability to pay any loss, the buyer might consider personally insuring the goods. The same principle applies to a seller. If full payment has not been received for goods already delivered, and if the seller retains a security interest, the seller should obviously either require proof of insurance from the buyer or personally insure the goods.

20:6   Risk of Loss

The basic UCC provisions dealing with *risk of loss* are §§ 2-509 and 2-510. There are other relevant provisions, and some of them will be discussed briefly here. The purpose of the UCC provisions is to provide clear guidelines to determine when the risk of loss passes from the seller to the buyer. The party who bears the risk of loss is obligated, as between the buyer and the seller, to take the loss and to try to collect from a warehouser or carrier who was responsible for the loss or from an insurer. In studying the specific risk of loss provisions, bear in mind that their application ordinarily results in the risk of loss being placed on the party who was in the best position to avoid the loss. Thus, for example, the risk of loss remains on a merchant who has relinquished possession of the goods. Also bear in mind that, in the absence of a breach of contract, the risk of loss usually passes at the same time title does.

 The parties may agree to allocate the risk of loss in a manner different from that provided by UCC § 2-509. In addition, the parties may agree that the risk of loss shall be divided between them [UCC § 2-303]. For example, where there is a substantial possibility that some loss may occur, the parties might seek an equitable sharing of the risk by means of such an agreement.

In allocating the risk of loss, the UCC distinguishes between three types of contracts: (1) contracts involving shipment of the goods by carrier; (2) contracts involving goods held by a bailee and delivered without moving; and (3) all other sales contracts.

Contracts Involving Shipment by Carrier   When goods are to be shipped by carrier, the risk of loss normally passes at the same time as title, as already discussed. Thus, in shipment contracts, the risk of loss passes to the buyer when the seller has duly delivered the goods to the carrier. In destination contracts, the risk of loss passes to the buyer when the goods have reached the destination and have been duly tendered to the buyer [UCC § 2-509(1)].

Goods Held by Bailee   Situations in which delivery of the goods from the seller to the buyer is to be made without removal of the goods from the actual possession of a bailee, normally a warehouser, are governed by UCC § 2-509(2), in conjunction with UCC § 2-503(4). In general, under these provisions risk of loss passes to the buyer when he is given or acquires effective means of control of the goods. Thus, risk of loss will pass to the buyer on his receipt of a negotiable document of title or on the bailee's acknowledgment of the buyer's right to possess the goods. If the seller gives the buyer a nonnegotiable document of title, or if the seller simply gives the buyer a written direction to the bailee to deliver the goods, risk of loss does not pass to the buyer until he has had a reasonable time to present the document or direction. During this time, the buyer may make a timely objection to a nonnegotiable document of title or a written direction. If the buyer does object, risk of loss does not pass until the seller either delivers a negotiable document of title or obtains the requisite acknowledgment from the bailee of the buyer's right of possession. The bailee may refuse to honor a nonnegotiable document or to obey a written direction. If he does object, risk of loss does not pass to the buyer.

Other Transactions Goods may be delivered in other ways, which are not covered by the foregoing rules. For example, the buyer may pick up the goods at the seller's place of business, or the seller may personally deliver the goods. In such cases, the time when risk of loss passes depends on whether the seller is a merchant. If the seller is a merchant, then risk of loss passes only on the buyer's actual receipt of the goods. Otherwise, the risk passes to the buyer when the seller tenders delivery of the goods, regardless of whether the buyer actually takes them.

EXAMPLE: Assume Hurvitz sells Ricolli a television set and makes the set available for Ricolli to take home. Ricolli requests Hurvitz to keep the set while Ricolli goes on vacation. During Ricolli's vacation the set is stolen. If Hurvitz is a merchant, the loss falls on him, since Ricolli never actually received the set. If Hurvitz is not a merchant, the loss falls on Ricolli, since tender of delivery was made.

The following case illustrates how one court determined risk of loss in a contract and what difficulties arose in making the determination.

Caudle
v
Sherrard Motor Co.
525 SW2d 238 (1975)
Texas Court of Civil Appeals

FACTS: In 1972 Caudle contracted to purchase a house trailer from Sherrard Motor Company in Denison, Texas. While the trailer was being readied, Caudle was called back to his Dallas office on business. Caudle told Sherrard he would return and take possession later. Two to four days later the trailer was stolen from Sherrard's place of business, and Caudle refused to pay. Sherrard sued for the contract price and won. Caudle appealed.

ISSUE: Had the risk of loss passed from Sherrard to Caudle?

RESULT: Under UCC § 2-509(3) Sherrard, a merchant, bore the risk of loss because Caudle, the buyer, had not taken physical possession of the goods.

REASONING:

*   *   *

It is plaintiff's contention that the risk of loss had passed to the defendant before the trailer's disappearance under [UCC § 2-509(2)(b)] which provides:

> Where the goods are held by a bailee to be delivered without being moved, the risk of loss passes to the buyer . . . on acknowledgment by the bailee of the buyer's right to possession of the goods.

Plaintiff contends that it was acting as a bailee while the trailer remained on its premises and that by executing the contract, it had acknowledged the defendant's right to possession of the trailer. Plaintiff further argues that because it did not agree to deliver the trailer to Caudle in Dallas, the trailer was to be delivered to Caudle "without being moved." These arguments, however, erroneously assume that the plaintiff is a bailee under the Code. It is apparent that the drafters of the Code contemplated a common law commercial bailee, such as a warehouseman, when using the term "bailee" in [UCC § 2-509(2)]. . . . Implicit in [various UCC provisions] is the concept that the party who issues [documents of title] and acknowledges the buyer's right to possession of the goods be in the business of storing goods for hire—a commercial bailee. This is not true here. We conclude, therefore, that the plaintiff was not a bailee under the Code. Hence, [UCC § 2-509(2)] does not control the determination of whether the risk of loss had passed to the defendant.

Plaintiff contends further that . . . the terms of the contract for the sale of the trailer provided that the risk of loss passed to the defendant when the contract was signed by the parties.

The pertinent clause of the sales contract states:

> No transfer, renewal, extension or assignment of this agreement or any interest hereunder, and no loss, damage or destruction of said motor vehicle shall release buyer from his obligation hereunder.

We hold that this language is insufficient to constitute a "contrary agreement" between the parties pursuant to [UCC § 2-509(4)]. A contract which shifts the risk of loss to the buyer before he receives the merchandise is so unusual that a seller who desires to achieve this result must clearly communicate his intent to the buyer. . . . This clause was apparently intended to fix responsibility for loss *after the defendant had taken possession* of the trailer. [Court's emphasis.] . . . We, therefore, conclude that it was not the intention of the parties to transfer risk of loss of the trailer *prior to delivery of possession to the buyer.* [Court's emphasis.] To hold otherwise would be to set a trap for the unwary. If parties intend to shift the burden of the risk of loss from the seller to the buyer before delivery of the goods, then such must be done in clear and unequivocal language.

It is defendant's contention that pursuant to [UCC § 2-509(3)] the risk of loss remained with the plaintiff because he had not taken actual physical possession of the trailer. We agree. That section provides,

> In any case not within Subsection [1] or [2], the risk of loss passes to the buyer on his receipt of the goods if the seller is a merchant; otherwise the risk of loss passes to the buyer on tender of delivery.

To determine if this section applies, the following questions must be resolved: (1) was the plaintiff a merchant and (2) did the defendant receive the trailer? The plaintiff is a merchant under Article 2 of the Code as it "deals in goods of the kind . . . involved in the transaction [UCC § 2-104(1)]. The language "receipt of the goods" is defined in the Code as "taking physical possession of them" [UCC § 2-103(1)(c)]. It is undisputed that the defendant never took physical possession of the trailer; therefore, he had not received the goods. Accordingly, we hold that the risk of loss did not pass to the buyer before the trailer was stolen. . . .

. . . Strong policy reasons support this approach. The party in control is in the best position to handle properly the goods, to contract for shipment with a reliable carrier, and to insure the goods. This theory is particularly applicable when the buyer is not a merchant and is unfamilar with the problems of handling the goods. . . .

. . . [A] merchant who is to make delivery at his own place of business continues to maintain control over the goods and can be expected to carry insurance to protect his interest in them. On the other hand, the buyer has no control over the goods and may not have had the foresight to obtain insurance on the undelivered merchandise. . . .

Akin, Judge.

Effect of Breach   If either the buyer or seller is in breach of the contract of sale at the time goods are lost, the risk of loss is on the breaching party [UCC § 2-510]. Under this section the breaching party bears the risk of loss even if the other party would have borne it had there been no breach. Therefore, if the seller breaches the contract by tendering or delivering goods that do not conform to the contract requirements, so that the buyer has the right to reject the goods, the risk of loss remains on the seller until the defect is cured or until the buyer accepts the nonconforming goods. Similarly, if the buyer has the right to revoke his prior acceptance of goods and exercises that right, he may treat the risk of loss as having rested on the seller from the beginning. However, the buyer can pass the risk of loss back to the seller in this way only to the extent of any deficiency in the buyer's effective insurance coverage.[3] If the buyer repudiates or otherwise breaches the contract after conforming goods have been identified to the contract, the seller may treat the risk of loss as resting on the buyer for a commercially reasonable time, but, again, only to the extent of any deficiency in the seller's effective insurance coverage.

20:7 Sale on Approval; Sale or Return

Sometimes a buyer and seller agree that the buyer will retain the right to return goods to the seller even if there is nothing "wrong" with the goods. Such arrangements are undertaken for good commercial reasons. For example, an appliance seller may want the buyer to try out a refrigerator in the home and will give the buyer the right to return the refrigerator if the buyer decides not to keep it. This is called a *sale on approval*. Or, a jeweler might purchase diamonds for resale with the right to return any diamonds that he or she is unable to sell. This is called a *sale or return*. Whether a sale is a sale on approval or a sale or return depends on whether the goods are delivered primarily for use (sale on approval) or for resale (sale or return) [UCC § 2-426(1)].

Both types of sale present problems of title and risk of loss that are not readily answered by UCC §§ 2-401, 2-508, and 2-509. What if the jeweler's store burns down and the stones are lost? Can the jeweler's creditors reach the diamonds that appear to be simply inventory? What if the refrigerator is stolen? Can the consumer's creditors reach the refrigerator? In both cases, physical control of the goods has passed to the buyer, and yet common sense suggests that the seller may not necessarily have parted with title and risk of loss. Sections 2-326 and 2-327 of the Code address the special problems of sale on approval and sale or return in a manner that is consistent with the broad principles of the Code.

Sale on Approval In a sale on approval, neither title nor risk of loss passes to the buyer until the goods are accepted by the buyer. The contract may provide a specified period within which the buyer must either accept or return the goods. If no period is specified, the buyer will be allowed a reasonable time within which to act. Failure to notify the seller of the decision to return the goods within a reasonable time constitutes acceptance. The buyer's actions or statements may indicate acceptance, but the fact that the buyer tries the goods does not constitute acceptance. If the buyer decides to return the goods, the return is at the seller's risk and expense. However, a merchant buyer must follow any reasonable instructions of the seller [§ 2-327(1)]. It follows that goods held on approval are subject to claims of the seller's creditors until the

---

[3] Performance and breach of sales contracts, including situations in which the buyer may reject goods or revoke a prior acceptance of goods, are discussed in Chapter 22.

buyer accepts the goods. Until the buyer does so, the goods are owned by the seller [UCC § 2-326(2)]. After the buyer does accept the goods, however, they are subject to the claims of the buyer's creditors.

Sale or Return In a sale or return transaction, title and risk of loss pass to the buyer in the same manner as they would in an outright sale. In other words, once proper delivery has been made, the risk of accidental loss or damage to the goods rests on the buyer, and any return of the goods is at the buyer's risk and expense. The time for return may be specified in the contract. If it is not, a reasonable time is allowed [UCC § 2-327(2)]. It follows that goods held on sale or return are subject to the claims of the buyer's creditors rather than those of the seller's creditors [UCC § 2-326(2)]. If the goods have not been paid for, the seller may arrange for protection from the claims of other creditors by taking a security interest in the goods.[4]

 The UCC provides that any "or return" term of a contract for sale is to be treated as a separate contract for sale that contradicts the sale aspect of the contract [UCC § 2-326(4)]. This provision, read in conjunction with the statute of frauds and the parol evidence rule [UCC §§ 2-201, 2-202], requires that, if a written agreement is involved or if the price of the goods is $500 or more, the "or return" term must be contained in a written memorandum. Whenever anything is put in writing, therefore, even if it is only the purchase order, any right to return unsold goods must also be put in writing.

Consignment Sales A seller may attempt, while retaining title to goods, to sell those goods to a merchant who deals in that type of goods and plans to hold the goods for resale. The seller's intent may be to finance the retailer while retaining a security interest in the goods. The seller may "reserve title" in the sales contract. Or the seller may structure the transaction as a consignment sale. In a consignment, one party, the consignor, delivers the goods to another party, the consignee, and the consignee has a duty either to sell the goods on behalf of the consignor or return them to the consignor. The consignee is, in effect, a sales agent for the consignor.

In either situation the retailer's (consignee's) creditors may be misled as to the ownership of the goods apparently held as inventory in the retailer's place of business. The UCC provides that such goods are subject to the claims of the retailer's creditors, like goods held on sale or return [UCC § 2-326(3)]. This is so regardless of the label the parties themselves put on the transaction.

There are, however, certain exceptions to this rule. The goods are not subject to claims of the retailer's creditors if (1) state law requires a sign indicating the seller's (consignor's) interest be posted at the retailer's place of business and the seller complies with the law; (2) the retailer's creditors generally know that the retailer is substantially engaged in selling the goods of others; or (3) the seller has complied with the filing provisions concerning secured transactions in Article Nine of the Uniform Commercial Code.

---

[4] Creditors' rights and remedies are discussed in detail in Chapter 31.

As a practical matter, the only effective way for a seller to retain rights in goods "sold" on credit to a retail merchant is to comply with the provisions on secured transactions. Posting a sign is ordinarily not an available alternative because many states do not have sign laws, and proving that the retailer's creditors knew he or she was selling the goods of others is likely to be extremely difficult in a suit against another creditor. The Code has removed most apparent advantages of consignment or reservation of title sales.

20:8   Rights of Third Parties

The discussion so far has focused on the relationship between the buyer and the seller. A sales transaction, however, can involve third parties whose rights may conflict with those of the immediate seller and buyer. For example, a seller may sell the same goods twice. A buyer may resell goods to which he or she did not have good title. The theory and reasoning of these problems involves balancing the interests of true owners against the reasonable expectations of those who buy goods in the course of commerce.

Rights of Bona Fide Purchasers   Early in the chapter you were introduced to the basic principle that, ordinarily, a person cannot transfer a better title to goods than he himself has. An exception arises when a person has *voidable title* to goods. The title may be voidable for any of the various reasons that contract law renders a contract voidable.[5] For example, the sale may have been procured through fraudulent misrepresentation. If the buyer's title is *voidable*, the original seller may recover the goods from the buyer. However, if the buyer has transferred the goods to a good faith purchaser for value (a *bona fide purchaser*), the original seller's right to recover the goods is cut off. The person with voidable title has the power to transfer a good title to a good faith purchaser for value [UCC § 2-403(1)].

EXAMPLE: Assume that Cain sells a load of lumber to Wills, who pays for it by check. If the check is dishonored for insufficient funds, Cain has the right to rescind the contract and recover the lumber from Wills. But if Wills has already resold the lumber to Kahn, and if Kahn was a good-faith purchaser for value, then Cain cannot recover the lumber from Kahn. Cain would still have a right of action against Wills for the purchase price, but title to the lumber would remain in Kahn.

A bona fide purchaser, by definition, must make a purchase for value in good faith. Value may consist of any consideration sufficient to support a simple contract [UCC § 1-201(44)(d)]. In most cases, therefore, there is no issue as to whether value has been given. There may, however, be an issue as to the purchaser's good faith. It will be recalled that the UCC imposes a different

---

[5] Voidable contracts are discussed in Chapter 9. Factors that render a contract voidable are discussed in Chapter 12.

standard of good faith on merchants than it does on nonmerchants. In the case of an ordinary consumer, good faith merely requires simple honesty. Basically, this means that a consumer must not have been aware of the rights of the original seller to the goods. In the case of a merchant, good faith also requires the observance of reasonable commercial standards [UCC § 2-103(1)(b)]. Therefore, a merchant might be denied status as a good-faith purchaser in a case in which a nonmerchant would be accorded such status. For example, if a nonmerchant purchased a watch for $100 that normally would sell for $200, and if he had no notice or knowledge of the ordinary price, he might be classified as a good-faith purchaser for value. A jeweler, however, would probably not be so classified. While payment of $100 for a $200 watch does constitute value, it also indicates a lack of good faith on the jeweler's part.

Entrustment of Goods to or Retention of Goods by Merchant Seller Any entrustment of the possession of goods to a merchant who deals in goods of that kind gives the merchant the power to transfer all rights of the entrustor to a buyer in the ordinary course of business [UCC § 2-403(2), (3)]. The classic illustration of this rule is the repair situation. Assume that Jake takes his radio to Carol's shop to have it repaired. Carol, whose business includes not only radio repair but also the sale of new and used radios, sells Jake's radio to Lee, a customer who entered the shop during normal hours to purchase a radio. Under the UCC, Lee has good title to the radio. This illustration also demonstrates the purpose behind the rule. A person who buys goods from a merchant whose business it is to sell those goods reasonably expects that the merchant had the right to sell them. If a buyer were required to investigate the merchant's title or authority to sell the goods, ordinary commercial intercourse would be seriously hampered.

This entrusting rule is also applied in situations in which a buyer of goods leaves them in the seller's possession. If Christina buys a bicycle from Barry's bicycle shop and pays cash, she obtains title to it. In the event of a dispute between Barry and Christina, she would recover. But assume that she asks him to keep the bicycle at his store until the following day, when she will pick it up. If, later that same day, Carl comes into the store and purchases the same bicycle in the ordinary course of business, Christina cannot recover the bicycle from him. Christina's allowing Barry to keep the bicycle permitted him to transfer good title to Carl.

Note that the buyer takes only the rights that the person who entrusted the goods to the merchant had. Thus, a buyer in the ordinary course of business does not acquire title to stolen goods, because the entruster would have had no rights in the goods. It should also be noted that the buyer who, in the ordinary course of business, buys goods from a person engaged in selling such goods takes the goods free of any security interest held in the goods by third parties [UCC § 9-307(1)].

The following case, which involves a sale of entrusted goods, illustrates how one court determined whether a purchaser was a buyer in the ordinary course of business.

Mattek

v

Malofsky

165 NW2d 406 (1969)

Wisconsin Supreme Court

FACTS: Mattek authorized Frakes, a used-car dealer in Menasha, Wisconsin, to display her 1964 Plymouth automobile on Frakes' lot. Frakes placed his dealer's plate on the car and sold it to Malofsky, a used-car dealer in Appleton, Wisconsin, for $1,750. No certificate of title was delivered. Mattek sued Malofsky to recover the Plymouth. Mattek won, and Malofsky appealed.

ISSUES: (1) Does the entrustment doctrine of UCC § 2-403(2) apply to sales between merchants, and (2) is an automobile dealer who buys a used car from another dealer without obtaining or inquiring about the certificate of title to the car a "buyer in the ordinary course of business" within the meaning of § 2-403.

RESULT: Section 2-403(2) applies to sales between merchants, but an automobile dealer who fails to observe reasonable commercial standards of the trade cannot be a buyer in the ordinary course of business.

REASONING:

*   *   *

We think the provisions of [UCC § 2-403] are applicable to sales between merchants. We come to this conclusion because the purpose of [UCC § 2-403(2) and (3)] is to protect a person from a third-party interest in goods purchased from the general inventory of a merchant regardless of that merchant's actual authority to sell those goods. This section does not expressly or by implication restrict such protection of a sale by a merchant to a member of the consumer public. If the policy of negotiability of goods held in the inventory of a merchant is to be promoted, it would seem to apply between merchants where merchants buy from one another in the ordinary course of business. The protection is afforded to "a buyer in the ordinary course of business," and by other provisions of the Uniform Commercial Code the term "buyer" includes a merchant.

In [UCC § 1-201(9)] a buyer in the ordinary course of business is defined as "a person who in good faith and without knowledge that the sale to him is in violation of the ownership rights or security interest of a third party in the goods buys in ordinary course from a person in the business of selling goods of that kind but does not include a pawn broker." Good faith is defined in [UCC § 1-201(19)] to mean "honesty in fact in the conduct or transaction concerned." This definition applies to a member of the consumer public only, because in [UCC § 2-103(1)(b)] "'good faith' in the case of a merchant" is defined to mean "honesty in fact and the observance of reasonable commercial standards of fair dealing in the trade." In addition, [UCC § 2-104(3)], relating to the general standard applicable to transactions between merchants charges each merchant with the "knowledge or skill of merchants."

Consequently, a merchant may be a buyer in the ordinary course of business under [UCC § 2-403] from another merchant if he meets four elements: (1) Be honest in fact, (2) be without knowledge of any defects of title in the goods, (3) pay value, and (4) observe reasonable commercial standards. In the observance of reasonable commercial standards, however, a merchant is chargeable with the knowledge or skill of a merchant.

We think Malofsky was not the buyer in the ordinary course of business within the meaning of [UCC § 2-403]. Although the delivery of the automobile to Frakes, a used-car dealer, constituted an entrustment, Frakes could by subsequent sale pass title to a buyer in the ordinary course of business. However, Malofsky as a merchant was not a buyer in the ordinary course of business because he was chargeable with the knowledge that the registration law [required delivery of a certificate of title on sale of a used car]. Malofsky should have known the used automobile had a certificate of title outstanding and that Frakes was required to give him such certificate of title. Under the standards set forth in [UCC § 2-104(3)], applicable to transactions between merchants, Malofsky is chargeable with this knowledge and his failure to procure a certificate of title or some evidence of title was unreasonable as a matter of law. Evidence of custom or usage of automobile dealers contrary to the statute cannot be used to defeat the rights of a third party whatever the value of such evidence may be in adjusting disputes between dealers. . . .

. . . We think . . . the Motor Vehicle Code must be construed with the [UCC] and it is proper to refer to the Motor Vehicle Code to determine what a used-automobile dealer is supposed to know or what knowledge he is chargeable with when he claims to be a buyer in the ordinary course of business. . . .

Hallows, Chief Justice.

Rights of Seller's Creditors The discussion here concerns the rights of the creditors of a seller who sells goods but retains possession of them and then becomes insolvent or is otherwise in financial difficulty. If a creditor has seen the goods in the seller's possession after the sale and perhaps even extended credit to the seller on the supposition that the seller owned the goods, the question is whether the buyer or the seller's creditors have priority. Under the UCC, a seller's creditor may treat a sale or an identification of goods to the contract as void if the seller's continued possession of the goods is fraudulent (against the creditor) under any rule of law of the state where the goods are located. However, a merchant-seller's retention of possession of goods in good faith and current course of trade for a commercially reasonable time after a sale or identification is not fraudulent [UCC § 2-402]. For example, it would not be fraudulent for a buyer to leave goods in the seller's possession until a contract for delivery can be arranged. In such a situation, the buyer would have priority over any of the seller's creditors.

20:9   Fraudulent Conveyances and Bulk Transfers

A *fraudulent conveyance* is a transaction by which a property owner attempts to hinder or defraud his creditors by placing the property beyond the creditors' reach. He or she does so by conveying (transferring) the property to someone else.

EXAMPLE: Art owns goods worth over $15,000, and he is indebted to Jake and Tom in amounts totaling $10,000. To avoid paying these debts, Art agrees with Bob, his brother-in-law, that he will sell the goods to Bob for $10,000 and then depart. The sale is made, and Art leaves town with the money. Jake and Tom are victims of a fraudulent conveyance.

All states have enacted statutes intended to protect creditors like Jake and Tom. Under these laws, creditors can obtain relief from a fraudulent conveyance by suing the transferor (the original debtor, who made the conveyance). In connection with that lawsuit the creditors can either (1) have the conveyance set aside entirely or (2) have the property taken from the transferee (the person who received it) and held under the court's control until all parties' rights have been decided.[6]

A creditor's right to relief depends primarily on whether the transaction in question constitutes a fraudulent conveyance. The most important factor in making this determination is whether the parties had fraudulent intent, which is the intent to hinder or defraud the transferor's creditors. It is hard to prove actual fraudulent intent, so the law recognizes what are known as *badges of fraud*. The existence of several of the badges in a given transaction leads to the presumption that the parties acted with fraudulent intent. These badges of fraud include the following:

• Transferor's indebtedness when the conveyance was made
• Lack of fair consideration for the conveyance
• Family or other close relationship between the transferor and transferee
• Transferor's retention of possession of the property
• Litigation involving the transferor that is pending or threatened at the time of the conveyance
• Secrecy or concealment in connection with the conveyance

Bulk Transfers   From the viewpoint of a merchant's creditors, a particularly worrisome type of transaction is one in which the merchant quietly sells his

---

[6] Creditors' rights and remedies are discussed in detail in Chapter 31.

business (the major asset of which is often the stock in trade) and then disappears without paying the creditors. A transaction of this type is often not a fraudulent conveyance as previously discussed because the buyer has frequently paid a fair consideration and is innocent of any fraudulent intent. Article 6 of the UCC is intended to give creditors some protection in this situation by regulating the conduct of what are known as *bulk transfers.*

A bulk transfer is a transfer that meets all the following criteria:

- Transfer is made in a single transaction
- Property transferred is a major part of the transferor's materials, supplies, merchandise, or other inventory
- Transfer is not made in the ordinary course of the transferor's business
- Transferor's principal business is the sale of merchandise from stock

Farming activities are not covered by Article 6. This means that a farmer's sale of his crop to a single buyer (a common occurrence) is not a bulk transfer. If a business sells goods but also provides services, as might be true of an air conditioning business, for example, the applicability of Article 6 depends on whether the business is primarily sales-oriented; if it is, Article 6 applies to a sale of all or most of the business's inventory or other goods.

Article 6 Requirements   The Article 6 requirements are fairly simple. When a bulk transfer is going to be made, the transferor must first prepare a list of his creditors, showing names, addresses, and (if known) the amounts owed or claimed to be owed to each one [UCC § 6-104]. The list is given to the transferee. Also given to the transferee is a schedule that describes all the property being transferred. The transferee must keep the list and schedule for six months after the transfer or file them in a public office.

The heart of Article 6 is the requirement that before a bulk transfer takes place, all known creditors of the transferor must receive a written notice about the transfer. For most transfers the transferee gives the notice, which must be either delivered personally or sent by registered or certified mail. The notice has to be given at least ten days before either the transferee's taking possession of or his paying for the transferred goods, whichever occurs first [UCC § 6-105]. The content of the notice is prescribed (see UCC § 6-107), and either a short form or a long form can be used. The long form is required if all the transferor's debts will not or may not be paid in full as they become due. As a practical matter, the short form is rarely used; because the form states that all debts *will* be paid as they fall due, it can be interpreted as the transferee's independent promise to pay the transferor's creditors.

 Any businessperson involved in a bulk transfer should try to make sure that all pertinent requirements are complied with. Qualified legal counsel should be consulted as to any doubts about the requirements or, for that matter, about whether the contemplated transaction falls within the scope of Article 6 at all.

Effect of Noncompliance   If a bulk transfer is made without compliance with the requirements of Article 6, the transfer is "ineffective" against any creditor of the transferor [UCC § 6-104(1)]. This means that the creditor has the same remedies that exist under the fraudulent conveyance statutes, discussed previously. Some states have enacted an optional section of Article 6 (§ 6-106), which requires a bulk transferee to see that the consideration received by the transferor is properly applied to payment of the transferor's creditors. Courts in a few of these states have interpreted § 6-106 to mean that if the consideration received in a bulk transfer is *not* properly applied to the transferor's debts, the transferee can be held personally liable for up to the fair market value of the property.

Key Concepts and Terms

- Title to goods represents ownership of goods. Under the Uniform Commercial Code title does not determine who bears the risk of loss in a sales transaction.

- Article 7 of the UCC deals with documents of title (bills of lading and warehouse receipts) issued by carriers and warehousers. A document of title may be negotiable or nonnegotiable; if negotiable, it represents a right of possession and title to goods.

- Title to goods that have been identified to the contract can pass in any manner explicitly agreed on by the parties. In the absence of such an agreement, title passes when the seller completes his performance with respect to physical delivery of the goods. The time when this occurs depends on whether the contract is a shipment contract, a destination contract, or a contract not requiring moving of goods.

- A buyer obtains an insurable interest in existing goods once they have been identified to the contract. A seller has an insurable interest so long as he or she has title to or any security interest in the goods.

- Risk of loss is normally borne by the party who is in the best position to prevent the loss. It is determined by the type of contract involved. These types are (1) contracts involving shipment by carrier, (2) contracts involving goods held by a bailee and delivered without moving, and (3) all other sales contracts. In contracts involving shipment by carrier, the risk of loss passes to the buyer either when the seller delivers the goods to the carrier or when the goods have reached their destination, depending on whether the contract is a shipment contract or a destination contract. In contracts involving goods being held by a bailee and delivered without moving, risk of loss passes when the buyer acquires effective means of control of the goods. In other transactions, risk of loss passes on the buyer's actual receipt of the goods from a merchant seller, or on a nonmerchant seller's tender of delivery to the buyer.

- When one party breaches the contract, the risk of loss is on that party, at least to the extent of any deficiency in the other party's insurance.

- In some sales contracts the buyer has the right to return the goods. If goods are purchased under a contract of this type primarily for the buyer's own use, it is a sale on approval. If goods are delivered primarily for resale, it is a sale or return. A sale's status as a sale on approval or a sale or return affects the time when title and risk of loss pass, as well as the right of the buyer's and seller's creditors to reach the goods.

- A bona fide purchaser is a person who makes a purchase in good faith and gives valuable consideration for the goods. A person with voidable title may transfer good title to a bona fide purchaser.

- If the owner of goods entrusts them to, or leaves them in the possession of, a merchant who deals in goods of that kind, the merchant may transfer the entrustor's rights in the goods to a buyer in the ordinary course of business.

- If a seller retains possession of goods that have been sold, the seller's creditor can ignore the sale, giving the creditor priority over the buyer, if the seller's retention is fraudulent against the creditor.

- A fraudulent conveyance is a conveyance of property intended to hinder or defraud the transferor's creditors. State statutes have been enacted to protect creditors against fraudulent conveyances.

- A bulk transfer is the transfer, in a single transaction and not in the ordinary course of business, of a major part of the inventory or other goods of a transferor whose principal business is the sale of merchandise from stock. Bulk transfers are governed by Article 6 of the UCC, which requires (1) preparation of a list of the transferor's creditors, (2) preparation of a schedule of the property being transferred, and (3) advance notice to creditors about the transfer.

- Badge of Fraud
- Bailee
- Bill of Lading
- Bona Fide Purchaser
- Bulk Transfer
- Buyer in the Ordinary Course of Business
- C.I.F.
- C&F.
- Certificate of Title
- Consignment Sale
- Destination Contract
- Document of Title
- Entrustment
- Ex-Ship
- F.A.S.
- F.O.B.
- Fraudulent Conveyance
- Insurable Interest
- Negotiable Document of Title
- Reservation of Title
- Risk of Loss
- Sale on Approval
- Sale or Return
- Shipment Contract
- Title
- Warehouse Receipt

Questions and Case Problems

1. Finch contracted to purchase a helicopter from Ace Aviation, a helicopter manufacturer and seller, with a delivery date of July 1. On June 15, Ace notified Finch that she could pick up the helicopter at Ace's plant on July 1. Finch responded

that she would be unable to do so and asked Ace to hold it until August 1. Ace replied that it did not have available storage facilities, but that the helicopter could be stored in a hangar at a nearby airport if Finch agreed and paid the storage charge. Finch agreed, and the helicopter was delivered to the airport on July 1, with the instructions to deliver it to Finch on demand. On July 2, the airport notified Finch that the helicopter was in its possession pending further instructions from her. On July 3, the helicopter was destroyed in a fire. Who should bear the loss?

2. Roth telephones Jenkins and places a purchase order for 20 calculators at a total price of $1,000. Roth requests that the calculators be shipped from New York, where Jenkins maintains his business, to Roth's business address in Boston. Jenkins packs the calculators in a carton, places a label indicating the carton's contents on its side, and mails the carton by fourth-class mail. He takes out no insurance, and he places an incorrect zip code on the carton. The carton does not arrive, and Roth refuses to make payment. Jenkins sues for the purchase price. What is the decision?

3. Clay buys a car from Akins, a used car dealer, for $750, but leaves the car on the lot while she goes to have lunch. While she is gone, Akins agrees to sell the car to Dahl for $700 cash, and Dahl leaves in the car to obtain the cash. Dahl never returns. He resells the car to Gomez for $600. Clay sues to recover the car. How should the case be decided?

4. Multiplastics agrees to specially manufacture and sell 40,000 plastic pellets to Arch Industries. Arch breaches the contract by failing to accept delivery when the pellets are tendered, and Multiplastics stores the pellets in its plant. The plant burns down one month later. Multiplastics does not have insurance on the pellets, and it sues Arch for the contract price. What is the result?

5. Chamberlin, a mobile home dealer, sells Crowder a new camper unit for $1,757.74. Crowder pays by check and loads the camper onto his pickup truck, even though the camper is too large for a proper fit. The next day Crowder sells the camper unit to Hollis, another mobile home dealer, for $500. Hollis does not ask why the camper does not fit the truck and does not ask Crowder for any evidence of title. Crowder's check to Chamberlin is not honored by the bank. Chamberlain sues Hollis to recover possession of the camper unit. What is the outcome?

6. Sanchez, an interior decorator, agrees to decorate and furnish McClure's home. Under the agreement, Sanchez places various items of furniture in McClure's home on a trial basis. The parties agree that once the entire decorating plan is completed to McClure's satisfaction, a sales contract will be executed for those items of furniture McClure wishes to keep, and the rest will be returned. After the furniture has been in McClure's house for two months, he obtains a loan from State Bank, using the furniture as collateral. McClure and Sanchez then sign a sales contract for the furniture, under which McClure agrees to pay in installments. Again the furniture is used as collateral. McClure defaults on both the loan and the installment payments, and both State Bank and Sanchez claim the right to levy on the furniture. Whose claim should be upheld?

7. Selma Hayes stores her refrigerator at Warren's Warehouse, and she receives a warehouse receipt that provides for "delivery to Selma Hayes." Hayes later sells the refrigerator to Gary Cobb. She endorses the warehouse receipt with the notation, "deliver to Gary Cobb." Cobb accepts the warehouse receipt, but he makes no attempt to take possession of the refrigerator. One week later the

warehouse burns down and the refrigerator is destroyed. Cobb demands that Hayes refund his money. Should she do so?

8. During divorce proceedings, Menyhart buys the Continental Coiffures Beauty Salon from Rogers, his wife, giving Rogers a promissory note for $7,000 as part of the purchase price. Later, while the bulk of the debt is still unpaid, Menyhart sells the salon business to Yarbrough, and neither party attempts to comply with the requirements of UCC Article 6. Menyhart disappears with the sale proceeds. Rogers seeks to have the sale invalidated on the ground that it violated Article 6. Does Article 6 apply? Why or why not? What would be the significance, if any, of detailed evidence as to the type of business carried on at the salon?

9. What is the practical effect of the *Hughes* (see page 344) decision? Is Hughes obligated to pay Al Green, Inc., for the automobile? If Al Green, Inc., had borne the risk of loss, would it be in breach of the sales contract for the automobile? Who was in the superior position to anticipate and insure against the risk?

21 Warranties

> *The purpose of [products] liability is to insure that the costs of injuries resulting from defective products are borne by the manufacturers that put such products on the market rather than by the injured persons who are powerless to protect themselves.*
>
> Justice Traynor, *Greenman v Yuba Power Products, Inc.,*
> 59 Cal 2d 57, 27 Cal Rptr 697, 377 P2d 897
> (California Supreme Court, 1963)

21:1 Introduction

The manufacture and sale of goods confers great benefit to sellers and buyers. However, the enterprise creates risk of injury to buyers and others if the goods are defectively designed or manufactured. When people are injured—economically or physically—because a product fails to meet expectations, courts may be called upon to adjudicate the conflict which arises out of the injury. The variety of theories and laws that govern these types of claims falls under the general area of law called *product liability.*

Product liability is a phrase that has recently come into common use and that indicates the liability of the manufacturer, processor, or seller of a product for injury caused by a defect in or condition of the product. Some attorneys specialize entirely in products liability litigation. In fact, some attorneys devote their entire practices to product liability in a particular area, such as aviation product liability, automotive product liability, and medical product liability. Product liability applies to a broad spectrum of disciplines—engineering, physics, chemistry, and even medicine. It has been said that no other area of the law is as difficult because product liability involves the relationship of humans and machines and the extent to which as a matter of social policy the law will make producers and distributors of products liable to persons injured by those products.

Theories of Liability   The manufacturer or seller of a defective product may be held liable for injuries resulting from the defect under three theories of liability: (1) breach of warranty under the Uniform Commercial Code, (2) negligence, and (3) strict liability (see Chapter 6). They are frequently applied in combination, and one, two, or all three theories may be found in a single case.

21:2   UCC Warranties

A sales warranty is a promise that the good sold has certain qualities or conditions. The promise may be expressly made as a part of the bargain, or it may be implied as a matter of law. Virtually all goods sold are sold subject to some form or forms of warranty. Thus the warranty is a common feature of commercial life. An understanding of warranty law helps unravel the reason for certain marketing and sales practices. In addition, it helps the businessperson plan to avoid misunderstanding and conflict in sales.

The basic distinction between an express and an implied warranty is the manner of creation. An *express warranty* arises from some representation made by the seller. In the sale of a new toaster, for example, the seller may have said that the toaster was free of defects in workmanship. This representation may be enforced as an express warranty. An *implied warranty* is one that has been imposed on the seller by law. In the case of the toaster, there would be an implied warranty of merchantability, which means suitability for the ordinary uses for which the toaster was manufactured. Various express and implied warranties are treated in more detail later in this chapter.

The rise of warranties, and particularly of implied warranties, has largely displaced the ancient doctrine of caveat emptor, which means "let the buyer beware." The doctrine of caveat emptor expresses the rule that buyers purchase at their peril and that it is incumbent on them to ascertain beforehand any defects in the purchased goods. This doctrine has been eroded not only by the development of implied warranties, but also by the development of related concepts such as unconscionability (see Chapter 12).

The UCC contains several sections dealing with warranties. The sections that follow consider express warranties, the implied warranties of merchantability and fitness for a particular purpose, and the warranty of title.

21:3   Express Warranties [UCC § 2-313]

An express warranty may be oral or written and may be created in various ways. The seller need not use the word "warranty" or any other formal word. If his words or conduct amount to an express warranty, he is bound by that warranty, even if he never intended to make a warranty.

Under pre-code law, it was held that a representation constituted an express warranty only if the buyer actually relied on the representation. The UCC changed this rule, and the buyer's reliance on any representation is generally not essential. Instead, the UCC requires that the representations be "part of the basis of the bargain." Under this approach, the mere fact that certain representations were made is generally sufficient to lead to the conclusion that they were part of the basis of the bargain, unless the seller can prove otherwise.

A representation, in order to constitute an express warranty, need not be made simultaneously with the conclusion of the bargain. It may be made during the course of negotiations. Moreover, under some circumstances representations that are made after the sale, without further consideration from the buyer, may be considered express warranties. Under the UCC, a sales contract can be modified without consideration [UCC § 2-209] A representation made subsequent to the sale may therefore be treated as a modification of the contract. However, not every such representation will be considered a warranty. To be a warranty, the representation must still be part of the basis of the bargain, and most postsale representations are unlikely to be so classified, the bargain having already been made.

Affirmation of Fact or Promise   Any affirmation of fact or promise made by the seller to the buyer that relates to the goods and is part of the basis of the bargain creates an express warranty that the goods shall conform to the affirmation or promise. Such an affirmation or promise may be made in various ways. For example, statements made in a newspaper advertisement, if read by the buyer, might amount to an express warranty.

Statements concerning the value of the goods or concerning a seller's opinion or recommendation of them are considered to be only "puffing" and not express warranties.[1] Considerable problems may be encountered in determining whether a particular representation is one of fact or of opinion. Such factors as the specificity of the statement, the buyer's reliance on it, and the buyer's knowledge or lack of knowledge concerning the product all may bear on a court's determination.

 It is always risky for a seller to make statements that cannot be substantiated. The clear trend is toward considering borderline statements as affirmations of fact and therefore as express warranties. Even if a seller is ultimately vindicated in his contention that a statement was mere puffing, it may be only after years of expensive litigation and at the expense of a specific customer and the seller's good will.

The following case represents a typical fact situation in which customer disappointment about the value of a product led to litigation.

Hall

v

T. L. Kemp Jewelry, Inc.
322 SE2d 7 (1984)
Court of Appeals of North Carolina

FACTS: On May 25, 1982, plaintiff went into T. L. Kemp Jewelry Store in Chapel Hill, North Carolina, to look for an anniversary present for his wife. Plaintiff expressed interest in a gold bracelet with diamonds and emeralds marked for sale at $2,650. On May 28, 1982, plaintiff returned

---

[1] Statements of fact and statements of opinion, including dealers' puffing, are discussed in Chapter 12.

to the jewelry store and purchased the bracelet for $1,900 plus tax. During negotiations for the bracelet plaintiff explained that he usually dealt with a wholesale jeweler and was inexperienced in dealing with a retail jeweler. He expressed a willingness to pay a retail price so long as the value of the jewelry was commensurate with the purchase price. The owner assured the plaintiff that the gold and stones were of "excellent quality." Plaintiff said, "If I have $2,000.00 worth of jewelry, let's wrap it up." Defendant supplied plaintiff with an appraisal, for insurance purposes, stating that the bracelet had a value of $2,650.00. In the following two months plaintiff sought and received appraisals of the bracelet from other jewelers; these jewelers appraised the bracelet at $900 and at $595. When plaintiff sought to return the bracelet and rescind the purchase, defendant refused.

ISSUE: Did the jeweler's assurances of value constitute an express warranty under UCC § 2-313?

RESULT: No. The jeweler's statements were merely opinion and did not constitute an express warranty of the value of the bracelet.

REASONING:

*   *   *

In order to overcome a motion for summary judgment as to this issue the plaintiff must present evidence tending to prove that defendant made: (1) an express warranty as to a fact or promise relating to the goods, (2) which was relied upon by the plaintiff in making his decision to purchase, (3) and that this express warranty was breached by the defendant. . . .

G.S. 25–2–313(2) provides:

> It is not necessary to the creation of an express warranty that the seller use formal words such as "warranty" or "guarantee" or that he have a specific intention to make a warranty, but an affirmation merely of the value of the goods or a statement purporting to be merely the seller's opinion or commendation of the goods does not create a warranty.

The question we must answer is whether the statements as to value rose to the level of a warranty or whether they were merely opinion. The distinction between an affirmation or a description from mere sales talk or opinion or puffing is hazy. . . . 5 Williston on Sales § 17–5 (4th ed. 1974). The law recognizes that some sellers' statements are only sales palaver and not express warranties. Thus expressions such as "supposed to last a lifetime" or "in perfect condition" do not create an express warranty. . . . Our review of the case law of this state revealed no case where an opinion as to value, standing alone, was sufficient to amount to an express warranty. This does not necessarily mean that value could never become expressly warranted, but it suggests that in the ordinary course of business, a statement as to value is not considered an express warranty. No special circumstances appear in this case which would separate defendant's statements as to value from those of other merchants in an ordinary transaction. We find defendant made no express warranty as to the value of the bracelet. . . .

Hill, Judge.

Description of Goods   Any description of the goods that is made part of the basis of the bargain creates an express warranty that the goods shall conform to that description. A description need not be by words. Technical specifications and blueprints, for example, provide a more exact description than language. A warranty based on description is an important one, because goods are often offered for sale or ordered by reference to descriptive or generic names. For example, an agreement to sell "portland cement" carries a warranty that the cement delivered shall conform to the requirements for portland cement. The warranty arises when the seller makes a statement descriptive of the goods sold or when the buyer orders goods of a specific kind.

The following case illustrates how a court determined whether a description of goods in an advertisement was a warranty. Notice also in this case the recurring issue of whether a statement about a product is a statement of fact or a mere statement of opinion.

Interco Inc.

v

Randustrial Corp.
533 SW2d 257 (1976)
Missouri Court of Appeals

FACTS: Interco's shoe division occupied 21 buildings in St. Louis. In Building No. 3 the first floor was extremely rough, making it difficult to move merchandise. In 1971, a Randustrial representative recommended application of Sylox, a Randustrial product, because of its flexibility. Sylox was applied and proved satisfactory. In 1972, Interco experienced a similar roughness problem on the second floor of Building No. 1. Interco applied Sylox to the floor without consulting Randustrial. Due to floor movement ("give"), Sylox proved ineffective. Sylox had worked on the other building's floor because that floor had less movement. Interco filed suit against Randustrial. Interco claimed breach of an express warranty created by the following catalog description of Sylox: "Sylox is a hard yet malleable material which bonds firm to wood floors for smooth and easy hand-trucking. Sylox will absorb considerable flex without cracking and is not softened by spillage of oil, grease or solvents." A jury returned a verdict for Randustrial, and Interco appealed.

ISSUE: Was the catalogue product description part of the basis of the bargain so as to constitute an express warranty under UCC § 2-313?

RESULT: The words used in the description were factual and were used to induce purchases and are, therefore, an express warranty.

REASONING:

*   *   *

Both parties agree that [UCC § 2-313] is applicable to the facts of this case. . . .

We have noted that Interco claims the existence of a warranty as to Sylox, and Randustrial argues the absence of a warranty. We disagree with Randustrial's contentions in this regard. Although Randustrial contends its reference to Sylox in its sales catalogue did not constitute an express warranty, if the words used in the catalogue constitute a description or an affirmation of fact or promise about Sylox and became a part of the basis of the bargain, an express warranty was created. . . .

Randustrial also asserts that there could be no breach of warranty because Interco had failed to test the material before applying it to Building No. 1 and had failed to seek advice from Randustrial on its application. The uncontradicted evidence was that the cause of the breakup of the Sylox was the movement in the floor. There was nothing vague in Interco's evidence as to the intended use of Sylox. The evidence was palpable that Interco wanted something to withstand flex without breaking. The catalogue stated that "Sylox will absorb considerable flex." Thus, there was a description or affirmation of fact or "warranty" regarding Sylox giving rise to the purpose for which it was purchased by Interco. This was not mere puffing of a product. Interco was entitled to take the catalogue description of Sylox at its face value and plain meaning. There was no need to consult Randustrial or seek its advice regarding the use of Sylox. Any suggestion that Interco was at fault for not having tested the product or sought consultation is fatuous, for the catalogue description made no such requirement. . . .

Randustrial's argument that Interco failed to prove reliance on any warranty is also not felicitous. There is no mention of reliance in [UCC § 2-313]. And the comments to that section of the U.C.C. reveal that the concept of reliance as required in pre-U.C.C. warranty cases was purposefully abandoned. . . . The unchallenged evidence was that Interco's Manager of Facilities Engineering read the catalogue description which stated that Sylox would "absorb considerable flex"; that his testimony was that "the literature says that it [Sylox] absorbs considerable flex. Based on that I was assuming that it would do the job." The U.C.C. requires no more than what took place here. The statement "absorbs considerable flex" became "part of the basis of the bargain." The fact that Interco relied to some extent on its past experience with Sylox in Building No. 3 is not determinative of any issue, as no particular reliance on an express warranty is necessary. . . .

The fact that the language read by Interco was contained in a catalogue and was basically an advertisement does not preclude a finding that it is a warranty. A brochure, catalogue or advertisement may constitute an express warranty. . . . However, the catalogue advertisement or brochure must have at least been read, . . . as the U.C.C. requires the proposed express warranty be part of the basis of the bargain. . . . Randustrial does not dispute the fact that Interco had read the catalogue.

Randustrial [argues] that the statement that Sylox "will absorb considerable flex" merely reflects the seller's opinion of the goods and creates no warranty. . . . [UCC § 2-313] specifically excludes a seller's mere opinion or commendation from being interpreted as an express warranty. . . . [However,] the language chosen by the seller in his advertising must be interpreted in favor of the buyer in order to restrict "untruthful puffing of wares." . . .

An important factor is whether the seller assumes to assert a fact of which the buyer is ignorant or whether the seller merely expresses an opinion on which the buyer may be expected to have an opinion and be able to express his own judgment. . . .

. . . It is manifest that the words were meant to induce purchases through the assurance that considerable flex would be absorbed and were not mere opinion. The words were an affirmation of fact within the meaning of [UCC § 2-313]. . . .

Gunn, Judge.

A *warranty of conformity* to description does not arise if a sale of specific items is involved. For example, assume that Robin offers to sell Charles "a Stradivarius violin" but does not show Charles any particular violin. Here, a warranty of conformity to description would arise. However, if Robin shows Charles a violin, states that it is a Stradivarius, and offers to sell it to Charles, there is no warranty of conformity to description. If the violin is not in fact a Stradivarius, Charles may not claim breach of warranty (although he might be able to obtain rescission of the contract on grounds of fraud, misrepresentation, or mutual mistake; see Chapter 12).

Sample or Model   Any sample or model that is made part of the basis of the bargain creates an express warranty that the whole of the goods shall conform to that sample or model. To illustrate, a potato seller opens a bag, shows some of the potatoes to a potential buyer, and then states that the rest of the potatoes are as good as those examined. The seller has made a warranty of conformity to sample.

The point must be made here that a sample is different from a model. The difference is that a sample is drawn from the bulk of the goods to be sold, while a model is individually constructed and is generally used when the goods are not available for inspection. The potatoes in the example above are a sample. A model might be used when a very large object is not readily available. The courts generally permit greater variation from a model than they do from a sample.

21:4   Implied Warranties: Merchantability; Fitness for a Particular Purpose

Implied warranties are imposed by operation of law to promote high business standards and to discourage sharp dealings. The UCC imposes two types of implied warranties: a warranty of *merchantability*, and a warranty of *fitness for a particular purpose*. These warranties reflect the fact that, as noted in an old English case, a "purchaser has the right to expect a saleable article answering the description in the contract."[2]

Implied Warranty of Merchantability [UCC § 2-314]   A sale of goods by a merchant who deals in goods of that kind usually carries with it a warranty that the goods are suitable for the ordinary purpose for which they are to be used. This is the implied warranty of merchantability. Goods do not have to be perfect to be merchantable. The warranty is essentially one of general fitness. For example, some goods are merchantable if they are of fair, average quality. The warranty is applied to merchant sellers only. It does not apply to a casual seller such as a vendor at a garage sale. The warranty is also inapplicable if the seller has disclaimed it, as discussed later in this chapter.

The UCC specifically provides that the sale of food or drink, whether for consumption on the premises or elsewhere, is subject to the implied warranty of merchantability. As applied to food, the warranty generally requires that the food be wholesome and not contain foreign objects. Some courts have held that the presence of natural objects in food does not constitute a breach of warranty. This distinction has sometimes resulted in unjust decisions.

EXAMPLE: Amy breaks her tooth on a hard object in a walnut-cream cheese sandwich. If the object were a piece of glass, a court would find the warranty of merchantability has been breached, and Amy would probably be able to recover damages. However, if a piece of walnut shell were in the sandwich, a court may find that the warranty of merchantability has not been breached, and Amy would not be able to recover damages.

Many courts, however, have discarded the distinction between foreign and natural objects. These courts focus instead on what a consumer should reasonably expect to find in the particular food.

The warranty of merchantability also applies to goods sold in the manufacturer's original package, even though they may not have been

---

[2] *Gardiner v Gray*, 171 Eng Rep 46, 47, 4 Camp 144 (King's Bench, 1815).

inspected by the retailer. A can of beans, for example, cannot be inspected by the seller, but if it contains insects, the seller will have breached the warranty of merchantability. It should be noted that the wholesaler who sold the beans to the retailer will have breached the warranty to the retailer, and the manufacturer will have breached the warranty to the wholesaler.

Fitness for Particular Purpose [UCC § 2-315] An implied warranty of fitness of goods for a particular purpose arises when the seller has reason to know that there is a particular purpose for which the goods are required and that the buyer is relying on the seller's skill or judgment to select suitable goods. This warranty applies to sales by nonmerchants as well as merchants. In practice, however, the warranty usually involves a merchant seller, since a buyer normally does not rely on a nonmerchant seller's knowledge.

The warranty of fitness for a particular purpose involves two conditions: (1) that the seller has reason to know that the buyer intends a particular use, as distinguished from an ordinary use, for the goods; and (2) that the seller knows that the buyer is relying on the seller's skill and judgment in selecting the goods. The essence of the warranty is the buyer's reliance on the seller's expertise in selecting the right product for the buyer's intended use. A major factor in determining whether a warranty of fitness for a particular purpose should be implied is therefore the knowledge possessed by the respective parties. Where the seller is clearly much more knowledgeable than the buyer, the warranty is likely to be implied. Where the buyer's knowledge is equal or superior to the seller's, there probably is no such warranty.

EXAMPLE: A purchased bricks from B to build a fireplace, and the bricks proved unsatisfactory for that purpose. If A were a homeowner inexperienced in building fireplaces, and B were a merchant familiar with bricks and their uses, and A had told B of the intended purpose and asked B to recommend a suitable brick, then a court would find an implied warranty of fitness of the bricks for the intended purpose. If, however, A were in the business of building fireplaces and A had specifically requested the type of brick involved, then a court would not find any implied warranty of fitness for the particular purpose. In other words, the buyer who provides his or her own specifications cannot later claim to have relied on the seller's expertise.

 Most people tend to think of warranties in terms of new products, but warranties may also exist with respect to used goods. A seller of used goods should therefore be aware that a court may find an implied warranty of merchantability or fitness for a particular purpose. If the seller does not want to warrant the goods, he or she should take clear steps to disclaim these warranties, as discussed in 21:4.

The following case illustrates that compliance with the warranty of merchantability does not always ensure the buyer's satisfaction. Consider whether the result would have been different if the purchaser had informed the seller that she intended to eat the pork without cooking it. Note how the court treats the breach of warranty and strict liability theories together.

Hollinger

v

Shoppers Paradise of New Jersey, Inc.
340 A2d 687 (1975)
New Jersey Superior Court, Law Division

FACTS: Mrs. Hollinger and her children contracted trichinosis from some pork chops she had cooked. Mrs. Hollinger filed suit against Shoppers Paradise, the seller, seeking recovery on theories of strict liability in tort and breach of warranty of merchantability. At the trial there was evidence that trichinosis is caused by parasitic worms called trichinae and that proper cooking is the only way to ensure that pork is completely free of trichinae. The trial court ruled in favor of the seller.

ISSUE: Does the presence of a defect that is inherent in a food product as it is usually sold render the product unmerchantable under UCC § 2-314?

RESULT: A food product may be reasonably fit for sale, and merchantable under § 2-314, even if it normally contains a defect which must be cured by the consumer.

REASONING:

* * *

. . . [R]ecovery for [either] strict liability [or] breach of implied warranty of merchantability [does not require] proof of negligence by the defendant. Liability is established if the evidence shows that the product was not reasonably fit for the ordinary purposes for which it was sold and such defect proximately caused injury to the ultimate consumer. . . . It seems clear that these principles are applicable to the retail sale of food products. . . . Thus, in the instant case, if plaintiffs show that the pork was not reasonably fit for eating when it was sold and that the defect therein caused their injuries, they may recover by reason of either breach of warranty or strict liability theories, which are considered together for purposes of analysis. . . .

Two reasonable inferences which could be drawn from the sale of the pork chops to Mrs. Hollinger and the subsequent illness of her and her family are that the meat was unfit for consumption and that this unfitness proximately caused plaintiffs' injuries. However, to infer that the product was unfit upon reviewing the consequences of its use is not to say that it was not *reasonably* fit at the time of sale for its ordinary and intended purpose. [Court's emphasis.] Raw pork is a unique product in that it may contain an inherent defect (trichinae) which is undetectable by the seller but curable through preparation by the consumer. The fact that there is a danger of illness as a consequence of eating uncooked or underdone pork is a matter of common knowledge which courts in other jurisdictions have recognized and of which this court takes notice. . . . It follows that the ordinary and intended purpose for raw pork is consumption after *proper cooking by the consumer* and that if the chops in question were reasonably fit at the time of sale for such use Shoppers Paradise may avoid a finding of strict liability or breach of warranty. [Court's emphasis.] . . .

. . . New Jersey has been in the forefront of jurisdictions extending protection to consumers by imposing strict liability in tort. . . . Recovery is based on considerations of policy rather than actionable conduct by the defendant. These considerations are identified in [*Cintrone v Hertz Truck Leasing*]:

> . . . Warranties of fitness are regarded by law as an incident of a transaction because *one party to the relationship is in a better position than the other to know and control the condition* of the chattel transferred. . . . [This factor makes] it likely that the party acquiring possession of the article will assume it is in a safe condition for use and therefore refrain from taking precautionary measures himself. [Court's emphasis.] . . .

In the case of raw pork the factual premise upon which [this] policy consideration rests is not present. Because of the character of the product it is impossible for the seller to detect the presence of the latent defect. . . .

. . . Since the presence of trichinae in raw pork can be cured *but only by the consumer*, the rationale for absolving the helpless seller from strict liability for damages caused by the parasite is [compelling]. [Court's emphasis.] . . . For the foregoing reasons it is the opinion of the court that the policies compelling application of strict liability are not applicable in the case of a consumer contracting trichinosis from pork chops. This is consistent with the holding that Mrs. Hollinger failed to properly cook the meat served on October 10, 1971, and leads to the conclusion that plaintiffs have failed to prove as a matter of law that defendant sold a product not reasonably fit for its ordinary and intended purpose. For these reasons the motion of Shoppers Paradise for dismissal of the complaint is granted.

Rosenberg, Superior Court Justice.

21:5 Warranty of Title [UCC § 2-312]

A contract for the sale of goods includes a seller's warranty that he or she has good title, the transfer is rightful, and the goods shall be delivered free of any security interest (see Chapters 29 and 30) or other encumbrance of which the buyer, at the time of contracting, has no knowledge. The purpose of these warranties is clear. A buyer has the right to expect that the seller can convey a good title. If the seller cannot do so, the *warranty of title* has been breached. For example, a seller of stolen goods cannot convey a good title, and a buyer could claim breach of the warranty of title and recover the money paid to the seller.

In addition, if the seller of goods is a merchant who regularly deals in goods of the kind, the seller warrants that the goods are free of any rightful claim of patent or copyright infringement by a third person. Interestingly, however, the warranty is reversed if the seller sells products for which the buyer has supplied specifications. In that event, the buyer must be responsible to the seller for any claims of third persons that the goods produced and sold violate a copyright or a patent. Thus, in both events, the party who is in control of the specifications of the product bears ultimate liability for violating the intellectual property rights of others.

21:6   Exclusion or Modification of Warranties [UCC § 2-316]

Express and implied warranties may be excluded or modified by the seller's disclaiming them. The courts look with disfavor on *disclaimers of warranty*, especially in cases involving consumers. The UCC to some extent reflects that disfavor. The UCC seeks to protect buyers from contracts in which unexpected language excludes or modifies warranties.

The rules governing warranty disclaimers in UCC § 2-316 are neither designed nor interpreted as loopholes for evasion of a seller's warranty obligations. The courts insist that sellers comply strictly with the methods of disclaimer specified in these rules. Even when a seller has complied, under certain circumstances courts have held that disclaimer provisions are unconscionable under UCC § 2-302.[3] In addition, a warranty disclaimer that would be effective under the UCC might be unenforceable because of other applicable state or federal legislation, as discussed in Section 21:10. Furthermore, a buyer who is prevented by a disclaimer from claiming breach of warranty may sue on tort theories of negligence or strict liability.

Disclaimer of Express Warranties [UCC § 2-316(1)]   The UCC makes express warranties much more difficult to disclaim than implied warranties. Under the UCC, a seller's words or conduct indicating that there is an express warranty are interpreted as being consistent with other words or conduct indicating that the warranty does not exist or is limited, as long as this interpretation is reasonable. If this interpretation is not reasonable, then the exclusion or limitation of the express warranty is totally ineffective unless the parol evidence rule [UCC § 2-202] compels a different conclusion.

The above provision typically comes into play when the seller has allegedly made oral warranties, but the written contract disclaims all warranties. The parol evidence rule protects a seller when a buyer falsely claims that the seller

---

[3] Unconscionability is discussed in Chapter 12.

made oral warranties. If the written contract was intended by the parties as the final expression of their agreement, the buyer cannot offer evidence of the oral warranties to prove that they were breached. This rule would seem to indicate that a written disclaimer of express warranties would prevail over prior oral express warranties. In practice, however, prior oral express warranties are often accepted as evidence in court. For example, a court may find that the written contract was not intended as the final expression of the parties' agreement, that the oral warranty is consistent with the written disclaimer, that the disclaimer is unconscionable, or that its inclusion in the contract was fraudulent.

The effect of UCC § 2-316 as it has been interpreted is that a seller is indeed protected against claims of oral warranties if the seller can convince the court that they are false. If, on the other hand, the court believes the buyer's testimony concerning oral warranties, it can find a way to refuse to give effect to the seller's written disclaimer.

Disclaimer of Implied Warranties [UCC § 2-316(2), (3)]   Implied warranties are easier to disclaim than express warranties, but the UCC does specify procedures designed to ensure that the buyer is aware of such a disclaimer. Under the UCC, the implied warranty of merchantability may be excluded or modified in whole or in part only by language that mentions "merchantability." A disclaimer of the warranty of merchantability need not be in writing, but if it is, the disclaimer must be conspicuous. To exclude or modify any implied warranty of fitness, the exclusion must be in writing *and* conspicuous. For example, all implied warranties of fitness may be disclaimed by the conspicuous statement, "There are no warranties which extend beyond the description on the face hereof."

The UCC provides alternative methods of excluding *all* implied warranties. One method is the use of expressions like "as is" or "with all faults." Another method is the use of other language which in common understanding calls the buyer's attention to the exclusion of warranties and makes plain that there is no implied warranty. Most courts have held that "as is" disclaimers must be conspicuous, although the UCC does not specifically so require. The UCC also permits implied warranties to be excluded or modified by course of dealing, course of performance, or usage of trade.

To be conspicuous, a disclaimer must be so written that a reasonable person against whom it is to operate ought to notice it [UCC § 1-201(10)]. Many warranty disclaimers have been held ineffective because they were not conspicuous. In assessing conspicuousness, courts have considered such factors as the disclaimer's location in the document and the size and color of the type. For example, a printed heading (1) in capital letters, (2) in contrasting type or color, and (3) placed on the front of a form contract is considered conspicuous. The same heading might not be considered conspicuous if placed on the back of the form, because a customer is unlikely to look there. Similarly, a misleading heading will not be effective even though capital letters are used. For example, a reasonable person would not expect to find a disclaimer of warranty under the heading "WARRANTY," and the courts would find that disclaimer to be ineffective.

The courts are clearly concerned that unscrupulous sellers may use disclaimer provisions to evade responsibility for the proper functioning of the products they sell. With that fact in mind, a seller who desires to limit warranties should do so by means of a carefully worded, prominently placed, and fair provision. The seller might also have the buyer sign a statement certifying that the buyer has read the warranty disclaimer provision. Such an approach helps to eliminate the reasons for distrusting disclaimers.

Disclaimer of the Warranty of Title [UCC § 2-312]   The warranty of title may be excluded or modified by specific language. For example, if the seller notifies the buyer that the property being sold has a lien on it, the warranty of title will not apply to that lien, but it would apply to all other liens of which the seller does not notify the buyer. The warranty of title may also be excluded or modified by circumstances that give the buyer reason to know that the seller does not claim title or is selling only the right or title that he may have. For example, the circumstances of a foreclosure sale (a resale of property after the initial buyer has defaulted and the seller has retaken possession of the property) might indicate to the buyer that the person making the sale did not warrant the title to the goods or their freedom from encumbrances.

Limitation of Remedy for Breach of Warranty [UCC § 2-719]   As an alternative to disclaiming warranties, some sellers prefer to limit the remedies available in the event of a breach of warranty. In other words, a buyer may be allowed only certain remedies for the breach. The UCC permits a seller to limit his responsibility only to repairing or replacing defective goods or parts. The UCC also provides that a seller may limit the damages that the buyer can claim, or exclude consequential damages. However, such a limitation is invalid if it is unconscionable, and limitation of consequential damages for personal injuries caused by consumer goods is presumed to be unconscionable. In addition, if circumstances cause a limited remedy to fail in its essential purpose, the buyer may have recourse to any other remedy provided by the UCC. For example, if repeated repair attempts are unsuccessful, a court may find that the warranty fails in its essential purpose. In such a case, a consumer may demand and be granted a refund.

 A seller should be wary of using repair or replacement warranties as a means of limiting potential warranty liability. Such warranties may be effective as limitations in commercial transactions, but they often fail when they are included in consumer sales contracts. When a consumer is involved, a court may find a repair or replacement clause to be unconscionable.

Effect of Opportunity to Examine Goods   If the buyer, before entering the contract, examined the goods or a sample or model of them to his or her satisfaction, or refused to examine the goods, there is no implied warranty with regard to defects that an examination ought to have revealed—that is, open or visible defects. This rule does not apply if the seller has merely offered

TABLE 21.1
Disclaimers of Warranty

Section	Warranty	Method of Exclusion or Modification
2-312	Title/Against Infringement	1. Specific language or circumstances give the buyer reason to know.
2-313	Express Warranty	1. Words of express warranty will be read consistently with language that negates or limits express warranty; 2. If a conflict arises, express warranty prevails over negation or limitation.
2-314	Merchantability	1. Language must mention merchantability and, if written, must be conspicuous; 2. "As is" or "with all faults" is sufficient; 3. Course of dealing or usage of trade can modify; 4. Opportunity for examination of goods, which would have revealed defects, was refused by buyer.
2-315	Fitness for a Particular Purpose	1. Language must be written and conspicuous; 2. "There are no warranties which extend beyond the description on the face hereof"; 3. Items 2, 3, and 4 under Merchantability.

to let the buyer examine the goods. Rather, the buyer must actually examine the goods, or the seller must demand that the buyer examine them. The provision concerning examination does not apply to express warranties.

21:7 Cumulation and Conflict of Warranties [UCC § 2-317]

A sale of goods may be accompanied by several warranties, both express and implied. Under the UCC these warranties are interpreted as being consistent with each other and cumulative wherever possible. When the warranties cannot be interpreted as being consistent, the intention of the parties determines which warranty is dominant. The UCC sets forth rules to assist a court in determining the parties' intention. The essence of these rules is that the more specific warranty generally prevails over the less specific. For example, technical specifications prevail over an inconsistent sample, model, or description; a sample prevails over an inconsistent general description; and express warranties prevail over inconsistent implied warranties, except for the implied warranty of fitness for a particular purpose.

 The rules for determining priority between inconsistent warranties are designed for situations in which the seller has in good faith made warranties that turn out to be inconsistent. If the seller has led the buyer to believe that all the warranties can be performed, the seller will be prevented from relying on inconsistency as a defense to a breach of warranty action.

21:8   Privity Requirements

Under what is known as the doctrine of *privity of contract*, a buyer can sue only the immediate seller for breach of warranty. This doctrine is being rejected in many courts. Most states now permit a buyer to bring a breach of warranty action not only against the immediate seller, but also against intermediate sellers and the manufacturer. For example, a defective bicycle purchased by an adult may cause injury to a child, and the purchaser may be able to hold the manufacturer liable for the defect.

Rights of Third Persons [UCC § 2-318]   Consumers other than the purchaser are generally permitted to sue sellers and manufacturers. The UCC has three alternative provisions on warranty actions by third persons. Each state chooses one of the alternatives when it adopts Article 2 of the code.

Alternative A extends warranty protection to family members and guests of the buyer who may reasonably be expected to use, consume, or be affected by the goods. Alternative B extends warranty protection to *all* persons who may reasonably be expected to use, consume, or be affected by the goods. Alternatives A and B are limited to personal injury. Alternative C extends warranty protection to the same persons as Alternative B, but includes *any* injury caused by the breach of warranty. To the extent the UCC alternative adopted by a state does not expressly give warranty protection to a person other than the buyer, the UCC remains neutral on extension of sellers' warranties to nonbuyers.

21:9   Product Liability:
Negligence Theory and Strict Liability

Thus far this chapter has dealt primarily with breach of warranty and the loss that results in the value of the product itself. Consider the example of the toaster again: a new toaster that does not work obviously is not worth very much. The breach of warranty with respect to the toaster has left the purchaser with a product considerably less valuable than that for which he bargained. Assume, however, that the defect in the toaster resulted in an electrical malfunction that caused a fire that, in turn, injured the purchaser and damaged her home. The purchaser would then demand not only a refund or replacement for the toaster, but also monetary damages for the personal injury and property damage. Here, the law of negligence and strict liability may be applied along with the law of warranties. The purchaser may claim damages in any of these three areas. She might bring a breach of warranty action. She might also bring a negligence action, claiming that the toaster was not manufactured with reasonable care. Or, the purchaser may seek to recover from the manufacturer under the theory of strict liability, which relieves the purchaser of the need to show negligence.

Negligence   In product liability suits based on *negligence*, the standard of care required is the same as in other cases based on negligence (see Chapter

6). That standard of care as applied to products liability is that a manufacturer, processor, or seller has a duty to use the care, skill, and diligence regarding the product that a reasonably careful, skillful, and prudent person would use in the same or similar circumstances. In negligence suits, the manufacturer or distributor is liable only where he fails to exercise the care that is reasonable under the circumstances. Absolute perfection and perfect safety are not required.

Negligent Design   A manufacturer of goods has a duty to use reasonable care in designing a product that could be dangerous if not used as the manufacturer intended. The question of liability often comes down to whether the cost of improving safety is less than the probable cost of an injury multiplied by the likelihood of injury. If a product designer might have greatly decreased the probability or extent of a injury by making a relatively costless or inexpensive design change, negligence may be found.

Duty to Warn of Danger   The manufacturer or seller has a duty to warn of a danger where (1) a product is dangerous when put to its normal and foreseeable use; (2) the danger in using the product is, or should be, known to the manufacturer or seller; and (3) the danger is not obvious, known to, or readily discoverable by the user. The basis of this duty is the manufacturer's superior knowledge of the dangerous characteristics of the product—that is, the manufacturer is considered to know everything about the product and therefore is obligated to inform prospective users of any dangerous qualities in the product.

Multiple Defendants   A person injured by a defective product has a variety of potential defendants. These may include the manufacturer of the defective product, the designer, the manufacturer of a component part, the seller of the product, or the testing company that endorsed the product.

Strict Liability   Suits against a manufacturer or seller to recover for product-caused harm are most often based on the theory of strict liability in tort.[4] Under the *Restatement (Second) of Torts* § 402A (1965), the seller of any product that is in a defective condition "unreasonably dangerous to the user" is liable for injury to the ultimate user, even though the seller has exercised "all possible care" in the preparations and sale of the product. This liability remains with the seller even though the ultimate user of the product has not actually purchased the product from, or entered into a contractual relationship with, the seller. Although relatively new in its application in product liability cases, the doctrine has been favorably received and there is a strong trend toward its acceptance.

The first decision establishing strict liability in a products case was *Greenman v Yuba Power Products, Inc.*[5] In that case, the California Supreme Court

---

[4] The tort theory of strict liability is discussed in Chapter 6.
[5] 59 Cal 2d 57, 27 Cal Rptr 697, 377 P2d 897 (1963).

expressly decided that a manufacturer was strictly liable in tort when a machine that it placed on the market, knowing it was to be used without inspection for defects, proved to have a defect that caused injury. The court ruled that it was not necessary for the plaintiff to establish an express warranty. The court observed that implicit in the product's presence on the market was a representation that it would safely do the job for which it was built. "Under these circumstances," said the court, "it should not be controlling whether plaintiff selected the machine because of the statements in the brochure, or because of the machine's own appearance of excellence that belied the defect lurking beneath the surface, or because he merely assumed that it would safely do the jobs it was built to do." Since 1963, the date of the *Greenman* decision, the doctrine of strict liability for products cases has been accepted in most states.

To recover for injuries, a person must show that the product was defective. In deciding whether a product was unreasonably dangerous, or defective, courts have indicated the product may have been defective for at least one of three reasons: "(1) it may have been fabricated or constructed defectively in the sense that the specific product was not at the time of sale by the maker or other seller in the condition that the market intended it to be; (2) it may have been improperly designed; and (3) purchasers and those who are likely to use the product may have been misinformed or inadequately informed, either about the risks and dangers involved in the use of the product or how to avoid or minimize the harmful consequences from such risks."[6] The plaintiff must also prove that the product was defective when it left the control of the manufacturer or seller.

The Expert Witness In years past, attorneys facetiously referred to an expert as "anyone from out of town." While the definition may still hold in certain cases, it is the expert's testimony on which the outcome the modern product liability case depends. Such cases often involve a manufacturer's failure to design and equip a product with a safety device to protect users from danger. Special training and background qualify the *expert witness* to provide a reasoned opinion as to whether a particular product was safely designed in accordance with the way people generally think and would normally use the product. Product liability, a subject studied in many engineering schools and psychology departments, is concerned primarily with what is termed "safety engineering" or "human factors." A "human factors expert" or "safety engineer" or "safety psychologist" frequently acts as an expert witness in product liability cases.

Defenses The principles of contributory negligence and assumption of risk (see Chapter 6) may be applied in defending a product liability suit. Under the defense of contributory negligence, the manufacturer or seller of a defective product is not ordinarily liable to persons who, by their own negligent conduct, contributed to their injuries.

---

[6] Keeton, *Product Liability and the Meaning of Defect*, 5 St Marys L J 30, 33–34.

Under the theory of assumption of risk, the person who voluntarily chooses to use a product with full knowledge of the risks and dangers involved assumes the risks.

Another defense is the consumer's failure to follow the manufacturer's instructions if the product requires assembly of component parts according to those instructions.

EXAMPLE: In a product liability suit for a death caused by the collapse of scaffolding purchased from a manufacturer, the manufacturer was not liable because the victim and others who assembled the scaffolding failed to follow the instructions and plans furnished by the manufacturer. The court noted that the scaffolding was not assembled according to the manufacturer's instructions; as a result of improper assembly the scaffolding braces bent, causing the scaffolding to collapse.

Warranties and Tort Theories of Action   If a plaintiff has sustained physical or economic injury as a result of using a defective product, theories of warranty and tort action may be used to seek redress from the seller or manufacturer. The following two cases illustrate this point well. The *Amway* case shows the practical problems of proving facts with sufficient certainty. The *Spring Motors* case analyzes the theoretical overlap between warranty law and strict liability law.

Thomas

v

Amway Corp.

488 A2d 716 (1985)

Supreme Court of Rhode Island

FACTS: In September 1976 plaintiff purchased from defendant a bottle of liquid soap. Shortly after using the product her skin became severely inflamed and red blotches developed over a large portion of her body. Her skin remained inflamed for over a year; the itching was so intense that she was often forced to leave work early. When the blotches finally cleared up, in August of 1978, they left marks all over her body. She died on May 28, 1980, from other causes. Evidence was presented to the effect that she had never had a skin condition prior to September 1976.

The trial judge dismissed the case on a motion for a directed verdict, ruling that the plaintiff's proof was insufficient, as a matter of law, to support any theory of recovery. The plaintiff appealed.

ISSUE: Can plaintiff recover under a theory of warranty or tort?

RESULT: No. The trial evidence was insufficient to support a theory of breach of an express or an implied warranty or of negligence or strict liability.

REASONING:

* * *

Breach of Implied Warranty of Merchantability

The plaintiff's allegation of a breach of implied warranty is premised on [UCC] § 2–314, which discusses the merchantability of goods. A review of the evidence fails to demonstrate any negation of the requirements of merchantability by defendant, Amway. This implied warranty is breached when a product of fair average quality does not pass in the trade and is unfit for the ordinary purpose for which it is used, which in this case was the cleansing of the body. . . .

The plaintiff did not present any evidence from which a jury reasonably could have inferred that Nature Shower was a liquid soap that would not pass without objection in the trade. Nor did plaintiff offer proof to show that Nature Shower was not of fair average quality or fit for the ordinary purpose of cleaning. The plaintiff has merely proven the happening of an occurrence; she demonstrates that she developed a skin condition following the use of Nature Shower in September 1976 but has not proved the causal nexus between the happening of the occurrence and the alleged breach of the implied warranty of merchantability. The plaintiff is not bound to exclude every other possible cause of her condition but she is required to show that the probable cause was the soap. . . .

Breach of an Express Warranty

[UCC] § 2–313 sets forth the necessary requisites of proof in order to prevail on a claim for a breach of an express warranty by affirmation or promise. The plaintiff contends that the label on Nature Shower expressly warranted that its use "leaves skin feeling silky clean . . . Gentle for all uses" and that "everyone in the family will enjoy the convenience of this versatile body cleanser for bathing, showering and handwashing." The plaintiff asserts that this express warranty was breached because she suffered a rash after using this product.

Although the trial justice's assertion that "it [Nature Shower] can be gentle but result in a rash" is inherently contradictory, especially when read in conjunction with the "for all uses" language, he was correct in directing a verdict on defendant's behalf with respect to this issue. The plaintiff who claims breach of express warranty has the burden of proving that the statements or representations made by the seller induced her to purchase that product and that she relied upon such statements or representations. . . . In the case at bar, defendant had not printed on the bottle that the product would not produce a rash, thus plaintiff had no representation to rely upon. As the trial justice properly noted, "[t]here is no evidence in this case that Mrs. Thomas made her bargain on anything contained on the container." Without this evidence, we affirm the trial justice's decision that plaintiff cannot recover for breach of express warranty. . . .

Negligence or Strict Liability

. . . [S]ufficient evidence did not exist from which the jury could have found or reasonably inferred negligence in the design, manufacture, testing, or inspection of the liquid soap, nor was there sufficient evidence of a defect. *Ritter v. Narragansett Electric Company*, 109 R.I. 176, 283 A.2d 255 (1971). In *Ritter* we held that one can only be liable in negligence if the plaintiff has met his burden of introducing credible evidence that the defendant knew, or had reason to know, of a defective design or that he was negligent in failing to test or inspect the product prior to sale.

Furthermore, he must prove that this defect proximately caused the injury.

In a strict liability action, the plaintiff has the burden of proving a defect in the design or manufacture that makes the product unsafe for its intended use, and also that the plaintiff's injury was proximately caused by this defect. . . .

The plaintiff in the case at bar has failed to meet her burdens of proof in both negligence and strict liability. The evidence which she presented does not sufficiently prove that the product was unreasonably dangerous and that its alleged defect caused her injury. She has merely shown that the use of the product resulted in injury, but she has not proved the necessary proximate relationship between either the defect and the injury or between the negligence and the injury. Although we do permit inferences of fact to be drawn from circumstantial evidence, we believe that to permit the jurors to infer from the circumstantial evidence in this case that there had to be something in the product that caused the injury is to permit them to engage in mere speculation.

For similar reasons, we also find that the trial justice was correct in granting a directed verdict on the count of failure to warn in both negligence and strict liability. In negligence, the defendant only has a duty to warn if he had reason to know about the product's dangerous propensities which caused plaintiff's injuries. . . . Under strict liability, a seller need only warn of those dangers that are reasonably foreseeable. If he does not provide such a warning, then the product is rendered defective. . . .

Plaintiff has not sufficiently proved that there was something in Nature Shower which caused her rash. Without more evidence establishing the foreseeability of the dangerous condition and the nexus between this condition and the injury, we find one cannot reasonably infer that defendant had a duty to warn. . . .

Bevilacqua, Chief Justice.

Spring Motors Distributors, Inc.
v
Ford Motor Co.
489 A2d 660 (1985)
Supreme Court of New Jersey

FACTS: Plaintiff, a commercial buyer of automotive motors, complained that motors it purchased from defendant contained transmission defects that caused plaintiff to sustain a loss of benefit of its bargain and consequential damages. The trial court found that plaintiff could not sue under the UCC warranty sections because the action had not been brought within the four-year statute of limitations for a contract action. Plaintiff also sued under common-law strict liability theory, which is subject to the six-year statute of limitations for tort actions.

The written warranty accompanying the sale of the motors stated that seller agreed to replace or repair defective parts under certain conditions. In addition, it stated: "To the extent allowed by law, this WARRANTY IS IN PLACE OF all other warranties, express or implied, including ANY IMPLIED WARRANTY OR MERCHANTABILITY OR FITNESS." Furthermore, the warranty expressly stated: "Under this warranty, repair or replacement of parts is the only remedy, and loss of use of the vehicle, loss of time, inconvenience, commercial loss or consequential damages are not covered."

ISSUE: Does the UCC permit commercial traders to limit the availability of a tort action for economic loss?

RESULT: Where commercial traders have allocated a risk of loss through warranty provisions of a sales contract, the court will not permit an action in strict liability for economic loss.

REASONING:

*   *   *

As the preceding cases demonstrate, the U.C.C. rules pertaining to the sale of goods overlap the doctrine of strict liability for placing a defective product in the stream of commerce. One reason for the overlap is that strict liability, in this regard, evolved from implied warranties of fitness and merchantability under the U.C.C. and its predecessor, the Uniform Sales Act. Those warranties originated as a matter of social policy to compensate consumers who sustained personal injuries from defective food. . . . Neither the ALI, which published the *Restatement (Second) of Torts*, nor the permanent editorial board of the U.C.C., which operates as a joint project of the ALI and the Commissioners on Uniform State Laws, has undertaken to resolve the overlap between strict liability as declared in section 402A and the breach of warranty provisions under the U.C.C. . . .

From the perspective of the injured party, strict liability generally provides a more congenial environment than contract principles, which may prevent recovery because of a lack of privity with the manufacturer. In addition to privity, the Code retains two other requirements that may pose considerable obstacles to a buyer. The first requirement is that of notice to a seller of a breach of warranty, [UCC] § 2–607(3); the second arises from the seller's ability to limit or disclaim liability to an innocent purchaser. [UCC] § 2–316. A buyer who does not deal directly with a manufacturer cannot negotiate over the terms of a disclaimer and might find it impossible to give the manufacturer notice of the breach of warranty following an injury. . . . Strict liability, on the other hand, circumvents the technical requirements of the U.C.C. with respect to privity, notice, and limitation of damages. Avoiding those requirements is particularly important for persons outside the distributive chain who sustain physical damage caused by a defective product.

By comparison, the U.C.C. emphasizes the simplification of the law governing commercial transactions and the expansion of commercial practices through agreement. . . . Underlying the U.C.C. policy is the principle that parties should be free to make contracts of their choice, including contracts disclaiming liability for breach of warranty. Once they reach such an agreement, society has an interest in seeing that the agreement is fulfilled. Consequently, the U.C.C. is the more appropriate vehicle for resolving commercial disputes arising out of business transactions between persons in a distributive chain.

The problem is ascertaining where on the spectrum to place a cause of action brought by a commercial entity, or even a consumer, for purely economic loss. . . .

The considerations that give rise to strict liability do not obtain between commercial parties with comparable bargaining power. . . . Furthermore, perfect parity is not necessary to a determination that parties have substantially equal bargaining positions. . . . Suffice it to state that Spring Motors had sufficient bargaining power to persuade Ford to install Clark transmissions in the trucks that were the subject of the contract.

Insofar as risk allocation and distribution are concerned, Spring Motors is at least as well situated as the defendants to assess the impact of economic loss. Indeed, a commercial buyer, such as Spring Motors, may be better situated than the manufacturer to factor into its price the risk of economic loss caused by the purchase of a defective product. . . .

Presumably the price paid by Spring Motors for the trucks reflected the fact that Ford was liable for repair or replacement of parts only. By seeking to impose the risk of loss on Ford, Spring Motors seeks, in effect, to obtain a better bargain than it made. In such a context, the imposition of the risk of loss on the manufacturer might lead to price increases for all of its customers, including individual consumers. . . . As between commercial parties, then, the allocation of risks in accordance with their agreement better serves the public interest than an allocation achieved as a matter of policy without reference to that agreement.

Delineation of the boundary between strict liability and the U.C.C. requires appreciation not only of the policy considerations underlying both sets of principles, but also of the role of the Legislature as a coordinate branch of government. By enacting the U.C.C., the Legislature adopted a carefully-conceived system of rights and remedies to govern commercial transactions. Allowing Spring Motors to recover from Ford under tort principles would dislocate major provisions of the Code. For example, application of tort principles would obviate the statutory requirement that a buyer give notice of a breach of warranty, [UCC] § 2–607, and would deprive the seller of the ability to exclude or limit its liability, [UCC] § 2–316. In sum, the U.C.C. represents a comprehensive statutory scheme that satisfies the needs of the world of commerce, and courts should pause before extending judicial doctrines that might dislocate the legislative structure.

Pollock, Judge.

21:10   Federal Legislation

The problem of providing a consistent and equitable allocation of the risk of loss from defective products is addressed by federal law as well as by the UCC, state consumer protection law, and state tort law. For the most part, federal law is oriented toward the protection of consumers rather than commercial buyers. Two major pieces of federal legislation are the Magnuson–Moss Warranty Act and the Consumer Product Safety Act of 1972. In addition, federal legislation regulates specific industries and trade practices.

Magnuson–Moss Warranty Act   The Magnuson–Moss Warranty Act (15 USC §§ 2301–2312) was Congress' response to a general belief that consumer warranties were often misleading, difficult to understand, and even more difficult to enforce. The act establishes certain requirements that must be met whenever a written warranty is given in connection with a sale of a consumer product (any tangible personal property normally used for personal, family, or household purposes) that costs $15 or more.

Under the act, a written warranty is (1) any written affirmation of fact or promise, made in connection with the sale of a consumer product, that the material or workmanship is defect-free or will meet a specified level of performance over a specified period of time; or (2) any written undertaking, made in connection with the sale of a consumer product, to refund, repair, replace, or take other remedial action if the product fails to meet the specifications set forth in the undertaking.

The act does not require that any warranty be given on a consumer product. If, however, a warranty is given, (1) it must be phrased in simple and readily understandable language, (2) it must be made available for the purchaser's inspection prior to the sale, and (3) it must be clearly and conspicuously designated as either a *full or a limited warranty*. A full warranty must meet the following minimum standards: (1) the warrantor must remedy any defects or malfunctions of the product within a reasonable time, and without charge; (2) the warrantor may not impose any limitation on the duration of any implied warranty; (3) the warrantor may not exclude or limit consequential damages for breach of any warranty, unless such exclusion or limitation conspicuously appears on the face of the warranty; and (4) if the warrantor is unable, after a reasonable number of attempts, to remedy a defect or malfunction in the product or one of its parts, the warrantor must give the consumer the option of a refund or replacement of the product or part. All other written warranties under the act are considered limited warranties.

A seller may not disclaim or modify any implied warranties on a consumer product (1) if a written warranty is given on the product or (2) if, within 90 days of the sale, the seller and consumer enter into a service contract for the product. However, if a written warranty is limited to a reasonable duration, then implied warranties may be similarly limited, provided the limitation is conscionable and is clearly and prominently stated on the face of the warranty.

The act encourages the use of informal dispute settlement procedures and also provides for its enforcement by judicial proceedings.

Consumer Product Safety Act of 1972   The federal *Consumer Product Safety Act* provides that the designer, manufacturer, and seller of a defective consumer product may be sued in federal court by an injured customer. Private individuals may bring suit to enforce consumer product safety rules that apply to substantial product hazards. The act also contains civil and criminal penalties, provisions for injunctions, and even a provision for seizure of the offending products. The act provides for inspections of the manufacturing site, the storage site, or the conveyance used for distribution of products. The act establishes record-keeping requirements for manufacturers, private labelers, and product distributors.

Consumer Product Safety Commission   To administer the Consumer Product Safety Act, Congress established an independent regulatory agency, the *Consumer Product Safety Commission* to establish consumer product safety standards. Any requirement of such a standard must be reasonably necessary to prevent or reduce an "unreasonable risk of injury" associated with the product. Acting in accordance with the rules governing administrative law generally, as discussed in Chapter 3, the commission sets standards for performance, composition, contents, design, construction, finish or packaging, and labeling of a consumer product. Labeling is especially important because it is visible to the consumer. The commission requires that a consumer product be marked with or accompanied by clear and adequate warnings or instructions.

 Manufacturers, distributors, or retailers who learn that a product does not comply with a safety rule, or that it has a defect that creates a substantial risk of injury must immediately notify the Consumer Product Safety Commission. The commission can then order the manufacturer, distributor, or retailer to notify all buyers, to offer repair, replacement, or refund, without charge, and to reimburse the consumer for any reasonable and foreseeable expenses incurred.

EXAMPLE: Blanco Automotive Company's engineers determine there is a danger in the design of the company's 1978 Turtle Car, of which 35,000 have been sold. After two years on the market, numerous accidents are occurring because of a defective braking mechanism. Blanco must immediately notify the Consumer Product Safety Commission, notify all Turtle purchasers, and arrange to repair the defect free of charge.

Key Concepts and Terms

- Product liability refers to a type of tort litigation in which a plaintiff seeks recovery from a manufacturer, processor, or seller for injury resulting from a defective product. Liability may arise from any one, or a combination, of three theories of liability: (1) negligence, (2) breach of warranty, and (3) strict liability.

- A sales warranty is a promise that the object sold has certain qualities or conditions. A warranty may be express or implied and may exist with respect to new and used goods alike.

- The warranty of title is a warranty that the seller has good title and the goods are rightfully transferred free of encumbrances of which the buyer is unaware. This warranty may be excluded or modified by specific language or under certain circumstances.

- An express warranty is an oral or written representation that is part of the basis of the bargain. An express warranty may be created by the seller's affirmation of fact or promise, description of goods, or exhibition of a sample or model of the goods. Statements of the product's value or the seller's opinion do not create express warranties.

- The implied warranty of merchantability is a warranty that goods sold are suitable for their ordinary purposes. Every sale of goods, including the sale of food or drink, by a merchant who deals in goods of that kind generally includes this warranty.

- An implied warranty of fitness arises if the seller has reason to know that the buyer is relying on the seller's skill or judgment to select goods suitable for the buyer's particular purpose.

- Any disclaimer of a warranty must be made in strict compliance with the UCC requirements. If a seller has made an express warranty *and* a disclaimer, the warranty and disclaimer will both be given effect unless it is unreasonable to do so, in which event the disclaimer is inoperative.

- An implied warranty of merchantability may be disclaimed only by language that mentions merchantability. If the disclaimer is written, it must be conspicuous. A disclaimer of an implied warranty of fitness must be written and conspicuous. Alternatively, all implied warranties may be excluded by a sale of goods in which the term "as is" or "with all faults" is used.

- A seller may limit a buyer's remedy for breach of warranty by being responsible only for repairing or replacing defective parts and by excluding consequential damages. These limited remedies are invalid if they are found to be unconscionable or to fail in their essential purpose.

- A buyer's examination of, or refusal to examine, the goods prior to entering into a contract prevents the existence of any implied warranty with respect to defects that an examination ought to have revealed.

- Multiple warranties are interpreted as being consistent and cumulative whenever possible. When they are not consistent, the parties' intent determines which warranty applies, with the more specific warranty generally prevailing over the less specific.

- The UCC has alternative provisions concerning warranty rights of third persons, but it generally remains neutral concerning such rights. Many courts have rejected or limited the doctrine of privity of contract, and have extended warranty rights to nonbuyers.

- Recovery for injuries is based on the theories of negligence, strict liability, and breach of warranty. When a negligence theory is asserted, the plaintiff must show that the manufacturer or seller failed to exercise reasonable care as to the product. Under a strict liability theory, liability may be proven simply on the plaintiff's showing that the product was "unreasonably dangerous to the user." Under a breach of warranty theory, the plaintiff must show existence of a warranty, breach, and injury.

- Defenses against a product liability lawsuit may be based on the general principles of contributory negligence and assumption of risk. Failure to follow instructions in the use or assembly of a product may also constitute a defense.

- The outcome of most products cases depends on the testimony of experts who examine the product and the industry standards, then render a reasoned opinion as to whether a particular product was properly manufactured or designed.

- The Magnuson–Moss Warranty Act contains requirements of disclosure and content with respect to written warranties on consumer products. Some states have statutes that also deal with warranties on consumer products.

- Breach of Warranty
- Consumer Product Safety Act of 1972
- Consumer Product Safety Commission
- Design Defect
- Disclaimer of Warranty
- Duty to Warn
- Economic Injury
- Expert Witness
- Express Warranty
- Fitness for a Particular Purpose
- Full Warranty

- Implied Warranty
- Limited Warranty
- Magnuson–Moss Warranty Act
- Merchantability
- Negligence
- Opportunity to Examine
- Privity of Contract
- Product Liability
- *Restatement (Second) of Torts* § 402A
- Strict Liability
- Warranty of Conformity
- Warranty of Title
- Warranty Against Infringement

Questions and Case Problems

1. Bundy, an experienced printer, needs a new press. He visits Quality Presses, which specializes in the sale of printing presses. Bundy sees two machines there, an Alpha and an Omega, but he does not see either one print. Quality's president advises Bundy that the Alpha would best suit Bundy's printing needs. Bundy reads a brochure, put out by the Alpha's manufacturer, which states that the Alpha can do up to "7,000 impressions an hour" and has a "superior inking system and precise inking controls." Bundy eventually buys an Alpha press from Quality. The purchase contract contains a disclaimer, in boldfaced capital letters, which states that the seller makes no express or implied warranties and expressly excludes any implied warranties of merchantability or fitness. Bundy's Alpha turns out to be a "lemon." It cannot do more than 5,000 impressions an hour, its printing quality is inconsistent, and it breaks down frequently. Finally, Bundy sues Quality for breach of express and implied warranties. What is the result?

2. In March 1973, Kavanaugh read a newspaper advertisement for a secondhand 1956 Cessna airplane. He met with Keenan, the owner, to discuss buying it. Keenan gave Kavanaugh an engine and propeller logbook detailing the mechanical repair and flight history. Kavanaugh carefully perused the logbook; it stated that on May 16, 1972, the engine had a major overhaul in which new mechanical parts were placed in it in conformity with the manufacturer's engine overhaul manual. Based on this information Kavanaugh bought the plane. On December 5, 1973, the engine lost power and began to shake violently in flight, and Kavanaugh made an emergency landing. The engine had to be completely overhauled. In the process, it was discovered that the 1972 overhaul had not included new parts and had been performed in a defective manner. Kavanaugh sued Keenan for the cost of the overhaul, claiming breach of express warranty. Was there a breach of express warranty?

3. Sowards buys a used coal truck from Childers & Venters. The seller knows that the buyer intends to use the truck to haul coal. The sales contract is a printed form, the first paragraph of which states that the sale is subject to the terms and conditions "set forth below and upon the reverse side hereof." The words, "and upon the reverse side hereof," are in bolder print than the rest. The back of the form is headed "PROVISIONS," under which are eleven numbered paragraphs. All except the eighth paragraph are in identical type. The eighth paragraph is in larger, bolder type, and disclaims any implied warranty of merchantability and any implied warranty of fitness for a particular purpose. The truck turns out to be unsuitable for hauling coal, and Sowards refuses to pay for it. Childers & Venters sues Sowards for the purchase price. How should the case be decided?

4. Plaintiff paid a fee for the use of defendant's raquetball court for one hour. During the first 15 minutes of play, the roof began to leak, forming a puddle of water on the floor of the court. Plaintiff slipped while playing, crashed into a wall, and injured his foot. He filed suit claiming negligence and breach of an implied warranty of fitness of the raquetball court. Can he recover on the negligence claim? On the warranty claim? Why or why not?

5. BB & B bought a used tractor from Dravo. BB & B obtained a warranty, handwritten into the form sales contract, which provided that "This price includes new, rebuilt engine and to carry 1500 hours of 100 percent engine warranty." BB & B sold their rock-crushing business, including the tractor, to German. German was presented a copy of the warranty and relied on the tractor engine being within the warranty time. When the tractor engine failed, German took it to BB & B, who replaced the engine with a rebuilt one and sought payment. German raised the warranty as a defense to payment. Is German entitled to enforce the express warranty against BB & B? Against Dravo?

6. Mays buys a new Ford pickup truck from a Ford dealer. Ford's warranty provides for free repair of any parts found defective within the earlier occurrence of 12 months or 12,000 miles. The warranty excludes any other express warranty and limits any implied warranty of merchantability or fitness to the 12-month/12,000-miles duration. About five weeks after the purchase, Mays notices unusual noise and vibration. During the next five months the dealer makes seven or eight repair attempts and replaces various parts, but nothing eliminates the problem. Finally, it is discovered that the truck's frame is bent. Since a distorted frame can cause excessive wear to all moving parts, Mays returns the truck. Ford refuses to do anything other than repair the truck, and Mays sues. Should he be awarded a refund of the purchase price?

7. Tam sees a picture of a pair of gray hiking boots in Nance's mail order catalog and orders the boots. When they arrive, the boots are not the same color as illustrated in the catalog; they are slightly darker. Has Nance breached any warranties? What if the product involved were paint, or the catalog had stated that actual colors might differ slightly from the illustration?

8. The High Velocity Gun Shop sells a shotgun to Mr. Sport. The shotgun has a "hair trigger" (not common to this type of gun), but High Velocity neglects to warn Sport about this. While Mr. Sport is using the shotgun, it discharges prematurely due to the "hair trigger," resulting in injuries to a child. Is the gun shop subject to liability for the child's injuries on any theory?

9. Loveless Products markets a new hair dye that is safe when used on the scalp, but contains certain chemicals that could cause burns to the eyes. The label on the dye states that it is intended solely for use on the scalp, but no specific warning is made about the hazard to the eyes. Betty purchases the dye, uses it on her eyebrows and a drop gets into her eye, causing severe injury. Can Betty recover from Loveless on a strict liability theory?

10. Plaintiff was injured when a defective gear mechanism locked and threw plaintiff from a bicycle purchased from defendant. Plaintiff asserts a product liability claim against defendant based on violation of the Magnuson–Moss Warranty Act. The Magnuson–Moss Warranty Act provides that

> [A] consumer who is damaged by the failure of a supplier, warranter, or service contractor to comply with any obligation under this chapter, or under a written

warranty, implied warranty, or service contract, may bring suit for damages and other legal or equitable relief. . . .

Can plaintiff sue under this provision?

11. What is the Consumer Product Safety Act of 1972, and how does it affect manufacturers or distributors of consumer products? What type of enforcement procedures does the act contain? Whose responsibility is it to administer the act? Discuss.

22 Performance; Remedies for Breach

22:1 Introduction

A contract of sale imposes basic obligations on both seller and buyer. The seller's basic obligation is to deliver goods that conform to the contract, and the buyer's basic obligation is to accept and pay for those goods [UCC §2-301]. The UCC provides specific rules for determining when the performance of these obligations is sufficient. Those rules are discussed in this chapter. Various rules discussed in preceding chapters also relate to the subject of performance. For example, the subject of delivery was considered to some extent in connection with transfer of title and risk of loss (Chapter 20), as was the seller's obligation to deliver goods that conform to any warranties (Chapter 21).

The parties' respective obligations sometimes are not clearly established in the contract. Some terms may be left open; the parties may intentionally leave some particulars of performance to be specified later by one or the other party [UCC § 2-311]. Or, the contract may be silent as to obligations. When the contract is silent, general contract principles, as well as principles of interpretation set forth in the UCC, are used to determine the parties' respective obligations. Again, some of these rules of interpretation, such as the rules with respect to course of performance, course of dealing, and usage of trade, have been considered earlier (Chapter 16).

The most important factor to consider in determining what the parties' obligations are—and therefore whether the parties have performed those obligations—is the contract itself. Bear in mind that the parties may alter by agreement most obligations that would otherwise be imposed under the code, except for the obligation of good faith that the code imposes in the performance or enforcement of all contracts. For merchants, the obligation of good faith includes the observance of reasonable commercial standards of fair dealing.

Sales contracts, like all other kinds of contracts, are sometimes breached. When one party fails to perform, the other party is entitled to one or more of the various remedies permitted by the UCC. Along with performance, these remedies will be discussed in this chapter.

22:2 Seller's Obligation

The seller's primary obligation consists of (1) a proper tender, or offer, of delivery of (2) *conforming goods* to the buyer. A *tender of delivery* is proper when it is made in accordance with the provisions of the contract and with the applicable provisions of the UCC. Goods are conforming when they comply with the obligations under the contract [UCC § 2-106(2)].

The seller must deliver the goods at the time and place specified in the contract. If the contract is silent as to the time and place for delivery, delivery must be made within a reasonable time [UCC § 2-309(1)] and ordinarily at the seller's place of business [UCC § 2-308]. The seller must tender delivery of the goods at a reasonable hour, must give the buyer reasonable notice of the tender, and must keep the goods available for the period reasonably necessary to enable the buyer to take possession [UCC § 2-503(1)].

As discussed earlier (see Chapter 20), the place and manner of delivery often are indicated by the use of shipping terms. To make a proper tender under a shipment contract, the seller must (1) put the goods in the carrier's possession, (2) make a reasonable contract for their transportation, (3) deliver to the buyer any document necessary to enable him to take possession, and (4) promptly notify him of the shipment [UCC § 2-504]. In the case of a destination contract, as well as a contract involving goods held by a bailee, delivery may take place in one of the following ways: (1) the seller's giving the buyer a negotiable document of title; (2) the seller's receiving the bailee's acknowledgment of the buyer's right to possession; or (3) the seller's giving the buyer a nonnegotiable document of title or a written direction to the bailee to deliver the goods, unless the buyer seasonably objects (objects within a reasonable time), to such a tender [UCC § 2-503(3)–(5)].

Sufficiency of Seller's Performance At common law, the *perfect tender* rule required the seller to make a tender of delivery that conformed in all respects to the contract requirements. In theory the UCC retains the perfect tender rule as a basic standard of performance, granting the buyer the right of rejection "if the goods or the tender of delivery fail in any respect to conform to the contract" [UCC § 2-601]. However, in actual practice the UCC generally requires only substantial performance by the seller (see Chapter 18). The UCC also contains several exceptions to the basic rule.

One exception, perhaps the most important one, permits a seller to *cure* a nonconforming delivery under some circumstances [UCC § 2-508]. In other words, if the seller, prior to the time set for performance, makes a delivery of nonconforming goods, he or she is permitted to rectify the improper tender by delivering conforming goods before the time for performance expires. To exercise this right, the seller must seasonably notify the buyer of the intention to do so. Another situation to which this exception would apply is the buyer's making a surprise rejection of goods for nonconformity. If the buyer rejects a nonconforming tender that the seller had reasonable grounds to believe would be acceptable, the seller may, with notice, have reasonable additional time to make a conforming delivery.

EXAMPLE: The seller of a hearing aid delivers a modified and improved version of the one ordered, thinking the buyer will accept this newer model. The buyer rejects it. The seller then has the right to cure the improper tender by delivering the hearing aid specified in the contract.

The following case illustrates how the courts apply the doctrine of cure as a practical matter. Note how the court's decision effectively prevented the buyer from rejecting the goods on the basis of a minor nonconformity.

Wilson

v

Scampoli
228 A2d 848 (1967)
District of Columbia Court of Appeals

FACTS: Scampoli purchased a television set from Wilson. When the set was delivered, Mrs. Kolley, Scampoli's daughter, noted that the picture had a reddish tinge. A service representative examined the set and told Mrs. Kolley that it would be necessary to take the chassis into the shop to determine the cause of the problem. Mrs. Kolley refused to allow him to take it, stating that she wanted a "brand new" set, not a "repaired" one. She later demanded a refund of the purchase price. Wilson refused, and Scampoli sued for a refund of the purchase price. The trial court ordered the contract rescinded and the purchase price refunded. Wilson appealed.

ISSUE: May a seller cure defective tender of goods by removing the goods and making minor repairs or adjustments to them?

RESULT: Yes. The seller may cure by repairing minor defects in the goods and need not replace the goods with new merchandise.

REASONING:

*   *   *

Appellant does not contest the jurisdiction of the trial court to order rescission in a proper case, but contends the trial judge erred in holding that rescission here was appropriate. He argues that he was always willing to comply with the terms of the sale either by correcting the malfunction by minor repairs or, in the event the set could not be made thereby properly operative, by replacement; that as he was denied the opportunity to try to correct the difficulty, he did not breach the contract of sale or any warranty thereunder, expressed or implied.

[UCC § 2-508] provides:

> (1) Where any tender or delivery by the seller is rejected because non-conforming and the time for performance has not yet expired, the seller may seasonably notify the buyer of his intention to cure and may then within the contract time make a conforming delivery.
>
> (2) Where the buyer rejects a nonconforming tender which the seller had reasonable grounds to believe would be acceptable with or without money allowance the seller may if he reasonably notifies the buyer have a further reasonable time to substitute a confirming tender.

A retail dealer would certainly expect and have reasonable grounds to believe that merchandise like color television sets, new and delivered as crated at the factory, would be acceptable as delivered and that, if defective in some way, he would have the right to substitute a conforming tender. The question then resolves itself to whether the dealer may conform his tender by adjustment or minor repair or whether he must conform by substituting brand new merchandise. . . .

Although the Official Code Comments do not reach this precise issue, there are cases and comments under other provisions of the Code which indicate that under certain circumstances repairs and adjustments are contemplated as remedies under implied warranties. . . .

While these cases provide no mandate to require the buyer to accept patchwork goods or substantially repaired articles in lieu of flawless merchandise, they do indicate that minor repairs or reasonable adjustments are frequently the means by which an imperfect tender may be cured. In discussing the analogous question of defective title, it has been stated that:

> The seller, then, should be able to cure [the defect] under subsection 2-508(2) in those cases in which he can do so without subjecting the buyer to any great inconvenience, risk or loss. Hawkland, Curing an Improper Tender of Title to Chattels: Past, Present and Commercial Code, 46 Minn.L.Rev. 697, 724 (1962). . . .

Removal of a television chassis for a short period of time in order to determine the cause of color malfunction and ascertain the extent of adjustment or correction needed to effect full operational efficiency presents no great inconvenience to the buyer. In the instant case, appellant's expert witness testified that this was not infrequently necessary with new televisions. Should the set be defective in workmanship or parts, the loss would be upon the manufacturer who warranted it free from mechanical defect. Here the adamant refusal of Mrs. Kolley, acting on behalf of appellee, to allow inspection essential to the determination of the cause of the excessive red tinge to the picture defeated any effort by the seller to provide timely repair or even replacement of the set if the difficulty could not be corrected. The cause of the defect might have been minor and easily adjusted or it may have been substantial and required replacement by another new set—but the seller was never given an adequate opportunity to make a determination.

Myers, Associate Judge.

A second exception to the perfect tender rule applies to *installment contracts* [UCC § 2-612]. Under the UCC, an installment contract is one that requires or authorizes the delivery of goods in separate lots to be accepted separately. The buyer may reject an installment only if the nonconformity substantially impairs the value of that installment and cannot be cured. Otherwise, the buyer must accept the installment, provided the seller gives adequate assurance that the nonconformity will be cured. Moreover, a nonconforming delivery of one or more installments will not be considered a breach of the entire contract unless the nonconformity substantially impairs the value of the whole contract. In other words, the UCC in essence adopts a standard of substantial performance with respect to installment contracts.

The UCC also adopts the substantial performance standard with respect to the third exception, which concerns deviations in shipping and delivery arrangements. Therefore, in a shipment contract, the buyer cannot reject a tender of delivery for such deviations unless he or she will suffer a material delay or loss on account of them [UCC § 2-504]. Where the agreed means or manner of delivery becomes unavailable or commercially impracticable, the seller may use a commercially reasonable substitute [UCC § 2-614].

Commercial Impracticability; Impossibility The UCC recognizes the fact that under some circumstances a party may find it impossible or commercially impracticable to perform a sales contract. Thus, a party need not perform the contract if performance "has been made impracticable by the occurrence of a contingency the nonoccurrence of which was a basic assumption on which the contract was made" [UCC § 2-615]. This is the doctrine of commercial impracticability. Despite the UCC's recognition of the doctrine, courts are reluctant to use it to relieve a seller of the obligation to perform. For example, most courts have rejected claims that increased costs excuse a seller from the obligation to deliver in accordance with the contract. One instance in which commercial impracticability *has* been recognized as an excuse for nonperformance is unanticipated failure of the source of supply if the contract called for the use of only a particular source. For example, under a contract to sell a crop growing on designated land, failure of the crop would excuse the seller's performance.

The destruction, before risk of loss passes to the buyer, of identified goods essential to the contract also excuses performance by the seller. If the loss is total, the contract is avoided; if the loss is partial, or if the goods have so deteriorated that they are no longer conforming, the buyer may either avoid the contract or accept the goods with an allowance in price [UCC § 2-613].

If commercial impracticability affects only a part of the seller's capacity to perform, he or she must perform to the extent possible. If the seller has more than one customer, some fair and reasonable manner must be adopted to allocate the available goods among the customers [UCC § 2-615].

22:3 Buyer's Obligations

The buyer's basic obligations are to accept and to pay for the goods [UCC § 2-301] Before doing so, however, the buyer ordinarily has the right to inspect the goods.

Inspection of Goods [UCC § 2-513]   The buyer generally has the right to inspect the goods, prior to acceptance or payment, at any reasonable place and time and in any reasonable manner. The parties may specify in the contract the place, time, or manner of inspection. The buyer must pay the expenses of the *inspection*, but he may recover the expenses from the seller if the goods are nonconforming and are rejected.

The parties may provide in their contract that payment must precede inspection. In any event, the code lists specific circumstances in which the buyer must pay before inspecting the goods, unless the parties have agreed otherwise. Thus, advance payment for inspection is normally required (1) if the contract provides for delivery C.O.D. (collect on delivery) or on other like terms, or (2) if the contract calls for payment against documents of title before the buyer actually receives the goods.

 The inclusion of a provision requiring payment prior to inspection obligates the buyer to pay even though the goods do not conform to the contract, unless the nonconformity appears without inspection [UCC § 2-512(1)(a).] The buyer's payment does not, however, mean that the buyer has accepted the goods. The buyer still retains the basic right to inspect the goods before acceptance and retains all remedies, such as rejection, that the code provides for nonconforming goods [UCC §§ 2-512(2), 2-606(1)(a).]

Acceptance of Goods [UCC § 2-606]   If the goods delivered by the seller conform to the contract, the buyer must accept them. If they do not conform, the buyer generally can reject them. *Acceptance* may be manifested by words, conduct, or both. The UCC specifies three methods: (1) if the buyer, after a reasonable opportunity for inspection, signifies to the seller that the goods are conforming or that they will be accepted despite some nonconformity; (2) if the buyer fails to make a timely rejection or to give the seller timely notice of rejection of the goods; or (3) if the buyer performs an act that indicates ownership (such as reselling or consuming the goods).

EXAMPLE: A buyer "picks up" a used car that he had agreed to buy from the dealer. The dealer had agreed to put the car "in good working order." As soon as the buyer drives away from the dealer's place of business he discovers that the brakes do not work properly. Instead of returning the car to the dealer immediately, the buyer takes the car home, attempts to fix the brakes, and continues to drive it for several days. The buyer will be held to have accepted the car, even though he could have rightfully rejected it.

When both conforming and nonconforming goods are delivered under a single contract, the buyer may wish to accept only those goods that conform. He may make such a partial acceptance, but is limited to acceptance of a commercial unit or units. A *commercial unit* is a single whole, the division of which would materially impair its character or value [UCC § 2-105(6)].

EXAMPLE: Valdez orders 100 cases of canned goods. If the cans are customarily sold by the case, Valdez could reject any cases that were nonconforming and accept those cases that were conforming. Valdez could not, however, break open a case and accept only a portion of its contents.

If the buyer accepts goods that are defective in some manner, he or she must notify the seller within a reasonable time after the defect is discovered or should have been discovered. Failure to notify the seller will bar the buyer from later pursuing any remedy.

Rejection or Revocation of Acceptance [UCC §§ 2-601–2-605, 2-608, 2-612, 2-711(3)]   When nonconforming goods are delivered, the buyer may accept the entire delivery and seek damages (see 22:7); he may make a partial acceptance under certain circumstances; or he may reject the entire delivery. In addition, under some circumstances the buyer may revoke an acceptance already made.

The buyer may revoke an acceptance if it was made on the reasonable assumption that the nonconformity would be cured by the seller and it has not been seasonably cured, or if the buyer accepted delivery without discovering the nonconformity and the acceptance was reasonably induced either by the difficulty of discovering the nonconformity before acceptance or by the seller's assurances. The nonconformity in the goods must "substantially impair" the value of the goods to the buyer [UCC § 2-608].

Theoretically, the buyer can reject delivery if the goods are nonconforming in any respect but may revoke acceptance only if the nonconformity substantially impairs the value of the goods to him. In practice, however, the absolute right of rejection is in many respects virtually indistinguishable from the right to revoke acceptance. Perhaps the major practical distinction is that sometimes acceptance with knowledge of a substantial nonconformity amounts to a waiver of that nonconformity and disallows the buyer from later trying to revoke the acceptance.

EXAMPLE: A buyer "picks up" the used car that she had agreed to buy "in good working order." As soon as she drives away from the dealer's place of business she discovers that the brakes do not work properly. Immediately she returns the car to the dealer. It is ambiguous whether the buyer has rejected the car or revoked acceptance of the car, but she probably has not accepted it. If, however, she had known of the problem with the brakes when she "picked up" the car, and took it without any assurance or expectation that the problem would be fixed, she would be held to have accepted it, and probably would not be permitted to revoke acceptance.

The buyer must give the seller timely notice of a rejection or revocation of acceptance. When rejection is based on a defect that is ascertainable by reasonable inspection, the buyer under certain circumstances must notify the seller of that defect. If the buyer does not, he or she cannot later rely on that defect to justify rejection (1) if the seller could have cured the defect or (2) when both parties are merchants, if the seller, after rejection, made a written request for a statement of defects from the buyer.

 As a practical matter, there are several reasons why a buyer ordinarily should not reject goods on the basis of a minor or technical nonconformity. First, the buyer usually needs the goods. Second, a court is not likely to look favorably on a rejection based on some minor deficiency. A court may, for example, hold the buyer's rejection improper on the ground that the buyer failed to permit the seller to cure. Finally, a buyer should always consider his or her business reputation. If a buyer acquires a reputation for rejecting goods without substantial reason, other businesspersons will be leery of dealing with him or her.

When a buyer is still in possession of the goods after rejecting them or revoking acceptance of them, he or she must hold them for a reasonable time and follow the seller's reasonable instructions concerning their disposition. If the seller gives no instructions, the buyer may store the goods for the seller, reship them to the seller, or resell them. The buyer may also resell the goods if the seller does not pay the buyer's expenses for inspection, receipt, transportation, care, and custody of the goods. If the buyer is a merchant, and if the seller has no agent or place of business at the market where the goods were delivered and rejected, the buyer must, in the absence of instructions from the seller, sell goods that are perishable or that may quickly decline in value. The manner in which a resale must be conducted is discussed in 22:6 and 22:7.

The following case illustrates the problem of proving substantial impairment and effective notice of revocation after acceptance of an automobile. In addition, the court considers the obligations of the buyer upon revocation.

Jackson

v

Rocky Mountain Datsun, Inc.
693 P2d 391 (1985)
Colorado Court of Appeals

FACTS: Plaintiff bought a new car from defendant dealer. During the first six months that plaintiff owned the car, it had to be towed to the dealer's shop for repairs at least seven times. Sometimes the car would not start.

Other times it would stop running and stall in traffic. Defendant's mechanics told plaintiff the car was a "lemon." The car was in the shop four of the first six months after purchase. In July, 1980, plaintiff brought the car in for servicing and was told that defendant would no longer work on the car. Plaintiff was provided a "loaner" car. Thereafter, she refused defendant's request that she pick up her own car and return the "loaner." In September, 1980, plaintiff advised defendant of her revocation of acceptance and demanded return of the amount she had paid on the purchase price of the car, plus various incidental damages. When defendant refused, plaintiff filed suit.

ISSUE: Has plaintiff successfully and justifiably revoked acceptance of the automobile so as to be entitled to return of the purchase price?

RESULT: Yes. Plaintiff was entitled to revocation and exercised the right to revoke in a proper and timely manner, and is therefore entitled to return of the purchase price.

REASONING:

*   *   *

The dealer argues that the trial court erred in concluding that the buyer had justifiably revoked her acceptance of the car because she failed to establish that the car's value was substantially impaired as a result of a nonconformity. We disagree.

Contrary to the dealer's suggestion here, in determining whether the value of goods are substantially impaired within the meaning of [UCC § 2-608], reference must be made to the effect of the goods' nonconformities upon the particular buyer asserting a right of revocation. . . .

Here, the evidence regarding the buyer's continuing difficulties with the car and the dealer's repeatedly unsuccessful attempts to repair it supports the conclusion that the value of the car to the buyer was substantially impaired as a result of its mechanical defects. . . .

Under [UCC § 2-608(1)(a)], a buyer is entitled to revoke acceptance if he accepts goods on the reasonable assumption that a nonconformity will be cured by the seller and the nonconformity is not "seasonably cured." Thus, a buyer is not required to provide a seller with an unlimited number of opportunities to cure a nonconformity before revoking acceptance under [UCC § 2-608].

In the present case, we conclude as a matter of law that the dealer was given an adequate opportunity to cure the car's defects prior to the time the buyer revoked her acceptance. . . .

Equally unmeritorious is the dealer's assertion that the buyer's notice of revocation of acceptance was ineffective because it was inconsistent with her continued use of the "loaner" car. She testified that the dealer's requests for the return of the "loaner" car were coupled with the demand that she pick up her car. Viewed in this context, the evidence of her refusal to return the "loaner" car was consistent with, rather than contrary to, the trial court's finding that she effectively notified the dealer of her intention to revoke acceptance.

We also reject the dealer's assertion that the buyer's notice of revocation was not effective because it did not set forth in detail the precise nature of the car's defects or nonconformities. [UCC § 2-608(2)] (Official Comment 5) states that:

> The content of the notice . . . is to be determined by considerations of good faith, prevention of surprise and reasonable adjustment. . . .

Here, the buyer repeatedly notified the dealer of the defective performance of the car, and the dealer made repeated attempts to repair it. Under these circumstances, it was not necessary for the buyer to set out in detail the car's nonconformities in her notice of revocation. . . .

The dealer further contends that the buyer was precluded from revoking her acceptance of the car because she was unable to deliver the car's certificate of title to the dealer. We disagree.

There is no requirement under the provisions of the UCC that on revocation of acceptance a buyer must deliver title to the goods to the seller. Indeed, under [UCC § 2-711(3)], on revocation of acceptance, a buyer retains a security interest in goods in his possession for any payment made on their price and may resell the goods in the same manner as an aggrieved seller. . . . And, where a buyer does not exercise his right of resale, generally all that is required is that the buyer assign to the seller all of his interest in the goods. . . .

The dealer does not assert here that it did not receive adequate notice of the resale of the car as required by [UCC § 2-706] nor that the plaintiff buyer did not account to the dealer for the amount the lender received for the car or that the lender received more for the car than was necessary to discharge the buyer's obligations under the installment sales contract. Hence, the dealer has not shown that it was prejudiced in any manner by the fact that the car was resold by the lender rather than directly by the plaintiff buyer. . . .

Van Cise, Judge.

Payment   The parties may specify the time and terms of payment, but unless otherwise specified payment ordinarily is due at the time of delivery [UCC §§ 2-310(a), 2-507(1), 2-511(1)]. The buyer may pay in any manner currently used in the ordinary course of business. Payment by check is a common and acceptable practice. The seller may demand payment in legal tender (actual cash) but must give the buyer any time reasonably necessary to procure the money. Dishonor of a check by the bank defeats the payment. In other words, the buyer is obligated to pay again if the check is not good [UCC § 2-511(2), (3)]. If the parties agree, the buyer need not pay with money [UCC § 2-304]. For example, the purchaser of a new car frequently trades in a used car as partial payment.

22:4 Anticipatory Repudiation and Assurance of Performance

The UCC follows the basic common law rule on *anticipatory repudiation* [UCC § 2-610]. This concept is that if one party, by words or actions, repudiates a performance due in the future (states or shows by his actions that he will not perform), as a result of which the value of the contract to the other party is substantially impaired, the innocent party can treat the repudiation as a breach. He may then choose among various courses of action: (1) he may, for a commercially reasonable time, await performance by the repudiating party, although if he waits longer than a commercially reasonable time, he cannot recover any damages that he should have avoided; (2) he may resort to any remedy for breach of contract (see 22:5–22:7), even if he has notified the repudiating party that he would wait for performance; or (3) regardless of whether the innocent party awaits performance or treats the repudiation as a breach, he may suspend his own performance until the matter is clarified one way or the other.

As noted in Chapter 18, an anticipatory breach must be unequivocal. Mere hesitation or ambivalence concerning performance does not constitute an anticipatory breach. It is difficult to determine when a party's words or actions in fact constitute an anticipatory breach of a contract. If one party ceases performance because he incorrectly concluded that the other party has committed an anticipatory breach, the first party may himself be found in breach of contract.

The UCC includes a provision designed to eliminate much of the uncertainty that surrounds anticipatory breach. This provision [UCC § 2-609] permits one party, when in doubt as to the other party's intention or ability to perform as promised, to demand adequate *assurance of performance*. Under this provision, when one party has reasonable grounds to be insecure about the other party's performance, the first party may demand in writing that the other party give adequate assurance of performance. Pending the receipt of this assurance, the demanding party may, if commercially reasonable, suspend his own performance. If his performance includes preparatory action, he may also suspend that action. For example, if a seller of specially manufactured goods had reason to doubt the buyer's ability to pay, the seller might make a written demand for assurance and stop manufacturing until the assurance was forthcoming.

UCC § 2-609 is used primarily in transactions between merchants. Between merchants, the reasonableness of grounds for insecurity and the adequacy of any assurance offered are determined according to commercial standards. Naturally, the reasonableness of both the demand and the assurance received will depend on the particular facts involved. The grounds for insecurity are often based on one party's apparently precarious financial situation. For example, if the buyer is behind in payments on the contract, the seller might demand an assurance of performance. Similarly, if the seller appeared to be on the brink of failure, the buyer might demand assurance of the seller's ability to deliver.

The ground for insecurity need not be related to the contract itself. For example, if the seller learned that the buyer was behind in payments to other creditors, it might be reasonable for the seller to demand an assurance of the ability to pay. If the goods involved were precision parts, and if the buyer learned that the seller was delivering defective precision parts to other buyers, the buyer might be justified in demanding assurance from the seller.

The adequacy of the assurance offered will also depend on the circumstances. In some situations a mere promise by the buyer or seller might be adequate. In other situations more might be demanded. For example, it might sometimes be reasonable to demand that the buyer deposit all or part of the purchase price in escrow. When the seller's ability to manufacture the goods is at issue, a demand for some proof of ability might be reasonable. The party on whom a justified demand has been made must give the assurance of performance within a reasonable time, not to exceed 30 days after receipt of the demand. Failure to provide the assurance within such time constitutes a repudiation of the contract.

The following case sets forth factors that a court considers in determining both the reasonableness of a demand for assurance of performance and the adequacy of the assurance given.

AMF, Inc.

v

McDonald's Corporation

536 F2d 1167 (1976)

United States Court of Appeals, Seventh Circuit

FACTS: In 1967 AMF and McDonald's agreed that AMF would install a model 72C computerized cash register in a McDonald's restaurant to evaluate it. In April 1968, a prototype 72C unit was installed in McDonald's busiest restaurant, located in Elk Grove, Illinois. In December 1968 and January 1969, McDonald's agreed to purchase 23 additional 72C's to be placed in McDonald's restaurants, with delivery to be made between February and June 1969. AMF had problems developing a reliable 72C. In February 1969, AMF revised the delivery schedule to between July 1969 and January 1970. The revised schedule was contingent on AMF's completion and satisfactory testing of a test unit being built at its Vandalia, Ohio, plant. On March 18, 1969, representatives of McDonald's and AMF met to discuss various problems, including the poor performance of the ELK Grove prototype 72C. At that meeting McDonald's suggested, and AMF agreed, that production of the other 23 units be suspended pending agreement on performance and reliability standards. In April 1969, the Elk Grove prototype was removed from McDonald's due to its poor performance. On May 1, 1969, representatives of McDonald's and AMF again met. At that time AMF did not have a working 72C, and, due to the inexperience of its Vandalia personnel, could not produce one within a reasonable time. The parties were unable to agree on reliability and performance standards, and McDonald's canceled the contract. The formal cancellation came on July 29, 1969. The reasons for cancellation were the poor performance of the prototype, the lack of assurances that a workable machine was available, and the unsatisfactory conditions at the Vandalia plant. AMF sued McDonald's for breach of contract. The trial court ruled in favor of McDonald's, and AMF appealed.

ISSUE: Did McDonald's have "reasonable grounds for insecurity" with respect to AMF's performance, justifying its cancellation of the contract?

RESULT: AMF's unsatisfactory performance, and its failure to provide adequate assurance of performance, justified the cancellation.

REASONING:

* * *

Whether in a specific case a buyer has reasonable grounds for insecurity is a question of fact. Comment 3 to UCC § 2-609. . . . On this record, McDonald's clearly had "reasonable grounds for insecurity" with respect to AMF's performance. At the time of the March 18, 1969, meeting, the prototype unit had performed unsatisfactorily ever since its April 1968 installation. Although AMF had projected delivery of all twenty-three units by the first half of 1969, AMF later scheduled delivery from the end of July 1969 until January 1970. When McDonald's personnel visited AMF's Vandalia, Ohio, plant on March 4, 1969, they saw that none of the 72C systems was being assembled and learned that a pilot unit would not be ready until the end of July of that year. They were informed that the engineer assigned to the project was not to commence work until March 17th. AMF's own personnel were also troubled about the design of the 72C, causing them to attempt to reduce McDonald's order to five units. Therefore, under [UCC § 2-609] McDonald's was entitled to demand adequate assurance of performance by AMF.

However, AMF urges that [UCC § 2-609] is inapplicable because McDonald's did not make a written demand of adequate assurance of due performance. In [a prior case] we noted that the Code should be liberally construed and therefore rejected such "a formalistic approach" to Section 2-609. McDonald's failure to make a written demand was excusable because AMF's [representative's] testimony and his April 2 and 18, 1969, memoranda about the March 18th meeting showed AMF's clear understanding that McDonald's had suspended performance until it should receive adequate assurance of due performance from AMF. . . .

After the March 18th demand, AMF never repaired the Elk Grove unit satisfactorily nor replaced it. Similarly, it was unable to satisfy McDonald's that the twenty-three machines on order would work. At the May 1st meeting, AMF offered unsatisfactory assurances for only five units instead of twenty-three. The performance standards AMF tendered to McDonald's were unacceptable because they would have permitted the 72C's not to function properly for 90 hours per year, permitting as much as one failure in every fifteen days in a busy McDonald's restaurant. Also, as the district court found, AMF's Vandalia, Ohio, personnel were too inexperienced to produce a proper machine. Since AMF did not provide adequate assurance of performance after McDonald's March 18th demand, [UCC § 2-609(1)] permitted McDonald's to suspend performance. When AMF did not furnish adequate assurance of due performance at the May 1st meeting, it thereby repudiated the contract under [UCC § 2-609(4)]. At that point, [UCC § 2-610(b)] permitted McDonald's to cancel the orders . . . , as it finally did on July 29, 1969. . . .

Cummings, Circuit Judge.

 UCC § 2-609 is designed for use in situations in which one party begins to have reasonable doubts concerning the other party's ability or intent to perform as promised. The section is designed to eliminate the necessity of having to guess, perhaps incorrectly. Any assurance that removes the uncertainty should be sufficient. A doubting party should, therefore, not be oppressive in the demands he or she makes. If the assurance demanded is out of proportion to the grounds for insecurity, a court might well find the demanding party's suspension of performance to constitute a breach of the contract.

Retraction of Anticipatory Repudiation As with contracts generally, a repudiating party may retract the repudiation at any time before performance is due. If, however, the aggrieved party has canceled the contract or otherwise materially changed position in reliance on the repudiation, the repudiation may not be retracted. The retraction must include any assurance of performance justifiably demanded by the aggrieved party [UCC § 2-611].

22:5 Remedies Generally

When one party to a sales contract breaches the contract, the other party is entitled to a remedy. The UCC specifies in detail various remedies available to the seller and the buyer. Before studying these remedies, it is important to take note of the underlying philosophy of the UCC: The remedies specified are to be liberally interpreted to the end that the innocent party is put in as good a position as if the other party had performed [UCC § 1-106]. Thus, the remedial provisions are not to be narrowly or technically interpreted. In addition, the code's provision of remedies is not meant to be exclusive. Unless the UCC otherwise provides, a party to a sales contract may pursue any general remedy available.

If the parties wish to do so, they can limit or modify the remedies that would otherwise be available under the UCC by including the limitations or modifications in the contract. The parties may also expressly agree that a remedy specified in a contract will be the exclusive remedy available. If they do not, the remedy will be considered optional. In addition, any limitation will not be given effect if it fails in its essential purpose, and any limitation or modification of remedies that is unconscionable is void [UCC § 2-719]. In other words, the UCC leaves the parties free to shape their remedies according to their particular requirements, but insists that they be reasonable. In the following case, for example, the federal appellate court refused to uphold a limited warranty of the seller to replace or repair the glass panels because, under the circumstances, the essential purpose of the warranty was defeated by the limitation.

R. W. Murray

v

Shatterproof Glass Corp.
758 F2d 266 (1985)
United States Court of Appeals, Eighth Circuit

FACTS: A subcontractor bought insulating glass panels from Shatterproof and installed them on the exterior of an office building owned by The Citadel, Limited. Soon, moisture accumulated between the dual panes of glass in the panels due to defects in a hermetic seal. About two-thirds of the panels had defective seals and consequently accumulated moisture. Shatterproof sold replacement panels to plaintiff but refused to supply them free of charge. Plaintiff sued for breach of express warranty. Shatterproof refused to replace the panels and claimed that plaintiff was barred from recovering the cost of labor and materials in replacing the panels by the following warranty provisions:

> . . . Shatterproof . . . warrants its insulating glass units for a period of twenty (20) years from the date of manufacture against defects in material or workmanship that result in moisture accumulation . . . resulting from failure of the hermetic seal. OUR EXCLUSIVE REMEDY AND THE LIMIT OF OUR LIABILITY UNDER THIS WARRANTY SHALL BE TO FURNISH A REPLACEMENT FOR ANY LITE FAILING TO MEET THE TERMS OF THIS WARRANTY . . . IN NO EVENT WILL WE BE LIABLE FOR SPECIAL, INCIDENTAL OR CONSEQUENTIAL DAMAGES OR MONEY DAMAGES IN EXCESS OF THE COST OF THE LITE. . . .

ISSUE: Does the limitation on consequential damages in the warranty bar plaintiff from recovering damages for the cost of labor and materials to remove the defective panels and install the replacement panels?

RESULT: The warranty failed of its essential purpose because the warranter failed to replace the panels satisfactorily.

REASONING:

*   *   *

The evidence supports jury findings that Shatterproof failed to replace defective panels within a reasonable time and is unable to supply replacement panels which would match the originals. Shatterproof concedes that, after 1979, it refused to supply replacements for failed panels free of charge. Further, at the time it sold replacement panels to plaintiffs, Shatterproof emphasized that it would probably not be able to supply replacements which would match the originals. In fact, the replacements did not match in color and, as plaintiffs' experts testified, the replacements were not commercially tolerable.

In *Givan v. Mack Truck, Inc.;* 569 S.W.2d 243 (Mo.App.1978), the court stated that a limited and exclusive warranty to repair or replace "fails of its purpose and is thus avoided under § 400.2–719(2) wherever the warrantor fails to correct the defect within a reasonable period; . . . " *Id.* at 247. Here, Shatterproof not only failed to replace the defective panels within a reasonable time, but was actually unwilling and unable to supply adequate replacements. Thus, plaintiffs established that Shatterproof's limited and exclusive warranty failed of its essential purpose under Missouri law.

The court in *Givan* discussed the effect of a failure of essential purpose on the damages available to the buyer as follows:

> Since . . . the limitation of remedy has failed of its essential purpose . . . all other contractual remedies are available. The most commonly applied formula for damages is stated in § 400.2–714(2) which gives the buyer "the difference at the time and place of acceptance between the value of the goods accepted and the value they would have had if they had been as warranted. . . . " . . . *Other remedies available include* the buyer's incidental and *consequential damages resulting from the breach,* § 400.2–715. *Givan v. Mack Truck, Inc., supra,* 569 S.W.2d at 247–48 (emphasis added).

The district court concluded that *Givan* established that consequential damages could be recovered, despite a contractual disclaimer of liability for such damages, when an exclusive or limited remedy fails of its essential purpose. Shatterproof contests this conclusion, arguing that a limitation of liability for consequential damages is valid unless unconscionable under MO.ANN.STAT. § 400.2–719(3). This section provides that "[c]onsequential damages may be limited or excluded unless the limitation or exclusion is unconscionable." *Id.*

We generally accord deference to the district court's interpretation of state law. . . . Here, the district court's construction of Missouri law is both reasonable and permissible. Accordingly, we conclude that consequential damages were recoverable since Shatterproof's limited and exclusive warranty failed of its essential purpose.

Plaintiffs assert that the damages awarded by the jury for the cost of labor and glazing materials to remove defective panels and install replacement panels were recoverable as direct damages under the "special circumstances" language of MO.ANN.STAT. § 400.2–714(2), because such damages flow as a natural consequences of the breach. . . . Shatterproof, on the other hand, argues that the removal and installation damages were not properly recoverable, because they are consequential damages under MO.ANN.STAT. § 400.2–715(2) and their warranty disclaimed liability for such damages. Since consequential damages were recoverable in this case despite the disclaimer, we need not determine whether the removal and replacement damages were direct or consequential in order to find that such damages were recoverable.

The availability of consequential damages also provides an alternative basis for a recovery of damages for panels which had not yet failed as of the time of trial. Due to the "checkerboard" problem caused by Shatterproof's inability to supply commercially tolerable replacements, Citadel suffered damages which could only be remedied by replacement of all the panels. The evidence reveals and common sense shows that Shatterproof had reason to know that Citadel would require panels of a matching reflectivity and color tint. Accordingly, losses caused by Shatterproof's inability to supply adequate replacements were recoverable as consequential damages. . . .

Ross, Circuit Judge.

The inclusion of a liquidated damages provision is a common way in which remedies are limited (see Chapter 20 for a discussion of liquidated damages provisions). Again, reasonableness is the key concern. The UCC permits the parties to a sales contract to agree to reasonable liquidated damages, but a provision for unreasonably large liquidated damages is void as a penalty [UCC § 2-718(1)].

Statute of Limitations [UCC § 2-725]   Under the UCC, an action for breach of a sales contract must be brought within four years after the cause of action has accrued. A cause of action normally accrues when a breach occurs, regardless of the innocent party's knowledge of the breach. For example, if the seller delivers nonconforming goods, a breach has occurred, a cause of action has arisen, and the four-year period begins to run. By agreement, the parties may reduce the period of limitations to not less than one year, but they may not extend the period. In most cases it is easy to apply the statute of limitations.

In a breach of warranty case, a cause of action accrues when tender of delivery is made, except when the warranty explicitly extends to future performance of the goods. Application of this rule may sometimes result in harsh decisions. Assume, for example, that a purchaser is injured by a defective product five years after the purchase. Because this is after the statute of limitations period, a personal injury action based on a theory of breach of warranty would be barred, even though the defect was unknown and undiscoverable prior to the injury. In light of that fact, injured persons often seek recovery in a tort action. Tort statutes of limitations are typically less than four years, but the period of limitations does not begin to run until the injury occurs. Thus, if a defective product caused an injury five years after its purchase, the buyer or other user would still have a potential tort action.

Not all courts have accepted such reasoning, however. Some courts have held that all actions, even personal injury actions, that arise out of a breach of warranty are governed by the UCC's four-year limitations period. Other courts have disagreed and have applied the tort statute of limitations. Still other courts have been influenced by the precise nature of the pleadings in the case. In other words, if the plaintiff classifies his action as one for breach of warranty, the UCC provision might be applied; if the plaintiff classifies his action as one in tort, the tort statute of limitations might be applied.

22:6   Seller's Remedies

The UCC provides the seller with a wide variety of remedies. The primary remedies to a buyer's breach are set forth in UCC § 2-703. If a buyer breaches a contract, the seller may (1) withhold delivery of the goods; (2) stop delivery of the goods; (3) identify to the contract finished goods that were not previously identified to it, and finish or salvage unfinished goods; (4) resell the goods and recover damages; (5) recover damages for nonacceptance or repudiation; (6) recover the price; or (7) cancel the contract. In addition, the UCC provides the seller with various remedies in the event of the buyer's insolvency.

The availability or desirability of any particular remedy will, of course, depend on the particular facts involved and the nature of the breach. For example, if the buyer's breach consists of an improper rejection of the goods, the seller cannot be expected to withhold delivery of the goods as a remedy. Or, if the buyer's breach consists of nonpayment for goods already delivered, several of the remedies provided by the code are simply inapplicable. This is not to say, however, that the seller must select only one remedy. The seller may pursue as many remedies as are appropriate and desirable in a given case.

Withholding or Stoppage of Delivery; Effect of Buyer's Insolvency [UCC §§ 2-702, 2-705]   The seller may withhold or stop delivery of goods if the buyer (1) repudiates the contract, (2) fails to make a payment when due, or (3) becomes insolvent.

The right to stop delivery extends until the buyer has either received the goods or obtained effective control of them. To stop delivery, the seller must notify the carrier or other bailee so that he can, by reasonable diligence, prevent delivery, and must surrender any negotiable document of title that has been issued for the goods. The seller cannot stop delivery if the buyer's right to possession has been acknowledged by a bailee other than a carrier, or if the buyer has a negotiable document of title. The seller cannot stop delivery of small shipments for any reason other than the buyer's insolvency.

A buyer's insolvency affects the seller's remedy in different ways, depending on the circumstances. The seller may demand cash payment on future delivery and payment for all goods previously delivered under the contract, even though the contract includes credit terms. If the goods have already been delivered to a carrier or other bailee for ultimate delivery to the buyer, the seller may stop delivery, provided he complies with certain requirements. If a seller discovers a buyer's insolvency after the goods have actually been delivered, the seller has a right to reclaim them within ten days after the buyer receives them. However, if the buyer made a written misrepresentation of solvency to the seller within three months prior to delivery, the ten-day limitation does not apply. If the buyer refuses to return the goods, the seller has no right to forcibly retake them. Note also that insolvency is often a prelude to bankruptcy proceedings. If the buyer does become involved in bankruptcy proceedings, the provisions of the bankruptcy act would take precedence over any provisions of the UCC and the seller's right to reclaim the goods might be defeated.[1]

Resale and Recovery of Damages [UCC § 2-706]   Resale and recovery of damages is the seller's primary remedy when the buyer's breach leaves the seller in possession of the goods. This remedy is available, for example, when the buyer's breach consists of repudiation of the contract or nonacceptance of the goods. If the seller resells the goods in a commercially reasonable manner, he or she may recover the difference between the resale price and the contract price, together with any incidental damages incurred, but less any expenses saved. Incidental damages might include expenses incurred in stopping delivery and returning the goods to the seller, and resale expenses [UCC § 2-710]

The goods may be resold at either a public or a private sale. If the resale is private, the seller must give the buyer reasonable notice of intention to resell. If the resale is public, the seller must notify the buyer of the time and place, unless the goods are perishable or may quickly decline in value.

Recovery of Damages for Nonacceptance or Repudiation [UCC § 2-708]
When the buyer's breach consists of nonacceptance or repudiation, the seller may resell the goods but is not obligated to do so. The seller has the option of seeking damages based on the difference between the market price of the goods at the time and place of tender and the unpaid contract price. The seller may also recover any incidental damages, but expenses saved as a result of the buyer's breach must be deducted. If the damages as computed under this contract-market price formula are inadequate to put the seller in as good a position as performance would have, then the seller may recover as damages the profit lost as a result of the buyer's breach, plus incidental expenses. This alternative measure of damages is designed for use in cases involving readily available standard-priced goods.

EXAMPLE: Lane sells encyclopedias at $500 per set. She makes a profit of $200 on each sale. She contracts to sell a set to Orloff, who wrongfully

---

[1] Bankruptcy is discussed in Chapter 32.

repudiates the contract. Lane then sells the set to a third person who intended to buy a set anyway. Lane will recover nothing if damages are based on the difference between resale price and contract price, or if damages are based on the difference between market price and contract price. Yet Lane clearly has lost $200, since the result of Orloff's breach is that Lane has made only one sale—and a profit of $200—whereas she would have made two sales—and a profit of $400—had Orloff not breached. In such circumstances, Lane would obviously seek recovery of damages measured by lost profits.

Recovery of Contract Price [UCC § 2-709]   If the buyer accepts the goods but fails to pay the purchase price, the seller may recover the price, together with any incidental damages caused by the breach. The seller may also recover the contract price in two other situations: (1) when the goods were lost or damaged within a commercially reasonable time after the risk of loss had passed to the buyer[2] and (2) when goods have been identified to the contract and the seller, after reasonable effort, is unable to resell them or the circumstances reasonably indicate an attempt to resell would be unsuccessful. These are the only three instances in which the seller may recover the purchase price as a remedy.

Unidentified or Unfinished Goods [UCC § 2-704]   The discussion of a seller's remedies thus far has proceeded on the premise that the goods involved have been finished and identified to the contract. Frequently, however, a buyer repudiates or otherwise breaches the contract before the goods have been identified to the contract. In this case the seller may identify the goods to the contract if they are in his possession and then seek appropriate remedies. To illustrate, assume that Johnson contracts to sell Kenny 500 pairs of socks of the 1,000 pairs he has in storage. If Kenny repudiates the contract, Johnson can designate 500 pairs as the subject of the contract. Johnson may then proceed to resell them or seek any other appropriate remedy under the UCC for Kenny's breach.

If the goods are unfinished when the seller learns of the buyer's breach, the seller has several options. He may resell any unfinished goods that were intended for the contract. Or, if it is commercially reasonable to do so, he may either (1) finish the goods and identify them to the contract or (2) stop manufacturing and resell the unfinished goods for their salvage value. The theory is that when unfinished goods are involved, the seller should act in such a manner as to lessen any damages flowing from the buyer's breach. Thus, the seller should choose whichever option is likely to result in the least damages.

Cancellation of Contract   Cancellation occurs when one party puts an end to the contract because of the other party's breach. A party may cancel the contract and still pursue any other available remedy, such as damages [UCC §§ 2-106(4), 2-720]. Thus on the buyer's breach, the seller may cancel the

---

[2] Risk of loss is discussed in Chapter 20.

TABLE 22.1
Summary of Sellers' Remedies

Remedy	Availability; Comments
Withholding or stoppage of delivery of goods [UCC §§ 2-702, 2-705]	Available if buyer repudiates the contract, fails to make payment when due, or becomes insolvent.
Resale of goods and recovery of damages [UCC § 2-706]	Available if buyer's breach leaves seller in possession of goods.
Recovery of damages for nonacceptance or repudiation [UCC § 2-708]	A contract-market price formula is used in cases where seller does not resell the goods.
Recovery of contract price [UCC § 2 2-709]	Available if (1) buyer has accepted the goods, or (2) goods are lost after risk of loss has passed to buyer, or (3) seller is unable to resell goods identified to the contract.
Resale of goods or finishing of goods and identification to the contract [UCC § 2-704]	Options as to unfinished goods. Seller must act so as to lessen damages flowing from the breach.
Cancellation of contract [UCC § 2-703]	May occur when buyer breaches contract; seller may also pursue other remedies.

contract and pursue any other remedy that may be appropriate under the circumstances.

The UCC distinguishes between cancellation and termination of a contract. Termination occurs when a party legally puts an end to the contract for some reason other than its breach by the other party. Termination has the effect of discharging all unperformed obligations that remain, although any rights based on prior breach or performance survive [UCC § 2-106(3)].

22:7 Buyer's Remedies

The buyer's remedies for a seller's breach are cataloged and described in several sections of the UCC. These remedies include (1) rejecting or revoking acceptance of goods when they are nonconforming (which is discussed in section 22:3); (2) reselling the goods under certain circumstances and in the same manner as the seller, as described in section 22:6; (3) obtaining substitute goods, called *cover;* (4) recovering damages under various circumstances; (5) requesting an order for *specific performance* or *replevin;* and (6) cancelling the contract. In addition, the buyer may always recover any part of the purchase price that has already been paid. Because the first two remedies have been treated elsewhere, only the last four will be discussed here.

Cover (UCC § 2-712) Cover, or the right to obtain substitute goods, is the principal remedy under the UCC when the seller's breach deprives the buyer of the goods for which he has contracted. The buyer's right to cover is the counterpart of the seller's right to resell, and both remedies are widely used. The buyer may cover by purchasing substitute goods from another source. The buyer's purchase must be made in good faith, without unreasonable delay, and in a reasonable manner. The buyer may then recover from the seller damages equal to the difference between the cost of cover and the contract price, plus incidental or consequential damages, less expenses saved by virtue of the seller's breach.

Cover is an optional remedy, and if the buyer elects not to cover he can later recover any consequential damages that could have been prevented by cover. However, cover is normally a desirable remedy, since it permits the buyer to obtain a substitute for the performance promised in the original contract.

Damages [UCC §§ 2-713-2-715]   As an alternative to cover, a buyer may merely seek damages for nondelivery or repudiation. If the buyer receives the goods and they are defective, he may accept them and seek to recover damages based on the nonconformity. The measure of damages depends on the alternative selected by the buyer. In all situations, the buyer may recover appropriate incidental or consequential damages.

The measure of damages for nondelivery or repudiation is the difference between the market price when the buyer learned of the breach and the contract price. When the buyer accepts the goods and seeks damages based on their nonconformity, the measure of damages is the loss resulting in the ordinary course of events from the seller's breach. Any reasonable manner of determining such damages may be used, but the most common measure is the difference between the value of the goods as accepted and the value they would have had if they had conformed to the contract. This measure is specifically prescribed for breach of warranty cases.

 While the discussion here is couched in terms of recovering damages, it is obviously preferable for the buyer and seller to reach an agreement on a reduced purchase price when defective goods are delivered and accepted. As a practical matter, it is sometimes difficult for the buyer to obtain a partial refund from the seller. The UCC, however, authorizes a buyer, on giving the seller notice of his intention to do so, to deduct the damages resulting from the breach from any part of the purchase price not yet paid [UCC § 2-717]. Therefore, a buyer who has accepted defective goods but has not yet paid the full price should consider exercising his right to deduct the damages when he makes his final payment.

The incidental damages that a buyer may recover include expenses reasonably incurred in inspection, receipt, transportation, and care and custody of goods rightfully rejected; any commercially reasonable expenses incurred in effecting cover; and any other reasonable expenses caused by the breach. Consequential damages are recoverable if the seller at the time of contracting had reason to know of the buyer's general or particular requirements and needs. In other words, consequential damages are recoverable if they are foreseeable, but are not recoverable if the buyer could have prevented them. Thus, the buyer must seek to minimize his damages, either by cover or other means.[3]

Specific Performance or Replevin [UCC § 2-716] Specific performance of a sales contract may be ordered if the goods involved are unique or "in other proper circumstances."[4] The UCC contains no specific requirement that the remedy at law be inadequate, although in most instances where specific performance is proper the remedy at law will be inadequate. Uniqueness is to be determined in light of the total situation. For example, output and requirements contracts that involve a particular or peculiarly available source or market may be the subject of an order of specific performance.

The UCC also grants the buyer the right to obtain possession of the goods under certain circumstances. This is called the right of replevin. The remedy of replevin is available only if the goods have been identified to the contract and only if cover is not reasonably obtainable.[5]

Cancellation of Contract The buyer's right to cancel the contract for a breach is the same as the seller's right in that regard. Thus, a buyer may cancel the contract and pursue other appropriate remedies.

---

[3] Consequential damages and the duty to minimize damages are discussed in Chapter 18.
[4] The circumstances under which specific performance will ordinarily be ordered are discussed in Chapter 18.
[5] Replevin is discussed in more detail in Chapter 31.

TABLE 22.2
Summary of Buyers' Remedies

Remedy	Availability; Comments
Rejection of nonconforming goods [UCC § 2-601]	May reject partial or entire delivery.
Resale of goods [UCC § 2-711(3)]	Available if seller's breach leaves buyer in possession of goods.
Cover [UCC § 2-712]	Buyer may also recover difference between cover and contract price.
Recovery of damages [UCC §§ 2-713–2-715]	If nondelivery, may recover difference between market price at breach and contract price; if nonconformity, may recover loss resulting in ordinary course of events. Incidental and consequential damages may be available.
Specific performance or replevin [UCC § 2-716]	Available if goods are existing and unique.
Cancellation of contract [UCC § 2-711(1)]	May occur where seller breaches contract; buyer may also pursue other remedies.

Key Concepts and Terms

- The seller's basic obligation is to deliver conforming goods. Under the perfect tender rule, the buyer has the right to reject a tender of delivery that is nonconforming in any respect. In practice, however, substantial performance by the seller is generally sufficient, and the seller has the right to cure an improper delivery under certain circumstances. The doctrine of substantial performance is also applicable to deviations from shipping and delivery arrangements.

- A seller may be excused from performance of the contract if it is commercially impracticable to perform or if goods essential to the contract were destroyed.

- The buyer's basic obligations are to accept and pay for conforming goods. The UCC specifies three methods by which acceptance may occur. These are (1) informing the seller that the goods are conforming or are acceptable despite some nonconformity; (2) failing to reject or give the seller notice of rejection within a reasonable time; or (3) performing any act that indicates ownership of the goods.

- The buyer generally may inspect the goods prior to acceptance or payment. Certain contracts require payment before inspection, but the buyer still has the right to inspect the goods before accepting them.

- Under the UCC a party, when in doubt as to the other party's intention or ability to perform, may demand adequate assurance of performance. The demanding party may suspend performance pending receipt of such assurance. Failure to provide the assurance constitutes repudiation of the contract.

- An action for breach of a sales contract must be brought within four years after the cause of action has accrued.

- The remedial philosophy of the UCC is that an innocent party should be put in as good a position as if the breaching party had performed. Therefore, in addition to remedies provided by the UCC, an aggrieved party may pursue any other available remedies.

- When a buyer breaches, the seller may pursue one or more of the following remedies: (1) withholding of delivery; (2) stoppage of delivery; (3) identification of goods to the contract, finishing of unfinished goods, or salvage of unfinished goods; (4) resale of goods and recovery of damages; (5) recovery of damages for nonacceptance or repudiation; (6) recovery of the price of the goods; or (7) cancellation of the contract. If the buyer is insolvent, the seller may also reclaim the goods under certain circumstances.

- The measure of damages recoverable by the seller varies depending on the remedy selected. Damages may be based on the difference between resale price and contract price, or the difference between market price and contract price, or on lost profits. Incidental damages are also recoverable.

- When a seller breaches, the buyer may pursue one or more of the following remedies: (1) rejection or revocation of acceptance; (2) resale; (3) cover (procurement of substitute goods); (4) recovery of damages; (5) specific performance or replevin; or (6) cancellation of the contract. The buyer may also recover any part of the purchase price that has been paid.

- The measure of damages recoverable by a buyer depends on the remedy selected. Damages may be based on the difference between the cost of cover and the contract price, the difference between the value of accepted non-conforming goods and the value of conforming goods, or on some other reasonable basis. Incidental damages are also recoverable, as are consequential damages that could not have been prevented.

- Acceptance
- Anticipatory Repudiation
- Assurance of Performance
- Commercial Unit
- Conforming Goods
- Cover
- Cure
- Incidental or Consequential Damages

- Inspection
- Installment Contract
- Perfect Tender
- Specific Performance or Replevin
- Stoppage of Delivery
- Tender of Delivery

Questions and Case Problems

1. Barrett orders carpeting from Venture on the following discount terms: five percent off the price of the order if paid within 60 days; four percent off if paid within 90 days. Venture ships carpeting that conforms to the order, but Venture's invoice sets out different discount terms: five percent off if paid within 60 days; no discount if paid within 90 days. Barrett objects and requests that Venture correct the nonconforming terms. When Venture refuses, Barrett rejects the carpeting. Barrett keeps the carpeting in its warehouse, where it is destroyed by fire three months later. Was there a contract? If so, was Barrett's rejection justified? On whom should the risk of loss fall?

2. Miller ordered and accepted delivery of a new station wagon with a heavy-duty trailer package that included extra-wide tires. Shortly after arriving home with the new car, Miller noticed that the spare tire was missing. He called the dealer and insisted on having the tire immediately. When the dealer told him no spare tire was available, Miller told the dealer he was revoking acceptance, that he was cancelling payment on the two checks that were tendered as the purchase price, and that the dealer could pick up the station wagon. The station wagon remained parked in front of Miller's house until the 10-day registration sticker expired and the local police towed the wagon away. The dealer sued for the purchase price. Miller claims that he revoked acceptance of the station wagon. What result? Would it matter to know that Miller's occupation required that he drive the wagon as much as 150 miles per day on Detroit freeways, and often in the early morning hours?

3. In 1967 Chapman, a plumbing contractor, purchased four kitchen units from Cervitor for installation in a university dormitory. The kitchen units were delivered in shipping crates on May 4, 1967. As was the custom in the construction industry,

the units were stored on the job site until the time for installation. On August 5, 1967, Chapman removed the units from the crates and installed them. The university's engineer inspected the units, noted several readily observable defects, and notified Chapman of his disapproval. Chapman then notified Cervitor that he was rejecting the units. Chapman reshipped the units to Cervitor, who refused to accept them. They were ultimately sold for storage charges. Cervitor sued Chapman for the purchase price. Who should win the case?

4. Tonka Tours contracted to buy a 52-foot houseboat from Chadima. The contract listed several repair items that were to be completed prior to closing. At the time of closing none of these had been done. Tonka was assured that the repairs would be made, however, and so proceeded with the closing. After the repairs were made, Tonka hauled the boat by truck to the lake on which Tonka intended to use the boat. During the first hour of Tonka's initial operation of the boat, both engines overheated and had to be shut off. Tonka then hauled the boat back to the original marina and authorized additional repairs. Two days later Tonka called, and then wrote, Chadima and informed him that it was "rescinding" the deal. Did Tonka effectively reject the tender of the boat?

5. Moss contracts to supply plumbing equipment to Devine for use in a building Devine is constructing. The contract requires payment to be made within 15 days of each delivery. Devine's payments are frequently late, and his indebtedness to Moss gradually increases to $25,000. Moss writes Devine a letter stating that further deliveries will be made only if (1) the past due amount is paid in full and (2) Devine deposits sufficient cash ($50,000) in escrow to guarantee payment for supplies yet to be delivered. Devine immediately sends Moss a check for $25,000, and informs Moss that he will not put $50,000 in escrow, but will make future payments on time. Moss refuses to make further deliveries, and Devine sues for breach of contract. What is the result?

6. In January, Reed contracted to purchase 1,000 hula hoops from Barry at a price of $3,000. Delivery was scheduled for June. In March, the bottom fell out of the hula hoop market, and Reed notified Barry that he was repudiating the contract. At that time Barry had spent $750 on production of the hoops, which were unfinished. Their salvage value was $500. In the hope that the hula hoop market would revive, Barry finished manufacturing the hoops, at an additional cost of $750. In May, the hula hoop market was still sinking, and Barry resold the order to another purchaser for $250. Barry then sued Reed for breach of contract. What damages should Barry recover?

7. McCoy contracts to buy ball bearings from Kemp. Delivery is to be made in nine equal shipments over a three-month period. The contract specifies that a delivery is satisfactory if no more than five percent of the ball bearings are defective. When the first shipment arrives, McCoy finds that eight percent of the ball bearings are defective, and he so notifies Kemp. Kemp offers to cure the nonconforming delivery by granting McCoy a five percent price reduction, but McCoy refuses. McCoy tells Kemp that "you are obviously unable to meet our specifications" and cancels the contract immediately. Kemp sues McCoy for breach of contract. How should the case be decided? What if a defective rate greater than five percent seriously impaired McCoy's ability to meet his contractual obligations to others? What, if anything, should McCoy have done differently?

8. Pasquale wants to purchase an airplane from L & H International, an aircraft dealer. L & H informs Pasquale that its credit situation requires a quick sale and therefore it is willing to sell the plane for $75,000, with $10,000 down. Pasquale

agrees, a contract is signed, and a down payment is made by check. The contract states that if the buyer breaches, the seller may keep the down payment as liquidated damages. Pasquale reneges on the contract and stops payment on its $10,000 check. Within a month, L & H sells the airplane to someone else for $89,000. L & H then sues Pasquale for the $10,000. What is the outcome of the case?

9. What is the primary remedy available to a seller in the event of a buyer's breach? To a buyer in the event of a seller's breach? Describe the requirements that must be met by the seller and buyer in pursuing these remedies.

10. Taylor buys a used heater. He becomes dissatisfied with the way it works and tells the seller so. He continues to use it for a while. Still dissatisfied, he decides to disconnect it and set it aside in a safe place. He also stops making payments. When the seller sues for the balance, Taylor claims he had never fully accepted the goods. Should his claim be upheld?

PART FIVE

Commercial Paper and Money Transfers

Introductory Comments

Virtually every commercial transaction involves a transfer of value from one person to another. Goods and services are paid for. Debts and accounts are settled. Businesses in one part of the country collect payment from businesses and customers in other parts of the country. These transfers require a dependable system for transferring payment.

Physical delivery of cash, of course, is a straightforward payment system. It is not, however, convenient or desirable in many circumstances. Cash can be stolen and easily used by the person who stole it; there is no inherent record of transfer. Cash must be obtained from a bank; it cannot be created on the spot. Cash requires physical transport. Moreover, while cash is useful for transferring value from one person to another, for example from A to B, it does not permit A to transfer value to B by requiring that C pay B. Commercial paper, and more recently electronic funds transfers, can be thought of as money substitutes that meet the needs of commerce for a flexible system of payments.

For many years commercial paper has been the lifeblood of business: promissory notes, checks, drafts, and other kinds of negotiable instruments remain indispensable to commercial transactions. Knowledge of the commercial paper law is essential to a businessperson. In addition, the advent of dependable wire and electronic technology has made possible the transfer of value without paper. This technology has both solved and created distinct legal problems. Because the rights of parties vary depending on the payment system used, the businessperson must understand the law associated with electronic funds transfers as well as the law regarding commercial paper.

The material in Chapters 23, 24, and 25 introduces the legal nature of commercial paper and provides the information necessary to use commercial paper intelligently. These chapters discuss the various types of commercial paper, the concept and the requirements of negotiability, the actual negotiation of commercial paper, the concept and rights of a holder in due course, and the liability of the various parties to commercial paper. Chapter 26 discusses the specific rights and liabilities arising out of the bank–customer relationship. Chapter 27 discusses the law governing electronic funds transfers and compares the rights and liabilities of parties to this type of payment system.

Although commercial paper law is treated as a distinct subject in these chapters, it is clear that commercial paper is not used in a vacuum. Checks, promissory notes, and other forms of commercial paper are used in connection with numerous types of transactions discussed in other parts of this book. For example, a note may be used in connection with a contract, a sale of goods, the sale of real property, or the extension of credit. In such situations, a person must have knowledge not only of the law that governs the underlying transaction, but also of the law that governs the use of commercial paper. An understanding of commercial paper, therefore, will enhance understanding of other aspects of business law.

23 Negotiable Instruments

23:1 Introduction

Commercial paper is a device for transferring value from one person to another. It is a money substitute. In addition, it may be a means of creating a debt. For example, a person may pay for goods by check. The check itself has value and may be used as a money substitute; it has value to the extent that it is likely to be honored and paid. That person may also pay for goods by signing a promissory note. The note, like the check, has value and may be used as a substitute for money. In addition, the note embodies a promise to pay money in the future; it creates a debt, and an extension of credit.

The key to understanding commercial paper law is to understand that the owner of commercial paper may have a right to payment that is greater than what he or she would have as a mere assignee of a contract right.

EXAMPLE: A agrees to paint B's portrait for $500. A assigns her rights in the contract to C. C, as an assignee, is entitled to the $500 if and only if A paints the portrait in accordance with the contract. If B, however, gave A a note for $500 and A gave the note to C, it is possible that B would be obligated to pay the note even if A never performed the contract. This potential for superior rights is what makes commercial paper significant.

Note that if B gave A $500 in advance, and A spent the money to buy something from C, B could not recover the money from C on the theory that A failed to paint the portrait and earn the money. Money "travels without baggage." You will find that commercial paper travels with less baggage than an ordinary contract right, but with somewhat more than money. Commercial paper travels with "carry-on baggage."

Commercial paper has been used for centuries. The law merchant, which was the medieval body of law governing business dealings, included rules governing the issuance of commercial paper.[1] These rules eventually became part of English common law, and today they are codified as Article 3 of the UCC. The UCC has changed the prior law in some respects; it has been said,

---

[1] The law merchant is discussed in Chapter 19.

CUSTOMER'S DRAFT

San Francisco ___, California___ July 15 ___ 19 81 ___ No. 1 ___

60 Days after date Pay To The Order of   **CROCKER NATIONAL BANK** $ 1,000.00

One thousand and No/100 _____ Dollars

Value received and charge the same to account of

To John Doe

San Francisco, CA

Account Number 01234

Jane Rowe

CANCELLED
11-8

FIGURE 23-1*   Draft

however, that it has made no radical changes in the law of commercial paper as that law has developed over the centuries. Thus, many of the rules embodied in Article 3 can be traced to the law merchant, and the principles of the law merchant may still be applied except where they are inconsistent with the UCC [UCC § 1-103].

23:2   Types of Commercial Paper

Commercial paper includes (1) orders to pay money and (2) promises to pay money. Under the UCC, an order to pay money may be classified as either a *draft* or a *check*, and a promise to pay money may be classified as either a note or a *certificate of deposit* [UCC § 3-104(2)].

Drafts   A draft, also known as a bill of exchange is a written order by one person (the *drawer*) directing another person (the *drawee*) to pay money to a third person (the *payee*). A typical draft is illustrated in Figure 23-1. Here, the drawer is Jane Rowe, the drawee is John Doe, and the payee is Crocker Bank.

Obviously, there must be some relationship between the drawer and the drawee, or the drawee would simply ignore the order. Often the drawee has funds belonging to the drawer, and the draft is used as a means of transferring those funds to the payee. In this regard, banks may be the greatest users of drafts, and they sell them to persons who want to transmit funds. If a person residing in one city wishes to make a payment in another city, he may do so by means of a bank draft. In exchange for his payment of money, the bank in the city of residence (the drawer bank) draws a draft on a bank in the city of payment (the drawee bank) directing that funds be paid to a specific party (the payee).

---

* The documents reproduced in Figures 23-1 through 23-4 were supplied through the courtesy of Crocker National Bank, San Francisco, California.

FIGURE 23-2 Check

Another frequently used draft, the *trade acceptance*, is used in connection with a sale of goods. A trade acceptance enables the seller to extend credit to a buyer and yet receive immediate payment. In a trade acceptance, the seller draws a draft directing the buyer to pay the seller at some future time. The buyer then accepts the draft by signing it, thereby becoming obligated to make the payment ordered. The seller then turns the trade acceptance into cash by negotiating it to a third party at a discount. Negotiation is discussed later in this chapter.

The drawee is not obligated to honor a draft until he or she accepts it by signing it. Once this is done, the drawee is known as the *acceptor*.

Checks A check is a specific form of draft. Its distinctive characteristics are that (1) it is always drawn on a bank and (2) it is always payable on demand. An example of a check is shown in Figure 23-2.

The various types of checks, and the duties of banks with respect to checks, are covered in detail in Chapter 26.

Notes A note, known also as a promissory note, is an unconditional promise by one party (the *maker*) to pay money to a second party (the payee). The basic distinction between a note and a draft is that in a note the maker promises to make payment himself, while in a draft the drawer orders another person—the drawee—to make payment. Thus, a note involves only two parties, the maker and the payee, while a draft involves three parties, the drawer, the drawee, and the payee. Promissory notes are used primarily in conjunction with credit transactions. Often the note is secured by some property of the maker. For example, the sale of real property may involve a note secured by a mortgage on the property; the installment sale of personal property may involve a note secured by the property sold; and other trans-

| LOAN NO. *1* | **R.R.** INITIALS | | *1/15/82* MATURITY DATE |

NOTE—SINGLE PAYMENT—INTEREST PAYABLE SEPARATELY

$2,500.00 _____ _San Francisco_____ ,California, _July 15___ ,198*1*

Six months after date ~~CANCELLED~~ _____after date

for value received, the undersigned _Jane Doe_ **11-8**_____ promise(s) to pay to **CROCKER NATIONAL BANK**,

or order, at its__ _Main_ _____ Office in _San Francisco___ , California, in lawful money

of the United States of America, the principal sum of

Two thousand five hundred and *xx*/*oo*_____Dollars,

plus interest, payable_ _monthly_____ , on the unpaid balance of said principal sum at the rate equal to 1/_20_ th of _one_ percent per day from date hereof until paid.

Upon default in payment of any interest hereon when due, the whole of said principal sum then remaining unpaid and all interest accrued hereon, at the option of the holder hereof, shall become immediately due and payable without demand or notice. Should any payment hereof not be made when due, the undersigned further promises to pay all costs of collection and a reasonable attorney's fee. If the undersigned is more than one, their covenants and obligations hereunder are joint and several and each hereby waives demand, diligence, presentment, protest and notice of every kind.

_0 Main Street_____   _Jane Doe_____
                ADDRESS

San Francisco CA _94000_
        STATE   ZIP CODE

_111-1112_ _____ **CANCELLED** _____
  TELEPHONE   **11-8**

50-9208 (REV. 10-77)

FIGURE 23-3 Note

actions may involve collateral notes secured by the maker's personal property. A simple note is illustrated in Figure 23-3.

Certificates of Deposit   A certificate of deposit is a specific type of note. It is an acknowledgement by a bank of the receipt of money, with the bank's promise to repay the money. Figure 23-4 is an example of a certificate of deposit.

Parties to Commercial Paper   In discussing the four types of commercial paper, reference has already been made to the essential parties—the drawer, drawee, maker, and payee. A person cannot understand the law of commercial paper without understanding the positions occupied by these parties. Special attention to the distinguishing characteristics of these parties is therefore warranted at this point, and definitions of these original parties to commercial paper follow. It should also be noted at this point that other parties may become involved in commercial paper, and these parties will be discussed at the appropriate places in the text.

Drawer: The person who creates a draft or a check by issuing a written order directing another person to pay money to a third person.

Drawee: The person upon whom a draft or check is drawn and who is directed by the draft or check to make payment.

FIGURE 23-4 Certificate of Deposit

Maker: The person who creates a note or a certificate of deposit by making a promise to pay money to another party.

Payee: The person to whom a commercial instrument directs the payment of money.

Negotiable and Nonnegotiable Commercial Paper   The terms "commercial paper" and "negotiable instruments" often are used interchangeably. It is important to note, however, that commercial paper can be nonnegotiable. Article 3 of the UCC applies to negotiable commercial paper. As a result, negotiable commercial paper is easily transferable, and holders in due course of such paper acquire certain special rights (see Chapter 24). Article 3 generally does *not* apply to nonnegotiable commercial paper; rather, such paper is treated as only a contract and is governed by the rules of contract law. As a result, nonnegotiable commercial paper is not easily transferred, and the holder in due course rules are not applicable. The utility of commercial paper lies in its ability to be transferred. Therefore, to serve as a substitute for money and a credit device, commercial paper must be negotiable. The rest of this chapter and the next three chapters will focus on negotiable instruments.

An instrument may create rights and obligations even though it is not negotiable. Also, the rights of the parties to a negotiable instrument may be affected by a separate agreement between them [UCC § 3-119]. (Such an agreement does not affect the rights of persons with no notice of it.) The resolution of a dispute as to the negotiability of an instrument does not necessarily have any bearing on the resolution of a dispute as to the rights of the parties under a separate agreement. In other words, a party may be unable to recover on an instrument but still be able to recover on the contract that gave rise to the instrument.

23:3   Requirements of Negotiability

The negotiability of commercial paper depends on its form. The instrument itself must contain all the essential elements of negotiability. Compliance with the statutory requirements is mandatory, and the parties may not alter these requirements by agreement. To be negotiable, an instrument must (1) be in writing and signed by the maker or drawer, (2) contain an unconditional promise or order to pay a *sum certain* in money, (3) be payable on demand or at a definite time, and (4) be payable to order or to bearer [UCC § 3-104(1)].

In Writing and Signed   A negotiable instrument must be in writing and signed by the maker or the drawer. The term "writing" includes printing, typewriting, or any other intentional reduction to tangible form [UCC § 1-201(46)]. Note, for example, that the negotiable instruments in Figures 23-1 through 23-4 contain both printed and handwritten matter. The requirement of a signature may be met in various ways. The signature may be handwritten, typed, printed, or made in some other manner. A person may sign his or her own name, use a trade or assumed name, or even use a symbol or mark, provided this is done with the intention of authenticating the writing [UCC §§ 1-201(39), 3-401]. A signature may also be made by an agent or other duly authorized representative [UCC § 3-403(1)].[2]

Unconditional Promise or Order to Pay [UCC § 3-105]   A negotiable instrument must also contain an unconditional promise or order to pay. A promise must be a definite undertaking to pay; mere acknowledgment of a debt does not constitute a promise. For example, an I.O.U. is not a promise. An order is a direction to pay. A simple authorization or request does not constitute an order. Nor do words such as "I wish you would pay." However, words of courtesy, such as "please," do not reduce an order to a simple request. Figures 23-3 and 23-4 are examples of promises to pay, while Figures 23-1 and 23-2 are examples of orders to pay.

The promise or order must be unconditional. That is, the promise or order to pay cannot be made contingent on the happening of some event. To be acceptable as a substitute for money or a credit device, a draft or promissory note must contain a definite and clear obligation to pay. A person must be able to tell from the instrument itself what obligations and rights it creates.

When an instrument is issued in conjunction with some other transaction, as when a promissory note is given as payment for a purchase, the instrument must not state that it is being issued on some condition related to the transaction. In the case of the promissory note given for payment, the note may refer to the sales agreement, but it may not state that it is subject to or governed by the underlying agreement. Such a statement would constitute a condition and render the note nonnegotiable.

Similarly, when a note or draft is drawn on an account that is maintained for a specific purpose, it is permissible to refer to the particular account to be debited, provided the reference does not amount to a condition. For example,

---

[2] The law of agency is discussed in Chapter 43.

the note or draft cannot state that it is to be paid only out of the particular fund. This statement is conditional, since the obligation to pay depends on the continued existence of the fund. The UCC makes an exception with respect to instruments issued by government entities. They are permitted to limit payment of an instrument out of a particular fund without destroying the instrument's negotiability.

Bank of Viola

v

Nestrick
390 NE2d 636 (1979)
Appellate Court of Illinois, Third District

FACTS: The *Liberty Advertiser*, a weekly advertising paper, signed a note to the Bank of Viola that stated:

> For value received, the undersigned promises to pay to the Order of Bank of Viola, Viola, Illinois, the principal sum of $15,8884.54 payable in installments Or as follows: Or *payable $80.00 per week from Jack & Jill contract* with interest at the rate of *8.00* per cent per annum from date until paid. [Italicized segments handwritten in original.]

At trial the defendant identified the "Jack & Jill" reference as an advertising contract with a store by that name.

ISSUE: Did the language referring to the Jack & Jill contract render the note non-negotiable?

RESULT: The reference does not explicitly limit payment to the proceeds of the Jack & Jill contract, and thus does not render the note non-negotiable.

REASONING:

*   *   *

. . . The statutory standard for determining whether a note is conditional is set forth in Illinois Revised Statutes, 1973, chapter 26, section 3 105(2)(b). Therein it states:

> "(2) A promise or order is not unconditional if the instrument

*   *   *   *   *   *

> (b) states that it is to be paid only out of a particular fund or source . . . ."

The drafters of this statutory section advise that the test set forth is merely a re-statement of prior law. . . . An excellent discussion of that prior law, the *Uniform Negotiable Instruments Act* is set forth by the supreme court of Alabama in *Rhodes v Schofield*, 1955 263 Ala. 256, 82 So.2d 236:

> " . . . it has been generally said . . . that an unqualified promise to pay is unconditional although coupled with 'an indication of a particular fund out of which reimbursement is to be made'; also that a 'promise to pay out of a particular fund is not unconditional'. The distinction between those two principals is not very clear. It is said at 7 *Am.Jur. 854*, Section 119: 'the courts seem[ed] to have experienced some difficulty in determining whether particular instruments require a payment to be made out of a particular fund. The true test in every case under the Uniform Act as well as the common law is whether the general credit of the maker or drawee accompanies the instrument. If it does, the instrument is negotiable (unconditional), otherwise it is not. (citations omitted) The wording of the particular instrument is not determinative of the question, but the intention of the parties as disclosed by the surrounding circumstances must also be considered. In this connection, it is to be borne in mind that the negotiability of bills and notes is favored in law, and whenever the promise can be held unconditional without doing violence to the ordinary meaning of the language used, it will be so held.' "

Thus, because current law merely restates prior rules, a promise will be held unconditional whenever it is possible to do so without doing violence to the ordinary meaning of the language used.

The current statute provides that a promise is not unconditional if the instrument states that it is to be paid *only* out of a particular fund or source. (Emphasis added.) This is in accord with prior law. . . . These cases consistently hold that the mere indication of a particular account, fund or source from which reimbursement is expected does not render an instrument conditional. Rather, reimbursement must be explicitly limited to a particular account, fund or source with such restrictive terms as "only", "exclusively", or "solely". . . .

Negotiability is favored in the law. . . . It follows that construing an instrument as unconditional is favored in the law. An instrument may be unconditional which indicates a particular account or fund or source from which reimbursement is expected. . . . A line of judicial precedents unbroken through this century requires words of explicit limitation before an instrument is said to be payable only out of a particular account, fund or source. Those words of explicit limitation are absent here. It does no violence to the statute or to the ordinary language of the instrument to conclude that this note is unconditional.

As set forth earlier, the mere wording of an instrument is not determinative of the issue. . . . Rather, the intention of the parties as disclosed by the surrounding circumstances must be considered, and the language of the instrument is but one of many probative elements considered in determining the intention which require the conclusion that this instrument was not conditional, but an unconditional promise to pay backed by the general credit of the maker. The face amount of the note was $15,884.54, and the handwritten portion provides that it is payable $80.00 per week from the Jack & Jill contract. Further, the note recites a due date of May 7, 1976. The court takes judicial notice of the fact that the year from the date of execution, May 7, 1975, until the due date, May 7, 1976, was but 52 weeks in length. Thus the maximum payment that could be paid before the due date would be $4,160.00. This amount is less than half the face amount of the note, to say nothing of interest which might accrue. Absent an extraordinary philanthropic motive on the part of the plaintiff bank, this arithmetic mandates the conclusion that the parties intended that the general credit of the defendant-maker would provide the means for payment when the balance of the note became due on May 7, 1976. . . .

Scott, Presiding Justice.

Sum Certain in Money [UCC §§ 3-106, 3-107] "Sum certain" refers to the amount to be paid and must be an amount that can be computed from the instrument itself. The amount may vary depending on the time of payment and still be considered "certain." An example of this is the payment of interest at a stated rate. The instrument may provide for different rates of interest before and after default, or it may provide for a stated discount or addition depending on the time payment is made, and still be negotiable. However, an instrument that called for interest payable "at the current rate" would be nonnegotiable, since the amount to be paid could not be determined from the instrument itself. The note in Figure 23-3 and the certificate of deposit in Figure 23-4 both provide for payment of interest at a stated rate.

There is one exception to the requirement that the sum certain be computable from the instrument itself. This exception is payment of costs of collection or an attorney's fee on default. The basic obligation (the principal and interest) must still be computable from the instrument, but the collection costs and attorney's fee may be determined from other sources. The note in Figure 23-3 contains a provision for payment of collection costs and attorney's fees in the event of default.

The UCC provides that "money" means a medium of exchange authorized or adopted by a domestic or foreign government as part of its currency [UCC § 1-201(24)]. Thus, an instrument that states the sum to be paid in a foreign currency is negotiable. Such an instrument may be paid either in the foreign currency or in dollars measured by the foreign currency, unless the instrument specifies that payment is to be made in the foreign currency.

 All these rules may appear highly technical, but their purpose is simple: The instrument itself must contain an unconditional obligation to make payment. With that in mind, a person drafting the instrument should ask two questions: (1) Is the obligation to pay absolute? (2) Can the obligation to pay be determined from the instrument itself, or must some other document be consulted? If the answer to either question is "no," the instrument is not negotiable. Any reference to the underlying transaction or to the fund out of which the instrument is to be paid must be phrased in such a way that it will not affect the unconditional nature of the obligation contained in the instrument.

Payable on Demand or at Definite Time [UCC §§ 3-108, 3-109]   The negotiable instrument must be payable on demand or at a definite time in the future. Instruments payable on demand, known as *demand instruments* or sight instruments, contain a provision that the instrument is payable on demand, payable at sight, or payable on presentation. Instruments that contain no time for payment are also payable on demand. Instruments that provide for payment at a definite time—known as *time instruments*—provide for payment on or before a stated date, at a fixed period after a stated date, or at a fixed period after sight. The instruments in Figures 23-1, 23-3, and 23-4 are time instruments; the check in Figure 23-2 is a demand instrument.

Under the UCC, an instrument that contains an acceleration clause meets the definite time requirement and is negotiable. An acceleration clause typically provides that on the happening of a certain event, such as the obligor's default, the obligation is immediately payable. The note in Figure 23-3 contains an acceleration clause. In some instances an instrument that contains an extension clause is also negotiable. An extension clause typically provides that on the occurrence of some event the time for payment is extended. To meet the definite time requirement, the extension clause must be exercisable only by the holder. An instrument that contains an extension clause exercisable by the maker or acceptor does not meet the definite time requirement unless the extension includes a definite time limit. Otherwise, the maker or acceptor would have the right to extend the time for payment indefinitely, making the instrument not payable at a definite time and thus nonnegotiable.

If an instrument is payable only on the happening of an act or event uncertain as to time of occurrence, it clearly does not meet the definite time requirement and is nonnegotiable.

The following case explores the definite time requirement of UCC § 3-109.

Smith

v

Gentilotti

359 NE2d 953 (1977)

Supreme Judicial Court of Massachusetts

FACTS: Plaintiffs, mother and son, sued the father's estate on a check drawn by the father, payable to the order of the son, and delivered to the mother when the son was an infant. The check was drawn November 25, 1969, and was postdated November 4, 1984. In addition, it was indorsed as follows: "For Edward Joseph Smith Gentilotti My Son If I should pass away The amount of $20,000.00 dollars Shall be taken from My Estate at death. S. Gentilotti 11-25-69." Evidence at trial revealed that the son was born November 4, 1964, that the father had given the mother more than $14,000 in checks and cash through the years and had inquired frequently as to whether she still had the check in question in the lawsuit. Both the mother and the father expected the check to be enforceable.

ISSUE: Does the check require payment at a definite time?

RESULT: The conditional language in the indorsement does not defeat the requirement that the instrument be paid at a definite time.

REASONING:

*   *   *

    . . . Under [UCC] § 3–104, the instrument in question is on its face a check drawn on a bank in Milford, Massachusetts, payable on demand, and a negotiable instrument. Its negotiability is not affected by the fact that it was postdated fifteen years; the time when it is payable is determined by the stated date. § 3–114(1), (2). The indorsement modifies the check by providing for acceleration of the time of payment and for direct payment by the drawer's estate. . . . The acceleration provision is authorized by § 3–109(1)(c). As for direct payment, the drawee bank was not authorized to pay the check more than ten days after the drawer's death, if it knew of the fact of death. § 4–405. Hence presentment to that bank was entirely excused as a futile gesture. § 3–511(2). . . . Thus, the provision for direct payment merely restates the result prescribed by law §§ 3–413(2), 3–507(1)(b). We need not consider the plaintiff's argument that the indorsement is a draft drawn on the drawer, effective as a note under § 3–118(a).

    The principal contentions of the defendant are, first, that the instrument sued on is not a negotiable instrument, and, second, that it is unenforceable for want of consideration or reliance. We hold that the instrument was a negotiable instrument. The plaintiffs, unless they have the rights of a holder in due course, took the instrument subject to the defense of want of consideration. §§ 3–306(c), 3–408. But the signatures were admitted, and in such cases "production of the instrument entitles a holder to recover on it unless the defendant establishes a defense." § 3–307(2). . . . The judge here did not find that the defense of want of consideration had been established, and neither his findings nor the stipulation and evidence compel such a finding. . . .

Braucher, Justice.

Payable to Order or to Bearer [UCC §§ 3-110, 3-111] To be negotiable, commercial paper must contain words that indicate that the original payee may transfer the paper to third parties. Such words are commonly called words of negotiability. Under the UCC, the words "order" and "bearer" are used to denote negotiability. Thus, to be negotiable, an instrument must be made payable to order or to bearer.

An instrument is payable to order if it is payable to the order of a specific person, to the order or assigns of a specific person, to a specific person or his order, or to the order of an unnamed person who is specified in the instrument with reasonable certainty. An example of this last condition is a draft payable to the order of "the mayor" of a particular city; the person is unnamed, but the person's identity is reasonably certain. The instruments in Figures 23-1 through 23-4 are all payable to order.

The term "bearer" means the person in possession of an instrument [UCC § 1-201(5)]. An instrument is payable to bearer if by its terms it is payable to bearer, to the order of bearer, to a specified person or bearer, to cash, or to the order of cash. An instrument is also payable to bearer when it uses any other words that do not purport to designate a specific payee.

On occasion an instrument is made payable "to order or to bearer." Under the UCC, such an instrument is payable to order, unless the bearer words are handwritten or typewritten. The presumption is that if the bearer words are printed, the maker or drawer of the instrument merely forgot to delete them when he inserted the name of the specific payee.

 The words "order" and "bearer" have clearly defined meanings and are intended to indicate that commercial paper is negotiable. An *order instrument* provides more protection than a *bearer instrument*, because the latter can be transferred from one person to another without *indorsement*. Since the rules are so clear in this regard, there is really no excuse for a mistake. Unless there is some compelling reason for not doing so, a drafter of commercial paper that is intended to be negotiable should always use the word "order" or the word "bearer."

The following case illustrates the basic requirement that the negotiability of an instrument must appear on the face of the instrument itself. The case is also noteworthy for its discussion of the reasons underlying this rule. In addition, the case exemplifies a situation in which the obligor successfully argued that the instrument was not negotiable, but still lost the case.

First State Bank
v
Clark
570 P2d 1144 (1977)
New Mexico Supreme Court

FACTS: M. S. Horne executed a $100,000 promissory note payable to R. C. Clark. The note provided that it could not be transferred, pledged, or assigned without Horne's written consent. At the same time Horne gave

Clark a letter authorizing Clark to pledge the note as collateral for a $50,000 loan that Clark intended to obtain from First State Bank. Clark obtained the loan and pledged the note, which was accompanied by Horne's letter of authorization. First State called Horne to verify his agreement to use of the note as collateral. When First State attempted to collect on the note from Horne, Horne refused to pay.

ISSUE: Is the note a negotiable instrument?

RESULT: The note is non-negotiable because the terms of negotiability cannot be discerned from the instrument itself.

REASONING:

*　　*　　*

Article 3 of the U.C.C. defines a certain type of readily transferable instrument and lays down certain rules for the treatment of that instrument and rules concerning the rights, remedies and defenses of persons dealing with it.

In order to be a "negotiable instrument" for Article 3 purposes the paper must precisely meet the definition set out in § 3-104, since § 3-104 itself states that, to be a negotiable instrument, a writing "must" meet the definition therein set out. Moreover, it is clear that in order to determine whether an instrument meets that definition *only the instrument itself* may be looked to, *not* other documents, even when other documents are referred to in the instrument. [Court's emphasis.] . . .

Section 3-104 thus requires that, in order to be a negotiable instrument for Article 3 purposes, one must be able to ascertain without reference to other documents that the instrument:

> (a) [is] signed by the maker or drawer; and (b) contain[s] an unconditional promise or order to pay a sum certain in money and no other promise, order, obligation or power given by the maker or drawer except as authorized by [Article 3]; and (c) [is] payable on demand or at a definite time; and (d) [is] payable to order or to bearer.

The note in question here failed to meet the requirements of § 3-104, since the promise to pay contained in the note was not unconditional. Moreover, the note was expressly drafted to be non-negotiable since it stated:

> This note may not be transferred, pledged, or otherwise assigned without the written consent of M. S. Horne.

These words, even though they appeared on the back of the note, effectively cancelled any implication of negotiability provided by the words "Pay to the order of" on the face of the note. Notations and terms on the back of a note, made contemporaneously with the execution of the note and intended to be part of the note's contract of payment, constitute as much a part of the note as if they were incorporated on its face. . . .

Counsel argue that § 3-119 applies and allows incorporating other documents to remove the defects on the face of the instrument. They argue that Horne's separate letter to Clark authorizing the pledging of the note to First State removed the conditions in the note and the express prohibition therein against its negotiability and rendered the note negotiable for Article 3 purposes. This is incorrect. An instrument which in and of itself does not meet the requirements of § 3-104 cannot be made negotiable for Article 3 purposes by reference to another document which purports to cure the defects in the note's negotiability. . . .

Section 3-119 and the Official Comments thereto go only to clarifying what the effect is of referring to other documents which may affect negotiability where such reference is on the face of *an otherwise negotiable instrument.* [Court's emphasis.] See U.C.C. § 3-119, Official Comment, Purposes. Neither § 3-119 nor any other U.C.C. section applies to allow the use of other documents to correct defects in otherwise *non-negotiable* instruments. [Court's emphasis.]

The whole purpose of the concept of a negotiable instrument under Article 3 is to declare that transferees in the ordinary course of business are only to be held liable for information appearing in the instrument itself and will not be expected to know of any limitations on negotiability or changes in terms, etc., contained in any separate documents. The whole idea of the facilitation of easy transfer of notes and instruments requires that a transferee be able to trust what the instrument says, and be able to determine the validity of the note and its negotiability from the language in the note itself. . . . Section 3-119 in no way implies or states, and neither do any comments thereunder, that an instrument non-negotiable on its face can be cured by reference to a document removing the defect which renders the instrument non-negotiable. . . .

Even though a note or instrument is not a "negotiable instrument" for Article 3 purposes, it may nevertheless be negotiable between the parties involved under ordinary contract law. . . . The Official Comments to § 3-119 which counsel have cited recognize this principle. E.G., U.C.C. § 3-119, Official Comment 3. The comments assert that even where an instrument *is* negotiable for Article 3 purposes the parties in any transaction are always bound by the totality of documents which are intended to form a contract between them, not just the terms set forth in one which happens to be a negotiable instrument. The same is true when the instrument does not meet Article 3 requirements. . . .

As between Clark and Horne, Clark had a contract right to pledge Horne's note to Clark as security. Clark had a contract right to negotiate the note. Thus the note was negotiable for Clark's limited purposes even though it was not an Article 3 negotiable instrument. Before accepting Clark's pledge, First State verified by direct conversation with Horne that Clark had Horne's authority to pledge the note as the letter permitted.

Horne in no way suggested that he had any offsetting defense to the validity of the note. . . .

. . . We have long recognized the possibility of estoppel in appropriate cases. . . . These cases clarify that equitable estoppel results from a course of conduct which precludes one from asserting rights he otherwise might assert against one who has in good faith relied upon such conduct to his detriment.

In the instant case the evidence clearly indicates that First State relied on the validity of Horne's note to Clark as a pledge to secure Clark's obligation to First State. . . . Horne knew he had an offsetting note from Clark which would in effect invalidate or cancel his obligation under the pledged note, but he failed to tell First State the true state of affairs. First State relied in good faith on Horne's conduct—his failure to reveal material facts—to First State's detriment. As a matter of law Horne cannot assert any defenses he has against First State arising from the material facts he failed to reveal. . . . [Since] there is no genuine issue as to any material fact regarding the genuineness of Horne's note and letter, summary judgment for First State against Horne was proper. . . .

Easley, Justice.

23:4 Effect on Negotiability of Omissions or Additional Terms; Ambiguities in Instrument

A note or draft is negotiable if it contains all the basic elements discussed in the preceding section. The omission of customary but nonessential matters does not effect its negotiability. For example, commercial paper often includes statements indicating where it was drafted and where it is payable, but the omission of such statements does not affect negotiability [UCC § 3-112(1)(a)].

The omission of the date generally does not affect negotiability. An undated instrument is not negotiable only when it is payable at a fixed period "after date," since it is neither payable on demand nor at a definite time. It can be made negotiable by insertion of the date [UCC § 3-115]. Antedated or post-dated instruments are also usually negotiable. The time when an antedated or postdated instrument is payable is determined by the stated date if the instrument is payable either on demand or at a fixed period "after date" [UCC § 3-114].

An instrument is obviously incomplete if it fails to state the name of the payee or the amount to be paid. If an instrument is otherwise complete, and if there are blank spaces for the insertion of such omitted items, it may be completed by a person with proper authority. Once completed, the instrument is then negotiable [UCC § 3-115]. For example, a signed but otherwise blank check may be filled in by any person authorized to do so.

The danger involved in signing a blank check cannot be overstated. The possibility always exists that the person to whom the check is given will insert an unauthorized amount and then promptly cash the check. Of course, the drawer (signer) of the check can always assert that he or she did not authorize the person to complete the check. The drawer may not, however, assert such lack of authorization against subsequent holders in due course (see 24:2 for definition of holder in due course). In other words, a holder in due course may enforce the check as completed [UCC § 3-407(3)]. While the drawer may seek recourse against the person who inserted the figure, that person often will be unable to repay the money.

Additional Terms in Instrument   An instrument, to be negotiable, generally may not contain any promise or order other than the promise or order to pay money [UCC § 3-104(1)(b)]. There are certain limited exceptions to this prohibition however. The more important exceptions are (1) a negotiable instrument can contain a provision granting the holder of the instrument the power to sell the collateral securing the obligation in the event of default; (2) a negotiable instrument may include a promise or power to maintain or protect the collateral or to give additional collateral under specified circumstances; and (3) a draft may include a provision stating that the payee's indorsement or cashing of the instrument acknowledges full satisfaction of the drawer's obligation [UCC § 3-112(1)].

Ambiguities in Instrument [UCC § 3-118]   The UCC provides specific rules for the resolution of certain ambiguities. Among the more important rules are the following: (1) when there is doubt as to whether an instrument is a draft or a note, the holder may treat it as either one; (2) in the event of a conflict, handwritten terms control typewritten and printed ones, and typewritten terms control printed ones; and (3) unambiguous words control figures, and figures control ambiguous words.

23:5   Methods of Transferring Commercial Paper

There are two basic methods of transferring commercial paper: (1) *negotiation,* which ordinarily involves indorsement, and (2) assignment. By its very nature a nonnegotiable instrument cannot be negotiated, but it may be assigned. Negotiable instruments can be transferred by either method.

The usual method of transferring negotiable instruments is by negotiation. This involves delivery of the instrument to the transferee, who is the person to whom the instrument is being transferred. The instrument is now negotiated, and the transferee becomes a holder and may qualify for the rights accorded a holder in due course. In this way, the transferee can actually acquire greater rights in the instrument than the transferor had.

A negotiable instrument may also be transferred by assignment. In an assignment, the transferee acquires only those rights that the transferor had. As discussed in Chapter 17, this means that any defense that could have been asserted against the transferor may also be asserted against the transferee.

Although the subject of defenses to negotiable instruments is covered in Chapter 24, an example now may help to illustrate the significance of the distinction between negotiation and assignment.

EXAMPLE: Barnes contracts to purchase a typewriter from McCoy and gives McCoy a promissory note as payment. McCoy never delivers the typewriter. If McCoy were to sue Barnes for payment of the promissory note, Barnes would have a good defense. If McCoy assigned the promissory note to a third party, who then sued Barnes, Barnes would still have a good defense. But if McCoy negotiated the promissory note to a holder in due course, who then sued Barnes for payment, Barnes would *not* have a good defense against that person.

Negotiation is obviously the preferable way to transfer a negotiable instrument.

23:6 Negotiation

Negotiation is the transfer of an instrument in such form that the transferee qualifies as a *holder*. Under the UCC, a "holder" is a person who is in possession of an instrument drawn, issued, or indorsed to him, to his order, to bearer, or in blank [UCC § 1-201(20)]. An instrument payable to order is negotiated by delivery of the instrument with any necessary indorsement, which is the transferor's signature. An instrument payable to bearer is negotiated simply by delivery of the instrument to a holder; no indorsement is required [UCC § 3-202(1)]. As a practical matter, however, the transferee of a bearer instrument often requires that the transferor indorse it. There are important practical reasons for requiring indorsement of a bearer instrument. First, indorsement is a means of identification of the transferor. Second, indorsement under some circumstances obligates the indorser to pay the instrument if it is subsequently dishonored. (These circumstances are considered at length in Chapter 25.)

To allow an effective negotiation, an indorsement must be written on the instrument itself or on a paper so firmly affixed to the instrument that it becomes a part of the instrument. This paper is called an *allonge*. The indorsement must also convey the entire instrument. An indorsement that attempts to convey a portion of the instrument operates only as a partial assignment; the transferee does not become a holder [UCC § 3-202(2), (3)].

Instruments Containing Incorrect Name [UCC § 3-203]   If an instrument is made payable to a person under a misspelled name or under a name other than his own, he may indorse it in the incorrect name, in his own name, or in both names. The preferable procedure is to sign both names, and any person paying or giving value for the instrument may require indorsement in both names.

Multiple Payees [UCC § 3-116]   Checks and other negotiable instruments are often made payable to more than one person. If an instrument is made payable to A *or* B, it can be negotiated by either payee; only one payee's indorsement is necessary. If an instrument is made payable to A *and* B, it can be negotiated by both parties; both payees' indorsements are required. An instrument made payable to A *and/or* B is treated as the equivalent of A *or* B.

Transfer of Order Instrument Without Indorsement   As noted earlier, negotiation of an order instrument normally requires indorsement. An attempted negotiation of an order instrument without indorsement is ineffective, and the transferee does not qualify as a holder. However, if the transferee has given value for the instrument, he has the right, enforceable by an action for specific performance, to have the unqualified indorsement of the transferor [UCC § 3-201(3)].

When a customer has deposited an instrument with a bank but neglected to indorse it, the bank may supply the customer's indorsement. The bank may also place a notation on the instrument that it was deposited by the customer or credited to his account. This notation is effective as the customer's indorsement. However, if the instrument contains words such as "payee's indorsement required," the bank may not supply a missing indorsement [UCC § 4-205(1)].

Rescission of Negotiation [UCC § 3-207]   Negotiation of a negotiable instrument may be rescinded on much the same grounds as those on which a contract generally may be rescinded. Thus, negotiation may be rescinded on the grounds of infancy or other incapacity, fraud, duress, mistake, or illegality. However, a negotiation may not be rescinded if the instrument has subsequently been transferred to a holder in due course. As a practical matter, therefore, the right of rescission is of little real value.

23:7   Types of Indorsements

There are four basic kinds of indorsement: (1) special, (2) blank, (3) restrictive, and (4) qualified. Each type of indorsement has the effect of transferring title to the instrument. Each type also has the effect of creating certain warranties. And, with the exception of qualified indorsements, each type has the effect of guaranteeing payment under certain circumstances.

The choice of indorsement has important consequences. Use of a particular type of indorsement may transform an order instrument into a bearer one, and vice versa. The indorsement may condition the right of the indorsee (person to whom the instrument is negotiated) to receive payment on the instrument. Also, the type of indorsement used always determines the method in which the indorse may further negotiate the instrument. The various kinds of indorsements will now be considered in detail.

Special Indorsements [UCC § 3-204(1)]   A special indorsement specifies the person to whom or to whose order it makes the instrument payable. For example, "Pay to Jack Levy," followed by the indorser's signature, is a special indorsement. Further negotiation of the instrument therefore requires the indorsement of the special indorsee. A special indorsement thus has the effect of maintaining the order character of the instrument. If the instrument was originally a bearer instrument, a special indorsement transforms it into an order instrument.

Unlike the instrument itself, indorsements need not have words of negotiability. "Pay to Jack Levy" has the same effect as "pay to the order of Jack Levy." In either case, the instrument can be negotiated further only with the indorsement of Jack Levy.

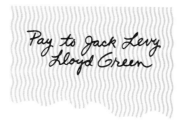

FIGURE 23-5 Special Indorsement

Blank Indorsements [UCC § 3-204(2), (3)] A blank indorsement is one that specifies no particular indorsee. A blank indorsement of an order instrument has the effect of transforming it into a bearer instrument. A bearer instrument that is indorsed in blank remains a bearer instrument. The effect in either case is the same: The instrument may thereafter be negotiated by delivery without indorsement by any person who has possession of it. For example, a check made payable to the order of Lloyd Green is an order instrument. If Lloyd Green simply signs his name on the back, his signature is a blank indorsement. The check becomes a bearer instrument; no additional indorsement is needed to negotiate the check again.

FIGURE 23-6 Blank Indorsement

 A negotiable instrument with a blank indorsement is as easily transferred as cash. Blank indorsements should therefore be used with extreme caution. When one is making a bank deposit, for example, a check should be indorsed in blank only in the teller's presence. Under no circumstances should a check intended for deposit be indorsed in blank prior to

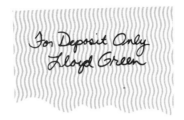

FIGURE 23-7   Restrictive Indorsement: For Deposit

entering the bank, unless the words "for deposit only" are included in the indorsement. For example, if a payee writes a blank indorsement on a check and goes to the bank to deposit it, but the check is blown out of her hand and found by someone else, the finder can then cash the check.

The holder of an instrument may convert a blank indorsement into a special indorsement by writing the name of a new payee over the signature of the indorser in blank. This has the effect of making the instrument an order instrument. For example, if a check payable to Jane Roe is indorsed "Jane Roe" and delivered to John Doe, it has been transformed from an order instrument to a bearer one. John Doe may reconvert it into an order instrument by writing "pay to John Doe" above Jane Roe's signature.

Restrictive Indorsements [UCC §§ 3-205, 3-206]   A restrictive indorsement is one that in some way limits the purpose of the indorsement. It may limit the use that the indorsee may make of the instrument or it may specify the circumstances under which the indorsee is entitled to payment. The UCC recognizes four different kinds of restrictive indorsements: (1) indorsements "for deposit" or "for collection," (2) conditional indorsements, (3) indorsements for the benefit or use of the indorser or another, and (4) indorsements prohibiting further transfer.

Indorsements "for deposit" or "for collection" are by far the most common restrictive indorsements. "For deposit" indorsements are commonly used when depositing checks in bank accounts. They have the effect of ensuring that the funds from the instrument will be used as directed, that is, credited to the indorser's account. An indorsement "for collection" is similar; it directs the indorsee (usually a bank) to collect on the instrument for the indorser. "Pay any bank" is a form of indorsement used by banks in the collection process and has the same effect as a "for collection" indorsement.

A conditional indorsement is simply an indorsement that conditions the order to pay on the occurrence of some act or event. Conditional indorsements are used in situations in which the indorser negotiates the instrument to the indorsee as payment for some act to be performed by the indorsee. If the indorsee fails to perform that act, then he has no right to recover on the instrument. Recall that the instrument itself may not make the obligation to pay conditional; if it does, the instrument is not negotiable. An indorser,

FIGURE 23-8   Restrictive Indorsement: For Collection

FIGURE 23-9   Conditional Indorsement

FIGURE 23-10   Trust Indorsement

however, may condition the obligation to pay without affecting the instrument's negotiability.

Indorsements for the benefit or use of the indorser or another are commonly known as trust or agency indorsements. As the name implies, these indorsements are used where an instrument is negotiated to one person, but is intended for the use of another person. For example, a check might be indorsed to a guardian for the use of his ward. In a trust indorsement, the transferee must apply the funds as directed by the indorsement. Any subsequent transferees of the instrument need not do so, unless they have knowledge that the original transferee in some way breached the restrictive indorsement.

An indorsement that prohibits further transfer of the instrument really imposes no restriction at all, because the attempted limitation on further negotiation is given no effect. An indorsement "pay to John Doe only" is treated as the equivalent of the indorsement "pay to John Doe."

The various kinds of restrictive indorsements have certain common consequences. First, a restrictive indorsement cannot prevent further negotiation of the instrument. Second, with some exceptions noted later, the indorsee and any subsequent transferee must apply any funds paid for the instrument to the purpose or in accordance with the condition stated in the indorsement. Third, if the indorsee and any subsequent transferees do abide by the terms of the restrictive indorsement, they may qualify as holders or holders in due course of the instrument.

Banks handle negotiable instruments, especially checks, in large numbers, and it is impractical for them to check the effect of all restrictive indorsements. In recognition of that fact, the UCC sets out special rules governing banks' handling of restrictively indorsed instruments. A bank may disregard any restrictive indorsement except that of the bank's immediate transferor. As a practical matter, this means that a "for deposit only" indorsement needs to be honored only by the bank in which the check is deposited. Other banks involved in the process of collecting on the check need not honor the restrictive indorsement.

Qualified Indorsements [UCC § 3-414(1)]   A qualified indorsement is one that contains the words "without recourse." The effect of this indorsement is that the indorser is not liable for payment of the instrument in the event that the party primarily responsible for it defaults. A qualified indorsement is used when the indorser wants to transfer a check to the indorsee, but does not want to guarantee that there are sufficient funds in the drawer's account to pay the check. For example, if an attorney receives a child-support check from one parent to be forwarded to the other parent, who is the attorney's client, the attorney may make a qualified indorsement of the check to the client. If the check is ultimately dishonored by the bank, the client of course may seek recourse against the other parent, but the attorney cannot be held liable on the check.

Key Concepts and Terms

- Commercial paper is paper that represents cash value in commercial transactions. It is used as a substitute for money and as a credit device. Examples of commercial paper are orders to pay money (drafts and checks) and promises to pay money (notes and certificates of deposit). Commercial paper may be either negotiable or nonnegotiable, but only negotiable instruments are easily transferable.
- An order is a direction to pay. A promise is a definite undertaking to pay.
- A draft is a written order by one person (the drawer) directing another person (the drawee) to pay money to a third person (the payee). Bank drafts and trade acceptances are examples of commonly used drafts.
- A check is a specific form of draft. It is always drawn on a bank and is always payable on demand.
- A note, also known as a promissory note, is an unconditional promise by one party (the maker) to pay money to a second party (the payee). Real

estate mortgage notes, installment notes, and collateral notes are examples of commonly used notes.

- A certificate of deposit is a specific type of note. It is an acknowledgment by a bank of the receipt of money, with the bank's promise to repay the money.

- To be negotiable, an instrument must (1) be in writing and signed by the maker or drawer, (2) contain an unconditional promise or order to pay a sum certain in money, (3) be payable on demand or at a definite time, and (4) be payable to order or to bearer.

- Omission of customary but nonessential terms does not affect the negotiability of an instrument. Under some circumstances, an incomplete instrument may be completed, after which it becomes negotiable.

- Commercial paper may be transferred by negotiation and by assignment. Negotiation is the usual and preferable method. Negotiation is the transfer of an instrument in such form that the transferee qualifies as a holder. An order instrument is negotiated by delivery of the instrument with any necessary indorsement. A bearer instrument is negotiated by delivery alone.

- An indorsement is the signing over of an instrument. There are four basic kinds of indorsement: (1) special, (2) blank, (3) restrictive, and (4) qualified.

- A special indorsement specifies the person to whom or to whose order it makes the instrument payable. A specially indorsed instrument remains or becomes an order instrument.

- A blank indorsement is one that specifies no particular indorsee. An instrument indorsed in blank remains or becomes a bearer instrument. A blank indorsement may be converted into a special indorsement by writing the name of a new payee over the blank indorsement.

- A restrictive indorsement is one that in some way limits the purpose of the indorsement. There are four different kinds of restrictive indorsements: (1) indorsements "for collection" or "for deposit," (2) conditional indorsements, (3) indorsements for the benefit or use of the indorser or another, and (4) indorsements prohibiting further transfer.

- A qualified indorsement is one that contains the words "without recourse." This indorsement relieves the indorser from any liability for payment of the instrument in the event of default.

- Acceptor
- Bearer Instrument
- Certificate of Deposit
- Check
- Demand (Sight) Instrument
- Draft (Bill of Exchange)
- Drawee
- Drawer
- Holder
- Indorsement
- Maker
- Negotiation
- Note (Promissory Note)
- Order Instrument
- Payee
- Sum Certain
- Time Instrument
- Trade Acceptance

Questions and Case Problems

1. In connection with a divorce proceeding, Kathy and Joel Fox enter a property settlement agreement that calls for Kathy to pay Joel $100,000. Kathy executes an installment note promising to pay Joel "$100,000, at the rate of $5,000 per month, in accordance with the property settlement entered into by the parties, the terms of which settlement are incorporated herein by reference." Joel promptly writes the following on the back of the note: "I hereby authorize Carl Ross, my attorney, to make all collections on this note, and I assign a one-third interest in this note to Carl Ross. /s/ Joel Fox." Is the installment note a negotiable instrument? Does Joel's writing constitute an indorsement? If so, what kind?

2. Pylant issued a check to Brannon. On the face of the check appear the following words: "For $10,000.00 Distressed Mdse to be totalled 4/17/83." Pylant asserts that this notation was made to acknowledge an understanding between Pylant and Brannon that the check was not to be negotiated by Brannon until Brannon had removed certain merchandise from Pylant's warehouse. Does the notation on the check, together with the extrinsic agreement, make the check nonnegotiable?

3. Berger writes out a check to "cash" and delivers it to Macias. Macias signs the check on the reverse side and gives it to Deborah Bonds. Bonds writes "Pay to Deborah Bonds" above Macias' name, then signs her name below that of Macias and gives the check to Aiso. Aiso loses the check, and Art Rubin finds it. Rubin writes, on a separate piece of paper, "For deposit only to account of Art Rubin. /s/ A. Rubin," and staples the paper to the check. Describe the effect of these various transactions.

4. Leroux signs the following document:

   May 3, 1979

   To whom it may concern:

   I have this day borrowed $5,000 from: Helen Keyes $5,000 to be paid on demand.

   Is the document a negotiable instrument?

5. Thomas gave Dozier a $20,000 promissory note. The note, when delivered, provided for "interest at the annual rate of _____ percent." The note also provided for payment of "attorney's fees of $_____ in the event of default." The parties orally agreed that Dozier could use the note as collateral for a bank loan and could enter the rate of interest charged by the bank as the rate of interest on the note. Dozier obtained a loan from State Bank at an annual rate of interest of 12 percent. She then wrote "12" in the blank space provided for interest in the note. The blank space provided for attorney's fees was never completed. Is the note a negotiable instrument?

6. Kelly contracts to purchase some wheat from Bonnelli, with delivery to be made within three months. Kelly wishes to pay by means of a negotiable instrument. He wants to deliver the negotiable instrument to Bonnelli now, but wants it to become payable only at the time when actual delivery of the wheat is made. What options are available to Kelly?

7. Knight writes a check naming Wolfe as payee. Wolfe indorses the check "without recourse" and delivers it to Sims, who pays Wolfe cash. The check is subsequently dishonored by the bank. Sims demands her money back from Wolfe. Must Wolfe repay the money? What if Wolfe and Sims had orally agreed that Wolfe would repay the money in the event of dishonor?

8. A cashier's check is an instrument drawn by a bank on itself, whereby the bank also accepts a primary obligation to pay. The purchaser of the cashier's check normally negotiates the check to a third party. Is this kind of instrument more like a note or a draft?

9. What is a *trade acceptance?* Illustrate the use of this instrument.

10. Lawyers often refer to a lawsuit to enforce payment of a negotiable instrument as a suit "on the instrument" or "on the check." What concept is embodied in this expression?

24 Holder in Due Course

24:1 Introduction

The holder in due course doctrine is an essential part of the law of negotiable instruments. Under the doctrine, a transferee of an instrument who qualifies as a *holder in due course (HDC)* takes the instrument free of most traditional contract defenses. The doctrine facilitates orderly commercial transactions. Its purpose and importance are best illustrated by applying it to a fact situation.

EXAMPLE: Martin contracts to sell a load of plywood to Lucy. Lucy pays Martin with a promissory note on which Lucy is the maker and Martin is the payee. Martin never delivers the plywood, but he still demands that Lucy pay the promissory note. Obviously, Lucy need not do so. If Martin sues her, she has a valid defense based on Martin's breach of the underlying contract. Assume, however, that Martin has sold the note to Nicole, who thereby acquires the status of an HDC. Nicole can demand that Lucy pay the note, even if Martin has not delivered the plywood. Lucy cannot assert Martin's breach of contract as a defense against an HDC.

From the example, it can be seen that the holder in due course doctrine facilitates the transfer of negotiable instruments. A transferee of a negotiable instrument wants to be assured of payment, regardless of any disputes between the obligor and the original payee. The holder in due course doctrine, by limiting the defenses that can be raised against an HDC, effectively assures the HDC's right to payment. The position of an HDC can be contrasted with that of an assignee under ordinary contract law. An assignee has no greater rights than the assignor had. Any defenses that could be raised against the assignor can also be raised against the assignee. By contrast, an HDC *does* acquire greater rights than the transferor had. Certain defenses that can be raised against the transferor cannot be raised against the HDC.

Commercial paper is used widely in commercial transactions. A negotiable instrument often changes hands several times before it is ultimately paid. For example, a farmer may wish to purchase supplies on credit, to be paid for several months later out of the proceeds of the season's crop. The retailer selling the supplies may be unable to extend credit for that long. To solve the problem, a trade acceptance (discussed in Chapter 23) or a note may be used. The farmer, by accepting the trade acceptance or executing the note, becomes obligated to make payment to the retailer several months in the future. However, neither party expects payment to be made to the retailer. Both parties expect that the retailer will sell the instrument to a third party, such as a bank or other lending institution. Typically, this third party purchases the instrument from the retailer at a discount; that is, the third party pays the retailer an amount less than the amount payable on maturity. In the same manner, the purchaser of this instrument may also purchase other instruments at a discount from other parties. Naturally, the purchaser of these instruments expects to be paid when they are due, and does not want to become embroiled in controversies between the original parties to the various instruments it has purchased. The HDC doctrine in most cases permits the purchaser to do exactly what all parties intended: to collect on the instrument when due, regardless of any breakdown in the relationship between the original parties to the instrument.

Classes of Holders   Under the UCC, there are three classes of holders of negotiable instruments: (1) simple holders, (2) holders for value, and (3) holders in due course. A simple holder is a person who possesses a negotiable instrument drawn, issued, or indorsed to him, to his order, to bearer, or in blank. In other words, a simple holder is one who has possession and good title to the instrument. A holder for value is, as the name implies, one who has given value for the instrument. What constitutes *value* is discussed later in this chapter. A holder in due course is one who has given value *and* who meets the other requirements for HDC status; all of these requirements are discussed later. Only an HDC is accorded special protection under the UCC. Other holders take the instrument subject to any defenses that could be asserted by the drawer or maker of the instrument[1] against the initial payee.

Because many legal disputes have arisen as to whether a particular person qualifies as an HDC, the bulk of this chapter is devoted to a discussion of the requirements for HDC status. Consideration will also be given to the rights acquired by an HDC.

Consumer Credit Transactions   The holder in due course doctrine is generally inapplicable to consumer credit transactions as a result of state and federal rules. These rules are discussed at the end of this chapter. For present purposes, simply bear in mind that the holder in due course doctrine applies primarily to commercial transactions not involving consumers.

---

[1] The term "drawer" refers to one who draws a check or other draft. A "maker" is one who signs a note as the party primarily liable on it. The term "obligor" refers to the party who must actually pay an instrument. Therefore, the maker of a promissory note is an obligor. However, the drawee is ordinarily the obligor on a check or other draft, rather than the drawer. This is so because after the instrument has been drawn and accepted, it is the drawee who is primarily liable on it.

24:2 Requirements for Holder in Due Course Status

A holder must meet each of the following requirements to qualify for the status and protections accorded to a holder in due course: He must take the instrument (1) for value, (2) in *good faith*, (3) without notice that it is overdue or has been dishonored, and (4) without notice of any defense against or claim to it [UCC § 3-302(1)]. These requirements, which will be considered in detail in the following sections, have been the subject of much litigation.

A holder's status as an HDC is determined either at the time the instrument is negotiated to him or at the time he gives value for it, whichever occurs later. Once a holder qualifies as an HDC he remains an HDC, even though he later acquires knowledge of some defense or claim or learns that the instrument is overdue or has been dishonored.

EXAMPLE: Adam Attorney purchased a word processing system from Computers Incorporated and executed a promissory note payable to Computers Incorporated as payment. Computers Incorporated in turn negotiated the promissory note to Office Financiers, which has not yet given value for the note. Adam Attorney later rescinds the purchase contract on the ground that the word processing system is defective. If Office Financiers learns of Adam's repudiation before giving value, Office Financiers can no longer qualify as an HDC because it learned of a defense to the note prior to giving value. It is not enough that Office Financiers had agreed to give Computers Incorporated value for the note before learning of the defense; the value must actually have been given. If, on the other hand, Office Financiers gives value before receiving any notice of Adam's rescission of the contract, Office Financiers does qualify as an HDC.

Holder Through Holder in Due Course   Under some circumstances the holder of an instrument may obtain the rights accorded to an HDC without meeting the requirements for HDC status. A provision of UCC Article 3 known as the "shelter provision" provides that the transferee of an instrument acquires the rights the transferor had in the instrument [UCC § 3-201(1)]. Therefore, if the transferor is an HDC, the transferee automatically acquires the rights of an HDC. For example, if an HDC of a promissory note gives the note to another person, that person is not an HDC, since she did not give value for the note. The person does, however, have the rights of an HDC because the transferor had such rights. Through this transfer, the transferee becomes what is known as a *holder through holder in due course*. The rights of an HDC may be transferred in succession this way. That is, a holder through holder in due course can in turn make a transfer to another person, and that person will acquire the rights of an HDC.

There are two situations to which the shelter provision does not apply. It does not apply to a transferee (1) who was a prior holder and, while a holder, had notice of a defense or claim against the instrument; or (2) who was a party to any fraud or illegality affecting the instrument. These exceptions are designed to prevent a holder from improving his position by first transferring the instrument to an HDC and then reacquiring the instrument.

EXAMPLE: Machine Corporation contracts to sell machinery to Factory Company, with delivery to be made in 30 days. Unknown to Factory Company, Machine Corporation has no intention of delivering the machinery. Factory Company executes a promissory note payable in 45 days as payment. Machine Corporation sells the note at a discount to an HDC, then later repurchases the note from the HDC. Although Machine Corporation's transferor was an HDC, Machine Corporation does not acquire the rights of an HDC, since Machine Corporation was a party to a fraud affecting the instrument.

Payee as Holder in Due Course [UCC § 3-302(2)] Prior to the UCC, the courts disagreed as to whether the original payee of a negotiable instrument could be an HDC. The UCC specifically provides that a payee can be an HDC. This rule is of limited practical importance because (1) if the drawer or maker of an instrument has some defense against enforcement of the instrument, the payee will almost always have notice of that defense and thus will not qualify as an HDC; and (2) if the obligor has no defense against the instrument, the payee will ordinarily be entitled to recover on it whether he is an HDC or not. In some circumstances, however, the original payee may take the instrument without knowing that a defense or claim exists. It is in this situation that the payee's HDC status is important. To illustrate, assume that Aaron defrauds Michael into signing a check payable to Peter. Peter, in good faith and without notice, pays Aaron for the check. In such a situation Peter, the payee, would qualify as an HDC, even though Michael had a good defense against Aaron.

24:3 Value

A holder in due course must give value in exchange for the instrument. A holder has given value if (1) the act (payment or other performance) that constitutes the consideration has been performed, (2) the holder has acquired a security interest in or a lien on the instrument (other than by legal process), (3) the holder has taken the instrument in payment of or as security for a prior debt, (4) the holder has given a negotiable instrument for the instrument taken, or (5) the holder has made an irrevocable commitment to a third person [UCC § 3-303].

The important thing to remember about the value requirement is that the value must actually have been given. Value is thus quite distinct from consideration. A promise to perform some act may constitute consideration for the negotiation of a negotiable instrument, but it does not constitute value for purposes of qualifying as an HDC. Value has been given only when the promised action is actually taken.

EXAMPLE: Berk negotiates a promissory note to Fowler in exchange for Fowler's promise to rewire Berk's house. Fowler never rewires the house. Fowler's promise to rewire constitutes consideration. However, he has not given value because he did not rewire the house.

The rationale for the value requirement is that the holder who has not given value may avoid any loss by simply rescinding the contract. In the above example, Fowler may simply rescind the contract and not rewire the house.

Partial Performance of Consideration Where a holder has only partially performed the agreed consideration, he has given value only to the extent of his performance. For example, Duran promises to pay $5,000 for a note, with the money to be paid in five equal monthly installments. After making two payments, Duran learns of a defense against the instrument. Duran has given value for 40 percent of the note. Therefore, she may qualify as an HDC of a 40 percent interest but cannot qualify as an HDC with respect to the remaining 60 percent.

Prior Debt as Value A holder takes for value when he takes the instrument as payment of or security for a prior debt. For example, if A extends credit to B, and B later transfers a promissory note to A in payment of the debt, A has taken the note for value. This is so even if the debt is not yet due and even if the debt is that of a third person. For example, if B gives A a promissory note as security for C's debt to A, then A takes the instrument for value.

Bank Deposits [UCC §§ 4-208, 4-209] A bank may qualify as an HDC on the basis of a bank deposit if the bank has given value for the deposit. This rule can be clarified by the following situation. When a customer of one bank deposits a check drawn on another bank, the customer's bank, which is the depositary bank, commonly credits the customer's account and places the check in the collection process. The check ultimately reaches the drawee bank and, in most cases, is paid. If the drawee bank finds that the check is not payable for some reason—such as the drawer's having insufficient funds in her account or having issued a stop payment order—the bank will not pay the check. Rather, it will send the check back to the depositary bank. The question then arises as to whether the depositary bank qualifies as an HDC and is entitled to insist on payment.

Under the UCC, if the depositary bank's customer has withdrawn the funds represented by the check, the bank qualifies as an HDC (assuming it meets the other HDC requirements). It has given value for the deposit. However, the mere crediting of a customer's account does not constitute the giving of value. If the check is dishonored, the bank can always debit the customer's account, therefore sustaining no loss.

EXAMPLE: Green maintains an account in State Bank. On June 1 the balance is $500. On June 2 Green deposits a check for $400 drawn on County Bank, increasing his balance to $900. On June 3 Green withdraws $425 from his account, lowering his balance to $475. On June 4 State Bank is notified that there are insufficient funds in the drawer's County Bank account to pay the $400 check. State Bank has not given value on that check. Since Green still has $475 in his account, the bank can debit his account for the $400 represented by the County Bank check, and it loses nothing in the transaction.

To determine whether funds have been withdrawn, the principle of first-in, first-out (FIFO) is applied. Under this rule, it is presumed that money is withdrawn from an account in the same order in which it is deposited. Note that the bank may be a holder through an HDC if the depositor was an HDC.

24:4 Good Faith

The requirement of good faith that permeates the UCC has been discussed in previous chapters. To qualify as an HDC, a holder of an instrument must meet the same basic test of honesty. The good-faith requirement is a subjective one in that it focuses on the holder's actual state of mind. The fact that a reasonable person might have been suspicious under similar circumstances does not prevent a finding of good faith if the holder in fact was not suspicious. The determination of good faith always depends on the particular facts and circumstances in a given case.

Although good faith is a separate requirement for HDC status, the courts usually consider good faith in connection with claims that the holder had knowledge or notice of some defense to or defect in the instrument. If a holder had notice of a defense, it will generally be found that he acted in bad faith.

The following case analyzes the good-faith requirement in a context in which a payee is found to be a holder in due course.

<hr>

Taves

v

Griebel

363 NW2d 73 (1985)

Court of Appeals of Minnesota

FACTS: Ryan owed Taves $18,500. In partial payment of the debt, Ryan delivered three checks to Taves as payee. Two checks, each for $1,500, were delivered in October of 1981, and one, for $10,000, was delivered in November of 1982. The checks were drawn by Griebel, a business associate of Ryan, on account of Rex International, Inc. Griebel had delivered the checks to Ryan without having filled in the payee or the amount, but with instructions to Ryan to pay the salary for a Rex employee and to pay rent on some farmland. Griebel stopped payment on all three checks. After the $10,000 check did not clear in 1982, Taves called Ryan and learned of the circumstances of the checks. Taves then sued Griebel on the checks.

ISSUE: Was Taves a holder in due course of the checks?

RESULT: Yes. Taves took the checks in good faith and without notice that Ryan was not authorized to make him the payee.

REASONING:

*   *   *

A holder in due course (HDC) takes an instrument:

    (a) for value; and
    (b) in good faith; and
    (c) without notice that it is overdue or has been dishonored or of any defense against or claim to it on the part of any person.

Minn.Stat. § 336.3–302(1) (1982). It is conceded that Taves took the checks for value. Griebel contends that Taves does not meet the latter two conditions of HDC status.

Good Faith

"Good faith" is a subjective rather than an objective determination. Minn. Stat. § 336.1–201(19) (Uniform Commercial Code Comment). The issue is honesty of intent rather than diligence or negligence.

> Some term it the 'white heart, empty head' test. It is not sufficient that there be circumstances or suspicions such as would put a careful purchaser upon inquiry. We have traditionally held that subjective good faith is simply 'the honest belief that [your] conduct is rightful.' [Citations omitted] . . .

Griebel claims that Taves lacked honesty of intent because he accepted checks drawn on corporate accounts in payment of his loans and because the second two checks were accepted following a stop payment order by the same drawer. These facts do not impugn Taves' good faith.

Taves never learned of Ryan's dishonesty until after speaking with Griebel. The evidence clearly showed that he blindly trusted Ryan. While the loans were outstanding, Taves conducted other business with Ryan on the assumption that he would eventually be repaid. Ryan told Taves that the loans were for the Rex hotel and for a farming project; Taves was not dishonest in accepting repayment from those corporate sources. He believed that he acted properly. His conduct was consistent with his testimony. There are no facts from which to infer that Taves lacked good faith.

Notice

A person has notice of a fact when:

    (a) he has actual knowledge of it; or
    (b) he has received a notice or notification of it; or
    (c) from all the facts and circumstances known to him at the time in question he has reason to know that it exists.

Minn.Stat. § 336.1–201(25) (1982). There was no actual or communicated notice to Taves that Ryan was not authorized to make him payee. Griebel contends that the first stop payment order, standing alone, gives notice that something was amiss. Failure to inquire why payment is stopped may be negligence and lack of diligence, but it is not "notice" of what he might discover. . . . Since the law does not impose a duty on the holder to discover why a check has been dishonored, a failure to inquire may not be construed as notice.

Griebel also claims that the third-party check itself was notice to Taves; that Taves should have contacted Ryan upon receipt of the check and made a full inquiry as to the agreements or understandings between Ryan and Griebel and the two corporations, and that Taves had no right to assume that Ryan was acting properly. This precise matter was taken up by *Eldon's.* In that case, attorney Drexler was not authorized to make a personal stock purchase from Merrill Lynch with a check drawn on Eldon's. The court explained:

> The fact that Merrill Lynch was the named payee on the check drawn by Eldon's did not in and of itself constitute 'notice' that Drexler was using the check improperly. Significantly, there were no other identification or designation marks on the check to indicate or give notice that it was drawn in payment for stock for Eldon's. . . . Merrill Lynch was entitled to conclude that Drexler, known to be an attorney, had lawfully obtained and was delivering the instrument to discharge the debt incurred by his own stock purchase. Merrill Lynch was not required to surmise that the check, rather than being a payment for Drexler's legal services, was being misused.

. . . In the present case, Griebel entrusted checks payable in blank to Ryan without imposing any limitations on check faces whatsoever. Taves had been conducting business with Ryan under the assumption that he was honest. Nothing suggested to Taves that the checks were misused. . . .

Courts are often confronted with the obligation of applying rules to determine which of two relatively innocent persons must suffer a loss due to misconduct of a third person. The instant case is such a situation. The Minnesota cases dealing with situations such as the one at bar have indicated that the loss must fall on the drawer rather than upon the payee (or other holder) because it was the drawer who created the situation and opportunity for defalcation by its agents. . . .

Taves took the checks in good faith. He was not on notice that the checks were misused. Griebel continued to give checks payable in blank to Ryan after he became aware that Ryan was misusing them. Taves was a holder in due course. . . .

Wozniak, Judge.

24:5 Lack of Notice That Instrument Is Overdue or Dishonored

Another qualification for HDC status is that the holder must take the instrument without notice that it is overdue or has been dishonored. Under the UCC, a person has notice not only when he has actual knowledge or notice, but also when the facts and circumstances known to him give him reason to know [UCC § 1-201(25)]. In other words, the issue of whether a holder has notice is determined by an objective standard (what a reasonable person would know under the circumstances), rather than a subjective standard (what the holder actually knew). Problems arise often concerning the holder's duty to determine whether an instrument has been dishonored. The following case analyzes the rationale for not placing a burden on the holder to make such a determination.

Money Mart Check Cashing Center, Inc.

v

Epicycle Corp.
667 P2d 1372 (1983)
Supreme Court of Colorado

FACTS: Money Mart cashes payroll and government checks for a fee. Epicycle issued a payroll check to an employee, then ordered a stop payment on the check when it realized the check had been issued in error. Meanwhile, Money Mart cashed the check for the payee/employee. Money Mart deposited the check, sending it through normal banking channels. The check was returned marked "Payment Stopped." Money Mart sued Epicycle on the check.

ISSUE: Did Money Mart have "notice" of the fact that payment had been stopped on the check or that the payee had obtained the check improperly?

RESULT: No. Money Mart lacked such notice and is a holder in due course.

REASONING:

*   *   *

. . . A person has "notice" of a fact when:

"(a) He has actual knowledge of it; or
(b) He has received a notice or notification of it; or

(c) From all the facts and circumstances known to him at the time in question he has reason to know that it exists."

[UCC] Section 4–1–201(25). . . . As can be seen, tests other than "actual knowledge" may be used in determining whether a person is a holder in due course. . . . There is no allegation that Money Mart had received notification of the defenses, so we must now determine whether Money Mart had "reason to know" of them.

The County Court referee found that Money Mart had no reason to know of the defenses because there was nothing inherently suspicious in the transaction and Money Mart had no duty to inquire about any possible defenses or ensure that the check was good. The Superior Court held that Money Mart's failure to inquire about the validity of the check constituted negligence. However, there is nothing in the Uniform Commercial Code and nothing in the record to support such a conclusion.

A determination of whether a holder has "reason to know" is based upon "all the facts and circumstances known to him." A person "knows" of a fact when he has "actual knowledge" of it. [UCC] Section 4–1–201(25)(c). The question therefore is whether Money Mart had actual knowledge of facts giving it reason to know that a defense existed. There is nothing to distinguish the facts of this case from any other of the thousands of checks that Money Mart and others cash each year: A man came to Money Mart to cash his paycheck; Money Mart is in the business of cashing paychecks; the face of the check disclosed nothing to raise even a suspicion that there was something wrong with it.

It has often been held that where an instrument is regular on its face there is no duty to inquire as to possible defenses unless the circumstances of which the holder has knowledge are of such a nature that failure to inquire reveals a deliberate desire to evade knowledge because of a fear that investigation would disclose the existence of a defense. . . . There is nothing in using a check-cashing service instead of a bank that would lead to a rule imposing different standards on the two kinds of institutions. . . .

Rovira, Justice.

Under the UCC, a holder has notice that an instrument is overdue if at the time he purchases it or otherwise acquires it he has reason to know (1) that any part of the principal amount is overdue, (2) that there is an uncured default in payment of another instrument of the same series, (3) that acceleration of the instrument has been made, (4) that he is taking a demand instrument after demand has been made, or (5) that he is taking a demand instrument more than a reasonable length of time after its issue [UCC § 3-304(3)].

The notice provided by some of the above circumstances is largely self-explanatory. If an instrument is payable on May 31, and a holder purchases it on June 1; she clearly has notice that the instrument is overdue. If an instrument is payable in installments, the fact of default on a prior installment should also put a prospective purchaser on notice that the instrument is overdue. It should be noted, however, that knowledge of a default in the payment of interest does not constitute notice that an instrument is overdue, since such defaults are fairly common and are often tolerated in commercial transactions [UCC § 3-304(4)(f)].

Unlike time instruments, a demand instrument has no stated time for payment. For this reason it is often more difficult to determine whether a purchaser had notice that a demand instrument was overdue. If a purchaser knows that payment has been demanded but has not been made, he has notice. In other situations, it is presumed that a demand instrument is overdue after a reasonable amount of time has passed. With respect to checks, a reasonable time is presumed to be 30 days. With other instruments, the determination of a reasonable time depends on the nature of the instrument, the usage of the trade or business, and the facts of the particular situation.

 If a prospective purchaser has any doubt as to whether a demand instrument is overdue, the prudent course of action is to investigate the matter before making the purchase. In this regard, it is often possible for the prospective purchaser to contact the obligor on the instrument and clarify any doubts that may exist.

24:6 Lack of Notice of Defense or Claim

A holder must take the instrument without notice of any defense against or claim to the instrument to qualify as an HDC. A defense exists if the maker or drawer of the instrument has a valid reason for refusing to pay the initial payee. A claim exists if a third party asserts ownership of the instrument. An objective standard is used in determining whether the holder had notice, although the subjective element of good faith also figures prominently.

The UCC lists several factors that either do or do not constitute notice [UCC § 3-304]. Sometimes the notice appears from the instrument itself. For example, if the amount payable has obviously been altered, a prospective purchaser should be suspicious and is put on notice that a defense probably exists. In other cases knowledge of the underlying transaction may put the purchaser on notice. For example, if the purchaser of an instrument knows that the original payee has breached his contract with the obligor, the purchaser has notice. Regardless of the nature of the notice provided, the basic issue remains the same: In light of all the facts and circumstances known to the holder at the time of purchase, did he know or have reason to know that a defense or claim existed? Consideration will now be given to some of the specific factors that the courts consider in determining what constitutes notice of a defense or claim. These are (1) the existence of irregularities in the instrument, (2) knowledge that an obligation is voidable or discharged, (3) knowledge of an extremely large discount in the purchase price of the instrument, (4) knowledge of the transferor's past business practices, and (5) knowledge of a close connection between the holder and the transferor.

Incomplete or Irregular Instruments   A purchaser has notice if an instrument is incomplete or otherwise irregular and the irregularity creates doubt as to the instrument's validity, terms, or ownership. To create such a doubt, an irregularity must relate to a material factor in the instrument. For example, visible evidence of forgery or failure to fill in the amount payable would constitute notice. Whether an irregularity constitutes notice depends on how material the irregularity is.

EXAMPLE: Brock purchases a promissory note. The original date of January 1, 1981, has been crossed out and January 1, 1982, has been inserted. The note originally specified interest at eight percent, but the figure "8" has been lined out and the figure "15" inserted. The instrument states that the obligation is "payable _____days after sight," and that payment is to be made in the "city of New York, state of _____]." This note contains both material and immaterial omissions and irregularities. The change in date does not put Brock on notice of a potential defense, since mistakes in date are common, particularly at the start of a new year. The change in interest rate, however, does put him on notice because the change constitutes a material change in the obligation evidenced by the note. Similarly, the failure to fill in the blank as to time of payment is material because it makes the instrument nonnegotiable, the instrument not being payable on demand or at a definite time. The failure to fill in the blank concerning the state is not material because specifying the place of payment is nonessential. It is reasonable to assume, anyway, that the state of New York was intended because the city of New York is specified.

Obligation Voidable or Discharged   The purchaser of an instrument may not qualify as an HDC if he takes the instrument with notice that the obligation of any party is voidable or that all parties have been discharged. For example, if the original payee fraudulently induced the execution of the instrument, the obligation is voidable. If a purchaser has knowledge or notice of facts indicating such fraud, he cannot qualify as an HDC. Here, good faith figures prominently in determining whether such notice existed. A purchaser ordinarily does not have to inquire, but he may not ignore the obvious. If the purchaser knows facts that should alert him to the possibility that the obligation is voidable, he must inquire or be found guilty of bad faith.

Discounted Instruments   Negotiable instruments are commonly purchased at less than the face price. Thus, the mere fact that an instrument is offered for sale at a discount does not constitute notice. It is the purchase of an instrument at an extremely large discount that might indicate both a lack of good faith and notice of a defense. This is particularly true if other suspicious circumstances are also present.

Knowledge of Transferor's Past Business Practices   A prospective purchaser of a negotiable instrument generally has no obligation to ask about the reputation or past business practices of the transferor. The fact that the transferor may have engaged in some questionable dealings in the past does not necessarily indicate that there is anything wrong with the instrument in question. However, the transferor's past business practices may constitute one factor that should be considered in conjunction with all the other factors in determining whether the purchaser took the instrument without notice of defenses and in good faith.

 A prospective purchaser of a negotiable instrument should never ignore indications of defects in the instrument. Failure to make reasonable inquiry may lead to difficulty in obtaining payment on the instrument and possibly to a lawsuit. If the purchaser can prove good faith and lack of notice, he or she may win the lawsuit. However, the entire problem may possibly be avoided if inquiries are made about the transferor's prior dealings before buying the instrument.

Close Connection Between Transferor and Holder   The existence of a close business relationship between the transferor and the purchaser is one factor that the courts consider on the issues of notice and good faith. Notice exists if the relationship is so close that the purchaser must have known of the facts giving rise to the defense.

The following case illustrates a close and continuing relationship between the transferor and the purchaser. Note how the issues of good faith and lack of notice are jointly discussed as one basic element to be met by an HDC.

Slaughter

v

Jefferson Federal
Savings & Loan Asso.
361 F Supp 590 (1973)
United States District Court, District of Columbia

FACTS: Monarch Construction Corporation engaged in a scheme to defraud homeowners in the District of Columbia. Monarch representatives, by misrepresentations and high-pressure sales tactics, induced owners of deteriorating inner-city houses to sign home improvement contracts. The prices charged were excessive, usually double or more than double the fair value. Lapin, a previous employee of Monarch, obtained first trust deed financing for the contracts from either Jefferson Federal Savings &

Loan Association (Jefferson) or Montgomery Federal Savings & Loan Association (Montgomery). The homeowners, some illiterate and many of limited education, were hurried through settlement proceedings and often signed papers without reading them.

Between 1964 and 1965, Jefferson made 171 loans to Monarch customers. Jefferson received the loan applications and the underlying home improvement contracts from Lapin, who was ostensibly acting as the homeowners' agent. Jefferson's appraisal committee, consisting of experienced real estate officers familiar with values and financing, viewed the homes. The settlement sheets sent to Jefferson frequently contained indications of irregularity or inconsistency with the underlying contract. Montgomery made loans to Monarch customers in much the same manner, making 31 loans in 1964. Montgomery's president knew home improvement costs, inspected many of the homes, and reviewed the settlement sheets. Despite the indications of irregularities, neither Jefferson nor Montgomery ever investigated or inquired about Monarch or Lapin.

A number of homeowners sued Jefferson and Montgomery, seeking recission and restitution of money paid.

ISSUE: Under the circumstances, were defendants prevented from attaining the status of holder in due course by "willful ignorance" of the possible defenses plaintiffs had to payment of the instrument?

RESULT: Yes. Defendants had sufficient information to put them on notice of such defenses.

REASONING:

*   *   *

Neither Jefferson nor Montgomery . . . was, however, a party to the fraud practiced on these homeowners nor did they have direct knowledge of its existence. Accordingly, as a defense against plaintiffs' claims the defendants have each interposed that they hold plaintiffs' notes in due course. If the claim of holder in due course prevails, defendants are, of course, immune from [plaintiffs'] defenses to the notes. . . . The burden of proof rests always on the one claiming to be a holder in due course. . . . A holder, to sustain this burden, must demonstrate that he meets the standards set forth in [UCC § 3-302], which provides in pertinent part:

Holder in Due Course
(1) A holder in due course is a holder who takes the instrument
    (a) for value; and
    (b) in good faith; and
    (c) without notice . . . of any defense against . . . it on the part of any person.

In dispute here is whether the instruments were taken in good faith and without notice of any defense to them. Good faith is defined as "honesty in fact in the conduct or transaction concerned." [UCC § 1-201(19)]. Willful ignorance or failure to inquire may negate good faith. . . . A person has "notice" of a fact when (a) he has actual knowledge of it; or (b) he has received a notice or notification of it; or (c) from all the facts and circumstances known to him at the time in question he has reason to know that it exists. [UCC § 1-201(25)].

The cases are sparse and uninstructive as to the duty of a first trust lender such as Jefferson or Montgomery. From the briefs and arguments, the issue here boils down to the following query: Where the holder is himself the original lender, as in these instances, can he insulate himself from the underlying transaction and thus, because he knows nothing and makes no inquiry, claim the good-faith status that is at the foundation of a holder in due course's immunity from defenses that are otherwise available to the borrower? While payees such as Jefferson and Montgomery may be holders in due course, [UCC § 3-302(2)], they must meet all of the requirements of 3-302. The inquiry must turn to an analysis of the case in the light of modern commercial realities.

It is necessary to avoid the obvious tendency to view this question in the light of hindsight. . . . The record is, moreover, devoid of proof that either Montgomery or Jefferson followed procedures that diverged from other responsible first trust lenders refinancing to aid home improvement purchases. Each case must rest on its own facts to determine whether or not the holder holds the note in due course. There is no rule of thumb to be automatically applied.

In concluding that Jefferson and Montgomery were not holders in due course, the Court has weighed the totality of the circumstances shown by the proof. It must be borne in mind that neither of these concerns stand in the same position they could readily urge if, as part of their general business, they had occasionally written a first trust loan generated by Monarch. Their volume of Monarch business was in each case continuous and substantial. Their representatives knew that Monarch's contracts were being written on marginal properties in the ghetto areas of the city; that many of Monarch's customers were of limited intelligence and as a class, were apt to be heavily burdened with consumer and other debt measured by their apparent income levels; and that many were being refinanced out of other satisfactory notes of reputable financial institutions having lower interests rates and lower monthly payments. Their trained real estate men saw the properties and the work being done and had access to the contract charges they were helping to finance.

Rather than make obvious inquiry into Lapin's bona fides and the contract requirements and settlement adjustments, they chose to be ignorant by trying to insulate themselves from the realities of their activity. The contracts and settlement sheets were at their disposal and revealed both internal irregularities and contradictions between the two documents. They were on notice that Lapin had ties with Monarch as he repetitively peddled loans to them. They were thus chargeable with a heavy duty to be assured that his purported representation of the borrower was aboveboard, for he was obviously acting for two principals whose interest could well be in conflict. . . . Given their superior knowledge of building costs and financial matters and the opportunity they had to observe and to question, plus the obvious need to inquire which the circumstances presented, they cannot rely on their self-induced ignorance to put themselves into a position of holders in due course. In short, there were many warnings of irregularity which even limited inquiry would have readily disclosed.

Jefferson and Montgomery may not in the light of these irregularities and indicia of fraud be heard to suggest that the proof as to a particular plaintiff does not put them on precise notice of misrepresentation and unconscionable dealing. All of the plaintiffs were targets of the fraud. The education, understanding, recollection and details of each borrower's dealings vary, but the pattern is overwhelmingly apparent, and had either of these associations taken appropriate precautions, under the circumstances presented they would have ceased facilitating Monarch's scheme, and none of the plaintiffs would have been serviced regardless of the particular course of their individual dealings with Monarch. Of course, if there is notice as to one defense or good faith is not shown, all defenses to the transaction are valid. [UCC § 3-306]. . . .

This is an equitable proceeding and the Court must consider the obvious commercial realities presented by the record before it. Indeed the Uniform Commercial Code itself recognizes something less than actual notice may suffice to destroy the holder in due course defense. The Court finds the commercial realities persuasive in determining that Jefferson and Montgomery did not act in good faith, and were on notice because they "should have known." These sophisticated financial institutions were concerned solely with the sufficiency of their security. But they were not dealing with comparably sophisticated borrowers experienced in commercial matters. The borrowers, many of whom were semiliterate, had no clout. They were threatened with loss of their homes if they raised any question and went forward, sometimes with enormous sacrifice, resigned in their ignorance to pay off unjustifiable charges to keep a roof over their heads. Where lenders facilitate consumer credit financing they must be held to a high standard of inquiry to make certain their services are not being misused by unscrupulous merchandisers such as Monarch. . . .

Gesell, District Judge.

 The judgment in the above case was reversed on appeal in *Slaughter v Jefferson Federal Savings & Loan Association*, 538 F2d 397 (United States Court of Appeals, District of Columbia Circuit, 1976). The appellate court agreed that Monarch and its agents were guilty of fraud, but concluded that Jefferson and Montgomery acted in good faith and without notice.

Note, however, that Jefferson and Montgomery were tied up in litigation for over five years (from January 1971, when the action was originally brought, to mid-1976, when the appeal was decided). Consider also the possible damage to Jefferson's and Montgomery's reputations as a result of the protracted litigation. All this might have been avoided if they had made some investigation into the nature of Monarch's and Lapin's dealings.

24:7 Rights of Holder in Due Course

When a holder seeks payment from the obligor of a negotiable instrument, two categories of defenses may be used: (1) *personal (limited) defenses* and (2) *real (universal) defenses.* When a person qualifies as an HDC, only real defenses may be asserted against him by the obligor. Personal defenses, which consist of most of the traditional defenses to contract actions, may not be asserted against an HDC unless the person asserting one of them has personally dealt with the HDC.

Real Defenses [UCC § 3-305]   As a matter of public policy, the drafters of the UCC (and the states enacting it) decided that certain defenses should be universally available. These are called real defenses. Real defenses include minority status (under legal age) to the extent it is a defense to a contract (see Chapter 13), discharge in bankruptcy or other insolvency proceedings (see Chapter 32), and any other discharge of which the holder has notice when he takes the instrument (see Chapter 25).

Forgery of the obligor's name and material alteration of the instrument are also real defenses. Therefore, the obligor can claim that the signature on the instrument was not his or that a material part of the instrument was altered. In the case of material alteration an HDC may enforce the instrument according to its original terms, but not as altered [UCC §§ 3-404, 3-407].

Certain other traditional contract defenses are classified as real defenses if they make the obligation entirely void, as opposed to merely voidable. These defenses are incapacity (other than minority), duress, and illegality. The drafters of the UCC felt that the extent to which these defenses should be assertible against an HDC was largely a matter of local policy. Therefore, the law of the particular state must be checked to determine when, if ever, these defenses make a contract absolutely void, and thus when they may be asserted against an HDC.

There is a similar UCC provision with respect to fraud.[2] Fraud in the inducement is considered a personal defense not available against an HDC. This means that most types of fraud, such as misrepresentation, are unavailable as a defense. Fraud in the execution of a contract may, however, be asserted as a defense against an HDC. This means that the obligor can contend that he was tricked into signing the instrument. To prevail on such a claim, the obligor must show that he or she was induced to sign the instrument

---

[2] Fraud as a defense to a contract action is discussed in Chapter 12.

without knowing and without reasonable opportunity to know its character or essential terms. In other words, the test is that of excusable ignorance of the writing's contents.

Personal Defenses [UCC § 3-306] Personal defenses may not be raised against an HDC, but they may be raised against any person who is not an HDC or a holder through an HDC and takes the instrument. For example, if the holder of the instrument fails to meet the requirements for HDC status, the obligor on the instrument may assert both real and personal defenses against the holder. Personal defenses include all defenses other than those classified as real defenses. They consist largely of traditional contract defenses, such as lack of consideration, nondelivery, breach of warranty, and unconscionability. Lack of capacity, duress, illegality, and fraud are also personal defenses except to the extent that they qualify as real defenses, as discussed earlier.

Rights of Holder Not Qualifying as Holder in Due Course The rights of an ordinary holder of a negotiable instrument are generally determined according to basic contract law. Where the holder is not the original payee, the holder has the rights of an assignee. Both real and personal defenses may be asserted against a holder. If there are no defenses available, then the holder can, of course, recover on the instrument.

24:8 Limitation of Holder in Due Course Doctrine in Consumer Credit Transactions[3]

The holder in due course doctrine functions well in business transactions among those who understand the doctrine. It permits negotiable instruments to be freely and quickly transferred among holders. In consumer transactions, however, the doctrine has been used unscrupulously.

EXAMPLE: Karen buys a refrigerator from Ace Appliances on credit and signs a promissory note payable to Ace. Ace immediately negotiates the note to a bank at a discount. Shortly afterward, the refrigerator breaks down. When Karen goes to Ace to complain and demand repair of the refrigerator, she learns that Ace has gone out of business. She then stops making payments on the note. The bank sues her, and she asserts breach of warranty as a defense. Because the bank is an HDC of the note and Karen's defense is a personal one, the defense will be disallowed against the bank. In effect, Karen must continue paying on the note. She has a potential breach of warranty action against Ace, but the action is worthless because Ace is no longer in business. In short, Karen is left with a malfunctioning refrigerator and the obligation to continue paying for it.

Abuse of the doctrine led to demands for legislation to protect consumers in these transactions. In response, most states passed laws limiting the applica-

---

[3] Consumer credit and credit protection generally are discussed in Chapter 28.

tion of the holder in due course doctrine in consumer transactions. These laws vary widely in their effect. Some laws prohibit the use of negotiable instruments in consumer financing, requiring instead the use of instruments labeled "consumer paper." Other laws eliminate the holder in due course doctrine in consumer transactions. Still other laws provide varying measures of lesser protection for consumers.

In 1975 the Federal Trade Commission (FTC) promulgated a trade regulation rule that effectively abolished the holder in due course doctrine in most consumer credit transactions [16 CFR §§ 433.1, 433.2]. The FTC rule requires that any consumer credit contract contain a prominent notice stating that any holder of the contract is subject to all claims and defenses that the consumer could assert against the seller. The net effect of the rule is the abolition of the holder in due course doctrine in such transactions. The FTC rule also has the effect of prohibiting "waiver of defenses" clauses. Under a waiver of defenses clause a consumer agrees not to assert against an assignee any claims or defenses he could have asserted against the original seller.

The FTC rule applies to two kinds of transactions: (1) consumer transactions in which the purchaser signs a promissory note payable to the seller, which the seller then negotiates to a third party; and (2) consumer transactions in which the seller arranges for a direct loan from a third party to the consumer, with the proceeds of the loan being used to pay for the purchase. The rule has national application. Thus, the holder in due course doctrine is inapplicable to most consumer credit transactions. It must be remembered, however, that the FTC rule does not apply to business transactions, to real property transactions, or when payment is made by check. The holder in due course doctrine remains in full effect with respect to these transactions.

The *de la Fuente* case, which follows, explains the change in the law wrought by both the FTC and Texas' consumer protection law. The Texas law represents a typical state legislative approach to commercial paper in the consumer sale context.

---

de la Fuente

v

Home Savings Asso.
669 SW2d 137 (1984)
Court of Appeals of Texas, Corpus Christi

FACTS: In late April of 1978 Gonzales, a representative of Aluminum Industries, Inc., visited the de la Fuente home to sell aluminum siding. As a result, on May 3, 1978, the de la Fuentes executed a number of documents, including a contract and a promissory note for improvements to their home. The contract amount was $9,138.24, to be paid in 96 monthly installments of $95.19 and with an annual percentage rate of 12 percent. The contract granted a lien on their home. At trial defendant claimed to be a holder in due course of the note secured by the lien.

Aluminum Industries was no longer in business. The de la Fuentes had claims good against Aluminum Industries.

ISSUE: Is defendant a holder in due course free of the claims against Aluminum Industries?

RESULT: No, defendant is not a holder in due course.

REASONING:

*   *   *

. . . [A]ppellee was [not] entitled to the protection of a holder in due course of a negotiable instrument, because (1) the holder in due course doctrine has been abolished in consumer credit transactions by FTC regulations; and, (2) the appellee did not conform to the notice requirements of the Texas Credit Code so as to cut off the rights of action and defenses of the buyer. The note in question contained a notice in bold face type which reads in part:

NOTICE

ANY HOLDER OF THIS CONSUMER CREDIT CONTRACT IS SUBJECT TO ALL CLAIMS AND DEFENSES WHICH THE DEBTOR COULD ASSERT AGAINST THE SELLER OF GOODS OR SERVICES OBTAINED PURSUANT HERETO OR WITH THE PROCEEDS HEREOF. . . .

This FTC Rule, subjecting the holder of the note to the claims and defenses of the debtor, is in direct conflict with the doctrine of the holder in due course. The Federal Courts have stated, without so holding, that the effect of this FTC Rule is to abolish the holder in due course doctrine. . . .

The FTC, in its Statement of Basis and Purpose, specifically named the holder in due course doctrine as the evil addressed by [the FTC Rule]. "[A] consumer's duty to pay for goods and services must not be separated from a seller's duty to perform as promised . . . " 40 Fed.Reg. 53,506, 53,523 (November 18, 1975). The FTC intended the Rule to compel creditors to either absorb the cost of the seller's misconduct or return them to sellers. 40 F.R. at 53,523. The FTC "reach[ed] a determination that it constitutes an unfair and deceptive practice to use contractual boiler plate to separate a buyer's duty to pay from a seller's duty to perform." 40 F.R. at 53,524. The effect of this Rule is to "give the courts the authority to examine the equities in an underlying sale, and it will prevent sellers from foreclosing judicial review of their conduct. Seller *and creditors* will be responsible for seller misconduct." 40 F.R. at 53,524 (emphasis added). It was clearly the intention of the FTC Rule to have the holder of the paper bear the losses occasioned by the actions of the seller; therefore, the benefits of the holder in due course doctrine under TEX. BUS. &

COM.CODE ANN. § 3.302 are not available when the notice required by the FTC in [its Rule] is placed on a consumer credit contract. . . .

Kennedy, Justice.

Key Concepts and Terms

- There are three classes of holders of negotiable instruments: (1) simple holders, (2) holders for value, and (3) holders in due course (HDCs). Only HDCs are accorded special protection under the UCC.

- To qualify for HDC status, a holder must take the instrument (1) for value, (2) in good faith, (3) without notice that it is overdue or has been dishonored, and (4) without notice of any defense against or claim to it. A holder through holder in due course usually obtains the rights accorded an HDC. The payee of an instrument may be an HDC.

- Value must actually be given to qualify for HDC status. A mere promise does not constitute value. A holder may give value in several ways, the primary way being by performance of the agreed consideration.

- A transferee must take the instrument in good faith to qualify as an HDC. The good-faith test is a subjective one and requires honesty. The good-faith requirement is generally considered in conjunction with the requirements concerning notice.

- A holder has notice (1) when he or she has actual knowledge or notice or (2) when the facts and circumstances known to him give him reason to know. The existence of notice is thus determined by an objective standard.

- To take as an HDC, the transferee must take the instrument without notice that it is overdue or has been dishonored. Notice exists if the purchaser has reason to know (1) that any part of the principal amount is overdue, (2) that there is an uncured default in payment of another instrument of the same series, (3) that acceleration of the instrument has been made, (4) that he or she is taking a demand instrument after demand has been made, or (5) that he or she is taking a demand instrument more than a reasonable length of time after its issue.

- To take as an HDC, the transferee must take the instrument without notice that there is a defense or claim against it. Notice is based on whether, in light of all the facts and circumstances known to the purchaser at the time of purchase, she knew or had reason to know that a defense or claim existed. Among the factors considered are the existence of irregularities or omissions in the instrument, knowledge of the transferor's past business practices, and the existence of a close relationship between the transferor and the holder.

- Two kinds of defenses may be raised against a holder by the obligor of a negotiable instrument: real defenses and personal defenses. Real defenses include minority, discharge in insolvency proceedings, any other discharge of which the holder has notice, forgery, material alteration, certain forms of incapacity, duress, illegality, and fraud in the execution. All other defenses are personal. Real defenses may be raised against an HDC, but personal defenses may be raised against an HDC only if the obligor has personally dealt with the HDC. A holder *not* qualifying as an HDC has the rights of an assignee and takes the instrument subject to both personal and real defenses.

- Most states have passed laws limiting application of the holder in due course doctrine in consumer transactions. These laws vary widely in their effect. The FTC has promulgated a rule that effectively abolishes the holder in due course doctrine in most consumer credit transactions involving sale of goods or services. The FTC rule does not apply to business transactions, to real property transactions, or when payment is made by check.

- Dishonor
- FIFO
- FTC Rule
- Good Faith
- Holder
- Holder for Value
- Holder in Due Course

- Holder Through a Holder in Due Course
- Notice
- Obligor
- Personal (Limited) Defenses
- Real (Universal) Defenses
- Stop Payment
- Value

Questions and Case Problems

1. Charles was the guardian for his seven-year-old son, Chad. Chad was the beneficiary of his grandfather's life insurance. The insurance company issued a check for $30,588.39 payable to "Charles, Guardian of the Estate of Chad, a Minor." Charles deposited the check in his personal checking account; over several months he and his wife spent the money for their own benefit. Chad's new guardian sued the bank, claiming it took the instrument with notice of Chad's claims against the instrument. The bank claims to be a holder in due course. Who prevails?

2. Akins agrees to sell his corn crop to Sweeney. As payment, Sweeney executes a promissory note payable to Akins. Akins pledges the note to Rogers as security for a loan. Akins defaults on the loan, and Rogers demands payment on the note from Sweeney. Sweeney responds that Akins has not delivered the corn. Rogers has Akins indorse the note, then sues Sweeney for payment. What is result of the lawsuit?

3. On March 9, 1981, Peter deCoote executed a promissory note payable to Ginny Dorg. The note provided that it was to be paid in 36 equal installments, "payable monthly after date beginning _____1, 1981, and on the first day of each month thereafter." Dorg sold the note to a bank. Does the bank qualify as a holder in due course?

4. Stereo Sales, Inc., sells equipment to Holmes for making stereo tapes from master tapes. Holmes pays $3,000 down and executes a $3,000 promissory note for the balance due. Stereo sells the note to National Bank for $500. Stereo's contract with Holmes requires it to furnish him master tapes weekly, from which Holmes is to produce individual tapes for resale to Stereo. Stereo never furnishes any master tapes and eventually goes out of business. Holmes refuses to pay the note and National Bank sues. At trial Holmes raises the defense of fraud, and National Bank

claims it is a holder in due course. Holmes proves that Stereo has sold National Bank 30 other notes at similar discounts and that the makers of 25 of those notes have defaulted and claimed breach of contract by Stereo. How should the case be decided?

5. Wheeler wrote a check payable to Eagle for $20,298 in payment of a masonry subcontract. Eagle promptly cashed the check at Vail National Bank, where it had an account. Prior to cashing the check, Vail called Wheeler's bank and was told there were sufficient funds in Wheeler's account and that there was no stop payment order on the check. Two days later, when Vail presented the check for payment, the check was dishonored because of a stop payment order given by Wheeler. Vail Bank sued Wheeler, claiming to be a holder in due course. Wheeler argued that Vail cannot have HDC status because it had not followed "good banking practices" when it cashed the check. What decision?

6. Egan signs two blank checks. Irving steals the checks and fills in the blanks. Irving cashes one check at his bank on Friday. The bank is notified the following Tuesday that Egan's bank has dishonored the check. Irving cashes the second check at his bank on Wednesday. That check is also dishonored. Irving's bank sues Egan for payment of the checks. Must Egan pay? Does Egan have any defenses?

7. Warren executes a $3,000 promissory note payable to Yvonne as payment for roofing his house. Yvonne gives the note to her son Ben as a birthday present. Ben negotiates the note to Owen, his bookie, as payment of a $2,000 gambling debt. Owen gives the note to his friend Jennifer as a wedding present. Jennifer sells the note to Marie for $2,500. Marie negotiates the note to Bill as payment for furniture, which he fails to deliver. Which of the parties qualify for the rights of a holder in due course? Which parties do not? Why?

8. Max executes a note payable on demand to Pat. One month later Pat demands payment, but Max refuses to pay. Two weeks after that, Pat sells the note to Wally at a 30 percent discount. Wally is unaware of the prior demand and does not know Max. One week later, Wally sells the note to Ann at a 25 percent discount. Ann is unaware of the prior demand, but she does know that Max has frequently defaulted on similar notes. Are Wally and Ann holders in due course? Would the time within which demand is generally made on similar notes have any bearing on the decision?

9. Payne, a college-educated businessperson, signs a promissory note payable to Industrial Supplies, Inc. and State Bank. Payne delivers the note to Industrial, which indorses the note and sells it to State Bank at a 20 percent discount. Payne refuses to pay the note and is then sued by State Bank. At trial Payne claims that State Bank is not a holder in due course. Payne also claims that Industrial tricked her into signing the note by misrepresenting it as an order for supplies and that she did not read the note before signing it. The trial court enters judgment for State Bank. Payne appeals. Should the judgment be affirmed or reversed on appeal?

10. In July 1981 Cathay delivered to Asian a check for $200,000, made payable to Asian International, Ltd., in full payment for equipment sold by Asian to Cathay. The president and the treasurer of Asian then indorsed the check to the order of Fort, and Fort deposited the check in his account with Merrill Lynch. Merrill Lynch credited the funds to Fort's account and received payment from the payor bank. When Asian sued Merrill Lynch for conversion of (wrongful dealing in) the check, Merrill Lynch claimed to be a holder in due course as a depositary bank. Asian claimed Merrill Lynch is not a bank. What result?

25 Liability of Parties

25:1   Introduction

A negotiable instrument may be transferred many times before it is paid. Ordinarily, the obligor, who is normally the drawee or the maker of the instrument, pays the ultimate holder according to the terms of the instrument, and the instrument is *discharged*. If the obligor fails to pay, however, the holder may be entitled to payment from other parties to the instrument.

A party to the instrument may have primary liability or secondary liability to the holder. A person is primarily liable if the terms of the instrument itself require him to pay. Since the maker of a note and the acceptor of a draft are required by the terms of the instrument to pay, they have primary liability. A person is secondarily liable when the obligation to pay arises only if the person with primary liability fails to pay the instrument. Since drawers and indorsers, the *secondary parties*, must pay when the *primary parties* do not, drawers and indorsers have secondary liability.

Furthermore, the liability of the parties is based either on contract or on warranty. Contract liability arises when a person signs an instrument and thereby undertakes either a primary or secondary liability to pay it. Warranty liability is imposed by statute—the UCC; warranties are implied by law in every transfer of a negotiable instrument. The rules governing the liability of both primary and secondary parties, including both contractual and warranty liability, are discussed in detail in this chapter. In addition, the liability of certain special types of parties and the liability on instruments containing forged signatures is examined. Finally, the chapter considers the various ways in which the parties to a negotiable instrument may be discharged from liability.

In studying the materials that follow, bear in mind that the rules are often applied to complex transactions.

EXAMPLE: East Electronics as drawer executes a draft drawn on Creative Credit as drawee, with South Suppliers named as payee. South indorses and sells the draft to Money Company, which in turn indorses and sells the draft to North Bank. North presents the draft to Creative for payment, but Creative refuses to pay. North obviously does not want to sustain the loss, so it will look to one of the other parties for payment. Should North demand payment from Money Company, its immediate transferor; from South, the original payee; or from East, the drawer? If North demands and receives payment from Money Company, can Money in turn demand payment from either South or East? What if North never notified Money, South, or East of Creative's refusal to pay? The answers to all these questions have a bearing on which party, if any, must make payment to North, and which party must suffer the loss caused by Creative's nonpayment.

The rules themselves are also complex. After studying this chapter the reader may wish to return to the preceding example to determine the liability of the various parties involved.

25:2   Contractual Liability of Primary Parties

The term "primary party" refers to the maker of a note and to the acceptor of a draft. Makers and acceptors have the same liability in an action based on contract. Recall, however, that a drawee is not an acceptor until he or she accepts the draft—that is, until he puts his signature on the face of the draft. Prior to acceptance, the drawee has no obligation to the payee or to any subsequent holder to honor the instrument [UCC §§ 3-409(1), 3-410(1)].

The maker or acceptor of a negotiable instrument has an absolute obligation to pay according to the terms of the instrument. If the instrument is incomplete when signed, the maker or acceptor undertakes to pay it when it is completed as authorized. Moreover, the maker or acceptor conclusively admits the payee's existence and capacity to indorse. The maker or acceptor cannot, for example, later assert that the payee was a minor incapable of negotiating the instrument [UCC § 3-413].

The primary party's obligation continues until payment is actually made or until the statute of limitations has run. A statute of limitations is a law that specifies the period of time within which a person can bring an action. Thus, the primary party remains liable until he pays the holder or until the holder can no longer bring a lawsuit to compel payment. There is one exception to this rule. A maker or acceptor of an instrument payable at a specific bank is discharged from liability if (1) the instrument is not presented for payment when due, (2) the bank becomes insolvent during the delay in presentment, and (3) the maker or acceptor is thereby deprived of funds maintained in the bank [UCC § 3-502(1)]. This exception is rarely, if ever, of any practical importance.

EXAMPLE: Lake executes a draft directing Carter as drawee to pay $1,000 to Watson. The draft is payable at State Bank. Carter accepts the draft by signing it. Watson does not present the draft for payment until six months after the due date. Unless the bank has become insolvent during the delay, Carter as acceptor is still obligated to make payment.

25:3   Contractual Liability of Secondary Parties

Secondary parties to negotiable instruments include drawers and indorsers [UCC § 3-102(1)(d)]. Their contractual liability is secondary in the sense that they are obligated to make payment only if the primary parties fail to do so. There is, however, a marked difference between the potential liability of drawers and that of indorsers. If a drawee refuses to accept the draft or if the drawee accepts it but later refuses to pay it, the drawer usually is as liable as a primary party. An indorser, however, is liable only if there has been compliance with the rules governing presentment and notice of *dishonor*. These rules generally require the holder to present an instrument to the primary party for payment when due. This is called *presentment*. Sometimes, presentment of a draft to the drawee with a request that he accept it is also required. If the instrument is not accepted or payment is refused, the instrument is considered dishonored, and the holder or indorser must notify secondary parties of that fact. The rules governing presentment and notice of dishonor are discussed more fully in 25:4. Noncompliance with these rules discharges the indorser's liability.

Drawer's Liability [UCC § 3-413(2)]   The drawer is liable for payment of a draft if the drawee–acceptor refuses to make payment. This rule stems from the fact that most drafts call for disbursement of the drawer's funds held by the drawee. Usually, the drawer's liability continues until payment is made or until the statute of limitations has run. In other words, if the drawee–acceptor refuses to pay, the drawer is, for practical purposes, treated the same as a primary party. Like the primary party, the drawer conclusively admits the payee's existence and capacity to indorse [UCC § 3-413(3)].

Although the drawer is in many respects treated like a primary party, the UCC does make distinctions between a primary party's liability and a drawer's liability. The most important distinction is that the drawer is liable only if the primary party—the drawee—acceptor—fails to pay. A second distinction, which has little practical effect, is that the drawer's liability is technically conditioned on due presentment and notice of dishonor. However, delay in presentment or notice of dishonor will discharge the drawer only if the drawee becomes insolvent during the delay [UCC § 3-502(1)]. Most drafts are drawn on banks, so a drawer is discharged from liability under the same circumstances as a maker or acceptor—that is, if the bank fails during the delay.

A drawer does have a more practical way of avoiding secondary liability. The drawer may disclaim liability by drawing the draft "without recourse."

Indorser's Liability [UCC § 3-414]   An indorser (other than a qualified indorser) is liable on the instrument if the party primarily obligated to make payment fails to do so. The indorser's liability, like the drawer's, is conditioned on the holder's due presentment, the primary party's dishonor, and notice of dishonor by either the holder or the indorser. For an indorser, unlike the drawer, these requirements have real meaning. Failure to meet the requirements discharges the indorser from the contractual obligation to pay the instrument.

EXAMPLE: Tamura executes a draft directing County Savings to pay $500 to Global Products. County Savings accepts the draft. Global then indorses the draft to Fast Financing. When Fast Financing seeks payment from County Savings, County refuses to pay. Fast Financing may turn either to Global as indorser or to Tamura as drawer for payment. However, while Fast Financing must comply with the requirements concerning presentment and notice of dishonor to hold Global liable, it does not need to comply to hold Tamura liable because she is the drawer.

When an instrument is dishonored by the primary obligor, the holder may demand payment directly from any indorser. Indorsers are generally liable to one another in the order in which they indorse, which is presumed to be the order in which their signatures appear on the instrument. In other words, the first indorser is liable to all subsequent indorsers, the second indorser is liable to all indorsers except the first, and so on.

Like a drawer, an indorser may disclaim contractual liability on the instrument by indorsing the instrument "without recourse."

25:4   Requirements of Presentment, Dishonor, and Notice of Dishonor

An indorser's contractual liability is strictly conditioned on the holder's compliance with the UCC requirements concerning presentment, dishonor, and notice of dishonor. This means that the holder must demand payment or acceptance by the primary party in a timely manner and, on the primary party's refusal to pay or accept, the holder must give timely notice of the refusal to secondary parties.

Necessity of Presentment [UCC § 3-501(1)]   Presentment consists of a demand for acceptance or payment made by the holder on the maker, acceptor, or drawee. Drafts can be presented for acceptance, but all negotiable instruments must ultimately be presented for payment.

The purpose of presenting a draft for acceptance is simply to obtain the drawee's agreement to pay the draft and thus to insure his primary liability. For example, if the holder of a time draft has any doubts as to the drawee's willingness to pay it when due, she can allay these doubts by presenting the draft for acceptance at any time prior to the due date.

Some drafts *must* be presented for acceptance. *Presentment for acceptance* is required (1) if the draft so provides, (2) if the draft is payable elsewhere than at the drawee's residence or place of business, or (3) if the draft's date of payment depends on such presentment. The holder has the option of presenting any other time draft for acceptance, but he may not present other demand drafts for acceptance.

Time of Presentment [UCC § 3-503]   The time when an instrument must be presented for either acceptance or payment depends on whether it is a time or a demand instrument.

Presentment for acceptance of a time instrument, if it is required, must be made on or before the due date. *Presentment for payment* must be made on the due date. If the time for payment is accelerated, the instrument must be presented for payment within a reasonable time after the acceleration. A demand instrument must be presented for acceptance or payment within a reasonable time unless it is payable after sight. In that case it must be either presented for acceptance or negotiated within a reasonable time after date or issue, whichever is later.

The UCC provides guidelines for determining what is a reasonable time. The nature of the instrument, any usage of banking or trade, and the facts of the particular case are all relevant. The code states that certain time periods are presumed to be reasonable in the case of uncertified checks, which are most checks (see Chapter 26 for a discussion of the various types of checks). To hold a drawer liable, a holder should present the check for payment or initiate bank collection within 30 days. To hold an indorser liable, a holder should present the check for payment or initiate bank collection within seven days after the indorsement.

 The UCC provisions concerning the time for presentment are detailed and complex. A holder of an instrument should remember three basic rules. First, a time instrument should be presented for payment on the date due. Second, a demand instrument should be presented for payment or negotiated to another party as quickly as is reasonably possible. Third, failure to make a timely presentment for acceptance or payment will discharge all indorsers from liability on the instrument. Therefore, a businessperson handling a large volume of negotiable instruments should adopt internal procedures designed to avoid delay in the negotiation and presentment of those instruments.

Manner of Presentment [UCC § 3-504] Presentment may be made in various ways. It may be made in person, by mail, through a clearinghouse, or through a collecting bank. When presentment is not made in person, the time when the demand for acceptance or payment is actually received is considered the date the presentment is made. Presentment must be made at the place specified for acceptance or payment. If the instrument does not specify any place, then presentment may be made at the place of business or residence of the party from whom payment or acceptance is demanded. When two or more obligors are involved, presentment may be made to any one of them.

Dishonor of Instrument [UCC § 3-507] Dishonor of a negotiable instrument (except a draft) consists of nonpayment by the primary party after due presentment. A draft is dishonored either by nonacceptance or by nonpayment [UCC §§ 3-505, 3-506]. This is not to say that the maker or acceptor must make payment immediately after being presented with the instrument. Reasonable examination to ensure that the instrument is properly payable is permissible, and the primary party may take certain steps, such as requiring reasonable identification from the holder, to ensure that payment will be made to the right person.

Notice of Dishonor [UCC § 3-508]   When an instrument has been dishonored, notice of such dishonor may be given by the holder to any party potentially liable on the instrument.

EXAMPLE: Laura executes a promissory note payable to Adam. Adam indorses the note to Karen, who indorses the note to Craig. Craig presents the note to Laura for payment, but she refuses to pay. Craig gives timely notice of the dishonor to Karen, who in turn gives timely notice to Adam. Since both indorsers of the instrument have been given notice, both remain liable for payment.

Such notice may also be given by a potentially liable party to any other potentially liable party. Notice must be given to all indorsers of the instrument or they are discharged from liability for payment, although it need not be given in order of indorsement. If the holder or indorser is a bank, it must give notice before its midnight deadline (see Chapter 26). Any other holder or indorser must give notice before midnight of the third business day after dishonor or receipt of notice of dishonor from another party. The notice may be oral or written, and it may be given in any reasonable manner. Written notice is given when it is sent and will be considered given even if it is not received.

 A holder should give written notice to all potentially liable parties whenever it is feasible to do so. In that way the holder has the most assurance of being able to prove that notice was given and of ultimately receiving payment. If the holder gives notice only to the immediate transferor, he runs the risk that other indorsers will not receive timely notice and will be discharged. If the holder gives oral notice, he runs the risk of being unable to satisfactorily prove that notice was ever given.

Situations Excusing Compliance with Presentment and Notice Requirements [UCC § 3-511]   Under some circumstances a failure to comply or a delay in complying with the presentment and notice of dishonor requirements is excused. The holder may then hold indorsers liable on the instrument despite lack of presentment or notice. These circumstances include the following:

Waiver of presentment or notice. An indorser may waive the right to require presentment or notice of dishonor. Such a waiver may be expressed or implied, oral or written. Negotiable instruments often contain a waiver provision excusing presentment or notice.

Inability to make presentment or give notice. It may be impossible, even though he exercises reasonable diligence, for a holder to present the instrument to the primary party or to give the indorser notice of the primary party's dishonor of the instrument. If so, the presentment or notice is entirely excused. To avail himself of this excuse, a holder must (1) use reasonable diligence to make presentment or give notice or (2) show that reasonable diligence would have been unsuccessful. Moreover, where presentment or notice is still possible after a delay caused by circumstances beyond the holder's control, such presentment or notice must be made or given. The delay is then excused, but a complete failure to make presentment or give notice would not be.

Actions of indorser. A party who, as a result of his own conduct, has no right to require or reason to expect that the instrument will be honored is not entitled to presentment or notice. For example, if the party has himself dishonored the instrument or has countermanded payment, presentment or notice is excused. Moreover, if the party indorsed the instrument after its "maturity," notice of dishonor is not necessary to hold that party contractually liable [UCC § 3-501(4)].

Death or insolvency. The death or insolvency of the maker, acceptor, or drawee excuses the holder from making a presentment. It does not, however, excuse him from giving notice of dishonor to the indorser.

Refusal of acceptance or payment. If payment or acceptance has been refused for some reason other than the lack of proper presentment, presentment is excused. For example, an anticipatory repudiation by the maker or acceptor would excuse formal presentment. Again, however, the holder is not excused from giving notice of dishonor.

The following case illustrates how a court determined whether presentment and notice were excused under the circumstances.

Silk

v

Merrill Lynch, Pierce, Fenner & Smith, Inc.
437 So2d 112 (1983)
Supreme Court of Alabama

FACTS: In November 1981 Silk accepted four checks, totalling $37,500, from Warrior Energy Corporation, drawn on Central Bank. At Warrior's request, Silk agreed not to deposit the checks until Warrior had sufficient funds in the account to cover them. In early February Silk indorsed the checks and deposited them into a Merrill Lynch (M-L) cash management account (CMA). M-L credited Silk's CMA and deposited the checks with its bank, which then presented the checks to Central Bank for payment. Central dishonored the checks for insufficient funds. M-L's bank noted the dishonored checks on M-L's bank record on February 11, 1982, but M-L did not debit Silk's CMA. On March 1, 1982, Silk used all the funds in his CMA, including the $37,500, to purchase stock on margin. On April 15, 1982, M-L notified Silk of the dishonored checks and debited his margin account. Fearful of a margin call, Silk sold the stock, which subsequently rose in price. Silk sued M-L for wrongfully debiting his CMA account, claiming lack of timely notice of dishonor.

ISSUE: Did Merrill Lynch make a timely notice of dishonor, or is it excused from doing so?

RESULT: Notice of dishonor was not necessary because the instrument was overdue when Silk indorsed it.

REASONING:

*   *   *

Merrill Lynch submits that it complied with the notice of dishonor requirements of § 7–3–508(2), by giving notice of the checks' dishonor before midnight of the third business day after it allegedly received notice of the dishonor. Merrill Lynch further posits that under the circumstances of this case, however, the notice of dishonor requirement was not applicable, citing § 7–3–501(4), which reads: "Notwithstanding any provision of this section, neither presentment nor notice of dishonor nor protest is necessary to charge an indorser who has indorsed an instrument *after maturity*." (Emphasis added.)

The term "maturity" is not defined within the definitional provisions of the Uniform Commercial Code (UCC). Referring to decisions of courts from other jurisdictions as guidance in our interpretation as to what constitutes "after maturity," we have located but one case . . . [In] that case, the New Jersey Superior Court ruled: . . .

> "Plaintiff's argument that no notice of dishonor was required because allegedly the indorsements made by defendants were made 'after maturity,' see NJSA 12A:3-501(4), lacks merit. The last cited section applies only where the indorsement was made after the instrument was 'overdue', a situation which did not exist in this case where the draft was indorsed by defendants within three days of its date of issue and 18 days before it was presented for acceptance. Here defendants had indorsed the draft before, not after, maturity." . . .

Construing the phrase "after maturity" to mean "overdue," as did the New Jersey court, appears reasonable. The term "overdue," though not specifically defined, is nonetheless employed in sections of the UCC relative to checks which give it a more precise meaning. For example, one of the requirements for a holder in due course status is that the holder must take an instrument "without notice that it is overdue." § 7–3–302. An instrument is considered overdue after more than a "reasonable length of time after its issue," which is presumed to be thirty days. § 7–3–304(3)(c). Paragraph 7 of the Official Comment states in pertinent part: "The 'reasonable time after issue' is retained from original section 53, but paragraph (c) adds a presumption, as that term is defined in this act (7–1–201), that a domestic check is stale after thirty days." Indeed the thirty-day period is but a rebuttable presumption. One treatise on commercial paper notes:

> "Section 3–501(4) provides as an absolute that an endorser taking an instrument after maturity is not entitled to fulfillment of the conditions precedent of presentment, notice or protest. No doubt this is based upon the rationale that the endorser could assume dishonor at that time. For demand instruments the maturity of which is a reasonable time after issuance, it may become debatable whether the endorser endorsed after maturity. For a check, Section 3–304(3)(c) creates a presumption that a holder has notice that the check is overdue if taken more than thirty days after issuance or date. This does not fix thirty days as presumptive of maturity except by indirection. Further, the presumption is rebuttable and, in any event, does not apply to noncheck drafts or to demand notes. Courts might reasonably develop a rule of thumb that endorsers who endorse any demand instrument after thirty days have the burden of showing that the instrument had not 'matured' when they took it." . . .

It is argued by the Silks that the checks were not indorsed after maturity because presentment on February 4, 1982, was pursuant to a verbal agreement between the drawer and the payee that the checks would not be presented when originally issued. This Court has held, however, that a demand instrument may not be altered or varied as to its maturity date by a parol agreement between the parties to the instrument. . . .

Maddox, Justice.

25:5 Warranty Liability

The holder of a negotiable instrument may seek payment from a secondary party by claiming that there was a breach of warranty. Two types of warranties exist with respect to negotiable instruments: *transfer warranties* and *presentment warranties.* Transfer warranties arise whenever an instrument is transferred for consideration. Presentment warranties arise whenever an instrument is paid or accepted. Liability based on warranty is often discussed as an aspect of indorsers' liability. This is somewhat misleading because both transfer and presentment warranties arise even in the absence of an indorsement. Therefore, a person who, without indorsement, transfers or obtains payment on an instrument that is payable to bearer may be held liable for breach of warranty, although such a person could not be held liable as an indorser. The possibility of obtaining payment from a person who has not indorsed the instrument is one advantage of seeking recovery on a breach of warranty theory. A second advantage is that the requirements concerning presentment, dishonor, and notice of dishonor do not apply to actions for breach of warranty. Thus, a holder may be able to recover from an indorser without meeting those requirements.

EXAMPLE: Nelson, an HDC of a check, presents it for payment, but the drawee bank refuses to pay because the original payee's signature is forged. Nelson fails to give Oakes, who indorsed the check over to Nelson, notice of the dishonor. Nelson cannot obtain payment from Oakes based on an indorser's contractual liability, since failure to give notice of dishonor discharges that liability. As will be seen, Nelson could obtain payment from Oakes based on Oakes' breach of transfer warranties.

Claims of breach of warranty arise most often in cases involving forged, stolen, or altered instruments. For example, a businessperson who frequently uses promissory notes may maintain a supply of preprinted notes. Someone could steal one of the notes, fill it in and forge the businessperson's name as maker, and negotiate it to another person. The note may be negotiated several times before finally being presented to the ostensible maker for payment. The ostensible maker may pay it and later discover that it was a forgery, or may note the forgery immediately and refuse payment. In either case, litigation is likely to result, and the courts must determine which of the various parties who handled the instrument must suffer the loss. The warranty rules are utilized in resolving such cases.

Similar allocation of loss problems arise in the case of stolen or altered instruments. If A writes a check payable to B, but C steals and cashes the check, who should bear the loss? What if the check passes through several hands before it is finally presented for payment at the bank where A maintains her account? What if a person alters a check and obtains payment of a greater amount than the check was written for? Again, the warranty rules are relied on to determine which of the various parties handling a stolen or altered instrument must ultimately bear the loss.

In general, the warranty rules tend to allocate loss to the person who was in the best position to avoid the loss. Of course, the person who forged, stole, or altered an instrument should ultimately bear the loss, but that person is seldom, if ever, available. The loss must therefore be placed on some innocent party. As discussed below, the protections accorded to the holder of such an instrument are substantially greater than those accorded to a party who makes payment on the instrument. The reason that a maker or drawee has less protection is that a maker or drawee is more likely to know that an instrument has been forged, stolen, or altered than is a holder in the chain of possession. In other words, among innocent parties the maker or drawee is in the best position to have avoided the loss.

UCC warranty provisions are contained in Articles 3 and 4 [UCC §§ 3-417, 4-207]. In the event of a conflict between the provisions, those of Article 4 govern.

Transfer Warranties [UCC §§ 3-417(2), 4-207(2)]   A transferor who transfers a negotiable instrument for consideration makes five warranties to the immediate transferee. These warranties are (1) that he has good title to the instrument and the transfer is rightful; (2) that all signatures are genuine or authorized; (3) that the instrument has not been materially altered; (4) that no defense of any party is good against him (or, in the case of a qualified indorser, that he has no knowledge of such a defense); and (5) that he has no knowledge of any insolvency proceeding, involving the maker, acceptor, or drawer. In addition, if the transfer is by indorsement, the transferor makes the same warranties to any subsequent holder who takes the instrument in good faith.

The most important of the transferor's warranties are the warranties of good title, genuine signatures, and lack of *material alteration.* Taken together, they amount to a guaranty that the instrument itself is not a forgery, that the signatures of the indorsers are not forgeries, that there have been no material changes made in the instrument, and that the transferor is a rightful holder of the instrument. If, for example, it should turn out that the maker's signature on a note was forged, the warranty of genuine signatures would be violated. Consequently, any transferee of this note could recover for breach of warranty from his immediate transferor, as well as from any previous transferors who indorsed the instrument.

Presentment Warranties [UCC §§ 3-417(1), 4-207(1)]   Each person who obtains payment or acceptance of a negotiable instrument, as well as any prior transferor of the instrument, makes three warranties to the person who in good faith pays or accepts the instrument. These warranties are (1) that the holder has good title, (2) that he has no knowledge that the maker's or drawer's signature is unauthorized, and (3) that the instrument has not been materially altered. These warranties are considerably narrower than the warranties made on transfer.

There are exceptions to the second and third warranties that benefit an HDC. Because these exceptions are complex, they will not be discussed here. Suffice it to say that their basic effect is to eliminate the warranties when payment or acceptance is obtained by an HDC from the maker, drawer, or acceptor.

The presentment warranties do not guarantee that all signatures are genuine. The warranty of good title is basically a warranty only that indorsements are genuine, since a forged indorsement cannot transfer title. The warranty of good title does not, however, guarantee that the instrument itself is not a forgery. The obligator's signature may be forged without violating the warranty of good title. Furthermore, the person presenting the instrument for payment only warrants that he has no knowledge that the obligor's signature was forged. Without proof that the holder had this knowledge, an obligor who pays a forged instrument cannot recover for breach of warranty from the person receiving payment. The reason for this rule is quite simple: As between two innocent parties, the one in the best position to have avoided the loss should bear the loss. A maker or drawer should know his signature; similarly, a drawee should ordinarily know the signature of his drawer. Those parties are therefore in a better position to detect a forged instrument than is a transferee of the instrument.

EXAMPLE: Abraham maintains a checking account at State Bank. Louise steals one of Abraham's checks, makes it out for $100 payable to herself, and forges Abraham's signature. Nicole, with no knowledge of the forgery, cashes the check, then obtains payment on the check from State Bank. On discovering the forgery, State Bank cannot seek repayment from Nicole. State Bank has Abraham's signature on file and could have verified the signature and detected the forgery before it made payment to Nicole. Nicole, on the other hand, had no way to verify the signature.

25:6   Liability of Agents, Accommodation Parties, and Guarantors

The UCC contains various rules concerning the liability of certain special types of parties, known as *agents, accommodation parties,* and *guarantors.* These parties are special in that they sign the instrument either on behalf of or to lend support to some other party to the instrument.

Agents [UCC § 3-403]   Under the UCC, no person is liable on a negotiable instrument unless his signature appears on the instrument. A signature may, however, be made by an agent or other authorized representative. An agent is a person who is authorized to act for another; the person for whom an agent acts is known as the principal (see Chapter 43).

When an agent names the principal and clearly signs in a representative capacity, there is no question as to who is liable on the instrument. It is clear that the principal is liable and the agent is not. Problems do arise, however, when an agent fails to disclose clearly that he is signing in a representative capacity. In such a situation, the agent is personally liable on the instrument.

To avoid personal liability, the agent must disclose two facts in the instrument: (1) the name of the principal and (2) the fact that the agent has signed in a representative capacity. All subsequent holders are then put on notice that the principal, and not the agent, is liable for payment. If the instrument discloses neither fact, the agent is personally obligated to all holders of the instrument. If the instrument shows one of the facts, the agent is liable to all parties except those who dealt directly with the agent. For example, if the original payee dealt with the agent and knew that the agent was acting only on behalf of the principal, the agent is not liable to the payee, but the agent is liable to all subsequent holders of the instrument.

 The UCC sets forth two methods of clearly indicating that an agent has signed in a representative capacity only. An agent for an individual should sign in this manner: "Peter Pringle by Arthur Adams, Agent." When signing on behalf of a corporation or other organization, an agent should name the organization and both the name and office of the agent. For example, "Ace Corporation by Arthur Adams, Treasurer," would be sufficient.

If the instrument does not contain the principal's name, the principal is not liable on it even though the agent intended to execute the instrument on behalf of the principal.

Accommodation Parties [UCC § 3-415] An accommodation party is one who signs a negotiable instrument in any capacity for the purpose of lending his name to another party to the instrument. To illustrate, assume that Kirk wants to purchase a television set on time, but the retailer will not extend credit to him. Helen, Kirk's mother, agrees to help out by signing a promissory note. The retailer then agrees to make the sale and accept the note. Helen is the accommodation party, and Kirk is the accommodated party. Although the retailer expects payment from Kirk, she now knows that she can look to Helen for payment if Kirk defaults.

An accommodation party is liable in the capacity in which he signed the instrument. For instance, Helen, as an accommodation maker of the note in the example just given, has basically the same liability as any other maker of a negotiable instrument. This rule is subject to certain exceptions, however. The accommodation party is discharged from liability to the holder (1) if the holder releases the accommodated party from liability or grants an extension of time to make payment (assuming that the holder knew of the accommodation party's status), or (2) if he unjustifiably impairs any collateral given to secure payment of the instrument. If the holder wishes to take either of these actions without discharging the accommodation party, he must either obtain the accommodation party's consent or else expressly reserve his rights against the accommodation party [UCC § 3-606]. To return to our illustration, this means that if the retailer wants to grant Kirk an extension of time to pay the note without discharging Helen, the retailer must either obtain Helen's consent to the extension or must expressly reserve his right to obtain payment from Helen.

Like agents, accommodation parties do not always disclose clearly that they are signing as accommodation parties.

When the instrument does not disclose a party's status as an accommodation party and the instrument is being held by an HDC who took the instrument without notice of the accommodation, the accommodation party cannot take advantage of the exceptions to liability just discussed. In other cases, an accommodation party who proves his status may take advantage of the exceptions; accommodation status may be proved by oral proof.

The UCC specifically provides that an indorsement that is not in the chain of title (an indorsement by someone with no apparent interest in the instrument) is notice of its accommodation character. For example, if a check is made out to Jones as payee, but is indorsed first by Wilson, then by Jones, all subsequent takers of the instrument are on notice that Wilson signed as an accommodation party. In addition, certain words of guaranty are, as will be discussed, clear indication that a party has signed an instrument as an accommodation party rather than as the party primarily liable for payment.

The following case discusses two issues: (1) whether the accommodation parties were properly permitted to prove their status as such and (2) whether the payee's actions toward the accommodated party had the effect of releasing the accommodation parties from liability. Consider what steps the payee might have taken to avoid the result in the case.

Lee Federal Credit Union
v
Gussie
542 F2d 887 (1976)
United States Court of Appeals, Fourth Circuit

FACTS: As consideration for a $30,000 loan, Ernest Lee executed a promissory note payable to Lee Federal Credit Union (Credit). At Credit's request, Warnetta Gussie and Kwang Rowe signed the note as co-makers. The loan, granted in 1971, became delinquent in June 1972. In August 1972, Lee gave Credit a check for $4,900, which was postdated to October. Credit deposited the check in October, but it was dishonored for insufficient funds. Credit never informed the co-makers of its acceptance of the postdated check or of the delinquency on the note. After the check was dishonored, Credit made attempts to collect from Lee. In August 1973, after learning that Lee had filed for bankruptcy, Credit notified Gussie of the delinquency and demanded payment. Gussie refused, and Credit sued Gussie, who in turn sued Rowe. The trial court concluded that both Gussie and Rowe were accommodation makers whose liability had been discharged and it entered judgment in their favor.

ISSUE: Is oral evidence admissible at trial to prove a party's accommodation status?

RESULT: Oral evidence may be admitted if the holder of the instrument had notice of the accommodation.

REASONING:

*   *   *

It is clear from the evidence that both Gussie and Rowe signed the note in question "for the purpose of lending [their] name[s] to another party to it," namely Ernest Lee. As such, they were accommodation parties within the meaning of [UCC § 3-415(1)]. Credit contends that the oral evidence as to the accommodation status of the co-makers should have been excluded since the face of the note reveals that they signed it as makers without any reservation of rights. Therefore, according to Credit, they are liable in the same manner and to the same extent as Ernest Lee. Section [3-415(3)] provides to the contrary, however. It reads:

> "As against a holder in due course and without notice of the accommodation oral proof of the accommodation is not admissible to give the accommodation party the benefit of discharges dependent on his character as such. In other cases the accommodation character may be shown by oral proof."

While Credit may have been a holder in due course, the district court found as a fact, which is not clearly erroneous, that Credit knew that the co-makers on the note were in fact accommodation parties, so Credit could not have been a holder in due course "without notice of the accommodation." This is one of the "other cases" mentioned in [§ 3-415(3)] in which "the accommodation character may be shown by oral proof." Thus, the oral evidence as to the status of the parties was properly admitted.

The question then becomes whether the actions of Credit in relation to the note were sufficient to discharge Rowe and Gussie from any further liability. We are of opinion they were. [UCC § 3-606] provides that:

> "(1) The holder discharges any party to the instrument to the extent that without such party's consent the holder
> (a) without express reservation of rights releases or agrees not to sue any person against whom the party has to the knowledge of the holder a right of recourse or agrees to suspend the right to enforce against such person the instrument or collateral or otherwise discharges such person, except that failure or delay in effecting any required presentment, protest or notice of dishonor with respect to any such person does not discharge any party as to whom presentment, protest or notice of dishonor is effective or unnecessary . . . "

In the instant case, Credit accepted Ernest Lee's post-dated check and, without notice or reservation of rights, extended the time of payment from the date the note had become delinquent until October when the check became payable. Such extension of time was granted without the consent of the accommodation parties and they were thus relieved of further liability upon the note. Credit, by its extension of time, at the very least, had "agree[d] to suspend the right to enforce against" Ernest Lee. [UCC § 3-606(1)(a)].

We recognize it is at least arguable that the agreed extension of time may not have been binding upon Credit and that it may have been able to institute proceedings against Lee prior to the date the check became payable. Yet, under the UCC in Virginia, it is the agreement which is controlling and not whether that agreement is necessarily binding. . . . The evidence clearly indicates that Credit agreed to extend additional time for payment on the note to Ernest Lee in exchange for the postdated check which he tendered in August. This agreement, having been reached without the consent of either Rowe or Gussie, was sufficient to relieve them from further liability. . . .

Widener, Circuit Judge.

An accommodation party is not liable to the accommodated party. Moreover, if an accommodation party pays the instrument, he or she may sue the accommodated party for reimbursement.

Guarantors [UCC § 3-416]   A guarantor is a particular kind of accommodation party. When there are two or more makers or acceptors, the use by one of words of guaranty indicates that that party is an accommodation party. The words "payment guaranteed" subject the signer to primary liability. A payment guarantor promises that if the instrument is not paid when due, he will pay it. The words "collection guaranteed" mean that the signer will pay an overdue note, but only after the holder has obtained and unsuccessfully attempted to collect on a judgment against the primary obligor, or has proved that such a proceeding would be useless. Words of guaranty which do not specify payment or collection are interpreted as a payment guaranty. The liability of a guarantor is primary in nature. This is so even when the guaranty is given on behalf of a secondary party.

25:7   Liability on Instruments Containing Forged Signatures[1]

A person whose signature has been forged on a negotiable instrument is not liable for payment of that instrument [UCC § 3-404]. A person whose name has been forged to an instrument can, however, later ratify (approve) it and thereby become liable on it, although such ratification is a rare occurrence.

Under the UCC, a forged signature operates as the signature of the forger. Thus, a forged instrument can still be negotiated. For example, assume that A executes a promissory note and forges B's name as maker. B is not liable on the note, but A is. The note can be negotiated from one party to another, and a holder in due course may acquire good title. When the time comes to seek payment, however, B probably will refuse, and A probably will not be found.

The above example deals with forgery of the obligor's signature. Forgery of a necessary indorsement has different consequences. Order paper (any negotiable instrument payable to order) requires an indorsement to be negotiated. A forged indorsement is, for purposes of negotiating the instrument and transferring title, no indorsement at all. Because a forged indorsement does not transfer title, the person acquiring under a forged indorsement cannot

---

[1] A bank's liability for payment of a forged check is discussed in Chapter 26.

become a holder or an HDC. Thus, he in turn is incapable of transferring good title to the instrument.

There are certain exceptions to the rule that a forged indorsement is ineffective. Two noteworthy exceptions are known as the *impostor rule* and the *fictitious payee rule*.

Impostor Rule [UCC § 3-405(1)(a)]   An impostor is a person who pretends to be someone he is not. For instance, if Adams pretends to be Murphy, he is an impostor. A person who impersonates another usually does so for dishonest purposes. One purpose might be to obtain possession of a negotiable instrument made payable to the person impersonated. Expanding on the example above, assume that Quincy owes money to Murphy, whom he has never met. Adams, knowing this, pretends to be Murphy and induces Quincy to issue a note (payable to Murphy) and give it to Adams. Adams now has the note and obviously intends to negotiate it to some innocent party. To do so, he must forge Murphy's name. This would ordinarily render the negotiation invalid and relieve Quincy of the obligation to pay on presentment. The UCC, however, recognizes that Quincy, who issued the note to an impostor, was in a better position to avoid the loss. In such circumstances an indorsement by any person in the name of the named payee is effective. If Adams indorses Murphy's name and negotiates the note to Wilson, Wilson can demand payment from Quincy (assuming that Wilson is not a party to the scheme). Moreover, if Adams should lose the note, any person who finds it can forge Murphy's indorsement and demand payment from Quincy. Thus, the UCC places the risk of loss on the person who permitted the impostor to obtain the instrument.

Fictitious Payee Rule [UCC § 3-405(1)(b), (c)]   The fictitious payee rule is that an indorsement by any person in the name of the named payee is effective. This rule applies when a negotiable instrument is made out to a payee with the intention that the payee have no interest in the instrument. The maker or drawer may himself intend that the payee have no interest; or an agent or employee of the maker or drawer, intending that the payee have no interest, may supply the name to the maker or drawer.

The fictitious payee rule is usually applied to situations involving business fraud. In a typical situation the obligor, or his employee, intends to pocket the money. He draws a check made payable to a fictitious payee with the intention of forging the payee's name and pocketing the proceeds. For obvious reasons the UCC places the risk of loss in such situations on the maker or drawer. If the obligor himself perpetrated the fraud, he can scarcely complain about being forced to pay. If the obligor's employee perpetrated the scheme, the obligor must pay because his carelessness permitted the employee to carry out the scheme. As between the obligor and the holder, the obligor was in the better position to prevent the loss.

The following case illustrates the application of the "Fictitious payee" rule where the payee is not a fictitious person. Note the policy reasons relied on by the court.

Fidelity & Casualty Co.

v

First City Bank
675 SW2d 316 (1984)
Court of Appeals of Texas, Dallas

FACTS: Johns, an employee of First National Bank, requested the bank's accounting department to prepare cashier's checks payable to Rock Island Bedding Co. and to Berry Industries, Inc. The request appeared normal because the bank was collecting debts owed Rock Island and Berry and remitting large checks to those firms regularly. Johns, however, intercepted 18 checks totaling $903,300, forged the indorsements of those firms, and deposited them at First City Bank. First City Bank accepted the checks, indorsed them "P.E.G." (prior endorsements guaranteed) and presented them to First National. First National paid the checks and recovered from its insurer, Fidelity. At trial, Fidelity sought to hold First City liable for the loss.

ISSUE: Did Johns' signature pass good title to the checks under the "Fictitious Payee Rule" of UCC § 3-405?

RESULT: Yes. The forged indorsement passes good title because Johns supplied the name of the payee intending that the named payee have no interest in the instrument.

REASONING:

*   *   *

As a general rule, forged endorsements are ineffective to pass title or to authorize payment. . . . As [UCC § 3-404(a)] provides, "Any unauthorized signature is wholly inoperative as that of the person whose name is signed. . . . " Thus, First City, as the collecting bank, warranted to First National, the payor bank, that it "ha[d] a good title to the item or [was] authorized to obtain payment or acceptance on behalf of one who ha[d] a good title." § 4.207(a)(1). Since the endorsement of the payee was not genuine or authorized, the collecting bank, First City, ordinarily would be liable to the payor bank, First National, for breach of warranty. . . . There is an exception to this general rule. Section 3.405(a)(3) provides:

(a) An indorsement by any person in the name of a named payee is effective if:

(3) an agent or employee of the maker or drawer has supplied him with the name of the payee intending the latter to have no such interest.

The general purpose of the Code is to allocate the loss, among innocent parties, to the person who is closest to the individual causing the loss and who, presumably, has the best opportunity to prevent it. . . . Thus, § 3.405 allocates the loss to the employer of the faithless employee:

> The principle followed is that the loss should fall upon the employer as a risk of his business enterprise rather than upon the subsequent holder or drawee. The reasons are that the employer is normally in a better position to prevent such forgeries by reasonable care in the selection or supervision of his employees, or, if he is not, is at least in a better position to cover the loss by fidelity insurance; and that the cost of such insurance is properly an expense of his business rather than of the business of the holder or drawee.

§ 3.405, Comment 4. . . . The effect of the section is to render a forged endorsement effective to transfer title. By shifting the loss to the drawer, the section precludes a collecting bank's liability on a § 4.207(a)(1) warranty and a drawee's liability to its customer under § 4.401. . . . Since First National was both drawer and payor, § 3.405(a)(3) provides First City a defense to Fidelity's cause of action.

. . . An employee "supplies" the name of the payee if he "starts the wheels of normal business procedure in motion to produce a check for a nonauthorized transaction." . . . Johns testified by deposition that he created false balances in the customers' accounts by submitting false invoices and, further, that the customers were not entitled to the funds represented by the eighteen checks. The checks would not have been issued but for Johns' deceit. Thus, Johns clearly "supplied" First National with the name of the payee.

Fidelity argues that § 3.405(a)(3) is inapplicable to the transactions because the payees were actual customers of First National. We disagree. "It is immaterial whether a person with the name of the payee actually exists or whether the name is in fact a wholly fictitious name." . . . The controlling factor is whether the underlying transaction is bona fide. . . .

Although First National may have been indebted to the payees at the time the checks were drawn, the checks were issued only because of Johns' fraudulent actions; thus, the transactions were not bona fide. In this respect, we distinguish [those cases] in which the employees intercepted checks that represented "legitimate and bona fide payments due and owing." . . .

Additionally, the evidence proves that Johns "intend[ed the payee] to have no . . . interest" in the checks. § 3.405(a)(3). Although the actual existence of the payee is relevant to the issue of intent. . . . Johns repeatedly testified by deposition that at the time he prepared the check request forms he intended the payees to receive no interest in the funds. . . . Fidelity offered no conflicting summary judgment evidence. Accordingly, we hold that First City proved, as a matter of law, the applicability of § 3.405(a)(3). . . .

Sparling, Justice.

25:8   Discharge of Parties

The UCC provides various ways in which parties may be discharged from liability on an instrument. A discharge may relieve one or more individual parties from further liability, or it may relieve all parties from liability. Certain methods of discharge (such as discharge of an indorser for noncompliance with the presentment and notice requirements) have already been discussed. Other important methods of discharge will be discussed here.

Payment [UCC § 3-603]   The normal method of discharge is by payment. When the party primarily liable on the instrument (the maker or the drawee–acceptor) pays the holder of the instrument, all parties are discharged from further liability on the instrument. If a secondary party makes payment, that party is discharged. Other parties who may be liable to the party making payment are not discharged.

EXAMPLE: Arnold executes a promissory note payable to Brenda. Brenda indorses the note to Carl, who in turn indorses it to Dana. If Arnold pays Dana, all parties are discharged. If Brenda pays Dana, Brenda and Carl are discharged, but Arnold remains liable. If Carl pays Dana, he is discharged, but Arnold and Brenda remain liable.

When only partial payment is made, the party doing so is discharged only to the extent of the payment.

 A party who pays an instrument in full may require that the instrument be given to him. This should always be done, since a negotiable instrument retains its negotiable character even after all parties have been discharged. No discharge is effective against a subsequent holder in due course who takes the instrument without notice of the discharge. The way to prevent an instrument from being fraudulently renegotiated is to take possession of the instrument when making payment on it.

Cancellation or Renunciation [UCC § 3-605]   The holder may discharge liability by canceling the instrument in several ways. The holder may cancel the instrument in its entirety. This discharges all parties from liability. The holder may also discharge an individual party by canceling the party's liability or by giving the instrument to the party. Cancellation may be accomplished in any manner that is apparent on the face of the instrument or in the indorsement. For example, the indorser is discharged if the holder strikes out the indorser's signature. The holder may also renounce his rights in writing, which means that he may state in writing that he gives up his right to receive payment from a party or parties.

Impairment of Right of Recourse or of Collateral [UCC § 3-606]   As just noted, the holder might discharge an individual indorser from liability by striking that indorser's signature. In addition, a party is discharged from liability if the holder of the instrument releases any other party against whom the first party has a right of recourse. Therefore, the holder's discharge of an indorser has the effect of discharging any indorsers subsequent to that indorser. The provision may apply to other parties to the instrument as well. For example, assume that a note is issued payable to Shani. Shani indorses the note to Brad, who in turn indorses it to Alyssa. At this point Shani and Brad are both secondarily liable to Alyssa, and Shani is secondarily liable to Brad. If Alyssa releases Shani from liability, that release also has the effect of discharging Brad.

 A businessperson might want to prevent the above result for various reasons. For example, Alyssa's release of Shani might be part of a business transaction between the two. Since Brad is not a part of that transaction, Alyssa would have no reason to release him. There are two ways in which a holder may release an individual indorser from liability without also discharging subsequent indorsers. The holder may obtain the consent of the subsequent indorsers, or the holder may expressly reserve his rights against the subsequent indorsers. Therefore, Alyssa can either secure Brad's consent to the release of Shani, or Alyssa can release Shani with an express reservation of rights against Brad. Brad then remains potentially liable to Alyssa, and Shani remains potentially liable to Brad. The only liability that has then been discharged is Shani's potential liability to Alyssa, which was Alyssa's intent.

The holder also discharges any party if he unjustifiably impairs any collateral given for that party's benefit. Such a discharge usually involves an accommodation party. If an accommodated party has given the obligor collateral to insure payment, the obligor's return of the collateral to the accommodated party would be an *unjustifiable impairment* and would discharge the accommodation party. To prevent such a discharge, the obligor can either secure the accommodation party's consent or can make an express reservation of rights.

Material Alteration [UCC § 3-407]   A material alteration of the instrument by the holder discharges from liability to the holder any party whose contract is thereby changed. That party, however, remains liable to a subsequent holder in due course. The subsequent HDC may still enforce the instrument against any party according to its original terms.

Key Concepts and Terms

- A primary party is the person who has an absolute obligation to pay the instrument. Primary parties include makers of notes and acceptors of drafts. A drawee is obligated to honor the instrument only after he or she has accepted it.
- A secondary party is a person who is obligated to pay the instrument if the primary party fails to do so. Secondary parties include drawers and indorsers.
- Generally, the holder of an instrument must present it to the primary party for payment when due; sometimes, the holder of a draft must also present

the draft to the drawee with a request that he accept it. If the instrument is not accepted or payment is refused, the instrument is considered dishonored, and the holder or potentially liable indorsers must notify secondary parties of that fact.

- The act of presenting an instrument and demanding acceptance or payment is called presentment. All negotiable instruments must be presented for payment; some drafts must be presented for acceptance. Generally, presentment must be made no later than the due date on a time instrument and within a reasonable time on a demand instrument.

- Dishonor consists of the obligor's nonacceptance or nonpayment after due presentment. Notice of dishonor may be given by the holder to any potentially liable party, and by any potentially liable party to any other potentially liable party. A bank must give notice before its midnight deadline. Other holders or indorsers must give notice before midnight of the third business day after dishonor or receipt of notice of dishonor.

- Compliance with the presentment and notice requirements is not required if (1) the indorser has waived compliance; (2) the holder is unable to comply; or (3) the indorser, as a result of his own conduct, has no right to require or reason to expect that the instrument will be paid. Presentment is not required if the obligor is dead or insolvent, or if payment or acceptance has been refused for some reason other than lack of proper presentment.

- Negotiable instruments carry five transfer warranties and three presentment warranties. The more important transfer warranties are the warranties of good title, genuine signatures, and lack of material alteration. The most important presentment warranty is the warranty of good title. These warranties arise even in the absence of indorsement, and noncompliance with presentment and notice requirements does not discharge warranty liability. Transfer warranties provide greater protection than presentment warranties.

- An agent is a person who is authorized to act for another; the person for whom an agent acts is known as the principal. An agent may sign an instrument on behalf of the principal, thereby obligating the principal. To avoid personal liability to pay the instrument, the agent must disclose (1) the name of the principal and (2) that the agent has signed in a representative capacity.

- An accommodation party is a person who signs a negotiable instrument in any capacity for the purpose of lending his name to another party to the instrument. An accommodation party who uses words of guaranty such as "payment guaranteed" or "collection guaranteed" is a guarantor. An accommodation party is generally liable in the capacity in which he signed the instrument. He is discharged from liability if the holder takes certain actions that have the effect of increasing the risk to the accommodation party. To avoid discharging an accommodation party, the holder must either secure the accommodation party's consent or make an express reservation of rights.

- A person whose signature has been forged is not liable for payment of a negotiable instrument, but the forger himself is liable. A forged instrument can be negotiated, but an instrument bearing a forged indorsement generally cannot be negotiated. A forged indorsement of a payee's name is effective if (1) the instrument was issued to an impostor (impostor rule) or (2) the instrument was issued with the intention that the payee have no interest in the instrument (fictitious payee rule).

- A discharge may relieve individual parties from further liability, or it may relieve all parties from liability. The usual method of discharge is by payment. Other methods of discharge include cancellation or renunciation, impairment of right of recourse or of collateral, and material alteration. No discharge is effective against a subsequent holder in due course who takes the instrument without notice of the discharge.

- Accommodation Party
- Agent
- Discharge
- Dishonor
- Fictitious Payee Rule
- Guarantor
- Impostor Rule
- Material Alteration

- Presentment
- Presentment for Acceptance
- Presentment for Payment
- Presentment Warranties
- Primary Parties
- Secondary Parties
- Transfer Warranties
- Unjustifiable Impairment

Questions and Case Problems

1. The holder in due course of a promissory note brought suit against Joyce Alves, an indorser. Alves had indorsed the note pursuant to the terms of a divorce separation agreement wherein she promised to "assign" her interest in the note to her husband. In her indorsement, however, she used the following language:

    Pay to the order of Keith R. Alves.

    /s/ Joyce Ann Alves

    Can Joyce present evidence of the separation agreement to prove that the transfer was an assignment rather than a negotiation? To disclaim contractual liability as an indorser?

2. Pamela forges Milt's name as maker of a promissory note payable to Pamela. Pamela indorses the note and sells it to Trudy. Trudy indorses the note and makes a gift of it to David. David presents the note to Milt for payment. Milt refuses to pay. One week later David tells Trudy of the dishonor. Is either Pamela or Trudy liable to David? If Milt had paid David, would any of the parties have been liable to Milt?

3. Young and Angelo, partners in a bakery, borrow $15,000 from State Bank and execute a 90-day promissory note for the debt. May also signs the note under the words, "Collection guaranteed." One week before the note is due Angelo informs the bank that she and Young have terminated their partnership, that Young has assumed all liabilities of the business, that Angelo does not want the note extended, and that Angelo will not sign a renewal note. The bank president gives Young an informal 60-day extension to pay the note. Young never pays, and State Bank sues Angelo and May on the note. Is either one liable? Discuss.

4. Blass, as president of Kaleo, Inc., executed a note to Bank on behalf of Kaleo for $83,000. Blass also signed the note, in his personal capacity, on the reverse side.

Shortly thereafter, Blass resigned as president. His successor, McNulty, agreed to indemnify him for any losses on the note. McNulty then negotiated extensions of the note and a substantial increase in the interest rate. Blass was not informed of the extensions and changes in the terms of the note. Within a few months both Kaleo and McNulty filed for bankruptcy. Bank sought to hold Blass to his contractual liability on the instrument. Is Blass liable to the bank?

5. Sally buys some sheep from Omar and pays him with a check for $500. She asks him to hold the check for two weeks, so that she can place sufficient funds in her bank account. Omar holds the check three weeks, then indorses it to Gennet as payment for work that Gennet performed on Omar's ranch. Gennet intends to deposit the check in her savings account the next day, but there is a blizzard and she is snowed in for two weeks. When she finally deposits the check, it is dishonored for insufficient funds. She seeks reimbursement from both Omar and Sally, but they claim that Gennet's delay in presenting the check absolved them of all liability. Are they correct?

6. Lambert sells supplies to City Hardware and accepts a promissory note as payment. The note states, "We promise to pay. . . ." Immediately above the signature the makers are identified as, "City Hardware and/or Robert Schwartz, Owner." The note is signed, "Robert Schwartz, President." The note is not paid when due, and Lambert sues Schwartz. Schwartz denies liability, claiming that he signed as an agent only. Is Schwartz in fact liable?

7. McCoy is the bookkeeper for Sam's Market. Knowing that she has insufficient funds in her bank account, McCoy writes a $2,000 check payable to Sam's Market and cashes it from the current day's receipts. She places Sam's Market's indorsement on the check as she is authorized to do. The check is given to Sano as payment for supplies. The check is dishonored by the bank, and Sano sues Sam's for the $2,000. Sam's denies liability on the ground that Sano failed to give the market notice of dishonor. How should the case be decided?

8. The following is the front of a promissory note:

November 7, 1987

I, Martha Macon, promise to pay $2,000 to the order of Paula Payee on November 7, 1988, with interest at 7.9% per year.

/s/ Martha Macon
/s/ Fred Friend

The back of the note says, "Pay to Fisher Corp. /s/ Martha Macon." On November 7, 1988, Fisher makes demand for payment from Martha. By early December Fisher concludes that Martha will not pay and it realizes that Fred has not been given notice of dishonor. Is Fred liable as a maker? As an accommodation party?

9. Magee, an employee of Snug Harbor Realty Company, is responsible for examining and initialing for payment invoices submitted to the company. The initialed invoices are forwarded to the company's bookkeeper for preparation of checks payable to the company's creditors. The checks are sometimes given to Magee for delivery to the payees. Magee forges the payees' indorsements on some checks, and the checks are paid by the drawee bank and charged against Snug Harbor's account. When Snug Harbor learns of the forged indorsements, it sues the bank. The bank argues that the fictitious payee rule relieves it of liability. Should the bank's position be sustained?

10. Bragg as maker and Sands as accommodation maker execute a promissory note payable to Cruz. The face of the note contains the following provision: "Present-

ment for payment and notice of dishonor are hereby waived." Cruz indorses the note and negotiates it to Elliott, who in turn indorses the note and negotiates it to Quoc. When the note is due, Bragg requests and receives a one-month extension from Quoc. Bragg eventually defaults and Quoc sues Sands, Cruz, and Elliott. The defendants claim that they have been discharged from liability as a result of (1) the extension of time and (2) the failure to give them notice of dishonor. How should the case be decided?

26 Bank Deposits and Collections

26:1 Introduction

Banks serve individuals and the business community by providing financial services. Among the most important of these services is the system of checking accounts and check payment and collection services. Despite the growth of electronic transfers, checks remain a major method of transferring value between individuals, businesses and customers, and debtors and creditors. It is important, therefore, to understand the rights and obligations associated with the check payment system.

Chapters 23, 24, and 25 examined the legal rules associated with creation and transfer of commercial paper under Article 3 of the UCC. This chapter focuses primarily on checks and the check collection system. The law governing the collection of checks is primarily Article 4 of the UCC, which has been enacted in all 50 states. Article 4 establishes (1) a time schedule for collecting and paying checks and (2) the framework of the relationship between banks and their customers. These can be varied by agreement between a bank and its customer. The bank's duty to act in good faith and to use ordinary care in its processing of checks, however, cannot be eliminated by agreement.

Definitions [UCC §§ 4-104, 4-105]   For purposes of this chapter, a "customer" is a person or an entity that has an account with a bank or for whom a bank has agreed to obtain payment on checks. A customer is said to draw a check by writing it out, after which that customer is referred to as the drawer of the check. The bank on which the check is drawn and which must ultimately pay the check is known as the *payor bank*, while the bank with which the check is initially deposited by a customer is the *depositary bank*. The party in whose favor a check is drawn is the payee. When the payee deposits the check—that is, when he delivers it to a bank with instructions that the amount of the check be credited to his account—he becomes a *depositor*.

26:2   Deposits; Relationship Between Bank and Depositor

A deposit may consist of cash, of a check, or of certain other drafts and orders. Depending on the mutual intent of the bank and its customer, any given deposit can be general or specific.[1]

Most deposits are general. A general deposit is, in effect, a loan by the depositor to the bank, and it is payable on demand. As soon as a general deposit of money is made, title to that money passes from the depositor to the bank. If the customer deposits a check, however, the deposit is of a *right* to money rather than of money itself. The deposit does not become one of money—so that title passes to the bank—until the check has been accepted and paid by the payor bank. Thus, for example, if a check is returned unpaid due to lack of sufficient funds in the drawer's account, the check is still the depositor's property. Therefore, the depositor (rather than the bank) must proceed against the drawer to obtain the amount of money represented by the check.

Every deposit is regarded as general unless it is made special by agreement between the parties. The distinctive feature of a special deposit used to be that when the depositor demanded it, the bank had to return exactly what had been deposited, rather than its equivalent. Today, a special deposit is one made for a special purpose that, in effect, prevents the bank's use of the deposited money. For example, a corporation might make a special deposit to establish a fund for the redemption (buying back) of some of its outstanding stock.[2]

Relationship Between Bank and Depositor   The relationship between the bank and its customer is multi-faceted. It is, of course, a voluntary contractual relationship. With respect to a general deposit, the relationship is one of creditor and debtor, which is consistent with the bank's acquisition of title to a general deposit. With respect to a special deposit, the relationship is more like one of bailment[3] because the deposited money does not become part of the bank's general assets.

In addition, there is an agency relationship (see Chapter 43) between a bank and its depositor. For example, the depositary bank acts as the depositor's collection agent when the depositor deposits a check that is drawn on a different bank. Moreover, a bailment relationship exists even as to what will

---

[1] The discussion in this chapter focuses on deposits in checking accounts. Bear in mind, however, that deposits can also be made in other types of accounts. For example, depositors often deposit money in savings accounts. The traditional form of savings account is the passbook account, which pays a low rate of interest but allows withdrawals at any time. Money can also be deposited for fixed terms ranging from 30 days to a number of years. A typical example is the treasury bill account, which has a 26-week term. Term accounts pay higher rates of interest than passbook accounts, but depositors incur a substantial penalty if they have to withdraw their money before the end of the term.

[2] A corporation's redemption of its stock is discussed in Chapter 46.

[3] A bailment arises when one person has temporary possession of, but not title to, another person's property. Bailments are discussed in Chapter 34.

become a general deposit when, for example, a merchant places a sack containing her business receipts for the day in a bank's night deposit box.

 Some banks attempt to limit their liability with respect to night deposits by requiring that the depositor agree to accept the full risk of any loss until the deposit has been verified by a bank employee the next day. Courts in a number of states have held that these agreements violate public policy, and so have refused to enforce them.

26:3   Checks and Checklike Drafts

When a person buys goods or services, there may or may not be an immediate assignment of the person's money to the seller, depending on how the person pays for the goods or services. If he or she pays in cash, there is an immediate assignment to the seller. If, however, the buyer pays by check, there is *not* an immediate assignment to the seller of money that the buyer has on deposit with the payor bank.

A check is merely a demand draft drawn on a bank; it is an order to a drawee bank to pay money. The seller receives only a provisional credit to his account when he deposits the check. Thus, the credit becomes final—and an actual transfer of money has occurred—only after the payor bank has received and paid the check. For this reason, the seller holding the check has no rights against the payor bank if that bank refuses to pay the check; the seller's only recourse is against the drawer.

Types of Checks   The check that an individual or business usually draws is an ordinary check. This is simply a draft drawn on a bank and to be paid on demand out of the drawer's account with that bank. An ordinary check that bears a date later than the date on which the check was drawn is a *postdated check*. A postdated check is valid, and it is payable on or after the date indicated on it. A drawer might postdate a check to be certain that sufficient funds will be on deposit to cover the check. Postdating a check is not wrongful unless it is done to defraud.

At times, a party being paid by check is unwilling to accept the risk that an ordinary check will not be paid. Special types of checks are available to meet this need. These include certified checks, cashier's checks, banker's checks, and traveler's checks.

A *certified check* is a check that the payor bank has agreed in advance to pay, so that it must ordinarily be paid even if there are insufficient funds in the drawer's account. The check is presented to the payor bank by either the drawer or the payee. After satisfying itself that the check is valid and that the drawer has sufficient funds in his account to cover it, the bank stamps the check "certified" or "accepted." The object of having a check certified is to make the check the equivalent of money.

A *cashier's check* is a check drawn by a bank on itself. Its strength lies in the fact that it is the obligation of the bank. A *banker's check* is similar to a cashier's check except that the check is drawn on another bank rather than on the drawer bank.

A *traveler's check* is purchased for later use by a customer who does not want to carry cash. It is similar to a cashier's check in that it is drawn on the payor bank (or other issuing organization, such as American Express). It differs from a cashier's check in that (1) the name of the payee is left blank, to be filled in later when the customer uses the check and (2) the customer signs the check twice—once when purchasing it and again when using it. The customer's second signature makes the check both negotiable and the equivalent of money.

Checklike Drafts   At one time so-called "thrift institutions" such as savings and loan associations and credit unions could offer a higher rate of return on money deposited with them than banks could. At the same time, banks were not permitted to pay interest on money deposited in checking accounts. The result was that people turned to banks for checking account services, but they often deposited their savings with thrift institutions. Much of that has changed in recent years with the partial deregulation of banks, interest rates, and financial services. Today, banks offer interest-bearing checking accounts, while the thrift institutions offer checklike services to their depositors. The result is that some people who once relied exclusively on conventional checks now use drafts drawn on thrift institutions instead.

A checklike draft drawn on a savings and loan association is called a *negotiable order of withdrawal (NOW)*. This instrument is much like a check except that it is not drawn on a bank. A draft drawn on a credit union is known as a share draft.

NOW and share drafts fall within the scope of instruments governed by Articles 3 and 4 of the UCC. Courts have tended to be expansive in the application of these Articles to checklike instruments. It is likely, therefore, that courts will decided that the checklike drafts that money market funds currently allow their depositors to write are also governed by Articles 3 and 4.

26:4   The Collection Process

The holder of a check is the party (1) having possession of a filled-out check and (2) having the right to payment on the check. The payee, who is the initial holder, first indorses the check.[4] The payee can then (1) attempt to cash the check, usually by presenting it to the payor bank and requesting payment; or (2) deposit it in his or her account; or (3) give it to somebody else, who becomes the new holder. At some point a holder usually deposits the check, and the depositary bank then attempts to obtain payment on the check from the payor bank.

In essence, the *collection process* is the means by which a check deposited in one bank but drawn on another is paid. Thus, if a drawer and payee are both customers of the same bank, collection does not occur if the payee deposits

---

[4] The payee indorses the check by signing his or her name on the back. A depositary bank will not ordinarily accept an unindorsed check for deposit although, to avoid delay, Article 4 allows the bank to add any needed indorsement. Indorsements are discussed in more detail in Chapter 23.

the check with that bank. The bank simply deducts the amount of the check from the drawer's account and adds it to the payee's account.

The holder of a check usually deposits the check in a bank other than the payor bank. The check must then be physically transferred back to the payor bank, which is accomplished through one or more interbank transfers. Because it is possible that the payor bank will *dishonor* the check when it receives it, the depositary bank accepts the deposit "subject to collection." The bank, acting as the depositor's agent, then begins the collection process. Meanwhile, the bank makes a *provisional settlement* of the check. This means that the bank gives the depositor's account a provisional credit for the amount of the check. A provisional credit is a credit that can be reversed later if the check is not paid. The provisional credit that the bank gives does not become final until enough time has passed for the depositary bank to have received either a notice of dishonor or return of the unpaid check.

 Generally, a depositary bank will neither allow its customer to withdraw money that has been only provisionally credited to his or her account nor pay checks drawn against the credit. Exceptions are often made, however, for valued customers whose credit is known to be good.

A depositary bank can send a check directly to the payor bank for payment. However, the route is usually less direct. If the depositary and payor banks are in different parts of the country, the check is apt to pass through two of the 13 Federal Reserve Banks (FRBs) located across the country.

EXAMPLE: Williams, a resident of Show Low, Arizona, draws a check on her account at the Show Low branch of First Arizona Bank. The payee named in the check is Zebco, a Pennsylvania company. Zebco deposits the check in its account at Colonists Bank in Philadelphia. The route then taken by the check might be as follows: Colonists sends the check to the FRB serving Philadelphia, which sends it to the FRB serving Phoenix, Arizona, which sends it to First Arizona's headquarters bank in Phoenix, which sends it to the First Arizona Show Low branch.

Banks in the collection chain other than the depositary and payor banks are called *intermediary banks.* The term "collecting bank" refers to any bank in the collection chain other than the payor bank. Thus, Colonists Bank and all the intermediary banks in the above example are collecting banks. Just as the customer who deposits a check receives a provisional credit for it from the depositary bank, each collecting bank receives a provisional credit from the bank to which it transfers the check.

Clearinghouses Because of the large flow of checks in major urban areas, banks in many cities have formed what are known as *clearinghouses.* Each day, every bank that is a member of a clearinghouse (1) sends to the clearinghouse all checks received by it and drawn on other member banks and (2) receives from the clearinghouse, in a single package, all checks that are drawn on that member bank and received by the clearinghouse from other member banks. The clearinghouse makes a single daily settlement with each member bank for checks handled by the clearinghouse that day. If the total amount of all checks sent by a member is more than the total of the checks received by it, the clearinghouse pays the member the difference. In the opposite situation, the member bank makes a payment to the clearinghouse.

26:5   Rights and Duties of Collecting Bank

Whenever a check is deposited with other than the payor bank, there will be at least one collecting bank, and often there will be more than one. Article 4 imposes certain requirements on each collecting bank and, for that matter, on the customer who deposits the check in the first place.

General Duty of Ordinary Care; Midnight Deadline [UCC §§ 4-104, 4-107, 4-202]   Article 4 lists five specific collection tasks that each collecting bank must perform with ordinary care. For example, the bank must use ordinary care in sending a check to the next bank in the collection chain, whether the check is moving toward the payor bank or, if the payor bank has refused to pay the check, toward the collecting bank's transferor. This ordinary care requirement applies to such matters as the method by which a check is physically transferred and the choice of intermediary banks or other agents, if such a choice exists.

Each collecting bank must also process the check within a reasonable time. Generally speaking, the bank satisfies this requirement if it meets its *midnight deadline.* The midnight deadline is midnight of the banking day following the banking day on which a bank receives a check. To allow a more uniform work flow, Article 4 permits each bank to set an afternoon hour of 2 p.m. or later as a cutoff hour for the processing of checks on any given day.

EXAMPLE: Valley Bank, which is open for business between 9 a.m. and 5 p.m. on weekdays, has set 3 p.m. as its cutoff hour. At 2:30 p.m. on Friday, June 6, Valley receives for collection check #501 drawn on Prairie Bank. At 3:30 p.m. on the same day it receives check #703, also drawn on Prairie. Valley has until midnight on Monday, June 9, to send check #501 to Prairie or to another collecting bank, but it has until midnight on June 10 to complete its processing of check #703.

Warranties of Customer and Collecting Bank [UCC § 4-207]   Article 4 lists the warranties that collecting banks and customers are deemed to make whenever they transfer a check and receive provisional credit for it. A collecting bank warrants, among other things, (1) that its title to the check is good, (2) that all indorsements on the check are genuine or authorized, and (3) that the check has not been materially altered. These warranties are in favor of the transferee collecting bank and each collecting bank that comes later in the collection chain. Warranties of a similar type, but in favor of the payor bank, are deemed to be given by each customer or collecting bank that obtains payment of a check.[5]

The distinction between the two types of warranties is, in essence, that warranties of the first type operate as a check moves from the depositary bank to the payor bank, while those of the second type operate as the "payment" moves back along the chain to the depositary bank. In practice, instead of there being any actual transfer of payment for every individual check, each collecting bank simply allows its provisional settlement of the check to become final. This occurs automatically with the passage of time unless the payor bank revokes the settlement.

The Article 4 warranty provision has the effect of placing on the depositary bank the burden of making sure that all indorsements on a check are valid. This policy is logical since the depositary bank can investigate the validity of indorsements more easily than intermediary banks or the payor bank can. Thus, if a payor bank has paid a check that has a forged indorsement, the bank is usually liable to the drawer if the drawer has given timely notice about the error. The payor bank will then seek recourse from the collecting bank from which it received the check, claiming breach of warranty. This process will be repeated back along the collection chain until it reaches the depositary bank. That bank's recourse is against the customer who deposited the check.

 Any claim for breach of one of these warranties must be made within a reasonable time after the claimant's discovery of the breach. If a claimant delays beyond a reasonable time, the party who would otherwise be liable is discharged to the extent of any loss suffered by that party because of the delay.

EXAMPLE: On August 1, State Bank learned that a $1,000 check it paid had carried an unauthorized indorsement. The check had been indorsed by Tom Horn and deposited by him in his account with First Federal Bank. During the month of August, Horn maintained more than $1,000 in his First Federal account, but on September 2, he closed the account and left for parts unknown. If State does not assert a breach of warranty claim against First Federal until September 15, First Federal will probably not be liable for the $1,000. State will have failed to act within a reasonable time, and First Federal will have suffered potential loss as a result. Had the claim come during August, First Federal could have recovered from Horn, but now it cannot do so.

Charge-Back or Refund [UCC § 4-212]   If a collecting bank that has given a provisional credit on a check fails to receive a final settlement of the check, the bank has the right to *charge-back* (reverse) the credit given to its customer or to obtain a refund from its customer. For example, if a depositary bank has provisionally credited its customer's account and the check is returned due to

---

[5] Bear in mind that both types of warranties discussed here are the same warranties that exist with respect to the transfer or obtaining of payment or acceptance of *any* negotiable instrument. The warranties are discussed in greater detail in Chapter 25.

insufficiency of funds in the drawer's account, the bank can deduct the amount of the check from the customer's account. The following case applies the midnight deadline rule to a bank's exercise of the charge-back right.

Manufacturers Hanover Trust Co.
v
Akpan
398 NYS2d 477 (1977)
New York City Civil Court

FACTS: On Monday, August 18, Akpan, the defendant, deposited a $2,500 check drawn by Lawrence on her account with Branch 102 of the plaintiff, Manufacturers Hanover Trust Company. On August 19, the check was received by the payor bank, and it was not paid due to insufficient funds in Lawrence's account. The payor bank returned the check to Manufacturers' headquarters bank that day. On August 22, Akpan drew a check for $2,490 on her account at Branch 102 and received cash for it. On Monday, August 25, Branch 102 first received notice from Manufacturers' headquarters bank that the $2,500 check had been returned. Branch 102 notified Akpan at once and informed her that her account had been charged for that amount. Apparently because there was little or no money left in the account, Manufacturers then sued Akpan to obtain the refund allegedly due it.

ISSUE: Did the bank exercise ordinary care in returning the check to Branch 102 to meet its midnight deadline?

RESULT: The bank failed to exercise ordinary care and, therefore, did not give timely notice of the dishonor to the depositor.

REASONING:

*   *   *

Plaintiff's first theory of liability is based on [UCC § 4-212], which gives a collecting bank (plaintiff) a remedy of charge-back if it has made a provisional settlement with its customer which fails by reason of dishonor. But this remedy is conditioned on the requirement that the bank, by its midnight deadline or within a longer reasonable time after it learns of the facts, [return] the item or sends notification of the facts. . . .

Thus, applying the midnight deadline rule in the instant case, plaintiff would have had to have given notice to Mrs. Akpan by midnight of Wednesday, August 20, . . . in order to exercise its right of charge-back. Notice was not actually given until Monday August 25, . . .

Plaintiff relies on [UCC § 4-106] which states that a separate office of a bank is considered a separate bank for the purpose of determining time limits under Articles 3 and 4 of the U.C.C. But even considering Branch 102 as a separate bank and not bound by information of the check's dishonor had by [Manufacturers's headquarters bank], this cannot be construed to mean that the midnight deadline rule first began to run on Monday, August 25, . . . when Branch 102 first received notice of the dishonor.

The official comment #4 to [UCC § 4-106] seems to deal with a situation such as in the instant case.

"Similarly, the receipt of a stop payment order at one branch should not be notice to another branch . . . , *although in circumstances in which ordinary care requires the communication of a notice or order to the proper branch of a bank, such notice or order would be effective at such proper branch from the time it was or should have been received.*" [Court's emphasis.]

Ordinary care required in the instant case that notice be sent to Branch 102 by the midnight deadline of [Manufacturers's headquarters bank] on midnight Wednesday. Such notice would be effective at the time Branch 102 *should have received notice;* thus the midnight deadline for Branch 102 was midnight Thursday. [Court's emphasis.] Since notice of dishonor was not sent to defendant within the midnight deadline, the remedy of charge-back is unavailable. . . .

Imperato, Judge.

26:6   Duties of Payor Bank

A payor bank has the general duty of paying a valid check drawn on it if the drawer has sufficient funds in his account at the time the bank receives the check. UCC § 4-302 provides, in essence, that a payor bank must make a provisional settlement of a check before midnight of the day of receipt. The bank then has until its midnight deadline to (1) pay the check; (2) return the check; or (3) if the check is not being either paid or returned, send a notice of dishonor. A returned check or notice of dishonor is sent to the collecting bank from which the payor bank received the check. If the payor bank fails to take the required action in time, it is liable for the amount of the check unless it has a valid defense, such as breach of a warranty.

Final Payment of Checks; Posting [UCC §§ 4-109, 4-213]   The term "final payment" refers to the time when the settlement of a check by the payor bank becomes final, rather than being merely provisional. Article 4 lists various events, the occurrence of any one of which constitutes final payment. For example, final payment occurs (1) when the payor bank pays a check in cash,

(2) when it has completed the *posting process,* or (3) when it fails to revoke a provisional settlement made by it earlier.

The term "posting process" refers to the usual procedure by which the payor bank (1) decides to pay a check and (2) records the payment. Examples of steps, one or more of which can constitute posting, are (1) verifying any signature, (2) determining whether the drawer has sufficient funds in his account to cover the check, and (3) stamping the check "Paid."

Charging Customer's Account; Order of Payment [UCC §§ 4-303, 4-401] When a payor bank receives and pays a check drawn by its customer, the bank charges the customer's account for the amount of the check. As is discussed in more detail below, the bank has the right (1) to pay a check even though the customer has insufficient funds in his account to cover the check, (2) to pay an altered check, (3) to pay a check that has been completed by someone other than the drawer, and (4) to pay in any order convenient to it checks from the same account that it receives at the same time. A payor bank's payment of a check drawn on insufficient funds in the drawer's account creates an overdraft, which is a negative amount in the drawer's account. Bear in mind that the bank is under no obligation to pay a check if the payment will create an overdraft. The bank's *right* to pay the check exists because the check is deemed to carry the drawer's promise to reimburse the bank.

If a check has been altered as, for example, by having the amount of the check increased, the bank can charge the customer's account for the original amount of the check. The bank can also pay and charge the customer's account for a check that was completed by someone other than the drawer, as long as the bank has not been notified that the completion is improper.

EXAMPLE: Axel gives Katrinka a check to cover the cost of groceries that Katrinka is going to buy. Axel dates and signs the check, and he writes in the name of the local supermarket as payee, but he leaves the amount blank. After completing her shopping, Katrinka completes the check by filling in the amount of her shopping bill. Unless Axel's bank has notice that Katrinka's completion of the check is improper, it can and probably will pay the check as written.

A payor bank does not necessarily receive checks in the same order in which the checks were drawn. Also, and particularly with respect to a high-activity account, the bank might receive at the same time a number of checks drawn on the same account. Article 4 gives the bank the right to pay the checks in any order convenient to the bank.

Wrongful Dishonor [UCC § 4-402]   A bank that wrongfully dishonors a customer's check is liable to the customer for damages proximately caused by the wrongful dishonor. The term "proximate cause" means a primary cause from which a particular loss followed as a natural and direct consequence, and without which the loss would not have occurred. If a dishonor occurs because of a mistake, the customer can recover only the actual damages sustained. If dishonor occurs for a reason other than mistake, such as if the bank acted intentionally and without a good reason, the customer can also recover punitive damages.[6]

Whether particular loss suffered by a customer is proximately caused by a wrongful dishonor is a question of fact that must be determined in each case. That question, as well as the related problem of computing the amount of money that the customer should be awarded, can be troublesome, as the following case illustrates.

American Fletcher Nat. Bank & Trust Co.
v
Flick
252 NE2d 839 (1969)
Indiana Appellate Court

FACTS: Flick sued American Fletcher Bank for damages arising from American Fletcher's dishonor of checks drawn by Flick. Flick had operated a used-car business, and the checks were drawn on his business account. He sought $125,000 for damages to his credit and business standing, for loss of business income, and for mental suffering.

ISSUES: What evidence is required to establish (1) whether loss, injury, or harm was proximately caused by a wrongful dishonor, and (2) what amount of damages is recoverable?

RESULT: The law presumes some harm to a customer's credit and business standing from a wrongful dishonor, but only nominal damages can be recovered unless there is evidence linking claimed substantial loss with the dishonor.

REASONING:

* * *

. . . [W]e hold that when a bank wrongfully dishonors its customer's business check there arises a presumption that the customer's credit and business standing is thereby harmed. . . . The primary reason for the recognition of this presumption is that a wrongful dishonor renders the existence of *some* harm to the customer's credit and business standing so probable that it makes legal sense as well as common sense to assume the existence of such harm unless and until the adversary comes forward with some evidence to the contrary. [Court's emphasis.] Although we are

---

[6] Punitive damages are awarded to a person not as compensation for actual loss suffered, but as a civil penalty against a wrongdoer and to deter similar wrongful acts by others.

not prepared to go as far as did [the court in a Pennsylvania case], the following statement from the opinion is a recognition of the high probability of such harm:

> In the modern world the financial credit of a man, particularly of one engaged in commercial pursuits, is a much prized and valuable asset. Although laboriously built it is easily destroyed. The banks of the country, through which the great volume of our commercial business is transacted, have a deserved reputation for accuracy and care in the conduct of their affairs. Hence when a check of a depositor is refused at the counter of his bank, that portion of the commercial world, greater or less, that comes within the sphere of his transactions, promptly imputes the blame to him rather than to the bank. . . .

The rationale of the [above case], however, does not hold true as to such other "consequential" losses or injuries as may be conceivably sustained as a proximate result of wrongful dishonor. Additional harms, injuries or losses, such as those alleged by Flick, are susceptible of evidentiary proof, both as to their actual existence and as to their extent. Flick here has failed to bring forth sufficient evidence to show that loss of income or other expense, harm or injury, if any, was proximately caused by the wrongful dishonor. He, therefore, cannot recover for such alleged loss, expense, harm or injury. He is . . . restricted to recovery for the harm to his credit and business standing, which harm is established by way of the unrebutted presumption heretofore discussed. . . .

Having found only the harm to credit and business standing compensable in this case the question which remains is whether there was sufficient evidence to justify any more than nominal damages. We think not and therefore plaintiff may only recover nominal damages. . . .

The law presumes that at least nominal damages result from a harm. . . . Therefore, plaintiff is entitled to at least nominal damages for the harm to his credit and business standing. . . . We recognize that the amount of damages appropriate for harm to credit and business standing is difficult to prove. When it is found that a harm has been caused and the only uncertainty is as to the dollar value of the harm, there can rarely be good reason for refusing, on account of such uncertainty, any damages whatever. . . . However, there must be some evidence on which to base an award of *substantial* damages. [Court's emphasis.] . . .

In our case, Flick completely failed to present any evidence that the wrongful dishonor proximately caused the substantial damages which were alleged. The evidence is undisputed that shortly after April 15, 1965, the bank returned three of Flick's checks because of insufficient funds in Flick's account. It is also undisputed that some time after April 15, 1965, Flick's business at Morris Street Auto Sales declined, he sold fewer autos, his income declined, he eventually began to lose money, and that his used car lot was closed in the fall of 1966. There is nothing in the record, however, linking these undisputed facts with the dishonor of the checks. There is nothing in the record which indicates that anyone other than the payees on the checks and Flick had knowledge of the dishonored checks or *could* have had any knowledge of said checks. [Court's emphasis.] There is nothing in the record to indicate that the checks caused any action or inaction by any other party. To the contrary, there is affirmative evidence in the record indicating that there were reasons other than the dishonor for the decline of Flick's business. We hold that appellee Flick is entitled to recover only nominal damages. . . .

Sullivan, Judge.

Stale Checks [UCC § 4-404]   A check is regarded as being stale six months after the date of the check. A payor bank is not required to pay a stale check (other than a certified check), although it can do so as long as it acts in good faith. In practice, most banks will not pay a stale check without first consulting the drawer, but exceptions are made under some circumstances. For example, a bank receiving a stale dividend check drawn by its corporate customer will ordinarily pay it at once, realizing that the corporation wants payment to be made.

26:7   Stop-Payment Orders

A *stop-payment order* is an order directing that a payor bank not pay a particular check. UCC § 4-403 gives each customer the right to stop payment on a check drawn by him. To be effective, the order must be received by the payor bank early enough to give the bank a reasonable time to act on it. An order is too late if the bank has taken any one of various actions listed in § 4-303 before receiving and having a chance to act on the order. For example, the order is too late if the bank has already paid or certified the check, or if it has completed the posting process. What constitutes a reasonable time if none of the events listed in § 4-303 has occurred depends on the circumstances. For example, if a customer gives her bank a stop-payment order, but the bank cashes the check when the payee presents it at that bank 90 minutes later, the bank has probably had sufficient time for processing and acting on the order. The same would not be true if the check were presented for payment only several minutes after the bank's receipt of the stop-payment order.

 A person who fears that a stop-payment order might not be processed in time to stop a particular check can create an overdraft situation by withdrawing most of the money from his account, thus leaving insufficient funds to cover the check in question. This procedure is risky in view of the bank's right to pay a check drawn on insufficient funds. The safer practice is to close the account and withdraw everything from it, although the customer must then make other arrangements for outstanding checks that *are* to be paid.

A stop-payment order can be oral or in writing. An oral stop-payment order is effective for only 14 calendar days unless the order is confirmed in writing within that period. A written order is effective for six months, but it can be renewed at the end of that period, and again following subsequent six-month periods if the drawer believes that the check might still be in circulation. In this regard, recall that a payor bank has the right to pay a stale check, although it is not required to do so.

A bank that pays a check despite having received a timely stop-payment order is liable to the customer for any damages that the customer suffered as a result. Article 4 states that the customer must prove both the existence and the amount of damages, although some courts say that the measure of damages is automatically the amount of the check unless the bank shows that the customer suffered a lesser loss. Note in the following case, however, that even if the bank fails to follow the stop payment order, it succeeds to the rights of the holder who presented the check for payment.

Parr

v

Security Nat. Bank
680 P2d 648 (1984)
Court of Appeals of Oklahoma

FACTS: On September 14, 1981, Parr wrote, dated, and mailed check #949 for $972.96 to Champlin Oil Co. On September 15, 1981, she called the bank and ordered payment stopped on the check. Parr gave the bank her account number, the check number, the date, the payee, and the amount of the check. A 50 percent error was made in identifying the amount of the check. On September 16 she went to the bank and executed a written stop-payment order. The written order was also in error as to amount. On September 17, 1985, the bank paid check #949. When Parr filed suit the bank defended that Parr's error relieved them of liability.

ISSUE: Was the bank liable for failure to stop payment on the check?

RESULT: Yes. The check was described with sufficient accuracy so as to obligate the bank to follow the order.

REASONING:

*   *   *

Section 4–403(1) of the Uniform Commercial Code . . . contains the applicable law on stop payment orders:

> A customer may by order to his bank stop payment of any item payable for his account but the order must be received at such time and in such manner as to afford the bank a reasonable opportunity to act on it prior to any action by the bank with respect to the item described in Section 4–303.

It is appropriate to examine the purpose of this section before construing it. The policy underlying § 4–403 is found in Comment 2 following the section:

> The position taken by this section is that stopping payment is a service which depositors expect and are entitled to receive from banks notwithstanding its difficulty, inconvenience and expense. The inevitable occasional losses through failure to stop should be borne by the banks as a cost of the business of banking.

Security National contends that whether a stop payment order has been received "in such manner as to afford the bank a reasonable opportunity to act" should be determined *after* examining how the defendant bank handles stop orders. This interpretation has found favor among highly respected legal authorities, but not among the majority of courts that have addressed this issue.

Both groups acknowledge § 4–403(1) has not changed the common law rule that a stop payment order must identify the check with "reasonable accuracy." It is from this premise that courts have determined whether the description is reasonably accurate without consideration of the defendant/bank's computer program. . . .

In *Delano v. Putnam Trust Co.* . . . , a single digit error in the amount of $100.00 did not prevent recovery where customer supplied bank with the correct check number, date, payee, and account number of the check. The bank's computer program required an exact match of check amount before it would stop payment. Court held bank had received sufficient information to allow it a "reasonable opportunity to act" on the stop payment order. Court stated the bank had a duty to inform its customer of the need for precision in reporting the amount before it could rely on customer's error to relieve it of liability. . . .

In *FJS Electronics, Inc. v. Fidelity Bank* . . . , Court allowed customer to prevail even though its 50 cent error in check amount prevented bank's computer from acting on stop payment order. The bank asserted § 4–403 "should be read to require compliance with the procedures of a particular bank, regardless of what they are and regardless of whether the customer has been made aware of them." . . . Court determined that the drafter's policy stated in Comment 2 to § 4–403 precluded such an interpretation. They reasoned:

> Fidelity made a choice when it elected to employ a technique which searched for stopped checks by amount alone. It evidently found benefits to this technique which outweighed the risk that an item might be inaccurately described in a stop order. This is precisely the type of inevitable loss which was contemplated by the code drafters and addressed by the comment quoted above. The

focus of § 4–403 is the service which may be expected by the *customer*, and a customer may expect a check to be stopped after the bank is given reasonable notice. A bank's decision to reduce operating costs by using a system which increases the risk that checks as to which there is an outstanding stop payment order will be paid invites liability when such items are paid.

We find this analysis, as well as that in *Delano, supra*, persuasive. We hold Parr described her check with reasonable accuracy, and Security National had a reasonable opportunity to act on the stop payment order.

We are aware of the burden this may place on Oklahoma banks. However, the industry has two alternatives to avoid liability if banking procedures necessitate an exact description of an item: (1) notify the customer at the time a stop order is given, or (2) seek a legislative amendment to § 4–403.

We recognize Parr received the benefit of having her debt paid to Champlin Oil and will recover from Security National for failure to stop payment. To avoid this possibility of unjust enrichment, § 4–407(b) subrogates the payor bank [Security National] to the rights of the payee [Champlin] against the maker [Parr]. In such a suit, an award of attorney's fees and costs to Security National would be proper under 12 O.S.1981 § 936, as Champlin would have been suing Parr on an open account if Security National had stopped payment on the check. . . .

Reynolds, Judge.

26:8   Bank's Liability as to Forged or Altered Check

A *forged check* is one on which what appears to be the signature of the drawer or indorser has actually been written by someone else, acting without authorization. Forged drawer signatures usually occur after an unauthorized person has obtained possession of one or more blank checks belonging to somebody else. Since checks that have already been drawn are often accessible to more people than blank checks are, forged indorsements are more common than forged drawer signatures. At times, however, the signatures of both the drawer and the indorser can be forgeries. For example, a person can obtain someone else's blank check and draw the check payable to a legitimate payee, forge the drawer's signature and the payee's indorsement, and then attempt to cash the check at the payee's bank.

An *altered check* is one on which the words or numbers written by the drawer have been changed by someone else. For example, what was drawn as a $100 check might be altered to call for the payment of $1,000, or the drawer's intent in postdating a check might be frustrated by someone else's alteration of the date.

The payor bank is under no duty to pay a forged or altered check. Indeed, the bank can be liable to its customer, the drawer, if it does so [UCC § 4-406].

This liability is not automatic, however, and it might not exist at all if the customer has failed to perform the duties imposed on him. Assuming that the payor bank has paid a check and charged the drawer's account, the check will eventually be returned to the drawer, usually with a periodic statement showing the activity in the drawer's account during the period covered by the statement. Most banks send out statements and canceled checks to their customers monthly. If a statement and the checks are not sent to the customer, they are at least made available for the customer's inspection. The customer is required to use reasonable care and promptness to examine the statement and checks, discover any forgery of signature or any alteration of a check, and notify the bank.

If the bank can show that the customer failed to perform this duty and that the bank suffered loss as a result, it is not liable to the customer with respect to the forgery or alteration. Also, if the customer fails to notify the bank about a forgery or alteration within 14 days after having access to the check and statement, the bank is not liable with respect to its later good-faith payment of any checks that are forged or altered in the same way by the same person.

EXAMPLE: Althea works for Gibson Co. in the accounting department. She has access to Gibson's blank checks. Each month Althea writes a check naming herself as payee and forges the drawer signature authorized for the Gibson account. Gibson receives its statement and canceled checks each month, but Althea's unlawful activity goes undiscovered for eleven months. Because of the 14-day rule, the bank is liable on only the first two forged checks at most, and it could be liable on only the first one, depending on the timing.

The above rules by which the payor bank can escape liability on a forged or altered check do not apply if the customer can show that the bank failed to use ordinary care in paying the check. Lack of ordinary care can be established by proof that the bank's procedures are below standard or that the bank's employees failed to exercise reasonable care in processing the check. For example, a bank receiving a check for payment is generally expected to verify the drawer's signature. It does so by comparing the signature on the check with the drawer's signature on the bank's signature card. If the check appears to have been altered, the bank should contact the drawer before paying it. A bank can also violate the ordinary care requirement by paying a check bearing a facsimile drawer signature if the bank has authority only to pay checks on which the drawer signature is handwritten.[7]

Even if a bank failed to use ordinary care, it is not liable on a forged drawer signature or an alteration if the customer does not discover and report the forgery or alteration within one year after the check and statement are made available to him. In the case of a forged indorsement, the customer has three years in which to discover and report it. The reason for the longer period is that the customer himself is apt to be unaware that an indorsement is a forgery

---

[7] A facsimile signature is placed on a document with a stamp or signature plate. Businesspeople often use facsimile signatures on routine correspondence, and sometimes they also use them on checks.

until the matter is brought to his attention by the party who was supposed to have received payment on the check.

Under some circumstances, a payor bank that has paid a forged or altered check can also escape liability because of a provision of UCC Article 3. UCC § 3-406 prevents the drawer from recovering against the bank if the drawer's negligence was a substantial contributing factor in allowing the forgery or alteration to occur. For example, an employer who leaves blank checks in an unlocked drawer that is easily accessible to employees who are not authorized to handle checks is apt to find it difficult to recover from the bank for payment of a check forged by an employee.

 Employee dishonesty is a chronic problem for many businesses. If possible, duties connected with keeping a business checking account should be divided among several employees. One employee might be made responsible for blank checks, while another is made responsible for inspecting bank statements and canceled checks. If facsimile signatures are used on checks, a third employee should be responsible for the stamp or signature plate.

26:9   Customer's Death or Incompetence

The drawer of a check might die or be declared by a court to be mentally incompetent after he has drawn the check, but before it is paid by the payor bank. With one exception discussed below, UCC § 4-405 provides that a bank loses its authority to accept, collect, or pay a check only when the bank (1) becomes aware of the death or adjudication of incompetence of its customer and (2) has a reasonable chance to act on that knowledge. Until those conditions are met, any collecting or payor bank can process the check in the usual manner.

The exception to the above rule is that regardless of a bank's knowledge of its customer's death, during the ten-day period following the date of death the bank can pay or certify checks drawn by the customer. The reason for this exception is that holders of recent checks should be permitted to obtain payment without having to assert their claims (for the amounts of the checks) against the deceased drawer's estate.[8] The only limit on this ten-day rule is that any person claiming an interest in the estate, such as a relative or creditor, can order the bank to stop payment on all the deceased drawer's checks or on one or more specific checks.

EXAMPLE: Jake was of limited means, and he owed $10,000 to Smoot and $15,000 to Hawley. On January 10, Jake drew a check for $10,000 payable to Smoot, and he sent Smoot the check. Jake died on January 12, and it is apparent to Hawley that the value of Jake's estate is less than $15,000. Hawley can order the payor bank to stop payment on Smoot's check, even though the bank could otherwise have paid it until at least January 22. By so doing, Hawley can increase the value of Jake's estate, which constitutes the fund available for paying Jake's creditors.

---

[8] The liability of a decedent's estate for the decedent's debts is discussed in Chapter 40.

26:10   Privacy of Bank Records

The financial records that banks compile and maintain on their customers are confidential by nature, and most customers would prefer that the records not be publicly disclosed. Accordingly, banks have the general duty not to disclose financial information about their customers without the customers' authorization or consent. This authorization or consent, when given, usually arises from a customer's naming a bank as a credit reference. As the following case illustrates, however, there can be circumstances under which a bank *should* disclose confidential information about one of its customers.

Richfield Bank & Trust Co.

v

Sjogren
244 NW2d 648 (1976)
Minnesota Supreme Court

FACTS: Mr. and Mrs. Sjogren borrowed money from Richfield Bank & Trust Company. The loan, which was to be repaid in 90 days, was obtained so that the Sjogrens could buy air purification units from National Pollution Eliminators, Inc., which had a checking account with Richfield. The loan was handled exclusively by Michael Thompson, Richfield's loan officer. Thompson was the only bank officer who handled National Pollution's account, and he was an active member in National Pollution's business affairs. He also knew that National Pollution was insolvent and would be unable to supply the purification units (which it intended to buy using the money received from the Sjogrens), but he did not disclose this information to the Sjogrens. The Sjogrens failed to repay the loan, and Richfield sued them. The Sjogrens' defense was that the transaction had been induced by Richfield's fraudulent concealment of material information.

ISSUE: Must a bank disclose to a customer the insolvent status of another customer with whom he or she is transacting business?

RESULT: The bank is obligated to disclose the insolvent status if necessary to avoid furthering a fraud of which it has actual knowledge.

REASONING:

*   *   *

The determination of whether the facts of this case fall within a category of "special circumstances" which would justify imposing on the bank the duty to disclose the financial condition of its depositor, National

Pollution, is complicated by the principle that a bank is generally under a duty not to disclose the financial condition of its depositors. . . .

In the [cases supporting this principle], however, the banks did not have actual knowledge of any fraudulent activities. . . . The clear implication is that if the bank actually knew that its depositor was insolvent and engaged in fraudulent activity at the time of the transaction, then it would have been under a duty to disclose this fact, since, . . .

> [t]here is a moral duty of banks to the community in which they do business to use reasonable care in seeing that their depositors are not committing a fraud upon the public.

Thus, the instant case can be distinguished from those cases holding that a bank may not disclose the financial condition of its depositors if it can be shown that Richfield Bank had *actual knowledge* of the fraudulent activities of its depositor, National Pollution. [Court's emphasis.]

In determining whether Richfield Bank had actual knowledge of fraudulent activity, it should be noted that knowledge of insolvency is not necessarily equivalent to knowledge of fraud. It is well settled that an insolvent purchaser, buying on credit, is not bound to disclose his financial condition to the seller if he has a reasonable expectation of being able to pay for the goods. . . . If, on the other hand, a party is so insolvent that he has no reasonable expectation of fulfilling his contract obligations, then it is fraud for that party to fail to disclose his insolvency before entering the contract. . . .

Applying this principle to the instant case, the determinative question is whether Richfield Bank, through its loan officer, Michael Thompson, actually knew that National Pollution was so irretrievably insolvent that it had no reasonable expectation of fulfilling its obligations under the contract with respondents. If Richfield Bank knew only that National Pollution was insolvent, it would not have actual knowledge of fraud and thus would not be under a duty to disclose the financial condition of its depositor to respondents.

The jury specifically found (1) that National Pollution's officers knew that they could not fulfill their contractual obligation to respondents; and (2) that Michael Thompson knew of the pertinent financial condition of National Pollution and of the actions, concealment, and representations of the officers of National Pollution in the conduct of their business in relation to the respondents. These findings are adequately supported by the record, which included substantial evidence as set forth herein, clearly demonstrating Thompson's extensive personal participation in an intimate knowledge of the affairs of National Pollution. Based on this evidence, the conclusion that Thompson actually knew that National Pollution had no reasonable expectation of fulfilling its contractual obligations is compelling.

Therefore, we hold that under the unique and narrow "special circumstances" of this case, in which the bank had *actual knowledge* of the fraudulent activities of one of its depositors, it had an affirmative duty to disclosure those facts to the respondents before it engaged in making the loan to respondents which furthered the fraud. [Court's emphasis.] . . .

MacLaughlin, Justice.

Federal Legislation   In 1970 Congress enacted legislation requring all insured banks (banks insured by the Federal Deposit Insurance Corporation) to maintain on their customers certain financial records that Congress viewed as having "a high degree of usefulness in criminal, tax, and regulatory investigations and proceedings" [12 USC § 1829b]. This legislation did not limit the federal government's access to the records so maintained, and the result was that federal agencies could often obtain financial records on any customer by merely requesting them. This situation was alleviated somewhat when, in 1978, Congress enacted the *Right to Financial Privacy Act* (REPA) [12 USC §§ 3401 et seq.].

The REPA does not prevent federal access to the financial records maintained by banks. It does, however, specify alternative procedures that a government agency must follow, and it limits the use of any information that an agency obtains. Some of the procedures give the customer the right to advance notice and an opportunity to be heard before records concerning him are disclosed. Note, however, that most customer rights in this regard are bypassed if the requesting agency determines that a delay in gaining access would create (1) a danger of physical injury to a person (2) serious property damage, or (3) a person's flight to avoid prosecution. Another important exception to customers' rights under the REPA is that nothing in the act prevents the disclosure of financial records in accordance with the procedures authorized by the Internal Revenue Code.

Key Concepts and Terms

- A draft is a negotiable instrument that is a written direction to pay a stated amount of money. A check is a draft payable by a bank on demand.
- Most bank deposits are general. A special deposit arises only by special agreement between the bank and its depositor.
- The relationship between a bank and its depositor is usually one of creditor and debtor, although the bank acts as the depositor's agent in such activities as obtaining payment on deposited checks.
- The collection process is the means by which payment on a check deposited in a collecting bank is obtained from the payor bank. It is governed by Article 4 of the UCC. The depositor receives only a provisional credit until final payment has been made.
- A collecting bank has a duty of ordinary care in its processing of a check. Generally, the bank must meet its midnight deadline. This means that the

bank must process the check before midnight of the banking day following the banking day on which it received the check.

- "Charge-back" refers to the right a collecting bank has to charge its customer's account for the amount of a check that was deposited by the customer and was dishonored by the payor bank.

- A payor bank has the general duty of paying valid checks drawn on its customer's account. It, too, must process checks within prescribed time limits.

- A payor bank that wrongfully dishonors a check can be liable to its customer for damages.

- The drawer of a check can, in effect, cancel that check by issuing a stop-payment order. A stop-payment order directs the payor bank not to pay the check in question.

- A payor bank that pays a forged or altered check can be liable to its customer for the amount of the check. Depending on the circumstances, the bank might then have recourse against the collecting bank from which it received the check.

- If a bank's customer dies or is declared incompetent, the bank's authority to pay checks drawn by the customer ordinarily ceases when the bank learns of the event. However, checks of a deceased customer can usually be paid for ten days after the death, regardless of the bank's knowledge.

- A bank cannot ordinarily disclose financial records about a customer without the customer's consent. The federal Right to Financial Privacy Act limits the federal government's access to such records.

- Altered Check
- Banker's Check
- Cashier's Check
- Certified Check
- Charge-back
- Check
- Clearinghouse
- Collecting Bank
- Collection Process
- Depositary Bank
- Dishonor
- Forged Check
- Intermediary bank
- Midnight Deadline
- Negotiable Order of Withdrawal
- Payor Bank
- Postdated Check
- Posting Process
- Provisional Settlement
- Right to Financial Privacy Act
- Stop-Payment Order
- Traveler's Check

Questions and Case Problems

1. On December 29, 1986, Almeda Homes, Inc. wrote two checks to Builders totaling $4,198.53. Almeda was experiencing financial difficulty at that time. On February 19, 1987, Builders requested Bank to issue cashier's checks in exchange for Almeda's business checks. Bank examined Almeda's account and issued two

cashier's checks totaling $4,198.53. That afternoon, Bank informed Builders it would not honor the cashier's checks. Bank stopped payment on February 22, 1987. Is Bank liable for the checks? See UCC § 4-303.

2. On June 1, 1986, Bank #1 certified a $60,000 check drawn by Hospital on its account at Bank #1. The check was payable to the order of Fred and Wanda Thornton. On June 8, 1986, Bank #1 stopped payment pursuant to a phone call it received from a representative of Hospital, who said the check had been lost. On July 16, 1981, the Thorntons indorsed the check and presented it to Bank #2, which credited the Thornton account and then permitted the Thorntons to withdraw the funds. When Bank #1 refused payment, Bank #2 sought payment of the check and damages under UCC § 4-402. Is Bank #1 a "customer" under UCC § 4-402 for purposes of recovering damages?

3. On March 2, Brewer drew a check for $204,000 payable to Meek. The check was drawn on Brewer's account at Bank #1. The next day Meek deposited the check in Bank #2. On March 4, when the check was presented to Bank #1, it was marked paid. At that time Brewer's account showed a balance sufficient to pay the check, but that included a provisional credit for a check for $123,000 deposited by Brewer but not paid. On March 11, 1981, the check Brewer had deposited was dishonored. Bank then refused to pay the $204,000 check. Meek claims that Bank is strictly liable as a payor bank that held the check beyond the midnight deadline. Bank claims it was under the mistaken belief that the account contained sufficient funds. Who wins?

4. Local 148 Welfare Fund (Fund) drew a check on its account at Bank payable to Donner, Dasher & Blitzen, a law firm representing a client in a lawsuit against Fund. Fund sent the check to its lawyer Smith to be used as payment in a settlement of the lawsuit. Smith forged the indorsement of the payee's name and then withdrew the proceeds and absconded. He was subsequently found dead from a bullet wound. Fund sought to recover the loss against Bank. The writing on the back of Fund's check appeared as follows:

> Pay to Special Account #012-04321
>
> /s/ Donner, Dasher & Blitzen
>
> For Deposit Only Special Account #012-04321

The account number was Smith's professional trust account. Donner, Dasher & Blitzen did not maintain a banking relationship of any kind with Bank. Should this writing put Bank on notice of the forgery?

5. A $13.50 check payable to a welfare recipient is drawn by Nassau County on its welfare account with Franklin Bank. The check is altered to increase the amount payable to $313.50, and it is then presented to Westbury Bank for payment. The alteration is not obvious from the face of the check, and Westbury cashes it. Westbury then sends the check to Franklin, which pays it. A Nassau County employee notices the alteration on receipt of the canceled check, and Franklin is notified promptly. How much, if anything, must Franklin recredit to Nassau County's account? Why? How much, if anything, can Franklin recover from Westbury? Why?

6. Marvel has a checking account with Pacific bank, and Fikes, a forger, obtains several of Marvel's blank checks. Fikes fills out one of the checks naming Palmer as the payee, and she forges Marvel's signature and Palmer's indorsement. Fikes

then presents the check for payment at North Shore Bank, at which Palmer has a checking account. North Shore pays the check, but five days later the check is returned, unpaid, to North Shore by Pacific due to the forgeries. At this time, Palmer has $150 in his North Shore account. North Shore charges Palmer's account for $275, the amount of the check, and advises Palmer by phone about the situation. Palmer comes to the bank and states that he does not know Marvel and that the indorsement is a forgery. The North Shore officer with whom Palmer talks does not believe him, and she calls over an armed guard to escort Palmer from the building. Palmer then reports the matter to the police. Over the next few days, North Shore, claiming insufficiency of funds, refuses to pay three checks drawn earlier by Palmer to pay creditors. The bank charges Palmer's account $5 for each returned check, and it then places in the hands of a collection agency the $140 debt it claims to be owed by Palmer. Palmer sues North Shore for wrongful dishonor of his three checks. Discuss the damages, if any, that Palmer should recover.

7. Granite Corporation draws a check payable to Overseas Corporation on its account with Hempstead Bank, to pay a business debt. Five days later Granite learns that Overseas has not received the check, so Granite issues a new check. Granite then writes to Hempstead, ordering it to stop payment on the first check. Thirteen months later a collecting bank presents the original check to Hempstead for payment. Although Granite does not have sufficient funds in its account to cover the check, Hempstead pays it anyway, and charges Granite's account. When Granite's president discovers the charge she is outraged, claiming that Hempstead should not have paid the check. Discuss the rights and liabilities of Granite and Hempstead with respect to the check.

8. In May of 1976, Industrial Corp. hired Julie as its new bookkeeper. Julie's responsibilities included keeping track of and paying Industrial's bills, and examining all bank statements and canceled checks. She paid Industrial's bills by preparing checks drawn on its account and adding a facsimile signature using a signature plate. All outgoing checks were supposed to be inspected and approved by Victor, Industrial's president, but Victor's usual examination was cursory at best. Often he did not look at the checks at all. On June 15, Julie prepared a check for $500, payable to a fictitious payee. She forged the payee's indorsement and deposited the check into her own account. The check was paid and returned to Industrial with the statement it received on July 1. On July 15, Julie forged another $500 check and, growing bolder due to the success of her scheme, between July 15 and December 20, she forged ten more checks for increasingly large amounts. The proceeds from all these checks found their way into Julie's account. On December 24, Julie resigned without notice and left the area. Industrial learned about what had happened as a result of its year-end audit. It sued its bank for $25,000, the total amount paid from its account on the twelve checks forged by Julie. How much, if anything, can Industrial recover from its bank? Why?

9. Vincent, who had a checking account with Highland Bank, died on June 24. On June 28, and before Highland was aware of its customer's death, Vincent's sister, Annette, appeared at Highland with one of Vincent's checks. The check was blank except that Vincent's signature was written on it, as drawer. Annette stated that Vincent wished to close his account, asked about the current balance in the account, learned that it was $1,500, and then wrote that amount on the check. She then added the date and her own name as payee, and indorsed the check. After verifying Vincent's signature on the check and Annette's identity, Highland

cashed the check. It later appeared that Annette had acted without proper authority. Drake, the executor (legal representative) of Vincent's estate sued Highland to recover the $1,500 paid to Annette. How much, if anything, can Drake recover for the estate? Why?

10. Johnson had a checking account with Trans-World Bank, but on September 20, 1982, he closed the account by withdrawing all funds from it. On July 19, 1983, Johnson, who still had blank checks from his old Trans-World account, used one of those checks to pay a grocery store bill. When the check was returned unpaid, marked "account closed," the supermarket notified the police department, which began an investigation. You are the manager of the Trans-World branch at which Johnson formerly had his account. A representative from the state district attorney's office visits you and states that Johnson will soon be arrested for having passed a bad check. She then asks you for information concerning the past and present existence and status of Johnson's account. Should you disclose this information? Why or why not?

27 Electronic Funds Transfers

27:1 Introduction

While checks, cash, and credit cards are the most common means of paying for goods and services, electronic funds transfers are the fastest growing payment method. An *electronic funds transfer* (EFT) is a transfer of money that is made by using an electronic terminal, a telephone, a computer, or magnetic tape—in other words, without the physical transfer of cash or the use of paper checks, negotiable instruments, or credit card receipts. EFT holds the potential of virtually replacing the check system within a few years. It is, therefore, as important for the businessperson to understand the rights and liabilities of parties to an EFT as it is to understand negotiable instrument law.

Negotiable instruments are governed by Articles 3 and 4 of the Uniform Commercial Code. Credit cards are governed by contract law, the federal Truth in Lending Act, and various state and federal consumer credit protection statutes, which are discussed in Chapter 28. Electronic funds transfers are governed by contract law and, in the case of consumer transactions with EFT, by the federal Electronic Funds Transfer Act.

The following case discusses the problem of whether a particular type of transaction is a negotiable instrument transaction subject to UCC Article 4 or an electronic funds transaction not subject to the UCC.

Houston Contracting Co.

v

Chase Manhattan Bank, N.A.
539 F Supp 247 (1982)
United States District Court, Southern District of New York

FACTS: Iranians' Bank maintained a demand deposit with defendant Chase Manhattan Bank. On Sunday, November 11, 1979, Iranians' transmitted a payment order to Chase by telex. It ordered Chase to

Pay to Houston Contracting Company A/C No. 00-0219-4 First National Bank of Houston Texas USA [Dollars] 300,000.

The telex was received by Chase but was not sent to Houston or to Iranians'. Because Iranians' account did not contain sufficient funds, Chase did not make the transfer. On November 14, 1979, the balance in Iranians' account was frozen by federal executive order. Chase did not communicate with either Iranians' or Houston concerning the payment order. Houston sued Chase, claiming Chase is liable for the amount of the payment order under UCC § 4-302 for failing to give notice of dishonor by the midnight deadline.

ISSUE: Is a telexed payment order a "demand item" subject to the midnight notification deadline of UCC § 4-302?

RESULT: No. An unsigned, non-negotiable telex payment order is not subject to Article 4 of the UCC.

REASONING:

*   *   *

The threshold inquiry is whether an unsigned telexed payment order is a "demand item" subject to the requirements of § 4–302. A "demand item" is nowhere defined in the UCC, there is no pertinent legislative history, and the precise issue before the court appears to be one of first impression. In resolving the issue, the court shall be guided by prior judicial applications of § 4–302 and by consideration of the underlying purposes of the relevant statutory provisions.

Although no court has considered whether an unsigned, non-negotiable telexed payment order is a "demand item" subject to the requirements of § 4–302, there is significant support for the proposition that negotiability is a requisite element of a "demand item." . . . Indeed, of the many cases construing § 4–302, not one has applied § 4–302 to anything other than "checks" and "drafts," which are negotiable instruments satisfying the strict definitional requirements of UCC § 3–104. . . . Moreover, no statutory policy favors the expansive interpretation of § 4–302 urged by Houston which would extend payor banks' obligations under that section beyond those obligations repeatedly recognized and enforced by courts. Payor banks have thus far been subjected to liability under § 4–302 for failure to provide timely notice of non-payment only with respect to negotiable instruments. To hold that an unsigned telex is the equivalent of a check or draft and to extend § 4–302 to the facts of this case would alter well-settled obligations, blur the well-defined distinctions developed under the UCC, and potentially disrupt the smooth, rapid functioning of commercial banking transactions which is a principal purpose underlying Article 4 of the UCC.

Gagliardi, District Judge.

27:2 Types of Electronic Transfers

Financial institutions are constantly evolving applications of technology to financial services. The following types of EFTs have become commonplace.

Point-Of-Sale Transfers (POS) The POS transfer permits the customer of a retail store to pay for goods or services by electronically debiting the customer's asset or credit account and crediting the retail store's account. The customer uses a plastic debit card and a code with a personal number identification for access to the account. For the consumer, the POS transfer eliminates bills and check writing. It also eliminates the use of the funds during the time it would have taken a check to clear the system. The merchant receives instant payment for the good or service and, under current payment law, incurs less risk of nonpayment.

Direct Deposit and Payment Electronic transfer of payments and deposits can be accomplished through the Automated Clearing House (ACH). The ACH permits the account holder to authorize a payee to receive periodic payments transferred from the drawer's to the payee's account. This authorization is given by the payee's bank to an ACH, which communicates the authorization to the drawer's bank and arranges automatic transfers in accordance with the agreement. This service can be provided for less than the cost of clearing a check, and it is becoming increasingly widespread. The United States Government is a major user of ACH for direct deposits of government payments. Insurance premiums, annuities, pensions, and payrolls also are commonly handled by direct deposit.

 A direct payment or deposit plan works well when it works properly. If a problem arises, however, it is usually best to cancel the authorization altogether, rather than to try to have the problem cured. Computers control these transactions, and it seems to be difficult for the people who work with the computer systems to fix "computer errors." Of course, a new authorization, reinstating the periodic payments or deposits, can be given after cancellation of the old one.

Pay-By-Telephone (PBT) Many banks permit customers to authorize by telephone the transfer of money between accounts or the payment of bills that are due periodically. This type of transfer is used most commonly when the amount of the transfer varies and it is not desirable to arrange in advance for an automatic regular payment.

Automated Teller Machines (ATM) Since their appearance in 1969 as cash dispensing machines, ATMs have become the most popular form of consumer EFT device. More than 50,000 are in place nationwide in banks, shopping centers, grocery stores, and university campuses. More than 100 million "debit" cards are held by consumers, primarily for use in ATMs. Until the mid-1970s state and federal laws governing the establishment of *branch banks* inhibited the spread of bank-owned ATMs in some states. To a great extent, however, the developments of ATMs that are owned by the retail establishment or that are shared by and accessible to several banks have resolved the branch banking problem.

ATMs are capable of performing a variety of banking services, including cash withdrawal from asset or credit accounts, deposits, balance inquiries, and transfers between accounts. ATMs make it possible to conduct many banking activities at convenient times and locations.

27:3   Consumer Transfers: The Electronic Funds Transfer Act

Most electronic funds transfers involving consumers and financial institutions, such as POS or ATM transfers, are governed by the federal Electronic Funds Transfer Act of 1979 (EFTA) (15 USC §§ 1693 et seq.), which went into full effect in 1980. The Act establishes the rights, liabilities, and responsibilities of consumers and financial institutions. It subjects EFTs to comprehensive regulation by the Federal Reserve Board through Regulation E (12 CFR §§ 205.1 et seq.).

The EFTA is a consumer protection statute and does not govern transfers between financial institutions and businesses or among businesses. Like other consumer protection legislation of the 1960s and 1970s, the EFTA emphasizes disclosure of information necessary to protect the unwary. In addition, it provides individual consumer rights, striking a balance between consumers' interest in information and safety and financial institutions' interest in avoiding burdensome regulation that would hamper the development of electronic payment systems. Thus, the EFTA's primary goal is to protect the consumer. In addition, the Act directs the Federal Reserve Board, in writing regulations, to "take into account, and allow for, the continuing evolution of electronic banking services and the technology utilized in such services" [15 USC § 1693b(a)(1)].

Definitions   The EFTA regulates financial institutions that offer electronic funds transfers involving an account held by a consumer. As used in the Act, "financial institution" includes banks, savings and loan institutions, credit unions, "or any other person who, directly or indirectly, holds an account belonging to a consumer" [15 USC § 1693a(8)]. Thus, it would include brokerage houses that permit electronic transfers by consumers to and from money market fund accounts. Under the Act, an electronic funds transfer is any transfer of funds, other than a transaction originated by a paper instrument, that (1) is initiated through an electronic terminal, a telephone, or computer or magnetic tape; and (2) orders or authorizes a financial institution to credit or debit an account. The types of accounts covered are demand accounts, savings accounts, and other asset accounts established primarily for personal, family, or household purposes.

The definition section of the Act poses interesting problems. For example, is a casual telephone call to the bank asking the bank to transfer funds from one account to another an "electronic funds transfer"? The Federal Reserve Board staff has taken the position that it is not if the bank is simply accommodating the customer on an occasional basis, as banks have done customarily for many years. The following case, one of the few appellate cases construing the EFTA, involves such a casual telephone transfer.

Kashanchi

v

Texas Commerce Medical Bank, N.A.
703 F2d 936 (1983)
United States Court of Appeals, Fifth Circuit

FACTS: On February 9, 1981, $4,900 was transferred from an account owned by plaintiff and her sister at defendant bank. The transfer was initiated by a telephone conversation between an employee of the bank and someone other than plaintiff or her sister. When plaintiff discovered the withdrawal on her bank statement on March 31, 1981, she sent a letter to the bank notifying the bank that the withdrawal was unauthorized. After the bank refused to recredit the account, plaintiff filed a lawsuit claiming violation of the Electronic Funds Transfer Act. The bank claims that a transaction of this nature is not governed by the Act.

ISSUE: Is a transfer of funds from a consumer's account, initiated by a telephone conversation between someone other than the owner of the account and an employee of the bank, an "electronic funds transfer" so that the EFTA governs the conflict?

RESULT: No. Such a transfer is not an "electronic funds transfer" if it is not made pursuant to a prearranged plan or agreement under which periodic transfers are contemplated.

REASONING:

*   *   *

The parties agree that the telephonic transfer that allegedly occurred in this case falls within the broad definition of "electronic fund transfers" in the Act. . . . Some of what Congress has given, however, it has also taken away. Excluded from the definition of an electronic fund transfer is

> any transfer of funds which is initiated by a telephone conversation between a consumer and an officer or employee of a financial institution which is not pursuant to a prearranged plan and under which periodic or recurring transfers are not contemplated. . . .

15 U.S.C. § 1693a(6)(E). . . . The question in this case is whether the telephone conversation was between the employee and a "consumer."

The Act defines a consumer as "a natural person." 15 U.S.C. § 1693a(5). If we were to apply this definition to the language in the exclusion, we would have to conclude that the withdrawal of the plaintiff's funds was excluded from the coverage of the Act since a natural person, even if the person was neither the plaintiff nor her sister, made the withdrawal. The plaintiff argues, however, that we should read the term "consumer" more narrowly in this portion of the Act; she would have us interpret the provision to exclude only transfers made by the account holder.

The plaintiff maintains that the legislative history of the Act supports her narrow reading of the exclusion. She points out that the House version of the bill used the word "holder," meaning "the individual who is recognized as the owner of the account by the financial institution where the account is held," . . . where the Senate version, eventually adopted by Congress as the EFTA, uses the word "consumer." The plaintiff would have us infer that the Senate intended the word "consumer" to be synonymous with "holder." There is no indication in the legislative history, however, that this is what the Senate intended. . . .

Further, the legislative history of the EFTA is consistent with the plain meaning of the language in the statute and with the presumption arising from Congress's disparate inclusion and exclusion of words of limitation. The plaintiff emphasizes that Congress designed the Act to provide a comprehensive scheme of federal regulation for all electronic transfers of funds. . . . Congress undoubtedly intended the Act's coverage to be broad; the Act itself provides that its list of electronic fund transfers is not all-inclusive. 15 U.S.C. § 1693a(6). Aware that computer technology was still in a rapid, evolutionary stage of development, Congress was careful to permit coverage of electronic services not yet in existence. . . .

. . . The absence of discussion about informal personal phone transfers would seem to indicate an intent not to cover these transfers, or at least an absence of congressional concern about them, in light of the extensive discussion throughout the hearings and reports of the other existing types of electronic transfers. It is highly unlikely that this silence was a result of congressional ignorance of the problem since these informal phone withdrawals presumably had been occurring since shortly after the time of Alexander Graham Bell. . . .

The plaintiff ignores the essential difference between electronic fund transfer systems and personal transfers by phone or by check. When the bank employee allegedly agreed to withdraw funds from the plaintiff's account, he or she presumably could have asked some questions to ascertain whether the caller was one of the account holders. The failure to attempt to make a positive identification of the caller might be considered negligence or a breach of the deposit agreement under state law. When someone makes an unauthorized use of an electronic fund transfer system, however, the financial institution often has no way of knowing that the transfer is unauthorized. For example, in order to make a transfer at an automatic teller machine, a person need only possess the machine card and know the correct personal identification number. The computer cannot determine whether the person who has inserted the card and typed in the magic number is authorized to use the system. What might be a withdrawal negligently permitted by the financial institution in one situation might not be a negligent action in the other. . . .

Randall, Circuit Judge.

The sections that follow examine the major provisions of the EFTA and compare them with the analogous provisions of the UCC governing paper transactions.

27:4 Disclosure [15 USC §§ 1693c, 1693d, and 1693e]

The EFTA requires financial institutions to provide written documentation at several stages of an EFT. A writing must be generated for the consumer when the contract for EFT services is entered, when an electronic terminal is used, and when preauthorized transfers are contemplated. In addition, a periodic statement of transactions must be provided.

Contract Terms   When a consumer enters into a contract for EFT services, the terms and conditions of the contract and the rights and responsibilities of the consumer must be disclosed in writing. Changes in the terms and conditions of the contract must be disclosed to the consumer within 21 days before they become effective, unless the change must be instituted immediately to protect the security of the system or the account.

Electronic Terminal Receipts   Each time an EFT is initiated at an "electronic terminal," a written receipt must be provided at that time to the consumer. The term "electronic terminal" includes POS terminals, ATM, and cash-dispensing machines, but not telephones. The receipt must set forth the amount involved, the date of the transaction, the type of transfer, the identity of the account, the identity of any third party from whom or to whom funds are transferred, and the location or identification of the electronic terminal involved.

Preauthorized Transfers   A consumer may contract with a financial institution to have transfers made to or from the account on a regular prearranged basis. This may be done through an ACH or between accounts at the same institution. When a preauthorized credit is made to the account, the financial institution must either notify the consumer of each credit, or agree with the consumer that notification will be given only if a preauthorized credit is not actually made to the account. Before a preauthorized debit may be made to the account, the authorization must be in writing, and a copy of the authorization must be given to the consumer. If the debit is to vary in amount from time to time, the payee or the financial institution must give the consumer reasonable advance notice of the amount and the date of the transfer.

Periodic Statements   The EFTA requires that the financial institution provide a statement, usually monthly, for each of the consumer's accounts accessible by EFT. The statement must set forth a record of transactions, the amount of fees or charges assessed for maintenance of the account, the balances of the account at both the beginning and the close of the period, and the address and telephone number to be used in case of error.

In effect, the documentation requirements of the EFTA fulfill the consumer's need for evidence of an EFT transaction analogous to that fulfilled by the UCC with respect to paper transactions. The UCC framers were not concerned specifically with contract disclosure to consumers, and so the UCC contains no provisions specifying what must be disclosed when a checking account is opened. However, UCC § 4-406 does require, in effect, that a bank make available to the consumer a periodic statement and the paid checks. The evidence of the amount, the payee, and the history of the check is inherent in the paper instrument, and the bank statement provides a record of the transaction.

27:5   Unauthorized Transfers

Unauthorized electronic funds transfers may be accomplished in a variety of ways. EFT cards and codes may be stolen and used. Imposters pretending to be bank employees may trick a customer into accessing an account. Computer "hackers" or bank employees may transfer funds surreptitiously. While paper payment systems leave a trail of evidence, making it relatively easy to identify who has been negligent and where the risk of loss should lie, electronic transfer systems do not. Yet the loss to a consumer or to the financial institution may be great.

The EFTA permits the financial institution to contract with the consumer to assume liability for an unauthorized transfer. The consumer can be held liable for all losses from an unauthorized transfer that would have been avoided had the consumer reported an unauthorized transfer appearing on a periodic statement within 60 days of its transmittal. The Act establishes a maximum liability of up to $500 if the consumer fails to report a lost or stolen card within two business days after learning of the theft or loss. Otherwise, liability is limited to a maximum of $50.

 Under the EFTA, a transfer is not considered an "unauthorized transfer" if it is made by a person to whom the consumer gave his or her access card or the means of accessing the account. Thus, the consumer takes the full risk for transfers made by people who breach trust by misusing the card.

Under the UCC the risk of loss of an unauthorized transfer is usually borne by the person in the best position to avoid the loss. In the case of an unauthorized transfer by a drawer's agent, that is the drawer; in the case of a theft of stolen order paper, that is the transferee who could have required identification; in the case of stolen bearer paper, that is the payee who could have ensured personal protection with a special indorsement. The EFTA provides more protection to the account holder by allocating loss to the financial institution even in situations in which the consumer was in a better position to avoid the loss. On the other hand, the EFTA gives strong incentives to the consumer to report loss or theft as soon as it is discovered, thereby reducing the financial institution's loss. It should be noted also that the financial institution usually is in the best position to avoid losses caused by its own employees.

27:6 Stop Payment; Reversibility

The "stop-payment" order of a check is simply a reversal of an order to make a payment before the order is obeyed. The order cannot be reversed, of course, after the check has been paid. The instantaneous nature of an EFT eliminates the "float" time during which effective reversal of a check can occur, and the EFTA does not provide for reversal of an EFT once it has been made. It does, however, permit a consumer to reverse a preauthorized transfer before the transfer is made. To do this, the consumer must notify the financial institution of the stop payment orally or in writing at any time up to three business days preceding the scheduled date of the transfer. The financial institution may request written confirmation of an oral stop-payment order.

27:7 Error Resolution

The EFTA establishes an error resolution process under which a consumer has 60 days after the transmission of a periodic statement to notify the financial institution that an error has been made. The notice must indicate the account holder's name and account number and explain why the consumer believes an error has occurred. The financial institution then has 10 days in which to investigate the error and send the results to the consumer. If an error did occur, the financial institution must correct the error within one day after discovery. If an error did not occur, the institution must notify the consumer within three days of that determination. If the financial institution provisionally credits the consumer's account within 10 days of the consumer's original notice, it may have up to 45 days to investigate and resolve the error.

 In choosing a payment method, the consumer should consider that, unlike the EFTA, the UCC contains no prescribed process for resolving errors in bank statements. An injured person may sue the bank for conversion or breach of contract if, for example, the bank fails to credit the account with a deposited item.

27:8   Damages [15 UCC §§ 1693m and 1693n]

The EFTA establishes civil liability for violating the Act. Any person who fails to comply with any provision of the Act may be liable for (1) any actual damages sustained by the consumer; (2) all costs of the action, including court costs and reasonable attorney's fees for successful consumer; and (3) statutory damages of $100 to $1,000 in an individual action, or up to the lesser of $500,000 or one percent of the net worth of the defendant in a class action.

Civil liability can be avoided if the defendant proves that the error was unintentional and that it maintained procedures designed to avoid such an error. Also, if the defendant notifies the consumer of its failure to comply with the Act, complies with the Act, makes the adjustment to the consumer's account, and pays the consumer's actual damages, no civil liability can be assessed. These rules encourage financial institutions to comply with the Act. In addition, criminal liability of up to $5,000 and one year's imprisonment may be assessed against a person who knowingly and willfully violates the Act.

27:9   Commercial Electronic Funds Transfers

Commercial electronic funds transfers account for a much larger dollar volume of payments than either checks or credit cards. It has been estimated that in 1980 more than $117 trillion was moved through wire transfers, most of which were made by banks and businesses rather than consumers. In contrast, about $19 trillion was moved by check and about $49 billion by credit card.[1] Virtually all of these "wire" transfers, which are electronic transfers, are excluded from coverage by the Uniform Commercial Code and state and federal electronic funds transfer law. Someday they may be covered by a comprehensive payments law, such as the draft Uniform New Payments Code. At the present time, however, commercial electronic funds transfers are governed by the common law of contract and tort and, indirectly, by state and federal regulation of the financial institutions involved in the transfers.

Commercial Wire Systems   There are several private wire transfer systems operated by banks and businesses. The major ones include FedWire, which is operated by the Federal Reserve Banks; BankWire, which is owned by major commercial banks; the Clearing House Interbank Payment System (CHIPS), which is operated by 12 major New York banks; and the Society for Worldwide Interbank Financial Telecommunications (SWIFT), an international communications network. In addition, wire transfers are made over public networks, such as the telex services offered by ITT. Some of these systems provide for settlement of accounts periodically; others provide only for communication among financial institutions.

---

[1] Scott, *Corporate Wire Transfers and the Uniform New Payments Code*, 83 Columbia Law Review 1664 (1983).

The Law Governing Commercial Wire Transfers   In varying degrees the wire transfer systems are based on contracts or customs that allocate the risk of error, fraud, and loss among users. When there is a failure to effect a transfer, or a transfer to the wrong party, or an uncertainty about whether a transfer has been received or completed, the parties either resolve the dispute or turn to the courts, which apply primarily common-law contract and tort principles to resolve the dispute.

There are surprisingly few appellate cases in this area. The following case represents one of the major recent ones. The court does not exclude the possibility that consequential damages are available for negligent failure to effect a wire transfer under common-law principles; however, the injured party must have acted prudently (mitigated the damages), and the defendant must have had reason to know the possible consequences of a failure to effect the transfer. In contrast, UCC § 4-103(5) limits damages for failure to exercise ordinary care in handling a check to the amount of the item; damages for the consequences of the loss are not available. So, while the UCC protects collecting banks from consequential damages when they lose checks, the common law turns on the facts of each case.

Evra Corp.

v

Swiss Bank Corp.

673 F2d 951 (1982)

United States Court of Appeals, Seventh Circuit

FACTS: Hyman-Michaels, plaintiff, entered into a contract for a ship charter that required plaintiff to make monthly payments "in advance" to the charterer's account in the Banque of Paris in Geneva, Switzerland. Plaintiff was on notice that the ship charterer would cancel the contract for failure to make timely payment. On April 25, 1973, plaintiff telephoned the Continental Bank in Chicago and requested it to transfer $27,000 to the ship charterer's account in Geneva. Continental telexed its London office, which telexed its correspondent bank in Geneva, the Swiss Bank Corporation (SBC), to transfer the funds to the Banque of Paris. Evidently, SBC's telex machine was out of paper, the message was not printed, and the order was not acted on. Consequently, the ship charterer did not receive payment and cancelled the contract, to plaintiff's economic disadvantage. Plaintiff sued SBC and Continental, claiming their failure to make the transfer was negligent and a breach of contract.

ISSUE: Is SBC liable to plaintiff for the consequences of its failure to transfer the funds?

RESULT: SBC is not liable for damages it could not have contemplated or that could more easily have been avoided by plaintiff.

REASONING:

*   *   *

The rule of *Hadley v. Baxendale*—that consequential damages will not be awarded unless the defendant was put on notice of the special circumstances giving rise to them—has been applied in many Illinois cases, and *Hadley* cited approvingly. . . . In [one such case], the plaintiff had delivered $200 to Western Union with instructions to transmit it to a friend of the plaintiff's. The money was to be bet (legally) on a horse, but this was not disclosed in the instructions. Western Union misdirected the money order and it did not reach the friend until several hours after the race had taken place. The horse that the plaintiff had intended to bet on won and would have paid $1650 on the plaintiff's $200 bet if the bet had been placed. He sued Western Union for his $1450 lost profit, but the court held that under the rule of *Hadley v. Baxendale* Western Union was not liable, because it "had no notice or knowledge of the purpose for which the money was being transmitted." . . .

[That case], we conclude, is authority for holding that Swiss Bank is not liable for the consequences of negligently failing to transfer Hyman-Michaels' funds to Banque de Paris; reason for such a holding is found in the animating principle of *Hadley v. Baxendale*, which is that the costs of the untoward consequence of a course of dealings should be borne by that party who was able to avert the consequence at least cost and failed to do so. . . .

. . . It was imprudent for Hyman-Michaels, having narrowly avoided cancellation and having (in the words of its appeal brief in this court) been "put . . . on notice that the payment provision of the Charter would be strictly enforced thereafter," to wait till arguably the last day before payment was due to instruct its bank to transfer the necessary funds overseas. And it was imprudent . . . for Hyman-Michaels, when it received notice of cancellation on the last possible day payment was due, to fail to pull out all the stops to get payment to the Banque de Paris on that day, and instead to dither while Continental and Swiss Bank wasted five days looking for the lost telex message. Judging from the obvious reluctance with which the arbitration panel finally decided to allow the *Pandora*'s owner to cancel the charter, it might have made all the difference if Hyman-Michaels had gotten payment to the Banque de Paris by April 27 or even by Monday, April 30, rather than allowed things to slide until May 2.

This is not to condone the sloppy handling of incoming telex messages in Swiss Bank's foreign department. But Hyman-Michaels is a sophisticated business enterprise. It knew or should have known that even the Swiss are not infallible; that messages sometimes get lost or delayed in transit among three banks, two of them located 5000 miles apart, even when all the banks are using reasonable care; and that therefore it should take its own precautions against the consequences—

best known to itself—of a mishap that might not be due to anyone's negligence. . . .

The rule of *Hadley v. Baxendale* links up with tort concepts in another way. The rule is sometimes stated in the form that only foreseeable damages are recoverable in a breach of contract action. . . . So expressed, it corresponds to the tort principle that limits liability to the foreseeable consequence of the defendant's carelessness. . . . The amount of care that a person ought to take is a function of the probability and magnitude of the harm that may occur if he does not take care. . . . If he does not know what that probability and magnitude are, he cannot determine how much care to take. That would be Swiss Bank's dilemma if it were liable for consequential damages from failing to carry out payment orders in timely fashion. To estimate the extent of its probable liability in order to know how many and how elaborate fail-safe features to install in its telex rooms or how much insurance to buy against the inevitable failures, Swiss Bank would have to collect reams of information about firms that are not even its regular customers. It had no banking relationship with Hyman-Michaels. It did not know or have reason to know how at once precious and fragile Hyman-Michaels' contract with the *Pandora*'s owner was. These were circumstances too remote from Swiss Bank's practical range of knowledge to have affected its decisions as to who should man the telex machines in the foreign department or whether it should have more intelligent machines or should install more machines in the cable department. . . .

Posner, Circuit Judge.

Unauthorized Transfers Another common problem arises when an unauthorized commercial wire transfer is made. This problem arose in a 1982 federal district court case.[2] The court held that defendant bank acted negligently when it received a wire transfer order and credited an account where the account number and the name of the account holder did not match up. An imposter had directed the shareholder service agent for a mutual fund to redeem $2 million worth of shares held by a trustee, and to wire the proceeds to a designated account at defendant bank. The designated account was not the account of the trustee. The credit enabled the imposter to obtain goods from the real account holder, who knew nothing of the fraud.

27:10 The Future of EFT Law

Since 1974 the National Conference of Commissioners on Uniform State Laws and the American Law Institute have cooperated on a major project to draft statutory rules governing all payment systems except cash. The pro-

---

[2] *Securities Funds Services, Inc. v American Nat. Bank & Trust Co.,* 542 F Supp 323 (1982).

posed Uniform New Payments Code creates a single set of rules to govern all payment systems, including checks, credit cards, debit cards, and EFT. The working premise of the drafters is that rights and liabilities of the parties to the transaction should not turn on which form of payment system is selected.

Some people argue that, since the technology is still developing, it is premature to establish a uniform set of rules. Others argue that consumer interests are better served if the applicable rule varies with different payment systems. For example, it may be sensible to permit reversibility of items on credit cards for a period of time, because the financial institution issuing the credit card has an ongoing contractual relationship with the retail merchants and can arrange to charge the item back against the merchant who has, for example, sold shoddy goods. It may be less sensible to permit reversibility of checks, where the holder/presenter of the check may not be known to the bank.

There seems to be little question, however, that the cost of processing checks, and even credit card slips, is driving financial institutions toward electronic funds transfers, and that increased attention will be devoted to the rights and liabilities of the parties to electronic transactions.

Key Concepts and Terms

- Electronic funds transfers are rapidly becoming a major means of paying for goods and services. The term refers to transfers of value that are made by using an electronic terminal, a telephone, a computer, or magnetic tape.

- EFTs are governed by the common law of contract and tort and by the Electronic Funds Transfer Act (EFTA); they are not governed by the Uniform Commercial Code.

- Many types of EFTs are evolving. Common types of EFTs are point of sale transfers, direct deposits and payment transfers, pay-by-telephone transactions, and automated teller machine transactions.

- The EFTA emphasizes disclosure of information to the consumer. The financial institution must provide written notice and documentation when the consumer enters into a contract for EFT services, uses an electronic terminal, or arranges a preauthorized transfer of funds. In addition, the financial institution must provide a periodic statement of the account.

- Under the EFTA, the consumer may have limited liability for an unauthorized transfer from an account, but no liability can be assessed if the consumer notifies the financial institution within two days after discovering the unauthorized transfer.

- The EFTA requires the financial institution to resolve conflicts involving error in the account in a timely manner, or to credit the account pending investigation and resolution.

- The EFTA provides for actual and statutory damages against a financial institution that does not comply with the Act.

- Automated Clearing House (ACH)
- Automated Teller Machines (ATMs)
- Branch Banks
- Electronic Funds Transfer (EFT)
- Electronic Funds Transfer Act (EFTA)
- Electronic Terminal
- Error Resolution Process
- Pay By Telephone (PBT)
- Periodic Statements
- Preauthorized Transfers
- Point of Sale Transfers (POS)
- Regulation E
- Reversibility
- Terminal Receipts
- Unauthorized Transfers
- Wire Transfer Services

Questions and Case Problems

1. Many observers regard home banking as a future trend in personal financial services. Home banking involves the use of the home television or home computer terminal to transmit orders to a financial institution. The order is transmitted over the telephone or cable television wires. Must a financial institution that provides such a service meet the requirement of the EFTA that it provide a terminal receipt following such a transaction? Is the transaction an electronic funds transfer? Is the home television or home computer a "terminal"?

2. Does receipt of a periodic statement showing an unauthorized transfer give notice to the consumer so that consumer has knowledge of the theft or loss?

3. In the *Evra* case (see page 539), why wouldn't Continental be liable for Swiss Bank Corporation's failure to effect the transfer of funds? See Chapter 43 on Agency.

4. Is it desirable to have uniform rules that cover credit transactions, checks, and electronic funds transfers? What are the advantages and disadvantages of a uniform set of rules?

5. What can a business firm do to prevent unauthorized transfers of funds from its accounts in a financial institution? What can a financial institution do to prevent such transfers?

6. Fred lent his 16-year-old son Jack his "Passport," a debit card issued by the Second National Bank. Fred authorized Jack to use the card to withdraw up to $25 per week for spending money while Jack worked one summer away from home. Jack used the card to withdraw $500 to pay for a new recreational motorcycle. When Fred learned of the unauthorized withdrawal, he demanded that Second Bank recredit the account on the ground that the withdrawal was made without authority and that he was not liable for the debts of his minor child. What result?

7. For many years the cost of the Federal Reserve System's check-clearing process was borne by the Fed. In the early 1980s the Fed began charging financial institutions for the service. Would you expect such a change to hasten or retard the growth of electronic funds transfers?

8. On a Thursday afternoon Helen went to the Third State Bank to withdraw $100 cash from her asset account. She intended to withdraw the cash using her debit card in one of the three ATMs located right outside the front door of the bank. Just before she inserted her card, a man in an official-looking uniform approached her and introduced himself as a bank employee. He asked her to insert her card and

code number in the ATM so that he could test the machine. She complied with his request. He then explained that something was wrong with the machine and asked her to use one of the other ATMs. She did. When she received her bank statement she discovered that $100 cash had been dispensed by the "broken" ATM and, presumably, taken by the person who had identified himself as a bank employee. Helen demands that the bank recredit the account and the bank refuses to do so. What result?

9. Increasingly, financial institutions "present" checks for their depositors by "truncating" them. In effect, the depositary bank holds the paper check and electronically transmits the information on the check to the payor bank for acceptance and payment. The check remains with the depositary bank and the payor bank does not return the actual check to the drawer. Does such a process create an electronic funds transfer for purposes of the Electronic Funds Transfer Act?

10. What is the "error resolution process" for the consumer checking process? Is it inferior to the error resolution process of the EFTA?

PART SIX

Creditor–Debtor Relationship

A creditor is worse than a master; for a master owns only your person, a creditor owns your dignity, and can belabour that.

Victor Hugo, *Les Miserables*

Introductory Comments

The creditor–debtor relationship is fundamental to American business. The relationship exists between two parties if one of them, the creditor, is owed money by the other, the debtor. A creditor or debtor can be an individual or a partnership, corporation, or other entity.

For most enterprises, the continual creation and paying off of debts is a common and necessary part of doing business. The business with enough cash to pay for all its needs is rare, as is the business that can survive without extending credit to its customers. Also rare is the individual who does not rely on credit. The American life-style would be greatly altered were we all to return to the practice of saving for desired goods and services before buying them.

To stay in business, a creditor must collect most debts. Therefore, the creditor's first concern is that these debts satisfy all legal requirements when they are created. Usually a debt owed by a business debtor is valid and enforceable. However, debts owed by "consumers"—individuals who buy for personal, family, or household purposes—may be a different matter. Consumer debts might not be as secure as business debts. For this reason, creditors may have a tendency to manipulate credit terms in their favor. To protect consumers from unfair and abusive credit practices, consumer credit protection laws have been enacted. These laws are discussed in Chapter 28, and the creditor who ignores them does so at his peril.

Another major concern of a creditor is whether the debts owed to him will actually be paid. Chapters 29 and 30 discuss how the creditor can reduce the risk somewhat by obtaining an interest, known as a security interest, in some of the debtor's property. If the debtor fails to pay, the creditor can take the property covered by the security interest, sell it, and use the sale proceeds to pay off the debt.

A creditor who lacks a security interest can still look to the debtor's property for payment of the debt. As discussed in Chapter 31, the creditor can sue the debtor, win a judgment, and then force the sale of some of the debtor's property so that the judgment can be satisfied. Before the judgment is obtained, the creditor might be able to tie up the debtor's property temporarily, regardless of who has possession of that property.

Clearly, creditors have many rights under the law, but debtors also have rights. Chapter 31 points out that some of a debtor's property cannot be reached by creditors at all; other property cannot be taken before the debtor has the chance to present his side of the matter in court. If a creditor violates a debtor's rights, the debtor can sue the creditor. The debtor might also recover an award of money damages.

Finally, what of the debtor who simply cannot pay all his debts? Chapter 32 covers the major options that are available to this debtor. One option is an agreement with creditors by which each creditor will accept less than what is actually owed. The debtor can also give his property to a neutral person, who sells it and pays off the creditors to the extent possible. If all else fails, the debtor can file for bankruptcy. The debtor's creditors may or may not be paid, but if the debtor is discharged in bankruptcy, most of his debts are extinguished, and he has the chance to make a fresh start in life.

28 Consumer Credit and Credit Protection

28:1 Introduction to Consumer Credit

Credit is the quality that attracts trust. In particular, it attracts trust in a person's intent and ability to pay money. In everyday terms, however, the term "credit" involves the loan of money.

A person is a "consumer" if he or she buys an item (or a service) primarily for personal, family, or household purposes. The goods or services bought for those purposes are known as *consumer goods* or *consumer services*. For example, a new family car is "consumer goods," while that same car bought for business use is not. The credit extended for the purchase of consumer goods or services is called consumer credit, and the transaction in which the extension of credit is made is a consumer credit transaction. The party extending credit is the *creditor*. The consumer or borrower party is the *debtor*.

The traditional source of borrowed money is the bank. Had banks remained the major source of consumer credit, extended on a transaction-by-transaction basis, it is possible that modern consumer credit law would never have developed. However, major banks now extend to consumers lines of credit that, through the magic of the bank credit card, can be used for any purpose whatsoever. Also, credit is routinely offered by many other entities, such as finance companies, retailers, and contractors that offer consumer-related services.

This widespread extension of credit has been referred to as the "consumer credit revolution." Its development was not without problems and abuses. One major problem was that credit terms could be worded or explained in many ways. For example, one lender might quote the interest rate on a loan to be "$10 per $100 per year," another might offer a "10 percent add-on" rate, and a third might offer "10 percent simple interest per year." These three offers may seem to be the same, but they actually differ in terms of the real cost of credit to the borrower. As a result, consumers found it difficult to shop intelligently for credit.

State Legislation Some problems relating to consumer credit were addressed in state statutes. These statutes, when they were enacted at all, tended to be spotty and inconsistent. For example, the requirements applying to small loans were often not the same as those applicable to installment sales (credit sales in which the buyer makes a series of periodic installment payments).

The first state-oriented, comprehensive statutory scheme involving consumer credit was the Uniform Consumer Credit Code (U3C). The U3C was first proposed in 1968 and was revised in 1974. It covers all the important areas of consumer credit, including disclosures of true credit terms, rate ceilings for interest and other charges, and creditors' rights. Similar to the U3C, but of somewhat broader scope and designed to be more in the consumer's favor, is the National Consumer Act (NCA). The NCA was proposed in 1970.

Neither the U3C nor the NCA is a state statute as such. The idea was that states would enact one or the other of the acts in entirety or at least in large part. What in fact happened was that only a few states enacted the U3C, and none at all enacted the NCA. A number of states have, however, extracted bits and pieces from both the U3C and the NCA for inclusion in their other statutes. The result is that even now, few states have comprehensive consumer credit codes.

Federal Legislation   States would likely have acted with greater authority in the consumer credit area had Congress not acted. In 1968, based on its constitutional authority to regulate commerce between the states, Congress enacted the *Consumer Credit Protection Act (CCPA)* [15 USC §§ 1601 et seq.]. The major focus of the CCPA as it was originally enacted was on disclosing the true cost of consumer credit. This coverage is part of Title I of the act, which is also known as the *Truth in Lending Act (TILA)*. Also included within the CCPA are provisions regulating equal credit opportunity, credit billing, and credit reporting.

Conflicts Between Federal and State Law   As a general rule, the CCPA "pre-empts the field" of consumer credit. This means that any state statute conflicting with a CCPA provision is ineffective, although only to the extent of the inconsistency. Some parts of the CCPA provide that a state statute is "inconsistent" only if it gives the consumer *less* protection than the federal statute does.

28:2   The Truth In Lending Act

Congress' broad purpose in enacting the TILA in 1968 was to promote the informed use of consumer credit by requiring the clear disclosure of credit terms to consumers in a consistent way. Key features of the act are (1) the disclosure requirements and (2) consumers' right to sue and recover damages from noncomplying creditors. These matters are discussed in detail in this chapter. First, however, it is appropriate to discuss the interpretation, coverage, and enforcement of the TILA, and to define some of the important terms used in the act.

Administrative Interpretation of TILA [15 USC § 1604]   The TILA is basically a framework of consumer credit protection law. This framework is filled out by regulations issued by the Board of Governors of the Federal Reserve System (the Board). These regulations are published first in the Federal Register and later in the Code of Federal Regulations (CFR).

The Board's TILA regulations are known as *Regulation Z* [12 CFR §§ 226.1 et seq.]. Regulation Z offers an authoritative interpretation of the TILA. For this reason, businesspersons (or their attorneys) must often look to Regulation Z for answers to specific TILA questions.

Both the TILA and Regulation Z impose many duties on creditors, and these duties can change somewhat each time the act or regulation is amended. Regulation Z is amended frequently. Although most large retailers and lenders keep up with the changes and are aware of and comply with the requirements that apply to them, the same is not true of many small businesses, such as "mom and pop" stores. Many operators of small businesses are still violating the TILA in various ways, often without even being aware that they are doing so. To aid these people and the consumer credit industry overall, Congress overhauled the Act with the Truth in Lending Simplification and Reform Act of 1980. The Reform Act was designed to facilitate creditor compliance with the law and to reduce the scope of liability for noncompliance. It requires the Board of Governors of the Federal Reserve System to promulgate model forms that, if used, put a creditor in compliance with the law. Although protection from TILA liability provides people with a powerful incentive to use these model forms, their use is not required. Similarly, tolerance ranges for numerical disclosures were authorized. Finally, civil liability for minor, technical deviations from the law was reduced significantly.

Transactions Covered [15 USC § 1603]   Generally speaking, the TILA and Regulation Z apply to all consumer credit transactions. Rather than stating its applicability in this way, however, the TILA sets forth the transactions to which it does *not* apply. These include (1) transactions involving extensions of credit primarily for business, commercial, or agricultural purposes; and (2) transactions in which the total amount financed is more than $25,000, unless a security interest is given in real property or a mobile home used as the consumer's main home.

Administrative Enforcement [15 USC § 1607]   The TILA is enforced by several different federal administrative agencies. The proper agency in a given case depends on the type of creditor involved. For example, an airline creditor's compliance with the TILA is the responsibility of the Civil Aeronautics Board. Generally, however, the TILA is enforced by the Federal Trade Commission (FTC). Under some circumstances, the FTC and other agencies can also require a creditor to reimburse a consumer for excess credit charges if the charges imposed were higher than the charges disclosed earlier by the creditor.

28:3   Truth in Lending Definitions

It is useful to understand certain key terms of the TILA and other parts of the CCPA.

Creditor [15 USC § 1602]: A creditor under the TILA is an individual or firm satisfying two criteria. First, the individual or firm must regularly extend consumer credit (1) that is payable in more than four installments or (2) for which a finance charge (defined below) will or may be required. Second, the individual or firm must be the one to whom the sale or loan contract initially requires payment of the debt arising from the transaction. For example, if Dobbs buys a new washing machine on credit from Ace Appliance Company and signs a promissory note in which he agrees to pay Ace for the machine, plus credit charges, in 12 monthly installments, Ace is a creditor under the TILA.

Also within the scope of "creditor" is a person who regularly arranges with others for extending consumer credit if (1) the credit is payable in more than four installments or a finance charge will or may be imposed and (2) the person actually extending credit is not also a "creditor." In addition, most issuers of credit cards are creditors for purposes of the TILA.

Debtor: Neither the TILA nor Regulation Z uses the term "debtor." Instead, they use either "consumer" or "obligor" to describe the person taking out a loan or buying goods or services on credit. For purposes of this chapter, "debtor" refers to a consumer who has entered into a consumer credit transaction, or intends to do so, and is the person obligated to pay the creditor later on.

Finance charge [15 USC § 1605]: Perhaps the most important TILA concept is that of the *finance charge*. The term "finance charge" refers to the cost of credit. Generally, the finance charge for a consumer credit transaction is the sum of all charges (1) payable by the consumer and (2) imposed directly or indirectly by the creditor in connection with the extension of credit. Specific types of charges that would be included in a finance charge are

- Interest
- Time-price differential (difference between cash price of item and total amount paid if item bought on credit)
- Charges payable under a point system (system requiring payment of a fee equal to a percentage of the loan being offered)
- Service or carrying charges
- Finders' fees
- Fees for most credit reports
- Premiums for some insurance protecting creditor in connection with the debt

Open-end credit; closed-end credit [15 USC § 1602]: Consumer credit as regulated by the TILA is either "open end" or "other than open end." *Open end* refers to a continuing credit arrangement, such as a charge account with a department store. Specifically, an "open-end credit plan" is a plan in which (1) the creditor reasonably expects repeated transactions; (2) the consumer can pay the balance on his account in full at any time without penalty; (3) the creditor can impose a finance charge from time to time on the outstanding unpaid balance; and (4) the creditor sets a credit limit, and the amount of credit available to the consumer at any time is the difference between that limit and the unpaid balance on the account. The typical bank or department store credit card is issued under an open-end credit plan.

Regulation Z uses "closed end" to describe a credit arrangement that is "other than open end." In essence, *closed-end credit* involves a single extension of credit. For example, if a person arranges to buy furniture under a credit arrangement made with the furniture dealer only for that specific transaction, the credit offered by the dealer would be closed end.

Annual percentage rate (15 USC § 1606): For a consumer to be able to compare different types of credit arrangements effectively, the cost of credit under each type of plan must be expressed in the form of some common term. The common term used in the TILA is the *annual percentage rate (APR)*. The APR is the cost of credit for one year, expressed as a percentage. It is usually simple to compute for an open-end plan. For example, a credit card plan might provide for a finance charge at the rate of 1.8 percent per month on the unpaid balance. This translates into an APR of 21.6 percent (12 times 1.8 percent).

For credit other than open end, computation of the APR is more complicated. As a practical matter, tables compiled by the Board are usually used for computing it with respect to a given transaction. The difference between the APR and what might appear to be the interest rate in a closed-end transaction can be illustrated as follows. A bank offers a loan at "$10 per $100 per year." This might appear to be a loan at 10 percent interest. However, assume that a consumer borrows $100 under these terms and repays it, with interest, in 12 equal monthly installments. The consumer has the use of the full $100 for only one month; the average amount of the bank's money she has during the year is about $50. The APR as determined under the TILA and Regulation Z is close to 20 percent.

28:4   Truth in Lending Disclosures

When consumer credit is extended, the creditor must make a number of disclosures to the consumer about the credit arrangement. This is a significant feature of the TILA. The specific disclosures required depend on whether the credit is open end or closed end, but certain general requirements apply to all disclosures.

General Rules Governing Disclosures [15 USC §§ 1631, 1632]   All information required to be disclosed by the TILA or Regulation Z must be disclosed clearly and conspicuously. The terms "finance charge" and "annual percentage rate" have to be more conspicuous than other terms or information. The purpose of these requirements is to prevent the creditor from using fine print, which most consumers will not read, and from burying the finance charge and APR information among other terms that might be more favorable. Numerical amounts must be expressed in figures, not words.

Cardholder agrees to pay Creditor the full amount of the New Balance on receipt of the monthly statement for the account. If not so paid, a **FINANCE CHARGE** will be added as explained below.

FINANCE CHARGE: A **FINANCE CHARGE** will be computed on the New Balance of your account as of the closing date shown on the statement by applying the PERIODIC RATE shown below (after first subtracting any unpaid **FINANCE CHARGES**).

ANNUAL PERCENTAGE RATE		PERIODIC RATE
Under $1,000	19.2%	1.60%
Over $1,000	12.0%	1.00%

If we receive full payment of your New Balance within 30 days after the statement closing date, no additional **FINANCE CHARGE** will be imposed on the New Balance.

New Balance: We compute the "New Balance" of your account by taking the balance you owed at the end of the previous billing cycle and subtracting any payments and credits received or credited during the present billing cycle.

Minimum Payment: You must make at least the Minimum Payment shown on your statement, computed as follows:

NEW BALANCE	MINIMUM PAYMENT
Less than $20	The amount of your New Balance
$20 to $500	$20 plus any amount past due
Over $500	4% of your New Balance plus any amount past due

Liability for Unauthorized Use: You may be liable for the unauthorized use of your credit card. You will not be liable for unauthorized use that occurs after you notify us at our address listed above, orally or in writing, of the loss, theft, or possible unauthorized use. In no event will your liability exceed $50.

In Case of Errors or Questions about Your Bill

If you think your bill is wrong, or if you need more information about a transaction on your bill, write us on a separate sheet at the address shown on your bill as soon as possible. We must hear from you no later than 60 days after we sent you the first bill on which the error or problem appeared. You can telephone us, but doing so will not preserve your rights.

In your letter, give us the following information:

- Your name and account number.
- The dollar amount of the suspected error.
- Describe the error and explain, if you can, why you believe there is an error. If you need more information, describe the item you are unsure about.

You do not have to pay any amount in question while we are investigating, but you are still obligated to pay the parts of your bill that are not in question. While we investigate your question, we cannot report you as delinquent or take any action to collect the amount you question.

Special Rule for Credit Card Purchases

If you have a problem with the quality of goods or services that you purchased with a credit card, and you have tried in good faith to correct the problem with the merchant, you may not have to pay the remaining amount due on the goods or services. You have this protection only when the purchase price was more than $50 and the purchase was made in your home state or within 100 miles of your mailing address. If we own or operate the merchant, or if we mailed you the advertisement for the property or services, all purchases are covered regardless of amount or location of purchase.

Open-End Credit Disclosures [15 USC § 1637] In an open-end consumer credit arrangement, there are two types of required disclosures. First, the creditor must disclose a number of facts to the debtor before an open-end account is opened. These disclosures cover the basic rights and duties of both the debtor and the creditor. They inform the debtor about when a finance charge will be imposed and how the charge will be computed (which includes a statement of the APR). Second, the creditor must make additional disclosures at the end of each billing cycle (usually a 30-day period) if money is owed on the account. The periodic disclosures inform the debtor about activity in the account during the billing period, the total outstanding balance on the account (including a separate showing of the finance charge), and when payment must be made to avoid additional finance charges.

Reproduced on the following pages are illustrative forms for an open-end account showing the required initial disclosures (Figure 28-1, at left) and periodic disclosures (Figure 28-2, below).

Closed-End Credit Disclosures [15 USC § 1638] The disclosures which the creditor is required to give to the debtor in connection with closed-end consumer credit are longer and more complex than those connected with open-end credit (see Figures 28-3, page 554, and 28-4, page 555). In fact, some creditors used to draw up what were really one-time credit arrangements in the form of open-end plans to avoid the tougher requirements. This practice was halted when Congress added to the definition of open-end credit the requirement that the creditor expect repeated transactions.

Account No.:   Statement No.:

Cardholder: Creditor:

PREVIOUS BALANCE	CHARGES	FINANCE CHARGE	PAYMENTS AND CREDITS	NEW BALANCE
$ _____	$ _____	$ _____	$ _____	$ _____

Minimum Payment Due: $

Closing Date:

To avoid all additional **FINANCE CHARGES,** pay the entire New Balance so that we receive it within 30 days after the above closing date.

Date	Transaction No.	Store	Description	Charges	Credits

FINANCE CHARGE is assessed on: $_____, which amount was the New Balance of your account as of _____, the closing date shown on your last statement (after first subtracting unpaid **FINANCE CHARGES**).

ANNUAL PERCENTAGE RATE		PERIODIC RATE
Under $1,000	19.2%	1.60%
Over $1,000	12.0%	1.00%

Send any Billing Inquiry, with account number, to:

ANNUAL PERCENTAGE RATE The cost of your credit as a yearly rate.	FINANCE CHARGE The dollar amount the credit will cost you.	Amount Financed The amount of credit provided to you or on your behalf.	Total of Payments The amount you will have paid after you have made all payments as scheduled.
%	$	$	$

You have the right to receive at this time an itemization of the Amount Financed.

☐ I want an itemization.   ☐ I do not want an itemization.

Your payment schedule will be:

Number of Payments	Amount of Payments	When Payments Are Due

Insurance

Credit life insurance and credit disability insurance are not required to obtain credit, and will not be provided unless you sign and agree to pay the additional cost.

Type	Premium	Signature
Credit Life		I want credit life insurance. _____ Signature
Credit Disability		I want credit disability insurance. _____ Signature
Credit Life and Disability		I want credit life and disability insurance. _____ Signature

You may obtain property insurance from anyone you want that is acceptable to (creditor). If you get the insurance from (creditor),   you will pay $ _____.

Security: You are giving a security interest in:

☐ the goods or property being purchased.

☐ (brief description of other property)

Filing fees $ _____   Non-filing insurance $ _____

Late Charge: If a payment is late, you will be charged $ _____ % of the payment.

Prepayment: If you pay off early, you

☐ may ☐ will not   have to pay a penalty.

☐ may ☐ will not   be entitled to a refund of part of the finance charge.

See your contract documents for any additional information about nonpayment, default, any required repayment in full before the scheduled date, and prepayment refunds and penalties.

_____

e means an estimate

ANNUAL PERCENTAGE RATE The cost of your credit as a yearly rate.	FINANCE CHARGE The dollar amount the credit will cost you.	Amount Financed The amount of credit provided to you or on your behalf.	Total of Payments The amount you will have paid after you have made all payments as scheduled.	Total Sale Price The total cost of your purchase on credit, including your downpayment of $ _____.
%	$	$	$	$

You have the right to receive at this time an itemization of the Amount Financed.

☐ I want an itemization.   ☐ I do not want an itemization.

Your payment schedule will be:

Number of Payments	Amount of Payments	When Payments Are Due

Insurance

Credit life insurance and credit disability insurance are not required to obtain credit, and will not be provided unless you sign and agree to pay the additional cost.

Type	Premium	Signature
Credit Life		I want credit life insurance. Signature
Credit Disability		I want credit disability insurance. Signature
Credit Life and Disability		I want credit life and disability insurance. Signature

You may obtain property insurance from anyone you want that is acceptable to (creditor). If you get the insurance from (creditor),   you will pay $ _____.

Security: You are giving a security interest in:

☐ the goods or property being purchased.

☐ (brief description of other property).

Filing fees $ _____   Non-filing insurance $ _____

Late Charge: If a payment is late, you will be charged $ _____/_____ % of the payment.

Prepayment: If you pay off early, you

☐ may   ☐ will not   have to pay a penalty.

☐ may   ☐ will not   be entitled to a refund of part of the finance charge.

See your contract documents for any additional information about nonpayment, default, any required repayment in full before the scheduled date, and prepayment refunds and penalties.

---

e means an estimate

As with open-end disclosures, the required closed-end disclosures are intended to advise the debtor about the significant financial and legal aspects of the credit arrangement. Generally, they are made before credit is extended, and they must be segregated from other information. In practice, a separate disclosure form is usually used. The form is slightly different depending on whether the closed-end credit transaction is a loan (Figure 28-3) or a credit sale (Figure 28-4).

 Figures 28-3 and 28-4 are examples of model disclosure forms for common consumer credit transactions. A creditor who uses one of the Board's forms, even with certain minor variations, will be considered to have complied with the disclosure requirements except as to any numerical disclosures. Most businesses should seriously consider using the Board's forms.

Since 1968, when the TILA was enacted, the courts have been called on to settle many disputes arising under the Act. A number of these cases have involved interpretation of the disclosure requirements. The case on pages 556–58 illustrates the judicial approach to truth in lending problems. Note how much emphasis the Court places on the Board's opinion about the disputed disclosure.

<hr />

Ford Motor Credit Co.
v
Milhollin
444 US 555 (1980)
United States Supreme Court

FACTS: Milhollin and several others, the respondents, bought cars from various Ford dealers on credit. The sales contracts were assigned to the petitioner, Ford Motor Credit Company (FMCC). Thus, FMCC, rather than the dealers, became the creditor. The front page of each contract contained the TILA closed-end disclosures. Not mentioned in the disclosures was the creditor's right to accelerate payment if the debtor defaulted. The respondents later sued the petitioner, claiming a violation of the TILA and Regulation Z. The district court held that a violation had occurred, and the Court of Appeals for the Ninth Circuit affirmed, although on the basis of somewhat different reasoning than the district court had used. The Supreme Court accepted the case for review because courts of appeals in other circuits had reached different conclusions on questions concerning the need to disclose acceleration rights.

ISSUE: Does the TILA require disclosure of acceleration terms in a loan?

RESULT: No. The courts will defer to the Federal Reserve Board staff recommendations on issues such as this.

REASONING:

* * *

The Truth in Lending Act has the broad purpose of promoting "the informed use of credit" by assuring "meaningful disclosure of credit terms" to consumers. . . . Because of their complexity and variety, however, credit transactions defy exhaustive regulation by a single statute. Congress therefore delegated expansive authority to the Federal Reserve Board to elaborate and expand the legal framework governing commerce in credit. . . . The Board executed its responsibility by promulgating Regulation Z, . . . which at least partly fills the statutory gaps. Even Regulation Z, however, cannot speak explicitly to every credit disclosure issue. At the threshold, therefore, interpretation of TILA and Regulation Z demands an examination of their express language; absent a clear expression, it becomes necessary to consider the implicit character of the statutory scheme. . . .

Respondents have advanced two theories to buttress their claim that [the TILA and Regulation Z] expressly mandate disclosure of acceleration clauses. In the district court, they contended that acceleration clauses were comprehended by the general statutory prescription that a creditor shall disclose "default, delinquency, or similar charges payable in the event of late payments," . . . and were included within the provision of Regulation Z requiring disclosure of the "amount, or method of computing the amount, of any default, delinquency, or similar charges payable in the event of late payments." . . . Before this Court, respondents follow the court of appeals in arguing that [Regulation Z] may be the source of an obligation to disclose procedures governing the rebate of unearned finance charges that accrue under acceleration. . . .

A fair reading of the pertinent provisions does not sustain respondents' contention that acceleration clauses are within their terms.

An acceleration clause cannot be equated with a "default, delinquency, or similar charg[e]." . . . In itself, acceleration entails no monetary penalty. . . . A "default, delinquency, or similar *charg[e],*" on the other hand, self-evidently refers to a specific assessable sum. Thus, within the trade, delinquency charges are understood to be "the *compensation* a creditor receives on a precomputed contract for the debtor's delay in making timely installment payments," . . . [Court's emphasis.] Acceleration is not compensatory; a creditor accelerates to avoid further delay by demanding immediate payment of the outstanding debt. . . .

The prepayment rebate disclosure regulation . . . also fails to afford direct support for an invariable specific acceleration disclosure rule. To be sure, payment by the debtor in response to acceleration might be deemed a prepayment within the ambit of that regulation. But so long as the creditor's rebate practice under acceleration is identical to its policy with respect to voluntary prepayments, *separate* disclosure of the acceleration policy does not seem obligatory under a literal reading of the regulation. [Court's emphasis.] [The regulation], therefore, squares with the position of the Federal Reserve Board staff that specific disclosure of acceleration rebate policy is only necessary when that policy varies from the custom with respect to voluntary prepayment rebates. . . .

It is a commonplace that courts will further legislative goals by filling the interstitial silences within a statute or a regulation. . . . But legislative silence . . . may . . . betoken permission or, perhaps, considered abstention from regulation. In that event, judges are not accredited to supersede Congress or the appropriate agency by embellishing upon the regulatory scheme. Accordingly, caution must temper judicial creativity in the face of legislative or regulatory silence.

At the very least, that caution requires attentiveness to the views of the administrative entity appointed to apply and enforce a statute. . . . Unless demonstrably irrational, Federal Reserve Board staff opinions construing the Act or Regulation should be dispositive. . . .

Finally, wholly apart from jurisprudential considerations or congressional intent, deference to the Federal Reserve is compelled by necessity; a court that tries to chart a true course to the Act's purpose embarks upon a voyage without a compass when it disregards the agency's views. The concept of "meaningful disclosure" that animates TILA . . . cannot be applied in the abstract. *Meaningful* disclosure does not mean *more* disclosure. [Court's emphasis.] Rather, it describes a balance between "competing considerations of complete disclosure . . . and the need to avoid . . . 'informational overload.' " . . .

The Federal Reserve Board staff treatment of acceleration disclosure rationally accommodates the conflicting demands for completeness and for simplicity. In determining that acceleration rebate practices need be disclosed only when they diverge from other prepayment rebate practices, the Federal Reserve has adopted what may be termed a "bottom-line" approach: that the most important information in a credit purchase is that which explains differing net charges and rates. . . . [The] court of appeals had no ground for displacing the Federal Reserve staff's expert judgment. . . .

Brennan, Justice.

28:5 Civil Liability for Truth in Lending Violations

The FTC and various other administrative agencies are responsible for enforcing the TILA. While administrative enforcement benefits the public at large, it often does little to help the individual consumer who is the victim of a violation of the act. For this reason, Congress included in the TILA a provision allowing consumers to sue and recover damages from noncomplying creditors.

Nature of Violation; Amount of Liability [15 USC § 1640] A creditor can be sued for a violation of the TILA itself or for a violation of Regulation Z. Among the types of violations that can and do occur are a creditor's failure to (1) make the required disclosures at all; (2) make accurate disclosures; (3) make disclosures at the proper time; or (4) furnish the debtor with other required information, such as the debtor's right to cancel certain credit transactions. It should be noted that the right to sue exists only for violations as to the more important disclosures.

An individual debtor who succeeds in a lawsuit against a creditor for violation of the TILA can recover (1) the amount of any actual damages or loss suffered; and (2) twice the amount of any finance charge imposed, but not less than $100 or more than $1,000; and (3) legal expenses, including reasonable attorney's fees. The effect of the TILA is that even if the finance charge involved is only several dollars, the successful debtor can recover at least $100. That is bad enough from the creditor's viewpoint, but the damages can be far higher in a class action. Recall that a class action is one begun by one or more debtors for the benefit of themselves and all others who have been harmed in the same way by the defendant's act, here, the creditor's violation. In a successful class action under the TILA, the damages recoverable are decided by the court. There is no minimum, but the total amount of damages awarded can be up to $500,000 or 1 percent of the creditor's net worth, whichever is less. Thus, any creditor having a net worth of $50,000,000 or more who violates the TILA can be liable for $500,000 in a class action.

Liability of Assignee [15 USC § 1641] A creditor who enters into a consumer credit transaction often assigns the contract with the debtor to another party, such as a bank or credit company, before the debtor has paid off the debt. If the creditor does so, the assignee has the right to receive the debtor's future payments. The assignee also gains all the creditor's other rights with respect to the contract, such as any security interest taken or retained in the debtor's property.

The effect of an assignment is to put the assignee in the original creditor's place. The TILA recognizes this fact and allows the debtor to sue the assignee for some violations of the act, even though the violation was actually made by the original creditor. The violations for which an assignee can be sued are those that are apparent from the disclosure statement. An example of an apparent violation is the failure to use such terms as "finance charge" and "annual percentage rate" as required in a disclosure statement.

Defenses Available to Creditors [15 USC § 1640] If a creditor (or assignee) is sued for a TILA violation, proof of any one of three different defenses offered by the creditor will succeed (cause the debtor to lose the lawsuit) even if a violation actually did occur. The first of these defenses is that the creditor acted to correct the error. This defense is available if (1) the correction is timely, (2) the debtor is notified about the error, and (3) adjustments are made to make sure that the debtor will not pay more than the finance charge (or dollar equivalent of APR) actually disclosed. A correction is timely if it is made within 60 days after the creditor discovers the error, before the debtor sues the creditor based on the error, and before the creditor receives written notice about the error from the debtor.

The second defense a creditor can assert is that he acted (or failed to act) because he relied on a Board rule or regulation, and that he did so in good faith. This right of reliance extends to the Board's interpretations of its rules and regulations, and also to any interpretation or approval given by an authorized Federal Reserve System employee. An authorized employee is one to whom the Board has given the authority to issue interpretations of regulations or approvals of particular conduct.

Finally, a creditor can successfully defend against a suing debtor by proving that the violation was (1) unintentional and (2) caused by a bona fide error that occurred even though the creditor followed procedures that should have avoided the error. Examples of bona fide errors are clerical, printing, and computer errors. An error that does *not* qualify is a mistake of law. For example, a creditor might fail to include a given fee in a disclosed finance charge because her attorney, after studying the TILA and Regulation Z, had incorrectly concluded that the fee need not be included. That omission is not an excusable bona fide error.

28:6 Consumer Leases

The TILA as originally enacted covered installment sales of consumer goods, but it did not cover leases of those goods. Abuses developed in the consumer products leasing industry. For this reason, Congress in 1976 enacted the Consumer Leasing Act (CLA) [15 USC §§ 1667 et seq.], which became part of the TILA.

Definitions [15 USC § 1667] A lease is a consumer lease under the CLA if (1) the subject of the lease is personal property; (2) the property is to be used by an individual mainly for personal, family, or household purposes; (3) the lease term is more than four months; and (4) the total amount that the lessee is to pay under the lease is $25,000 or less. "Lessor" under the act refers to an individual or firm regularly engaged in the consumer leasing business, either by making consumer leases or by offering or arranging for them. "Lessee" refers to a person who is offered a consumer lease or becomes obligated to pay under one.

If a consumer goods item is rented on a weekly basis, the fact that the lease term can extend for longer than four months if the lessee renews it each week does not make the lease a consumer lease.

Requirements as to Consumer Leases [15 USC §§ 1667a-1667c]   The CLA requires that the lessee be given a number of disclosures before signing a consumer lease. These disclosures advise the lessee about important terms of the lease. They cover such matters as periodic payments, other payments the lessee must make, warranties on and maintenance of the leased property, and termination of the lease.

In what is known as an open-end lease, the lease states that the property will have a given value at the end of the term. This is called the depreciated value. If the actual value of the property at the later date is less than the estimated depreciated value, the lessee must pay the difference. This difference can be substantial if, for example, the lessor originally sets an unrealistically high depreciated value. Since a lessor who does so can then count on receiving a large payment at the end of the lease term, he can offer deceptively low monthly rental payments. To curb abuses of this nature, the CLA limits the amount that the lessee can be obligated to pay at the end of the lease term.

Civil Liability [15 USC § 1667d]   A lessor who violates the CLA also violates the TILA. He can be sued by the lessee who was affected by the violation, just as a debtor can sue a creditor under the TILA.

28:7   Rescission of Credit Transactions

A consumer has a limited right to rescind certain credit transactions even if his only reason for doing so is that he changed his mind. The right applies (1) to some transactions in which the creditor receives a security interest in the consumer's home and (2) to some *home-solicitation sales.* These two classes of transactions are discussed below.

Security Interest Covering Dwelling [15 USC § 1635]   The creditor in a consumer credit transaction often requires some sort of security for the credit extended. The creditor can retain a security interest in property being bought by the debtor. Or, and perhaps in addition, the creditor can demand a security interest in other property owned by the debtor. The debt would then be secured in the sense that if the debtor defaults later on, the creditor can enforce the security interest. Typically, enforcement consists of the property being taken from the debtor and then sold so that the creditor can be paid. If the property in which a creditor takes a security interest is the debtor's main dwelling (which can be a mobile home), enforcement of the interest can result in the debtor's loss of the dwelling.

Because consumers sometimes rush into credit purchases without giving sufficient thought to possible consequences, Congress included in the TILA a cooling-off period with respect to certain transactions. Essentially, in most consumer credit transactions in which the credit will get a security interest in the debtor's main dwelling, the debtor has three days in which he can rescind the transaction. The three-day period begins either when the transaction takes place or when the creditor has delivered the material (more important) truth in lending disclosures and other required documents, whichever is later. Thus, for example, if a home improvement contract that grants the contractor a security interest in the house is signed on March 1, but the contractor does not deliver all the material disclosures until June 6, the homeowner has until midnight of the third business day after June 6 to rescind the contract. Even if the truth in lending disclosures have not been made, however, a debtor who waits too long will lose the right to rescind. In most cases the right expires when the dwelling is sold or three years after the contract is signed, whichever occurs first.

The major exception to the three-day rescission rule is that no right to rescind exists in the typical home mortgage situation, as where a bank's security interest in a dwelling secures repayment of money that the debtor borrowed to buy that dwelling.

Home-Solicitation Sales   Often, in what are known as home-solicitation sales, a consumer is emotionally overwhelmed by a door-to-door salesperson. The consumer signs a contract for the credit sale of goods or services that he may not really require or, more important, that he cannot really afford.

Many states addressed the problem of abuses in the home-solicitation sales business. For all practical purposes, these state statutes were preempted by the federal government when in 1974, the FTC adopted a trade regulation rule governing home-solicitation sales [16 CFR § 429.1]. The FTC rule allows a consumer to cancel most home-solicitation sales contracts any time within three business days after the contract is signed.

The FTC rule applies only to sales (1) to a consumer and (2) of consumer goods or services costing $25 or more. A sale need not actually be made in the consumer's home to qualify as a home-solicitation sale. Essentially, it is only required that (1) the seller or its representative personally seek the sale on a face-to-face basis and (2) the consumer's agreement or offer to purchase be made at a place other than the seller's place of business.

EXAMPLE: Brady is a salesman with AAA Home Insulation Company. He makes an unannounced visit to Lester's home, where he tries to interest Lester in insulation for Lester's house. Lester wants to think it over, and Brady leaves, promising to call later in the week. Several days later, Brady phones Lester and invites him to a local coffee shop. Lester accepts, and he signs a contract for insulation while at the coffee shop. This sale is a home-solicitation sale under the FTC rule.

The sale to Lester in the above example would also be a home-solicitation sale if, instead of having come unannounced, Lester had invited Brady to his house to make a sales presentation. However, it would not be a home-solicitation sale if, for example, Lester's initial contact with Brady had occurred when Lester stopped at AAA's sales office and inquired about insulation.

If the FTC rule applies to a sale, the consumer has certain rights and the seller has certain duties. The contract must conspicuously disclose the consumer's right to cancel the contract. The seller must also furnish a properly filled-out notice of cancellation. If the consumer elects to cancel, he or she merely signs and dates the notice and mails it to the seller. The seller must then return any payment made by the consumer and any promissory note signed by the consumer. The consumer must, of course, offer to return any goods delivered by the seller, although the consumer can keep the goods if the seller waits too long to pick them up.

 If the FTC rule applies, most sellers will not deliver any goods or services until the rescission period has ended. If the consumer needs the goods or services at once, he or she can sign a separate, *handwritten* statement waiving the rescission right.

28:8 Claims and Defenses Against Assignees

A credit sale of goods or services to a consumer can be handled entirely by the seller. This occurs when a consumer and seller enter into a retail install-ment contract, and the consumer then makes payments to the seller over the term of the contract. Frequently, however, the seller discounts the contract to a bank or other third party; that is, he assigns the contract to someone else. For example, if a contract requires the consumer to pay $1,000 over 12 months, the seller might assign the contract to a bank immediately and receive a smaller amount, say $900, from the bank. The consumer then would make payments to the bank.

In the traditional installment contract there is a *waiver of defenses* clause, which applies if the contract is assigned. The effect of this clause is that the consumer cannot assert against the assignee certain claims and defenses he could have asserted against the original seller. As a result, the consumer can be left with little or no recourse.

EXAMPLE: Harold buys a new car on credit, and Harold's contract includes a waiver of defenses clause. The dealer assigns the contract to a bank. The car turns out to be a lemon, but the dealer refuses to repair it properly or replace it. Having waived his defenses, Harold cannot withhold payment from the bank, even though the car may be entirely unsatis-factory.

In 1975 the FTC acted to protect consumers like Harold by issuing a trade regulation rule [16 CFR §§ 433.1, 433.2]. The rule does not prohibit the use of waiver of defenses clauses in installment contracts for the sale of consumer goods or services to consumers. Instead, it requires that any such contract include a prominent notice to the effect that anyone holding the contract is subject to all claims and defenses that the consumer could assert against the seller. The same requirement exists for a purchase money loan (loan for purchase of consumer goods or services) if the seller either refers the consumer to the lender or is related in some way to the lender. Thus, for example, if a seller routinely refers her credit customers to a particular finance company, the required notice must appear in the loan contract even though no actual assignment of the contract will occur.

Under the FTC rule, the maximum amount the consumer can recover from the assignee or purchase money lender is the amount already paid by the consumer on the assigned contract.

The following case illustrates the value of the rule to a consumer who has been defrauded.

Tinker

v

De Maria Porsche Audi, Inc.
459 So2d 487 (1984)
Florida District Court of Appeal, Third District

FACTS: In 1976 Tinker purchased an automobile from De Maria and financed the purchase through the Bank. De Maria's sales representatives alleged to Tinker that the auto was in good operating condition, that it had its original engine, and that it had never been in a collision. It turned out that the car had been purchased from an untitled owner and had been wrecked and determined to be a total loss by the previous owner's insurance company. Tinker ceased making payments on the car, claiming fraud in the inducement. The preprinted installment sales contract that Tinker had signed was prepared by Bank and contained the following notice:

NOTICE

ANY HOLDER OF THIS CONSUMER CREDIT CONTRACT IS SUBJECT TO ALL CLAIMS AND DEFENSES WHICH THE DEBTOR COULD ASSERT AGAINST THE SELLER OF GOODS OR SERVICES OBTAINED PURSUANT HERETO OR WITH THE PROCEEDS HEREOF. RECOVERY HEREUNDER BY THE DEBTOR SHALL NOT EXCEED AMOUNTS PAID BY THE DEBTOR HEREUNDER.

Bank sued Tinker for the payments remaining on the installment sales contract.

ISSUE: Does fraud by the seller cut off the rights of the third party financier to payment on the installment contract?

RESULT: Yes. The Bank took the installment contract subject to Tinker's defenses to paying De Maria.

REASONING:

*   *   *

Whether the jury's finding of fraud by De Maria is, as contended by Tinker, an absolute defense to the Bank's counterclaim for the balance owed on the contract, depends on the legal efficacy of the "Notice" provision which was included. Appellant expressed some uncertainty at trial as to how the provision operates.

The Notice is required by federal law in all consumer credit contracts made in connection with purchase money loans, such as installment sales contracts where the consumer executes the sales agreement together with a promissory note, both of which are, through a preprinted assignment clause, assigned to a bank which is closely affiliated with the seller. . . . The effect of the federal rule is to defeat the holder in due course status of the assignee institutional lender, thus removing the lender's insulation from claims and defenses which could be asserted against the seller by the consumer.

Prior to the passage of the rule, consumers were caught in a "no-win" situation when the seller failed to remedy the defect either because of its unwillingness or its disappearance from the market. The institutional lenders then took advantage of protections under the holder in due course doctrine when the consumer sought to assert seller misconduct as a defense to the creditor's suit for payment on the note. The rule is expressly designed to compel creditors to either absorb seller misconduct costs or seek reimbursement of those costs from sellers.

Although we have found no cases directly on the point, it is clear that not only does the Notice clause entitle the buyer to withhold the balance of the purchase price owed to the creditor when the seller's contractual duties are not fulfilled, but it gives the buyer a complete defense should the creditor sue for payment. The trial court correctly interpreted the law and accordingly gave a proper instruction:

> [I]f you find that the bank has proven [its counterclaim by the] weight of the evidence, then you must consider the . . . defenses offered by Mr. Tinker. If Mr. Tinker proves [fraud by the seller] then you must find in favor of Mr. Tinker and against the bank on its [counter] claim. . . .

> Ferguson, Judge.

28:9 Equal Credit Opportunity

In past years, the availability of credit to some persons depended on factors other than the persons' ability to repay. For example, a married woman often found it difficult to obtain credit of her own when she wanted it for reasons unrelated to her husband's credit rating. The lack of a credit history sometimes caused serious problems for a woman who was later widowed or divorced. The *Equal Credit Opportunity Act (ECOA)* [15 USC §§ 1691 et seq.] was added to the CCPA in 1974 in an effort to alleviate this problem and to allow aggrieved persons to recover damages for discriminatory credit practices. The ECOA is interpreted and expanded somewhat in Regulation B [12 CFR §§ 202.1 et seq.]. The act's scope is not limited to applications for *consumer* credit. For example, a denial of credit to a business because key people in that business are women violates the act.

Prohibited Conduct [15 USC § 1691] The ECOA prohibitions come into play at the time a person applies for credit. A creditor is forbidden to discriminate against any credit applicant on the basis of the applicant's race, color, religion, national origin, sex, marital status, or age (as long as the applicant is old enough to enter into a valid contract). Nor can a person be discriminated against because (1) all or part of his or her income comes from welfare, or (2) the person has, in the past, exercised any right under the CCPA in good faith.

These statutory prohibitions have been expanded in Regulation B, which lists information that a creditor cannot request from an applicant. For example, a creditor cannot require an applicant to disclose income from alimony or child support unless the applicant wants the creditor to consider that income in deciding on the applicant's creditworthiness. Nor can a creditor inquire about birth control practices, intentions about childbearing, or childbearing capability.

After setting forth the prohibited conduct, the ECOA lists creditor acts that do not amount to discrimination under the act. In essence, a creditor can

- Inquire about marital status if the creditor's purpose is to find out its rights with respect to particular extension of credit;
- Inquire about age or welfare source of income if the creditor's purpose is to find out the amount and likely continuation of applicant's income level;
- Use a credit system that considers age, if the system is valid;
- Inquire about or consider age of an elderly applicant if age is to be used by the creditor in favor of the applicant.

After credit has been applied for, the creditor must notify the applicant within 30 days as to the action taken on the application. If the action is adverse, the applicant is entitled to be told why. Adverse action includes a denial or revocation of credit and a refusal to grant credit substantially as requested by the applicant. If the applicant is already delinquent under an existing credit arrangement, however, the creditor's refusal to extend additional credit under that arrangement is not an adverse action under the act.

EXAMPLE: Doris holds a MasterCard credit card issued by the Ajax Bank, and she is behind on her payments to Ajax on the account. Doris requests Ajax to raise her credit limit. She also applies to the Bradley Bank for a Visa card. Both Ajax and Bradley deny Doris' requests. Bradley's denial is an adverse action under the ECOA, but Ajax's is not.

Although the ECOA itself does not say so, the legislative history of the act shows that Congress intends that the courts and the FTC, in enforcing the act, should look to the *effects* of creditor practices, not just to the creditors' motives or actual conduct.

Enforcement; Civil Liability [15 USC §§ 1691c, 1691e] Various federal agencies enforce the ECOA. The primary enforcing agency is the FTC.

The ECOA allows a credit applicant who has been discriminated against to sue the creditor for damages. If the applicant is successful he or she can recover both the amount of the actual loss and punitive damages (damages awarded as a penalty against the wrongdoer rather than to compensate the victim for the actual loss suffered). The court can award up to $10,000 in punitive damages to a plaintiff who sues on his own behalf. Far more is recoverable in a class action. A successful plaintiff is also entitled to recover the amount of the legal expenses in bringing the lawsuit, including reasonable attorney's fees.

 A creditor who acts (1) in good faith and (2) in accordance with instructions from the Board cannot be liable for violating the ECOA. An "instruction from the Board" can be in the form of a Board rule, regulation, or official interpretation. It can also be an interpretation or approval by an authorized Board employee.

28:10 Credit Cards and Credit Billing

It is commonplace to use a credit card instead of cash or a check to pay for goods or services. Predictably, this increased use of credit cards has been accompanied by various abuses. These abuses were addressed by Congress in 1970 when it added several sections [15 USC §§ 1642-1644] to the TILA, and again in 1974 when it enacted the Fair Credit Billing Act (FCBA) [15 USC §§ 1666 et seq.].

Issuance of Cards; Unauthorized or Fraudulent Use [15 USC §§ 1642-1644] Under the TILA, a credit card (other than a renewal card) can be isued *only* in response to a request or application for it. If a properly issued card is lost or stolen, the maximum amount the cardholder can be required to pay for unauthorized use of the card is $50. Unless the card issuer has taken a number of prescribed steps, the holder is not even liable for that amount. In no event is the cardholder liable for charges made *after* the issuer has been notified about the loss. As interpreted by Regulation Z the $50 limit on a cardholder's liability for unauthorized use of a card extends to most business credit cards.

Offsets [15 USC § 1666h] A holder of a bank-issued credit card often has money deposited in a checking or savings account with the issuing bank. If the cardholder is late in making payments on the card account, the bank may be tempted to deduct the amount owed to it on the card from the funds that the cardholder has in a checking or savings account. This procedure, known as an *offset* is forbidden by the TILA unless the cardholder has given advance written consent to it.

EXAMPLE: Jasper holds a Visa card issued by the Argo Bank. The total amount he owes on the Visa account is $1,200. Jasper also has $500 deposited with Argo in a savings account. Argo requires that at least $100 be paid each month on any Visa account having an outstanding balance of over $1,000. If Jasper fails to make the required monthly payment, it would be a simple matter for Argo to withdraw $100 from Jasper's savings account and apply it to the Visa account. However, unless Jasper has consented to an offset, his account is protected under the TILA provision.

Claims and Defenses Arising Out of Transaction [15 USC § 1666i]
Another potential problem of a customer's using a credit card issued by other than the seller is illustrated in the following scenario: Mason, a consumer, goes to a hardware store and buys a new power saw. He pays for it with his MasterCard, which was issued by Valley Bank. Two weeks later the saw proves to be defective, and Mason takes it back to the store. The dealer, who has already turned in the credit-card slip and been credited for the sale, refuses to take the saw back or do anything else to help Mason. Indeed, he claims that Mason's problems with the saw were caused by misuse. At this point, Mason has a useless saw that he has not yet even paid for. Valley Bank is equally unsympathetic to Mason's plight. It was not directly involved in the sale, having merely extended credit, and it wants to be paid.

The TILA eases the difficulties faced by cardholders like Mason in the above example. As to most transactions exceeding $50, the card issuer is subject to all claims and defenses (other than tort claims) arising out of the original transaction, up to the amount owed to the issuer on that transaction. The purpose of this TILA provision is not necessarily to penalize banks and other card issuers. Rather, the provision was included on the theory that the issuers can often force retailers and others honoring credit cards to do what is right, while the typical consumer cannot.

Credit Billing [15 USC §§ 1666-1666d]   As many holders of credit cards learn, mistakes can and do occur when the card issuer bills for credit extended. When that happens, a cardholder can find himself in an endless battle with a computer. The TILA includes provisions intended to offer some relief in this situation. Note that these provisions apply to billing in connection with *all* open-end credit, not just to credit-card accounts.

If the debtor under an open-end credit plan finds what he believes to be an error in a statement of his account sent by the creditor, the debtor has 60 days in which to notify the creditor about it, in writing. Assuming that the notice contains sufficient information, the creditor must then investigate the matter and either correct the error or advise the debtor why the disputed charge is correct. A creditor who fails to carry out these duties forfeits up to $50 of the amount owed by the debtor.

Other aspects of billing under open-end plans are also regulated by the TILA. These include (1) the length of time during which the amount due under a plan can be paid without further finance charge (the "free ride" period), (2) the prompt crediting of payments, and (3) the treatment of excess payments (people actually pay too much on occasion). A debtor who is affected by a creditor's violation of the credit billing requirements can sue and recover damages, as discussed in 28:5.

28:11   Credit Reporting

The most significant security that a consumer can offer when seeking credit is the likelihood that he or she will repay the debt. A prospective creditor asks two key questions: Can the consumer repay? If so, will he repay? Many businesses do not have the means to obtain credit information on their own. Instead, they usually turn to a credit reporting agency, also known as a credit bureau, to acquire the needed data. For a fee, the agency prepares a report outlining the credit history of the prospective debtor.

Because one's credit rating is so important, the consumer wants to be sure that information contained in a credit report is accurate. The consumer also wants to preserve privacy as much as possible. These considerations, among others, have been the subject of abuses and problems that developed in the credit-reporting industry over the years. As a result, in 1970 Congress enacted the *Fair Credit Reporting Act (FCRA)* [15 USC §§ 1681 et seq.]. The major purpose of the FCRA is to require credit-reporting agencies to obtain and distribute credit information in a way that is fair to consumers. Specific problems covered by the act include (1) the consumer's privacy; (2) the accuracy, relevance, and proper use of credit information; and (3) the consumer's access to and right to correct credit information concerning him.

The FCRA regulates credit-reporting activities concerning applications for employment and consumer-related insurance as well as applications for consumer credit. However, the primary focus of the discussion here is on the consumer credit aspect of the act.

Definitions [15 USC § 1681a]   For purposes of the FCRA, a credit-reporting agency is a *consumer-reporting agency.* This term refers to any person or firm that regularly gathers and evaluates credit information on consumers for the purpose of furnishing reports to others.

Perhaps at the heart of the FCRA is its definition of the term *consumer report.* Essentially, a consumer report is any communication (written or oral) that (1) is made by a consumer-reporting agency; (2) concerns specific matters listed in the FCRA; and (3) is or likely will be used as a factor in determining a consumer's eligibility for consumer credit, insurance, or employment. The "specific matters" referred to above are creditworthiness, credit standing, credit capacity, character and general reputation, personal characteristics, and mode of living. Among types of reports that are *not* consumer reports are reports containing information *only* about transactions between the consumer and the person making the report.

EXAMPLE: Clarence applies to Secaucus Bank for a loan, and he lists Williams, his landlord, as a credit reference. Secaucus contacts Williams. The only information Williams provides is that although Clarence has been a quiet tenant, he has often been late in paying his rent. This information given by Williams affects Clarence's credit rating, but it is not a consumer report within the scope of the FCRA.

Obsolete Information [15 USC § 1681c]   As a general rule, a consumer report must not contain obsolete adverse information. Under the FCRA, most adverse information is obsolete if it is more than seven years old. Examples of information to which the seven-year limit applies are criminal records, unpaid bills, and lawsuits against the consumer. The only exception to the seven-year limit concerns a consumer's bankruptcy; bankruptcy information is obsolete after ten years.

The restriction on obsolete information does not apply if a consumer report is to be used in connection with a credit transaction involving $50,000 or more. Thus, for example, a consumer report used by a bank in deciding whether to loan a consumer $75,000 to buy a new house can state the fact that the consumer was convicted of embezzlement 20 years earlier and that he was imprisoned for five years for that offense.

Distribution of Consumer Reports [15 USC § 1681b]   The FCRA limits the right of consumer-reporting agencies to furnish consumer reports to other persons. A report can be furnished as the consumer involved instructs in writing, or as a court may order. Otherwise, and excluding the furnishing of reports with respect to insurance, employment, and several other purposes listed in the act, a credit reporting agency can furnish a consumer report only under limited circumstances. This is illustrated in the following case.

Heath

v

Credit Bureau of Sheridan, Inc.
618 F2d 693 (1980)
United States Court of Appeals, Tenth Circuit

FACTS: Heath, a reform-seeking member of the union, claims that the Progressive Mine Workers Union of America requested from the credit bureau a "consumer report" in order to "embarrass, humiliate, and discredit" Heath in the eyes of the public and his co-workers and fellow union members. The credit bureau had allegedly prepared and delivered the report even though it knew the union requested the report for purposes not permitted by the Fair Credit Reporting Act. Heath sought actual and punitive damages.

ISSUE: Was the report a "consumer report" within the meaning of the FCRA?

RESULT: Yes. It was a "consumer report" even though there was no consumer relationship between Heath and the union.

REASONING:

*   *   *

. . . The essence of the trial court's ruling, and appellees' argument, is that there can be no consumer report in the circumstances alleged in this case: the statutorily permitted purposes to which the information must relate all concern consumer transactions; therefore, information supplied to a person not engaged in such a transaction cannot be a consumer report. Thus, bankruptcy information on Heath supplied to the union, even for the express purpose of harassment, cannot be a consumer report because Heath and the union were not engaged in a consumer transaction. This construction of the statute finds support in several cases. . . . But we think it springs from a mistaken premise—that applicability of the Act is governed entirely by the purpose of the person requesting the information.

We believe a critical phrase in the definition of consumer report is the second requirement: the relevant information must be "used or expected to be used or collected in whole or in part for the purpose of serving as a factor" with regard to enumerated transactions. This phrase clearly requires judicial inquiry into the motives of the credit reporting agency, for only it "collects" the information. Similarly, the term "expected to be used" would seem to refer to what the reporting agency believed. . . . Thus, if a credit bureau supplies information on a consumer that bears on personal financial status, but does not know the purpose for which the information is to be used, it may be reasonable to assume the agency expected the information to be used for a proper purpose. . . . Similarly, if at the time the information was collected, the agency expected it to be used for proper purposes, a transmittal of that information would be a consumer report. . . . Finally, even if the request for information was made under the false pretense of a proper purpose, data supplied would be a consumer report if the agency expected it to be used for the represented purpose.

By restricting the purposes for which consumer reports can be supplied to legitimate transactions involving consumers, we believe Congress meant to prevent intrusions into consumers' private affairs when no legitimate transaction was actually imminent. Indeed, an abuse frequently noted by members of Congress during consideration of the Act was the instance of a TV reporter acquiring such reports by giving a fictitious company name and false reasons for acquiring the report. . . .

Logan, Circuit Judge.

Disclosures to Consumers [15 USC §§ 1681g, 1681h, 1681m] The FCRA requires that both users of consumer reports and consumer reporting agencies make certain disclosures to consumers. Most consumers are quite aware of their own credit history in general terms, but they may be unaware of particular facts that creditors look to before extending credit. Often, the first clue a consumer receives that something is "wrong" with his or her credit history is a potential creditor's either denying credit or offering credit at a higher charge than the consumer had expected. Whenever either event occurs and the action was based on information in a consumer report, the user of the report (the potential creditor) must inform the consumer of that fact and provide the name and address of the consumer reporting agency that made the report. If consumer credit is denied or made more costly because of information obtained from *other than* a consumer-reporting agency, the consumer has only the right to learn the nature of the information. He is not entitled to learn its source.

Regardless of whether a consumer knows that a given consumer-reporting agency has prepared a consumer report on him or has information concerning him in its files, the consumer is entitled to a disclosure of certain information from the agency, on request. This information is (1) the nature and substance of all nonmedical information that the agency has on the consumer in its files, (2) the sources of that information, and (3) the identification of those to whom the agency has furnished any consumer report on the consumer (other than for employment purposes) within the last six months. These disclosures must be made during normal business hours. They can be given over the phone or to the consumer in person. A consumer visiting the consumer-reporting agency can bring along one other person, such as an attorney.

Disputed Accuracy of Information [15 USC § 1681i] A consumer may dispute the accuracy of an item of information in a consumer-reporting agency's file on him. If so, and if the consumer advises the consumer-reporting agency about it, the agency must generally investigate the matter. Information found to be inaccurate must be deleted promptly. Information that can no longer be verified must also be deleted.

If the agency's investigation fails to resolve the dispute, the consumer can file a brief statement presenting his side of the matter. The dispute must then be noted by the agency in any later consumer report it prepares on the consumer. The consumer's statement, or a summary of it, must also .be included with each later report. If the consumer requests it, the agency must also notify recent recipients of consumer reports about deleted or disputed items of information.

Compliance Procedures [15 USC § 1681e]   Consumer-reporting agencies are required to follow reasonable procedures (1) to avoid including obsolete information in any consumer report and (2) to furnish consumer reports only to those entitled to receive them. As a general matter, agencies must also follow reasonable procedures to assure the maximum possible accuracy of all information in reports prepared by them.

EXAMPLE: A bank requests a consumer-reporting agency to prepare a consumer report on Hansen, who has applied for a loan. The agency phones the local branch of a major retailer, states Hansen's name and address, and asks the retailer for whatever information on Hansen it has in its files. The retailer indicates that Hansen's credit rating is bad. Without any further information or investigation, the agency prepares a report stating that Hansen is a bad credit risk. The agency has violated the FCRA because it has not followed a reasonable procedure to maximize the accuracy of its information.

Enforcement; Civil Liability for Violation [15 USC §§ 1681n, 1681o, 1681s] The FTC is charged with enforcement of the requirements of the FCRA in most situations, just as it is the primary enforcement agency for other parts of the CCPA.

If a consumer-reporting agency or user of a consumer report fails to comply with any requirement of the FCRA, the affected consumer can sue and recover damages from that agency or user. The affected consumer can recover the amount of his legal expenses (including reasonable attorney's fees), as well as damages for actual injury to his individual credit.

If a consumer-reporting agency or user of a consumer report intentionally fails to comply with the FCRA, the consumer can also recover punitive damages in an amount that the court determines. Thus, there is no limit on the damages recoverable for intentional misconduct. In this respect, the FCRA differs from parts of the CCPA which do limit the damages recoverable. If the situation warrants it, the consumer may also be entitled to equitable relief, in the form of an injunction.

 If a user of a user of a consumer report or other consumer credit information is used for violating the user-oriented requirements, discussed earlier, the user is not necessarily liable even if the alleged violation is proven. The FCRA provides that no user will be liable if it proves that when the alleged violation occurred, it maintained reasonable procedures to assure compliance with the FCRA requirements.

Civil Liability for Defamation and Related Torts [15 USC § 1681h]   Before the FCRA (or any similar state legislation) was enacted, the usual approach taken by a consumer who had been wronged by incorrect information supplied by a credit-reporting agency was to sue for defamation,[1] invasion of privacy, or negligent reporting of information. A consumer-reporting agency, user of consumer credit information, or person furnishing information to a consumer-reporting agency can still be sued for these torts under the FCRA. Generally, however, the basis of the lawsuit is limited to false information furnished with malice of willful intent to injure the consumer. Thus, the plaintiff must prove more than just a willful violation of the FCRA. Essentially, the plaintiff must show that the person or entity sued acted in bad faith and that this bad faith was intentionally directed at the plaintiff.

 The FCRA does not cover the tort of commercial defamation. Essentially, this tort involves injury to one's business or business credit caused by the publication of inaccurate credit information. A lawsuit based on commercial defamation can still be brought, but the plaintiff's right to recover damages is based entirely on state law.

Key Concepts and Terms

- The federal government has enacted comprehensive legislation intended to protect consumers in their credit transactions. Statutes in some states provide similar protection, but usually on a less comprehensive basis.

- The federal Truth in Lending Act (TILA) helps consumers shop intelligently for credit by requiring that credit terms be disclosed in advance and in a consistent way.

- The nature of the required TILA disclosures depends somewhat on whether the credit involved is open end or closed end. More detailed disclosures must be made for closed-end credit than for open-end credit.

- A creditor who violates the TILA requirements can be liable to the consumer who was affected by the violation. If the consumer sues and wins, he or she recovers at least $100 plus legal expenses. The consumer also recovers the amount of any actual damages suffered.

- Certain leases of consumer goods are governed by requirements similar to those governing consumer credit transactions.

- A consumer has a three-day cooling off period in which to cancel a credit transaction if (1) the creditor acquires a security interest in the consumer's dwelling as part of the transaction and (2) the loan is for a purpose other than buying the dwelling. The same right applies to many home-solicitation sales.

- The assignee of an installment contract for the sale of consumer goods or services to a consumer is subject to the claims and defenses that the consumer could assert against the original seller. The same is true for some purchase money lenders.

---

[1] Defamation is the publication of false information that injures the name or reputation of another person. In this context, publication means disclosure to other than the person involved. For example, a credit agency publishes defamatory information about a consumer when it includes in a report given to a retailer the untrue statement that the consumer was recently convicted of a crime.

- A person cannot be denied credit on the basis of sex, marital status, age, or race. A creditor who discriminates on this basis can be liable for substantial damages.

- Numerous requirements exist as to the issuance to and use of credit cards by consumers. A cardholder has limited liability for unauthorized use of his card, and a card issuer is not immune from liability with respect to transactions in which its card was used.

- A consumer can question an item that appears on the periodic bill of the consumer's open-end credit account. If he does so, the creditor must investigate the matter.

- There are limits on the adverse information that can be included in credit reports on consumers, and the distribution of the reports is restricted. Consumers are entitled to learn about adverse information in credit files on them and to have inaccurate information corrected.

- A credit reporting agency that violates the statutory requirements can be liable to the affected consumer. The extent of liability depends on whether the violation was intentional. It can also depend on whether the agency acted maliciously toward the consumer.

- Annual Percentage Rate (APR)
- Closed-End Credit
- Consumer Credit Protection Act (CCPA)
- Consumer Goods and Services
- Consumer Report
- Consumer-Reporting Agency
- Creditor
- Debtor
- Equal Credit Opportunity Act (ECOA)
- Fair Credit Reporting Act (FCRA)
- Finance Charge
- Home-Solicitation Sale
- Offset
- Open-End Credit
- Regulation Z
- Truth in Lending Act (TILA)
- Waiver of Defenses

Questions and Case Problems

1. Sapenter owns two pieces of property. One is her home, on which she owes only a small amount to a bank. The other property is a six-unit apartment building on which Sapenter owes a large amount to Dreyco, a lender. Sapenter falls behind in her payments to Dreyco, and Dreyco threatens to enforce his security interest in the apartment building. To avoid having to enforce the security interest, Dreyco agrees to loan Sapenter additional money and to take a security interest in Sapenter's home. Sapenter soon falls behind once again, and Dreyco seeks to enforce his security interest in the home. Sapenter argues that since Dreyco never gave her any of the required TILA disclosures concerning the final loan, she can and wishes to rescind that transaction. Sapenter also sues Dreyco for damages for having violated the TILA. Can Sapenter rescind the loan transaction? Is she entitled to damages? Discuss the reasons for your answers.

2. On Thursday, Fred visited Vacuums Unlimited, where he talked with Kirby, a salesman. Kirby demonstrated a new Superflo machine and its attachments. Not entirely convinced, Fred left the store. The next day, Friday, Kirby visited Fred's home and demonstrated the machine there. Fred was won over. He paid Kirby $100 as a down payment and signed a contract for payment of the $900 balance, plus a finance charge, over the next 24 months. Not having read the contract carefully before signing it, Fred was unaware that it contained a printed waiver of any right Fred might have to rescind the contract. Kirby departed with the signed contract, leaving the machine and attachments with Fred. On Saturday, a friend advised Fred that Superflo products are overpriced and of poor quality. Vacuums Unlimited was closed on Sunday, but on the following Monday Fred called Kirby and said that he wanted to cancel the contract. Kirby declared that Fred had no right to do so. Fred failed to make any payments on the machine, and Vacuums Unlimited is now suing him. Fred defends on the basis that he should have been allowed to rescind the contract and get his $100 back. Is Fred correct? Why or why not?

3. Ken buys a new mobile home costing $15,000. He gives the dealer a $3,000 down payment and finances the $12,000 balance by signing an installment contract. The dealer immediately assigns the contract to a bank. After Ken has paid $500 to the bank on the contract, the mobile home turns out to have many design and manufacturing defects. Among other problems, the roof develops a bad leak, and Ken's uninsured $10,000 stamp collection is destroyed. Both the dealer and the mobile home manufacturer have gone out of business, so Ken turns to the bank. He (a) refuses to make further payments on the contract, (b) sues the bank for breach of warranty, and (c) also sues the bank for the value of the ruined stamp collection. What rights does Ken in fact have against the bank?

4. Jerry and Marcia Markham find a house they want to buy. They apply for a loan and a mortgage to be made to them jointly. The significance of the joint loan is that although the debtors intend to repay the loan together, each of them would be responsible for the full amount if the other did not pay. The bank turns down the loan because Jerry and Marcia are not married. Does this action of the bank violate the Equal Credit Opportunity Act?

5. Helen Harbaugh, a teacher, is married to John Harbaugh. Helen fills out an application for a Visa card to be issued by Continental Bank. In the application she states her name as "Mrs. John Harbaugh," and she also signs the application that way. Continental feeds the information into its computer for a credit check. The computer system used by Continental is such that courtesy titles such as Mr., Mrs., and Ms. are suppressed. Therefore, the name entered into the computer is John Harbaugh. The computer is unable to verify that John is employed as a teacher. Continental so advises Helen, who supplies the necessary information. Helen's employment is confirmed, and Continental issues two Visa cards, but in the name of John Harbaugh. Helen complains to Continental, but without success. Several months later, Continental advises John that the cards will be reissued and asks him to correct erroneous information. Helen and John send back a new application indicating that the applicant is "Helen Harbaugh." Again, two Visa cards are issued in the name of John Harbaugh. Helen sues Continental, claiming that it violated the Equal Credit Opportunity Act. Should she prevail? Why or why not?

6. Cody receives a Visa card in the mail from Tri-State Bank. Having been discharged in bankruptcy only a year before, Cody is happy to get the card, although he had

not applied for it. The letter accompanying the card states that Cody's credit limit is $1,100, and that his use of the card will constitute his acceptance of it. All the terms of Tri-State's credit arrangement are properly disclosed, but there are no instructions about what to do if the card is lost or stolen. Cody uses the card to pay a $100 car-repair bill. He then loses the card, and he does not notify Tri-State. Somebody else finds the card and runs up charges of $2,000 with it. A month later Cody receives a bill from Tri-State for $2,100. Cody fails to pay, and Tri-State sues him for $2,100. Discuss whether Cody is liable to Tri-State and, if he is, the extent of his liability.

7. Information Dynamics provides a service to merchants whereby it distributes information on microfiche concerning the check cashing history of customers whose histories are reported by merchant-subscribers to the service. Thus, a single merchant receives a large amount of information about the creditworthiness of potential customers. Does this violate the provisions of the Fair Credit Reporting Act, limiting consumer reports to persons who intend to use the information in connection with a credit transaction with the consumer about whom information is sought?

8. Retail Credit Company, a consumer-reporting agency, prepares an investigative consumer report on Mrs. Rasor. The report is done in connection with Rasor's application for health insurance that she needs to obtain a loan from the Small Business Administration (SBA). Retail Credit's agent spends about four hours investigating Rasor and ten other people. The report falsely states that Rasor has a reputation of "living with more than one man out of wedlock," that her reputation has suffered because of this fact, and that she drinks to excess. As a result of the report, Rasor is denied insurance by one company and is offered insurance by another only at an above-average premium rate. Rasor's SBA loan is also delayed. At Rasor's insistence, Retail Credit eventually conducts a second, more thorough investigation, which reveals that much of the initial report is incorrect. Rasor sues Retail Credit for damages. How should the case be decided?

9. Ackerley applies for credit with several retailers, but he is turned down each time. The first retailer, Atlas Lumber Company, refuses to explain why it is denying credit. The second retailer, Hercules Hardware Supplies, discloses that the reason for its action is an adverse consumer report that it has received from CBS Credit Bureau. Ackerley visits CBS, which refuses to show him anything in its file on him or even to discuss the matter. Ackerley sues Atlas, Hercules, and CBS for $200 in actual damages for lost wages. Each defendant moves for dismissal (asks the court to throw out the complaint against that defendant). Atlas, which had in fact relied on the adverse consumer report from CBS, argues that it was unaware of any requirements under the Fair Credit Reporting Act. Hercules argues that it complied with the law. CBS argues that it did not violate the law. CBS also argues that since Ackerley was unemployed, he suffered no actual damages. You are the judge. How will you rule on each defendant's motion? Why?

10. Colletti's car was repossessed by the Bank, which reported the repossession to TRW Credit Data, a credit reporting agency. TRW reported the information to creditor-subscribers who requested information about Colletti. Colletti insisted that the repossession was unlawful and requests that TRW withdraw the credit report, which is damaging to Colletti's credit rating. TRW refuses the request on the ground that the information is not inaccurate. Is TRW right? What recourse, if any, does Colletti have?

29 Introduction to Secured Transactions

29:1 Introduction

Credit is at the hub of most business transactions that involve more than a minor sum of money. This is as true for an ordinary consumer as it is for a multibillion-dollar corporation. People who extend credit, whether they are merchants, bankers, or others, can do so on the bare strength of the debtor's promise to pay or repay in the future. Transactions between friends or closely related parties are often handled this way. Commercial transactions, however, often are not. For his own protection, the commercial creditor requires more than a mere promise to pay.

The added protection the creditor seeks is the acquisition of some kind of interest in property owned by the debtor. That interest is known as a *security interest* if a creditor receives it to secure the payment of a debt. The interest can be in any kind of property or right that the debtor has. Here, however, the discussion concerns only security interests in the debtor's personal property or fixtures.[1] Thus, the essence of what is known as a secured transaction is the use of personal property or fixtures, known as the *collateral*, to secure the performance of an obligation. The obligation is usually one to pay money.

Article 9 of the UCC is the governing law of secured transactions in all states except Louisiana. Article 9 is a comprehensive scheme for regulating security interests. With several exceptions, it applies to *any* transaction that is intended to create a security interest in personal property or fixtures. Article 9 provides a relatively simple and unified system by which the large variety of modern secured transactions can take place with less cost and greater certainty than under the earlier law. In another sense, Article 9 balances the often conflicting goals of debtors and creditors. It seeks to protect the debtor from a creditor who demands too much control over the collateral or the right to seize the collateral at will, but it also protects the creditor from debtor wrongdoing.

---

[1] "Personal property" consists of almost all property that is not real property. "Real property" refers to land and improvements (houses or other buildings) erected on land. "Fixtures" are items of personal property that have been attached to real property. For example, a new furnace is personal property when it is delivered to a building, but it becomes a fixture when it is installed. Security interests in real property are discussed in Chapter 36.

Article 9, originally made available to the state legislatures in 1962, was substantially revised in 1972. The revised article is printed in Appendix B, and it should be referred to during the study of this chapter. Bear in mind that although many states have adopted the 1972 revision, some states have not. Also, some states have altered the official version of Article 9 by adding, modifying, or deleting particular provisions.

29:2   Relationship With Other Transactions

A few comments about how Article 9 relates to other areas of business law may make it easier to understand the concept of secured transactions.

Contracts   A contract can be defined as an agreement between parties by which each party receives something and gives up something else. Any agreement by which a security interest is created usually qualifies as a contract. Obviously, the opposite is not true; many contracts have nothing at all to do with secured transactions.

Sales   Sales are governed by Article 2 of the UCC, and most security interests arise in connection with sales on credit. "Credit" is the key to the distinction between the scope of Articles 2 and 9. Article 2 covers the pure sales aspects of a transaction (see Chapters 19 through 22), while Article 9 governs to the extent that, as security for the buyer's payment of the purchase price, the seller retains an interest in the goods sold. On those sales that do not involve credit, Article 9 does not apply at all. If a transaction cast in the form of a sale is actually intended to operate only as a secured transaction, Article 9 applies.

EXAMPLE: Bradley requires a short-term loan of $1,000 and is prepared to offer a security interest in his car as collateral. McDuff is willing to make the loan, but she knows nothing about security interests and distrusts them. Because of McDuff's attitude, Bradley sells the car to McDuff for $1,000, but the parties agree that Bradley can repurchase the car later on for the same amount plus interest. The "sale" is a secured transaction, and Article 9 governs the parties' rights and liabilities.

Commercial Paper   Article 3 of the UCC deals with the rights and relationship of parties of checks, promissory notes, and other commercial paper (see Chapters 23 through 25). Article 9 applies to these negotiable instruments to the extent that they are collateral in a transaction, such as where a negotiable document of title is pledged as security. If Article 3 conflicts with Article 9 in a particular situation, Article 9 governs.

Leases   A lease of personal property is usually not a secured transaction. The parties to a lease normally intend that the lessee possess and use the leased property during the lease term and then return it to the lessor. However, Article 9 applies if a lease is intended as security. A lease that includes an option to purchase the leased property is not necessarily a lease intended for security. If, however, the lessee can become the owner of the property for little or no additional consideration after he has complied with the mandatory lease terms, the lease *will* be considered to be one intended for security and will be governed by Article 9.

EXAMPLE: Johnson leases a vehicle valued at $20,000 from Smith Leasing Company. The sum of the required monthly payments during the lease term is $21,000, and Johnson can acquire title to the vehicle at the end of the term by paying an additional $100. Article 9 governs the parties' rights and liabilities because the transaction is deemed to be one intended for security.

29:3 Definitions

The study of secured transactions requires familiarity with a number of terms, all of which are defined or used in Article 9. "Secured transaction" and "security interest" were defined earlier in this chapter. Other important terms are explained below. Except as indicated, the official definitions appear in UCC § 9-105.

Collateral: The property in which a security interest exists.

Security agreement: Any contract or agreement that creates or provides for a security interest.

Debtor: The party who must pay or otherwise perform the obligation that is secured.

Secured party: The seller, lender, or other party in whose favor a security interest exists.

Purchase money security interest [UCC § 9-107]: Primarily, a security interest that secures payment of the purchase price of the collateral in which that interest exists. The interest can be retained by the seller who sold the collateral to the debtor on credit, or it can be granted to a lender who loaned the debtor the money to buy the collateral.

Attachment of security interest [UCC § 9-203]: The process by which a security interest becomes enforceable against the debtor, though not necessarily against other persons.

Perfection of security interest: The process by which a secured party acquires the maximum rights obtainable under Article 9 with respect to the collateral. "Perfection" is not defined in the UCC, but essentially, once a secured party has "perfected" his security interest, he has done everything to secure his rights. These rights are then superior to the rights of many other persons who may lay claim to the collateral.

EXAMPLE: Willard decides to buy a new car for personal use. The price of the car is $10,000, and since Willard has only $2,000, he visits his local bank. The bank agrees to lend Willard $8,000, and Willard agrees that, to secure the loan, the bank shall receive a security interest in the new car. This loan arrangement is a secured transaction in which Willard is the debtor and the bank is the secured party. The agreement between Willard and the bank is the security agreement, while the car qualifies as consumer goods and constitutes the collateral. The interest in the car that the bank receives is a purchase money security interest because the loan is used for buying that car. The bank can then perfect its interest as discussed later in this chapter.

29:4 Types of Collateral

Most security interests cover "personal property," a term that covers many different types of collateral. It is helpful to classify personal property as being tangible, quasi-tangible, or intangible. Each of these categories is then further subdivided under Article 9.

Tangible Collateral [UCC § 9-109] Literally, property is "tangible" if it is capable of being touched. Tangible collateral is property that has material substance, such as a piece of fruit, a book, or a car. For purposes of Article 9, tangible collateral is "goods," which is divided into four categories. The first is *consumer goods*, defined in UCC § 9-109 as goods that are used or bought primarily for personal, family, or household purposes. The second is *equipment*—goods used or bought primarily for business use, including farming or the practice of a profession. The third category is *farm products*—crops, livestock, or supplies used or produced in farming operations. The last category is *inventory*—goods held for sale or lease, or to be furnished under service contracts.

The actual or intended use of tangible collateral, rather than the nature of the collateral itself, determines its status under this scheme. For example, a new car bought for family use is "consumer goods," but if the car is bought by a traveling salesman for business purposes, it is "equipment." That same car is "inventory" while it is in the dealer's showroom or, for that matter, if it is bought by another dealer who intends to resell it.

Quasi-Tangible Collateral [UCC 9-105] "Quasi" means "as if," and collateral is quasi-tangible if it is represented by a piece of paper rather than by the property itself. Under Article 9 there are three categories of quasi-tangible collateral: (1) chattel paper, (2) documents, and (3) instruments. "Chattel paper" refers to one or more writings that are evidence of both a money obligation and a security interest in specific goods. A "document" is a document of title, which is any piece of paper commonly treated as adequate evidence that the person in possession of it has the right to hold and dispose of both the document and the goods it covers. An example is a warehouse receipt [see discussion in Chapters 20 and 34]. "Instruments" refers to commercial paper, such as checks, promissory notes, and certificates of deposit (see Chapter 23).

Intangible Collateral [UCC § 9-106] Collateral is intangible if it has no physical form. Intangible collateral is divided into the categories of accounts and general intangibles. An "account" is any right to payment for goods sold or services rendered if the right is not evidenced by either an instrument or chattel paper.

"General intangibles" is a catchall category for all personal property other than goods, accounts, chattel paper, documents, instruments, and money. Examples of general intangibles are the goodwill of a business and literary rights.

29:5 Excluded Transactions

Certain types of transactions are not governed by Article 9 even though they might appear to fall within its scope. The reason for many of the exclusions is that bodies of law outside the UCC adequately regulate these transactions.

Real Property [UCC § 9-104]   Article 9 applies if the collateral subject to a security interest is a fixture, but it does not apply to the creation or transfer of an interest in real property. Thus, Article 9 is inapplicable in the common situation where a person decides to buy a new house, obtains a loan to pay the purchase price, and signs a mortgage or similar instrument covering the property by way of security for the loan. Also outside the scope of Article 9 are leases of real property, transfers of the right to receive rent under leases, and statutory liens on real property. An example of a statutory lien on real property is a landlord's interest in the personal property of a tenant who has not paid the rent.

Accounts [UCC §§ 9-102, 9-104]   Many businesses must maintain inventories and replenish them as goods are sold. Sales are often on open account, leaving the businesses with accounts rather than cash. A common method by which these businesses obtain needed operating capital is through what is known as *accounts receivable financing.* One way a business does this is by assigning its accounts to its creditor as security for existing loans or future advances. Article 9 clearly applies to this type of transaction because a security interest would be created. However, Article 9 also applies to most *sales* of accounts or chattel paper. As a result, Article 9 also governs a second method of accounts receivable financing, by which a business needing capital sells its accounts outright to someone else.

It may be clear in a given situation that an assignment or sale of accounts is not made to obtain or secure financing. Article 9 recognizes this possibility by listing four types of transfers of accounts to which it does not apply: (1) a sale made as part of a sale of the business out of which the accounts arose, (2) an assignment for purposes of collection only, (3) a transfer of a right to payment under a contract if the transferee is the person who is also to perform the contract, and (4) a transfer of a single account to satisfy a prior debt.

Other Exclusions [UCC § 9-104]   Article 9 does not apply to transfers by government agencies. Other transactions to which it does not apply include any transfer of (1) a claim for employee compensation, (2) a claim under an insurance policy, (3) a tort claim, and (4) an interest in most types of bank accounts.

Creation and Perfection of Security Interest

29:6   Attachment of Security Interest

A security interest is created when it attaches. *Attachment* occurs when the last of the following three events have taken place, in any order: (1) the secured party has possession of either the collateral (see discussion below) or a written security agreement, (2) the secured party has given value, and (3) the debtor has acquired rights with respect to the collateral. Obviously, the debtor must also have incurred some sort of debt or other obligation. This requirement is implicit in, for example, the definition of "security interest" as an interest-securing payment or performance of an obligation.

Possessory Security Interests [UCC § 9-203]   In most secured transactions the parties intend that the debtor will retain possession of the collateral, at least prior to any default by the debtor. However, that is not always true. Sometimes, the debtor transfers possession of the collateral to the secured party, who holds it until the secured debt has been paid. The secured party is then said to have a *possessory security interest.* Most possessory security interests arise from *pledge* transactions. For example, a person might pledge shares of corporate stock as collateral for a loan. A possessory interest can attach without a written security agreement, although some sort of written agreement is often used. The debtor must, however, deliver the collateral to someone else. Delivery can be either to the secured party or to some third person who, by arrangement, is to have possession. Ordinarily, the debtor is entitled to regain possession only after the secured debt or obligation has been satisfied.

Rights and Duties of Secured Party in Possession [UCC § 9-207]   A secured party who has the collateral in his possession has certain rights. He can (1) repledge the collateral on terms that do not impair the debtor's right to redeem it; (2) use or operate the collateral to preserve it or its value; and (3) unless the collateral is consumer goods, use or operate the collateral to the extent allowed by the terms of the security agreement. A secured party in possession also has certain duties. He must take reasonable care of the collateral. Ordinarily, he must also keep it identifiable, although fungible collateral (such as grain) can be mixed with other property of the same kind. If the secured party fails to carry out these duties he is liable for any resulting loss.

Even though collateral is in the secured party's possession, the debtor must bear the risk of its being damaged or destroyed. This means that the secured party can charge the debtor with reasonable insurance expenses. The debtor can also be charged with taxes and other reasonable payments required in connection with the secured party's possession, preservation, or use of the collateral.

29:7   The Security Agreement [UCC § 9-203]

In the case of a security interest other than a possessory one, the debtor and secured party must enter into a written *security agreement* (see pages 591–92) before the interest can attach. In most cases the agreement must contain only (1) a description of the collateral and (2) the debtor's signature. If the collateral is either crops that will be or are being grown or timber that is to be cut, a description of the land involved must also be included in the agreement. However, most security agreements also contain other provisions.

Description of Collateral   The description of the collateral in a security agreement must be reasonably specific. Generally, a description is sufficient if it makes it possible to identify the property intended as security. As the following case illustrates, however, other potential collateral that the secured party may have intended to include will not be covered unless it is adequately described. Note how the parties' use of a preprinted agreement form contributed to their problem.

Mitchell

v

Shepherd Mall State Bank
324 F Supp 1029 (1971)
United States District Court, W.D. Oklahoma,
Bankruptcy Division

FACTS: Mitchell and his partner, the debtor, filed a petition in bankruptcy, and the bankruptcy judge in that proceeding found that a security interest held by Shepherd Mall State Bank covered equipment, inventory, accounts receivable, contract rights, and proceeds in the debtors' stores. The trustee in bankruptcy now seeks review of the correctness of that finding.

ISSUE: Does the security agreement adequately describe the collateral to include accounts receivable, inventory, and contract rights?

RESULT: No. The portion of the form dealing with these items appears only to classify the collateral, not to take a security interest in these items.

REASONING:

*   *   *

The relevant portions of the Security Agreement are set out below: ([italicized] portions indicate typewritten insertions on the form agreement) . . .

D. COLLATERAL

1. The security interest is granted in the following collateral:

   a. Describe collateral. . . . (4) If insufficient space to list all collateral, continue on separate sheets affixed hereto and signed for purposes of identification.
   See EQUIPMENT LIST *attached hereto and made a part hereof, describing equipment, furniture and fixtures located at Moore and Edmond stores.* (Description continued on 2 pages attached hereto).

2. Classify goods under (one or more of) the following Uniform Commercial Code categories:
   ☐ Consumer Goods
   ☒ Equipment (business use)
   ☒ Inventory
   ☒ Accounts Receivable
   ☒ Contract Rights

As can be seen from the material quoted above the collateral described ("equipment, furniture and fixtures") is not the same as the collateral classified. The list describing the "equipment, furniture and fixtures" makes no reference to either "Inventory," "Accounts Receivable," or "Contract Rights."

. . . [The court discusses financing statements filed by the bank. These statements described the collateral as including inventory and proceeds, accounts receivable, and contract rights. The court concludes that it is the security agreement, not the financing statement, that creates a security interest.]

Paragraph D1 of the security agreement quoted above which purports to describe the collateral is unambiguous. . . . However, it is not the sufficiency of the description which is questioned. The language of this paragraph is clear as to what is described.

It is the statement contained in Paragraph D2 of the security agreement which it is contended extends the security interest to the inventory, accounts receivable, and contract rights. . . . This printed paragraph attempts the impossible under the Code. It purports to classify accounts receivable and contract rights as goods. Goods, however, include only "consumer goods," "equipment," "farm products," and "inventory." . . . Accounts receivable and contract rights are otherwise defined in [UCC § 9-106].

Classifications under the Code are important to determine such questions as the place of filing, etc. . . . It is, however, not among the purposes of classification to describe or create the security interest. . . .

The printed form invited a misclassification, but should this error be permitted to render an otherwise unambiguous description of collateral uncertain? We think not. . . .

It could as well be said in the instant case that a third party would only be interested in the collateral as clearly designated by the form itself.

He would not be concerned with the classification made by the parties, and should not be required to read and interpret the paragraph which purports to deal only with classification. . . .

Daugherty, District Judge.

After-acquired Property [UCC § 9-204] *After-acquired property* is property that might or will come into the debtor's possession after the security agreement is signed. The parties to a secured transaction often want the collateral to include after-acquired property. For example, one holding a security interest in inventory wants that interest to cover new goods bought by the debtor to replace goods that are sold. Otherwise, the collateral might eventually disappear altogether.

Except where the collateral is consumer goods, the security agreement can provide that the security interest created extends to after-acquired collateral. The description of the collateral must be reasonably adequate, although the law in some states is that a specific reference to after-acquired property is unnecessary if the nature of the collateral is such that it will necessarily change, as is true of inventory. On the other hand, vagueness in an after-acquired property clause can lead to problems.

EXAMPLE: A security agreement covers "all farm equipment" owned by the debtor, as well as "all property similar to that listed above" that the debtor acquires later. Since the latter clause can include anything from a screwdriver or garden hoe to the largest of farm machinery, the secured party's security interest might not include a farm tractor that the debtor acquires later.

The rule about after-acquired property is somewhat more limited if the collateral is consumer goods. After-acquired consumer goods are not subject to the secured party's security interest unless the debtor acquires the additional goods *within ten days* after the secured party "gives value."

Other Optional Provisions   Most security agreements include far more than just a description of the collateral and perhaps an after-acquired property clause. Some of the various matters likely to be included or covered in a security agreement are listed below. As a practical matter, the secured party usually has superior bargaining power and is thus able to dictate the form and content of the agreement.

- Identification of parties
- Description of value given by secured party
- Grant of security interest
- Debtor's rights in collateral
- Secured party's rights in collateral

- Accelerated payment of secured debt
- Protection of collateral; risk of loss or damage
- Time and manner of satisfying secured obligation
- Debtor's waiver of rights and defenses
- Events of default
- Secured party's rights and remedies on debtor's default

Debtor's Waiver of Defenses [UCC § 9-206] A security agreement that covers a debtor's credit purchase of goods often includes what is known as a *waiver of defenses* clause. The purpose of the clause is to prevent the debtor from asserting certain claims or defenses against one to whom the secured party assigns the security interest (see Chapter 30). Bear in mind that a seller who takes a security interest in goods he has sold on credit often wants to be paid at once. He is also happy to pass on to someone else the risk and administrative cost involved in collecting the debt. The seller can achieve these goals by assigning the chattel paper (here, the security agreement and the buyer's promissory note) to a third party (the assignee). However, under general sales law a buyer can assert certain claims or defenses against the seller if there are problems under the sales contract. For example, a buyer might claim failure of consideration or breach of warranty (see Chapters 21 and 22).

If the seller assigns the chattel paper, the assignee would prefer not to be placed in the same position as the seller with regard to liability for performance of the contract. Often, the assignee will not have had anything to do with the original contract—he has only the buyer's promise to pay a given amount and a security interest in the collateral. This is why the waiver of defenses clause is desirable from the assignee's viewpoint. Without it, the assignee would be left open to a lawsuit by the buyer and might hesitate to accept the assignment from the seller in the first place.

Under Article 9, a waiver of defenses clause is enforceable by certain assignees. The assignee must have paid value for the assignment and have taken it in good faith. As the following case illustrates, the assignee must also have been unaware of the particular claim or defense that the buyer later asserts.

Massey-Ferguson Credit Corp.
v
Brown
547 P2d 846 (1976)
Montana Supreme Court

FACTS: Brown, the appellant, bought a harvesting machine from Dan Morrison & Sons, and as part of the transaction he traded in his old harvesting machine. Brown signed a security agreement in the form of a retail installment contract covering the transaction. Morrison immediately assigned the contract to Massey-Ferguson Credit Corporation, the respondent. The new machine turned out to be defective, and Morrison failed to repair it despite its agreement to do so. Morrison later went out of business, and Brown stopped making payments on the machine. Massey-Ferguson then enforced its security interest by taking the machine back and selling it to someone else for less than Brown had owed on it. Massey-Ferguson sued Brown for the amount still owed to it on the contract, and Brown counterclaimed for the value of his trade-in.

ISSUE: Is Brown precluded from raising his defense to payment in a lawsuit by the assignee of the credit contract?

RESULT: No. Brown's waiver of defense is not effective against the assignee because it did not take the contract without notice of defenses.

REASONING:

*   *   *

[We] now consider whether [the breach of the repair agreement] defense can be applied to respondent, seller's assignee. Respondent asserts the seller's breach is not an applicable defense against the assignee of this retail installment contract. Undeniably, appellant's signature appears on a contract which states:

> " . . . buyer(s) will not set up any claim, or defense which he may have against the seller as a defense . . . in any action . . . by the seller's assignee."

The enforceability of covenants of this type is governed by [UCC § 9-206(1)], which provides in pertinent part:

> " . . . an agreement by a buyer or lessee that he will not assert against an assignee any claim or defense which he may have against the seller or lessor is enforceable by an assignee who takes his assignment for value, in good faith and without notice of a claim or defense. . . . "

In our view, respondent Massey-Ferguson Credit Corporation cannot be considered among those whose protection is contemplated by [§ 9-206(1)]. The evidence shows that respondent's representative participated, at least to some degree, in making the sale by orally affirming the seller's promises to appellant buyer. It is clear from the exhibits that the contract was executed and assigned at about the same time and upon the same instrument, and the blank form sales contract employed was in this case furnished by respondent corporation. Under these circumstances, it has been held the assignee does not take the assignment "without notice of a claim or defense" and is therefore not entitled to the enforcement protection provided by [UCC § 9-206(1)]. We find [this rule to be] in strict accord with the purpose and policy behind this section of the Uniform Commercial Code, as explained in [a Kentucky case]:

"We consider it to be the policy of the Uniform Commercial Code to encourage the supplying of credit for the buying of goods by insulating the lender from lawsuits over the quality of the goods. But we conceive that the insulation was intended primarily for *financial institutions* rather than the manufacturer who finances his own sales. He needs no inducement to supply credit for the purchase of his goods because the whole object of his business is to sell his goods." . . .

Harrison, Justice.

A waiver of defenses clause is *not* effective with respect to the so-called "real defenses," which are the defenses that can be asserted against the holder in due course of a negotiable instrument. As discussed in Chapter 24, the real defenses include infancy, illegality of the transaction, certain misrepresentations, and discharge in bankruptcy.

 A waiver of *any* defenses might be unforceable by an assignee if the collateral is consumer goods. This is so because the Article 9 rule is subject to any statute or court decision that establishes a different rule for buyers of consumer goods. Statutes in some states invalidate waivers of defenses in consumer transactions. In other states, court-made law has the same effect. Moreover, as discussed in Chapter 28, a rule issued by the Federal Trade Commission requires that any sales contract for a credit sale of consumer goods conspicuously advise the debtor that, in effect, any assignee of the contract is subject to *all* claims and defenses that the debtor could assert against the seller. The only exception to this requirement concerns consumer goods bought with a credit card.

29:8   Secured Party's Giving of Value [UCC § 9-203]

A security interest cannot attach until "value has been given." This requirement concerns a duty of the potential secured party. Essentially, it means that in exchange for granting the security interest, the debtor must receive from the secured party consideration sufficient to support a simple contract. The value given can be a present extension of credit or a commitment to extend credit in the future. This is the value given in most secured transactions. In others, one might "give value" for rights acquired either (1) in exchange for partial or total satisfaction of a preexisting claim or (2) as security for a preexisting claim.

EXAMPLE: John owes Bill $1,000, but the debt is unsecured; that is, Bill has only John's promise to pay. John now signs a security agreement granting Bill an interest in certain property owned by John, as security for the debt. Bill now has a valid security interest. He has given value because the interest was granted as security for a preexisting claim.

SECURITY AGREEMENT

Agreement Number: Account Number:

Buyer: Seller:

Buyer hereby grants to Seller a security interest in the Collateral described below. Said interest is given to secure the performance and payment of a promissory note of even date herewith in the principal amount of $ _____, with interest at the rate of __% per annum on the unpaid balance, which note is given to Seller and is payable as therein provided.

Description of Collateral:

The above Collateral is classified as (check one or more):

☐ Consumer goods
☐ Equipment (business use)
☐ Inventory
☐ Accounts Receivable
☐ Contract Rights

The security interest herein granted also covers property of the same character as that described above which Buyer may hereafter acquire at any time until the termination of this security agreement, such after-acquired property being more specifically described as follows:

The names and addresses of all persons to whom notices required or permitted by law are to be sent are set forth below.

Buyer acknowledges that (1) Buyer has read both sides of this agreement and (2) Buyer has received a legible, completely filled-in copy of this agreement.

SEE OTHER SIDE FOR ADDITIONAL TERMS AND CONDITIONS

IN WITNESS WHEREOF, Buyer and Seller have executed this agreement on the _____ day of _____, 19__.

BUYER   SELLER

_____ By _____

_____   _____

_____   _____

TERMS AND CONDITIONS

1. <u>Payment</u>. Buyer shall pay to Seller the sum evidenced by the above-mentioned promissory note or any renewals or extensions thereof.

2. <u>Buyer's Covenant</u>. Buyer covenants that except for the security interest hereby granted, Buyer has, or on acquisition will have, full title to the collateral free from any lien, security interest, or claim. Buyer will, at Buyer's expense, defend any action that may affect Seller's security interest in, or Buyer's title to, the collateral.

3. <u>Proceeds</u>. Buyer hereby grants to Seller a security interest in and to all proceeds of the collateral, as defined by Article 9 of the Uniform Commercial Code as enacted in the State of _____. This provision shall not be construed to mean that Buyer is authorized to sell, lease, or dispose of the collateral without Seller's consent.

4. <u>Financing Statements</u>. At the request of Seller, Buyer will join in executing, or will execute as appropriate, all necessary financing statements in a form satisfactory to Seller, and will pay the cost of filing such statements.

5. <u>Location of Collateral</u>. Buyer will keep the collateral separate and identifiable at the address of Buyer shown herein, and Buyer will not remove the collateral from such address without the written consent of Seller.

6. <u>Alienation of Collateral</u>. Buyer will not, without the written consent of Seller, sell, contract to sell, lease, encumber, or otherwise dispose of the collateral or any interest therein until this security agreement and all debts secured hereby have been fully satisfied.

7. <u>Protection of Collateral</u>. Buyer shall keep the collateral in good order and repair, and Buyer shall not use the collateral in violation of any statute or ordinance.

8. <u>Insurance</u>. Buyer shall insure the collateral with an insurer acceptable to Seller against such casualties and in such amounts as Seller may require. Said insurance shall be for the benefit of Buyer and Seller as their interests may appear.

9. <u>Taxes and Assessments</u>. Buyer shall pay promptly when due all taxes and assessments levied on the collateral or on its use or operation.

10. <u>Default</u>. If Buyer fails to pay when due any amount payable on the above-mentioned note or on any other indebtedness secured hereby, or shall fail to observe or perform any of the provisions of this agreement, Buyer shall be in default.

11. <u>Remedies</u>. On any default, and at any time thereafter:

(a) Seller may declare all obligations secured hereby immediately due and payable and may proceed to enforce payment of the same and exercise any and all of the rights and remedies provided by law.

(b) Seller shall have the right to remove the collateral from Buyer's premises. Seller may require Buyer to assemble the collateral and make it available to Seller at any place to be designated by Seller that is reasonably convenient to both parties. For purposes of removal and possession of the collateral, Seller or its representative may enter any premises of Buyer without legal process, and Buyer hereby waives and releases Seller of and from any and all claims in connection therewith or arising therefrom.

12. <u>Effect of Seller's Waiver</u>. Failure of Seller to exercise any right or remedy, including but not limited to the acceptance of partial or delinquent payments, shall not be a waiver of any obligation of Buyer or right of Seller; nor shall it constitute a waiver of any other similar default subsequently occurring.

13. <u>Time as of Essence</u>. Time is of the essence of this agreement.

14. <u>Waiver of Defenses</u>. Buyer hereby waives as against any assignee of the security interest granted hereby any claim or defense which Buyer may have against Seller to the full extent permitted by law.

15. <u>Governing Law</u>. This agreement shall be construed according to the law of the State of _____ .

29:9   Debtor's Acquisition of Rights in Collateral

The requirement that a debtor have "rights" in collateral before a security interest in that collateral can attach is logical; a debtor cannot grant a security interest unless he himself has some rights in the property. A debtor has sufficient rights to grant a security interest if he has both title to and possession of the property, as where the debtor buys goods on credit and takes them home with him. However, the nature and extent of the debtor's rights need not be so obvious. Instead, it is generally enough that the debtor has some ownership interest in the property or some right to obtain possession of it.

EXAMPLE: Farmers Bank loans farmer Jones money to buy a new harvesting machine, and the parties sign a security agreement to cover the new machine. Jones then places an order for the machine with Acme Equipment Company, which has several, identical harvesting machines in stock. Since Farmers Bank has a signed security agreement and has given value, its security interest attaches as soon as Acme identifies a machine to the contract—in other words, as soon as Acme determines the particular machine that will be delivered to Jones. Attachment is not postponed until the time when Jones actually acquires possession of the machine.

29:10   Perfection of Security Interest

The attachment of a security interest gives the secured party only limited rights with respect to the collateral. Attachment does not protect the secured party against many other people who may acquire or claim some sort of interest in that collateral. As a result, the secured party ordinarily wants to maximize his rights by perfecting his interest. If he does so, his interest becomes superior (1) to unperfected interests arising earlier and (2) to some interests of others arising subsequently.

A security interest is perfected when (1) it has attached and (2) any required additional steps for perfection have been taken. *Perfection of security interest* occurs automatically at the time of attachment for some types of interests, but it usually requires something more. That "something more" consists of either the secured party's taking possession of the collateral, or the secured party's filing a financing statement. These requirements are discussed in the remainder of this chapter.

Perfection on Attachment [UCC § 9-302]   Article 9 lists several types of security interests that are, in effect, automatically perfected when they attach; that is, the secured party need not do anything more. The most important type of security interest that is perfected when it attaches is a *purchase money security interest* in consumer goods other than motor vehicles or fixtures.

The automatic perfection rule may worry a secured party since a given item bought by the debtor may or may not qualify as "consumer goods," depending on its use. For example, an armchair qualifies if it is bought for use in the debtor's home, but it does not qualify if it is bought for use in the debtor's office. The answer to this problem is that the secured party can take the debtor's word about the intended use of the goods, even if the debtor is lying.

 Although the secured party need not file to perfect a purchase money security interest in consumer goods, it is to its advantage to do so. As discussed in Chapter 30, filing can save an interest that would otherwise be lost if the debtor sells the goods to another consumer.

Perfection Through Possession [UCC §§ 9-302, 9-304, 9-305]   A secured party can perfect a security interest in certain types of collateral, including goods, money, instruments, and chattel paper, by taking possession of the collateral. Indeed, perfection of a security interest in money or most instruments other than those constituting part of chattel paper can be done *only* in this way. Perfection by possession is simple, but is not practicable in most cases. The result is that if some act of perfection is required, filing is the method generally used.

29:11   Perfection by Filing [UCC §§ 9-302, 9-304, 9-403]

Under Article 9, *filing* usually consists of the secured party's presenting a "financing statement" to the appropriate public official (filing officer) and offering the required filing fee. The filing officer then indexes the financing statement so that it can be located, and he holds the statement for public inspection. The purpose of filing is to give people other than the parties to a secured transaction a way to learn about the secured party's interest. For most types of collateral, filing either is mandatory to perfect a security interest or is optional in the sense that it can be done even though it is not necessary.

Financing Statement [UCC § 9-402]   Article 9 specifies the information that must be included in a *financing statement* if the statement is to be effective. For most types of collateral, the minimum required information is as follows:

- Names of debtor and secured party
- Addresses of debtor and secured party
- Statements showing types of collateral or describing collateral
- Description of land, if collateral is crops growing or to be grown
- Debtor's signature

A financing statement that substantially complies with the Article 9 requirements is effective even though it contains minor errors, as long as the errors are not seriously misleading to those reading the statement. An example of a financing statement is set forth in Figure 29-2.

 The description of the collateral in a financing statement need not be detailed, but if the description is too general and vague, the statement will be ineffective to perfect the secured party's security interest. Examples of descriptions that are suspect because they are too general are "all personal property," "all assets, regardless of type or description, now

FINANCING STATEMENT

This financing statement is presented to a filing officer for filing pursuant to provisions of Article 9 of the Uniform Commercial Code of _____ [*state*].

Debtor (or assignor)   Name: _____
                                        Address: _____
                                        _____

Secured party (or assignee)   Name: _____
                                        Address: _____
                                        _____

1. This financing statement covers the following types (or items) of property: _____ [*brief description of security*].
(Check Applicable Items)

2. (If collateral consists of goods which are or are to become fixtures) The above-described goods are affixed or are to be affixed to property located at:

Street & No.	Section	Known As	Block No.	City	County	State	Name of Record Owner of Premises
_____	_____	_____	_____	_____	_____	_____	_____

3. ☐ Proceeds of the collateral are also covered.

4. ☐ Products of the collateral are also covered.

Debtor (or assignor): _____ [*Signature*]

FIGURE 29-2

owned or to be bought in the future," and even "all equipment now owned or hereafter acquired." If an error is to be made, it is better from the secured party's viewpoint that the collateral be described in too much detail, rather than in too little.

The following case explores the difference between the description of the collateral necessary for a security agreement and the description of the collateral that is satisfactory in a financing statement.

American Restaurant Supply Co.
v
Wilson
371 So2d 489 (1979)
Florida District Court of Appeal, First District

FACTS: A security agreement described the collateral as "Food service equipment and supplies delivered to San Marcos Inn at St. Marks, Florida." The secured party claims that this description is sufficient to cover all food service equipment or supplies at the Inn or owned by the debtor.

ISSUE: Does the security agreement sufficiently describe the collateral?

RESULT: No. The description does not make possible the identification of the equipment and supplies in which the plaintiff claims a security interest.

REASONING:

*   *   *

A security interest cannot be enforced against the debtor or third parties unless the collateral is in the possession of the secured party or the security agreement contains a description of the collateral. . . . The description of collateral " . . . is sufficient whether or not it is specific if it reasonably identifies what is described . . . ." . . . Section 9–110, U.C.C. The Comment to Section 9–110 of the Uniform Commercial Code states that the test of sufficiency of a description " . . . is that the description do the job assigned to it—that it make possible the identification of the thing described."

Although [UCC Section 9–110] sets forth the test for sufficiency of the description of collateral in both the security agreement and the financing statement, a description of collateral sufficient for a financing statement might not be sufficient in a security agreement. This is because the financing statement and the security agreement serve different purposes.

The purpose of the financing statement is merely to provide notice of a possible security interest in the collateral in question. . . . [UCC Section 9–402] requires that the financing statement contain a description indicating the types of collateral in which the secured party may have a security interest. The description of collateral in a financing statement is sufficient if it reasonably informs third parties that an item in the possession of the debtor may be subject to a prior security interest, thus putting the parties on notice that further inquiry may be necessary. . . .

The security agreement is the contract between the parties; it specifies what the security interest is. Because of its different function, greater particularity in the description of collateral is required in the security agreement than in the financing statement. . . . A description of collateral in a security agreement is sufficient if the description makes possible the identification of the items in which a security interest is claimed.

The Comment to the Uniform Commercial Code, Section 9–208 . . . clearly indicates that the description of collateral in a security agreement is required to be more precise than in the financing statement. . . . The Comment to this Section states:

"2. The financing statement required to be filed under this Article (see Section 9–402) may disclose only that a secured party may have a security interest in specified types of collateral owned by the debtor. *Unless a copy of the security agreement itself is filed as the financing statement third parties are told neither the amount of the obligation secured nor which particular assets are covered.* Since subsequent creditors and purchasers may legitimately need more detailed information, it is necessary to provide a procedure under which the secured party will be required to make disclosure." [Court's emphasis]

Thus, a security agreement should describe the collateral with details sufficient for third parties to be able to reasonably identify the particular assets covered. . . .

Mills, Judge.

Place of Filing [UCC § 9-401]   The place where a financing statement is to be filed depends on the nature of the collateral described in the statement. For collateral of a given type, the proper place of filing varies among the states because Article 9 provides for three alternative schemes to govern the matter. Each scheme involves the use of local and state filing. "Local filing" means filing with a designated county officer, such as the county recorder. "State filing" means filing with the secretary of state. It should be noted, however, that under each of the three alternative schemes, financing statements covering most nonfarm business secured transactions are filed in a single place, the office of the secretary of state.

Outlined below are the requirements under the scheme adopted by a majority of the states:

Collateral	*Place of Filing*
• Consumer goods, farm equipment, or farm products	Generally, local filing in county of debtor's residence; if debtor is nonresident of state, local filing in county where collateral located
• Crops growing or to be grown	Local filing in county where land located *in addition to* local filing in county of debtor's residence, if different
• Timber, minerals, or fixtures	Local filing in county where land located
• All other collateral	State filing

The scheme adopted in a substantial minority of the states is similar to the one outlined above except that all state filing must be accompanied by local filing, usually in the county where the debtor's place of business is located.

If filing is done either in the wrong place or in not all the required places, but in good faith, it is effective for any collateral as to which the filing is proper. It is also effective against anyone who has actual knowledge about the contents of the financing statement.

Duration of Filing [UCC § 9-403]   A filed financing statement is usually effective to perfect the secured party's security interest for five years after the date of filing. Before that five-year period ends, the secured party can file a *continuation statement* to extend the effectiveness of his financing statement.

If a secured party fails to file a timely continuation statement, his security interest becomes unperfected and is not perfected again until he files a new financing statement. "Timely" means within six months before the financing or continuation statement then in force expires. In any period during which the security interest is unperfected, it becomes subordinate to the interests of all other parties who have perfected interests in the collateral.[2]

EXAMPLE: On January 1, 1978, Able filed a financing statement covering a debtor's inventory. He failed to file a continuation statement during the last half of 1982 but, on June 1, 1983, he realizes his error and files a new financing statement. Meanwhile, Baker perfected a security interest in the debtor's inventory on January 1, 1980, while Charlie perfected an interest in the same inventory on April 1, 1983. Able's interest is now subordinate to those of both Baker and Charlie.

Key Concepts and Terms

- A secured transaction is a transaction in which payment of a debt or performance of some other obligation is secured, and the security is an interest in the debtor's personal property or fixtures. Secured transactions are governed by Article 9 of the UCC.

- A security interest is created when it attaches. Attachment occurs when (1) the secured party has given value, (2) the debtor has acquired rights in the collateral, and (3) the secured party is in possession of either the collateral or a security agreement.

- The minimum requirements for a security agreement are that it be in writing, describe the collateral, and be signed by the debtor. Most security agreements cover many other aspects of the transaction.

- To maximize his rights in the collateral, the secured party must perfect his security interest. Filing a financing statement is the usual method of perfection.

- A filed financing statement perfects the secured party's security interest for five years. The secured party can extend the perfected status of his interest by filing a continuation statement.

---

[2] The priority of conflicting interests in the same collateral is discussed in Chapter 30.

- Accounts Receivable Financing
- After-acquired Property
- Attachment of Security Interest
- Chattel Paper
- Collateral
- Consumer Goods
- Continuation Statement
- Debtor's Waiver of Defenses
- Equipment
- Farm Products

- Filing
- Financing Statement
- Inventory
- Perfection of Security Interest
- Pledge
- Possessory Security Interest
- Purchase Money Security Interest
- Quasi-Tangible Collateral
- Security Agreement
- Waiver of Defenses

Questions and Case Problems

1. Define "security interest" as that term is used in UCC Article 9. Give an example of a simple secured transaction governed by Article 9.

2. What is the significance of the "attachment" of a security interest?

3. What does the holder of a security interest gain by perfecting that interest? How is perfection accomplished?

4. The collateral described in a security agreement is "all inventory, equipment, and other goods now owned or hereafter acquired" by Antenna Systems, the debtor. Antenna Systems later goes bankrupt, and a dispute arises between the secured party and the trustee in bankruptcy as to their rights in the following property of Antenna Systems: (a) confidential blueprints and technical data produced by the engineering staff in designing products for customers; (b) information in the form of bids, proposals, and cost estimates, all of which would be of value to other firms in the same business; (c) tooling (jigs, patterns, templates, and the like) used to reproduce parts of antenna systems; and (d) a supply of standard replacement parts. How much, if any, of the property listed in categories (a) through (d) is covered by the security interest? As to each class of items, why should those items be included or excluded?

5. On May 1, Sullivan signed a security agreement giving Wald a security interest in Sullivan's business equipment. Wald agreed to lend Sullivan $15,000, which Sullivan received on May 10. Wald also agreed to lend Sullivan an additional $25,000, to be secured by Sullivan's inventory and a new car that Sullivan intended to buy. Sullivan received the $25,000 on June 1, and he bought the new car on June 15. What was the date of attachment of Wald's security interest in (a) Sullivan's equipment, (b) Sullivan's inventory, and (c) the car?

6. What is a "financing statement," and what is it used for?

7. Wong obtains a loan from a finance company and uses the money to buy a car for personal use. As part of the transaction, Wong signs a security agreement that grants the finance company a security interest in the car. One month later the car is destroyed in an accident, and Wong's insurer sends her a check covering the loss. With the finance company's consent, Wong uses the insurance money to buy another car, but no new security agreement is signed. The finance company now claims that it has a security interest in the replacement car. Is its claim valid?

8. Lopes owes Garvey $1,500, and the debt is unsecured. Garvey learns that Lopes' business is doing poorly, and he wishes to protect himself by obtaining a security interest covering the debt. Lopes signs an agreement that grants Garvey a security interest in Lopes' car in exchange for Garvey's agreement to reduce the debt to $1,000. Later, a dispute arises as to whether Garvey has a valid security interest in the car; Lopes claims that he does not. Is Lopes correct?

9. Harrison grants to the local bank a security interest covering certain equipment and fixtures. The bank files an appropriate financing statement with the secretary of state, but it fails to file locally. Later, Harrison becomes indebted to both Starr and McCartney, each of whom made a search to determine the extent of existing security interests in Harrison's property before they extended credit and took security interests in the same equipment and fixtures covered by the bank's security interest. Starr searched locally and at the secretary of state's office, where he discovered the bank's financing statement. McCartney only checked in the county where Harrison lived and carried on his business; therefore, he did not find the financing statement. To what extent is the bank's security interest perfected as against Starr? To what extent is it perfected as against McCartney?

10. Jones, who operates his own machinist's shop, buys a new milling machine from Morton on credit. Jones signs a promissory note for the unpaid part of the purchase price. He also signs a security agreement that grants Morton a security interest in the new machine, and the agreement includes a waiver of defenses clause. One week later Morton assigns Jones' promissory note and the security interest to Chandler and receives a sum of money from Chandler in exchange. Two months after that the milling machine turns out to be defective, and Morton refuses to correct the defect or accept a return of the machine. Jones then stops making payments on the note held by Chandler, and Chandler sues Jones to recover the amount due. Jones argues that he should not have to pay because warranties covering the machine were breached. How should the court decide the case?

30 Rights of Parties to Secured Transactions

30:1 Introduction

Chapter 29 covers the concept of what a secured transaction is, as well as the manner in which a security interest in personal property or fixtures is created. Chapter 30 considers the rights of both secured parties and debtors that are also governed by Article 9 of the UCC. Article 9 establishes a system of priorities by which the relative rights of several secured parties, each of whom holds a security interest in the same collateral, can be determined. It allows a secured party to transfer his or her interest to someone else. It also sets forth detailed rules as to how a security interest can be enforced if the debtor defaults by failing to satisfy the secured obligation. Article 9 allows the debtor to transfer collateral that is covered by a security interest and it permits the debtor to reobtain possession of collateral that has been taken from him after a default. Article 9 also provides for recovering damages from a secured party who has acted improperly.

Priorities

30:2 Priorities

Priority refers to the superiority of one claimant's rights or interests over those of another. It involves the problem of resolving conflicting interests of different claimants who are all asserting rights in the same *collateral*.

The simplest method of determining priority would be to do so according to the order in which the interests in particular collateral arose. The UCC rejects this approach, however. Instead, the UCC favors certain claimants over others. The Article 9 priority rules are complex and riddled with exceptions. However, the basic factors used in determining priority are (1) the status of a particular claimant (who may or may not be a secured party) and (2) the time when a secured party claimant's security interest attached or was perfected. These factors are discussed in detail in this chapter.

30:3   Priorities Among Different Classes of Claimants

A number of different types or classes of claimants (in addition to the debtor) might claim rights in particular collateral. They include (1) unsecured creditors, (2) unperfected secured parties, (3) perfected secured parties, (4) subsequent buyers, (5) judicial lien creditors, and (6) statutory lien creditors. An *unsecured creditor* is one who holds a personal claim against the debtor and has no security interest in collateral. Whether a secured party's interest is perfected depends on whether the party took the required action (if any) to perfect the interest, as discussed in Chapter 29. A *subsequent buyer* is a person to whom the debtor sells the collateral. A *judicial lien creditor* is a creditor who has acquired a *lien* on the collateral through the judicial process, such as by attachment or execution.[1] A *statutory lien creditor*, on the other hand, is a creditor whose lien arose automatically under state law other than the UCC.

EXAMPLE: Linda has her car repaired at Blake's garage, and a state statute gives Blake a possessory lien (lien that requires continued possession to be effective) on the car for the cost of work done on it. If Linda does not pay Blake's repair bill and Blake refuses to release the car to Linda, Blake is a statutory lien creditor. If, on the other hand, Blake does release the car to Linda, Blake becomes an unsecured creditor. If Blake later sues Linda, is awarded judgment, and has the car seized under a writ of execution, Blake becomes a judicial lien creditor. And in the unlikely event that, after relinquishing possession, Blake persuades Linda to enter into a security agreement covering the car, Blake becomes a secured party, and he can then perfect his security interest.

Unsecured Creditors   As to particular collateral, the interest of an unsecured creditor is generally subordinate or junior to the interests of all the other classes of claimants listed above.

Unperfected Secured Creditors [UCC § 9-301]   Generally speaking, an unperfected secured party's interest is junior to that of (1) any perfected secured party, (2) any judicial or statutory lien creditor, and (3) many subsequent buyers.

Perfected Secured Creditors [UCC §§ 9-301, 9-307, 9-310]   As already noted, the interest of a perfected secured party in collateral is superior to that of both an unsecured creditor and an unperfected secured party. It is also usually superior to that of a judicial lien creditor. The priority of most statutory liens is governed by state or federal law outside the UCC. However, a *possessory* lien arising under state law in favor of a person who furnishes services or materials with respect to goods that are covered by a perfected security interest has priority over the perfected security interest.

EXAMPLE: Friendly Finance Company has a perfected security interest in Victor's expensive wristwatch. Victor leaves the watch with Jake for repair, and under the law Jake has a possessory lien on the watch for the

---

[1] A lien is any interest in property claimed by someone other than the owner. Attachment and execution are discussed in Chapter 31.

value of the work he does on it. If Victor does not pay for the repairs and Jake retains possession of the watch in accordance with his statutory right, Jake's lien is superior to Friendly's security interest. If, on the other hand, state law does not require Jake to retain possession of the watch to retain his lien, state law other than that which is laid out in the UCC will govern the question of priority between Friendly and Jake.

There are some circumstances in which a subsequent buyer has priority over perfected secured parties, as discussed in 30:8. Therefore, even though a secured party has done everything possible to maximize his or her rights in collateral, the right to priority can be lost if the collateral finds its way into the hands of a subsequent buyer.

Occasionally a secured creditor fails to perfect because it files the financing statement in the wrong place. Normally, such a secured party would lose out to a secured creditor who has perfected its security interest in the same collateral. As the following case illustrates, however, such a security interest may be good against a perfected secured party who had actual knowledge of the misfiled financing statement.

In Re Mistura, Inc.
705 F2d 1496 (1983)
United States Court of Appeals, Ninth Circuit

FACTS: The Marcuses sold a drug store to Mistura, Inc., taking back a security interest in the fixtures and personal property for the unpaid balance of the purchase price. They filed a financing statement on June 15, 1977. However, only the lien on fixtures, not the lien on personal property, was perfected because the statement was filed with the Maricopa County Recorder, rather than the Arizona Secretary of State, as required by Arizona law. Subsequently Mistura obtained a loan from McKesson. On September 5 McKesson properly perfected a security interest in the same collateral as the Marcuses. On September 12, 1980, the Marcuses filed a financing statement with the Secretary of State.

ISSUE: Is McKesson's security interest superior to the Marcuses?

RESULT: No. The Marcuses' good-faith filing in 1977 was effective against McKesson because McKesson had knowledge of the contents of the improperly filed financing statement.

REASONING:

*   *   *

[UCC § 9-401(2)] provides a careless creditor with some protection when a filing is made in good faith in an improper place. It provides:

> A filing which is made in good faith in an improper place or not in all of the places required by this section is nonetheless effective with regard to any collateral as to which the filing complied with the requirements of this article and is also effective with regard to collateral covered by the financing statement against any person who has *knowledge of the contents of such financing statement.* [Emphasis added]. . . .

Several courts have held knowledge of a creditor's prior security interest to be "knowledge of the contents of such financing statement." . . . This line of cases assumes that knowledge of the security interest provides the subsequent creditor with knowledge of the contents of the financing statement. Other courts, however, have reached the opposite result. . . .

It is clear that the courts have almost universally required actual, rather than constructive, knowledge of the general contents of the financing statement. However, the nature of the actual knowledge required varies substantially across a broad spectrum. To complicate matters, "the Code provides no further guidance as to where on the spectrum from 'should have found out' to 'actually eyeing the maverick [financing statement]' the correct solution lies." . . .

In the instant case, the bankruptcy court properly placed the burden of proof on the Marcuses to prove that McKesson had actual knowledge of the contents of the financing statement. However, it failed to further elaborate on the nature of the actual knowledge that was required to satisfy the provisions of [UCC § 9-401(2)]. We find that without this determination, and in light of the divergence of views on the requisite nature of actual knowledge required, the statute was not properly construed. . . .

Kilkenny, Circuit Judge.

30:4 Priorities Among Members of the Same Class

More than one security interest of the same type can exist in the same collateral. For example, two different creditors can hold unperfected security interests in the same property owned by the debtor. In that event, priority is given to the secured party whose interest attached first.

 Disputes between unperfected secured parties should never go to court. If creditor A is junior to creditor B under the above rule, A need simply file to perfect her interest before proceeding further against the debtor or the collateral. By so doing, A achieves priority over B.

Perfected Secured Parties [UCC § 9-312] The rule for determining the priority among two or more perfected secured parties is not quite so simple.

One might think that priority should be determined according to the order in which the parties perfected their interests. This was the rule under the original (1962) version of Article 9, but that rule can lead to injustice.

EXAMPLE: On January 1, Penny arranges with a bank for a loan, which is to be secured by Penny's jewelry. Penny signs a security agreement and financing statement, and the bank files the statement on January 2. However, the bank does not advance the loan proceeds until January 10, so that its security interest neither attaches nor is perfected until that date (date of giving value). Meanwhile, on January 5, Penny obtains a loan from a finance company, and on that date she gives the finance company possession of the jewelry as security. As a result, the finance company's interest is perfected on January 5, and the finance company has priority over the bank. This is so even though, before January 1, the bank may have made a careful search of the records in the proper office to learn whether Penny's jewelry was the subject of any existing security interest.

The rule as to the priority of perfected secured parties was changed in the 1972 revision of Article 9. Today, the general rule is that priority is given to the secured party who is the first to *either* file or perfect his interest. Hence, in the above example the bank has priority over the finance company because the bank filed first, even though the finance company was the first to perfect its interest.

An important exception to the general rule as to priority among perfected secured parties involves *purchase money security interests.* The priority of a creditor holding such an interest, who is known as a purchase money secured party, depends on whether the collateral is inventory. If (1) the collateral is *not* inventory; and (2) the purchase money secured party perfects the interest within ten days *after* the debtor takes possession of the collateral, the purchase money security interest has priority over other security interests in the same collateral, even if those other interests are perfected.

EXAMPLE: First National Bank has a perfected security interest in all of Brown's equipment, including after-acquired equipment. On January 1, Goldberg loans Brown money to buy a new machine and receives a security interest in the machine. Brown buys the machine and takes possession of it on January 3. On January 5, Hassad makes a loan to Brown. Hassad also takes a security interest in the new machine, and she perfects her interest on January 6. As long as Goldberg perfects his interest in the machine on or before January 12, he will have priority over both First National Bank and Hassad as to the machine.

A security agreement that covers *inventory* usually includes an after-acquired property clause because of the expected changes in the inventory. Since one holding a perfected security interest in inventory ordinarily expects to have top priority as to new inventory, the rule of "super-priority" for purchase money security interests discussed above is slightly different if the collateral is inventory. The purchase money secured party can still achieve priority over earlier perfected interests, but the requirements are stricter. First, the purchase money security interest must be perfected *before* the debtor receives possession of the new inventory to be covered. Thus, there is no ten-day grace period as there is for noninventory collateral. Second, the purchase money secured party must give a written notice containing prescribed information to every other secured party who has previously filed a financing statement covering inventory of the same type. The other secured parties must receive this notice before the debtor receives possession of the new inventory.

EXAMPLE: Reed holds a perfected security interest in Sam's inventory, and the security agreement contains an after-acquired property clause. Sam orders new inventory items from suppliers Jackson and Winfield, both of whom want purchase money security interests covering what they deliver. On August 1, Jackson files a financing statement covering his interest, and Jackson also sends a notice to Reed. The notice states that Jackson intends to acquire a purchase money security interest in described goods that will be delivered to Sam. Reed receives the notice on August 3. On August 10, Sam receives the shipments from both Jackson and Winfield. On August 15, Winfield files to perfect his interest, and he sends Reed an appropriate notice. Jackson's interest has priority over Reed's interest as to the goods Jackson shipped. However, Winfield's interest does not have priority over Reed's as to the goods Winfield shipped because Winfield filed and gave notice too late.

Transfer of Interests

30:5   Transfer of Security Interest

A secured party can transfer, or assign, the security interest to someone else, who is the assignee. Any assignment of a security interest involves three parties: (1) the original debtor; (2) the original secured party, who is the assignor; and (3) the assignee. An assignment gives the assignee all the rights that the assignor had before the assignment. The assignee in effect becomes the new secured party, and the original secured party is out of the picture concerning the collateral to which the assigned interest relates. Whether a given assignment of a security interest is valid and will serve its intended purpose is left to law outside the UCC. The assignment must satisfy the requirements of a valid contract, and there must be some sort of delivery to and acceptance by the assignee.

The underlying reason for the assignment of a security interest is often the assignor's need to secure his own financing. The assignor assigns his right to payment or performance of the secured obligation, and the assignment carries with it the security interest in the collateral that constitutes the security. The security interest cannot be assigned alone; that is, without the secured obligation.

Perfected Status of Assigned Security Interest [UCC §§ 9-302(2), 9-405]   If a security interest was perfected by the assignor before the assignment, the assignee need not file to continue the perfected status against creditors of the original debtor. Article 9 does, however, allow a *statement of assignment* to be filed, and it requires such filing under several circumstances that are not directly related to the assignment itself.

From the assignor's viewpoint, a reason for filing the statement is to have inquiries concerning the initial secured transaction addressed to the assignee, rather than to himself. Recognizing the fact that an assignment of a security interest often occurs at or near the beginning of a secured transaction, Article 9 allows an assignment to be disclosed in the original financing statement.

 The optional aspect of filing with respect to an assignment applies only between the debtor and the assignor (the original secured party). If, as is often true, the assignment itself is a new secured transaction, the assignee must take whatever steps are required to perfect his interest. The manner in which this is accomplished depends on the nature of the collateral. The usual method is filing, as discussed in Chapter 29.

30:6   Assignment of Account [UCC § 9-318]

Recall that Article 9 governs most *assignments of accounts*. To be considered at this point are the relative rights of the account debtor and the assignee when an account is assigned. The account debtor is the party who is obligated to pay the account, and he may or may not be the debtor in a secured transaction.

EXAMPLE: Allen owes money on an open account he has with Moss, a merchant from whom Allen buys business supplies and equipment from time to time. Since there is no security agreement in force between Allen and Moss, Moss is an unsecured creditor. Moss needs financing, so she assigns most of her accounts, including Allen's, to a lender as security for a loan. In this situation, Allen is the account debtor regardless of what, if anything, Moss does with the account. However, since only Moss and the lender entered into a secured transaction, only Moss is the "debtor" in that transaction.

The contract between an account debtor and his or her creditor might prohibit any assignment of the account. This contract term cannot be enforced against an assignee. On the other hand, the assignee's rights against the account debtor are subject to all the terms of the contract and to any claim or defense arising from that contract. The assignee's rights are also subject to any other claim or defense the account debtor has against the assignor if the claim or defense arose before the account debtor was notified about the assignment. The only limit on the account debtor's rights in this regard arises if and to the extent that the account debtor has agreed to waive certain defenses.

After the assignment of an account, the account debtor and assignor may find it necessary or desirable to change the terms of the contract between them. As long as any change is made in good faith and in accord with reasonable commercial standards, the assignee is also bound by the change. A major exception to this rule is that no change can alter the assignee's right to payment that has already become due. Note also that such a modification can constitute a breach of the contract between the assignor and the assignee.

EXAMPLE: Gray, a general contractor, was the successful bidder on a government construction contract. Gray entered into a subcontract with Stuart, a plumber, to do the plumbing work on the project. Before Stuart even began work, he assigned his right to payment under the subcontract to EZ Finance Company as security for a loan. After Stuart has completed ten percent of his work under the subcontract, the government agency that contracted for the project is ordered to cut its expenses as part of an effort to balance the federal budget. The agency modifies the project by reducing its scope, one result being that the need for plumbing work is cut in half. Gray and Stuart can modify the subcontract as reasonably required without EZ's participation or consent. EZ will be bound by the terms as modified except to the extent that the modification attempts to affect EZ's right to payment for the ten percent of the plumbing work already done. However, depending on the terms of the assignment agreement between Stuart and EZ, Stuart may be liable to EZ for breach of contract.

Article 9 recognizes the plight of an account debtor who pays the assignor because he is unaware or merely suspects that an assignment has been made. If the account has, in fact, been assigned, must the account debtor pay again, this time to the assignee? The answer is that until he is properly notified about the assignment, the account debtor can continue making payments to the assignor, regardless of the assignment.

30:7   Transfer of Collateral [UCC §§ 9-205, 9-311]

A debtor's rights in collateral can be transferred voluntarily or involuntarily. A sale of a security interest is an example of a voluntary transfer; an attachment of the property is an example of an involuntary transfer. Under Article 9 a security interest is not invalid or fraudulent against other creditors simply because the security agreement allows the debtor to sell all or part of the collateral, or requires the debtor neither to replace sold collateral nor to account for the sale proceeds. Article 9 takes this approach to validate and offer some flexibility as to what are known as floating liens on changing inventory.[2]

The Article 9 provisions referred to above do not mean that a debtor and secured party cannot include coverage about the debtor's transfer rights in the security agreement. Most security agreements do cover the matter. For example, the agreement can forbid any sale or other transfer of the collateral. Any such prohibition is effective between the debtor and secured party.

---

[2] A "floating lien" covers new inventory as the debtor acquires it, but the lien is lost as old inventory is sold. Thus, at any given time the lien covers whatever inventory the debtor has at that time.

EXAMPLE: Gustav buys a new bulldozer for business use with funds advanced by Rotkopf for that purpose. Gustav grants Rotkopf a security interest in the bulldozer, and the agreement states that Gustav cannot sell the machine until the secured obligation has been discharged. The agreement also makes any sale in violation of this restriction an "event of default." While Rotkopf's security interest still exists, Gustav sells the machine without notice to or the consent of Rotkopf. Rotkopf can now declare Gustav to be in default and can pursue any of the available remedies.

On the other hand, the security agreement can *permit* sale of the collateral, and most merchant debtors would be unable to remain in business without that permission. The permission to sell can be expressed in broad terms, or the agreement can require that specific consent be obtained for each planned sale. The agreement can also require the debtor to notify the secured party about each sale.

Continuation of Security Interest [UCC § 9-306(2)] The general rule, subject to various exceptions, is that a security interest continues in collateral after its sale by the debtor unless the sale was authorized (agreed to) by the secured party. The secured party also acquires a security interest in the identifiable proceeds from the sale regardless of whether the sale was authorized. A critical issue is apt to be whether a particular sale was authorized. Problems arise when authorization was not express but, arguably, could be implied from the parties' past dealings. The following case illustrates this situation. It also shows that if the debtor makes an unauthorized sale, the secured party may be able to sue the buyer for conversion (wrongful taking) of the collateral.

Hedrick Savings Bank
v
Myers
229 NW2d 252 (1975)
Iowa Supreme Court

FACTS: Hedrick Savings Bank, plaintiff, had loaned money to Eckley, a rancher, from time to time. The loans were secured by a security interest covering all of Eckley's livestock, and the security agreement stated that Eckley would not sell any of the livestock without plaintiff's written consent. Despite this provision, Eckley frequently did sell livestock without plaintiff's consent. During 1968 and 1969 he sold 96 animals to defendant Myers. Hedrick sued Myers for conversion of those animals.

ISSUE: Did the Bank waive its right to its lien by impliedly consenting to the sale of the animals?

RESULT: Yes. The Bank impliedly consented to the sale.

REASONING:

*   *   *

The controlling statute [UCC § 9-306(2)] contains this:

> "Except where this Article otherwise provides, a security interest continues in collateral notwithstanding sale . . . by the debtor *unless his action was authorized by the secured party in the security agreement or otherwise,* and also continues in any identifiable proceeds including collections received by the debtor." [Court's emphasis.]

. . . [The] sole issue is whether plaintiff . . . impliedly consented to the sale of the [96] animals.

Since such authorization was not given in the security instrument, the implied consent must be found, if at all, in the "or otherwise" provision of the statute. The trial court found such authorization in the course of dealing between plaintiff and Eckley. The crucial question is whether a course of dealing may constitute authority to sell in violation of the express prohibition of the security agreement. . . .

We hold there is substantial evidence to support the trial court's finding that, from the very beginning of plaintiff's relationship with Eckley, sales of livestock pledged as collateral were made to various dealers. Plaintiff had knowledge of this, raised no objection, accepted checks from these sales for credit to Eckley's account, and clearly relied on Eckley's honesty to properly account for the proceeds. This established a course of dealing from which the trial court could find, as it did, implied authority to sell to defendants in the challenged transactions. . . .

We rely on [an earlier Iowa case] for the principle that evidence of a course of dealing has relevance in interpreting agreements under the [UCC]. . . . Taking [that case] one step further, we now hold a prior course of dealing may, upon proper proof, constitute authority to sell pledged collateral under [UCC § 9-306(2)]. As used in the statute, "otherwise" should be construed to include a prior course of dealing. . . .

LeGrand, Justice.

30:8   Rights of Purchaser of Collateral

As discussed above, a secured party who authorizes the debtor's sale of collateral loses the security interest in that collateral when the sale is made. Even if a sale is *not* authorized, the secured party can still lose either the security interest or the right to priority, depending on the buyer's status.

Buyers Taking Free of Perfected Security Interest: Buyers in Ordinary Course of Business [UCC § 9-307] *Buyers in the ordinary course of business* (other than those buying farm products from farmers) are the major class of subsequent buyers who take free of security interests, whether or not those interests are perfected. The following case illustrates the requirements that one must meet to qualify as a "buyer in the ordinary course of business." Note that, for all practical purposes, a sale must be from inventory if the buyer is to qualify.

Bank of Utica

v

Castle Ford, Inc.
317 NYS2d 542 (1971)
New York Supreme Court, Appellate Division

FACTS: Worden ran a car sales business. He obtained financing from plaintiff, the Bank of Utica, which was granted security interests covering all of Worden's cars. Under the financing arrangement, a separate "chattel mortgage" (which is the same as a security agreement) was signed for each car as Worden obtained it. In 1967 Worden bought a 1965 Oldsmobile to offer for sale in his business, and he signed a chattel mortgage covering the car. The mortgage forbade Worden to part with possession of the car or to use it except for display for sale to a buyer in the ordinary course of business. Worden later sold the car to Castle Ford, defendant, which was another car dealer. Castle asked Worden if he had any "floor plan financing arrangement," and Worden said that he did not and that the car was fully paid for. Worden later went bankrupt, leaving the Bank of Utica unpaid. The bank then sued Castle to recover the Oldsmobile or its value.

ISSUE: Was Castle, the buyer, a "buyer in the ordinary course of business" who could take free of Bank's security interest?

RESULT: Yes. Castle met the requirements of a buyer in the ordinary course of business.

REASONING:

*   *   *

Uniform Commercial Code, section 1-201(9), provides " 'Buyer in ordinary course of business' means a person who in good faith and without knowledge that the sale to him is in violation of the ownership rights or security interest of a third party in the goods buys in ordinary course from a person in the business of selling goods of that kind but does not include a pawnbroker." Section 9-307(1) thereof provides "A buyer in ordinary course of business . . . takes free of a security interest created by his seller even though the security interest is perfected and even though the buyer knows of its existence." . . .

[The trial court] held that since Castle is an automobile dealer, it was not a buyer in ordinary course of business within the meaning of the above quoted sections, and hence that plaintiff's security interest in said vehicle gave it prior rights therein as against Castle. The court reasoned that . . . another dealer in motor vehicles was not a purchaser in ordinary course of trade when it bought a vehicle from a fellow dealer. With this conclusion we cannot agree. . . .

. . . The nature of Castle's business is immaterial under present law, so long as it was not a pawnbroker. As to Castle, the question is merely, did it buy the vehicle in good faith and without knowledge of the violation of plaintiff's security interest therein? . . .

"Good faith" is defined in the statute in general as "honesty in fact in the conduct or transaction concerned" [UCC, §1-201(19)], and "in the case of a merchant [it] means honesty in fact and the observance of reasonable commercial standards of fair dealing in the trade" [UCC, § 2-103(1)(b)]. It may be argued that as a dealer Castle should have been aware that vehicles of other dealers are often under financing plans and that it should not have taken Worden's word that none existed with respect to the vehicle in question, but that it should have investigated the official records of financing statements and lien filings concerning the existence of such security agreement. The answer to such argument, however, is that even if Castle searched the records of such filings and learned that plaintiff had a lien interest in this vehicle, it would not have been warned against buying or forbidden to buy, for by the express terms of the statute. . . . Castle could buy the vehicle free of plaintiff's lien interest provided that he otherwise acted in good faith, that is, without knowledge that Worden was not authorized to sell the vehicle. . . . There is nothing in the record to show that the details of the particular loan from plaintiff to Worden upon this vehicle were filed, as opposed to the general financing statement filed by plaintiff in 1965. Failure of Castle to search the official records does not constitute bad faith nor charge it under these circumstances with notice that Worden lacked authority to make the sale. . . .

Witmer, Justice.

Buyers Taking Free of Perfected Security Interest: Buyers of Consumer Goods [UCC § 9-307]   A buyer of consumer goods may take free of a security interest, even though it is perfected. This occurs if (1) the buyer gives value; (2) the goods are bought for the buyer's personal, family, or household purposes; and (3) the buyer is unaware of the security interest. However, this rule does *not* apply if, before the sale, the secured party filed a financing statement covering the goods. This exception might seem to wipe out the "general rule," but recall from Chapter 29 that filing is not required to perfect a purchase money security interest in most consumer goods.

EXAMPLE: Baldwin, a consumer, buys a refrigerator from appliance dealer Godsey, and he grants Godsey a purchase money security interest. While Godsey's interest still exists, Baldwin sells the appliance to Walton, another consumer, for a fair price. If Walton does not know about Godsey's security interest, she takes the appliance free of that interest unless Godsey has taken the unusual step of filing.

Buyers Taking Free of Unperfected Interest [UCC § 9-301]   Any subsequent buyer of collateral who takes the collateral free of perfected interests, as discussed above, also takes free of unperfected interests. However, Article 9 also gives many other buyers priority over unperfected secured parties. A buyer of farm products in the ordinary course of business qualifies for this priority. Also qualifying are most buyers *not* in the ordinary course of business, as long as any such buyer (1) gives value, (2) is unaware of the security interest, and (3) receives delivery of the collateral (assuming that delivery is possible).

EXAMPLE: Rose operates a machine shop and owns various machines used in his business. Gosnell holds an unperfected security interest in all of Rose's machines. Rose sells a machine to Spencer for a fair price and delivers the machine the same day. Unless Spencer knows about Gosnell's interest, that interest is junior to Spencer's rights in the machine.

Default; Enforcement of Security Interest

30:9   What Constitutes Debtor's Default; Secured Party's Remedies

Article 9 does not specify what constitutes a debtor's *default*. Instead, the matter is usually covered in the security agreement. A typical agreement lists various events, the occurrence of any one of which will be treated as an event of default. The most usual event of default is the debtor's failure to discharge the secured debt by paying it. Examples of other common events of default are (1) the debtor's having misrepresented an important fact in his credit application, (2) the debtor's being a party in a bankruptcy proceeding, (3) damage to or destruction of the collateral, and (4) the death of the debtor or a key person in the debtor's business.

Secured Party's Remedies on Default [UCC § 9-501]   The occurrence of a default does not necessarily mean that the secured party will take any action adverse to the debtor. Rather, it gives the secured party the *right* to act if desired. When a default has occurred, the secured party is apt to consider the nature and extent of the default and the nature of the underlying transaction itself before deciding what, if anything, to do. For example, a business debtor's failure to pay an installment on time can signal the debtor's approaching bankruptcy. The same default by an individual debtor who signed a security agreement covering consumer goods may reflect no more than an oversight on the debtor's part.

Assuming that a secured party wishes to act after a default, Article 9 provides certain remedies. Within prescribed limits, the security agreement can also provide for other remedies. Essentially, there are three approaches the secured party can take: (1) he can sue the debtor for the amount owed on the debt, just as he could do if the debt were unsecured; (2) he can foreclose on the collateral; or (3) he can obtain possession of the collateral and then take one or more of several available actions. The first of these three options is not governed by Article 9, and the second is referred to only in a general way (see 30:10). However, the third option is covered in detail (see 30:11).

30:10   Foreclosure [UCC § 9-501]

Foreclosure is a process by which a debtor's rights in collateral are extinguished. A secured party who desires to exercise the right to foreclose frequently does so under an acceleration clause in the security agreement. An acceleration clause provides that on the debtor's default, the secured party can declare the entire debt to be due.

The most common method of foreclosure following a debtor's default under a security agreement consists of the secured party's commencing a suit for foreclosure in an appropriate court. If the secured party wins the suit, the collateral is ordinarily disposed of in a judicial sale, which is a sale carried out under the court's supervision.[3] The secured party might want to buy the collateral at the judicial sale. Article 9 appears to give the secured party this right, but it does not clearly say so.

30:11   Repossession of Collateral [UCC 9-503]

The *self-help* provision is a key feature of Article 9. Unless the security agreement provides otherwise, the secured party has the right to *repossess* the collateral following the debtor's default. The secured party can repossess privately, without a court's assistance, if repossession can be carried out without a *breach of the peace*. The following passage from a New York court's opinion[4] illustrates what constitutes a "breach of the peace."

---

[3] Under what is sometimes referred to as strict foreclosure, the secured party obtains possession of the collateral and simply retains it in satisfaction of the secured obligation. The secured party's retention of the collateral is discussed in 30:13.

[4] *Cherno v Bank of Babylon*, 282 NYS2d 114 (New York Supreme Court, Special Term, 1967).

. . . The classic definition of breach of the peace is "a disturbance of public order by an act of violence, or by an act likely to produce violence, or which, by causing consternation and alarm, disturbs the peace and quiet of the community." . . . Thus, when in the course of repossession, the conditional vendee received a black eye, it was a question for the jury whether a breach of the peace had occurred, . . . and when padlocks on a building are broken there is such force and violence as to constitute a violation of [a criminal statute] . . . and, presumably, a breach of the peace. Here, however, the bank's employees entered by use of a key, unauthorizedly obtained. Such an entry, the [debtor's] consent aside, would constitute a breaking. . . . But, breaking or not, there was nothing in what they did that disturbed public order by any act of violence, caused consternation or alarm, or disturbed the peace and quiet of the community. Nor was the use of a key to open the door an act likely to produce violence; indeed, it produced from the landlord only (1) a call for the police and (2) a request to the bank employees that they leave the key when they were through. Under the circumstances that existed during the time the bank's employees entered the premises, there was as a matter of law no breach of the peace. . . .

A secured party who intends to repossess collateral usually prefers not to give the debtor advance notice of the intention. Given notice, the debtor might hide the collateral or otherwise attempt to put it beyond the secured party's reach. Article 9 does not include a notice requirement, and most courts have not imposed such a requirement either.

 States vary significantly on what repossession actions constitute a breach of the peace. Typically, repossessing an empty automobile on the street does not breach the peace; breaking into a residential garage usually does. It is important for a business that employs self-help repossession to be thoroughly familiar with the attitude of state courts on the subject.

Consumer Goods   Article 9 makes no distinction between self-help repossession of consumer goods and self-help repossession of other types of collateral. However, the repossession of consumer goods may also be governed—and limited—by other state law concerning consumer credit protection or retail installment sales.

Resort to Judicial Process   If the debtor resists an attempted repossession of collateral after default (so that the repossession cannot be done without a breach of the peace), the secured party can seek judicial assistance. The procedure that the creditor should follow depends on state law other than the UCC.

30:12   Disposal of Collateral After Default [UCC § 9-504]

If a debtor has defaulted and the secured party has repossessed the collateral, the secured party has the right to dispose of the collateral. The most common disposition method is sale of the collateral.

Article 9 imposes only two requirements with respect to how a sale of repossessed collateral is carried out. First, the secured party must generally give the debtor "reasonable notification" about the sale. Notice to the debtor is not required only if (1) after the default, the debtor waived the right to notice; or (2) the collateral (a) is perishable, (b) threatens to decline rapidly in value, or (c) is of a type normally sold on a recognized market. Unless the collateral is consumer goods, if the notice requirement applies, the secured party must also notify any other secured party who claims an interest in the collateral.

The second requirement for a sale of repossessed collateral is that all terms of the sale must be *commercially reasonable*. The price received for the collateral is the sale term most apt to be challenged, but the focus of Article 9 is on the overall procedure used, rather than merely on the price. For example, in one case,[5] the court held that the procedure followed in a sale was commercially reasonable even though inventory with an estimated retail value of over $3,000,000 was sold for $300,000. Interestingly, $300,000 was the exact amount owed to the secured creditors!

 UCC § 9-501(3) provides, in effect, that although a security agreement cannot include the debtor's waiver of his right to a commercially reasonable sale after default, the agreement *can* set forth reasonable standards for measuring the secured party's actions in carrying out a sale. If the collateral can be easily classified and is generally treated in a uniform way, it may be to the secured party's advantage to include standards for disposition in the agreement. That simple act might avoid a lawsuit later in which the debtor claims that the disposition made was not commercially reasonable.

Repossessed collateral can be sold at either a private sale or a public sale. The distinction between the two types of sales is that a public sale is advertised to the public, while a private sale follows private negotiations between the secured party (who repossessed the collateral) and the buyer. A public sale is usually required if the secured party wants to buy the collateral (which he often wants to do since nobody else will pay an adequate price for it). This is because in a private sale the secured party is allowed to buy only limited types of collateral. Regardless of the type of sale and who the purchaser is, the purchaser acquires all the debtor's rights in the collateral. The purchase also has the effect of ending the secured party's security interest and any subordinate security interest or lien.

30:13 Secured Party's Retention of Collateral [UCC § 9-505(2)]

Experience has shown that the parties are often better off if a resale of repossessed collateral can be avoided. Recognizing this fact, Article 9 allows the secured party to retain collateral other than certain consumer goods, in full satisfaction of the secured debt. A secured party who wants to retain the

---

[5] *Re Zsa Zsa Ltd.*, 352 F Supp 665 (United States District Court, S.D. New York, 1972).

collateral instead of sell it must notify the debtor of that intent. If the collateral is other than consumer goods, the secured party must also notify any other secured party claiming an interest in the collateral. If anyone to whom a notice must be sent objects within 21 days to the secured party's retention of the collateral, the secured party must sell the collateral instead of retaining it.

Consumer Goods [UCC § 9-505(1)] Article 9 gives added protection to a debtor who has acquired a substantial equity in repossessed consumer goods. The secured party must sell or otherwise dispose of the goods within 90 days unless, after default, the debtor waives this requirement. The extent of the debtor's protection depends on whether a purchase money security interest is involved. If so, the mandatory disposal rule applies if the debtor has paid 60 percent or more of the cash price of the goods. In the case of other security interest, the rule applies if the debtor has paid 60 percent or more of the loan.

EXAMPLE: Edward buys a new car for $8,000, paying $2,000 down and borrowing $6,000 from a bank. The bank has a purchase money security interest in the car. Edward later defaults, and the bank repossesses the car. If Edward has reduced the debt by at least $2,800, the bank cannot retain the car in satisfaction of the debt without Edward's consent ($2,800 plus $2,000 down payment equals $4,800, which is 60 percent of $8,000). If, however, Edward had paid cash for the car and later obtained a $6,000 loan from the bank using the car as collateral, the bank would have a security interest in the car, but not a purchase money security interest. Edward would then need to have paid at least $3,600 on the debt (60 percent of $6,000) before he would have the right to automatic sale or other disposal of the car after repossession.

30:14 Debtor's Right of Redemption [UCC § 9-506]

Unless the debtor has signed a written waiver after the default, he or she can redeem the collateral (regain possession of it). To do so, the debtor must offer (1) to fulfill all obligations secured by the collateral, and (2) to pay the expenses reasonably incurred by the secured party in connection with the repossession.

"All obligations secured by the collateral" can consist of only the amount past due, which might be a single installment payment. However, if the security agreement contains an acceleration clause that the secured party elects to enforce, the debtor has to come up with the entire outstanding balance plus interest. As a result, the right of *redemption* is often of little relief to the debtor; a person who cannot make a single payment often lacks sufficient resources to pay off the entire debt.

While there is rarely much doubt about the amount of the secured obligation, there may be a question about repossession expenses. A dispute can involve not only whether a given expense is reasonable, but also whether that expense is even one incurred in connection with the repossession. A secured party who demands more than he should from a redeeming debtor can be liable for conversion of the collateral.

EXAMPLE: Boris bought a car with money loaned by a bank, and he gave the bank a security interest in the car. Boris later moved to a neighboring state, and still later he became delinquent in his payments to the bank. The bank then arranged with Ajax, an automobile recovery bureau, to repossess the car. Instead of repossessing the car, Ajax merely located Boris, arranged for him to make the back payments, and allowed him to keep the car. Ajax then billed the bank $130 for its services. Later, Boris was again in default, Ajax was again ordered to repossess the car, and this time Ajax did so, at an expense of $90. In an attempt to redeem the car from Ajax, Boris offered to pay $350 ($90 plus the principal and interest due on the loan). On the bank's orders, Ajax demanded $480 ($350 plus the $130 billed to the bank earlier), which Boris refused to pay. The bank is liable to Boris for conversion of the car because the $130 is not an amount incurred in connection with the repossession.

The redemption right continues to exist until the secured party (1) disposes of the collateral, (2) enters into a contract for its disposition, or (3) has discharged the debt by retaining the collateral. The last of these three events cutting off the redemption right raises the question of whether a creditor can block redemption by simply deciding to retain the property. For the answer, recall that even if the 60 percent rule for consumer goods does not apply, the secured party must notify the debtor of his or her intent to retain repossessed collateral, and that the debtor then has 21 days in which to object. Thus, the debtor's right to redeem cannot be blocked in this way unless the debtor fails to object in time to the secured party's proposed retention of the collateral.

30:15   Distribution of Proceeds; Deficiency Judgment [UCC § 9-504]

Article 9 establishes the order by which the proceeds received by a secured party from a nonjudicial sale of repossessed collateral are to be distributed. The proceeds are applied first to the reasonable expenses that the secured party incurred in connection with the repossession. Any surplus is then applied to satisfaction of the secured debt. After that, any remaining surplus is applied to satisfy debts secured by any subordinate security interest in the collateral that was sold, but only if the holder of the subordinate interest makes a written demand for payment. In the unlikely event that there is still a surplus after payment according to the above schedule, the debtor is entitled to it, and the debtor cannot waive this right.

Article 9 does not apply to disposition of the proceeds from a judicial sale of the collateral. However, under state law, the result is usually about the same as for nonjudicial sales.

Deficiency Judgment [UCC § 9-504]   Although the debtor may receive some of the proceeds from a sale of repossessed collateral, he rarely does so. A more likely situation is that the proceeds are insufficient even to pay off the secured debt. The debtor is then liable to the secured party for the deficiency unless the parties have agreed to the contrary. Few debtors have sufficient bargaining power to persuade a potential secured party to abandon the right to a deficiency judgment.

EXAMPLE: Rossi buys a business machine from Mangione, incurring a secured debt. The machine is later repossessed and sold by Mangione at a time when the amount of the debt, plus interest, is $5,000. Mangione incurs reasonable repossession expenses of $500. The parties' rights to the sale proceeds depend on the price received. If the price exceeds $5,500, Rossi is entitled to the excess. If it is less than $5,500, Mangione can sue Rossi to recover the difference between $5,500 and the actual sale price.

Right to Deficiency Judgment If Secured Party Retains Collateral [UCC § 9-505]   Since retention of repossessed collateral constitutes satisfaction of the debt in full, the retaining secured party loses any right he otherwise would have had to recover a deficiency judgment. This fact may be significant if the value of the collateral is less than the amount outstanding on the debt, a common situation in the case of some types of collateral.

 The secured party can also lose the right to a deficiency judgment or, indeed, the right to sue on the secured obligation, by holding repossessed collateral for an unreasonable time. Note that unless the 60 percent rule for consumer goods applies, Article 9 does not specify *when* a notice of proposed retention of collateral must be sent.

EXAMPLE: Ahab was in default on his car loan after paying off less than 60 percent of the debt. Lawrence, the lender, repossessed the car, held it for four months, and then sued Ahab on the promissory note. The case was not tried until 27 months after the repossession. During that 27-month period Lawrence had possession of the car but neither gave notice of intent to retain it nor attempted to sell it. Due to Lawrence's inaction, Ahab's debt probably would be discharged. In effect, Lawrence would be deemed to have elected to retain the collateral even though he never gave the required notice.

30:16   Secured Party's Liability to Debtor [UCC § 9-507(1)]

Article 9 protects a debtor who will be or has been harmed by a repossessing secured party's failure to carry out his duties. For example, the debtor can apply to a court for an order preventing the secured party from disposing of the collateral in a commercially unreasonable manner. If an improper disposition has already been made, the debtor can recover damages from the secured party. The measure of damages set forth in Article 9 is the loss suffered by the debtor due to the improper disposition. This loss is the difference between the proceeds received by the secured party and the proceeds that should have been received. If the secured party cannot show that the proceeds received reflected the proper value of the collateral, the proper value will be presumed to be at least the amount of the debt secured by that collateral. This presumption has the effect of preventing the secured party from obtaining a deficiency judgment.

EXAMPLE: Union Bank repossesses collateral and sells it for $10,000 without notifying Andrews, the debtor, of the sale. The outstanding balance on the secured debt is $15,000. Union then commences an action to recover the $5,000 deficiency. Unless Union can prove that only $10,000 would have been received, even if Andrews had been notified about the sale, the value of the property will be presumed to be $15,000. Andrews is thus entitled to recover $5,000 in damages, which cancels Union's deficiency.

State law other than the UCC may allow the recovery of damages other than simply those based on the debtor's "loss." For example, the debtor might be able to sue the secured party for *conversion*, which is the wrongful taking of property. The measure of damages for conversion is the value of the property at the time of the conversion, less the unpaid balance of the purchase price. Obviously, these damages can be significantly greater than the debtor's provable loss.

Consumer Goods [UCC § 9-507(1)]   If the collateral is consumer goods, the damages recoverable by the debtor are not limited to the loss suffered because of the secured party's noncompliance with the Article 9 requirements. Instead, the *minimum* amount that the debtor is entitled to recover is, depending on the nature of the transaction (1) the credit service charge plus ten percent of the debt or (2) the time price differential plus ten percent of the cash price.

EXAMPLE: Mildred agrees to buy a new car for personal use from Valley VW. The price is $5,000. Mildred pays $1,000 down and agrees to pay off the balance in 36 monthly payments of $150. The deferred payment price is hence $6,400 (36 times $150 plus the $1,000 down payment), and the time–price differential is $1,400. Mildred defaults and Valley VW repossesses the car and sells it without notifying Mildred. Mildred can recover at least $1,900 ($1,400 plus ten percent of $5,000) in damages from Valley VW.

Punitive Damages   *Punitive* (or exemplary) *damages* are awarded to a victim as a civil penalty (a penalty paid to a private individual rather than to a governmental subdivision) for a wrongful act, rather than to compensate the victim for losses. Article 9 does not specifically provide for punitive damages. However, they may be recoverable under non-UCC state law if a secured party acted with malice or reckless disregard of the debtor's rights, as is illustrated in the following case.

Davidson

v

First Bank & Trust Co.
609 P2d 1259 (1976)
Oklahoma Supreme Court

FACTS: Davidson was in the marble-cutting business and had owed money
to his bank, First Bank, for a number of years. The Bank effectively
transferred the business to Sneed, whom it had suggested as a business
partner for Davidson, in the manner described in the opinion. At trial,
Davidson sought punitive damages against the Bank for its conduct as a
secured creditor.

ISSUE: Was the Bank's method of disposing of the collateral so egregious as
to warrant imposition of punitive damages?

RESULT: Yes. The Bank's course of conduct of the sale completely disregarded Davidson's interests.

REASONING:

*   *   *

. . . At the suggestion of Bank, Davidson contacted a man named Sneed
to work with him to enable his marble-making business to operate in a
profitable manner. At this time Davidson executed a promissory note and
security agreement in favor of Bank which provided for monthly payments with a final balloon payment at the end of the year.
. . . [I]n November of 1972, Bank, because of differences between
Davidson and Sneed, attempted to foreclose before the note was in
default. The problems were resolved however, and Bank refinanced the
note in a similar manner, payable by Davidson only.
The situation between Davidson and Sneed did not improve and they
had a falling out in the early fall of 1973. Sneed removed a portion of the
marble-making equipment from Davidson's shop, some of which he
claimed to own, and opened a competitive marble-manufacturing business across the street. The volume of equipment taken is in dispute, but
Sneed admits "borrowing," with Bank's permission, the two major pieces
of equipment owned by Davidson. Because of the loss of this equipment,
Davidson was effectively put out of business and he defaulted on the
last balloon payment due November 15, 1973.
Bank obtained entry to the shop through Sneed and on November 21,
1973 took possession of the remaining property secured by the agreement. On November 21, 1973, Bank executed its "Notice of Sale under

Security" listing items to be sold at public auction on December 6, 1973 at 10:00 A.M. The notice did not cover all items of property listed on the security agreement. Although the secured items were unique and there was no ready market for marble-making equipment in Yale, Bank posted only three notices of sale in Yale. This was the extent of its commercially reasonable advertisement. At the time of the sale, the front door of the building remained locked and when no prospective buyers appeared, Bank's employees left the store. Bank did not credit Davidson's account on date of sale; it retained the repossessed equipment until after Davidson filed his original petition. The items were eventually sold to Sneed privately some four months later without notice to the public or to Davidson. Sneed paid Bank $1,000 for the equipment, less than 1/4 of the stipulated value at time of sale.

On December 20, 1973 Davidson initiated the present suit against . . . Bank for conversion of property by means of a wrongful taking of the equipment. . . .

Trial was had to a jury. Davidson went to the jury on the theory that Bank had converted the property because it "was not sold in a commercially reasonable manner." It was stipulated by the parties [that] the value of the property equaled the balance remaining unpaid on the note in the amount of $4,285. The jury was instructed that if it found conversion by commercially unreasonable sale, the court would determine the actual damages and if it found such conversion by Bank was malicious and with wilful intent to deprive Davidson of his property, punitive damages would be proper. The jury found the issues in favor of Davidson. . . .

We agree with the opinion and result of the [intermediate appellate court] holding the jury was properly instructed as to punitive damages. If repossessed property is sold in a commercially unreasonable manner there is a conversion, the actual damages being the difference between the value of the property and the proceeds of the sale. If there is a conversion, and the actions are malicious or wilful, punitive damages may be awarded by the jury under existing statutory and case law. . . .

Numerous cases, not decided under the U.C.C., have awarded punitive damages for actions involved in repossession of collateral where aspects of malice, fraud, or oppression are shown. Although the U.C.C. does not favor punitive damages, these jurisdictions have applied rules of damages, including punitive, in proper cases under aggravated circumstances. See [a Colorado case] where punitive damages were permitted against a bank who refused to return plaintiff's tools that had been wrongfully repossessed. [A federal case] allowed punitive damages for unlawful repossession of a car where plaintiff was given no notice of repossession and was not in default. [A Texas case] allowed punitive damages five times that of actual damages where defendant had sold plaintiff's furniture before actual repossession. [A Washington, D.C. case] allowed punitive damages for wrongful repossession under the U.C.C. . . .

. . . Bank's cavalier manner in its dealings with Davidson is sufficient evidence to send the question of punitive damages to the jury. As pointed out in Davidson's brief, the entire sequence of events involved in the sale was improper. The Bank did not give proper notice of the items to be sold. The only justification Bank gave for its failure to pursue a likely market for sale of the equipment is that it did not want to spend the money. On the sale date Bank's officer did not open the front door or even attempt a sale. Bank permitted Sneed to borrow items belonging to Davidson prior to default on the note in order that Sneed could open a competing business. Bank retained the collateral after default for several months without crediting it against Davidson's note. The final sale was made to Sneed for a price less than 1/4 the stipulated value of property at time of sale. These facts are evidence of the tortious conduct upon which the jury based its award of punitive damages. . . .

Doolin, Justice.

Key Concepts and Terms

- The priority of conflicting interests in collateral depends on the status of the claimants. As between two perfected secured parties, the first either to file or to perfect his interest usually has priority over the other.
- A secured party can assign the secured obligation to someone else, and such an assignment carries the security interest with it. Similarly, one holding an account can sell or assign that account.
- A debtor can sell collateral that is subject to a security interest, although the sale may be a breach of the contract with the secured party.
- A secured party who authorizes sale of the collateral loses his or her security interest in it. A seller's security interest, even if perfected, is also often lost if the collateral is sold to a consumer or buyer in the ordinary course of business.
- A debtor defaults when he or she acts in violation of the security agreement. Failure to discharge the secured debt or to make timely payment on it is the most common default.
- After default, the secured party can (1) sue on the debt, (2) foreclose on the collateral, or (3) repossess the collateral.
- Repossessed collateral must generally be sold or otherwise disposed of in a commercially reasonable manner. At times, the secured party can retain the collateral in satisfaction of the debt. The debtor has the right to redeem repossessed collateral within a limited period.
- If repossessed collateral is sold, the sale proceeds are applied first to the repossession expenses and then to the secured debt. The debtor is entitled

to any surplus. The secured party can recover a deficiency judgment if the sale's proceeds are insufficient to discharge the debt.

- A secured party who fails to carry out the duties imposed on him can be liable to the debtor for damages, which may include punitive damages.
- In a number of ways, Article 9 gives credit buyers of consumer goods protection that is not enjoyed by other classes of debtors.

- Assignment of Account
- Breach of the Peace
- Buyer in Ordinary Course of Business
- Collateral
- Commercially Reasonable
- Conversion
- Default
- Deficiency Judgment
- Foreclosure
- Inventory
- Judicial Lien Creditor

- Lien
- Priority
- Purchase Money Security Interest
- Redemption
- Repossession
- Right of Redemption
- Self-help Repossession
- Statement of Assignment
- Statutory Lien Creditor
- Subsequent Buyer
- Unsecured Creditor

Questions and Case Problems

1. What is the general rule governing the priority of two or more secured parties, each of whom holds a perfected security interest in the same collateral? In your opinion, is this rule fair? Why?

2. Huff leased a truck from Nevada National Bank under terms that, in effect, gave Bank a security interest. In earlier transactions between Huff and the Bank, Huff was consistently behind in his payments. This pattern of behavior continued with respect to the truck. For two years Bank tried to keep the transaction going rather than repossess the truck. Finally, when Huff's insurer cancelled the insurance policy on the truck and Huff was one and a half months behind in its payments, Bank repossessed the truck without warning, causing significant disruption to Huff's business. Huff claims that in its course of dealing, by accepting consistently late payments, Bank waived its right to repossess without notifying Huff that strict compliance with the lease would be required. Bank argues that the lease agreement permitted repossession on default. What result?

3. On November 15, 1977, Don purchased a diamond wedding ring set from Clark Jewelers for $14,420. He made a $5,000 down payment and agreed to pay the balance within 90 days. Maricharles, who had accompanied Don to the jeweler, was personally fitted and received the diamond rings as an engagement gift from Don the same day. Don executed a purchase money security agreement on the rings in favor of Clark Jewelers, but Maricharles was not a party to the agreement. Don failed to make further payments on the rings, and then declared bankruptcy. Clark Jewelers then sued Maricharles to foreclose on the diamond rings. Maricharles claims that Clark knew of the gift of the collateral (rings) to her. Clark claims that she took the rings subject to Clark's security interest. Is Clark entitled to the rings?

4. What is a deficiency judgment? Under what circumstances does a secured party who has repossessed collateral lose the right to obtain a deficiency judgment?

5. Delta's truck, which Delta bought and used for business purposes, is in Able's garage for repairs. The repairs are completed, but Delta cannot pay the repair bill. Able elects to retain possession of the truck until the bill is paid, as state law allows him to do. Meanwhile, several others are also asserting interests in the truck. Those claimants, listed in the order in which their claims against Delta arose, are as follows: Baker, who loaned Delta money to start her business and who holds a promissory note signed by Delta; Charlie, who also loaned Delta money and took a security interest covering all of Delta's equipment, including after-acquired equipment, but did not perfect his interest; and Eagle, who sold Delta the truck on credit and perfected a security interest in it. Discuss the relative priority of the claims of Able, Baker, Charlie, and Eagle.

6. PCA held an unperfected security interest in all of farmer York's farm equipment, and the security agreement contained an after-acquired property clause. On April 1, Carson sold York a new tractor on credit, retaining a security interest in it. York took delivery of the tractor on April 2. On April 5, PCA filed to perfect its security interest, and Carson filed on April 10. As between PCA and Carson, who has priority with respect to the tractor? How would your answer differ, if at all, if York were a merchant rather than a farmer, and Carson had sold York inventory items instead of a tractor?

7. Builder Bob has an open account with Mitchell, a merchant. At Bob's insistence, the contract between Bob and Mitchell provides that Mitchell cannot assign his right to receive payment from Bob. Hard times befall Mitchell, however, and to secure needed financing he assigns all his accounts to Anderson. At that time, Bob owes Mitchell $10,000. Bob is not advised about the assignment, and he pays Mitchell $8,000 on the account. Mitchell then departs, leaving many unpaid creditors in his wake. Anderson now informs Bob about the assignment, directs that payments be made to him (Anderson), and advises Bob that he currently owes $10,000 plus interest. Is Bob liable to Anderson? If so, for how much?

8. White, who sells cars full-time, sells yachts on the side from an office in her home. White does not have a merchant's license as is required by state law. She does have business cards bearing an appropriate firm name, her home phone number, and the name of a yacht manufacturer. White had sold several yachts in the past. A bank loans White money to purchase a new yacht, takes a security interest in the boat, and perfects that interest. White displays the boat at a boat show and later moors it at a nearby lake. Stanley sees the boat at the lake and buys it from White for personal use. White defaults on her loan from the bank, and the bank sues Stanley for conversion of the yacht. Should the bank prevail? Why or why not?

9. Donald buys a new car from BMC Motors, and BMC retains a security interest in the car. Donald is often late in his payments. Several times he phones BMC to ask for more time to make particular payments, and on each occasion he withholds payment until he receives written notice that an extension has been granted. Once again Donald is behind on a payment, and once again he phones BMC for an extension. Donald is told that he will be notified by letter as to the pattern of payment expected in the future. While awaiting the notification, Donald takes the car to a garage for an oil change and leaves it there. BMC's employee goes to the garage, lies to the attendant, saying that Donald consented to repossession, and starts to drive off in the car. Donald walks up at that moment, guesses what is

happening, shouts at the driver to stop, and hurries toward the car. However, BMC's employee "floors it" and leaves with haste. As she does so, the left rear wheel of the car passes over Donald's foot, crushing it. Donald sues BMC for damages. Should he prevail? Why or why not? In your answer, discuss the propriety of the repossession and the nature of any damages to which Donald is entitled.

10. Well-Bilt, a furniture manufacturer, repossesses certain furniture from Morton, a dealer, after Morton's default under the agreement between them. At the time the unpaid balance of the secured debt is $50,000. The wholesale value of the repossessed furniture is $60,000, and its retail value is about $100,000. Well-Bilt gives Morton eight days' advance notice that the furniture will be sold privately. Before the sale date, Well-Bilt contacts one possible buyer for the furniture, and the prospect expresses some interest. On the sale date, Well-Bilt buys the furniture for $35,000. Well-Bilt sues Morton for the $15,000 deficiency, and Morton counterclaims (sues Well-Bilt) for damages, alleging that the sale was improper. How should the court decide the case? Why?

31 Creditors' Remedies; Debtors' Rights

31:1 Introduction

A debt is satisfied, and the debtor is discharged, when the debt no longer exists. A creditor usually intends that the debtor will pay off the debt voluntarily, and most debts are satisfied this way. Depending on the nature of the debt, payment can be made either in a lump sum or in installments over a period of time. All is well as long as the debtor pays on time. Sometimes, however, this does not happen, and the creditor must then look for a way to collect the debt.

The creditor's available remedies can be classified as being either nonjudicial or judicial. A nonjudicial remedy is one that the creditor can use without outside help, while a judicial remedy involves some sort of participation by a court.

Nonjudicial Remedies The most common nonjudicial remedy is the use of what are known as *dunning letters*. Strictly speaking, a dun is no more than a persistent demand for payment. In practice, however, dunning letters reflect an attempt to shame or coerce the debtor into paying up. Under the federal Fair Debt Collection Practices Act [15 USC §§ 1692 et seq.], there are limits on the allowable use of dunning letters.

If a creditor's collection efforts fail, the creditor himself may be able to seize certain of the debtor's property. This nonjudicial remedy is usually available only to a creditor who has a security interest in the property to be seized, as discussed in Chapter 30. If this remedy is not available, the creditor must turn to a judicial remedy.

Judicial Remedies A creditor's basic judicial remedy is a lawsuit on the debt. In the complaint filed against the debtor, the creditor alleges that the debtor owes a specific amount of money and requests that the court issue a judgment ordering the debtor to pay that amount. If the creditor loses, the alleged debt is discharged in the sense that a court has found that no enforceable debt exists. If the creditor wins, he obtains a judgment against the debtor for a specific amount. That amount becomes a new debt, replacing the old one.

A creditor who obtains a judgment against a debtor becomes a *judgment creditor;* being judgment creditor gives him or her rights with respect to property owned by the debtor. During the course of the lawsuit, however, the debtor may have disposed of property. To avoid this problem, the creditor can obtain rights in some of the debtor's property at once, using what is known as a *prejudgment remedy.* But prejudgment remedies are available only for any debtor's property that is not exempt from the claims of creditors. Moreover, misuse of a prejudgment remedy wrongs the debtor and may enable the debtor to recover damages from the creditor. Finally, prejudgment remedies have been limited in recent years by federal statutes and court decisions that liberally intepret debtors' constitutional rights.

31:2 Definitions

Certain terms occur frequently in a discussion of creditors' remedies. A familiarity with these terms at the outset will make discussion in the rest of this chapter easier to understand.

Bond: A written contract between one person (the principal) and a surety company (the surety) for the benefit of a third person (the obligee). A *bond* is basically a promise that the principal will perform a stated duty owed to the obligee, and that if he fails to do so, the surety will pay the obligee up to a stated amount of money. The language of the bond is often quite specific as to exactly how and when the surety will be liable. One "posts" a bond by obtaining it from a surety company (for a fee) and filing it with the proper person, who, in the law of creditors' remedies, is usually the clerk of a court.

Default: The failure to perform a duty or obligation. With respect to the creditor-debtor relationship, the most common default is a debtor's failure to pay a debt at all or in the proper manner. For example, if a person buys new furniture on credit and obligates herself to pay the furniture dealer in monthly installments over the next two years, the person is in default if she fails to pay an installment on time.

Unsecured creditor: A creditor who has only the debtor's promise to pay. An unsecured creditor has no rights with respect to any specific property owned by the debtor. The debt may be evidenced by a signed, written document such as a promissory note. Alternatively, the debt may exist only on the creditor's books, such as when goods are sold on open account (buyer orders goods or services; seller delivers them and later bills buyer).

Secured creditor: A creditor who has a security interest in property owned by the debtor. Ordinarily, the security interest is created when the debt is created.[1]

Lien: An interest in certain property, usually arising in connection with a debt of the property owner, that gives the lienholder a right to the property if the debt is not paid. The debt often involves the property on which the lien is claimed, but it does not have to. A lien can be consensual, statutory, or judicial. A mortgage securing repayment of the loan used to buy a home is an

---

[1] Security interests in personal property are discussed in Chapter 29. Security interests in real property are discussed in Chapter 36.

example of a consensual lien. A statutory lien is one granted by statute, such as the lien on a car granted to a mechanic who worked on the car but was not paid. A judgment lien, defined below, is an example of a judicial lien. The priority of one lien over another depends on the status of the lienholder. One lien is said to be junior to a second lien if the second lienholder's rights in the property are superior to those of the first lienholder. For example, a judicial lien is usually junior to a statutory lien.

<u>Money judgment</u>:   A court's judgment by which the loser of a lawsuit is ordered to pay a stated amount of money to the winner.

<u>Judgment debtor</u>:   A person against whom a money judgment has been issued.

<u>Judgment lien</u>:   A lien on the property of one against whom a money judgment has been issued. The lien is in favor of the person who successfully sued the property owner. In most states it covers only the debtor's real property, but its coverage includes real property that the debtor acquires after the judgment is issued.

<u>Encumbrance</u>:   A right or interest in real property held by someone other than the property owner. A person encumbers his property when he creates or allows the creation of an *encumbrance* on it. The most common example of an encumbrance is a mortgage.

<u>Insolvency</u>:   The situation in which the value of a person's assets other than exempt property is less than the total amount of his debts.

<u>Consumer</u>:   An individual who buys goods or services primarily for personal, family, or household purposes.

<u>Retail installment contract</u>:   A contract for the credit sale of goods or services to a consumer. The contract requires payment of the price of the goods or services, plus the credit charges, in periodic installments.

31:3   Exempt Property

A defaulting debtor could be left with nothing if a creditor could look to all the debtor's property for satisfaction of the debt. To protect some debtors, statutes in every state provide that certain property is not subject to the claims of the property owner's creditors. This property is known as *exempt property*. The rationale for the exemption statutes is that if a debtor is left with something, he or she will continue to be able to support a spouse and children and hence not burden society by going on welfare.

 Exemption statutes do not apply to a creditor's claim to property on which the creditor holds a security interest. The grant of a security interest is a voluntary act in that the debtor can encumber exempt property with a security interest if he chooses to do so. As a practical matter, the grant of a security interest is often required if the debtor is to obtain desired credit. Thus, the only real voluntary aspect of the transaction is apt to be the debtor's decision to buy on credit rather than wait until he can pay cash for desired goods or services.

Persons Protected   Only a debtor who falls within the class of debtors described in an exemption statute can take advantage of the statute. Typically, the debtor must be an individual, rather than a corporation, partnership, or other business.

The *homestead exemption* exempts the debtor's home, or some part of it, from claims of creditors. In most states the homestead exemption statute states the maximum dollar amount of the exemption. In such states, the exemption usually is applied only to the value of the property in excess of outstanding loans secured by the property. Thus, a $40,000 exemption fully covers a debtor's interest in a $100,000 home if the home is encumbered by a $20,000 first mortgage and a $40,000 second mortgage. Some states exempt a specific amount of land as a homestead, such as 40 acres in the country, rather than a dollar value amount of land.

If the value of homestead property exceeds the exempt amount, the rights of creditors to reach that excess value depend on state law. In some states, the creditor can do nothing as long as the debtor continues to use the property as his home. In other states, the property can be split, if possible, and creditors can force a sale of the part not covered by the exemption, to satisfy debts. In still other states, creditors can force a sale of the entire homestead, as long as the debtor receives the exemption amount out of the sale proceeds.

EXAMPLE: Haller's home is worth $100,000, and the homestead exemption amount in her state is $30,000. Haller owes $20,000 on a loan secured by the home. She is in default on unsecured debts totaling $80,000. If Haller's unsecured creditors can force a sale of the home, only the sale proceeds in excess of $50,000 (homestead exemption amount plus amount of mortgage lien) can be subjected to the creditor's claims.

Other Exempt Property   The exemption statutes in most states also cover personal property, up to stated value limits. Types of personal property apt to be listed in such statutes include (1) wages or salary; (2) tools and equipment used in the debtor's trade or occupation; (3) the debtor's automobile; (4) household goods and furniture; (5) food and clothing; and (6) some insurance proceeds, pensions, and related benefits. In addition, many exemption statutes allow the debtor to exempt other property of his choice, as long as the total value of the property he selects does not exceed the amount specified in the statute.

Claim of Exemption   Some exemptions must be claimed by the debtor, while others take effect automatically. The governing statute states what, if anything, the debtor must do to claim a particular exemption. For example, the homestead exemption statutes in some states require the homeowner to claim the exemption by filing a "declaration of homestead" in the office of the local county recorder. Generally, the exemption is automatic if a statute does not specifically require the debtor to do anything.

31:4   Execution

Execution is a remedy that is available only to a creditor who has already obtained a money judgment. Its purpose is to assist the creditor in obtaining satisfaction of the judgment debt. In essence, nonexempt property is taken from the debtor and sold, and the sale proceeds are paid to the judgment creditor.

Procedure The procedure followed in an execution is closely governed by state statute, but the usual procedure is along the following lines. First, the creditor obtains a writ of execution, which is a court order directed to the county sheriff and ordering him to "levy on" property belonging to the judgment debtor. The writ states the dollar amount of the judgment against the debtor. In theory, the sheriff "executes the writ" by locating nonexempt property owned by the debtor and in the debtor's possession, and then levying on enough of the property so that when the property is later sold, the debt can be satisfied. In practice, the creditor locates the property and leads the sheriff to it. In most states, the sheriff must look first to the debtor's personal property. If not enough personal property can be found, then the sheriff can levy on real property.

What constitutes an effective levy on property depends on the nature of the property. Strictly speaking, a *levy* is an interference with an owner's possession of his property. The traditional form of levy for personal property that is easily moved is a seizure of the property. In the case of other property, a levy can consist of the sheriff's taking control of the property in some other manner. For example, the sheriff might order the debtor not to either use or move a large machine. Similarly, a physical seizure is usually not required for a levy on real property. Property that has been levied on is considered to be in the sheriff's custody even if the property has not actually been moved. The debtor can get the property released from the sheriff's custody by posting a bond in which the debtor, as principal, promises to preserve the property and deliver it as and when ordered by the court to do so.

The next step in the typical execution process is the execution sale. The property levied on is sold to the highest bidder at a public auction held for that purpose. Advance public notice of the sale must be given, and a personal notice to the debtor may be required as well. The judgment creditor is often the buyer at the sale although, in some states, he or she is not permitted to buy at an execution sale.

The proceeds from the sale are applied first to payment of the expenses incurred in carrying out the execution and sale. The judgment creditor can be paid next under some circumstances, but if the property sold was subject to a prior lien that, under state law, must be satisfied out of the sale proceeds, the judgment creditor will be paid after that lien is satisfied. Also, it is not uncommon for several different judgment creditors to have caused writs of execution to be issued, so that the property sold was levied on under more than one writ. In that event, the priority of the judgment creditors is determined according to the order in which the creditors obtained their writs. In the rare event that any sale proceeds are left over after all judgment creditors have been paid, the balance is paid to the judgment debtor.

The final step in the execution process involves what is known as the return of execution. The return is a report prepared by the sheriff in which the sheriff outlines exactly what he did to obey the original writ.

Property Subject to Execution   The particular types of property that can be levied on under a writ of execution depend on state exemption statutes and other statutes relating specifically to execution. As a general rule, all nonexempt real and tangible personal property can be levied on. Intangible property or property interests that usually *cannot* be levied on include (1) contract rights; (2) tort claims; (3) promissory notes (a note itself is tangible, but the right to its payment is not); (4) rights to the cash value of life insurance policies; and (5) patents, copyrights, and licenses.

The issue of what property can be levied on arises in many contexts. The following case involves the question of whether an equitable interest in property can be the subject of execution. In reading the case, bear in mind that the real estate sales contract gives the buyer an equitable interest in the property; at the closing, the legal title of the seller is joined with the equitable interest of the buyer to give the buyer the full ownership interest.

Farmers State Bank
v
Slaubaugh
366 NW2d 804 (1985)
Supreme Court of North Dakota

FACTS: Slaubaugh, a farmer, failed to make payment on notes to the Bank. The Bank initiated action to reduce the claim to a judgment. The sheriff executed a notice of levy and notice of sale of Slaubaugh's real estate. Slaubaugh then filed a claim for exemption of property from the sale. He claimed that he had merely an equitable interest in the property by virtue of a contract for deed.

ISSUE: Can a judgment creditor levy execution against property to which the debtor has only an equitable interest?

RESULT: Yes. Although in common law only legal title could be subject to execution, state statute permits execution against equitable interests.

REASONING:

*   *   *

There is no question that Slaubaugh, as vendee under the contract for deed, obtained an equitable interest in the property. When a vendor sells real estate under a contract for deed he retains legal title, while the vendee acquires equitable title to the property. . . .

It is true that at common law only property to which a debtor has legal title is subject to execution. . . . Thus, in the absence of a statutory provision to the contrary, an execution operates only on legal rights and titles, and not on equitable interests. Courts have taken the view that execution is available to reach equitable interests of a judgment debtor where the applicable statute provides in broad language that all property of the debtor shall be subject to levy. . . .

[A North Dakota Statute] indicates exactly what property is subject to execution in North Dakota: "All . . . property, both real and personal, *or any interest therein,* of the judgment debtor not exempt by law, and all property and rights of property seized and held under attachment in the action are subject to execution." [Emphasis added.]

Past decisions of this court have made it clear that an equitable interest in property, whether real or personal, is subject to execution, levy, and sale.

In [an 1887 case, this] court, in construing [a statute] containing language virtually identical to [the present statute], held that an equitable interest in the stock of a corporation was subject to levy and sale under execution.

This court [has] held that while the mere docketing of a judgment created no lien on the equitable interest under a contract for deed, such an interest could be levied upon under an execution. . . .

Vande Walle, Justice.

Effect of Execution Sale; Debtor's Redemption Right   A valid execution sale satisfies the judgment debt to the extent of the amount that the judgment creditor actually receives. If, as is often true, the sale proceeds are insufficient to satisfy the debt fully, the balance of the debt remains.

A debtor can redeem (regain possession of) his property that was sold at an execution sale if the applicable execution statute provides for redemption. If the redemption right exists, the debtor exercises it by offering to pay the amount received by the sheriff at the execution sale, plus interest and expenses related to the sale. The governing statute specifies (1) the person to whom the offer is submitted, 2) how the purchaser at the execution sale recovers whatever he or she paid, and (3) the time period during which redemption is permitted.

Relief from Execution   Irregularities (mistakes) can and do occur in the process of carrying out an execution. For example, the creditor who sought execution might not have had a final judgment in her favor, so that she had no right to a writ of execution; or the sheriff might have levied on the wrong kind of property; or an execution sale might have been held without proper notice or at an improper place.

A debtor who has been wronged by an irregularity can often recover damages. If the right to sue for damages does not exist or could not compensate the debtor adequately, the debtor might be able to apply for other appropriate relief from the court that issued the writ of execution. Depending on how far the execution proceeding has gone and on the governing state law, the debtor may be able to persuade the court to grant relief, such as (1) canceling the writ, (2) temporarily enjoining execution (forbidding execution until the debtor presents his argument against it in court), (3) compelling a resale of the property levied on, or (4) ordering that the property be returned to the debtor.

31:5   Postjudgment Garnishment

A judgment creditor must find a remedy other than execution if the writ of execution is returned unsatisfied. That is, the sheriff might not have been able to levy on any of the debtor's property, or the proceeds from the sale of what property was levied on might have been insufficient to satisfy the judgment debt. Money is still owed to the judgment creditor in either case. To alleviate this problem, statutes in most states provide an additional remedy that becomes available if execution has proved to be ineffective. This remedy is known by different names in different states, but for present purposes it is referred to as *postjudgment garnishment.*

Garnishment is ordinarily a prejudgment remedy in that a creditor uses it *before* obtaining a judgment against the debtor. The distinctive feature of garnishment is that it applies to the debtor's property that is in somebody else's possession. Postjudgment garnishment is thus a means by which a creditor can obtain satisfaction of a judgment debt through property that, although owned by or owed to the debtor, is in the hands of a third person. The third person might be a bank or similar institution in which the debtor has money on deposit, or it might be the debtor's employer who holds wages or salary owed to the debtor but not yet paid to him. Other property that might be subject to postjudgment garnishment includes insurance proceeds payable to the debtor and money or other property due the debtor under a deceased person's will.

31:6   Attachment and Garnishment Generally

A defaulting debtor might have nonexempt property at the time the creditor sues him on the debt, but the creditor has no guaranty that the debtor will have that or other nonexempt property later, when the creditor obtains a judgment. Thus, a prudent creditor wants to do something to tie up the debtor's property *before* he obtains a judgment against the debtor. The processes by which the creditor can do so are known as *prejudgment remedies.* The remedies are so called because they are available before judgment. Two of the most common prejudgment remedies are *attachment* and *garnishment.* These remedies are available in most states and are governed by state statutes.

Attachment and garnishment are distinguishable, although in some states "attachment" is used in such a way as to include garnishment within its scope. For present purposes, the differences between the two remedies are threefold. First, attachment affects property owned by the debtor and in his possession, while garnishment affects property owed by *or owed to* the debtor and in the possession of someone else (known as the garnishee). Second, attachment involves a levy on the property while garnishment does not. Third, attachment creates an attachment lien on the property while, in at least some states, garnishment does not create a lien.

Purposes Attachment and garnishment have several purposes. The primary purpose of each remedy is to allow an unsecured creditor to obtain an immediate lien on or interest in some of the debtor's property. The nature of that lien or interest is such that it prevents the disposal or dissipation of property that can ultimately be sold on execution to satisfy the debt. Also, the lien or interest is superior to some other liens or interests covering the same property.

EXAMPLE: Hood is in default on unsecured debts owed to both Scarlett and Tuck. Tuck sues Hood in 1980, but, believing Hood to be an honorable fellow, he does not attach any of Hood's property. Scarlett sues in 1981, and he immediately attaches Hood's forest retreat. If Tuck obtains a judgment against Hood in 1983, his judgment lien on the forest retreat is junior to Scarlett's earlier attachment lien.

Another reason a creditor attaches or garnishes the debtor's property is to try to pressure the debtor into paying up. Litigation is expensive, and both parties will save money if the legal action on the debt (the principal action) can be dropped at an early stage. Also, since the debtor is often deprived of the use of attached or garnished property, the debtor's desire to get the property back might force him to pay.

 Some attorneys believe that attaching or garnishing an individual debtor's property is not always wise. Their theory is that the attachment or garnishment may irritate the debtor and cause him to defend himself in the principal action, thus making it impossible for the creditor to obtain a default judgment.[2]

Procedure Generally The procedure to be followed for both attachment and garnishment varies somewhat from state to state. Outlined below is the procedure under typical statutes of the *traditional* type. Bear in mind, though, that the discussion of debtors' constitutional right to notice and a hearing (see 31:11) must also be read for a complete picture.

Attachment Procedure The first step taken by a creditor who wants to attach the debtor's property is to prepare an attachment affidavit. An *affidavit* is a written statement of facts, the truth of which is sworn to by the person signing the affidavit, called the *affiant*. An attachment affidavit identifies the debtor, describes the nature and amount of the debt, and states one or more

---

[2] A default judgment is a judgment for the plaintiff that is issued when the defendant fails to answer the complaint or otherwise defend himself. Creditors favor default judgments because they can be obtained quickly and with little expense.

of the grounds for attachment that are set forth in the statute. A common ground is the affiant's belief that the debtor is about to dispose of his nonexempt property or to move it outside the court's jurisdiction. In most states, the creditor must also obtain an attachment bond. The purpose of the bond is to give the debtor some protection if the attachment turns out to have been improper.

The affidavit and bond are filed with the clerk of the court. If the creditor has already begun the principal action (or is filing a complaint against the debtor at the same time), the clerk issues a writ of attachment. The writ is similar to a writ of execution in that it directs the sheriff to levy on the debtor's nonexempt property. The writ usually describes the particular property to be levied on.

The sheriff then "executes the attachment," which means that he levies on the property. The levy is accomplished in the same way as a levy of execution. Thus, for example, the sheriff need not necessarily physically seize and remove bulky property, and under some statutes he need not remove the property at all, no matter how movable it is. In most jurisdictions the debtor must be personally served with a written notice about the levy, even if the debtor was present when the levy was made. Finally, the sheriff prepares a return of the writ, describing exactly what he did.

Once property has been attached, the attachment continues until further order of the court. If the creditor ultimately wins in his lawsuit against the debtor, the attached property is then subject to execution and sale to satisfy the judgment debt.

Garnishment Procedure   Garnishment is similar to attachment in that it is begun by the creditor's preparing an affidavit and, in most states, obtaining a garnishment bond. The garnishment affidavit differs from an attachment affidavit in that it identifies the garnishee and states the creditor's belief that the garnishee is holding some of the debtor's nonexempt property (which includes money owed to the debtor).

The creditor files the affidavit and bond with the clerk of the court, and the clerk issues a writ of garnishment. The writ has the effect of bringing the garnishee into the proceeding as an additional defendant. It is served on the garnishee, and that service establishes the court's jurisdiction over the garnishee. The garnishee then must answer the writ; in effect, he admits or denies that he possesses any of the debtor's property. Assuming that the garnishee has some of the debtor's property, the creditor can use various means to discover the nature and extent of that property. In the meantime, the garnishee must hold and preserve the property until the court's further order; the garnishee cannot give the property to the debtor. As with attachment, if the creditor later obtains a judgment against the debtor, the garnished property (or the proceeds from its sale) can eventually be applied toward payment of the debt.

31:7   Property Subject to Attachment or Garnishment

Property can generally be attached or garnished if that property is subject to execution. In some states, though, a creditor can also attach or garnish property that is *not* subject to execution. The fact that the property is already encumbered by one or more liens held by others is not a bar to attachment or garnishment.

Real Property   Real property can be and often is attached. The debtor need not necessarily own the property outright. For example, he might have only a life estate, which means that the ownership of the property will automatically pass to someone else when the debtor dies. Real property is usually not, however, subject to garnishment.

Personal Property   Virtually all nonexempt tangible personal property can be attached or garnished. Also subject to attachment and garnishment under some statutes are many types of intangible personal property, such as shares of stock in a corporation.

If the intangible property to be garnished is a debt, the debt must have present, rather than future, existence. For example, if a debtor owns rental property, the creditor can garnish currently owed rent and past due rent, but she cannot garnish rent that is not yet due. Under most statutes, the debt must also be for a fixed amount. Thus, for example, a tort claim on which the victim has not yet obtained a money judgment is usually not subject to garnishment because the amount of the damages payable to the victim is unknown. Note in the following case the problem of determining whether a debt is liquidated or unliquidated.

Hinote's Home Furnishings, Inc.
v
Olney & Pederson, Inc.
700 P2d 1208 (1985)
Court of Appeals of Washington

FACTS: Hinote's obtained a judgment against Olney & Pederson, a construction firm. Hinote's then applied for and obtained a writ of garnishment against Mr. and Mrs. Isaman as debtors of Olney & Pederson. The Isamans answered the writ by stating that to the best of their knowledge they owed nothing to Olney & Pederson. Olney & Pederson had built a house for the Isamans. Some of the features of the house were included in the base price; others were "extras." Olney & Pederson kept poor records and went out of business a month after completing the Isaman house. At the time of the garnishment it was clear that the Isamans owed Olney & Pederson something for "extras," but the amount was unascertained until trial.

ISSUE: Was the Isamans' debt sufficiently certain that it would be garnished?

RESULT: Yes. The debt was sufficiently concern as to constitute a liquidated debt that could be garnished.

REASONING:

* * *

It is well settled in Washington that an unliquidated claim is not subject to garnishment. . . . However, what is perhaps less well settled is what constitutes an unliquidated claim. Washington courts have expressly defined an unliquidated claim for the purposes of awarding prejudgment interest but not for determining whether a claim is subject to garnishment.

In [a 1968 Washington case], the court held that a "liquidated" claim for prejudgment purposes is:

> one where the evidence furnishes data which, if believed, makes it possible to compute the amount with exactness, without reliance on opinion or discretion.

The court adopted Professor McCormick's explanation of the application of this definition . . . :

> Under this view, only those claims would be termed "unliquidated" where the exact amount of the sum to be allowed cannot be definitely fixed from the facts proved, disputed or undisputed, but must in the last analysis depend upon the opinion or discretion of the judge or jury as to whether a larger or a smaller amount should be allowed. . . . In short, it is the character of the claim and not of the defense that is determinative of the question whether an amount of money sued for is a "liquidated sum."

It follows from the foregoing that, where the amount sued for may be arrived at by a process of measurement or computation from the data given by the proof, without any reliance upon opinion or discretion after the concrete facts have been determined, the amount is liquidated and will bear interest. . . .

This definition of an unliquidated claim for prejudgment interest purposes is virtually identical to the [following] definition of such a claim for garnishment purposes . . . :

> It is also to be observed that there is considerable diversity of opinion as to what constitutes an unliquidated claim within the rule that unliquidated claims are not attachable or garnishable. But generally, claims for an amount depending upon a standard of measure not a matter of opinion may be attached or garnished. Likewise, claims on accounts between parties, which are uncertain merely because such accounts, which are not subject to any matter of opinion, are unsettled and unadjusted, are not ordinarily, for that reason, exempt from process. . . .

In [a 1973 Washington case], the exact amount of the increased costs, which were allegedly due to poor management, strikes, accidents, etc., could not be definitely fixed. Here, however, the exact amount owed could be easily computed. All that was at issue was whether certain items were "extras"; the exact cost of each "extra" was fixed and not in dispute. Counsel for Isaman conceded this at trial. The only determination made by the trial judge was whether an item constituted an "extra", not how much each "extra" was worth. We hold that Olney & Pederson's claim against Isaman was liquidated and, therefore, it was subject to garnishment by Hinote's. . . .

Scholfield, Acting Chief Judge.

Money   Money found in the debtor's possession can be attached, although the right of attachment does not usually extend to money that the debtor has in his pockets at the time of the levy. Most people do not keep any sizable amount of money lying around, however. If a debtor has money, it is apt to be either deposited in a bank or owed by an employer. Both bank deposits and unpaid wages are subject to garnishment. Indeed, most garnishees are either banks in which debtors have checking or savings accounts, or employers. The law of some states allows a continuing garnishment of unpaid wages, thus making it unnecessary for the creditor to obtain and serve a new writ of garnishment each time the debtor is due to be paid.

31:8   Relief from Attachment or Garnishment

Procedural irregularities can occur in an attachment or garnishment just as in an execution. For example, the creditor may make a false statement in the affidavit, or may fail to state an adequate ground for the attachment or garnishment. In such cases, the debtor can apply to the court in the principal action for relief. If, for example, there has been excessive attachment, the debtor might ask the court to dissolve the attachment as to part of the property. The debtor may also be able to recover damages for wrongful attachment or garnishment.

Bond to Release Property   The debtor usually has the right to post a bond to obtain the temporary release of his property, even if there has been no irregularity in an attachment or garnishment. Most bonds of this type provide that, in effect, the debtor will produce the property if the judgment in the principal action is against him. If the debtor does not produce the property, the surety is liable for the value of that property. Some bonds operate as a full release of the property, however. Under a bond of this type the debtor promises to pay any judgment against him, and if he fails to do so, the surety pays.

31:9   Repossession

Attachment and garnishment are not the only prejudgment remedies available to some creditors. A creditor who has some interest in particular personal property can attempt to repossess that property through use of a somewhat different remedy. The name of this additional remedy varies, depending on the governing state statute. For example, it is called replevin in some states, claim and delivery in others. For present purposes, *replevin* is used to describe all these remedies.

Replevin is a legal remedy by which the creditor seeks a judgment that specific property must be returned to the creditor, rather than a money judgment. It is also a prejudgment remedy in that the creditor can reobtain possession of the property at once, rather than having to wait until the case is decided.

The interest in particular property that gives rise to a creditor's resort to replevin is usually based on a credit sale of goods. The creditor sells goods to the debtor under a contract that lists various events, the occurrence of any one of which constitutes a default by the debtor. A common default is the debtor's failure to pay on time. The typical contract then provides that if a default occurs, the creditor is entitled to repossess the property.

Under Article 9 of the UCC, an interest retained by a seller of goods on credit is a security interest. As discussed in Chapter 30. Article 9 provides for self-help repossession. In essence, the creditor can repossess goods using his own private means if the repossession can be carried out peacefully. Motor vehicles are often repossessed in this way. However, self-help repossession of goods that are in the debtor's home or place of business is often difficult; peaceful repossession is impossible if the debtor refuses to allow the creditor entry. It is at this point that the creditor turns to replevin.

Traditional Replevin Procedure   The typical replevin procedure was quite simple before 1969 when, as a result of a series of important cases (see 31:11), the procedure became more complex. The traditional procedure is similar to attachment in many ways. The creditor prepares an affidavit in which he describes the basis of his claim, the particular property in which he has an interest, and the nature of that interest. He presents this affidavit and an appropriate bond to the clerk of the court. The clerk then issues the writ, which directs the sheriff to levy on the specific property described in the writ. The sheriff executes the writ by seizing the property. He retains custody of the property for several days; during that period the debtor can reobtain possession of it by posting a bond. If the debtor fails to post a bond, the sheriff delivers the property to the creditor. The sheriff then prepares and files his return of the writ. Meanwhile, the creditor retains the property until a court hears the case and issues a judgment stating to whom the property should go.

Today, the replevin procedure in most states includes the above steps. However, it also provides for advance notice to the debtor and for the debtor's opportunity to be heard. The discussion in 31:11 must be read for a complete picture of replevin under modern practice.

31:10 Restrictions on Garnishment of Wages

Compensation for personal services owed to but not yet paid to an employee by his employer has long been a favorite target of garnishing creditors. This is because the typical employer is easily identified and found, and the amount of compensation due is easily determined. Also, many debtors have little or no other nonexempt property that the creditor can turn to.

"Wages" (including salary and any other form of money compensation for personal services) is exempt to some extent in virtually all states. The need for this exemption arose because garnishment of all or a major part of a debtor's wages often led to the debtor's bankruptcy. The state exemption statutes are far from uniform, however, with the result that they serve their purpose effectively in only some states.

Federal Legislation Generally [15 USC §§ 1671, 1675, 1677] The federal government entered the picture in 1968 when Congress enacted the Consumer Credit Protection Act (CCPA). Most of the CCPA directly concerns credit offered to individuals for personal, family, or household purposes, as discussed in Chapter 28. However, Title III of the CCPA [15 USC §§ 1671 et seq.] imposes restrictions on the garnishment of wages.

The Title III restrictions apply to wages paid to all employees throughout the United States. These restrictions have no effect on any state statute that prohibits garnishment of wages altogether or restricts garnishment more than the federal law does, but state statutes that provide less protection are, in effect, superseded by the federal law.

Restriction on Amount Garnished [15 USC §§ 1672, 1673] With several exceptions, the maximum amount of a person's weekly wages that can be garnished is the lesser of (1) 25 percent of the person's disposable earnings for that week or (2) the amount by which the person's disposable earnings for that week exceed 30 times the federal minimum hourly wage. If an employee is paid other than by the week, the wages are translated into a weekly wage to determine the limits on garnishment.

For purposes of the CCPA, "disposable earnings" is compensation for personal services minus any amount that the employer is required to withhold.

EXAMPLE: Alfred takes home $150 per week (his gross earnings, less deductions for social security and federal and state income taxes). Wilfred takes home $260 per week. Assuming that the federal minimum wage is $4 per hour, the maximum amount of Alfred's weekly wages that can be garnished is $30 ($150 minus 30 times the minimum wage, which is less than 25 percent of $150). The maximum amount of Wilfred's weekly wages that can be garnished is $65 (25 percent of $260, which is less than $260 minus 30 times the minimum wage).

The garnishment limits do not apply at all to any order of a bankruptcy court or to any debt for state or federal taxes. Also, the limits are considerably higher if the debt involved is a support order issued by a court. For example, up to 65 percent of the disposable earnings of a divorced person can be garnished for payment of overdue alimony and child support.

Discharge of Employee [15 USC § 1674(a)] Since garnishment generates administrative expenses that must be paid by the garnishee, employers do not like to have the wages of their employees garnished. Indeed, garnishment often used to lead to the employee's being fired. The CCPA limits this practice by prohibiting the discharge of an employee due to garnishment of wages for any *one* debt.

 A businessperson should be aware that the federal discharge prohibition has been interpreted to mean that if the maximum allowable amount of an employee's wages has already been garnished for one debt, service of a writ of garnishment on the employer in connection with a second debt is not a second garnishment within the meaning of the discharge rule. The rationale for this interpretation is that since the employee no longer has any disposable earnings subject to garnishment, the employer could not comply with the second writ, even if it wanted to.

Enforcement; Civil Liability [15 USC §§ 1674(b), 1676] The Wage and Hour Division of the Department of Labor enforces the federal restrictions on garnishment of wages. An employer who wrongfully discharges an employee because of a garnishment can be fined, imprisoned, or both. However, the CCPA is silent on the question whether that employer can also be sued for damages by the discharged employee. Different courts have reached contrary results on this question.

31:11   Debtors' Constitutional Rights

The Fourteenth Amendment to the United States Constitution, as interpreted by the courts, is the source of a vast body of law. Much of the litigation based on the amendment has stemmed from its *due process clause*, which provides that no state shall "deprive any person of . . . property, without due process of law."

Until 1969, the creditors' remedies discussed earlier in this chapter were thought not to violate due process requirements; the legal atmosphere was favorable to creditors. This favorable atmosphere collapsed abruptly in 1969 when the United States Supreme Court issued the following landmark decision.

Sniadach

v

Family Finance Corp.

395 US 337 (1969)

United States Supreme Court

FACTS: Family Finance Corporation, the respondent, sought to garnish the wages of Sniadach, the petitioner, in connection with a $420 debt. Sniadach received no advance notice about the garnishment, and none was required under the governing Wisconsin statute. Sniadach's employer stated that it had under its control wages of $63.18 owed to Sniadach but not yet paid to her. The employer agreed to hold one-half of the unpaid wages subject to the court's order.

ISSUE: Does the Wisconsin garnishment proceeding statute violate Sniadach's right to due process under the Fourteenth Amendment?

RESULT: Yes. The statute permits deprivation of property without a prior opportunity to be heard.

REASONING:

*   *   *

The Wisconsin statute gives a plaintiff 10 days in which to serve the summons and complaint on the defendant after service on the garnishee. In this case petitioner was served the same day as the garnishee. She nonetheless claims that the Wisconsin garnishment procedure violates that due process required by the Fourteenth Amendment, in that notice and an opportunity to be heard are not given before the . . . seizure of the wages. What happens in Wisconsin is that the clerk of the court issues the summons at the request of the creditor's lawyer; and it is the latter who by serving the garnishee sets in motion the machinery whereby the wages are frozen. They may, it is true, be unfrozen if the trial of the main suit is ever had and the wage earner wins on the merits. But in the interim the wage earner is deprived of his enjoyment of earned wages without any opportunity to be heard and to tender any defense he may have, whether it be fraud or otherwise.

Such summary procedure may well meet the requirements of due process in extraordinary situations. . . . But in the present case no situation requiring special protection to a state or creditor interest is presented by the facts; nor is the Wisconsin statute narrowly drawn to meet any such unusual condition. Petitioner was a resident of this Wisconsin community and [personal] jurisdiction was readily obtainable. . . .

In this case the sole question is whether there has been a taking of property without that procedural due process that is required by the Fourteenth Amendment. . . . [The] right to be heard has little reality or worth unless one is informed that the matter is pending and can choose for himself whether to appear or default, acquiesce or contest. . . . In the context of this case the question is whether the interim freezing of the wages without a chance to be heard violates procedural due process.

A procedural rule that may satisfy due process for attachments in general . . . does not necessarily satisfy procedural due process in every case. . . . We deal here with wages—a specialized type of property presenting distinct problems in our economic system. We turn then to the nature of that property and problems of procedural due process.

A prejudgment garnishment of the Wisconsin type is a taking which may impose tremendous hardship on wage earners with families to support. Until [enactment of the CCPA] which forbids discharge of employees on the ground that their wages have been garnished, garnishment often meant the loss of a job. Over and beyond that was the great drain on family income. . . .

Recent investigations of the problem have disclosed the grave injustices made possible by prejudgment garnishment whereby the sole opportunity to be heard comes after the taking. . . .

The leverage of the creditor on the wage earner is enormous. The creditor tenders not only the original debt but the "collection fees" incurred by his attorneys in the garnishment proceedings. . . .

Apart from those collateral consequences, it appears that in Wisconsin the statutory exemption granted the wage earner is generally insufficient to support the debtor for any one week.

The result is that a prejudgment garnishment of the Wisconsin type may as a practical matter drive a wage-earning family to the wall. Where the taking of one's property is so obvious, it needs no extended argument to conclude that absent notice and a prior hearing . . . this prejudgment garnishment procedure violates the fundamental principles of due process. . . .

Douglas, Justice.

The *Sniadach* decision is limited to garnishment of the wages of an individual. More significant to creditors was the underlying legal theory, known as the *Sniadach* doctrine, that a debtor is entitled to notice and an opportunity to be heard before property can be taken, even if the taking is not necessarily permanent and will ultimately be judged by a court.

Developments since Sniadach   It did not take the courts long to extend the *Sniadach* doctrine to garnishment of a consumer's bank account. Later, the Supreme Court extended the doctrine to cover garnishment of a corporate debtor's bank account. This decision made it clear that businesses also have due process rights that must be observed. Other courts extended the *Sniadach* doctrine to cover attachments. And in the case of *Fuentes v Shevin*[3] the Supreme Court declared unconstitutional the taking of consumer goods under a writ of replevin issued without the debtor's having been given advance notice or an opportunity to be heard.

Creditors have not lost all the battles, however. For example, the remedy of postjudgment garnishment without advance notice and a hearing has withstood constitutional attack. The reason is that a postjudgment garnishment order is based on a court's judgment that itself was issued in a proceeding during which the debtor's due process rights were observed. Execution without advance notice and a hearing can be defended on the same basis. And in

---

[3] 407 US 67 (1972).

another Supreme Court case,[4] the Court suggested that a statute allowing a debtor's property to be seized before judgment without advance notice and a hearing is not unconstitutional if the statute (1) requires the creditor to post a bond, (2) requires the creditor to file an affidavit alleging personal knowledge of specific facts forming a basis for the seizure, (3) requires a judge to decide whether the writ should be issued, (4) allows the debtor to recover the property by posting a bond, and (5) gives the debtor the right to a hearing immediately after the seizure.

The constitutional questions relating to creditors' remedies have not all been answered yet. In general, the *Sniadach* line of cases has not been extended to the self-help repossession provisions of Article 9. When judicial process is used as a prejudgment remedy, the principles described above provide guidance.

Nature of Due Process Required   Obviously, a full trial is not required before a debtor's property can be attached, garnished, or replevied. The requirement of a full trial would have the effect of eliminating the prejudgment remedies altogether. In an effort to comply with due process requirements, most states have amended their attachment, garnishment, and replevin statutes to include what is known as a "show cause" procedure. In essence, the creditor obtains from the court an order addressed to the debtor and directing the debtor to show why a writ of attachment, garnishment, or replevin should not be issued. The debtor then has a specified time in which to answer the order. He or his attorney can appear before the court for this purpose, and if the debtor makes a sufficient showing, the writ is not issued. As a practical matter, it should be noted that this sort of procedure can weaken the creditor's position substantially because it gives the debtor time to put his property beyond the creditor's reach in any number of different ways. Some state statutes address this problem by allowing a debtor's property to be seized without notice under limited circumstances and providing for a hearing very soon afterward. The courts have reached different conclusions about whether statutes of this last type are constitutional.

 Not all state statutes have been amended or replaced to comply with the constitutional principles laid down by the Supreme Court. Any creditor who seeks to attach, garnish, or replevy property under a statute not providing for advance notice to the debtor and some sort of hearing must realize that the action might be challenged on constitutional grounds, and that the challenge might succeed.

31:12   Wrongful Attachment, Garnishment, or Execution

An attachment, garnishment, or execution and sale can be wrongful in a number of different ways. For example, the creditor might have used the remedy for an improper purpose or have made a false statement in his

---

[4] *Mitchell v W. T. Grant Co.,* 416 US 600 (1974).

affidavit; the sheriff might have levied on exempt property or property having a value far exceeding the amount of the debt; or an execution sale might have been held without proper notice to the debtor.

If a wrongful act has occurred, the debtor can recover damages from whoever was responsible for or carried out the act. The proper defendant is often the creditor, sometimes the sheriff, and at times both the creditor and the sheriff. The debtor's right to damages for wrongful attachment or garnishment does not require him having prevailed in the principal action. Indeed, his right to damages can arise before a judgment is even issued in that action.

Measure of Damages   If there has been a wrongful attachment, garnishment, or execution, the debtor is entitled to be compensated for loss. Naturally, the debtor has the right to have property returned (or, in a garnishment, to have the garnishment dissolved). If the property cannot be returned, the debtor receives its value, determined as of the time of the seizure.

The recovery of the property or its value only returns the debtor to his or her original position, rather than compensating for any loss suffered. Depending on the circumstances, the debtor might also be able to recover damages for such factors as (1) the debtor's loss of use of the property; (2) damage to or depreciation of the property; (3) lost business profits, including a lost opportunity for an advantageous sale of the property; (4) injury to the debtor's credit rating, and (5) the debtor's mental suffering and humiliation.

If the creditor (or, rarely, the sheriff) is found to have acted with malice, the debtor may also be able to recover punitive damages. Malice in this context means that the wrongdoer intentionally acted against the debtor and with an evil purpose. For example, an attaching creditor, whose primary purpose is supposed to be obtaining security for her debt, acts maliciously if her real purpose is to drive the debtor out of business by tying up the debtor's inventory.

Nature of the Legal Action   Several approaches may be available to a debtor who is the victim of wrongful attachment, garnishment, or execution. First, the debtor may be able to sue the surety named in the bond that the creditor had to file with the attachment affidavit. Note, however, that the maximum amount the surety can be required to pay under the bond will rarely be enough to cover an award of punitive damages. Second, the debtor usually can sue the creditor or sheriff directly in connection with a wrongful attachment, garnishment, or execution. In some states the debtor must show that the defendant acted with malice, while in others the debtor must show only that an impropriety occurred.

Finally, the debtor may be able to sue for the tort of either *malicious prosecution* or *abuse of process*. The basis for malicious prosecution is that the creditor never should have sued the debtor in the first place, so the creditor never had the right to attach or garnish any of the debtor's property. The basis for abuse of process is that the creditor intentionally used a proper legal procedure for an improper purpose. For example, the creditor may have had the right to sue on the debt and to obtain a writ of attachment against the debtor's property, but he is liable for abuse of process if his purpose in attaching the property was to vex and harrass the debtor, rather than to obtain security for the debt.

The following case involves the issue of whether punitive damages should be available to a plaintiff in a wrongful garnishment case.

Moon
v
Tower Grove Bank & Trust Co.
691 SW2d 399 (1985)
Missouri Court of Appeals

FACTS: The Moons sued the Bank, alleging wrongful garnishment of two bank accounts. The Bank originally had sued the Moons under a promissory note allegedly co-signed for a daughter. The Bank obtained a default judgment. However, the summons in the case was defective in that it mistakenly named Elijah Moon as "Elizah Moor." Because of this and other defects, the Bank had the default judgment set aside and sued again. This time the Bank arranged for so-called "postcard notice," changing "Moor" to "Moon" but retaining the misspelled name "Elizah." The Bank obtained another default judgment and then effected execution and garnishment against the Moons' bank accounts.

ISSUE: Are punitive damages available against the Bank on these facts?

RESULT: No. There is insufficient evidence of malice to support punitive damages.

REASONING:

*   *   *

. . . After viewing the evidence in the light most favorable to plaintiffs, we find nothing to indicate any element of wantonness or bad motive on the part of bank or attorney necessary to support a punitive damage award. There was no evidence bank or attorney knew the judgment was void at the time they effected garnishment or that they were aware what they did was wrongful. Postcard notice was the standard procedure to reset a cause in the magistrate court. . . .

In wrongful garnishment actions in Missouri two types of malice have allowed recovery of punitive damages: actual malice and legal malice. In actual malice, the action is motivated by hatred or ill will. Legal malice has been defined as the intentional doing of a wrongful act without just cause or excuse in reckless disregard of the rights of others. . . . However, demonstration of a simple good faith mistake or ignorance as to the wrongfulness of the act constitutes a defense to the award of punitive damages. . . .

To justify punitive damages based on legal malice, Missouri courts have stated there must be some element of bad motive or wantonness. This means the defendant not only must have intended to do the wrongful act, but that he knew it to be wrongful when he did it. . . . If, on the other hand, defendant has acted in good faith on the honest belief his act is lawful, he is not liable for punitive damages, although he may have been mistaken as to the legality of his act. . . .

In the instant case, bank through its attorney garnished property following a default judgment which was void for lack of personal jurisdiction. Bank set aside the first default judgment after learning names were misspelled. It reset the cause and issued postcard notice, retaining one spelling error. A second default judgment was taken.

The evidence viewed most favorably to plaintiffs indicates bank's garnishment of accounts (through its attorney) was based on the mistaken assumption that the second default judgment was valid. To support the submission of punitive damages, there must be substantial evidence bank knew the judgment was void at the time the garnishment was run. . . . The evidence reveals nothing other than good-faith error. Accordingly, the trial court did not err in refusing to submit punitive damages to the jury. . . .

Crist, Judge.

31:13 Wrongful Repossession

If a creditor has the debtor's property seized under a writ of replevin and the replevin is wrongful, the debtor can recover damages from the creditor. In a replevin action, the creditor can obtain possession of the debtor's property before the court issues a judgment, but that judgment, when issued, determines which party ultimately receives the property. If the judgment is in the creditor's favor, the debtor will not ordinarily have suffered any loss for which he is entitled to compensation. If the debtor wins, however, the replevin judgment will usually attempt to serve at least two functions. The first function is to return the parties to their positions before the replevin proceeding was begun. The second function is to compensate the debtor for his loss.

To serve its first function, the typical replevin judgment in favor of the debtor requires the creditor to return the replevied property or, if the property cannot be returned, to pay the debtor the value of the property. That value is determined as of the time when the property was seized. As to the second function, the debtor can have suffered the same types of loss that can occur with wrongful attachment or garnishment. All aspects of the loss that the debtor has proved are added up, and the total is listed in the judgment as the damages that the creditor must pay. In addition, if the creditor is found to have acted maliciously, the judgment can include an award of punitive damages against the creditor. For example, the creditor might have obtained the writ of replevin even though he knew that he had no actual right to do so. Or, having innocently replevied property, the creditor might have refused to return the property after having discovered that it belonged to someone else.

Key Concepts and Terms

- A debt is satisfied when it has been paid off or otherwise ceases to exist.
- A debtor who fails to make a payment is in default. The creditor can then sue on the debt and obtain a money judgment. The creditor can then obtain satisfaction of the judgment by execution, postjudgment garnishment, or both. Before the judgment is issued, the creditor might be able to attach or garnish the debtor's property.
- Certain property of individuals is exempt from the claims of creditors. Exempt property cannot be subjected to attachment, garnishment, or execution.
- Execution involves a seizure of a judgment debtor's nonexempt property, the sale of that property, and the application of the sale proceeds toward satisfaction of the debt.
- If execution is ineffective to satisfy a money judgment, the creditor can use postjudgment garnishment to obtain property or money that, although owned by or owed to the debtor, is in someone else's possession.
- After a creditor has sued on a debt, but before he has recovered a judgment, the creditor can attach nonexempt property in the debtor's possession or garnish the debtor's nonexempt property in the possession of somebody else. Both attachment and garnishment deprive the debtor from using the property and can lead to execution on the property later, when the creditor has obtained a judgment against the debtor.
- A creditor who has an interest in particular property owned by a defaulting debtor can sue the debtor in replevin to obtain title to that property. A creditor suing in replevin can obtain possession of the property before a final judgment is issued.
- Federal law limits the amount of an employee's wages that can be garnished. It also protects the employee against being discharged by his employer due to a single garnishment of wages.
- Many debtors have the constitutional right to be notified in advance and to be able to present their side of disputes with creditors before their property can be taken from them in connection with their debts.
- A debtor can usually reobtain possession of property that has been levied on, garnished, or replevied by posting a bond. If an attachment, garnishment, replevin, or execution is improper, the debtor may be able to apply to the court for appropriate relief. He may also be able to recover damages from whoever committed the impropriety.

- Abuse of Process
- Affiant
- Affidavit
- Attachment
- Bond
- Due Process Clause
- Dunning Letter
- Encumbrance
- Execution
- Exempt Property
- Garnishment

- Homestead Exemption
- Judgment Creditor
- Levy
- Lien
- Malicious Prosecution
- Postjudgment Garnishment
- Prejudgment Remedy
- Quasi in Rem Jurisdiction
- Replevin
- Return of Execution

Questions and Case Problems

1. What is the difference between a judicial remedy and a nonjudicial remedy? State an example of both a judicial and a nonjudicial remedy that a creditor might use against a defaulting debtor.

2. Define and distinguish execution, attachment, garnishment, and replevin according to your understanding of those terms as they are used in this chapter.

3. Lakeshore Motor Freight obtained a default judgment against Glenway Industries for $8,193.80. In a judgment debtor examination, Lakeshore learned that Glenway's only asset was a breach of contract claim for two million dollars then pending in a federal court. Lakeshore sought execution against the contract claim. Is this the type of property against which a creditor can execute? What problems are posed by permitting such execution?

4. Kearney bought two certificates of deposit from Glendale Federal Savings and Loan. The CDs were taken in Kearney's name "in trust for the benefit of Mary L. Wormley." Wormley was a client of Kearney's and an heir of an estate for which he had served as attorney. Unibay served a writ of garnishment against Glendale to obtain $31,000 of the debt represented by the CDs. Under relevant state law a bank account held in this form is treated as a revocable trust. Is it subject to garnishment by Unibay?

5. Plunkett is injured, and his new car is slightly damaged, when Fouts runs a red light and hits Plunkett's car. Fouts carries no automobile liability insurance. It appears that his only asset of any value is his car, which was not damaged in the accident. Plunkett sues Fouts for damages and wins a $2,000 default judgment when Fouts fails to appear in court. Plunkett now seeks to levy execution on Fouts' car so that it can be sold to satisfy the judgment. Discuss the likelihood of Plunkett's success in this effort.

6. Johnson obtains a $5,000 money judgment against Roberts, and Roberts fails to pay it. Roberts owns relatively little property. Indeed, her only nonexempt property currently in her possession is an oil painting that has an appraised value of $2,000. However, Roberts does have $10,000 deposited in a savings account at a local bank. How can Johnson obtain satisfaction of his judgment against Roberts?

7. Lorenzo works for Metropolitan Opera Association. His gross wages are $300 per week, and Metropolitan deducts $80 per week for Social Security and state and federal income taxes, as it is required to do by state and federal law. On April 1, 1982, Metropolitan was served with a court order requiring it to withhold $100 per week from Lorenzo's wages and to pay the $100 to Lorenzo's former wife as overdue alimony and child support. These payments are to continue until Metropolitan receives a further order from the court. Meanwhile, GMAC, one of Lorenzo's creditors, has sued Lorenzo on a debt and been awarded a judgment for $300. Execution turned out to be ineffective, so GMAC proceeded under the state postjudgment garnishment statute. On June 1, 1982, a writ of garnishment was served on Metropolitan, but Metropolitan refused to withhold any of Lorenzo's wages for GMAC, claiming that federal law forbids any additional withholding. GMAC now seeks a court order requiring Metropolitan to withhold $55 from Lorenzo's wages each week and to pay it to GMAC until the $300 judgment has been satisfied. Assume that the federal minimum wage is $4 per hour. Is GMAC entitled to garnish $55 per week from Lorenzo's wages? Why or why not? If not, how much can GMAC garnish? Why?

8. Peebles sues Clement for $4,000 on an overdue debt, and she seeks to attach some of Clement's property without advance notice or a hearing. In accordance with the state attachment statute, Peebles (a) signs an affidavit in which she states her belief that Clement is about to remove his property from the state, (b) obtains an attachment bond in double the amount claimed in the legal action, and (c) files the affidavit and bond with the clerk of the court. The clerk then issues a writ of attachment, and the sheriff levies on some of Clement's nonexempt property. The state statute provides that Clement can (a) recover the property by filing his own bond in double the amount of Peebles' claim; or (b) ask the court to dissolve the attachment, at which point he is entitled to a hearing on the matter. Instead of taking either of these two steps, however, Clement asks the court to dismiss the attachment altogether, claiming that the procedure followed by Peebles violated his constitutional rights. You are the judge. How do you rule on Clement's request?

9. Overmyer Company, a warehouse firm, contracts with Frick Company for the installation of refrigeration equipment, and Overmyer signs a promissory note covering the cost of the work. Frick completes its work, but Overmyer fails to make required payments on the note. Frick then files statutory liens covering some of Overmyer's property. Overmyer wants the liens to be removed and its time for payment on the promissory note to be extended. Attorneys for Overmyer and Frick meet and agree to a new promissory note that includes a clause whereby Overmyer waives its right to notice and a hearing before its property can be attached if it defaults on the new note and is sued by Frick. After the note is signed, Frick releases the liens it had filed. Overmyer defaults on the new note, and Frick sues Overmyer on the note and obtains a writ of attachment against Overmyer's property without advance notice or a hearing. Overmyer applies to the court for relief from the attachment, claiming that its right to due process was violated. How should the court rule? Why?

10. CFI holds two promissory notes signed by Mr. and Mrs. Howard in connection with the Howards' purchase of new furniture. The Howards default on the notes, and CFI repossesses the furniture, sells it, and applies the sale proceeds to the debt. The receipt given to the Howards when their furniture was repossessed has "paid in full" written across the bottom. CFI sues the Howards on the balance it

claims to be still due on the notes, and it is granted a default judgment. The next day, CFI obtains a writ of execution, and the sheriff seizes the Howards' car, after being directed to it by CFI's agent. At the time, Mrs. Howard protested vigorously and produced the "paid in full" receipt, but to no avail. The Howards later claim damages from CFI for the wrongful taking of the car. Did the seizure of the car constitute wrongful attachment?

32 Debtor Relief

32:1 Introduction

"Debtor relief" has many different meanings. It can refer to the rights of a debtor (1) who is billed incorrectly for credit extended to him in the past (see Chapter 28) or (2) whose property has been seized by or for the benefit of his creditors (see Chapters 30 and 31). Debtor relief also involves the options available to a debtor who cannot pay his debts. The more important of these options are discussed in this chapter.

A person who needs debtor relief in the sense the term is used here is often *insolvent.* This means that the value of all the debtor's assets, other than exempt property is less than the total amount of his debts. As an insolvent debtor fails to pay the debts on time, he finds himself under increasing pressure from his creditors. The debtor looks for a way to escape his indebtedness, and as discussed in the rest of this chapter, there are various approaches available to him.

Relief Short of Bankruptcy

32:2 Simple Forms of Debtor Relief

Relatively simple methods by which debtors might be able to find relief include informal agreements with creditors, debt consolidation loans, and professional debt counseling.

Informal Agreements   A debtor who cannot make current payments on his debts can contact his creditors, inform them of his problems, and attempt to work out an acceptable solution. For example, a creditor might allow the payment period to be extended or even reduce the amount of the debt. Although any agreement of this nature is apt to be unenforceable due to lack of consideration, many creditors will accept and perform the agreement if the debtor seems honest and it appears likely that payment will be made eventually.

Debt Consolidation Loans   A debt consolidation loan is a new loan obtained by a debtor and intended to provide him with money to pay off all or the most pressing of his creditors. In essence, the debtor substitutes a single new debt for a number of old ones. The new loan is repayable over a long enough term so that, in theory, the debtor can make the required payments out of his regular income.

The major problem with consolidation loans is that many debtors who require the loans are unable to qualify for them. Moreover, even if a debtor can qualify, the rate of interest might be so high that the debtor only postpones his predicament until the time he defaults on the new loan.

Professional Debt Counseling   In some states a debtor can seek help from a professional debt counselor in preparing a plan for paying his debts. The counselor might contact some of the creditors in the course of working out the plan and might be able to obtain concessions as to time of payment and perhaps even the amount to be paid. The plan sometimes provides for the debtor to make periodic payments to the counselor, who then pays the creditors.

If debt counseling is to work, the debtor must have enough regular income, property that can be sold, or both so that he can make the payments. Also, most debt counselors charge a fee. Therefore, unless one or more creditors can be persuaded to reduce the size of their claims, the debtor ends up paying more than he was obligated to pay before visiting the counselor. It is for this reason that a majority of the states prohibit the offering of certain debt-counseling services on a fee basis.

32:3   Composition with Creditors

The term *composition with creditors* refers to a contractual arrangement between a debtor and at least two of his creditors. The parties enter into an agreement under which the creditors agree to accept less than is actually due, as full satisfaction of the debts owed to them. A single agreement includes both a composition and an extension if it provides for the debtor to pay less than was originally due over a longer period than was originally planned.

Advantages and Disadvantages of Composition   From a debtor's viewpoint, the major advantage of a composition with creditors is that the debtor can retain his property rather than having to give it up at once, as is required under most other debtor relief arrangements. Other advantages are that by not declaring bankruptcy (which is the main alternative to composition), the debtor (1) leaves the bankruptcy option open for possible use at a later time and (2) avoids whatever stigma may be associated with bankruptcy. To creditors, the main advantage of a composition is that because the procedure is relatively simple and does not generate court costs, trustees' fees, and other administrative expenses, more money is available for payment of debts than is available under other arrangements. This advantage is especially important to unsecured creditors since, as discussed later in this chapter, they often receive little or nothing in a bankruptcy proceeding.

The major disadvantage of a composition arrangement is that unless all the debtor's creditors accept and sign the agreement, nonassenting creditors can cause problems. For example, nonassenting unsecured creditors might be able to force the debtor into bankruptcy (see 32:7). In addition, although composition is theoretically available to any debtor, creditors are more receptive to it if the debtor is a business that can be expected to continue as the creditors' customer.

Validity and Effect of Composition Agreement   At least two creditors must sign a composition agreement since the creditors' promise to each other that each will abide by the agreement (for their mutual benefit) constitutes the consideration for it. Perhaps the most important requirement of a valid composition agreement is that all the parties must act in good faith. All signing creditors need not be treated equally, but the treatment of each one must be disclosed and agreed to by all. Thus, for example, if the debtor secretly agrees to give a special advantage to one creditor, the agreement cannot be enforced against the other creditors.

A valid composition agreement is binding (1) on all the signing creditors, between themselves, and (2) between the debtor and each of those creditors. The debts covered by the agreement are discharged as soon as the agreement has been performed, and any new promise by the debtor to pay more on one of those debts requires new consideration. A composition agreement can also be binding on a creditor who, while not having signed the agreement, accepted his share of payments made under it.

EXAMPLE: Pierce, Lynch, and Fenner are Bean's creditors. All four parties prepare a composition agreement that provides for the satisfaction of the debts owed to Pierce, Lynch, and Fenner at the rate of 75 cents on the dollar. At the last minute Fenner decides not to sign the agreement, but Bean pays her in accordance with the agreement anyway, and Fenner keeps that payment. The debt owed to Fenner is now considered to be fully satisfied, and Fenner cannot sue to recover the unpaid part (25 percent) of the original debt owed her.

32:4   Assignment for Creditors

An insolvent debtor might wish to avoid bankruptcy even though he is not able to persuade enough of his creditors to agree to a workable composition arrangement. An option that might be available to this debtor is an *assignment for creditors*, also known as an assignment for the benefit of creditors. In essence, a debtor wishing to make an assignment for creditors transfers all or much of his property to another person, who is called the *trustee*. The trustee then liquidates the property (converts it to cash by selling it) and distributes the cash among the debtor's creditors.

Comparison with Composition Arrangement   An assignment for creditors is similar to a composition arrangement in that it usually allows creditors to receive more than they would in a bankruptcy case. However, it differs from a composition in a number of ways. Significant distinctions are that (1) the assent of all or most creditors is not required, (2) an assignment is a sufficient ground for the debtor's involuntary bankruptcy (see 32:7) and (3) debts are usually satisfied only to the extent of the payments actually made to creditors.

Governing Law   Assignments for creditors developed under the English common law. They are now governed by statute in a number of states, although common-law assignments are also permitted in some of those states. Where a choice exists, most assignments are of the common-law type because they are usually simpler, quicker, and cheaper than statutory assignments. Common-law assignments also impose fewer restrictions on the debtor. For example, a typical state statute (1) requires a detailed disclosure of the debtor's assets and business dealings, (2) limits the choice of the trustee, (3) states how creditors are to be notified and must present their claims, and (4) governs the distributions to the creditors.

Procedure   A debtor who wishes to make an assignment for creditors prepares a written instrument. Among other things, this instrument (1) designates the trustee; (2) describes the property being assigned; (3) identifies the creditors and debts; and (4) within any applicable statutory limits, instructs the trustee as to how distributions to creditors are to be made.

In practice, the trustee is often one of the debtor's creditors. The property that the debtor can assign to the trustee is any property that the debtor could legally sell or give away. Ordinarily, the debtor assigns all of his nonexempt property, although he can assign exempt property as well. The debtor can, of course, assign only whatever interest he has in his property. If, for example, a creditor holds a lien covering some of the property, that lien is usually not affected by the assignment.

 UCC § 9-301 provides a major exception to the above rule concerning lien-holders. A perfected security interest under Article 9 is enforceable against the trustee, consistent with the rule. However, the trustee's rights, in his or her capacity as trustee, are superior to those of someone holding an unperfected interest.[1]

EXAMPLE: Jean operates an electronic repair shop, and Zenith Corporation is one of her creditors. Jean grants Zenith a security interest covering some of her equipment, and Zenith does not take the steps required to perfect its interest. Jean then makes an assignment for creditors, and the

---

[1] The perfection of security interests under UCC Article 9 is discussed in Chapter 29. The priority or ranking of different claims to the same property is discussed in Chapter 30.

property transferred to the trustee includes the equipment covered by the security interest. If Zenith had perfected its interest, the trustee would take the equipment subject to that interest. Since Zenith did not perfect, however, its rights in the equipment are now subordinate to the trustee's rights. For all practical purposes, Zenith has lost its lien.

Once an assignment has been made, the trustee ordinarily liquidates the property and distributes the cash. Administrative expenses (including the trustee's fee) are paid first, and claims against the debtor for taxes are paid next. The remaining cash is available for distribution to the creditors. Secured creditors must normally be paid first. In a common-law assignment, the assignment document can specify the order and extent of each unsecured creditor's participation in the distribution. All unsecured creditors must be treated equally under a typical assignment for creditors statute.

Validity of Assignment   An assignment for creditors generally does not take effect until the trustee and at least some of the debtor's creditors have consented to it. Trustee consent is rarely a problem since the debtor usually obtains it before making the assignment. As for creditors, they are presumed to have consented to the assignment. This means that if an assignment is otherwise valid, it will take effect unless all or at least most of the creditors object to it.

The basic requirement of a valid assignment for creditors is that the debtor act in good faith. In particular, the debtor must not act with intent to hinder or defraud his creditors.

EXAMPLE: Dawes, an insolvent debtor, indicates to his creditors that he is assigning all his nonexempt property to a trustee, for the creditors' benefit. In fact, Dawes only assigns some of that property, and he conceals the remainder of it. Dawes has acted fraudulently, and the assignment can be set aside by a court if one of the creditors applies for that relief.

Effect of Assignment   After an assignment for creditors becomes effective, the debtor cannot revoke it, and he has no further interest in the assigned property. Because of this lack of interest, creditors cannot levy on or garnish the property; as discussed in Chapter 31, attachment, garnishment, and execution are available only with respect to property owned by or owed to the debtor.

Unfortunately for the debtor, an assignment for creditors discharges only those debts that are paid in full by the trustee. Thus, the debtor can emerge with some of his debts untouched and others merely reduced in amount. It is for this reason that assignments for creditors are used primarily by corporations; after all its property has been assigned, a corporation is an empty shell, and its remaining debts are uncollectible.[2]

---

[2] The immunity of shareholders from corporate debts is discussed in Chapter 47.

Bankruptcy

32:5 Introduction to Bankruptcy

Bankruptcy is a statutory procedure by which (1) a debtor places his or her assets under a court's control, after which (2) either the assets are sold for the benefit of creditors or a plan for the debtor's financial rehabilitation is prepared and executed, and (3) the debtor can be discharged from liability on all or some of the unpaid debts. The goals of the bankruptcy laws are to give the debtor a "fresh start" in life, free from debt, and to apply the debtor's property fairly and equitably for the benefit of the creditors.

Governing Law   The United States Constitution [Article I, § 8] grants to Congress the power "to establish . . . uniform laws on the subject of Bankruptcies throughout the United States." The first modern federal bankruptcy act was enacted in 1898. The 1898 act was amended from time to time, and it remains the law today as to bankruptcy cases commenced before October 1, 1979. In 1978 the 1898 act was replaced by the current Bankruptcy Code [11 USC §§ 101 et seq.].

Overview of Bankruptcy Code   The Bankruptcy Code is divided into eight chapters, numbered 1 through 15 (odd numbers only). Chapters 1, 3, and 5 contain general provisions, most of which apply to all bankruptcy cases. Of the remaining five chapters, the important ones for present purposes are Chapters 7, 11, and 13, each of which concerns a different type of bankruptcy case. The distinction between the coverage of these three chapters is discussed throughout the remainder of this part of the book. However, a brief description of the three different types of bankruptcy cases here will make the later discussion easier to understand.

Chapter 7 (liquidation):   Chapter 7 covers what is known as straight bankruptcy. Distinctive features of a Chapter 7 case are that (1) the debtor in effect washes his hands of his financial problems by turning them over to a court and (2) creditors seek payment of their claims primarily from assets that the debtor already has, rather than from the debtor's future earnings. In a Chapter 7 case, the debtor's nonexempt assets are taken from him and liquidated, after which the creditors are paid to the extent possible from the fund created by the *liquidation.* The bankruptcy court can then order that many of the debtor's debts are discharged, even if all the creditors have not been paid.

Chapter 11 (reorganization):   Chapter 11 involves the reorganization and financial rehabilitation of business debtors. It is intended to be attractive to a financially troubled business at a time when effective reorganization of the business is still possible. The business debtor in a Chapter 11 case usually retains possession of its assets. A key feature of a Chapter 11 case is the preparation of a *rehabilitation plan,* which is done under the court's supervision. The plan provides for the continued operation of the business and the payment of all or at least some of its debts over an extended period. Thus, the primary source of payments to creditors is the debtor's future income.

Chapter 13 (adjustment of debts of individual with regular income): Chapter 13 applies only to individual debtors who have limited debts and a regular source of income. Its focus is on getting an individual back on his financial feet rather than salvaging a business. A key feature of a Chapter 13 case is the preparation of a rehabilitation plan by which all or some of the debtor's creditors will be paid, primarily out of the debtor's future income. For the debtor, an attractive feature of Chapter 13 is that if the debtor makes all the payments required under the plan, the court can order the discharge of more of the debts than can be ordered discharged in a Chapter 7 case.

32:6 Bankruptcy Courts and Officers; Creditors and Other Interested Parties

A bankruptcy case is heard by and carried through under the supervision of a bankruptcy judge. Each federal judicial district has its own bankruptcy court.

Trustees The trustee carries out much of the actual administration of most bankruptcy cases. A trustee is required in Chapter 7 and Chapter 13 cases. A trustee is not required in a Chapter 11 case, although the court may appoint a trustee. If there is no trustee in a Chapter 11 case, the debtor remains in possession of the estate and is called a *debtor in possession.*

The trustee's role is to marshal the assets of the debtor and preserve those assets for the benefit of the unsecured creditors. To this end the trustee, or the debtor in possession, has many powers. For example, he or she can sue and be sued and, with the court's approval, can hire attorneys, accountants, and other professionals to assist as needed. The trustee's fee and the fees of others hired by the trustee in that capacity are paid out of the estate. Since these payments are made before any creditors can be paid, the fees reduce the amount that the creditors receive.

Creditors Under the Bankruptcy Code a creditor is someone (including a government entity such as the Internal Revenue Service) holding against the debtor a claim that arose before what is known in a bankruptcy case as the "order for relief." Persons not falling within this definition are not "creditors" under the Bankruptcy Code, even though they have valid claims against the estate. For example, a person who sells goods or services to the trustee after the order for relief is not a "creditor"; his claim falls within the category of administrative expenses.

Committees In a Chapter 7 case the creditors can elect a committee of three to eleven unsecured creditors to consult with and make recommendations to the trustee. The purpose of the committee is to ease communications between the debtor, the trustee, and the creditors. In a Chapter 11 case there must be at least one committee of unsecured creditors, and the court appoints it.

Additional committees are also permitted, to represent various creditor interests.

Custodians Another class of persons recognized in the Bankruptcy Code is referred to collectively as *custodians*. A custodian is someone (other than the debtor) who has possession of all or most of the debtor's property. An example is the trustee under an assignment for creditors. A custodian must usually deliver the property to the bankruptcy trustee, although the court can allow the custodian to remain in possession if that would better serve the creditors' interests.

Parties in Interest The term *party in interest* refers to any person, group, or entity having an interest in a bankruptcy case. The debtor, the trustee, all creditors, and creditors' committees are all parties in interest.

32:7 Commencement of Bankruptcy Case

A bankruptcy case is commenced by filing a petition with the bankruptcy court, specifying the particular chapter (Chapter 7, 11, or 13) under which relief is requested. The case can be commenced either voluntarily or involuntarily. A voluntary case is one in which the debtor files the petition. In an involuntary case, the petition is filed by one or more creditors.

In a voluntary case, the filing of the petition constitutes the order for relief. In an involuntary case the order for relief, if any, comes later on, after the court has decided not to dismiss the case.

Eligible Debtors Whether relief under a particular chapter of the Bankruptcy Code is available to a given debtor depends on that debtor's status. With the exception of insurance companies, banks, and several other specific businesses, any person can be a debtor under Chapter 7 or 11. The term "person" in this sense means an individual, a partnership, or a corporation.

Eligibility for Chapter 13 relief is more restricted. The relief is available only to individuals other than stockbrokers or commodity brokers. The individual (or couple, if a husband and wife file together) must have less than $100,000 in unsecured debts and less than $350,000 in secured debts. In addition, the individual must have a regular source of income that is large enough to allow a substantial payment to creditors under a Chapter 13 plan.

EXAMPLE: Until recently, John earned $125,000 per year as a business executive. He is currently unemployed, however, and the prospects for a new job comparable to his old one are poor. Mary, his wife, has never worked outside their home and has no marketable skills. John and Mary's unsecured debt is $75,000 and their secured debt is $357,000. John and Mary cannot file under Chapter 13. Not only is their secured indebtedness too high, but they also lack a regular source of income.

Involuntary Cases An involuntary bankruptcy case can be commenced only under Chapter 7 or 11, and against an eligible debtor. There are, however, several restrictions as to allowable debtors in addition to those discussed above. For example, an involuntary petition cannot be filed against a farmer. There are also restrictions as to the creditors who can file an involuntary petition. If the debtor has 12 or more different creditors, any three or more creditors who together hold unsecured claims of at least $5,000 can file. If there are fewer than 12 creditors, any one creditor who has an unsecured claim of at least $5,000 can file. In determining whether there are fewer than 12 creditors, creditors who are the debtor's employees or are insiders (persons or entities closely related to the debtor) are not counted.

EXAMPLE: Washington Corporation is indebted to Adams, Jefferson, Madison, and nine others, one of whom, Polk, is the president of Washington Corporation. Since Polk is an insider, he would not be counted as a creditor for filing purposes. Therefore, an involuntary petition can be filed by less than three of the creditors. The unsecured debts owed to the named creditors other than Polk are as follows: Adams is owed $6,000, Jefferson $4,000, and Madison $2,000. Adams can file alone, and Jefferson and Madison can file together. If it is only Jefferson who wants to force Washington into bankruptcy, Jefferson must persuade one or more other creditors holding at least $1,000 in unsecured claims to join him on the petition.

 Even though a petition for involuntary bankruptcy has been filed, the debtor can continue to use, acquire, and dispose of his property until the court orders otherwise. The court can, however, appoint a temporary trustee if that is necessary to preserve the debtor's property.

The debtor can oppose the involuntary bankruptcy petition by filing an answer to it. If no answer is filed, the court orders relief under Chapter 7 or 11, as requested in the petition. If the debtor does file an answer, the court must hold a hearing to determine whether either of two prescribed grounds for involuntary bankruptcy exists. The first ground is that the debtor is "generally not paying" his debts as they become due. The other ground is that, within 120 days before the petition was filed, a custodian was appointed or took charge of all or most of the debtor's property.

 If neither ground for involuntary bankruptcy is shown to exist in the hearing on an involuntary petition, the court can order the petitioning creditors to pay the debtor for legal expenses and a reasonable attorney's fee. In addition, any petitioner who is found to have acted in bad faith (with evil intent toward the debtor) can be ordered to pay damages to the debtor.

32:8   Dismissal of Bankruptcy Case

The bankruptcy court has jurisdiction over all matters arising in or related to bankruptcy cases. The court is not required to accept that jurisdiction in any given case, however. Instead, it can dismiss the petition. For example, if a debtor is negotiating an out-of-court settlement with most of her creditors and there are only several dissenting creditors who have filed a petition, the court might dismiss the petition on the ground that the parties' interests would be better served in that way. A bankruptcy case can also be dismissed "for cause." For example, the court can dismiss a Chapter 13 or voluntary Chapter 7 case because of the debtor's unreasonable delays or because the debtor failed to pay required legal fees. Among the prescribed grounds for dismissal of a Chapter 11 case is a continuing loss to or reduction of the estate, coupled with no reasonable likelihood that the business debtor can be financially rehabilitated.

The dismissal of a case operates to return everything to its status before the case was commenced. For example, if a custodian has delivered property to the trustee and the case is dismissed, that property is returned to the custodian. Under some circumstances a case filed under one chapter of the Bankruptcy Code can be converted to a case under a different chapter.

32:9   The Bankruptcy Estate; Exemptions

The bankruptcy estate is created automatically on the commencement of a bankruptcy case. It consists of all property and property interests that the debtor owned at the time of commencement. Among the many types of property or property interests included in the estate are (1) real property, and liens on real property, such as a mortgage held by the debtor as mortgagor; (2) unpaid wages; (3) tangible personal property; (4) rights to sue other people; (5) interests in patents or trademarks; and (6) the right to a tax refund.

It is immaterial that a specific property item is covered by a lien or is only partly owned by the debtor. For example, if a debtor and his brother are equal co-owners of a house on which there is a mortgage, the debtor's half-interest in the house is included in the estate. Also included is any property the estate acquires after the case commences. For example, if a bankruptcy petition is filed on August 1 and the estate includes corporate stock, dividends paid on the stock after August 1 go to the estate. In addition, the estate includes (1) all property that is delivered to the trustee by a custodian, (2) all property that the trustee obtains through exercise of his power to avoid prepetition transfers, and (3) some property that the debtor acquires after filing the petition.

Exemptions   A basic purpose of the Bankruptcy Code is to give debtors a fresh start. An individual debtor can retain basic necessities by filing a list of them that he claims to be exempt. Each listed item automatically becomes exempt unless a party in interest objects, in which event the court determines the exempt status of that item. Once property is exempt, it is not subject to creditors' claims with respect to most debts arising before the case was commenced.

Any individual debtor can claim available exemptions under *both* general state law (see Chapter 31) and federal law other than the Bankruptcy Code. Examples of property that is exempt under federal nonbankruptcy law are Social Security benefits and veterans' benefits. Some debtors have the option of claiming instead the exemptions set forth in the Bankruptcy Code itself. These exemptions include

- Up to $7,500 for debtor's equity (value, less total amount of liens) in homestead (main residence);
- Up to $1,200 for motor vehicle;
- Up to $200 per item for household furnishings and goods, clothing, appliances, books, and many other consumer goods (property held for personal, family, or household use);
- Up to $400, plus unused portion of homestead exemption, for *any* property;
- Up to $750 for professional books or tools of trade;
- Reasonable alimony or child-support payments received by debtor.

For purposes of the federal exemption scheme, the value of any property item is that item's fair market value. Obviously, a debtor who has a choice will select the exemption scheme that benefits him the most. To give the states some control over exemptions claimed by their citizens, the Bankruptcy Code provides that each state can forbid its citizens from selecting the federal scheme.

If a husband and wife file a bankruptcy petition together, *each* spouse can exercise the exemption right as to his or her property. Unless state law bars selection of the Bankruptcy Code exemption scheme, one spouse can select the Bankruptcy Code scheme while the other claims exemptions under state law and federal nonbankruptcy law.

Debtor's Power to Avoid Certain Liens   An individual debtor might own property that could be claimed to be exempt if it were not covered by a lien. For example, before the bankruptcy case was commenced, a creditor might have sued the debtor and obtained a judicial lien[3] on property that, while not exempt under state law, could be claimed as exempt under the Bankruptcy Code. The debtor can avoid (have set aside) any judicial lien on that property. He can also avoid any nonpossessory, non-purchase-money security interest[4] covering certain items if the lien of the security interest prevents the property from being claimed as exempt. This right applies to professional books, tools of trade, and prescribed health aids, and to many, but not all, types of consumer goods.

In a Chapter 7 case the individual debtor has a *right to redeem*. In essence, if consumer goods have been (1) exempted or (2) abandoned by the trustee (see 32:14), the debtor can avoid a lien on the property by paying the lienholder the value of the property.

---

[3] A judicial lien is an interest in property arising from judicial process. An example is an attachment lien, discussed in Chapter 31.

[4] A security interest is nonpossessory if the debtor, rather than the creditor, is in possession of the property. The interest is a non-purchase-money one if it was *not* acquired (1) in connection with the sale of the property covered by the interest and (2) by either (a) the lender whose loan was used to buy the property or (b) the seller. For example, if a person buying a new car on credit is required to give the car dealer one security interest covering the car and another covering the person's household furniture and appliances, both security interests are nonpossessory, but only the interest covering the furniture and appliances is a non-purchase-money one.

A debtor's waiver of his right to avoid a lien or security interest, or to redeem property, is unenforceable in a bankruptcy case. Also unenforceable under some circumstances is a debtor's waiver of his right to claim an allowable exemption. Therefore, a creditor should not rely on such a waiver.

A well-advised insolvent debtor may use the state and federal exemptions to shelter as many assets as possible from creditors' claims in bankruptcy. If a debtor plans carefully, he may exchange non-exempt assets for exempt assets in advance of bankruptcy. When this happens, creditors often seek to avoid the exemption on the ground that the debtor has acted fraudulently. As the following case illustrates, the federal bankruptcy courts consistently have upheld the debtor's right to acquire exempt assets in anticipation of bankruptcy.

In Re Levine
40 BR 76 (1984)
United States Bankruptcy Court, S.D. Florida

FACTS: Debtor borrowed $90,000 on a line of credit from Bank to invest in a home reconstruction project. The loan was secured by a mortgage on Debtor's personal residence. All funds invested by Debtor in the project were derived from drawing down the line of credit. When Debtor anticipated possible personal bankruptcy, he persuaded his partner in the investment project to buy him out for $100,000. Debtor then used the $100,000 to repay Bank and reduce the line of credit secured by Debtor's personal residence. When Debtor declared bankruptcy he claimed the entire value of his residence as homestead, which was permissible under state law.

ISSUE: Can the trustee in bankruptcy impose a lien on Debtor's homestead property because Debtor paid a loan secured by the property with non-exempt assets on the eve of bankruptcy?

RESULT: No. Such an exchange of non-exempt for exempt property does not constitute fraud on the creditors.

REASONING:

*   *   *

The homestead exemption law is found in the Florida Constitution Article X, Section 4:

> There shall be exempt from forced sale under process of any court, and no
> judgment, decree, or execution shall be alien thereon, . . . the following
> property owned by head of a family: (1) a homestead, . . .

The legislative intent of this language is unambiguous: "There shall be
exempt." . . . Both the Supreme Court of Florida and the Florida Legislature have deemed the homestead exemption to be sacred, strongly and
emphatically dictating that it is not to be tampered with. The sanctity of
this exemption in Florida is reflected in numerous decisions. . . .

Although the Florida Courts have recognized limited exceptions permitting a violation of the homestead protection, the exceptions are
strictly construed. They are uniformly an equitable attempt to rectify
otherwise heinous and unjust circumstances. In imposing an equitable
lien on otherwise exempt property, there is generally a finding of "rep-
rehensible conduct," which describes the action giving rise to the need
for the equitable remedy, such as the acquisition of exempt property by
the use of tortiously acquired funds.

For example, in [one case] the Defendant, an employee of a bread
company, embezzled funds from his employer and placed those funds
into his homestead prior to filing bankruptcy. . . .

In the final analysis, the Court must determine whether on its face, a
pre-bankruptcy transfer of property from non-exempt to exempt status
constitutes a fraud on creditors or is a transfer made with intent to hinder,
delay or defraud them. In that regard, the case law is almost universal in
favor and recognition of this right to engage in such pre-bankruptcy
planning. The legal authority for this position is found to exist in jurisdictions throughout the country and represents the overwhelming weight
of authority.

In [a 1983 bankruptcy case], the Court held:

> Before the Bankruptcy Code was adopted in 1978 it had been urged that
> property obtained in such last minute conversions be ineligible for exemption. . . .
> The Code however, adopts the position that the conversion of non-exempt to
> exempt property, without more, will not deprive the debtor of the exemption
> to which he would otherwise be entitled. . . . The result which would obtain if
> debtors were not allowed to convert property into allowable exempt property
> would be extremely harsh, especially in those jurisdictions where the exemp-
> tion allowance is minimal. . . .

The Trustee argues that the mere act of converting property from nonexempt to exempt status is a badge of fraud and is prohibited. This Court
does not agree. To make such a conclusion would require an implication
of fraud. If it is generally held to be legitimate, how can this Court imply
from the transfer an intent to defraud? . . .

The cases cited by the Trustee do nothing to alter this Court's conclusion with respect to the weight of authority on this issue. . . .

Further, this Court does not agree . . . that the congressional intent
contained in the legislative history behind § 522 should be disregarded,

in light of the wealth of case law to the contrary. This Court believes the statement contained in the legislative history to § 522 was based upon Congress' recognition that the transfer of assets from non-exempt to exempt is a recognized and approved method of pre-bankruptcy planning. . . .

The other cases cited by the Trustee are all easily distinguished and do not support a contrary view. . . .

In conclusion, the Trustee has failed to demonstrate through evidence in this case a factual scenario that constitutes a fraud sufficient to warrant an equitable lien or a finding of fraud under § 548 of the Bankruptcy Code. When reduced to its simplest form, the Trustee has attempted to convince this Court that a pre-bankruptcy transfer of nonexempt to exempt property is an ipso facto fraud and an intent to hinder and delay creditors. To accept that proposition this court would be required to ignore the substantial body of Florida law, together with the well reasoned opinions of the various other courts throughout this country. The Trustee has failed to show a right to relief in this cause and therefore judgment shall be entered for the Defendant. . . .

Weaver, Bankruptcy Judge.

32:10   Administration of Bankruptcy Estate

After a bankruptcy case has commenced, the debtor must file a list of his creditors with the court. Usually, he must also file a schedule showing his assets and debts, and a statement about his financial affairs. The list and schedule are used as the basis for a notice concerning the case. The notice is sent to each creditor. After notice has been given, the trustee schedules a meeting that each creditor can attend in person or by sending an agent, such as an attorney. There are frequently other meetings as well. For example, an unsecured creditors' committee in a Chapter 7 case might meet informally with the trustee to discuss the administration of the estate.

The debtor is required to cooperate with the trustee in all respects. Thus, the debtor must surrender to the trustee all estate property and related documents, and he must appear at the meeting of creditors. At the meeting, the debtor must answer relevant questions directed to him by the trustee or by any creditor. If an individual debtor fails to cooperate as required, the court can deny granting a discharge of his debts.

Duties of Trustee   The trustee or debtor in possession must disclose any information about the estate and its administration that a party in interest requests, unless the court orders otherwise. The trustee (but not a debtor in possession) must also investigate certain aspects of the debtor's affairs. The scope of this investigation is limited to financial affairs in Chapter 7 and most

Chapter 13 cases, but it is broader in a Chapter 11 case and a Chapter 13 case in which the debtor conducts a business.

One of the trustee's primary duties in a Chapter 7 case is to collect all the estate property and liquidate it. The debtor's duty to give up property in his possession has already been mentioned. To assist the trustee in obtaining other property, the Bankruptcy Code requires that most estate property in someone else's possession when the petition is filed be delivered to the trustee. If the property cannot be delivered, then its value must be. This requirement extends not only to custodians (who hold all or most of the debtor's property), but also to others holding any property of value. Generally, any debt owed to the estate must also be paid to the trustee. The trustee also has two years after the filing of the petition in which to exercise any right to sue that has passed to the estate. In addition, the court can order an attorney or accountant who has information about the debtor's property or financial affairs to disclose certain of that information to the trustee.

In a Chapter 11 or 13 case the trustee does not usually liquidate the estate property; the purpose of the proceeding is to rehabilitate the debtor. However, the trustee must obtain possession of the property in the manner discussed above if he is to assess and administer the estate properly.

Trustee's Use of Estate Property   The court can authorize the temporary continuation of the debtor's business in a Chapter 7 case. In contrast, in a Chapter 11 or 13 case the debtor's business can be continued *unless* the court orders otherwise. A trustee or debtor in possession who is continuing a business has the right to use, sell, or lease most estate property in the ordinary course of that business. This right is superior to any provision in a contract or lease that would cause a debtor's interest in property to be terminated or modified because of the debtor's being the subject of a bankruptcy proceeding. This means that a contract or lease provision of this type is unenforceable against a trustee or debtor in possession.

32:11   Automatic Stay; Relief from Stay

As soon as a bankruptcy petition is filed, a number of acts and proceedings involving the debtor or his property are automatically stayed, or postponed. Included among the acts and proceedings that are stayed by the filing of a bankruptcy petition are

- Commencement or continuation of any civil action against the debtor
- Enforcement against the debtor or estate property of any judgment obtained before the bankruptcy petition was filed
- Any act to obtain possession of estate property
- Any act to create, perfect, or enforce any lien against estate property
- Any act to collect a claim against the debtor if the claim arose before the petition was filed
- In a Chapter 13 case, most efforts to collect on any debt for consumer goods from a codebtor (other person, often a family member, who is also liable on the debt)

The purpose of the *automatic stay* is to give the debtor a breathing spell from his creditors by stopping all their efforts to collect from or harass him. Bear in mind, though, that some acts or proceedings are *not* covered by the automatic stay. These include (1) the commencement or continuation of a criminal prosecution against the debtor, (2) the collection of alimony or child support from other than estate property (such as from the debtor's wages), and (3) the perfection of certain security interests within the ten-day grace period provided by UCC § 9-301 (see 30:4).

Relief from Stay   An automatic stay is terminated by dismissal of the bankruptcy case. Also, any party in interest can request the court to grant relief from a stay. The court has 30 days in which to act on the request, and it can hold a hearing on the matter. If, within that 30-day period, the court does not order the stay to be continued, the stay terminates as to the requesting party.

 The court decides whether a particular proposal for modifying a stay or providing other relief will give the party in interest adequate protection. However, it is the trustee (or debtor in possession) who actually submits the proposal to the court. A failure to submit a proposal can result in the court's granting broader relief to the petitioning creditor than it might otherwise have done.

32:12   Bankruptcy Trustee's Avoidance Powers

One of the most significant powers held by the trustee in a bankruptcy case is the power to avoid several types of transactions that occurred before the bankruptcy petition was filed. These *avoidance powers* extend to *prepetition transactions* that were both voluntary and involuntary from the debtor's viewpoint. The powers exist to allow the trustee to nullify the effect of transactions that, on the eve of bankruptcy, operated to dissipate the estate. Among the general types of transactions that the trustee can avoid are (1) transactions that certain other creditors could avoid, and (2) *preferential transfers.*

Transactions Avoidable by Other Creditors   11 USC § 544(a) is known as the *strong-arm clause.* Under it, the trustee is given the rights of several types of creditors, the most important being a creditor who has a judicial lien (such as an attachment lien, as discussed in 31:6) on the debtor's property on the date the bankruptcy petition was filed. There does not have to be an *actual* creditor or an actual lien in the case; the trustee's status is that of a hypothetical creditor. He is simply given whatever rights and powers a judicial lienholder would have under the governing state law. The strong-arm power is primarily intended to avoid prepetition transfers of unperfected security interests.

EXAMPLE: On September 1, Acme Corporation granted to Delta, one of Acme's creditors, a security interest covering Acme's inventory. On October 1, Acme filed a bankruptcy petition, and as of that date Delta had made no attempt to perfect its security interest. Since a judicial lien has priority over an unperfected security interest under state law, which is UCC Article 9, the trustee can avoid the security interest, meaning that the interest is invalid against the trustee. The result would be the same if Delta had attempted to perfect its interest but had done so improperly.

Note in the following case that the trustee's power to avoid an unperfected security interest is independent of the trustee's knowledge of the interest.

In Re Measure Control Devices, Inc.
48 BR 613 (1985)
United States Bankruptcy Court, E.D. New York

FACTS: Prior to instituting bankruptcy proceedings, Measure Control purchased an injection molding machine and granted a purchase money security interest to Creative Bath Products ("Creditor"). Creditor filed a UCC-1 financing statement in the office of the Nassau County Clerk. There is no record of a filing of the financing statement in the office of the New York Secretary of State in Albany. Following the sale of Measure Control's assets, trustee sought to void Creditor's interest in the proceeds of the sale on the ground that its security interest was not properly perfected. Creditor argued that since the trustee had actual notice of the Nassau County filing prior to the sale, its security interest was perfected on principles of "good faith" as provided by UCC § 9-401(2).

ISSUE: Does the trustee's knowledge of the existence of the security interest prior to the sale preclude her from avoiding it on the ground that it was not perfected under state law?

RESULT: No. According to federal bankruptcy statutes an unperfected security interest is null and void against a trustee in bankruptcy.

REASONING:

*   *   *

The injection molding machine listed as collateral in the security agreement was used or bought for use primarily in the debtor's business. It is thus classified as equipment within the meaning of UCC § 9-109(2). To perfect an interest in equipment, UCC § 9-401(1)(c) is explicit in requiring a UCC-1 financing statement be filed with New York's Secretary of State, as well as with the applicable County Clerk. UCC § 9-401(1)(c) states in pertinent part:

(1) The proper place to file [a financing statement] in order to perfect a security interest [in equipment] is as follows:

* * * *

(c) in the department of state and in addition, if the debtor has a place of business in this state and in only one county of this state, also in the office of the filing officer of such county. . . .

Section 544(a) of the Bankruptcy Code (the "strong arm" clause), allows a trustee in bankruptcy to avoid liens and security interests against the debtor's estate which were not properly perfected under state law before the debtor filed for bankruptcy.

Section 544(a) states in pertinent part:

(a) The trustee shall have, as of the commencement of the case, and *without regard to any knowledge of the trustee* or of any creditor, the rights and powers of, or may avoid any transfer of property of the debtor or any obligation incurred by the debtor that is avoidable by—

(1) A creditor that extends credit to the debtor at the time of the commencement of the case, and that obtains, at such time and with respect to such credit, . . . a judicial lien whether or not such a creditor exists. . . . (Emphasis added).

The trustee is thus, accorded by statute, the status of a lien creditor without notice. . . .

The creditor here, did not file a UCC–1 financing statement with the Secretary of State. Accordingly, its security interest was not perfected within the meaning of UCC § 9–401(1)(c). . . . Nevertheless, the creditor contends that since the filing in the County was made in good faith and since the trustee had actual notice of the filing its security interest was perfected by virtue of UCC § 9–401(2). That section provides in pertinent part:

A filing which is made in good faith in an improper place or *not in all of the places required* by this section is nevertheless . . . *effective* with regard to collateral covered by the financing statement *against any person who has knowledge* of the contents of such financing statement. (Emphasis added).

This argument is apparently addressed to the court's equitable powers which pursuant to § 105 of the Bankruptcy Code are, indeed, broad. But, § 105 does not give bankruptcy courts the authority to contravene statutory provisions of the Bankruptcy Code. . . . UCC § 9–401(2) is inapplicable to this case since the Bankruptcy Code explicitly gives the trustee the status of a lien creditor without notice.

In summary, since the creditor's security interest was never perfected, it is null and void as to the trustee in bankruptcy. The trustee can, therefore, avoid the lien under § 544(a). Consequently, it should be stricken as a lien against the proceeds of the sale of the asset in question. . . .

Duberstein, Chief Judge.

Preferential Transfers [11 USC § 547]   In essence, a prepetition transfer is perferential if it gives the transferee an advantage over other creditors. The Bankruptcy Code gives the trustee the power to avoid certain prepetition transfers even if they were legally valid. This power, when exercised, promotes the equal treatment of creditors. Its existence is intended to discourage creditors from racing to the courthouse to dismember a debtor during his slide into bankruptcy. For example, a creditor is less likely to obtain an attachment lien against a debtor who is about to file a bankruptcy petition if the creditor knows that the trustee can avoid the attachment as a preferential transfer.

As the following case indicates, a transfer is avoidable as being preferential only if prescribed requirements are met. Note the court's discussion about (1) a debtor's presumed insolvency before a bankruptcy petition is filed and (2) the question of whether the act of perfecting a security interest is an avoidable transfer.

In Re Butler
3 BR 182 (1980)
United States Bankruptcy Court, E.D. Tennessee

FACTS: Butler, the debtor, filed a bankruptcy petition on November 19, 1979. Earlier, Butler had granted a security interest in a bulldozer he owned to a creditor, the defendant. The creditor perfected its interest on November 1, 1979. The trustee, wishing to sell the bulldozer free of the creditor's lien, commenced a proceeding to avoid that lien.

ISSUE: Was the creditor's perfection of the security interest only 18 days before the debtor's bankruptcy a preference voidable by the trustee?

RESULT: Yes. All of the elements of a voidable preference were present.

REASONING:

*   *   *

It is the trustee's contention that defendant's perfection of its security interest just eighteen days before the filing of the bankruptcy case constitutes a preferential transfer and is voidable under [the Bankruptcy Code].

The code allows the trustee to recover transfers, either securing or paying antecedent debt, within a prescribed period of time before the bankruptcy case. It replaces [complex provisions of the 1898 act].

The six elements of a preference under [the Bankruptcy Code] are:

(1) a transfer of property of the debtor;
(2) to or for the benefit of a creditor;
(3) for or on account of an antecedent debt;
(4) made while the debtor was insolvent;
(5) made within 90 days before the date of the filing of a petition; and
(6) that enables the creditor to receive more than he would have received if the transfer had not been made and the case were a liquidation case under Chapter 7.

There was a requirement [in the 1898 act] that the creditor receiving the preference have reasonable cause to believe that the debtor was insolvent.

Congress in its wisdom has chosen to eliminate the reasonable-case-to-believe test from the ordinary preference situation. The goal of equality of distribution among creditors becomes paramount. Whether or not a preferred creditor had knowledge of the debtor's insolvency, with one exception which is not relevant in this proceeding, will no longer be relevant in a proceeding to avoid a preference.

Congress has simplified the trustee's burden in preference actions in another way. [The Bankruptcy Code] grants the trustee a presumption of insolvency during the 90 days before bankruptcy. Under [the 1898 act], proof of insolvency was always difficult. Reconstructing the debtor's books and records was never an easy matter. Yet it was unusual when a debtor was not insolvent for the 90 days before bankruptcy.

The presumption of insolvency in the Code recognizes this, but permits the creditor against whom the action is pending to come forward with evidence of solvency. . . .

Under [the Bankruptcy Code] a transfer is deemed to be made when it takes effect between the parties, if it is perfected no more than 10 days after it takes effect. If it is perfected more than 10 days after it takes effect, the transfer is deemed made when it is perfected. . . .

In the present proceeding the court finds that "transfer" of property of the debtor occurred within 90 days of the filing of the petition. It was for the benefit of defendant and involved an antecedent debt.

The creditor put on no proof to overcome the presumption of debtor's insolvency. The proof indicated, in fact, that debtor was insolvent. The proof further showed that in a Chapter 7 case the only asset for creditors will be the proceeds from the sale of the dozer. Defendant will receive a pro rata share. The "transfer" would enable the defendant to get all of the proceeds. This would be "more" than he would receive in a liquidation case under chapter 7. . . .

Kelly, Bankruptcy Judge.

The Bankruptcy Code also lists various transfers that the trustee *cannot* avoid as being preferential. Several of these exceptions involve situations in which, because the debtor received something of value at the time of transfer, the estate suffered no net loss. Other exceptions exist because of the importance of certain creditor interests. For example, the debtor's payment of a debt incurred in the ordinary course of business is often not an avoidable preference if the debt was incurred no more than 45 days before the date of payment. In addition, the trustee's avoidance powers may be limited by any state law that, in effect, allows a grace period for the perfection of interests in property.

EXAMPLE: Abbott Corporation sells a piece of equipment to Costello Company on credit and reserves a security interest in the equipment. The equipment is delivered to Costello on July 10. UCC Article 9 provides that if Abbott perfects its interest by July 20, Abbott's interest is superior to that of a lien creditor whose lien arose between July 10 and the date of perfection. If Costello files a bankruptcy petition on July 13 and Abbott perfects its interest on July 19, the trustee cannot use the strong-arm clause to avoid the interest.

Another important limit on the trustee's avoidance powers concerns the right of one who sells goods to a debtor on credit to reclaim those goods if the debtor was insolvent when he received the goods. For example, UCC Article 2 gives the seller the right to reclaim under this circumstance, as long as he does so within ten days after the debtor received the goods. If, in addition to complying with the ten-day requirement, the seller demands reclamation in writing, the Bankruptcy Code allows the seller to reclaim the goods even though a bankruptcy petition concerning the debtor has been filed in the meantime.

Finally, although the trustee can generally recover the property involved after a transfer has been avoided, he cannot do so if the property has passed from the original transferee to one who, in essence, paid for the transfer to him and was unaware that the prior transfer could have been avoided by the trustee.

32:13   Creditor's Claims Under Bankruptcy Code

The Bankruptcy Code classifies creditors' claims as being either secured or unsecured. A claim can be secured only if the creditor holds a lien on property of the bankruptcy estate. Here, "lien" means a judicial lien, a statutory lien, or a security interest.[5] A given claim is considered to be secured *only* to the extent of the value of the property covered by the lien when the bankruptcy petition was filed.

EXAMPLE: A secured creditor is owed $100,000 by the debtor, but the value of the estate property covered by the security interest was only $60,000

---

[5] Judicial and statutory liens are discussed in Chapter 31. Security interests are discussed in Chapters 29 and 30 (personal property) and 36 (real property).

when the debtor's bankruptcy petition was filed. As far as the bankruptcy case is concerned, the creditor has a secured claim for $60,000. The remaining $40,000 of the debt is treated as an unsecured claim.

It is possible for a lienholder's *entire* claim to be treated as an unsecured claim in a bankruptcy case. This situation occurs if the lien has been avoided.

Presentation and Allowance of Claims   After a bankruptcy proceeding has commenced, each creditor can present his claim against the estate by filing a document, known as a *proof of claim*, in which the claim is described. In a Chapter 11 case, the list of creditors filed by the debtor is treated as a proof of claim covering most claims. If a creditor fails to file a proof of claim, the debtor can file one on the creditor's behalf; the debtor's reason for doing so is that otherwise the claim might not be discharged.

 In a Chapter 7 case there can be no distribution to a creditor who has not filed a proof of claim (or had one filed on his behalf). While filing is not required, a creditor should usually file in a Chapter 7 case unless there is no prospect of receiving a distribution from the estate.

Generally, only the holders of *allowed* claims can participate in distributions from the bankruptcy estate. An allowed claim is one that the court recognizes as being valid. Filing a proof of claim (or listing a claim in a Chapter 11 case) automatically leads to that claim being allowed unless a party in interest objects. Ordinarily, if there is an objection, the court holds a hearing on the matter. At the hearing the court determines the amount of the claim and allows or disallows the claim in whole or in part.

The court must disallow most claims that are unforceable against the debtor, such as claims that are barred by the state statute of limitations. A claim must also be disallowed to the extent that it can be offset against a debt owed by the creditor to the debtor. Thus, for example, if Williams, the debtor in a bankruptcy case, owes Jensen $500, but Jensen owes Williams $100, Jensen's claim for $500 will be reduced to $400 before being allowed. Note that the allowance of a creditor's claim does not necessarily mean that the creditor will receive *any* parment, let alone payment of her entire claim. The allowance merely means that the creditor might receive something and, in effect, sets an upper limit on what she can receive.

32:14   Distributions Under Chapter 7

The policy of the Bankruptcy Code is to treat creditors equally, but examination of the rules governing distributions to creditors reveals the Orwellian nature of the equality: some creditors are clearly more equal than others. In a Chapter 7 case, secured claims must be satisfied first. Whatever remains in the estate is paid to unsecured creditors, but some types of unsecured claims must be paid before others.

Secured Claims   Under bankruptcy law a claim is secured only to the extent of the value of the property covered by the lien. A secured claim—or the secured part of a claim—is fully satisfied in a bankruptcy case if the property covered by the lien is released to the lienholder or if the lienholder is allowed to pursue the nonbankruptcy remedies available under state law. The result is that a secured claim can have been satisfied before the distribution phase of a Chapter 7 case. For example, property of little value to the estate might have been abandoned to the lienholder.[6] Or, the lienholder might have been permitted to enforce the lien by way of relief from the automatic stay.

To the extent that the secured claims have not already been disposed of in the above or other, related ways, the first step in the Chapter 7 distribution process is settlement of those claims. Ordinarily, the trustee either delivers the property covered by the liens to the lienholding creditors or, more often, sells the property and distributes the sale proceeds, less costs of the sale, to those creditors. When the trustee sells the property, he usually sells it free of the creditor's liens; the Bankruptcy Code allows him to do this under prescribed circumstances.

Unsecured Claims   The distribution to creditors holding unsecured claims would be simple if the assets remaining in the estate after the satisfaction of secured claims were merely divided among the unsecured creditors pro rata (in proportion to the amount of the creditors' claims). However, the Bankruptcy Code recognizes special circumstances that warrant exceptions to this policy. The exceptions are achieved primarily by means of a system of priorities. Under this system *all* higher ranking claims must be paid in full before anything can be paid on lower ranking claims.

The six types of priority claims, listed in their order of rank, are briefly described as follows:

- Administrative expenses
- Debts incurred after an involuntary petition was filed, but before the order for relief
- Certain wages owed to the debtor's employees, up to $2,000 per employee
- Certain contributions to the debtor's employee benefit plans
- Prepetition deposits of money for the purchase or lease of undelivered consumer goods or services
- Federal, state, and local taxes

Another set of priorities governs the distribution of the money, if any, that is left in the estate after all priority unsecured claims have paid in full. Again, higher ranking claims are paid in full before lower ranking claims receive anything, and distributions are made pro rata for claims of a given rank if full

---

[6]   An example of property having little value to the estate is a machine that, although worth $1,500, is covered by a lien to secure a $2,000 debt. As discussed in the next paragraph of the text, since the lienholder would get the machine or the proceeds from its sale in any event, the trustee saves time and administrative expense by merely abandoning the machine (giving up the estate's interest in it), which allows the creditor to enforce its lien.

payment cannot be made. The ranking under this final set of priorities is as follows, in the order listed:

- Allowed unsecured claims for which the creditors filed proofs of claim in time, or had acceptable excuses for filing late
- Allowed unsecured claims for which proofs of claim were filed late and without acceptable excuse
- Interest on claims already paid, for the period between the filing of the petition and the date of payment of the claims

The debtor is entitled to any money left over after all the above claims have been paid. As a practical matter, unsecured creditors whose claims are not entitled to priority usually receive little or nothing on their claims in a Chapter 7 case. Thus, there is almost never anything for the debtor.

32:15   Chapter 11 Plans

The goal of a Chapter 11 case is to restructure the debtor's finances so that the business can be continued and creditors can be paid in full, or at least in part, over an extended period. The restructuring is done through a plan that governs the creditors' rights with respect to the debtor and the debtor's property. When a plan is approved and in place, all creditors are bound by its terms. Depending on the terms of the plan, the debtor gets back all of its property to use in running the reorganized business.

During the 120 days after the order for relief is filed, the debtor in possession has the exclusive right to propose a plan to the court. Under some circumstances, such as when a court appoints a trustee, other parties may propose Chapter 11 plans for the debtor. After the plan is filed, its terms are disclosed to all the creditors, and their acceptance of the plan is then solicited.

Plan Requirements   A Chapter 11 plan must divide the creditors' claims into classes of substantially similar claims. Claims in each class must be treated equally. In addition, the plan must specify which classes of creditors are *impaired classes* and how they will be treated. A class is impaired if its rights are altered under the plan. Within the broad guidelines of the Code, the debtor has great flexibility in structuring a Chapter 11 plan.

Acceptance and Confirmation of the Plan   The plan cannot be put into effect unless it is accepted by each impaired class of creditors. A class accepts the plan if creditors representing one-half of the creditors and two-thirds of the dollar value of the claims in the class accept the plan. Unimpaired creditors are assumed to have accepted the plan.

EXAMPLE: The claims in a given class, and the creditors holding those claims, are as follows: $600 (Groucho), $400 (Chico), $300 (Harpo), and $200 (Zeppo). If Groucho and Zeppo vote to accept a proposed Chapter 11 plan, Chico votes to reject it, and Harpo does not vote, the class has accepted the plan (two out of three voting claims voted to accept; $800 is two-thirds of $1,200).

A court will confirm the plan if the plan is proposed in good faith and meets the requirements of the Code. However, impaired classes that do not accept the plan must be treated in a "fair and equitable" manner. This provision is called the "cram-down provision" of the Bankruptcy Code. In addition, all classes of creditors must receive no less than they would in a Chapter 7 liquidation. Finally, the plan must appear financially sound and likely to succeed.

32:16   Chapter 13 Plans

A Chapter 13 case differs from a Chapter 11 case in a number of ways. For example, the focus is on getting an individual debtor back on his financial feet, rather than on salvaging a business that is in financial difficulty. The debtor files the proposed payment and rehabilitation plan; under no circumstances can creditors file a plan. There is no requirement that claims be divided into classes, and the consent of unsecured creditors is not required for confirmation of a plan.

Plan Requirements   To be confirmed, a Chapter 13 plan must satisfy a number of requirements. Among the provisions that must be made in the plan are

- Submission to the trustee's supervision and control of all or part of the debtor's future income, as necessary to execute the plan
- Full payment, by means of later cash payments, of all priority claims, except as any holder of a priority claim otherwise agrees
- If the plan classifies claims, equal treatment for each claim within a given class
- Repayment over not more than a three-year period, although the court can approve up to a five-year period

The Bankruptcy Code lists additional types of provisions that can, if desired, be included in a Chapter 13 plan. Thus, a plan can

- Modify the rights of holders of all secured claims except those secured *only* by the debtor's principal residence
- Modify the rights of holders of all unsecured claims
- Provide for curing of a default and continuation of payments on a debt, such as a home mortgage, on which the last payment is due after termination of the plan
- Reject any executory contract or unexpired lease
- Provide for the payment of any claim from exempt property
- Provide for the redelivery of estate property to the debtor, either when the plan is confirmed or at a later time

Confirmation of Plan   The court must hold a confirmation hearing. At the hearing any party in interest can object to confirmation, although it is only the secured creditors holding allowed claims who must accept the plan (or receive other treatment, as discussed below). The major requirements for confirmation of a plan are, briefly, that (1) the debtor pay all required legal fees; (2) the plan have been proposed in good faith; (3) the plan be such that, consistent with his or her duty to support dependents, the debtor should be able to make payments under and otherwise comply with the plan; and (4) the planned distributions to unsecured creditors are not less than what those creditors would receive under Chapter 7.

If one or more secured creditors refuse to accept a Chapter 13 plan, the plan can still be confirmed, but only if the interest of each nonaccepting secured creditor is satisfied in one of two ways. The first of these "cram-down" alternatives is that the debtor can simply surrender the property covered by each nonaccepting secured creditor's lien to that creditor. The second option available to the debtor is that the plan can provide that the nonaccepting secured creditor (1) retains his lien and (2) will receive property having a present value (value as of the effective date of the plan) not less than the allowed amount of his claim.

EXAMPLE: Brown, the debtor in a Chapter 13 case, conducts business as a sole proprietor. Brown owes $5,000 to Curb Corporation, which holds a security interest in a machine that, although worth only $2,000, is essential to the continuation of Brown's business. Curb refuses to accept Brown's Chapter 13 plan. The plan can be confirmed if it provides that Curb will (1) keep its security interest in the machine and (2) receive either (a) later periodic payments or (b) other property, such as Brown's old car, as long as the present value of the deferred payments or other property is at least $2,000.

32:17   Discharge of Debtor; Reaffirmation of Debts

A *discharge* in a bankruptcy case means that the debtor is free from further liability on certain debts. For an individual debtor, the object of *any* bankruptcy proceeding is to obtain a discharge. A corporate or partnership debtor can receive a discharge only in a Chapter 11 case. Bear in mind, however, that some debts *cannot* be discharged, and other debts *will not* be discharged under certain circumstances. Debts that cannot or might not be discharged are discussed below. To be considered first, though, are the circumstances under which any type of discharge can be granted.

Grant of Discharge   The Court grants a discharge in a Chapter 7 case unless the trustee or a creditor objects. If an objection if made, the discharge will not be granted if any one or more of a number of specific facts are found to exist. Among the listed facts are the following:

- Debtor is not an individual
- Within one year before the petition was filed, debtor transferred or concealed property with intent to hinder or delay a creditor
- Debtor concealed, destroyed, falsified, or failed to keep or preserve adequate records as to his financial condition or business affairs

- Debtor failed to explain any loss of assets satisfactorily
- Debtor refused to obey a lawful order of the bankruptcy court
- Debtor was granted a discharge under Chapter 7 or 11 (or Chapter 13 under some circumstances) in a case commenced within six years before the petition in the present case was filed

Generally, confirmation of the rehabilitation plan in a Chapter 11 case discharges the debtor. In a Chapter 13 case, the court ordinarily grants a discharge after the debtor has completed all payments under the Chapter 13 plan. If the debtor failed to make all payments under the plan, the court can still grant what is known as a *hardship discharge.* The requirements for a hardship discharge are that (1) the debtor failed to complete payments under the plan due to a reason beyond his control, (2) unsecured creditors received at least as much as they would have received in a Chapter 7 case, and (3) modification of the plan is impracticable.

EXAMPLE: A confirmed Chapter 13 plan requires the debtor to pay the trustee $150 per month for 36 months, for the benefit of the creditors. Thus, the total amount to be paid by the debtor is $5,400. After the debtor has made payments for 20 months, she is disabled in an accident and forced to leave her job. Her income is reduced to half of what it was before and, for the indefinite future, will consist only of disability compensation and related benefits. As a result, the debtor pays the trustee only $75 per month for the last eight months of the plan. The court can grant a hardship discharge if unsecured creditors have received what they would have received under Chapter 7.

If the debtor has not paid at least 70 percent of the unsecured claims when a Chapter 13 hardship discharge is granted, the debtor cannot receive a discharge in a later Chapter 7 case commenced within six years after commencement of the earlier Chapter 13 case.

Debts Not Discharged   Certain types of debts that are not discharged in a Chapter 7 case. Examples of such debts are fines or penalties imposed by government entities, most unpaid taxes, most unpaid student loans, and unpaid alimony or child support.

Other types of debts will not be discharged if, and only if, the creditors involved object to discharge and make an adequate showing that one of the Bankruptcy Code's grounds for exception from discharge exists. The most significant debt of this type is one that the debtor incurred by using a written statement that (1) was false in one or more important respects, (2) concerned the debtor's financial condition, (3) was reasonably relied on by the creditor, *and* (4) was intended to deceive the creditor. A typical example of a statement of this type is an application for a loan or other credit. Of the four listed requirements, the one that often determines the dischargeability of the debt is the creditor's reasonable reliance on the statement. Thus, for example, a creditor's failure to convince the court that his reliance on a false financial statement was reasonable under the circumstances will lead to the debt's being discharged.

If a creditor challenges the discharge of a consumer debt (debt incurred by individual for personal, family, or household purposes), but the court discharges the debt anyway, the creditor must usually pay the debtor's legal expenses for the dischargeability proceeding.

If the debtor has completed his payments under a Chapter 13 plan, the only allowed debts provided for by the plan that are not discharged are (1) debts for alimony or child support and (2) certain long-term obligations (such as a loan secured by a home mortgage), the last payment of which is due after the last payment under the plan.

Reaffirmation of Debt   A debtor reaffirms a debt if, after a bankruptcy case has commenced, the debtor agrees to pay a creditor on a debt that is dischargeable in the case. Because the existence of *reaffirmation* agreements can hinder or even prevent a debtor's fresh start after a bankruptcy proceeding, the Bankruptcy Code imposes several requirements as to these agreements. For example, the agreement must be made before any discharge is granted, and the debtor can cancel the agreement within 30 days after making it. If the debtor is an individual, the court must inform the debtor about his right not to make the agreement. Also, the court must approve any reaffirmation of a consumer debt that is not secured by real property. This approval generally requires a finding that the reaffirmation does not impose an undue hardship on the debtor or a dependent and that it is in the debtor's best interest.

Key Concepts and Terms

- Insolvency is the situation in which the total amount of a debtor's debts exceeds the total value of those of the debtor's assets that can be reached by creditors.
- An individual debtor can sometimes relieve his financial difficulties by obtaining a debt consolidation loan or using the services of a debt counselor.
- A business debtor can be relieved from some of its indebtedness if it can persuade all or most of its creditors to agree to a composition arrangement, which reduces the debtor's total indebtedness and, if performed, discharges the debts. Otherwise, the debtor might still avoid bankruptcy by making an assignment for creditors, which discharges debts to the extent that they are paid.
- Bankruptcy is a form of debtor relief by which the debtor places his assets under judicial control, after which either the assets are liquidated and sold for the benefit of creditors by the trustee, or a plan for the debtor's financial rehabilitation is prepared. Bankruptcy is governed by the federal Bankruptcy Code.
- A bankruptcy case is commenced by filing a petition with the bankruptcy court. The debtor files the petition in a voluntary case, while one or more creditors file in an involuntary case. A voluntary petition can be filed under Chapter 7 (liquidation of assets), Chapter 11 (reorganization and financial

rehabilitation of business debtor), or Chapter 13 (financial rehabilitation of certain individual debtors). An involuntary petition can be filed only under Chapters 7 or 11.

- The court can dismiss any bankruptcy case for cause, and it must dismiss an involuntary case if either of the two statutory grounds for involuntary bankruptcy does not exist.

- The bankruptcy estate consists of all the debtor's property and property interests. It is usually administered by the trustee. Individual debtors can exempt certain property from the estate.

- When a bankruptcy petition is filed, creditors' efforts to collect on debts owed by the debtor are automatically stayed. The court can terminate or modify the stay as to a particular creditor on request.

- The trustee has the power to avoid certain prepetition transfers involving the debtor's property, including (1) transfers that some actual or hypothetical creditors could avoid under state law, and (2) preferential transfers. A preferential transfer is one that gives a creditor greater benefits than the creditor would receive if the transfer had not been made.

- Creditors' claims are secured or unsecured. A claim is secured if the creditor has a lien on property of the bankruptcy estate, and the claim is secured only to the extent of the value of that property. Claims are presented by the filing of proofs of claim in most cases.

- The right and extent to which a given creditor shares in the distributions in a Chapter 7 case depends on the status of the creditor's claim as secured or unsecured and, as to an unsecured claim, the ranking of the claim in the statutory scheme of priorities.

- A Chapter 11 plan is intended to allow the debtor to remain in business. A Chapter 13 plan is intended to give the individual debtor a fresh start while, at the same time, making it possible for him to pay at least some of his debts.

- A Chapter 11 or 13 plan must be confirmed by the court before it can be executed, and confirmation will be withheld unless the plan meets detailed statutory requirements.

- An individual debtor will usually receive a discharge from most of his debts. Some debts cannot be discharged, however, and others will not be discharged under certain circumstances.

- A debtor can, but need not, reaffirm a debt that will be discharged. Strict requirements apply to any reaffirmation by an individual debtor, especially as to consumer debts.

- Allowable Claims
- Assignment for Creditors
- Automatic Stay
- Avoidance Power
- Bankruptcy
- Best Interest of Creditors
- Composition with Creditors
- Custodian
- Debtor in Possession
- Discharge of Debtor

- Hardship Discharge
- Insolvency
- Liquidation
- Parties in Interest
- Preferential Transfer
- Proof of Claim

- Reaffirmation of Debt
- Rehabilitation Plan
- Reorganization
- Right of Redemption
- Strong-Arm Clause
- Trustee

Questions and Case Problems

1. What are the advantages and disadvantages of bankruptcy, as compared against other forms of debtor relief from the viewpoint of (a) creditors and (b) debtors?

2. The Bankruptcy Code has been criticized as providing a loophole for deadbeats because it allows people to avoid debts that they are capable of paying. Do you agree with this criticism? Why or why not?

3. Define "secured claim" and "unsecured claim" as those terms are used in the Bankruptcy Code. What, if any, advantages does the holder of a secured claim have over the holder of an unsecured claim? What is the significance of a claim's being allowed?

4. Meyers files a voluntary bankruptcy petition, and among his assets he lists a pickup truck that is worth $1,650, but which is covered by a nonpossessory, non-purchase-money security interest in Credithrift's favor, securing a debt of $2,500. Meyers works as a forklift operator at a factory, and he uses the truck for commuting to and from work. Credithrift applies to the court for relief from the automatic stay so that it can enforce its lien on the truck; it has evidence that the truck is depreciating at the rate of $75 per month. In response, Meyers claims that the truck is a tool of his trade and that Credithrift's lien should be set aside. (a) What, if any, relief from the automatic stay should be granted to Credithrift? Why? (b) Is Credithrift's lien avoidable by Meyers? Why or why not? (c) If the court decides, rightly or wrongly, that Meyers' argument lacks merit, how else, if at all, can Meyers obtain the release of the lien on his truck?

5. The Laurinburg Oil Company filed for bankruptcy and received an automatic stay against suits by creditors. The state of North Carolina seeks a ruling by the court to lift the stay and permit it to sue for a civil injunction against the company. The state alleges that the company maintains a waste disposal facility that is filled beyond its capacity and constitutes an environmental health hazard under state and federal pollution laws. The action by the state, if successful, would require the company to expend substantial funds to restore the facility to a condition in which it will no longer violate environmental pollution laws. Should the bankruptcy court lift the stay for a suit of this nature?

6. On June 1, Scopes gave up on his cabinet-making business and filed a bankruptcy petition under Chapter 7 of the Bankruptcy Code. Earlier the same year Scopes had bought some new equipment on credit, as follows. On January 1, he bought a radial arm saw from Bryan and gave Bryan a security interest covering the saw. Bryan perfected that interest on January 5. On February 1, Scopes bought a lathe from Darrow. Darrow was granted a security interest in the lathe but did not perfect that interest until March 15. Scopes defaulted on his payments to Bryan and Darrow, and both creditors acted to protect their interests. On April 1, Bryan repossessed the saw, as he had the right to do under his contract. On April 15,

Darrow repossessed the lathe. The bankruptcy trustee now seeks to recover both the saw and the lathe for the bankruptcy estate. She argues that both Bryan and Darrow received the benefit of preferential transfers that she, the trustee, has the power to avoid. Discuss what rights, if any, the trustee has with respect to the two pieces of equipment.

7. Curtis and his wife, the debtors in a Chapter 13 case, file a proposed payment plan in which they divide their unsecured debts into two classes: (1) unpaid child support owed to Curtis' former wife and (2) all other unsecured debts. Under the Curtis plan, the unpaid child support will be paid in full, but the other unsecured creditors will receive only 10 cents on the dollar. For payment of these debts, the plan calls for Curtis' employer to make direct payment to the trustee, at the rate of $75 per month out of Curtis' wages, for 18 months. Curtis' net earnings are $787 per month, and he estimates that the total of his recurring monthly expenses is $700. At the confirmation hearing Curtis states that his wife is pregnant and that he will have to pay some, if not all, of the costs of childbirth; that he had no prospect of a wage increase; and that his employer is unsympathetic and is apt to fire him if payments under the plan extend beyond 18 months. The trustee objects to the Curtis plan, claiming that it was not proposed in good faith and that the 10 percent payment to the second class of unsecured creditors is too low. She proposes to file an alternate plan for the court to consider. (a) Should the court allow the trustee to file an alternate plan? Why or why not? (b) Should the Curtis plan be confirmed? Why or why not?

8. In 1981 Jones applied for a $1,700 loan from Merchants Bank. In the space on the loan application provided for the listing of existing debts, Jones stated the following: (1) "auto loan from United Bank," with no amount stated, (2) "F&M," with no amount stated, (3) "Am Cr?—$250," and (4) "MasterCard," with no amount stated. Merchants checked with a local credit bureau about Jones' credit rating, and it then made the loan. In 1982 Jones applied to Merchants for a second loan, for $1,000, and this time he left the space for listing existing debts blank. In early 1983 Jones applied to Merchants for a $4,000 loan to pay off the earlier two loans and provide Jones with needed capital. Again, Jones left blank the space on the application provided for the listing of debts, although he was indebted to Merchants and several other creditors at the time. Later in 1983 Jones filed for bankruptcy under Chapter 7. The case has proceeded to the point where the court is ready to grant Jones a discharge. Merchants Bank argues that because of Jones' failure to list his debts on the 1983 loan application, the $4,000 debt owed to it should not be discharged. Should the $4,000 debt be discharged? Why or why not?

9. Stephens files a petition for relief under Chapter 7. Among Stephens' debts is a debt of $550 owed to BFC, a loan company. The debt is secured by a non-possessory, non-purchase-money security interest in certain of Stephens' household goods, worth $500. After the meeting of creditors, Stephens visits BFC seeking a new loan of $1,000. BFC agrees to make the loan, but only if Stephens reaffirms the $550 debt. Stephens does so and obtains the new loan. At no time did the court approve the reaffirmation or even receive a copy of the loan agreement in which it was made. Discuss any ways in which, under these facts, BFC has or might have violated requirements of the Bankruptcy Code. Can BFC enforce Stephens' reaffirmation? Why or why not?

10. On the day an involuntary bankruptcy petition was filed against him, under circumstances in which he would have anticipated the impending bankruptcy,

Greenwalt made a $50,000 transfer to a bank account held by Brandy Enterprises. Brandy Enterprises was a partnership created by Greenwalt for the benefit of his stepchildren. Greenwalt operated as the manager of Brandy Enterprises and wielded all control over it. The stepchildren had no prior knowledge of the deposit. One stepchild regularly signed checks in blank on the account and gave them to Greenwalt. Does this transfer meet the requirements that a creditor must prove to prevent a debtor's discharge in a Chapter 7 bankruptcy proceeding?

PART SEVEN

Property

Introductory Comments

Property is one of the most important areas of business law. The reason for its significance is readily apparent. All businesses buy, sell, and lease property, and otherwise engage in a host of property transactions in the course of their daily activities. Property is the measure of success in our society, and its acquisition is the means by which businesses grow and prosper.

There are two basic classes of property: land and buildings, which are called real property; and movable things and intangibles, which are known as personal property. While most of the other chapters in this book involve property or property rights, the material in the following chapters analyzes the law applicable specifically to these classes of property. The basic concepts of property law are introduced in Chapter 33. Succeeding chapters discuss bailments and personal property leases (Chapter 34; the purchase and sale of real property (Chapter 35); mortgages and deeds of trust (Chapter 36); the landlord–tenant relationship (Chapter 37); premises liability (Chapter 38); regulation and control of land use (Chapter 39); and trusts, wills, and estate administration (Chapter 40).

There are few broadly applicable or unifying doctrines in property law, and at times property law appears to bear little relation to modern economic or social conditions. The principal reason for this state of affairs is that property law has its origin in feudal England, with its peculiar system of land tenure dating back hundreds of years. This is not to say, however, that property law is totally of English origin; laws affecting property in many states reflect other historical antecedents. For example, community property laws in several western states can be traced to the laws of Spain and Mexico.

Perhaps another reason why property law is not based on broadly applicable doctrines is that the law has been adapted over the years to meet changing economic, political, and social conditions in the United States, and it continues to be refined by the courts today. For example, the courts are now frequently using contract principles in deciding property cases, whereas in the past property law and contract law were considered quite distinct—each with its own peculiar doctrines and rules. As older property law doctrines fail to meet the needs of modern times, new rules are being fashioned and adopted.

Despite the complexities of property law, it remains one of the most fascinating and important areas of business law. It incorporates and reflects history, economics, and politics. For this reason, studying property law is vital not only in terms of its usefulness in guiding the conduct of business, but also in terms of understanding the most important underpinning of the nation's economy.

33 Introduction to the Law of Property

33:1 Introduction

The meaning of "property" depends on how the term is used. What is property in one situation might not be considered property in another. In one sense, the term refers to the right of possessing, enjoying, and disposing of a thing, ordinarily to the exclusion of others. In another sense, it refers to a thing that can be owned. The meaning of "property" can also depend on the particular circumstance in which it is used. For example, it is sometimes used to mean land rather than buildings or other improvements on that land.

Property, a property right, or an interest in property can be tangible or intangible. Property can consist of land, buildings, or articles of personal use. The term includes all animate objects that are capable of appropriation or manual delivery. It also includes obligations, debts, products of labor or skill, and all other things of value.

There are two fundamental classes of property: (1) land and that which is attached to land, all of which is called *real property*, and (2) movable or intangible things, which are called *personal property*.

Constitutional Protection of Property Rights Property is specifically protected by the Constitution of the United States. Indeed, some historians have asserted that the fundamental impetus for the adoption of our constitution and the failure of the initial form of government after independence, under the Articles of Confederation, was precisely the lack of suitable protection to property owners. The Fifth Amendment to the Constitution provides, "No person shall be . . . deprived of life, liberty, or property, without due process of law; nor shall private property be taken for public use, without just compensation."[1] The Fourteenth Amendment to the United States Constitution prohibits the states from denying any person the due process of law or the equal protection of the laws.

---

[1] The power of government to take property for public use by eminent domain or other similar proceedings is discussed in Chapter 39. The Constitution is reprinted in Appendix A.

33:2 Ownership of Property

All property has an owner, whether public or private. Ownership and property are interrelated concepts. Ownership of something is the right of one or more persons to possess and use it to the exclusion of others, and property is the "something" that can be owned, including what is known as the "bundle of rights" incident to ownership. For example, one can own an idea (which is intangible personal property) just as one can own a parcel of land (real property).

Incidents of Ownership   The ownership of property is either absolute or qualified. It is absolute when a single person (sole owner) has absolute control over the property and can use or dispose of it according to his pleasure, subject only to the general laws in force. Ownership is qualified when property is shared with one or more persons, when the time of its enjoyment is deferred, or when its use is restricted.

Special Rights Based on Ownership   In the absence of statute or case law to the contrary, the owner of real property has the right to its surface and to everything permanently situated beneath or above it.[2] Every property owner is entitled to what is called *lateral* and *subjacent support*, which is what his land receives from adjoining property. This right is subject to the right of the adjoining property owner to make excavations on the land for construction or other improvements, as long as the walls of the excavations have been properly braced.

The occupants of property have rights to the natural condition, level, and purity of all streams, lakes, and ponds which their property adjoins. If rights to the use of waters are based on ownership of property bordering a natural body of water, they are called *riparian rights*. Riparian owners are usually entitled to the reasonable use of water from such bordering or adjacent bodies of water. In some western states, however, a riparian owner's use of the water may be limited under what is called the *prior appropriation doctrine*. The effect of the doctrine is that a riparian owner located downstream can, because of his or her prior use of a given quantity of water, have acquired the right to continue receiving that amount of water.

Under the common law, a property owner was deemed to own the land and the property under it to the center of the earth and above it to infinity in space. Violation of the airspace above an owner's property was deemed to be as much a trespass as entry on the land without the owner's permission. Obviously, the needs of commercial, military, and private air traffic have made inroads on the strict common-law theory. However, property owners may still have remedies available to protect against unreasonable interferences with their use and quiet enjoyment of the airspace above their property.

Owners of property also enjoy rights to air, light, and a view unobstructed by neighboring property. If a proposed or new building on adjoining property

---

[2] Not all countries view ownership in a similar fashion. In Mexico, for example, ownership of property does not extend to subsurface minerals; they belong to the state.

blocks any of these rights, the affected property owner might be able to obtain an injunction, or even damages under certain circumstances.

Fixtures   When property becomes permanently attached to land, it is called a *fixture*. Under the common law, fixtures could not be removed from the land by a tenant or other temporary occupant; rather, the fixtures became part of the property owned by the landlord. An early exception to the rule of fixtures was recognized to allow a tenant to remove *trade fixtures*, those installed to carry on a trade or business. This exception encouraged economic investment for trade. The tenant remained liable, however, for material damage caused by removing trade fixtures. Today, most states have liberalized the rules governing fixtures. A person can generally remove from leased premises any property, whether or not used in a trade or business, so long as the removal does not cause substantial damage.

33:3   Possessory Interests in Property

There is an often-repeated adage to the effect that possession is nine-tenths of the law. There is much truth to this statement because the law does protect the possessor of property for many different purposes. However, possession is distinguishable from ownership. Both terms denote dominion and control over property, but ownership denotes *title* to the property while possession denotes the right to use the property. For example, a landlord owns property, while a tenant enjoys its possession for a period of time.

Possession generally requires both physical control of property and the intent to control it. When the law deems a person to be in possession and in fact he or she is not, the person is said to be in *constructive possession* of the property. For example, an owner of a mountain cabin who uses the cabin only during the winter is in constructive possession of it during the rest of the year.

A person who possesses property usually prevails against all claimants but the true owner. The following classic case illustrates the distinction between possession and ownership, and how this distinction affects property rights. Note that the party seeking damages was not the owner but was only in possession of the property. Indeed, while the question of ownership was raised, it was not dispositive of the issues in the case. Rather, the inquiry focused on the property rights of two parties neither of whom owned the disputed property.

Anderson

v

Gouldberg

53 NW 636 (1892)

Minnesota Supreme Court

FACTS: Anderson sued to recover possession of 93 pine logs or their fair market value. Anderson claimed he cut the logs and hauled them to a mill, where they were taken by the defendants. The defendants contended that Anderson did not own the logs and had no authority from the owners to cut them.

ISSUE: Can a person who obtains possession of property through trespass recover the property from someone who wrongfully takes the property from that person?

RESULT: A trespasser's title is good against anyone except the true owner or someone with authority from the true owner.

REASONING:

* * *

It is settled by the verdict of the jury that the logs in controversy were not cut upon the land of the defendants, and consequently that they were entire strangers to the property. For the purposes of this appeal, we must also assume the fact to be . . . that the plaintiffs obtained possession of the logs in the first instance by trespassing upon the land of some third party. Therefore the only question is whether bare possession of property, though wrongfully obtained, is sufficient title to enable the party enjoying it to maintain replevin [a legal action in which the plaintiff seeks the return of specific property rather than damages] against a mere stranger, who takes it from him. . . . When it is said that to maintain replevin the plaintiff's possession must have been lawful, it means merely that it must have been lawful as against the person who deprived him of it; and possession is good title against all the world except those having a better title. Counsel says that possession only raises a presumption of title, which, however, may be rebutted. Rightly understood, this is correct; but counsel misapplies it. One who takes property from the possession of another can only rebut this presumption by showing a superior title in himself, or in some way connecting himself with one who has. One who has acquired the possession of property, whether by finding, bailment, or by mere tort, has a right to retain that possession as against a mere wrongdoer who is a stranger to the property. Any other rule would lead to an endless series of unlawful seizures and reprisals in every case where property had once passed out of the possession of the rightful owner.

Mitchell, Justice.

Interests and Estates in Property The concept of property is based on the legal concept of *estates* in property. Both of these concepts developed at a time when land was the only property of substantial value. Thus, interests in property were historically referred to as estates in land. As personal property was accumulated and became more important, the system of estates or interests in land was applied to personal property as well. Although the types of estates and the terms used to distinguish among the classes of property apply primarily to real property or land, they have general applicability to personal property for purposes of the discussion in this chapter.

An *estate* is an interest in property that is of a given duration or time. An interest can be a present or a *future interest*. The owner of a *present interest* has the right to the immediate possession of property, while the owner of a future interest has the right to the possession of property at some future time.

Fee Simple The term *fee simple* refers to an estate or interest in property of potentially infinite duration with no restrictions. Under the common-law system of land-holding, the fee simple ownership was the closest to absolute ownership that could exist. Usually, when one speaks of ownership of property, without qualification or restriction, it is the fee simple to which reference is being made.

Life Estate A *life estate* is an interest in property limited in duration to the lifetime of a particular person or persons. This limitation distinguishes the life estate from the other estates. A life estate is usually limited to the lifetime of the holder of the estate, but it can be limited to someone else's life.

The holder of a life estate, who is known as a *life tenant*, is entitled to all income from the property during the life tenancy. If the tenancy is in real property, the life tenant can exploit the natural resources so long as the exploitation does not permanently damage the interests of those who will enjoy the property on termination of the life estate. The life tenant must preserve the property, maintain it, and keep structures in good repair, but is under no obligation to improve it. The life tenant must pay all ordinary taxes on the land during the existence of the life estate. When a life tenant dies, the property reverts to the owner or the owner's heirs, or passes to a third person as designated by the grantor of the life estate.

Future Interests A *future interest* is a property interest that will come into existence at some time in the future. The term is somewhat misleading in that the *interest* must have present existence, even though *possession* is postponed to some future time. If the property owner has disposed of less than his entire estate for a period of time, his remaining interest is called a *reversion*. For example, if an owner conveys a life estate, his future interest on termination of the life estate is the reversion. The owner has not fully conveyed the estate and is entitled to its return. If, instead, a person granting a life estate *has* disposed of his entire interest in the property, he has given a third person the right of possession and ownership on termination of the life estate. This interest is known as a *remainder*.

Nonfreehold Estates The common law developed certain estates that conveyed possession and use but retained ownership in the grantor. These estates were known as *nonfreehold estates;* today they are called leaseholds. Leaseholds,

FIGURE 33-1 Examples of Present and Future Interests

1. The Fee Simple: From O "to A and his heirs forever"

A owns all interests. The notation "and his heirs forever" indicates a fee simple estate; it confers no interest on A's possible heirs.

2. The Life Interest and a Reversion: From O "to A for life"

A owns a life interest and is called the life tenant. O owns a reversion and is called the reversioner. On A's death, O's interest becomes a fee simple again. If A outlives O, O's heirs inherit the reversion interest and take in fee simple at A's death.

3. The Life Interest and a Remainder: From O "to A for life, then to B"

A owns a life interest and is called the life tenant. O owns a remainder and is called the remainderman. On A's death B takes in fee simple. If A outlives B, B's heirs inherit B's remainder interest and take in fee simple at A's death.

and the rights and duties of the grantor (landlord) and grantee (tenant) are discussed in detail in Chapter 37.

33:4   Concurrent Ownership of Property

Any of the estates in property discussed above may be held by a single individual or concurrently by two or more persons. For example, a fee simple, life estate, or other type of estate may be owned by two or more people. The major forms of concurrent ownership are (1) tenancy in common; (2) joint tenancy; (3) partnership ownership[3]; (4) condominium or cooperative ownership; and (5) forms of marital ownership, such as tenancy by the entireties.

Tenancy in Common   A *tenancy in common* is a tenancy shared by two or more persons (*cotenancy*) in which each tenant is considered to be an owner of a separate and distinct share of the property. The property itself is not physically divided, but the interest of each tenant in common is transferable. Statutes in many states provide that an interest created in favor of several

---

[3] Partnerships are discussed in Chapter 44.

persons is an interest in common unless it is acquired by them as partners or is declared in its creation to be a *joint interest.*

Each tenant in common has the right to possession and enjoyment of all of the property, with the other tenants. When one tenant in common dies, his interest passes as he wishes to the beneficiary of his estate or to his heirs. The surviving tenants in common have no *right of survivorship*—that is, they do not automatically acquire the deceased tenant's interest.

Joint Tenancy *Joint tenants* are in effect owners of undivided shares in property. That is, each joint tenant owns the entire property, subject to the interests of the other joint tenants. This kind of estate, as distinguished from the tenancy in common, has survivorship as one of its incidents. Under the doctrine of *survivorship,* the death of one joint tenant causes his interest to pass automatically and immediately to the remaining joint tenants without ever becoming a part of his probate estate.

A joint tenancy can be created between or among two or more persons. In fact, there can be an unlimited number of joint tenants. On the death of each one, the estate belongs to the survivors until only one is left; the tenant who lives the longest takes the estate as the absolute owner. Since joint tenants possess undivided property as one fictitious entity, most states require that their interests in the property be equal in all respects. They must take the property at the same time, by the same instrument, with identical interests, and with an undivided right to possess the whole property, and not merely a portion of it. If these four *"unities" of time, title, interest, and possession* are not present, a joint tenancy cannot be created. The joint tenancy can be severed at any time by one joint tenant destroying one of the four unities as, for example, by conveying his interest in the property or by giving up possession. When a joint tenancy is severed, it becomes a tenancy in common and the right of survivorship is destroyed.

The absence of the right to survivorship is the principal feature distinguishing a tenancy in common from a joint tenancy. Tenants in common are each presumed to own an equal share, but equal shares are not required. Thus, for example, Lewis may convey a one-fourth undivided interest in certain property to Nicholas and a three-fourths undivided interest in the same property to Melissa, as tenants in common. Both Nicholas and Melissa have the right to possession of the whole property. Any rental income from the property goes one-fourth to Nicholas and three-fourths to Melissa. On the sale of the property, the proceeds are divided in the same fashion.

Rights and Duties of Cotenants Each tenant in common or joint tenant is equally entitled to the possession and enjoyment of the entire cotenancy property. A cotenant may not exclude another cotenant from any part of the property. As long as a tenant in possession does not exclude another cotenant, he is entitled to use and occupy every part of the property without paying any amount to the other cotenant. However, in some states one cotenant must account to other cotenants for the reasonable rental value of the property and for profits derived from the use of property that permanently reduces its value.

A tenant in common or a joint tenant may convey his interest in the property to a third party or may agree with the other cotenants to a *voluntary partition* or division of the land among themselves. The tenants may also seek what is known as *judicial partition,* by which a court either divides or sells the property through court order and then adjusts all the parties' claims. A joint tenant cannot convey his interest by will since his interest ceases on his death.

The rights of cotenants are discussed further in the following case.

Gillmor

v

Gillmor

694 P2d 1037 (1984)

Supreme Court of Utah

FACTS: Plaintiff and defendant, who were cousins, were tenants in common of approximately 33,000 acres in three counties in Utah. Defendant used the land to graze sheep and cattle to the point that addition of cattle or sheep by plaintiff would cause overgrazing of the land. Defendant refused to alter his operation or reduce the size of his herd when plaintiff so requested. Plaintiff sued for the value of defendant's use of the land during the time which plaintiff was excluded from use.

ISSUE: Did defendant's use of the land constitute a wrongful exclusion of plaintiff from her right to possession as a cotenant?

RESULT: Yes. Defendant's continued use of the land after plaintiff's request was an impermissible "ouster" of plaintiff.

REASONING:

* * *

The law is that a cotenant may sue for his share of rents and profits from common property if he has been ousted from possession of the common property. . . . The defendant argues that the trial court did not find that the defendant ousted the plaintiff. The trial court did not specifically use that term in its findings of fact and conclusions of law, but it did find that the defendant had both exercised exclusive use and possession and had also excluded the plaintiff from use of the common properties.

Mere exclusive use of commonly held properties by one cotenant is not sufficient to establish an ouster. A tenant in common has the right to use and occupy the entire property held in cotenancy without liability to other cotenants. Each cotenant has the right to "free and unobstructed possession . . . without liability for rents for the use and occupation thereof." . . . That one cotenant is not liable to his cotenant for rents for the occupancy of the common property is elemental. And this is true even though [the cotenant] uses it and derives income therefrom, as where he occupies . . . or farms a piece and takes the crops; or uses it for storage purposes; as long as he does not interfere with the cotenant's right to likewise occupy, use and enjoy. . . .

However, a cotenant who ousts another cotenant or acts in such a fashion as to necessarily exclude a fellow cotenant, violates the rights of that cotenant. . . . To establish a right to share in the rents and profits from the common property, it must be established that a cotenant has used the property so as to "necessarily exclude his cotenant." . . .

Exclusive use means more than one cotenant using the entire property; it requires either an act of exclusion or use of such a nature that it necessarily prevents another cotenant from exercising his rights in the property. . . .

The defendant contends that the trial court erred in finding that the defendant had exercised exclusive possession and use of the common properties in such a manner as to exclude the plaintiff from using the land. We disagree. The plaintiff sought to graze livestock on the land to the extent of her interest, but was effectively prevented from doing so. She sent defendant a letter expressing her intent to graze her livestock on the properties in proportion to her ownership and requested that the defendant accommodate her plans by altering his operations accordingly. The defendant refused to respond and continued to graze the lands to their maximum capacity. He even acknowledged that additional grazing would have damaged the range land. The defendant asserts that at various times he or his attorney invited the plaintiff onto the lands, but he never indicated any intention to alter his operations so as to accommodate the plaintiff's use of the land. Had the plaintiff grazed her livestock on the common properties while defendant's livestock was also there, the land would have been overgrazed. Indeed, the defendant admitted that if the plaintiff had attempted to put additional sheep on the land, he would have sought an injunction to prevent damage to the land. . . .

Stewart, Justice.

Marital Estates   A form of concurrent ownership limited to property owned by husband and wife is called a *tenancy by the entireties*. It is similar to joint tenancy in that it includes the right of survivorship. It is different from joint tenancy in that neither husband nor wife can destroy or sever the tenancy without the other's consent. Many states do not recognize this type of estate, and others restrict its use. The tenancy by the entireties usually takes the form of a transfer to husband and wife. Thus, where a conveyance is made to a husband and wife and a third person, the husband and wife would take their interest in tenancy by the entireties, and the third party would take his interest in the property as a tenant in common. This derives from the traditional common-law view of the husband and wife as one person. A tenancy by the entireties can be terminated only (1) if one spouse conveys his or her interest to the other, (2) if both spouses convey their interests to a third party, (3) on the death of one spouse, or (4) on divorce.

Another type of marital estate is that of *community property*. Community property has been adopted by eight states: Arizona, California, Idaho, Louisiana, Nevada, New Mexico, Texas, and Washington. The law of community property is derived from the civil law of Spain, France, and Mexico, whose laws were applied in the eight community property states before they joined the United States. Although modern community property law varies from state to state, the central idea is that a community interest of husband and wife exists in most property acquired during marriage regardless of which spouse actually acquired the property.

Community property is similar to both joint tenancy and tenancy in common. As with joint tenancy, each spouse owns an undivided interest in community property, and the interest of each spouse in the property is equal. As in a tenancy in common, there is no right of survivorship; a spouse may dispose of his or her interest in community property by will. However, most states have enacted statutes by which the community property interest of one spouse who dies without a will passes in whole or at least in part to the surviving spouse. Finally, it should be noted that community property does not extend to property owned by one spouse before marriage or acquired after marriage by gift or inheritance. Unless such property is *commingled* with or treated as community property, it remains the *separate property* of the particular spouse.

33:5 Nonpossessory Interests in Property

Certain relationships between owners of property and others can create interests in property that are not possessory. The basic types of nonpossessory interests are (1) easements, (2) profits, and (3) licenses.

Easements An *easement* is a person's interest in somebody else's land which gives the person the right to use the land in some fashion. An easement is always distinct from the possession of the land itself, for it does not convey title to the land.

EXAMPLE: A utility company has an easement to run power lines over another's property. The utility only enjoys a limited right to use the land for a specific purpose. It has no right to possession of the property.

An easement can be created (1) voluntarily, (2) by necessity, (3) by implication, or (4) by prescription. Creation by the first three is discussed below; prescriptive easements are discussed later in the chapter.

A property owner can voluntarily convey an easement to another person. In such a case, the owner must grant the easement by means of a deed that meets the formal requirements of the statute of frauds (see Chapter 15). An easement can also be created voluntarily by *reservation*. For example, an owner of property might convey part of it to another but keep an easement for himself to benefit his remaining property.

An *easement by necessity* is created when, for example, one parcel is divided into two lots and access to one lot can be had only by crossing the other. An easement by necessity can arise only if (1) the boundaries of the property over which the easement is claimed are fixed and certain; (2) the original parcel was owned at some time by a common owner; (3) there is a strict necessity for the easement's existence, such as no other access to a public road; and (4) the necessity arose when one parcel of land was severed from another. An easement by necessity terminates as soon as the necessity terminates.

An *easement* can also arise *by implication* under certain circumstances. For example, if a person owns two adjacent pieces of property and uses one as a roadway to benefit the other, an implied easement will arise if the parcel benefited is later conveyed. The deed does not have to convey the easement; it will arise by implication due to the former owner's use over a continuous period of time.

Another type of easement is an *easement appurtenant*. An easement appurtenant is created when the owner of land grants to another some right to use the land, for the benefit of the grantee's land. The land benefited is called the dominant estate, while the land to which the easement is attached is the servient estate.

EXAMPLE: Henry owns a lot on Georgian Bay and has divided it into two parcels for sale. He conveys one to Clara and retains the other. At the time Henry conveys the land to Clara by deed, he also grants her an easement for access over his remaining parcel. The grant is an easement appurtenant since Clara owns the land benefited by the easement. Clara's parcel is the *dominant estate*; Henry's is the *servient estate*.

An easement that is not appurtenant is called an *easement in gross*. Easements in gross are said to be of personal benefit to the easement holder.

EXAMPLE: Con Edison obtains an easement from Farmer Dittle to run high-voltage power lines across Dittle's land to utility consumers in New York. Because this easement will benefit Con Edison itself rather than its real property (Con Edison acquires only the right to build and maintain power lines across Dittle's property), the interest is an easement in gross.

The periods of potential duration of an easement are the same as those of estates in lands. Therefore, an easement can be in fee simple, for life, or for a period of years, or it can terminate on the occurrence of a specified event. An easement in gross, being personal, is good only for the life of the easement holder.

Scope and Termination of Easements   The scope of an easement created by express grant is determined by the terms of the grant. The right to an easement includes the right to do what is necessary for its full enjoyment, but no more than that. For example, one holding a road easement may repair the road when necessary, but he is not permitted to go beyond making repairs to making improvements (such as widening and paving what was a gravel road) unless the owner of the servient estate consents.

Whenever circumstances may appear to terminate an easement, termination will occur only if the parties intended those circumstances to result in termination. Otherwise, the easement will continue to exist. If an owner of an easement discontinues its use and intends to abandon it, the easement will be extinguished. Mere nonuse, without acts indicating an intent to abandon, is insufficient to extinguish an easement by grant, but may extinguish a prescriptive easement if nonuse extends for a certain statutorily prescribed period of time. Adverse use by the owner of a servient estate can also extinguish an easement. For example, if a servient estate owner constructs a fence blocking an old road used for access to another's property, such adverse use over an extended period of time might extinguish the easement. In addition, an easement can be terminated by (1) the owner's acquisition of the servient estate, or (2) a written release signed by the easement holder and the owner of the servient estate.

Profits A *profit* is the right to take off or from another's land something that is part of the property, such as minerals, crops, timber, or even wild animals living on the land. A profit is thus one person's nonpossessory interest to acquire possessory rights in something on another's property. When a profit is granted, an easement will be implied to aid in taking the profit. For example, if Wellesley, the owner of 1,000 acres of prime timber land, sells the timber to McAvoy, the latter has a profit, together with an easement to go on the timber land and remove the timber.

Licenses A *license* is a privilege to go on another's property and to do acts that otherwise would constitute trespass. The license is different from an easement because a license is revocable by the grantor. For example, if Zadok tells Brodie that he may hunt and fish on his property, Brodie has a license. If Brodie shows up to fish and Zadok obstructs his passage, this act revokes the license and Brodie has no claim against Zadok. A license is usually presumed to be personal and nonassignable. However, if the parties so intend, it may be made transferable.

33:6 Transfer of Property by Deed

A *deed* is an instrument by which a property owner, called the grantor, conveys property to a purchaser or other transferee, called the grantee. The deed has the legal effect of transferring to the grantee title to an interest in land and buildings or other structures situated on the property. Deeds are generally classified on the basis of different title covenants or guaranties undertaken by the grantor. These covenants protect the grantee against problems that might occur after title has been transferred.

Originally, under feudal law, conveyances occurred in a ceremonial, physical transfer of property called *livery of seisin*, with both parties on the land. No written instrument was required in the ceremony. In 1536, the Statute of Uses was enacted in England by which a conveyor of property could transfer title by document. In 1677, the Statute of Frauds was enacted in England. It provided, among other things, that no estate could be created or transferred except by an instrument in writing signed by the grantor. This statute caused documentary transfers to be absolutely necessary and in this way established the foundation for our modern system of deeds and conveyances.[4]

To satisfy the modern statute of frauds, which has been codified by every state, a deed must be in writing and signed by the grantor. A deed must sufficiently identify the parties to the transaction and identify the property conveyed with reasonable certainty.

Title to property passes on actual or constructive delivery of a valid deed describing that property. *Actual delivery* occurs on the physical delivery of the instrument to the grantee by the grantor with the intent to pass title. *Constructive delivery* occurs if it is evident that, by his words and conduct, a grantor intends to relinquish all control and ownership of a deed or property, even though the deed or property might still be in his possession. The recording of a deed by a grantor in the appropriate county *registry of deeds* raises a presumption that the deed was delivered. However, recording is not considered delivery under the law; the grantee's subsequent acceptance of a deed after recording will ordinarily be considered legal delivery. Therefore, when a grantor has delivered a deed with intent to transfer title and the grantee has accepted delivery, title to the property becomes vested in the grantee. A simple redelivery or cancellation of the deed at this time does not restore the property to the grantor.

A deed cannot be delivered conditionally to a grantee. However, a deed can be given to a third party to be held pending the happening of a certain event, after which it is to be delivered unconditionally to the grantee. In such a case, the instrument becomes effective as a conveyance on the second delivery, when title actually passes. The third party holds the deed in what is called "*escrow.*" Escrow is explained more fully in Chapter 35.

EXAMPLE: A typical residential sale entails the conditional delivery into escrow of a deed to the property to be sold, contingent on the purchaser's performance of various acts, including payment of the purchase price. When these conditions have been performed and the purchase price is paid into escrow, title to the property is delivered to the purchaser out of escrow and the purchase price is transferred to the seller.

 Under the law, a deed is simply an evidence of title. Its loss, destruction, assignment, redelivery, or other disposition has no effect on the title or ownership of the property conveyed.

---

[4] The statute of frauds as it pertains to contracts is discussed in Chapter 15.

Description of Property   No particular method of land description is required to convey property by deed. To be effective, any description used must identify the property with reasonable certainty. If a description is ambiguous, the general rule is that the grantor did not intend to convey anything and that no property was actually transferred. Although property is sometimes described by street and number, reference to adjacent property, or the historical name of property, there are four methods of land description that are primarily used. They are (1) rectangular coordinates, (2) parcel maps, (3) metes and bounds, and (4) courses and distances.

Under the system of *rectangular coordinates* as used in federal surveys, particularly in the western United States, land is divided into square townships that are six miles on each side, and identified by reference to a principal meridian, which runs longitudinally, and a principal base line, which runs latitudinally. Each township is composed of 36 sections, each containing one square mile, or 640 acres. Each township is further subdivided into quarter-quarter sections, each containing 40 acres. Thus, for example, a boundary line might be described in part, using rectangular coordinates, as "running in a north–south direction and being 150 feet east of the northwest corner of the northeast quarter" of a particular section in a particular township.

When a tract of land is subdivided, the subdivider ordinarily files a *parcel map* in the appropriate public office. The parcel map becomes a public record in which each parcel in the subdivision is identified by number. When a parcel is sold, the description in a deed will refer to the parcel map and be identified by its number.

Property can also be described by the location or identity of natural or artificial monuments, such as rocks, trees, fence posts, and stakes located on the periphery of affected property. The distance along the peripheral lines of property between two monuments is described in feet, yards, or meters. Such a description in a deed giving distances is called a description by *metes and bounds*.

Property can also be described by reference to directions on a compass and distances in such directions. For example, a deed may describe a particular piece of property, beginning with "monument A, then north 150 feet, then west 150 feet, then south 150 feet, then east 150 feet, then back to the place of beginning." Such directions, based on the points of the compass, are called *courses and distances*.

General Warranty Deed   The type of deed that gives the grantee the most protection is called the general *warranty deed*. By a general warranty deed, the grantor warrants (guarantees) the title against defects arising both before and during his ownership of the property. The grantor warrants that he has the estate he purports to convey and the authority to convey it, and that there are no physical or title encumbrances outstanding against the property.

The law has developed various guaranties of the grantor's title and ownership to protect the purchaser of property. These guaranties are commonly referred to as covenants for title and are incorporated into the general warranty deed. They include (1) the *covenant for seisin*, which is a guaranty that the grantor owns the property to be conveyed; (2) the *covenant of the right to convey*, which is a guaranty that the grantor has a right to convey the property; (3) the *covenant against encumbrances*, which is a guaranty that there are no mortgages, tax liens, easements, or other encumbrances outstanding against the property to be conveyed; (4) the *covenant of quiet enjoyment*, which is a guaranty that the purchaser will not be disturbed in the future by the grantor or others who may claim an interest in the property; and (5) the *covenant for future assurances*, which is a guaranty that the grantor will do all acts within his power necessary to make the purchaser's title good. Breach of any of these covenants may entitle the grantee to damages for losses arising from the breach.

Special Warranty Deed The *special warranty deed* is more limited in the number of covenants that the grantor gives. Under the special warranty deed, the grantor warrants (1) that the title is free of defects that arose during his ownership of the property, (2) that he has the estate that he purports to convey, and (3) that the estate is free from physical or title encumbrances that may have been created by him.

 In the past, most deeds of conveyance were general warranty deeds. In recent years, there has been a steady trend against the use of such deeds, particularly in large cities. Banks and lending institutions almost invariably refuse to give any warranties, and well-advised businesspersons will do the same. A deed without guaranties requires the purchaser to satisfy himself about the sufficiency of title before the transaction is completed, and it precludes future claims that could arise against the grantor, except in case of fraud. The grantee ordinarily protects himself by obtaining "title insurance."

Quitclaim Deed A grantor who conveys property by a *quitclaim deed* does not make any warranties with respect to title. The effect of a quitclaim deed is limited to transferring to the grantee whatever interest, if any, that the grantor has in the land. In some states, so-called *bargain and sale deeds* are used in lieu of quitclaim deeds, but there is no real difference between them.

Recording of Deeds In some circumstances, the same interest in property will be conveyed to more than one person. If a dispute develops between or among conflicting interests, the law must have a fair and predictable method of deciding who will win. Today, the recording acts adopted in every state establish priorities among multiple grantees of the same interest in property. Recording acts are designed to protect innocent purchasers, while affording grantors a procedure to protect title to their property and to provide a permanent record of land transactions.

Under the recording acts, which vary significantly from state to state, any instrument evidencing an interest in property can be recorded. The grantee presents the instrument at a clerk's office or registry of deeds in the county where the land is located. A permanent copy of the instrument is made, and it is thereafter filed according to the date and time of presentation. The original deed is returned to the grantee. A reference to the deed is also usually made in some sort of index, arranged either alphabetically by name (grantor–grantee and grantee–grantor indexes) or according to the location of the property (tract index). These indexes are keyed by date and page number to the volumes of copied instruments so that a deed can be located if the name of either party or the property's location is known.

The act of recording gives notice to the entire world of the existence and contents of a recorded deed or instrument. Obviously, not everyone has actual notice of a deed or its recordation. The primary significance of recording acts is that they are the basis of constructive notice. This means that although a person might not actually know of a deed's existence, the opportunity to learn about it exists, and the person can be charged with knowledge of its contents.

33:7 Other Methods of Acquiring or Transferring Property

Property can be acquired through occupancy, transfer, gift, will, or purchase. All these methods imply voluntary acts by owners to part with their property. Other methods of acquiring property also exist by which ownership is transferred through use, either adverse or in opposition to the rights of the true property owner. Title to property so acquired is gained through *adverse possession*. Lesser rights to the use of property can be acquired through prescriptive easements.

Adverse Possession Public policy protects established interests in property, but it also favors the productive use of property. Adverse possession is a method of acquiring title to property based on possession. To establish title by adverse possession, a claimant must show possession that (1) is actual, (2) is open, (3) is either hostile to the true owner's rights or based on a claimed right, (4) is exclusive, and (5) lasts during the period of time required by statute.

The basic theory of adverse possession is simple. If after a specific number of years a property owner has not taken legal action to eject one who has been occupying his or her property without consent, the owner is prevented from bringing an action, and title passes to the person in possession. Bear in mind, however, that the statutes governing adverse possession vary considerably from state to state.

The elements of adverse possession are discussed and analyzed in the following case. Note how, under the facts of the case, the requirements of adverse possession may be implied by the fact of possession of another's property.

Naab

v

Nolan

327 SE2d 151 (1985)

Supreme Court of Appeals of West Virginia

FACTS: In 1976 the Nolans had their property surveyed and discovered that the Naabs' garage extended 1.22 feet onto their property. Nolan requested that Naab tear down the garage. The Naabs' refused, claiming that the garage was there when the Naabs bought the property in 1973. It had been erected in 1952 by a previous owner of the Naabs' property. West Virginia has a 10-year statute of limitations in adverse possession cases.

ISSUE: Have the Naabs established adverse possession over the property on which the garage is situated?

RESULT: Yes. All of the elements of adverse possession under West Virginia law are present.

REASONING:

*   *   *

An elementary principle of property law states that the owner of a burdened premise is bound by the actions or inactions of his predecessors in title. The record discloses that the predecessors in title of both the Naabs and the Nolans accepted the erection of the concrete garage and accompanying gravel driveway sometime before 1952. The record also indicates that when the Fultons placed a concrete slab at the entrance to the alley from the driveway, no complaint was registered by the Nolans' predecessors in title.

Thus, this Court is faced with a situation where a driveway and small garage have existed for almost a generation before any complaint was made that the driveway and garage encroached on another's property. [The West Virginia statute], which gives a person ten years to assert his ownership to land, is a statute of limitations that is indicative of the legislative desire to settle disputes and quiet title to real property within that period.

The doctrine of adverse possession is firmly established in our property law and accompanies [the West Virginia statute of limitations] in settling land disputes equitably and efficiently. This doctrine enables one who has been in possession of a piece of real property for more than ten years to bring an action asserting that he is now the owner of that piece of property even when title rests in another. In [another case] this Court stated:

> One who seeks to assert title to a tract of land under the doctrine of adverse possession must prove each of the following elements for the requisite statutory period: (1) That he had held the tract adversely or hostilely; (2) That the possession has been actual; (3) That it has been open and notorious (sometimes stated in the cases as visible and notorious); (4) That possession has been exclusive; (5) That possession has been continuous; (6) That possession has been under claim of title or color of title.

The circuit court found by a preponderance of the evidence the existence of facts sufficient to establish title by adverse possession in that portion of the Nolans' lot occupied by the Naabs' garage. We agree with the court's decision.

Element one, unquestionably, is present. The survey clearly indicated that the garage occupied a portion of the appellants' lot. Such physical dominion is sufficient to satisfy the first adverse or hostile element. This same fact of exercising physical dominion over a portion of the lot satisfies the second requirement, that the possession be "actual." . . .

The third requirement, that possession be open and notorious, requires that the acts asserting dominion over the property "must be of such a quality to put a person of ordinary prudence on notice of the fact that the disseisor is claiming the land as his own." . . . Proof of actual knowledge on the part of the true owner is not ordinarily required. . . . The fourth element in proving a successful transfer of title to property by adverse possession does not defeat the sporadic use of the property by others; it only need be the type of possession that would characterize an owner's use. The record does not indicate that anybody but the appellees and their predecessors in title ever used the garage.

Possession is continuous when the preponderance of the evidence shows continuous possession by one asserting adverse possession for the statutory period of ten years. It is uncontradicted that the Naabs and their predecessors in title have occupied the garage at least since 1952.

The sixth and final requirement for successful assertion of title by adverse possession has also been met. A claim of title is generally nothing more than the disseisor's entering upon the land with the intent to claim it as his own. The appellees fulfilled this requirement when they proceeded as if they had title to that portion of the Nolans' lot upon which the garage was located. No permission was either asserted or proved. The circuit court, therefore, was correct in finding that the Naabs had acquired title to the land on which their garage sits. . . .

Per Curiam.

Prescriptive Easements   Just as title to property can be acquired by adverse possession, an easement can be acquired by what is known as prescription through adverse use. The elements required for obtaining easement rights by prescription are similar to those involved in adverse possession. The scope of a *prescriptive easement*, however, is measured by the extent of the actual, adverse use of the property over which the easement is acquired. For example, if a pathway is acquired by prescription, the easement is generally limited to foot traffic, or at most bicycle traffic; certainly, the easement holder may not drive a dump truck along the pathway. This limit on prescriptive easements is quite different from the permissible uses of property acquired by adverse possession, where no such restrictions apply. For example, if title to property is gained through adverse possession by the possessor's herding cattle for the required number of years, her rights are absolute. She can stop herding cattle and build condominiums on the land or use it for any other lawful purpose.

     An owner can protect his rights in a variety of ways to prevent prescriptive easements from arising. He can block off his land from time to time, thereby breaking the continuity of use. He can also give users written permission to use the property for a stated purpose at stated times. This permission negates one of the elements required to establish a prescriptive easement. Finally, the owner can go to court to stop the use by injunction within the time limit specified by law.

Key Concepts and Terms

- The ways by which property can be acquired include occupancy, transfer, gift, will, and purchase.
- Property can be tangible or intangible and can constitute land, buildings, or articles of personal use. "Property" includes animate objects, obligations, debts, products of labor or skill, and all other things of value.
- The two basic classes of property are (1) land and that which is attached to land, called real property; and (2) movable things or articles, called personal property.
- All property has an owner, either public or private. Ownership carries with it the right to dispose of and create lesser interests in property.
- The ownership of property is either absolute or qualified. It is absolute when a single person has absolute dominion and control over the property and can use or dispose of it according to personal pleasure, subject only to general laws in force. The ownership of property is qualified when it is shared with one or more persons, when the time of enjoyment is deferred, or when its use is restricted in some fashion.
- Property rights are specifically protected by the United States Constitution and by the laws of every state. The Fifth Amendment to the United States Constitution prohibits the deprivation of property without due process of law or the taking of property for public use without just compensation. The Fourteenth Amendment provides in part that a person may not be deprived of property without due process of law.

- An estate in land is an interest in property of a given duration or time. The principal types of estates that exist are (1) fee simple, (2) life estate, and (3) nonfreehold estate. A future interest is a property interest that comes into existence at some time in the future.
- An estate in property can be held by a single individual or concurrently by two or more persons. The major forms of concurrent ownership are (1) tenancy in common; (2) joint tenancy; (3) partnership ownership; (4) condominium or cooperative ownership; and (5) forms of marital ownership, such as tenancy by the entireties.
- A cotenancy is a property interest in which ownership interests are shared. Types of cotenancy include (1) a joint tenancy, (2) a tenancy in common, (3) a tenancy by the entireties, and (4) the community interests of husband and wife.
- Property is usually transferred by deed. A deed is an instrument made by a grantor of property in favor of the grantee, the person to whom the property is conveyed. Deeds are generally classified on the basis of different title covenants or guaranties undertaken by the grantor. The most common deeds are the general warranty deed, the special warranty deed, and the quitclaim or bargain and sale deed.
- A deed must be in writing and signed by the grantor. The deed must sufficiently identify the parties to the transaction and the land conveyed, and it is not effective until it is delivered.
- Land is usually described by one of the following methods: (1) rectangular coordinates, (2) parcel maps, (3) metes and bounds, and (4) courses and distances.
- A property owner can also grant to someone else a nonpossessory interest in the property. The basic types of nonpossessory interests are (1) easements, (2) licenses, and (3) profits.
- Adverse possession is a method of acquiring title to property based on possession. To establish title by adverse possession a claimant must show possession that (1) is actual, (2) is open and notorious, (3) is either hostile to the record owner's rights or is based on a claim of right, (4) is exclusive, and (5) lasts during the period of time prescribed by statute.
- An easement, which is a person's interest in somebody else's land that gives the person the right to use the land, can be acquired by prescription or adverse use.

- Actual Delivery
- Adverse Possession
- Bargain and Sale Deed
- Community Property
- Constructive Delivery
- Constructive Possession
- Courses and Distances

- Deed
- Dominant Estate
- Easement
- Estate
- Fee Simple
- Fixture
- Future Assurances

- Future Interest
- Joint Tenants
- Lateral (Subjacent) Support
- License
- Life Estate
- Livery of Seisin
- Metes and Bounds
- Nonfreehold Estate
- Parcel Map
- Partition
- Personal Property
- Prescriptive Easement
- Present Interest
- Prior Appropriation Doctrine
- Profit
- Quiet Enjoyment
- Quitclaim Deed
- Real Property
- Rectangular Coordinates
- Registry of Deeds
- Remainder
- Reversion
- Right of Survivorship
- Riparian Rights
- Servient Estate
- Special Warranty Deed
- Survivorship
- Tenancy by the Entireties
- Tenancy in Common
- Unities of Time, Title, Interest, and Possession
- Warranty Deed

Questions and Case Problems

1. Delamirie finds a ring with a valuable stone and takes it to Armory for appraisal. Armory retains the ring, and takes the stone from the setting. When Delamirie demands the ring's return, she is offered the setting minus the stone. Delamirie sues Armory for the return of the stone. How should the case be decided? Why?

2. Lewis sells Lester the Boca Grande Residential Hotel for $100,000 in cash. The terms of sale do not mention fixtures, such as stoves, refrigerators, rugs, curtain rods, and bathroom and light fixtures, which Lewis placed on the property during his ownership. Lewis wants to remove these from the hotel but Lester objects, claiming that the items are fixtures which pass with the real estate under the conveyance. To whom do the items belong?

3. Truax and Ajax purchase a dairy and hold title to the property as tenants in common. Ajax takes possession of the farm, while Truax continues to reside in a distant city. The dairy becomes very profitable under Ajax. Is Truax entitled to share in the proceeds? If so, to what degree? If Ajax leases the land to Cardax for $1,000 per month, is Truax entitled to a portion of the rental? If Ajax commences a farming operation on the property, growing corn and other grains, is Truax entitled to share in the proceeds of sale? If Ajax constructs new buildings on the property to maintain the dairy and farming operations, must Truax contribute to the cost of construction? If Ajax wants to leave the dairy and farming business, may he sell the property on his own, or must he obtain the consent of Truax? Suppose that Truax objects to the sale of the dairy; what can Ajax do?

4. William and Catherine lived together, in a house owned by them as tenants in common, without the benefit of marriage. On William's death, his widow and heir, Arlene, claims one-half the rental value of the house. Arlene argues that Catherine's possession of the home is adverse to her so as to warrant an accounting for and the payment of rent. What result?

5. Compare and contrast ownership with possession of property.

6. Buller prepares a deed conveying her ranch to Roberts and instructs a friend, Powell, to give the deed to Roberts. Can Buller recall the deed before it is given to Roberts? Is it possible for Roberts to take title before the deed has been handed over to him?

7. Why is an easement called a nonpossessory interest in property?

8. Franks builds a fence on property she thinks she owns, but it is actually 15 feet within her neighbor Nunes' lot. After the prescribed statutory period has expired, does Franks acquire the strip by adverse possession? If Franks and Nunes both agree on the location of the fence, but each erroneously thinks it is built on the property line, when in fact it is entirely on Nunes' property, does Franks acquire title after expiration of the applicable statutory period?

9. RKO Theater and a bank are neighbors. A public sidewalk runs in front of the two buildings. The bank owns the land under the sidewalk, but since the theater had been built its employees have used the sidewalk to maintain and change the marquee. For 21 years the theater has used the sidewalk for this purpose. Has the theater acquired an easement? If so, what kind? Can a court order the bank not to interfere with the theater's use of the sidewalk?

10. In 1940 Schlagel purchased a tract of land from Baumgart. Sometime later Baumgart and Schlagel agreed orally to extend the back boundary line of the property in exchange for the payment of $200. Schlagel planted fruit trees, mowed the grass, operated an archery range, and conducted other activities indicating ownership of the tract throughout the years since 1940 in the belief that he owned the property. Schlagel now seeks to establish adverse possession in accordance with Pennsylvania's 21-year statute of limitations. Is Schlagel's possession sufficiently "hostile" within the meaning of the doctrine of adverse possession?

34 Bailments and Leases

Bailments

34:1 Introduction

A *bailment* is a legally recognized relationship that arises when one person delivers personal property to another on condition that the property be returned. The person who owns the property and turns over possession of it is called the bailor. The person to whom possession is given is the bailee. The principal elements of every bailment are (1) the bailor's delivery of property into the bailee's lawful custody or possession, (2) the bailee's acceptance of the property, and (3) the bailee's obligation to restore it to the bailor. Examples of particular bailment transactions include lending or leasing personal property for cleaning, repair, or the performance of services; delivering goods on commission for sale; and pledging personal property as security for a debt. A bailment also arises when goods are stored in a warehouse or transported by a common carrier.

Most bailments are created by express agreement. A bailment agreement can be oral or written, and it may or may not be supported by consideration. A bailment can also be implied by the parties' acts, however. For example, an implied bailment is created when a person deposits clothes with a dry cleaner. A written contract in such a situation is not ordinarily signed by the parties, it being understood that the clothes will be returned to the owner after they are cleaned. In addition, the law implies a bailment in certain situations. These bailments are known as involuntary or *constructive bailments*.

EXAMPLE: The captain of a fishing vessel unintentionally hauls in traps belonging to a commercial lobsterman and keeps them on board until the boat's return to port rather than throwing them back into the water. The captain is an involuntary bailee of the lobster traps. If, instead, the captain obtained possession of the traps through fraud or trickery, the bailment would be a constructive one.

Classes of Bailments   Bailments are generally classified according to the duties and liabilities of the parties. The three classes of bailments are (1) those for the sole benefit of the bailor, (2) those for the sole benefit of the bailee, and (3) those for the mutual benefit of both parties. By way of example, a bailment for the sole benefit of the bailor is created when the owner of a trailer stores it free of charge on a truck dealer's lot near his home. A bailment for the sole benefit of the bailee is created when a used-car dealer parks another's antique car in a display area of his car lot to attract customers. A *bailment for the mutual benefit* of both parties is created when one person leases a car from another. Bailments for the sole benefit of either the bailor or bailee are generally gratuitous, while bailments for the mutual benefit of both parties involve compensation and are known as bailments for hire.

The various elements of a bailment are discussed in the following case.

Stubbs

v

Hook

467 NE2d 29 (1984)

Court of Appeals of Indiana, First District

FACTS: Hook owned an airplane which he kept in a tie-down space he rented annually from Stubbs' Aviation Service. The airplane was parked in a space designated by Stubbs and located at the end of a 2,500-foot grass runway. Stubbs furnished the tie-down equipment, which consisted of brackets set in the ground linked to chains with manual fasteners that anyone could open. Stubbs possessed a set of keys for the airplane and moved it occasionally both by using the key and manually. Hook retained keys to the airplane. One day Hook arrived to pay his rental fee and was told that his airplane had been damaged two or three weeks earlier. The damage, which was located on the upper part of the right wing and on the engine cowling, appeared to have been caused by a ground vehicle. Hook claimed Stubbs was a bailee and was liable for the damage.

ISSUE: Did a bailment contract exist between Hook and Stubbs?

RESULT: No. There was no bailment relationship between the two.

REASONING:

* * *

A bailment is an agreement, either express or implied, that one person will entrust personal property to another for a specific purpose and that when the purpose is accomplished the bailee will return the property or the bailor will reclaim it. . . . In an action based upon breach of a bailment contract, proof that the property was received by the bailee in good condition and was damaged prior to being returned to the bailor raises an inference the bailee was negligent. . . . This rule is a recognition of the bailee's duty to exercise reasonable care to protect the bailor's property. . . .

In order for a bailment to exist, the bailed property must be delivered into the bailee's exclusive possession and accepted by the bailee. . . . It is essential to the creation of the relation of bailor and bailee that there be a delivery of the property to the bailee. In order to constitute a sufficient delivery in any given case, it is the general rule that there must be such a full transfer, either actual or constructive, of the property to the bailee as to exclude the possession of the owner and all other persons and give to the bailee, for the time being, the sole custody and control thereof.

We have not found any Indiana cases that apply this rule to factual situations analogous to the case at bar. Hook cites several cases from other jurisdictions for the proposition that rental of a tie-down space creates a bailment. In some of these cases, the parties agreed a bailment existed, . . . and in others, the possession issue was not raised, . . . therefore they are not applicable to the case at bar. However, a South Dakota case is exactly on point with the case before us.

In *Nelson v. Schroeder Aerosports, Inc.,* . . . the owner of an airplane sought to recover damages his plane sustained in a storm. He had rented a tie-down space from the defendant-airport operator. The plaintiff retained the keys to his airplane and allowed a third party access to it. Apparently, the plaintiff's case was predicated on the theory that the defendant negligently failed to properly anchor the aircraft prior to the storm, although the tie-downs were secure. The trial court directed a verdict for the defendant, which was affirmed on appeal, on the grounds that a bailment did not exist because the plaintiff had not relinquished exclusive control of the aircraft.

The only factual distinction between *Nelson* and Hook's case is that Stubbs had a set of keys for the airplane. Nevertheless, Hook retained keys to the aircraft and allowed a third party access to it. Therefore, the trial court erroneously concluded a bailment existed that put the burden of proof and ultimately the responsibility for the damage on the defendants. . . .

Robertson, Judge.

34:2 Termination of Bailments

A bailment can be terminated in a number of ways. For example, the parties can terminate a bailment by mutual agreement at any time, or one party might be able to rescind the bailment contract. A bailment for a stated period terminates at the end of that period; one for a specific purpose terminates when that purpose is accomplished. Destruction of the property may also terminate a bailment. Further, if a bailee acts improperly with respect to bailed property, the bailment may be terminated by operation of law, and any attempt by a bailee to sell or substantially abuse or misuse the bailed property automatically terminates the bailment in most states and entitles the owner to recover the property.

34:3   Rights and Liabilities of Bailor and Bailee

The rights, duties, and liabilities of a bailor and a bailee between one another are fixed by state statute or common law unless modified by the terms of a valid contract between them. The bailment contract determines the parties' specific rights and duties.

Title to Property and Right of Possession   On the creation of a bailment, title to the property remains in the bailor. Unauthorized acts by the bailee, such as a sale of bailed property to an innocent purchaser, do not affect the bailor's title, except in the situation where the bailor "entrusts" goods to a merchant who sells the goods to a buyer in the ordinary course of business. The entrustment doctrine is explored in Chapter 20. During the bailment, the bailee controls the property and can prevent others from possessing it. So long as the bailee acts within the purpose of a bailment, the bailor has no right to retake possession of the property without the bailee's consent.

Return of Bailed Property   On termination of a bailment, the bailee must return bailed property or account for it according to the terms of the bailment. A bailee who refuses to return property, disposes of it in an unauthorized manner, or uses it for purposes not contemplated in the bailment can be held liable to the bailor for damages. In most cases, the bailee must return the identical goods bailed. However, in the case of fungible goods, such as wheat, coffee, barrels of oil, or canned goods, a return of the same quantity as originally bailed is sufficient; each unit of the bailed property is the same as every other. Some bailment agreements include an option to purchase the bailed property. These options are often used in lease transactions. If the bailee exercises the option, the transaction becomes a sale and the bailee does not have to return the bailed property.

Bailee's Duty of Care   The degree of care required of a bailee depends on the class or type of bailment. When the bailment is for the bailor's sole benefit, without any compensation to the bailee, the bailee is answerable for loss or damage only if he is grossly negligent. When a bailment is mutually beneficial to both parties, the bailee is held responsible for ordinary negligence. When it is for the bailee's sole benefit, as in the case of a simple loan of property without compensation, the bailee must exercise the highest degree of care and will be held liable for even slight negligence resulting in loss or damage to the property. Distinctions in the duty of care among the three classes of bailments have been abolished in some states. There, all bailees must exercise ordinary care over bailed property depending on its nature, value, and quality; the circumstances under which it was deposited; and the terms of the bailment agreement. A few types of bailees, such as common carriers and innkeepers, are held strictly liable for loss or damage of bailed property on the grounds of public policy.

Burden of Proof   To recover for loss or damage to bailed property, the bailor must generally prove that the bailee breached his or her duty of care. In most states, the bailee's negligence is presumed if the bailee either is unable to redeliver bailed property at all or redelivers the property in a damaged condition. In these states, the bailor need only establish that a bailment was created, that bailed property was delivered in good condition, and that the bailee failed to return the property in the same condition at the end of the bailment. The bailee must then prove otherwise to avoid liability for the loss or damage. The rationale behind this rule is that the bailee is always in a better position to offer proof of his own care for bailed property than is the bailor to offer proof of the bailee's negligence.[1]

The following case illustrates the bailor's burden of proof and why bailment is considered a special relationship in the law. Consider the burden of proof and the presumption of negligence, and compare these with the requirements of proof in normal negligence cases.

Bernstein

v

Noble

487 A2d 231 (1985)

District of Columbia Court of Appeals

FACTS: In February 1984 Noble ordered a stereo tuner from a store in Maine and directed that it be shipped to his apartment in Bernstein's apartment building. The tuner was delivered to the apartment building on February 20 by UPS. The building receptionist signed a receipt for the tuner and placed the tuner on a shelf in a small room next to her desk. Access to the room was limited, and there were bars on the windows. When the night receptionist came on duty the tuner was still in the small room. Sometime during the night, however, it was removed from the room. The next day, the box the tuner came in was found outside the apartment building, but the tuner was missing. Noble sued Bernstein, alleging negligence in a bailment relationship.

ISSUE: Has the plaintiff shown a "prima facie case of negligence" in a bailment?

---

[1] Negligence and the burden of proof are discussed generally in Chapter 6.

RESULT: Yes. The necessary elements of a bailment relationship existed, and plaintiff has shown a prima facie case.

REASONING:

*   *   *

The creation of a bailment requires that possession and control over an object pass from the bailor to the bailee. . . . In this jurisdiction, a plaintiff may establish a prima facie case by showing the bailment and loss of his property. . . . Establishment of a prima facie case raises a presumption or inference of negligence on the part of the bailee; this presumption controls the result by rule of law where there is no evidence presented in rebuttal. . . . When a defendant comes forward with evidence to rebut the presumption, the evidence destroys the inference as a controlling rule of law but does not destroy its probative weight as an inference of fact. . . . In any bailment case, a bailee may establish that a loss of property was not due to a lack of proper care on his part, or he may offer affirmative proof that as bailee he exercised the degree of care which the particular bailment called for, although he may be unable to explain or justify the loss. But whatever defense he offers presents no more than a question of fact. . . .

A landlord may properly occupy the dual position of landlord and bailee. . . . [T]he nature of the bailment will determine the proper standard of care which the bailee must exercise. If the bailment is gratuitous, the liability would be limited to acts of gross negligence, willful acts, or fraud, . . . and in this jurisdiction, when a bailment is for hire, an exculpatory clause contained within a contract will also serve to limit liability to only those acts of gross negligence, willful acts, or fraud. . . . Such clauses are, however, construed against the landlord. . . .

In the instant case the landlords provided the locked room for packages received for tenants. Thus the relationship between the landlords and Noble with respect to the package in the room was that of bailor and bailee. . . . A bailment for hire was created when Mrs. McLean placed the package for Noble on the shelf. . . . The landlords were therefore required to exercise ordinary care, and proof by Noble of delivery and failure to produce the tuner established a prima facie case. . . .

Rogers, Associate Judge.

Limits on Liability   Frequently, bailees insert provisions in bailment agreements limiting their liability to specified amounts. If the terms of the contract are clearly called to the bailor's attention, or if the facts are such that the bailor is chargeable with notice of the terms (as, for example, by a large sign posted at a parking lot and limiting its liability), the limit on liability set forth in the bailment contract will be upheld, at least as to claims based on negligence or breach of contract. However, provisions that excuse or limit a bailee's liability for willful injury to bailed goods are usually held to violate public policy, and they are rarely enforced by the courts. In some states, liability-limiting provisions are declared unlawful by statute.

Bailee's Lien   A bailee who has worked on an article or performed some other act in reference to it by which its value has been enhanced has a lien on the property for the value of his reasonable services. This lien allows the bailee to keep the property until he is reimbursed for his labor and expenses.

EXAMPLE: A film editor edits 39,000 feet of exposed film to make a finished product of approximately 5,000 feet for the bailor. The bailor then fails to pay the editor the agreed amount for her services. The editor has a bailee's lien covering the film footage remaining in her possession.

A *bailee's lien* traditionally has been limited to keeping bailed property until payment of the lien. Most states provide by statute for the public sale of bailed property after notice to the bailor that the property will be put up for sale due to nonpayment. A bailee who fails to follow any of the statutory requirements in enforcing the lien can be liable to the bailor for conversion of the property.

Bailor's Duty of Care   The extent of a bailor's obligation depends primarily on the class of the particular bailment. In every bailment the bailor has a minimum obligation to refrain from knowingly delivering property that is likely to imperil the bailee's life or property. Where a bailment is purely gratuitous and for the bailee's exclusive benefit, as where articles are loaned without compensation, a bailor's only duty is to inform the bailee of any known defects. In a bailment for hire or for the mutual benefit of both parties, the bailor is held to a higher degree of responsibility. Although a bailor of this type is not ordinarily an insurer against injuries to the bailee for defects, he is held to a high degree of care to examine the property before it is bailed. Frequently he is regarded by the courts as impliedly warranting the reasonable suitability of the property for its intended use. If injury results from defective bailed property, the bailor can be liable for breach of this implied warranty. The bailor can also be liable for injuries caused by a defective condition in bailed property if the defect was known or was discoverable through the exercise of due care.

Rights and Liabilities as to Third Persons   If a third person damages or unlawfully obtains possession of bailed property, either the bailor or the bailee can maintain a damages action against the third person. If the bailor sues and recovers damages, the bailee is prevented from doing so, and vice versa.

Because the bailee has possession and control of bailed property, liability for injuries resulting to a third person normally falls on the bailee rather than the bailor, whose responsibility terminates with his relinquishment of control over the property. Thus, if a bailee tries to repair bailed property but does so negligently, he can be held liable for resulting injury or damage to third persons. However, the bailor will be held liable for injuries to a third person if the bailor has been negligent in entrusting a dangerous article to a person who he knows is unfamiliar with its dangerous character or is incompetent to operate it safely. For example, if a leased machine or motor vehicle is likely to cause injury to third persons unless operated with care and skill, the lessor (bailor) can be liable in damages for injuries inflicted by the bailee if he knows the bailee is incompetent or reckless. Likewise, a bailor who negligently furnishes a bailee with property that is not reasonably fit and proper for its known or intended use can be answerable to a third person injured from the use of the property. If, however, a third person is contributorily negligent, or if the third person's injuries result from obvious defects in the bailed article or defects that are unknown to the bailor, the bailor is not liable.

34:4   Special Bailments

Bailments are sometimes classified as being either ordinary or special. Ordinary bailments include those previously discussed in this chapter. Special bailments include those involving warehousers, common carriers, and innkeepers. These bailments are for the mutual benefit of both parties and in many respects are subject to the same rules that govern ordinary bailments. However, special bailments affect the public interest in such a way that, for reasons of public policy, the law has imposed on the special bailee a somewhat different liability from that imposed on the ordinary bailee. It should be noted that special bailees may and frequently do act as ordinary bailees and are treated as such whenever the reasons for their exceptional liability do not exist.

Consignors and Factors   A consignment is a transaction in which goods are delivered by their owner to another who is an agent to sell the goods. It is also called a bailment for sale and a bailment coupled with an agency to sell and, as such, is a special bailment. Delivery under a consignment is made with the understanding that the recipient (consignee) will either sell the property for the supplier (consignor) and remit the proceeds, or return the goods if a sale has not been made. The *consignor* retains title to the goods until a sale is made to a third party. The consignee never becomes personally liable for the purchase price except in the sense that he must account for the proceeds of any of his sales. When a consignee makes a sale, title to the goods flows immediately to the purchaser from the owner. By their nature, consignment transactions thus allow a supplier to sell goods through a merchant who is unwilling to accept risk. In a consignment, risk of loss is ordinarily placed on the consignor until the goods are sold to a third party, unless, of course, the consignment contains a provision to the contrary.

If a consignee is engaged in the business of selling goods, he is called a *factor* or commission merchant. A factor is an agent who is employed by another to sell property for him. The factor is vested by the owner with the possession or control of the property or with authority to receive payment from the purchaser for the property sold. In most states, the conduct of factors and other consignees is regulated by statutes known as Factors' Acts or

Traders' Acts. These acts govern the sale of consigned goods and the rights of purchasers. The UCC also governs the rights of purchasers of goods entrusted to a merchant who deals in goods of a particular kind.

Finders of Lost and Abandoned Property   Many states have enacted statutes that set forth procedures, usually involving advertising and the posting of notices, by which a finder of lost property can acquire title to it. Ordinarily, a person who finds lost property does not become its owner. Rather, the finder is a bailee who must exercise the same degree of care required of any other bailee. A person cannot claim to be a finder if goods are not in fact lost.

A finder of lost property is not entitled to compensation for his or her services but may be entitled to reimbursement from the owner for any expenses incurred in protecting or preserving the property or in advertising for the owner. The finder has a duty to restore the goods to the owner if known, and if unknown, to make reasonable efforts to locate the owner. The finder also has a duty to exercise reasonable care in ascertaining the right or identity of any person claiming to be the true owner. Thus, a finder can be liable to the owner if he carelessly gives found property to someone claiming to be the owner without making reasonable inquiries to determine the validity of the claim.

A finder of abandoned property obtains title to the goods. For example, goods that are discarded into an outdoor trash bin are assumed to be abandoned rather than lost. Title can be obtained by taking possession with the intent of possessing the property.

34:5   Warehousers

A *warehouser* stores bailed goods and merchandise for compensation. State and federal regulations have been enacted to regulate the warehouse business. In the states, the warehousing business is governed by common-law rules involving bailments and by statute, particularly Article 7 of the UCC. The federal government has enacted the United States Warehouse Act [7 USC §§ 241–273], which regulates the storage of agricultural products.

Warehouse Receipts   Under the UCC, a warehouser must issue and deliver a warehouse receipt for goods received for storage. The warehouse receipt acknowledges that the warehouser has received certain described property from the owner or depositor; it creates the bailment contract. Transfer of property stored in a warehouse can be made by a transfer of the warehouse receipt rather than by a physical transfer of the goods. This is so because in ordinary commercial transactions, a warehouse receipt is regarded as a symbolic representation of the property stored. The receipt can also modify the ordinary rules of liability that the law imposes on warehousers.

Warehouser Liability and Standard of Care   UCC § 7–204 provides that a warehouser is liable in damages for loss of or injury to goods caused by the failure to exercise reasonable care. What constitutes reasonable care depends on the circumstances, including the nature and value of the goods stored, their exposure to injury or loss, and the means taken to prevent the injury or loss. All warehousers are generally obligated to store goods in a place that is reasonably safe from dangers, both inside and outside the premises, and reasonably fit for goods of the type accepted. A warehouser's obligation with respect to the safekeeping of goods begins when control of them is assumed, and it terminates on their delivery to the proper person. In case of theft, the warehouser must show that the loss was caused by an event beyond his control, giving proof of the circumstances of the theft and some evidence of due care on his part.

 Not being an insurer of stored goods, the warehouser is not automatically liable for loss of bailed property. The UCC requires a warehouser to exercise the degree of care in relation to stored goods that a reasonably careful person would exercise under like circumstances.

Measure of Damages   The measure of damages in an action by an owner or depositor of warehoused goods against the warehouser is full compensation for the loss. If all the goods have been lost, recoverable damages are measured by the market value of the merchandise as reflected in the warehouse receipt. If goods have been damaged, the amount recoverable is the difference in value between the goods in the condition delivered to the warehouser and their value in the damaged condition on redelivery.

Limit on Liability   Warehouse receipts frequently contain clauses limiting the warehouser's liability in case of injury to or loss of stored goods. Unless a state statute governs the matter, courts usually uphold provisions limiting liability to an agreed valuation of the property. However, a limit on liability does *not* apply if the warehouser has willfully or intentionally damaged or injured the goods, or if the warehouser has converted them for personal use.

 Despite their general tendency to uphold liability-limiting provisions in storage contracts or warehouse receipts, as mentioned above, courts have ruled that stipulations totally relieving the warehouser from the consequences of his own negligence are invalid. The UCC provides that damages for loss of or damage to stored goods can be limited by the terms of the warehouse receipt or storage agreement. The receipt or agreement can set forth a specific liability per article, item, or unit of freight. However, any such receipt or storage agreement must provide the bailor an opportunity to request an increased valuation with a corresponding increase in rates. The UCC further permits reasonable conditions as to the time and manner of presenting claims to be included in the warehouse receipt or tariff.

34:6   Common Carriers

A *common carrier* engages in the business of transporting persons or property from place to place for compensation. It is a bailee with respect to property entrusted for delivery. Common carriers are extensively governed and controlled by federal and state statutes, as well as by the UCC. Since 1887, carriers engaged in interstate commerce have been regulated and controlled by the Interstate Commerce Act [49 USC §§ 1 et seq.]. The *Carmack Amendment* of 1916 is a portion of the Interstate Commerce Act. It codifies the common-law rule that a common carrier, although not an absolute insurer of goods transported, is liable for damage or loss to the goods unless the carrier can show that damage was caused by (1) an act of God, (2) a criminal act, (3) an act of the shipper, (4) action by a public authority, or (5) the inherent nature of the goods themselves [49 USC § 20(11)].

Under the Carmack Amendment, the initiating carrier is liable for the full amount of any damage to goods when they are in the care of the initiating carrier, any of the connecting carriers, or the delivering carrier. The initiating carrier's liability as an insurer ends when the final carrier ceases to act as a carrier and either assumes the role of warehouser or delivers the goods to the consignee.

The federal Bills of Lading Act of 1916 [49 USC §§ 81–124] governs bills of lading issued by common carriers for the transportation of goods in interstate or foreign commerce. Intrastate shipments and bills of lading are regulated by Article 7 of the UCC.

Carrier Liability and Duty of Care A common carrier's liability for loss, damage, or destruction of goods in transit is that of an insurer. That is, the carrier is strictly liable for loss, and no showing of its negligence is necessary unless one of the statutory or common-law exceptions applies. This rule of *strict liability* generally pertains regardless of whether a shipment is interstate (and thus subject to federal law) or intrastate (and thus subject to state law). However, limits on liability are common, and the parties can agree to reasonable limits as long as they do not violate public policy.

Freight Forwarders The *freight forwarder* is a person or firm in the business of assembling or consolidating goods that are consigned by shippers and are smaller than a carload, and then arranging for their shipment by a carrier for ultimate delivery to the intended consignees. The freight forwarder does not transport the goods, but acts as an agent or broker working with a carrier, which does the actual transporting. In receiving goods from shippers and in turn delivering them to a carrier, the freight forwarder is both consignee and consignor. Unless a freight forwarder also offers carrier services, it is not aware of the identity of the original consignors whose goods have been consolidated or of the ultimate consignees to whom the goods are being shipped. When the carload of consolidated goods arrives at its destination, it is broken up into the original shipments by the carrier and then delivered to the intended consignees.

34:7 Innkeepers

The business of innkeeping is as old as civilization and has a law of its own. As has been the case with other branches of the law, the rules governing innkeepers have necessarily been broadened in their application by the ever-changing conditions of modern life. The number of persons living in places other than the traditional home, either temporarily for business or pleasure, or indefinitely, has made the hotel business one of the country's largest industries.

The relationship between an innkeeper and a guest is a mutual one involving reciprocal rights and obligations. In most states many duties and obligations of both innkeepers and their guests are regulated by statute. Under a typical statute the innkeeper must furnish accommodations and exercise proper care for the safety and tranquility of the guest. In turn, a guest must observe recognized proprieties and refrain from conduct that would be offensive to other guests or bring the hotel into disrepute. Although an innkeeper's rates and charges can be fixed by contract between the parties, they are generally the same for all guests and must be just and reasonable.

Innkeeper Liability and Duty of Care   Under the common law, an innkeeper was practically an insurer of his guests' property. Today, most states have reduced the innkeeper's liability to that of an ordinary bailee. Most states also limit the extent of an innkeeper's liability, either to a stated amount for each piece of luggage or to a stated total for all other property, unless the innkeeper contractually agrees to assume a greater liability. If a guest desires to impose on an innkeeper liability in excess of the limit imposed by statute, the guest must notify the innkeeper of the nature and value of the property sought to be protected.

 Most state statutes that limit liability apply to money, jewelry, or other valuables that are to be kept within a hotel's safe or the guest's room. Under these statutes, unless the guest deposits articles of value in a hotel's safe or gives notice as to their value and existence, the innkeeper is usually absolved of any liability for loss.

Innkeepers' Liens   Under the common law, innkeepers were given a lien on their guests' property for the amount of reasonable charges furnished. That is, if a guest failed to pay, the innkeeper could assert a lien over the guest's property. In most states, the common-law lien has been codified, and innkeepers have the power to enforce their liens by court action or by sale of the property after a prescribed length of time. If a statutory lien enforcement procedure is prescribed, it is ordinarily exclusive and must be followed. Despite the increasing due process protections given owners of property before it may be taken or sold (as discussed in Chapter 31), for example, the constitutionality of these lien statutes has been upheld against contentions that they permit the taking of property without due process of law or without just compensation.

Leases of Personal Property

34:8   Introduction

The *leasing of personal property* plays a prominent and vital role in the American economy. Billions of dollars' worth of new and used goods and equipment are under lease today. It has been estimated that 70 percent of all computers, 30 percent of all passenger cars, 60 percent of all office equipment, 50 percent of all railroad cars, 25 percent of all aircraft, 15 percent of all ships, and 10 percent of all machinery and furniture are under lease.

A personal property lease entails the temporary transfer of possession and use of one's property for compensation to another, who agrees to return the property at a future time. The lease is a type of bailment and is generally governed by the rules of law applicable to bailments. The parties to a personal property lease used to be referred to as the lessor and the hirer, but today they are more commonly referred to as the lessor and the lessee.

Various types of leases are commonly used by the business community. The lease that is ultimately chosen depends, of course, on the circumstances of the leasing transaction and the parties' needs. Leases offer many advantages to a business. Since leasing does not require a large outlay of cash, working capital remains free for other uses. This freed working capital can improve the appearance of the lessee's short-term financial position as indicated on its balance sheet. Leasing is also preferable when permanent ownership is not desired, such as when a product is in a high technology field and is likely to become rapidly obsolete. Leases are also attractive to businesses that are subject to frequently changing government regulations or when property is likely to wear out or need constant repair. Leasing may be particularly attractive to a business experiencing a cash shortage. In this situation, leasing offers the additional advantages of conserving credit; the business can maintain its cash position by not having to pay a down payment in a purchase that is financed by a loan. Another financial benefit is more favorable tax treatment in that the business can often deduct larger sums for rentals than it could deduct for depreciation on a purchase. Finally, leasing can also be advantageous if the lessor provides other services such as accounting, maintenance, or repair. Bookkeeping is simplified in this situation, since the lessee's only expense is rent.

The following case involves the problem of when a lease terminates.

Fallon County

v

Brindley
687 P2d 722 (1984)
Supreme Court of Montana

FACTS: Brindley rented a Caterpillar Model 435 pull-type scraper from Fallon County on October 15, 1979. Brindley signed a lease contract and paid one month's rent of $500 in advance. The lease required Brindley to return the scraper to the County at the end of the desired rental period, and at the end of the pre-paid one-month period Brindley attempted to transport the scraper back to the Fallon County storage yard. Brindley winched the front wheels of the scraper up and chained the scraper to his truck. About 24 miles down the road, the scraper separated from the truck and sustained major structural damage; it was wrecked and virtually destroyed. The County sued Brindley, claiming, among other types of damages, continued rental of the scraper.

ISSUE: Did the lease terminate on the date of the accident?

RESULT: Yes. The lease terminated with the destruction of the subject matter of the lease.

REASONING:

*   *   *

[Montana law] provides: *"When hiring terminates. The hiring of a thing terminates . . . by the destruction of the thing hired."* This section and its predecessor apply to all things hired. In [a 1971 case] we held that [this statute] controlled termination of the lease of a "skidder" machine. In [a 1967 case] the statute controlled termination of a lease of premises in a building.

Absent a contractual provision to the contrary, the lease terminates by law upon the destruction of the thing hired. Only express agreement to the contrary can preclude operation of the statute. . . . No such agreement exists in this case.

In [the 1967 case], the only factual issue presented, other than damages, was whether a building that had been partially gutted by fire was repairable or destroyed. Lessor argued that the building was destroyed and plaintiff's lease terminated by operation of law. This Court set forth two tests for determining whether [the statute] applied.

The first test which the Court labeled an "untenability" test, is essentially a test for fitness for use:

> Under this test the thing hired is considered destroyed: 'When destruction of the demised premises is of such a nature that it cannot be used for the purposes for which it was rented and cannot be restored to a fit condition by ordinary repairs, made without unreasonable interruption of the lessee's use.' . . .

Under the second test, the Court considered the thing destroyed "if the cost of restoration . . . as it was immediately before the fire is more than one-half of the value of the property at the time of the fire." . . .

The Court held that under both tests the evidence lead to the conclusion that the building was destroyed. The Court observed that "parts of respondent's business were located in both buildings. A destruction of even the 'so-called' north building would be sufficient to terminate the lease under the statute involved." . . . Under both the fitness-for-use and cost-of-repairs tests, "destruction" can mean less than complete obliteration.

The record here indicates that the scraper's fitness for use ceased when it separated from Brindley's truck and "sustained serious structural damage." The County's complaint alleged that the "scraper was wrecked and virtually destroyed" by the accident. Commissioner Lang testified that the scraper was not fit for use, but that he had not investigated the cost of repairs. The record is silent as to the salvage value of the scraper, the cost of repairs, or how long it might take to return the scraper to fitness for use. . . .

Weber, Justice.

Regulation of Leases   The leasing of personal property is generally governed by the rules of law applicable to bailments. It is not ordinarily deemed to be within the scope of Article 2 of the UCC, which governs sales transactions. The applicability of the UCC to lease transactions, however, is undergoing rapid change, particularly through decisional law. Many states now apply the sales provisions of the UCC to leases, either directly or by analogy. Leases that are actually secured transactions continue to be regulated by Article 9 of the UCC (see Chapter 29). In addition, various states and the federal government have enacted statutes that regulate the leasing of personal property, particularly the leasing of motor vehicles. For example, in 1976 the federal government enacted the Consumer Leasing Act [15 USC §§ 1667a–1667e], which protects any lessee who has entered a "consumer lease" for a period exceeding four months for a total contractual obligation not exceeding $25,000.[2]

34:9   Rights and Liabilities of Lessee and Lessor

A lessee of personal property has a duty to use ordinary care to preserve the leased property safely and in good condition. This duty can be expanded or diminished by contract. Except to the extent that the duty has been modified by contract, a lessee who fails to exercise ordinary care must repair all damage to the property caused by this failure. The lessee must also bear all expenses naturally arising in the use of the property, such as the cost of diesel fuel for a leased bulldozer. As for the lessor, unless his duties have been modified by contract, he is obligated to repair all deterioration of and damage to the property not caused by the lessee. He may also be responsible for reimbursing the lessee for any expenses that the lessee incurred for repair work after having given the lessor sufficient notice that the work was necessary.

Liability for Defects in Leased Property   A lessor is obligated to put leased property into a condition fit for the purpose for which it is leased. If the lessor fails to do this, the lessee can pay for the work necessary to repair the defects after giving proper notice, and then recover his expenses. The lessor can be liable to the lessee for personal injuries, as well as property damage, resulting from the lessor's negligence. A lessor can also be liable to third persons injured by leased property that was defective at the time of delivery to the lessee.

---

[2] Consumer leases and the Consumer Leasing Act are discussed in Chapter 28.

A lessee or third party injured due to a defect in a leased article is confronted with many theories of liability on which an action against the lessor can be based. Negligence, discussed in Chapter 6, is the traditional remedy, but problems of proving negligence impair its effectiveness. In addition, defenses, such as assumption of the risk or contributory negligence, may bar or limit recovery in an action based on negligence. For these reasons, the modern trend is to hold purchasers or suppliers of products or other goods strictly accountable to intended users. As discussed below, one avenue open to an injured lessee or third party is recovery on an implied warranty theory, the basis of which is that a leased product must be (1) fit for the purpose for which it is intended and (2) of merchantable quality. Another avenue has been the imposition of strict liability in tort by which sellers and manufacturers of products are held strictly liable for injuries caused to users of these products regardless of fault.

Breach of Warranty Traditionally, warranty protections extended only to sales transactions. Increasingly, however, warranties have been extended to bailments and leases. Since nearly every state has adopted the UCC, cases now arise in which the express and implied warranty protections of the UCC are also sought to be applied. As discussed in Chapter 21, the warranties imposed by the UCC are both express and implied. UCC § 2-314 imposes on sellers certain implied warranties independent of the contract between the parties. UCC § 2-315 provides a warranty of fitness when a buyer relies on a seller's skill or judgment in selecting suitable goods. UCC § 2-316 provides that disclaimers inconsistent with express warranties will not be given legal effect. Finally, UCC § 2-318 lists those persons who receive warranty protection in personal injury cases.

The difficulty of applying the UCC warranty protections directly to leased transactions is that the UCC applies expressly to sales and not leases. Under Article 2 of the UCC, a buyer from a merchant seller is entitled to a warranty of merchantability, including a warranty that goods are fit for the ordinary purposes for which they are used. In contrast, in a lease situation there is no express warranty of merchantability under the UCC. The following case illustrates the situation in which an injured person argued that the Article 2 warranty provisions should apply to a lease transaction or bailment for hire. Consider whether the court's reasoning is persuasive.

Bona

v

Graefe
285 A2d 607 (1972)
Maryland Court of Appeals

FACTS: Bona was injured when the brakes of a power golf cart failed during its use on a golf course. Bona sued Royce, the owner–lessor of the cart, and Graefe, the golf course manager–sublessor, alleging breach of warranty. The trial court entered a directed verdict in favor of Royce and Graefe.

ISSUE: Are the warranties of the Uniform Commercial Code available to the lessee of personal property?

RESULT: No. The legislature did not intend the Code to be applicable to leases of personal property.

REASONING:

*   *   *

Perhaps no uniform act was the subject of more extensive study and debate prior to its adoption than the Uniform Commercial Code (the UCC). . . . The express warranty provisions of § 2-313 and the warranty of fitness implied by § 2-315 are parts of Article 2 of the UCC, which is clearly limited to sales of goods. Bona would have us read the sections as being also applicable to bailments for hire. Perhaps one answer to this contention, like A. P. Herbert's Lord Mildew's, is that if the draftsmen had intended the sections to apply to leases of goods as well as to sales, they should have said so. . . .

It seems anomalous to us that many authors of the texts and commentaries seem to take the stance that there should be no differentiation between sales and bailments under Article 2 of the UCC, reasoning either by analogy or by interpretation. . . .

For us to accept Bona's contention would take us beyond the limits of judicial restraint and into the area of judicial legislation. . . .

Concededly, a few courts have read UCC § 2-315 as being applicable to cases where a chattel is the subject of a lease rather than a sale. . . . Most frequently these are instances where the arrangements are equivalent to the purchase price plus interest, or a purchase is contemplated at the end of the lease period, and the lessee assumes obligations more consistent with ownership than with bailment. . . .

Another class of bailor–bailee cases is bottomed on strict liability in tort, . . . although on occasion, passing reference may be made to the implied warranties of the UCC. . . .

There is a third type of case in which one who leases goods has been held to have impliedly warranted either under common law concepts or by analogy to the UCC the suitability of the chattel leased. . . .

Other cases may give lip service to breach of warranty but usually require proof coextensive with that required in a negligence action. . . .

Another case to which we have been referred which applied UCC thinking to the lease of a chattel . . . also involved an injury suffered by the lessee of a golf cart when there was a brake failure. There the court struck down a disclaimer contained in a lease, analogizing the lease to a sale, by applying UCC § 2-316 and § 2-719. . . .

Maryland seems never to have adopted what has been the general rule elsewhere: that the bailor of a chattel to be used by the bailee for a particular purpose known to the bailor impliedly warrants the reasonable suitability of the chattel for the bailee's intended use of it. . . .

Consequently, the liability of the lessor of a chattel, as distinguished from that of a vendor, if it is to be imposed at all in Maryland, must be imposed in a tort action for negligence. It is not enough for a plaintiff to prove that a lessor failed to make proper inspections; he must prove either that the lessor knew of the defect or that a reasonable inspection, if made, would have disclosed the defect. . . .

Singley, Judge.

Strict Liability in Tort   The doctrine of strict tort liability imposes on sellers and manufacturers strict liability for injuries caused to a user of products regardless of fault.[3] The doctrine of strict liability often offers an injured bailee the most convenient path for recovering damages for injuries caused in the lease of a product. Strict liability in tort is particularly useful in situations in which parties have contractually eliminated warranties of fitness or merchantability; in these cases it may offer an injured lessee or third party the only path for recovery of damages. Under the doctrine of strict liability in tort, one who, as lessor, leases a product that is (1) defective and (2) dangerous to the user is liable for harm if the lessor is engaged in the business of leasing such products and if the product is expected to and does reach the consumer without substantial change in its condition. The injured person must prove that (1) the leased article was the cause of the injury, (2) the defect existed at the time the product left the lessor's possession and control, and (3) the defect made the article unreasonably dangerous.

The following case illustrates a lessor's liability under the doctrine of strict liability in tort for defects causing personal injuries. Note the difference between the expansive opinion and reasoning of the California Supreme Court in this case and the more narrow, strict constructionist opinion of the Maryland Court of Appeals in the previous case, *Bona v Graefe*, concerning the applicability of the UCC warranty protections to lease transactions. Consider whether the Maryland court would have been as receptive as the California court to a contention that strict liability applies to leases as well as sales.

Price

v

Shell Oil Co.
466 P2d 722 (1970)
California Supreme Court

FACTS: Price, an airline mechanic, sustained injuries when a ladder on a tank truck he was climbing split into segments. The ladder was part of a truck leased to his employer by Shell Oil Company. A suit was brought

---

[3] Product liability is discussed in Chapter 21.

against Shell, and Price's case was submitted to the jury on the theory of strict liability in tort. The jury returned a verdict against Shell Oil.

ISSUE: Is the doctrine of strict liability in tort available to lessees of personal property?

RESULT: Yes. The doctrine of strict liability is available to lessees of personal property under the same circumstances it would be available to buyers of goods.

REASONING:

*   *   *

We hold in this case that the doctrine strict liability in tort which we have heretofore made applicable to sellers of personal property is also applicable to bailors and lessors of such property. . . .

Shell contends that the trial court erred in submitting the case to the jury on the issue of strict liability. It argues that it is not a manufacturer, distributor or retailer of gasoline trucks. On the contrary, Shell asserts that in the present circumstances it was a bailor or lessor [with] . . . no greater duty than that of exercising ordinary care. In support of this contention Shell notes that section 408 of the *Restatement Second of Torts* "continues to hold" *lessors* of personal property liable only for negligence although section 402A now imposes strict liability upon sellers of such property. From this premise Shell argues that the *Restatement* did not intend to apply strict liability to lessors.

The rule is now settled in California that "A manufacturer is strictly liable in tort when an article he places on the market, knowing that it is to be used without inspection for defects, proves to have a defect that causes injury to a human being." . . . A retail dealer, being an "integral part of the overall producing and marketing enterprise" . . . is similarly liable. . . . We have given this rule of strict liability a broad application. . . .

Such a broad philosophy evolves naturally from the purpose of imposing strict liability which "is to insure that the costs of injuries resulting from defective products are borne by the manufacturers that put such products on the market rather than by the injured persons who are powerless to protect themselves." . . . Essentially the paramount policy to be promoted by the rule is the protection of otherwise defenseless victims of manufacturing defects and the spreading throughout society of the cost of compensating them. . . .

[W]e can perceive no substantial difference between *sellers* of personal property and *nonsellers*, such as bailors and lessors. [Court's emphasis.] In each instance, the seller or nonseller "places [an article] on the market, knowing that it is to be used without inspection for defects. . . . " In the light of the policy to be subserved, it should make no difference that the party distributing the article has retained title to it. Nor can we see how the risk of harm associated with the use of the chattel can vary with the legal form under which it is held. Having in mind the market realities and the widespread use of the lease of personalty in today's business world, we think it makes good sense to impose on the lessors of chattels the same liability for physical harm which has been imposed on the manufacturers and retailers. The former, like the latter, are able to bear the cost of compensating for injuries resulting from defects by spreading the loss through an adjustment of the rental. . . .

[We are not] dissuaded from our above conclusion by Shell's somewhat oblique argument that the *Restatement Second of Torts* in section 408 imposes on *lessors* of personal property liability only for negligence while in section 402A it imposes strict liability only on *sellers* of such property. [Court's emphasis.] This is no more than saying what is obvious—that the doctrine of strict liability as articulated in the *Restatement* was not made applicable against lessors or bailors. As we have explained, we think it should be, . . . even though the authors of the *Restatement* refrained from expressing such a view.

For the above reasons, we are of the opinion that the doctrine of strict liability in tort should be made applicable to bailors and lessors of personal property in the same manner as we have held it applicable to sellers of such property. . . .

However, since we reason by analogy, we make clear that the doctrine should be made applicable to lessors in the same way as we have made it applicable to sellers. . . .

Sullivan, Justice.

Key Concepts and Terms

- A bailment is the relationship that is created when one person deposits his or her property with another person. The person who owns the property and turns over possession of it is the bailor. The person to whom possession is given is the bailee.

- The principal elements of every bailment are (1) the bailor's delivery of property into the bailee's lawful custody or possession, (2) the bailee's acceptance of the property, and (3) the bailee's obligation to restore it to the bailor.

- A bailment does not involve any change in title to or ownership of the bailed property, but only a change in regard to possession.

- On termination of bailment, the bailee must return bailed property or account for it according to the terms of the bailment.

- Exceptions to the rule requiring the bailee to return bailed property arise in bailments of fungible goods and in those coupled with an option to purchase.

- Bailments are generally classified as (1) those for the sole benefit of the bailor, (2) those for the sole benefit of the bailee, and (3) those for the mutual benefit of both parties.

- To recover for loss of bailed property under a bailment for the mutual benefit of both parties, the bailor need only establish (1) that a bailment was created, (2) that the bailed property was delivered in good condition, and (3) that the bailee failed to return the property in the same condition at the end of the bailment. The bailee is presumed to have been negligent and must prove otherwise.

- Special bailments are for the mutual benefit of both parties and affect the public interest in such a way that the law has imposed on the bailee somewhat greater liability than that imposed on the ordinary bailee. Examples of special bailees are warehousers, carriers, and innkeepers.

- A common carrier transports property (and people) from place to place for compensation. Common carriers are generally strictly liable for loss or damage to property delivered to them unless they can show that the loss or damage was caused by means beyond their control.

- The personal property lease is a type of bailment and is generally governed by the rules of law applicable to bailments. The parties to a personal property lease are commonly referred to as the lessor and the lessee.

- A personal property lessor is obligated to put leased property into a condition fit for the purpose for which it is leased. The lessor's liability for defects in leased property may be based on negligence, breach of warranty, or strict liability in tort.

- A lessee has the duty to use ordinary care to preserve leased property safely and in good condition.

- Bailee's Lien
- Bailment
- Bailment for Mutual Benefit
- Breach of Warranty
- Carmack Amendment
- Common Carrier
- Consignor
- Constructive Bailment
- Consumer Lease
- Factor
- Freight Forwarder
- Lease
- Special Bailment
- Strict Liability
- Warehouse Receipt

Questions and Case Problems

1. Mrs. Brown brings her drapes in good condition to Howard's Laundry for cleaning. When she picks them up, they have shrunk. The laundry's efforts to stretch the drapes are unsuccessful. Was a bailment created? If so, what must Mrs. Brown prove to recover for damages sustained to her drapes?

2. Weinberg holds a "Parkard" issued by the Wayco Petroleum Company, entitling him to park his automobile in the company's five-story garage. The card states

that the holder is licensed to park one automobile at his own risk, that he should lock his car, and that Wayco will not be responsible for the car or its contents. Entrance to the self-park garage is gained by placing the "Parkard" in a mechanical device that opens the entrance gate. No specific space is assigned to Weinberg, and he can park anywhere in the garage. One night, after Weinberg parks his car, the car is broken into and personal property is stolen. Was a bailment created? Is Wayco liable to Weinberg? Would the result be different if an attendant were on duty who retained ignition keys and parked the vehicles?

3. Plaintiff left his disabled automobile unattended in a parking lot overnight. On the next day he called Autohaus to arrange for repairs and took his car keys to Autohaus. The automobile was towed to Autohaus' lot. Autohaus employees then locked the car and placed the keys inside the service department. When the work was complete and Wright arrived at Autohaus to claim his automobile, there was damage to the body, the radio and audio equalizer were missing from the interior, and numerous items were missing from the trunk. At plaintiff's request, Autohaus repaired the car and replaced the radio but indicated that payment for these expenses would be plaintiff's responsibility. Plaintiff claims Autohaus is liable for the damage as a bailee of the automobile. What result?

4. Southeastern Steel hires Luttrell to weld the engine of an air compressor which was damaged when water froze in the cooling system. Before delivering the compressor to Luttrell, employees of Southeastern remove various parts, but they leave oil, and possibly gasoline and ether, in the compressor. Following the custom of the welding trade, Luttrell makes no examination of the engine before welding. The contents ignite, causing an explosion with resulting injuries to Luttrell, who sues Southeastern Steel for damages. Was a bailment created? If so, what duty did Southeastern Steel owe to Luttrell? How should the case be decided?

5. Hollins contracted with AATCO to have his automobile transmission replaced. While his car was in AATCO's shop, it was stolen. The car had been parked in a locked building, and the building was surrounded by a chain link fence with a locked gate. However, although it was AATCO's usual practice to remove the key from the ignition of each car being worked on, the key had been left in Hollins' car the night it was stolen. When Hollins came to pick up his car, he was informed of the theft and told that the car had been found at a salvage yard; the engine, transmission, tires, accessories, and hood had been removed, and the body of the car had been burned. Hollins sues AATCO as a bailee. Can AATCO successfully argue that, under the circumstances, it was not negligent?

6. Skate Escape operates a roller skate and bicycle rental business. Hall rented a pair of skates from Skate Escape to go roller skating with friends. She fell almost immediately after putting on the roller skates, and upon examination she found that one of the axles was bent. She was hospitalized with a broken ankle and missed a period of time from work. The rental contract for the skates provided:

> BY HIS ACCEPTANCE AND REMOVAL OF BIKES AND/OR SKATES FROM LESSOR'S LOCATION, CUSTOMER AGREES BIKES AND/OR SKATES ARE IN ACCEPTABLE OPERATING CONDITION, AND THAT LESSOR MAKES NO WARRANTIES, EXPRESS OR IMPLIED, IN CONNECTION THEREWITH.

Does this language exclude Hall's suit for negligence relating to the condition of the bailed property?

7. On the eve of an extended trip to Europe, Kraut, a collector of rare Russian enamels, places approximately 300 of her acquisitions, valued at $731,000, in

storage with Morgan, a commercial storage company. The enamels are later stolen from Morgan's warehouse. After advertising that she will pay a reward for their return, Kraut recoups most of the stolen items by paying an unidentified intermediary $71,000. Can Kraut recover from Morgan the ransom and other expenses paid to recover the stolen art? Why?

8. Mrs. Caranas leaves her purse containing $5 in cash, credit cards, and ten pieces of jewelry worth $13,000 in the restaurant of the Hilton Hotel, where she and her husband are lodging. A busboy finds the purse and gives it to the hotel cashier, who later gives it to a man who came to claim it. The claimant was not Mr. Caranas. The Caranases sue the hotel for their loss. Was a bailment created? What is the extent of the hotel's liability?

9. How does the duty of care applicable in ordinary bailment/lease situations differ from the duty of care of a warehouser or a common carrier?

10. Sister Stang is killed in an automobile accident when the tire on a leased car in which she is riding blows out, causing the accident and her death. Should her representatives be permitted to recover against the lessor under the doctrine of strict liability in tort? Would it make any difference if the lessor were not in the business of leasing vehicles on a regular, continuous basis? Would it make a difference if the driver of the car rented it for one day rather than for a longer term?

35 Purchase and Sale of Real Property

35:1 Introduction

The purchase of real property—and buildings—either by businesses or by individuals usually involves the investment of substantial sums of money for relatively long periods of time and the transfer of valuable assets. Indeed, the purchase of a home ordinarily represents the average American's largest single purchase.

The purchase and sale of real property is governed primarily by state law. However, federal laws also apply to some extent. These laws are limited to specific national problems for which individual state remedies have been inadequate. For example, the Real Estate Settlement Procedures Act [12 USC §§ 2601 et seq.] standardizes the disclosure of financial information required in connection with a sale of residential property. The Interstate Land Sales Full Disclosure Act [15 USC §§ 1701–1720] governs the sale or lease of subdivision lots by developers throughout the country. It requires sub-divisions to be registered and detailed records and property reports to be filed.

The procedures involved in selling residential property are basically the same as those involved in the sale of commercial real estate, which is property purchased by a business or for business purposes. In most states, the typical home purchase or simple commercial real estate transaction involves (1) a brokerage contract, (2) preliminary negotiations with a prospective purchaser, (3) the deposit receipt, (4) a contract of sale, (5) a mortgage or other security instrument, (6) a survey or other investigation of the property, (7) title insurance, (8) drafting of documents, and (9) the closing in escrow. Except for mortgages, which are discussed in Chapter 36, these matters are discussed in this chapter. Additional considerations in commercial real estate transactions include the type of financing to be used, tax problems, and the structure of the entity that is to acquire title to the property.

If property is to be acquired by individuals or by a married couple, all parties must consider how title to the property will be held. For example in states where the law of community property applies, a husband and wife may acquire the property as the separate property of either spouse, as community property, or in joint tenancy. For both individuals and businesses, therefore, the choice of the purchasing entity, or how title will be held, is a vital concern. This decision may affect the degree to which property will be taxed, the liability of owners, and the ease of transferability. The form of ownership which is ultimately chosen depends on the purchaser's needs, the reasons for acquiring the property, and the advantages one form of ownership offers over the others.

 The form of ownership (how title to the property being acquired will be held) should be determined during the initial stages of a purchase. For a business, how title is held can vitally affect its liability, taxation, or the ease with which it can undertake future property transactions. Property can be purchased by one or more individuals, a partnership, a joint venture, a corporation, or a trust. Convenience and simplicity of ownership, as well as the ease of transfer, may dictate that the name of an individual be used to acquire property. In other situations, the limited liability of corporations or their more favorable tax structure might favor acquisition by a corporation. Occasionally, it may be desirable to use a third person otherwise unconnected with the purchase as the purchasing entity. For example, if several tracts of land are being acquired for development, confidentiality may be most important, requiring the purchase of property in this fashion.

35:2 The Brokerage Contract

Most sales of residential and commercial property are handled through brokers. A real estate broker is an agent of the buyer or the seller and is ordinarily compensated by that party.[1] The broker may neither acquire an interest adverse to the principal nor make a profit other than the commission to which he is entitled, unless, of course, the principal acquiesces or consents to a different arrangement.

 Most sellers of residential property are well aware that the broker is entitled to a commission on completion of the sale. In most states, however, a broker is said to earn a commission when a buyer "ready, willing, and able to buy on the seller's terms" is found. Therefore, in these states it is possible for a broker to legally earn a commission even though a sale was never actually closed. Sellers are thus advised to obtain a written agreement from the broker that provides for payment of the broker's commission only "if, as, and when" title passes to the purchaser.

The Listing Agreement The rights and obligations of the seller and the real estate broker are ordinarily set forth in a *listing agreement*. This is a contract of employment that gives the broker limited authority to act on the owner's

---

[1] The agency relationship is discussed in Chapter 43.

behalf to sell the property. In return, the broker is entitled to a commission contingent on the performance of the services within the terms of the listing agreement.

There are five basic types of listing agreements in general use in the real estate brokerage business.

1. The *exclusive authorization and right to sell contract* gives the broker the sole right to sell property listed. Even if the owner sells the property, the broker is still entitled to the agreed commission.

2. An *exclusive agency contract* gives the broker taking the listing the exclusive right to act as an agent to sell the owner's property. The owner promises the broker that the property will not be listed with any other agent during the period of time the exclusive agency contract is in effect. However, since the owner is not an agent, he or she may sell the property without being obligated to pay the broker a commission on the sale.

3. In certain situations, a *nonexclusive agency contract* is used with specific commencement and termination dates stated. As the name implies, the broker under contract does not have the exclusive right to represent the owner. If specific dates are included in the contract, the agency begins and ends at a certain time.

4. In contrast, an *open listing*, which is very similar to the nonexclusive agency contract, requires no termination date. An open listing may be terminated at any time before sale of the property without the owner incurring any liability to the broker.

5. Finally, the *net listing* is used occasionally for an owner who has determined the selling price of the property but is willing to let the broker make whatever can be made on the sale by trying to sell it for more. In other words, the seller fixes a price for the property and the broker may sell it for more money. The price differential becomes the broker's commission. This type of listing assumes, of course, that the seller knows the market, knows how much the property is worth, and has full faith in the broker selected. If not, there is a potential for fraud; for this reason the net listing is used less often than the other types of agreements.

A somewhat related type of contract used by real estate brokers is known as a *multiple listing agency contract*. This is a device used by a group of brokers to obtain a wider market for the sale of property. Property is listed, usually on a weekly basis, among the subscribing brokers, all of whom thus have a quick and easy reference to most of the property being sold in any given area. The multiple listing usually entails an exclusive agency contract with the broker.

35:3 Preliminary Negotiations

When a potential buyer indicates to a broker or directly to the seller an interest in purchasing property offered for sale, negotiations usually begin between the parties, particularly in the more complicated residential and commercial transactions. Normally, the broker acts as an intermediary. In some cases, the broker conducts all of the negotiations, while the seller merely ratifies the agreement reached with the purchaser. In other cases, attorneys representing the parties conduct the negotiations and draft all of the pertinent documents involved in the sale. During negotiations, the parties must agree on all of the terms of the purchase and sale. They must consider such problems as the mode of paying the purchase price, tax consequences, the status of fixtures or personal property, the time in which possession is to be transferred, and who must pay for repairs or bear the burden of loss prior to closing. Important questions should be anticipated by the parties.

 The purchaser and seller should thoroughly discuss and agree on all of the pertinent details of the contract of sale, thus preventing future disputes as to the meaning of terms, and even litigation in case the sale falls through.

Representations and Warranties   Representations and warranties play an important role in the sale of real property. A major purpose of representations and warranties is to furnish information about the property that will help the purchaser decide whether to buy the property and to protect the purchaser from future surprise as to what has actually been purchased. A *representation* is a statement of fact or opinion during negotiations that induces one of the parties to enter into the contract of sale. A warranty is basically a promise made by the seller that a certain fact relating to the property or the contract of sale is or will be as it is stated or promised to be.

If there is a breach of a representation, the affected party may be able to void the contract, unless the breach has been waived. In contrast, if there is a breach of a warranty, the contract remains binding and the injured party is entitled only to damages.

Seller's Considerations   There are a variety of factors that the seller should consider in negotiating a contract of sale. During negotiations, the seller must be assured that once the terms of the contract have been reached and the contract is signed, it will be binding on the parties. In addition, if representations and warranties are to be made, the seller should limit their scope and restrict the time period during which they will be effective. If the purchaser is deferring payment of a portion of the purchase price, the seller should set forth the specific provisions of the financing agreement and the parties' obligations.

A seller should also take into account the tax consequences of a real estate transaction. For income tax purposes, a gain or loss is not recognized until there is a sale, exchange, or other disposition of property. A gain or loss is measured as the difference between (1) the amount realized, such as cash and other property received; and (2) the adjusted basis of the property, including the seller's cost, acquisition expenses, and certain other expenses such as the cost of constructing a building that the seller erected on the property. If a seller can postpone a gain (or sometimes a loss), he might obtain substantial tax savings.

The most commonly used methods of deferring gain or loss are installment sales and *"like kind" exchanges* of property between a purchaser and seller. For example, a seller can elect to postpone reporting income, and thus defer taxes, when the transaction is structured so that installment payments are received from the purchaser beyond the year of sale. In this fashion, gain is spread out over several tax years, and tax liability is reduced.

Sellers of residential housing commonly take advantage of a federal tax law that permits them to defer income and hence reduce taxes. If a seller purchases and uses a new principal residence within a prescribed period (currently 24 months) after the date of sale, gain is recognized only to the extent that the sale price of the old residence exceeds the cost of the new one. Taxation of the rest of the gain is deferred, even though a profit has been made by the seller within the particular taxable year.

Purchaser's Considerations   In buying a particular piece of property, the purchaser should be concerned with the price, how and to what extent it will be financed, the amount of debt to be incurred, and the costs of financing.[2] In negotiating the purchase of real property, the purchaser, unlike the seller, will want as many conditions in the contract as possible to assure that the property will meet his requirements in every respect. The purchaser should insist that (1) the property not be threatened or adversely affected by eminent domain or natural disaster on the closing date; (2) the seller's representation and warranties, if any, be true on the closing date; (3) the seller comply with all of his agreements on or before the closing date; and (4) that the property be properly zoned and that no proposed zoning change occur before the date set for closing. A purchaser should condition the sale on the receipt of satisfactory evidence that adequate utilities, including water and sewer, are available to service the property. The purchaser might also want to include a condition that any necessary easements be obtained. Obviously, the matters covered by some of these conditions may appear to be remote, but no one would like to be the purchaser of a piece of property, for example, that is under water on the closing date as a result of an unexpected flood, without being protected by appropriate conditions in the contract of sale. In negotiating the contract of sale, the purchaser should remain flexible, always bearing in mind the principal objectives in purchasing the property. If these objectives are met the sale should be concluded; if not, the purchaser should not enter into a contract of sale or should withdraw from negotiations.

35:4   Purchase Price and Deposit Receipt

Perhaps the most important aspect of any sale is the purchase price and how it will be determined. A total dollar amount ordinarily forms the basis of most residential and commercial transactions. Price may be determined by the total area of the property to be sold, calculated on a per-acre or per-

---

[2] Mortgages and deeds of trust used in financing the purchase of land and buildings are discussed in Chapter 36.

square-foot basis. If area is used as the means of determining price, the contract of sale should include the total number of acres of square feet to be included within the purchase. In other transactions, portions of property to be sold may be more valuable than other portions. For example, different zoning classifications may apply to different portions of property to be sold. In such cases, it may be advantageous for the purchaser to allocate the purchase price among the various portions of the property according to their relative value. Such an allocation can affect subsequent taxation of the property or may even affect the profits to be made when the various portions are sold in the future.

Deposit Receipt   In most residential and commercial real estate transactions handled by a broker, the prospective purchaser makes the seller an offer, accompanied by a deposit, also known as *earnest money*, that is later credited to the purchase price. The document by which the offer is made, and which shows the amount of the deposit, is called a *deposit receipt*. After the prospective purchaser signs the deposit receipt, the seller can accept or reject the offer. If the offer is accepted, a contract is ordinarily prepared and signed, and the transaction is then concluded in escrow. It should be noted, however, that in some states the deposit receipt is the only contract between the parties. It becomes a contract in these states when the seller signs it, thus showing his acceptance of the offer.

In the purchaser's offer there should be no material variance between the terms and conditions set forth in the listing agreement by which the property is offered for sale and those contained in the deposit receipt. Because the owner in most cases will already have indicated the terms of sale, the purchaser will not usually vary his offer significantly from the terms and conditions of the listing, except perhaps for the purchase price. These procedures as to offers, of course, are more applicable to the ordinary sale of residential housing than to more complicated commercial transactions in which extensive negotiations between the parties usually precede an offer or deposit receipt.

In the ordinary, uncomplicated real estate transaction in which the broker acts as an intermediary between the parties, the deposit receipt used in a given locality is a standard form. The form often provides that if a purchaser fails to pay the balance of the purchase price or to complete the purchase as provided in the receipt, any amounts paid on deposit by the purchaser can be retained by the seller as liquidated damages. Some deposit receipts also provide that the broker retain as a commission a portion of the forfeited deposit. Note, however, that in some states the seller must return to the buyer any amount over the actual damages suffered by the seller and caused by the buyer's breach. Of course, if the seller either refuses or fails to perform, the purchaser is entitled to the return of his deposit.

The following case illustrates the legal effect of the deposit receipt in a state where a valid deposit receipt constitutes a binding contract between the purchaser and seller. Note that the breach of a deposit receipt can subject the offending party either to damages or specific performance of the contract.

Meyer

v

Benko
55 Cal App 3d 937 (1976)
California Court of Appeal

FACTS: The Meyers wanted to purchase the Benkos' home. The parties
executed a signed deposit receipt that named the sellers and buyers,
identified the property being sold, specified a price of $23,500, detailed
the method of financing, and allocated various incidental costs and
duties. The deposit receipt also required the seller to do any necessary
work at his expense. The purchase price was apparently somewhat below
the market value. As a condition to guaranteeing the Meyers' loan, the
Federal Home Administration (FHA) required that a new roof be installed.
Both parties refused to pay for the cost of the roof, and the loan
commitment lapsed. The Meyers then filed suit seeking specific performance of the contract and alleging that despite the fact that they had
performed all of the conditions precedent to the conveyance of the
property, the Benkos' refused to convey the property.

ISSUE: Did the deposit receipt constitute a contract between the Meyers and
the Benkos?

RESULT: Yes. The deposit receipt constituted a valid, enforceable contract.

REASONING:

*   *   *

Every contract requires the mutual assent or consent of the parties. . . .
The existence of mutual consent is determined by objective rather than
subjective criteria, the test being what the outward manifestations of
consent would lead a reasonable person to believe. . . . Accordingly, the
primary focus in determining the existence of mutual consent is upon
the acts of the parties involved. In the case at bar, this focus is directed
toward the Deposit Receipt and related documents, and the actions of
the parties during the period of time encompassing the execution of these
documents.

The utilization of the objective test of mutual consent demonstrates
that the Deposit Receipt is in fact a contract. The fact that this document
was signed by *both* parties indicates that the parties entered into an
enforceable agreement. [Court's emphasis.] . . . Although the parties
introduced conflicting testimony as to whether or not the terms of the
Deposit Receipt were explained to the defendants before they signed that

document, this evidence was not sufficient to establish a lack of mutual consent. "The general rule is that when a person with the capacity of reading and understanding an instrument signs it, he is, in the absence of fraud and imposition, bound by its contents, and is estopped from saying that its explicit provisions are contrary to his intentions or understanding." . . . In addition, the material factors common to a contract for the sale of real property are contained within the terms of the Deposit Receipt. The Deposit Receipt named the sellers, named the buyers, identified the property being sold, and specified the price for which that property was being sold. Further, it detailed the method of financing the transaction, as well as providing an allocation of various incidental costs and duties. The presence of these material factors upon the face of the document raises two inferences, both of which indicate the existence of mutual consent. First, these factors indicate that the parties had proceeded beyond the stage of mere preliminary negotiations and into the stage of actual contract formation. Moreover, the presence of this material in the document gave notice to the subscribing parties, notably the defendants, that they were entering into a binding contract by subscribing their signatures upon that document. The evidence introduced by the defendants relating to their lack of knowledge about the implications of the terms contained in the Deposit Receipt fails to rebut these inferences. Finally, the execution of the escrow instructions, whose terms substantially mirrored those found in the Deposit Receipt, further demonstrates the mutual consent of the parties to those terms as a binding commitment.

In toto, the various facts discussed above lead to the inescapable conclusion that, based upon an objective test of contract formation, the parties mutually assented to the formation of a contract on the terms and conditions set forth in the Deposit Receipt. Accordingly, pursuant to the term obligating the seller "to pay for . . . FHA appraisal and . . . to do any necessary work at his expense," the defendants were bound to pay for the new roof.

We take note of the fact that our resolution of this case is consistent with the general view that such deposit receipts constitute binding and enforceable contracts. . . .

Stephens, Judge.

35:5 The Contract of Sale

After the terms of sale have been negotiated, the purchaser and seller must enter into a formal contract unless the deposit receipt serves as a contract, as discussed above. The importance of this document cannot be overstated. Because each sale is unique, a special contract is ordinarily required, particularly in commercial transactions. The contract should be prepared by an attorney and signed by all parties concerned.

Land Contract   The most common type of sale contract used is the *land contract*. Under it, one party agrees to convey title to real property to the other party on the satisfaction of specified conditions set forth in the contract. While the form of the land contract varies from state to state, many of the basic provisions are similar.

The land contract is ordinarily executory in nature. That is, the terms and conditions specified in the contract must be performed by either or both of the parties in the future. These obligations generally include (1) the seller's delivery of a deed on his receipt of all the purchaser's payments and (2) the seller's turning over possession of the property to the purchaser. Usually the purchaser is allowed to take possession after the contract has been signed, but before delivery of the deed. At times, however, the purchaser receives possession only after title has been transferred and all the conditions of sale have been performed. In this event, the land contract will often provide for such matters as the use of the property during the pendency of the sale and the right to rents or profits generated by the property during that period.

Land contracts often include basic representations and warranties covering such matters as the marketability of title and the absence of pending condemnation proceedings. These representations and warranties are usually made by the seller. In certain circumstances, a seller might make representations or warranties as to the existence of leases and tenants, pending litigation, special assessments, building permits, or the assessed valuation of the property.

Many contracts include provisions for the award of damages in case of breach, and a fixed (or liquidated) damages clause is often used for this purpose. This clause provides that in the event of breach or default by one party, a specific sum is to be awarded to or retained by the other. In some states, liquidated damages clauses of this type will be enforced as written. In other states, where statutory provisions against forfeitures are strictly enforced, damages on breach will be awarded only to the extent that they have been actually incurred, regardless of what a liquidated damages clause might provide.

Description of Property   A precise description of the property to be sold is ordinarily included in every land contract. Note, however, that if a survey or other independent determination of the boundaries has not been made, a purchaser should not necessarily rely on a description furnished by the seller. In this regard, many land contracts provide that the purchaser is buying a specified number of acres, "more or less." If the purchaser requires a certain minimum acreage and is found to be getting less than that, he should be given the right to terminate the contract or to receive a pro rata deduction in the purchase price.

 If an accurate description of the property is not available, or if the parties agree that a survey will be made before the closing, it is wise to provide in the contract of sale that the description used at the closing will be based on the survey.

Time of the Essence   In many land contracts, time is "of the essence." This means that one party's performance at or within the time specified in the contract is essential to the performance required of the other party. Therefore, the purchaser must comply strictly with the provisions regarding the time of payment. If he does not, he can forfeit all rights, and the seller can be relieved of his obligation to perform.

Time-of-the-essence provisions are ordinarily created either by express stipulation of the parties in the contract of sale or by implication, depending on the circumstances of the transaction. Even when time is not made expressly or impliedly of the essence, a contract can be rescinded if one party fails or refuses to perform within a reasonable time. This rule governs the time fixed both for paying the purchase money and for conveying title to the property. Thus, for example, if parties have agreed to the payment of the purchase price and delivery of the deed on a particular day, they will be bound by the agreement, and time will be of the essence in that agreement.

Risk of Loss   In many states, once a contract has been signed, the risk of loss passes to the purchaser unless there is an agreement to the contrary. Thus, for example, damage to property from flood, hurricane, or even condemnation passes to the purchaser after the land contract has been signed. To avoid assuming this risk, a purchaser can (1) include a provision that all risk of loss before closing will be borne by the seller; (2) include specific covenants to limit the seller's use of the property before closing, thereby decreasing the risk of loss; and (3) require the seller to repair or restore the property if it is damaged before the closing.

In other states, the *Uniform Vendor and Purchaser Risk Act* has been enacted. The act provides that during the pendency of a sale the purchaser in possession bears the risk of loss of improvements, buildings, or other structures, as well as loss of land by eminent domain. Under the act, therefore, it is the purchaser's *possession* of the property, rather than his having simply signed the contract, that shifts the risk of loss to him.

 The contract should specify who bears the risk of loss, when the risk passes to the purchaser, and who purchases insurance against the risk of loss. Each party should be certain that insurance is adequate to cover a full loss of the property.

Distinction Between Land Contract, Deed, and Option to Purchase   A land contract for particular property gives the purchaser what is called equitable ownership of the property. In contrast, a deed gives the purchaser legal title to the property. An option to purchase is simply an owner's continuing offer to sell property on his or her stipulated terms. An option ripens into a contract of sale if and when it is exercised by the purchaser on the terms and within the time stipulated.

Doctrine of Merger A purchaser's acceptance of the seller's deed in accordance with a land contract constitutes completion of the contract and all its terms, unless the contract provides otherwise. Consistent with this principle, when the purchaser accepts a deed, the land contract and deed are said to merge. The effect of this merger is that the seller is discharged of all contractual duties to the purchaser except those contained in the deed itself. Thus, for example, a purchaser who has bargained for some right in the contract of sale may learn that unfortunately the right has been lost by default on acceptance of the deed. To avoid this result, the parties must see to it that all warranties, representations, or conditions contained in a contract of sale are fully performed before the deed is accepted.

35:6 Establishing Title

An agreement to sell and convey property is in effect a legal agreement to sell a title to the land. Unless there is a provision in a land contract indicating the specific type of title to be provided, the law ordinarily implies that the seller will convey a good or *marketable title* to the purchaser. As a general rule, "good title" is synonymous with "marketable title."

What constitutes a marketable title may sometimes be difficult to determine. The basic requirements are (1) that there be no doubt about the true ownership or status of the property; (2) that the title be free of any reasonable objection of a reasonable purchaser; and (3) that the title be free of encumbrances, liens, or other charges on the property unless these are accepted by the purchaser.

 The purchaser of real property should not blindly rely on the seller's representation or warranty that he or she has a good, marketable, or even insurable title to the property. As soon as possible after the parties have signed the contract of sale, the purchaser should have the title searched and should obtain a preliminary title report of the seller's title.

Title Search The product of a title search is a title report containing an *abstract of title*. The abstract of title contains (1) a brief description of the land and structures to be conveyed, (2) a list of the various grantors who have conveyed the property in the past, (3) the essential elements of each instrument or deed affecting the land, and (4) a conclusion about the present status of the title.

 Purchasers of property are generally unaware that a title company does not guarantee that its search is accurate. Only by asking (and paying) for title insurance (discussed below) does a purchaser get this guaranty. Without title insurance, the purchaser must bear the risk of loss from problems such as the title searcher's overlooking a lien on the property or making an honest mistake in describing the boundaries.

Title Insurance Title insurance insures the purchaser against loss or damage due to defects, liens, and other encumbrances on his title that are not specifically excepted from or excluded by the policy. Title insurance differs from other forms of insurance in that it insures title as of the date of the policy against loss due to existing or past occurrences. Most other types of insurance insure against loss resulting from future events.[3] Every policy of title insurance basically contains (1) a description of the property, (2) the name of the insured, (3) the amount of loss insured, (4) the extent of coverage, (5) the exclusions from coverage, (6) general exceptions, and (7) conditions and stipulations.

 It must be stressed that a title insurance company does not *cure* a defective or unmarketable title. Nor in most states is a title insurance company under a duty to point out title defects or encumbrances to the purchaser. A title insurance company is only bound to protect the purchaser against loss as a result of defects and encumbrances. It is therefore of utmost importance for the purchaser to have complete confidence in the title insurance company selected, to understand fully the type of title policy issued, and to review, when appropriate, the status of the property with either an attorney or title insurance company personnel.

35:7   Closing

The sale of property involves many details. Just as the seller should not be required to deliver a deed until payment is received, the buyer should not risk payment without first receiving the deed to the property or some obligation to deliver it. A purchaser must either be assured in the contract of receiving marketable title, or obtain title insurance. Liens, encumbrances, and other charges against property must be settled as agreed between the parties. Prorations of rents, taxes, assessments, insurance premiums, and interest charges must be made. Documents must be drafted and signed by the parties. Carrying out all these steps takes time. During the time required to carry them out—and to make sure that they *are* carried out—the property is put "in escrow." This means that the seller in effect places the property in the hands of a third party, who delivers the property to the purchaser when all the conditions of sale have been performed.

Escrow   The deposit of an instrument or document in *escrow* is usually referred to as the opening of the escrow, although it is also called the "beginning of the escrow" or "going into escrow." The term "close of escrow" is used when the escrow conditions have been performed by all of the parties so that the third party must deliver the deed to the purchaser and the purchase money to the seller.

   Creation of an escrow requires (1) an agreement as to the subject matter, (2) an escrow agent, (3) delivery of documents to the escrow agent, (4) performance of the required acts by the seller and purchaser, and (5) transfer of title and payment of the purchase price out of escrow.

---

[3] The various types of insurance are discussed in Chapter 41.

Escrow Agent   The third party in an escrow arrangement is called the *escrow agent.* The agent is both an agent of and a trustee for the parties, with limited powers. Before the close of escrow, the escrow agent is no more than a depositary for the property. The agent must strictly comply with the terms of his instructions. When the agent has done so, he becomes a trustee of both the party for whom the various instruments or funds are held and the party to whom they are to be delivered.

Escrow Instructions   The duties of the escrow agent are usually set forth in escrow instructions. In some states there is only one set of instructions governing the agent's conduct. In other states there can be two sets of instructions, one prepared and signed by the purchaser, the other by the seller. Often, printed instructions are prepared by corporate escrow agents or title companies who handle escrows and other real estate transactions for purchasers and sellers. Since the escrow agent is bound by the instructions, it is imperative that they be clearly drafted, to avoid confusion or misunderstanding.

Performance of Escrow Conditions   The parties to an escrow must strictly comply with the terms and conditions of the escrow. The doctrine of substantial performance (see Chapter 18) does not apply. This means that title to the property being sold will not pass until there has been full performance of the escrow agreement terms. If escrow instructions specify the time for performance, the escrow agent has no authority to accept performance after that prescribed time limit. In short, if either party fails to perform according to the terms of the sales contract and the escrow instructions, the escrow will not be closed and title to the property will not be transferred. When the time fixed for performance expires, a party who *has* fully performed can withdraw from the agreement and terminate the escrow if the other party has failed to perform as agreed.

The following case involves the liability of an escrow agent who failed to follow escrow instructions.

Akivis

v

Brecher

492 NYS2d 316 (1985)

New York Supreme Court, Kings County

FACTS: A real estate contract provided that, within 60 days after closing, the seller would remove the contents of a commercial building and leave the building "broom-clean." To insure that performance, the seller was to leave $5,000 in escrow. The escrow agent was instructed to pay the seller the $5,000 if the building contents were removed as promised; if they were not removed, the escrow agent was to pay the buyer $12.00

per day from the $5,000 until the contract was performed. The escrowee (escrow agent) paid the $5,000 to the seller without personally inspecting the building to see that the contract was performed.

ISSUE: Is the escrowee liable to the buyer for the cost of removing the materials and cleaning the building?

RESULT: Yes. The escrowee breached the terms of the escrow and is liable for the damage to the buyer.

REASONING:

*   *   *

An escrow agent becomes the trustee of both parties after receipt of the funds or instrument in question. . . . An escrowee is required to hold the funds to insure strict compliance with the condition. . . .

Additionally, absent an agreement to the contrary, the escrowee may not await an agreement of the parties of compliance with the condition and may be surcharged for late release of the escrowed item upon such insistence. . . . An escrowee must make an independent determination of compliance with the condition, except under circumstances where compliance is beyond the escrowee's ability to do so. In that event he may be required to bring an action for a court determination of compliance. . . .

In the case at bar in the answer, the escrowee acknowledged receipt of the fund in his answer and also indicated that he disbursed the fund to the sellers upon receipt of notice of compliance. There is no indication that the attorney made an independent inspection or other valid independent determination of such compliance. This court holds that the attorney is personally responsible for such that an independent inspection would have shown.

If the parties did not physically remove their possession from the premises, the attorney is liable for the lesser of $12.00 a day until removal, or the cost of removal.

In making that determination, the damages chargeable against the escrowee is limited to those necessarily *inherent* to the removal. [Court's emphasis.] . . .

Kramer, Justice.

Title and Right of Possession to Deposits in Escrow   The escrow agent obtains no title to the subject of the escrow. Legal title to the property to be sold, for example, remains in the seller until the escrow conditions are performed. Similarly, the deposit of a deed in escrow does not pass title to the purchaser until all the escrow agreement terms have been performed. However, at the time the contract of sale is signed and a deed deposited in escrow, the purchaser acquires an equitable interest in the property. In such a case, if a purchaser has fully performed all of the obligations under the contract of sale, as well as all of the escrow terms, but the seller dies before the escrow is actually closed, the law resorts to a legal fiction known as the doctrine of relation-back. The theory is that the delivery of legal title to the purchaser relates back to the time the equitable title was acquired. This allows the transfer of the property to be made. The doctrine of relation-back is an exception to the general rule that escrow does not convey title before all of the conditions have been performed.

Termination of Escrow Before Closing   A party to an escrow has no right to withdraw from the escrow before expiration of the time period fixed for performance of the conditions unless (1) the other party consents or (2) the escrow agreement provides otherwise. If an escrow is terminated in this way, the delivery of the deed in escrow is ineffectual.

Closing Statement   When all of the terms and conditions of the contract of sale have been completed, the escrow is closed by the escrow agent. At this time, a *closing* statement is prepared in which the details of the transaction are listed. These details include (1) the purchase price of the property, (2) obligations chargeable to each party, (3) proration of taxes, (4) charges or payments to be shared by the seller and purchaser, (5) the title company's charges, (6) real estate broker's commission, (7) insurance, and (8) loan payments.

Real Estate Settlement Procedures Act   The federal *Real Estate Settlement Procedures Act* [12 USC §§ 2601 et seq.] governs some aspects of residential real estate sales throughout the United States. The act is intended to make sure that sellers and purchasers of residential housing that is designed for occupancy by one to four families will receive disclosures showing all the costs of the transaction. These disclosures cover such matters as the cost of financing the transaction, the cost of title insurance, prepayment rights and penalties, and the proration of insurance and taxes on the property. At the same time, the act protects the parties from unnecessarily high charges caused by abusive practices, especially by lenders. A standard form must be used for the disclosures. The form clearly itemizes all charges imposed on the parties in connection with the transaction.

35:8   Remedies

The purchaser of property under a land contract has several remedies against a seller who wrongfully fails or refuses to perform the contract or to convey the kind of title required to be conveyed. If the seller is able but unwilling, or refuses, to convey title to the property sold, the purchaser can seek specific performance of the contract. In other cases, the purchaser can bring an action for damages. A damages action is particularly appropriate if the seller is unable to convey the property according to the terms of the contract because of a defect in or lack of title to the property. If a seller defaults under an executory contract, if the contract is invalid, or even if property has been destroyed or so materially damaged as to relieve the purchaser from the contract, the purchaser can ordinarily recover the payments or deposits he made on the contract (but not damages) so long as he himself is not in default.

The damages that a purchaser can recover for the seller's breach of a land contract are only those that, in fairness, can be considered to have either arisen from the breach or been contemplated by both parties when the contract was made. In other words, if a seller wrongfully breaches the contract, the measure of the purchaser's damage is the loss that he has sustained as a result of the breach. The burden is on the purchaser to show the amount of damages caused by the seller's breach. A purchaser who cannot do so is limited to a recovery of nominal damages. In some states, the purchaser is entitled, as general damages for the seller's wrongful failure or refusal to convey, to recover the difference between the actual value of the property and the agreed price, plus any payments that may have been made.

Seller's Remedies   The seller has a variety of remedies if the purchaser has breached the provisions of a land contract. If the contract has been signed and then breached by the purchaser the seller can seek (1) damages for the contract price or (2) specific performance to require the purchaser to pay the amount due under the contract. If the purchaser has been allowed possession under the terms of the contract, the seller can elect to declare the contract at an end and bring an action to recover possession.

Rescission   A contract of sale can be rescinded at any time before closing on the consent of all the parties to the agreement. However, one party's neglect, refusal, or failure to perform permits the other party to rescind the contract, as long as he or she does so within a reasonable time after the other party's default. In other circumstances, a contract for the sale of property can provide that the obligations of both parties depend on the happening of certain events; if the events do not occur, neither party is obligated to perform and the contract stands rescinded.

The purchaser under a land contract may be entitled to rescind the agreement for (1) the seller's material default in performing obligations, (2) fraud, (3) mistake in inducing the signing of the contract, or (4) a defect in the seller's title. In some states, the purchaser can also rescind if improvements on the property are accidentally destroyed or an eminent domain proceeding (see Chapter 39) commences before the property is conveyed.

Rescission must be evidenced by some positive act or words. The right to rescind can be lost by unreasonable delay. Furthermore, rescission can be waived if what is actually an invalid contract is treated by the parties as being valid and enforceable.

"As Is" Sales   In the past, most real estate transactions were *"as is."* That is, no implied warranties of condition or fitness were imposed, and the doctrine of *caveat emptor* ("let the buyer beware") prevailed. Any representations and warranties contained in the contract of sale terminated at the closing with the conveyance of the deed. Today, only a minority of states still apply the caveat emptor doctrine in the sale of residential housing. The modern trend is to hold the seller liable for damages or injuries that are caused by defects and arise after title has been conveyed and possession transferred.

The following case illustrates what one court considered to be the implied warranties in the sale of residential housing. Consider the court's rationale for imposing these warranties and why the traditional doctrine of caveat emptor is no longer appropriate to residential housing.

McDonald

v

Mianecki

398 A2d 1283 (1979)

New Jersey Supreme Court

FACTS: The McDonalds purchased a new home built by Mianecki. The well water used in the home failed to meet state standards of potability. The water had a bad odor and taste, and it caused clothes, dishware, and utensils to become stained when washed. A device installed by Mianecki to remove impurities after the McDonalds had moved in proved inadequate. Eventually, the McDonalds sued Mianecki for damages, alleging breach of an implied warranty of habitability because of the impure well water.

ISSUE: Does the builder-seller of a new house impliedly warrant that it is fit for habitation?

RESULT: Yes. The doctrine of implied warranty of habitability applies to such a construction-sale contract.

REASONING:

*   *   *

Prior to the mid-1950's the ancient maxim of *caveat emptor* ("let the buyer beware") long ruled the law relating to the sale of real property. Thought to have originated in late sixteenth-century English trade society, the doctrine was especially prevalent during the early 1800's when judges looked upon purchasing land as a "game of chance." . . . The maxim, derived from the then contemporary political philosophy of *laissez faire*, held that a "buyer deserved whatever he got if he relied on his own inspection of the merchandise and did not extract an express warranty from the seller." . . .

According to one commentator . . . [:]

> After World War II . . . the building industry underwent a revolution. It became common for the builder to sell the house and land together in a package deal. Indeed, the building industry outgrew the old notion that the builder was an artisan and took on all the color of a manufacturing enterprise, with acres of land being cleared by heavy machinery and prefabricated houses being put up almost overnight. Having learned their law by rote, however, the lawyers tended to insist that *caveat emptor* nonetheless applied to these sales.

In light of this modern day change in home buying practices, it is not surprising that increased pressure developed to abandon or modify the ancient doctrine. . . .

The reasoning underlying the abandonment of *caveat emptor* in the area of home construction is not difficult to fathom. Tribunals have come to recognize that "[t]he purchase of a new home is not an everyday transaction for the average family[;] . . . in many instances [it] is the most important transaction of a lifetime." . . . Courts have also come to realize that the two parties involved in this important transaction generally do not bargain as equals. The average buyer lacks the skill and expertise necessary to make an adequate inspection. . . . Furthermore, most defects are undetectable to even the most observant layman and the expense of expert advice is often prohibitive. . . . The purchaser therefore ordinarily relies heavily upon the greater expertise of the vendor to ensure a suitable product, . . . and this reliance is recognized by the building trade. . . .

Aside from superior knowledge, the builder-vendor is also in a better position to prevent the *occurrence* of major problems. [Court's emphasis.] . . . As one court has stated, "[i]f there is a comparative standard of innocence, as well as of culpability, the defendants who built and sold the house were less innocent and more culpable than the wholly innocent and unsuspecting buyer." . . .

It is not in expertise alone that the builder-vendor is generally superior. In the vast majority of cases the vendor also enjoys superior bargaining position. . . . Standard form contracts are generally utilized and "[e]xpress warranties are rarely given, expensive, and impractical for most buyers to negotiate. Inevitably the buyer is forced to rely on the skills of the seller." . . .

The application of an implied warranty of habitability to sellers of new homes is further supported by the expectations of the [parties]. Clearly every builder-vendor holds himself out, expressly or impliedly, as having the expertise necessary to construct a livable dwelling. It is equally as obvious that almost every buyer acts upon these representations and expects that the new house he is buying, whether already constructed or not yet built, will be suitable for use as a home. . . .

For the reasons set forth herein, we conclude that (1) the doctrine of implied warranty of habitability applies to the construction of new homes by builder-vendors whether or not they are mass-developers, and

(2) potability of the water supply is included within the items encompassed by the implied warranty. *Caveat emptor* is an outmoded concept and is hereby replaced by rules which reflect the needs, policies and practices of modern day living. It is our conclusion that in today's society it is necessary that consumers be able to purchase new homes without fear of being "stuck" with an uninhabitable "lemon." *Caveat emptor* no longer accords with modern day practice and should therefore be relegated to its rightful place in the pages of history. . . .

Pashman, Judge.

The implied warranties of *habitability*, condition, or fitness do not apply to commercial transactions. Here, the traditional rule is still applied, and the purchaser takes the property "as is."

 The purchaser of commercial property should either order a careful inspection by qualified experts before a contract is signed, or insist that a satisfactory inspection be made a condition of the sale. For example, a contract might require that before closing, the seller of a commercial building remedy all defects, including any fire, health, or building code violations. If this is done, there should be no question as to the parties' obligations if defects are discovered during the pendency of a sale or after the sale has been concluded.

Key Concepts and Terms

- The purchase and sale of real property is governed primarily by state law. However, certain federal laws have been enacted to govern specific national problems for which individual state's remedies are inadequate. These laws include the Real Estate Settlement Procedures Act and the Interstate Land Sales Full Disclosure Act.
- In most states the typical residential purchase or simple commercial transaction involves (1) a brokerage contract, (2) preliminary negotiations, (3) the deposit receipt, (4) a contract of sale (unless the deposit receipt serves as the contract), (5) a mortgage or other security arrangement, (6) a survey or other investigation of the property, (7) title insurance, (8) drafting of documents, and (9) the closing in escrow.
- The sale of residential and commercial property is handled exclusively through brokers in most states. The contract between a broker and a property owner is governed by the laws of agency.
- The rights and obligations of the seller and real estate broker are ordinarily set forth in a listing agreement. This is an agency contract of employment giving the broker limited authority to act on behalf of the owner to sell the property.

- The purchaser's written offer, accompanied by a deposit to be credited to the purchase price, is generally called the deposit receipt. The deposit receipt is an offer that the seller can accept or reject.

- Except in states where the deposit receipt serves as the contract after the seller's acceptance, the land contract is the most common type of contract used for a sale of real property. Under the land contract, one party agrees to convey title to real property to the other on the satisfaction of specified conditions set forth in the contract.

- The deposit of an instrument or document with a third party for the purpose of exchanging papers, documents, deeds, or other instruments, as well as money, is called an escrow. The deposit of these instruments in escrow is usually referred to as the opening of the escrow. When all the conditions have been performed by all the parties, so that the escrow agent is required to deliver the deed to the purchaser and the purchase money to the seller, the escrow is closed.

- The duties of the escrow agent are normally set forth in escrow instructions. The escrow agent must act specifically in accordance with the instructions given. The instructions should be clearly drafted to avoid confusion or misunderstanding as to what is required before the escrow will be closed.

- The purchaser of property under a land contract has several different remedies against a seller for the wrongful failure or refusal to perform the contract or to convey the appropriate title. These remedies include (1) specific performance of the contract, (2) reformation or rescission of the contract, and (3) the recovery of damages.

- Remedies of a seller of property when provisions of a land contract have been breached by the purchaser include (1) the recovery of damages; (2) specific performance of the contract; and (3) if the purchaser has been allowed possession of the property under the terms of the contract, recovery of possession of the property.

- Traditionally, real estate was bought and sold "as is." Today, many states hold sellers of residential property liable for damages and injuries that are caused by defects and arise after title has been conveyed and possession transferred. These implied warranties of habitability, condition, or fitness do not apply to commercial transactions; the traditional rule still applies to those transactions.

- Abstract of Title
- Closing
- Deposit Receipt
- Earnest Money
- Escrow
- Escrow Agent
- Exclusive Agency
- Exclusive Authorization and Right to Sell Contract

- Land Contract
- Like-Kind Exchange
- Listing Agreement
- Marketable Title
- Merger Doctrine
- Multiple Listing Agency Contract
- Net Listing
- Nonexclusive Agency
- Open Listing

- Real Estate Settlement Procedures Act
- Representation
- Time Is of the Essence
- Title Insurance
- Uniform Vendor and Purchaser Risk Act
- Warranty of Habitability

Questions and Case Problems

1. Ziminski lists property that he wishes to sell with Trade Properties, a real estate company, at a selling price of $100,000. Zwas, a salesman for Trade Properties, advertises the property and shows it to potential buyers. Zwas introduces Falk, a potential buyer, to Ziminski. A binder is drafted, and both Falk and Ziminski sign it. Ziminski binder is drafted, and both Falk and Ziminski sign it. Ziminski insists that a clause be inserted in the binder that his acceptance is subject to the approval of his attorney. The broker agrees, and the clause is inserted. Later, Ziminski's attorney disapproves of the deal, and the whole thing falls through. Trade Properties sues Ziminski for its commission. How should the case be decided?

2. Rose entered into an agreement with a realtor, Schroeder, listing a service station and bulk plant for sale. The agreement provided that if Schroeder found a buyer "ready and willing" to purchase the property on "such other terms and price" as the seller might accept, a 10 percent commission would be due. The listing selling price was $185,000. Several months later, the realtor presented an offer for $175,000 from a buyer. The terms of the proposed financing in the offer were quite complicated. Schroeder explained to Rose that the balloon payment on the financing would be about $30,000. Based partly on this assertion, Rose accepted the offer. Later Rose calculated the financing terms himself and discovered that the balloon payment would be much larger, probably $100,000, because the monthly payments were insufficient to meet the interest and principal due. Rose decided not to close the deal. Schroeder sues Rose for her commission. Rose claims that Schroeder is not entitled to a commission because she breached a fiduciary duty to Rose when she stated an erroneous balloon payment amount. What result?

3. The Brewers list their home with Lewis Real Estate. Lewis finds Myers, a suitable prospective broker who is willing to meet the Brewers' terms. The parties sign a "binder deposit" and Myers puts $200 in escrow with Lewis. The binder provides that if Myers fails to enter into a formal sales contract, the Brewers have the right to retain the deposit as liquidated damages. Thereafter, Myers changes her mind and refuses to enter into a contract of sale. Because they cannot find another buyer who will pay the same price that was offered by Myers, the Brewers sue her for the difference between what she offered and the ultimate selling price. The Brewers contend that Myers gave them the option of either accepting the $200 deposit as liquidated damages or suing the buyer for actual damages. Is Myers liable for the seller's actual damages? Why?

4. Chapman entered into a real estate contract to buy property from the Hoseks and made a $7,000 earnest money deposit. She seeks to rescind the contract on the ground of fraud, claiming that the seller, the listing broker, and the selling broker misrepresented to her that flood insurance was not needed for the property. Moreover, she claims, they concealed from her that during heavy rains the house and the area immediately surrounding it flooded, rendering the house inaccessible. Can Chapman rescind on this basis?

5. The Brooks sell their house to the Rouses. In the "Acceptance of Purchase Offer" the sellers represent and warrant to the broker and to any subsequent purchaser that the property and its improvements, equipment, and facilities are "in good, proper, satisfactory, and functional working order and condition." After the sale, the purchasers discover that the septic tank leaks, the air conditioning equipment is defective, and the swimming pool and basement leak. The Rouses sue the sellers for breach of express warranties and contract. The trial court dismisses the suit, finding that the clause in the sales contract merged with and was extinguished by the deed, which contained no such warranties. Was the trial court correct in its decision? Why?

6. Smith enters into a written contract to sell his house to Jones, with title to pass on the closing of escrow in 45 days. The contract calls for Jones to pay the purchase price into escrow on or before December 31. Jones offers the money on January 1, one day late. On Smith's refusal to perform, can Jones now enforce the contract?

7. Convey purchases a cold storage plant from Capitol Savings under an installment land contract. Under the terms of the contract, Convey is not given legal title to the property until the final installments are paid, but he is given possession and use of the plant. After he acquires possession, the plant collapses, and it will take $15,000 to rebuild it. Who bears the risk of loss?

8. Discuss and distinguish a land contract, option to purchase, and deed.

9. On September 15, Mallen gave A-1 Escrow Company a deed naming Dube as grantee of Mallen's river property. Mallen orally instructed A-1 to give the deed to Dube if Dube pays $5,000 on or before December 15. On October 1, Mallen decides to cancel the transaction and recall the deed from A-1 because she no longer wants to sell to Dube. Is she legally entitled to do this? If Dube had given A-1 $5,000 on September 30, would the result be different?

10. Ern-Roc Homes builds a house and sells it to the Sanjs. The contract of sale provides the usual guaranties, including a guaranty against roof leakage "due to defective materials and/or installation." The guaranty is for one year from the time of closing of title. A few months after buying the home, the Sanjs sell it to Gomes, and they assign Ern-Roc's guaranties along with it. When the house develops roof trouble within the one-year period, Gomes contacts Ern-Roc and asks it to do the repair work. Ern-Roc refuses, claiming that guaranties made to the first purchaser were not meant for subsequent purchasers. Ern-Roc also points to a provision in the original contract with Sanj, which states: "It is expressly understood and agreed that the purchaser will in no event assign this contract without the written consent of the seller." If Gomes were to sue Ern-Roc, who would win the case? Why?

36 Mortgages and Deeds of Trust

A client came into a lawyer's office and said:
  "Is this a lawyer's place?"
  "Yes, I am a lawyer."
  "Well, Mr. Lawyer, I need a paper made."
  "What kind of paper?"
  "Well, I think I want a mortgage. Why, you see, I bought some land from Angus McPherson and I want a mortgage on it."
  "Oh no, you don't want a mortgage; what you want is a deed."
  "No, Mr. Lawyer, I want a mortgage. Why, you see, I bought two pieces of land before and I got a deed for both of them and another fellow came along with a mortgage and took the land; so I think I'd better get a mortgage this time."[1]

36:1 Nature, Form, and Elements of the Mortgage

The *mortgage* is the instrument that, traditionally, has been used to create a security interest in real property. In early English law, the mortgage took the form of an absolute conveyance of land. A debtor, the *mortgagor*, conveyed land to a creditor, the *mortgagee*, on the condition that the mortgage would become void—and the creditor would reconvey the land to the debtor—on performance of the obligation. The date of maturity was called the "law day." By a provision in the mortgage known as the *defeasance clause*, payment of the debt on law day defeated the mortgage and put ownership back in the mortgagor. However, if the debtor did not pay the debt before the law day, the creditor became the absolute owner of the mortgaged property. The mortgagor's failure to pay the mortgage indebtedness when due automatically extinguished all his interest in the property; legal title to the mortgaged property then passed to the creditor. It was not unusual for a mortgagor to fail to pay the mortgage debt, especially since execution of the mortgage gave the creditor the right to possession of the land and to the profits generated from its use. The land was "dead" in the sense that it gave no return to the debtor. In fact, in England the word "mortgage" meant "dead pledge" (mort=dead, gage=pledge).

The hardships resulting from the forfeiture or loss of mortgaged property prompted courts of equity to give protections to the mortgagor so that he could regain or redeem the property. A body of law developed by which the debtor

---

[1] Adapted from M. Brown, *Wit and Humor of Bench and Bar*, 352 (1899), quoted in Henkel & Seltzer, "Acceleration Clauses in Mortgages: Misuse During Periods of Tight Money," 17 *Am Bus L J* 441 (Winter 1980).

could do so by repaying the debt within a reasonable time after breach of any of the mortgage conditions. This right to save property after its forfeiture was called *equity of redemption*. With the adoption of the debtor's right to redeem the mortgaged property after forfeiture, creditors were placed at a disadvantage. They could no longer count on receiving payment or obtaining the security by a certain time. To remedy this situation, a procedure evolved for *foreclosure* of (cutting off) debtors' rights. The creditor would petition a court of equity to foreclose on mortgaged property, seeking a decree that required the debtor to repay the debt by a fixed date. If the debt was not paid, the debtor's equity of redemption would be barred forever.

Title Versus Lien Theory of Mortgages   Because the law of mortgages developed in courts of both law and equity, modern mortgages have a dual character: the mortgage is a conveyance, yet it is also a lien to secure the payment of debt.

EXAMPLE: D owns property worth $20,000. He wants to borrow $10,000 from C. In turn, C wants some security for the money he is about to loan. D executes a promissory note to C by which he promises to pay $10,000 to C with interest. At the same time, D gives to C a mortgage on the land to secure the obligation of the note. The mortgage gives C a claim against D's land for repayment of the loan. The mortgage will be recorded in the appropriate public office where the property is located. The note will not be recorded since it does not create any interest in land; it is not a document of title but merely a promise. Thus, in a broad sense the mortgage encompasses two documents. The first is a promissory note by which D becomes obligated to pay C a sum of money. The second, the actual mortgage, gives C a security interest in the property to ensure D's performance of the obligation. D is said to hold the *equity* in the property now, whereas before the mortgage he held title.

Most states have modified the strict, legal *title theory*, which views the mortgage as a conveyance. Most states follow the equitable or *lien theory*, which holds that a mortgage does not convey the legal title to land but simply creates a lien to secure payment of the mortgage debt. Under this theory, a mortgage vests title in the mortgagee only to protect his interest and give him the full benefit of the security, but for no other purpose. The mortgagor retains title until foreclosure and ordinarily is entitled to possession and use of the mortgaged premises, as well as to the rents and profits generated by the property. However, the mortgage may also permit possession by the mortgagee.

Form and Elements of the Mortgage   A mortgage must be in writing, and it must bear the signature of the mortgagor. It must also be based on a legal and valid consideration.[2] Any interest in real estate can be made the subject of a

---

[2] Consideration is discussed in Chapter 11.

mortgage, so long as the interest is sufficiently described. A mortgage on land includes all of the structures and improvements on the land, including those made after the conveyance of the mortgage, unless the mortgage instrument excludes structures and improvements.

Under the modern view of mortgages, the debt secured by a mortgage is the primary obligation between the parties. The mortgage is incidental to the indebtedness. Hence, the existence of a valid obligation is an essential element of a mortgage. If there is no valid obligation to be secured, the mortgage is of no effect.

EXAMPLE: Morton gives a mortgage to Crabbe to secure payment of a gambling debt. Later, the debt is declared invalid. Because the underlying debt is invalid, the mortgage also is invalid.

In some states, every transfer of an interest in real property (other than in trust) made only as security for the performance of another act is considered to be a mortgage. If the purpose of an instrument is to secure a debt, it does not matter what particular form the transaction takes. In these states, therefore, a deed intended as security is treated as a mortgage.

36:2   Types of Mortgages and Security Transactions

There are many types of security transactions in real property. The previous section explained the basic theory of a mortgage. This section examines the various types of mortgages and other security interests in real property.

Deeds of Trust   The *deed of trust* (or *trust deed*) is used in many states exclusively in lieu of mortgages. It is functionally identical to a mortgage. Deeds of trust may be given as security for the performance of an obligation, and they must contain the elements of a valid mortgage. The distinctive feature of a deed of trust is that the property that is to stand as security is conveyed by the debtor to a trustee for the creditor's benefit, rather than directly to the creditor. Thus, there are three parties to a deed of trust: (1) the trustor (debtor; also known as the trust deed mortgagor), (2) the trustee, and (3) the beneficiary (creditor). The trustee's powers and duties are fixed by the trust deed, and the trustee occupies a fiduciary relationship to both the beneficiary and the trustor. What the trustee eventually does with the property depends on whether the trustor pays the secured debt.

EXAMPLE: D (trustor) conveys title to her property to T (trustee) to secure a debt owed by D to B (beneficiary). If D performs her obligation, T reconveys the property to D. However, if D defaults in performance, T can sell the property and apply the sale proceeds to satisfy the debt owed to B.

With a trust deed, legal title actually passes to the trustee and remains there until either the debt is paid or the trustee sells the title to a purchaser at a default sale. However, in many states, although the trust deed actually transfers title, it is *regarded* as simply a mortgage with the *power of sale*. The trustee has only the title necessary to fulfill the terms of the trust. Until a sale becomes necessary, the trustee's title lies dormant. In the meantime, the trustor is entitled to possession and can convey or encumber the property subject to the trust deed. On payment of the debt, the trustee's interest in the property ceases even though no reconveyance of the title is made.

The deed of trust ordinarily contains a *default clause* providing that all sums secured by the deed shall immediately become due and payable at the beneficiary's option if the trustor defaults in payment of the underlying debt. If the trustor defaults and the beneficiary so demands, the trustee is obligated to sell the property. After the property is sold the trustee must apply the proceeds of the sale first to pay off the loan or debt; the balance, if any, is given to the trustor. The trustee then delivers a trustee's deed to the purchaser of the property.

Equitable Mortgages An *equitable mortgage* is a mortgage that, although technically invalid as a mortgage because it fails to satisfy one or more legal requirements, is treated as a mortgage by the courts. This means that if a mortgage is defective for some reason, the courts can, in effect, cure the defect. The result is that almost every express written agreement by which one party clearly indicates an intention to make particular property a security for a debt creates an equitable, enforceable lien on the property.

EXAMPLE: Jim and Rose, a married couple, gave Gene a mortgage to secure a debt for $10,000. The mortgage was carelessly prepared: (1) it was signed by Jim but not by Rose, although they jointly owned the property; (2) it inaccurately described the property as being located in a neighboring state, although the location of the property was obvious from the terms of the mortgage; and (3) it was never recorded. Despite these defects, the instrument will be enforced against Jim and Rose as an equitable lien or mortgage.

Various remedies exist to enforce equitable mortgages. In some states a legal proceeding can be brought to establish and foreclose an equitable mortgage. Another remedy is a proceeding to reform and enforce a defective mortgage. A proceeding to obtain specific performance is also possible.

The following case illustrates a court's willingness to find an equitable mortgage even in the face of a deed that appeared to grant an outright ownership interest.

Silas

v

Robinson
477 NE2d 4 (1985)
Appellate Court of Illinois, First District

FACTS: In 1985 Silas and Robinson, who were sisters, took title to property as joint tenants. Robinson lived on the property and rented out the second floor. In 1980 Silas filed an action for partition of the property and an accounting for Robinson's occupancy and the rents collected. Robinson claimed, in defense, that she and her sister intended Silas' interest as a security interest, not an ownership interest, in the property. There was evidence at trial that Robinson made monthly payments to Silas of $135.00.

ISSUE: Was there an equitable mortgage between the parties?

RESULT: Yes. The transaction was intended as a security interest, which the court enforces as an equitable mortgage.

REASONING:

*   *   *

Every deed conveying real estate, which shall appear to have been intended only as a security in the nature of a mortgage, though it be an absolute conveyance in terms, shall be considered as a mortgage." . . . "Any evidence tending to show that the purpose and intention of the parties of the transaction was that of a loan and security is admissible. . . . Thus, all of the circumstances surrounding the transaction are relevant to the parties' intent . . . Relevant factors to determine whether the deed absolute in form was intended to be a mortgage include the relation of the parties, the circumstances surrounding the transaction, the adequacy of consideration, and the situation of the parties after the transaction. . . . Although proof of an equitable mortgage must be clear, satisfactory and convincing, it is not necessary that there be no conflict in the evidence presented. . . .

The facts proved here amply establish that Robinson and Silas intended that the deed to both of them in joint tenancy would serve as security for Silas' loan to Robinson, which Robinson would repay in full at the rate of $135 per month. In addition, the evidence showed that Robinson managed and rehabilitated the property, by paying for repairs, real estate taxes, and insurance, and by occupying a portion of the premises and renting out the remainder. Silas, in contrast, contributed virtually nothing in repairs, maintenance, or taxes, nor did she attempt to occupy or otherwise take advantage of the benefits of ownership of the property. In short, both sisters regarded the premises as belonging to Robinson alone and considered Silas' initial contribution of $3,200 as a loan to Robinson so that she could purchase the property. As a result, the evidence clearly established that Silas' interest was an equitable mortgage which, once satisfied, obligated Silas to quitclaim the property to Robinson.

Silas also argues that there was never a mortgage between the sisters because according to Silas "conveyances of real estate cannot be by insinuation or oral agreement" but instead "must be in writing, clear and absolute." Here, however, Silas misunderstands the nature of an equitable mortgage. . . . No writing was required, however, since an equitable mortgage can be found on the basis of parol evidence. . . .

Next, Silas urges that there was no mortgage because none was ever recorded as required by statute. . . . Silas neglects the obvious, however, since the statutes also provide that a deed absolute in form is to be considered a mortgage if it appears that the parties intended it to serve only as a security. . . . Accordingly, a recorded deed which names two sisters as joint tenants may be treated as an equitable mortgage where the circumstances surrounding their transaction so indicate.

In addition, Silas claims that there was no mortgage because Robinson never signed any instrument agreeing to pay Silas on a definite date. There was no requirement that any part of the agreement be in writing. . . . The evidence presented . . . clearly established a debt relationship between Robinson and Silas, which was sufficient to find the creation of an equitable mortgage. . . .

Lastly, Silas argues that there was no mortgage because title to real property can be transferred only in writing, not in parol, and must sufficiently describe the property. We note once more that the theory of equitable mortgage takes into account all attendant circumstances, not merely the form of the deed or conveyance. . . .

Romiti, Justice.

Purchase Money Mortgages   A *purchase money mortgage* is a mortgage given by a purchaser to the seller of property to secure payment of the purchase price of the property conveyed. The mortgage must be given at the same time the deed is delivered to be regarded as a purchase money mortgage.

EXAMPLE: Doris purchases a piece of property from Blake for $20,000. She gives Blake $10,000 in cash and, at the same time, a promissory note and mortgage for the balance. Because the mortgage is given to secure the purchase of the property being bought, it is a purchase money mortgage.

A mortgage need not necessarily be given to a seller to make it a purchase money mortgage. In some states it can be given to anyone—such as a bank—advancing the purchase money.

Open-End Mortgages   An *open-end mortgage* permits a debtor to borrow money at will in the future using real estate as security, and normally without any expense or delay. In other words, the open-end mortgage is a mortgage given to secure a present loan or debt as well as future loans by or debts due to the same lender; it is a mortgage to secure both present and future advances of money. These mortgages have been frequently used to secure building or construction loans.

Under an open-end mortgage the lender agrees to lend money to the borrower. The borrower in turn agrees to use the loan proceeds to construct the facility in question. To provide security for repayment of the loan, the borrower executes and delivers to the lender a mortgage deed covering the land on which the facility is to be constructed. The lender then advances installments of the loan to the borrower as the work progresses on the facility. In this manner, the lender minimizes the risk of his or her investment by insuring that the loan is in fact used to increase the value of the mortgaged land; it also relieves the borrower of having to invest funds until they are needed. The borrower is also assured of a continuing supply of capital and avoids the expense and inconvenience of obtaining a new loan when additional sums are needed. Moreover, the borrower pays interest only on the amount of the loan outstanding. The use of future advance financing also benefits the lender. It promotes additional borrowing since it minimizes the bother and cost of frequent individual loans. It permits the lender to retain the right to disburse the loan in installments as the value of the mortgaged property increases rather than requiring the lender initially to disburse the entire amount of the loan at a time when the value of the land securing the loan might be less than the amount to be disbursed.

 The use of an open-end mortgage for future advances is relatively common in real estate financing to provide working capital for business enterprises. Financing of the construction of a shopping center, a commercial housing project, or a manufacturing plant is a typical example of a transactions involving such a loan.

Second Mortgages   A property owner who has previously granted a mortgage to secure a debt can give another, or second, mortgage on the same property to the extent of his remaining interest. Indeed, there can be a second, a third, and a fourth mortgage all covering the same property.

EXAMPLE: Bill buys a piece of property from Clarence for $20,000. Bill pays Clarence $10,000 in cash and gives him a purchase money mortgage for the balance. Later, Bill wants to build an addition to his home. He borrows $5,000 from Hope and gives her a second mortgage on the property. This second mortgage is inferior in terms of rights and priorities to the first mortgage. If Bill needs still more money for another project and can arrange for another loan secured by his property, the third lender will receive a third mortgage. The third mortgage will be inferior to both the first and the second mortgages.

Second mortgages are relatively common in real estate sales, financing, and business construction. They are used by banks to secure homeowner loans and by other financial institutions that extend credit. In building construction, they play a prominent role in the financing or refinancing of multimillion-dollar projects. Although first mortgages take priority over second mortgages, in practice all mortgages are paid off simultaneously. Only in the event of default and foreclosure do the priorities come into play, entitling the first mortgage to be satisfied first, out of the proceeds of sale.

Wraparound Mortgages   In recent years, there has been a renewed use of a real estate financing device, first used in the 1930s, known as the *wraparound* *mortgage*. The wraparound mortgage is a second mortgage (or trust deed) securing a promissory note, the face amount of which is the sum of the existing first mortgage liability *plus* the cash advanced by the second mortgagee. The wraparound borrower must make payments on the first mortgage debt to the wraparound lender, who in turn makes payments on the first mortgage debt to the first mortgagee. The interest rate on the wraparound note is normally higher than the interest rate on the underlying debt, since a wraparound mortgage is used generally in a high-interest period. The lender receives interest on the full amount of the wraparound note instead of just on the amount of additional funds or credit loaned. This is so despite the fact that the lender has actually loaned (or extended credit on) only the amount of the additional funds.

Disguised Security Transactions   Security transactions involving real property that are not evidenced by a mortgage or deed of trust are a long-standing problem in mortgage law. In most states, the law is that a disguised security transaction, understood by the parties to secure a debt, will be given the effect of a mortgage. For example, a creditor might require a debtor to grant her land by absolute deed under an oral agreement or tacit understanding that the land will be reconveyed only if the debtor pays the debt when it is due. Or, a creditor might obtain from a debtor an absolute deed to real property and give her some sort of unrecorded agreement to reconvey the property on receiving payment of the debt. The written agreement to reconvey could take the form of (1) an option to repurchase, (2) an unconditional contract obligating the grantee to reconvey and the grantor to repurchase, or (3) a lease-back to the grantor with an option to repurchase at or before the end of the lease term. Some contracts or options provide for the deposit in escrow of a deed of reconveyance.

The above transactions are all designed to eliminate the equity of redemption and the necessity of foreclosure in case the debtor defaults. Besides avoiding the expense and delay involved in foreclosure, the creditor often expects to gain other advantages that cannot be obtained with a regular mortgage. These include a right to possession of the property before default, the ability to prevent the debtor from further encumbering the property, and the possibility of enlarging the creditor's security interest to cover future advances to the debtor without the execution of a new security instrument.

All of these transactions, which are absolute conveyances on their face but are intended only to be security for debt, will be regarded by the courts as mortgages. If the purpose of a conveyance is security, it will be treated by the parties and the courts as a mortgage, even though the parties might have agreed or understood that the debtor should have no right to redeem. The right to redeem after default is an inseparable incident of the mortgage relationship.

36:3 Mechanics' Liens

Mechanic's Liens   A *mechanic's lien* is a security interest in real property that arises as a matter of statute. Most state mechanics' lien statutes give such a lien to a person who has performed labor or furnished materials or equipment contributing to the improvement of property at the owner's request. A mechanic's lien provides a means by which the payment of certain debts incurred by a property owner can be enforced. The right to the lien depends on the specific terms of the appropriate statute; that is, a mechanic's lien cannot exist unless it is expressly created by statute. A lien claimant acquires a lien superior to the rights of the property owner and any subsequent purchaser. A mechanic's lien is similar to a mortgage in that it is a lien on real property. It differs from a mortgage in that it is not given as security for a debt but, rather, arises because of the performance of labor or the furnishing of material to benefit the property.

A mechanic's lien is not enforceable in most states unless the claim of lien has been *perfected* within the statutory period and in the manner provided by law. The initial step in perfecting a claim is to give preliminary notice to the owner, stating in general terms the kind of labor or materials furnished, the value, and the name of the person to whom the items were furnished. The claim is then recorded in a prescribed public office in the locality where the property is situated. If the debt is not paid, the lien can be foreclosed. The lien foreclosure procedure follows the procedure used in foreclosing a mortgage. In most states, a mechanic's lien has priority over all liens that attach after the mechanic's lien claimant first performed work or furnished materials. A mechanic's lien can be waived by failing to perfect it in the proper manner.

Although no two state mechanic's lien statutes are identical, most statutes are similar to either the New York statute or the Pennsylvania statute. Under the New York system, a lien of a subcontractor or materialman is based on and subordinate to the contractor's rights. This means that the lien is dependent on and limited by (1) the amount that remains due the contractor at the time the subcontractor or materialman serves notice on the owner (that he has furnished or is about to furnish labor or material) or (2) the amount that may become due the contractor after this time. Under the Pennsylvania system, the lien of the subcontractor or materialman is a direct lien and does not depend on the existence of any indebtedness due from the owner to the contractor.

36:4   Rights of Parties; Use and Enjoyment of Property

The interests of the mortgagee and mortgagor in property are for many purposes considered separate and distinct. Under the law, the mortgagee has no control over mortgaged property. However, the mortgagee has the right to protect his separate interest and to this end may obtain insurance or pay off prior liens that affect his interest. The mortgagor must preserve the mortgaged property for the purpose of the security for which it was originally pledged, and it is customarily his duty to pay taxes and assessments levied on the property. If the mortgagee pays these taxes or assessments to protect his interest, he is entitled to be reimbursed for the amounts so paid, which means that he can add the amounts to the mortgage debt.

Acceleration Clauses   Mortgages, deeds of trusts, and the underlying promissory notes commonly provide for acceleration of the indebtedness on any failure to pay a required installment of principal or interest. In addition to acceleration for failure to pay installments, the instruments might permit acceleration at the option of the mortgagee or trust deed beneficiary if the borrower sells the property or further encumbers it. Some acceleration clauses provide that on certain conditions or the happening of specified events, the entire balance due on the debt "shall immediately become due and payable," but most clauses provide that in that event, the holder of the note or the mortgagee "may, at his option, declare," the entire unpaid balance immediately due and payable.

A *due-on-sale clause* is an acceleration clause that authorizes a mortgagee or trust deed beneficiary to accelerate the entire loan balance if and when the owner (mortgagor or trustor) sells or conveys the property. These clauses have been used by lenders as a means of increasing the interest rates on loans that are below current rates. Frequently, a lender will offer to waive enforcement of the clause only if the interest rates on the loan are increased. The practical effect of a lender declaring the balance of a loan due is to restrict the owner's ability to sell the property securing the loan. Consequently, the due-on-sale clause has been attacked as constituting an unreasonable restraint on the sale of property. In the 1970s there was considerable litigation over the enforceability of these clauses.[3] Federal legislation in 1982, however, resolved most of the controversy surrounding due-on-sale clauses in favor of their enforceability.

Rights to Possession of Mortgaged Property In lien theory states, the mortgagee is not entitled to possession of the mortgaged property except through foreclosure and purchase or on agreement of the parties. The same is true of the trustee or beneficiary under a deed of trust. A mortgage can, however, contain an express provision giving the mortgagee certain rights, such as the right to take possession of or manage the property, to pay expenses, and to collect rents and profits. A mortgagee can also take possession with the mortgagor's implied consent. The mortgagee (or trustee under a deed of trust) in all these situations is known as a *mortgagee in possession* and is subject to certain rules governing his duties and conduct toward the mortgagor.

Ordinarily, the mortgagor remains in possession of mortgaged property. As legal owner, the mortgagor can use it as he pleases. Nevertheless, in most states, if the mortgagor's use of the property is so excessive or unreasonable as to be wasteful, the mortgagee can recover damages, obtain an injunction, or initiate other legal proceedings.

"Waste" is a special term in law that refers to conduct that causes physical damage to or destruction of property. It includes both "voluntary waste," such as excessive cutting of timber or removal of minerals or permanent structures, and "permissive waste," such as not keeping the property repaired properly. A mortgagor might also engage in "financial waste" by failing to pay taxes or to pay off other liens, thus impairing the mortgagee's security.

---

[3] See, for example, *Fidelity Federal Sav. & Loan Asso. v de la Cuesta*, 458 US 141 (1982), in which the Supreme Court ruled that the due-on-sale clauses of federal savings and loan associations were governed only by federal law.

36:5   Priorities

The general principle expressed in the maxim "first in time, first in right" applies to mortgages. Under this rule, any lien or encumbrance that attaches to mortgaged property after the execution of a mortgage is subject to the mortgage. For example, a mortgage on property given to secure a loan for the construction of a building on the property is superior to the liens of laborers and materialmen who later enter into contracts with the property owner and furnish labor and materials used in the construction. It is beyond the power of the mortgagor to disturb this priority. On the other hand, a mortgagee's interests and rights are subject to any outstanding interest in the mortgaged property acquired before the execution of the mortgage. In determining the priority of several mortgages on the same property, they are generally ranked in order of their creation, the first in time standing first in order. This order of priority is, however, altered by state recording laws, discussed below.

Recording Laws   Mortgages, like deeds to property, can be and usually are recorded in the appropriate public office. In most states, the right to record a mortgage is purely statutory and must be exercised in accordance with the terms of the statute.

Most state recording systems give priority to the person whose mortgage is first recorded. Thus, mortgage priorities are similar to the rules governing the priorities of deeds, discussed in Chapter 33. In other words, if an owner mortgages a property twice, the first mortgage recorded will be given priority over all other mortgages or liens, unless the mortgagee knew of these other mortgages or liens at the time of recording. In a minority of the states, the mortgage takes effect when executed, not when recorded. Thus, where two mortgages are executed on the same day, the fact that one is recorded before the other does not necessarily give it priority in these states. In the absence of other facts, both claims would be equal.

An exception to the general rule of priorities is applied to purchase money mortgages, which usually are entitled to preference over all other claims or liens arising through the mortgagor. The reason frequently advanced for this rule is that the execution of the deed and the mortgage are regarded as simultaneous acts, so that no claim or lien arising through the mortgagor can attach before the mortgage.

36:6   Payment and Discharge; Equity of Redemption

Payment of the indebtedness secured by real estate must be made at the time and in the manner provided in the mortgage or other security instrument. Usually, all or most of the debt is paid in periodic installments, but the instrument can also call for payment in a lump sum on the maturity date. A payment or offer of payment of all that remains owing on the maturity date extinguishes the mortgage lien and discharges the debt. When the debt is paid, the mortgagee customarily signs—and in some states records—a release, acknowledging payment and satisfaction of the debt. Bear in mind, however, that although the mortgagor must pay the debt *by* the maturity date, he generally has no right to pay the entire debt *before* it is due unless a mortgage provision or an agreement between the parties authorizes such payment. Indeed, there is often a *penalty for prepayment* because of the loss of interest that the mortgagee may suffer.

Equity of Redemption   Under the common law, a mortgagor's failure to pay the mortgage debt on the exact date on which it matured—the law day—extinguished the mortgagor's right and title to the mortgaged property and made the mortgagee's title absolute. This harsh rule not only became a common theme of melodrama, but it also received the early attention of courts of equity, which soon developed equitable principles to reverse this result. They first developed the equitable or lien theory of mortgages. The courts then developed what is known as the "equity of redemption." It offered a defaulting debtor a way to avoid forfeiting his title by allowing him to pay the debt at any time before actual foreclosure of the mortgage. Today, this right exists in all states.

EXAMPLE: Don purchased a mountain lot. To finance the purchase, he obtained a loan from his local bank and gave in return a promissory note and mortgage for $10,000. He subsequently defaulted on payments. At the time of default, Don owed $2,500. Before the bank initiates foreclosure proceedings to terminate his interest in the property, Don can pay—or offer to pay—the bank the total amount then due under the mortgage, thereby redeeming the property.

It is important to note that, for reasons of public policy, the right of redemption cannot be waived or relinquished by agreement. Any agreement that is made to waive or relinquish this right is void.

36:7   Foreclosure

A mortgagor's failure to pay off the mortgage debt or to perform other contractual duties can result in sale of the mortgaged property and the mortgagor's loss of his equity of redemption. The process by which this is done is called *foreclosure*. As discussed in detail below, two kinds of foreclosure procedures are in general use: (1) foreclosure by sale pursuant to judicial decree and (2) foreclosure by private sale without judicial intervention. The latter procedure is customarily referred to as *power of sale* or *nonjudicial foreclosure*. In most states, mortgages and deeds of trust contain a clause providing that, on default, the mortgagee or trustee can sell the property to satisfy the debt. In other states, foreclosure is commonly accomplished only through judicial action.

Foreclosure by Judicial Action   Foreclosure by judicial action begins with a proceeding brought against the mortgagor. At the proceeding, the mortgagor is given the opportunity to raise defenses that might prevent foreclosure. If the court determines that there has been a default and that the mortgagee has a right to foreclose, a decree or judgment is entered stating the amount due the lender and specifying a period in which the borrower can redeem the property by paying off the whole obligation. The decree provides that a specified period of notice be given to the public that the property is to be sold at public auction. This notice, which is published in a newspaper, must include a description of the property and the time, place, and terms of sale, as well as the officer named to conduct the sale.

The mortgagee is customarily permitted to bid at the auction, and in practice the mortgagee is often the only or the highest bidder. A mortgagee who successfully bids no more than the unpaid amount of the obligation secured by the mortgage need not pay anything at all; the bid price is merely applied to the mortgage debt. If the court approves the propriety of the sale, the officer who conducts it must execute a deed to the purchaser.

Foreclosure Through Power of Sale Sale under a power contained in a mortgage or deed of trust is the other established mode of mortgage foreclosure. In states where such foreclosures are recognized, the sale is made without recourse to the courts, although statutes prescribe the manner of advertising and conducting the sale. The sale must be made strictly in accordance with the power conferred and with the terms of the mortgage or deed of trust. The advantage of the power of sale to the creditor derives from the right to choose between the alternatives of foreclosure by court action or the trustee's sale. In this manner, a creditor can avoid the delay and expense of a judicial foreclosure proceeding. While the mortgagor usually has a statutory right to redeem the property after judicial foreclosure and sale, there is no such right of redemption once the property is sold pursuant to a power of sale.

Power of sale foreclosures afford mortgagees greater efficiency and substantial savings. At the same time, important rights of the mortgagor are sacrificed. The mortgagor is forced to give up substantial judicial protection where the only recourse is a personal action against the mortgagee to enjoin a sale, to undo it, or to seek damages after its completion.

A nonjudicial foreclosure sale is open to many abuses. For example, a mortgagee might not make a good faith effort to realize from the sale any more than the amount of the debt, despite the fact that the mortgagor might have considerable equity in the property. The mortgagee might also foreclose through the power of sale only for a technical default, based on conduct that the court in a judicial foreclosure might overlook. Finally, a mortgagee might sell the property after a default with respect to fraudulent or usurious terms in the mortgage contract, terms that a court would refuse to enforce in a judicial foreclosure.

The general rule is that in the absence of fraud, mistake, or unfairness, the fact that the sale price received in a foreclosure sale was low is not a sufficient ground to invalidate the sale unless (1) the price was grossly inadequate and can be considered unconscionable or (2) additional circumstances affected the regularity of the sale.

EXAMPLE: A mortgagor sues to have a foreclosure sale set aside. He alleges that the mortgagee, who successfully bid on the property, was unjustly enriched due to the low price bid. However, the mortgagor fails to allege any fraud or irregularity surrounding the sale. The court will probably refuse to set the sale aside.

Consider in the following case how easily the power of sale was accomplished as compared to judicial foreclosure requiring court approval.

Outpost Cafe, Inc.

v

Fairhaven Savings Bank
322 NE2d 183 (1975)
Massachusetts Appeals Court

FACTS: In 1972 Outpost Cafe, Inc. was in breach of one or more of the conditions contained in a mortgage of certain premises. Outpost Cafe had given the mortgage to the Fairhaven Savings Bank in 1970. On January 16, 1973, the bank, pursuant to a power of sale contained in the mortgage, conducted a duly advertised sale and sold the premises to the highest bidder. The purchaser put down a deposit in accordance with the terms of the sale and entered into a memorandum of sale with the attorney for the bank. Six days later, on January 22, 1973, Outpost Cafe tendered to the bank an amount in excess of the amount then due under the terms of the mortgage. The bank refused to accept the tender. Outpost Cafe then sued to redeem. By this time the bank had executed but had not yet delivered a deed of the premises to the purchaser at the foreclosure sale. The pertinent state statute provided that a mortgagor could redeem mortgaged property after a breach of condition unless the land had been sold pursuant to a power of sale contained in the mortgage deed.

ISSUE: Did a "sale" occur, within the meaning of the state statute, so as to foreclose the mortgagor's right to redeem?

RESULT: Yes. A sale occurred, even though the deed had not been transferred.

REASONING:

*   *   *

The disposition of this case turns on when "the land has been *sold* pursuant to a power of sale contained in the mortgage deed" . . . and on when a "*sale* [occurs] pursuant to a power contained in the mortgage"

. . . [Court's emphasis.] The defendant and the purchaser contend that the premises were "sold" within the meaning of those sections at least as early as the time when they executed the memorandum of sale at the foreclosure sale; the plaintiff contends that a "sale" is not complete until a deed is delivered to the purchaser at the foreclosure sale and that it may redeem the premises at any time prior to the delivery of such a deed.

An auction sale is complete, in the generally understood sense, when the auctioneer signifies his acceptance of the highest bid. . . .

If we were to be guided solely by the ordinary principles of statutory construction, we would unhesitatingly conclude that the premises in this case were "sold" within the meaning of [the statute] on the date of the foreclosure sale and that the plaintiff's tender came too late because not made until after the equity of redemption had been barred by virtue of the concluding provision of [the statute]. We believe that a careful analysis of the pertinent cases leads to the same conclusion. . . .

Grant, Justice.

Single-Action Rule   Under what is known as the single-action rule, when a mortgagor defaults, the mortgagee usually institutes a single action for the collection of the mortgage debt and foreclosure of the mortgage. This is required by statute in some states; in these states, a separate action for either kind of relief bars the other kind.

Deficiency Judgments   A mortgage foreclosure sale reduces the mortgage debt by an amount equal to the sale price, minus the expenses of the foreclosure and sale. For example, if a mortgagee is owed $25,000 on the mortgage, the foreclosure sale raises $22,000, and the cost of the foreclosure and sale is $2,000, the mortgage debt is reduced by only $20,000, leaving a deficiency of $5,000. Because the mortgagor is personally liable for the mortgage debt due to the promissory note that accompanies the mortgage, the mortgagee is at least theoretically entitled to a personal judgment against the mortgagor for the amount of the deficiency. In some states, a mortgagee can obtain a personal judgment for the debt in the foreclosure judgment itself; the amount raised by the foreclosure sale is applied to satisfy this personal judgment. In other states, no personal judgment is entered until the sale reveals the shortfall.

In the following case the court reviews the history of deficiency judgments and the use of equitable principles in ruling on requests for a deficiency judgment against the debtor following foreclosure.

Arnold
v
Melvin R. Hall, Inc.
478 NE2d 696 (1985)
Indiana Court of Appeals, First District

FACTS: In December 1981, the Arnolds entered into a contract with Hall, Inc. to purchase Petroleum Services of Gosport, Indiana, for $135,000. That price included real estate, buildings, and improvements valued at $100,000 and tools, equipment, fixtures, stock, and inventory valued at $35,000. In the same instrument, the Arnolds also acknowledged the receipt of a $14,800 loan from Hall. As payment, the Arnolds immediately deeded to Hall a 103.5-acre tract of land which the parties valued at $65,000. Additionally, the Arnolds agreed to pay monthly installments of $1,066.37 commencing on January 7, 1982. The Arnolds satisfied their installment obligations more or less regularly until February 1983. In April 1983, Hall filed a complaint seeking foreclosure. On October 27, 1983, the trial court entered a foreclosure order and deficiency judgment against the Arnolds. On November 3, 1983, the remaining personal property was sold. After the costs of the sale were deducted, the sheriff reported a net profit of $15,441.75 to be applied to the outstanding debt. On December 8, 1983, the real property was sold at the sheriff's sale. Hall, the lone bidder at the sale, bid $54,000 for the realty. The net profit from the sale was $53,355.35. This left a total deficiency of $15,805.31, which Hall then sought to collect from the Arnolds.

ISSUE: Is Hall entitled to a deficiency judgment?

RESULT: No. In the absence of evidence that the property's value is less than the remaining debt, a mortgagee who purchases at the foreclosure sale is not entitled to a deficiency judgment.

REASONING:

*   *   *

For more than a decade, Indiana courts have followed the tenets set down by our supreme court . . . [which], through an application of equitable principles, [has] held that in all but a few specific situations a conditional land sale contract should be viewed as an equitable mortgage. . . . Consequently, in those situations the appropriate remedy for the vendor confronted with a defaulting purchaser is that provided by the mortgage foreclosure statutes. . . . This was, in fact, the remedy pursued by Melvin R. Hall, Inc. Thus, it is essential that we examine the parameters of the mortgage foreclosure remedy in order to resolve the issue raised by the Arnolds.

Traditionally, foreclosure of mortgages and other liens on real estate has been an equitable remedy. As early as the reign of James I, equity began to intervene to protect mortgagors from the harsh results often visited upon them by the law courts. . . . In Indiana, a suit to foreclose remains essentially "an appeal to the equity powers of the court." . . .

In addition to his equitable remedy of foreclosure, a mortgagee is generally entitled to the legal remedy of a deficiency judgment for the balance of the debt remaining following the foreclosure sale. Of course, once equity took jurisdiction of the suit to foreclose it could also consider the availability of a deficiency judgment. . . . This it did pursuant to the general rule of equity that "where a court of equity obtains jurisdiction of an action, it will retain it, and administer full relief, both legal and equitable, so far as it pertains to the same transaction or the same subject-matter." . . . When equity exercised its jurisdiction over requests for the legal remedy of a deficiency judgment it applied equitable principles. . . . One state which applies equitable considerations to requests for deficiency judgments is Florida. Although Florida now has a statute which expressly permits this approach, it is clear that Florida courts would apply equitable considerations independent of any statute. . . . In determining the availability of a deficiency judgment in a particular case, the Florida courts examine a wide range of equitable considerations. Particularly important is who purchased the property at the foreclosure sale and how much was paid for it. . . . Where the mortgagee purchases the property at the foreclosure sale for less than the outstanding debt, equity dictates that he be denied a deficiency judgment. . . .

We think equity and established public policy require a similar result in Indiana. . . . [O]ur supreme court [has] invoked equitable principles to prevent forfeiture in all but a few cases of defaulting vendees. . . . In fact, equity first interceded in mortgage foreclosures to protect mortgagors from the forfeitures which often occurred in the law courts. . . . A similar situation is presented to us by this case. Melvin R. Hall, Inc. received substantial payments from the Arnolds prior to their default on the land contract obligation. It also acquired the real estate at the foreclosure sale. If, in addition, Melvin R. Hall, Inc. receives a deficiency judgment it will, in effect, reap a double recovery. Such a result is clearly violative of equity. . . . Consequently, equity and public policy demand that, absent evidence that the property's value is less than the total remaining deficiency, a mortgagee/vendor who purchases the property at the foreclosure sale is not entitled to a deficiency judgment. . . .

Ratliff, Presiding Judge.

During the Depression, mortgage foreclosure sales routinely failed to raise enough money to cover the mortgagors' debts. As a result, mortgagees in great numbers obtained personal judgments against debtors seeking to recoup deficiencies. In response to this, many states enacted *antideficiency judgment statutes* that prohibit to some degree a mortgagee's ability to obtain a personal judgment against the mortgage debtor after foreclosure and sale. Most antideficiency judgment statutes do not absolutely bar mortgagees from obtaining a *deficiency judgment.* For example, some statutes place substantial burdens of proof on mortgagees seeking deficiency judgment. Whatever their provisions, antideficiency judgment statutes have the effect of making deficiency judgments after mortgage foreclosure relatively rare today.

Rights of Purchasers and Other Lienholders   The doctrine of *caveat emptor* ("let the buyer beware") applies to both kinds of foreclosure sales discussed above. A purchaser at a foreclosure sale must determine the validity of the title that is acquired, although he can be entitled to relief if he has been misled by fraud or mistake and was not contributorily negligent. If a foreclosure sale is invalid for any reason for which the purchaser is not responsible, the purchaser then stands in the position of a mortgagee and can institute another foreclosure proceeding.

In the absence of any binding stipulation in the mortgage or deed of trust regarding the distribution or application of the proceeds of a foreclosure sale, a court having jurisdiction of the proceeding can determine the order of priority of various liens on the property and give specific directions as to the distribution and application of the proceeds. Generally, the proceeds must first be applied to the mortgage debt. Any surplus that remains after the discharge of the mortgage debt and other liens on the property must be paid to the mortgagor.

36:8 Redemption from Sale

After foreclosure of a mortgage by public sale, the *equitable* right of redemption ends, as discussed previously. However, in approximately 25 states, a *statutory* right of redemption exists. The statutes granting this right vary greatly from state to state, but they all prescribe a period after a foreclosure sale during which a mortgagor can reacquire his property by paying a sum computed in accordance with the statutory formula. Statutes in a few states also provide that the mortgagor can remain in possession during the statutory redemption period. Note that this right of redemption, called the redemption from sale, is quite distinct from the equity of redemption that is entirely cut off by a foreclosure. Because the right to redeem after a foreclosure sale is purely statutory, it can be exercised only in the manner prescribed by statute. Exercise of the right generally defeats any rights acquired by a purchaser at the foreclosure sale and restores the title to the property as though no sale had been attempted. That is, the purchaser at a foreclosure sale buys the property subject to any statutory right of redemption.

36:9　Receivers

In most states a receiver can be appointed to take charge of mortgaged property at the request of the mortgagee, to protect the mortgagee's interest. In practice, receiverships are usually requested only during foreclosure proceedings, and the court does not always grant the request. For example, the inadequacy of security for the mortgage debt is not, without more, a ground for appointing a receiver unless a statute provides otherwise. In some states the mortgagee can claim the rents, income, and profits of the mortgaged property after the mortgagor defaults and the mortgagee is given a right to the appointment of a receiver to take charge. In other states the mortgagor's insolvency, combined with the insufficiency of the security to pay the debt, can be the ground for appointing a receiver, at least when the mortgagor is in default. Appointment of a receiver is especially appropriate if these factors are combined with a danger of loss, waste, destruction, or serious impairment of the property.

A court has the power to appoint a receiver to manage a mortgagor's business. Here, too, the circumstances of each case will determine whether the appointment is proper and should be made.

36:10　Transfer of Mortgaged Property and Mortgage Debt

A mortgagor's interest in mortgaged property can be sold and conveyed at any time. When a mortgagor sells mortgaged property, he loses all control over it, but his liability under the mortgage continues. If the purchaser actually assumes and agrees to pay the mortgage debt, he becomes liable for the debt not only to the mortgagor but also to the mortgagee.

 Most sellers of real property take it for granted that if there is a debt still owing on the property, the purchaser takes complete responsibility for payment of that debt. This is not always true. Liability on the debt depends on whether the buyer takes the property "subject to" the mortgage or "assumes" it. In the "subject to" approach the property alone stands as security for the debt; the buyer undertakes no personal liability. When a buyer "assumes" a mortgage, however, he agrees to make the payments and becomes personally liable to the mortgagee for the mortgage debt. Of course, if state law does not permit deficiency judgments, this distinction makes little difference.

Transfer of Mortgage and Debt　Just as a mortgagor can convey his or her interest in mortgaged property, the mortgagee can transfer or assign the mortgage and secured debt. When a valid transfer or assignment is made, the transferee receives the mortgagee's rights and powers just as though he had been named in the mortgage. For example, the transferee can foreclose the mortgage on the mortgagor's default. In lien theory states, where a mortgagee's interest is a lien and for security purposes only, a transfer of the mortgage debt automatically operates as a transfer of the lien securing it. This is so because under the lien theory a mortgage has no independent existence. That is, it only reflects the debt, and cannot be separated from it.

Key Concepts and Terms

- The modern mortgage is both a conveyance and a lien to secure the payment of debt.
- Most states have adopted the equitable or lien theory of mortgages. This is the theory that a mortgage does not convey legal title to land but only creates a lien to secure payment of the mortgage debt.
- A security transaction in real property creates an interest in the property to secure the performance of an obligation. Mortgages and deeds of trust are the instruments used in most security transactions. A security transaction that is not evidenced by a mortgage or deed of trust but is understood by the parties to secure a debt will be given the effect of a mortgage.
- Any kind of interest in real property can be made the subject of a mortgage. A mortgage on land generally covers all structures and improvements on the land, including those made after the mortgage transaction.
- The owner of property who was previously granted a mortgage to secure a debt can give one or more junior mortgages on the same property to the extent of his remaining interest.
- The interests of the mortgagee and mortgagor in property are separate and distinct. The mortgagee has no control over mortgaged property and is not entitled to possession either before or after the mortgagor defaults, unless authorized by the mortgage. The mortgagor must preserve the mortgaged property to protect the mortgagee's security interest.
- The equity of redemption gives a defaulting mortgagor the right to pay the mortgage debt at any time before foreclosure. This right cannot be waived or relinquished by agreement because of the strong public policy favoring it.
- Foreclosure of a mortgage entails the sale of the mortgaged property and termination of the mortgagor's equity of redemption. It can occur when the mortgagor fails either to pay the secured debt or to perform other duties imposed on him by the terms of the mortgage. The basic foreclosure procedures are (1) sale pursuant to a judicial decree and (2) private sale without judicial intervention.
- Statutes in about half the states provide for redemption from sale. These statutes allow a mortgagor to redeem his property after a foreclosure sale by paying a sum computed according to the statutory formula within a prescribed time after the sale.
- A receiver is a person or entity appointed by the court to protect the rights of a mortgagee whose security in mortgaged property is threatened. A receiver can be appointed to manage a mortgagor's business.
- A mortgagor can convey his interest in the mortgaged property at any time. If he does so he loses all control over the property, but his liability under

the mortgage continues. A purchaser who actually assumes and agrees to pay a mortgage debt becomes liable for the debt not only to the mortgagor but also to the mortgagee.

- A mortgagee can assign the mortgage and mortgage debt.

- Antideficiency Judgment Statute
- Assumption of Mortgage
- Caveat Emptor
- Deed of Trust
- Defeasance Clause
- Deficiency Judgment
- Due-on-Sale Clause
- Equitable Mortgage
- Equity of Redemption
- Foreclosure
- Law Day
- Lien Theory

- Mechanic's Lien
- Mortgage
- Mortgagee
- Mortgagor
- Open-End Mortgage
- Power of Sale
- Prepayment Penalty
- Purchase Money Mortgage
- Single Action Rule
- Surplus
- Title Theory
- Wraparound Mortgage

Questions and Case Problems

1. Compare and contrast the title and lien theories of mortgages. Determine whether your state is a title theory or a lien theory state.

2. Boardwalk Corporation proposes to erect a five-story building in New York City, and hopes to seek financing from its regular construction financier, Builders Bank. Boardwalk estimates that the total cost of the project will be $10 million. It would prefer to receive only $2 million initially and to draw the balance of the loan in subsequent installments as dictated by the progress of the project. Since cost overruns are almost inevitable, Boardwalk wants to ensure that the financing is sufficiently flexible to permit the extension of credit beyond the initial $10 million without undue cost or delay. Builders Bank is prepared to deal with Boardwalk if the firm can provide sufficient security of real property to cover not only the $10 million primary indebtedness, but also an unsecured note in the amount of $100,000 executed previously by Boardwalk in favor of the bank on a previous construction job. How can this transaction best be structured?

3. Lake Hillsdale Estates (Hillsdale) borrowed $198,301 from Louisiana Savings Association (Savings) and secured a note for that amount with a deed of trust in favor of Savings. After Hillsdale's default on the note, the trustee sold the property in accordance with the trust instrument. Savings purchased the property at the foreclosure sale for $85,530. Savings then sought a deficiency judgment against Hillsdale. Hillsdale counterclaimed, asking the court to (1) set aside the sale on the ground that the trustee failed to secure an adequate price, and (2) deny Savings a deficiency judgment on equitable grounds. What result?

4. On February 12, 1982, Pezzimenti bought property from Cirou for $550,000. Pezzimenti executed a note and a mortgage in favor of Cirou to secure the purchase price, less a down payment of $100,000. The payments were approximately $5,400 a month. Over the succeeding 10 months, Cirou had the following

experiences with the mortgage: first, Cirou learned by accident that Pezzimenti had transferred the property by quitclaim deed. Second, a $22,000 mechanics' lien was filed against the mortgaged property. The mortgagor obtained release of the lien, but then refused to pay the mortgagee's attorney's fees on the matter, as required by the mortgage. Third, the property insurance almost lapsed and was restored only through efforts of the mortgagee. Fourth, the mortgagor attempted to reduce the amount of a mortgage payment by $98, an amount equal to a rental payment not yet due to the mortgagor from the mortgagee. Mortgagee refused to accept the reduced mortgage payment and sought judicial foreclosure on the property. Mortgagor argues that foreclosure is improper because the breach was minor and technical and did not impair the security of the mortgage. If you were the judge, would you grant foreclosure?

5. Wisconsin Wire Works conveys mortgaged premises to Megao Development Corp. without the consent of the mortgagee, Mutual Federal. The mortgage provides for acceleration of the balance due if the mortgagor "shall convey away" the mortgaged premises. Mutual Federal initiates a proceeding to foreclose the mortgage, seeking to enforce the due-on-sale acceleration clause. How should the court decide the case?

6. Compare and contrast the equity of redemption and the statutory right of redemption from sale.

7. Gerdin saw a notice of a foreclosure sale by the Princeton State Bank on some property that he had once owned. Out of curiosity, he went to the sale. There he found that the Princeton State Bank's attorney and the sheriff were the only other people at the sale. The attorney, Hoffman, told Gerdin that the bank would bid $55,000 for the property, and if Gerdin bid more he would get the property. Gerdin immediately went to the Princeton State Bank and arranged for financing to buy the property for $10 more than the Bank's bid. At no time did the Bank or its attorney reveal to Gerdin that there was a $50,000 tax lien on the property which had not been extinguished by the foreclosure sale process. Gerdin bought the property and then learned that the total of the purchase price and the tax lien far exceeded the value of the property. He seeks to have the sale set aside on the ground that Hoffman and the Bank had a duty to disclose the existence of tax liens. Should the Bank have such a duty?

8. First Federal forecloses and sells real property owned by Molds. It later seeks a deficiency judgment and the appointment of a receiver for the property during the period of redemption. First Federal alleges that the property will depreciate in value during the period of redemption and for that reason a receiver is required. Does depreciation in value constitute waste and a sufficient basis on which the appointment of a receiver may be made?

9. Potwin State Bank agreed to finance the construction of houses by Warrant. The mortgage expressly stated that it was given to include security for future advances. During the construction of various houses by Warrant, labor and materials were furnished by contractors. Mechanic's liens attached after the mortgage was recorded but before various advances were made under the mortgage. Ultimately, the bank foreclosed on the mortgage, seeking priority over the mechanic's lien claimants. Do the mechanic's liens take priority over the mortgage advances?

10. Compare and contrast judicial foreclosure and foreclosure through a power of sale.

37 Landlord and Tenant

37:1 Introduction; Types of Tenancies

Many people rent rather than own the real property on which they live. This has traditionally been true for young people during their early years away from their parents' home. It has become increasingly true for many older, established people as well. This chapter discusses the relationship that exists when a person who owns real property rents that property to someone else.

The renting of real property is based on a form of contract called a *lease* or a rental agreement. This is true whether the contract is oral or in writing. The person who gives possession and use of real property to the other is known as the landlord, or *lessor*. The person who receives possession of the property and has use of the premises during the term of the lease is the tenant, or *lessee*.

If a landlord–tenant relationship exists, the tenant's interest or estate is called a leasehold. Leaseholds are generally classified according to their duration as (1) a tenancy for years, (2) a periodic tenancy or tenancy from year to year, (3) a tenancy at will, or (4) a tenancy at sufferance.

Tenancy for Years A *tenancy for years* is one in which the beginning and end are fixed in advance. The term is a misnomer because the tenancy can be for a certain number of days, weeks, months, or years. The chief difference between a tenancy for years and other tenancies is that it expires at the end of a stated period without the need for either party to give notice of its expiration or termination. A lease can be created for as long a period as desired unless there is a statute that limits the maximum years of a particular lease.

Periodic Tenancy A *periodic tenancy* continues for successive periods of the same length of time—weekly, monthly, or yearly, as long as the beginning of the tenancy is certain. It is terminated by notice at the end of one of the periods. A periodic tenancy may arise by implication. This occurs if property is leased with no specific termination date, but provision is made for periodic payments of rent. In such a case, the tenant has a periodic tenancy measured by the rental periods. For example, if a tenant rents an apartment beginning January 1 and pays rent monthly, a periodic tenancy (month-to-month) has been created.

Tenancy at Will   In a *tenancy at will* the tenant has a right to possession of premises for an indefinite period. A tenancy at will terminates at the will of either the landlord or the tenant.

Tenancy at Sufferance   A *tenancy at sufferance* is an unlawful possession of property. For example, a tenant who occupies the premises without the landlord's consent after the stated period of tenancy has expired is a tenant at sufferance. One who obtains possession of property without the owner's permission is also considered to be a tenant at sufferance. A tenancy at sufferance lasts only until the landlord takes steps to evict the tenant or seeks to regain possession. If a landlord gives either express or implied consent to a tenant's *holding over* after the expiration of a lease, this consent may be sufficient to transform the tenancy at sufferance into a tenancy at will or, under certain circumstances, into a periodic tenancy.

As the following case illustrates, a tenant at sufferance is still a tenant, and there is a landlord–tenant relationship. Thus, the landlord may have obligations to the tenant that would not be owed to a mere trespasser.

Rivera

v

Santiago
495 A2d 1122 (1985)
Appellate Court of Connecticut

FACTS: In October 1983 defendant landlord sent a notice to quit to plaintiff tenant. In January 1984 plaintiff filed a complaint seeking to compel defendant to make repairs under a Connecticut statute that affords judicial relief to tenants. Under the statute, "landlord" is defined as "the owner, lessor, or sublessor of the dwelling unit or the building of which it is a part," and "tenant" is defined as "the lessee, sublessee or person entitled under a rental agreement to occupy a dwelling unit to the exclusion of others or as is otherwise defined by law." Defendant claims that plaintiff cannot bring the action because there is no landlord–tenant relationship.

ISSUE: Is a tenant at sufferance a tenant for purposes of the statute governing the landlord's obligation to make repairs?

RESULT: Yes. The relationship of landlord and tenant continues after a notice to quit, although the rental agreement has terminated.

REASONING:

*   *   *

The issuance by a landlord of a notice to quit is an unequivocal act terminating the lease agreement with the tenant. Termination of the lease does not terminate the tenancy since, upon service of a notice to quit, a tenancy at sufferance is created. . . . In the present action, the plaintiff became a tenant at sufferance on October 24, 1983, when she was served with a notice to quit. Nonetheless, the landlord-tenant relationship continued.

The statutory obligations of the landlord and tenant continue even when there is no longer a rental agreement between them. After a notice to quit has been served, for example, a tenant at sufferance no longer has a duty to pay rent. He still, however, is obliged to pay a fair rental value in the form of use and occupancy for the dwelling unit. . . . A landlord also is required to fulfill his statutory obligations, even after a notice to quit has been served on the tenant and a summary process case is begun. . . . In that case, funds paid into court during the pendency of a summary process action for use and occupancy were properly partially distributed to hold over tenants in order to reimburse them for sums spent in discharge of obligations imposed on the landlord by virtue of General Statutes § 47a–7. . . .

Although General Statutes §§ 47a–14h and 47a–7 use the terms "tenant" and "landlord," there is no provision which requires that the relationship between the parties be based solely on a rental contract. The wording of the statutes militates against such a narrow construction. "A statute is to be construed so that all its parts have meaning. . . ." . . .

General Statutes § 47a–[14h(g) provides that "[t]he court, in ordering interim or final relief, may order that accrued payments of rent or *use and occupancy* held by the clerk be used for the repair of the building or be distributed in accordance with the rights of the parties." (Emphasis added.) Under Connecticut law, use and occupancy, by definition, is an amount equal to fair rental value and payable during the pendency of a summary process action. . . . It is the amount to which the landlord is entitled after the rental agreement has been terminated but while a tenancy at sufferance exists. Use of that phrase in the statute indicates that a tenancy at sufferance falls within the court's jurisdiction pursuant to the statute. . . .

Stodolink, Judge.

37:2   The Lease Agreement

A lease transfers a right to possession of property from the property owner to a tenant who, in turn, gives some consideration (usually rent) to the owner. Thus, a lease is both a conveyance and a contract for the possession of property. Leases are generally governed by the same principles that govern other contracts. There must be a delivery and acceptance of the lease, and the lease must contain the names of the contracting parties and a description of the leased premises. A lease must also be supported by consideration. Fraud or mutual mistake, or other illegality, can invalidate a lease.

While no particular legal terminology is required to make a lease, the document must (1) express an intention to establish the relationship of landlord and tenant; (2) include provisions for the transfer of use and possession of the property and its reversion to the landlord at the end of the term; and (3) state the boundaries of the property, the term of the leasehold, the agreed rent, and how and when the rent is to be paid.

Oral Leases   A landlord–tenant relationship can be created orally in most states. However, if the term of an oral lease exceeds the period set forth in the state statute of frauds, which affects oral contracts, the lease is unenforceable and might even be invalid, depending on state law.

Other Relationships Distinguished   The leasehold is the only interest in real property that confers a right to possession. Other interests, such as easements and licenses, entitle the holder to use another's land but do not entail the transfer of possession. For example, a typical billboard agreement gives the advertiser the right only to erect a billboard on another's property; since it does not entail possession, a landlord–tenant relationship is not created.

Covenants and Conditions   A *covenant* is an undertaking by one of the parties to a lease to do or not to do a particular act, and most leases include express covenants. For example, a lease may include covenants by which the tenant promises to use the property only for a specific purpose and the landlord promises to make needed repairs and to ensure the tenant's quiet enjoyment of the property. The covenant of "quiet enjoyment" refers to the tenant's right to possess and use the property without interference by the landlord.

Covenants are classified as independent or dependent. An independent covenant is one that can be enforced or performed despite the other party's failure to perform his own covenant or obligation. For example, assume that L covenants under a lease to paint a house and T covenants to pay rent for the right to occupy that house. If L fails to paint the house, T must still continue to pay rent. L's breach of his covenant does not excuse T from paying rent since the covenants are independent. T's remedy is to sue L for damages for failing to paint the house.

A dependent covenant is an obligation that constitutes consideration for another obligation undertaken by the other party. If one party fails to perform, the other party is relieved of the obligation under his covenant. For example, a tenant's covenant to pay rent is dependent on a landlord's performance of the covenant for quiet enjoyment; an act by the landlord that interferes with the tenant's enjoyment or possession of the property can suspend the tenant's obligation to pay rent.

Most leases also include "conditions," which are qualifications or restrictions. For example, a lease provision that premises are to be used for "bakery and associated purposes and traffic in food and beverages and for no other purposes" is a *condition*. If the tenant changes the use of the premises from a bakery to a nightclub, the condition is breached and the landlord can forfeit the lease or obtain a court order prohibiting the tenant from violating it.

The most significant difference between covenants and conditions lies in the remedies available to either party in case of breach. The remedy for breach of a covenant is usually an action for damages. In contrast, a party usually cannot recover damages for breach of a condition. Instead, the breach can result in forfeiture of the lease.

37:3 Possession of Premises

Some states follow what is usually termed the English rule as to the possession of leased premises. Under this rule the landlord must provide the tenant with possession of premises at the beginning of the agreed term, even to the extent of ousting anyone who may already be in possession. Other states follow the so-called "American rule." This rule is that unless a provision to the contrary is included in the lease, a landlord must give the tenant only the legal right to possession at the beginning of the term, not necessarily actual possession. In these states, the landlord does not have to put the tenant in possession as against an intruder or other party. The realities of modern leasing, however, are such that most tenants are actually put in possession of leased property at the inception of the agreed term. Moreover, both the Model Residential Landlord–Tenant Code and the *Restatement (Second) of Property, Landlord and Tenant*, recognize that a landlord is obligated to provide the tenant with actual possession except to the extent that the parties agree otherwise. A landlord breaches this obligation if a third party is in possession on the date the tenant is entitled to possession of the leased property.

Peaceful and Quiet Enjoyment The essence of the landlord–tenant relationship is the tenant's right to have the peaceful and quiet use of real property throughout the duration of the tenancy. This right, based on the *covenant for quiet enjoyment*, is contained in most written leases and rental agreements. The covenant for quiet enjoyment protects the tenant against physical expulsion, interference by the landlord, or other acts threatening the tenant's beneficial enjoyment of the premises. In short, the covenant operates to guarantee that the tenant will have possession of the property throughout the lease term.

Landlord's Reversionary Interest For all practical purposes, the tenant is the absolute owner of the leased premises during the lease term. The landlord's rights are confined to his reversionary interest in the premises. At the end of the term, the tenant must vacate and surrender the premises to the landlord unless the tenant has an option to purchase and exercises it in a timely fashion. The landlord does not have to request that the tenant vacate. However, a tenant can remain in possession after the original term ends if (1) he or she pays rent to the landlord and (2) the landlord accepts the rent. The tenant will then be considered either a periodic tenant or a tenant at will.

Eviction An *eviction* is any act by a landlord that deprives the tenant of possession, expels him from the premises, or deprives him of enjoyment of the premises. The wrongful eviction of a tenant will terminate the tenant's obligations under the lease and entitle him to recover damages. Eviction can be actual, as where it occurs because of the landlord's affirmative act. As discussed below, however, eviction can also be constructive.

Constructive Eviction A *constructive eviction* is the landlord's substantial interference with the tenant's possession that (1) renders the premises unfit for the purposes for which they were leased or (2) deprives the tenant of the enjoyment of the premises. To establish a constructive eviction, there must be (1) a substantial interference and (2) abandonment of the premises by the tenant. For example, if a landlord fails to furnish heat, light, or other utilities, the tenant is constructively evicted if forced to abandon the property as a result. In certain cases, constructive eviction has also occurred because of a landlord's failure to make repairs or alterations required by the terms of the lease or by public authorities.

EXAMPLE: Dr. Peters, a psychotherapist, rents an office from Rockrose Associates for professional use. Under the lease, the landlord is required to soundproof the office. He fails to do so, and over a period of three months, neighboring tenants' noise interferes with the doctor's sessions with her patients. Under the doctrine of constructive eviction, Dr. Peters is relieved of paying rent if she abandons the premises.

Retaliatory Eviction A landlord is prohibited from evicting a tenant as retaliation for the tenant's complaints to a governmental agency as to the condition of a dwelling, its habitability, or housing code violations. If a retaliatory motive can be imputed to the landlord, the tenant cannot be evicted; if he is, he may be entitled to damages. Retaliation is difficult to prove, particularly if a landlord waits several months after a tenant's complaint before initiating eviction. To lighten the burden of proof, some states have enacted statutes that provide for a presumption of retaliatory motive if the landlord commences an eviction proceeding within a specified period of time after the tenant has complained to a governmental agency. If the landlord's dominant purpose is retaliation for the tenant's exercise of his lawful rights, however, a *retaliatory eviction* will be found regardless of the time period involved.

37:4 Use and Enjoyment of Premises

During the term of a lease, the tenant has the sole and exclusive right to occupy and control the premises. A tenant may use leased property in the same manner as the owner might have done and for any lawful purpose or business that does not injure the landlord's interest. As discussed above, however, parties to a lease can restrict the uses to which leased property can be put, so long as these restrictions are not contrary to law or public policy. A tenant does not have the right to remove, destroy, or even alter buildings or make other improvements without the landlord's consent.

A lease usually covers all the property and fixtures that are essential or reasonably necessary to the full use and enjoyment of the property. Thus, if use of a portion of a building not included in the lease is necessary to the enjoyment of the leased portion, an easement or privilege passes to the tenant. A right-of-way for access to leased property, including the right to use steps, halls, stairways, and elevators, is ordinarily implied. A landlord may or may not be required to furnish water, lights, heat, and other utilities, depending on the terms of the lease.

Tenant's Use of Premises   A tenant must take care not to damage leased premises. The tenant is responsible to the landlord for all property damages that the tenant causes intentionally or negligently. A tenant is not responsible for depreciation in value of the property as a result of ordinary wear and tear, in the absence of an agreement to the contrary.

If a tenant creates a nuisance that affects other tenants or third parties on leased premises, or if he uses property unlawfully, he may be subject to an eviction even though there is no specific agreement between the parties dealing with these subjects. A nuisance occurs if the tenant's conduct substantially interferes with the enjoyment by other tenants or third persons of their own property. In rental apartments, for example, the most common nuisances are noise during the usual hours of sleep and harassment of cotenants. A nuisance does not arise if conduct only annoys an apartment manager. For example, if a tenant fails to make prompt rental payments, argues with a manager, demands repairs of property, or complains about other things, his conduct might not be a legal nuisance, even though it would certainly be aggravating to the parties involved.

Change of Use   It is not uncommon for the landlord to insist on inserting a clause in the lease restricting a tenant's use of the premises. Landlords do this in order to control the uses to which leased property may be put. The violation of a lease clause limiting the use of property can result in a forfeiture of the lease, constitute grounds for an injunction, or be the basis of an award of monetary damages.

Improvements and Alterations   Unless a lease provides to the contrary, neither the landlord nor the tenant is obligated to make specific improvements or alterations to leased property. Either party can make minor improvements or alterations that do not materially change the condition of the premises. Leases frequently provide that improvements, alterations, or additions made by one of the parties shall be the property of the landlord and shall remain on the property at the termination of the lease.

 At times, a tenant's right to remove improvements or additions is expressly authorized or prohibited by the lease. Some leases cover this matter by use of broad terms, such as "improvements" and "additions." Whether or not a particular improvement or addition will in fact be covered depends on the specific language used. To avoid future problems, any lease—and especially a lease of business property—should specify as precisely as possible what improvements or additions the tenant will (or will not) be permitted to remove.

37:5   Condition of Premises; Repairs

Under the common law a landlord was not responsible for the condition of leased premises at the beginning of a lease. The tenant took the premises as they were, with all their faults. This rule developed from the view that a lease is a conveyance—a sale for a term—to which the principle of "let the buyer beware" applied. It was perhaps best typified by the language of one court, which stated that "fraud apart, there is no law against letting [leasing] a tumbled-down house, and the tenant's remedy is upon his contract, if any.[1] In the absence of express warranty, statute, fraud, or misrepresentation by a landlord, the tenant traditionally has been required to take property as he finds it, with all known defects or those that can be ascertained by reasonable inspection.

Landlord's Obligation to Repair   In the absence of statute or an agreement to the contrary by parties to a lease, there is no implied covenant by a landlord to repair leased property during the lease term. In some states, however, statutes have changed the landlord's obligations to undertake repairs of rented or leased premises. Under these statutes, a residential landlord must put premises into a condition fit for human occupancy and must repair subsequent dilapidations other than those attributable to the tenant. If a landlord fails to make repairs within a reasonable time after notice, a tenant can either make the repairs himself or vacate, thereby discharging himself from further obligations under the lease.

Implied Warranty of Habitability   In most states, the common-law rule that a landlord is under no obligation to maintain premises in a reasonable state of repair is giving way to other legal doctrines that impose affirmative duties on landlords to furnish habitable premises at the commencement of a lease or rental agreement. This duty is based on what is called the implied *warranty of habitability*. The warranty extends primarily to premises used for residential rather than commercial purposes, and it applies during the entire term of the lease rather than only at its inception.

If a landlord breaches the implied warranty of habitability, a tenant can rescind the lease, vacate the premises, offset the costs of repair against the rent due, or seek money damages. In many states, a tenant's remedy of offsetting repair costs against rent is regulated by statute. In determining

---

[1] *Robbins v Jones*, 15 CB [NS] 221, 240 (1803).

whether a landlord has breached the implied warranty of habitability, several criteria are used by courts. These include

- Whether the defect is a violation of any applicable housing code or building or sanitary regulations
- Whether the defect affects a vital facility
- Potential effect of the defect on safety and sanitation
- Length of time the defect has persisted
- Age of the structure
- Amount of the rent
- Whether the tenant has waived the defect
- Whether the tenant was in any way responsible for the defect

In addition, some states have imposed an implied warranty of habitability by statute.

The following case is representative of judicial reasoning about the implied warranty of habitability. Consider the court's reasoning and why it held that the common-law rule must give way to the modern approach that imposes on the landlord a duty to place premises in a habitable condition.

Green

v

Superior Court of San Francisco
517 P2d 1168 (1974)
California Supreme Court

FACTS: Sumski, the landlord, commenced an eviction action against his tenant Green, seeking possession of leased premises and $300 in back rent. Green admitted that he had not paid the rent, but he defended the action on the ground that Sumski had failed to maintain the leased premises in a habitable condition. Some of the more serious defects described by Green included (1) the collapse and nonrepair of a bathroom ceiling; (2) the continued presence of rats, mice, and cockroaches on the premises; (3) the lack of any heat in four of the apartment's rooms; (4) plumbing blockages; (5) exposed and faulty wiring; and (6) an illegally installed and unsafe stove.

ISSUE: Is there an implied warranty of habitability in residential leases?

RESULT: Yes. California law implies such a covenant, the breach of which excuses the nonpayment of rent.

REASONING:

*   *   *

At common law, the real estate lease developed in the field of real property law, not contract law. Under property law concepts, a lease was considered a conveyance or sale of the premises for a term of years, subject to the ancient doctrine of caveat emptor. Thus, under traditional common-law rules, the landlord owed no duty to place leased premises in a habitable condition and no obligation to repair the premises. . . . These original common-law precepts perhaps suited the agrarianism of the early Middle Ages which was their matrix; at such time, the primary value of a lease lay in the land itself and whatever simple living structures may have been included in the leasehold were of secondary importance and were readily repairable by the typical "jack-of-all-trades" lessee farmer. Furthermore, because the law of property crystallized before the development of mutually dependent covenants in contract law, a lessee's covenant to pay rent was considered at common law as independent of the lessor's covenants. Thus even when a lessor expressly covenanted to make repairs, the lessor's breach did not justify the lessee's withholding of the rent. . . .

In recent years, however, a growing number of courts have begun to re-examine these "settled" common-law rules in light of contemporary conditions, and, after thorough analysis, all of these courts have discarded the traditional doctrine as incompatible with contemporary social conditions and modern legal values. This emerging line of decisions, along with a veritable flood of academic commentaries, demonstrates the obsolescence of the traditional common-law rule absolving a landlord of any duty to maintain leased premises in a habitable condition during the term of the lease.

The recent decisions recognize initially that the geographic and economic conditions that characterized the agrarian lessor–lessee transaction have been entirely transformed in the modern urban landlord–tenant relationship. We have suggested that in the Middle Ages, and, indeed, until the urbanization of the industrial revolution, the land itself was by far the most important element of a lease transaction; this predominance explained the law's treatment of such leases as conveyances of interests in land. In today's urban residential leases, however, land as such plays no comparable role. The typical city dweller, who frequently leases an apartment several stories above the actual plot of land on which an apartment building rests, cannot realistically be viewed as acquiring an interest in land; rather, he has contracted for a place to live. . . .

Modern urbanization has not only undermined the validity of utilizing general property concepts in analyzing landlord–tenant relations, but it has also significantly altered the factual setting directly relevant to the more specific duty of maintaining leased premises. . . . Contemporary urban housing and the contemporary urban tenant stand in marked contrast to this agrarian model.

First, the increasing complexity of modern apartment buildings not only renders them much more difficult and expensive to repair than the living quarters of earlier days, but also makes adequate inspection of the premises by a prospective tenant a virtual impossibility; complex heating, electrical and plumbing systems are hidden from view, and the landlord, who has had experience with the building, is certainly in a much better position to discover and to cure dilapidations in the premises. Moreover, in a multiple-unit dwelling repair will frequently require access to equipment and areas solely in the control of the landlord.

Second, unlike the multi-skilled lessee of old, today's city dweller generally has a single, specialized skill unrelated to maintenance work. Furthermore, whereas an agrarian lessee frequently remained on a single plot of land for his entire life, today's urban tenant is more mobile than ever; a tenant's limited tenure in a specific apartment will frequently not justify efforts at extensive repairs. Finally, the expense of needed repairs will often be outside the reach of many tenants for "[l]ow and middle income tenants, even if they were interested in making repairs, would be unable to obtain any financing for major repairs since they have no long-term interest in the property." . . .

In addition to these significant changes, urbanization and population growth have wrought an enormous transformation in the contemporary housing market, creating a scarcity of adequate low cost housing in virtually every urban setting. This current state of the housing market is by no means unrelated to the common-law duty to maintain habitable premises. For one thing, the severe shortage of low and moderate cost housing has left tenants with little bargaining power through which they might gain express warranties of habitability from landlords, and thus the mechanism of the "free market" no longer serves as a viable means for fairly allocating the duty to repair leased premises between landlord and tenant. For another, the scarcity of adequate housing has limited further the adequacy of the tenant's right to inspect the premises; even when defects are apparent the low income tenant frequently has no realistic alternative but to accept such housing with the expectation that the landlord will make the necessary repairs. Finally, the shortage of available low cost housing has rendered inadequate the few remedies that common-law courts previously have developed to ameliorate the harsh consequences of the traditional "no duty to repair" rule.

In most significant respects, the modern urban tenant is in the same position as any other normal consumer of goods. . . . Through a residential lease, a tenant seeks to purchase "housing" from his landlord for a specified period of time. The landlord "sells" housing, enjoying a much greater opportunity, incentive and capacity than a tenant to inspect and maintain the condition of his apartment building. A tenant may reasonably expect that the product he is purchasing is fit for the purpose for which it is obtained, that is, a living unit. Moreover, since a lease contract specifies a designated period of time during which the tenant has a right to inhabit the premises, the tenant may legitimately expect that the premises will be fit for such habitation for the duration of the term of the lease. It is just such reasonable expectations of consumers which the modern "implied warranty" decisions endow with formal, legal protection. . . .

Tobriner, Judge.

Tenant's Obligation to Repair Under the common law, a tenant was obligated to make certain repairs that were necessary to prevent waste or decay of the premises. Today, under the terms of most long-term leases, it is customary for the tenant to make *all* necessary repairs and to restore or reconstruct the premises after damage by fire or other causes. Beyond this, a tenant, particularly a residential tenant, is not obligated to make repairs in the absence of an agreement to do so in the lease. In any event, a tenant is not bound to make substantial or lasting repairs or improvements, such as putting on a new roof or constructing buildings on the property.

37:6 Rent

Rent is the consideration paid by a tenant to a landlord for the use and occupation of the leased property. The amount and terms of rent payment are usually stipulated in the lease. If the lease does not contain a provision as to rent, the law implies a promise by the tenant to pay the reasonable value of his use and occupation of the property.

As long as a lease is in existence, rent must be paid. This is true even if the lessee refuses to take possession of the leased property or takes possession but later abandons the premises. Unless the abandonment is justified, as in the case of damage or destruction of the property or a constructive eviction, the landlord can even leave the property vacant in some states and recover rent periodically during the remainder of the term. Under this view, which is contrary to the general rule that damages be mitigated a landlord is not obligated to find a new tenant or relet property so long as the lease continues and the tenant has unjustifiably abandoned the property.

 Leases usually favor the landlord. Often, they place heavy burdens on a tenant who does not fulfill his terms of the bargain. For example, in some states a lease can provide that the tenant's failure to pay rent on time permits the landlord to accelerate the entire rent due for the rest of the term, even under a multiyear lease. A business tenant often has greater bargaining power than an individual who is trying to rent residential premises. The tenant should use that power to persuade the landlord to delete or alter provisions that are unduly burdensome.

Late Charges Under most commercial and residential leases, late charges can be imposed when the tenant fails to pay the rent when due. Unquestionably, the imposition of a late charge induces the tenant to pay rent on time. Although interest can be added to any payment that is late, late charges might not be valid if an arbitrary sum is set for the late payment with little or no regard to the amount or duration of the delinquency. A sum that fairly compensates the landlord and at the same time is not excessive is usually considered to be valid.

Security Deposits Often the lease requires the tenant to deposit some form of security, usually cash, before the lease term commences. The deposit secures the tenant's obligation to perform under the lease. Security deposits are commonly used since other, older common-law remedies, such as the landlord's physical taking of the tenant's personal property in the event of default, have been abolished or restricted by statute.

Taxes and Other Payments In most states, a tenant is not obligated to pay real estate taxes assessed against leased property. Unless this duty is transferred by the terms of the lease, it must be met by the landlord.

37:7 Assignment and Subletting

An *assignment* of a lease is the lessee's transfer of his or her entire interest in the leased premises for the entire unexpired term of the original lease. In the absence of a statutory provision or a restriction in the lease, a tenant for a definite term has the right to assign his interest without the landlord's consent. When a valid assignment is made, the assignee succeeds to all the tenant's interests and to the benefit of all covenants and agreements made by the landlord. In turn, the assignee must perform all of the original tenant's duties. That is, the assignee must pay rent, taxes, or other sums of money to the original landlord as required under the terms of the original lease. The assignee's duties terminate when the lease expires or when the assignee reassigns the lease to a third party.

Subletting A tenant under a lease for a definite period has the right to sublet the premises (lease the premises to someone else) in the absence of statutory prohibitions or restrictions imposed by the lease itself. The relation between the sublessor (original tenant) and sublessee is that of landlord and tenant, and their rights are governed by the terms of the sublease. The only limit on the right to sublet is that premises may not be sublet for a use that is either inconsistent with the terms of the original lease or injurious to the premises. For example, a tenancy at will cannot be sublet to another without the landlord's consent since the landlord can terminate the original lease at any time. When property is sublet, the sublessee acquires no greater rights in the use and enjoyment of the premises than were enjoyed by the original lessee.

 Subletting does not remove the tenant's liability to the landlord for the payment of rent or the performance of the agreements or covenants contained in the original lease. In addition, the tenant is liable to the landlord for damage to the premises caused by the sublessee's negligence or wrongful acts.

Limits on Assignment and Subletting   Often, leases prohibit the tenant from assigning or subletting without the landlord's consent. In the absence of other provisions in the lease, a landlord may refuse to consent to a sublease or assignment. Therefore, some leases also contain provisions that the landlord's consent will not be arbitrarily or unreasonably withheld. In determining whether a particular refusal by a landlord is unreasonable or arbitrary, a key factor is whether the landlord will be assured that the principal terms of the lease, particularly those as to the payment of rent, will be met if the premises are assigned or sublet.

EXAMPLE: A tenant requests the landlord to consent to a sublease of the leased premises. The landlord refuses, although he does not object to the nature of the proposed sublessee's business. In fact, his refusal to consent is based on his desire to rent directly to the proposed sublessee under a new lease, at a higher rent. If the original tenant agrees to guarantee the sublessee's obligations under the terms of the original lease, a court will probably find that the landlord's refusal to consent is unreasonable.

37:8   Termination of the Lease

A lease can be terminated for several reasons. The most common is the expiration of the agreed term. However, a lease can also end by (1) forfeiture, as where a tenant fails to meet his obligations under the lease in breach of a condition; (2) rescission by one party; or (3) agreement between the parties. A lease can also terminate if the premises are destroyed or rendered uninhabitable. Ordinarily, the death of either the tenant or the landlord does not terminate a lease.

Whether the breach of a condition in a lease will terminate the lease or give one party the right to rescind or cancel the lease depends on the provisions of the lease itself and how vital or essential the breached provision is. For example, late payment of rent is not ordinarily a ground for the termination of a lease unless it is expressly made so by a provision in the lease.

A tenant loses all interests in the property upon surrendering the leased property. A surrender generally occurs only if the lease is terminated by agreement of the parties.

Termination by Notice   Most states have enacted statutes that explicitly set forth the procedures by which a leasehold tenancy can be lawfully terminated. Under a typical statute, the landlord must give what is called a *notice to quit* in order to terminate a periodic tenancy—one from year to year or month to month—if the term of the tenancy is not definitely fixed. The same rule is applied to tenancies at will. A notice to quit is not necessary in the case of any lease that fixes the time of its termination since the lease terminates automatically on expiration of the lease term.

37:9   Renewal of Lease; Holding Over

A landlord is not bound to renew a lease unless there is an express agreement in the lease to do so. Similarly, the tenant is not bound to accept a renewal. This is not to say, however, that the terms of a lease cannot be renewed or extended after the lease expires. Provision for renewal or extension is frequently in the form of an option, which the tenant can exercise by giving the landlord proper notice, as discussed below. If the renewal provision in the lease does not set forth the terms of the renewal, the terms of the original agreement will generally govern.

The purpose of the requirement that the tenant give the landlord notice of his intention to exercise a renewal option is to enable the landlord to rent the property to someone else if the present tenant does not renew. Therefore, the tenant must give the notice before the expiration of the present lease term. A tenant's renewal notice need not be in writing; it can be oral or it can be implied by a tenant's holding over. However, the notice must accept the renewal privilege as offered. The landlord can treat any attempt to change the lease terms offered by the option to renew as a rejection of the option. For example, a notice from a tenant that she will remain one year after expiration, when she has an option to renew for four years, can be treated as an invalid notice, which terminates the lease on its original expiration.

Holding Over by Tenant   A tenant has no right to "hold over" (remain in possession of the leased premises after the termination of the lease, without the landlord's consent). A landlord can choose either to waive a holdover or to treat the tenant who holds over as a trespasser. If the landlord does allow the tenant to remain, the tenant can be a tenant at sufferance, a tenant at will, a periodic tenant, or a tenant for a definite term, depending on both the circumstances of the case and the statutes in effect.

When a landlord neither assents to the tenant's holding over nor agrees to an extended or renewal term, the tenant is liable to the landlord for unlawful occupancy of the premises. The measure of damages that the landlord can recover is generally the rental value of the property for the period of the tenant's wrongful possession, although some states permit the recovery of greater damages or the imposition of penalties.

37:10   Landlord's Remedies; Damages

There are a variety of remedies by which a landlord can regain possession of leased premises or obtain money damages after a lease is forfeited, a condition is breached, or the lease expires. Some state statutes permit the landlord to reenter the property if the tenant has vacated and abandoned it; other states require that the landlord take court action first. The landlord can also seek to evict a tenant who, for example, breaches a condition by holding over after the expiration of a lease or rental agreement or by failing to pay rent.

Every state provides for a summary eviction procedure by which the landlord can recover possession of leased property quickly and at low cost.

This procedure is often called *unlawful detainer*, which is so named because the tenant remains in possession contrary to the lease. In a summary proceeding, the landlord must prove that the lease has expired or that the tenant has breached a condition or covenant. The tenant is usually permitted few defenses, although in some states the tenant can raise any breaches by the landlord, particularly the breach of the implied warranty of habitability.

A landlord can also sue to have the tenant ejected to regain possession of leased property. Unlike the eviction procedure, *ejectment* does not take precedence over all other civil litigation and might not come to trial for some time. During the pendency of an ejectment action, the tenant is entitled to possession. For these reasons, most landlords prefer the summary eviction procedure to a suit in ejectment.

Landlord's Lien   Many states have statutes that allow a lien on a tenant's personal property that is located on leased premises. This lien is referred to as a landlord's lien. In some states there is a general landlord's lien on all the tenant's personal property, giving the landlord priority over other creditors. Because no right of possession is conferred, however, the landlord must institute judicial proceedings to foreclose the lien if the rent is unpaid. In other states, the landlord is authorized to enter premises peaceably and seize certain types of property that belong to the tenant, and to hold them as security for the unpaid rent. If a statute of this type permits seizure of a tenant's property without prior notice or the tenant's right to be heard at a judicial hearing, it is apt to violate the tenant's constitutional right to due process of law.[2] In fact, some states have extensively rewritten landlord lien statutes in an attempt to satisfy due process requirements. Where the statutes authorize a hearing and court order before a landlord can seize property, and the landlord is authorized only to hold, but not dispose of, a tenant's property until court order, they satisfy due process requirements.

Landlord's Duty to Mitigate Damages   Under the common law, if a tenant abandoned possession of property without legal justification, the tenant's obligations under the lease continued without change. Indeed, since the most important obligation of the tenant was the payment of rent, the common law did not impose on the landlord the duty of reletting the premises. On the contrary, the landlord could permit the premises to remain vacant and sue the tenant for the unpaid rent as it accrued. A landlord could even arbitrarily refuse to accept a new tenant, even one suitable and responsible in every way.

The privilege enjoyed by landlords not to minimize damages has given way in many states to a more modern view similar to that in the law of contracts. In these states, a landlord has the duty to make reasonable efforts to reduce his damages by reletting leased premises after a tenant's abandonment. This view conforms to contract principles in which a party to a contract must mitigate damages following a breach of the other party. It is also based on the modern theory that a lease of real property is more in the nature of a

---

[2] The constitutionality of statutes that allow seizure of property without notice and a hearing is discussed in more detail in Chapter 31.

commercial contract than a conveyance of an estate or interest in land. Therefore, if a landlord is allowed to reenter premises after they are abandoned by a tenant, the landlord must usually use reasonable efforts to procure a new tenant. If the landlord does not do this, the tenant might be relieved of his obligation under the lease as well as his duty to indemnify the landlord for loss of rent.

EXAMPLE: The Lamberts rented an apartment in Lefrak City. When they were unable to pay rent, they vacated the apartment and requested that the landlord apply their security deposit to the rent owed. The apartment remained vacant for 17 months. Finally, the landlord filed suit, claiming rent due during the remaining rental term under the lease until the apartment was rerented. If the landlord fails to establish that he acted in good faith to rerent their apartment, a court is apt to find that the landlord is entitled only to three months' rent; three months being a reasonable period of time in which to rerent.

Key Concepts and Terms

- The rental of real property is based on a form of contract that is most commonly referred to as a lease or rental agreement. The person who owns real property and leases it to someone else is known as the landlord or lessor. The person who receives possession and has use of the premises during the term of a lease is the tenant or lessee.

- A leasehold is generally classified according to its duration as (1) a tenancy for years, (2) a periodic tenancy, (3) a tenancy at will, or (4) a tenancy at sufferance.

- A lease is usually in writing, but it can also be oral in most states. If the term of an oral lease violates a state's statute of frauds, however, the lease is unenforceable.

- In most states, the landlord must actually put the tenant in possession of leased property at the beginning of the agreed term. The very essence of the landlord–tenant relationship is the right to have the peaceful and quiet use of property throughout the duration of a tenancy. This right is guaranteed by the landlord's covenant for quiet enjoyment, which is contained in most written leases and rental agreements.

- During the term of a lease, the tenant is the owner of the leased premises for all practical purposes. The landlord's rights are confined to his reversionary interests in the premises. At the end of the tenancy, the tenant must vacate and surrender the premises to the landlord.

- An eviction consists of any act by a landlord that (1) deprives the tenant of possession, (2) expels him from the property, or (3) deprives him of its enjoyment. The wrongful eviction of a tenant by the landlord not only terminates the tenant's obligations under a lease, but also entitles the tenant to recover damages.

- A landlord is generally not responsible for the condition of leased premises at the beginning of a lease period. The tenant takes the premises as they are, with all their faults. However, in some states, a residential landlord must, under what is called the implied warranty of habitability, put premises into a condition fit for human occupancy and repair all subsequent dilapidations other than those attributable to the tenant.

- Rent is the consideration paid by a tenant to a landlord for the use and occupation of real property under a lease. As long as a lease is in existence, rent must be paid. In some states, even if leased property is damaged or destroyed, the obligation to pay rent continues.

- An assignment of a lease is the transfer of a tenant's entire interest in leased premises to a third person for the entire unexpired term of the original lease. In the absence of a statutory prohibition or restriction in a lease, a tenant has the right to assign or sublet his interest without the landlord's consent.

- A sublease is a leasing of premises by the original tenant to someone else. It differs from an assignment in that the original tenant (the sublessor) retains an interest in the property.

- A lease can be terminated (1) through forfeiture on the tenant's failure to meet his obligations under a lease, (2) by recission or agreement between the parties, and (3) under some circumstances by an occurrence that causes the premises to be destroyed or otherwise made uninhabitable. Ordinarily, the death of a lessee or lessor does not terminate a lease.

- A lease can usually be renewed or extended after the expiration of the original time set forth in the lease agreement.

- A tenant has no right to hold over (remain in possession of leased premises after the termination of a lease) without the landlord's consent.

- In many states, statutes grant to a landlord a lien on the tenant's personal property located on leased premises. However, the statute does not give the landlord the right to possession of the tenant's property. The landlord must institute judicial proceedings to foreclose the lien in cases of unpaid rent.

- The major remedy that a landlord has to regain possession of leased property is a summary eviction procedure, known in most states as unlawful detainer.

- Under the common law, if a tenant abandoned possession of the leased property, the tenant's obligations continued under the lease, and the landlord was not required to mitigate damages. Today, most states require a landlord to minimize damages by making a reasonable effort to relet premises after a tenant's abandonment.

- Assignment
- Condition
- Constructive Eviction
- Covenant
- Covenant for Quiet Enjoyment
- Ejectment
- Eviction
- Holding Over
- Lease
- Lessee
- Lessor
- Mitigation of Damages
- Notice to Quit
- Periodic Tenancy

- Rent
- Retaliatory Eviction
- Security Deposit
- Sublease
- Tenancy at Sufferance
- Tenancy at Will
- Tenancy for Years
- Unlawful Detainer
- Warranty of Habitability

Questions and Case Problems

1. Klingensmith leases an office to Burke under a year-to-year lease. At the end of the second year, Burke moves out without giving Klingensmith any notice. Is Burke liable for another year's rent?

2. Chris Whitney rents a warehouse for storage of high explosives. Shortly after the lease is signed, most of the warehouse is destroyed by a hurricane. Is the lease terminated by this event?

3. The Isaacsons lease farmland from the Richards under a lease that provides that they will be granted the "first right of refusal to purchase the premises." Later, the Richards convey the property, valued at more than $60,000, to their son for $20,000 and the son's promise that he will care for his mother after his father's death and keep the farm in the family. The Isaacsons then bring an action against the Richards for specific performance of the right to purchase under the "first refusal" provision in the farm lease. What is the result?

4. Tappa leases store space in a shopping center from Linke for a rental of $6,000 per year. Eight months after occupying the space, Tappa's retail permit is revoked by the city. As a result, Tappa is forced to vacate the store. Is Tappa entitled to stop paying rent for the remaining period of the lease? Discuss.

5. Kolea leased a garage to store automobiles. One year after he occupied the premises, the building was completely destroyed by an accidental fire. Kolea later refused to pay rent, contending that the fire excused him from continuing to perform his obligations under the lease. Although the lease did not contain a provision as to the tenant's obligations in the event of the building's destruction, the landlord sought to hold Kolea liable for the rent. How does a court determine whether Kolea ought still be liable for rent?

6. Why shouldn't a material breach of the lease always excuse performance, as in contract law? What if the tenant, or the landlord, has spent a substantial amount of money improving the property under a long-term lease? Is this different from a contract situation where the breaching party has expended large amounts of money in reliance on the contract?

7. Duvall rents an apartment on a month-to-month basis. She complains to the landlord about a broken lock, a leaky roof, lack of hot water, a leaking toilet and pipes, cockroach infestation, and hazardous floors and steps. The landlord does nothing. Duvall repairs some of the malfunctions on her own and deducts the cost from her rent. Eventually she stops paying rent because the other repairs are not made. The landlord then sues her for the back rent and for possession of the premises. What is the outcome?

8. Brenda rented an apartment from Reicher Enterprises in Baltimore. Before renting the apartment, she made an inspection of it and noticed chipped and cracked paint throughout. The landlord promised to paint and fix up the apartment after she moved into it, but he never did so. Later, one of Brenda's daughters became

seriously ill from eating the chipped and cracked paint, which was lead-based. The child suffered blindness, retardation, and other neurological handicaps. Brenda sued the landlord for the injuries to her child. How should the case be decided?

9. Weber rents a berth at the dock of John's Pass Seafood Company to moor his fishing boat. Under the lease, Weber agrees to indemnify John's Pass from all liability occasioned by the use of the dock, even if the injury is caused by John's Pass' negligence. One night, a fire on a nearby vessel moored to the same dock spreads to Weber's boat. Weber sues John's Pass for the damage to his boat, charging it with negligence in failing to provide fire extinguishers and other firefighting equipment required by a local ordinance. John's Pass points to the exculpation clause by way of defense to the lawsuit. Is John's Pass liable to Weber? Why or why not?

10. Sommer rented an apartment to Kridel for a two-year term. Before she even moved in, Kridel notified Sommer that she would be unable to take possession of the apartment. Later, Sommer told a third party who was interested in renting the apartment that it was unavailable. Sommer then sued Kridel for the total amount due under the lease. Who should win the lawsuit? Why?

38 Premises Liability

38:1 Duties to Invitees

The traditional rule is that the liability of a landowner for injuries to a third person entering his land depends on whether the third person was an invitee, a licensee, or a trespasser at the time of the accident. Today, the courts rely less on these classifications of the injured person. The modern view is based on the landowner's reasonable care to protect third persons from injury. It is useful, nevertheless, to examine the roles of an invitee, a licensee, and a trespasser.

An *invitee* is a person who is invited, directly or impliedly, by the landowner to enter the land for some purpose of interest or advantage to the owner. The *Restatement (Second) of Torts* § 332 (1965) defines an invitee as either a public invitee or a business visitor. A public invitee is a person who is invited to enter land as a member of the public for a purpose for which the land is held open to the public. A *business visitor* is a person invited to enter land for a purpose directly or indirectly connected with business dealings with the landowner. People who accompany invitees are usually held to have the same status as invitees. For example, one spouse accompanying the other, a nephew accompanying an uncle, or a friend accompanying another friend is usually considered to be an invitee so long as the prime person is an invitee.

A landowner owes to each invitee the duty to exercise ordinary and *reasonable care* to maintain the premises in a reasonable safe condition for its intended use. At a minimum, the landowner must warn the invitee of dangers that are not obvious and that are known to the owner, or that the landowner could have discovered with reasonable diligence. However, this duty does not extend to cleaning up "natural accumulations" of snow or ice. The invitee must anticipate the dangers caused by such conditions. Then again, if the landowner does undertake to clean away snow or ice accumulations and acts negligently in the cleaning operations, such negligence may be deemed the legal cause of the injury, and he will be held liable. It should be noted that in some states there are statutes that require the removal of ice or snow.

Invitees to a store are owed a duty in the area in which the selling or business occurs, as well as at the entrances and exits of the store. Also, where a business is operated in connection with another store or parking lot, the duty to keep the premises reasonably safe extends to approaches connecting the store to the other store or its parking lot.

A public employee—a police officer, fire fighter, or other public servant—is usually classified as an invitee on the theory that, in the scope of employment, he or she goes onto property to enforce and to look after a property owner's interests.

 A person who is *not* in direct or exclusive control of the land may be liable to invitees for the condition of the premises. For example, the operator of a market who rents space from an adjacent service station for parking is under a duty to exercise reasonable care to keep the parking lot in a safe condition.

38:2   Duties to Licensees and Adult Trespassers

Broadly defined, a *licensee* is a person who is invited or permitted by the landowner to enter the property for his or her own convenience, pleasure, or benefit, or for purposes that are not connected with the landowner's interests. Licensees, for example, may be business visitors who were initially invitees but who have strayed from that part of the premises to which they were invited or authorized to enter: door-to-door salespersons, process servers, social guests, and visiting relatives. A landowner is under no duty to inspect and prepare the premises so they will be safe for the licensee's reception. However, where (1) there is a known dangerous condition, (2) the landowner can reasonably anticipate that the licensee will not discover or realize the danger, and (3) the landowner invites or permits the licensee to enter or remain on the premises without exercising reasonable care either to give warning or to make the condition reasonably safe, the landowner can be liable for the licensee's injury.

Furthermore, the landowner owes a licensee, at least if his presence on the premises is known or reasonably should have been known, the duty to use reasonable care not to injure him by affirmative acts—the duty to refrain from unreasonably dangerous active conduct that might be harmful to the licensee.

Adult Trespassers   A *trespasser* is a person who enters another's premises without license, invitation, or other right to do so created by the landowner's consent. Traditionally, a landowner owes trespassers no duty to keep his premises in a safe condition for their use and, as a general proposition is not responsible for a trespasser's injury resulting from a defect of the premises. A landowner is obligated only to refrain from willfully or wantonly injuring a trespasser.

38:3   Child Trespassers and Attractive Nuisance

Most states accept the view that under certain circumstances a landowner may be held responsible for injury caused by dangerous conditions on the premises to children who trespass, even though the landowner would not be liable if the injured person had been an adult trespasser. The expression *attractive nuisance* is the legal shorthand description used by courts to designate this type of case. The principle of liability has been known by other names, such as the "turntable" doctrine, the "infant trespasser," "dangerous instrumentality," "playground" rule, and "the trap" theory. Nonetheless, the basic principle is that one who has or creates on his own premises a condition that may reasonably be expected to be a source of danger to children is under a duty to take those precautions that a reasonably prudent person would take to prevent injury to young children whom he knows to be accustomed to be there, or who may be expected to be attracted to his land.

EXAMPLE: A four-year-old boy drowns in an open excavation ditch that was partially filled with muddy water, and his parents sue defendant landowner to recover damages for their son's wrongful death. The court is apt to apply the doctrine of attractive nuisance, reasoning that there was a danger that a young child might suddenly come on the excavation and fall in without discovering it in time to avoid it, especially if the child was running.

The attractive nuisance doctrine reflects a struggle between two conflicting interests: on the one hand, the interest of society in preserving the safety of its children and, on the other hand, the interest of landowners in using their land for their own purposes with reasonable freedom. The younger the child, the more likely will a condition be held to be an attractive nuisance. Unattended vehicles, swimming pools, pits, explosives, and machinery have all been held in particular cases to qualify as attractive nuisances. To be a child trespasser, the child must be so immature as to be unable to recognize the danger involved. In practice, children above the age of 14 years seldom qualify.

Some courts have expressed the view that the doctrine is applicable only if the injury is caused by an artificial condition on the land or by a structure that was placed on the land. This view is based on the idea that it is the responsibility of the parents or guardians to protect children from dangers posed by natural conditions.

38:4   Modern Viewpoint as to Landowner's Duties

Increasingly, courts are rejecting the principle that the standard of care owed by a landowner should be based on the status—as an invitee, a licensee, or a trespasser—of a person who comes on the premises. The now-classic California Supreme Court opinion in *Rowland v Christian*, 443 P2d 561 (1968), provides the reasoning that has been adopted by many states. In *Rowland*, the court abolished the status distinction governing the duties to invitees, licensees, and trespassers, and adopted a rule of "reasonable care" under all circumstances. The court stated:

> Without attempting to labor all of the rules relating to the possessor's liability, it is apparent that the classifications of trespasser, licensee, and invitee, the immunities from liability predicated upon those classifications, and the

exceptions to those immunities, often do not reflect the major factors which should determine whether immunity should be conferred upon the possessor of land. Some of those factors, including the closeness of the connection between the injury and the defendant's conduct, the moral blame attached to the defendant's conduct, the policy of preventing future harm, and the prevalence and availability of insurance, bear little, if any, relationship to the classifications of trespasser, licensee and invitee and the existing rules conferring immunity. . . . The proper test to be applied to the liability of the possessor of land . . . is whether in the management of his property he has acted as a reasonable man in view of the probability of injury to others, and, although the plaintiff's status as a trespasser, licensee, or invitee may in the light of the facts giving rise to such status have some bearing on the question of liability, the status is not determinative.

Some state and local statutes, as well as government building codes and regulations, have a direct bearing on the maintenance practices of landowners, particularly where businesses are conducted. Failure to follow these standards may be shown to amount to failure to have exercised reasonable care. Note in the following case the importance of building codes and regulations in providing evidence of negligence.

Nixon
v
Mr. Property Management Co.
690 SW2d 546 (1985)
Supreme Court of Texas

FACTS: R.V.M., age 10, was abducted from a sidewalk outside her family's apartment complex. Her assailant dragged her to the Chalmette Apartments, located diagonally across from her home. He took her into a vacant apartment, raped her, and locked her in a closet. There was evidence that the apartment unit was in dilapidated condition, with broken windows and the front door off the hinges, in violation of a city ordinance specifically requiring that doors and windows of a vacant apartment be secured to prevent unauthorized entry. Plaintiff sued the building owner and the management firm for negligence.

ISSUE: As a matter of law, could defendants' failure to maintain the premises render them liable in negligence to R.V.M.?

RESULT: There is sufficient evidence that a court could find plaintiff's injuries to be the foreseeable and proximate result of defendants' breach of duty.

REASONING:

*   *   *

Duty

In this case, the question of what duty Mr. Property owed to R.M.V. is answered by the ordinance. This ordinance legislatively imposes a standard of conduct which we adopt to define the conduct of a reasonably prudent person. . . . The unexcused violation of a statute or ordinance constitutes negligence as a matter of law if such statute or ordinance was designed to prevent injury to the class of persons to which the injured party belongs. A reasonable interpretation of this ordinance is that it was designed to deter criminal activity by reducing the conspicuous opportunities for criminal conduct. In fact, Mr. Property's president testified that one reason vacant apartment units should be secured is to prevent this type of criminal activity. An ordinance requiring apartment owners to do their part in deterring crime is designed to prevent injury to the general public. R.M.V. falls within this class. Since the ordinance was meant to protect a larger class than invitees and licensees, and since R.M.V. committed no wrong in coming onto the property, these premise liability distinctions are irrelevant to our analysis. . . .

If the trier of fact concludes that Mr. Property violated the ordinance without a valid excuse, Mr. Property is negligent per se. This does not end our inquiry; we must still determine if there is a material fact issue on the question of proximate cause.

Proximate Cause

A material fact issue exists in this case as to whether Mr. Property's negligence, if any, proximately caused R.M.V.'s injuries. The two elements of proximate cause are cause in fact and foreseeability. . . .

Cause in fact denotes that the negligent act or omission was a substantial factor in bringing about the injury and without which no harm would have been incurred. . . .

[W]e conclude that a reasonable inference exists that, but for Mr. Property's failure to comply with the ordinance regarding maintenance of its apartment complex, this crime would have never taken place. There is evidence that the assailant took R.M.V. "directly to a vacant apartment," the inference being that the assailant was acutely aware of the vacant unit's existence and embarked upon his course of criminal conduct at this particular time and place knowing that this unit was an easily accessible place in which to perpetrate this assault in isolation. . . .

Finally, we turn to the question of foreseeability. Foreseeability means that the actor, as a person of ordinary intelligence, should have anticipated the dangers that his negligent act created for others. . . . Usually, the criminal conduct of a third party is a superseding cause relieving the negligent actor from liability. However, the tortfeasor's negligence will not be excused where the criminal conduct is a foreseeable result of such negligence. Texas courts follow this rule. . . .

The evidence is replete with instances of prior violent crimes occurring at Chalmette Apartments. This record certainly provides evidence that further acts of violence were reasonably foreseeable. Evidence of specific previous crimes on or near the premises raises a fact issue on the foreseeability of criminal activity. . . .

In [a New Jersey case] the New Jersey Supreme Court affirmed a jury award for an assault victim and against the apartment owner. On the issue of foreseeability, the court stated:

> There was ample evidence that criminal activity affecting the Monroe Street building was reasonably foreseeable. More than one witness testified to the high incidence of crime in the neighborhood. Plaintiff's own, unchallenged testimony related an attempted theft within the building. Against this background, the jury could readily view the absence of a lock on the front entrance— an area outside an individual tenant's control—as exemplifying a callous disregard for the residents' safety in violation of ordinary standards of care. Since there was sufficient evidence for concluding that the mugging was a foreseeable result of the landlord's negligence, the jury's finding of liability was warranted. . . .

[Another] case involving a kidnap from a bank parking lot and subsequent murder . . . is especially instructive on this point. In [that case], the court held that the widow failed to allege sufficient facts of previous crimes to meet the test of foreseeability, but it remanded to allow her to amend. When the case was again appealed, . . . the court said allegations that the bank was in high crime area including allegations of similar crimes on or near the facility were sufficient to state a cause of action for negligence.

Although there is no evidence that previous rapes had occurred at Chalmette Apartments, this is not a prerequisite to finding a material fact issue on foreseeability. . . . With a litany of prior crimes, including other violent and assaultive crime, at Chalmette Apartments, and with deposition testimony that vagrants frequented the area, a material fact question exists on the foreseeability of this crime as it relates to the proximate cause issue. . . .

Hill, Chief Judge.

It is important to note that in the *Nixon* case, the Texas Supreme Court did not do away with the distinction among invitees, licensees, and trepassers. In effect, it carved out an exception to that method of analyzing premises liability problems. Only nine or ten states have abandoned the status-classification scheme in favor of negligence analysis. Nevertheless, like the Texas court, many courts have found circumstances—attractive nuisance, unreasonably dangerous conditions, involuntary trespass—where negligence analysis is used instead of traditional analysis.

38:5   Stores and Other Places of Business

Any person in possession of commercial premises—a store, office, bank, hospital, or public building—has a duty to exercise ordinary care to maintain the premises in a reasonably safe condition for customers and members of the general public who are properly on the premises. This duty applies to all parts of the store or business premises where the customer may properly go, such as entryways, doors, floors, aisles, and steps, and even extends to conditions such as lighting and displays. The rationale is that the customer has a right to feel safe from all dangers and defects while on commercial premises.

Self-Service Marketing   Self-service marketing poses certain inherent problems. In particular, customers in the self-service situation may create risks to other customers by not handling merchandise as a salesperson would. Merchandise may drop on the floor and break, or be placed precariously back on a shelf. If dropped merchandise does not immediately come to the attention of employees, it can present an opportunity for someone to slip and fall.

Merchants are under a duty to display goods in such a way that they will not (1) fall and injure a customer, (2) topple if a customer using care attempts to take an item from the top of the display, or (3) generally be placed in a manner that would threaten to injure a store's visitors. Some conditions that have been identified as unreasonably dangerous are displays protruding into an aisle or passageway, falls of a display onto a customer, and hazards presented by floor debris.

The Slip-and-Fall Case   Objects and slippery substances on the floor can easily cause customers to slip and fall, often with very substantial injury. The owner of commercial premises has a duty to exercise care to keep the floors free from litter or debris, even when the debris is brought into the store by customers. To fulfill this duty, the storekeeper must exercise reasonable care to inspect and clean the premises to make sure that fallen items do not remain on the floor. What constitutes "reasonable care" depends on the circumstances. Usually, the mere presence of debris on the store's floor and the fact a patron fell do not necessarily mean the storekeeper failed to exercise proper care. The key to liability is whether the storekeeper knew, or ought to have known, of the floor's condition. The storekeeper is deemed to have actual knowledge of a dangerous condition, such as a floor spill, if he or his employee caused the condition or observed it.

To be liable, a storekeeper does not always need *actual* knowledge of the spill. A storekeeper may be deemed to have what is termed *constructive notice* of a condition. This means that he should have, or could have, discovered the dangerous condition if he had exercised reasonable care. For example, if a substance has remained on the floor for a long enough time that the storekeeper should have discovered it, he will be deemed to have constructive notice of its existence. This notice is sufficient to establish liability. In determining what constitutes a storekeeper's constructive notice, the courts have looked to several factors. Among these factors are (1) the number of customers who use the store, (2) the type of merchandise displayed, and (3) the location of the spill or other debris. For example, the operator of a busy supermarket should know that customers handling displayed produce often drop bits of produce on the floor of the area.

Where the method of doing business, as in the case of self-service supermarkets, tends to produce hazards because of large numbers of customers handling or dropping merchandise, the courts have sometimes said that constructive notice may exist even when the item on the floor was there for only a short time.

 The prudent retailer recognizes that customers are likely to injure themselves. Management of this risk requires that the retailer establish regular and appropriately frequent inspection routines, that employees be instructed as to how to deal with a danger or an injury, and that merchandizing displays be constructed with an eye toward avoiding potential injury.

Negligent Premises Design   An emerging basis of premises liability is the failure to exercise due care in the design of a building. This failure is illustrated in the following decision. Note that a psychologist's expert testimony helped establish the unsafeness of the defendant's premises.

Watt
v
United States
444 F Supp 1191 (1978)
United States District Court for the District of Columbia

FACTS: A visitor was injured when she fell on steps at the Smithsonian Institution. She sued the federal government, alleging that her fall had been caused by the negligent design of the steps.

ISSUE: May an injured person recover damages for negligent design of a building?

RESULT: Yes, if the injury was a proximate result of a design that posed an unreasonable risk to the person.

REASONING:

*   *   *

The plaintiff, Hazel D. Watt, a resident of New York, New York, had visited the Museum [of History and Technology] with her daughter and departed through the north door at about 2:45 p.m. on April 16, 1975, a sunny, clear and dry day. The two crossed a concrete sidewalk and curving asphalt driveway and entered the fountain area, descending two small steps. They were then standing on the uppermost of three levels of semicircular granite platform steps. The daughter, Ann Wiechmann, proceeded to the street to summon a taxicab while the plaintiff remained standing in the position just described. After waiting awhile, the plaintiff decided to join her daughter on the street and walked to the right a short distance when she suddenly fell and fractured her right elbow. The plaintiff was wearing shoes with a 1½" heel, composition soles, rubber heels, and equipped with rubber preservers at the toe and heel.

The semi-circular platform steps around the circumference of the fountain are constructed of variegated granite. The riser of each step is approximately 5 3/8 inches high and the tread is approximately 10 feet deep. On April 16, 1975, there were no cautionary signs warning pedestrians of the existence of the platform steps, nor were there stripes or other markings at the edge of the platform steps. The plaintiff's fall occurred at the edge of the top platform step.

The plaintiff alleges that the pedestrian walkway around the fountain was unreasonably dangerous because of the difficulty presented in visually detecting the presence of the platform steps. Additionally no warning was posted to alert pedestrians of the existence of the platform steps. The plaintiff's allegations include negligence in the design, construction and maintenance of the platform steps and a failure to exercise reasonable care.

The plaintiff testified that she did not see and was not aware of the presence of steps as she walked along the top platform step. She was looking ahead but not at the ground. She was aware that she was at a slightly higher elevation than the street, but it was not apparent to her that the downgrade was accomplished by steps rather than a ramp.

Expert testimony was presented by both parties. A psychologist and human factors specialist called by the plaintiff testified that the variegated granite presented a visual dilemma because of its texture and because the sharp edges of the rectangular platform blocks with grouting between them do not provide a contrast to the edge of the step. A person should be able to distinguish a step when three or four strides away, and at the area where the fall occurred, one does not receive a visual cue of the existence of a step until only one stride away.

An architect testified that the fountain area is designed so as to invite people to walk through but it is unsafe. A change in grade creates a hazard and unless steps are uniform and readily discernible, they are defectively designed. . . .

By a preponderance of the evidence, the plaintiff proved that the platform steps in the fountain area were designed so as to create a hazard for a pedestrian. It is difficult to distinguish that a step is present because of the sameness of color and inability to discern the edges. It is hazardous not to indicate different levels. The platform steps were defectively designed because of the inability to detect their presence, and the government architects who approved the design showed a want of reasonable care. The architects' negligence is imputed to the defendant. . . .

It is the opinion of the Court that the negligence of the defendant's architects in approving a faulty design of platform steps was the proximate cause of the plaintiff's injury and that the architects knew and recognized the hazard at the time approval was given so that the defendant had actual notice of the defect. . . .

Curran, District Judge.

38:6   Defenses

Common defenses in a premises liability suit are (1) contributory negligence and (2) the geographical limitation of the landowner's duty. *Contributory negligence* is the failure of a person to exercise reasonable care for his own safety. Under ordinary circumstances, persons are obliged "to see what there is to see."

The extent to which the premises were used by the plaintiff before and at the time of an injury has a bearing on the question of his contributory negligence. A plaintiff is more likely to be found to be contributorily negligent if he conducts his movements in a manner that is unlike that of others who use the premises. For example, if a store patron ignores a safe, well-used route to her destination and uses an unlighted route, she may be contributorily negligent.

Geographical Extent of Duty   Another factor examined by courts in considering the liability of a landowner is whether the injury occurred in a portion of the premises that was designated and prepared to accommodate customers and was an area in which the customer might reasonably be expected to be. The owner's duty of care extends only to portions of the premises where the customer might reasonably be expected to travel; the duty does not extend to premises reserved for use only by the storekeeper or employees, such as shipping rooms and warerooms, and areas that are marked "private" or "employees only." Therefore, a business owner will not be liable if a customer is injured while on these premises.

A businessperson who is in charge of premises that are open to the public should post "private" or "employees only" signs for all areas to which the general invitation to the public does not extend.

38:7   Liability for Injury on Leased Premises

In most states, landlords are not liable for injury sustained by a tenant on leased premises. However, there are exceptions to this general rule. Liability can be imposed if (1) a landlord knew of a dangerous condition or should have known of it and failed to inform the tenant; (2) the landlord concealed a dangerous condition; (3) the landlord made repairs in such a negligent fashion that the tenant was injured; (4) the injury occurred in a common area or an area in the landlord's possession; or (5) the lease or rental agreement specifically provided that the landlord would make a designated repair, and he failed to do so, resulting in a tenant's injury.

If the landlord leases part of the property to different tenants, and reserves other parts, such as common entrances, halls, stairways, and utility or service rooms for the common use of all the tenants, the landlord must exercise reasonable care to keep these reserved areas safe. As the following case illustrates, a landlord can be liable to a tenant, members of a tenant's family, or third persons for injuries resulting from the landlord's negligence.

Macke Laundry Service Co.

v

Weber

298 A2d 27 (1972)

Maryland Court of Appeals

FACTS: Bruce Weber, about 3½ years old, wandered alone into the laundry room of an apartment building where he lived with his parents and was severely injured when he placed his left hand in the drive mechanism of a clothes dryer. The dryer was owned by Macke Laundry Service, which operated and serviced the equipment in the laundry room. Bruce's mother sued both the landlord and Macke.

ISSUE: Is Bruce someone to whom the landlord and the laundry service owed a duty?

RESULT: Yes. Bruce was an invitee on the premises.

REASONING:

* * *

There is substantial authority for the proposition that when a landlord sets aside areas for the use of his tenants in common, he owes the duty of reasonable and ordinary care to keep the premises safe for his invitees. . . .

. . . The duty stems from the responsibility engendered in the landlord by his having extended an invitation, express or implied, to use the portions of the property retained by him. . . . Such an invitation extended to a tenant includes the members of his family, his guests, his invitees and others on the land in the right of the tenant. . . . It has been held that a child on the land at the invitation of the child of the tenant is entitled to the benefit of the landlord's obligation in this respect. . . . There is an important qualification to the rule as to the duty of the landlord. His responsibility for the reasonably safe condition of premises retained under his control is limited to the confines of his invitation to use them, express or implied. It does not extend to the use of such premises for an unintended purpose. . . .

Our decisions have consistently held a landlord liable for improper maintenance of facilities or for failure to remedy defects in equipment over which he retains control and furnishes for common use by his tenants. . . .

Although a landlord owes no greater duty of care to a child than to an adult, . . . [the landlord] knew or should have known that the laundry room was readily accessible to children, a circumstance which made what might otherwise have been a theoretical hazard an actual danger to a person unable to comprehend it. . . .

Here, it is clear that the facilities installed in the laundry room were provided for the use of tenants, who were invitees. There is no evidence that such use was restricted to adults, or that entry was in [any way] restricted to adults and children accompanied by adults. On the contrary, there was testimony that the door was always open, and was usually propped open by one of the trash cans which were customarily stored there.

On these facts, Bruce was neither a trespasser nor a bare licensee: he was an invitee, to whom a duty of reasonable care was owed. This duty was breached when the guard which normally shielded the drive mechanism on the back of the clothes dryer fell off, or was taken off and never replaced, despite the fact that Mrs. Weber and two of her neighbors testified that they had reported the condition by calling the "service number" which appeared on the dryer. It was the breach of this duty which was the sole cause of Bruce's injury. . . .

Macke urges on us the argument that when Bruce chose to go behind the dryer, he became a trespasser or mere licensee. . . .

We do not see it quite that way. There was uncontroverted testimony that the laundry room in Building No. 2 was used for the collection of trash, for the storage of certain of the tenants' effects, that the door was always open, and was frequently propped open, and that there had been a problem with children playing there. There was testimony that if clothing dropped behind the dryer, it was necessary to go behind the dryer to retrieve it. Although Mrs. Weber's testimony may have been wanting in explicit technical terminology, there was enough for the jury to conclude that she did her laundry in Building No. 1 because she was apprehensive about the manner in which laundry equipment had been installed in Building No. 2. Even apart from the testimony as regards the telephone calls about the absence of the guard from the drive mechanism—and the existence of such calls was denied by Macke—there was certainly enough for the jury to conclude that the defendants failed to meet the standards of care required to make the premises safe for the tenants. . . .

Jingley, Judge.

Liability for Crimes of Third Persons The general rule is that the landlord–tenant relationship does not impose a duty on a landlord to protect a tenant from criminal activities of third persons. Under this rule the landlord is not an insurer of a tenant's safety against crime. For a landlord to be liable for injuries that result from criminal activities, it must be shown that he breached contractual or statutory obligations or was negligent in keeping the premises safe. In some states, statutes and regulations requiring a landlord to maintain "safe premises" have been interpreted to mean that the landlord has a duty to keep the premises safe only in the sense of being free from physical defects likely to cause injury, but not to require the landlord to take security measures against criminal activities. Bear in mind, however, that there is an increasing trend for courts to impose on landlords the duty to protect tenants against criminal activities of third persons. These cases have involved fact situations where the landlord knows of repeated criminal behavior on the premises and fails to warn the tenant or take appropriate security measures.

EXAMPLE: A tenant breaks his lease because of repeated burglaries and attempted burglaries of the apartment through a sliding glass door. The landlord, knowing why she lost the last tenant, rerents the apartment to a new tenant without revealing the history of burglaries and without taking measures to secure the sliding glass door. If the tenant suffers injury from burglary, the landlord may be held liable for having breached a duty to warn and to protect the new tenant.

Landlord's Liability to Third Persons In most states, landlords are not liable to third persons for injury caused by the condition or use of leased premises if the premises are under a tenant's full control and were in good condition when leased. However, the fact that a tenant occupies leased premises when an accident occurs does not automatically relieve the landlord of liability for injury or damage to third persons that results from his own negligent maintenance of the premises. Indeed, there are many circumstances under which a landlord can be held liable to third persons injured as a result of the condition or use of the leased premises. If the landlord has authorized his property to be used in such a manner as to endanger and injure a third person, the landlord is answerable for the consequences. Liability can even extend to owners or occupants of adjoining or neighboring property or to users of an adjacent public highway injured through some act or omission attributable to the landlord.

A landlord's duties and liabilities to persons who are on leased property with the tenant's consent are the same as those owed to the tenant himself. An important exception, frequently termed the public purpose rule, applies when there is a lease involving the use of premises by the public: A business patron's rights to recover for injuries from defects in leased property are not necessarily limited to the rights of the tenant. Courts in many states have held that where property leased for a public purpose is not safe for the purpose intended, and the owner knew or should have known of the unsafe conditions through the exercise of reasonable diligence, the owner is liable to patrons on the premises for injury that results from these conditions.

Exculpation Clauses   Many leases contain provisions that excuse the landlord from liability for injury or damage, even when the injury or damage is caused by the landlord's own negligence. These provisions are called exculpatory or exculpation clauses. In most states this type of limit on a landlord's liability is generally permitted in commercial leases, but it is invalid and cannot be enforced in residential leases.

 If a landlord's negligence involves a failure to fulfill a statutory duty, an exculpation clause will often not be enforceable to avoid liability even under a commercial lease.

Tenant's Liability to Third Persons   When property is leased in a condition suitable for its ordinary and contemplated use by the tenants, it is the tenant—and not the landlord—who is liable to a third person on or off the property for injuries caused by a condition or use that is under the tenant's control. The tenant's liability to third persons or the public continues to exist even though the landlord has agreed to keep the premises in repair.

If a business patron or customer is injured on leased premises, the tenant is usually liable for injuries caused by a negligent act or the tenant's failure to correct a defect or dangerous condition on the premises. A proprietor of a public place of business is bound to keep such premises in a safe condition and to use ordinary care to avoid accident or injury to those entering the premises on business. The fact that the proprietor is a tenant does not lessen her duty to keep the premises reasonably safe for customers.

Key Concepts and Terms

- The common-law approach in determining a landowner's liability to persons injured on his land is to measure liability according to the status of the entrant at the time of the accident as an invitee, a licensee, or a trespasser. In some states, the status distinctions have been abolished and the courts have adopted a rule simply that a landowner must exercise "reasonable care" under all circumstances.

- An invitee is a person who has been directly or impliedly invited by the landowner to enter the land for a purpose of advantage to the owner. A landowner owes invitees the duty to exercise ordinary care to maintain the premises in a safe condition or at least to warn of dangers that are not obvious.

- A licensee is a person who is invited or permitted by the landowner to enter the property for his own convenience, pleasure, or benefit, or for purposes not connected with the landowner's interests. While a landowner has no duty to inspect or prepare the premises so they will be safe for a licensee, the landowner does have a duty to warn a licensee of a known dangerous condition.

- A trespasser is a person entering another's premises without invitation or permission. He is owed only a duty not to be willfully or wantonly injured by the landowner.

- Under the attractive nuisance doctrine, one who has or creates a condition on his premises that may be a source of danger to children is under a duty to take those precautions that a reasonably prudent person would take to prevent injury to young children who he knows go onto his land or who may be expected to be attracted by the condition.

- Merchants are under a duty to display their goods so they will not fall and injure a customer, so the merchandise will not topple if a customer using care attempts to take an item from the top of the display, and so that the merchandise is not placed in a manner that would threaten injury to those visiting the store.

- The owner of commercial premises has a duty to exercise reasonable care to keep the floors free from litter or debris, even when the debris is brought into the store by other customers.

- When property is leased in a condition suitable for its ordinary and contemplated use by the tenant, the tenant—and not the landlord—is usually liable to a third person on or off the property for injuries caused by a condition or use of the property under the tenant's control.

- Liability can be imposed on a landlord for injuries to a tenant if (1) the landlord knew of a dangerous condition or should have known of it and failed to inform the tenant; (2) the landlord concealed a dangerous condition; (3) the landlord made repairs in a negligent manner, causing injury to the tenant; (4) an injury occurred in a common area or one in possession of the landlord; or (5) the lease or rental agreement specifically provided that the landlord would make a designated repair, and he failed to do so, later causing a tenant to be injured.

- Attractive Nuisance
- Business Visitor
- Constructive Notice
- Contributory Negligence
- Exculpation Clause
- Geographical Extent of Duty
- Invitee
- Licensee
- Negligent Design
- Reasonable Care
- Slip-and-Fall
- Trespasser

Questions and Case Problems

1. One January evening, Larry steps out of his car in the parking lot of a supermarket. Although snow has not fallen for several days, the parking lot is still covered with snow and ice. Larry slips and lands on his hip, sustaining severe injuries. He sues the supermarket for negligence. What is the result and why? Would the supermarket be liable if Larry was parking in the supermarket lot to attend a motion picture three blocks away? Discuss. How would liability be affected if Larry had parked in the supermarket lot because he intended to use the market's restroom, but not to purchase anything? Discuss.

2. One night a thief attempts to burglarize Margie's home. He falls into Margie's partially completed swimming pool and is severely injured. If Margie had failed to erect a fence or post any warning or lights around the pool, is she subject to liability for the thief's injuries?

3. In *Nixon v Mr. Property* (see page 800), if there had been no city ordinance, would R.V.M. have been able to recover under traditional premises liability rules? Explain the argument for either permitting or denying her recovery.

4. Large piles of slag accumulate on Jack's mining property, which is unfenced. The neighborhood children play on the piles, although Jack has posted a "DANGER NO TRESPASSING" sign. One of these children, Jason, age seven, is injured when he cuts himself on the slag. Is Jack liable for Jason's injuries?

5. Allen sees Tim, a trespasser, on a part of his land previously free from trespassers. Tim is about to come in contact with dangerous machinery which Allen maintains on his land. Allen has time to shut off the power but fails to do so and Tim is injured. Is Allen liable to Tim? Discuss.

6. Emily operates a gas station. One of her customers inadvertently spills water in the men's room, making the entrance very slippery. However, no one complains to Emily about the condition until several hours later, when John slips and falls, hurting his back. John was not a customer of the service station, but a 12-year-old child on his way home from school. Is Emily subject to liability for John's injuries?

7. Seymour, a door-to-door salesman, suffers a broken leg when he trips on a step of Carol's front porch. Carol was not at home at the time, but she knew that the step needed repair and that the danger was not readily visible. Is she liable for Seymour's injuries?

8. MacAdam Cement Company maintains large piles of sand on its premises for use in making concrete. The sand is impure and often contains sharp pebbles and bits of glass. Over the weekend, the premises are unattended. A fence and "NO TRESPASSING" signs have been erected. Several ten-year-olds climb through the

fence one weekend and are cut while playing in the sand piles. Is the cement company subject to liability for their injuries?

9. Harry is walking on a city sidewalk adjoining Alison's property. (a) Assume that Harry is struck by a branch falling from a native tree located on Alison's property. If Alison has never inspected the tree to make sure it is safe, is she subject to liability for the injuries resulting to Harry? (b) If Harry is struck on the head by a baseball hit in a game being played on Alison's land, is she subject to liability for his injuries?

10. A landlord of a small commercial shopping center rented space in his building to a state mental health clinic. The landlord was advised that some of the clinic patients might be violent and assault others. The landlord took no security measures. He sent out a newsletter to tenants indicating that a mental health clinic would be a new tenant, but he did not mention the possibility of assault. Some tenants were aware of the nature of the clinic from reading the newspaper, and they took reasonable precautions. If a tenant who did not in fact know of the danger were assaulted by a patient, would the landlord be liable?

39 Regulation and Control of Land Use

[T]he general rule at least is, that while property may be regulated to a certain extent, if regulation goes too far it will be recognized as a taking.

Justice Oliver Wendell Holmes,
Pennsylvania Coal Co. v. Mahon, 260 US 393, 415 (1922)

39:1 Introduction

In America, decisions about the use of land traditionally were left to individual property owners. This practice reflected the strong value placed on property rights and the recognition that some land-use decisions could best be made by the owner. In the twentieth century, however, Americans have shown an increased willingness to subject land-use decisions to government regulation for the public good. This chapter examines the legal mechanism for land-use control.

Police Power   A state regulates the use of land under the authority of what is known as its *police power.* The United States Constitution does not specifically provide for the exercise of this power by the states; rather, it is one of the unspecified powers reserved to the states or the people by Article X of the Constitution. The police power of states is quite distinct from other constitutional provisions, such as the Fifth and Fourteenth Amendments, which require compensation for private property taken for *public use.* When property is reasonably regulated pursuant to the police power and the property owners are not actually deprived of its use, the payment of compensation is not required. The reason is that no *taking* has occurred.

Nuisance   Before the advent of zoning laws and other laws aimed particularly at the use of land, application of the nuisance doctrine was the primary means by which property use was regulated. A *nuisance* in this context is an invasion of another person's interest in the use and enjoyment of his property. A nuisance is termed a private nuisance when it interferes with the private use of property. For example, a property owner who constructs a 400-foot tower, installs a loudspeaker on top of it, and then plays loud music at night has created a private nuisance. A nuisance is a public nuisance when it interferes with a right enjoyed by the general public. An example of a public nuisance is a property owner's pollution of a stream used by an entire community, so that it is no longer fit for drinking or swimming. The right to relief from a nuisance is based on the idea that one must use one's property so as not to injure that of another. An individual who is harmed by a private nuisance can sue for relief from the nuisance. The appropriate relief is a court order requiring that the nuisance be eliminated. The general rule is that only a government entity can sue for relief from a public nuisance.

39:2   Eminent Domain

The state's right to take private property for public use is known as the right of *eminent domain*. The procedure involved is variously called an eminent domain action, an appropriation action, or a condemnation proceeding. The power of eminent domain is based on the concept that privately owned property is held subject to the state's right to take it if the public would benefit more by its public use than by its private use. The power of eminent domain is not granted by the United States Constitution. Instead, it is an inherent power of the states. It is limited only by the Fifth Amendment, which requires that property owners be compensated for property taken for public use. Every state has a statute that gives the right of eminent domain to a variety of public and semipublic authorities and organizations. The specific procedure for taking property varies from state to state.

Public Use   Since eminent domain is the right to take property for public use, a taking for private purposes violates the constitutional rights of the owner. A public use is one that promotes the general interests of the community as a whole and furthers a legitimate purpose of government. Once the taking of property is deemed to be for a public use, however, the fact that private persons can or will receive benefit from it is not sufficient to take away the characteristics of a public use.

The following case illustrates the situation in which property was to be taken under the power of eminent domain and then used or managed by private entities. Consider the property owner's argument that the proposed taking was unconstitutional.

Berman

v

Parker

348 US 26 (1954)

United States Supreme Court

FACTS: The District of Columbia Redevelopment Act of 1945 was enacted for the purpose of redeveloping substandard housing and blighted areas in the District of Columbia. The District of Columbia Redevelopment Land Agency was empowered to acquire real property by eminent domain. An owner of property that was used as a department store claimed that because his property was commercial property, rather than unsafe or unhealthy slum housing, the property could not be taken in connection with the redevelopment of the area. He also contended that his property was being illegally taken since, under the terms of the statute, the property would be redeveloped by a private agency rather than by a public one.

ISSUE: Does the exercise of eminent domain over plaintiff's property constitute an impermissible taking under the Fifth Amendment?

RESULT: No. If the taking is for a public purpose, in the broad sense, and the landowner receives just compensation, the Fifth Amendment is not violated.

REASONING:

*   *   *

We do not sit to determine whether a particular housing project is or is not desirable. The concept of the public welfare is broad and inclusive. . . . The values it represents are spiritual as well as physical, aesthetic as well as monetary. It is within the power of the legislature to determine that the community should be beautiful as well as healthy, spacious as well as clean, well-balanced as well as carefully patrolled. In the present case, the Congress and its authorized agencies have made determinations that take into account a wide variety of values. It is not for us to reappraise them. If those who govern the District of Columbia decide that the Nation's Capitol should be beautiful as well as sanitary, there is nothing in the Fifth Amendment that stands in the way.

Once the object is within the authority of Congress, the right to realize it through the exercise of eminent domain is clear. For the power of eminent domain is merely the means to the end. . . . Once the object is within the authority of Congress, the means by which it will be attained is also for Congress to determine. Here one of the means chosen is the use of private enterprise for redevelopment of the area. Appellants argue that this makes the project a taking from one businessman for the benefit of another businessman. But the means of executing the project are for Congress and Congress alone to determine, once the public purpose has been established. . . . The public end may be as well or better served through an agency of private enterprise than through a department of government—or so the Congress might conclude. We cannot say that public ownership is the sole method of promoting the public purposes of community redevelopment projects. What we have said also disposes of any contention concerning the fact that certain property owners in the area may be permitted to repurchase their properties for redevelopment in harmony with the overall plan. That, too, is a legitimate means which Congress and its agencies may adopt, if they choose.

In the present case, Congress and its authorized agencies attack the problem of the blighted parts of the community on an area rather than on a structure-by-structure basis. That, too, is opposed by appellants. They maintain that since their building does not imperil health or safety nor contribute to the making of a slum or a blighted area, it cannot be swept into a redevelopment plan by the mere dictum of the Planning Commission or the Commissioners. The particular uses to be made of the land in the project were determined with regard to the needs of the particular community. The experts concluded that if the community were to be healthy, if it were not to revert again to a blighted or slum area, as though possessed of a congenital disease, the area must be planned as a whole. It was not enough, they believed, to remove existing buildings that were insanitary or unsightly. It was important to redesign the whole area so as to eliminate the conditions that cause slums—the overcrowding of dwellings, the lack of parks, the lack of adequate streets and alleys, the absence of recreational areas, the lack of light and air, the presence of outmoded street patterns. It was believed that the piecemeal approach, the removal of individual structures that were offensive, would be only a palliative. The entire area needed redesigning so that a balanced, integrated plan could be developed for the region, including not only new homes but also schools, churches, parks, streets, and shopping centers. In this way it was hoped that the cycle of decay of the area could be controlled and the birth of new slums prevented. . . . Such diversification in future use is plainly relevant to the maintenance of the desired housing standards and therefore within congressional power. . . . Property may of course be taken for this redevelopment which, standing by itself, is innocuous and unoffending. . . . If owner after owner were permitted to resist these redevelopment programs on the ground that his particular property was not being used against the public interest, integrated plans for redevelopment would suffer greatly. . . . But as we have already stated, community redevelopment programs need not, by force of the Constitution, be on a piecemeal basis—lot by lot, building by building.

It is not for the courts to oversee the choice of the boundary line nor to sit in review on the size of a particular project area. Once the question of the public purpose has been decided, the amount and character of land to be taken for the project and the need for a particular tract to complete the integrated plan rests in the discretion of the legislative branch. . . .

The rights of these property owners are satisfied when they receive that just compensation which the Fifth Amendment exacts as the price of the taking. . . .

Douglas, Justice.

Persons and Interests Entitled to Compensation   To be entitled to compensation in an eminent domain proceeding, a property owner must show a taking of property or a property interest that he owned. For example, a leasehold is a property interest that cannot be taken or damaged for public use without compensation. A lienholder and the owner of an unexercised option to purchase land also possess property rights which cannot be taken by the government without compensation.

The only compensation allowable in most states is the value of property actually taken, plus the amount, if any, by which the value of the owner's adjacent property is decreased. "Adjacent property" as used here refers to that which remains after a taking of less than all the owner's property, as where a strip of land running through a farm is condemned for highway purposes. The compensation for damage to adjacent property is known as *severance damages*. No compensation is allowed for consequential losses, such as lost business opportunities, inconvenience, or the mere frustration of a landowner's plans. Nor is compensation allowed for the operating equipment or merchandise of a business, even though the taking terminates a successful commercial enterprise on the premises. However, in some states the owner of a business can be compensated for the loss of goodwill, which consists of the benefits accruing to the business as the result of its location or reputation.

Valuation of Property The measure for valuing condemned property in most states is its fair market value. An important rule in this process is that the property be measured by the value of its *highest and best use*. In urban areas, the highest and best use of a home is obviously use as a dwelling. As to other types of property, the highest and best use is not so easily determined. Consequently, an appraiser is ordinarily employed to determine the value of property and its highest and best use. The use ultimately determined can make a tremendous difference in valuation and the payment of compensation.

 The rule in most states is that the highest and best use of property encompasses not only its present use but also any other use to which it could be put to make it more valuable. Thus, the potential use of property can be considered even though the land may be vacant at the time of the taking.

39:3 Zoning

Zoning is a relatively recent concept in the regulation of land use. The earliest zoning laws, enacted in 1914 in New York, were intended to protect the public against nuisances and land uses that were dangerous to the public's health. The United States Supreme Court upheld the states' right to enact zoning laws in 1926.[1] Today, the state is still the only entity with authority to impose and enforce zoning restrictions, either directly or through local or municipal authorities to which the power has been delegated.

Zoning Ordinances A zoning ordinance generally consists of two parts: (1) a map showing the location of the various zones or districts and (2) a text

---

[1] *Euclid v Ambler Realty Co.* 272 US 365 (1926).

setting out the rules applicable to each zone with general information about the rules and their administration. The term "zone" does not necessarily mean that only one area is set aside for each use. Rather, several widely separated areas covered by a zoning ordinance can have the same general use. Most zoning ordinances include structures, use, or area regulations that govern such matters as the height, location, setback (the minimum permissible distance for a building to be located from the boundary of the property), and minimum floor space of buildings, as well as lot sizes and parking requirements.

Spot Zoning   Spot zoning designates relatively small parcels of land for a use different from that governing the surrounding area, even though all of the land is of the same character. Spot zoning is generally invalid because it violates the requirement that a particular zoning ordinance apply to all property within a particular zone. Where spot zoning is valid, it can result in either economic hardship to the affected property owner (by decreasing the value of the property) or economic advantage (by granting the owner a special privilege not given to others similarly situated).

Contract Zoning   Contract, or conditional, zoning is zoning that is done on the condition that the owner of the affected land execute a contract or covenant restricting the use of the land in certain ways specified in the contract. Contract zoning is thus a method of land-use control whereby a locality can tailor land use to particular tracts of land, permitting an owner to develop land in ways that do not harm the surrounding district or zone as a whole, without the need for spot zoning.

EXAMPLE: A landowner wishes to build a light manufacturing plant on a lot zoned for residential use. If the owner agrees to provide a park surrounding the plant to protect nearby houses, the locality may agree to rezone the land for light industrial use. The owner would execute the covenant in favor of the locality, which in turn would agree to rezone the land.

Floating Zones   Another method of achieving flexibility in land-use planning is use of the "floating zone." A floating zone is a zone that, when created, exists only in the abstract. That is, the land to be included in the zone is neither described in the zoning ordinance nor shown on the zoning map. Particular land is included in the new zone later, by amendment to the general zoning ordinance, after a landowner has made a request for it.

EXAMPLE: A zoning ordinance creates a limited industrial district, setting forth the requirements, conditions, and uses permitted. No land in the affected locality is placed within this limited industrial district. Later, a property owner whose tract is in a residential district applies for rezoning to this limited industrial use. Because the limited industrial district can be located anywhere within the locality, it is a floating zone, and the owner's application can be approved.

Adoption of Zoning Ordinances   Zoning ordinances are normally enacted by municipalities and other local government entities. Various boards or commissions are usually created by these ordinances and are given the power to establish administrative rules and regulations governing the procedure to be followed in zoning cases. The zoning board can also recommend the adoption of district boundaries and appropriate regulations to be enforced in these districts.

Enforcement of the zoning ordinances can be entrusted to a zoning board or commission or to a specified administrative official, such as a zoning officer or building inspector who also may be given the power to issue building permits. If proposed construction, submitted to the zoning officer or building inspector for review, meets the requirements of a particular zoning ordinance, the permit is usually granted. If the requirements of the zoning ordinance are not met, the permit is usually granted. If the requirements of the zoning ordinance are not met, the permit is usually denied and the applicant permitted to make suitable modifications. An applicant can also seek judicial relief or appeal the denial of an application for a building permit to the zoning board or board of review.

The following case demonstrates the scope of the zoning power. Note the extent to which social and moral values can be regulated by zoning ordinances, and consider the views expressed in the dissent.

Belle Terre

v

Boraas

416 US 1 (1974)

United States Supreme Court

FACTS: Belle Terre, a village of 220 homes inhabited by 700 people on Long Island's north shore, adopted a zoning ordinance that prohibited more than two unrelated persons from occupying a "one-family" house. Six unmarried university students, three male and three female, leased a home for their own use and claimed to be "one family." The owners of the house and the students were served by the village with an order to remedy the violation of the zoning ordinance. The students then brought an action in court, challenging the constitutionality of the zoning ordinance. They contended that it violated equal protection of the law and their rights of association, travel, and privacy.

ISSUE: Does the ordinance deny the owners and the students their right to equal protection of the law or violate their rights to association, travel, or privacy under the Constitution?

RESULT: No, the ordinance does not run afoul of any of these Constitutional protections.

REASONING:

Douglas, Justice.

*   *   *

The present ordinance is challenged on several grounds: that it interferes with a person's right to travel; that it interferes with the right to migrate to and settle within a State; that it bars people who are uncongenial to the present residents; that it expresses the social preferences of the residents for groups that will be congenial to them; that social homogeneity is not a legitimate interest of government; that the restriction of those whom the neighbors do not like trenches on the newcomers' rights of privacy; that it is of no rightful concern to villagers whether the residents are married or unmarried; that the ordinance is antithetical to the Nation's experience, ideology, and self-perception as an open, egalitarian, and integrated society.

We find none of these reasons in the record before us. It is not aimed at transients. . . . It involves no procedural disparity inflicted on some but not on others. . . . It involves no "fundamental" right guaranteed by the Constitution, such as . . . the right of association, . . . the right of access to the courts, . . . or any rights of privacy. . . . We deal with economic and social legislation where legislatures have historically drawn lines which we respect against the charge of violation of the Equal Protection Clause if the law be "reasonable, not arbitrary"' . . . and bears "a rational relationship to a [permissible] state objection." . . .

It is said, however, that if two unmarried people can constitute a "family," there is no reason why three or four may not. But every line drawn by a legislature leaves some out that might well have been included. . . .

A quiet place where yards are wide, people few, and motor vehicles restricted are legitimate guidelines in a land-use project addressed to family needs. This goal is a permissible one. . . . The police power is not confined to elimination of filth, stench, and unhealthy places. It is ample to lay out zones where family values, youth values, and the blessings of quiet seclusion and clean air make the area a sanctuary for people. . . .

Justice Marshall, dissenting.

*   *   *

My disagreement with the Court today is based upon my view that the ordinance in this case unnecessarily burdens appellees' First Amendment freedom of association and their constitutionally guaranteed right to privacy. Our decisions established that the First and Fourteenth Amendments protect the freedom to choose one's associates. . . .

Constitutional protection is extended, not only to modes of association that are political in the usual sense, but also to those that pertain to the social and economic benefit of the members. . . . The selection of one's living companions involves similar choices as to the emotional, social, or economic benefits to be derived from alternative living arrangements. . . .

The instant ordinance discriminates on the basis of just such a personal lifestyle choice as to household companions. It permits any number of persons related by blood or marriage, be it two or twenty, to live in a single household, but it limits to two the number of unrelated persons bound by profession, love, friendship, religious or political affiliation, or mere economics who can occupy a single home. Belle Terre imposes upon those who deviate from the community norm in their choice of living companions significantly greater restrictions than are applied to residential groups who are related by blood or marriage, and compose the established order within the community. The town has, in effect, acted to fence out those individuals whose choice of lifestyle differs from that of its current residents. . . .

A variety of justifications have been proffered in support of the village's ordinance. It is claimed that the ordinance controls population density, prevents noise, traffic and parking problems, and preserves the rent structure of the community and its attractiveness to families. As I noted earlier, these are all legitimate and substantial interests of government. But I think it clear that the means chosen to accomplish these purposes are both overinclusive and underinclusive, and that the asserted goals could be as effectively achieved by means of an ordinance that did not discriminate on the basis of constitutionally protected choices of lifestyle. The ordinance imposes no restriction whatsoever on the number of persons who may live in a house, as long as they are related by marital or sanguinary bonds—presumably no matter how distant their relationship. Nor does the ordinance restrict the number of income earners who may contribute to rent in such a household, or the number of automobiles that may be maintained by its occupants. In that sense the ordinance is underinclusive. On the other hand, the statute restricts the number of unrelated persons who may live in a home to no more than two. It would therefore prevent three unrelated people from occupying a dwelling even if among them they had but one income and no vehicles. While an extended family of a dozen or more might live in a small bungalow, three elderly and retired persons could not occupy the large manor house next door. Thus the statute is also grossly overinclusive to accomplish its intended purposes. . . .

By limiting unrelated households to two persons while placing no limitation on households of related individuals, the village has embarked upon its commendable course in a constitutionally faulty vessel. . . . I would find the challenged ordinance unconstitutional. But I would not ask the village to abandon its goal of providing quiet streets, little traffic, and a pleasant and reasonably priced environment in which families might raise their children. Rather, I would commend the town to continue to pursue those purposes but by means of more carefully drawn and even-handed legislation. . . .

Variances   It is difficult to draft a general zoning ordinance that takes into account all the existing shapes, sizes, and peculiar conditions of every lot in a city or other locality. For this reason, most zoning ordinances provide for relief to affected property owners by way of a *variance* from a general zoning ordinance. The criterion for granting a variance is usually a hardship imposed on the property owner due to a unique or peculiar aspect of his lot. A variance must not result in substantial detriment to the public health, safety, or welfare, and it must not depart substantially from the comprehensive plan.

EXAMPLE: A zoning ordinance requires a 20-foot building setback from the street. Because of the shallowness of a particular lot, which was laid out before the enactment of the zoning ordinance, it is not practicable for the owner to set back a new building 20 feet. This is a proper case for a variance. However, if the shallow lot had been created *after* the enactment of the zoning ordinance, the difficulty would be self-created, and a variance would probably not be granted.

Nonconforming Uses   A *nonconforming use* is a use of property that (1) exists at the time a particular zoning ordinance is enacted and (2) is not permitted in the newly created zone. Nonconforming uses are recognized and allowed to continue both to facilitate the adoption of comprehensive zoning plans (by eliminating nonconforming users' need to challenge the zoning) and to protect the nonconforming users' property rights. A zoning ordinance can, however, provide that a given nonconforming use must terminate after a specific period of time. For example, a period of years may be granted a property owner for the removal of a junkyard located in an area newly zoned for residential use.

Discrimination and Exclusionary Zoning   The control and restriction of land through zoning is a legitimate use of the police power to provide for the general health and welfare of the community. Obviously, this power can be abused. Land-use controls, such as minimum lot sizes, minimum floor space, bans on apartments, limits on the number of bedrooms, and building moratoriums can discriminate against minorities or low-income groups, or even exclude them from entire neighborhoods. For example, limits on the number of bedrooms can tend to discriminate against and exclude families with children. Land-use controls that are discriminatory and exclude specific individuals or groups from communities are invalid. On the other hand, if a zoning scheme is not aimed at specific groups but is reasonably related to community needs, it will usually be upheld.

EXAMPLE: A locality adopts a system of land-use planning that permits only high-priced single-family dwellings to be built and requires that they be built on large lots. The stated purpose of the zoning is to keep property taxes at a low level. However, since the effect of the zoning will be to exclude low-income and middle-income families, the zoning will probably be declared to be invalid if it is challenged in court.

39:4   Inverse Condemnation

In certain circumstances, property can be damaged or taken for public use by government action without a formal taking or eminent domain proceeding. For example, a particular zoning ordinance might so restrict an owner's use of property as to render it of no value for any purpose, or noise from a municipally owned airport might so interfere with an owner's use and enjoyment of property that the property could be considered taken by the municipality. This inadvertent taking is called *inverse condemnation*—the owner is deprived of use of his or her property to the extent that it may as well be condemned. A property owner can seek compensation by filing an inverse condemnation action. An action of this type is also known as a reverse condemnation proceeding since it is the same as an eminent domain proceeding, except that it is initiated by the property owner rather than by a governmental entity.

The following case illustrates inverse condemnation. Note the scope of the court's ruling and the types of government action that may or may not constitute a taking of property.

Griffin Development Co.
v
City of Oxnard
703 P2d 339 (1985)
Supreme Court of California

FACTS: In 1979 Griffin completed construction of a 72-unit apartment complex in the City of Oxnard. When built, the complex complied with all city standards applicable to apartments and condominium projects. Such projects were not then subject to special standards. In 1980 the city adopted new standards applicable to new condominium projects. Through ordinance and resolution, the city applied these new standards to condominium conversions as well. The regulations require a special use permit from the city as a prerequisite to conversion; anyone wishing to convert apartments to condominiums must meet the standards which apply to the construction of new condominium projects. Among the standards is the requirement that parking be provided at a ratio of two spaces in a garage per dwelling unit and must be located no further than 50 feet from the unit served. In addition, visitor parking must be provided at a ratio of one space per unit and must be located no more than 100 feet from the unit. Griffin sought a special use permit to convert its apartment complex to condominiums. The permit was denied for lack of parking, among other reasons. The cost to Griffin of complying with the standards for new condominiums would be prohibitive.

ISSUE: Does the city's regulation of condominium conversions so limit Griffin's use of its property as to constitute an impermissible "taking" under the Fifth Amendment or to violate its right to due process?

RESULT: No. The ordinance does not violate Griffin's right to due process of law or constitute an impermissible taking under the Fifth Amendment.

REASONING:

*   *   *

[Griffin's] underlying argument is simply that [a condominium] conversion involves no "change in use" but, rather, a mere change in the form of ownership. . . .

Properly framed, the question raised is whether regulation of condominium conversions (which may or may not involve structural alterations) is consistent with the requirements of due process. In [an earlier case] we restated the basic due process limitations on regulations affecting property interests: " 'So far as the requirement of due process is concerned, and in the absence of other constitutional restriction, a state is free to adopt whatever economic policy may be reasonably deemed to promote public welfare, and to enforce that policy by legislation adapted to its purpose. The courts are without authority either to declare such policy, or, when it is declared by the legislature, to override it.' " . . .

The vast majority of cities and counties in California has adopted comprehensive schemes of land use regulation. Except where such regulations have infringed upon fundamental constitutional rights or relied on suspect classifications such as race, they have generally been upheld in the face of due process and equal protection challenges. Against this background, California courts have consistently treated condominium conversion regulation as a legitimate exercise of the police power. . . .

The standard of judicial review with respect to economic regulation has been clearly established: "[L]egislation regulating prices or otherwise restricting contractual or property rights is within the police power if its operative provisions are reasonably related to the accomplishment of a legitimate governmental purpose." . . .

Griffin in this case does not claim that the Oxnard condominium conversion ordinance restricts any fundamental right, such as freedom of expression or privacy. Rather, it asserts only that its property interests are adversely affected by the city's denial of a special use permit to turn apartments into condominiums. . . .

Prefatory to our examination of the goals of the ordinance, we note that one obvious purpose in requiring a special use permit for condominium conversions is "to maintain a healthy rental housing inventory." [We have] acknowledged that such restrictions on removal of units from the rental housing market through condominium conversion—even though conversion may not involve a "change in use" in the sense that appellant is apparently using the phrase—possess an "independent police power source and purpose." . . .

However, beyond the special purpose of preserving an adequate supply of rental housing, the ordinance shares with many other forms of land use control—zoning, height restrictions, etc.—the basic goal of assuring high standards of construction and adequate facilities in developing residential areas. Rationales behind specific standards which differ from those applicable to apartments are set forth in a memorandum from the city's planning director to the city attorney. For example, with respect to the requirement that each unit have two parking spaces in a covered garage not more than 50 feet from the unit, the planning director stated: "Auto ownership statistics reveal that the average owner occupied unit has more than one auto. The City's experience with residential crime shows that a high percentage of such activity occurs in multi-family projects having carports or other open parking and seems to be directly related to auto burglary." . . .

Griffin has specifically challenged the application of these standards to condominium conversions, arguing that such conversions are merely a change in the form of ownership. Because the conversion involves no "change in use" it is claimed to be unreasonable to apply the standards because they are not sufficiently related to the public welfare. However, this "change in use" approach simply ignores the legitimate concerns which may prompt a city to regulate condominium conversions. The city could reasonably conclude that over a period of time owner-occupied condominiums would serve a segment of the local population with distinct needs. Indeed, the planning director indicated this underlying concern in his memorandum: "Regulations which have been developed recognize the basic differences between owner occupied and rental housing. Oxnard and other cities have experienced that in the conversions of units for sale as condominiums, the buyer of that unit has sole discretion with respect to how the unit is occupied, whereas in a rental situation, the manager has a substantial degree of control over the occupancy. Therefore, our condominium standards are necessary to protect not only the buyer of that unit but to protect against overcrowding and impacts that adversely affect other units in the same complex."

. . . [T]he police power "extends to objectives in furtherance of the public peace, safety, morals, health and welfare and 'is not a circumscribed prerogative, but is elastic and, in keeping with the growth of knowledge and the belief in the popular mind of the need for its application, capable of expansion to meet existing conditions of modern life.' " . . . A city's desire to "grow at an orderly pace and in a compact manner" is clearly encompassed within the concept of "public welfare" . . . , as is a city's attempt to preserve what it regards as an adequate supply of rental housing.

Our examination of Oxnard's condominium conversion regulations plainly indicates legitimate governmental purposes. Moreover, the operative provisions of the regulations are directly and reasonably related to these goals. We conclude, therefore, that the regulations—reasonably related to legitimate governmental purposes—are a valid exercise of the city's police power.

Griffin also contends that the city's condominium conversion ordinance, as applied, results in a confiscatory "taking" of property. A land use measure may be unconstitutional and subject to invalidation "only when its effect is to deprive the landowner of substantially all reasonable use of his property." . . . Under this test, Griffin has failed to make out even a colorable claim that application of the ordinance results in a "taking." Griffin is free to continue to rent its apartments, unaffected by the ordinance; the regulations apply only to its plans to convert the apartments to condominiums.

Moreover, this case does not resemble those in which a city effects a taking through an overly zealous effort to eliminate an existing nonconforming use. We have held that in such cases the city may pursue two constitutionally equivalent alternatives: "It can eliminate the use immediately by payment of just compensation, or it can require removal of the use without compensation following a reasonable amortization period." . . . In the instant case, however, the city has in no sense attempted to eliminate an existing nonconforming use; the ordinance plainly does not affect Griffin's continuing use of the 72-unit structure as an apartment complex.

Any finding of a "taking" in this case would necessarily be based upon the claim that the regulations result in a diminution of the value of Griffin's property. However, . . . most land use regulations have "the inevitable effect of reducing the value of regulated properties." . . . Such reduction in property value does not, by itself, render a regulation unconstitutional. . . .

Kaus, Justice.

39:5 Landmarks and Historic Buildings

The preservation of the nation's cultural resources has been a public concern almost since the founding of the Republic. For example, in 1816 the City of Philadelphia prohibited private development in the Independence Square area, and later in the century, to preserve the Gettysburg battlefield, the federal government declared it a national monument. Today, there is government action at all levels to preserve landmarks and historic buildings.

The preservation of historic structures generally is accomplished by one of two methods. The first is direct governmental intervention through the power of eminent domain, which establishes public ownership of historic buildings. Landmarks and structures taken in this fashion require compensation to the affected landowner. The second method involves indirect action through zoning regulations, requiring private owners to preserve their property in a specific fashion; it does not necessarily involve the taking of property.

The principal question involved in governmental regulation of landmarks through zoning is whether the restrictions imposed constitute a taking for which compensation must be paid. If a regulation deprives an owner of all reasonable uses of his property, then it can be said that a taking has occurred for which compensation is required. In contrast, if an ordinance permits some uses, the property is not considered to have been taken and the owner need not be compensated.

Most state and local preservation statutes empower a "preservation commission" to designate a geographical area or an individual building as a historic site. The owner is then denied the right to demolish or renovate any buildings involved, especially their facades. While most ordinances of this type permit an owner of a historic structure to apply for a permit to demolish or alter the building, this permission is usually denied as inconsistent with the preservation agency's basic function.

Federal Landmark Preservation   Early in this century, Congress enacted the Antiquities Act of 1906 [16 USC §§ 431–33]. This act empowered the President to declare historic landmarks, structures, and other objects of historic or scientific interest located on federal land to be national monuments. Landmarks such as the Statute of Liberty and the Edison Laboratory were designated national monuments pursuant to this act. In 1935, the Historic Sites, Buildings, and Antiquities Act [16 USC §§ 461 et seq.] was adopted to identify and preserve cultural resources in the United States. Today, the preservation of landmarks and historic buildings is governed by the National Historic Preservation Act of 1966 [16 USC §§ 470 et seq.]. This act establishes a review process that federal agencies must follow in assessing the effect of their programs on districts, sites, buildings, or other structures that are included in a listing prepared by the Secretary of the Interior. This listing, known as the National Register of Historic Places, serves as a guide for implementing national historic preservation policy. Any property that has national historical significance or commemorative value is eligible for the registry. The Advisory Council on Historic Preservation coordinates the national historic preservation program and regulates the impact of federal agency actions on National Register properties.

39:6   Federal Regulation of Land Use

The role of the federal government in land-use control has been primarily to provide financial aid to cities and states for development and urban renewal. Obviously, many other types of federal legislation designed to preserve clean air, eliminate water pollution, or regulate noise, for example, vitally affect the uses to which land can be put. Moreover, legislation enacted by the federal government often parallels similar legislation adopted by the states. Indeed, it is not uncommon for a particular project to be the subject of regulation by several government entities, ranging from the localities themselves to federal agencies. For example, an *environmental impact statement* may be required at all levels of government before a project may be approved. Different aspects of federal regulation of land use will now be discussed.

National Environmental Policy Act (NEPA)   A major piece of federal legislation that vitally affects the use of land throughout the United States is the *National Environmental Policy Act of 1969 (NEPA)* [42 USC §§ 4321 et seq.]. The purpose of NEPA is to establish procedures by which environmental concerns that are created by proposed government projects are identified and then thoroughly analyzed. Accordingly, whenever a federal agency proposes "legislation and other major federal actions significantly affecting the quality of the human environment," it must prepare an environmental impact statement and file it with the proposal. No particular federal agency has the power to enforce the act. Instead, because the act provides that the impact statements must be made available to the public, the public at large has the right of enforcement.

NEPA is specifically directed at projects that involve a major federal action. Examples of "major federal actions" are government construction projects, the granting of federal permits for private projects (even if no federal funds are involved), and the issuance of federal mortgage insurance and loans.

Coastal Zone Management Act   The Coastal Zone Management Act of 1972 [16 USC §§ 1451 et seq.] authorizes a national program for the management, use, protection, and development of natural resources along the nation's coasts. The program establishes standards for public and private uses of land and waters in the coastal zone, and it provides funds to coastal states to develop and implement their own coastal management programs. These state programs must consider ecological, cultural, historic, and aesthetic values, as well as the need for economic development of the lands in question.

Federal Land Policy and Management Act   In 1976, Congress enacted the Federal Land Policy and Management Act [43 USC §§ 1701 et seq.]. The act repealed many outdated and archaic public-land laws. The law now requires that the Secretary of the Interior prepare and maintain an inventory of all public lands, including their resources and uses.

Wilderness and Open-Space Preservation   Every year at least two to three million acres of open space or farmland in the United States are developed to accommodate the growth of industry and expanding urban areas. About one-third of the land lost is prime agricultural land. It is only in recent years that the federal government has begun to respond to this situation. For example, before 1964 there were no statutorily designated wilderness areas. Any areas that did receive protection for their wilderness qualifications were protected by the federal government only pursuant to administrative action within a particular federal agency or, less formally, on a regional basis by the Department of the Interior. The Wilderness Act of 1964 [16 USC §§ 1131 et seq.] created the national wilderness preservation system and established several wilderness areas as components of that system. The act also requires the Department of the Interior to review areas previously set aside by administrative action to determine whether they should also be included in the wilderness system.

39:7 Private Land-Use Restrictions

There is a long history of regulation of land through private restrictions. One of the earliest forms of land-use control was the *restrictive covenant*. Sellers of property used restrictive covenants to impose limits on purchasers as to the type of improvements that could be built on land sold, to restrict the use of land to specific purposes, and even to specify to whom property could or could not be sold. A restrictive covenant is usually imposed directly by the seller on a purchaser of property. In this way, there can be no question that the purchaser is aware of the restriction and is bound by it.

Another type of private restriction is called an *equitable servitude*. Although just as binding on property owners as a restrictive covenant, the equitable servitude differs in that the restriction is not necessarily mentioned in a particular deed. For example, a developer of a residential tract might file in the appropriate public office a subdivision map, plat, or other document containing all the pertinent data about the development, as well as specific restrictions. The owner of a lot in the subdivision—and all future owners—are bound by the restrictions. They are considered to have constructive notice of the restrictions so long as their deed refers to the existence of the map or plat. In fact, however, an owner often does not realize that the use of his property is restricted until he has attempted to use his property in a way that is contrary to the restriction imposed and is then restrained in court by other property owners.

Creation of Restrictive Covenants Any landowner can impose restrictions on, the use of land that he conveys to others so long as the restrictions are not unlawful or against public policy. Restrictive covenants are generally treated as covenants running with the land. This means that the duty to perform the covenants—as well as any right to take advantage of them—passes to those who may purchase the property in the future.

Restrictive covenants are primarily used to maintain a general scheme, plan of design, or purpose on the land on which the restrictions are placed. They are most frequently imposed on residential property. The object of restricting the type of building to be built and the use to which the land is put is to ensure purchasers of lots within a subdivision, for example, that the use and enjoyment of their land for residential purposes will not be affected by the development of commercial activities in the neighborhood. Likewise, a person who buys or builds a home will be assured through the use of restrictive covenants that his property will not be depreciated by subsequent construction of inferior structures on adjoining lots.

 Frequently, restrictive covenants are imposed on land to protect a seller from competition by the purchaser. The owner of a tract of land on which a business is maintained may want to sell a part of the land and yet prevent the new owner or subsequent purchasers from engaging in a competing business on the property. Restrictions of this type are valid and, as long as they are not unreasonable and do not amount to an undue restraint of trade, they are enforced. They are normally limited to a period of years, however.

Extinguishment of Restrictions   Restrictive covenants can be extinguished by mutual agreement, abandonment, waiver and acceptance, or changes in the character of a neighborhood that would make enforcement of the restrictions unjust.

Enforcement of Covenants   Restrictive covenants are special forms of contract, and damages for their breach are governed by the general law of damages in contract actions. They can also be enforced through injunctive relief. Moreover, an owner of land on which restrictions have been imposed can seek declaratory relief to determine whether or not a proposed use of land violates the restrictions or whether the restrictions have been extinguished.

The following case illustrates the use of restrictive covenants as a private land-use control. Note that restrictive covenant cases often strike at the heart of difficult and important social issues.

Gregory
v
State Dept. of Mental Health
495 A2d 997 (1985)
Supreme Court of Rhode Island

FACTS: Plaintiff's property abuts a wooded lot that is owned by defendant and targeted for development as a group home for six mentally retarded persons. The real estate owned by plaintiff and defendant is subject to the following restrictive covenant:

> Said lot is also conveyed subject to the following restrictions: That only a single one-family dwelling house, not to exceed 2½ stories in height, and other buildings incidental thereto, shall be built or placed thereon; . . . that said premises shall be used for private residential purposes only."

Plaintiff obtained an injunction to prohibit construction of the group home on the ground that its placement in the neighborhood would violate the "single one-family dwelling" and "residential purposes only" language contained in the restrictive covenant.

ISSUE: Is a group home for mentally retarded adults a "single one-family dwelling" used for "residential purposes"?

RESULT: Yes. The group home is within the requirements and the spirit of the restrictive covenant.

REASONING:

*   *   *

In construing the terms of a restrictive covenant, we are mindful of the oft-repeated maxim that restrictive covenants are to be strictly construed in favor of the free alienability of land while still respecting the purposes for which the restriction was established. . . . Further, we have held that cases involving the interpretation of restrictive covenants must be decided on a case-by-case basis since they "present such a wide spectrum of differing circumstances." . . .

Here, the covenant itself contains no definitions of either "single-family dwelling" or "residential." The task presented to this court, then, is the narrow one of construing the meaning of these terms. As in statutory construction, these words should be given their plain and ordinary meaning unless a contrary intent is discernible from the face of the instrument. . . .

Case law from other jurisdictions is voluminous with respect to the definitions of the terms "single-family dwelling" and "residential" found in restrictive covenants, with the overwhelming majority supporting the inclusion of group homes within their scope. Two recent cases are particularly illustrative. In [one], the Nebraska Supreme Court was faced with a restrictive covenant that provided:

> "No lot shall be used except for *residential purposes.* No building shall be erected, altered, placed or permitted to remain on any lot other than one detached *single family dwelling* not to exceed two and one-half stories in height, and a private garage." [Court's emphasis] . . .

The court pointed out that a building used for residential purposes is one in which people make their homes as opposed to one in which a business is conducted. In reaching the conclusion that a group home for five mentally retarded women would be a residential use of the property, the court found determinative that the group home would be a permanent residence for the women, that they would share the common areas, prepare and eat meals together, and have houseparents who would teach them "the skills which are normally taught and performed in a residence such as taking care of the house, cleaning, preparing meals and money management." . . .

In determining the scope of the term "single-family dwelling," the court looked to other jurisdictions and quoted the following language from the Minnesota Supreme Court:

> "From the outside, the home looks like all the other single-family homes in the neighborhood. The residents live in a family-type setting and call the dwelling their home." . . .

The court then concluded that in appearance and use, the proposed group home would not violate the terms of the restrictive covenant.

In [a New York case], the restrictive covenant in issue limited construction to "single family dwellings and outbuildings" and provided that "no part of said property nor any of the buildings to be erected thereon shall be used for any business purpose whatsoever. . . . " The homeowners' association in that case sought to block the establishment in its neighborhood of a community residence for eight mentally disabled adults. The court recognized that the term "family" does not always delineate a "traditional, biological concept" and focused its inquiry on whether "in theory, size, appearance and structure the group residence emulated the traditional family unit." . . . The court then examined the goals of the group-home movement and determined that where the primary object was to create a relatively permanent environment "operating as a single household unit" with a set of houseparents, and which "as much as possible bears the generic characteristics of the traditional family," the community residence satisfied the requirements of the restrictive covenant. . . .

We are thoroughly persuaded that the group home proposed for Cooke Drive will not contravene the requirements or the spirit of the restrictive covenant the Gregorys seek to enforce. The purpose of the covenant, the preservation of the quality of life and character of the neighborhood, is in no way threatened by the presence on Cooke Drive of a home, carrying on the day-to-day activities of all the other homes, with its only significant distinguishing feature being that the members of the household are disabled to varying degrees by mental retardation. . . .

Kelleher, Justice.

Key Concepts and Terms

- The regulation of land use is performed by most states or localities pursuant to their police power.
- The right to take property for public use is known as the right of eminent domain. This right is inherent in government and is based on the concept that privately owned property can be taken for public purposes for the public's benefit.

- If property is taken for public use or is damaged by governmental action, either with or without a formal taking or eminent domain proceeding, the owner is entitled to compensation. The procedure by which a property owner tries to obtain just compensation in a case not involving a formal taking is commonly referred to as inverse condemnation.

- The measure of damages for property taken in eminent domain is its fair market value. In determining fair market value, the highest and best use of the property is considered.

- Zoning is an important technique in regulating land use. Zoning regulations may fix the height of buildings, the character of materials, methods of construction, and the separation of residential districts from industrial and commercial areas.

- A zoning ordinance generally consists of (1) a map showing the location of the various zones and (2) a text setting out the rules applicable to each zone and information about their administration.

- The federal government regulates the use of land indirectly through agencies. The federal government has also enacted legislation such as the National Environmental Policy Act, the Coastal Zone Management Act, and the Federal Land Policy and Management Act, which vitally affect all public lands and resources.

- Restrictive convenants are private land-use restrictions that impose limits on purchasers of property to protect the seller or neighboring landowners.

- Condemnation Proceeding
- Eminent Domain
- Environmental Impact Statement
- Equitable Servitude
- Highest and Best Use
- Inverse Condemnation
- National Environmental Policy Act (NEPA)
- Nonconforming Use
- Nuisance
- Police Power
- Public Use
- Restrictive Covenant
- Severance Damages
- Taking
- Variance
- Zoning

Questions and Case Problems

1. Between 1966 and 1970 Canal Authority exercised the power of eminent domain to acquire land for a Cross-Florida Barge Canal. The property was condemned and title taken in fee simple by the Canal Authority. Subsequently, the project was abandoned as unfeasible. The condemned landowners claim that, since the public purpose for which the land was taken has been frustrated, the taking is no longer for a public purpose. They argue that they should be entitled to return of their land. What do you think of this argument? Does it matter that the land was acquired in good faith? Would it matter if the Canal Authority had resold the property? What is the better rule?

2. Analyze the following statements:

a. "It is time that we apply the clear and unmistakable lesson of the past 50 years: Zoning has been a failure and should be eliminated! Governmental control over land use through zoning has been unworkable, inequitable, and a serious impediment to the operation of the real estate market and the satisfaction of its consumers."

b. "It's absurd and tragic that the national goals of stimulating more and better housing in a desirable housing environment are being frustrated by local goals of limiting housing. It is equally inexcusable that federal policies to encourage business and development and competition are being impeded by local policies that operate to discourage them."

3. Sundell owns land on the shore of a lake. The town of New London operates a sewage treatment plant that discharges nutrient-laden effluent into a brook upstream from Sundell. Ample evidence indicates that algae bloom in the lake, causing it to emit foul odors and to become less capable of supporting fish life. There is also ample evidence to show that the algae are the result of the town's activities. Is this a nuisance? Can the city be enjoined? Has Sundell's property been taken? Can he bring a successful action in inverse condemnation for the taking of his rights to enjoy the lake and lakeshore?

4. The Cleburne Living Center (CLC) sought to lease a residence to use as a group home for the mentally retarded. It was informed that the city regarded the facility as a "hospital for the feebleminded" and required a special use permit, which it denied CLC. CLC claims that the requirement of a license violates the right of the proposed residents to the equal protection of the law under the Fourteenth Amendment of the Constitution because it draws a distinction between retarded and nonretarded citizens that does not substantially further an important governmental purpose. What result?

5. The Agins own a five-acre parcel of unimproved land in a California city. Recently the city adopted a zoning ordinance that placed the land in a residential planned development and open-space zone, permitting the Agins to build no more than five single-family residences on the tract. The Agins sue for damages, alleging inverse condemnation. They assert that the city has taken their property without just compensation and they seek a declaration that the zoning ordinance is unconstitutional. What should the court rule?

6. The Stovers, as a protest against high taxes, hung tattered clothing, old uniforms, underwear, rags, and scarecrows in their front yard. After several years, a city ordinance was enacted prohibiting the erection and maintenance of clotheslines or devices for hanging clothes or other fabrics in a front or side yard abutting a street. Provisions were included for the issuance of a permit in certain circumstances. The Stovers were refused a permit on the grounds that they had sufficient other property for the maintenance of a clothesline. When they continued to maintain the clothesline, they were arrested, tried, and convicted of violating the ordinance. Should their conviction be upheld? Is the ordinance a proper exercise of municipal power?

7. The city of Petaluma, California, responding to a 25 percent growth rate over a period of two years, instituted a comprehensive five-year housing and zoning plan that fixed the housing development growth rate at 500 dwelling units per year. The plan also directed that building permits be divided evenly between the east and west sections of the city, and positioned a 200-foot-wide "green belt" around Petaluma to serve as the boundary for urban expansion during the plan's term. Two property owners sue the city. They attack the plan as an unconstitutional

infringement of their freedom to travel and a violation of their right to due process of law. The city defends its plan as a reasonable exercise of its police power in preserving the rural character of Petaluma and pacing its growth at an orderly rate. How should the case be decided?

8. Penn Central wanted to lease air rights above its Grand Central Terminal in New York City to UGP Properties, Inc. UGP planned to construct a 55-story office tower above the site. Plans drawn up by a noted architect complied with the city's zoning requirements. Since Grand Central Terminal had previously been designated as a landmark and the city block a "landmark site" under New York City's landmarks preservation law, the property owner was required to apply to the Landmarks Preservation Committee for administrative approval. After a hearing, the necessary certificates were denied by the Commission. Penn Central sued New York City claiming that the application of the landmarks law had (1) resulted in a taking of its property without just compensation in violation of the Fifth and Fourteenth Amendments to the United States Constitution and (2) arbitrarily deprived them of property without due process of law. Should New York's landmarks preservation law be upheld?

9. Shady Acres is a small, unincorporated community 15 miles from a large city. All the residences in Shady Acres are ranch and split-level homes. A social action group from the city purchases five acres of land for construction of low-income housing units in Shady Acres. The local citizens become apprehensive about overcrowded schools and an increase in the crime rate. Eventually they force a revision of the local zoning ordinance. Local land, formerly zoned for multiple dwellings, is rezoned to permit only single-family dwellings. The owner of the land on which the low-income housing units were to be built sues to have the law declared unconstitutional. Decide the case.

10. The Cottonwood subdivision includes restrictive covenants in deeds for residential property prohibiting (1) the erection of any structure other than a detached single-family dwelling and a private garage and (2) the keeping of livestock and fowl, with the exception of small birds or animals kept as pets. Bagley constructs a home in Cottonwood and then wants to build a three-horse stable and tack room on an adjoining lot. Her plan calls for a one-story concrete block structure. What are the rights of Bagley's neighbors? Can Bagley build her stable and tack room?

40 Trusts, Wills, and Estate Administration

40:1 Estates and Estate Planning

The property a person owns at any given time comprises his "estate." This estate will vary in nature and amount until the person dies. One's estate is augmented and consumed in the normal course of events. For example, a person's estate is reduced slightly when she spends money on groceries and then eats them. The part of a person's estate that is not consumed or destroyed must be passed on to some other person or entity. This passing on *can* occur during the property owner's lifetime; otherwise, it *will* occur at death.

The simplest means by which a living person can dispose of property is by outright gift. A person who gives a gift is a *donor;* a recipient is a *donee.* From the donor's viewpoint, the major objection to disposition by gift is that a gift is absolute. That is, the donor gives up not only the right to receive any benefits from the property given, but also all power to control the property or its use in the donee's hands. Another potential shortcoming of making a gift is that due to age, health, or spending habits the donee might be incapable of using the gift in the manner intended by the donor.

In recognition of these and other problems, the legal system provides a device, known as a *trust*, by which a living donor can dispose of property and still retain some control over it. The legal system also allows a property owner to make a will, by which he can decide who is to receive the property after death. Gifts, trusts, and wills are the basic tools used in *estate planning*. If a person dies leaving property not disposed of by will, or one of the other means available, the property is distributed to the persons and in the manner provided by state statute.

Estate Planning Estate planning is an activity by which one's estate is identified, increased if possible, and later disposed of according to the owner's wishes, all with minimum loss through taxation. These goals are pursued through a comprehensive plan that requires a carefully drafted will and can also include the use of such devices as gifts, life insurance, and trusts.

Because of its tax-limiting function, estate planning is often thought to be of concern primarily to the wealthy, but this view ignores the property-disposition function of the planning. In fact, estate planning can serve people of only moderate means. For example, an estate plan that calls for the purchase of life insurance might create an estate where none would otherwise exist, or a plan might help a person prepare for retirement by providing for an individual retirement account. An estate plan can also make adequate provision for the continuation or orderly transfer of a business after the owner's death.

Trusts

40:2   Introduction to Trusts

A trust is a device whereby legal title to property is separated from the right to benefit from ownership of the property. Thus, the power to control and manage property can be given to someone skilled in property management, and the right to the income and benefit from the property can be given to someone else, the true beneficiary. The need to make such a separation arises most often in the family context, where parents may wish to transfer property for the benefit of their children but defer transferring full ownership until the children are older. Or a person may wish to give sufficient property in trust to provide someone an income for life, and then direct the next disposition of the property.

The creator of the trust is called the *settlor* or *trustor*. The subject matter of the trust, the property, is called the *res* or *corpus*. The trustor transfers the legal title to the *trustee* and imposes on the trustee the obligation to hold the property for the benefit of the *beneficiary*. The trustee's interest is called the legal interest, and the beneficiary's interest is called the beneficial, or *equitable*, interest.

The trustee can be either a private person or an institutional trustee, such as a bank. Ordinarily, the trustee receives a fee, which may be paid out of the trust income, but otherwise the trustee is not entitled to benefit from the income or value of the property.

Most trusts cannot continue indefinitely. When a trust terminates, the property held in trust must pass to someone, called a *remainderman*. The remainderman may be a beneficiary, in which case the beneficiary becomes a remainderman—and acquires legal title in addition to the equitable interest—when the trust terminates. However, the remainderman often is someone other than the beneficiary.

EXAMPLE: Brown creates a trust under which the local bank is the trustee, Brown's husband is the income beneficiary, and Brown's son is the remainderman. Brown's husband will receive the income generated by the trust property during the duration of the trust. When the trust terminates, the trustee will transfer the trust property to Brown's son, who will then hold it free of any trust.

A trust can be created by more than one person, as where a husband and wife are the trustors, and there can be more than one trustee, as where an individual and bank are made joint trustees. There are often multiple beneficiaries and remaindermen. Moreover, the same person can assume more than one role under a trust. For example, Brown in the above example might have named her son as trustee, herself and her husband as beneficiaries, and her son as remainderman.

If the same person is the only trustee, beneficiary, and remainderman there can be no trust; the equitable and legal ownership of the trust property has merged in that person.

Purposes   Trusts are used for various purposes. Many trusts are created to reduce the trustor's income tax, the estate tax payable by the trustor's estate after his death, or both. Other purposes include avoiding probate, providing income to people who would be unsuitable recipients of outright gifts, and obtaining the services of a trustee who is an expert at managing property of the type that is the subject of the trust.

Types of Trusts, Generally   Trusts can be classified in many different ways. For example, a given trust can be express or implied, private or charitable, or revocable or irrevocable. It can have been created either while the trustor was living or after his or her death.

Express and Implied Trusts   An *express trust* is created intentionally by the trustor. Most trusts are of this type. The trust is a private express trust if the beneficiaries are private persons, usually relatives or close friends of the trustor. It is a charitable trust if the beneficiary is a charitable organization, such as a church, a school, or the Red Cross.

An *implied trust* is one created by operation of law to correct what would otherwise be an unfair situation. It can be either a *resulting trust* or a *constructive trust.* A resulting trust is one in which title to property is acquired by someone other than the person who gave the consideration for the property, for the latter's benefit but without an express trust or intent that there be a gift. For example, if Benny buys a piece of land for his own benefit, but he has Rochester, his valet, named as the new owner in the deed, a court is apt to charge Rochester with the duties of a trustee with respect to the land since Benny is entitled to the beneficial interest in it.

A constructive trust arises when a party has obtained money or other property by fraud or similar wrongdoing, such as violation of a confidential relationship. If, for example, Benny in the above example had directed Wilson, his attorney, to handle the real estate transaction and to have title to the property placed in Benny's name but, in fact, Wilson had arranged to have title placed in his own name, a court would probably find that Wilson holds the property in a constructive trust, with Benny as the beneficiary.

The basic duties of the trustee are essentially the same whether a trust is express or implied, except to the extent that additional duties are provided for in the document creating an express trust. Usually, however, the duty of the "trustee" of a constructive trust is to transfer legal title to the property to the beneficiary.

Revocable and Irrevocable Trusts A revocable trust is one that can be revoked. A trust is irrevocable unless the trustor specifically reserves the right to revoke the trust. Often such a reservation has adverse tax consequences.

Living and Testamentary Trusts A trust that is created to take effect during the life of the trustor is called a *living trust,* or an *inter vivos* trust. One that is created to take effect at, or after, the death of the trustor is called a *testamentary trust.* The law of wills requires, in effect, that a trust created to become effective at death be created in a will or in an acceptable will substitute, such as a life insurance policy.

Spendthrift Trusts At times a trustor wants to provide for a beneficiary who, because of his many creditors, his unwise spending habits, or both, should not be given even the limited rights of a beneficiary under a normal express trust. This problem can be solved by including in the terms of the trust what is known as a spendthrift provision. The distinctive feature of a trust containing such a provision is that the beneficiary's interest in the trust cannot be assigned, voluntarily or involuntarily, to someone other than the beneficiary. For example, the beneficiary cannot assign to a creditor his right to receive income from the trust, and the creditor is powerless to reach that income by judicial means until the income has been paid to the beneficiary. Once the income has been paid, the beneficiary can, of course, do whatever he wants to with it. Note in this regard that if a spendthrift provision is *not* included in a trust, a beneficiary generally can assign his interest in the trust, and creditors can reach that interest, although statutes in some states limit the creditors' right somewhat.

40:3 Creation of an Express Trust

No particular formal words or acts are required to create a valid express trust. There are, however, a number of general requirements. First, the trustor must intend to create the trust and must be legally capable of doing so. For example, neither a child nor a person who has been declared to be mentally incompetent can create a valid trust. Second, there must be both a legally capable trustee who is willing to act in that capacity and at least one beneficiary. However, the fact that the person who is named as trustee by the trustor turns out to be unwilling to serve or incapable of serving does not invalidate an otherwise valid trust; a court has the power to appoint a new trustee.

The third requirement of a valid trust is that there be a res of the trust. It can be money, other personal property, real property, or any combination of different types of property. Some states recognize what are known as life insurance trusts, under which there is no actual trust property until the insurance proceeds are paid after the trustor's death.

A fourth requirement is that the beneficiaries be described clearly enough to be identified with reasonable certainty. Although any person or entity capable of owning property can be a trust beneficiary, the trust instrument must at least guide the trustee as to the identity of the intended beneficiaries. Finally, the trust must have a legal purpose and not violate public policy. For example, if a trustor names his daughter as the beneficiary of a trust but requires that she divorce and cease living with her husband before she can receive trust income, the trust is invalid as being contrary to the public policy favoring marriage.

Trust Agreement Although a trustor can create a living trust orally, the usual and better practice is to use a written instrument for that purpose. In the trust instrument the trustor sets forth all the desired terms concerning the trust. A typical trust agreement covers such matters as

- Identification of trustor, trustee, beneficiaries, and remaindermen
- Purpose of trust
- Description of trust property
- Trustee's powers and duties in managing trust
- Trustor's retained powers with respect to trust property, including power to modify or revoke trust
- Distributions of trust income to beneficiaries
- Duration of trust; terminating events

The trust agreement is signed by the trustor, and the trustee's written acceptance of the trust is often attached. Other formalities are required only to the extent dictated by the type of property being transferred to the trust. For example, if real property is being transferred, the agreement might have to satisfy certain formal requirements so that it can be recorded in the county recorder's office.

40:4 The Role of the Trustee

By definition, the trustee's basic duty is one of trust. A fiduciary relationship exists between the trustee and the beneficiaries, which means that the trustee is held to a high level of honesty and good faith in managing the trust property.

State statutes give trustees certain powers and impose on them certain duties and responsibilities, but for the most part, these statutes apply only to the extent that they do not conflict with the terms of the trust instrument. That is, when the trustor creates the trust he has the right to establish the trustee's required performance.

Trustee's Powers The trustee's primary responsibility is to manage the trust property. To do so, he must have certain powers with respect to the property. Powers typically granted by law or the trust instrument include the power to

- Invest trust property
- Sell, exchange, or lease trust property
- Enter into other contracts with respect to trust property
- Mortgage trust property
- Distribute trust income to beneficiaries

Trustee's Duty to Account and Pay Taxes   After a trust has been created and the trustee has acquired the trust property, the trustee is required to account for that property for as long as he serves as trustee. The trustee should have records of all receipts of money and other property, all transactions involving the trust property, and all distributions and other disbursements from the trust.

Ordinarily, trust property generates income, which is subject to state and federal income taxation. A trust is treated as a separate entity for tax purposes, and state and federal statutes include specific provisions governing the taxation of its income. The trust can deduct expenses in managing the trust and trust income that is distributed to beneficiaries. The trustee is responsible for preparing and filing needed tax returns and paying any tax due.

Allocations Between Principal and Income   Under the terms of the typical trust, the trustee must distribute trust income, or at least some part of trust income, to the beneficiaries. The trustee might also receive money or other property that, although received because of the trustee's legal ownership of the trust property, does not really constitute income. Receipts of this type are credited to principal rather than income, and they are frequently required to be retained by the trustee and added to the trust property. The result is that the trustee must decide how each receipt is to be allocated between principal and income; depending on the nature of the trust property, this can be a major duty. Trusts also have expenses, and the trustee must make a similar allocation for each expense. Note that the beneficiaries benefit to the extent that a given receipt is allocated to income or an expense to principal. Conversely, allocating a receipt to principal or an expense to income benefits the remaindermen by increasing the property that they will receive when the trust terminates.

The manner in which the trustee carries out the allocation duty is governed by any instructions set forth in the trust instrument. To the extent that there are no instructions, the trustee must act in accordance with state statutory and case law. State law varies on this subject, although over half the states have enacted the Uniform Principal and Income Act in either its original (1931) or revised (1962) version.

In most states, a trustee is permitted to allocate between principal and income at his own discretion if the trustor has given the trustee that power. Some allocation decisions faced by a trustee holding this power are simple. For example, if the trust property consists of money that the trustee has invested in a certificate of deposit, the periodic interest payments received obviously constitute income. However, a large portion of the property currently being held in trusts in the United States is corporate stock. The dominant rule is that cash dividends from stock are treated as income; stock dividends are treated as principal.

Level of Skill Required   Some trustees lack special property management skills, while others are property management specialists. A trustor's intentions often can best be met by his naming two trustees. One trustee would be a friend or relative who is aware of personal relationships between the trustor and the beneficiaries and remaindermen, the other a professional person.

 An unskilled trustee must use the same degree of care and skill that a reasonably prudent person would use in managing his own property and affairs. A trustee who has special qualifications is held to the standard set by others having similar qualifications. For example, if the trust property consists of a stock portfolio, a professional stock advisor named as trustee would be held to a higher standard of skill in managing the portfolio than would a trustee not having those credentials.

The trustee who violates the duty to manage the funds prudently may be assessed, or *surcharged,* the loss to the trust. Rarely, if ever, has a court surcharged a trustee for obtaining only a moderate return. It is more likely that the trustee will be surcharged for taking too much risk. Therefore, trustees tend to be risk-averse, and return on trust funds is rarely robust. Even where the trustee loses principal by failing to diversify or otherwise avoid loss, it may be protected if the trustor has authorized the trustee's course of conduct.

United States Trust Co.
v
Bohart
495 A2d 1034 (1985)
Supreme Court of Connecticut

FACTS: In 1943 Richard P. and Elsie Ettinger established a trust for the benefit of Bohart, their granddaughter. Ettinger was the founder, president, and major shareholder of Prentice-Hall, a publishing firm, and Prentice-Hall stock was the principal asset of the trust. In 1965 Ettinger resigned as trustee and appointed plaintiff as a corporate trustee. Bohart was to be an income beneficiary until she reached the age of 35. Because she died before reaching that age, the entire trust principal became payable to her children. The trustee sought judicial approval of its accounting. The Bohart children claim the trustee breached a fiduciary duty in failing to diversify the trust assets. The evidence showed that when the Trust Company became trustee, Prentice-Hall stock sold for about $18.50 a share. By January 1970 the stock had climbed to $52.00. Over the next few years the stock fluctuated wildly, and upon distribution of the trust in 1979, the stock was worth approximately $24.00 a share.

ISSUE: Did the trustee violate its fiduciary duty by failing to sell the stock and diversify the trust assets?

RESULT: No. The trustee's investment strategy did not violate its fiduciary duty.

REASONING:

*   *   *

The gravamen of the defendants' claim is that the plaintiff was negligent in failing to diversify the trust assets by selling Prentice-Hall stock before its 1972–1973 decline. The trial court refused "to charge [the plaintiff] for possible fluctuations of the market that from hindsight might have resulted in the sale of stock at its highest peak" and held that the plaintiff had not acted improperly in retaining the stock.

The law governing the duties of a trustee respecting investment of trust assets is well settled. Generally, a trustee must act with the care of a prudent investor. . . . A trust agreement may, however, "specifically permit trustees to invest in speculative or otherwise hazardous investments." . . . When a trustee has been vested with such discretion, liability attaches only if the discretion is abused. . . .

The record in this case reveals that the plaintiff was accorded the discretion to act as it did. The second paragraph of the trust agreement provides in relevant part: "The Trustee is specifically authorized to continue to hold the property as received from the Settlors. . . . " As the trial court found, one of the settlors' motivations for creating a trust composed almost exclusively of Prentice-Hall stock was to preserve family control of the company. Moreover, Mr. Ettinger saw no need to diversify the trust portfolio during the twenty-two years he served as trustee. While, in retrospect, the value of the trust could have been maximized had the plaintiff divined the downward course of the stock market in the 1970's, we cannot say that it abused the discretion specifically granted it in continuing to hold Prentice-Hall stock. "A trustee is neither the insurer nor the guarantor of the value of a trust's assets. A trustee's performance is not judged by success or failure, and while negligence may result in liability, a mere error in judgment will not." . . .

Peters, Chief Justice

Conflicts of Interest   The trustee's duty of good faith requires that he keep trust property and affairs separate from his other property and affairs. In particular, the trustee must avoid self-dealing, and the prudent trustee avoids even an appearance of self-dealing. For example, it is unwise for a trustee to purchase trust property for herself or another client, even if the price is fair. The trustee violates her trust if she purchases that property at less than a fair price.

40:5   Duration of Trust; Modification or Revocation

A trust continues to exist until its purpose has been accomplished or until the terminating event specified in the trust instrument occurs. Many trusts are structured so that they terminate after a set period of time or after the death of the beneficiaries.

A charitable trust can continue indefinitely, but a private trust cannot. Specifically, a private trust cannot violate what is known as the *rule against perpetuities.* In essence, the duration of a trust is limited to 21 years plus a period measured by the death of a designated individual or the last death of a designated group of people. Every interest in the trust must pass to a definite person within the time limit. As a practical matter, a parent usually can create a trust for the benefit of unborn grandchildren, but not the children of unborn grandchildren. The limitation prevents private trusts from continuing indefinitely.

EXAMPLE: Evert creates a trust in which her son, Connors, is the initial beneficiary. Connors is to receive the trust income until he dies, after which the trust property is to be divided among Connors' children. The share of any minor child will be held in the trust until that child reaches the age of 21. This arrangement will not violate the rule against perpetuities, even though it is not presently possible to know how many children Connors will have at the time of his death. However, the trust *would* violate the rule if Evert's great-grandchildren, rather than her grandchildren, were the remaindermen. This is so because property ultimately intended to pass to the child of a currently unborn grandchild could pass later than 21 years after the death of any currently living person.

There are limits on who can be the "designated persons" for purposes of the rule against perpetuities. These persons should be reasonably easy to identify. For practical purposes, the broadest designation a trustor can use is "all my heirs, currently living" or words to that effect.

Modification or Revocation   Once a trust has been created, the trustor can neither modify the trust terms nor revoke the trust unless he has reserved those rights in the trust agreement. The power to modify which, for practical purposes, includes the power to revoke, is attractive to the trustor because it allows him to reacquire all or part of the trust property whenever he wishes.

Not so attractive are the adverse tax consequences of these powers. If the trustor retains the power either to modify or to revoke the trust (1) the trustor will probably be taxed on trust income, thus negating possible income tax savings and (2) even if the power is not exercised, the mere existence of the power means that the trust property will probably be included in the trustor's estate for estate and inheritance tax purposes when he dies. To some extent, these results can be prevented by making the trust irrevocable. However, many people lack enough financial security to dispose of their property irrevocably.

A partial solution to the above problem is use of what is known as a Clifford trust, which is a short-term irrevocable trust. A Clifford trust takes advantage of the fact that under federal law and the law of many states the trustor is not taxed on the income of an irrevocable trust having a term of over 10 years even if, after the trust terminates, the trustor will reacquire the trust property as remainderman. The same tax advantage results if, instead of setting a period longer than 10 years, the trust agreement provides that the trust will terminate on the death of the beneficiary. However, the Clifford trust may be less attractive in the future as a means of avoiding tax, depending on what Congress does in the name of tax reform.

Wills

40:6   Introduction to Wills

A *will* is a statement, usually written, by which a person indicates how his property is to be disposed of after his death. Making a will is a voluntary act; nobody can be forced either to make one at all, or to make one providing for any particular scheme of distribution.

The person making a will is referred to as the *testator* (male) or *testatrix* (female). Persons to whom property is to pass under the will are the beneficiaries. The person who has the duty of actually making the distributions of property according to the will is commonly referred to as the *personal representative*.[1] A person who dies without having made a valid will is said to have died *intestate*. His property is distributed according to a fixed statutory scheme.

Purposes of Will   Although the primary purpose of a will is to allow the testator to declare the intended distribution of his property, a will can also serve other purposes. For example, the testator can use his will to create a testamentary trust if he does not wish property to pass to beneficiaries outright soon after his death. He can designate the personal representative of his choice and perhaps one or more alternate representatives as well. He can also indicate his desires as to who should be appointed guardian of his minor children.

Types of Gifts   A gift provided for in a will is referred to as a *devise* if the gift is real property. The terms *bequest* and *legacy* refer to gifts of personal property. The beneficiary receiving a devise is known as a *devisee*, while a *legatee* is one receiving a legacy or bequest.

---

[1] The traditional title of a personal representative designated by the testator in his will is *executor* (male) or *executrix* (female). A person appointed by the court, either because the testator failed to designate anyone or because of intestacy, was traditionally known as the *administrator* (male) or *administratrix* (female). "Personal representative" is commonly used today in place of the traditional terms.

A legacy can be specific, general, or residuary. A *specific legacy* is one of particular property that is identified in the will, such as "Aunt Matilda's ivory brooch." A *general gift* is one that is not described specifically; an example is "the sum of $10,000 to Hobbs, my faithful butler." A *residuary gift* is one of all or part of the residue of the estate, which is the property left over after all priority claims against the estate have been paid and all specific and general gifts have been distributed.

 Every will should include a clause disposing of the residuary estate. Otherwise, the residuary property will pass as if the testator had died intestate, which can result in distributions that the testator did not intend.

Will Beneficiary's Death   If the beneficiary named in a will does not survive the testator, the gift can *lapse* (be canceled). Whether a particular gift will lapse depends in part on the testator's stated intent, if included in the will, and on the language used by the testator.

EXAMPLE: In his will, Jacob left his summer cottage to "my beloved daughter Melinda or her estate" and his vintage MG sports car to "my son Jack." The will contains no specific language as to the lapse of either gift. Jacob, Melinda, and Jack die together in a plane crash. According to the general rule, the gift to Jack has lapsed; the MG will be retained by Jacob's personal representative and added to the residuary estate. However, because of the words "or her estate," the summer cottage will pass to Melinda's estate.

The rule as to lapsed gifts has been modified in many states by what are known as *antilapse statutes*. The scope of these statutes varies, but in essence the statutes prevent lapses by specifying to whom property left to a deceased beneficiary is to go.

40:7   Requirements of a Valid Will

The key requirements of a valid will are that (1) the testator have testamentary intent and testamentary capacity when the will is made, (2) all required formalities be observed, and (3) the will not be made as a result of undue influence. These and related requirements concerning wills are governed by state statutes, and the statutes vary somewhat among the states. There is some uniformity in that over one-fourth of the states have enacted the Uniform Probate Code.

Testamentary Intent   Testamentary intent is simply the intent to provide for the distribution of one's property after death. It is normally stated in a will. Otherwise, it can sometimes be presumed, either from the language used in a document that is offered as a will or from the testator's acts or statements at the time he signed the document.

Testamentary Capacity   *Testamentary capacity* is the power to make a valid will. First, a person must be of at least the age specified by statute; a child lacks testamentary capacity. Second, the person must be "of sound mind," meaning that he or she must be mentally competent. While one's age is a fact that can be determined objectively, one's mental competence is not. A person can have testamentary capacity even though lacking sufficient mental competence to operate a business or even to sign a valid deed. Generally speaking, testamentary capacity exists if a testator is aware of the following basic facts:

- Nature and extent of his property
- Effect of making a will
- Instrument being signed is his will
- Manner of disposition provided for in will
- Natural objects of his bounty and their relationship to him

The term "natural objects of his bounty" refers to those persons who, because of their close relationship to the testator, would reasonably be expected to share in the estate.

The required level of mental competence must exist only at the time the testator signs the will. For example, a will is not invalidated if the testator becomes senile later on. Nor is a will invalid because the testator was mentally disordered at some time before (but not when) he signed the will.

Formal Requirements   Some states recognize a *nuncupative* (oral) will if (1) it is later reduced to writing by a witness and (2) the testator declared it during his last illness. Generally, however, a will must be in writing and signed by the testator.

Most wills are prepared by someone other than the testator, often an attorney. A will of this type, often referred to as a *formal will* must always be signed by the testator or at his direction. Some states require that, while signing, the testator declare aloud that he is signing his will. This act is known as *publication of the will.*

One or more *attesting witnesses* must also sign a formal will in most states. The number of witnesses required depends on state law, as does the exact procedure to be followed. For example, in some states the witnesses must observe the testator signing the will, while in other states the testator need only declare that the document is his will and that he has signed it. The main purpose for requiring attesting witnesses is that later, after the testator's death, the witnesses can state that the testator actually signed the will and that he did so voluntarily. The witnesses are also expected to satisfy themselves that the testator is mentally competent to make a will. They are not expected to read the will, and under the law of many states, they cannot be beneficiaries under the will.

The simplest type of written will is a *holographic,* or handwritten, will, which is recognized in many states. The holographic will must be entirely handwritten and signed by the testator. A handwritten date is also required in some states. Any typing on the document invalidates the will, as does any writing by a person other than the testator. The advantage of a holographic will is that no witnesses are required. The requirement is dispensed with because forgery of an entire document is far more difficult than forgery of only a signature.

The purpose of formality in wills law is to satisfy the court that the testator intended the instrument to be legally effective and that the instrument embodies the testator's true testamentary intent. Attorneys create office rituals for executing wills so that all formalities are met and so that the will can be probated. Often, however, testators do not use an attorney and instead attempt to dispose of their property at death in a manner that does not fully comply with the wills statute. Courts, then, are faced with the prospect of denying a person's will for lack of technical formality. The following case involves such a problem.

Faith

v

Singleton
692 SW2d 239 (1985)
Supreme Court of Arkansas

FACTS: Mrs. Joyner, who was 80 and faced hospitalization, went to the home of her neighbors and asked them to type the following document, which Joyner then signed and the neighbors witnessed:

> State of Arkansas
> County of White
>
> I, the undersigned, do hereby request, at the time of my death, that Calvin Britton, Route 5, Searcy, Arkansas, who has lived and care for me for years, have my home and all the furnishings as long as he wants, or as long as he shall live. I further request that only one other person reside in the home with him, not an entire family. Then, at Calvin Britton's death, the home, property and furnishings can be sold and all proceeds from the property is to go to my brothers and sisters and Thomas Joyner's (Deceased) brothers and sisters in equal parts.

Apparently all will formalities were met except that Mrs. Joyner specifically denied that she wanted a will, stating "I want a piece of paper fixed up so I can sign it and Calvin will have a place to live."

ISSUE: Does the document Mrs. Joyner signed fail as a will for lack of publication?

RESULT: No. The document can operate as a will, even if Mrs. Joyner did not wish to call it a will.

REASONING:

*   *   *

Whether the instrument is in fact a will is the question before us. A will is a disposition of property to take effect upon the death of the maker of the instrument. . . . To be valid as a will an instrument must be executed with testamentary intent, or *animus testandi*. . . . That merely means the intention to dispose of one's property upon one's death. By looking to the four corners of the instrument, we determine that intent. . . . It is a question of law for the court to determine from the face of the instrument whether the writer intends to make a testamentary disposition. . . .

No doubt Mrs. Joyner intended to dispose of her property on her death, and the instrument clearly sets out what she wanted done. That is enough to qualify it as a will, so far as intent is required. Although Mrs. Joyner said, for whatever reason, that she did not want a will, a will is precisely what she dictated and executed. As Justice Oliver Wendell Holmes stated: "We must think things not words. . . . " Oliver Wendell Holmes, "Law in Science and Science in Law," *Collected Legal Papers*, p. 238 (1921). "If what the testator does sign proves to be what the law declares is a testament, and witnesses duly attest it, they have attested a will, though neither the testator nor the witnesses knew that the law declared the writing to be a will." . . . A person may act *animo testandi* without knowing that he is making a will, and it is immaterial what kind of instrument he thinks he is making, if only he manifests a clear intent to dispose of his property after his demise and observes the statutory formalities. . . .

The appellees also argue that other reasons should prohibit probate. First, it is contended that the formalities of execution were not followed because Tennie Joyner did not declare the instrument to be her will. [An Arkansas Statute] provides in pertinent part: "The testator shall declare to the attesting witnesses that the instrument is his will . . . " The requirement that the testator declare the instrument to be a will is called publication. In [an 1853 Arkansas case], publication was defined:

> Publication under the statute is necessary to give effect to a will; but it means that the testator, having capacity to make a will, shall understand that the instrument which he is about to execute, is a testamentary disposition of his property, and that he shall, at the time, communicate to the witnesses, that he does so understand it. The statute says he shall *declare* it; but . . . no particular form of words is necessary, and that it would be unwise, if not unsafe, to speculate upon the precise mode of communication, as every case must depend upon its own peculiar circumstances. The fact of publication therefore, is to be inferred or not, from all the circumstances attending the execution of the will; all that is said and done as part of the *res gestae*.

It is not required that a testator recite precisely the words "this is my will," although that is obviously the preferred practice. Publication can be inferred from acts and circumstances. . . .

The appellees wish to void Mrs. Joyner's last requests by asking us to strictly construe the technical requirements of [the Arkansas Statute]. Where there is no indication of fraud, deception, undue influence, or imposition, this court avoids strict technical construction of statutory requirements in order to give effect to the testator's wishes. . . . It is not disputed that Tennie Joyner understood that she was making a testamentary disposition of her property nor is it disputed that that was communicated to the witnesses and they understood. Tennie Joyner's intentions and desires were clear. . . .

Hickman, Justice.

Undue Influence The term *undue influence* refers to influence or pressure that substitutes the wishes of another for those of a testator regarding the disposition of his property. Undue influence invalidates a will. Requiring a testator to sign a will at gunpoint is an obvious example of undue influence, but usually the influence is more subtle. The following case indicates the required elements of undue influence and presents a classic example of facts leading to the presumption of its existence.

In Re Estate of Nelson
274 NW2d 584 (1978)
South Dakota Supreme Court

FACTS: Nelson died leaving as his only heirs a brother, a sister, and a nephew. In wills signed before October 1953, Nelson had left most of his estate to his three heirs. Through a series of three later wills, however, the provision made for the heirs was decreased, ever-increasing amounts of the estate going instead to Theodosen, Nelson's attorney. Nelson's final will, signed in 1956, made Theodosen the sole beneficiary, completely disinheriting the heirs.

ISSUE: Is the 1956 will a product of undue influence by Theodosen, Nelson's attorney?

RESULT: Yes. Theodosen's dominant position raises the presumption of undue influence, and that presumption is not rebutted by the evidence.

REASONING:

*   *   *

Influence, to be undue, must be such as to destroy the free agency of the testator and substitute the will of the person exercising it for that of the testator. . . . Its essential elements are (1) susceptibility of the testator to undue influence; (2) opportunity for the exercise of undue influence; (3) disposition to exert undue influence; and (4) a result in the will showing the effect of such undue influence. . . .

Where a confidential relationship exists between a testator and a beneficiary, the beneficiary actively participates in the preparation and execution of the will, and the beneficiary unduly profits in the will, a presumption of undue influence arises. . . . The establishment of facts giving rise to the presumption also establishes a prima facie case which can sustain a finding of undue influence. . . . The presumption of undue influence remains even though the beneficiary introduces evidence rebutting the presumption. . . .

The proponents [those who hold that the will is valid] argue that the presumption of undue influence does not exist in the present case. We do not agree. Theodosen and Nelson were not social friends. Their only relationship was that of attorney–client. That relationship is a confidential relationship. . . . Theodosen admits that he drafted the January 24, 1956 will and was present when it was executed. This will devises and bequeaths all of Nelson's property "to my friend, John M. Theodosen . . . , and leaves "nothing to any of my relatives." [Personal instructions accompanying the will] give Theodosen the discretion to turn over the property he [receives under the will] to a charitable corporation. These facts give rise to a presumption of undue influence and, in this case, sustain a finding of undue influence.

The proponents argue, however, that the presumption was conclusively rebutted at trial. They claim that two of the essential elements of undue influence, susceptibility and opportunity, are lacking. Again we disagree.

Although Nelson was mentally astute until his death, Theodosen, by virtue of his legal training and confidential relationship, held the dominant position. He allowed Nelson to give him [broad discretionary powers as a trustee] in the first will. In 1955 after office hours on New Year's Eve, Theodosen drafted another will giving himself all the property. . . . Finally, in 1956, Nelson gave Theodosen all of his property . . . with personal instructions involving broad discretion. . . . Theodosen encouraged complete confidence in his legal advice by never refusing to write himself into the will and never insisting that Nelson seek independent legal advice if he (Nelson), in fact, did want to make such a disposition.

Added to this is the fact that pre-Theodosen wills provided for Nelson's sister, brother, and nephew. Within four years of Nelson's first dealing with Theodosen they were totally disinherited. While these relatives are not considered the natural objects of the testator's bounty, . . . their gradual disinheritance by Nelson in wills drafted by Theodosen demands close judicial scrutiny. . . . The pattern of the wills indicates an inability by Nelson to resist Theodosen's influence. . . .

There are additional facts pointing to undue influence by Theodosen. Theodosen was the attorney for Nelson's sister Fern when each will was drafted and while Fern was disinherited. Theodosen was named executor in all the Nelson wills; a practice that was apparently standard in Theodosen wills for many other decedents. Theodosen was present at the execution of all the wills, and was alone in his office with Nelson before the witnesses arrived to execute the final will. The will remained in Theodosen's safe and was under his control until admitted to probate.

While the presence of any of these facts standing alone may not have been enough to establish undue influence, taken together they clearly create a presumption of undue influence. The evidence presented was insufficient to rebut the presumption. No evidence was presented indicating that Theodosen took no unfair advantage of his dominant position. A prima facie case of undue influence was established and it required a finding of undue influence. . . .

Zastrow, Justice.

40:8   Modification or Revocation of a Will

A will can be modified or revoked at any time by the testator. There are also certain events, the occurrence of any of which can operate as an entire or partial revocation.

Testator's Voluntary Acts   Most wills include a clause to the effect that the testator is revoking all prior wills. Whether or not this clause is included, a new will, if valid, automatically revokes all prior wills made by the testator, at least to the extent that the prior wills are inconsistent with the new one. If a new will is invalid, however, the next preceding valid will remains in effect.

EXAMPLE: On June 15, 1975, Tom signed a will, and all required formalities were observed. Eight years later, in July of 1983, Tom directs his attorney to prepare a new will since he has decided to make major changes in the distribution of his estate. Tom signs the new will on July 29, 1983, but, due to an oversight, only one attesting witness signs the will, although state law requires two. Tom dies in September 1984. The 1983 will is invalid, and Tom's estate will pass under the 1975 will.

A testator can revoke a will by destroying or obliterating it. He can make a partial revocation by obliterating the provisions desired to be revoked. In many states, the testator can also revoke his will by using a separate instrument as to which the formalities required for the will itself are observed. For example, if three attesting witnesses are required to sign a formal will, three witnesses must also sign a separate document revoking that will.

The usual and safest method of modifying a will is use of a *codicil*. A codicil is a separate instrument, executed with the same formalities as the will, in which the testator states the desired changes. The changes can consist of additions, deletions, altered language, or any combination of these. The advantage of the codicil procedure is that it saves the time and expense required for preparation of a new will, although execution of a new will is recommended if changes are numerous or substantial. There is no limit on the number of codicils a testator can execute.

Revocation by Operation of Law   Certain events are so closely related to the likely intended disposition of a person's property that if one of them occurs, the disposition provided for in an existing will is automatically altered. Events of this type include the testator's marriage or divorce, and the birth of his child. The exact effect of such an event varies, depending on state law. The testator's marriage revokes his existing will in some states. In most states, the testator's divorce operates to delete any devise or legacy to the former wife. A child born after the execution of a will that omits any reference to that child is generally entitled to the share of the parent's estate that the child would take if the parent had died intestate, that is, without a valid will.

40:9   Disclaimer; Spouse's Right to Take Against Will

A beneficiary is not required to accept the property that would otherwise pass to him under a will. For example, the beneficiary might prefer that the subject of a specific legacy pass to the residuary beneficiary rather than to himself. A more common situation is that unnecessary adverse tax consequences would result from the beneficiary's acceptance of property as specified in the will.

EXAMPLE: Harry's will establishes a testamentary trust under which Sam, Harry's son, is the life beneficiary and Gloria, Sam's daughter, is the remainderman. If Sam disclaims (refuses to accept) his interest in the trust, the trust property will pass directly to Gloria.

State law and, in many instances, federal tax law govern both the timing and the manner of making an effective disclaimer of an interest under a will.

Election to Take Against Will   A testator can disinherit most of the natural objects of his bounty. He can leave nothing or only a token gift to children, parents, siblings, or other relatives. The only practical requirement in this regard is that the intent to disinherit a close relative should be stated in the will. Otherwise, the relative might be able to successfully claim that he or she was *pretermitted*, or unintentionally overlooked by the testator, in which event the relative will receive an intestate share of the estate.

The person one cannot effectively disinherit under the law of most states is one's spouse. Under a typical statute, the surviving spouse has the right to accept the provision made for him or her in the will (which might be no provision at all) or, instead, to elect to take a share of the estate, as prescribed in the statute. For example, the statute might give the survivor the right to one-third of the estate. An election to take against the will must be made within the time limits specified by state law.

 There can be legitimate estate planning reasons for disinheriting a spouse. Potential tax savings is the major one. A spouse who is disinherited as part of an estate plan should be aware of and in agreement with the plan.

Administration of Estates

40:10   Probate

Probate is the process by which a testator's will is offered to a court after his death to determine that the will is valid. The person offering the will, usually a close relative of the testator, and often the personal representative named in the will, is known as the proponent.

In most instances, having a will admitted to probate is a simple matter. If the attesting witnesses are available, they can testify that the testator signed the will voluntarily and that they believed him to be mentally competent at the time. If the witnesses are not available, the proponent must prove that their signatures on the will are valid. Some states recognize and have statutes providing for what are known as self-proving wills. The advantage of this kind of will is that, if all the special statutory requirements are met, the probate court accepts the genuineness of the will without proof. The practical advantage of this procedure is that, at the time of probate, the proponent does not need to locate and produce the attesting witnesses or produce specimens of their signatures for purposes of comparison.

After a will has been admitted to probate, the court officially appoints the personal representative by issuing what are known as letters testamentary. Ordinarily, the person or entity designated by the testator is appointed. If no designation was made, the court usually appoints a close relative or friend of the testator.[2]

Will Contests   A will contest arises when one or more persons, referred to as contestants, claim that a will being offered for probate is invalid. A person must, to be eligible as a contestant, have an interest in the estate, and the interest is usually one that will be adversely affected if the will in question is admitted to probate. Typically, the contestant is somebody who was either disinherited or treated less generously in the will than he had expected.

---

[2] Strictly speaking, the term "letters testamentary" refers only to the written authority given to an executor or executrix; the authority given to a personal representative who was not designated by the testator is known as "letters of administration."

The grounds for a will contest might be that the will was revoked, superseded by a later will, or the result of undue influence. Alternatively, a contestant might claim that the entire will is a forgery or that the testator lacked testamentary capacity when he executed it.

Once a will has been contested, the probate court holds a hearing, which is much like a regular trial. The purpose of the hearing is to determine whether the will being offered is valid or, if several wills have been offered, which (if any) is the valid one.

 A testator can attempt to discourage beneficiaries from contesting his will by including in the will what is known as an in terrorem clause. Such a clause, valid in most states, provides that a beneficiary who contests the will forfeits his or her interest as beneficiary. If the will contestant is successful, however, the in terrorem clause falls with the invalid will.

40:11   Intestate Succession

When a person dies either without leaving a valid will or leaving a will that fails to dispose of all of his or her property, the property not passing under a will is distributed according to the state laws governing *intestate succession.* Every state has such laws, although they are not uniform. For example, if a person dies intestate leaving a surviving spouse and children, they will receive the entire estate under the law of most states, but the manner in which the estate is divided among them varies. Division of the estate between the surviving spouse and children, while seemingly fair on first impression, can cause hardship for the spouse.

EXAMPLE: Chris dies intestate, leaving his unskilled wife, Juliene, and two minor children. Under state law, Chris' modest estate is divided in half. One share goes to Juliene, while the other is divided between the children. Because of the children's minority, their shares are held for them in trust until they reach majority. Juliene must support herself and raise the children, but the half of Chris' estate being held for the children is unavailable to her. Juliene's interest—as well as Chris' probable intent had he considered the matter—would have been better served if Chris had left a will naming Juliene as the sole or principal beneficiary.

If a person dies intestate leaving a spouse but no children, the spouse will receive the entire estate. If there are children but no surviving spouse, the children receive the property. Intestacy laws also cover the situation in which one dies leaving neither a spouse nor any children. Relatives who might then receive all or part of a decedent's estate include parents, grandchildren, and siblings, depending on state law. If no surviving heir or ancestor of one who dies intestate can be found, the decedent's estate escheats (passes to) the state.

Appointment of Personal Representative   An intestate estate is administered by a personal representative appointed by the probate court. The appointee is apt to be the same person the court would appoint if the decedent had left a will.

40:12   Role of the Personal Representative

The role of a personal representative is somewhat similar to that of a trustee in that a person acting in either capacity manages and is accountable for someone else's property. The major distinctions are that (1) a decedent's estate will be closed after all required administrative procedures have been carried out, while a trust usually exists for a longer time; and (2) the personal representative is often also a beneficiary, while a trustee usually has no personal interest in the trust property. Despite any interest he or she has in the estate, the representative owes to others interested in the estate a high level of honesty and good faith in carrying out the duties of the position.

Steps in Administering Estate   The steps taken in administering a decedent's estate depend on state law, as does the required procedure for taking them. Important functions of the personal representative include the following:

- Inventorying estate, which might require appraisals
- Collecting debts owed to decedent
- Locating heirs and others interested in estate
- Notifying creditors, to allow submission of claims against estate
- Preparing and filing required tax returns
- Settling claims against estate
- Distributing estate property in accordance with will or intestacy laws
- Accounting for all estate property

A personal representative who fails to carry out his duties properly and consequently causes loss to the estate can be personally liable to the estate for that loss. Personal representatives usually post a bond, which is paid for by the estate, to cover this potential liability.

After all required actions have been taken, the personal representative petitions the court to be discharged. When the petition is granted, the representative is free of further duties concerning the estate, and the estate is closed.

Distributions to Beneficiaries   A person's being named as a will beneficiary does not necessarily mean that he will receive any part of the estate. One reason is that a number of other claims must be paid out of the estate before anything can be distributed to beneficiaries. Included among these priority claims are the following, commonly payable in the order listed:

- Funeral expenses
- Administration expenses (legal expenses; compensation of personal representative and attorney)
- Family allowance (amount paid under state law to surviving spouse or for benefit of children for purchasing necessities during period of administration)
- Amounts owed to federal government, such as income and estate taxes

- Medical expenses for decedent's last illness
- Amounts owed to state and local governments
- Other valid debts of decedent

The priority claims can consume the entire estate, leaving nothing for *any* beneficiaries.

Another situation that prevents a beneficiary from receiving property in accordance with the terms of a will is what is known as *ademption* of the gift. Ademption occurs under either of two general circumstances. The first is that the specific property described in the will is not part of the estate. The property might never have existed at all or it might have been consumed, lost, destroyed, or transferred earlier.

The second circumstance that can give rise to an ademption is an earlier gift by the testator to the beneficiary. Assume, for example, that in 1981 Walt signs a will leaving $10,000 to his niece, Pat; in 1982 Walt gives Pat $5,000; and in 1983 Walt dies. Should Pat receive $10,000 from Walt's estate? Or should the 1982 payment be treated as a partial satisfaction of the gift provided for in the will? The answer generally depends on the testator's intent, which is a question of fact that the probate court must decide.

A beneficiary might also lose his share of an estate because of *abatement*. A legacy can abate (be eliminated) when, after the priority claims have been paid, there is sufficient property left in the estate to cover only some of the devises and legacies. The testator's expressed intent governs as to which gifts abate first. If the testator failed to express any intent about the matter, the general rule is that residuary gifts abate first, followed by general gifts. If some but not all gifts of a given class can be made, the beneficiaries of that class take on a pro rata basis.

EXAMPLE: Horace's will provides for the following gifts: his company stock to Glenda, his wife; $20,000 to his son, Jack; $10,000 to his daughter, Jill; and the residue of his estate to a charitable organization. After all priority claims have been paid, Horace's estate consists of the stock and $6,000. Glenda will receive the stock, Jack $4,000, and Jill $2,000; the charity will receive nothing.

40:13   Avoiding Probate

The term "avoidance of probate" refers to ways in which a property owner can transfer property by means other than a will. It does not involve entire elimination of the probate procedure. If a testator leaves a will, that will must go through probate, although some states provide for short, simple probate procedures for certain small estates. What a testator can do, however, is arrange his affairs so that most of his estate passes independent of the will.

Purposes   There are several reasons why a person might want to avoid probate. Cost is one factor. The fees payable to such people as the personal representative and the attorney often depend on the size of the estate. Another factor is privacy. Probate is a public proceeding, and a person might wish to avoid public disclosure of the size or nature of his estate, or of the manner in which he chose to distribute it.

Methods Effective methods of avoiding probate include a testator's use of gifts, trusts, life insurance, and joint tenancy. The estate plan for a given estate often contemplates the use of more than one of these methods.

Since a gift is absolute, property given away during the testator's lifetime cannot pass under the testator's will. The same is true as to any property transferred to a living trust that has not been revoked by the time the testator dies. If a testator names his estate as the beneficiary of his life insurance policy, the insurance proceeds will be distributed according to the will. If, however, the beneficiary is a close relative, such as the testator's spouse or child, the proceeds will pass directly to the beneficiary. The distinctive feature of joint tenancy, which is a type of co-ownership of property, is that when one joint tenant dies, title to his interest in the property passes automatically to the surviving joint tenant or tenants.

40:14 Federal and State Taxation

The period required for the administration of a decedent's estate can be lengthy, especially for a large estate. During this time the estate can earn income, which is taxable. For example, the estate might receive interest on certificates of deposit, dividends on stock, or rental income. The estate is a separate entity for federal and state income tax purposes, and special rules govern its income tax liability. The personal representative is responsible for preparing and filing needed tax returns and paying any tax owed. The representative will usually also have to prepare and file final personal income tax returns on behalf of the decedent.

Federal Estate Tax Depending on its size, an estate might be subject to a federal estate tax. Any tax due is paid out of the estate, before distributions to beneficiaries are made. The personal representative is responsible for preparing and filing the estate tax return and actually paying the tax.

Federal tax used to be payable on even relatively small estates, but changes in the tax laws have tended to eliminate the estate tax as a significant factor in estate planning for many people. Estate planning for larger estates considers the various deductions available under federal law. The marital deduction is the most significant one for many people. A person's entire estate can pass free of estate tax if the estate is left to the surviving spouse. Bear in mind, however, that the surviving spouse's estate, as increased by any amount left to the survivor by the spouse who died, will be taxed when the survivor dies.

 Regardless of the available credits and deductions, if the bulk of an estate consists of a business, the business might have to be sold to generate enough money to pay the federal estate tax unless adequate estate planning has been done to provide another source of the needed money.

State Estate and Inheritance Taxes   Most states also tax decedents' estates, either directly or indirectly, and these taxes are independent of and in addition to the federal estate tax. Because states usually allow fewer and smaller exemptions and deductions from the tax than are available under federal law, the state tax bill is often higher than the federal bill, even though the tax rate is lower.

The majority of states provide for an inheritance tax. The tax is imposed on and paid by each beneficiary after he has received estate property. The amount of tax due depends on both the size of the gift and the beneficiary's relationship to the decedent. For example, on a gift of a given amount or value, the surviving spouse will pay less tax than a sibling of the decedent, and the sibling will pay less than a beneficiary not related to the decedent. Some states impose an estate tax instead of inheritance taxes. Like the federal estate tax, a state estate tax is paid by the personal representative before any of the estate property is distributed to the beneficiaries.

Key Concepts and Terms

- Estate planning helps a person to acquire an estate and dispose of it as he or she wishes, while keeping loss through taxes to a minimum.
- A trust is a basic estate planning device. Different goals can be achieved by using different types of trusts.
- A living trust is normally created by the trustor's execution of a trust agreement, while the terms of a testamentary trust are included in the trustor's will.
- A trustor is the person who establishes a trust. A trustee is the person who holds the legal title to trust property and is responsible for its management. The beneficiary is the equitable owner of the property and ordinarily receives the income generated by it.
- A trustor can reserve the right to modify or revoke a trust.
- The duration of a private trust, even if irrevocable, is limited by the rule against perpetuities.
- A will is a person's declaration, usually written, of how he wants his estate to be distributed after his death.
- A will is invalid if (1) the testator lacked testamentry capacity, (2) the will was the result of undue influence, or (3) required formalities were not observed.
- A testator has the right to revoke or modify his will at any time, but he can do so only in the manner permitted by law.
- A beneficiary can disclaim his interest under a will, and a testator's surviving spouse can elect to take against the will.
- A decedent's will is admitted to probate after the probate court finds that the will is valid. A will contest occurs if one or more people interested in the estate challenge the validity of a will being offered for probate.
- If a person dies intestate, his estate is distributed according to a state statutory scheme.

- The personal representative of a decedent's estate has the duty of administering the estate in the manner provided by law and in the decedent's will.

- A person can avoid having his property pass through probate by careful use of trusts, gifts, life insurance, and joint tenancy.

- A decedent's estate is taxed on its income. The federal government also imposes a tax on the estate itself, while most states tax beneficiaries after they have received distributions from an estate.

- Abatement
- Ademption
- Administrator, Administratrix
- Antilapse Statute
- Beneficiary
- Bequest
- Codicil
- Constructive Trust
- Corpus
- Equitable Interest
- Estate Planning
- Executor, Executrix
- General Gift
- Holographic Will
- Inter Vivos Trust
- Intestate Succession
- Lapse
- Legacy

- Living Trust
- Nuncupative Will
- Personal Representative
- Pretermitted Heir
- Probate
- Remainderman
- Res
- Residue
- Resulting Trust
- Revocable Trust
- Settlor
- Surcharge
- Testamentary Capacity
- Testamentary Trust
- Testator, Testatrix
- Trustee
- Trustor
- Undue Influence

Questions and Case Problems

1. Michael Uliscni died, survived by his only child, Holly, who was born out of wedlock. By court order Holly had been declared Uliscni's daughter. When Uliscni's will was drawn, Uliscni told his attorney that he had no children. The attorney then drafted the following clause, which was included in the will: "I do hereby specifically disinherit any and all persons who are or claim to be my heirs at law." Apparently, Uliscni and Holly had no personal relationship at all. Holly claims to be a pretermitted heir. What factors would a judge consider in evaluating her claim? 372 N.W.2d 759

2. Herschel Allgood, who lived in California, asked his mother, Aletha, to arrange for him to purchase a specific plot of land in Mississippi. He intended eventually to move back to Mississippi and live on the land. Aletha took the property in her own name; when Herschel sent monthly mortgage payments, Aletha cashed the checks and made payments herself. Eventually, Aletha and Herschel had a falling out, and Herschel now sues, claiming that a constructive trust should be imposed

on the property to his benefit. Aletha claims that since record title was taken by her in her name, and she made all payments on the mortgage, the record title stands. What result? 473 So.2d 416

3. Why it is advisable for a person who has signed a will to review that will periodically?

4. Why might a person want to avoid having her property pass under her will or according to the intestate succession laws, and how can this goal be achieved? If a decedent's property does not pass through probate, is that property also ignored for federal estate tax purposes? Explain.

5. Jones is a widower who has two adult children, Allen and Robert. He decides to write his own will, and in the will he wants to disinherit Allen, leave half of his estate to Robert, and leave the other half of his estate to a charity. Jones begins typing a document reflecting these wishes, but the typewriter jams after he has typed the first paragraph, and he writes out the rest of it by hand. He then signs and dates the document. Later that day Jones has both Allen and Robert sign the document as attesting witnesses, but he neglects to inform either son that the document is his will. Six months later Jones dies, and the document is discovered. Allen, Robert, and the charity each claim one half of Jones' estate. How should the estate be divided, and why? Include in the answer any assumptions you have made about the governing state law.

6. The trust property held by a trustee includes 100 shares of Intex Corporation. The trust agreement requires the trustee to distribute trust income each year to the beneficiaries, and it gives the trustee full discretion in allocating receipts and expenses between principal and income. In 1983 Intex declares a two-for-one stock split, with the result that the trustee receives an additional 100 shares of Intex stock. The trustee allocates the new shares to principal, and one of the beneficiaries petitions the court for relief. He argues that the shares should be allocated to income and distributed to him and the other beneficiaries. Should the court interfere with the trustee's action? Why or why not? Would your answer be different if the trust agreement were silent on the matter of allocation? Why?

7. Wilma created a living trust under which she was to receive all trust income until she died. The trustee, a bank, was also authorized to "invade the principal" (make distributions to Wilma out of the trust principal) at the bank's discretion. On Wilma's death, trust income and, at the trustee's discretion, principal are to be paid to Stanley, Wilma's son. On Stanley's death, the trust is to terminate, and the trust property is to be distributed in equal shares to those of Wilma's eight nieces and nephews listed on a separate schedule to be given to the trustee. Two years after creating the trust Wilma signed a will in which general legacies were made to one niece and one nephew, the others not being mentioned, and Stanley was named as the residuary legatee. Wilma died recently, and the trustee never received the separate schedule indicating the trust remaindermen. The trustee now petitions the court for instructions as to the proper interpretation of the trust agreement. Specifically, the trustee wants to know to whom it will be transferring the trust property after Stanley's death. (a) Why would the trustee seek resolution of this question now, even though the trust will not terminate until the unknown future date of Stanley's death? (b) How should the court answer the trustee's question? Why?

8. Your great-aunt Emily was 94 when she signed her first and last will two years ago. At the time, Emily lived in a rest home and had a nurse to assist her in most of her activities. You visited Emily regularly and talked with her. Usually she

recognized you and could carry on a rational conversation, but at times you had to identify yourself, and conversation on those days was difficult. From time to time Emily got her relatives' names mixed up, and she often seemed to be able to recall early events in her life with greater clarity than later ones. Emily died recently, and you discover that in the will she named you as her personal representative and principal beneficiary. Emily's only other heirs are Enid, her niece, and Joe, her nephew. Both Enid and Joe are to receive small bequests under the will, and neither is happy about it. Nevertheless, you offer the will for probate, and Enid and Joe promptly contest it. (a) What is the likely basis of Enid and Joe's claim? (b) What do Enid and Joe stand to gain by contesting the will? (c) As the proponent, what facts do you want to have brought out at the probate hearing? Why? (d) Do Enid and Joe have anything to lose by contesting the will? Explain.

9. Lisa, a widow, has a son, Ralph, and a daughter, Nancy, but she sees little of them since they do not live nearby. Lisa has no other close relatives. For a number of years Lisa has entrusted the management of her property to Maurice, her attorney and advisor. Maurice suggests that Lisa should have a will. After considering the matter, Lisa decides to leave most of her estate to Nancy, with small bequests to Ralph and Maurice. Maurice, who is to be Lisa's personal representative, attempts to convince Lisa that Nancy is unworthy of her mother's bounty because of her immoral lifestyle and radical political views, but Lisa holds firm. She instructs Maurice to draft a will for her signature. Maurice does so, but he intentionally reverses the status of Ralph and Nancy so that Ralph is named as the principal beneficiary. Lisa signs the typed will without reading it, and all required formalities are observed. Soon afterward Lisa dies. How should Lisa's estate be distributed? Why? How, if at all, would your answer differ if Lisa had read the will before signing it?

10. Garfield signed a formal will in which he named his cousin, Odie, the principal beneficiary, and in which he specifically disinherited his son, Nermal. Later, Garfield had a change of heart and decided to substitute Jon, his friend and protege, as the principal beneficiary. Garfield handwrote and signed a codicil making the change, and he sent the document to his attorney with instructions to have it typed. Two days later, while on his way to the attorney's office to sign the typed codicil, Garfield was run over by a truck and killed. Odie and Nermal are Garfield's only surviving relatives. Who, among Odie, Jon, and Nermal, will receive all or the bulk of Garfield's estate? Why?

PART EIGHT

Insurance

Introductory Comments

Insurance is one of the largest industries in the United States. Billions of dollars are spent in this country every year on insurance to protect businesses and individuals from the various risks of loss.

The business of insurance is conducted by large corporations operating in this country on a nationwide basis. Despite the national scope and range of the insurance industry, the regulation of this industry has been left largely to the states. The federal government does regulate special areas of insurance, such as securities issued by insurance companies, but it is prevented by law from intervening in the industry's purely intrastate functions. The states retain the power to charter insurance companies, oversee rates, fix the terms of insurance policies, regulate agents and brokers, and monitor a host of other activities undertaken by the insurance industry.

Although the concept of insurance evolved to protect commercial and individual endeavors and could therefore be written in any form, most insurance is now issued in standard form policies written by the insurance companies themselves. These policies are drafted by experts experienced in providing an apparently wide range of coverage tempered by countless exclusions. It is no accident, therefore, that the complex language of most insurance policies is largely incomprehensible to the typical policyholder. A facetious remark about insurance policies that "the front page giveth but the back page taketh away" is neither inaccurate nor inappropriate.

For most individuals insurance represents, after the purchase of a home, perhaps the next largest investment or expenditure they will make during their lifetime. For most businesses, insurance is a key item that must be carefully planned to protect the owners and their assets from risk of loss or liability. For these reasons, insurance is one of the few subject areas that must be discussed and analyzed as a separate unit within business law as a whole.

Chapters 41 and 42 introduce the law of insurance. Chapter 41 focuses on the concept of insurance, the types of risks for which insurance can be purchased, the nature of the insurance business, and how the industry is regulated. In Chapter 42, the various types of commercial, medical, liability, and homeowners' policies are discussed and analyzed. These two chapters provide a solid foundation on which the prudent, well-informed businessperson can base decisions to purchase business and personal insurance.

41 Introduction to the Law of Insurance

41:1 Nature of Insurance

In essence, insurance is an agreement by which one party (the insurer) for a consideration (the premium) promises to pay money to another (the insured or the beneficiary) if a specified event takes place. The event is usually one that causes either (1) the death or injury of a person or (2) the damage, loss, or destruction of property. The written instrument that sets forth the contract of insurance is the policy. As a rule, insurance companies use a standard form of insurance policy for the various types of insurance they offer. Amendments, additions, or deletions to the standard policy are called endorsements or *riders*. In the case of conflicting provisions, an endorsement or rider prevails over a contrary policy.

An insurance contract can be entered into only by someone capable of contracting under insurance law. In the absence of a statute to the contrary, insurance contracts are like other contracts in regard to the capacity of the parties to the contract. Therefore, any individual adult or association of individual adults can make a contract for insurance on property. Similarly, any business has the power to insure the lives of its key employees or officers whose duties and responsibilities are such that a financial loss to the business would result from their death.

Even if a person who wants insurance is insurable or otherwise eligible for insurance, the insurer retains the power to choose with whom it will do business. Any insurance company can decline to issue or renew a policy for any reason it deems proper. However, many states have enacted antidiscrimination statutes that prevent insurers from refusing to issue or renew policies on the basis of an applicant's race, national origin, occupation, age, residence, or similar characteristics. Some statutes also prohibit the cancellation of insurance policies except for nonpayment of premiums or, in regard to automobile insurance, for the loss of a driver's license or vehicle registration.

 An insured can lose the right to collect insurance benefits from an insurance company if he fails to meet his obligations under the insurance policy. These obligations include providing adequate information about the insured person or thing, paying premiums on time, promptly notifying the insurance company about losses covered by the insurance, and cooperating with the insurance agent when a claim is made.

41:2 Kinds of Insurance

It is not unusual for a business to have several insurance policies at the same time to protect against the common risks associated with the operation of the business. There are so many kinds of insurance available today that protection can be bought against almost any conceivable risk or loss. Because risks and losses are always present in the conduct of business or during the course of an individual's lifetime, insurance has become a major planning and preventive tool. It can maintain the integrity or continuity of a business or the assets of an individual when loss occurs.

Consider a hypothetical corporation, BB&S, Inc., that manufacturers electronic games in California. Bill and Jill Brooks and Ken Smith own all the corporation's stock, in equal shares. Most of the electronic components used by BB&S in the manufacture of its games are made out of state or are imported from abroad. The company employs 50 workers in its plant, which was recently expanded and remodeled. During the past year, the company was plagued by a run of bad luck that would have driven ordinary mortals out of business:

(1) Components imported from abroad were lost at sea, while another shipment of components from New York was destroyed when the plane in which they were being transported crashed.

(2) It was discovered that the title to the property purchased by BB&S for its plant expansion was defective. The company was forced to pay an additional sum to perfect its title.

(3) A fire at the BB&S plant caused the company to shut down operations for two weeks. As a result, the company suffered considerable loss of profits.

(4) Vandals broke into the BB&S warehouse and stole 25 electronic games and caused $50,000 worth of damage to the building itself.

(5) A visitor to the plant slipped on a silicon chip, cracked her head, and broke both arms and a leg. She required immediate hospitalization and emergency surgery.

(6) The bookkeeper employed by BB&S embezzled $10,000 to pay gambling debts.

(7) The driver of a BB&S delivery truck negligently struck another vehicle, causing injuries to that vehicle's driver. The BB&S truck, while being driven back to the plant, was hit by an uninsured motorist.

(8) Ken Smith became very apprehensive about illness after his brother died, although a physical examination showed that Ken was in perfect health. In turn, Bill and Jill became concerned that they would have no money to purchase Ken's interest in the company should he suddenly die.

(9) Three employees of BB&S were injured on the job due to unrelated work-site hazards.

(10) All 50 employees went out on strike for two weeks, demanding that BB&S improve safety conditions at the plant.

(11) A purchaser of a BB&S game suffered severe burns when he tried to extinguish a fire that broke out in the game due to a short circuit.

(12) Bill Brooks suffered a concussion after being hit with a baseball bat during a practice session of the company's softball team.

All of the business activities, risks, or losses included in the above example can be covered by insurance. Of course, there are many other kinds of insurance regularly used by both businesses and individuals that are designed to cover peculiar needs or activities. Other less common forms of insurance can also be obtained to meet unusual or uncommon risks. Clearly, insurance coverage is limited only by the ingenuity or creativity of the potential insureds and by the willingness of an insurer to accept the risks.

The most common and widely used kinds of insurance are life, health, automobile, and property insurance. These types are discussed briefly below.

Life Insurance　Life insurance is essentially a contract to pay a specified sum, in a lump sum or in installments, either to the person named as the *beneficiary* or to the estate of the insured when the insured dies. Among the kinds of life insurance available are (1) ordinary life, (2) limited-payment life, and (3) term life. Under an *ordinary, or straight, life insurance policy,* the insured must pay premiums throughout his or her life. A limited payment policy requires that premiums be paid during a limited period, such as 10, 15, or 20 years, or until the death of the insured, whichever occurs first. *Term insurance* continues only for a stated period, usually five years. Under level term policies, the benefits payable on the insured's death remain the same—or level—during the term of the policy. The policy can be renewed for additional periods up to age 65, at a higher premium with each renewal since the risk of death increases with the age of the insured. Under decreasing or reducing term policies, the benefits payable gradually decline during the term of the policy. For example, the face value of a policy purchased by a 20-year-old person would decrease through-out his life to zero at age 65. The annual premiums would remain constant because the increased risk of death as the insured ages is offset by the decline in face value of the insurance.

One type of decreasing term insurance is what is known as *credit life insurance.* This is carried by a debtor on his life in connection with a specific credit transaction, and the creditor is named as the beneficiary. The debtor pays the premium, as part of his cost of obtaining the credit. Since the purpose of credit life insurance is to make sure that the creditor is paid, the amount of insurance starts out as the amount of the debt and is reduced as the debt is paid off in installments.

Many life insurance policies include investment features in addition to providing for the payment of benefits when the insured dies. For example, an ordinary life insurance policy with a savings feature allows an insured to borrow against his policy or surrender it for a cash payment. The policy's cash surrender value and the amount that can be borrowed against the policy depend on the total amount of the premium payments that have been made. Endowment policies are another form of investment through insurance. Under this type of policy an insurer pays the insured a fixed sum as guaranteed income when he attains a specified age. If the insured dies before the termination of the endowment period, payments are made to the beneficiaries.

Accident and Health Insurance   Accident insurance covers accidental injury or death from specified perils and under stated conditions. Health, medical, and hospitalization insurance is designed to pay at least part of an insured's expenses that arise from sickness, disability, and hospitalization.

Property Insurance   *Property insurance* covers a great variety of risks. The most common is fire. Fire insurance is a contract by which the insurer agrees to pay the insured a specified amount for loss of or damage to designated property caused by fire. It may include other kinds of insurance as well. Most states have what is known as the standard fire policy, which is a standard contract of insurance prescribed by statute. Frequently, fire insurance policies also insure against damage from (1) wind, hail, and other forces of nature; (2) smoke; and (3) faulty plumbing or plumbing fixtures.

Another kind of property insurance is burglary, robbery, and malicious mischief insurance. It is designed to protect the insured from loss resulting from those crimes.

Title insurance covers the risk or loss due to a defect in the title to property (see Chapter 35).

 A businessperson can protect her business by carrying business interruption insurance and strike or labor dispute insurance to insure against losses that arise from these events. She can also obtain fidelity insurance to insure against losses due to embezzlement or other dishonest acts by employees.

Liability Insurance   Liability insurance is designed to indemnify the insured against liability, loss, or damage on account of the specific acts, conduct, or conditions specified in the policy. For example, products liability insurance protects the producer or manufacturer of goods against losses that result from damages claims filed by users of the goods. The hazards covered by such a policy are usually described as accidents arising out of the handling or use of goods or products manufactured, sold, or distributed by the insured.

Several distinct classes of risks are frequently covered in the same policy. For example, the typical automobile insurance policy covers not only the car but also liability to third persons in connection with the use of the car. Thus, an automobile insurance policy might include (1) "bodily injury" (personal injury) and property damage liability insurance, which protects against personal injuries or property damage sustained by third persons; (2) collision insurance, which protects against damage to the insured vehicle regardless of fault; (3) "comprehensive insurance," which protects the insured from losses due to theft of or certain damage to the vehicle; and (4) uninsured motorist protection, which protects the insured against bodily injuries caused by an uninsured or hit-and-run driver. Automobile insurance can also include medical payments coverage, which provides for accident-related medical and hospital expenses of the insured or any occupant of his car.

No-fault Insurance *No-fault insurance,* although only recently instituted for automobiles, is not a recent concept. No-fault insurance has been adopted by every state, as well as by the federal government. It takes the form of workers' compensation, unemployment insurance, and Social Security.[1] In the last ten years, various no-fault automobile insurance systems have been adopted by approximately 25 states. Under these plans, payments for automobile accident losses are made to injured parties without a determination of fault. Although details of no-fault insurance vary considerably from state to state, the fundamental concept is that an injured person can recover at least some compensation directly from his own insurance company (or from the government, under some plans), instead of having to wait for a determination of fault or legal responsibility for an accident and then collect accordingly. Most plans eliminate or curtail the payment of benefits for general damages such as pain and suffering. However, most no-fault plans *do* retain conventional tort liability as the basis for compensation in cases of serious injury.

Types of Insurance Policies A specific type of policy can be obtained once a person has decided on the kind of insurance needed. Available policies can be classified as being (1) open, (2) valued, (3) commercial block, (4) running, (5) floater, and (6) master.

An open, or unvalued, insurance policy sets forth only a description of the property covered under the policy. The insurer is obligated to pay the actual value of the property up to but not exceeding the stated policy limits.

EXAMPLE: A farmer buys a cotton crop insurance policy. The policy does not fix a value on the insured crop but only provides that (1) the insurer's liability shall not exceed the amount set out in the application for insurance and (2) the amount of insurance depends on the average price per unit actually received for cotton harvested or on the average daily cotton exchange quotations for a specified six-month period. This insurance policy, which does not carry a specific value, is an open policy.

In contrast, a valued policy is one in which the parties have agreed on the value of the insured property in the event of future loss, or the value is fixed by state statute.

A *commercial block policy* insures against several basic but different types of risk as to commercial property. These risks include fire, theft, burglary, water damage, and liability.

A running policy provides continuous or successive insurance that will vary from time to time as to the amount of coverage. This type of policy is used to

---

[1] Workers' compensation is discussed in Chapter 50.

cover an insured's inventory that fluctuates in quantity (and hence value) from day to day. Often associated with a running policy is a floater policy. The distinctive feature of a floater policy is that the insured property is covered as it is moved from one place to another. Thus, for example, a merchant's running policy would cover inventory while it is in the store. However, the merchant might have to obtain a floater policy to cover specific inventory items that are moved elsewhere, as would occur when customers are allowed to remove items from the store to try them out before buying them.

Often, an insured's business or profession requires several policies of insurance of the same type, covering different risks. In such situations a master policy is used. Master policies contain certain general terms, which are incorporated by reference in certificates of insurance issued later. Using a master policy avoids the specific inclusion of detailed policy provisions and general terms in each subsequently issued certificate.

A common example of the use of a master policy is *group insurance*, which is the coverage of a number of individuals by a single policy. Group policies for life or medical insurance are a common fringe benefit of most businesses. The premiums may be paid in whole or in part by the employer. In group insurance the general practice is to issue individual certificates based on a master policy. The master policy itself insures nothing; only the combined terms of the master policy and the certificate of insurance constitute the insurance contract.

The law applicable to group insurance differs from that governing individual policies. For example, the group insurer has no duty to check individually the insurability of each person in a group policy. An insured is bound by the provisions stated in the master policy and not necessarily in the certificate of insurance. Ordinarily, group life insurance is written as term insurance and the premiums are adjusted annually based on each year's experience. Group policies usually limit an employee's coverage to the time or duration of employment.

 Employees are often concerned about continuing group coverage after they terminate their employment. Most group policies provide conversion to individual coverage. It is important that both the employer and the departing employee know how and when conversion can be made. An employer should also ascertain the deadline for a departing employee to apply for conversion. An employer who fails to give timely and accurate information on how and when to take advantage of a conversion privilege can be liable for lost benefits.

Reinsurance   To protect against huge potential losses under existing insurance policies, most insurers take out what is in effect insurance on their own insurance. This system is known as *reinsurance*. It is a common practice in the insurance industry. Through reinsurance, insurers contract with other companies (reinsurers) for indemnification for all or part of their potential policy losses which might have to be paid under original insurance contracts. In this manner, insurance companies reduce their potential liabilities and apportion risks of loss.

As with other types of insurance, the liability of the reinsurer depends on the terms of the reinsurance contract. In most states, reinsurance contracts and the business of reinsurance are strictly regulated by law. Normally, a reinsurance policy covers the same time period as the original insurance policy that it reinsures. Because reinsurance is primarily an indemnity system, a reinsurer is not liable unless the insurer actually pays an insured's claim.

Reciprocal Insurance *Reciprocal insurance* is a system in which individuals, partnerships, or corporations, none of which is an insurance company, agree to indemnify each other against certain kinds of losses. The participants, who are referred to as reciprocal insurers, all contribute money to a fund that is maintained for paying claims. Each reciprocal insurer thus becomes both an insurer and an insured at the same time. The practice of creating reciprocal insurance arrangements is limited mostly to businesses that would otherwise have to pay prohibitively large premiums for needed insurance. By use of reciprocal insurance, the businesses can obtain the insurance coverage they need. If there is money left in the fund after the expiration of the indemnity period agreed on, the businesses also share in the distribution of the fund.

41:3 Insurance Companies

In practically all states, statutes have been enacted which, while varying widely in their terms and provisions, provide elaborate systems for the formation and regulation of insurance companies. An insurance company has only the powers that are conferred by one of these statutes. The corporate powers of a life insurance company organized under the laws of one state, for example, cannot be enlarged by the laws of any other state in which the company may be permitted to do business.

A company organized to transact insurance can carry out its activities in the usual and necessary manner as governed by its charter or articles of incorporation (see Chapter 45). For example, an insurance company that is chartered to insure all kinds of property against fire or other casualty can insure against loss by burglary. However, it cannot engage in a transaction or business that is not expressly permitted by its charter and not reasonably incidental to the purposes for which it is organized.

Types of Insurance Companies In general, there are three kinds of insurance companies: stock, mutual, and mixed. A stock insurance company is a corporation in which the initial capital investment is made by subscribers to the stock. The business is then conducted by a board of directors elected by its stockholders, and the distribution of earnings or profits as between stockholders and policyholders is determined by the board of directors. A stock insurance company has also been tersely defined as one in which stockholders contribute all the capital, pay all the losses, and take all the profits!

A mutual insurance company is a cooperative enterprise whose members (the policyholders) maintain a dual relationship with the company: They are both insurers and insureds. Not only do they contribute to the payment of losses but they are also entitled to receive payment in case of death or other loss and to share in the company's profits. By a system of premiums or assessments, the members contribute to a fund from which losses and liabilities are paid. After these payments are made, any profits from this fund are divided among the members in proportion to their interest.

Policyholders in mutual companies are not generally regarded as stockholders of such companies. Thus, an important difference between stock companies and mutual insurance companies is that stockholders of stock companies have the legal right to elect directors and officers while members of a mutual company do not have that right.

Mixed companies, as the term implies, possess the characteristics of both of the other two types.

There are other types of insurance organizations, more limited in scope, that must be mentioned. These are rating bureaus and advisory organizations. Their functions are distinct from those of regular insurance companies, and they are generally regulated by state statutory provisions applicable exclusively to them. A rating organization exists for the purpose of establishing rates, rating plans, or rating systems. These rates, plans, or systems are then used by insurance companies in establishing the premiums they will charge. An advisory organization prepares forms, makes underwriting rules, or collects and furnishes loss and other statistical information to insurers or rating organizations. An advisory organization acts only in an advisory capacity; it does not establish rates. An insurer can be a member of a rating or an advisory organization and participate in its management. It can also subscribe to the services of rating or advisory organizations of which it is not a member.

Lloyd's of London   At this point it is appropriate to discuss the well-known *Lloyd's of London*, which differs from other insurance companies in a fundamental way. Lloyd's is the oldest insurance organization in existence. The key word here is "organization," for Lloyd's is not a single company. Instead, insurance is written on all types of risks—except ordinary life insurance—by a syndicate or group of individuals, each of whom is personally liable to the extent of the risk assumed. The total membership of Lloyd's exceeds 18,000 wealthy private individuals from 60 countries organized into 436 syndicates. The syndicates range in size from a few individuals to several hundred. Business is offered to these syndicates by approximately 265 brokerage firms that scout around the world for insurance opportunities. For example, assume that an oil company wants to insure its new multimillion-dollar oil tanker. The risk of loss is so great that no single insurer will assume the whole risk. Through Lloyd's, the tanker can be insured by members of a syndicate, and each member becomes potentially liable only for a portion of the tanker's value if it is lost.

41:4   Insurance Agents and Brokers

The business of buying and selling insurance is conducted primarily by insurance agents, brokers, and other persons who act as representatives of buyers or sellers. An *insurance agent* is a person authorized to represent an insurer in dealing with third persons in matters relating to insurance. The agent owes a permanent allegiance to and sustains a continuing relationship with the insurance company he or she represents. There are various kinds of insurance agents; frequently, the term is defined by state statute.

In contrast, an *insurance broker* acts as a middleman between the insured and the insurer. The broker is not employed by a specific company but instead hires out to the public and solicits insurance business from the public.

The principles of the law of agency apply to the relationship between insurance companies and their agents.[2] An insurance company, like any other principal, is liable for the acts of its agents done within the scope of their authority.

Lazzara

v

Howard A. Esser, Inc.

604 F Supp 1205 (1985)

United States District Court, Northern District of Illinois

FACTS: Lazzara handled his insurance needs through Esser. In 1974 Esser recommended that Lazzara increase his automobile insurance coverage to $1 million, which Lazzara asked Esser to procure for him. Esser procured the insurance but inadvertently left a $150,000 "gap" between the primary insurance for $100,000 and the $250,000 deductible for the secondary coverage. When Lazzara sustained a judgment for $510,000, he had to pay the $150,000 gap. Lazzara sued the two companies that insured the loss, claiming Esser was their agent for whom they bear liability.

ISSUE: Was Esser an agent of the insurance companies or a broker?

RESULT: Esser was acting as a broker for Lazzara, not as an agent of the companies.

REASONING:

* * *

The Illinois courts have . . . defined an insurance broker as "one who procures insurance and acts as middleman between the insured and the insurer, and solicits insurance business from the public under no employment for any special company, but, having an order, places the insurance with the company selected by the insured, or, in the absence of any

---

[2] The general rights and liabilities of agents are discussed in Chapter 43.

selection by him, with the company selected by such broker." . . . An insurance agent, on the other hand, has a fixed and permanent relation to the company he represents and has certain duties and allegiances to such companies. . . .

Whether a person is an agent or a broker is determined by his acts or what he does. . . . A four-prong test has been developed to determine whose interest a broker is representing:

1. Who set him in motion first?
2. Who could control his actions?
3. Who pays him?
4. Whose interest was he to protect?

. . . Although the question of whether an insurance broker is the agent of the insured or insurer is generally one of fact, where the evidence shows clearly he is the agent of the insured, it becomes a question of law. . . .

In the present case, the documents before this Court clearly show that Esser was acting as Lazzara's broker for the purpose of procuring the insurance. As in [previous cases], Esser was set in motion by Lazzara. Also, Lazzara was the person who could control Esser's actions. It was Lazzara who ordered Esser to obtain the $1 million insurance policy. Esser was contacted and directed by Lazzara to protect the interests of Lazzara, not the insurers.

Moreover, that Esser received its commission checks from Aetna and Reliance is not a factor that supports Esser's assertion that it did not act as Lazzara's broker. The contracts between Esser and Aetna and Reliance provided that the commissions would be derived from the premiums paid by Lazzara, as required by Illinois law. . . . In fact, for at least the first premium payment, Lazzara paid Esser the premium, who in turn paid the insurance companies, *after* deducting its commission.

For renewal premiums, both insurance companies provided a plan whereby they would directly bill the insured and then pay Esser its commission out of the premiums received. Esser had admitted in its complaint that the policies were renewed through it. Even if Esser took advantage of this plan, however, the plan was merely one of convenience for both Esser and the insurers and does little to demonstrate that Esser was an agent for the insurers for the purpose of *procuring insurance.*

Furthermore, nothing in the pleadings or record justifies finding an agency relationship between Esser and the insurers for the relevant purpose at issue here, i.e., for the purpose of procuring and renewing insurance. Esser has given no evidence of a "fixed or permanent" relationship between itself and the insurers. . . . Esser was permitted to solicit from any potential insured it desired. Neither company placed restrictions on the number of carriers for which Esser could act as a broker. Neither company required that Esser broker a particular amount of business annually. Esser, and not the insurers, was responsible for the accounting and payment of premiums, and Esser was not paid a salary, but was compensated by commissions earned when insurance was purchased by an insured Esser had solicited. . . .

Rovner, District Judge.

41:5　Duty to Follow Instructions in Good Faith

Both an insurance agent and an insurance broker must act in good faith. They must confine their acts to the actual authority granted to them. For example, the insurance agent must obey her company's instructions and use due care and reasonable diligence in transacting the business entrusted to her. If an agent or broker departs from instructions or breaches the duties entrusted to him, he can be liable for losses sustained. Thus, if an insurance company, which is entitled under the terms of a policy to cancel or reduce a risk, directs its agent to cancel the policy but the agent fails to do so, the agent can be liable to the insurer for any amount that the insurer later has to pay under the policy.

The following case illustrates the general obligations of an insurance broker and the circumstances under which a broker or an insurance company can be held liable to an insured for the broker's acts that are beyond the scope of his authority. The same principles apply to agents.

Lewis

v

Michigan Millers Mut. Ins. Co.
228 A2d 803 (1967)
Connecticut Supreme Court

FACTS:　Lewis, plaintiff, obtained from Michigan Millers Mutual Insurance Company, defendant, a liability insurance policy covering premises Lewis owned on Dixwell Avenue in New Haven. After the policy had been issued, Lewis' insurance broker, Bretzfelder & Cahn, Inc., misconstrued certain instructions and transferred the policy coverage from the Dixwell Avenue property to other property Lewis owned, on Read Street. Later, Lewis was sued by a woman who claimed to have been injured on the Dixwell Avenue property. Lewis requested that the insurance company defend her, as it had agreed to do in the policy. The insurance company refused, asserting that at the request of Lewis' broker, it had transferred the policy coverage from the Dixwell Avenue property to the Read Street property. After the insurer refused to defend, the lawsuit against Lewis was eventually settled. In the present action, Lewis sought to recover from the insurer the amount of the settlement, plus the reasonable cost of her attorney's fee.

ISSUE: Did Cahn, the broker, have the authority to transfer the plaintiff's insurance coverage?

RESULT: No, Cahn lacked such authority.

REASONING:

*   *   *

When procuring insurance for a person such as the plaintiff, a broker becomes the agent of that person for that purpose. . . . Once that purpose is accomplished, however, and the insurance is procured, the agency relationship between the insured and the broker terminates, and the broker is without any authority to do anything which further affects the insured unless expressly or impliedly authorized by the insured to do so. . . .

From an application of the above principles to this case, it is apparent that, when Cahn sought and obtained the renewal policy for one year covering the Dixwell Avenue property, it acted as the plaintiff's agent. It is equally apparent that once the policy was issued, Cahn ceased to be the plaintiff's agent. At this point, in the absence of a new conferral of authority on Cahn by the plaintiff, Cahn could not affect the existing contract of insurance between the plaintiff and the defendant covering the Dixwell Avenue property. Some six months after the renewal policy had been issued and the agency relationship had ceased, the plaintiff notified Cahn that her mail was to be referred to the Read Street address. The finding is unclear as to whether the plaintiff, by this notification, intended to have Cahn in turn notify the defendant of this change of mailing address. Even if we assume, however, that it was the plaintiff's intention to once again utilize Cahn as her agent, this time for the limited purpose of having Cahn inform the defendant of the change of mailing address, this agency did not empower Cahn to procure a binding transfer of liability coverage from the Dixwell Avenue property to the Read Street property. Cahn was not expressly or impliedly authorized by the plaintiff to request such a transfer. Nor did it have the apparent authority to seek and obtain the transfer on the plaintiff's behalf. Apparent authority is that semblance of authority which a principal, through his own acts or inadvertences, causes or allows third persons to believe his agent possesses. . . . To fix the principal's liability for the agent's act, it must be shown either that the principal, by his own acts, causes the mistaken belief that the agent had the requisite authority or that the principal knowingly permitted the agent to engender that belief. . . . Also, of course, the third party must have acted in good faith on the false appearance created by the principal. . . . In the present case, the plaintiff did not hold Cahn out to the defendant as possessing the authority to obtain the endorsement, nor did she knowingly permit Cahn to act as having such authority. Indeed, the plaintiff did not even learn of Cahn's actions until the endorsement transferring coverage was a fait accompli. At that point she expressly protested the transfer. There is no evidence that the defendant relied on anyone other than Cahn before it issued the endorsement. In the absence of actual knowledge to the contrary, it was bound to know that Cahn's authority to represent the plaintiff had terminated six months earlier when the renewal policy was issued. . . . It was not justified in relying solely on Cahn's request to transfer the plaintiff's coverage. The "[a]pparent power of an agent is to be determined not by his own acts but by those of the principal." . . . Here, the plaintiff neither did anything nor knowingly allowed anything to be done which would justify the defendant's acquiescence to Cahn's request to issue the endorsement transferring coverage.

The facts found do not support the conclusion reached by the trial court that Cahn had the authority to procure the endorsement on behalf of the plaintiff. Thus, the endorsement did not deprive the plaintiff of insurance coverage on the Dixwell Avenue property. . . .

Thim, Associate Judge.

41:6 Duty to Procure Insurance

An insurance agent or broker must exercise good faith and reasonable diligence to procure insurance on the best terms obtainable. If an agent or broker is employed to keep up insurance, the failure to do so by either renewing an expired policy or properly maintaining an existing policy can render the agent or broker liable to the client for losses sustained. However, if insufficient information is given and, for that reason, no policy is procured, the agent or broker would not be liable for failing to procure insurance since there was actually no valid contract to procure. If insurance cannot be obtained, the agent or broker must notify the client within a reasonable time. Failure to do so can render the agent or broker liable for damages suffered by the client for lack of insurance.

The losses or damages that an aggrieved client can claim when an agent or broker fails to obtain insurance vary from state to state. In most states the damages are equal to the amount that would have been due under a policy had one been obtained. Where no loss occurs, the measure of damages is the amount paid as the premium.

The following case illustrates that, in some states, an agent or broker can be liable for any loss—even lost profits from the interruption of business—sustained when he fails to obtain insurance as he is supposed to do.

Joseph Forest Products, Inc.

v

Pratt

564 P2d 1027 (1977)

Oregon Supreme Court

FACTS: Joseph Forest Products requested Pratt, its insurance agent, to obtain fire insurance on a pole-treating plant. Pratt agreed to do so, and Joseph paid the required premium. Pratt failed to obtain the insurance. During the period in which coverage was supposedly in effect, Joseph's plant was damaged by fire. Joseph sued Pratt for damages to its plant, equipment, and inventory, as well as damages for lost profits. The trial court ruled that Pratt was liable only for the amount that would have been due under the insurance policy had it been obtained; it did not allow Joseph to recover consequential damages for lost profits.

ISSUE: Is Joseph Forest Products entitled to consequential damages against Pratt for Pratt's failure to procure insurance?

RESULT: Yes, to the extent the damage is provable and was foreseeable at the time of the application for the insurance.

REASONING:

*   *   *

An insurance agent or broker who agrees to procure insurance for another for a fee but fails to do so may be liable for any damage resulting from his omission. Liability may be based upon a breach of contract or upon negligence, or upon both, depending upon the particular circumstances of the case. Normally, causation requirements will limit any recovery to that which the plaintiff would have received through the insurer if coverage had been provided. However, if the plaintiff is able to prove that additional consequential damages resulted from the agent's failure to obtain coverage, he will then be entitled to recover those consequential damages as well. . . .

As a general rule the liability of the agent with respect to a loss, by reason of his breach of duty, is that which would have fallen on the company had the insurance been properly effected, *together with such other damages as proximately result from the breach*, and less the amount of unpaid premiums or cost of the insurance. . . . [Court's emphasis.]

An insurance broker is the agent of the insured in negotiating for a policy, and owes a duty to his principal to exercise reasonable skill, care, and diligence in effecting insurance. Thus he may be held liable where he has breached a contract to procure insurance for his principal. And while such broker is not obligated to assume the duty of procuring a policy, without consideration for his promise, he must exercise ordinary care in the performance of such duty when assumed, the promise to take the policy being a sufficient consideration. He is charged with the exercise of reasonable care and skill in making inquiries and obtaining information concerning the responsibility of the insurer with whom [he places] the risk, and is liable for *any loss* occasioned by such want of care. [Court's emphasis.]

If a broker or agent of the insured neglects to procure insurance, or does not follow instructions, or if the policy is void or materially defective, through the agent's fault, he is liable to his principal for any loss he may have sustained thereby. . . .

It is true that, as defendant points out, some courts have stated that agents and brokers will be liable for losses only up to the limits of the policy applied for. This statement is correct as a general rule because, even if he were insured, the plaintiff's losses would have been covered only to the extent of the policy limits. . . . However, the rule has no application to additional, consequential losses sustained, not by reason of the occurrence of the contingency insured against (such as fire, theft, etc.), but by reason of defendant's breach of contract or negligent failure to secure coverage (such as loss of profits due to unnecessary delay in obtaining reimbursement for the original loss). We can discern no reason for creating a special exception to normal liability concepts because the case involves an insurance agent. . . .

Howell, Justice.

Compensation   An insurance agent's right to compensation from an insurance company for selling and writing insurance depends on the terms of the contract existing between the agent and the company. Insurance brokers and agents have a general lien on all policies they procure for their principal—and on all money they receive on such policies—for payment of amounts owed to them for commissions, disbursements, and advances.

41:7   Regulation of Insurance Business

The power to organize an insurance company and conduct the insurance business is not a right. Rather, it is a privilege granted by each state, subject to certain conditions. The business of insurance is one that is affected with a public interest. As such, it is a proper subject of state regulation and control. Thus, each state can regulate the relations between insurer and insured, as well as the internal affairs of insurance companies operating within the state.

The power to regulate the insurance business is very broad. It extends to all persons seeking to engage in the insurance business. For example, state law can confine the business of insurance to corporations. State law can also prescribe reasonable conditions to the conduct of the insurance business by individuals as well as corporations.

Most states have enacted statutes that create regulatory entities, such as insurance boards, superintendents, or commissioners. These boards and officials regulate and supervise the transaction of insurance business to protect the public interest, make uniform rates, execute the insurance laws, and see that violations of the insurance laws are dealt with properly. In some states, the superintendent or commissioner of insurance is given the power to revoke, withhold, or refuse to renew an insurance company's license.

The states' right to regulate and control insurance companies includes the right to manage their dissolution. Indeed, if a company cannot financially continue its operations, it can be dissolved at the instance of the state. Once dissolution proceedings have commenced, or after expiration or forfeiture of an insurance company's charter, the company cannot legally issue an insurance policy. Many states permit the appointment of a receiver in proceedings for either (1) the liquidation and dissolution or (2) the rehabilitation or reorganization of an insurance company. The difficulties encountered in the forced liquidation or reorganization of insurance companies that have assets and liabilities in two or more states led to the adoption by many states of the Uniform Insurers Liquidation Act or statutes patterned after that act. The purpose of the uniform act is to secure equal treatment for all creditors regardless of the state in which they do business.

Federal Regulation of Insurance   For many years insurance was held not to constitute commerce within the meaning of the United States Constitution. Consequently, the industry was left relatively free from federal intervention even though business was conducted on an interstate basis. In 1944, however, the United States Supreme Court held that fire insurance transactions that cross state lines do constitute interstate commerce and are subject to regulation by Congress under the commerce clause. This decision[3] clearly represented a potential change in the regulation of the insurance industry. To nullify the decision, in effect, Congress enacted the McCarran–Ferguson Act [15 USC §§ 1011-1015]. By and large, the act limits the federal government's power to regulate the insurance industry.

 Although the federal government is precluded by the McCarran–Ferguson Act from regulating insurance, Congress can still regulate specific practices of the insurance industry through laws affecting *all* businesses and industries. For example, loans extended by insurance companies or certain insurance sales practices that involve credit must conform to the standards set forth in the federal truth in lending laws, as discussed in Chapter 28.

---

[3] *United States v South-Eastern Underwriters Asso.*, 322 US 533 (1944).

Key Concepts and Terms

- An insurance policy is a contract by which, in consideration of periodic payments called premiums, an insurer promises to pay the insured or a beneficiary a sum of money if an event specified in the policy occurs.
- Different types of insurance cover different risks. These risks include (1) an insured's death, accidental injury, or illness; (2) the damage or destruction of the insured's property; and (3) the insured's becoming liable to some other person.
- Insurance policies can be classified as being (1) open, (2) valued, (3) commercial block, (4) running, (5) floater, or (6) master.
- The three main types of insurance companies are stock companies, mutual companies, and mixed companies.
- The business of buying and selling insurance is primarily carried on by insurance agents and brokers. Agents are employed by and represent specific insurance companies. Brokers are not employed by specific companies; they hold themselves out for hire to and solicit insurance business from the public at large. Agents and brokers must act in good faith and must follow instructions given by their clients. Insurance companies are bound by all acts and contracts of their agents within the scope of their authority.
- The insurance industry is regulated primarily by state law. Specific matters that are regulated or controlled include premiums, provisions of insurance policies, and the conduct of insurance agents and brokers. Federal regulatory powers are limited by the McCarran–Ferguson Act.

- Beneficiary
- Commercial Block Policy
- Credit Life Insurance
- Group Insurance
- Insurance Agent
- Insurance Broker
- Lloyd's of London
- McCarran–Ferguson Act
- No-fault Insurance
- Ordinary (Straight) Life Insurance
- Property Insurance
- Reciprocal Insurance
- Reinsurance
- Rider
- Term Insurance

Questions and Case Problems

1. Consider the following statements:

a. "The liability insurance system that the automobile insurance companies have developed in the United States to deal with accidental loss and injuries does not work well. For years there have been complaints that automobile insurance company performance is unsatisfactory. Criticism extends from specific company practices, such as arbitrary and unfair cancellation and nonrenewal actions, to rejection of the basic premise—insurance against negligently caused losses—on which the present system of automobile insurance has been erected. The system is slow, incomplete, and expensive. The companies and organizations involved in furnishing this service to the public in many respects do a poor job."

b. "The basic difficulty with the present automobile insurance system is that the insured event is too complicated, turning as it does on legal liability. You can be paid for a traffic accident only by traversing tricky terrain. First you must claim against the other driver's insurance company. . . . Second, you must claim that the other driver was at fault and that you were free from fault. . . . Third, you must claim for a totally uncertain amount which includes not only your out-of-pocket loss for medical expenses and missed wages, but also payment for so-called pain and suffering."

In light of these criticisms should no-fault insurance be adopted by all states? Why? To what extent should tortfeasors—and thus their insurers—be liable for injuries and death caused by their negligence or willful misconduct?

2. Stoll, an insurance broker, contacts Collegiate Manufacturing with suggestions for additional insurance. Stoll advises Collegiate to protect itself against fire loss by a policy to provide coverage for the company's fluctuating inventory. Collegiate agrees and Stoll places the insurance. However, the policy insures the inventory only up to a maximum limit of liability that is less than its market value. Collegiate's president fails to read the policy and is thus unaware of the limitation. A fire subsequently occurs, causing $394,000 in damage, but Collegiate receives only partial payment of $280,000, the maximum due under the policy. Collegiate sues Stoll for $114,000—the excess of the loss over the payment—because of Stoll's alleged negligent failure to provide adequate coverage. Stoll denies any negligence and alleges as a defense Collegiate's contributory negligence in failing to advise itself of the protection under the policy. Stoll also asserts that in any case, the coverage that Collegiate thought had been provided is not available from any company Stoll represents. How should the case be decided?

3. Commercial Insurance, through its agent, Leonard, insures an automobile belonging to Ingalls. After issuing the policy, Commercial investigates Ingalls and learns that the automobile is used by Ingalls' son who is deemed by Commercial to be a poor risk. Commercial writes to Leonard, stating that it is canceling Ingalls' insurance policy; it also notifies Ingalls of the cancellation. However, Leonard tells Ingalls to disregard the cancellation and that the insurance is still in effect. Ingalls tells Leonard that if the insurance is not in effect, he will buy insurance elsewhere, but relying on Leonard's statements, Ingalls does not purchase other insurance. Later, the automobile is damaged. Commercial denies liability on the ground that it had previously canceled the policy. Is Ingalls entitled to recover under the policy? Is Leonard liable to Ingalls?

4. Often the situation arises in which a party has discussed insurance coverage with a broker and left the broker's office with the impression that insurance will be procured, when in fact it has not been procured and the insurance broker does not think sufficient instruction has been given. If a loss occurs, the uninsured customer attempts to hold the broker liable for failure to procure insurance. What kind of evidence of an undertaking would you want before holding a broker liable under those circumstances?

5. Burdette purchased "blanket" fire insurance policy for his restaurant and other buildings on the restaurant premises to cover up to $242,000 in loss. After the restaurant was destroyed, Burdette learned of the "coinsurance" clause in his contract, which limited coverage on any one building to 90% of the replacement value of the building. Burdette claims he did not know the building was not fully

covered by the "blanket" policy and seeks to hold the agent liable for the uncovered amount. Burdette admits he did not read the policy but claims he relied on the agent to procure full coverage. What result?

6. How does Lloyd's of London differ from other insurance companies?

7. In February 1968, a hot water heater owned by Karam exploded, damaging a leased building in which Karam was operating a Laundromat. Two actions for property damage were instituted against Karam and his liability insurer. The actions were settled for $18,500 with the insurer paying $10,000 and Karam paying $8,500. Karam then sued Darbonne, his insurance agent. When Karam had originally sought insurance, he had asked the agent to obtain property damage liability coverage for $100,000. Darbonne had intended to obtain insurance in this amount, but by mistake she had obtained only $10,000 coverage. The invoice sent to Karam by Darbonne billing for the property damage liability coverage indicated that the agent had obtained $100,000 in property damage liability coverage. Is the agent liable to Karam for her failure to obtain adequate liability insurance coverage? If so, in what amount?

8. DiMicco met with an employee of Buckingham-Wheeler Insurance Agency to discuss the placing of insurance on a 20-foot boat that was approximately eleven years old. After the meeting, the agency's employee advised DiMicco that he would insure the boat for $5,000. The employee did this despite the fact that he knew that the insurer would not issue a policy on a boat having a value of $5,000 or greater or a boat that was older than three years of age without a survey as to its condition. Some weeks after the meeting the boat was damaged in a storm and sank. DiMicco sought to recover for her loss. Can the insurance company deny coverage? Is the insurance agency liable to DiMicco? Is the agency liable to the insurance company? Who must pay for the loss?

9. Farmers Mutual issues an insurance policy to George Bechard in connection with George's ownership of a Chevrolet truck. The policy provides the usual liability coverage. It also provides for the payment of benefits to or for the benefit of any person who, while driving or riding in the truck, is killed or injured in an accident. However, a rider to the policy specifically states that accident insurance benefits will not be paid "for death while driving the truck in the course of a person's employment." Mutual's agent tells George that he "is covered" regardless of the circumstances under which he is driving the truck at any time. George is later killed in an accident that occurs while he is driving the truck in the course of his business. His widow claims the accidental death benefit under the policy, but Mutual denies liability, pointing to the rider. Is Mutual bound by the statement of its agent? Should George's widow recover the death benefit?

10. Myles buys a ferryboat at an auction for $2,850. He then seeks to insure it against loss. He knows that the former owner had insured the boat for $100,000. He also knows that other, similar ferries are quite valuable and that he bought his boat at a bargain price. Under these circumstances, is it proper to insure the vessel for $100,000? Should Myles disclose his purchase price to the insurer? Discuss.

42 The Insurance Contract and Coverage

42:1 Formation and Validity of Insurance Contracts

The relationship between an insurer and an insured is purely contractual. A contract of insurance is a voluntary contract, and competent persons can make whatever contract for insurance they see fit to make, provided the contract does not contravene any law or public policy.

A contract of insurance—or any renewal of it—must be assented to by both parties either in person or through their agents. As with other contracts, there must be a meeting of the minds of the parties on the essential terms and elements of the contract. These terms include (1) the subject matter to be insured, (2) the risk insured against, (3) the commencement and period of the risk undertaken by the insurer, (4) the amount of insurance, and (5) the premium and time at which it is to be paid.

The first step in creating an insurance contract is applying for insurance. The application is an offer or proposal for a contract; it must be accepted by the insurer before a contract of insurance—the policy—is issued. Insurance companies are not compelled to accept every application presented and can stipulate what terms and for what period of time the risks will be accepted. An acceptance makes the insurance binding and effective. Ordinarily, notice of acceptance of the application is sent to the applicant. Neither the delivery of an insurance policy nor the prepayment of the premium is necessary for a valid contract unless the parties so stipulate. Frequently, however, especially in the case of *life insurance*, prepayment of the initial premium is required. When this is the case, an insurance contract is not completed, nor is the risk assumed by the insurer, until payment is made.

Pending formal acceptance of an application, an insurance company can issue a contract for temporary insurance. Temporary insurance covers someone or something for a reasonable time until either a policy can be written or its issuance approved. Temporary insurance is usually evidenced by a binding slip or an interim receipt referred to as a *binder*. A binder differs from an application for insurance in that a binder is itself a contract, albeit an informal one. In view of its informal nature, a binder need not express all the elements of a contract, such as the rate of premium or even the name of the insurer, and it can be an oral agreement.

Although it is usual to name the insured in an insurance policy, it is not essential; the insured can be described in ways other than by name. So long as an insurance company is not misled as to the applicant's identity, it cannot avoid the risk by claiming that the name or description of the insured is not that stated in the policy. For example, the validity of a renewal policy of fire insurance issued to a corporation is not affected by the fact that the insured corporation has changed its name without the insurer's knowledge.

The risk under an insurance policy usually attaches as of the time agreed on or understood by the parties. "Attachment of the risk" refers to the time after which the insurer will be liable for loss or damage under a policy. In some circumstances, the time at which a contract of insurance becomes effective—and the risk attaches—is regulated by statute.

An insurance policy must generally specify the period during which the insurance is to continue. If an exact time period is specified, that specification governs. If no time is expressly indicated, surrounding circumstances can be considered to determine the duration of coverage.

The following case illustrates that there is no contract for insurance until the basic requirements of contract have been satisfied.

McKenzie & Mouk, Inc.

v

Hall

467 So2d 1220 (1985)

Court of Appeal of Louisiana, Second Circuit

FACTS: In December 1981 Hall's sister, Green, went to McKenzie & Mouk Insurance Agency and inquired about auto insurance for Hall. An employee quoted a premium price of $99.00 for six months. The employee filled out a binder-application form, which Green did not sign. Green gave the agency a check for $99.00 and received a receipt. The application was submitted to an insurance company that checked Hall's driving record and advised the agency that it would require a premium of $343.00 for the six-month period. The agency wrote Mrs. Green a note explaining this and advised her to "Please call us and advise us if you wish to keep the policy and we will mail it on to you." Green claims she called and said she did not want the insurance. The agency claims it never heard from her. Now it sues for the additional fee plus late charges.

ISSUE: Is Green obligated to pay the additional charge?

RESULT: No. Neither Green nor Hall ever agreed to pay the additional charge for the insurance.

REASONING:

*   *   *

An application for coverage merely constitutes a contractual offer, and the insurance contract is not completed until the application is accepted by the insurer. . . . When it was determined by the insurance company to whom the application was submitted that a higher premium should be charged, the insurance agency, apparently recognizing that there was no agreement for the issuance of a policy at a higher premium, wrote Mrs. Green asking her if she wished to keep the policy and, if so, to so advise the agency. In effect, the agency was making a new offer or counteroffer to the defendant to issue a policy at a higher premium. As this court stated in *Rigdon v. Marquette Casualty Company,* . . . while a contract of insurance ordinarily is effected by an offer by the one seeking insurance and an acceptance by the insurance company, such is not always the case:

> An offer or a counteroffer to insure may be made by an insurer to a proposed insured. Thus, where the company, instead of accepting an application for insurance, makes a counteroffer or proposition, this may be accepted or rejected by the applicant, or proposed, insured at his pleasure. Until accepted, the proposal does not become a contract. *The acceptance of such a proposal must be shown by some act binding on the party accepting beyond a mere mental resolution to that effect.* (Emphasis Added)

Whether Mrs. Green specifically advised the agency that she did not want the policy or whether Mrs. Green never contacted the agency is immaterial. In either event, the new offer or counteroffer was never accepted by the defendant or his representative. There was never any agreement on the part of the defendant or his representative to pay the higher premium. The fact that the insurance company elected to issue a policy at a unilaterally established premium cannot serve to establish any obligation on the part of the defendant to pay the higher premium.

The defendant paid the premium he agreed to pay and is liable for nothing more. . . .

Hall, Judge.

42:2   Insurable Interest

An *insurable interest* is necessary to the validity of an insurance contract. If no insurable interest exists, the contract is void. A distinction must be made between property insurance and life insurance in determining what amounts to an insurable interest. In regard to property, anyone has an insurable interest who derives a benefit from the property's existence or would suffer loss from its destruction. This is true whether or not the insured has title to, a lien on, or possession of the property. For example, a contractor who agrees to construct or repair a building for a stipulated price has an insurable interest in the building, as do persons furnishing materials for use in the work. The owner of the building has an insurable interest to the extent of its value, even though the loss, in the absence of insurance, would fall on the contractor.

Life or Health Insurance   Every person has an insurable interest in his own life. He may insure it in good faith for the benefit of his estate or any person. However, a person cannot have an insurable interest in the life of another unless he has a reasonable expectation of benefit or advantage from the continuance of the other's life. In all cases there must be a reasonable relation between the parties—pecuniary or blood or affinity—that gives rise to an expectation of benefit or advantage from the continuance of the insured's life. Clearly, the essential element in determining whether an insurable interest exists in a life or health insurance policy is good faith. It should not be obtained for the purpose of speculating on the hazard of a life in which the insured has no interest.

Key Employee Insurance   It is generally recognized that a business has an insurable interest in the lives of its key officers or employees and has the power to obtain insurance on their lives. For example, a small, closely held corporation can purchase *key employee insurance* and name the company as beneficiary with the intention that it will use the proceeds to purchase the insured's interest in the firm. The mere existence of the relationship of employer and employee is not sufficient in itself to give the employer an insurable interest. It must further be shown that there is a reasonable expectation that the employer would realize a substantial pecuniary gain through the continued life of the employee, or sustain a substantial pecuniary loss if the employee dies.

Credit Life Insurance   A creditor has an insurable interest in the life of his debtor, at least for the amount of the debt and the cost of carrying the insurance on the debtor's life. This interest is subject to the limitation that the amount of the policy must not be so disproportionate to the amount of the debt (plus the cost of carrying the insurance) as to justify the conclusion that the policy is essentially a wagering or speculative one. For example, a credit life policy for $3,000 is really a *wagering policy* and is void if the insured's debt is only $70.

The following case discusses and analyzes the concept of insurable interest in life insurance. It explores most of the relationships in which an insurable interest can exist. Consider whether the reasoning of the court is persuasive.

Mutual Savings Life Ins. Co.
v
Noah
282 So2d 271 (1973)
Alabama Supreme Court

FACTS: Donald Noah was named as the beneficiary in three policies of insurance issued by the Mutual Savings Life Insurance Company on the life of his brother, William Noah. The policies were in force when William died, but the insurer refused to pay the amounts due except for partial payment under a burial insurance policy. It contended that Donald Noah lacked an insurable interest in the life of his deceased brother. Donald filed a declaratory judgment action against the insurance company seeking to have the court declare that the insurer was obligated to pay the death benefits and the balance of the burial benefits prescribed under the policies, plus accidental death benefits provided in all three.

ISSUE: Is brotherhood a sufficient blood relationship to constitute an insurable interest?

RESULT: Yes. The brother–brother relationship is sufficient to support an insurable interest.

REASONING:

*   *   *

Several reasons have been assigned as the basis for the insurable interest requirement, both of which are grounded upon public policy considerations: a policy taken out by one for his own benefit on the life of another, in whom he has no insurable interest is, in substance, a wagering contract; and such a policy may hold out a temptation to the beneficiary to hasten by improper means the death of the insured. . . .

Certain blood relationships have been held sufficient, in and of themselves to negate the supposition that the beneficiary would take out such a policy for the purpose of wagering on the insured's death, or that such a policy would entice the beneficiary to take the insured's life, and in such cases the relationship alone is said to create an insurable interest. This is true notwithstanding the fact that the beneficiary may have no reasonable expectation of pecuniary advantage through the continued life of the insured or consequent loss by reason of his death, which would otherwise be required in order to find an insurable interest.

The relationship of husband and wife has been held to be sufficiently close to give either an insurable interest in the life of the other. . . . The parent–child relationship has been accorded the same status as that given to husband and wife. . . .

On the other hand, the following relationships have been held not to create an insurable interest on the basis of such relationship alone. Cousin and cousin; . . . the wife of his wife's brother . . . ; aunt and niece . . . ; aunt-in-law and niece . . . ; niece and uncle. . . .

The specific issue presented in the case under review is whether one has an insurable interest in the life of his brother by virtue of the relationship alone. While realizing that this issue is one of first impression in Alabama, and that other jurisdictions are in conflict on this matter, a review of the holdings of other states has convinced this court that the vast majority and best reasoned holdings support the proposition that the brother–brother relationship will, in and of itself, support an insurable interest. . . .

As to what blood relationships are sufficiently close to support an insurable interest, that of brothers is admittedly a borderline case. . . .

The reason most often assigned as the basis of a holding that such relationship will, in and of itself, support an insurable interest is that the natural love and affection prevailing between the two and the expectation that one will render the other aid in time of need is sufficient to overcome any wagering contract argument, as well as any impulse to hasten the death of the insured. This rationale was well stated in [an Arkansas case] as follows:

> "Brothers are so closely related that they are naturally interested in the preservation of the life of each other. Generally, they will lay down their life for each other. As a rule they care for each other in illness to the extent, if necessary, of furnishing all needed comforts and medicinal aid. It would be contrary to human nature for them to speculate on the death of each other, so it may well be that their contracts for insurance on the life of each other should not be classed as wagering contracts."

This view was adopted by Kentucky in [a case] wherein the court stated that an insurable interest may arise from blood relationship alone without regard to whether the beneficiary has any pecuniary interest in the life of the insured or is dependent upon him. If blood relationship alone constitutes an insurable interest, certainly, the court reasoned, the relationship of one brother to another, is sufficiently close for that purpose. The court concluded as follows:

> "[W]here the relationship . . . is so close as to preclude the probability that mercenary motives would induce the sacrifice of life to gain the insurance, the element of pecuniary consideration is not deemed essential to sustain the validity of the policy." . . .

In addition to the cases cited above a number of other jurisdictions have held the blood relationship alone sufficient. . . .

Perhaps the facts of the instant case tend to contradict the closeness and mutual love and affection which the above holdings attribute to the brother–brother relationship, but this court does not write for this case alone. The holding of this court today will govern all future cases, not just the exceptional one where the natural love and affection common to the brother–brother relationship may be missing. . . .

Heflin, Chief Justice.

42:3 Premiums

An insurance *premium* is the consideration paid by an insured to an insurer for undertaking to indemnify the insured against peril. The premium and the time at which it is to be paid are essential terms of the insurance contract. The gross premium ordinarily includes the net premium and the loading. The "net premium" is the amount required by the insurer to provide the insurance coverage itself. The "loading" is an amount added to the net premium to cover administrative and other costs, such as brokers' commissions, medical examinations, and the processing of applications.

Policy premiums are calculated on the basis of the relation between the risk of loss and the value of the object insured. For example, as the value of insured property increases, so does the premium. An insurer will determine what the likelihood is that a loss to insured property will occur and what it will have to pay to the insured on such a loss. Of course, a host of variables, such as the location of the property, its value, the nature of the business, how property is used, and its age, would all go into an insurer's calculations of the premium.

Premiums for life insurance are based on mortality tables, interest rates, and administrative expenses required to carry on the business of insurance. Mortality tables are statistical tables that show the probable life expectancy of a normal person according to sex and age. Knowing life expectancy, the insurance company can then compute the interest it will receive on the investment of the premiums paid during the expected life of the insured. This interest, plus the reserves required by law to be maintained by insurance companies, must equal the total required policy or death payments at the assumed mortality rate. In other words, a portion of the premium is theoretically reserved or set aside by the insurer and another portion is invested. These reserves, when added to the interest on the investments over the expected life of an insured as statistically shown in the mortality tables, must equal the face value of the policy to be paid on the insured's death. Any surplus represents the profits made by the insurer.

A statement of the premium, or a statement of the basis and rates on which the final premium is to be determined and paid, is a necessary part of the policy. A binder need not, however, specify the rate of premium or basis for its computation; an agreement to pay the premium or customary rate is implied.

Self-Insurance   Purchasers of liability and other types of insurance can often save on their premiums by electing to absorb an initial part of a loss through a "deductible." This is a specified amount of monetary damage that an insured must pay first, before the insurer will cover the loss in excess of that amount. The use of this or other devices by which an individual or business voluntarily chooses to bear either a part of, or the entire, risk is sometimes called *self-insurance*. Obviously, it is not insurance in the traditional meaning of the word, since it really signifies the *absence* of insurance.

 Because there are so many kinds of insurance available, an individual or business should consider whether certain risks or losses could very well be self-insured either because the probability of their occurrence is low or the premiums that would be charged are too high to justify coverage.

Return of Premium   As a general rule, an insurer is entitled only to such a reasonable premium as the risk carried warrants. A person is entitled to a return of the premium (1) in the case of overinsurance; (2) when the contract is voidable due to the insurer's fraud or misrepresentation; (3) when the contract is voidable because the insured was ignorant of certain facts through no fault of his own; or (4) when, by any default of the insured other than actual fraud, the insurer did not incur any liability under the policy.

42:4   Risks and Coverage

An insurer is at liberty to select the character of the risk it will assume. All foreseeable losses or risks can be insured against except those for which issuance of insurance would be against public policy or prohibited by statute, or those occasioned by the insured's own fraud or misconduct. Within these limits, the parties can make such contracts as they choose and can qualify or limit the liability assumed. Almost any contingent or unknown event that can injure a person having an insurable interest or create a liability against him can be insured against. Of course, the insurer is not liable except on proof that a loss is within the terms of the policy, for these terms determine the measure of the insurer's liability.

 The essence of insurance is that the greater the hazard, the higher the cost. That is why insurance companies investigate how business property is used before they agree to issue an original policy. It is also why they include provisions that suspend or limit insurance coverage when an insured increases the risk without notifying the insurer. Often an insured will mistakenly believe that the provisions of an insurance policy cover all the risks he wants to be insured. An insured must take the time to understand what is and is not being covered under any policy. If essential risks or losses are excluded, additional coverage should be obtained.

42:5   Notice and Proof of Loss

Insurance policies ordinarily contain provisions requiring the insured to give timely notice to the insurer of a loss or occurrence arising under the terms of a policy. The purpose of a provision for notice is to allow the insurer to review its rights and liabilities as well as to afford it an opportunity for investigation and possible settlement or payment of a claim. The insured's failure to give timely notice will not relieve the insurer of liability under a policy unless the insurer is substantially prejudiced by the provision.

The time for giving notice or making proof of loss does not begin to run until the insured has knowledge, or is charged with notice, of the loss or event on which his rights are based. Thus, where the beneficiary of a life or accident policy is ignorant of the existence of the policy, delay in giving notice or furnishing proof of loss is excused until a reasonable time after her discovery of the policy's existence. An insured can be excused for delay or failure to give notice where it appears that she believed that an accident or injury was not covered by the policy or that she was not liable for the accident in question.

 No matter what type of insurance policy an individual or business buys, there are time limits incorporated within the policy. These deadlines are not only easily overlooked, but they are often misunderstood. For example, few people realize that the clock continues to run even while negotiations for settlement are continuing with an insurance company. Most insureds, in the absence of legal advice, may not know whether a deadline is approaching or whether an insurer has waived a deadline, as discussed below. Unless the insurer has specifically waived a deadline, it is better to commence litigation before the time expires rather than to wait for the insurance company to act, only to discover that a deadline for filing a claim or commencing litigation has passed, precluding recovery under the policy.

Policy provisions concerning notice or proof of loss can be expressly waived by the insurer or its authorized agent. A waiver will be implied from (1) conduct amounting to a recognition of liability, such as proceeding with payment of a loss or settlement of a claim; (2) the insurer's failure to object to an attempted notice or proof of loss; or (3) the facts of the case, under some circumstances.

Note in the following case the importance of complying precisely with all requirements of the insurance contract.

Miles

v

Iowa National Mutual Ins. Co.
690 SW2d 138 (1985)
Missouri Court of Appeals

FACTS: On December 4, 1977, Miles' building exploded and was consumed by fire. On January 12, 1978, Miles submitted a proof of loss to Iowa National. On March 16, 1978, Iowa National's attorney wrote to Miles, returning the proof of loss and notifying Miles that the proof of loss was defective. Miles died on November 26, 1978. On March 21, 1979, the attorney for Miles' estate wrote Iowa National asking for an explanation of the rejection of the proof of loss. Iowa National explained the company's position: Miles, having made no reply to the return of the proof of loss, had in effect, accepted the company's rejection; and because he made no attempt to submit a corrected or amended proof of loss, the company considered him to have thereby abandoned the claim, precluding any further claim under the policy. The policy required that adequate proof of loss be supplied within 60 days of the loss.

ISSUE: Did the insured fail to submit a proof of loss necessary to sue on the claim under the insurance policy?

RESULT: Yes, the insured failed to perform in accordance with the condition of the policy.

REASONING:

*   *   *

In an action on an insurance policy, a plaintiff insured must *plead* performance of the conditions of the policy requiring the insured to act or must show a sufficient excuse for nonperformance. . . . A requirement that plaintiff also *prove* that which he is required to plead is implicit. Thus, an element of the insured's case is proof of compliance with (or the occurrence of) the policy's conditions for which plaintiff may substitute proof of an excuse for nonperformance. In a case where submission of a proof of loss is required by the policy, the plaintiff may excuse his nonperformance by proving, for example, a denial of liability by the insurer before the time for submitting the proof of loss has expired obviating the need to present a proof of loss on the claim. . . . Plaintiff may also show substantial performance or compliance with the proof of loss condition thus excusing literal performance. . . . The purpose of the proof of loss is to furnish to the insurer the facts of the case necessary to a determination of its liability. . . . In showing either the company's early denial of liability or substantial performance, of course, plaintiff is demonstrating a lack of prejudice to the insurer arising from plaintiff's failure to file a formal proof of loss. . . .

Courts of this state do not favor forfeitures, and conditions in an insurance policy barring action by the insured unless he has fully complied with the terms of the contract are "most strongly" construed against the insurance company. . . . In the case of the policy provision requiring the insured to furnish the company a proof of loss, the company must walk a straight and narrow path, else it will waive the requirement. A waiver may be inferred from the conduct and course of dealing of the insurer leading the insured to believe that proofs of loss are unnecessary. . . . Even the act of the fire insurer subjecting the insured to an examination under oath as to the occurrence may constitute a waiver. . . . The company waives submission of a proof of loss by denial of all liability before the time for filing the proof expires, as we noted above. It may waive literal compliance by failing to request a verified statement from the insured who within two weeks of the event made a recorded telephonic report of the accident and was available and had willingly complied with other specific requests. . . . Once the company has waived the proof of loss condition, it may not revive the condition or withdraw its waiver and insist upon compliance with the provision without the insured's consent. . . .

Moreover, even where the insured has furnished the company with something purporting to be a timely proof of loss, the company has the duty of advising the insured of any defect or insufficiency in the submission. . . . The company may not neglect to object to a defective proof of loss until plaintiff's case comes to trial long after the period for submission of the proofs has expired and then deny liability on some other ground. . . .

The only safe and fair course for an insurer to follow when presented with a defective proof of loss is promptly to return the proof of loss to the insured, advising the insured of its defects and insufficiencies and extending to the insured a reasonable time to cure the defects. In this case, the defendant insurance company did exactly that and nothing more or less. After specifying the deficiencies in the submitted proof of loss, Mr. Bott's March 16, 1978, letter to the insured implicitly invited or at least clearly left it up to Miles to submit a new or corrected proof of loss.

Where the insurer rejects a proof of loss and calls to the policy holder's attention the inadequacies of the submission, the ball is in the insured's court, and he must act to comply with the conditions of the policy or not at his own risk. In this case, the insured did nothing between April, 1979 and his death in November, perhaps because in the meantime the matter was under investigation by a federal grand jury and the less he said the better. Nevertheless, Miles and his representative had ample time to submit an amended proof of loss or to protest the company's rejection of the January 12, 1978, proof of loss and to assert that it was correct and proper. They never did. Had they done so, the question here would be quite different.

In any event, the insurer here did all that it should have done under the circumstances, and its action rejecting the proof of loss was not shown by plaintiff's evidence to be a denial of the claim. . . .

Nugent, Judge.

42:6 Rights and Obligations of Parties After Loss

Insurance policies usually provide that the insurer has the right to investigate, negotiate, and settle any claim or suit as it deems proper. A policy might also contain a clause that prohibits the insured from voluntarily assuming any liability or interfering in settlement negotiations without the insurer's consent. The purposes of this provision is to prevent collusion and to give the insurer complete control of the defense or compromise of a suit or claim.

Duty of Insurer to Act in Good Faith   An insurer's obligation of good faith and fair dealing is implied in every insurance contract to protect an insured from unwarranted liability. This obligation requires an insurer to settle a claim against its insured even though the express terms of the policy do not impose such a duty. Therefore, an insurer is required to make an intelligent evaluation of a settlement offer in good faith by considering the interests of the insured equally with its own. This evaluation should be based on a reasonable investigation by persons qualified to make a decision respecting the risk involved.

When there is a great risk of a recovery beyond the policy limits so that the most reasonable manner of disposing a claim is a settlement which can be made within policy limits, good faith requires the insurer to settle the claim. Its unwarranted refusal to do so constitutes a breach of the implied covenant of good faith and fair dealing. An insurance company that acts outrageously to deprive an insured of policy benefits runs the risk of having to pay far more than the policy requires. Its conduct could amount to a tort, which can result in punitive as well as compensatory damages. A wrongful refusal to settle may also constitute a violation of a state consumer protection statute. In at least one state, for example, an insurance company's refusal to deal in good faith has been held to constitute a violation of the state's ban of unfair or deceptive practices by all businesses.

Duty of Insurer to Defend   Most policies of liability insurance contain a clause that obligates the insurer to defend the insured against all lawsuits covered by the policy, even though they might be groundless, false, or fraudulent. If there is doubt as to an insurer's duty to defend, as might exist if there is an ambiguous exclusionary provision in the policy, the courts will generally decide in the insured's favor.

An insurer's unjustified denial of liability and unwarranted refusal to defend a suit against the insured constitutes a breach of its contract, and the insured is thereby released from the obligation of leaving the management of litigation to the insurer. The insured can defend on his own account and make any reasonable compromise of the action. An insurer that wrongfully refuses to defend can be obligated to pay the amount of a judgment rendered against its insured, or of any reasonable settlement made by the insured in good faith (although ordinarily not more than the face amount of the policy).

Duty of Insured to Cooperate   In most liability insurance policies there are provisions that require the insured to cooperate with the insurer in such matters as attending hearings and trials, securing and giving evidence, obtaining the attendance of witnesses, and assisting in making settlements. An insured is required to disclose information reasonably demanded by the insurer to enable it to determine whether it should settle a claim against the insured or whether there is a genuine defense. If an insured breaches a cooperation provision after the insurer has exercised reasonable diligence in securing the insured's cooperation and the insurer is substantially prejudiced by the breach, the insurer has a defense against liability on the policy.

42:7 Proceeds and Beneficiaries

The beneficiary is the person entitled to the proceeds of insurance when the loss, damage, or liability insured against arises.

Ordinarily, the term "beneficiary" refers to the person designated in a life insurance policy as the one who is to receive the benefits that become payable when the insured dies. Should a beneficiary predecease an insured, the right to receive the proceeds depends mainly on the nature of the interest that the deceased beneficiary had. If the policy does not provide for the beneficiary's death and does not reserve the right to change a beneficiary, the named beneficiary has a vested right, which passes to his estate on his death. This right cannot be divested (taken away) by the insured or other owner of the policy (except by permitting the policy to lapse).

EXAMPLE: Morton takes out a life insurance policy and names his wife, Betty, as beneficiary. The policy provides that Morton can waive the right to change or revoke the beneficiary, and Morton chooses to waive this right. Morton's irrevocable designation of Betty gives her a vested and absolute interest in the policy proceeds that cannot be divested by Morton without her consent.

If a life insurance policy permits a change of beneficiary by the insured, but no other beneficiary is named after the designated beneficiary predeceases the insured, the proceeds of the policy are payable to the estate or legal representative of the insured. A beneficiary of a life insurance policy who murders or feloniously causes the death of an insured forfeits rights under the policy.

As a general rule an insured under any type of insurance policy is limited to recovery of the amount set forth in the policy. Also, if an insured accepts payment of a lesser amount, he cannot recover an additional sum later by showing, for example, that both parties supposed that another insurer was liable for a portion of the loss. On the other hand, if the payment of a loss is procured by the insured's fraud, the insurer can recover the amount it paid. Likewise, an insurer that has made a payment under an erroneous belief induced by mistake of fact is entitled to restitution from the beneficiary even though the insurer contributed to the mistake.

An insured must demand payment if the insurer fails to pay promptly. If an insurer fails or refuses to pay, an insured is generally limited to recovering the proceeds of the policy, plus interest. Special damages are not ordinarily awarded, although some courts are now moving in the direction of allowing additional damages, including even mental and emotional distress caused by the insurer's failure to pay. After an insurer grants the insurer a release from any further obligation to pay, the release is binding on the insured unless it was induced by false representations or fraud.

42:8   Assignment or Transfer of Policy

An insurance policy can be assigned by the insured to a third person, to the insurer, or to the beneficiary. Assignment can be made to secure a debt owed by the assignor to the assignee, to create a trust, as a gift, or for any other legitimate purpose. Unless the assignment is a gift, it generally must be supported by consideration. An ordinary life insurance policy cannot be assigned without the beneficiary's consent. As a general rule, an assignee acquires no greater rights by virtue of the assignment than the assignor enjoyed.

 Insurance policies often require that the insurer be notified about and consent to an assignment. Ordinarily, in the absence of a contrary provision in the policy, an assignee's rights are lost if the insured violates the policy terms, as by failing to obtain the insurer's consent to the assignment.

No particular language is necessary to make a valid assignment. Unless required by statute or the policy terms, an assignment need not even be in writing.

42:9   Conditions, Concealment, Representations, and Warranties

Insurers can impose any *conditions* on their obligations, so long as the conditions are clearly expressed and are not contrary to law or public policy. Conditions in insurance law are of two kinds—precedent and subsequent. A *condition precedent* is a condition that must be performed before an insurance contract becomes effective. It calls for the happening of some event or the performance of some act after the terms of the contract have been agreed on, but before the contract becomes binding on the parties. In a life insurance policy, for example, a typical condition precedent is that the policy shall not take effect until delivery and payment of the first premium during the good health of the applicant.

A *condition subsequent* is a condition that must be present after the risk insured against has attached. For example, a provision in a jewelry store owner's burglary policy that the insured keep 75 percent of the value of the inventory in a safe when the store is closed is a condition subsequent, the breach of which relieves the insurer of liability.

Concealment   Each party to an insurance contract must communicate to the other, in good faith, all facts within his knowledge that are material to the contract and that the other party has no means of ascertaining. A party's failure to communicate what he knows, and ought to communicate, is *concealment.* Concealment of matters that are material to the risk invalidates the policy. The test of materiality is whether a fact, if truly stated, might reasonably have influenced the insurer in its decision to reject or accept the risk, or to charge a higher premium.

Keeping secrets about a business is often a wise idea. However, it can be costly when an insurance company is kept in the dark. Generally, it is to the insured's advantage to notify the insurer of developments that may affect the risks or the premiums. For example, a change in the structure or ownership of a business, or an improvement that reduces risk, might entitle an insured to a reduced premium. If the insurer is not notified, the insured would not be eligible for lower premiums. When altered circumstances *increase* risks, warranting higher premiums, failure to notify the insurer of the change could lead to retroactive added premiums at best; at worst, it could lead to rejection of otherwise valid claims.

Representations and Misrepresentations A *representation* is an oral or written statement given by the insured to the insurer before the contract is made. The statement consists of factual information that is intended or necessary to enable the insurer to determine whether it will accept the risk and at what premium. Representations are either affirmative or promissory. Affirmative representations are allegations of fact as they exist at the time they are made; promissory representations refer to what is to happen during the term of the insurance policy.

A representation can be false and yet not have been made with an intent to deceive. In contrast, a misrepresentation is a statement as a fact of something that (1) is untrue, (2) is known to be untrue, and (3) *is* made with an intent to deceive. A misrepresentation can also be a statement that an insured claims is true without knowing it to be true, and which has a tendency to mislead.

EXAMPLE: Broyles bought a car on May 11, 1977. At the same time, he purchased a life insurance policy from Ford Life Insurance Company. Broyles signed a health statement on the application, declaring that he was in "good health" to the best of his knowledge. A place for listing exceptions to or limits on the general statement of health was left blank. In fact, as early as July 1976, Broyles knew he was suffering from some kind of blood disorder. He died of leukemia on October 8, 1977. Broyles had not known that he had leukemia when he applied for the life insurance. However, because he had known that he had a blood disorder, his statement as to his good health was untrue and, as such, was a misrepresentation.

 If there is a deliberate concealment or misrepresentation in obtaining an insurance policy, the insurer will normally not have to pay for a loss. Even if the insurance contract is valid to begin with, failure to provide current information about a risk can preclude or diminish recovery for a loss. It is not at all unusual for business insurance policies to require the policyholder to promptly report changes in operations, fluctuations in inventory, relocation of the business, and other conditions that might increase the risk of loss. Therefore, the insured should carefully read the policy to ascertain what risk is insured and what information needs to be communicated on a continuing basis to the insurance company.

Warranties   A *warranty* is a statement, description, or undertaking by an insured that appears in the insurance policy and relates to the risk insured against. For example, a provision of a burglary policy by which the insured agrees to install certain locks on the insured premises is an express warranty. A warranty must appear on the face of a policy or be incorporated in some fashion into the policy.

At this point a distinction must be made between a warranty and a representation. A warranty is part of the completed contract, whereas a representation is made during the formation of a contract and is not necessarily incorporated into the policy itself. In other words, a representation tends to induce the insurer to assume the risk more readily, whereas a warranty is a written stipulation in the policy on which the validity of the contract depends. A warranty can be breached regardless of the insured's intent. Breach of a warranty prevents recovery under the insurance policy, even if the warranty does not relate to a matter that is material to the risk. However, a misrepresentation must relate to a material matter and must have been willfully and knowingly made with an intent to defraud in order for an insurer to be relieved of liability.

42:10   Waiver and Estoppel

In all types of insurance, a party to the contract can waive or be estopped from asserting policy provisions. Waiver and estoppel, which are defined below, are frequently applied in insurance law in favor of the insured or beneficiary to prevent a rescission by the insurer or a forfeiture of the policy. Both doctrines are also applicable in favor of the insurer, however. That is, the insurer can claim that the insured forfeited his policy because of waiver or estoppel.

The terms *waiver* and *estoppel* designate different legal concepts, although in many insurance cases estoppel is used in a vague sense, making its meaning practically synonymous with waiver. Generally, waiver is a voluntary act that implies an abandonment of a right or privilege. Estoppel has been so loosely used as to make it difficult to define. Essential elements of estoppel are the misleading of a party who is entitled to rely on the acts or statements in question, and a consequent change of position to that party's detriment. Thus, any agreement, declaration, or course of action on the insurer's part that leads an insured honestly to believe that by conforming to it his policy will not be forfeited, followed by due conformity on his part, will estop (prevent) the insurer from declaring a forfeiture, even though the insurer may claim that the policy has been forfeited under the express provisions of the contract. It can be seen, therefore, that a distinction does exist between waiver and estoppel, but this distinction is not as clear as the definitions indicate them to be and, in fact, many courts use these terms interchangeably.

The following case illustrates the use of the estoppel doctrine in insurance law. The court's opinion analyzes the limits of the doctrine in the sense that estoppel cannot be used to create or fashion terms of an insurance contract where none previously existed.

Pearce

v

American Defender Life Ins. Co.
330 SE2d 9 (1985)
North Carolina Court of Appeals

FACTS: On June 4, 1968, American issued a life insurance policy to Pearce, providing a $20,000 death benefit. Pearce purchased additional coverage of $40,000 for accidental death. The $40,000 rider specifically excluded accidents caused by flight on aircraft otherwise than as a commercial passenger. In 1971 Pearce entered the U.S. Air Force and undertook flight training. At that time Pearce advised American of his flight status and asked for clarification of the policy coverage. A representative from American's policyholder service office responded in a letter, clearly stating that the policy and rider excluded flight only in time of war. On July 24, 1979, Pearce died in an accident involving military aircraft. His beneficiary sued to enforce the $40,000 accident rider.

ISSUE: Did American "waive" the limitation under the accidental death rider?

RESULT: No, the erroneous statement from the policyholder service office did not create new coverage through waiver.

REASONING:

*   *   *

We begin our analysis by pointing out that the policy provision in question, which excepts from coverage death resulting from travel in an aircraft if the insured is a flight crew member, is unambiguous. Plaintiff does not contend that the policy, considered as written, independent of the exchange of letters in 1971, obligates defendant to make payment to plaintiff under the Accidental Death Rider. Plaintiff's claim, instead, is that defendant is estopped from relying on the aircraft exception, or that defendant has waived that portion of the insurance contract, or that that portion of the insurance contract was modified by the exchange of letters in 1971.

The doctrines of "waiver" and "estoppel," although related, are conceptually distinct. Waiver is "the voluntary, intentional relinquishment of a known right," . . . while estoppel "refers to an abatement raised by law of rights and privileges of the insurer where it would be inequitable to permit their assertion." . . . Waiver is available only when the evidence shows that the insurer *intentionally* relinquished its rights under the insurance contract. . . . Estoppel, on the other hand, "necessarily implies prejudicial reliance of the insured upon some act, conduct, or nonaction of the insurer." . . . Our courts have often held that forfeiture provisions in an insurance contract may be waived by the insurer, or that the company may, because of its conduct, be estopped from relying on such provisions so as to avoid its obligations under the policy. . . . While these doctrines sometimes have been relied upon to prevent forfeiture, the rule is well settled that . . .

> The doctrines of implied waiver and of estoppel, based upon the conduct or action of the insurer, are not available to bring within the coverage of a policy risks not covered by its terms, or risks expressly excluded therefrom; and the application of the doctrine in this respect is, therefore, to be distinguished from the waiver of, or estoppel to deny, grounds of forfeiture.

. . . "The theory underlying this rule seems to be that the company should not be required by waiver and estoppel to pay a loss for which it charged no premium. . . ." . . .

In the instant case, the Accidental Death Rider provides for the payment of an additional $40,000 in the event the insured dies as the result of an accident, and expressly exempts from coverage death resulting from an accident involving an aircraft on which the insured serves as a crew member. We think it clear that application of the doctrines of waiver or estoppel on these facts would essentially rewrite the policy, extending coverage to a risk expressly excluded therefrom, and obligating defendant to pay a loss for which it charged no premium. This we cannot do. . . .

Hedrick, Chief Judge.

42:11 Cancellation

Cancellation is commonly regarded as the right to rescind, abandon, or abrogate a contract of insurance. An insurance contract is not susceptible to cancellation or rescission only in part, at least without the consent of both the insurer and the insured. The cancellation of an insurance policy does not affect any rights that have already accrued under the policy in favor of the insured or a third person. Thus, for example, an insurer cannot avoid liability for a loss by giving notice of its election to terminate the policy *after* the loss has occurred.

Both the form and the sufficiency of a notice of cancellation are determined by policy provisions. Most insurance policies contain provisions allowing cancellation at the request of the insured. For example, an insured's mere physical surrender of the policy does not necessarily terminate the contract. Fire insurance policies and other contracts of insurance on property, in addition to the common provision for cancellation of the policy on the insured's request, generally provide that the insurer can cancel by giving notice to the insured within a prescribed period, usually five or ten days, and returning the unearned portion of the premium paid by the insured. The reason for this provision is to allow the insured ample opportunity to negotiate for other insurance to replace the canceled policy.

Both the insurer and the insured can cancel or rescind an insurance policy on the basis of fraud or misrepresentation. An insured's right to rescind a policy for fraud must be exercised promptly after the insured learns of the fraud. The insurer must give notice that the policy is canceled and must pay back or offer the insured the premiums paid.

42:12   Incontestability Provisions

Life insurance policies usually contain provisions commonly referred to as *incontestability clauses.* An incontestability clause provides that the policy cannot be contested after a certain passage of time. There are two kinds of clauses, one providing that the policy shall be incontestable after a particular date and the other providing that the policy shall be incontestable after a specified period of time. The latter type, which usually designates the period as one or two years, is in general use. The intent of both types of incontestability clauses is to fix a limited time within which an insurer must discover and assert any grounds it may have for rescinding a policy issued by it. Legislation in all but two states—Missouri and Rhode Island—requires that life insurance contracts have incontestability clauses.

If a policy contains an incontestability clause, the insurer must take legal action within the specified time period either by suing to cancel or rescind the policy, or by setting up misrepresentation or fraud in the procurement of the policy as a defense in an action brought by the insured or the beneficiary.

Key Concepts and Terms

- The relationship between an insurer and an insured is purely contractual. A contract of insurance must describe (1) the subject matter to be insured, (2) the risk insured against, (3) the commencement and period of the risk undertaken by the insurer, (4) the amount of insurance, and (5) the premium and time at which it is to be paid.

- Negotiations for the purchase of insurance are ordinarily initiated when a person fills out an application. The application itself is not a contract; it is only an offer. It must be accepted by the insurer before an insurance contract is created.

- A binder is a receipt that an insurer can issue to the insured. It provides temporary insurance coverage.

- An insurance premium is the price at which the insurer agrees to carry the risk insured against. As such, it is the consideration paid by the insured for the insurance.

- An insurer is at liberty to select the character of the risk it will assume. Subject to this right, all foreseeable losses or risks can be insured against unless (1) insuring them is contrary to public policy or prohibited by statute or (2) they are losses caused by the insured's own fraud or other misconduct.

- The insurer is not liable except on proof that a loss within the terms of a policy has occurred.

- An insurable interest is necessary to the validity of an insurance contract. In regard to property, anyone has an insurable interest who derives a benefit from its existence or would suffer loss from its destruction. In regard to life insurance, every person has an insurable interest in his own life. To have an insurable interest in another's life, a person must have a reasonable expectation of benefit or advantage from the continuance of the other's life.

- Most insurance policies require the insured to give timely notice to the insurer of a loss or occurrence arising under the terms of the policy. The purpose of such a provision is to allow the insurer to (1) review its rights and liabilities and (2) investigate claims and perhaps settle them.

- An obligation of good faith and fair dealing on the insurer's part is implied in every insurance contract. This obligation requires an insurer to settle a claim against its insured in an appropriate case even though the policy does not expressly impose such a duty.

- The beneficiary is the person entitled to the proceeds of insurance when the loss, damage, or liability insured against arises. Ordinarily, "beneficiary" refers to the person designated in a life insurance policy as the one who is to receive the benefits that become payable when the insured dies.

- An insured can recover only the amount set forth in his insurance policy. An insured cannot recover additional sums after payment of a loss has been made.

- In all types of insurance, a party to the contract can waive or be estopped from asserting policy provisions. Waiver and estoppel are frequently applied in insurance law in favor of the insured or the beneficiary to prevent the insurer's cancellation of the policy.

- Attachment of the Risk
- Beneficiary
- Binder
- Concealment
- Condition Precedent
- Conditions
- Condition Subsequent
- Deductible
- Estoppel
- Incontestability Clause
- Insurable Interest
- Key Employee Insurance
- Life Insurance
- Loading
- Net Premium
- Premium
- Proof of Loss
- Representation
- Self-insurance
- Wagering Contract
- Waiver
- Warranty

Questions and Case Problems

1. Jesse buys a used Cadillac for $4,100. A comprehensive insurance policy on the car is issued by an insurer. Three days later, the car is stolen. On processing the theft claim, the insurer discovers that Jesse had purchased a stolen vehicle. It then disclaims liability on the ground that Jesse had no insurable interest in the vehicle. Does Jesse have an insurable interest in the stolen car?

2. Prior to October 1964, Mrs. King and her husband owned real property and the building on it, in which they operated a grocery store. On October 12, 1964, Mr. and Mrs. King conveyed the real property to their daughters. For the next several years the daughters and their husbands cared for the Kings and helped run the grocery store. The proceeds from the store were placed in a special bank account and used to meet the Kings' needs. In February 1967, Aetna Insurance Company issued a policy to Mrs. King insuring her against any loss she might sustain from the destruction of the building and its contents by fire. In December 1967 the store and all of its contents were destroyed by fire. Aetna denied Mrs. King's claim for loss on the ground that at the time of the fire she did not have an insurable interest in the store and its contents. How should this case be decided?

3. Dr. Pappas owned an old log-frame house on which he purchased fire insurance in the amount of $5,000. Later, Dr. Pappas deeded the property to his then 6-year-old son. He later purchased an additional fire insurance policy, but never gave notice to either insurance company that he had deeded the property to his son. The house was subsequently completely destroyed by fire. Did the doctor have an insurable interest in this property? Would the fact that the doctor paid for the rehabilitation and remodeling of the home, prior to its loss, have any bearing on the question of insurable interest? Would the doctor's probable control over the insured property during his son's minority affect his insurable interest? Assume that the second insurance company knew at the time its policy was issued that the doctor did not have title to the house. Should a duty to investigate and ascertain the property's true status be imposed on that company? If the insurance company had known that the doctor did not have title to the insured property at the time the policy was issued, should it be estopped or prevented from asserting the doctor's lack of insurable interest?

4. When Oliver's family sold the family farmland to a logging company, the company gave Oliver permission to remove two well-preserved log cabins from the land for restoration in another site. It was understood that if Oliver could not move the cabins, the logging company would destroy them. Oliver sought and obtained fire insurance on the cabins. On Halloween pranksters set fire to the cabins and destroyed them. When Oliver filed a claim, the insurance company refused the claim on the ground that Oliver lacked an insurable interest in the cabins. What result?

5. Walker contracted with Fisher to trim Walker's trees. On the same day Walker called her insurance agent and stated she would like to have an accident policy on Fisher. The agent agreed to issue the policy. The policy was effective for one day and named Fisher as insured and Walker as beneficiary with her relationship to the insured shown as "employer." The premium of 85 cents was paid by Walker. The policy provided in part for accidental death benefits of $10,000. While trimming trees at Walker's residence, Fisher sustained an accidental bodily injury from which he later died. Did Walker have an insurable interest in Fisher's life?

Would the result be different if Walker were named only as a nominal beneficiary and at the suggestion of the agent who did not know Fisher's nonfamily status?

6. Carlos Huff, Sr., died from multiple stab wounds. Earlier that year an insurance company had issued a $10,000 policy on his life with his 17-year-old son as the named beneficiary. The insurance company refuses to pay on the ground that the son feloniously caused the decedent's death. The state statute provides that "No person who is convicted of or pleads guilty to a violation of [aggravated murder, murder, or voluntary manslaughter] shall in any way benefit by the death." The son was adjudicated as a juvenile and his case was never transferred to adult court. Thus he was never charged with any of the named crimes. Moreover, he claims that while he stabbed his father to death, he did so to defend his mother, whom his father was strangling. Can he recover on the insurance policy?

7. When James Robinson's 16-year-old son died, the death certificate stated, "there were no marks on body that indicated violence; apparently died from natural causes." About seven months before, Robinson had applied to Reliable Life Insurance Company for a life policy on the boy, naming himself as beneficiary. The application stated that the boy had not been treated by a doctor in the past five years, had not had any illness or injury within the past five years, and had never been hospitalized at all. The facts, discovered by Reliable after the boy's death, were that Robinson's son had suffered from sickle-cell anemia for several years, and less than two years earlier had been hospitalized for two weeks for intestinal hemorrhaging and sickle-cell anemia. The false medical history prompted Reliable to refuse to pay on the policy. The statute applicable to the case provided that false statements in an application for life insurance would not void coverage unless the insurer showed that the matter or thing represented was material to the risk "or actually contributed to the contingency or event on which said policy became due and payable." Should Reliable have to pay the face amount of the life policy?

8. Distinguish between conditions and representations. Why are they so important in the law of insurance?

9. In his application for life insurance, Bunn indicated that he was married and that he did not contemplate a change in occupation or foreign travel. At the time the application was made, however, Bunn was not married, although he had been living with a woman for 15 years and was the father of her two children. Later, Bunn married the woman and left for work in Vietnam. He died there one year later. The insurer denied liability under the policy on the ground that Bunn made two material misrepresentations in his application for the policy. Were both representations material? Should the policy be declared void?

10. Johnston was arrested and taken into custody by state police during a raid at the Tally Ho Restaurant. Johnston claimed that he had innocently wandered into a gambling and stag party, and the state dropped all charges against him. However, Johnston's name had appeared in several newspaper stories in connection with the illegal party and police raid. He sued Tally Ho for negligence in allowing the party, seeking damages for injury to his reputation and business standing. Tally Ho requested its insurer, PMA, to defend the action under the terms of its liability policy. PMA refused, and Tally Ho joined PMA as a third-party defendant in the action. PMA's insurance policy provided as follows:

> "The company will pay on behalf of the insured all sums which the insured shall become legally obligated to pay as damages because of Coverage A (bodily injury) or Coverage B (property damage) to which this insurance applies, caused

by an occurrence, and the company shall have the right and duty to defend any suit against the insured seeking damages on account of such bodily injury or property damage, even if any of the allegations of the suit are groundless, false, or fraudulent."

Is Johnston's claim for damage to his reputation and business standing covered by the "property damage" clause of the policy? Does PMA have a duty to defend Tally Ho? Johnston also alleged in his complaint that he was "set upon and arrested by the police." He did not allege specifically that any bodily injury resulted, and he did not claim damages for bodily injury. Does the mere use of the words "set upon and arrested" mean that Johnston was physically injured, obligating the insurance company to defend Tally Ho?

PART NINE

Business Organizations

Introductory Comments

Business in the United States encompasses all economic activity pursued for profit. All business organizations—whether they are sole proprietorships, partnerships, or corporations—have this purpose. Success depends in part on the form and structure of the business enterprise. Obviously, while success in business is not necessarily guaranteed simply because one form of organization has been adopted over another, the careful crafting of a business does enhance the likelihood of its success.

The law of business organizations is rooted in the law of agency. Agency establishes the relationship between the principal and the agent, the one who acts for the principal. This relationship is at the core of the employee–employer relationship, the partnership relationship, and the relationship between a corporation and its officers and employees.

The chapters in this part discuss the basic types of business organization and cover how they are formed, how they are managed, and how they operate. These chapters provide the business law student with a basic understanding of the legal doctrines affecting the most important business entities.

The common law of agency is discussed in Chapter 43. General and limited partnerships are discussed in Chapter 44. Also discussed in Chapter 44 are other similar forms of businesses, such as joint ventures, which have many partnership characteristics yet differ from partnerships in fundamental ways. Chapters 45 through 47 present the law of corporations, including corporate management and finance (Chapter 46) and the rights of shareholders (Chapter 47). Chapter 48 focuses on the franchise, which, although not a type of business organization, is a common and vital form of business enterprise. The final chapter in this part, Chapter 49, is based on all the materials discussed in Chapters 44 through 48. It analyzes the most important factors to be weighed in the formation of a new business, how these factors affect the conduct of business, and their relative merit.

Students may find it helpful to focus on the basic issues with which all business organizations must deal: (1) formation, (2) control, (3) management, (4) transferability of ownership, (5) liability, and (6) duration. An appreciation of how these issues are handled with respect to the sole proprietorship, the partnership, the corporation, and the franchise—and how they may differ for each—will help the student work successfully in the business environment and use the knowledge gained in this text productively.

43 Agency

43:1 Introduction

"Let every eye negotiate for itself and trust no agent." So stated William Shakespeare in one of his works. While such advice may have been good counsel in the bard's time, in our modern economy it is virtually impossible to transact business in the absence of agents or the *agency* relationship. Because the use of agents is pervasive in commercial life, it is essential that the businessperson know (1) how to create an agency relationship, (2) how to conduct business using agents, and (3) how to terminate an agency. This chapter is designed to meet these goals.

An agency arises when one person, the principal, enlists the services of another person, the agent, to manage a business or perform a transaction in the principal's name or on his behalf subject to the principal's control. Agency is a *fiduciary relationship*, meaning one of trust or confidence. Any person having the capacity to act may do so through an agent. Once an agency has been established, the acts of the agent become those of the principal.

There are three different kinds of agents: general, special, and universal. A general agent is authorized to perform all activities connected with the projects or tasks for which he is hired. A special agent is authorized to perform only specific activities under particular instructions. A universal agent is authorized to transact all of the principal's business and to do all acts that the principal can delegate; thus, a universal agent is an unlimited general agent.

43:2 Creation of Relationship

The agency relationship is ordinarily created by agreement between the principal and the agent. An agency is created and authority is actually conferred very much as any other contract is made (see Chapters 10 through 15). As between the principal and agent, there must be a meeting of minds in establishing the agency, as well as the consent of both the principal and the agent. The principal must intend that the agent act for him, and the agent must intend to accept the principal's authority and act on it.

While the creation of an agency relationship arises from mutual consent, it is not essential that a formal or written contract be signed by the parties. Thus, although an agency is often express, it can also be implied, based on the conduct of the parties or how they represent their relationship to other persons with whom business is conducted. Bear in mind, too, that the language used in an agreement between persons does not necessarily determine the legal nature of their relationship. Rather, the intention of the parties is controlling. If business performed by one person on behalf of another is essentially in the nature of an agency, an agency relationship is created regardless of what the parties call that relationship. Conversely, the mere use of the words "agent" or "principal" will not necessarily give rise to an agency if the persons do not intend to act as principal and agent.

Agency by Estoppel and Necessity   Two kinds of agencies that are not created by contract are agency by estoppel and agency by necessity. An *agency by estoppel* is created when one person permits another to act for him and, by so doing, causes third persons to reasonably believe that an agency has been created. This relationship between the parties is called an agency by estoppel because the courts will not permit one person who has held out another as his agent to deny the existence of an agency later, during litigation.

Agency by necessity comes into existence when an emergency arises that makes it necessary or proper for one person to act for another without having express authority to do so. The emergency must be a real one; it is not sufficient that the agent only believes that an emergency exists. An agent's authority under this doctrine terminates as soon as the agent has performed the emergency services and has communicated with the principal that certain acts have been performed on his behalf.

43:3   Authority of Agent

The essence of the agency relationship is the authority of the agent to act for and bind the principal. The source of the agent's authority is always the principal. An agent can have (1) actual authority or (2) apparent or ostensible authority. *Actual authority* is express or implied authority granted to the agent by the principal. Express authority, as the name implies, means authority expressly conferred by the principal on the agent. Implied authority is not actually given by the principal to the agent. Instead, it is the authority the agent uses to do whatever acts are incidental, necessary, usual, or proper to the exercise of the express authority actually delegated to him. An agent is usually deemed to have the implied authority to perform business on the principal's behalf in accordance with the general custom, usage, and procedures in that business.

EXAMPLE: Paul, the owner of a used-car lot, contracts with Eric to manage the lot for him and to sell cars for a commission. In operating the lot, Eric begins a marketing campaign that includes newspaper advertising. Eric has the implied authority to contract for advertising because it is a customary part of conducting a used-car business.

Apparent Authority *Apparent* or *ostensible authority* is authority that, although not actually granted to the agent by the principal, the principal knowingly permits the agent to exercise, or that the principal holds the agent out to third persons as possessing. Thus, if a principal conducts business so as to cause third persons to reasonably believe that the agent possesses authority to act in the principal's name with regard to particular matters, the principal will be bound by the agent's acts within the scope of that apparent authority as to a third person who in good faith reasonably believes that the agent has such authority. For the doctrine of apparent or ostensible authority to be invoked, the following must be established: (1) the principal in some way manifested consent to the exercise of such authority, or at least has knowingly permitted the agent to carry out particular activities; (2) the third person acted reasonably and in good faith in believing that the agent was acting with the principal's authority; and (3) the third person relied on this authority and would suffer injury or loss if the transaction was not binding on the principal.

The following case illustrates the way in which these elements establish the authority of an agent. As the case shows, determination of apparent or ostensible authority is made by examining the actions of the principal, not the actions of the agent. An agent's assumption or representation that he or she has the authority does not create apparent authority.

R. H. Kyle Furniture Co.

v

Russell Dry Goods Co.
340 SW2d 220 (1960)
Kentucky Court of Appeals

FACTS: Kyle Furniture Company sued Russell Dry Goods to recover $1,767.15 for goods alleged to have been sold and delivered to Russell on the order of its manager, Clyde Thomas. Russell contended that it had never bought the goods and that they had not been delivered to its store. It further argued that its manager had lacked the authority to buy the goods and that it was therefore not liable for their cost. The trial court ruled in Russell's favor, holding that it did not have to pay.

ISSUE: Is Russell liable as a principal for the purchase price of the goods ordered by Thomas?

RESULT: Yes. Russell clothed Thomas with the apparent authority to order the goods.

REASONING:

*   *   *

The questions are whether Thomas bought the merchandise for himself and other persons or for the [dry goods] store, of which he was the manager, and whether the plaintiff [Kyle Furniture] could rely upon the apparent or ostensible authority of Thomas to buy the merchandise for the [store].

H. T. Burdette, one of plaintiff's traveling salesmen, testified that Thomas first purchased certain items of furniture on October 12, 1955. They were shipped to the store and charged to the company. There were several other like transactions before February 29, 1956, when Thomas and he discussed the proposition of setting up a special furniture department on the second floor of the Russell building. He submitted a stock order amounting to $2,471.40, subject to being confirmed by Cal Turner. Turner declined to approve it, as "he was not ready to go in the furniture business." There were several isolated orders given by Thomas which were duly shipped and charged to the dry goods company before an order was given on April 28, 1956, for an assortment of rugs, carpeting, dishes, lawnmowers, electric fans and furniture. The order aggregated $1,767.15. It was sent in as having been sold to the dry goods company and its account was charged. When the truck arrived at Russell Springs with the shipment, the store was on fire or had already burned down. At Thomas' request, the goods were taken to his garage and unloaded there. This is the account sued on.

. . . The first information the plaintiff had of any limitation upon Thomas' authority was a letter from Cal Turner, president of J. L. Turner and Company, declining to pay the account sued on. . . .

Thomas testified that all of the purchases had been made for himself personally or clerks in the store or friends at wholesale prices. He admits having made a little profit on some of the shipments, but whether for himself or the store is not revealed. . . . Thomas insisted that Burdette knew these were personal transactions. He stated that he would personally pay Burdette for the shipments when he came around on his visits. . . . Burdette denied this and many other affirmative statements. Thomas did not remember anything at all about the particular shipment involved here being received. Other than the evidence of the truckman, the record is silent as to what became of the merchandise.

Cal Turner testified that Thomas and all other managers of his various subsidiary stores had been positively denied authority to make any purchases of stock.

The defendant undertook to show that furniture was not handled in the store. This apparently was to prove that the plaintiff should have known Thomas was not buying the merchandise as stock for the store. But a long-time clerk testified that it had carried in stock household articles, wallpaper, rugs, mattresses, bed springs and, at one time, window fans and some chairs made in a local factory. This tended to show that the defendant did not confine its operations strictly to "dry goods."

The court sustained an objection to an inquiry of the plaintiff's credit manager concerning the custom in the business world to rely upon the authority of the manager of a store to buy merchandise. The witness avowed that store managers normally have full authority to purchase merchandise, and this is generally relied upon. We think this evidence was competent. The evidence had a tendency to prove a presumption of agency. . . .

Authority to contract on behalf of the principal may arise from a usage or custom of business. . . .

It is within well-settled law that the plaintiff, as principal, is bound by the notice or knowledge of its salesman, Burdette, although it was not actually communicated to his company. . . . And further, though it was competent for the principal to limit the authority of an agent, the restriction on the authority of Thomas to buy merchandise for the store is not binding on the plaintiff, for there was no evidence that it had notice or knowledge thereof; and the directive was ineffective to limit the agent's apparent authority in this transaction or relieve the company of an obligation to pay for the merchandise. . . . Therefore, the defendant is bound on this contract of purchase, if it was made by Thomas within the implied or ostensible scope of his authority as manager of the store, unless plaintiff's salesman knew or had reason to know that he was exceeding his authority in ordering the goods on the credit of the company. This is so well recognized that citation of law is scarcely required. . . .

As stated in some of the cases summarized, it would be impossible for persons to deal safely with corporations if in each case they were required at their peril to determine the exact scope of the authority of such agents as managers and superintendents; hence, they are justified in relying upon the apparent or implied authority of such agents. We think that is sound law. The term "apparent or implied authority" would not likely apply to the purchase of goods wholly outside the character or line of merchandise carried, e.g., the manager of a men's clothing store buying a large quantity of drugs. In the instant case, the stock of the defendant's country store was not limited to "dry goods," which is generally defined as textile fabrics. . . . It was undenied that the Russell store had previously stocked articles similar in character to those contained in this order. The purchase could well be regarded as having been made in the ordinary and usual course of the business, even though the purchases may have been specially made for individual customers. . . .

Stanley, Commissioner.

Power of Agent to Bind Principal The scope of an agent's power to bind the principal depends largely on the powers that the principal has conferred on the agent. Common sense plays a large role in determining the extent of an agent's powers and his authority in any given case. For example, an agent's power to make a contract extends only to contracts that are usual and customary in the business or trade involved. An agent's normal contractual powers clearly would *not* include the authority to modify an agreement after its execution, to waive its conditions, or otherwise to diminish the obligations of the other contracting party.

Authority to borrow money on the principal's credit may be the most important—and also most dangerous—authority that a principal can confer on an agent. This authority does not exist even for a general agent unless it has been expressly given or is necessarily implied by the character of the business.

 An agent who has the slightest doubt as to the propriety of an authorized activity should bring all facts of the prospective transaction to the principal's immediate attention and request written clarification of the action authorized by the principal. In this way, the agent could avoid being accused at a later time of exceeding the scope of authority or acting adversely to the principal's interests.

Subagents Sometimes a principal expressly authorizes an agent to delegate authority to another person. This person, called a *subagent*, then represents the principal as if he were directly appointed by the principal. An agent's authority to create a subagency can be implied if the nature of the business is such that the principal can reasonably contemplate that the agent's authority will be exercised through subagents. Whether subagents can be appointed is determined on a case-by-case basis. The customs or usage of a particular trade or business are important considerations. If a particular business is ordinarily conducted through subagents, it may be presumed that the principal has impliedly authorized their appointment and use. If a principal has placed personal trust or confidence in the agent, however, the agent's authority cannot be delegated to another without the principal's consent.

43:4 Ratification of the Agent's Acts

The principal is not bound by acts exceeding the scope of an agent's authority. A principal can, however, ratify acts that were done in excess of the agent's authority, or even acts that were done by a person who purported to be an agent but actually was not. If the principal does ratify, the rights and duties of all parties concerned are just the same as if the agent—or would-be agent—had had proper authority when the act was done.

To constitute a valid *ratification*, the principal's approval must be given with full knowledge of all facts pertinent to the transaction. A principal's mere acceptance of the benefits derived from the agent's unauthorized acts will not amount to a ratification if the principal has not been supplied with all material facts. The principal must either adopt or reject the entire transaction. He cannot avail himself of those acts that are beneficial and repudiate those that are detrimental.

Ratification as Express or Implied   Ratification of an unauthorized act can be express (either orally or in writing) or implied from the acts or conduct of the principal subsequent to the act. Although particular formalities are not usually required for ratification, it should be noted that to bind the principal, the form of ratification must be of equal dignity to what the original authorization would have been. That is, if the original authorization to create an agency had to be in writing, such as authorization to sell land, then the ratification also must be in writing. However, it need not be a formal document, nor need it necessarily be addressed or delivered to the other party to the contract.

Ratification may arise from the principal's silence as well as from the principal's affirmative act or statements.

EXAMPLE: Without authorization, Alice makes a contract to sell a truckload of George's tractors to Acme Company for a good price. George learns about the contract and, without saying anything, delivers the tractors to Acme. By his conduct, George has ratified the unauthorized contract that his agent made.

Implied ratification is also created by a principal's failure to repudiate an agent's unauthorized act within a reasonable time. The principal cannot simply wait, retain the benefits of an unauthorized act or contract if it should turn out to be profitable, and yet retain a right to repudiate the act. In other words, the principal must decide whether to ratify or repudiate, and then act promptly on that decision; to promote stability in commercial transactions, it is highly important that persons who transact business with one another act with the knowledge that they will be bound by their actions.

43:5   Rights, Duties, and Liabilities of Principal and Agent

The range of an agent's duties toward the principal are determined by the scope of the authority conferred by the principal. The agent is under a duty to act only as authorized, and an agent who exceeds that authority becomes liable to the principal for damages that result from the unauthorized acts. The agent has a duty to obey all reasonable instructions of the principal. Where the instructions are clear and precise, they must be followed exactly.

An agent, as a fiduciary, has the obligation to disclose to the principal all facts relevant to the agency. For example, if the principal has instructed the agent to sell property on certain specified terms or at a particular price, and the agent later learns that other or more advantageous terms or a better price could be obtained, the agent is obligated to communicate this to the principal. An agent also has a duty not to act against the principal by serving or acquiring any private interest in his capacity as an agent. For example, an agent cannot engage in competition with the principal or gain any unfair advantage or secret profit in an agency transaction. Furthermore, an agent cannot furnish to others or use for himself, in opposition to the principal, any information received confidentially from the principal or acquires in the course of the agency. The following case illustrates the situation in which an agent breached his fiduciary duties to the principal.

Douglas
v
Aztec Petroleum Corp.
695 SW2d 312 (1985)
Texas Court of Civil Appeals

FACTS: In February 1980 Aztec's president, Seib, engaged Douglas to buy a block of oil and gas leases for Aztec. For his services, Douglas was to receive $5,000 plus an assignment of an overriding royalty interest in the leases obtained. Aztec sent Douglas a check for the $5,000 and additional checks, for a total of $343,557.35. Douglas obtained the leases at a lesser price, then altered photocopies of checks to the lessors in a manner that obscured the amounts and the payees of the checks. The actual checks, as they cleared the bank, indicate payment for many personal items, such as boats, cars, and dental bills. When Aztec refused to grant Douglas the overriding royalty interest in the leases, Douglas sued. Aztec argued that Douglas is not entitled to the interest because he did not perform in "an honest and forthright manner," as provided in the contract.

ISSUE: Did Douglas' deception of his principal excuse Aztec from paying Douglas the agreed upon compensation?

RESULT: Yes. Douglas' actions constituted a breach of fiduciary duty of an agent to a principal.

REASONING:

*   *   *

It is uncontroverted that Douglas was Aztec's agent. An agency is a fiduciary relationship. . . . The law requires more of a fiduciary than arms-length marketplace ethics. He owes his principal loyalty and good faith; integrity of the strictest kind; fair, honest dealing; and the duty not to conceal matters which might influence his actions to his principal's prejudice. . . . He is obligated to exercise a high degree of care to conserve his principal's money and to pay it only to those entitled to receive it. . . . He must keep his principal's funds as a separate and identifiable account. . . . The agent must make an accounting to his principal of any money that has come into his possession because of his agency. . . . "A fiduciary has no right to make merchandise of the confidence reposed in him." . . .

Douglas' own testimony is a startling catalogue of violations of almost every fiduciary duty. It is undisputed that a substantial portion of the funds advanced did not go for the purposes stated in the agreement, the purchase of oil leases. Douglas admits spending large sums on two new cars, a boat, and other personal expenses almost immediately after getting Aztec's money. He admits failing to account honestly. He confesses forging receipts and altering checks to "plug in" whatever figures were necessary to add up to the $343,000 entrusted to him and to conceal the diversion of his principal's money. As justification he urges a secret kickback agreement with Aztec's president. As we have said previously, an estoppel cannot arise from such facts.

Appellant Douglas argues that Special Issue No. 1, which asked the jury if he "had failed to complete his services to Aztec in an honest and forthright manner," is not a distinctly tort issue. Therefore he contends Aztec waived recovery in tort since no tort issues were requested or submitted. However, this argument ignores the applicable principle that no waiver results, and indeed no issue should be submitted, if the evidence conclusively establishes an independent ground of recovery. . . . "An issue is conclusively established when the evidence is such that there is no room for ordinary minds to differ as to the conclusion to be drawn from it." . . . The evidence in this case overwhelmingly and conclusively demonstrates Douglas' breach of trust. Douglas' own testimony establishes it. We therefore conclude that Douglas' breach of fiduciary duty is established as a matter of law. It is a fundamental principle of our law that an agent who acts adversely to his principal or otherwise breaches his fiduciary obligation is not entitled to compensation for his services. . . . In [a 1974 case] the court cited with approval sec. 469 Restatement of Agency which states:

> An agent is entitled to no compensation for conduct which is disobedient or which is a breach of his duty of loyalty; if such conduct constitutes a wilful and deliberate breach of his contract of service, he is not entitled to compensation even for properly performed services for which no compensation is apportioned.

The override represented compensation due Douglas for "honest and forthright" performance of his agency, a duty imposed on every fiduciary. The court's judgment that Douglas is not entitled to the overriding royalty interest is based upon conclusive evidence of his willful breach of fiduciary duty. The court's denial of the override to Douglas is a proper legal consequence of his established infidelity. . . .

Bass, Justice.

Agent's Duty to Hold Money or Property   Money or property held by an agent is held in trust and must be applied for the purposes of the agency. The agent is under a duty to use reasonable care to protect the principal's property by keeping it in a safe place and protecting it from being lost, destroyed, or stolen. Money or property that the agent receives for the principal must be paid promptly to the principal.

Payment made to an agent who has authority to collect payment is equivalent to payment to the principal. This payment is complete when the money is delivered into the agent's hands and discharges any indebtedness the third person owes the principal. The debt is considered paid even though the agent may subsequently misappropriate the money or fail to turn it over to the principal.

Agent's Duty to Exercise Reasonable Care and Skill   An agent must exercise reasonable care and skill in the discharge of his agency. "Reasonable skill" is that skill possessed by persons usually engaged in the same occupation or business. Accordingly, an agent who represents himself as having particular skills and talents in a field assumes an obligation to exercise the care and skill that persons of similar expertise in the same field would have. Errors of judgment *not* due to the agent's lack of reasonable skill will not render the agent liable to the principal.

Principal's Rights   The principal is entitled to all rights and benefits that result from an agent's authorized acts on behalf of the principal. If the principal is named as the contracting party, a third person is bound by a contract made by an agent in the name of the principal and is liable to the principal to the same extent as he would be if the principal had contracted with him directly.

Principal's Duty to Agent   The primary duties of the principal to the agent are those that arise from the agency contract. The principal has a duty to compensate, reimburse, and indemnify the agent for services rendered or money expended in the transaction of agency business. The amount of the agent's compensation for services should be firmly fixed in the agency agreement. If it is not, the law will imply a promise on the principal's part to pay the agent a reasonable amount for those services.

In the absence of contractual provisions to the contrary, a principal is obligated to pay a sales agent commissions on any bona fide sale to a solvent purchaser. This is usually true even if the principal subsequently refuses to fill the order or the customer refuses to receive the goods or pay for them. The exception to this rule is that if the principal has reserved the right to reject orders, the agent is not entitled to the commission on orders rejected.

Remedies   A principal whose agent violates or threatens to violate the duties of the agency relationship has several available legal remedies. These remedies include a lawsuit against the agent (1) for breach of the agency contract or for failure to perform it properly; (2) for money received by the agent for the principal but not turned over by the agent; (3) for a tort, such as fraud or other dishonesty; or (4) for an accounting. In addition to these judicial remedies, the principal can also discharge the agent, rescind or cancel the agency contract, or simply refuse to pay the agreed compensation.

An agent also has remedies against the principal. The agent can, for example, sue to recover compensation that is owed to him for services rendered. An agent who is wrongfully discharged can sue the principal for damages.

43:6   Rights, Duties, and Liabilities as to Third Persons

In relation to third persons, the principal is bound by and liable for all acts performed by his agent within the actual or apparent scope of the agent's authority. This rule of liability is based not on agency principles but on those relating to the law of employer and employee. The principal can also be held liable for the torts an agent commits in the course and scope of his employment, even though the principal did not authorize, ratify, participate in, or even know of the misconduct. Liability for an agent's torts is grounded on the employer–employee principle of *respondeat superior*.[1]

Knowledge and Notice   A principal is chargeable with and bound by knowledge or notice that his agent receives from a third person while the agent is acting within the scope of his authority. Notice chargeable in this way is called *constructive notice*. A principal who has constructive notice of a fact is treated just as if he had actually received the notice. Stated another way, the principal, not the third person, has to bear the responsibility for the agent's failure to communicate. The theory is that between two innocent persons—the principal and the third person—the one setting the situation in motion should suffer the legal consequences of a wrongdoer. The imputation of the agent's knowledge to the principal has been applied in a variety of business situations. For example, an agent's knowledge of the contents of a contract can be imputed to the principal.

 Depending on the scope and purpose of an agency, it may be essential that the principal be fully and currently informed about all or at least some circumstances, as they arise, relating to the subject matter of the agency. If so, when the agency is created, the agent should be instructed as to (1) what information relating to his or her actions is to be commu-

---

[1] The doctrine of respondeat superior is further discussed in Chapter 50.

nicated to the principal and (2) how the communications are to be made. The instruction should be in writing. It can be part of the contract creating the agency if a written contract is used.

Liability of Agent   An agent who negotiates and signs a contract with a third person on behalf of a principal is ordinarily not personally a party to the contract and does not intend to be personally liable under it. The agent will not be personally liable if (1) signing the contract is within the scope of the agent's authority and (2) the agent's status as an agent is known to the third person. The agent's status is usually disclosed by his signing the contract in a representative capacity, such as "National Hardware Service, by John Jacobs, Agent." If, however, nothing in the contract indicates an agency relationship between the agent and his principal, the agent might be held liable as one of the contracting parties. Furthermore, if an agent purports to act in his agency capacity in making a contract with a third person, but is actually acting without or in excess of his authority, the agent is personally liable for any damages suffered by the third person due to the agent's act.

Agent's Tort Liability   Regardless of the agency relationship, an agent is liable for any torts he commits. The agent's tort liability is based not on a contractual relationship between the principal and agent, but simply on the legal rule that every person must act in a manner that will not be harmful to another. The fact that the principal may *also* be liable for the agent's torts does not excuse the agent from liability; they can be liable jointly.

43:7   Undisclosed Agency

If the other party to a transaction conducted by an agent knows that the agent is acting for a principal and knows the principal's identity, the principal is said to be disclosed. If a third person knows or has reason to know that the agent is, or may be, acting for a principal but is unaware of the principal's identity, the principal is said to be partially disclosed. If the third person has no notice whatsoever of the fact that the agent is acting for another person, the principal—as well as the agency relationship—is said to be *undisclosed*.

Concealment of the identity of a principal is a common and sometimes necessary practice in business. For example, concealment of the identity of the true purchaser of realty may be a wise—and perfectly legal—business technique to prevent business competitors from bidding on the same property. Furthermore, concealment of a principal's true identity might enable the principal to take actions without having to be concerned with the personal feelings of some third person.

Liability of Principal and Agent   In an undisclosed agency situation in which the principal fails to perform as agreed, the other party has the option of holding either the agent or the principal (assuming discovery of the principal's existence and identity) liable and has a reasonable time in which to decide whom to sue. After deciding, he or she must abide by the decision even though there is ultimately no satisfaction of the liability.

To avoid the possibility of personal liability on a contract, an agent must, when the contract is made, disclose not only the agency relationship but also the principal's identity. The effect of an agent's failure to do so is illustrated in the following case.

Mawer-Gulden-Annis, Inc.
v
Brazilian & Columbian Coffee Co.
199 NE2d 222 (1964)
Illinois Court of Appeals

FACTS: Mawer sued Brazilian & Colombian Coffee and its president, Weinshenk, seeking damages for the value of olives that Mawer had ostensibly sold and delivered to Brazilian. In entering into the transaction with Mawer, Weinshenk did not disclose that he and his company were acting for an undisclosed principal on whose behalf the goods were purchased. At trial, Brazilian contended that it did not purchase the olives in its own right. Brazilian argued that it was acting as a food broker and that Mawer should have known the identity of its principal from the bills of lading. The trial court found Brazilian and Weinshenk liable, and they appealed.

ISSUE: Did Brazilian adequately disclose the identity of its principal so as to avoid liability on the contract entered into on behalf of the principal?

RESULT: No. Brazilian had a duty to bring the fact of its agency and the identity of its principal to the attention of the buyer, so as to give actual notice of the agency.

REASONING:

*   *   *

Defendants denied they purchased the goods in their own right or for an undisclosed principal but stated that their function was as food brokers representing plaintiff in the sale wherein they would obtain a customer for plaintiff. They further state that the goods were actually delivered by plaintiff to the customer defendants obtained for the plaintiff. . . .

In the instant case the trial court, upon hearing and weighing the evidence, and passing upon the credibility of the witnesses, found that Brazilian did not disclose the name of its principal at the time of contracting. We cannot hold that these findings were against the manifest weight of the evidence especially when in its letter of June 20, 1961, . . .

eight days after the confirmation and delivery, Brazilian, through Weinshenk, its president, writes, "The writer tried to contact you several times by phone and vice versa to give you the name of the buyer, but as your B/L 0OZ 3990 (the bill of lading) indicates, you delivered these goods to our customers, Pantry Queen Food Products Company, and therefore you should have invoiced them for this merchandise directly."

In [an early Illinois case] the court said:

> "It is a settled rule in verbal contracts, if the agent does not disclose his agency and name his principal, he binds himself and becomes subject to all liabilities, express and implied, created by the contract and transaction, in the same manner as if he were the principal in interest. . . . And the fact that the agent is known to be a commission merchant, auctioneer, or other professional agent, makes no difference. . . . "

The duty is upon the agent, who wishes to avoid liability, to disclose the name or identity of his principal clearly and in such a manner as to bring such adequately to the actual notice of the other party, and it is not sufficient that the third person has knowledge of facts and circumstances which would, if reasonably followed by inquiry, disclose the identity of the principal. . . . The reason for the rule is [the] necessity for disclosing who the principals are to give the contracting party the opportunity to make inquiry as to the fact, and then to determine whether he is satisfied that such persons are the principals of the agent, and if they are, then whether such party is willing to extend credit to such principals. . . .

The defendant's argument that the plaintiff is chargeable with knowledge of the principal from the fact that the carrier allegedly called and spoke to the shipping clerk regarding the olives and that the bill of lading made out by the shipping clerk showed Pantry Queen as the consignee, when taken together with the fact that defendant is generally known as a broker, is untenable.

Even if we assume plaintiff, from the above circumstances, had learned the identity of the principal, such information was not so timely as to relieve defendant of liability. To avoid personal liability, disclosure of the principal must be made at the time of contracting, otherwise either the agent or the subsequently disclosed principal may be held. . . . Defendant, not having informed plaintiff of the customer for whom it was purchasing, therefore, contracted as a principal, and cannot now complain if it is held liable as such. . . .

Kluczynski, Justice.

43:8 Duration and Termination of Agency

Duration of an agency relationship is determined by the agency agreement. If no time is specified, the agency relationship will expire at the end of a reasonable time or on completion of the purpose of the agency.

Principal's Power to Revoke   The principal's power to revoke an agent's authority is not absolute. That is, actions of an agent could continue to bind a principal as to third persons after the principal has revoked the agent's authority if the third person does not know of the revocation and relies on the continued existence of the agency.

 Disputes and litigation can be prevented if a principal who has revoked his or her agent's authority notifies any persons who have dealt with the agent that the agency relationship no longer exists.

Termination by Operation of Law   In some situations an agency is said to be terminated "by operation of law," meaning simply that the circumstances are such that in the interest of fairness the law automatically terminates the agency. These circumstances include (1) the death of the principal or agent; (2) either party's inability to continue to perform, such as due to illness; (3) loss or destruction of the subject matter of the agreement; and (4) a change in business conditions, value of the subject matter, or identity of the principal.

43:9   Power of Attorney

A *power of attorney* is a written instrument by which a person, acting as a principal, appoints another as his agent, conferring on that person the authority to perform certain acts on his behalf. The writing is sometimes also called a letter of attorney. The word "attorney" is used simply to designate a particular type of principal–agent relationship. An agent acting under a power of attorney is referred to as an attorney in fact and may or may not be an attorney at law.

Some states require a power of attorney to convey real property or any interest in it to be prepared with the same formalities as a deed or mortgage (see Chapters 35 and 36). Some states also require these powers of attorney to be recorded with a designated public official.

Types of Powers   The purpose of a power of attorney is to serve as tangible evidence of the agent's authority to third persons with whom the agent may deal. A power of attorney can be *general*, which means that the agent is authorized to act in any manner consistent with the general business or purposes of the principal. It can also be *special*, which means that the agent can act only to perform specified tasks. A power of attorney can also be partly general and partly special.

EXAMPLE: Prince wants to sell tracts 1, 2, and 3 of his property. He can grant a sales agent a general power (sell any or all of the tracts to whoever will pay the best price) or a special power (sell tract 1 to Jones for no less than $10,000). However, Prince can also grant a partly general and partly special power (sell tracts 1 and 3 to whoever will pay the best price, but sell tract 2 only to Balboa for no less than $15,000).

The following case illustrates a typical use of the power of attorney and some of the problems associated with its use. Note that the power of attorney is virtually always revocable and, as an agency relationship, terminates on incompetence of either party. Thus, it is not an ideal method of solving the problem of managing the assets of an incompetent family member. The usual alternative is the judicial appointment of a legal guardian and conservator, which creates a fiduciary relationship not necessarily based on consent. In addition, as the case discusses, some states permit a "durable" power of attorney.

<hr>

Peterson

v

Peterson

700 P2d 585 (1985)

Court of Appeals of Kansas

FACTS: In order to help his 85-year-old mother arrange her financial affairs, Charles Peterson met with Mrs. Peterson's attorney and arranged for his mother to create a series of irrevocable trusts for the disposition of her property at death. In addition, she signed papers granting Charles the "irrevocable" power of appointment. About a month after creating the trusts and power Mrs. Peterson sought a court order nullifying the trusts and the power on the ground that she was not advised of their irrevocable nature. The court found no basis for nullifying the irrevocable trusts.

ISSUE: Is an "irrevocable" power of attorney irrevocable?

RESULT: No. A power of attorney is an agency relationship that can be revoked by the principal.

REASONING:

*   *   *

Plaintiff next argues that in Kansas a "durable" power of attorney remains in effect, if the proper wording is used, even if the person giving the power of attorney becomes incapacitated, K.S.A. 58–610 *et seq.*, but that an "irrevocable" power of attorney would violate public policy and cannot exist.

A power of attorney is defined . . . as "an instrument in writing by which one person, as principal, appoints another as his agent and confers upon such agent the authority to act in the place of the principal for the avowed purposes set forth in the instrument." The general rule of agency is that "[t]he power to revoke an agent's authority at any time is not affected by the fact that there is an express or implied contract between the agent and the principal that such agency is irrevocable. . . . "

. . . Since it is deemed contrary to public policy to have an agent forced on a principal against his will, unless a power of attorney is coupled with an interest, it is revocable by the principal at will. The interest of the agent is subject to a reserved power of revocation which is implicit in the power of attorney. . . .

In order to render effectual the termination of an agency, notice of the termination must be given to the affected parties. . . .

Amy Ruth Peterson filed the petition in this case on December 16, 1981, and prayed for the revocation of this power of attorney. If that was not adequate notice of revocation, and we think that it was, she then gave notice of revocation by separate written statement on September 3, 1982. This power of attorney qualified as a durable power of attorney under K.S.A. 58–610 *et seq.*, which has nothing to do with its revocation but provides that it shall continue in effect if the principal becomes incapacitated. The capacity of Amy Ruth Peterson was never questioned and so was never an issue in this litigation. She could, and did, revoke this power of attorney by the filing of the petition herein, and the district court erred in holding the power of attorney to be irrevocable. . . .

Wahl, Judge.

Interpretation of Power of Attorney   The key rule in interpreting a power of attorney is that the parties' intention as it existed when the power was granted is controlling. Furthermore, powers of attorney are strictly construed. This means, for example, that a given instrument will be held to grant *only* those powers that are specified in it. For these reasons, any power of attorney should set forth as many of the important aspects of the agency being created as possible, including the following:

- Status of the principal, such as whether an individual or a business entity
- Type of power of attorney being granted
- Nature of the property and property rights that are to be subject to the power
- Nature of the ownership of the property that is to be subject to the power
- Scope and extent of powers granted
- Effective date of the power, and its duration

Some powers of attorney set forth the manner in which the power being granted is to be executed. If this is done, the attorney in fact must act precisely as directed.

Key Concepts and Terms

- Agency is a fiduciary relationship. It arises when one person (the principal) confides to another (the agent) the management of a business or performance of a transaction to be carried out by the agent in the principal's name and subject to the principal's control. Any person or organization having the capacity to act can act through an agent.

- The agency relationship ordinarily is created by agreement of the principal and agent. The agreement is often express, but it can also be implied if the relationship can be reasonably inferred from the surrounding circumstances.

- Agency can be created when a person permits another to act for him and, by so doing, causes third persons to reasonably believe that an agency has been created. This is called agency by estoppel.

- Agency by necessity is an agency that is created in certain emergency situations in which it is proper for one person to act for another without having the express authority to do so.

- Under the doctrine of apparent or ostensible authority, if the principal conducts business so as to cause third persons to reasonably believe that the agent possesses authority to act in the principal's name, the principal will be bound by the agent's acts. Determination of ostensible authority is made by examining actions of the principal, not the agent.

- A principal sometimes expressly authorizes an agent to delegate the agent's authority to another person, a subagent. The subagent then represents the principal as if he had been directly appointed by the principal.

- Ratification is a principal's adoption of his agent's prior act, which did not bind the principal but was done or professed to be done on his account. It can be express (orally or in writing) or implied from the acts or conduct of the principal subsequent to the act.

- An agent must obey all reasonable instructions of the principal and is required to exercise the utmost good faith, loyalty, and honesty toward the principal. He must also exercise reasonable care and skill. The principal has the duty to compensate, reimburse, and indemnify an agent for services rendered or money spent in the transaction of agency business.

- The principal is liable for torts performed by the agent within the actual or apparent scope of the agent's authority. The agent is also liable for his torts.

- The extent to which an agent conceals the identity of the principal determines whether the agency is disclosed, partially disclosed, or undisclosed.

- Duration of an agency is determined by agreement between the principal and agent. If no time is specified, the agency expires at the end of a reasonable time or on completion of the purpose of the agency. An agency can also be terminated by operation of law.

- A power of attorney is a written instrument by which a person, acting as principal, appoints another as his agent, conferring on the agent the authority to perform certain acts on the principal's behalf.

- Agency
- Agency by Necessity
- Apparent (Ostensible) Authority
- Constructive Notice
- Fiduciary Relationship
- General Power
- Implied Authority
- Power of Attorney
- Ratification
- Respondeat Superior
- Special Power
- Subagent
- Undisclosed Agency

Questions and Case Problems

1. Rosen visits Deporter Tours. She brings with her a brochure published under the name of World Trek, advertising an African safari. Deporter agrees to arrange for Rosen to join the safari, which is to begin in Cairo. Rosen pays $1,200 for the tour, and Deporter forwards that sum, minus a ten percent commission, to World Trek. Because Rosen plans to tour Europe on a casual and unscheduled basis for several months before joining the safari, she and Deporter exchange contact addresses. Rosen goes about her travels, and she receives no further word about the safari. On the starting date for the safari, she turns up in Cairo but finds no sign of the safari nor anyone who has even heard of World Trek. Rosen subsequently learns from Deporter that the meeting place for the safari was changed to Nairobi, and that World Trek had been unable to contact her to let her know. This happened because Deporter had failed to communicate Rosen's contact address to World Trek. Rosen sues Deporter for recovery of the $1,200 tour price, claiming that the agency breached its agreement to arrange the tour and thus prevented her from going on the safari. How should the case be decided?

2. Grimes meets Artug at a party where he offers to help Artug find a publisher for Artug's new book "solely as a friend." Grimes forgets about his promise and does nothing to find a publisher for the manuscript. Has an agency relationship been created? Is Grimes liable to Artug for breach of contract?

3. Delta Corp. is in the business of servicing mobile-home purchase contracts. For a fee, it handles the collection of monthly payments from mobile-home buyers. Delta acquires these accounts by making agreements with dealers in mobile homes, or with the banks that financed them. Donald is a Delta representative in Arizona, and he has authority to solicit accounts from banks and dealers. The president of Western Coach Corporation, a retail seller of mobile homes, tells Donald that she knows of a Texas company that has a portfolio of $2 million in mobile-home contracts that it wants to sell. Donald sees an opportunity to place these contracts in banks with which Delta does business. Thus, he agrees to pay Western Coach Corporation five percent of the gross charges in transferring this portfolio, as a "finder's fee," and he and Western Coach sign a contract to this effect. Subsequently, Delta Corporation refuses to pay the five percent to Western Coach, denying that Donald had any authority to bind it to any such agreement. Did Donald have this authority? Why?

4. Ralph's business manager receives a check payable to Ralph. The manager indorses Ralph's name on the check, cashes it, and keeps the money. Ralph sues the bank for the amount of the check. How should the case be decided?

5. Bozza and Ruzzo ran a trucking business in a corporate form. In May 1981 they purchased a Kenworth truck in the corporation name. In June 1981 they reported

the truck stolen and filed a proof of loss with the corporation's insurance carrier, Excess. Excess' adjuster, Campos, investigated the loss and arranged for two drafts, each in the amount of $7,375, to be issued payable to Ruzzo-Bozza Trucking, Inc. Before the checks were delivered, Bozza called Campos, explained that he suspected Ruzzo would abscond with the insurance money, and asked them to to tell him when the checks were ready so that he could accompany Ruzzo to get them. Campos, nevertheless, delivered the checks to Ruzzo, who exchanged them for cashier's checks and absconded with the money. The corporation now sues Excess, the insurance company, for the amount of the checks. Excess claims that Ruzzo had the apparent authority to accept the checks for the corporation. What result?

6. Shelby was a business owner and a long-time customer of the bank. He dealt mostly with Slepekis, a vice president of the bank. Slepekis arranged a legitimate loan for Shelby. At the last minute Shelby did not need the money, but Slepekis persuaded him to borrow the money anyway and then to lend it to Slepekis. Shelby did so. Slepekis then lost his job and failed to repay the money to Shelby. When the bank called the loan, Shelby repaid it. Shelby now sues the bank, alleging that the bank is liable in respondeat superior for Slepekis' fraud against Shelby. What result?

7. Brunner, an onion farmer, engaged Horton to market his 1987 crop. On a commission basis, Horton assumed the job of arranging transportation, selecting buyers, setting prices, collecting the net proceeds of the sales, and paying Brunner. Horton arranged for Valdez Brokerage to buy the onions. Valdez was not well known in the industry, and Horton had been advised of problems with Valdez's operation. Horton did not disclose these problems to Brunner until almost a month after the last shipment of onions to Valdez. When Valdez failed to pay for the onions, Brunner sued Horton for breach of the fiduciary duty. How should the case be decided?

8. Williams is a sales representative for Ace Co, a publisher of books for the medical profession. Her job is to visit doctors, hospitals, and other potential customers and solicit orders for books from Ace's line. She is paid a 25 percent commission on all sales. On leaving Dr. Boyd's office after making an unsuccessful sales presentation, Williams notices a valuable painting on the wall of Boyd's waiting room. Angered by her failure to make a sale, Williams defaces the painting. Boyd discovers who ruined his painting and sues Ace for its value. Is Ace liable for Williams' act?

9. Janet frequently buys heavy machinery from various suppliers for the Kendall Construction Co., of which she is the general purchasing agent. Two months after she leaves that job, Janet buys two tractors from a former supplier without stating that the tractors are not being bought for Kendall. After defaulting on the purchase, Janet is sued by the supplier, who also sues Kendall. Discuss the liability of all the parties.

10. Crestview Co. authorizes Haven to buy a new generator for the company plant. Haven enters into an agreement with Genco and signs the agreement, "Crestview Company, by its agent Haven." Can Genco enforce the agreement against Crestview? Against Haven?

44 Partnerships, Limited Partnerships, and Special Ventures

44:1 Nature and Formation of Partnerships

The partnership is a common form of business organization. Many of the doctrines of partnership law developed in Europe under the law merchant during the Middle Ages and in England under the common law. In the United States, most of these doctrines are now codified in the *Uniform Partnership Act* (UPA), which was originally drafted in 1914. The UPA has been adopted in every state except Georgia and Louisiana. Because of the widespread applicability of the UPA throughout the United States, the discussion of partnership law in this chapter will be based on it.[1]

A partnership is an association of two or more persons to carry on a business for profit as co-owners [UPA § 6]. A partnership can be formed for any purpose that is not in violation of law or public policy; it can be formed for a single transaction or for a continuing series of transactions.

There are various types of partnerships, each creating different powers and liabilities for partners. The types that will be discussed in this chapter are general partnerships and limited partnerships.

Among *general partnerships*, a distinction is made in some states between trading or commercial partnerships on the one hand, and ordinary or nontrading partnerships on the other. A trading partnership is one that engages in buying or selling. In contrast, a nontrading partnership is one that is not organized for trade or commerce. Partnerships organized for the practice of a profession, such as law, are examples of nontrading partnerships. Although the UPA seems to have abolished these categories, courts in some states have made distinctions between members of trading and nontrading partnerships in regard to such matters as their power both to borrow money and to sell personal property on behalf of the firm.

Creation of Partnership   A partnership is created by a contract between or among the parties (the intended partners). The parties must expressly agree to unite their property and services as co-owners to carry on a business for profit

---

[1] The complete text of the UPA is reproduced in Appendix D.

and to share the profits and losses in stated proportions. The contract must be based on valid consideration.

A partnership agreement regulates the duties of the partners and can include virtually any provision desired by them. Certain partnership agreements must be in writing to be effective. For example, an agreement that provides for mandatory continuance of a partnership for more than one year is within the statute of frauds (see Chapter 15) and must be evidenced by a written document. Other partnership agreements do not need to be in writing. For example, an agreement authorizing the partners to deal in real estate need not be in writing insofar as the rights of the partners as to one another are concerned.

 It is suggested that any partnership agreement be in writing so that the partners' understanding of their mutual rights and duties is preserved and protected. If a partnership agreement is not in writing, it may be very difficult to prove that an oral agreement among the partners existed if, for example, one of the partners dies.

Other Business Relationships Compared   In some ways partnerships resemble other forms of business and other types of relationships. Thus, a partnership has certain elements in common with an agency relationship, a joint venture, a corporation, a nonprofit association, the relationship between joint owners of property, and even a trust. At the same time, a partnership has characteristics that are clearly distinguishable from these other relationships. Some of these similarities and differences will now be discussed briefly.

The primary distinction between a partnership and an agency (see Chapter 43) is that a partnership consists of co-owners. Although an agent can receive a share of the profits of the principal's business as compensation for services, the agent is not an owner.

A *joint venture* resembles a partnership in that its members associate as co-owners in a business enterprise, agreeing to share profits and losses. However, a partnership ordinarily engages in a continuing business for an indefinite or fixed period of time, whereas a joint venture is formed for a single transaction or a limited series of transactions.

Unlike a partnership, a corporation is always treated as an artificial person created by law separate and distinct from its shareholders (see Chapter 45). Shareholders of a corporation are not personally liable for corporate debts, and no shareholder or corporate officer can bind the corporation without authorization from the board of directors. In contrast, each partner has the power to bind each fellow member of the partnership. Each partner is individually liable both for debts and obligations of the partnership and for acts of copartners that are within the scope of their authority.

Employment relations are also readily distinguishable from partnerships. Unlike a partner, for example, an employee is not empowered to exercise management or control over the work being performed. An employee usually works for a fixed compensation and does not share in the profits and losses of the employer's business as does a partner. Finally, an employee is not viewed as having a fiduciary relationship with his or her employers, whereas a relationship of trust always exists between partners.

Who Can Be Partners   In general, any person or entity capable of making a contract can be a partner. Since UPA § 2 is rather broad in its definition of "person," individuals, other partnerships, corporations, and business associations all have the capacity to become partners. Under the UPA a corporation can become a partner, although it might be limited in doing so by state corporation laws. A minor can become a partner, but his contract of partnership might not be valid, with the result that his potential liability as a partner might not be enforceable.

Silent Partners   Occasionally, a partnership is formed in which one or more of the members do not want to be associated publicly with the partnership. These members are known as *silent partners*, and their connection with partnership business is ordinarily concealed. Silent partners sometimes take an active part in partnership affairs, but often they do not.

Junior and Senior Partners   The terms "junior partner" and "senior partner," while frequently used in law firms and other professional partnerships, generally have no special legal significance other than that which is given the terms in the partnership agreement. In at least one state, it is provided by statute that partners can, by written agreement, establish various classes of partners, such as senior partners, junior partners, and managing partners, and that they can also establish various classes of nonpartner employees.

44:2   Partnership Property

All property brought into a partnership or acquired by it is partnership property [UPA § 8(1)]. Property acquired with partnership funds is also partnership property. Under UPA §§ 8(3) and 8(4), real property can be acquired in the partnership name. In every state, the personal property of a partnership is owned by the partnership itself and not by the partners individually.

Conveyance of Property   Partnership property can be conveyed only in the partnership name [UPA § 8(3)]. Title to real property that is in the names of all of the partners individually can be conveyed if all the partners sign the conveyance; this passes all of their rights to such property [UPA § 10(5)].

Any partner can convey title to real property by a conveyance signed on behalf of a partnership if title to the property is in the name of the partnership [UPA § 10(1)]. Of course, such a conveyance must also be within the authority of the partner. A conveyance of partnership property by a partner, even though made without authority, cannot be recovered by a partnership if the property has been conveyed for value and the purchaser lacks knowledge or notice that the partner exceeded his authority.

If title to property is in the name of one or more of the partners, a partner in whose name the title stands can convey title. Thus, for example, if property

TABLE 44-1
Partnership Property

Acquisition	1. Contributed by partners 2. Acquired with partnership funds 3. Given to partnership
Title	In partnership, not individual partners
Conveyance	1. By partner with authority, in partnership name 2. By all partners if title to real property is in names of all partners individually 3. Unauthorized conveyance not recoverable from bona fide purchaser without knowledge or notice
Rights	Use by partners for partnership business
Form of ownership	Tenancy in partnership

owned by the Santa Fe partnership is held in the name of Fremont, legal title can be conveyed by Fremont in her own name. However, under UPA § 10(3), a partnership may recover property that is conveyed this way unless it is otherwise bound by the partner's acts.

Although the UPA regulates the sale of real property, it does not specifically deal with the sale or conveyance of personal property. These transactions are handled by the partners under their general powers to enter into contracts within the customary scope or purpose of partnership business.

Property Rights of Partners   The property rights of an individual partner include (1) the interest in the partnership; (2) the right in specific partnership property held in tenancy in partnership; and (3) the right to participate in management.

A partner's interest in the partnership is his share of the profit and surplus [UPA § 26]. A partner can dispose of his interest in a partnership by selling it to another partner. A partner can also transfer his interest in the partnership to a third person. However, a third person to whom the interest is assigned cannot become a partner without the consent of the existing partners. Indeed, the conveyance of a partner's interest does not entitle the assignee to (1) interfere in the management or administration of partnership business, (2) require any information or account of partnership transactions, or (3) inspect the partnership books [UPA § 18(g)]. The assignee is entitled only to receive the profits to which the assigning partner would otherwise be entitled.

Tenancy in Partnership   Real property that is owned or acquired by a partnership is held under what is called a *tenancy in partnership* [UPA § 25(1)]. Under UPA § 25(2), the characteristics of a tenancy in partnership are that (1) each partner has an equal right to use the property for partnership purposes in the absence of an agreement to the contrary; (2) a partner does not possess in any specific item of partnership property an interest that can be voluntarily sold, assigned, or mortgaged; (3) a creditor of a partner cannot proceed against any specific item of partnership property; and (4) on the death of a partner, the partnership property vests in the surviving partners for partnership purposes and is not subject to the right of survivorship.[2]

44:3 Powers of Partners

The general powers of partners are largely defined by the rules of law applicable to agents. In fact, the law of partnership has been called a branch of agency law. In one sense, every partner is a principal. However, for all purposes within the scope of a partnership's business, every partner is also a general and authorized agent of the partnership as well as an agent of all the other partners.

The powers of partners are governed largely by the provisions of the UPA and by the terms of the partnership agreement. Under UPA § 18(c), all partners possess an equal right in the management and conduct of the partnership business, even though some partners may receive a larger percentage of the profits. The conduct of a partnership is usually decided by a majority of the partners. Majority rule does not apply to an act that, by the partners' agreement, must be consented to by all the partners. Also, UPA § 9(3) provides that certain acts usually require the consent of all the partners. These acts are

- Assigning partnership property for the benefit of creditors[3]
- Disposing of partnership goodwill
- Doing any act that would make it impossible to carry on the ordinary business of the partnership
- Consenting to the entry of a court judgment against the partnership
- Submitting a partnership claim or liability to arbitration

Scope of Authority   A partner's status as such gives him the authority to act as an agent for the partnership in transactions within the usual course of partnership business [UPA § 9(1)]. The partner need not obtain express permission from other partners to transact partnership business. For example, a partner can use the partnership's assets to pay its debts, and she can enter into contracts in the name of the partnership and bind the firm by these contracts. A partner also has the authority to sign bills and notes or other debt instruments on behalf of the firm, and to collect, release, compromise, and pay claims or debts due the partnership.

A partner's act does not always bind the other partners or the partnership. If, for example, a partner acts without authority on a matter not within the apparent scope of partnership business, neither the partnership nor the other partners are bound by the act unless the other partners later ratify it. Partners can also restrict their authority as agents of the firm. They can even place secret restrictions on one another's authority, and these restrictions will bind

---

[2] The right of survivorship is discussed in Chapter 33.
[3] Assignments for the benefit of creditors are discussed in Chapter 32.

all the partners and any other person who may have knowledge of them or be under a duty to make an inquiry in this regard. Secret restrictions usually do not, however, apply to third persons who deal with the firm and have no knowledge about them.

44:4   Rights and Duties of Partners

The relationship existing among partners is one of trust. They each have an obligation to exercise the utmost good faith and integrity in their dealings with one another with regard to partnership affairs. This relationship, which is a fiduciary one, requires a partner to share with the partnership (1) all business opportunities clearly related to the subject of partnership operations and (2) any personal profit or advantage that he gains from dealings that involve partnership property and affairs. If a partner has promised to devote full time to the partnership business, the partner's time is considered to be a partnership asset. Hence, a partner cannot render services to any other employer, even one that does not compete with the partnership, without the consent of all other partners. If a partner does so, the salary he receives can be considered partnership income.

The rights and duties of partners among themselves are specified in considerable detail by the UPA. Under the UPA, each partner can

- Share equally in the profits of the firm [UPA § 18(a)]
- Receive repayment of his contributions, whether by way of capital or advances to the partnership profits [UPA § 18(a)]
- Receive indemnification on payments made on behalf of the firm or for personal liabilities incurred [UPA § 18(b)]
- Receive interest on advances and on capital contributions [UPA §§ 18(c), (d)]
- Share in the management and conduct of the business [UPA § 18(e)]
- Have access to the firm's books and records [UPA § 19]
- Have a formal accounting of partnership affairs [UPA § 22]

These rights can be changed by agreement. For example, all the partners can agree to vest the management of the partnership in one or more of the partners or change the general rules about the distribution of profits or sharing of losses. The principle of majority rule can be changed by agreement to require the unanimous decision of partners on certain matters. The partners can also agree to give themselves the right to expel a partner under certain circumstances.

Partners' rights are complemented by a series of duties. Under the UPA, each partner has a duty to

- Contribute toward losses sustained by the partnership [UPA § 18(a)]
- Work for the partnership without remuneration other than a share of profits [UPA § 18(b)]
- Submit to a majority vote when differences arise among partners as to the conduct of the firm's business [UPA § 18(b)]

- Share with other partners any information regarding partnership matters [UPA § 20]
- Account to the firm for any profit derived from any partnership transaction or from the use of partnership property [UPA § 21]

Profits and Losses   Each partner is entitled to an equal share in the profits of the partnership [UPA § 18(a)]. Unless there is an agreement to the contrary, partners share equally in the profits, even though they may have contributed unequally to capital or services. The sharing of profits can be controlled by an express agreement among the partners, or by an agreement that may be implied from the partners' conduct. Note, however, that a contractual provision limiting only the *salaries* of partners does not limit the partners' rights to participate in the profits of the firm over and above operating expenses. A partner's breach of a partnership agreement, whether or not committed in bad faith, does not cause loss of the right to share in partnership profits. However, a partner who refuses to contribute funds essential to the operation of a partnership business can be excluded from participation in the profits. If a partner abandons the business, he can also forfeit some or all of his share of the profits.

UPA § 18(a) provides that unless there is an agreement to the contrary, each partner must contribute toward the losses sustained by a partnership according to his share in the profits. If partners do make a different agreement among themselves as to how losses shall be apportioned, the agreement will be controlling as among the partners. An agreement can provide any reasonable basis for apportioning losses. For example, a partnership agreement can provide that losses shall be shared on an equal basis, or it can limit the liability of particular partners as to losses.

Distributions and Compensation for Services   Each partner can be reimbursed for all expenses paid or incurred in the ordinary conduct of partnership business, plus interest [UPA §§ 18(b), (c)]. However, no partner is entitled to compensation for services on behalf of a partnership except with the consent of all other partners [UPA § 18(f)]. The reason for this rule is that ordinarily a partner is obligated to devote his services to the partnership, giving it all his time, skill, and ability. Therefore, unless there has been some agreement among the partners covering the matter, no partner has any right to a greater share of the partnership profits simply because he has rendered services. The only exception to this rule is that on dissolution, a surviving partner is entitled to reasonable compensation for services in winding up the partnership affairs.

 Ordinarily, provisions of a partnership agreement will expressly regulate the duty of partners to render services to the partnership. It is therefore important to review the partnership agreement to determine the exact nature of a partner's obligation in that regard. This is also true if a partner engages in outside activities for his own benefit. There is nothing inherently fraudulent or against public policy in permitting a partner to engage in his own business pursuits while he is a member of a partnership.

However, he must (1) act in good faith toward the other partners and (2) not violate any agreement among the partners preventing him from engaging in the enterprise in question.

Repayment of Contributions   Each partner is entitled to be repaid for contributions of capital or advances to the partnership property [UPA § 18(a)]. Capital consists of the money that the partnership agreement requires each partner to contribute for starting the business. An advance is an amount paid in by the partner in excess of the investment specified in a partnership agreement. If one partner has contributed a larger amount to the capital of the firm than another, the repayments will be made in the same proportion in which the capital was furnished.

Books and Records   One of the ordinary duties of partners is to keep accurate books and records showing the firm's accounts. On demand, partners must present full and complete information to any other partner on all matters affecting the partnership business [UPA § 20]. Each partner is entitled to access to the partnership books and records at all times. These records must be kept at the principal office of the partnership business [UPA § 19]. When a partner dies, his personal representative has the same rights with respect to access and inspection of partnership books as the partner himself would have had.

Right to Accounting   Under the UPA, each partner has the right to a formal *accounting* as to partnership affairs. This right arises if a partner is wrongfully excluded from the partnership business or its property by the other partners [UPA § 22(a)], if the right to an accounting exists under the terms of any agreement among the partners [UPA § 22(b)], or whenever other circumstances make it just and reasonable [UPA § 22(d)]. Every partner must also account to the partnership for any benefit and hold for it any profits derived without the consent of the other partners from any transaction connected with the formation, conduct, or liquidation of the partnership.

A partner who requests an accounting and does not receive it can sue for an accounting. It is not necessary that a partner cause the dissolution of the partnership to get an accounting. However, to be entitled to a court-ordered accounting, the partner must show that he is in fact a partner and that the transaction giving rise to the demand is connected with the formation, conduct, or liquidation of the partnership.

Liabilities   Given the many rights and duties imposed on partners, it is clear that the potential for litigation between members of a partnership is considerable. A partner can be liable to another partner if he neglects to give a partnership all his time, skill, and ability, or if he neglects to use his knowledge, skill, and ability to promote the common benefit of the business. A partner can also be liable for failing to perform services agreed to be performed, for wrongfully engaging in an enterprise other than partnership business, and for not paying another partner compensation that is due the latter for services rendered the partnership. Finally, a partner can be liable to one or more other partners for breach of the fiduciary relationship that is inherent in a partnership, and for personal injuries and property damage.

Under general partnership law, a legal action cannot be maintained among partners with regard to partnership transactions unless there has been an accounting or settlement of partnership affairs. Under this rule, a partner cannot ordinarily sue to recover (1) a share of the partnership profits, (2) a share of the proceeds of a sale of partnership property, (3) compensation for services rendered, or (4) damages for breach of certain general provisions of a partnership agreement. However, it is frequently possible to avoid the effects of this rule; many states have enacted statutes that permit actions between partners in cases where they would not be maintainable under the common-law rule.

44:5 Liability to Third Persons

The liability of a partner for the acts of his copartners is founded on principles of agency. The UPA prescribes the nature of the liability. Under UPA § 15(b), partners are jointly liable for all debts and obligations resulting from partnership transactions. In regard to liability for torts, partners are jointly and severally liable for torts committed in the course of partnership business. This means that a third person suing for a tort can either sue all of the partners jointly or sue any one partner individually [UPA §§ 13, 15(a)].

Under the doctrine of mutual agency, any member of a partnership is liable for torts even in the absence of participation, ratification, or knowledge. That is, an injured party can single out a partner and hold him liable, even if he was not personally involved in the commission of the tort. However, if a tort requires a showing of malice or wrongful intent, each partner sought to be held liable must also be shown to have acted with malice or to have possessed wrongful intent.

 A silent partner who participates in the profits of a partnership is subject to the same liability as active partners. The law does not permit a silent partner to share secretly in the profits of a firm without taking his share of the risks and without bearing his share of the losses as to third persons. Thus, for example, a creditor is entitled to recover from all the partners, including silent ones, even though one partner might hold herself out as the sole owner of a business and in spite of any agreement entered into among the partners purporting to limit liability.

Torts of Employees   The UPA does not specifically provide that a partnership is liable for the torts of an employee. Rather, it provides that the law of agency applies [UPA § 4(3)]. This rule makes the partnership liable for the torts of employees—as agents of the partnership—committed within the scope of their employment. The members of the partnership are also liable for these torts, and this liability is joint and several. However, if an employee commits a tortious act *outside* the scope of his employment, neither the partnership nor the partners will be held liable.

Conversion and Misapplication of Funds If a partner, acting within the scope of his apparent authority, receives money or property from a third person and misapplies it, the partnership is liable for the loss [UPA § 14]. UPA § 14 also provides that a partnership will be liable if property received by it in the course of its business is misapplied by any partner while it is in the partnership's custody. This rule represents a codification of the common law, which made all partners liable for a conversion of property committed by one member of the firm while acting within the scope of his authority.

Partners are jointly and severally liable for everything chargeable to the partnership due to misapplication of funds [UPA § 15(a)]. Therefore, if one partner converts a third person's money or property, the person can sue all of the partners jointly or any one partner individually. However, neither the partnership nor innocent partners are liable for a conversion or misapplication of funds that does not occur in the course of the firm's business. Thus, for example, if a partner in a law firm embezzles money, the other partners are not liable since the embezzlement was not done in the course of proper partnership business.

Fraud and Misrepresentation Fraud and fraudulent representations of one partner in the course of partnership business bind the partnership and render it liable. This is so even though other partners are innocent of any participation in the fraud. The reason for this rule is found in the general principle of the liability of firms and partners for unlawful acts committed by their agents within the general scope of their agency. The rule imposing civil liability on an innocent partner for the fraud of a copartner is especially applicable where the innocent partner receives the benefit of the fraudulent conduct.

Indemnification Because all partners are jointly liable for partnership debts and obligations [UPA § 15(b)], each partner may be required to pay the entire amount of such a debt or obligation himself. When one partner has so paid off a debt or obligation that is jointly owed by the partners, the UPA requires the partnership to indemnify the one who paid. UPA § 18(b) provides for indemnification whenever a partner has made payments or has incurred personal liabilities in the ordinary and proper conduct of partnership business, or for the preservation of its business or property. If a partnership is itself unable to indemnify a partner, the obligation falls on all the other partners.

Criminal Liability The rule in some states is that a partnership cannot commit a crime since it is not a legal entity. In many states, however, a partnership can be found to have committed a crime, through the acts of one or more of the partners. The penalty in those states is a fine levied against the partnership's property.

A partner is, of course, individually liable for his criminal act, and if all the partners participate in the act they are criminally liable as well. However, a partner who does not participate in criminal conduct involving other partners will not be held criminally liable. That is, one partner's criminal conduct does not automatically make other partners liable too.

Partnership by Estoppel   In certain circumstances, parties can be held liable as partners as against third persons, even though a partnership does not exist between the parties. Under the UPA, one who has allowed or caused others to believe that he is a partner can be estopped to deny the relationship [UPA § 16(1)].

EXAMPLE: Anderson, the sole proprietor of a retail fabrics business, approaches Zale for a loan. Anderson tells Zale that Goodson is a partner in Anderson's business. Goodson knows about Anderson's statements but does not advise Zale to the contrary, although she could easily do so. Zale relies on Goodson's credit and status in the community in extending the loan to Anderson. Insofar as this loan is concerned, Goodson is estopped from denying that she is a partner with Anderson. Goodson can be held liable to Zale for the amount of the loan as if she were in fact a partner in Anderson's business.

Liability of Third Person to Partnership for Injuries to Partner   Unlike a corporation, which is generally permitted to recover damages for a negligent injury to one of its employees, a partnership usually has no right to recover damages from another person for injuries inflicted on one of the partners. The reason for this rule is that a partner is not considered an employee of the partnership, so no right of action can arise.

EXAMPLE: Armstrong and Sharp are partners doing business as United Steel Supply Company. While on partnership business, Armstrong is injured by Grune's negligent act. Armstrong can recover damages from Grune for loss of income. However, since Armstrong is not considered an employee of United Steel, United Steel cannot recover damages from Grune for its lost earnings and profits due to Armstrong's injury.

44:6   Dissolution of Partnership

"Dissolution of a partnership" is the change in the relation of the partners that is caused by any partner ceasing to be associated in the carrying on of the business [UPA § 29]. *Dissolution* is not in itself a termination of the partnership or of the rights and powers of partners. Many of these rights and powers continue during the winding up process that follows dissolution. Although various terms have been applied to the process leading up to the final settlement of all partnership affairs, the term "dissolution" designates that point in time when the partners cease to carry on the business together. The term is thus distinguishable from "winding up" (or "liquidation" as it is also called), which is the process of settling partnership affairs after dissolution, and "termination," which is that point in time when all the partnership affairs are completely wound up.

Causes of Dissolution   UPA § 31(1) provides that, even without any violation of a partnership agreement, dissolution is caused by (1) the termination of the definite term or particular undertaking specified in the partnership agreement, (2) the withdrawal of a partner when no definite term or particular undertaking is specified; (3) the mutual consent of all the partners before or after the termination of a specified term or undertaking; or (4) the expulsion of a partner if expulsion is carried out in accordance with the provisions of the partnership agreement. Dissolution is also caused by any event that makes it unlawful for the partnership to be carried on or for its members to carry on in partnership [UPA § 31(3)]; by the death of any partner [UPA § 31(4)]; and by the bankruptcy of any partner or the partnership itself [UPA § 31(5)]. In addition, dissolution can occur if a partner withdraws at any time in violation of the partnership agreement and the circumstances do not permit dissolution under any other provision of the UPA [UPA § 31(2)].

The various causes of dissolution are discussed separately below. It should be noted, however, that the most common potential causes of the dissolution of a large partnership are the death or withdrawal of a partner. As a practical matter, these causes have been eliminated in many large partnerships. The partnership agreements of law, accounting, and stock brokerage firms frequently provide that there will be no dissolution on the death of any individual partner or on his withdrawal, such as by retirement. The validity of these agreements has been authorized by statute in a number of states.

Expiration of Term; Completion of Purpose [UPA § 31(1)(a)]

A partnership agreement can provide that the partnership is to last for a stated period of time, such as one year or two years. If so, the partnership is dissolved when the stated time expires. Similarly, the agreement can state that the partnership is to last until a certain project is completed; completion of the project dissolves a partnership of this type. Note, however, as discussed below, that any partner can effectively end the partnership relationship before its intended term expires. Conversely, on the expiration of a partnership term, the partners can decide to continue the partnership business. If they do, their rights and duties remain the same as they were on the expiration date [UPA § 23].

Withdrawal [UPA §§ 31(1)(b), 31(2)]

Dissolution of a partnership by withdrawal can be accomplished at any time even if it violates an agreement among the partners [see UPA § 31(2)]. Thus, although a given partnership is to exist for a specific period of time, or for the accomplishment of a particular purpose, it can be dissolved by the withdrawal of any partner even at a moment's notice.

The right to dissolve a partnership at any time is deemed implicit in a partnership at will. A withdrawing partner is not liable to other partners even though dissolution of a partnership results in loss to the other partners. However, the right to dissolve a partnership at will must be exercised in good faith. If a partner acts in bad faith—as by attempting to appropriate for personal use some special advantage or opportunity that may more properly belong to the partnership—this would be treated as a wrongful dissolution.

If a partnership is for a fixed term, dissolution by withdrawal constitutes a violation of the partnership agreement. Thus, although the withdrawing partner has the *power* to dissolve the partnership in this way, he does not have the *right* to do so. Accordingly, the withdrawing partner in this situation can be held liable to the other partners for any losses caused by the dissolution.

The following case illustrates how a partner's withdrawal causes the dissolution of a partnership. Consider the duties of partners during dissolution and why the partner in this case was deemed to have breached his fiduciary duty to the other partners even though his withdrawal constituted a proper basis for dissolution.

Lavin

v

Ehrlich

363 NYS2d 50 (1974)
New York Supreme Court

FACTS: Ehrlich was one of three partners in a neighborhood tax preparing business. Ehrlich managed the business, and the other two partners were essentially investors. In a letter to the other partners, Ehrlich announced his immediate withdrawal from and dissolution of the partnership. Later that same month, he contracted to buy the storefront property in which the partnership operated its business. He then took title to the building and refused to negotiate a new lease with the partnership, which he considered dissolved. The partners sued Ehrlich, contending that he could not unilaterally dissolve the partnership and that he had further breached his fiduciary duties in buying the property. The displaced partners sought a court order holding that Ehrlich held the property in a constructive trust for the partnership.

ISSUE: Did Ehrlich breach his fiduciary duty to his partners?

RESULT: Yes. Ehrlich was obligated to offer the partnership the opportunity to purchase the building.

REASONING:

*   *   *

A neighborhood tax preparing business depends on many of the same clients returning each year. To this end, the location of the business is important and forms part of its goodwill. Were a partner in the business to buy in his own name the building housing it and then eject the partnership at the end of the lease, that would be an intolerable breach of fiduciary relationship. . . . But, what if that partner first serves notice to dissolve the partnership before buying the building; can he still be held to the same duties to his partners?

[Plaintiffs Lavin and Dillworth] first assert that Ehrlich could not unilaterally dissolve the partnership in contravention of the express withdrawal provisions of the partnership agreement. A contract provision does permit a withdrawing partner to give the others first option to buy him out on terms to be mutually agreeable, and failing in that gives him the right to sell to a stranger. However, there is no stranger poised to buy, nor is there any indication that one portends. Indeed, the provision on withdrawal is at best an agreement to agree. Accordingly, the agreement is not in point here.

Ehrlich argues that the agreement provides no specific term of life for the partnership, and so it is a partnership at will, to be dissolved at the insistence of any partner. . . . This is true, and Ehrlich's letter . . . effectively triggered the dissolution of the partnership, and should have set the winding up in motion towards final termination.

However, this dissolution did not free Ehrlich of all fiduciary relationship to the partnership. "On dissolution the partnership is not terminated, but continues until the winding up of the partnership affairs is completed." . . . There may be a relaxation of a partner's duties to his co-partners in relationships that look to the future of the newly dissolved partnership. . . . But, in dealings effecting the winding up of the partnership and the proper preservation of partnership assets during this time, "the good faith and full disclosure exacted of partners continues." . . .

Moreover, the Court is satisfied on the record that Ehrlich instituted and carried on negotiations for the building's purchase during the vital partnership tenure, and completed them later, without offering the ultimate deal to his partners. The opportunity to purchase the property and insure continued possession of the goodwill asset embodied in the location should have been offered to the partnership. Ehrlich breached his fiduciary duty in not making that offer and in appropriating this important partnership asset to himself. . . .

At the bottom, Ehrlich is doing something hopefully achievable from a technical standpoint, but sadly lacking in equity. He was the actual conductor of the business. He went out and grabbed the building, and now hopes, with this maneuver and his possession of the list of names and past tax return files (which he has undisputedly) to capitalize on the partnership location and goodwill to the exclusion of his partners. We cannot accept his strategy. . . .

Bertram Harnett, Justice.

Mutual Consent [UPA § 31(1)(c)]   A partnership can be altered, modified, or dissolved by mutual agreement. A partnership formed under an agreement that does not contain a provision as to its duration lasts no longer than as mutually agreed by the partners. Moreover, even if the time for the dissolution of a partnership is specified in the partnership agreement, the partners can mutually agree to dissolve their relationship before that time. This may be accomplished either by an express agreement for dissolution or by conduct implying an intention to dissolve the partnership. Partners can also agree on terms of a dissolution differing from those originally provided in the partnership agreement. If they do so, the specific dissolution agreement controls, and all the partners are bound by it.

Expulsion of Partner [UPA § 31(1)(d)]   The expulsion of a partner in accordance with a provision in the partnership agreement authorizing expulsion causes a dissolution of the partnership. If the agreement lists specific grounds for expulsion, one or more of those grounds must be shown to exist before an expulsion is justified. The expelling partners are not liable for any losses that the expelled partner sustains as a result of the expulsion. The other partners can be liable, however, if the expulsion is made in bad faith or without any right to expel as authorized by the partnership agreement. If a partner is expelled pursuant to an express provision of a partnership agreement, the remaining partners have the right to continue the business.

Death of Partner [UPA § 31(4)]   The death of a partner causes dissolution of a partnership regardless of whether the partnership is at will or for a fixed period of time. As in the case of dissolution by other causes, the death of a partner does not *terminate* the partnership until its affairs are wound up by the surviving partners. Note, however, that partners can provide by agreement that the partnership shall *not* be dissolved by the death of a partner. Indeed, partners can even set forth the terms by which the partnership will be continued by the surviving partners after the death of one or more of the copartners. For example, it is common for partners to agree that their surviving partners shall have the right or option to purchase a deceased partner's interest in the firm on specified terms and conditions.

Dissolution by Judicial Decree [UPA § 32(1)]   In certain circumstances, a judicial declaration can dissolve a partnership. A court shall, on application by or for a partner, decree dissolution of a partnership in any one of the following instances: (1) when a partner has been declared insane or shown to be of unsound mind; (2) when a partner becomes incapable of performing his part of a partnership contract; (3) when a partner has been guilty of misconduct that prejudicially affects the carrying on of the business; (4) when a partner willfully or persistently commits a breach of the partnership agreement or otherwise so conducts himself that it is not reasonably practical to carry on the business in partnership with him; (5) when the business of the partnership can be carried on only at a loss; and (6) for other circumstances that may render dissolution just and equitable.

A suit for dissolution of a partnership is equitable in nature. A court can consider all of the facts and circumstances before granting or withholding relief. Usually, a court orders partnership assets sold and the proceeds applied to payment of all partnership debts. The balance remaining is then applied to repay each partner's contributions, and to pay current earnings according to each partner's share of the partnership profits [UPA § 40]. If there are no partnership debts, a court can order distribution of the partnership assets "in kind," which means distribution of the assets themselves rather than the proceeds from their sale. If there are losses, or if partnership liabilities exceed assets available for distribution, each partner must contribute according to his share of the profits [UPA § 18(a)]. If a partner has not contributed the full share of capital that he originally agreed to, he must pay his share before other partners are required to make up any losses sustained. If one of the partners is insolvent or refuses to contribute his share of the losses, the remaining partners must make up his share proportionately. They will then have the right to sue the defaulting partner to enforce his contribution [UPA §§ 40(d)–(f)].

 When partners fall out, it may be wiser for them to invoke judicial dissolution under UPA § 32 and seek an accounting, than to try to divide up the assets of the partnership on their own. If one partner does not want to dissolve the partnership under court supervision, at the very least the partners should consider obtaining an independent audit of the partnership's worth.

Misconduct and Breach of Agreement   The UPA provisions dealing with misconduct are drafted in such broad language that they can cover a wide variety of frictions among partners [see UPA §§ 32(1)(c)–(f)]. Because of the difficulty in defining just what misbehavior or what degree of misconduct would authorize judicial dissolution, courts are often cautious about dissolving a partnership for misconduct. They ordinarily require a showing of gross misconduct or willful neglect of partnership obligations before they will grant a decree of dissolution. For example, dissolution will not be decreed for a partner's lack of courtesy to firm customers or for friction among partners that does not affect the success of the business. Nor will dissolution be ordered for trifling causes or temporary grievances involving no permanent mischief. However, if one partner has been guilty of misconduct that is markedly injurious to the interests of an innocent partner, this misconduct will be regarded as sufficient ground for dissolution.

Dissolution can also be decreed if a partner's conduct is inconsistent with continuation of the partnership, if a partner's misconduct materially interferes with the business, or if a partner willfully breaches the partnership agreement. Moreover, the wrongful exclusion of one partner by one or more of his copartners from participation in the business or the management of the partnership amounts to misconduct and constitutes a ground for judicial dissolution.

Admission of New Partner   The UPA does not appear to make the admission of a new partner a cause for dissolution. For example, the admission of a new partner is not listed either as a cause of dissolution or as a ground for obtaining a judicial decree of dissolution [see UPA §§ 31, 32]. Moreover,

UPA § 18(g) provides that one cannot become a member of a partnership without the consent of all the other partners, thus apparently recognizing the admission of a partner into a continuing partnership.

Effect of Dissolution   When a partnership dissolves, the general agency of one partner for his copartner ceases. The mutual agency is prolonged to a limited degree only until the affairs of the partnership are wound up. In other words, after dissolution no partner has any power whatsoever to act for or bind the others. Dissolution does, however, leave each of the partners with an equal duty and an equal power to do whatever is necessary to collect the debts due the partnership and to adjust, settle, and pay its debts. Moreover, dissolution of a partnership terminates the authority of a partner to act for the partnership except in limited circumstances [UPA § 33]. However, a partner does not lose his authority insofar as it may be necessary for the winding up of partnership affairs.

The dissolution of a partnership works an absolute revocation of all implied authority in any of the partners to bind the others to new contracts or obligations. In addition, if a partner dies or withdraws without violating the partnership agreement, and the business of the partnership is to continue without a winding up and liquidation, the withdrawing partner is entitled to the value of his partnership interest at the time of dissolution. This value is ascertained either by provisions in the partnership agreement or by agreement of the parties. Ultimately, the partnership interest represents the partner's proportionate share of the profits and surplus of the business. The following case reflects some of the problems associated with valuing the partner's share on dissolution.

Lange
v
Bartlett
360 NW2d 702 (1984)
Court of Appeals of Wisconsin

FACTS: Art Lange and Bert Bartlett worked together for several years on a part-time basis installing swimming pools. In 1972, they verbally agreed to form the partnership "Pool Boys" and began operating the business full-time. This arrangement continued until April of 1975 when Lange told Bartlett that he no longer wanted to participate in the partnership. It is clear that Lange was not expelled as a partner; rather, he retired from the partnership. Bartlett eventually offered Lange $3,000 in payment for Lange's share of the partnership; Lange refused this offer. Subsequently, in 1978, Lange sued to recover his share of the partnership.

ISSUE: Is the withdrawing partner in a business that is to continue after dissolution entitled (1) to profits that accrue to the continuing firm during the time between the dissolution and the settlement of his partnership interest, or (2) to interest on the value of his partnership interest at dissolution?

RESULT: The withdrawing partner may elect to take either profits or interest.

REASONING:

* * *

When a partner dies or retires, the partnership is dissolved. . . . However, the partnership is not terminated upon dissolution; it continues until the wind-up of the partnership affairs are completed. . . .

It is at this juncture, the point of dissolution, that the retiring partner makes an election. He can either force the business to "wind-up" and take his part of the proceeds, sharing in profits and losses after dissolution, or he can permit the business to continue and claim as a creditor the value of his interest at dissolution. . . . The determination of whether the retiring partner consented to or acquiesced in the continuation of the business is a question of fact. . . .

Thus, the first task for a trial court faced with making a settlement of a former partner's account after dissolution is to determine what election the retiring partner made at the point of dissolution. Every partnership dissolution causes a wind-up rather than a continuation unless the outgoing partner "consents" to a continuation. Distinguishing in the first instance whether a wind-up or a continuation is at hand is critical simply because the settlement of the former partner's account differs depending on whether it is a wind-up or a continuation.

For instance, if a trial court determines that a business was engaged in a wind-up, the former partner receives the value of his or her interest at the date of liquidation or final settlement. . . . In other words, the outgoing partner shares in both profits *and losses* until termination. . . . The former partner, therefore, does not take as a creditor. The outgoing partner gets a share of the profits, if any, only after all of the other creditors have been paid and only until termination. . . . Termination is the point in time when all of the partnership affairs are wound up. . . .

Continuation, however, effects a totally different settlement of the former partner's account. The outgoing partner can agree, at the time of dissolution, that the business will be continued. If the outgoing partner elects to allow the business to continue, then that partner has a second election—to receive either interest or profits from the date of dissolution—in addition to the value of his or her interest in the partnership. . . . This "second election" can be made only by the former partner; it cannot be made by either the continuing partner or the trial court. The profits garnered from continuation are different from the profits at wind-up simply because, in a continuation, the outgoing partner is not responsible for the debts of the continuing partnership. The outgoing partner, instead, takes as a creditor.

Although this election may seem somewhat onesided as the retiring partner is no longer involved in the business, it "serves as "a species of compulsion . . . to those continuing the business . . . to hasten its orderly winding up.' . . . The second election rests partly on the use of the outgoing partner's assets in the conduct of the business." . . . The right to a share of the profits exists only until the final accounting has been made. . . . Once judgment is entered, then the former partner gets interest on the judgment, at the legal rate, until paid. . . .

Finally, we reach a contention by Bartlett which is found to be a common complaint in partnership dissolution in our research of cases across the country. Bartlett strenuously argues that the business has greatly expanded since Lange left in 1975. He claims it is not the intent of the statutes to allow Lange to reap profits from aspects of the business which were not operating at the time of the partnership dissolution. Bartlett is incorrect. [The applicable statute] states that the retiring partner may opt, in lieu of interest, for "profits attributable *to the use of his right in the property of the dissolved partnership. . . . "* (Emphasis added.) This figure may differ from year to year depending upon Bartlett's use of partnership property. Lange's partnership property includes not only the tangible assets but also any goodwill in the "Pool Boys" name and reputation prior to dissolution that would have contributed to the success of Bartlett's sauna, spa and hot tub business.

We conclude that regardless of the expended effort on behalf of Bartlett, Lange is still entitled to a share of the partnership profit from the day of dissolution. However, a court can take into account the substantial labor and management services made by the continuing partner and deduct that amount before arriving at the figure of what profit is due the former partner. . . .

Brown, Presiding Judge.

Liability for Obligations of Dissolved Firm   The dissolution of a partnership does not dissolve the existing liabilities of any partner [UPA § 36(1)]. The right of third persons to enforce obligations and contracts binding on a firm at the time of its dissolution usually continues after the termination of a partnership. Regardless of the reasons, a partner who leaves a firm remains liable to the partnership's creditors for all existing debts of the firm to the same extent as if he or she had remained with the partnership. Creditors can agree not to hold a partner liable on his withdrawal from a firm, but they are not required to do so. Thus, a retiring partner cannot absolve herself from liability for firm debts contracted while she was a member of the firm in the absence of an agreement on the part of a creditor [see UPA § 36(2)]. She cannot be held liable for future debts.

When the business of a dissolved partnership is continued by former partners, creditors of the old firm are creditors of the persons or partnership continuing the business [UPA § 41]. This rule applies in a variety of situations, such as when a partner retires and transfers his interest to other partners or to third persons. It also applies if all but one partner retire and the retiring partners assign their rights to the continuing partner. However, if a new firm doing business under an old firm's name is composed of entirely different persons, it is not liable for the old firm's debts.

A person admitted as a partner into an existing partnership is liable for all the obligations of the partnership that arose before his admission, as though he had been a partner when the obligations were incurred [UPA § 17]. This liability can, however, be satisfied only out of partnership property. It must be emphasized that UPA § 17 applies only to one who enters an *existing partnership*. Thus, for example, one who enters into a partnership with a person who had done business as a sole proprietor does not become liable for the prior debts of the business at the time it was carried on as a proprietorship, and those debts cannot be satisfied out of partnership property.

Notice of Dissolution   To protect innocent third persons, the law imposes on partners the duty of giving *notice of dissolution* of a partnership. Otherwise, they run the risk of being bound to third persons by the subsequent exercise of the authority that they have given to each other as partners. Therefore, under this rule, members of a dissolved partnership continue to be liable to those with whom they have previously dealt as partners and who have no notice or knowledge of the dissolution of the firm, and who in good faith continue to act in the belief that the firm is still in existence [UPA § 35(1)]. For this reason, and as part of any dissolution, a retiring partner generally publishes notice of withdrawal from a firm to protect against future debts incurred by the partners continuing the business.

Both the character and the sufficiency of a notice of dissolution that will be effective to relieve a partner from liability depend in large part on whether the person receiving the notice has had former dealings with the firm. Those who have had actual dealings with the firm are entitled to direct notice of the dissolution. Those who have known of the existence of the firm but have not dealt with it are entitled merely to constructive or general notice. UPA § 3(2) recognizes that notice can be given verbally, by delivery through the mail, or by other means of communication to the recipient's place of business or residence. To avoid liability for contracts with persons who know of a partnership's existence but have not learned of its dissolution, the fact of dissolution must be advertised in a newspaper of general circulation in the place at which the partnership business was regularly conducted [see UPA § 35(1)(b)(II)].

Continuation in Business   The effect of dissolution is to permit a partnership to operate until it is wound up. However, when dissolution is caused by breach of a partnership agreement, those partners who have not caused the dissolution can continue the business in the same name, provided that they pay the partner who caused the dissolution the value of his interest [UPA § 38(2)(b)]. Moreover, dissolution does not necessarily cause the liquidation of a firm where there has been an agreement among the partners stating that it does not do so. The remaining partners can also continue to operate a partnership if one partner has been expelled pursuant to the terms of a partnership agreement.

44:7   Winding Up

Winding up means the administration of assets of a partnership for the purpose of terminating the business and discharging its obligations. Included in the winding up or liquidation of partnership affairs are (1) the performance of existing contracts, (2) the collection of debts or claims due the firm, and (3) the payment of partnership debts. The right to carry out the winding up is given either to partners who have not wrongfully dissolved the partnership or to the legal representative of the last surviving partner [UPA § 37]. Moreover, any partner or his legal representative can have a partnership wound up by court decree. If a partnership is ended by mutual consent or by the expiration of its term, the right to wind up is vested in all partners, and each is under a duty to liquidate partnership affairs.

Liquidating Partners   The partners who have the right to do the winding up can agree that one or more of them shall act as *liquidating partners.* Those who remain in charge of the business during the winding up period occupy a fiduciary relationship to the other partners until the winding up is complete. If partners cannot agree as to who shall wind up, a court can appoint a receiver.

A liquidating partner is considered to have all the power that is necessary for the final settlement of the partnership's affairs. If other partners expressly give their consent, the liquidating partner has broad power to incur obligations. For example, a liquidating partner can incur obligations that are necessary to complete existing contracts after the partnership is dissolved, and he can borrow money to pay partnership debts. However, there are limits to a liquidating partner's powers. For example, a liquidating partner is the sole agent of a partnership *only* for purposes of winding it up. Thus, he normally lacks the power to incur obligations that will bind the firm or the other partners as individuals. He also lacks the power to enter into new contracts or new business on behalf of the firm.

UPA § 18(f) provides that if a partnership is being wound up because one of the partners has died, a surviving partner is entitled to reasonable compensation for his services in winding up the partnership's affairs. This rule, which is an exception to the usual rule that no partner is entitled to remuneration for acting in the partnership business, is included in the UPA because the death of a partner necessarily leaves the entire burden of winding up on the survivors. In certain circumstances, a court might award compensation to the partners who have performed more than their share of work in winding up and liquidating the partnership.

Application of Assets to Liabilities   In settling accounts among partners after dissolution, the liabilities of the partnership rank in order of payment as follows: (1) those owing to creditors other than partners; (2) those owing to partners for other than capital and profits; (3) those owing to partners in respect to capital; and (4) those owing to partners in respect to profits [UPA § 40(b)]. These statutory rules for the distribution of assets apply only in the absence of an agreement among partners on the same subject matter.

After the payment of liabilities, any surplus can be applied to pay in cash the net amount owing to the partners [UPA § 38(1)]. When a partner leaves a firm voluntarily, or involuntarily without assigning his interest to the other partners, he is entitled to receive an amount equal to the value of his interest at dissolution. The same rule applies when a partner dies, except that the decreased partner's share goes to his estate.

44:8 Limited Partnerships

Limited Partnerships are entities created by state statutes. They were developed to facilitate commercial investments by those who wanted a financial interest in a business but did not want all the responsibilities and liabilities of partners. In recent years, most states have adopted the *Uniform Limited Partnership Act* (ULPA), which governs the rights, duties, and obligations of limited partnerships. The ULPA was first promulgated in 1916, and the original act was superseded in 1976 by a revised act. The 1916 text, which is reproduced in Appendix E, will probably not be replaced in all states for a number of years. However, the 1976 revised text, reproduced in Appendix F, forms the basis of the discussion of limited partners in this chapter.

A limited partnership is a partnership formed by two or more persons having as its members one or more "general partners" and one or more "limited partners." A general partner is a partner who assumes the management responsibilities of the partnership and full personal liability for the debts of the partnership. A limited partner is a partner who makes a contribution of cash or other property to the partnership and who obtains an interest in the partnership in return. The limited partner, whose liability for partnership debts is also limited, is not active in management.

A person can be both a general partner and a limited partner in the same partnership at the same time. In this case, the partner has in respect to his contribution as a limited partner all the rights he would have if he were not a general partner [ULPA § 303].

44:9 Formation of Limited Partnership

There are certain requirements for the formation of a limited partnership. These requirements concern the certificate of limited partnership that the partners must execute. The certificate sets forth the name of the partnership, the general character of its business, the location of its principal place of business, the name and address of each partner and his capital contributions, a designation of which partners are general and limited, and the respective rights and priorities, if any, of the partners [ULPA § 201]. A copy of the certificate must be filed in the office of the Secretary of State [ULPA § 201; see also §§ 204, 206]. The certificate can be amended or canceled by following similar formalities [ULPA § 202]. If a certificate contains false statements, anyone who suffers a loss by relying on it can hold liable (1) any person who signed the certificate and who knew of the erroneous statements or (2) any general partner who should have known of the erroneous statements, even if he lacked actual knowledge of them [ULPA § 207(1)].

The purpose of the certificate is to give all potential creditors notice of the limited liability of the limited partners. The ULPA requires at least substantial compliance in good faith with these requirements. If there is no substantial compliance, the purported limited partner can be held liable as a general partner. However, a purported limited partner can escape liability as a general partner if, on ascertaining the mistake, he promptly renounces his interest in the profits of the business or in other compensation he receives [ULPA § 304].

44:10 Rights and Liabilities of Limited Partners

The rights of a limited partner are substantially the same as those of a partner in a general partnership, except that the limited partner has no right to take control of the business. Thus, a limited partner has the right of access to the partnership books, the right to an accounting as to the state of the partnership business, the right to inspect the partnership's tax returns, and the right to receive other information regarding the affairs of the partnership as is just and reasonable [ULPA § 305].

In contrast to the liability of a partner in a general partnership for partnership debts, a limited partner has *no* personal liability for partnership debts [ULPA § 303]. The maximum loss that a limited partner can sustain is the amount of his investment in the limited partnership. However, if a limited partner is also a general partner, or if he takes part in the management and control of the business, the limited partner then becomes liable as a general partner [ULPA § 303(a)].

44:11 Termination of Limited Partnership

Under ULPA § 801, a limited partnership can be dissolved (1) at the time or on the happening of the events specified in the certificate of limited partnership, (2) on the written consent of all partners, and (3) in the event of a general partner's withdrawal. In certain cases, dissolution of a limited partnership does not have to occur on the withdrawal of a general partner if there is at least one other general partner and the certificate of limited partnership permits the business to be carried on by the remaining general partner. A limited partnership can also be dissolved by court order on application by or for a partner whenever it is not practicable to carry on the business in conformity with the partnership agreement [ULPA § 802].

The following case involves the problem faced by the limited partners when the general partner dissolves the partnership without their consent. It demonstrates the importance of providing some mechanism in the limited partnership agreement for the limited partners to select another general partner to carry on the business when the general partner dissolves the limited partnership.

Roeschlein

v

Watkins
686 P2d 1347 (1983)
Colorado Court of Appeals

FACTS: In 1976 a limited partnership was formed for the purpose of assuming a 20-year lease on a mobile home park. Later, Watkins, the general partner, decided unilaterally to dissolve and wind up the partnership without the consent of the limited partners.

ISSUE: Does unilateral dissolution of a limited partnership breach the general partner's fiduciary duty to the limited partners?

RESULT: No. The general partner does not have a fiduciary duty to continue the business or to permit the limited partners to find a general partner to continue the business.

REASONING:

*   *   *

Plaintiffs . . . argue that it was error to dismiss their claim against Watkins based upon breach of what they assert was a common law fiduciary duty imposed upon him over and above those duties which devolved upon him by virtue of the partnership agreement and the Uniform Partnership Act. We find no merit to this contention.

A general partner, in winding up partnership affairs, owes his limited partners a common law fiduciary duty of good faith, sound business judgment, candor, forthrightness, and fairness.

Plaintiffs assert that, under this common law standard, Watkins, who was the sole general partner, breached his fiduciary duties by failing to disclose his intent to dissolve and wind up the limited partnership sufficiently in advance so as to allow the limited partners to replace him with a new general partner. No statutory authority has been cited for such a duty, and none appears to have been contemplated by the articles of limited partnership. The Partnership Agreement provides:

> Limited Partners representing two-thirds (2/3) of the Limited Partnership interest in a partnership shall have the right to remove the existing General Partner(s) and elect a new General Partner(s).

It further provides:

> If all General Partners have been adjudicated bankrupt or made assignments for the benefit of creditors, the Limited Partners representing a majority of the Limited Partnership interest in the Partnership may elect a successor General Partner.

No reference is made in the articles of limited partnership to a right of the limited partners to elect a successor general partner upon resignation of the sole remaining general partner, or to a duty placed upon the general partner requiring him to notify the limited partners of his intent to retire from the general partnership. Here, the articles of partnership do not require such a duty, and we decline to impose such a duty upon the general partners of limited partnerships. Such an imposition would be in clear contradiction of the plain meaning of the articles of partnership. . . .

The position of the limited partners is best understood by considering [the applicable statute], which states in part:

> In the absence of any statement in the certificate to the contrary or the consent of all members, a limited partner, irrespective of the nature of his contribution, has only the right to demand and receive cash in return for his contribution. . . .

Smith, Judge.

 Note that, as in the *Roeschlein* case, the partnership agreement usually is drawn by the general partner before the limited partners are signed on as investors. Only when the limited partners have sufficient negotiating power can they effectively impose protective provisions.

Settlement and Distribution of Assets [ULPA § 804]   Various priorities must be observed in settling a limited partnership's accounts after dissolution. On dissolution, assets are to be distributed first to creditors in satisfaction of liabilities of the limited partnership; next, to partners and former partners in satisfaction of liabilities for distributions under ULPA §§ 601 and 604; and last, to partners first for the return of their contributions and secondly in proportion to their interest in the partnership. Of course, the members of a limited partnership can include in the partnership agreement different priorities for distribution on winding up of partnership affairs.

44:12   Joint Ventures

A joint venture is an association of persons with the intent to engage in and carry out a single business venture for profit. The joint ventures combine their efforts, property, money, skills, and knowledge without creating a partnership or corporation; each participant stands in the relation of principal as well as agent to each of the others with an equal right to control the means employed to achieve the common purpose of the venture.

A joint venture is very similar to a partnership. Indeed, the rights, duties, and liabilities of joint venturers are often tested by the same rules as those that govern partnerships. However, there are important differences between these two types of business relationships. Perhaps the most significant difference is the single—or ad hoc—nature of a joint venture. In contrast, a partnership is usually formed to conduct a continuing business. Other differences include the eligibility of a corporation for membership in a joint venture but not ordinarily in a partnership, and the fact that joint venturers, unlike partners, can sue each other for damages without resorting to an accounting.

Convenience and expediency have made joint ventures a popular form of enterprise. Today, joint ventures are an almost necessary means of acquiring the great concentration of economic resources, knowledge, and skills required for such large-scale construction projects as public buildings, highways, bridges, dams, and even nuclear reactors. Joint ventures have also been used for the exploitation and development of natural resources, for joint participation in public offerings of stocks and bonds, for commercial shipping ventures, and for the development and sale of real estate subdivisions. Joint ventures also offer certain benefits when used as vehicles for tax-oriented investments, such as real estate or oil and gas projects, because they are taxed as partnerships rather than as corporations.

44:13 Elements of a Joint Venture

The relationship of joint venturers is created when two or more persons combine their money, property, or time in the conduct of some particular line of trade or for some particular business deal. The first requirement for the creation of a joint venture is the parties' intent to create the enterprise. This intent is usually manifested by contract, although little formality is required. The relationship of joint venturers can, however, be created by oral agreement, or its existence can be inferred from the conduct of the parties and from other facts and circumstances surrounding their association.

The second requirement is that all participants combine their property, money, labor, knowledge, or skills in some common undertaking. The contributions of the parties need not be equal or of the same character, but there must be a contribution by each participant of something benefiting the enterprise. Facts showing the joining of funds, property, or labor in a common purpose to obtain a result for the benefit of all parties, in which each participant has a right to direct the conduct of others, is often considered evidence that a joint venture exists.

A third requirement for creating a joint venture is that each person have equal control over the enterprise. There must also be a community of interest in the subject matter of the joint venture. Moreover, a joint proprietary interest in property used pursuant to a joint venture must be shown in some states. In other states, it is only necessary to have a joint interest in the objects and purposes of the venture. The fourth requirement is an agreement among the venturers to share profits.

In addition to satisfying the above requirements, a joint venture must be limited to a single undertaking. It is this characteristic that is most often used to distinguish a joint venture from a partnership. An enterprise must be of limited scope and duration in order to constitute a joint venture. In certain circumstances, however, associations organized for diversified operations of a continuing nature have been recognized as joint ventures. The following case illustrates the elements necessary for the formation of a joint venture and shows that although parties might change the structure of the business, a joint venture relationship will not necessarily end if the parties intend it to continue.

Tate

v

Ballard

68 NW2d 261 (1955)

Minnesota Supreme Court

FACTS: Tate and Ballard formed an association to purchase and operate a factory. Both advanced money toward the purchase price of the plant and for working capital. Later, a corporation was formed to carry out the venture. Still later, Tate sued for dissolution of the association and for an accounting on the ground that the parties had been engaged in a joint venture. Ballard denied that a joint venture had been created. At trial, the court ruled in favor of Tate and held that Ballard was indebted to Tate for $4,000 by the terms of their joint venture agreement.

ISSUE: Did the parties continue to be engaged in a joint venture after they incorporated the business?

RESULT: If the corporation was formed for the purpose of carrying on the joint venture, then the business retained its character as a joint venture.

REASONING:

*   *   *

A joint venture ordinarily is created where two or more persons agree to combine their money, property, time, or skill in a business operation and share in the profits of the enterprise in some fixed proportion. We have held that four prerequisites are essential to its formation, i.e., (1) contribution of money, property, time, or skill, not necessarily in equal proportions, by each of the parties; (2) joint proprietorship and mutuality of control of the subject matter of the venture; (3) an agreement for sharing of profits, though not necessarily the losses, arising from the venture; and (4) a contract express or implied establishing the joint venture relationship. . . . [Ballard] concedes that in the instant case there is evidence sufficient to establish the elements of *contribution* and *sharing of profits* but asserts that there is none which would support the essential findings of *contract* covering the venture or *joint proprietorship and control* of the subject matter thereof. [Court's emphasis.]

With respect to the contract prerequisite, [Ballard] contends that the formation of the corporation and transfer of all assets to it effectively terminated any relationship of joint venture which may have existed prior thereto and converted the status of the parties to that of ordinary corporate stockholders. However, it has been held that formation of a corporation to which the assets of a joint venture are transferred is not inconsistent with the continuance of the joint venture relationship between the parties if it can be established that such was their intent. . . . As expressed in [another case], "The fact that joint adventurers may determine to carry out the purpose of the agreement through the medium of a corporation does not change the essential nature of the relationship."

It is clear from these principles that the purpose or intent of the parties in the formation of the corporation is important in determining whether the joint venture continued thereafter. Such intent may be gathered from the actions of the parties as well as their expressions. Here there was testimony that the corporation was formed primarily for the purpose of saving taxes and thus increasing profits. No corporate meetings of either stockholders or directors were ever held. No minute books were submitted. The enterprise was thereafter conducted by the parties in the same manner as it was before formation of the corporation. . . . All of such factors lend reasonable support to the trial court's determination that the joint venture relationship continued after the formation of the corporation and that the latter merely constituted an instrument to facilitate and further the operation of the former. . . .

As to the issue of joint or mutual control, defendant argues that the evidence establishes that [Tate] merely controlled the plant at Clovis, while the corporation exercised the over-all proprietary control of all the assets, and that hence this essential prerequisite to joint venture was absent. It must be recalled, however, that the mutuality of control required is that of the parties to the venture and that in this respect, a comparison of the rights of [Tate] with those of the corporation, as suggested by defendant, would not be the determinative factor. Further, a disparity in the exercise of actual control as between the parties to a joint venture does not negate such a venture where, as here, the parties through the exercise of their rights as corporate stockholders, or otherwise, may, if desired, each exercise an equal measure of control therein. . . .

Gallaher, Justice.

44:14 Rights and Liabilities of Joint Venturers

The rights and duties of joint venturers depend primarily on the terms of the contract by which the relationship was brought into existence. Joint venturers are also affected by general principles of contract and partnership law. The most basic of these is the principle that the relationship of joint venturers is fiduciary in nature. The law imposes on joint venturers the obligation of loyalty to the joint concern and of the utmost good faith, honesty, and fairness in their dealings with each other with regard to matters pertaining to the enterprise.

Profits and Losses   In the absence of an agreement to the contrary, joint venturers are entitled to a share of the profits equal to their shares in the business, as set forth in the joint venture agreement. This is true even though contributions of the participants differ in kind or in amount.

Joint venturers are also bound to share losses resulting from an enterprise, if it is so provided in their contract or required by law. A participant in a joint venture who fails to pay his share of sustained losses can be sued for contribution by his associates. For that matter, a joint venturer can also subject himself to liability for damages by failing to contribute his share toward the payment of expenses or to perform other obligations to further the goals of the business.

Property Rights   Unless otherwise agreed, property purchased with the funds of a joint venture or with its profits belongs to all the participants for the purposes of the enterprise. A joint venturer who holds or acquires title to property for the venture is a trustee for the other participants, even if the property was purchased with his own funds. Therefore, a joint venturer who retains or appropriates for personal benefit property belonging to the venture, or who acts in any other way to deprive the associates of the benefit of such property, becomes liable for breach of fiduciary duties. Similarly, a joint venturer who purchases or leases property related to the enterprise without full disclosure to the other associates, or who mismanages assets of the enterprise, will be liable to the others.

Withdrawal   A party to a joint venture cannot unilaterally withdraw from or abandon the enterprise before its purposes have been attained. One who does so can be liable to the other parties to the venture for damages resulting from the withdrawal. If, in addition, the withdrawing party then acts independently with respect to the subject matter of the joint venture, he can be compelled to share the benefits with the other parties.

Liability to Third Persons   Each joint venturer has the power to bind the others and to subject them to liability to third parties in matters that are within the scope of the venture. This is consistent with the general rule that each member of a joint venture acts as both principal and agent within the apparent scope of the venture and for its benefit. As to third persons who deal with a member of a joint venture in good faith and without any knowledge of any limit on his authority, the law presumes that the venturer has been accorded the power to bind his associates. Consequently, associates can be liable to third persons even where they have expressly agreed among themselves that no liability should arise.

Key Concepts and Terms

- A partnership is an association of two or more persons to carry on as co-owners a business for profit. It is a voluntary association by agreement, and it is governed by the Uniform Partnership Act in most states. A contract, either express or implied, is ordinarily essential to the formation of a partnership.

- All property brought into a partnership or acquired by it with partnership funds is partnership property. Title of property so acquired can be conveyed only in the partnership name.

- The property rights of an individual partner include rights in specific partnership property, the interest in the partnership, and the right to participate in management.

- A tenancy in partnership arises when property is acquired by a partnership, regardless of whether title was taken in the names of all the partners or in the name of only one. Each partner has an equal right to use the property for partnership purposes. On the death of a partner, property held in tenancy in partnership vests in the surviving partners for partnership purposes; it is not subject to the right of survivorship.

- All partners possess an equal right in the management and conduct of partnership business. Questions that affect a partnership are usually decided by a majority of the partners.

- Each partner is entitled to an equal share in the profits of the partnership unless the partners have agreed to a different arrangement. Losses are also to be shared by all partners equally or in agreed proportions.

- Every partner is not only a principal but also a general and authorized agent of the partnership. The authority of a partner to act as an agent for a partnership is limited to transactions within the scope of the partnership business or within the apparent scope of a partner's authority.

- Among themselves, partners are fiduciaries. An obligation of the utmost good faith and integrity is imposed on partners in their dealings with one another with regard to partnership property and affairs.

- Partners are jointly liable for all debts and obligations that result from partnership transactions. Partners are jointly and severally liable for torts committed in the course of partnership business.

- Dissolution is a change in the relation of the partners caused by any partner's ceasing to be associated in the conduct of the business. Dissolution is followed by winding up of the business, and later by its termination.

- "Winding up" means the administration of a partnership's assets for the purpose of terminating the business and discharging its obligations. It entails the performance of existing contracts, the collection of debts or claims due the firm, and the payment of partnership debts.

- In settling accounts among partners after dissolution, creditors (other than partners) are ordinarily given priority. After these creditors have been paid, debts owing to partners may be paid. Any surplus is then distributed to the partners as return of capital and profits.

- A limited partnership is a partnership formed by two or more persons having as its members one or more general partners and one or more limited partners. It is governed by the Uniform Limited Partnership Act in most states. The general partner assumes the management responsibilities of the partnership and full personal liability for its debts. Each limited partner makes a contribution of cash or other property to the partnership and obtains an interest in the partnership in return. A limited partner, whose liability for partnership debts is limited, cannot be active in management.

- A joint venture is an association of persons with the intent to engage and carry out a single business venture for profit.

- There are generally four essential elements to the formation of a joint venture: (1) an intent to create a joint venture; (2) an agreement to combine property, money, labor, knowledge, and skills in a common undertaking; (3) a right to joint control; and (4) an agreement for the sharing of profits.

- Accounting
- Dissolution
- General Partnership
- Joint Venture
- Limited Partnership
- Liquidating Partner
- Notice of Dissolution
- Partnership by Estoppel
- Silent Partner
- Tenancy in Partnership
- Uniform Limited Partnership Act (ULPA)
- Uniform Partnership Act (UPA)

Questions and Case Problems

1. Paboogian purchases a dental building with his own money but puts title to it in the name of his partnership. Does the building thereby become partnership property? Would the result be different if Paboogian had purchased the building with partnership funds?

2. How is a general partnership formed? How does the formation of a limited partnership differ from that of a general partnership?

3. Holmes signs a loan agreement with the Tenth City Bank to borrow $1 million for a partnership. Unknown to the bank, the partnership agreement provides that no single partner can borrow funds for the partnership without the written consent of all partners. Can the bank enforce the loan agreement against the partnership? On learning of the loan, partner Mendes notifies the Tenth City Bank that she will not be liable on any subsequent partnership debts. Will this notice relieve Mendes of further liability?

4. Potter and Hercule are partners. During a business trip for the partnership, Potter negligently operates his car and injures Tobin. Can Tobin recover from Hercule for Potter's negligent conduct?

5. Tinker, Tabay, and Vargas form a partnership for a three-year period to manufacture a new perfume. Six months later, Tinker elects to dissolve the partnership. Is Tinker liable to the other partners for any damages resulting from dissolution of the partnership? After dissolution, the remaining partners continue to operate the business in the firm name. Can Tinker sue her former partners for compensation accruing after she withdrew from the partnership? Is Tinker liable for debts acquired by the partnership after her withdrawal?

6. Discuss the various causes of the dissolution of a partnership. What is the difference between a partnership's "dissolution" and the winding up of its affairs?

7. Gratch purchases a warehouse with his own funds but records title in the name of a partnership of which he is a partner. Later, in a dispute with the partnership, Gratch alleges that he never intended that the building be partnership property. If the partnership shows that it urgently needed this type of warehouse, is it likely to prevail? If so, why?

8. Shawn, England, and May begin work on an idea to create a "thunder-lizard doll." The doll represents an imaginary lizard that England used in Oklahoma on a radio program about the weather. Eventually, the doll idea develops into a proposed book about Oklahoma weather. England writes a manuscript, Shawn has it typed and edited, and May does the art work. Before completion of the book, Shawn is ejected from the venture. Shawn then sues England and May for an accounting of the profits. England and May contend that a partnership existed only as to the lizard doll idea and that it ended when that idea was dropped. Is Shawn entitled to an accounting? Why?

9. Does property owned by a partnership differ from property owned by individual partners but used for partnership purposes? If so, how?

10. In what ways does a joint venture resemble a partnership? In what ways is it different?

45 Introduction to Corporations

The corporation is a creature of the State. It is presumed to be incorporated for the benefit of the public.

Hale v Henkel,
201 US 43 (United States Supreme Court, 1906)

A business corporation is organized and carried on primarily for the profit of the shareholders.

Dodge v Ford Motor Co.,
197 NW 668 (Michigan Supreme Court, 1919)

45:1 General Comments

A corporation is a form of business enterprise that exists as a legal entity separate from the individuals who own or manage it. The owners, known as shareholders, are recognized by the law as distinct from the corporation and, as such, are not liable for the corporation's debts and obligations. A corporation, unlike a partnership (see Chapter 44), has an indefinite existence because an owner's corporate shares can be transferred when he dies. A corporation is managed by officers and directors who are charged by law with specific duties to the corporation and to its shareholders. In short, a corporation has (1) a separate identity, (2) continuity of existence, (3) limited shareholder liability, (4) free transferability of ownership rights, (5) centralized management, and (6) limited powers through its officers and directors.

Traditionally, the power to incorporate is held by the state under its general corporation laws. These statutes prescribe the corporate structure and the relationships between management and shareholders, between the majority and minority shareholders, and between classes of shareholders. They also set forth limits of management accountability.

Model Business Corporation Act The Model Business Corporation Act (MBCA) provides state legislators, lawyers, and law review commissions with a working model for the revision and modernization of state corporation laws. The MBCA, which is set out as Appendix C to this book, is the result of the American Bar Association's efforts to draft both a federal corporation law and a state model corporation law. It has been adopted in whole or in part by at least 35 states. Because the MBCA is used so widely as a model for state corporation laws, reference will be made to it throughout this and the other chapters on corporations.

Corporate Charter   A company doing business as a corporation is given rights or privileges by the state. The instrument that conveys them is called a corporate charter. Besides these rights and privileges, the charter embraces the state constitution and other statutes that affect the corporation in the state where it is organized. The charter governs the course and conduct of the corporation's business and delineates the proper scope of its activities. The charter is also referred to as the articles of incorporation or the certificate.

45:2   Classes and Types of Corporations

The corporation is the dominant form of business enterprise in the United States. Although corporations represent less than ten percent of the existing business enterprises in number, they employ three-fourths of the nation's labor force and control or own a similar percentage of our national wealth. Most economic activity in the country can be attributed to the large, publicly held corporations. Their size and power have given them the ability to exert great influence on the conduct of society. Corporations may be classified as public, private, or quasi-public. These classes are discussed below.

Public Corporation   A public corporation is a corporation that is created for public purposes connected with the administration of government. An incorporated school district and an incorporated municipality are examples of public corporations. Local taxes largely support local public corporations.

Private Corporation   A private corporation, in contrast to a public one, is a corporation created to earn profits for its owners (profit corporation) or to raise funds for charitable purposes (nonprofit corporation). The three most common types of private corporations are the incorporated sole proprietorship, the close corporation, and the publicly held corporation. The characteristics of each type are discussed below.

Incorporated Sole Proprietorship.   As its name suggests, the incorporated sole proprietorship is a corporation that is owned and operated by one person. This person is the director and chief executive officer of the corporation. He is answerable only to himself as long as his actions are within the limits of the law.

Close Corporation.   A *close corporation* has three distinctive features: (1) it is owned by a small number of shareholders, (2) it does not sell its stock to the general public, and (3) its officers and directors are ordinarily shareholders. Often, a close corporation is owned by a family and is operated as a partnership.

Publicly Held Corporation.   A publicly held corporation is a corporation that sells and trades its shares and issues debt obligations to the general public. The nation's largest corporations are publicly held. Because it is the most prevalent form of corporation, the publicly held corporation is the basis of discussion in the rest of this chapter and in the other chapters on corporations.[1]

Other types of private corporations are formed for specific advantages or benefits enjoyed by their owners. These include the Subchapter S corporation, the holding company, the professional corporation, the foreign corporation, and the multinational corporation.

Subchapter S Corporation. A *Subchapter S corporation* is a close corporation that has elected to be treated as a sole proprietorship or partnership for income tax purposes under the Internal Revenue Code. The term "Subchapter S" is derived from the particular subdivision of the Internal Revenue Code that permits this type of taxation and sets forth the eligibility requirements for this tax status. The Subchapter S provision exempts the corporation from paying corporate income tax and allows the shareholders to be taxed on corporate earnings and to deduct corporate losses directly. Consequently, the Subchapter S corporation avoids the "double taxation" levied on a normal corporation. This double taxation arises because when a normal corporation distributes money or property to its shareholders, the amount of money or the fair market value of the property is taxed as a dividend to the shareholders, but before the distribution it was also taxed as a part of the corporation's profits.

The eligibility requirements under the Internal Revenue Code for Subchapter S corporations are quite technical. In general, a corporation is eligible if it has no more than 35 individual shareholders, has no more than two classes of stock outstanding, and is a domestic corporation. Furthermore, the Subchapter S corporation must derive its income primarily from an active business enterprise, not from passive investment.[2]

Holding Company. A *holding company* is a corporation that owns interests in one or more other corporations. The extent to which it owns these interests varies. A holding company can be organized and operated for the sole purpose of holding a controlling interest, and in this sense, it is a supercorporation that dictates the policies and programs of those corporations in which it owns stock. A holding company can also be an ordinary business enterprise that quite incidentally owns stock in another corporation. Another common type of holding company is a large enterprise at the top of an organizational pyramid that owns all the stock and controls the management of its constituent companies or operating divisions.

Professional Corporation. Accountants, dentists, doctors, lawyers, and other professionals are allowed to incorporate under the laws of many states and by the federal government under the Internal Revenue Code. The professional corporation is formed to obtain the benefits flowing from corporation status: limited liability and federal income tax advantages. State statutes governing professional corporations, however, usually restrict stock owner-

---

[1] The "publicly held" corporation should not be confused with the "public" corporation; "publicly held" refers to the fact that the corporation *is owned by* the public, not that it is *operated for* the public, as is a public corporation.

[2] Corporate taxation and the consideration of this factor in selecting the type of business organization is discussed in Chapter 49.

ship to individuals licensed in that state, and they generally forbid a professional corporation from conducting its activities except through professionals.

<u>Foreign Corporation.</u>   A *foreign corporation* is a corporation that is created by or organized under the laws of another state or country. Thus, a corporation organized under the laws of one state and operating in another state is a foreign corporation in the latter state. Of course, a corporation transacting business in another state must have the required certificate of authority to do business in that state. Otherwise, it cannot enforce its claims against that state's residents in the state's courts. The same is true for a corporation organized in a foreign country and doing business in the United States.

 Meeting certain requirements to transact business in another state does not involve the same expense or red tape that incorporation in the home state does, but it is inconvenient and can be easily overlooked. Therefore, if business is to be conducted in another state, it is wise to ascertain whether any of these requirements exist before transacting business in that state and to take the appropriate steps to meet those requirements.

Multinational Corporations   Corporations organized under the laws of a state often do business in foreign countries. Corporations formed in other countries also engage in business in the United States. A corporation might manufacture products in this country and sell them directly abroad; or it might obtain raw materials in one country, produce a finished product in the United States, and then market the goods elsewhere. When corporations engage in business in this manner, they are referred to as multinational corporations.

Most of the larger multinational corporations are actually comprised of several constituent companies called subsidiaries. A single, controlling (parent) corporation directs all the activities of the subsidiaries. Multinational corporations that operate in this fashion have three basic characteristics: (1) central control by the parent corporation, (2) a common production and marketing strategy for the entire enterprise, and (3) integration of operations among the subsidiaries and affiliates with the parent.

Quasi-Public Corporation   A *quasi-public,* or public service, *corporation* is a corporation that owes a duty to the public because it has special privileges conferred by the state. These privileges include having freedom from competition and enjoying certain powers of a public nature, such as the power of eminent domain (see Chapter 39), to enable them to discharge their duties for public benefit. In exchange for having freedom from competition, quasi-public corporations are closely regulated and subject to strict governmental scrutiny. For example, power companies and telephone companies are typical quasi-public corporations, and they are closely regulated in such areas as plant expansion and rate increases.

45:3   Promoters

The modern business corporation does not come into being spontaneously. Someone must conceive and initiate the business and bring together people interested in the enterprise. This person is generally referred to as a *promoter,* one who takes part in the formation of a new corporation.

A promoter is not the same as an incorporator. A promoter can aid in establishing a corporation without actually participating in its formation or signing any incorporation documents. He need not be related to the corporation as an officer, director, or shareholder. A promoter's activities can be divided into (1) discovery, (2) investigation, and (3) assembly. Discovery is finding the business opportunity; investigation is analyzing the proposed business to determine its economic feasibility; assembly is bringing together property, money, and personnel to set the business in motion.

A promoter's work begins long before the corporation is organized. The promoter looks for the capital needed to achieve the purposes set forth in the proposed articles of incorporation. He brings together the potential shareholders, aids in procuring stock subscriptions, and sets in motion the machinery that leads to formation of the corporation itself.

Once the corporation is formed, the promoter does not necessarily lose his character as such. If a person continues to perform the acts that characterize promoters, such as inducing persons to subscribe to capital stock or invest in the corporation's securities, his relationship to the corporation as a promoter continues.

Compensation of Promoters   The states have not adopted a uniform approach to compensating promoters for services rendered before incorporation. In some states, in the absence of a provision in the articles of incorporation or statutory provisions, a corporation is not liable to its promoters for services rendered or expenses incurred before incorporation unless the corporation later expressly agrees to make such payments. Under this view, an implied promise to reimburse a promoter cannot be imputed to the corporation, since the corporation did not exist when the services were rendered or the expenses incurred. In other states, a promise to pay a promoter is implied, particularly when the promoter performs necessary and reasonable services in obtaining a charter, in securing stock subscriptions, or in otherwise perfecting the organization. This rule for reimbursing a promoter for preincorporation expenses is based on the notion that it would otherwise be difficult to organize a corporation. No one would render any services, however essential, if the corporation's obligation to pay could not be imputed to it once it comes into existence. Regardless of which approach is adopted by the states, after a corporation has been organized, it can authorize payment of compensation to promoters [MBCA § 22].

Duties and Liabilities of Promoters   A promoter stands in a fiduciary relationship to the prospective corporation and to the subsequent stock subscribers. The promoter must exercise the utmost good faith in dealing with the corporation and its shareholders. He must fully disclose all material facts and fully advise the corporation and its shareholders of any interest that may in any manner affect them. A promoter will not be allowed to benefit by any secret profit or advantage gained at the expense of the corporation or its shareholders unless all material facts have been disclosed. Compensation to promoters for services must be made on the basis of full disclosure as well. For example, a promoter who secretly profits through the sale of property to a corporation has committed a fraud on the corporation and its shareholders. The promoter may be required to account for the profit or return it to the corporation.

In the absence of a statute to the contrary, if a promoter makes a contract for the benefit of a corporation before the corporation exists, the promoter is personally liable on it. This is also true when a promoter conducts the ordinary affairs of a business in the nature of a corporation before it is legally organized or qualified to do business. Of course, the corporation can later enter into a new contract with the same creditor or the same contracting party, thereby releasing the promoter from liability.

 A promoter frequently enters into contracts on behalf of a corporation before it is legally born. Unless the promoter has obtained a corporation's formal ratification of preincorporation contracts as soon as the incorporation is official, the promoter will remain personally liable under the contracts.

The issue in the following case is a promoter's liability for certain conduct in connection with a corporate property transaction. Consider why the court held the promoter liable.

Park City Corp.

v

Watchie

439 P2d 587 (1968)

Oregon Supreme Court

FACTS: Watchie acquired options to purchase 965 acres of property for $729,000. He then interested a group of investors in buying the property and acted as a trustee on their behalf. The investors were interested only in holding the property as an investment for later resale, not for development. Watchie organized a corporation to develop the property. After forming the corporation, Watchie, as the investors' trustee, entered into a contract with the corporation to buy the property owned by the syndicate for $1.4 million. None of the corporation's stock subscribers had been advised that the property had been previously acquired by the investors for one-half the purchase price, nor were they advised of Watchie's relationship as trustee for the group. Although extensive plans were made for developing the property acquired by the corporation, development was never carried out. Ultimately, the corporation sued Watchie for violating his fiduciary relationship as a promoter by realizing such a large profit on the sale of the property to the corporation. At trial, the court ruled that the corporation failed to prove the allegations of its complaint against Watchie.

ISSUE: Did Watchie violate his fiduciary duty to the shareholders of the corporation?

RESULT: No, Watchie did not breach his duty because he did not benefit personally from the transaction and did not scheme with the seller to overcharge the corporation.

REASONING:

* * *

Plaintiff's cause of suit is based upon a doctrine originally formulated in this country in the Massachusetts case of Old Dominion Copper Mining & Smelting Co. v. Bigelow, 1909, 203 Mass. 159, 89 N.E. 193. . . . We read that case to hold that the promoter of a corporation owes to the corporation, and its subsequent subscribers of stock, a fiduciary duty. This duty is violated if he schemes to and does secretly acquire property or the right to buy property which he knows the corporation will require and sells it to the corporation, while he still retains control of the corporation, at a secret profit which is not disclosed to the later subscribers or to an independent board of directors of the corporation. In that event the corporation may bring an action to recover the secret profits. Oregon has adopted this theory in [a 1908 case]. The doctrine is generally recognized. . . .

The best expression we have found of the precise rule which delineates the particular kind of factual situation in which the corporation is permitted the remedy of the recovery of secret profits is in [the 1908 case], and it is this:

> If two or more persons associate themselves for the purpose of purchasing property, and one of them represents to the others that particular property can be bought for a designated price, which he procures to be paid by the associates, when in truth the purchase is for a less sum, and he has received the difference between the two sums, no doubt he may be compelled to account for such differences, though the property may be worth all that was paid for it. The same principle applies as against promoters of corporations. Hence, if any of them has a secret contract for the purchase of property, the terms of which are more favorable than those disclosed by him, or an agreement that he shall have stock in the corporation without paying therefore, any advantage which he thereby obtains is a fraud on the other shareholders and upon the corporation, and he will not be permitted to retain it. . . . And he may be compelled to account for such difference without rescission of the contract. . . .

Plaintiff's complaint alleged facts which would bring the case within the factual situation covered by the rule just quoted. As before mentioned, the allegations of the complaint are limited to charges that Watchie was the promoter of plaintiff corporation; that he personally contracted to buy the Skyline property, that he formed plaintiff corporation and while he was in the complete control of it, sold the property to the corporation for double his own purchase price and that Watchie "did not disclose to either the Board of Directors or the stockholders of plaintiff corporation that [Watchie] would make a profit of $729,000, by reason of said contract." These are the pertinent allegations of the complaint.

The evidence does not sustain the allegations. In the complete transaction, as described in the evidence, the property was bought by the Seattle syndicate. It was not bought with the scheme or design of selling it to this or any other persons or corporation but it was held for sale at the price specified. Contrary to the allegations, Watchie did not participate in any part of the profit made by the Seattle syndicate in the contract for the sale of the property, except for the commission paid to H. R. Watchie & Associates, Inc. In the contract with plaintiff corporation, Watchie was named as the vendor. But he was acting, admittedly, only as the trustee for the Seattle syndicate. He was not the true vendor or the recipient of any of the profits, as alleged. Nor is there any evidence that at any time, Watchie as an individual or as trustee schemed to over-load the profit on unsuspecting subscribers . . .

Sloan, Justice.

45:4 The Process of Incorporation

The right to act as a corporation is a privilege conferred by state law. A corporation comes into existence only by complying with statutory requirements of the state in which it is incorporated. No corporation can exist without the state's authorization.

 When owners of a business incorporate, they create a legal entity having the capacity to contract and incur debts on its own. To achieve freedom from personal liability for corporate debts, the owners, directors, and officers must comply with the requirements set out in the corporation laws of the state of incorporation. Noncompliance can mean suspension of the corporation and potential personal liability of the shareholders, officers, and directors for corporate debts.

Incorporation ordinarily begins when owners of a business file articles of incorporation with a designated state official, such as the Secretary of State [MBCA § 55]. In a few states, a copy of the articles must also be filed locally, in the county where the corporation's principal office is to be located or where it owns property. The state official with whom articles are filed determines whether they are in the proper form and are entitled to be filed. When articles conforming to the provisions of the state corporation law are presented, the state official must file them and then issue a certificate of incorporation [MBCA

§ 55]. Most states require payment of an incorporation fee before a corporation is permitted to conduct business.

The statutory requirements as to the form and content of the articles of incorporation must be substantially followed. Most states require articles of incorporation to contain certain minimum provisions as set out in the applicable corporation law, which is the law of the place where the corporation is to be organized [MBCA § 54]. Articles of incorporation are usually required to contain the following information: (1) corporate name, (2) corporate purpose, (3) corporation's specific business, (4) location of principal office, (5) name of designated agent for service of process, (6) number of directors, and (7) capital structure [MBCA § 54].

In some states, even though statutory requirements are met, a corporation might still not be qualified to do business. For example, the election of corporate officers, the subscription and payment of capital stock, and other steps may also be necessary. Accordingly, under state statutes of this type, if nothing more is done than filing articles of incorporation in the proper office, no corporation will come into existence. In other states, the existence of a corporation is deemed to commence at the time the articles of incorporation are filed with the state and a certificate of incorporation issued [MBCA § 56]. This is true even though such statutes may also require some form of organizational procedure or meeting before the corporation can actually conduct business [MBCA § 57].

After the articles of incorporation have been filed with the state and a certificate of incorporation issued, the corporate board of directors usually holds a meeting to complete all of the steps necessary to its organizational structure [MBCA § 57]. At this time, the corporation elects corporate officers and adopts governing rules, which are called *bylaws.* The corporation also (1) obtains authorization to open bank accounts, (2) complies with qualifications for doing business in other states if necessary, (3) obtains approval to lease or purchase property, (4) ratifies promoter contracts, and (5) obtains approval to issue stock and debt securities.

Bylaws Every corporation has the power to enact bylaws that govern its internal operation. Bylaws supplement the articles of incorporation and contain details of corporate administration, management, and internal operating procedures. Bylaws must be consistent with all state laws and with the articles of incorporation.

The initial bylaws are adopted by the board of directors. The power to alter, amend, or repeal bylaws or to adopt new bylaws, subject to repeal or change by action of the shareholders, is vested in the board of directors unless that power has been reserved to the shareholders in the articles of incorporation [MBCA § 27].

Corporate Name A name is particularly important to the existence of a corporation. The name designates the corporation in the same manner as the name of an individual designates the person. Thus, each corporation must have a name by which it is to do all legal acts, to sue and to be sued. Under

MBCA § 8, a corporate name cannot contain any word or phrase indicating or implying that the corporation is organized for any purposes other than those specified in the articles of incorporation. For example, a marine supply corporation cannot call itself a marine shipbuilding corporation. Moreover, a corporate name cannot be the same as or deceptively similar to the name of any other corporation organized or doing business in the state. A corporation may, however, obtain another corporation's written consent to use a similar or identical name. A corporation resulting from a merger or consolidation can take the same name as that used in the state by any of its predecessors.

The right to use a corporate name is as much a part of the corporate charter as any other privilege. A significant part of the value of a corporate name is usually that which derives from the rights accorded by the law of trade names, trademarks, and service marks (see Chapter 54).

To protect corporate names, MBCA § 9 provides that the exclusive right to use a particular name can be reserved by (1) any person intending to organize a corporation, (2) a domestic corporation intending to change its name, (3) a foreign corporation intending to apply for a certificate of authority to transact business in the state, (4) any foreign corporation authorized to transact business in the state and intending to change its name, and (5) any person intending to organize a foreign corporation that will do business in the state. The reservation is made by filing an application with the state to reserve a specified corporate name. If the name is available for corporate use, the state reserves it for the applicant's exclusive use for 120 days. The name can then be registered with the state by filing an application for registration and paying a registration fee [MBCA § 10].

Seal   Under the common law, a corporation could act only by its seal. This technical rule has given way. Today, in the transaction of business, a seal is no more necessary to validate the acts and contracts of a corporation than it is to validate those of an individual. However, it is sometimes desirable to adopt a seal so that all corporate contracts or other acts can be attested to with the seal. The presence of the seal establishes that the instrument to which it is affixed is the act of the corporation, and it is evidence of the proper execution of a contract and that the seal was affixed by proper authority.

Corporate Domicil and Place of Business   One's "domicil" is the place where one lives. The term refers to a relationship that the law creates between an individual—or a corporation—and a particular locality, state, or country. Sometimes the terms "domicil" and "residence" are used synonymously, but the two are actually different in meaning. For example, a person who resides in Florida for the winter but has a permanent home in New York is domiciled in New York, not Florida. Similarly, a corporation can transact business in Florida, and even maintain an office there to further its business, without being domiciled there.

A corporation's domicil belongs exclusively to the state in which it is created. Since a corporation exists only by reason of the law of the state where it is incorporated, it must dwell in that state and cannot migrate at will from state to state. These general rules do not mean, however, that a corporation's existence will not be recognized in other places. A corporation can qualify to transact business in any other state unless otherwise prohibited by law. Certainly, it can transact business in interstate commerce without undue interference from any state other than that of its incorporation.

For nearly 50 years, the state of Delaware has been unofficially recognized as the most desirable corporate domicil. Its liberal promanagement corporation laws and favorable court decisions in cases involving corporations have attracted business enterprises from all over the world. Forty percent of the companies listed on the New York Stock Exchange are domiciled in Delaware, and over 200 of the 500 largest industrial corporations in America are incorporated in this state.

45:5 Defects in the Formation Process

A corporation created in strict compliance with all the mandatory legal conditions for incorporation is termed a *de jure corporation*—a lawful corporation. It is a separate legal entity and possesses all the attributes or powers incident to a corporation. Such attributes include (1) limited liability, (2) continuity of life, (3) the power to sue and be sued, (4) the power to hold and convey property, (5) the capacity to contract, and (6) the right to exercise other corporate powers. The right of a de jure corporation to exist and act cannot be successfully attacked directly by the state or by any other party. In other words, the law recognizes the corporation character of a de jure corporation.

Occasionally, however, incorporators fail to or improperly perform one or more of the formal requirements for incorporation. In this situation, the corporation lacks de jure status. It does not possess all the attributes and powers ordinarily enjoyed by a corporation that fully complies with the requirements of the law.

In a few states a defective corporation is regarded as a nullity—as though no corporation had been formed at all. For example, lawsuits based on contractual obligations or torts can be defended on the basis that no corporation exists; conveyances made by the defective corporation can also be invalidated. Moreover, associates, shareholders, incorporators, or any other officers of what was purported to be a corporation may be sued and held personally liable on "corporate" obligations.

De Facto Corporation   In many states, a corporation that has not obtained de jure status but has complied sufficiently to be given corporate status against third parties is recognized as a *de facto corporation*. A de facto corporation is an apparent corporate organization, asserted to be a corporation by those running the business, and actually acting as such, but it lacks the legal sanction of the law and corporate status against the state.

As a general rule, a de facto corporation comes into existence when a de jure corporation has not been created because of some irregularity or defect in its formation or because of some failure to comply with the conditions of a state incorporation law. A de facto corporation will be held to exist if there is

(1) a valid law under which the corporation might be incorporated, (2) a bona fide attempt to organize under that law, and (3) an actual exercise of corporate powers.

Under Section 56 of the MBCA a corporation comes into existence only when the certificate of incorporation has actually been issued. If an individual or group of individuals assumes to act as a corporation before the certificate has been issued, they can be held liable under MBCA § 146 for all debts and liabilities incurred. Under the MBCA and in those states that have adopted similar provisions, if a corporation's articles have been approved and a certificate of incorporation has been issued, a valid corporation will be presumed to have been formed, except in certain actions brought by the state.

Corporation by Estoppel In certain circumstances, an organization that cannot be either a de jure corporation or a de facto one can still be regarded between the parties to a given transaction as a corporation. That is, an organization that has not complied with state statutes and can in no sense be deemed even a de facto corporation for any purpose can obtain corporate status by virtue of an estoppel. The effect of the estoppel is to prevent one or more persons from denying the existence of the corporation. For example, if a person transacts business with an entity holding itself out as a corporation, the entity can be estopped from denying corporate existence if disputes over the transaction occur later. In some states, a corporation must have at least a de facto existence before it can be estopped to deny its existence. In other states, if an entity represents itself as a corporation, it can be estopped from denying corporate existence regardless of its true status.

The following case illustrates how the MBCA has affected the concept of de facto corporations and corporations by estoppel. Consider the court's reasoning in its decision that the model act eliminated these concepts. Note also the precise point at which, according to the court, a corporation comes into existence.

Robertson

v

Levy

197 A2d 443 (1964)

District of Columbia Court of Appeals

FACTS: Robertson entered into an agreement with Levy for the latter to form a corporation and purchase Robertson's business. Levy submitted articles of incorporation to the state on December 27, 1961, but they were rejected on January 2, 1962. Despite the rejection, Levy began operating the business as a corporation. Robertson sold his assets to the corporation and received an installment note in return. A certificate of incorporation was finally issued on January 17, 1962. In June 1962, the corporation ceased doing business, and Levy stopped making payments on the note. Robertson sued Levy personally for the balance due on the note.

ISSUE: Does the failure to incorporate render Levy personally liable on the note signed on behalf of the corporation?

RESULT: Yes. Levy bears personal liability for the note.

REASONING:

* * *

The case presents the following issues on appeal: Whether the president of an "association" which filed its articles of incorporation, which were first rejected but later accepted, can be held personally liable on an obligation entered into by the "association" before the certificate of incorporation has been issued, or whether the creditor is "estopped" from denying the existence of the "corporation" because, after the certificate of incorporation was issued, he accepted the first installment payment on the note.

The Business Corporation Act of the District of Columbia . . . is patterned after the Model Business Corporation Act. . . .

For a full understanding of the problems raised, some historical grounding is not only illuminative but necessary. In early common law times private corporations were looked upon with distrust and disfavor. This distrust of the corporate form for private enterprise was eventually overcome by the enactment of statutes which set forth certain prerequisites before the status was achieved, and by court decisions which eliminated other stumbling blocks. Problems soon arose, however, where there was substantial compliance with the prerequisites of the statute, but not complete formal compliance. Thus the concepts of de jure corporations, de facto corporations, and of "corporations by estoppel" came into being. . . .

One of the reasons for enacting modern corporation statutes was to eliminate problems inherent in de jure, de facto and estoppel concepts. Thus [MBCA §§ 56 and 146] were enacted as follows:

> [MBCA § 56]. Effect of issuance of incorporation.
>
> Upon the issuance of the certificate of incorporation, the corporate existence shall begin, and such certificate of incorporation shall be conclusive evidence that all conditions precedent required to be performed by the incorporators have been complied with and that the corporation has been incorporated under this chapter, except as against the District of Columbia in a proceeding to cancel or revoke the certificate of incorporation.
>
> [MBCA § 146]. Unauthorized assumption of corporate powers.
>
> All persons who assume to act as a corporation without authority so to do shall be jointly and severally liable for all debts and liabilities incurred or arising as a result thereof.

The first portion of [MBCA § 56] sets forth a *sine qua non* regarding compliance. No longer must the courts inquire into the equities of a case to determine whether there has been "colorable compliance" with the statute. The corporation comes into existence only when the certificate has been issued. Before the certificate issues, there is no corporation de jure, de facto or by estoppel. . . .

The authorities which have considered the problem are unanimous in their belief that [MBCA §§ 56 and 146] have put to rest de facto corporations and corporations by estoppel. Thus the Comment to . . . the Model Act, after noting that de jure incorporation is complete when the certificate is issued, states that:

> Since it is unlikely that any steps short of securing a certificate of incorporation would be held to constitute apparent compliance, the possibility that a de facto corporation could exist under such a provision is remote.

Similarly, Professor Hornstein in his work on Corporate Law and Practice [observes] that: "Statutes in almost half the jurisdictions have virtually eliminated the distinction between de jure and de facto corporations. . . ."

The portion of [MBCA § 56] which states that the certificate of incorporation will be "conclusive evidence" that all conditions precedent have been performed eliminates the problems of estoppel and de facto corporations once the certificate has been issued. The existence of the corporation is conclusive evidence against all who deal with it. Under [MBCA § 146], if an individual or group of individuals assumes to act as a corporation before the certificate of incorporation has been issued, joint and several liability attaches. We hold, therefore, that the impact of these sections, when considered together, is to eliminate the concepts of estoppel and de facto corporateness under the Business Corporation Act of the District of Columbia. It is immaterial whether the third person believed he was dealing with a corporation or whether he intended to deal with a corporation. The certificate of incorporation provides the cut off point; before it is issued, the individuals, and not the corporation, are liable.

Turning to the facts of this case, Penn Ave. Record Shack, Inc. was not a corporation when the original agreement was entered into, when the lease was assigned, when Levy took over Robertson's business, when operations began under the Penn Ave. Record Shack, Inc. name, or when the bill of sale was executed. Only on January 17 did Penn Ave. Record Shack, Inc. become a corporation. Levy is subject to personal liability because, before this date, he assumed to act as a corporation without any authority so to do. Nor is Robertson estopped from denying the existence of the corporation because after the certificate was issued he accepted one payment on the note. An individual who incurs statutory liability on an obligation under [MBCA § 146] because he has acted without authority, is not relieved of that liability where, at a later time, the corporation does come into existence by complying with [MBCA § 56]. Subsequent partial payment by the corporation does not remove this liability. . . .

Hood, Chief Judge.

45:6 Corporate Powers and Functions

State laws give generous powers to corporations to enable them to engage in business activities. For example, MBCA § 4 gives a corporation the following rights and powers:

- Right to sue and be sued
- Right to acquire or sell real or personal property
- Right to hold, acquire, or dispose of shares of stock
- Ability to make contracts and become liable on them
- Power to mortgage corporate property
- Right to lend money and guarantee obligations of others
- Right to become a partner of others
- Power to compensate employees
- Right to pursue a nonprofitable objective
- Right to be treated as a separate entity or person
- Right to perpetual existence
- Right to make donations for the public welfare or for charitable, scientific, or educational purposes
- Right to pay pensions and to establish profit-sharing and other incentive plans for corporate directors, officers, and employees

In addition, MBCA § 3 provides that a corporation can engage in any lawful business purpose except banking or insurance.

A corporation has express powers to perform any act authorized by its articles of incorporation or by the general corporation laws of the state of incorporation. If a corporation does not insert provisions relating to corporate powers in its articles of incorporation, it usually means that the corporation has elected to have comprehensive powers to meet the objectives of incorporation. In most states, moreover, corporations also have implied powers to do whatever is reasonably necessary to promote their purposes and aid their express powers unless these powers are prohibited by common or statutory law [see MBCA § 4(q)].

45:7   Ultra Vires Acts

An act of a corporation that is beyond its express or implied powers is said to be *ultra vires*—beyond corporate powers. Ultra vires acts can arise when a corporation acts outside the powers granted in its articles of incorporation or beyond the powers granted under a state corporation law. The ultra vires doctrine seeks to preserve (1) the public's interest that a corporation will not exceed the powers granted to it, (2) the shareholders' interest that their capital will not be subjected to risks not contemplated by the articles of incorporation, and (3) the obligation of all persons dealing with a corporation to take notice of the limits on its power.

The ultra vires doctrine has been used by corporations as a defense. That is, corporations have sought to avoid obligations on the ground that corporate powers were exceeded in undertaking those obligations. The modern trend is to reject this kind of assertion, whether it is urged for or against a corporation, if it will result in legal wrong or inequity. Therefore, in many states—and in the MBCA—the availability of the ultra vires defense is limited [MBCA § 7].

In the following case, the court discusses why a corporation's making charitable contributions is not ultra vires. Consider the court's discussion of the ultra vires doctrine and its application to the facts of the case.

A. P. Smith Mfg. Co.

v

Barlow
98 A2d 581 (1953)
New Jersey Supreme Court

FACTS: A. P. Smith, a corporation, contributed regularly over the years to local charities. In 1951 the corporation's board of directors adopted a resolution appropriating $1,500 to Princeton University. When this action was questioned by shareholders, the corporation sought to have a court determine the propriety of its contribution. At trial, the court ruled that the contribution was proper and constituted a lawful exercise of corporate powers.

ISSUE: Did the charitable contribution constitute an *ultra vires* act of the corporation?

RESULT: No. A contribution of this nature is a lawful exercise of the corporation's implied and incidental powers.

REASONING:

*   *   *

The [trial court], in a well-reasoned opinion . . . , determined that a donation by the plaintiff The A.P. Smith Manufacturing Company to Princeton University was *intra vires* [within its powers]. . . .

The company was incorporated in 1896 and is engaged in the manufacture and sale of valves, fire hydrants and special equipment, mainly for water and gas industries. . . . Over the years the company has contributed regularly to the local community chest and on occasions to Upsala College in East Orange and Newark University, now part of Rutgers, the State University. On July 24, 1951 the board of directors adopted a resolution which set forth that it was in the corporation's best interests to join with others in the 1951 Annual Giving to Princeton University, and appropriated the sum of $1,500 to be transferred by the corporation's treasurer to the university as a contribution towards its maintenance. . . .

The objecting stockholders have . . . acknowledged that for over two decades there has been state legislation on our books which expresses a strong public policy in favor of corporate contributions such as that being questioned by them. Nevertheless, they have taken the position that (1) the plaintiff's certificate of incorporation does not expressly authorize the contribution and under common-law principles the company does not possess any implied or incidental power to make it. . . .

In his discussion of the early history of business corporations Professor Williston refers to a 1702 publication where the author stated flatly that "The general intent and end of all civil incorporations is for better government." And he points out that the early corporate charters, particularly their recitals, furnish additional support for the notion that the corporate object was the public one of managing and ordering the trade as well as the private one of profit for the members. . . . However, with later economic and social developments and the free availability of the corporate device for all trades, the end of private profit became generally accepted as the controlling one in all businesses other than those classed broadly as public utilities. . . . As a concomitant the common-law rule developed that those who managed the corporation could not disburse any corporate funds for philanthropic or other worthy public cause unless the expenditure would benefit the corporation. . . . During the 19th Century when corporations were relatively few and small and did not dominate the country's wealth, the common-law rule did not significantly interfere with the public interest. But the 20th Century has presented a different climate. . . . Control of economic wealth has passed largely from individual entrepreneurs to dominating corporations, and calls upon the corporations for reasonable philanthropic donations have come to be made with increased public support. In many instances such contributions have been sustained by the courts within the common-law doctrine upon liberal findings that the donations tended reasonably to promote the corporate objectives. . . .

. . . [W]e have no hesitancy in sustaining the validity of the donation by the plaintiff. There is no suggestion that it was made indiscriminately or to a pet charity of the corporate directors in furtherance of personal rather than corporate ends. On the contrary, it was made to a preeminent institution of higher learning, was modest in amount and well within the limitations imposed by the statutory enactments, and was voluntarily made in the reasonable belief that it would aid the public welfare and advance the interests of the plaintiff as a private corporation and as part of the community in which it operates. We find that it was a lawful exercise of the corporation's implied and incidental powers under common-law principles . . . As has been indicated, there is now widespread belief throughout the nation that free and vigorous nongovernmental institutions of learning are vital to our democracy and the system of free enterprise and that withdrawal of corporate authority to make such contributions within reasonable limits would seriously threaten their continuance. Corporations have come to recognize this and with their enlightenment have sought in varying measures, as has the plaintiff by its contribution, to insure and strengthen the society which gives them existence and the means of aiding themselves and their fellow citizens. Clearly then, the appellants, as individual stockholders whose private interests rest entirely upon the well-being of the plaintiff corporation, ought not be permitted to close their eyes to present-day realities and thwart the long-visioned corporate action in recognizing and voluntarily discharging its high obligations as a constituent of our modern social structure. . . .

Jacobs, Justice.

45:8 Corporate Tort and Criminal Liability

A corporation can commit and be held liable for almost every kind of tort. The fact that a business is incorporated is not a defense in a tort action. Moreover, the agency rule of respondeat superior (see Chapter 43) is also applicable to corporations. Under this rule, a corporation can be held liable for the torts and other wrongful acts of its officers, directors, agents, or employees, so long as the wrongdoer is acting within the scope of his authority or the course of his employment.

Fraud Corporations can also be held liable for the fraud and deceit of their officers and agents acting within the scope of their corporate authority or employment. A corporation's liability for fraud extends to false statements in certificates, reports, or documents required to be filed with a governmental entity. This is particularly true if the required documents are the sort on which others are to rely and act.

Criminal Liability   It was long held under the common law that a corporation could not be prosecuted criminally. Today, however, a corporation can be held criminally liable for the acts of an officer or employee acting within the scope of his employment. To hold a corporation liable, it is not necessary to show that the criminal acts of an officer or employee were expressly authorized or approved. Indeed, a corporation cannot even escape liability by claiming that it specifically prohibited its officers and employees from violating the law.

A corporation can be punished by fine or by seizure of its property. Because it might be more difficult to punish corporations than to punish individuals, a state can impose different punishment on a corporation than is imposed on an individual for the same criminal offense. For example, a state can properly impose the penalty of mandatory dissolution on a corporation in addition to the penalties imposed on individuals. However, states cannot impose different degrees of punishment for the same act because doing so would violate the constitutional right of equal protection under the law.

45:9   Consolidation and Merger

Various changes can be made in the structure of a corporation. These changes include merger, consolidation, and changes in capital stock. A *merger* is the absorption of one or more corporations into another corporation [MBCA § 71].

EXAMPLE: The Crestview Steel Corporation seeks a merger with its competitor, the Bay Iron Corporation. At a meeting of Crestview's board of directors, the vice-president for corporate acquisitions proposes various merger alternatives. These merger proposals are as follows:

1. The first proposal involves a merger by mutual agreement between Crestview and Bay Iron in which Bay Iron shares would be converted into Crestview shares. Bay Iron shareholders would either exchange their existing shares for Crestview shares or would be paid in cash for the value of their Bay Iron shares. Under this alternative, Bay Iron shareholders could continue their investment and could share in Bay Iron's potential growth through their ownership of Crestview shares. Bay Iron would cease to do business as a separate company, however; it would merge with Crestview.

2. The second proposal entails Crestview's formation of a new corporation—the Brannan Steel Corporation. Under this alternative, Crestview would merge Bay Iron by mutual agreement into Brannan Steel by exchanging Brannan stock for the outstanding Bay Iron stock. Dissenting shareholders would be paid the value of their shares. In this manner, Crestview would avoid fusion with Bay Iron but would end up controlling Bay Iron by virtue of its ownership of Brannan Steel. This transac-

tion would be a typical three-party merger. Under this plan, former Bay Iron shareholders would not acquire any Crestview shares.

3. The third merger proposal involves the gradual acquisition of Bay Iron by Crestview. This alternative would be particularly advantageous if Bay Iron shares were depressed or underpriced in the stock market. Under this type of merger, Crestview would purchase a large block of Bay Iron stock at favorable prices. It would then make a cash offer to Bay Iron shareholders to purchase additional shares in order to give it a majority position in Bay Iron. If this tender offer were successful, Crestview would acquire control of Bay Iron, although it would not necessarily purchase all outstanding Bay Iron stock. Some Bay Iron shareholders might not tender their shares to Crestview for purchase. Once in control of Bay Iron, however, Crestview could then propose a merger to Bay Iron's board of directors, which Crestview would control. Under this merger, Bay Iron's minority shares—owned by those who did not tender or sell their stock to Crestview during its tender offer—would be converted into cash.

The merger proposals illustrated in the above example are but three of the many different types of corporate changes in structure and ownership. They are all legitimate business transactions resulting in the merger of one or more corporations.

A *consolidation* is the unification of two or more corporations to form a single new corporation [MBCA § 72]. Merger and consolidation are similar in that both reach a similar result. That is, the surviving corporation issues stock for the stock of the absorbed corporations and has the assets of all the combined companies. Every state corporation law contains procedures for merger and consolidation. Either procedure is usually accomplished by action of the boards of directors of the affected corporations. Approval by the required percentage of the shareholders, usually one-half to two-thirds of the shares of the affected companies, is also required [see MBCA §§ 71-77].[3] There is an exception to the prerequisite of shareholder approval of a merger or consolidation: approval is not necessary if one corporation holds an overwhelming majority of the stock of another corporation, usually 90 or 95 percent [see MBCA § 75]. For example, merger of a subsidiary corporation can be accomplished by vote of the boards of directors of the corporations involved.

De Facto Mergers   A de facto merger is a transaction that for all practical purposes is a merger but is treated as a sale of assets. In certain situations it is possible for a corporation to cast an intercorporate transaction as a sale of assets rather than a merger, thus preventing a dissenting shareholder from blocking the sale or from receiving the fair value of his shares owned. To remedy this situation, some courts have developed the de facto merger doctrine. Under this doctrine, shareholders who dissent to the sale of assets are given both the opportunity to receive payment of the fair value of their shares and appraisal rights to determine that fair value. In those states that have adopted the MBCA, the problem of de facto mergers has largely ceased to exist. The reason is that

---

[3] The rights of shareholders in mergers are discussed in Chapter 45.

MBCA § 79 specifically requires shareholder approval for a sale of assets and gives dissenting shareholders the same right to fair payment for shares owned that they have in a merger or consolidation [see MBCA §§ 80, 81].

Rights and Liabilities of Successor Corporations   Most states provide that the property, powers, and assets that belong to constituent or merged companies at the time of a consolidation or merger pass to the successor corporation (the corporation formed by the consolidation or merger). Even in the absence of a statutory provision, the effect is usually the same.

The extent to which liabilities of the constituent or merged corporations pass to the successor corporation varies from state to state. In some states, the successor's liability is limited to the amount of property or assets it received. In other situations, when a successor corporation merely continues the business of merged or consolidated corporations, the successor can be held liable for *all* of the old corporation's debts, regardless of the amount of property received. In some states this rule is broadly applied, at least with a consolidation. Therefore, when a debtor corporation ceases to exist, the consolidated corporation is answerable to all the old corporation's liabilities. In still other states, liability for the obligations of a corporation that has transferred all its assets to another corporation through consolidation, merger, or otherwise has been imposed by statute. Of course, if a corporation's assets are transferred to a new corporation for the specific purpose of defrauding creditors, the new corporation is held liable for the debts and liabilities of the old corporation, even though these obligations may have come into existence after the transfer.

A consolidated or merged corporation can also be liable for taxes imposed on a predecessor. For example, a consolidated corporation can be held liable for paying a federal tax that one of its constituent corporations was obliged to pay before consolidation.

45:10   Dissolution and Liquidation

The *dissolution* of a corporation is an event that necessarily leads to termination of the corporation's existence. A corporation's articles of incorporation can limit the lifetime of the corporation to a specified term. If so, the corporation is dissolved—and its existence terminates—when the specified term expires. The dissolution and termination of a corporation can also occur either voluntarily or by what is known as judicial liquidation. Judicial liquidation is involuntary dissolution that is brought about by petition to a court filed by either the corporation's shareholders or its creditors.

 The dissolution of a corporation does not relieve officers and directors from responsibility to the corporation's creditors. All states have enacted statutes that hold directors and officers responsible for winding up company affairs, including the payment of debts and taxes.

Voluntary Dissolution   In many states, the majority of a corporation's shareholders can seek and obtain a dissolution. In states that have adopted the MBCA, a corporation can be voluntarily dissolved by the written consent of all its shareholders [MBCA § 83]. A corporation can also be voluntarily dissolved by its incorporators before the business commences or any shares are issued [MBCA § 82], or by the act of the corporation itself when authorized by the board of directors and approved by the shareholders [MBCA § 84].

Involuntary Dissolution or Liquidation   Many states have enacted statutes providing in general terms for involuntary dissolution of a corporation by action of a specified number of proportion of its shareholders. This procedure is referred to as the *liquidation* of assets or business of a corporation, rather than a corporation dissolution. However, for all intents and purposes, liquidation is the same as dissolution.

The MBCA provides for the liquidation of a corporation in a legal action by a shareholder when it is established that (1) the directors are deadlocked in the management of corporate affairs, (2) the shareholders are unable to break the deadlock, and (3) irreparable injury is being caused by the deadlock [MBCA § 97]. MBCA § 97 also provides for the liquidation of a corporation's assets and business when shareholders are deadlocked in voting power and have failed, for a period that includes at least two consecutive annual meetings, to elect successors to directors whose terms have expired or would have expired on the next election.

Most states also provide by statute for involuntary dissolution or liquidation under the following circumstances: (1) when the directors or those in charge act in an illegal, oppressive, or fraudulent manner; (2) when corporate assets are being misapplied or wasted; (3) when an election or appointment of directors is invalid; or (4) when a corporation has abandoned its business, or the corporation's objectives have fully failed or are entirely abandoned [see MBCA § 97(4)].

In most states, when a corporation is dissolved or liquidated, a trustee or receiver is appointed to oversee the process. Trustees are authorized to enforce a corporation's contractual rights and to meet its obligations that were created prior to dissolution or liquidation. Trustees can also engage in any new transaction incidental to their winding up of corporate affairs. For example, they can compromise and settle claims or convey corporate property for this purpose, and they can distribute the corporation's assets. In this regard, the trustees are merely agents of the corporation and its shareholders.

When a corporation is dissolved, its assets are first used to pay the debts and claims asserted against it by creditors. Secured creditors are entitled to be satisfied from secured property. The remaining assets can then be distributed among the shareholders. Distributions made to shareholders on liquidation of a corporation are referred to as liquidating dividends.

Key Concepts and Terms

- A corporation is a legal entity created by law. It is separate and distinct from the individuals who own or manage it. The owners of a corporation have limited liability. Debts and liabilities incurred by a corporation belong to the corporation and are not attributed to the shareholders. Management of a corporation is centralized in the officers and directors, who are charged with specific duties to the corporation and its shareholders.

- The common characteristics of corporations include (1) separate identity, (2) continuity of existence, (3) limited shareholder liability, (4) free transferability of ownership rights, (5) centralized management, and (6) limited powers.

- Corporations can be organized for many purposes, public and private. Three common forms in the United States are the incorporated sole proprietorship (the one-person corporation), the close corporation, and the publicly held corporation.

- A promoter is a person who initiates a corporation and brings together persons interested in the enterprise. The promoter must exercise the utmost good faith in dealing with the corporation and its shareholders both before and after incorporation.

- The right to act as a corporation is a special privilege conferred by state law. A corporation comes into existence only by complying with statutory requirements of the state in which it is incorporated.

- Once articles of incorporation have been filed and accepted by the state, a certificate of incorporation is issued and corporate existence commences.

- A corporation that has been regularly created in strict compliance with all the mandatory legal conditions for incorporation is a de jure corporation. A de jure corporation is a separate legal entity and possesses all of the attributes or powers incident to a corporation.

- A corporation has express powers to perform any act authorized by the articles of incorporation. In most states, corporations also have implied powers to do whatever is reasonably necessary to promote their express purposes and aid their express powers.

- An act of a corporation that is beyond its express or implied powers is said to be ultra vires. Ultra vires acts can occur when a corporation acts outside the powers granted in its articles of incorporation, or beyond the powers granted under a state corporation law.

- A corporation can be held liable for the torts of its officers, directors, agents, and employees acting within the scope of their authority or the course of their employment. In many states, a corporation can also be held criminally liable.

- Changes can be made in corporate structure by such acts as merger or consolidation. A merger is the absorption of one or more corporations by another corporation. A consolidation is the unification of two or more corporations to form a single new corporation.

- Property, powers, and assets belonging to a constituent or merged corporation at the time of a consolidation or merger pass to the new or successor corporation. In many states, liabilities of a predecessor corporation pass to the successor as well.

- A corporation can be terminated by (1) voluntary dissolution, or (2) liquidation of the corporation by a court on petition of either the shareholders or the creditors.

- Bylaws
- Close Corporation
- Consolidation
- Corporation by Estoppel
- De Facto Corporation
- De Jure Corporation
- Dissolution
- Foreign Corporation
- Holding Company
- Liquidation
- Merger
- Promoter
- Quasi-Public Corporation
- Subchapter S Corporation
- Ultra Vires

Questions and Case Problems

1. The Wilmington Memorial Company sells cemetery markers and monuments, in competition with the Silverbrook Cemetery Company, which sells and erects markers in conjunction with its cemetery operation. Silverbrook's charter provides that it can "sell personal property of every kind and may make all contracts and do all acts necessary" to run its cemetery. Believing that the marker business is beyond Silverbrook's corporate powers, Wilmington sues to enjoin Silverbrook from engaging in this business. How should the court decide the case?

2. Architect Howe enters into a contract with Boss for services to be performed for a corporation not yet formed. When the contract is made, Boss signs it as follows: "Edwin A. Boss, agent for a Minnesota corporation to be formed who will be the obligor." Howe performs services worth $38,000 but is paid only $14,500. The corporation is never formed. Howe sues Boss for the balance. Is Boss personally liable? Why?

3. Preston purchases a tract of land for $240,000. Later she forms a corporation and sells the same land for $350,000. Is the sale proper? Can this question be answered without additional facts? If not, what additional facts must be disclosed?

4. On April 9, 1980, Bowers and Division 8, Inc. entered a subcontracting agreement which provided that Division 8 was to furnish the labor and materials necessary to fabricate and install aluminum windows and entries on a construction project for which Bowers was the general contractor. Division 8 was unable to complete the contract, and on January 9, 1981, it attempted to assign it to Altura. Division 8 notified Bowers by letter that it had ceased to operate as a glassing contractor and that it had sold all contracts to Altura. Crownover attached a handwritten note to the letter requesting that all future checks from Bowers be made payable to "Altura Glass Co." Crownover signed the note "Pres. Jack Crownover." The assignment to Altura was accepted by Bowers. On January 13, 1981, Bowers issued a check payable to "Altura Glass Company, Inc." which Altura accepted. Altura was later unable to complete the work, forcing Bowers to hire another subcontractor. Bowers contends that Crownover should be liable on the contract because on January 9, 1981, when Crownover accepted assignment of the subcontracting agreement, Altura did not have a certificate of incorporation. Although the necessary documents had been mailed to the secretary of state on January 9, 1981, the certificate was not issued until January 12, 1981. What result?

5. How do Subchapter S and close corporations differ from publicly held corporations?

6. Life Science produced a dangerous pesticide called Kepone at its plant in Virginia. Moore and Hundtofte were the managing officers directly responsible for operations. In 1973 and 1974, Life Science failed to file an annual report with the state or to pay certain franchise taxes. Consequently, the corporation was dissolved on June 1, 1975. Despite dissolution, Moore and Hundtofte continued to manufacture Kepone as though Life Science were still a viable corporation. On August 11, 1975, they applied for reinstatement of Life Science's corporate status, and the application was approved two days later. Before reinstatement, however, the federal government fined the corporation and the two directors for violation of certain safety regulations. Moore and Hundtofte opposed the fine, arguing that they were not personally liable. They contended that the reinstatement of Life Science's corporate status in August related back to June, validating as corporate acts all actions taken in its name by the two officers in the interim. Are Moore and Hundtofte personally liable?

7. In 1967 Ortiz was injured at work by a defective punch press. Ortiz filed suit against Amsted, based on the following chain of events: In 1956, after the machine was manufactured and sold by the Johnson Machine and Press Corporation (Johnson), Johnson was acquired by Bontrager Corporation. The physical assets of Johnson were transfered to Bontrager, and Johnson became a mere "shell" corporation with no assets. The "shell" was maintained by Bontrager in order to continue the Johnson trade name. In 1962 Amsted acquired the principal assets of Bontrager, including a manufacturing facility, equipment, the trade name, customer lists, and the single share of existing stock of the Johnson Corporation. After the acquisition of its assets by Amsted, Bontrager remained in existence a short time and then dissolved, distributing the proceeds of the sale (its major asset) to its shareholders. The purchase agreement between Bontrager and Amsted specifically recited that Amsted would not assume any liability of Bontrager and that Bontrager would be solely responsible for all its existing liabilities. At all times the plant in which the machine that injured Ortiz was manufactured continued in operation producing punch presses. Should Amsted be held answerable for Ortiz's injuries?

8. A group of hotel and restaurant owners, supply companies, and several other businesses organized an association to attract conventions to Portland, Oregon. The association financed its activities by contributions from members. Hotel members were asked to deal only with suppliers who paid their assessments. Implementation of the agreement by hotel members to curtail purchases from nonpaying suppliers was a violation of federal law, the Sherman Antitrust Act. The Hilton Hotels Corporation, one of the members of the association, had a corporate policy prohibiting such discrimination against suppliers. Indeed, the Hilton policy was to purchase supplies solely on the basis of price, quality, and service. The manager of the Portland Hilton was clearly aware of this policy and was determined to carry it out to the letter. On two occasions, he called the hotel's purchasing agent into his office and told him plainly that Hilton would not take part in any boycott. Despite his instructions to the contrary, the purchasing agent met with a supplier and threatened loss of Hilton business until the supplier paid the association assessment. Later Hilton Hotels was criminally prosecuted for this violation of the Sherman Act. Was Hilton guilty? Can the hotel be held liable for the criminal acts of its agent, even when the agent acted contrary to his instructions?

9. The United States Coast Guard's observations of an oil refinery led to a prosecution of the oil company for polluting coastal waters. The law under which the

corporation was prosecuted authorized the imposition of a fine or imprisonment. After a trial, the oil company was given a suspended fine and placed on probation for six months. As a condition of probation, the company was required to set up a pollution prevention program. Less than delighted with the terms of probation, the oil company went back into court contending that it could only be given a fine. Can the corporation properly be placed on probation, or is it only subject to a fine?

10. Duffy, a promoter for a corporation not yet formed, enters into a contract with Mann on behalf of the corporation. The contract obligates the corporation to employ Mann for two years. Later, the corporation is formed and Mann commences work on the date specified in the contract. One month after beginning work, Mann is fired. He sues both Duffy and the corporation for breach of contract. How should the case be decided?

46 Corporate Management and Finance

46:1 Introduction to Corporate Management

Every corporation is governed by a board of directors. The board represents the corporation in all business matters; it has the authority to transact all ordinary business within the scope of its articles of incorporation. The directors are responsible for all corporate decisions, and they exercise this decision-making power in meetings usually held at times fixed by the articles of incorporation or the corporate bylaws.[1]

The board's powers are conferred by state corporation laws. Under the MBCA, the directors are authorized to

- Approve a change in the corporation's registered office or registered agent [MBCA § 13]
- Establish the time of payment of stock subscriptions [MBCA § 17]
- Establish the selling price of corporate stock [MBCA § 18]
- Establish the value of noncash contributions received for shares of stock [MBCA § 19]
- Adopt or change bylaws [MBCA § 27]
- Fill vacancies on the board [MBCA § 38]
- Declare dividends [MBCA § 45]
- Remove officers [MBCA § 51]
- Propose amendments to the articles of incorporation [MBCA §§ 58, 59]
- Approve any plan of merger or consolidation [MBCA §§ 71, 72]
- Recommend the sale of substantially all corporate assets [MBCA § 79]
- Recommend corporate dissolution to shareholders [MBCA § 84]

In addition to exercising these statutory powers, the board makes decisions about the expansion of business, the development of new products, and the nature and extent of corporate borrowing.

The board of directors uses its powers to run the corporation at large. Directors may oversee the conduct of corporate officers and the course of corporate

---

[1] The election of directors is discussed in Chapter 47.

business. Internal management, however, is almost always left to the corporate officers, with the board acting as a reviewing body of the actions taken by the president or the chief executive officer. For this reason, it can be said that the boards of most large, publicly owned corporations have no real, independent power in the day-to-day corporate activities. This view of the board's functions is supported by MBCA § 35, which provides that the business and affairs of a corporation shall be managed *under the direction* of the board.

Executive and Audit Committees The board of directors usually meets officially only a few times each year. Business requiring the board's attention between board meetings is conducted by the executive committee. Normally, an executive committee consists of the chief executive officer of the corporation, one or two inside directors, and one or two outside directors. Under MBCA § 42, an executive committee can exercise all the authority of the board of directors, but it cannot sell major corporate assets, issue stock, or declare dividends.

Another useful committee often appointed by the board of directors is the audit committee. This committee generally reviews the corporation's financial statements with independent auditors. An audit committee may also inquire into the financial practices of the corporation, its accounting practices, and financial reporting. At times it may even evaluate the corporation's financial statements in terms of their content and readability.

46:2   Directors

Most publicly held corporations have two types of directors: inside directors, who are officers of the corporation and full-time employees, and *outside directors*, who are not corporate employees. Inside directors have specific knowledge of corporate operations, while outside directors, who are usually unaffiliated with the corporation, do not. In certain circumstances, an outside director might have a business or professional relationship with a company, as, for example, an investment banker or a lawyer. In closely held corporations, outside directors are often friends or relatives of the principal shareholders. The New York Stock Exchange requires newly listed companies to have at least two outside directors because they help to serve as independent checks on management.

Corporate directors are obligated to be well informed of corporate affairs. The fact that a director is inactive does not excuse him from this obligation. A director must take the initiative to stay informed and to question suspect actions. Otherwise, he may be subject to personal liability.

46:3   Powers and Duties of Officers and Directors

The business of a corporation is conducted through its officers and directors. They are the corporation's agents.[2] Officers and directors are required to act in the utmost good faith, giving to the business the benefit of their care and judgment, and to exercise their powers solely in the interests of the corpora-

---

[2] The agency relationship is discussed in Chapter 43.

tion and its shareholders. Officers and directors must also act only within the scope of their authority, as is expressly conferred by the corporation.

 The question of the exact extent of an officer's authority often arises. This authority can be express, as conferred by the corporation; implied; or apparent, based on what the officer appears to be authorized to do in the regular conduct of business. Since the authority of an officer or employee might affect business dealings with a corporation, it is wise to raise the question of his or her authority before an agreement is made; otherwise, the agreement could later turn out to be illusory.

President   The president of a corporation is vested with authority in various ways. In some states, the president derives authority by statute or from the corporation or board of directors. In these states the president has no inherent powers to act for the corporation. The fact that a president owns a majority of the corporate stock or otherwise controls the corporation does not vest the president with any additional authority.

Other states take the broader view that the president is the general manager of corporate affairs and has authority to act for the corporation. This authority allows him to perform all acts within the scope of corporate business and within the scope of his usual duties. He also has implied authority to do any act appropriate in the ordinary course of business. This implied authority does not extend to acts beyond the general scope of the ordinary business of the corporation or for his own benefit. That is, a president who is entrusted with the management of the entire business has not necessarily been delegated all corporate rights and powers, but only the business he is authorized to transact in the name of the corporation.

The following case illustrates the extent of a corporate president's authority to act for or contract on behalf of the corporation. Consider the limits imposed on the officer's authority.

Templeton

v

Nocona Hills Owners Asso.
555 SW2d 534 (1977)
Texas Court of Civil Appeals

FACTS: Templeton entered into a one-year employment contract as manager of the Nocona Hills Country Club. The agreement was signed both by her and by the president of the club, but it was never ratified by Nocona's board of directors. Shortly after a change in ownership, Templeton was discharged by the general manager for disloyalty. She brought suit against the country club to recover the amount she would have received had the written contract been honored.

ISSUE: Did the corporation president have authority to enter into an employment contract on behalf of the corporation?

RESULT: No. The president had neither inherent nor actual authority to bind the corporation.

REASONING:

*   *   *

The authority of an officer to contract for a corporation may be actual or apparent. In Texas, by statute, the board of directors of a corporation, not its president, is charged generally with the duty of managing the corporation's affairs. . . . Consequently, actual authority of the president to contract on behalf of the corporation must be found either in specific statutes, in the organic law of the corporation, or in a delegation of authority from the board of directors formally expressed, or must be implied from the nature of his position or from custom or habit of doing business. . . . As to express authority, there was no proof in this case of any of the provisions of the corporate charter or by-laws, and there was no attempt to prove that the board of directors or the shareholders had invested the president with any authority to make contracts on its behalf. . . . In fact, the only evidence concerning contracts on behalf of the corporation was [President] Jameson's testimony that only the board could authorize them, and that the board refused to approve the one in question here. As to implied authority, the settled rule in Texas is that a corporation president, merely by virtue of his office, has no inherent power to bind the corporation except as to routine matters arising in the ordinary course of business. . . . The execution of an employment contract binding the corporation to employ a person in a managerial position for a period of one year could not be considered a matter in the ordinary and usual course of appellee's business. . . . Especially is this true since the power to hire and discharge employees for [the corporation] was vested in a general manager rather than in the president. Indeed, Jameson had not even taken office as president . . . when the contract was executed. Under the record in this case, we are impelled to the conclusion that appellant failed in her burden to establish that Mr. Jameson was invested with actual authority to make the contract sued upon.

There was likewise a failure to produce any evidence that Jameson had apparent authority to make the contract. . . . The record here contains no evidence of any act on the part of the corporation's board of directors or other authorized person which would lead any reasonable person to believe that Mr. Jameson was invested with the power to execute, without approval of the board of directors, a year's employment contract. . . .

Cornelius, Justice.

46:4   Compensation of Corporate Officers

A corporation may compensate its officers for services rendered by them on behalf of the corporation. This compensation can take various forms, including salaries, bonuses, stock options, and payments to pension or retirement plans. The manner and total amount of compensation ordinarily is determined by the board of directors, with some limitations. The board must act according to the procedures set forth in the articles of incorporation, the bylaws, the board's resolutions, or applicable state statutes. Furthermore, the board must award salaries that are reasonable and for services actually rendered. In determining whether compensation is reasonable, the total compensation package, including bonuses and other fringe benefits, must be analyzed. For example, spending corporate funds on costly fringe benefits might result in excessive total compensation, even though an officer's base salary is reasonable. The officer's work performance and the nature of the work in light of his qualifications, abilities, and responsibilities must also be examined. In this respect, an officer's contribution in helping a corporation withstand adverse financial circumstances may be considered. Other factors that should be looked at in determining a reasonable salary include the salary paid to other officers of the corporation, the salary paid to officers of corporations engaged in similar businesses, and the general financial condition of the corporation.

46:5   Fiduciary Duty of Officers and Directors

Officers and directors occupy a fiduciary relationship to the corporation and its shareholders. This means that they are bound in good conscience to act in the interests of the corporation and to guard those interests. The transactions of an officer or director for the corporation must be fair and honest. This rule [MBCA § 35] is followed in most states. If an officer or director makes a personal profit while acting in his fiduciary capacity, he may be compelled to account for and return those profits to the corporation.

If an officer or director becomes involved in a transaction against the interests of a corporation or its shareholders, the transaction is void unless (1) the facts of the transaction are disclosed; (2) the transaction is approved by a majority of the disinterested directors or the shareholders; or (3) the transaction, in the final analysis, is found to be fair and reasonable to the corporation [MBCA § 41].

In addition, officers and directors, by state law, have a duty to use reasonable care and diligence in performing their designated functions. This means that they must exercise the same degree of care and prudence that people prompted by self-interest generally exercise in their own affairs. In exercising reasonable care, a director can rely on information, reports, opinions, and statements prepared or presented by corporate officers or employees whom the director reasonably believes to be competent in the matters presented. A director can also rely on the specialized knowledge of lawyers, accountants, investment brokers, and board committees.

EXAMPLE: If the audit committee of the board meets regularly with the outside auditor, examines the audit report, reviews the management letter, asks probing questions, and has no reason to suspect negligence, error, or fraud on the part of the auditing firm, members of the audit committee are entitled to rely on the representations of the auditor. On the other hand, if the audit committee discovers serious discrepancies in the audit and fails to take appropriate action, including possibly a change of auditors, members of the committee could not defend themselves in an action for breach of the duty of care by arguing that they relied on the outside auditor.

46:6   Duty of Loyalty; Corporate Opportunities

Officers and directors owe a *duty of loyalty* to the corporation—the duty to refrain from participating in personal ventures that exploit their corporate position in any way. Corporate officials are obligated to expend their best efforts to promote the interests of the corporation and its shareholders and place those interests above their own personal gain. Thus, they must refrain from competing with the corporation, engaging in conflicts of interest, usurping corporate opportunities, or oppressing minority shareholders.

Corporate Opportunities   The duty of loyalty requires corporate officers to refrain from appropriating for personal benefit a business opportunity that properly belongs to the corporation. This is known as the *corporate opportunity doctrine*. Under the doctrine, corporate officials cannot divert to themselves opportunities in which the corporation has a right, property interest, or expectancy, or which should properly belong to the corporation. For example, an officer of a corporation is not permitted to use corporate property or assets to develop a business that would be in direct competition with the corporation. Furthermore, an officer or director cannot acquire property in which the corporation is itself interested or which is important to the corporation's business. Thus, for example, if a corporation has leased certain property, a director cannot buy that property.

   If an officer or director takes advantage of a corporate opportunity, he must turn over to the corporation all property or profits he acquires through the opportunity. In an appropriate case, damages can also be awarded to the corporation.

EXAMPLE: Acme Packers handled and prepared canned meat products. Acme sold all its output to other manufacturers who in turn sold the canned goods under different labels. Two Acme directors incorporated another company called Acme Fine Meats and began to market under this label products purchased directly from Acme Packers. Although Acme Packers was not engaged in the retail marketing of canned products, it could easily have done so because canned products are within its line of business. Thus, the directors of Acme Fine Meats unfairly acquired a business opportunity rightfully belonging to Acme Packers. All profits of Acme Fine Meats rightfully belong to Acme Packers and must be turned over to it.

The corporate opportunity doctrine appears to be easy to apply, but in most cases it is not. Proper application of the rule involves a two-step process. First, a court must determine whether the business opportunity in question is actually a corporate opportunity. If it is so determined, the court must then ascertain whether taking advantage of the business opportunity also was a breach of the officer's fiduciary duty to the corporation.

46:7 Liabilities of Officers and Directors

State corporation laws generally do not contain long lists of prohibited transactions. They impose few specific liabilities on officers and directors, and of these, most are applicable only to directors. For example, MBCA § 48 imposes liability on directors for a distribution to shareholders contrary to statute or charter restrictions. To avoid liability in this situation, a director who attends a board meeting at which an illegal action is taken must record a dissenting vote in the minutes of the corporation [see MBCA § 35]; if the action is approved by the board, the dissenter must file a written dissent with the corporate secretary immediately after the meeting adjourns to avoid liability.

To avoid liability in other situations, a director must observe the standard of care set forth in MBCA § 35. This standard is that a director must act in good faith in a manner reasonably believed to be in the best interests of the corporation and with such care as an ordinarily prudent person in a like position would use under similar circumstances. In performing his duties, a director can rely on information, opinions, reports, and statements of others. A director can also delegate certain functions to the officers and other employees of the corporation.

 When an officer or director assigns work to an employee, he or she might believe that legal responsibility is also transferred to the employee. This is not true. Officers and directors must apply the diligence, care, and skill an ordinarily prudent person would apply in the interests of the corporation and its shareholders. Thus, the fact that a particular corporate employee is primarily responsible for a particular corporate task does not relieve corporate officers or directors from personal liability for the employee's negligence.

In the absence of self-dealing, officers or directors are not usually liable for honest errors or mistakes in judgment. In this regard, courts, in refusing to impose higher standards of care on corporate officers or directors, have typically applied the sentiment that no man of sense would take the office if the law imposed on him a guaranty of the general success of the company as a penalty for any negligence.

If an officer or director violates any of the common-law or statutory duties owed to the corporation or the shareholders, he may be held personally liable.

For example, an officer or director can be held liable for engaging in a conflict of interest, seizing corporate opportunities, engaging in transactions unfair to minority shareholders, or otherwise acting to further an interest at the expense of the corporation or its shareholders.

46:8 Business Judgment Rule

One of the basic principles of the corporate system is that the corporation is managed by and acts through its board of directors. The board is primarily responsible for setting corporate policies in such matters as the declaration of dividends, the adequacy of executive compensation, the hiring and firing of employees, marketing, pricing, and mergers or acquisitions. The board is assumed to use unbiased business judgment and to be better equipped than courts would be in making these decisions. Consequently, when a court is confronted with a challenged business decision, it defers to the discretion of the directors. This is known as the *business judgment rule.* The rule arises out of judicial concern that highly qualified individuals will be reticent to serve as corporate directors if the law requires them to use a higher degree of care in the conduct of their office than that which is required of the reasonable, prudent person. The discretion of directors that is permitted by the rule was summarized many years ago by a court as follows: "Questions of policy management, expediency of contracts or action, adequacy of consideration, [and] lawful appropriation of corporate funds to advance corporate interests, are left solely to the [the directors'] honest and unselfish decision, for their powers therein are without limitation and free from restraint, and the exercise of them for the common and general interests of the corporation may not be questioned although the results show that what they did was unwise or inexpedient."[3] Courts have also invoked the business judgment rule to conserve judicial resources by not permitting every business decision to be reviewed or subject to challenge in court.

 The business judgment rule does not allow directors to abdicate all responsibility. As noted by one court that considered the relationship between the directors' duty of due care and the business judgment rule: "When courts say that they will not interfere in matters of business judgment, it is presupposed that judgment . . . has in fact been exercised. A director cannot close his eyes to what is going on about him . . . and have it said that he is exercising business judgment. Courts have properly decided to give directors a wide latitude in the management of the affairs of the corporation provided always a judgment, and that means an honest, unbiased judgment, is reasonably exercised by them."[4]

The following case examines the "business judgment" defense in the context of a law seeking to enforce the terms of a so-called "golden parachute" employment contract.

---

[3] *Pollitz v Wabash R. Co.,* 100 NE 721, 724 (New York Court of Appeals, 1912).
[4] *Casey v Woodruff,* 49 NYS2d 625, 643 (New York Supreme Court, 1944).

Koenings

v

Joseph Schlitz Brewing Co.
368 NW2d 690 (1985)
Court of Appeals of Wisconsin

FACTS: In the midst of a "takeover battle" by another firm, Schlitz Brewing Co. entered into "golden parachute" employment contracts with 70 key employees, including Koenings, an in-house attorney for Schlitz. The contract provided that, if the employee's workload dropped significantly, the employee could declare the contract terminated and collect the remaining salary due under the contract as liquidated damages. When the firm was acquired by Stroh, Koenings experienced a drop in his workload and exercised the "golden parachute" provision in the contract. When Schlitz refused to pay the remaining salary, Koenings sued for breach of contract.

ISSUE: Is the "golden parachute" provision a reasonable exercise of the board of directors' business judgment?

RESULT: No. The provision stipulating specific damages is an unreasonable penalty and is invalid as a matter of public policy.

REASONING:

* * *

Golden Parachutes

A golden parachute employment contract generally contains a continuation of salary provision for a stated time period after termination. A number of factual situations may trigger the opening of the parachute, or safe-landing provision of the contract, allowing the key employee to continue receiving a salary after termination of employment. The employee triggers the opening of the parachute when the target company, or takeover company, fires the employee, changes the employee's responsibilities, status, title, or forces relocation. The proliferation of friendly as well as unfriendly takeovers has led various corporate institutions to use these contracts. The terms of such employment contracts vary, but generally they include termination provisions and severance benefits that are triggered by a change in corporate control.

Golden parachute proponents utilize three basic arguments to support the validity of such contracts. Under the retention theory, it is argued that the contracts are necessary to attract and retain competent executives; the defensive theory holds that such contracts make the cost of a takeover so high that unwanted suitors are effectively warded off; lastly, the nondistraction theory holds that by guaranteeing financial security to senior executives who are subject to possible dismissal or reduction of responsibility by a change of corporate control, the executives are allowed to continue to work unburdened by concern for their own futures during the takeover, meanwhile insuring that they will still act in the stockholders' best interests. An added argument in favor of such contracts is that the dollar amounts due to the executives through these agreements are *de minimis* considered against the aggregate value of the takeover offer; thus, the contracts are proper. The validity of such executive contract benefits depends on their inherent reasonableness; they are more likely to be upheld if promulgated by a disinterested board of directors or a board committee. . . .

Reasonableness or Unreasonableness

The trial court applied a totality of circumstances test in this case to determine the reasonableness of the stipulated damages clause which is a question of law. . . . The trial court concluded that damages were easily ascertainable, that Wisconsin's black letter rule of mitigation of damages had to be applied and that the income earned by Koenings at Farmhouse had to be considered in determining his actual contractual loss. . . .

We hold that the trial court correctly applied the mitigation of damages factor and found the stipulated damages clause to be a penalty on public policy grounds. Public policy is a broad concept embodying the community common sense and common conscience. The molders of public policy are the people of this state. Three methods are generally employed to establish public policy: constitutional conventions and/or amendments, legislation and referenda. "[I]t is only when the people have failed to speak in these methods that the courts can be said to have power to make public policy by decision." Courts should proceed cautiously when making public policy determinations. The power to declare a contract or a contract clause void as being against public policy should be exercised only in cases free from doubt.

Koenings argues that his golden parachute agreement is valid under the business judgment rule. Most academic commentators condemn defensive manipulations such as golden parachutes, but they grudgingly acknowledge that federal courts usually resort to a mechanical application of the business judgment rule to uphold such defensive tactics. The common law business judgment rule provides that directors or officers will not be held liable for a breach of fiduciary duty to the corporation or its stockholders for a mistake of fact or law that causes harm to the corporation or its stockholders, if the directors acted in a good faith exercise of their business judgment. In the absence of fraud, bad faith, gross overreaching or abuse of discretion, good faith is presumed and courts will not interfere with the exercise of the business judgment by directors. Commentators abhor this laissez faire, mechanistic approach and argue that all defensive tools employed by directors should be scrutinized in the light of the benefit or detriment to the stockholders and the specific conflict of interest involved.

We believe that, in this context, the business judgment rule is archaic and unresponsive to fair treatment of stockholders. We agree with the academicians that tactics such as golden parachutes generally are in derogation of the fiduciary duties officers and directors owe to their stockholders. The effects of such tactics must be minimized. We agree with the scholars that management faced with merger suitors should maintain passivity and refrain from these types of activities. We hold that golden parachute contracts, as a matter of public policy, must have mitigation clauses. Because such contracts bear the taint of conflict of interest in favor of the management-beneficiaries to the detriment of the stockholders' interest, such contracts are unreasonable without a mitigation clause and are unenforceable on public policy grounds as a penalty. . . .

Moser, Judge.

It is important to note that the business judgment rule is not the highest standard used by the courts to evaluate the actions of corporate officers and directors. Under the federal securities laws, officers and directors of corporations that issue public securities are required to have significant legal, financial, and operational knowledge of the corporation. The liability of officers and directors under the federal securities laws is examined more closely in Chapter 53.

46:9 Indemnification and Insurance

Indemnification in the corporate context is a corporation's payment of an obligation or liability imposed on an officer or director. As such, it is the most common method of protecting corporate officers and directors against the cost of defending lawsuits and the imposition of personal liability. A corporation can pay the obligation directly, or it can make good the loss sustained by the corporate official.

Nearly every state has adopted a statute permitting indemnification. The MBCA provides for the indemnification of any corporate official, including any officer, director, employee, or agent who may be made party to litigation by reason of his position with the corporation [MBCA § 5]. Such a lawsuit might be brought by (1) a corporation; (2) a shareholder challenging the official's performance of duties; (3) a governmental agency; or (4) a private party for breach of contract, tortious conduct, or other violation of law.

Note that under the MBCA indemnification in derivative actions differs from that in third-party actions. A derivative action is one that is initiated by a shareholder on behalf of the corporation. In a derivative action indemnification is restricted to expenses, including attorney's fees. A third-party suit is an action brought for personal recovery in the plaintiff's own name. In a third-party action indemnification is allowed not only for expenses but also for judgments, fines, and amounts paid in settlement. The obvious policy reason for broader coverage of third-party claims is that in a third-party action the individual was presumably working in good faith for the corporate interests and therefore should be protected, whereas in a derivative action the officer or director allegedly violated a duty to the corporation.

The extent of indemnification depends on the corporate official's conduct. The common standard of conduct is that a corporate official must have acted in good faith and in a manner reasonably believed to be in, or not opposed to, the best interests of the corporation. For example, if a director meets the duty of loyalty to the corporation and the duty of care, indemnification is proper.

The amount of the payment also varies: a corporate official who is found to be liable for negligence or misconduct in the performance of his duty to the corporation may be indemnified for expenses only with court approval, but indemnification for expenses is automatic if he is found not to be liable.

In a criminal action, the corporate official may be entitled to indemnification if he had no reasonable cause to believe that his conduct was illegal.

Insurance   In recent years, another method of protecting directors and officers from liability has emerged. Many corporations now purchase liability insurance for their officers, directors, and other corporate officials. This insurance generally covers corporate officials against any loss arising from a claim against them in their official capacity. Loss is usually defined as any amount a director or officer is required or permitted to pay in regard to a legal liability for a wrongful act, including damages, judgment, settlements, and expenses incurred in defending suits.

Most liability insurance policies of this type contain exclusions or exceptions from coverage. There is usually no coverage for any claim against an officer or director based on a personal gain or profit to which the officer or director was not legally entitled. Therefore, most insurance will not protect an officer or director from breach of the duty of loyalty or from a conflict of interest. Also, the insurance usually will not protect an officer or director against expenses incurred in actions arising under the federal securities laws.

Corporate Finance

46:10   Introduction to Corporate Finance

There are two basic ways to finance a corporation. The first way, generally referred to as equity financing, is to issue shares of stock. The second way, referred to as debt financing, is to borrow money on the credit of the corporation. The broad term *securities* is used with respect to both types of financial arrangements.

In forming and operating a corporation, promoters, corporate officers, or directors must decide what percentage of the corporation's operating capital should be debt and what percentage should be obtained through the issuance of stock. The possible range of corporate financing may vary from an all-common stock capital structure to one in which common equity in minimal and the corporation's capitalization is represented primarily by debt securities or preferred stock. Obviously, various factors influence the decision as to how much stock should be issued and the extent to which the corporation should borrow funds for its operation. For example, a higher proportion of debt to equity signifies a greater risk to the corporation. If a corporation cannot pay its debt obligations, it may be forced into insolvency or bankruptcy.

Considerations involved in determining the most beneficial debt-equity ratio for a corporation include an assessment of the corporation's growth potential and earning capability, and the projected need for borrowed capital.

46:11 Equity Securities; Stock

The right of a corporation to issue stock is generally controlled by state law. Most state corporation laws require that the articles of incorporation specify whether one or more classes of stock will be issued, how many shares will be authorized, and the amount that must be paid in on stock subscriptions before the corporation can commence business. For example, under the Model Business Corporation Act (MBCA), the articles of incorporation must set forth the total number of shares that the corporation is authorized to issue, the classes of each share, and a statement of the preferences, limitations, and relative rights in regard to the shares of each class [MBCA § 54].

The amount of stock initially issued by a corporation is determined by the promoters or incorporators. This amount is also governed by practical business considerations and financing agreements. Once the amount of authorized capital stock has been established, it cannot be increased or decreased without amending the articles of incorporation, which requires shareholder consent [see MBCA §§ 58(d), 59]. Frequently, corporations initially authorize more shares than are immediately issued. Consequently, the corporate officers or directors, rather than shareholders, have control over this aspect of corporate financing. In such a case, the officers or directors can authorize the issuance of additional shares without shareholder approval if all of the authorized shares have not been issued.

Once a corporation complies with the statutory requirements governing the issuance of stock, it can issue all, part, or none of the stock authorized as it so chooses. Until shares of stock have actually been issued, they are called authorized or unissued shares [MBCA § 2]. Once issued, they are called issued or outstanding shares.

The capital of a corporation is its net worth. It is the total amount of money subscribed and paid in by the shareholders, plus all the gains or profits arising from corporate operations, minus any losses that have been sustained. Capital indicates the assets of a corporation—regardless of their source—that are used in the conduct of corporate business. Working capital is the difference between current assets and current liabilities. It is frequently used as a measure of a company's liquidity and capacity to meet its obligations as they fall due.

Types of Equity Securities   In most states, corporations are generally authorized by statute to issue two or more classes of stock that differ as to their respective rights and interests [see MBCA §§ 15, 16]. The most widely used classes of stock are *common* and *preferred*. The purpose in having different types and classes of securities is to allocate the risk of loss among shareholders. In addition, these classes are used to allocate control of the corporation through voting restrictions among shareholders and to establish participation rights in corporate proceeds either through profits or on liquidation.

Other commonly used classes of stock are par value and no-par value stock. The designation of a par value for stock originated from the requirement in early American corporation laws that the value of the outstanding stock must be specified in a total dollar amount. These laws were based on the requirement or assumption that corporations would not commence business until the stock had been fully subscribed or purchased. In contrast, no-par stock has no nominal or par value indicated on the face of the stock certificate. In 1979, amendments to the MBCA eliminated the concepts of par and no-par value.

Common Stock   Common stock, or common shares, confer the ordinary rights of a shareholder to participate in the control of a corporation, in the surplus and profits, and in the distribution of corporate assets on dissolution. Common stock is ordinarily exposed to the greatest risk because it is entitled to receive distributions only after all other claims have been satisfied. On the other hand, common shareholders also have the opportunity to reap the greatest rewards because they are entitled to all amounts available in excess of prior claims. Furthermore, common shareholders control the corporation. They affect the growth of earnings and assets by electing directors who make the fundamental decisions about corporate directions, operations, and investments. In addition, they determine indirectly through the election of directors which portion of corporate earnings or assets will be distributed to security holders as dividends and which shall be retained by the corporation for further investment and operations.

Preferred Stock   Preferred stock represents a type of corporate financing that provides a corporation with a security, coupling the flexibility of common stock with the limited obligation of the bond. The issuance of preferred stock is authorized by MBCA §§ 15 and 16. Preferred stock represents a type of ownership. Unlike common stock, however, preferred stock carries only limited or contingent voting rights. Voting rights may arise, for example, only in case of default in dividend payments or when the attributes of the preferred stock itself are to be changed. Preferred stock does not dilute the voting control residing in the common shareholder. It is thus an excellent financial tool, permitting participation in corporate profits while restricting participation in corporate operations.

EXAMPLE: Stanton has long operated the Crestview Company as a sole proprietorship. He wishes to pass the business on to his children, but he is worried about their ability to run it harmoniously together after he retires. Stanton believes that his daughter, Arcadia, is far more able than is his son, Morley, to run and manage the business. However, he wants Morley to benefit from company profits. Thus, Stanton incorporates Crestview and creates two classes of stock: common and preferred. The preferred shares are given no voting rights. He later transfers the common stock to Arcadia, effectively allowing her to control the corporation through the voting rights conferred on the common shares. Stanton gives Morley the preferred shares, enabling him to participate in the company's profits without the right to interfere in the affairs of the business. Thus, Stanton has ensured the continuity of the business by giving Arcadia voting control via the common stock. At the same time, Stanton has protected Morley by giving him the right to participate in corporate profits via the preferred stock.

The special character of preferred stock lies in its relationship to the common stock. Preferred shareholders normally have preference or first claim when dividends are declared. The favored position of preferred stock also extends to the disposition of assets on corporate liquidation.[5] This priority, however, exists only with reference to the common stock and does not affect the senior position of corporate creditors or bondholders. The preference given to preferred stock on liquidation has meaning and value only if corporate assets remain after creditors have been fully paid.

Fractional Shares   Most states, as well as MBCA § 24, authorize corporations to issue fractional shares, or scrip, entitling the holder to combine the fractional shares to acquire whole shares. In some states, the owners of fractional shares are entitled to vote, receive dividends, and participate in the distribution of corporate assets in the event of liquidation.

Acquisition and Redemption of Issued Shares   Any corporation can acquire shares originally issued by it [MBCA § 6]. In recent years, many large publicly owned corporations have purchased their own stock, often at premium prices. The acquisition of this stock has come largely in response to situations in which investors or other corporations have initially purchased large blocks of a corporation's stock, thereby posing potential takeover problems. To prevent the use of these large blocks in takeover bids, corporations have found it more prudent to acquire them in buy-back transactions. In a few cases, corporations have been sued for reacquiring such blocks from single large shareholders at premium prices. However, state and federal laws do not necessarily forbid the sale of shares back to a company or a corporation's acquisition of its own shares so long as full disclosure is made.

Redemption is the involuntary sale of stock by the owner to the issuing corporation for a fixed price. The fixed or call price at which the stock must be

---

[5] Disposition of assets on liquidation is discussed in Chapter 45.

redeemed is generally based on the value of the stock or is set forth in the stock certificate or redemption agreement. The power of a corporation to redeem its stock for retirement or cancellation must be authorized in the articles of incorporation or by appropriate state statute. Once shares are made redeemable, they are generally protected against subsequent impairment or repudiation, although in certain circumstances a corporation may modify redemption rights on shareholder approval [see MBCA §§ 58–60, 65].

It is a common practice for corporations to make preferred stock redeemable. Indeed, some issues of preferred stock or other securities *must* be redeemed. If so, the corporation usually establishes a *sinking fund* for this purpose, although the use of such a fund is not required in all cases [see MBCA §§ 15, 16]. To establish a sinking fund, a corporation sets aside funds from its net earnings at various intervals each year specifically to pay for redemptions. The amount of funds set aside is usually a percentage of the total amount of the preferred stock or other redeemable securities that have been issued and are to be redeemed.

46:12   Problems of Capital Formation

In financing a corporation through the issuance of capital stock, two basic questions emerge: (1) what type of consideration can be validly accepted by the corporation in payment for shares issued and (2) who determines whether valid consideration has been paid and what limits are placed on the discretion of those making this decision.

Stock Subscription Agreements   In the past, corporations were largely financed through stock subscriptions by which future shareholders agreed to contribute money or other assets for stock issued, or to be issued, by a corporation. These agreements are generally known as *subscription agreements* [see MBCA § 17]. Agreements made before the actual formation of a corporation have been termed preincorporation agreements.

The basic problem with preincorporation subscriptions is that a subscriber has no one with whom to contract, since the corporation does not yet exist. Courts in various states have adopted several solutions to resolve this problem. For example, in some states subscribers are deemed to have made a continuing offer in the subscription contract to purchase stock when the corporation actually comes into existence. The subscriber may withdraw an offer at any time until it is accepted. In other states, subscription agreements are deemed to be contracts among the subscribers for the benefit of the corporation. In these states, a subscription agreement cannot be revoked unless the corporation does not come into existence or does not fulfill the terms of the contract. Still other states have enacted laws that make subscriptions irrevocable for a given period of time. For example, under MBCA § 17, a subscription for shares is irrevocable for a period of six months unless otherwise provided by the terms of the subscription agreement or unless all the subscribers consent to the revocation of such a subscription.

Consideration for Shares   Although most states—and the MBCA—specify the types and amount of consideration for which stock can be issued, there are a variety of ways by which purchasers of stock have evaded paying full value. One method, for example, is to issue stock for less than its value as fixed by the board of directors. Stock issued for a lesser value has been called discount stock. In other cases, stock has been simply given away without any consideration whatsoever. This stock is called bonus stock. Stock has also been issued for inadequate consideration. Frequently, for example, property or services given to or rendered a corporation are greatly overvalued. Stock so acquired in this way is called *watered stock.*

Most states now strictly regulate all these practices. For example, MBCA § 18 provides that shares can only be issued for consideration as authorized by the board of directors, either at a fixed price, at a minimum price, or as based on a formula or other method for the determination of the price. Formula pricing methods are frequently used in connection with the issuance of additional shares of a class for which an active trading market already exists, and in competitive bidding transactions such as those used by many public utilities, where the exact price is fixed just before sale. Under MBCA § 19, the consideration for the issuance of shares can be paid in money, in other property, or in labor or services actually performed. However, neither promissory notes nor future services can be used to pay for shares issued by a corporation.

Despite these statutory provisions, problems still arise, particularly over the question of the proper valuation of property received by a corporation in return for shares issued. With discount or bonus stock there is simply a disparity between the value of stock and the money received by the issuing corporation. In such a case, it is relatively easy to establish that a corporation received insufficient consideration. However, with watered stock the primary question is how the valuation of the property was made in return for the issued stock. Obviously, cases can arise in which shares are issued for property or services rendered that seemingly bear little relationship to the value of the shares issued. In most states, as well as under MBCA § 19, the judgment of the board of directors or shareholders as to the value of consideration received for shares is conclusive in the absence of fraud.

 MBCA § 19 and similar provisions give considerable discretion to boards of directors whose judgment will generally be upheld by the courts in these matters. However, if fraud can be proved, all the parties involved in the transaction, including the shareholder who received the stock for the inadequate consideration and board members, can personally be liable in damages for the sums that the corporation should have received when it issued stock.

The following case illustrates the situation in which a promissory note was given in exchange for the issuance of a stock certificate that was to be delivered after payment of the note. Observe that the applicable state statute, patterned after MBCA § 19, provided that a promissory note would *not* constitute payment for the issuance of corporate shares.

Haselbush

v

Alsco of Colorado, Inc.
421 P2d 113 (1966)
Colorado Supreme Court

FACTS: Haselbush sued to cancel a note previously signed by him and given to Alsco, Inc. in return for the issuance of a stock certificate for 10,000 shares of Alsco stock. The certificate was never delivered to Haselbush but was held by the corporation pending payment of the note. The trial court upheld the validity of the note and awarded judgment in favor of the corporation.

ISSUE: Is the promissory note void for illegality?

RESULT: No. The corporation can enforce the promissory note, even though it violated state law by issuing stock in exchange for the note.

REASONING:

*   *   *

In seeking to have the note cancelled, Haselbush claims that issuance of the stock certificate and acceptance of the promissory note by Alsco was illegal and void under the Colorado Constitution, Article XV, Sec. 9 and [Colorado statutory law]. The pertinent part of Article XV, Sec. 9 of the Colorado Constitution reads as follows:

> No corporation shall issue stocks or bonds, except for labor done, services performed, or money or property actually received, and all fictitious increase of stock or indebtedness shall be void. . . .

[The pertinent Colorado statute] reads as follows:

> Neither promissory notes nor future services shall constitute payment or part payment, for shares of a corporation.

In [an earlier case] we held that Article XV, Sec. 9 of the Colorado Constitution is not a defense to an action (in this case a counterclaim) brought on a promissory note given for the stock of a corporation. The statute does not affect that holding and we adhere to the rule in that case.

The statute does not forbid the corporation from taking a note or obligation from a prospective stockholder. On the contrary, it impliedly recognizes the right to do so, but declares that no such note shall be considered as payment, and no certificate shall issue until the note is paid. . . . The issuance of the certificate, if in fact there was such here, does not affect the enforceability of the note.

Both the constitutional provision and the statute are aimed at preventing the watering of corporate stock. Their purpose is to prevent corporations from issuing stock without receiving full value, and so to prevent the diluting of the holdings of innocent stockholders, and the reliance by creditors on false or non-existent capital resulting from the issuance of watered stock. This purpose would not be served by holding, as Haselbush asks us to hold, that these provisions may be used to defeat an action by the corporation seeking to enforce payment on a promissory note given for the issuance of stock when the transaction has been made in good faith. . . .

Pringle, Justice.

46:13   Debt Securities; Bonds; Convertible Securities

Most corporations issue debt securities such as *bonds* and *debentures.* All corporate borrowing must be authorized by the board of directors or delegated by the board to the officers of the corporation. Shareholder approval is not ordinarily required to permit a corporation to engage in debt financing.

Debt securities are normally issued with a maturity date on which the principal amount is to be repaid. There is normally a fixed income rate on the principal amount borrowed. Holders of debt securities must be paid interest before any dividends can be paid to shareholders. Moreover, the principal must be paid before anything is paid to shareholders on corporate liquidation. Debt securities are redeemable at the option of the corporation. Occasionally, reduction in the amount of outstanding debt is required by the articles of incorporation. A corporation might even be required to maintain a sinking fund for this purpose.

The holders of debt securities are generally given no voting rights in the election of directors. In a few states, statutes provide that voting rights can be given to holders of debt securities if authorized by the articles of incorporation.

There are basic differences between stock (equity) and debt securities. Stock ordinarily includes voting rights, while debt securities do not. Owners of stock participate via dividends in corporate profits, and the dividends are roughly in proportion to the earnings of the corporation. In contrast, debt receives a fixed rate of interest that must be paid at specified times. On liquidation of a corporation, the holders of debt obligations receive up to the amount of their claims, whereas equity investors receive the residue. Finally, interest on debt is regarded as an expense for accounting purposes and taxation and is therefore deductible by the corporations. Dividends on stock constitute income and are not deductible.

Bonds   A bond is a corporate promise to pay a certain amount of indebtedness. It is secured by the assets of the corporation. A convertible bond carries with it the privilege of conversion into shares of stock at the bondholder's option. An income bond is a bond on which income is payable only if the income is available out of corporate earnings after interest on other corporate indebtedness has been paid. A participating bond—also called a profit-sharing bond—is a bond with a fixed rate of interest plus a right to participate in corporate earnings to the extent provided in the bond. Interest on a participating bond is a fixed charge and must be paid regardless of corporate earnings. In this respect, it differs from the income bond.

Indentures and Trustees   Bonds are generally long-term promissory notes. They contain more elaborate provisions than do simple promissory notes given by one individual to another in a commercial transaction. To enable an issuing corporation to borrow relatively small amounts on identical terms from a large number of persons, the obligation is channeled through a trustee, who administers the payment of interest and principal. The trustee also enforces other obligations on behalf of the bondholders as a group. The borrowing corporation contracts with a trustee through an instrument called an *indenture*. The indenture defines the assorted obligations of the borrower, the rights and remedies of the lenders, and the role of the trustee. The bond itself is simply a promise by the borrower to pay a specified amount on a specified date, plus interest, subject to the conditions spelled out in the indenture.

Trust Indenture Act of 1939   In 1939, Congress enacted the Trust Indenture Act [15 USC §§ 77aaa et seq.] to protect the interest of investors in notes, bonds, and other corporate debt obligations. The act is designed to protect investors by requiring certain trust indentures to conform to specific statutory requirements. Under indentures covered by the act, trustees have a great responsibility for the protection of investors. The act insures that investors will obtain the services of a trustee properly qualified to represent their interests. Under the act, if debt securities worth $1,000,000 or more are offered to the public, they must be issued pursuant to an indenture with a properly qualified trustee. Information must be provided relating to trustees in the indenture under which a debt security is to be issued.

Debentures   A debenture is similar to a bond in that it is a promise to pay a certain amount of indebtedness. Debentures differ from bonds in that no property is pledged as security. In other words, a debenture is an unsecured written corporate promise backed by the general credit of a corporation and not secured by any specific property.

 Not all bonds and debentures rank equally as claims on a corporation. Two frequently encountered variations are the mortgage bond and the subordinated debenture. Holders of the mortgage bond are secured as to the payment of principal and interest by a pledge or mortgage of described assets of the debtor. They have a prior claim to payment of their proceeds against other creditors with respect to the mortgaged property. The subordinated debenture has precisely the opposite effect for its holders. It effectively prevents repayment of the principal in the event of the corporation's liquidation or reorganization until all other creditors to whom it is subordinated are repaid in full.

Convertible Securities *Convertible securities* are equity or debt securities that can be changed into another type of security. For example, preferred shares are frequently made convertible into common shares at the option of the shareholder under specified terms. Bonds are also frequently made convertible into common stock. Convertible securities—whether originally equity or debt—are used primarily as a financing device when new risk capital requires some seniority over the holders of existing securities.

For investors, convertible securities offer some advantages over common stock or debt obligations, such as bonds and debentures. With a fixed income return, convertible securities provide a degree of safety and assured income that protects against a decline in common stock prices or a drop-off in corporate earnings. Convertible securities also provide an opportunity for the shareholder to participate in higher common stock prices if the market value of the security into which a preferred stock or debenture is convertible appreciates.

Key Concepts and Terms

- The board of directors is the governing body of a corporation. The board represents the corporation and has the authority to transact all ordinary business.
- Most publicly owned corporations have both inside and outside directors. The New York Stock Exchange requires newly listed companies to have at least two outside directors.
- The board of directors is primarily responsible for setting corporate policies. Where matters of business judgment are involved, directors meet their responsibility of reasonable care and diligence if they act honestly, in good faith, and with unbiased judgment.
- The officers and directors of a corporation are its agents, through whom the corporation functions and carries on its business.
- Officers and directors are fiduciaries both to the corporation and to the shareholders. They have a duty to avoid using inside information for personal advantage, to preserve corporate opportunities, and generally to be loyal to the corporation and its shareholders. In the absence of self-dealing, officers or directors are not usually liable for honest errors or mistakes of judgment.
- Officers and directors can be held liable under § 11 of the Securities Act of 1933, which requires them to have a significant legal, financial, and operational knowledge of a corporation whenever securities are registered with the SEC before they are issued and sold to the public.
- Officers and directors can be held liable under the Securities Exchange Act of 1934 for misstatements, misrepresentations, half-truths, or the omission

of material information in the offer or sale of any securities registered with the SEC. An officer or director can also incur civil and criminal liability under the 1934 act in connection with (1) applications, reports, or documents filed or required to be filed with the SEC; (2) statements as to stock ownership and transactions in such stock; (3) manipulation of securities prices; (4) use of manipulative and deceptive devices in the offer and sale of securities; and (5) concealing material information.

- Indemnification and insurance protect officers and directors against the cost of defending lawsuits and the imposition of personal liability.

- A corporation can be capitalized (financed) by issuing stock or borrowing on the credit of the corporation. "Securities" is the term used in connection with corporate financial arrangements, whether based on equity or based on debt.

- Common stock is the basic equity security. Ordinarily its owner is entitled to participate in the control of the corporation, in surplus and profits, and in the distribution of corporate assets on dissolution.

- Preferred stock is another type of equity security. It represents a type of corporate financing that couples the flexibility of common stock with the limited obligation of the bond. Preferred shareholders normally have preference over common stock when dividends are declared and in the disposition of assets on corporate liquidation.

- Most corporations can and do issue debt securities, such as bonds or debentures. A bond is a secured obligation of a corporation. When unsecured, the debt is called a debenture. The holders of debt securities are generally given no voting rights in the election of directors. Debt securities receive a fixed rate of interest that must be paid at specified times. On liquidation of a corporation, the holders of debt securities receive up to the amount of their claims.

- Convertible securities can be either equity or debt securities that can be changed into another type of security. Preferred shares and bonds are frequently made convertible into common stock at the option of the shareholder. Convertible securities—whether equity or debt—are used primarily as a financing device when providers of new risk capital require some seniority over the holders of existing securities.

- A corporation can acquire, redeem, retire, or cancel securities originally issued by it. Redemption is the involuntary sale of securities by the owner to the issuing corporation for a fixed price.

- Bond
- Business Judgment Rule
- Common Stock
- Convertible Securities
- Corporate Opportunity Doctrine
- Debenture
- Due Diligence
- Duty of Care

- Duty of Loyalty
- Indemnification
- Indenture
- Insider
- Outside Director
- Preferred Stock
- Prospectus

Questions and Case Problems

1. Arthur J. Goldberg, former Justice of the United States Supreme Court, observed that "contrary to legal theory, the board of directors of most of our large companies do not in fact control and manage their companies, nor are they equipped to do so." (*New York Times*, 29 Oct. 1972, Sec. 3, p. 1.) Are these views substantiated by the discussion in this chapter of corporate management and the duties of officers and directors? Should directors exert greater control over corporate management?

2. Richardson, the president and sole shareholder of a corporation, obtained a loan from Wiebke to meet her business payroll. Richardson gave Wiebke a promissory note, which she signed as an individual. The note did not mention the corporation although Wiebke believed that the loan was to be used in the corporation's business. On obtaining the loan, Richardson put it in her corporation's bank account. A ledger account entitled "Wiebke loan" was set up on the corporate books. Interest paid on the note was carried on the corporation's books as a corporate expense. Later, Richardson defaulted on the note, and Richardson went into personal bankruptcy. Wiebke then sued the corporation and sought to hold it liable. Who would win the lawsuit?

3. Woodtek purchased all the shares of Musulin Forest Products from Matt Musulin and his son. Woodtek's vice-president and general manager executed a promissory note in favor of Musulin. When the time came to pay the note, Woodtek contended that the vice-president had no authority to sign such a note for the corporation. It argued that the board of directors had not authorized the note in the first place and that Musulin should have inquired. Is Woodtek liable?

4. A group of Florida investors organize a corporation to operate a country club and golf course. At a shareholders' meeting, they discuss the possibility of acquiring land adjacent to the golf course, but the matter is not pursued by the corporation. Later, two of the corporation's largest shareholders—its president and vice-president—purchase the adjoining land and sell it for a substantial profit. A minority shareholder sues, charging that the officers have breached their fiduciary duty by taking a corporate opportunity for themselves. The shareholder claims that the officers must give to the corporation all the profits from the sale of the adjoining property. How should the case be decided?

5. Pablo is president and director of Hawaiian International Finances (HIF) and a director of Pablo Realty. On a trip to California in connection with her realty business, Pablo spots attractive real estate investment opportunities and brings them to the attention of the finance company. HIF's board of directors sends Pablo and three other directors back to California to investigate. Eventually, Pablo contracts on behalf of HIF to buy two parcels of land. The sellers are represented by brokers who subsequently split their commissions with Pablo, paying her a total of $22,000. When HIF finds out about these payments some months later, it sues to recover the sums. Must Pablo pay over to HIF the amount of her commissions received? Would the result be affected by the fact that Pablo received no compensation for serving as president and director of HIF?

6. Shelton, the branch manager of Alenco Company, promises Lanier a one-year contract and an annual compensation of $22,000 if Lanier will leave his present job and go to work for Alenco. Lanier accepts and when he starts work with Alenco he is presented with a new offer that differs significantly both in salary and commissions from the one originally offered by Shelton. Lanier therefore sues

Alenco for the salary due under the rest of his one-year contract. Alenco argues that Shelton does not have either express or apparent authority to hire anyone for a fixed term. It claims such contracts are against company policy. Alenco asserts that it is up to Lanier to ascertain the limits of Shelton's authority. Is Alenco liable to Lanier for the terms of the contract originally promised by Shelton?

7. Williams requests the U-Vend Corporation to install a hot-drink machine and a soda dispenser in the Radio Shack outlet that she manages. Williams signs a three-year lease for the machines. The lease designates Radio Shack Corporation as the lessee. Williams pays the first month's rent with a personal check, which she signs. Subsequent payments are made by bank money orders signed "Radio Shack Corporation" by various employees of the outlet. Eight months later, U-Vend receives a letter from the treasurer of Radio Shack, requesting that it remove the machine from its outlet since neither Williams nor anyone else had authority to order anything from it. Because Radio Shack continues to refuse to pay for the installed machines, U-Vend sues for damages for the remaining months of the three-year lease. What is the result?

8. Equitable Life held a note of Inland Printing Company that was secured by personal property and real estate. The note came due but was not paid. When Equitable looked for the property, it found that Inland had been sold to another company. Equitable then sued directors and officers of Inland on the ground that they had negligently wasted Inland's assets, resulting in damage to its creditors. Equitable did not assert any fraud or deceit on the part of the officers and directors. How should the case be decided?

9. Portage Plastics, a corporation with a high ratio of debt to equity, borrowed $12,500 from each of two persons who were not shareholders. The loans provided for payment of five percent of the net profits before taxes to the lenders instead of interest. Are the loans actually equity securities despite being termed loans?

10. Pinson reads an article in a newspaper that Minco, a company in which she owns stock, has discontinued its uranium explorations. Because of this article, Pinson sells her stock. At the same time, Durant, a director of Minco, believes a geologist's theory that uranium is indeed present on company property. He makes plans to have the company undertake additional tests. Without disclosing his plans, Durant buys Minco stock. Minco later makes a major uranium strike, causing the value of its stock to skyrocket. Pinson sues Durant for damages. Did Durant have a duty to Pinson or to others to disclose his inside information? To whom did he owe a duty of disclosure? Should Pinson be permitted to recover damages, although she now owns no Minco stock?

47 Rights and Liabilities of Shareholders

47:1 Introduction

A corporation is an entity that, for most purposes, is separate and distinct from its individual members or shareholders. Title to corporate property is held by the corporation as a separate entity and not by the shareholders. Shareholders have no power to represent a corporation or act for it in the transaction of its ordinary business, even when all or a majority of the corporation's stock is owned by a single individual.

As a general rule, corporations operate under the principle of majority rule. The holders of a majority of the shares with voting power control the corporation by electing the board of directors. The board of directors, in turn, also acts by majority vote in carrying out its duties and obligations.[1]

47:2 Shareholder Functions

The shareholders' principal function is to elect the board of directors [MBCA § 39]. By electing directors, shareholders indirectly control the actions of a corporation and determine its policies and goals. In addition to electing or removing directors, shareholders ordinarily exercise several other functions. They have the power to (1) adopt, amend, or repeal bylaws; (2) amend the articles of incorporation [MBCA § 59]; (3) approve loans to officers, as well as stock-option plans offered to directors, officers, or employees [MBCA § 20]; (4) approve extraordinary corporate matters or fundamental changes in the corporate structure, such as mergers or consolidations [MBCA § 73]; and (5) approve the dissolution of the corporation [MBCA § 84].

Annual Meetings The holding of an annual corporate meeting to elect directors is usually regulated by statute, the articles of incorporation, corporate bylaws, or common-law rules. Shareholder meetings are called, usually on an annual basis, to elect members to the board of directors, review the financial status of the corporation, and vote on various proposals submitted to the

---

[1] The rights, duties, and obligations of directors are discussed in Chapter 46.

shareholders. By statute, written notice must be given each shareholder, stating the place, day, and hour of the meeting [MBCA § 29]. The notice must be delivered to the shareholder not less than 10 nor more than 50 days before the date of the meeting. If a special meeting is called, shareholders must be informed of the purpose for which it is called. Moreover, if extraordinary changes, such as a merger, dissolution, or sale of corporate assets not in the regular course of business are contemplated, the shareholders must be given specific notice of the proposal before the meeting [MBCA §§ 73, 79, 84]. Any action taken at a meeting for which requisite notice has not been given is a nullity unless the notice requirements have been waived [MBCA § 144].

Quorum   A *quorum* is required for a valid shareholder meeting. Most states have enacted statutes specifying the percentage of shares constituting a quorum. For example, MBCA § 32 provides that a majority of the shares entitled to vote, represented in person or by *proxy* (discussed below), constitute a quorum at a meeting of shareholders. If a quorum exists, a vote of the majority of the shares present is sufficient to conduct business, unless the vote of a greater number is required to decide a particular matter.

Shareholder Proposals   To fully participate at an annual meeting, shareholders are given the right to propose corporate amendments, offer resolutions, speak for or against resolutions, and ask questions of the corporate officers present at the meeting. Proposals and questions have run the gamut from individual questions about corporate dividend policies to the offering of resolutions on voting procedures, location of corporate meetings, or other matters of interest to shareholders. In recent years, the actions of large publicly owned corporations have been seriously questioned, particularly through shareholder proposals or resolutions objecting to corporate policy that involves bribery practices, environmental protection, affirmative action, American foreign policy, or investment in South Africa. The right of shareholders to speak and to make such proposals are fundamental attributes of corporate ownership—so much so that the federal securities laws applicable to the solicitation of proxies, for example, require the inclusion of shareholder statements up to 200 words whenever their proposals are deemed to be proper subjects for shareholder deliberation.

47:3   Voting Rights

Unless a class of stock has been created without voting rights, each shareholder is normally entitled to one vote for each outstanding share owned. In many states, special statutory rules govern the voting of jointly held shares, shares held by fiduciaries, shares owned by minors, and shares held by other corporations.

Because of their size, most large corporations find it impractical to determine on the date of the meeting who the shareholders are, how many shares they have, and who is entitled to vote. Accordingly, the stock transfer books of corporations are frequently closed on a record date fixed for the determination of shareholder lists before the actual date of the meeting [see MBCA § 30]. Only the shareholders listed on this record date are eligible to vote at the next shareholder meeting.

Voting Agreements and Voting Trusts   A group of shareholders may agree to vote their shares in the same way. Such arrangements are called *voting or pooling agreements*. A more formal arrangement is termed a *voting trust*. In a voting trust shares are actually transferred to a trustee, who must vote under a legally enforceable trust agreement. Most states regulate voting arrangements and voting trusts.

Cumulative Voting   One of the most important contemporary issues concerning shareholder voting rights is *cumulative voting*. The purpose of cumulative voting is to give minority shareholders representation on the board of directors in proportion to the number of shares owned. Under cumulative voting, a shareholder can give one or more candidates seeking election to the board of directors as many votes as the number of directors to be elected multiplied by the number of votes to which each shareholder is entitled. Thus, for example, if a corporation is to elect five directors to its board, a shareholder owning 20 percent of the voting shares can elect at least one director under cumulative voting. She does so by casting up to all her votes for that one director, rather than splitting her vote among all five of the directorships to be filled. For minority shareholders, cumulative voting is most successful when a greater number of directors are to be elected. In such cases, fewer votes are needed by minority shareholders to elect at least one director. If minority shareholders were not afforded cumulative voting rights, they would have no representation on the board because minority shares would always be outvoted by the majority under straight voting principles.

The constitutional or statutory law of nearly half the states requires some form of cumulative voting. In other states, corporations are authorized to permit this type of voting in their articles of incorporation.

Large, publicly owned corporations recognize the power of minority shareholders under cumulative voting. To avoid that power, most of these corporations are incorporated in states that do not mandate cumulative voting. Some corporations have also attempted to limit the effect of cumulative voting by establishing classes of directors with staggered terms, thereby reducing the number of directors to be elected each year. The fewer the number of directors to be elected, the larger the minority interest must be to enable a shareholder to elect one director. Although the creation of classes of directors has been successfully challenged, particularly in states that require cumulative voting, the MBCA does authorize it [MBCA § 37]. However, this authorization is effective only if cumulative voting is not otherwise required, as under the optional provisions of MBCA § 33.

Proxies   If a shareholder grants authority to another to cast his vote at a shareholder meeting, both the authorized person and the instrument empowering him to cast a vote on behalf of another are called proxies. The word "proxy" is a contraction of "procuracy," the act of representing another person as an agent. The person granting the proxy is called the principal.

The shares of publicly owned corporations are usually held by a large number of shareholders who, for one reason or another, do not attend annual meetings. By giving their voting power to proxies, shareholders can exercise their voting rights at these meetings. Corporations also use proxies to obtain a quorum so that a lawful meeting can be held [see MBCA § 32].

A proxy is either general or limited. If a person is given a general proxy, he can vote on all corporate proposals, except on extraordinary matters such as fundamental changes in the articles of incorporation. If a special or limited proxy is given, however, the proxy can only vote in a certain manner or on certain specified matters as required by the principal. Since the proxy relationship is an agency relationship, it can be revoked by the principal at any time unless it has been made irrevocable. Under MBCA § 33, a proxy is valid only for eleven months unless otherwise provided.

Since publicly owned corporations are characteristically controlled or managed by holders of only a small percentage of the equity of such corporations, the use of proxies at shareholder meetings is essential to conduct corporate activity. If proxies were permitted to be solicited and obtained without explanation as to the matters to be voted on or the manner in which shares would be voted, shareholders effectively would have no voice in the operation of their corporation. Consequently, the solicitation of proxies by corporations or by shareholders, as well as their form and content, are stringently regulated both by the states and by the federal government. The SEC has established disclosure requirements that must be met prior to proxy solicitation. The proxy rules adopted by the SEC are closely patterned after the registration and disclosure procedures of the Securities Act of 1933.[2] The SEC rules require that shareholders be given the opportunity to specify the manner in which their shares are to be voted. Furthermore, proxy solicitations must not mislead shareholders. They must be accurate and complete to enable shareholders to make informed decisions in their capacity as voters. The regulations seek to ensure that shareholder meetings will be meetings of informed parties competent to deliberate on corporate matters and decide them by shareholder vote. In fact, it has been said that the SEC so designed its rules as to make proxies the closest practicable substitute for attendance at a shareholder meeting.

A proxy contest typically results from a conflict between current management and insurgent shareholders who are seeking corporate control. Often, a group of shareholders acquires a substantial position in a corporation and wants to control it through the election of a majority of the directors. This can only be done either by acquiring a majority of the voting shares or by soliciting a sufficient number of proxies from other shareholders to control the election. Proxies, therefore, are invaluable to each factions' efforts to elect its own slate of directors.

---

[2] Federal securities regulation is discussed in Chapter 53.

47:4   Preemptive Rights

One of the common ways by which a corporation raises more funds for its operation is by issuing additional stock. If a corporation does so, it can give its shareholders preferential treatment by permitting them to purchase the new stock ahead of other shareholders in proportion to the number of shares each shareholder owns. This privilege is called a *preemptive right*. It enables shareholders to maintain the existing ratio of their proprietary interest and voting power in a corporation despite the issuance of more stock.

Most states do not require corporations to grant preemptive rights to shareholders. For example, under MBCA § 26 shareholders have no such rights unless authorized in the articles of incorporation.

When a corporation issues new stock, each shareholder usually receives a *warrant*, or right to purchase the new stock. The warrant sets forth the requirements necessary to purchase one share, the price per share, and the warrant's expiration date. Because new shares are frequently offered below the current market price, such rights ordinarily have a market value of their own and may be actively traded on the stock market. In most cases, preemptive rights and warrants must be sold or exercised within a relatively short time before their expiration.

47:5   Inspection Rights

A fundamental right in corporation law is the right of shareholders to inspect the corporation's books and records. Although in some states only inspection of corporate share registers is permitted, the right of inspection is enforced in all 50 states by statute. The MBCA has a typical inspection provision. It requires each corporation to maintain particular records, grants to certain shareholders the right to inspect them on written demand, sets forth the penalty for violation of the inspection right, and authorizes courts to compel the production of records for inspection when a demand has been improperly denied [MBCA § 52].

The right of shareholder inspection is not absolute. It must be exercised with restraint and only for a proper purpose. A proper purpose is generally considered to be one that is lawful, made in good faith, reasonable, relevant to the shareholder's interest and status as a shareholder, and not inimical to the corporation. The three purposes that have been consistently held to be proper are (1) investigation of suspected corporate mismanagement; (2) determination of the value of corporate stock; and (3) communication with other shareholders. For example, in a proxy contest between management and dissident shareholders, inspection of the shareholder register is absolutely necessary if the dissidents are to communicate with other shareholders and solicit their proxies. Without access to the shareholder register, dissident shareholders would have little or no chance to successfully obtain proxies.

To exercise the right of inspection a shareholder must present a written demand to the corporation. The demand must comply with the requirements as to content and demonstrate that the demanding shareholder has the required proper purpose. Often, a demand for inspection is refused even though a proper purpose is evident. At this point, the shareholder must seek judicial enforcement of his inspection rights. The standard practice among large publicly held corporations is for management to deny shareholder demands for inspection unless ordered to do so by a court. Indeed, the right to inspect share registers containing the names and addresses of other shareholders has become the subject of more litigation than any other individual shareholder right.

 The right of inspection raises a number of potential problems. For example, it is not always clear who is a shareholder or what entities are corporations within the meaning of the rule. Problems also arise as to the specific books and records that are subject to inspection. Moreover, the right to inspect may not always include the right to copy, and the right of a shareholder to inspect may not extend to agents or other persons employed by the shareholder to assist in making an inspection. Finally, the right to inspect the records of a given corporation may not include the right to inspect the records of a subsidiary corporation even though it is wholly owned by the parent.

47:6   Dividend Rights

A *dividend* is an amount set apart by the board of directors from a corporation's net earnings and surplus funds for distribution to shareholders. The declaration and payment of dividends constitutes a normal and routine part of corporate business, and corporate directors ordinarily have the power to declare cash dividends and to determine their amount [see MBCA § 45]. Dividends are usually paid in cash, but they can also be paid in property, including the corporation's own shares.

There are two general prerequisites to the declaration of a dividend: (1) surplus earnings or corporate profits and (2) a resolution by the directors to declare a dividend. Consistent with the first of these requirements, a dividend cannot be declared and paid if the corporation is insolvent or if paying the dividend would make the corporation insolvent. Moreover, a corporation cannot make any dividend payment that would be contrary to a restriction in the articles of incorporation [MBCA § 45].

Bear in mind that just because a corporation has profits does not necessarily mean that the directors will distribute those profits to the shareholders. The directors have wide latitude in determining the circumstances under which dividends will be declared. While they can pay out profits as dividends, they can also plow them back into the business to ensure the corporation's health and growth.

At the time a dividend is declared, each shareholder of record is entitled to his share of the dividend. However, in modern corporate practice, corporations usually declare dividends payable to those who were shareholders of record on a specified date. Normally, the date of payment follows the date of declaration by one or two months. For example, a dividend notice that is dated

October 28, 1983, and states: "The directors of the Crestview Corporation have declared a regular quarterly dividend of 40 cents per share, payable on the 5th day of December, 1983, to the shareholders of record on the 20th day of November, 1983," will entitle only the shareholders listed on the record date, and not necessarily those owning Crestview stock either on the date of declaration or on the actual date of payment, to the dividend. Shares of stock sold or transferred on the various stock exchanges after the record date are termed *ex-dividend*, which means that they are sold without dividend rights.

Dividends can be paid in cash, as in the Crestview example above. However, they can also be paid in other forms, such as stock dividends, stock splits, and property dividends.

Stock Dividends A *stock dividend* is a dividend that is payable in the stock of the dividend-paying corporation. The corporation usually issues new stock for this purpose. Since the size of each shareholder's dividend—the amount of new stock the shareholder receives—is based on the number of shares already owned, the distribution does not affect any shareholder's proportionate interest in the corporation. To a large extent, stock dividends are psychological dividends since no assets of the corporation are actually distributed to shareholders. In fact, stock dividends do not increase the holding of shareholders in the distributing corporation. When a stock dividend is declared, the corporation simply transfers to its capital fund an amount of surplus earnings or profits that is equal to the value of the new stock; the corporation reduces its earned surplus by the same amount. This so-called "capitalization of surplus" does not alter the combined total of stated capital, paid-in surplus, and earned surplus on the corporate books. Although the transferred earnings to the capital fund may increase the aggregate value of all the capital stock, the increased equity is reflected merely by an increased number of shares. The book value of each share is diminished, but the ownership interest of each shareholder in the corporation remains unchanged.

Stock Split In a *stock split*, a shareholder receives two, three, or four times as many shares as previously owned. (In a reverse stock split, the actual number of shares owned by any shareholder is reduced in reverse proportion.) Unlike a stock dividend, a stock split adds *nothing* to the capital fund of a corporation. The split merely increases (or decreases, in the case of a reverse stock split) the total number of shares outstanding, reduces the unit value of each share, and may stimulate the trading of shares in the stock market by making the shares cheaper to buy. Unlike a stock dividend, a stock split must be authorized by an amendment of the articles of incorporation.

Property Dividends A property dividend is one paid in property belonging to the corporation. For example, a corporation in the liquor distribution business might pay a dividend in liquor. More often, the property paid as a dividend is shares of stock. The shares can be either of a subsidiary of the corporation or of an unaffiliated corporation. When a parent corporation distributes shares of a subsidiary to divest itself of ownership, the transaction is commonly referred to as a spin-off.

Preferred Dividends   Various classes of stock are often created to give shareholders different rights in the corporation. As discussed in Chapter 46, one of these classes is preferred stock. It is often used to give owners a dividend preference over the common shareholders. This preference is entirely a matter of contract and is generally set forth in the articles of incorporation or bylaws and on each stock certificate. Preferred dividends are generally payable only out of net earnings and at the discretion of corporate directors.

Cumulative Dividends   When a dividend is passed or omitted in any year because of deficiency in earnings, the shareholders lose any right to share in the profits for that year. However, this right is not lost if the corporation has provided for the cumulation of dividends on the stock. The right of preferred shareholders to cumulative dividends may differ from that of common shareholders if there is a provision authorizing such right in the corporation's articles of incorporation, the bylaws, or the stock certificates, or a guaranty of dividends issued by the corporation.

EXAMPLE: The earnings of the Crestview Corporation were down last year. Consequently, the board of directors voted to omit dividends on both the common and preferred stock. This year, the corporation's earnings are sufficient to pay dividends. Crestview's articles of incorporation provide for the payment of passed dividends on the preferred stock, but not on the common stock. Thus, in addition to a dividend for the current year, the preferred stockholders will also receive the omitted dividend that should have been paid last year. Both dividends will be paid out of current earnings. Because the common stock has not been given a similar right of cumulative or passed dividends, the common stockholders will receive a dividend only for the current year. The omitted common stock dividend from last year will not be made up out of current earnings.

47:7   Majority and Minority Shareholders

The power of majority shareholders to control a corporation imposes on them a duty to exercise good faith, care, and diligence in the control of corporate affairs and to protect the interests of minority shareholders. Majority shareholders cannot use their control to benefit themselves alone or to destroy the minority's interest. For example, majority shareholders may not, as against a minority shareholder, dissipate or waste corporate funds or profits. The majority must also act fairly and with due regard to the interests of the minority shareholders in the purchase or sale of property, in contracts with the corporation, and in all other dealings involving minority interests. In turn, minority shareholders must generally submit to the decisions made by the majority so long as the majority acts in good faith and within the limit imposed by law.

The reasons and public policy behind these general rules are apparent. There is an ever-present danger that majority shareholders will use their power, position, or inside information to further their own interests to the detriment of the corporation or minority shareholders. For example, majority shareholders could appoint themselves to key executive positions while denying employment to minority shareholders; they could pay themselves high salaries but refuse to declare dividends (which would also benefit minority shareholders).

To protect minority shareholders, some states have enacted statutes requiring the vote of two-thirds or three-fourths of the shares with voting power before fundamental corporate changes can occur. In other states, if a charter amendment or other fundamental change materially affects the rights of a particular class of stock, an affirmative vote of the shares of that affected class must approve the action, regardless of whether the shares of that class have any general voting power.

Extraordinary Corporate Transactions Shareholders have certain rights when a corporation participates in a merger, consolidation, or sale of assets. Under the common law, all these transactions (which are described in Chapter 45) require the unanimous consent of the shareholders. Therefore, dissenting shareholders could veto any proposed transaction of this type. In response to this inordinate power of minority shareholders, most states enacted statutes permitting a merger, consolidation, or sale of corporate assets on the affirmative vote of a majority of the voting shares of the corporations involved. For example, the MBCA authorizes a merger or consolidation [§§ 71–73], or a sale of substantially all corporate assets other than in the regular course of business [§ 79] after majority shareholder approval. The procedure set forth in most state statutes and in the MBCA also requires approval by the board of directors and notice to all shareholders.

Short-Form Merger The MBCA also permits what has been termed a short-form merger. In a merger of this type the owners of at least 90 percent of the shares can approve a merger in a summary manner without notice to or consent of minority shareholders [see MBCA § 75].

Dissenters' Rights To protect the rights of minority shareholders who object to a merger (other than a short-form merger), consolidation, or sale of assets, most states, as well as the MBCA [§§ 80, 81], give shareholders who dissent from such transactions the right to demand that the corporation pay them the fair value of their shares. For a shareholder to exercise this right, a written objection to the corporate transaction must be filed with the corporation before the shareholders vote on the proposed transaction. If the transaction is approved, the dissenting shareholders must be so advised and offered fair value for their shares. If a dispute arises as to what constitutes fair value, shareholders can seek a more impartial appraisal via judicial relief.

In the following case, the fundamental issue is the relationship of the majority and minority shareholders, and their rights and obligations with regard to a merger. The case illustrates how, although being careful to follow the statutory procedures, the majority shareholders still breached their fiduciary obligations to the minority shareholders, rendering the merger invalid.

Singer

v

Magnavox
380 A2d 969 (1977)
Delaware Supreme Court

FACTS: In 1974, North American Phillips Corporation incorporated North American Phillips Development Corporation (Development) for the purpose of making a tender offer for shares of the Magnavox Corporation. Development offered to buy all Magnavox shares for $8 per share. The directors of Magnavox voted to oppose the offer on the grounds of price inadequacy and so notified their shareholders. Later, the respective managements of Magnavox, North American, and Development compromised on their difference over the tender offer. They agreed to terms that included an increase in the offer price to $9 per share. Two-year employment contracts were signed with 16 Magnavox officers. As part of the agreement, Magnavox withdrew its opposition to the tender offer. Development then acquired approximately 84.1 percent of Magnavox's outstanding common stock. With Development firmly in control of Magnavox, the managements of these two companies then set about to acquire all equity interests in Magnavox through a merger. Development created T.M.C. Development Corporation for this purpose. The directors of Magnavox unanimously agreed to a merger with T.M.C. and scheduled a special shareholders' meeting to vote on the plan. The shareholders were told that approval of the merger was assured since Development's holding alone was large enough to provide the requisite statutory majority. The merger was approved at the shareholders' meeting. The Singers, who were minority shareholders, then filed an action in court alleging that the merger was fraudulent in that it did not serve any business purpose other than the forced removal of public minority shareholders from an equity position in Magnavox at a grossly inadequate price to enable North American, through Development, to obtain sole ownership of Magnavox.

ISSUE: Did the majority shareholders of Magnavox meet their fiduciary duty to the minority shareholders?

RESULT: No. The merger was conducted only for the purpose of "freezing out" the minority shareholders, not to advance the business of the corporation.

REASONING:

*   *   *

In this appeal it is uncontroverted that defendants complied with the stated requirements of [Delaware law]. Thus there is both statutory authorization for the Magnavox merger and compliance with the procedural requirements. But, contrary to defendants' contention, it does not necessarily follow that the merger is legally unassailable. We say this because, (a) plaintiffs invoke the fiduciary duty rule which allegedly binds defendants; and (b) Delaware case law clearly teaches that even complete compliance with the mandate of a statute does not, in every case, make the action valid in law. . . .

It is a settled rule of law in Delaware that Development, as the majority stockholder of Magnavox, owed to the minority stockholders of that corporation a fiduciary obligation in dealing with the latter's property. . . . The fiduciary obligation is the cornerstone of plaintiffs' rights in this controversy and the corollary, of course, is that it is likewise the measure of the duty owed by defendants.

Delaware courts have long announced and enforced high standards which govern the internal affairs of corporations chartered here, particularly when fiduciary relations are under scrutiny. It is settled Delaware law, for example, that corporate officers and directors . . . and controlling shareholders . . . owe their corporation and its minority shareholders a fiduciary obligation of honesty, loyalty, good faith, and fairness. . . .

Defendants concede that they owe plaintiffs a fiduciary duty but contend that, in the context of the present transaction, they have met that obligation by offering fair value for the Magnavox shares. And, say defendants, plaintiffs' exclusive remedy for dissatisfaction with the merger is to seek an appraisal. . . . We disagree. In our view, defendants cannot meet their fiduciary obligations to plaintiffs simply by relegating them to a statutory appraisal proceeding.

At the core of defendants' contention is the premise that a shareholder's right is exclusively in the *value* of his investment, not its *form*. [Court's emphasis.] And, they argue, that right is protected by [an] appraisal which, by definition, results in fair value for the shares. This argument assumes that the right to take is coextensive with the power to take and that a dissenting stockholder has no legally protected right in his shares, his certificate or his company beyond a right to be paid fair value when the majority is ready to do this. . . .

Plaintiffs allege that defendants violated their respective fiduciary duties by participating in the tender offer and other acts which led to the merger and which were designed to enable Development and North American to, among other things:

> [C]onsummate a merger which did not serve any valid corporate purpose or compelling business need of Magnavox and whose sole purpose was to enable Development and North American to obtain sole ownership of the business and assets of Magnavox at a price determined by defendants which was grossly inadequate and unfair and which was designed to give Development and North American a disproportionate amount of the gain said defendants anticipated would be recognized from consummation of the merger.

Defendants contend, and the [trial court] agreed, that the "business purpose" rule does not have a place in Delaware's merger law. . . .

Plaintiffs contend that the Magnavox merger was fraudulent because it was made without any ascertainable corporate business purpose and was designed solely to freeze out the minority stockholders. . . .

We hold . . . that a § 251 merger, made for the sole purpose of freezing out minority stockholders, is an abuse of the corporate process; and the complaint, which so alleges in this suit, states a cause of action for violation of a fiduciary duty for which the Court may grant such relief as it deems appropriate under the circumstances. . . .

Duffy, Justice.

Shareholder Deadlock   The operation and management of a corporation requires a high degree of mutual trust, respect, and cooperation. This is particularly true of corporations in which the principal shareholders also serve as corporate officers and directors. If dissension occurs among shareholders, conflicts invariably arise among officers and directors. If corporate control is evenly divided, dissension can lead to deadlock among directors, thereby obstructing even routine corporate business matters.

To remedy the situation, MBCA § 97 provides for the liquidation of a corporation when shareholders are deadlocked in voting power. Liquidation is authorized when shareholders have failed for a period including at least two consecutive annual meeting dates to elect successors to directors whose terms have expired or would have expired on the election of their successors. Many states have enacted similar legislation providing for dissolution in case of shareholder deadlock. Most statutes require that some irreparable harm or injury to the corporation be established before judicial dissolution is authorized. The statutes vary as to the person authorized to bring an action for dissolution, the type of deadlock that must exist, and the nature of the irreparable injury that the corporation must have suffered.

EXAMPLE: Sarah and her three children form a corporation for the purpose of holding the family farmlands. Later, when Sarah dies, the shareholders, her children, are plagued by conflict and animosity. No dividends are declared. The buildings fall into disrepair. There are numerous lawsuits between shareholders. The only effective legal remedy available to the children is to seek judicial dissolution based on deadlock and waste of corporate assets.

47:8   Shareholder Remedies

There are various remedies that a shareholder can use against or on behalf of the corporation in which he owns shares. First, of course, the shareholder can sue the corporation in his own right if he has sustained an individual loss that is separate and distinct from any loss suffered by other shareholders. However, the shareholder can also (1) file what is called a *derivative action* on behalf of the corporation or (2) file a representative or class action on behalf of himself and other shareholders if the number of persons interested in the action is too large for all to be joined as parties. Derivative and class actions are discussed below.

Derivative Action   A shareholder's derivative action is a legal action that a shareholder files, but that the corporation itself would normally be expected to file. Thus, since the action is brought on the corporation's behalf, the corporation is the real plaintiff, even though it is named as a defendant. The reason the shareholder files the action is that, for some reason, corporate management has refused to do so. For example, this refusal might occur when the wrong that the corporation has allegedly suffered—and on which the derivative action is based—involves management's own wrongdoing. Before a shareholder can successfully assert a derivative action, a demand must be made on the appropriate corporate official to bring the suit. If the official refuses the demand, the way is clear for the shareholder to proceed. A demand is not required if it is obvious that the demand would be futile, as, for example, when the claim is being made against the corporate directors themselves [see MBCA § 49].

The following case expresses the Delaware Supreme Court's position on the "demand futility" problem in the context of an arguably excessive employment contract with a dominant shareholder. Note that since a substantial number of major American firms are incorporated in Delaware, the pronouncements of Delaware courts on corporate law are very important.

Aronson

v

Lewis
473 A2d 805 (1984)
Supreme Court of Delaware

FACTS: Lewis, a shareholder of Meyers Parking System, Inc. [Meyers], brought a shareholder derivative action against Meyers and its board of directors. Lewis was seeking to redress a wrong to the corporation which, he alleged, the corporation suffered when it entered into a five-year, $150,000-plus "consulting" contract with Fink, who owned 47 percent of the stock and who selected each director and officer of the firm. Lewis claimed that the contract, and an additional interest-free $225,000 loan to Fink, constituted a waste of corporate assets and served no valid business purpose. Lewis neglected to make a demand on the board of directors before filing suit, and Meyer sought to bar the suit for failure to make such a demand.

ISSUE: Was Lewis required to make a demand on the board of directors?

RESULT: Yes. Lewis is excused from making such a demand only if the directors are not, in fact, sufficiently independent to exercise independent business judgment.

REASONING:

* * *

In our view the entire question of demand futility is inextricably bound to issues of business judgment and the standards of that doctrine's applicability. The business judgment rule is an acknowledgment of the managerial prerogatives of Delaware directors under Section 141(a). . . . It is a presumption that in making a business decision the directors of a corporation acted on an informed basis, in good faith and in the honest belief that the action taken was in the best interests of the company. . . . Absent an abuse of discretion, that judgment will be respected by the courts. The burden is on the party challenging the decision to establish facts rebutting the presumption. . . .

Our view is that in determining demand futility the Court of Chancery in the proper exercise of its discretion must decide whether, under the particularized facts alleged, a reasonable doubt is created that: (1) the directors are disinterested and independent and (2) the challenged transaction was otherwise the product of a valid exercise of business judgment. Hence, the Court of Chancery must make two inquiries, one into the independence and disinterestedness of the directors and the other into the substantive nature of the challenged transaction and the board's approval thereof. As to the latter inquiry, the court does not assume that the transaction is a wrong to the corporation requiring corrective steps by the board. Rather, the alleged wrong is substantively reviewed against the factual background alleged in the complaint. As to the former inquiry, directorial independence and disinterestedness, the court reviews the factual allegations to decide whether they raise a reasonable doubt, as a threshold matter, that the protections of the business judgment rule are available to the board. Certainly, if this is an "interested" director transaction, such that the business judgment rule is inapplicable to the board majority approving the transaction, then the inquiry ceases. In that event futility of demand has been established by any objective or subjective standard. . . .

Having outlined the legal framework within which these issues are to be determined, we consider plaintiff's claims of futility here: Fink's domination and control of the directors, board approval of the Fink-Meyers employment agreement, and board hostility to the plaintiff's derivative action due to the directors' status as defendants.

Plaintiff's claim that Fink dominates and controls the Meyers' board is based on: (1) Fink's 47% ownership of Meyers' outstanding stock, and (2) that he "personally selected" each Meyers director. Plaintiff also alleges that mere approval of the employment agreement illustrates

Fink's domination and control of the board. In addition, plaintiff argued on appeal that 47% stock ownership, though less than a majority, constituted control given the large number of shares outstanding, 1,245,745.

Such contentions do not support any claim under Delaware law that these directors lack independence. In [a 1971 case], the Court of Chancery stated that "[s]tock ownership alone, at least when it amounts to less than a majority, is not sufficient proof of domination or control." Moreover, in the demand context even proof of majority ownership of a company does not strip the directors of the presumptions of independence, and that their acts have been taken in good faith and in the best interests of the corporation. There must be coupled with the allegation of control such facts as would demonstrate that through personal or other relationships the directors are beholden to the controlling person. . . .

The requirement of director independence inhers in the conception and rationale of the business judgment rule. The presumption of propriety that flows from an exercise of business judgment is based in part on this unyielding precept. Independence means that a director's decision is based on the corporate merits of the subject before the board rather than extraneous considerations or influences. While directors may confer, debate, and resolve their differences through compromise, or by reasonable reliance upon the expertise of their colleagues and other qualified persons, the end result, nonetheless, must be that each director has brought his or her own informed business judgment to bear with specificity upon the corporate merits of the issues without regard for or succumbing to influences which convert an otherwise valid business decision into a faithless act.

Thus, it is not enough to charge that a director was nominated by or elected at the behest of those controlling the outcome of a corporate election. That is the usual way a person becomes a corporate director. It is the care, attention and sense of individual responsibility to the performance of one's duties, not the method of election, that generally touches on independence.

We conclude that in the demand-futile context a plaintiff charging domination and control of one or more directors must allege particularized facts manifesting "a direction of corporate conduct in such a way as to comport with the wishes or interests of the corporation (or persons) doing the controlling". . . . The shorthand shibboleth of "dominated and controlled directors" is insufficient. . . .

Moore, Justice.

In some states, statutes require shareholders in derivative actions who own less than a specified percentage or dollar amount of shares in the corporation to post security for the reasonable expenses incurred by the corporation. If this security for expenses is not posted, a derivative action could be dismissed despite the validity of the underlying claims. Moreover, a shareholder who initiates a derivative action without reasonable cause may be held liable to the defendants for the reasonable expenses, including attorney's fees incurred in their defense [MBCA § 49]. However, it should be noted that most states that have adopted the MBCA have excluded such provisions or have excluded attorney's fees from reasonable expenses. In addition, most states require that the shareholder have owned stock in the corporation at the time the allegedly wrongful action took place.

Class Action   As discussed in Chapter 2, a class action is an action that an individual brings for personal benefit *and* on behalf of others who have a similar interest in the outcome of the case. Class actions are especially useful in the corporate context, where it is practically impossible to join all share- holders of a widely held public corporation. By lumping claims together, a shareholder who would otherwise be without resources to engage in extended litigation is permitted to stand as a representative for many other shareholders who are similarly situated.

47:9   Shareholder Liability

One of the main reasons for establishing a corporation is to limit personal liability. Shareholders want to protect their personal assets by limiting their potential liability for business obligations to their investment in the corporation's capital stock. Because a corporation is a separate legal entity, distinct from its shareholders, shareholders generally are not liable for any of the corporation's obligations. In the absence of charter, constitutional, or statutory provisions to the contrary, this rule applies to liability for torts as well as to contractual obligations. Except as discussed below, the rule applies to a shareholder who owns a controlling interest, a majority, or even all of the stock of a corporation. It also applies to a shareholder that is itself a corporation.

Liability of Controlling Shareholders   There are some circumstances under which the corporate entity is disregarded and shareholders are held liable for corporate obligations. Courts have coined the phrase "piercing the corporate veil" to refer to this situation.

   Perhaps the most common circumstance in which the corporate identity is disregarded is that in which a corporation is merely an alter ego or business conduit of an individual or another corporation. Under what is known as the *alter ego doctrine*, liability may be imposed on a controlling shareholder if there is such unity of interest and ownership that the separation of the individual and the company has ceased to exist. The doctrine applies to the situation in which the corporate structure is a sham and the individual—not the corpora- tion—is doing business behind the corporate shield.

 The alter ego doctrine has been used to impose liability on an individual for torts such as fraud, as well as for debts and other contractual obligations. To avoid having the alter ego doctrine invoked and the corporate veil pierced, shareholders should keep their personal business carefully separated from that of the corporation. Personal funds or other assets should not be mingled with those of the corporation; all dealings with the corporation should be properly documented and kept at arm's length. A common trap is the controlling shareholders' neglect of corporate formalities. The shareholder who runs a corporation like a personal business is especially vulnerable. He or she frequently fails to hold required meetings and to keep adequate books and records. A creditor who finds a corporation unable to meet its obligation may discover and use this disregard of formalities to invoke the alter ego doctrine and obtain a judgment against the shareholder personally.

The following case illustrates the application of the alter ego doctrine and the circumstances under which a controlling shareholder might be held personally liable for corporate debts or obligations. Note the facts of this case and the reasons why the court declined to invoke the doctrine.

Holmes
v
Clow
533 SW2d 99 (1976)
Texas Court of Civil Appeals

FACTS: Holmes sued Mobile Modulars, Inc. and Del Clow, its president, to recover $2,062 for certain blueprints and design work for a housing project. Holmes based his action against Clow individually on the premise that Clow organized and controlled the corporation for his sole benefit and that the corporation was Clow's alter ego, created to defraud Holmes and other creditors.

ISSUE: Is Clow liable for the contracts of Mobile Modulars, Inc.?

RESULT: No. The facts present no basis for disregarding the separate legal entity of the corporation.

REASONING:

* * *

Generally speaking, the legal fiction of corporate entity may be disregarded where the fiction is used as a means of perpetrating a fraud or is relied upon to justify a wrong. . . . This rule, however, is an exception to the general rule which forbids disregarding corporate existence or entity and is not to be applied unless it is made to appear that there is such unity that the separateness of the corporation has ceased and the facts are such that adherence to the fiction would, under the particular circumstances, sanction a fraud or promote injustice. . . .

In order to warrant piercing the corporate veil, the courts generally require the presence of one or more of the following factual situations: (1) evidence that the corporate entity amounts to a fraud, promotes injustice or it is relied on to justify a wrong, (2) that it was inadequately capitalized, (3) that an individual controls and manages the entity in such a manner that it becomes his alter ego, and (4) that the corporate formalities were not adhered to by the corporation. Each case must rest on its special facts. . . .

First, we consider the question of the alleged fraud. There is nothing in the evidence indicating bad faith on the part of [Clow] in forming the corporation. Insofar as the record shows, the corporation was formed for the purpose of constructing a large number of houses under a specific F.H.A. commitment. [Clow] testified that prior to incorporation cost figures were prepared on the housing project and it was determined that the undertaking would be profitable. There is no evidence that [Clow] made any false representations to appellant or withheld facts concerning the corporation's financial condition. . . .

Next appellant contends that the corporation was underfinanced to the extent it constituted a fraud on persons dealing with it. The evidence shows that while the corporation had an authorized capital of $500,000.00, the sum of only $1,000.00 was paid in. The trial court found that the paid in capital was adequate at the time of incorporation in view of the fact that it had a commitment from a bank for an interim loan which the incorporators believed sufficient to cover its debts. There is no evidence that [Clow] or any other person misrepresented to appellant the extent of the capital of the company, nor is there any evidence that [Clow] personally received any benefit from the blueprints supplied by appellant. The trial court found that appellant failed to establish that [Clow] used the corporation as a sham to perpetrate a fraud, to avoid personal liability, or to avoid the effect of the statute. Subsequent events, namely the failure of the corporation, cannot afford the basis of finding fraud at the inception of the corporation. . . . It is incumbent upon the one seeking to pierce the corporate veil to show by evidence that the financial setup of the corporation is just a sham and accomplishes an injustice. . . . Under the circumstances, and keeping in mind that the burden of proof on the issue was on appellant, we do not feel that the evidence is such as to require us to hold that, as a matter of law, the corporate entity should be disregarded on the grounds that the financial setup was a mere sham.

Next, appellant contends [Clow] failed to adhere to the requirements concerning the operation of the corporation and that in so doing [Clow] assumed such control over the corporation as to make it, in effect, his alter ego. In this connection appellant argues that there is no evidence showing that corporate minutes were kept and there is no evidence showing that the board of directors ever approved the various corporate transactions. He further contends that the evidence conclusively shows [Clow] exercised control over the directors. As stated above, the only testimony before the trial court concerning the corporate operations was given by [Clow] and his wife. They both testified that while the corporate records could not be located, apparently due to the lapse of time, the directors met and approved all corporate transactions. They further denied that [Clow] exercised control over the directors and testified each director was afforded a right to vote his convictions. There is no direct evidence in the record to the contrary.

Generally speaking the courts will not disregard the corporate entity and treat it as the alter ego of an individual unless it is shown that there is such unity of interest and ownership that the individuality of the corporation and the owner or owners of its stock has ceased and that the observance of the fiction would sanction fraud or promote injustice. Bad faith in one form or another must be shown before the court will disregard the fiction of separate corporate existence. . . . Under the circumstances we do not think this court is required to hold as a matter of law that the corporate entity ceased to exist and became [Clow's] alter ego. . . .

Moore, Justice.

Watered Stock As discussed in Chapter 46, stock acquired in exchange for property or services at an overvaluation or at a discount is called watered stock. Use of watered stock is generally held to constitute a fraud on the corporation's creditors. A subscriber or purchaser to whom watered stock is issued is liable to creditors to the extent of the difference between the value of the shares and the amount actually paid for them. The rule in some states is that if overvalued property has been given to a corporation in exchange for its stock, a fraudulent intent to overvalue the property must be shown to establish a shareholder's liability [see MBCA § 19]. Other states, however, have adopted the "true value" rule, under which motive, intent, or good faith are disregarded. In such states, a shareholder is held liable for watered stock regardless of motive or intent.

Illegal Dividends Another exception to the rule of limited shareholder liability may come into play if dividends are illegally declared and paid by a corporation. In this situation, shareholders can be held liable to creditors to the extent of the illegal dividend. In some states, shareholders can be held liable on this basis only if (1) corporate debts existed at the time the dividends were declared, (2) the corporation was insolvent, and (3) the shareholders knew of the illegality of the dividend. Primary liability for illegal dividends is placed on the directors who declared them [MBCA § 48]. However, any director against whom a claim is asserted for wrongful payment of a dividend is entitled to contribution from any shareholder who knowingly received the dividend.

47:10   Transfer of Stock

Corporate stock is transferable, just as any other personal property is transferable. The power to transfer or dispose of stock is a right that is incident to ownership and can be limited only by statute or by a valid charter or contract provision. The transfer of stock is primarily regulated by Article 8 of the Uniform Commercial Code.

Regulations can be made respecting the mode and formal requirements of the transfer of stock. Restrictions on the power to transfer shares are sometimes imposed by provisions in a corporate charter or by general laws applicable to all corporations. However, such restrictions are strictly interpreted by the courts, and those contained in a corporate charter must be reasonable and not contrary to public policy.

A corporation's power to enact bylaws restricting the sale or transfer of stock generally is regulated by statute. In the absence of statutory authority, a corporation does not have the power, either through its bylaws or through other regulations, to prohibit the transfer or sale of its stock without consent or approval of the corporation, its directors, officers, or other shareholders. To be effective, any restriction on the transfer of stock must appear on the stock certificate itself. Any corporate law that unreasonably restrains a shareholder's ability to transfer corporate stock is against public policy and therefore invalid.

The generally authorized method of transferring is delivery of the stock certificate indorsed to a specific person by the owner named on the certificate. A stock certificate can also be indorsed in blank, which means that the name of the transferee is omitted. This type of certificate is called a *street certificate*. A person can hold a stock certificate in "street name," that is, without being named as the owner or transferee.

Stock can also be transferred by delivery of the certificate accompanied by a separate document containing a written assignment of the certificate or a power of attorney to sell, assign, or transfer the shares.

The purchaser of stock who has obtained its indorsement or who has complied with the reasonable requirements as to transfer is entitled to have the stock transferred in his name on the books of the corporation. This right is enforceable against the corporation and its transfer agents. A corporation may, of course, refuse to make a transfer on its books to protect itself from loss or fraud. It may require that the certificate be surrendered so that it can authenticate it or guarantee the signature of the transferor. If a corporation wrongfully refuses to transfer stock, the transferee can either maintain an action for damages or sue to compel the transfer.

Key Concepts and Terms

- Corporations operate under the principle of majority rule.
- Shareholders exercise control over a corporation through the election of the board of directors, which takes place at the annual shareholder meeting. A quorum is required for a valid shareholder meeting.
- Each shareholder is normally entitled to one vote for each share owned. Only shareholders listed in the books of a corporation on the record date are eligible to vote at a shareholder meeting.
- Cumulative voting is a device permitting shareholders to exercise power in a corporation directly proportional to the percentage of shares owned.
- A proxy is one's authorization to another to act for him or her in a certain manner or on specified matters. By means of the proxy, shareholders can exercise voting rights when they do not personally attend shareholder meetings.
- A shareholder is ordinarily given preemptive rights to purchase new stock issued by a corporation in proportion to the number of shares he owns.
- A fundamental right in corporation law is the right of shareholders to inspect the books and records of the corporation in which they own stock. The right of inspection can be exercised only for a proper purpose.
- A corporation may declare and pay dividends in cash, its own stock, or other property. Directors are given considerable discretion in declaring dividends.
- The owners of preferred stock often receive dividend preference over the common shareholders. Dividends on preferred stock are generally payable only out of net earnings.
- Shareholders have a variety of remedies to use against or on behalf of a corporation. An individual can sue in his own right, bring a class action, or file a derivative action to redress a wrong done to the corporation.
- A shareholder whose identity is indistinguishable from that of the corporation is personally liable for corporate obligations. This is the alter ego doctrine; the corporation is the alter ego of the shareholder. A shareholder could also be held liable to the corporation for holding watered stock. Directors and controlling shareholders may be held liable for the payment of illegal dividends.
- Corporate stock is inherently transferable. A shareholder's power to transfer or dispose of stock is a right that is incident to ownership and can be limited only by statute, contract, or the articles of incorporation.

- Alter Ego Doctrine
- Cumulative Voting
- Derivative Action
- Dividend
- Ex-Dividend
- Pooling Agreement
- Preemptive Right
- Preferred Dividend
- Proxy
- Quorum

- Stock Dividend
- Stock Split
- Street Certificate
- Voting Trust
- Warrant

Questions and Case Problems

1. The Securities and Exchange Commission has written as follows: "The traditional concept that boards of directors serve as a check on management and that the board is answerable to the shareholders by virtue of their elective power has been questioned in light of the fact that board elections are frequently a ratification of management nominees and that shareholders who wish to participate more fully in the affairs of their corporation are often frustrated and discouraged by the difficulty such participation entails under the present regulatory system." A contrary view has been stated as follows: "[T]here is no reason for [shareholders] to have any voice, direct or representational, in the catalogue of corporate decisions . . . on prices, wages, and investment. They are no more affected than nonshareholding neighbors by these decisions. . . . They deserve the voiceless position in which the modern development [has] left them." Can these two conflicting views be reconciled? Is it wise to give shareholders greater powers over the course and conduct of corporate affairs? Do not most shareholders in fact follow the so-called "Wall Street rule" that if the shareholder disagrees with management, he sells the stock? In what ways can shareholders influence management besides participation in the election of directors?

2. Ametco is a large multinational corporation with mining operations in South America. An organization that opposes American foreign investment purchases ten shares of Ametco's stock and then seeks to make certain proposals at Ametco's next annual meeting. These include a proposal that Ametco sell its investment in one Latin American country and a proposal that Ametco end the discharge of pollutants into the Pacific Ocean from its smelter in another South American country. Ametco denies that its smelter is polluting the Pacific. What can this dissident organization do to bring its proposals before other shareholders? What are Ametco's obligations to help the organization notify other shareholders of its proposals? Can Ametco prevent the organization from circulating to other shareholders proposals that Ametco believes to be false and injurious to its operations at home and abroad?

3. Mrs. Rettina owns a 20 percent interest in a lumber company. The other 80 percent interest is held by the company's managers, who also own 100 percent of a related business. Extensive intercorporate transactions occur between these two companies. Mrs. Rettina has received no dividend for several years despite handsome salaries and bonuses paid to management. What rights does Mrs. Rettina have and what may she do under the circumstances?

4. Erdman and three others each owned a 25 percent interest in a corporation. After working approximately 18 years, Erdman left the company but held on to his stock. Subsequently, the other three realized $40,000 from the sale of some investments the corporation had made while Erdman was still active. Then, despite declining profits, the three used the $40,000 to grant themselves retroactive salary increases and bonuses. Erdman sued, charging wrongful depletion of corporate assets and demanded a portion of the proceeds in the form of a dividend. How should the case be decided?

5. The board of directors of the Mayflower Hotel Corporation approved a proposed merger of the corporation into the Hilton Corporation. All nine Mayflower directors are nominees of Hilton, having been elected after Hilton acquired 56 percent of Mayflower's outstanding stock. A minority shareholder objects to the merger and seeks to block it in court. She contends that no quorum was present at Mayflower's meeting when the proposed merger was approved. Under the corporate bylaws, a quorum consists of five directors. At the meeting, six of the nine directors were present, but four of them were directly interested in the proposed merger. Mayflower's bylaws permit the counting of interested directors toward a quorum, but the minority shareholder argues that this provision is invalid. Should interested directors be counted toward a quorum? Should the merger be invalidated? Does § 41 of the MBCA affect the outcome? If the merger is upheld, what other rights does the minority shareholder enjoy?

6. Magline consistently showed a profit but never declared a dividend. At the end of the 1978–79 fiscal year, Magline's current assets totaled $3,000,000. The following year that figure increased to $4,000,000. Magline's·quick assets (cash and items quickly convertible to cash) exceeded current liabilities by more than $1,000,000. After repeated defeats at board meetings, two directors (who together owned 41 percent of Magline shares) sued to compel the payment of dividends. Magline's controlling shareholders argued that the company needed a large amount of working capital for diversification of its plant and product line. They also contended that Magline needed reserve funds in case it would have to renegotiate its government contracts. Should Magline be ordered to declare a dividend under the circumstances?

7. Prior to its merger with E. I. Du Pont de Nemours and Company, Conoco, Inc.'s board of directors negotiated "golden parachute" contracts with nine of its key officers. As a result of the merger, Du Pont owned all of the stock in the new corporation (New Conoco). After the merger was consummated, a bought-out shareholder of "Old" Conoco filed a derivative action on behalf of Old Conoco against various of its officers and all of its directors. The plaintiff alleged that the contracts were illegal, improper, without·a valid business purpose, a fraud upon Old Conoco, and a waste of corporate assets. Is this shareholder eligible to bring a derivative action of this nature?

8. Stamco Supply, Inc. is a "close corporation" having only a few shareholders. Grimme, the chief executive officer, and his family own and exercise a controlling influence in Stamco. On different occasions the corporation's board of directors, dominated by the Grimme family, voted to repurchase the shares held by Grimme's mother and also by Grimme's brother. No notice of repurchase was given to the remaining shareholders. Schroer, a minority shareholder who was neither an officer nor a director of Stamco, made a formal demand on the corporation to repurchase all common shares held by Schroer. When the demand was declined, she filed suit against the corporation to compel repurchase of her shares on the same terms as those given the controlling family group. Does the majority owe her a fiduciary duty to deal with her stock on the same basis as family-related stock?

9. The Campbells are the principal shareholders of Royal Development, a home-construction firm. The corporation issued to them 4,500 shares valued at $45,000 for which they paid $33,000 in cash and 25 lots. After commencing building on these 25 lots, Royal Development folded due to lack of funds. Mesa Lumber, which had sold Royal Development $5,000 worth of lumber and building supplies,

participated in the liquidation of Royal's assets but recovered very little. Mesa then sued Royal Development and the Campbells individually. Mesa claimed that the Campbells had grossly undercapitalized the corporation, had not paid the full subscription price for their stock, and had so intermingled their personal affairs with those of the company that the corporation had no existence separate and apart from them. To sustain its allegations, what must Mesa prove? Should the Campbells be held individually liable for the debts of their corporation?

10. The directors of Gaines Corporation send out a proxy solicitation on a proposed sale of Gaines to Life Investors, urging approval of the sale. The proxy statement mentions pending lawsuits that charged certain officers of Gaines with paying excessive commissions and fees in connection with acquisition and management of property. After the sale is approved, some minority shareholders sue for rescission. They claim that the proxy statement was defective because (1) it did not mention the fact that the pending lawsuits sought $2,000,000 in damages and that all of the directors and officers of Gaines were charged with fraud, self-dealing, and mismanagement and (2) management did not disclose in its proxy solicitation that the directors and officers of Gaines had a real personal interest in approving the sale because the sale would result in the abandonment of the lawsuits against them. Were all material facts disclosed to the shareholders? Can the sale of Gaines to Life Investors be rescinded? Is a derivative action proper in this case?

48 Franchises

48:1   Introduction

The system of franchising is relatively simple. Under a franchising agreement, the developer of a product or service *(franchisor)* grants another person *(franchisee)* an exclusive right (franchise) to market a product or service under the franchisor's trademark or trade name through a marketing plan in a specified area for a specified period of time. The franchise is not simply a license to sell a product or service—it entails a close, cooperative relationship between the franchisor and the franchisee. In addition, the franchisor's trade name or trademark identifies the franchisee as part of a larger business enterprise rather than as an independent retailer selling a unique product or service.

There are three basic types of retail franchises: (1) those in which the franchisor is a manufacturer whose basic operation is to distribute trademarked products, such as automobiles, trucks, or gasoline; (2) those in which the franchisor is a wholesaler whose basic purpose is to reduce the expenses involved in the flow of inventory in, for example, drugstores, hardware stores, and the automotive aftermarket; and (3) those in which the franchisor is merely a trademark holder and service sponsor to the retailer who conducts an enterprise, such as a fast-food or motel chain, under a common trade name using similar operating procedures. Retail franchises in which the franchisor is a manufacturer or wholesaler are commonly referred to as *distribution franchises*, while the franchises in which the franchisor is a service sponsor are ordinarily referred to as *business format franchises*.

In addition, franchises may be granted to franchisees to manufacture or process goods. Traditionally, for example, soft drink and beer companies franchise the bottling operation, permitting the bottler to resell at the wholesale level.

48:2   Franchisor–Franchisee Relationship

Franchising is a form of business organization that does not fall readily into the legal framework of agency, partnership, or corporation. It is not an independent contractor relationship.[1] In fact, a franchise relationship is a

---

[1] These relationships are discussed in Chapters 43 (agency) and 52 (independent contractor).

distinct legal form of business organization. The distinctive characteristic is that the franchisor exercises substantial control over the franchisee's business, yet the ownership risk of the enterprise falls primarily on the franchisee. In this way the franchisor expands the distribution network of the business using the capital contribution of the franchisee. In addition, the franchisor's distribution network consists of entrepreneurs who have a greater incentive to assure the success of the business than an employee or an agent would. The franchisee gains the benefits of brand identification, quality control, and market research that reduce the risk of the enterprise. The franchisor and the franchisee, however, remain two distinct and separate legal entities whose relationship is based primarily on contract.

Usually the franchisor offers the franchisee certain minimum services and legal rights. These services and rights are tied to a system of distribution or marketing that is used by all the franchisees. The distribution or marketing system regulates such matters as purchasing, merchandising, advertising, record-keeping, maintenance, supply, and business format. The franchisor may also train the franchisee's employees, supervise the franchisee, require the use of standardized operating manuals, control quality, and provide other expert services.

The franchisor's control over the franchisee is at the heart of the franchisor–franchisee relationship. This control is buttressed by a contractual requirement that the franchisee conform to the standard operating procedures as dictated by the franchisor under threat of losing the franchise. In a distribution franchise, the control exercised by the franchisor might be limited to those matters directly bearing on the product itself, such as storage, handling, display, or servicing. In a business format franchise, however, the franchisor's control extends to almost every aspect of the franchisee's business.

48:3   The Franchise Contract

Two documents are generally used in connection with the creation of a franchisor–franchisee relationship and the grant of a franchise. The first document is a *deposit receipt*, which is also known as a letter of intent, territorial binder, or letter of commitment. It is a temporary agreement in which the franchisor acknowledges receipt of a money deposit from the franchisee, ordinarily called a *franchise fee*, and agrees to perform certain acts leading to the signing of a *franchise contract*. Later, the parties sign the franchise contract, which is a far more detailed document. The contract spells out all the rights and liabilities of the parties.

 Under most franchise arrangements, a franchise fee is required at the time a deposit receipt or franchise contract is actually signed. The franchise fee may be payable in a lump sum or in installments, depending on the agreement between the parties. The businessperson is cautioned about the possibility that the franchise fee may also be "hidden" in payments that the franchisor requires for merchandise or services, in excess of the bona fide wholesale prices of the goods furnished to the franchisee. The fee could also be disguised as contributions to an advertising fund administered by the franchisor.

Clauses in franchise contracts usually stipulate that the franchisor will (1) provide managerial assistance to the franchisee, (2) assist in site selection, (3) conduct traning programs, and (4) provide operating manuals. In return, the franchisee agrees to run the business in a manner stipulated by the franchisor. Most contracts also specify that the franchisor will provide particular equipment, goods, or types of facilities.

The franchisee's commitments often extend to (1) the business organization and business practices of the enterprise, (2) the territory within which the business will operate, (3) the expected volume of products that will be sold, and (4) the services that will be provided in connection with the sale of goods.

Advertising   The advertising done for a franchise operation is generally originated by the franchisor. Some contracts provide that the franchisor bears the expense of this service. Under other contracts, the franchisee is obligated to pay for advertising, generally on the basis of a percentage of sales. A franchise contract may also provide that a certain percentage of the franchisee's gross sales be spent for advertising by the franchisor.

48:4   Duration and Termination of the Franchise

The terms of the franchise are determined by the franchise contract. Often, however, franchisees are at the mercy of the franchisor with regard to the termination of the contract. Many franchise contracts provide that the franchisor has the right to terminate at will. In addition, a contract may specify events, such as failure to meet sales quotas, that trigger termination. The courts, however, have implied an obligation to give reasonable notice to the franchisee. State statutes have buttressed this requirement in many states by providing that franchise contracts cannot be canceled arbitrarily if they have been performed in a reasonable and satisfactory manner.

Both state governments and the federal government have perceived a need for statutory protection of franchisees' rights in their contracts. For example, the federal *Automobile Dealer Day in Court Act* [15 USC §§ 1221–1225] prevents car manufacturers from terminating dealerships in bad faith. In addition, this act prevents automobile manufacturers from using the threat of terminating the dealership or associated new-car financing as a means of pressuring the dealer to accept cars, parts, accessories, and supplies.

A franchisor can, of course, terminate the franchise contract if the franchisee fails to discharge the duties required of him under the contract. For example, if the franchisee of an employment agency franchise agrees in the contract that the business will be conducted in a downtown office but in fact operates only as a telephone service from his or her home, the franchisor has good cause to terminate the contract.

Most franchise contracts contain notice provisions requiring the franchisor to give the franchisee reasonable notice of termination. The failure to comply with the notice requirement renders the termination invalid, and the franchisor may be liable in damages to the franchisee. The following case illustrates the limits that the courts tend to place on a franchisor's right to terminate a franchise contract, as well as the scope of the contract itself.

Shell Oil Co.
v
Marinello
307 A2d 598 (1973)
New Jersey Supreme Court

FACTS: In 1959, Shell Oil Company leased a service station to Marinello and entered into a written dealership agreement with him. The lease was for a one-year term and was regularly renewed in writing for the next 12 years. In 1972, Shell notified Marinello that it was terminating the lease and dealership agreement. Marinello sued to enjoin the termination. Shell maintained in court that it could terminate the lease under the rules of landlord and tenant law. Marinello argued that the dealership agreement and lease constituted a franchise and could not be terminated without good cause. The trial court agreed with Marinello, ruling that Shell could not terminate the lease without good cause.

ISSUE: Was the relationship between Shell Oil and Marinello a franchise within the meaning of the New Jersey Franchise Practices Act?

RESULT: Yes. The fundamental business relationship was a franchise.

REASONING:

*   *   *

We are in full agreement with the basic determination of the trial court that Shell had no legal right to terminate its relationship with Marinello except for good cause, i.e., the failure of Marinello to substantially comply with his obligations under the lease and dealer agreement. . . .

Shell argues that its lease of the service station premises to Marinello is independent of its dealer agreement with him, and that its legal rights as a landlord under the lease are absolute and cannot be restricted. This is pure sophistry. The two contractual documents are but part of an integrated business relationship. They were entered into simultaneously, [and] have the same commencement and expiration dates. . . .

The relationship between Shell and Marinello is basically that of franchise. The lease is an integral part of that same relationship. Our

Legislature, in enacting the Franchise Practices Act, has declared that distribution and sales through franchise arrangements in New Jersey vitally affect the general economy of the State, the public interest and the public welfare. . . . The Act prohibits a franchisor from terminating, cancelling or failing to renew a franchise without good cause, which is defined as the failure by the franchisee to substantially comply with the requirements imposed on him by the franchise. . . .

The Act does not directly control the franchise relationship herein since Marinello's last renewal antedates the effective date of the statue. . . . However, the Act reflects the legislative concern over long-standing abuses in the franchise relationship, particularly provisions giving the franchisor the right to terminate, cancel or fail to renew the franchise. To that extent the provisions of the Act merely put into statutory form the extant public policy of this state. . . .

Based on the foregoing, Marinello's franchise, including his lease, would have legal existence for an indefinite period, subject to his substantially performing his obligations thereunder. . . .

Sullivan, Justice.

48:5 Governmental Regulation of Franchising

Various approaches have been adopted by the states and the federal government to regulate franchises. Under certain circumstances, franchises have been deemed to be securities that are subject to the registration requirements under federal and state securities acts.[2] The federal mail fraud statute [18 USC § 1341] has also been applied to franchises.

In addition, franchising has been subject to regulation through the federal and state antitrust laws that govern price-fixing, price controls, tie-in buying, and market or territorial domination.[3] The antitrust laws prevent the franchisor from establishing the resale price of the product or service; however, these laws do permit most constraints on territory, quality, service provision, and sales quotas. A franchisor who wishes to restrain overpricing of its products often can do so by exercising these constraints. For example, if the franchisor requires a minimum sales quota, a franchisee will be constrained from charging a price for the goods that will not produce the desired quota. In addition, the antitrust laws prohibit the use of the franchise agreement as a means of creating or extending a monopoly or otherwise unreasonably restraining trade. For example, a fast-food franchisor may require that a highly popular brand of soft drink be sold by the franchisee. That is, it may tie the promise to use the soft drink to the right to use the franchisor's trademark. It may not do so,

---

[2] Securities regulation is discussed in Chapter 53.
[3] Antitrust legislation is discussed in Chapter 55.

however, if it owns the soft-drink firm, so that use of the trademark is tied to sale of the soft drink.

The most important federal legislation applicable to franchises is the *Federal Trade Commission Act*, which prohibits unfair or deceptive acts or practices in commerce [15 USC §§ 45(a)(1) and 45(a)(6)]. Under the authority of this act, the Federal Trade Commission (FTC) has adopted rules and regulations governing the sale of franchises and business opportunities [see 16 CFR Part 436]. These rules were adopted in response to widespread abuses in connection with the sale of franchises and business opportunity ventures throughout the country. They reduce the opportunity for deceptive practices by prohibiting certain acts and by requiring the disclosure of information relevant to a proposed sale of franchises. The rules set forth the circumstances under which a franchisor or franchise broker can make claims about the actual or projected sales, income, or profits of existing or potential outlets. They also impose other requirements on franchisors or franchise brokers for establishing franchises.

State Regulation of Franchising   Many states have enacted legislation relating specifically to franchising. This legislation generally authorizes legal action by a franchisee to recover damages for the franchisor's violation of the law. However, the provisions of these state laws vary. In some states these provisions are similar to the federal franchise laws. Laws of this type declare certain acts to be unfair and deceptive practices, or unfair methods of competition, and they require full disclosure of all pertinent information by franchisors before franchises can be sold. Other state laws incorporate principles of the federal securities and antitrust acts, requiring franchisors to register with the state agency before selling franchises, and perhaps requiring that a copy of the franchise prospectus or advertising material used to promote the sale of franchises be filed with a state regulatory agency. Still other state laws require only the franchisors deal with franchisees in good faith.

The various franchise laws adopted by the states are not consistent or uniform in approach. Indeed, even the basic definition of terms varies widely from state to state, depending on the particular regulatory approach used. For example, one group of states defines "franchise" on the basis of how much control is exercised by the franchisor and how closely the franchise is associated with the franchisor's marketing plan or system; in the absence of these features, a business venture is not deemed to be a franchise subject to state regulation. A second group of states defines "franchise" in terms of the common interest that the parties to a franchise contract have in the success of the business; typical statutory language in these states refers to "the community of interest among the parties" to a particular business arrangement. A third approach focuses on the mutual financial benefits in a business relationship and requires a continuing financial interest between parties in addition to the licensing of a basic marketing plan. A few states have attempted to define "franchise" in other terms. For example, in some states a franchise is defined as a continuing commercial relationship, while in others a franchisee's business must be substantially reliant on the franchisor for its supply of basic goods in order to constitute a franchise. Obviously, the applicability of a state's franchise legislation to a particular business arrangement or venture depends on the definition of terms, the purpose of the legislation, and the abuses sought to be remedied.

The following case illustrates how a court determines whether a particular business venture is a franchise. Bear in mind that the result might very well have been different had some other regulatory approach or definition of terms been in force.

People

v

Kline

110 Cal App 3d 587 (1980)

California Court of Appeal

FACTS: Under circumstances described below in the Court's analysis, Donald Kline was charged with and convicted of the unlawful offer and sale of a franchise in violation of the California Franchise Investment Law, the first franchise disclosure law enacted in the United States. The California law defines franchise on the basis of the control exercised over the franchisee and the existence of a marketing plan or system prescribed by the franchisor.

ISSUE: Was Kline's offer and sale of business opportunities a franchise within the meaning of the California statute?

RESULT: Yes. Even in the absence of a marketing plan, the total scheme of the enterprise indicated a franchise relationship.

REASONING:

*   *   *

In mid-1977 [Kline] formulated plans to establish a fast food chain which would sell hot dogs from portable kiosks under the name "Aunt Hilda's Pennsylvania Dutch Steamed Franks." He incorporated a company for this purpose, designated as National Food Service Marketing, Inc. . . .

In June 1977, [Kline] had begun regularly to patronize a restaurant in Tiburon, where he met James Shaul and Caroline Mushet with whom he discussed his plans for the Aunt Hilda's Pennsylvania Dutch Steamed Franks enterprise. He told Mushet that he intended to build many kiosks for the enterprise, and showed her blueprints for the kiosks.

In November 1977, Shaul told Mushet that [Kline] "was offering a very good price for his franchise," and suggested that they become involved in the enterprise as partners, with Shaul as manager and Mushet as investor. On November 21, 1977, Shaul, Mushet, and [Kline] met at Shaul's apartment to discuss the enterprise. [Kline] told Mushet that he was offering a franchise for $25,000 on a very short term basis, which he would soon sell for $40,000 and later would sell for $80,000. Shaul told Mushet that "it was a turn key operation." Mushet understood this to mean that "it was everything complete, ready to go, absolutely supplied and sustained and everything else." She was also told that the menu for the business "would be handled by an expert." She was given a "pro forma" outlining projected sales, operating expenses, payroll expenses, and profits for "Aunt Hilda's Pennsylvania Dutch Steamed Franks," and [Kline] handed Mushet a newspaper article about franchises and said that he was proposing a similar operation. She testified that, "as I understood it, he was going to have many many franchises. He was going to have a lot of Aunt Hilda's barns all over the place."

Mushet was not given specific details as to a marketing plan or system; both [Kline] and Shaul, however, told her that "everything would be supplied and managed and promoted by National Food Service Marketing." She understood that the day-to-day operation of the business was to be conducted by National Food Service Marketing, Inc., that there would be an ongoing relationship between [Kline's] corporation and her proposed partnership with Shaul, and that [Kline] was in complete control of the operation.

That very evening Mushet decided to enter into the proposed investment. Mushet and Shaul signed a handwritten "partnership agreement" drafted by [Kline] in which Mushet agreed to invest $50,000 in the partnership for the purchase of at least two "Aunt Hilda's Kiosks' Business Opportunities." They also signed as partners a "purchase agreement," also handwritten and drafted by [Kline], to purchase two "Aunt Hilda's Kiosks' Business Opportunities" for $25,000 each from National Food Service Marketing, Inc.

Mushet gave [Kline] $50,000 in two installments [Kline] later demanded more money from her, and on two occasions she loaned him funds totaling $15,000). . . .

[Kline] contends that the court erred, . . . because [he] did not sell or offer to sell a "franchise." . . . " 'Franchise' means a contract or agreement, either expressed or implied, whether oral or written, between two or more persons by which:

> (a) A franchisee is granted the right to engage in the business of offering, selling or distributing goods or services under a marketing plan or system prescribed in substantial part by a franchisor; and
>
> (b) The operation of the franchisee's business pursuant to such plan or system is substantially associated with the franchisor's trademark, service

mark, trade name, logo-type, advertising or other commercial symbol designating the franchisor or its affiliate; and

   (c) The franchisee is required to pay, directly or indirectly, a franchise fee.

[Kline] argues that the two "business opportunities" sold to the partnership formed by Shaul and Mushet did not as a matter of law constitute
a franchise . . . because there was no "marketing plan or system" and
even if so, it was not "prescribed in substantial part by a franchisor." . . .

   The contract or agreement which constitutes a "franchise" . . . may be
expressed or implied, oral or written. In the case at bench there was a written
contract binding the franchisor, National Food Service Marketing, Inc.,
[Kline's] corporation, to "total and continuing support" of the franchisee.
[Kline] had agreed orally to assist in advertising and to supply food and
supplies and menu planning, etc., through his corporation. The use of identifiable and distinctive kiosks at least implied a prescribed marketing plan or
system, and there was an expressed agreement to sell "Aunt Hilda's Pennsylvania Dutch Steamed Franks," surely an indication of a common marketing plan or system. [Kline] also promised that there would be an operational
plan which he had "pretty well worked out." He represented to a number of
people that he was organizing a national food franchise similar to other well-
known and successful national franchise. The whole scheme was [Kline's]
conception of an integrated operation prescribed and directed by him through
National Food Service Marketing, Inc., his corporation. By phrasing his
handwritten agreement in terms of sale of a "business opportunity" [he]
cannot avoid the requirement of registering this franchise sale.

   There was therefore ample evidence from which the trial court could
find all of the statutory elements of a franchise; as that court said: "The
whole aroma, the whole atmosphere around this sale clearly related to
the sale of other than just the kiosk. It was a sale, actually, of a franchise."

   [Kline's] argument that there must exist a fully prescribed and detailed
marketing plan or system in order to meet the definition of a registerable
franchise sale or offer is too narrow a statutory construction. The Legislature
expressed concern for the protection of prospective franchisees in enacting
the Franchise Investment Law. . . . In fact the specified intent of the law was
to prevent such a sale as made by [Kline], where the seller's failure to provide
full information "would lead to fraud or a likelihood that the franchisor's
promises would not be fulfilled." Therefore it is not appropriate to construe
the definition of [franchise] to fully developed franchise schemes. A sale for a
fee of a business substantially associated with the seller's trademark, service
mark, trade name, logotype, advertising or other commercial symbol, which
the seller represents *will constitute* a franchise and will include a marketing
plan or system *to be* prescribed in substantial part by the seller is the unlawful
sale of an unregistered franchise. [Court's emphasis.] . . .

                                                        Koford, Justice.

48:6   Franchisor's Liability for Acts of Franchisee

The franchisor is not liable to third persons for acts of the franchisee under most circumstances. This is so because franchising does not necessarily create an agency relationship in which the acts of the franchisee are imputed to the franchisor. However, if a sufficient degree of control and direction is exercised by a franchisor, an agency relationship may be created. In such cases, the franchisor can be liable to third persons for acts or omissions of the franchisee. In determining whether an agency relationship exists between a franchisor and franchisee under a franchise agreement, the right to control the business is an important factor. If the franchisor has the right to exercise complete control over the operation of the franchise, an agency relationship may exist, with the franchisor as the principal and the franchisee the agent.

In product liability cases the franchisor may be liable to a third person injured by a product supplied by the franchisor, despite the absence of control over the franchisee's business.[4] For example, if a person is injured by a defective automobile part he purchased from a franchisee, the franchisor or manufacturer can be held liable to the injured person regardless of the precise relationship of the franchisor and franchisee under the franchise agreement.

The liability of a franchisor for acts of the franchisee is exemplified in the case below. Note the circumstances under which the franchisor was held liable and the extent of the franchisor's control over the franchisee.

Kuchta

v

Allied Builders Corp.
21 Cal App 3d 541 (1971)
California Court of Appeal

FACTS: Kuchta contacted the Allied Builders Corporation concerning the construction of an outdoor patio and living area. Allied referred Kuchta to its franchisee, Ralph Weiner. A contract was signed with Weiner, naming him as the contractor. The contract required in part that all construction conform to local and state building codes. Weiner submitted building plans to the appropriate local agency, but they were disapproved. Without Kuchta's knowledge or consent, Weiner submitted other plans that complied with the regulations, and these were approved. However, Weiner built the patio and living area according to the original, noncomplying plans. When the local housing agency discovered what had occurred, Kuchta was required to demolish the patio and restore the area to its original condition. Kuchta then sued both Allied and Weiner

---

[4] Product liability is discussed in Chapter 21.

for damages. Allied defended, arguing that as the franchisor it was not liable for acts of its franchisee.

ISSUE: Was Allied liable for the wrongful actions of Weimer?

RESULT: Yes. Allied exercised such control over Weimer as to create an agency relationship between Allied and Weimer.

REASONING:

* * *

The law is clear that a franchisee may be deemed to be the agent of the franchisor. . . . In the field of franchise agreement, the question of whether the franchisee is an independent contractor or an agent is ordinarily one of fact, depending on whether the franchisor exercises complete or substantial control over the franchisee. . . .

In the case under review, there was evidence that Allied Builders exercised strong control over Weiner. The franchise agreement itself gave Allied Builders the right to control the location of the franchisee's place of business, to prescribe minimum display equipment, to regulate the quality of the goods used or sold, to control the standards of construction, to approve the design and utility of all construction, and to assign persons to see that the franchisee performed according to the franchisor's standards. Additionally, Allied enjoyed the right of inspection over the franchisee's plans and specifications, the franchisee's work in progress, and finished jobs, as well as the right to train Weiner's salesmen. Moreover, Allied Builders was entitled to share in the profits of the franchisee and to audit Weiner's books. These elements of control were sufficient to support an implied finding of agency. . . . Both the main office and the branch office answered their phone in the same manner, to wit, "Allied Builders." Both the franchisor and the franchisee did business under the same name at that time, to wit, Allied Builders System. The contract listed "Allied Builders System" as the contractor. Both offices employed common advertising in newspapers and in the yellow pages of the telephone book. Calls to the main office brought swift and certain reaction from the franchisee. Weiner represented to plaintiffs that the firm had been in business for over 50 years, which covered the entire span of Allied's experience in the building business. The plaintiffs' check for payment on the contract price was endorsed and deposited to the account of "Allied Builders System." Consequently, there was ample evidence that Allied Builders either intentionally, or by want of ordinary care, led third persons, including plaintiffs, to believe that the franchisee and Allied Builders were part of the same business operation.

While Allied Builders argues that no agency relationship existed by virtue of the franchise agreement, in that the agreement itself stated that no such agency relationship was created, the declarations of the parties in the agreement respecting the nature of the relationship are not controlling. . . .

Weiner was an agent or ostensible agent of Allied. It is clear that he acted in an important management position. Therefore, the only question remaining is whether a franchisor may be liable in punitive damages for a franchisee's fraud to the same extent as it would for the fraud of an employee, officer or manager.

The franchise agreement provided a plethora of controls and supervisory privileges on behalf of the franchisor. Allied enjoyed a right to cancel the franchise relationship at any time by reason of Weiner's insolvency, failure to maintain sufficient gross sales, or failure to comply with any contractual obligation, including Weiner's duty to comply with all building codes and to obtain necessary building permits. The most significant control an employer has over the acts of an official is the right to terminate his employment for misconduct. Allied had even this control over Weiner. Allied also required the franchisee to make a certain amount of gross sales yearly and the franchise royalty was based entirely upon gross receipts. Thus, Allied received a financial benefit from fraudulently induced contracts. In light of the foregoing indicia of control, it is difficult to distinguish between this agency relationship and that of any managerial official. Weiner may be equated in all respects with an employee, officer or manager. . . .

Kerrigan, Acting Presiding Justice.

Key Concepts and Terms

- Under a franchising agreement, the developer of a product or service (franchisor) grants another person (franchisee) an exclusive right (franchise) to market the product or service under the franchisor's trademark or trade name through a marketing plan in a given area for a specified period of time.

- The relationship between franchisor and franchisee combines features of the agency relationship and the independent contractor relationship. At the heart of the franchisor–franchisee relationship is the control the franchisor exercises over the franchisee, including control of site, methods of business operation, merchandising, record-keeping, and quality of the product or service.

- The franchise contract creates the franchisor-franchisee relationship, grants the franchise, and sets forth the parties' rights and duties.

- Termination of a franchise is governed by provisions in the contract and, in some states, by statute.

- Franchises have been regulated by the states and by the federal government through securities legislation, antitrust laws, and mail fraud statutes, as well as through specific franchise disclosure laws.

- Franchisors are ordinarily not liable to third persons for acts or omissions of the franchisee. However, if the franchisor exercises a sufficient degree of control and direction over the franchisee, an agency relationship may be created, rendering the franchisor liable for the franchisee's acts.

- Automobile Dealers Day in Court Act
- Business Format Franchise
- Distribution Franchise
- Federal Trade Commission Act
- Franchisee
- Franchise Contract
- Franchise Fee
- Franchisor

Questions and Case Problems

1. Analyze and discuss the various types of franchise regulatory approaches adopted by the states.

2. National Cleaners sells cleaning solvent to local dry cleaners and prescribes and enforces quality service standards. In return, a local subscribing dry cleaner is granted the right to display a regionally or nationally advertised symbol of quality. A fee is charged for the right to use this symbol. Is this arrangement a franchise? Do the definitions of franchise, as discussed in this chapter, affect the answer?

3. What distinguishes the franchise from other business relationships?

4. Seams is a large department store chain that advertises heavily in newspapers, magazines, and mail-order catalogs. The No-Leak Roofing Company rents space in one of Seams' stores under a typical department store lease and concession arrangement. No-Leak is a roof repair company that actively participates on a cooperative basis in Seams' local advertising program. Under the contract, No-Leak pays Seams a fixed minimum rent plus a percentage of gross sales. No-Leak must maintain certain types and levels of insurance and have all the necessary business permits. Although No-Leak does business under its own name, its invoices state that it is a Seams' authorized roofing contractor. Is this arrangement a franchise? Does the answer depend on the particular definition or approach to franchises in force in the state where No-Leak is doing business?

5. Why is the franchisor ordinarily not liable for wrongful acts of the franchisee? What is the determining factor of a franchisor's liability?

6. Why are franchise terminations particularly the subject of state laws?

7. Murphy sustains personal injuries while she is a guest at a Holiday Inn motel. The motel is operated by Betsy-Lynn Motor Corporation as a franchise. Holiday Inn does not own the premises on which the accident occurred. Can Murphy hold Holiday Inn liable for her personal injuries? Under what circumstances would Holiday Inn be liable?

8. Guild Industries granted area franchises for the distribution of furniture under its "Baby Butler" trade name. All the franchises granted were unsuccessful and were closed after the franchisees sustained substantial losses. Each of the product distribution schemes devised by Guild to be used by its franchisees was inherently

fraudulent. Representations made by Guild to prospective franchisees were false. The franchisees also encountered unanticipated costs which precluded realization of the promised profits. In view of these facts, what state and federal remedies exist to protect the public and prospective franchisees from Guild's business scheme? What remedies would be available to franchisees who have gone out of business, despite the representations and assurances of Guild Industries?

9. Gail Coty is injured while operating a meat-slicing machine on the premises of her employer, the Yankee Doodle Dandy Restaurant, a fast-food franchisee. She sues the franchisor for negligence, seeking damages for her personal injuries. The franchise contract imposes on the franchisee numerous restrictions relating to the operation of the restaurant. These restrictions are primarily geared toward protecting the Yankee Doodle trademark and the goodwill associated with it. The franchisor does not retain any day-to-day supervisory control, cannot hire or fire anyone, cannot stop work in the restaurant, and cannot give any orders to the franchisee's employees. Assuming that Gail could prove negligence, is the franchisor liable for the torts of its franchisee?

10. Mr. Steak, Inc., issued franchises for restaurants throughout the country. From 1962, all its franchise agreements prohibited the sale of alcoholic beverages on restaurant premises. A reprinting of the franchise forms in 1968 inadvertently omitted this clause, and various franchises were granted without it. As a result, 27 of the over 200 Mr. Steaks throughout the country served alcohol. The omission was later discovered and reinserted in the franchise forms. Following a slump in sales, Mr. Steak experimented in authorizing the sale of alcoholic beverages in certain of its restaurants; it even issued four written waivers of the prohibition clause. Another ten franchise operators started to sell liquor on their own without any waiver from Mr. Steak. However, when the owners of a Mr. Steak franchise in Colorado told the franchisor of their intent to sell alcohol, Mr. Steak refused to give its permission and sued to enjoin the breach of its franchise. How should the case be decided?

49 Considerations in Choosing a Form of Business Organization

49:1 Introduction

One of the most important, indeed fundamental, issues in launching a business venture is the form and structure the venture will take. In deciding which particular form of business to adopt, one should consider the advantages and disadvantages of each type of business entity. The purpose of this chapter is to aid the business student in evaluating the basic types of business organizations.

The selection of the best form of business organization depends to a large degree on the nature of the business itself, the general financial conditions and tax situations of the participants, the number of investors involved, the extent to which capital is required, and a host of other factors. In many cases, family relationships must also be considered.

The principal organizational structures for the conduct of business are the sole proprietorship, the partnership (see Chapter 44), and the corporation (see Chapters 45–47). That is not to say, however, that the choice of organization must be from among these basic forms of business enterprise. Other forms, such as the joint venture, business trust, real estate syndicate, or real estate investment trust, are commonly used for particular business purposes. A *joint venture*, for example, is often used to finance special-purpose investments and projects that may require large sums of capital, particularly in real estate development. Moreover, the basic forms of business enterprise are not uniform in nature or totally separate and distinct, either from a tax or a business point of view. This is particularly true of corporations, which can be one-person ventures, family corporations, or multinational giants with thousands of investors, employees, and managerial personnel. It is also true of the franchise (see Chapter 48), which is really a business relationship that can be operated by a partnership, a sole proprietorship, or a corporation. Despite the blending of one form with another, each type of business organization is subject to specific laws based on the nature, attributes, and requirements of its particular structure.

The determination of the best form of business—or at least the one most suited to a particular type of activity—is extremely important and carries serious legal and tax consequences for all participants. In some ventures, participants typically prefer certain forms of business over others. For example, the limited partnership is by far the most commonly used business entity in real estate because it offers investors both the limited legal liability of a corporation and the tax benefits of a partnership. On the other hand, many persons about to launch a business think only in terms of operating as a corporation. From an economic standpoint, the great appeal of the corporation stems from the fact that the law treats it as an entity separate and distinct from its shareholders. Moreover, there is great flexibility in structuring ownership through classes of stock and preferences. Nevertheless, it has often been remarked, "When in doubt, do not incorporate," because in many cases the partnership or sole proprietorship offers far more advantages than does a corporation.

As the following case shows, it is of vital importance for people in business to be aware of the many types of entities capable of doing business and to make certain that the entity chosen conforms to the legal criteria governing that business. Note that although the business here was characterized in one form by its participants, the court considered it to be an entirely different type of entity.

Rizzo

v

Rizzo

120 NE2d 546 (1954)

Illinois Supreme Court

FACTS: Rocco Rizzo, Sr., operated a business under the name of Rocco Rizzo & Co. Michael, the oldest son, went to work for his father in 1910; Joseph in 1913; Rocco, Jr., in 1916; and John in 1920. Each son performed definite duties for the business. Michael, the most experienced, was the general manager. None of them received wages, and all the profits were equally divided. In 1915, Rocco, Sr., retired from active participation. In 1929, the father deeded the business property to Michael, who paid no consideration for either the business or the building. After the death of Rocco, Jr., his estate claimed one-quarter of the business, contending that it was a partnership. The other brothers argued that the business was a sole proprietorship owned by Michael. At trial, the court found that the brothers had operated the business as a partnership from 1920 to 1931, when Rocco, Jr., died. Thus, his estate was entitled to a one-fourth interest in the partnership as of the date of his death. The court also ruled that the plaintiff was entitled to an accounting from the other brothers.

ISSUE: Was the business a sole proprietorship or a partnership?

RESULT: The practice of the Rizzo brothers indicates that they carried on the business as a partnership.

REASONING:

*   *   *

In the instant case the decree of the court in plaintiff's favor is predicated upon the existence of a partnership relation between plaintiff's deceased husband and his brothers. The requisites of a partnership are that the parties must have joined together to carry on a trade or venture for their common benefit, each contributing property or services, and having a community of interest in the profits. . . .

Defendants contend that the evidence establishes that Michael Rizzo was the sole proprietor of the business on the date of the death of plaintiff's decedent. In support thereof, defendants point out that the business was turned over to Michael in 1915 when his father retired, that the profits were merely the measure of compensation for the brothers, that Michael was regarded as the boss by persons dealing with the firm, and that a formal partnership contract had to be drawn up at the request of the bank in order to negotiate a loan in 1937, indicating that there was no partnership prior thereto.

The fact that Michael, as the oldest son, had more authority in the management than the other brothers does not of itself preclude the existence of a partnership, particularly in view of the custom in such closely knit immigrant families. In fact, Michael stated that the business was turned over to him because he was the oldest son. Furthermore, it is an accepted partnership practice that one partner may be charged with greater managerial responsibilities.

The fact that the brothers admitted that they all worked in the business, sharing equally in the profits and going without pay if there were none, tends to comply with the essential requirement for a partnership. That interpretation is enhanced by . . . the statement of an employee of 30 years that all the brothers were regarded as the owners.

Furthermore, the fact that the firm name, originally Rocco Rizzo & Co. had been changed to Rocco Rizzo Son & Co. when Michael entered the business, and was again changed to Rocco Rizzo Sons & Co., and was so listed in the telephone book and on the truck during the lifetime of Rocco, Jr., is further evidence of the existence of a partnership between the brothers as of 1931. Changes in the firm name to Jacob Shlem & Sons were deemed significant in establishing the existence of a partnership in [another case, in which] the sons also went to work in the family business.

Under the circumstances in the case at bar, therefore, there is ample evidence that the brothers, Michael, Joseph, John, and Rocco, Jr., were carrying on the business for their common benefit, each contributing his services and having an equal interest in the profits; hence, the finding of the master as approved by the chancellor, that the brothers were partners as of the date of the death of Rocco, Jr., could in no way be deemed to be manifestly against the weight of the evidence. . . .

Bristow, Justice.

The remaining sections of this chapter focus on factors that affect a businessperson's choice of the best type of business organization for a given enterprise. These factors are (1) creation of the organization and continuing requirements following its creation, (2) management, (3) compensation of the participants, (4) capital requirements, (5) duration of the business, (6) transferability of the business or rights in it, (7) personal liability of the participants, and (8) taxation. Bear in mind, however, that usually it is impossible for those about to launch a business venture to avail themselves of all the advantages of any form of business. Instead, the most important factors should be identified, and the advantages and disadvantages of each carefully analyzed. The form of business organization that most meets the needs of the participants should be ultimately chosen. When this is accomplished, the business will be far more likely to succeed than if the various factors discussed in this chapter are ignored and the form of business enterprise is chosen out of whim or for unimportant reasons.

49:2   Creation; Continuing Requirements

A sole proprietorship is the simplest business enterprise to form. It can be commenced at any time, usually by obtaining a business license and paying sales and other taxes. A written agreement is not necessary. Indeed, the states impose very few formal requirements that must be complied with before one can engage in business as a sole proprietor.

Forming a general partnership is also relatively simple. A written agreement is not ordinarily required. A partnership that will necessarily last longer than one year, for example, must be created by a written agreement because of the statute of frauds (see Chapter 15).

In a limited partnership, the partners must prepare and sign a certificate setting forth prescribed information, including a designation of which partners are general and which are limited (see Chapter 44). The certificate must be filed with a state official, usually the Secretary of State. The certificate may be amended or canceled by following similar formalities.

Once a sole proprietorship or partnership is formed, the states usually do not require it to disclose on a regular basis data or information concerning its operation. Partnerships are required to file an information tax return each year, but they are not otherwise subject to reporting requirements. The information return must disclose each partner's distributive share of the partnership income, gains, losses, deductions, and credits. Each partner must also disclose his share of these items on his own individual tax return.

Corporations   The requirements for organizing a corporation are more formal. Incorporation is a statutory process requiring strict compliance with the requirements. Every state requires a corporation to file its articles of incorporation before it can lawfully engage in business (see Chapter 45). Usually it must pay a filing fee. It must also pay a license fee to the state in which it desires to do business, even if it is not incorporated in that state, and an annual franchise fee for the privilege of doing business. In addition, a corporation must strictly comply with state and federal securities laws when issuing stock.

 The cost of forming a corporation, including legal fees, as compared with the cost of creating a sole proprietorship or partnership, may be quite high. The amount of the fees and taxes that a corporation must pay, the cost of filing reports and returns with the state or federal government, and the annual upkeep required of the corporation should not be casually overlooked when deciding which form of business venture is most appropriate.

Other formalities that a corporation must observe and that distinguish it from a sole proprietorship or partnership include annual shareholder and formal director meetings, notification to shareholders of various corporate actions, and the taking of detailed minutes of meetings conducted by the board of directors or the shareholders.

49:3   Management

The number of persons involved in a business, and the method by which it will be managed, are obviously important determinants of the appropriate type or structure of business organization. In a general partnership, the partners are all co-managers. Each partner has both the express and implied authority to bind the partnership in dealings with third parties. Each partner also has a technical and legal veto over the other partners as to partnership affairs. If there are many general partners, each capable of acting for the partnership as a whole, the business could lose its sense of purpose, going off in many directions. For this reason, the partnership agreement typically establishes a form of *centralized management* structure.

   In a limited partnership, the limited partners cannot participate actively in management. Accordingly, a limited partnership interest represents a passive investment, which may not meet the objectives of participants who want some control over their investment.

   The corporate form is much more suitable than a partnership to a business involving large numbers of people. The centralized management, through the election of directors by shareholders and, in turn, the appointment of corporate officers by directors, is often a major reason for incorporating. The ultimate power in a corporation usually resides in the shareholders who own the majority of the voting stock or are in a position to control the corporation; the minority interests may have little or no role in the active management of a corporation. This limitation on the role of minority shareholders is particularly significant when active owners want assurance that inactive owners will not interfere in the business. Therefore, to the extent that an enterprise requires a sophisticated management structure, the corporate form is probably the most preferable type of business organization.

Fiduciary Duties of Management   The legal obligations of partners or corporate managers to act in good faith must be considered when choosing a business form. In a partnership, for example, each partner is bound by the highest duty of loyalty to the other partners. A lesser standard of care is generally applied to corporate officers and directors. They are usually not liable for acts of ordinary negligence; they are presumed to have acted within the broad range of normal business judgment.[1] Clearly, this deference given to corporate management decisions by the courts can be a distinct advantage.

It should be noted, however, that the high standard of care applicable to partners is being more frequently applied to corporate managers in a growing number of states. In addition, the strict compliance required of corporate management to the federal securities laws (see Chapter 53) also tends to reduce the differences in the duty of care between the partnership and the corporation.

49:4 Compensation of Participants

Any assessment of the desirability of one business form over another must contain a comparative analysis of the compensation options available with the various types of business organizations. Compensation usually consists of any of the four following elements: (1) basic cash compensation or salary; (2) benefits under pension, retirement, or profit-sharing plans; (3) other fringe benefits, such as group insurance programs, club memberships, and business use of company automobiles; and (4) incentive compensation, which can be most meaningful in terms of both financial rewards and employee motivation.

The corporate form of business offers the most possibilities in terms of compensation. A corporate employee's compensation package can be structured to include all four of the elements listed above. Stock compensation and stock options, unavailable in other forms of business enterprise, are traditionally used as incentive compensation for executives. Furthermore, if a shareholder is also an employee of the corporation, he or she may be entitled to participate in an accident and health insurance plan and to receive group life insurance or other benefits. The shareholder-employee does not have to pay income tax on benefits paid by the corporation.

The compensation alternatives available to organizational forms other than the corporation are more limited. For example, a sole proprietor is not eligible to participate in a qualified pension plan under the *Internal Revenue Code,* because he cannot be both an employer and employee at the same time within the meaning of the law. Note, however, that the Internal Revenue Code does allow an individual to set aside and deduct up to a prescribed amount of

---

[1] The business judgment rule is discussed in Chapter 46.

income each year for retirement savings. In a partnership, health or life insurance and other benefits received by a partner might be considered compensation and treated as taxable income.

49:5 Capital Requirements

The choice of organization often depends on how much capital will be required to run the business and whether it will be necessary to retain capital. With a sole proprietorship and general partnership, these considerations might not play a vital role; a person or partnership can engage in business without operating capital and without the need to accumulate profits.

The corporate form offers the greatest ease and flexibility in obtaining capital. The various ways a corporation can raise capital, including issuing equity and debt securities, readily permit the transfer and readjustment of interests of those who own the business. Indeed, this may be the prime advantage to the corporate form. Therefore, to the extent that an enterprise seeks to take advantage of financing alternatives, the corporation can offer a significant advantage.

When capital is acquired through debt financing, the corporate form has an additional advantage in that the corporation, rather than the shareholders, will be held liable for corporate debt obligations. In some situations, however, this aspect of the corporate form is not significant because debt financing might not be available without incurring *personal liability*. For example, creditors of closely held corporations frequently require personal guaranties of the principal shareholders. As to a profitable partnership, on the other hand, a third party might very well extend credit to the partnership with recourse limited to the partnership assets; that is, without the partners being personally liable.

49:6 Duration of the Business

The intended *duration of a business* is another factor to consider in selecting a business structure. Most sole proprietorships terminate on the owner's death. Of course, the business can be taken over by a family member or an associate, or the assets can be sold to permit its continued existence.

Partnerships must be dissolved in order for the business to be terminated. The Uniform Partnership Act lists a number of acts or events that cause dissolution (see Chapter 44). Obviously, the existence of these many causes of dissolution and eventual termination should prompt potential partners to study their relationship in-depth from both the business and personal standpoints. For example, an otherwise successful partnership business might have to be terminated because of personality differences among the partners or simply because one partner dies. Therefore, uncertainty as to a partnership's duration might prompt those about to engage in a business to select another form of enterprise.

Generally, a corporation has perpetual life unless it is dissolved by the shareholders or by court order. If a corporate president or a shareholder dies, for example, a corporation's business is not automatically terminated.

49:7   Transferability of Ownership

A basic concern in the formation of any business is how easily the business (or rights in it) can be transferred or sold. A sole proprietorship is perhaps the easiest type of business to sell. Since a sole proprietor answers to no co-owner, the business can be sold at any time. In contrast, under § 18 of the Uniform Partnership Act, a partner in a general partnership cannot transfer his interest without the other partners' consent. (Such a limitation on the transferability of a partnership interest is often advantageous, particularly if all the participants actively contribute to the success of the business.) For a limited partnership, the partnership's required certificate can provide for the transferability of a limited as well as a general partner's interest.

Shares of corporate stock are generally transferable at any time by the shareholders. Free transferability is often an advantage in forming a business as a corporation, particularly if capital will be raised by issuing equity securities. Note, however, that restrictions similar to those of partnerships can be imposed to limit the transfer or sale of a shareholder's interest. For example, shareholders of a closely held corporation often enter into a restrictive agreement that prevents one shareholder from selling her interest without first offering it to the corporation or the other shareholders. The increasing recognition of special treatment for closely held corporations in state corporation laws has led many courts to be extremely tolerant of share transfer restrictions when challenged.

 Although the mechanics differ, *transferability of ownership* varies only slightly between the partnership and corporate forms. In both forms, the interests can be either freely transferable or restricted from transfer. Only in a limited number of situations will transfer limits be better adapted to the corporate form. Accordingly, the significance of this factor in selecting the form of enterprise should not be overestimated.

49:8   Liability of Participants

A businessperson's potential liability varies greatly from one business structure to another. The limited liability of corporate shareholders is often considered the primary advantage of the corporation. Because a corporation is an entity separate and distinct from its shareholders, shareholders are not normally liable for the corporation's obligations. They are liable only to the limited extent of their initial investment, which means that the maximum loss that they can sustain is the value of the stock they own.

There are, however, various judicially created doctrines that have been applied by the courts to extinguish limited shareholder liability. For example, it can be extinguished if a corporation is operated as an alter ego of the principal shareholder (see Chapter 47). Moreover, if a corporation has been inadequately capitalized, the corporate entity might be disregarded and the individual shareholders held personally liable. Although the courts will not casually disregard the corporate entity and impose liability on shareholders, the possibility of their doing so must be considered when choosing the most appropriate business entity.

In close corporations, limited liability of the shareholders may be illusory. Close corporations often receive bank or other loans on the condition that an individual shareholder cosign the promissory note, which makes him personally liable on the debt. Accordingly, at least until a corporate enterprise becomes well established and sufficiently stable in the eyes of creditors, the only protection against liability that the shareholders might have is their insulation from tort liability. The existence of this protection, without more, is not necessarily a valid reason for incorporating. A business venture, whether incorporated or not, can adequately protect itself against tort liability by obtaining various readily available types of insurance coverage (see Chapter 41).

Unlike a corporate shareholder, both a sole proprietor and a partner in a general partnership are individually liable for all obligations incurred by the sole proprietorship or partnership. In a partnership, each partner can also be liable for wrongful acts committed by one or more of the other partners.

Limited partnerships are often formed to protect investors against the potential liability that would exist with a general partnership. The liability of limited partners is akin to the liability of corporate shareholders in that a limited partner is not individually liable for the partnership's obligations. Instead, a limited partner's liability is limited to his or her stated contribution to the enterprise, provided the partnership agreement is publicly filed and various other rules are observed, including the absolute requirement that the limited partner take no part in the management of the business. A general partner of a limited partnership, in contrast, has unlimited personal liability for partnership obligations.

Of course, either a general or a limited partnership can purchase various types of insurance against the possible imposition of personal liability. However, the nature of a business may make it very difficult for a partnership to obtain *liability insurance*. For example, a fledgling partnership that manufactures an inherently risky product might have considerable difficulty in obtaining product liability coverage, or the cost of the insurance might be inordinately high.

49:9 Taxation

A business can be intentionally structured to create maximum tax savings. There is nothing unethical, immoral, or illegal about planning to minimize state or federal taxes. As the United States Supreme Court has observed, "The legal right of a taxpayer to decrease the amount of what otherwise would be his taxes, or altogether avoid them, by means which the law permits, cannot be doubted."[2]

All individuals in business, including sole proprietors, are subject to a graduated federal tax on their incomes. Each self-employed person must also

---

[2] *Gregory v Helvering*, 293 US 465 (1935).

pay self-employment tax on part or all of his income to help finance Social Security benefits. While Social Security taxes are withheld from the wages of employees, self-employed persons must pay the tax as part of the income tax.

Taxation of Partnerships and Corporations   Like sole proprietors, partners are taxed individually. The partnership files an information tax return which shows the partnership's income and deductions and their allocation among the partners. In turn, each partner reports his allocated share of income and deductions on his individual income tax return.

EXAMPLE: Yellin is a partner with three others in Olé Perfume Enterprise. Each of the four partners shares equally in the profits and losses. In its third year of operation, the partnership has a gross income of $400,000 with deductions of $200,000. Yellin must report on her own income tax return for that year gross income in the amount of $100,000 as her share of the partnership's gross income, but she can take deductions in the amount of $50,000. She must report the income of $100,000 regardless of how much is actually distributed to her.

In calculating his income tax, each partner must include on his own return his share of partnership income and deductions for the taxable year in which they are accrued by the partnership. It does not matter when partnership income is actually distributed to each partner; that is, even if part of the income is distributed during the next year, it must be reported the year it was earned by the partnership. Indeed, a partner is taxed on his proportionate share of partnership income even if *none* of the income is actually distributed.

The principal tax distinction between the corporation and the partnership is that a corporation is a taxable entity, separate and apart from its shareholders. As a result, income generated by a corporation can be taxed twice; once at the corporate level and again at the shareholder level.

EXAMPLE: The Brannan Corporation has earnings of $10 million on which it is taxed by the federal government. From these earnings Brannan distributes $2 million to its shareholders as dividends. The dividends received by the shareholders are also taxed as ordinary income when reported by the shareholders on their annual returns. Thus, $2 million of Brannan's earnings is taxed twice, once at the corporate level and once again when the distributed earnings are received as dividends by the shareholders.

In some states, shareholders are also burdened with an intangible personal property tax on their shares.

Ordinarily a corporation has a *separate legal identity* for tax purposes even if it is wholly owned by a single shareholder or by related shareholders. Therefore, no matter how decisive a sole shareholder's actions will be in determining those of the corporation, once the corporation is active as an entity and is more than the alter ego of the shareholder the two are separate taxpayers.

A business will ordinarily be subject to tax on the basis of its *actual* form and identifiable characteristics, rather than on the basis of its apparent structure. Thus, if a corporation is a sham, serving only as the alter ego of its principal shareholder, the corporate entity might be disregarded for tax purposes. Corporate earnings will then be attributed to the shareholders, who will be taxed in the same manner as other individuals. Similarly, a partnership that evidences a number of features characteristic of a corporation might end up being taxed as a corporation rather than as a partnership.

Accumulation of Income   A significant drawback to the partnership form is that accumulated or undistributed earnings usually must be allocated to the individual partners for tax purposes in the year they are earned. In contrast, the law allows a corporation to accumulate up to a prescribed amount of its earnings and profits without adverse tax consequences to the shareholders in most situations. Traditionally, the ability to accumulate earnings is one of the primary benefits flowing from corporate status.

Taxation of Joint Ventures   As discussed in Chapter 44, a joint venture is a combination of two or more persons seeking a joint profit in some specific venture without designating themselves as a partnership or a corporation. A joint venture is usually formed for the purpose of engaging in a single project that could require several months or several years for its completion, but in most other respects it resembles a partnership and embodies the idea of the mutual agency of its members. Ordinarily, joint ventures are taxable as partnerships. For example, if two corporations form a business and divide the profits and losses equally, the endeavor is a joint venture, the business is taxed as a partnership, and each corporation must report on its tax return its one-half share of the profits and losses earned from the joint venture.

Subchapter S Corporation   The final business entity that should be considered from the tax standpoint is the *Subchapter S corporation*, which is discussed in Chapter 45. To avoid the double taxation that would otherwise be imposed, as discussed above, certain corporations can elect to be taxed under Subchapter S of the Internal Revenue Code instead of under the regular rules governing the taxation of corporations. In effect, a Subchapter S corporation's income is taxed to the shareholders as though it had been distributed to them as a dividend at the end of the corporation's taxable year. Moreover, if the corporation suffers a loss, the loss is treated as the shareholders' loss. For all other tax purposes, the corporation is treated like any other corporation despite the Subchapter S election. Thus, by incorporating and electing to be taxed under Subchapter S, the owners of a small business can enjoy the benefits both of the corporation and the partnership. A Subchapter S corporation can be used to divide business income among children or other relatives for tax purposes without taking the money out of the corporation and without incurring the double tax liability. This often is a simpler, more feasible approach than the family partnership.

Key Concepts and Terms

- Selecting the most suitable form of business organization depends to a large degree on (1) the nature of the business, (2) the general financial condition and tax status of the participants, (3) the number of investors involved, (4) and the extent to which capital is required.

- The principal forms available for a business enterprise are the sole proprietorship, the partnership, and the corporation.

- To the extent that an enterprise requires a sophisticated management structure, the corporation is the most preferable form of business organization.

- A business organization must meet certain requirements imposed by the states before it can engage in business. A sole proprietorship or partnership must only apply for a business license and arrange for the payment of sales or other taxes. A limited partnership must file a certificate with the state. A corporation must meet formal requirements regarding incorporation and qualification and may also be required to comply with the requirements of the federal securities laws before stock or other securities may be issued.

- The amount of capital necessary to begin a business varies with its size. Accordingly, most sole proprietorships and partnerships engage in business without having to raise significant amounts of capital. A corporation, however, must generate capital and usually does so by selling shares or issuing debt securities. If flexibility in financing and capital formation are required, the corporation may be the preferable form of business organization.

- The longevity of a business depends on its form. A sole proprietorship usually terminates on the owner's death. Various acts or events may cause the dissolution and eventual termination of a partnership. A corporation can exist indefinitely, even if a shareholder dies or sells his shares.

- The ease of sale or transfer of ownership might be another determining factor. A sole proprietorship is the easiest type of business to sell. A partner cannot sell or transfer a partnership interest without the consent of the other partners. Corporate shares are ordinarily freely transferable at any time by the shareholders, although many smaller, close corporations do restrict the transfer or sale of shareholders' interests.

- The businessperson's personal liability is an important consideration in choosing the most suitable business form. A sole proprietor or general partner is individually liable for all business obligations and torts. A limited partner's liability extends only to the amount of the partner's contribution to the enterprise. Because a corporation is a separate entity under the law, shareholders are not normally liable for any corporate obligations or torts.

- Tax implications are yet another factor in deciding how to organize a business. Both a partnership and a sole proprietorship are treated similarly for income tax purposes. In contrast, income generated by a corporation and distributed as dividends is taxed twice—once at the corporate level and again at the shareholder level.

- Accumulation of Income
- Centralized Management
- Duration of Business
- Internal Revenue Code
- Joint Venture
- Liability Insurance

- Personal Liability
- Separate Legal Identity
- Subchapter S Corporation
- Taxation
- Transferability of Ownership

Questions and Case Problems

1. Dubois is the sole proprietor of a small explosives firm. The net profits of the business in 1980 were $200,000 and constituted the sole source of Dubois' income. Dubois expects that the profits of his business will increase at the rate of about five percent per year over the next ten years. The business has a small sales force and several manufacturing employees. There are two key employees whom Dubois is anxious to keep in the business. Dubois believes that he needs an annual income of about $65,000 per year to cover his living expenses and his federal and state income taxes. He has no other outside income. Should he incorporate? If so, what are the advantages and disadvantages?

2. Discuss the reasons why organizational and managerial structure are important factors to consider when forming a business.

3. Compare and contrast the question of liability in a corporation, a partnership, and a sole proprietorship.

4. Rolf and Amundsen are interested in starting a business to sell books by mail and public auction. They plan to have an inventory composed exclusively of books and to conduct the business out of their homes. They do not plan to hire any employees. Rolf and Amundsen each contribute approximately $50,000 for the acquisition of rare books and to borrow additional money on a short-term basis from banks. What type of business association should they form and why?

5. Willie and Hope Farmer run a successful lumber business. They want to expand production but do not have the necessary capital to do so. They are reluctant to take on additional debt because of their financial position and the prevailing high interest rates. Winston, who knows of the Farmers' expansion plans, contacts them to discuss possible investment in their business. She does not want to become involved in its management but would like some control over its affairs if she puts up money. What form of organization is most appropriate in this situation? Why?

6. On graduation from college, Bradley Condrake returns home to start a fish and poultry company. He has chosen this particular business venture because his father ran a similar enterprise for a long time. Bradley hopes to benefit from his father's connections with suppliers and outlets and to learn his marketing skills. However, Bradley's father, already retired, does not wish to participate actively in the business. He does plan to invest money and to participate minimally. During the initial stages of the business, Bradley does not plan to employ more than one or two part-time persons as the need arises. He has leased a building for the business with an option to purchase. He will purchase the equipment he will need, particularly refrigeration equipment, from other companies. What type of business organization should Bradley form? Why?

7. Drewes is attempting to form a business renting tools, machinery, and other items to the public. The initial capital needs are so great that Drewes must obtain

financing from outside investors or banks. Drewes prefers to manage the business herself but will consider letting one or more of the investors help her run the business. A major problem with a rental business is the potential liability for injuries to persons who rent equipment, and Drewes is concerned about this. She also realizes that she may gain tax benefits from the depreciation of the rental equipment and perhaps from the losses she might sustain during the first year or two of operations. In light of these circumstances, how should the business be formed? Why?

8. Smith works for an accounting partnership owned by Kelley and Galloway. He receives $1,000 per month in salary, travel expenses, and a bonus paid out of the firm's profits. Although Smith is held out to third persons as a partner, and contracts with third parties indicate that Smith is a partner, there is no partnership agreement and he has not contributed to any of the partnership assets. Smith becomes dissatisfied with the firm and leaves. He contends he is entitled as a partner to ten percent of the profits. What type of business arrangement had been created? Is Smith entitled to share in the profits?

9. Discuss the tax differences of the corporation, the Subchapter S corporation, and the partnership.

10. The Allen family owns and operates a pet shop. All three family members participate in the business and own the property on which they operate their store. The net profits are distributed equally to each family member who participates in the business. One of them reads an article about the wisdom of incorporating, but they decide that the business should continue as a family operation. Moreover, even though they would obtain limited liability on incorporation, they realize that no bank would extend the corporation credit without the individual guaranty of the shareholders. They do not foresee a substantial change either in the profits or losses of the business, and they do not have plans for a substantial expansion of the business. They are also somewhat interested in establishing a pension plan or disability insurance program but realize that if they incorporate this may be difficult with only three shareholders. Should the Allens continue their business as a partnership or should they incorporate? Why?

PART TEN

Employment Relationships

Introductory Comments

The material in this part of the book explores the traditional employer–employee relationship as well as the relationship between the employer and the independent contractor. Both relationships are, essentially, agency relationships subject to the principles of agency discussed in Chapter 43. The employer-employee relationship, while contractual in nature, is subject to the regulation of labor law. The independent contractor relationship is primarily contractual.

The traditional employment relationship is that of employer and employee. The distinction between status as an agent and status as an employee is sometimes blurred, but essentially it is that an employee is hired to work for and under the direct control of the employer, rather than to represent him. The basic rights and duties of employers and employees are discussed in Chapter 50.

Chapter 51 discusses two significant aspects of the employer-employee relationship that are regulated extensively by federal legislation. The first of these is labor relations, which involves the right of employees to organize and bargain collectively with their employer. The second is job discrimination, which, if left unchecked, operates to restrict people's employment rights and opportunities for reasons unrelated to their ability to do the work in question.

An independent contractor is a person who is hired to do a particular job. As discussed in Chapter 52, the employer's interest is in the completed job. Indeed, the distinguishing feature of an independent contractor relationship is the employer's lack of control over the means by which the contractor accomplishes the job. The relationship exists when, for example, a business contracts with an accounting firm for an audit of its books and preparation of its income tax returns. The accountant is so important an independent contractor from a businessperson's viewpoint that the relationship between the accountant and client is discussed in some detail, in Chapter 52.

The different employment relationships discussed in Part Ten are complex and involve many rights and corresponding duties and liabilities. Clearly, the more complete knowledge a businessperson has about the statutory and court-made law that governs the relationships, the better equipped that person will be to make reasoned decisions in the employment area and, in this way, to minimize future litigation.

50 Basic Rights and Duties in the Traditional Employer–Employee Relationship

50:1 Introduction

This chapter examines the traditional employment relationship, which exists between employer and employee. At one time, the terms "master" and "servant" were commonly used to indicate the relationship that exists when one person employs another. Today, the words "employer" and "employee" are used, although legal literature and judicial decisions still use the traditional terms at times.

In theory, every person has the right to contract for labor or services and to abandon employment if conditions of service are not satisfactory. Historically, however, for reasons of poverty, family, employment scarcity, or competition, an employee has had little choice but to accept employment on the terms and conditions offered by the employer. Laws made in recent years regulating employment and labor relations have attempted to alleviate some of the perceived inequities of the system.

50:2 The Employment Contract

The relationship of employer and employee is contractual in nature, and its creation is determined by principles governing the formation of other contracts (see Chapters 10 through 15). Employment contracts are often oral and informal. However, whether informal or not, every employment contract includes an implied provision of good faith and fair dealings between employer and employee and an implied provision that neither will do anything that will injure the rights of the other to receive the benefits of the agreement.

 Many firms have employee manuals to explain company policy, procedures, and employment terms and conditions. Under some circumstances, courts have held that the provisions of such a manual constitute a part of the employment contract. The firm may not have viewed the manual in that light. While a good manual can anticipate and clarify a wide range of questions, and therefore is a valuable tool for both employee and employer, it is important that steps be taken to clarify the precise nature of the manual. If the manual summarizes complex policies (for example, pension fund plans), this point should be made and the complete policy referenced. Many firms include a provision that explains the summary nature of the manual and the need to seek precise information in the personnel office.

50:3   Employee's Duties to Employer

An employee has certain duties to the employer that exist even if there is no contractual provision imposing them. These duties include reasonable skill, loyalty, and good faith.

Skill   An employee must use care and reasonable skill in managing or controlling any aspects of the employer's business for which he or she is hired. An employee who fails to exercise reasonable skill can be liable for damage caused to the employer by that failure.

Loyalty to Employer's Interests   An employee has the duty of furthering the employer's interests. The employee is not permitted either to engage in a business detrimental to that of the employer or to perform for personal benefit any activity that would have the effect of destroying the business. Nor can the employee use information obtained by virtue of his or her employment to further personal interests. For example, courts have held it a violation of an employee's duties (1) to engage or even participate in a business that competes with that of the employer (even outside working hours) or (2) to seek to obtain for personal use the employer's customer accounts.

 An employee's fiduciary duties not to engage in any conflict of interest as to the employer are not limited to officers, directors or other management personnel. Even rank-and-file employees have a duty not to do anything that interferes with an employer's interests. Bear in mind, though, that unless it is specifically prohibited, an employee *can* take on outside work after regular office hours as long as the work (1) is not inconsistent or an interference with the employer's business and (2) does not reduce the value of the employee's full-time services to the employer.

Employee's Duties as to Property Acquired in Connection with Employment   Generally, everything an employee acquires in connection with his or her employment, except compensation, belongs to the employer. This is true regardless of whether the acquisition is lawful or unlawful, or whether it is made during or after expiration of the term of employment. This basic rule is simply another expression of the agency rule (see Chapter 43) that an agent cannot use property that is the subject of the agency, or powers conferred on him, for his own benefit. Furthermore, if an employee creates something as part of his duties under the employment, the thing created is the employer's property, unless by agreement the employee retains some right in the product. For example, a chemist who discovers a formula—which may have great economic value—while conducting research for her employer during work hours is not entitled to ownership of the formula. The formula is the property of the employer.

The following case analyzes the problem of distinguishing between information that an employee takes wrongfully from a firm and information that is or has become a part of the employee's general knowledge.

Smith Oil Corp.

v

Viking Chemical Co.
468 NE2d 797 (1984)
Appellate Court of Illinois, Second District

FACTS: In September 1983 Rock Valley Oil & Chemical Company purchased the Smith Oil Corporation. Three employees, the defendants, immediately left the firm and were employed by a competitor, Viking Chemical Corporation. Smith sought an injunction against Viking and its employees using Smith's trade secrets. In particular, Smith sought to prevent the employees from using information that they recalled from Smith's supplier book or monthly sales report. Smith claimed that the information regarding customers, suppliers' prices, and costs is protected whether taken directly from the manuals or recalled independently by the employees.

ISSUE: Is such information a protected trade secret?

RESULT: No. Such information constitutes part of the general knowledge base of the employees.

REASONING:

* * *

A trade secret must be defined in terms of the facts of a particular case, with the following factors to be considered: (1) the extent to which the information is known outside of the employer's business; (2) the extent to which information is known by employees and others involved in the business; (3) the extent of the measures taken by the employer to guard the secrecy of the information; (4) the value of the information to the employer and his competitors; (5) the effort or money expended by the employer in developing the information; and (6) the ease or difficulty with which the information could be properly acquired or duplicated by others. . . . It is recognized, as a general rule, that the right of an individual to follow and pursue a particular occupation for which he is best trained is a fundamental right and that one who has worked in a particular field cannot be compelled to erase from his mind all of the general skills, knowledge and expertise acquired through his experience. . . .

First, we decide whether any of the disputed material is entitled to receive protection as a trade secret. Plaintiffs asserted a proprietary interest in the customers and sought to enjoin defendants from soliciting the sale of any product sold or worked on by defendants while employed by Smith, and from calling on any customer or former customer on Smith's customer list. The trial court found that the defendants Giovingo and Fedeli, through their employment with Smith, learned the names of many industrial oil or lubricant customers and became familiar with many people to contact and with the names of those customers but that the prior knowledge of customer needs, in and of itself, was not entitled to protection. We agree. An employer ordinarily has no proprietary interest in his customers, although he can protect confidential information by a reasonable restrictive covenant. . . . We note that in this case no restrictive covenant is involved.

The manifest weight of the evidence adduced at the hearing supports the conclusion that the customer sales reports were not trade secrets. There was evidence that the defendants did not need the plaintiffs' sales report because the customer would give the salesman the price he was paying previously in order to get a competitive price; that product and pricing information was routinely given out by Smith order clerks to customers over the phone; that the customer lists were not under lock and key and were available to any clerk or employee; that computer sales reports were not restricted as to access nor locked up; that the defendants knew who the major customers in the industry were from general experience and merely had to ask the customer to give him a copy of the blanket orders, price structure and names of the products he was buying in order to compete; and that customers commonly dealt with more than one supplier, depending on who made the best bid. While it is undisputed that knowing who the customers are and what their needs are is valuable business information, the trial court's conclusion that the salesman's knowledge comes under the category of general knowledge and not under the category of a protectable trade secret is supported by the manifest weight of the evidence. . . .

Next, plaintiffs assert a proprietary interest in defendants' general knowledge and skills acquired at Smith and sought to enjoin their use in other employment. The manifest weight of the evidence adduced at the hearing supports the trial court's holding that the defendants cannot be prevented from using their general blending or chemistry skills or sales skills even if obtained or developed at Smith; nor prohibited from making use of individual items of sales information contained in customer lists or reports which they may happen to recall from their independent recollection. . . .

Seidenfeld, Presiding Judge.

Employer's Profits or Earnings   An employee may be required to account for any secret profit, gift, gratuity, or benefit he receives in his capacity as an employee. The employee has the duty to exercise good faith toward the employer and cannot, without the employer's consent, retain profits or earnings received in performing the employer's business or participating in an undertaking that constitutes a breach of duty to the employer or conflicts with the employee's duties to the employer.

50:4   Employer's Duties to Employee

Duties an employer owes to an employee depend on the nature of the employment, provisions of the employment contract, and applicable statutes. An employer generally does not have the duty to provide specific work for the employee. Rather, he can use the employee's services when and how he chooses, so long as he compensates the employee according to the contract.

Employee's Welfare   An implied provision of employment contracts is that the employer will not add to the employment any new conditions involving dangers or inconveniences not within the employee's contemplation at the time he was hired. An employer's general duties are to ensure that the place at which the employee works is reasonably safe and to furnish suitable and safe tools and equipment. This becomes more imperative as the risk increases; the employer's standard of care for the employees' safety must be commensurate with the dangers of the business. Public policy as to care and protection of workers has undergone great change in recent times, and as discussed in 50:10, legislation has been enacted to protect employees' safety and health.

50:5   Employee Privacy

Privacy is an elusive right and one that, in the employer–employee setting, must constantly be balanced against the employer's right to conduct business profitably and successfully. Unlike his counterpart of 50 years ago, today's worker does not sell "his soul" to the employer; he sells only his labor. Nevertheless, federal Labor Department hearings have revealed that using cameras on assembly lines, denying access to records, monitoring employee's conversations (even in washrooms), and using lie detectors are common practices. Conflict between management's desire to control and monitor many aspects of employee life and, on the other hand, the employee's desire for greater self-expression and personal growth free of corporate influence is producing a decided shift toward individual rights.

Lie Detector Tests   The *polygraph*, or lie detector, is an electrical instrument that can measure and record on a graph certain physiological data concerning the person being tested. These data include blood pressure, pulse rate, respiration rate, and galvanic skin response (a measurement of relative skin conductivity). When a polygraph expert questions a person to whom the instrument is attached, the data are recorded. The expert can then examine the resulting chart (polygram) and determine with a high degree of accuracy which questions the individual has answered truthfully. Lie detector tests have long been the subject of controversy. Their use by employers has raised the serious question of invasion of employees' privacy and privilege against self-incrimination.

The giving of preemployment polygraph tests is the most controversial use of the polygraph in private industry. Proponents argue that it gives the employer both protection from employee theft and a cheap way of verifying employee truthfulness. Critics point to the lack of scientific support for the claims that the polygraph can screen dishonest employees from honest ones.

Many union contracts include bans on lie detector tests. Also, legislation in some states prohibits employers from *requiring* prospective employees to undergo lie detector tests, although they can request that applicants do so. In other states, legislation prohibits employers from even requesting a prospective employee to take any test purporting to determine honesty.

The courts have divided on the question of whether employees' right to refuse a polygraph test is protected by reason of public policy in the absence of legislation. Where states have legislated against the use of the polygraph, however, the courts have construed the legislation strictly, to fulfill the public policy of promoting employee privacy.

Employee Surveillance   An employer's surveillance of employees raises questions that can only be resolved on balancing the employer's and employee's interests in each case. An employee's personal mail when delivered to the place of business is a case in point. Routine mailroom procedures in many companies call for opening all letters, regardless of who the addressee is. If mail marked "personal" is opened by the employer and read without the employee's authority, some courts have found an unjustified intrusion into the private life of the employee. The employer has then been liable for damages.

 Employers who screen all incoming mail should expressly (and in writing) warn employees that their mail is subject to being opened. Such a warning can (1) discourage employees from having personal mail sent to the business and (2) remove any "expectation of privacy" that is essential to an invasion of privacy lawsuit.

Employee surveillance problems can also arise when an employer monitors an employee's telephone conversations. Federal law allows a person to record a conversation so long as the purpose is not to commit a crime or other injurious act. State legislation, however, may be more restrictive. In the absence of particular state or local restrictions, an employer can install a telephone-monitoring device on telephones in departments that deal with the general public. The justification for this practice is that it enables the employer to protect employees from abusive language by irate customers, and allows supervisors to better train and instruct employees on how to communicate with the public. When telephone monitoring is adopted by an employer, the employer should be completely open about it. This means that employees should be advised of the monitoring in advance, to preclude an invasion of privacy suit.

50:6 Injuries to Employees; Workers' Compensation

In the absence of statute, an employer is liable to an employee for injuries received in the course of employment if the injury results from the employer's negligence. The employer's duty is to use reasonable care to provide the employee with a safe working place and with safe tools and equipment. As in other negligence actions, what constitutes reasonable care depends on the surrounding circumstances. A problem from the employee's viewpoint is that the employer can assert defenses ordinarily applicable in negligence cases (see Chapter 6). Thus, the employee's contributory negligence might bar recovery. Also, the doctrine of assumption of risk applies on the theory that, by entering employment, the employee assumes ordinary risks. Moreover, under what is known as the *fellow servant doctrine*, an employer is not liable to an employee for injuries sustained solely as the result of the negligence of other employees.

In recognition of the problems that employees have when they try to recover from their employers for their injuries, most states have enacted *workers' compensation* legislation. This legislation, which is liberally interpreted by the courts, eliminates the need to prove negligence. Instead, the employee is granted the right to receive compensation for most employment-related injuries without regard to fault. A disadvantage of workers' compensation from the employee's viewpoint is that the amount of compensation that will be paid is limited.

Workers' compensation laws are administered primarily by administrative boards or commissions, rather than by the courts. The amount of compensation to be awarded in any given case is determined in accordance with a prescribed schedule, in an informal administrative proceeding. At that proceeding, the employer might resist the employee's claim by showing that (1) there was no injury or (2) the injury that did occur was either not as severe as claimed or was not job-related. The amount of compensation finally awarded is usually paid by the employer's workers' compensation insurance carrier. At times, however, the employer itself pays all or part of the award.

 In some states, an employee injured on the job must be compensated *solely* under workers' compensation legislation; he does not have the right to sue the employer for damages. In other states, however, the employee can elect whether to take the statutory workers' compensation coverage or waive that coverage and sue the employer for negligence.

Disability Resulting from Mental Stress   Mental or nervous disorders or disabilities resulting from employment-connected *physical* injuries and an accompanying trauma or shock to the nervous system are generally compensable, even though they cannot always be established by objective diagnostic procedures. They are compensable on the theory that the physical injury (however slight) is an identifiable and specific physical or disease-related "cause" for the mental or nervous disorder. The judicial viewpoint has been expressed in this regard that a psychoneurosis resulting from shock due to an accident constitutes a "violence to the physical structure of the body" within compensation statutes and is therefore compensable.[1]

Courts have had difficulty dealing with the situation in which the worker's disability was caused neither by a single injury to the worker nor by a single mental shock, but rather by emotional pressures produced by the job. The following decision, which could have far-reaching consequences, illustrates one court's approach to this problem.

Kelly's Case
477 NE2d 582 (1985)
Supreme Judicial Court of Massachusetts

FACTS: On Friday, August 19, 1977, Kelly's supervisor called her aside and told her the company was cutting back in her department and that she was being laid off. Kelly became quite upset and was upset over the weekend. On Monday, August 22, she was told that she could transfer to another department and work there as a foreperson. She did not like the idea and became depressed, developed chest pains, and was taken to a hospital, where she was put on medication. Kelly remained out of work for six weeks. When she returned to work in the new department, she again developed chest pains and was hospitalized with a psychiatric depression disorder. Based on her psychiatrist's testimony, the Workers' Compensation Board determined that she had been totally disabled since August 22, but that the disability did not arise out of or in the course of her employment. Kelly appealed.

ISSUE: May a disability that results from an employee's learning that she will be laid off from one department and assigned to another be said to arise out of and in the course of employment?

RESULT: Yes. As a matter of law, such a disability may arise out of the course of employment.

REASONING:

*   *   *

A disability arises out of and in the course of employment if it is "attributable to the 'nature, conditions, obligations or incidents of the employment; in other words, [to] employment looked at in any of its

---

[1] *Todd v Goostree*, 493 SW2d 411 (Missouri Court of Appeals, 1973).

aspects.' " . . . Thus, the question is whether the event that caused Kelly's disability was an incident of employment "in any of its aspects." We have no doubt that that event was such an incident, particularly in view of the long-standing principle that the workers' compensation statute should be construed, whenever possible, in favor of the employee so as "to promote the accomplishment of its beneficent design." . . . Kelly, then, is within the class of persons the Legislature sought to protect. . . .

We reject any contention that Kelly is not entitled to workers' compensation unless her emotional disability resulted from an unusual and objectively stressful or traumatic event. "Our decisions place injuries attributable to specific events at work within the business risks covered by the act, even when employment does not expose employees to an unusual risk greater than that experienced by the general public. . . . Furthermore, it is settled law that an employer takes his employee "as is," that is, with whatever peculiar vulnerabilities to injury the employee may have, and that "an identifiable incident or strain need not be unusual or severe to support compensation if the particular employee succumbs to it. . . .

. . . [W]hen an injury is attributable to a specific work-related event, as here, or a series of such events, rather than to gradual wear and tear, the employee need not show that the employment exposed him or her to an unusual risk greater than that experienced by the general public. "To be compensable, the harm must arise *either* from a specific incident or series of incidents at work, *or* from an identifiable condition that is not common and necessary to all or a great many occupations" (emphasis added). . . .

. . . We recognize that layoffs and job transfers are frequent events, and that emotional injuries are more prone to fabrication and less susceptible to substantiation than are physical injuries. Nevertheless, it is within the Legislature's prerogative to determine, as a matter of public policy, whether one of the costs of doing business in this Commonwealth shall be the compensation of those few employees who do suffer emotional disability as a result of being laid off or transferred, and it is also the Legislature's prerogative to say whether determination of the existence of such a disability is appropriately left to the expertise of the Industrial Accident Board. We construe G.L. c. 152, § 26, as providing that an employee who suffers emotional disability as a result of layoff or transfer is entitled to workers' compensation, and as vesting in the Industrial Accident Board the responsibility to make the relevant factual determination. . . .

O'Connor, Justice.

"Dual Purpose" Doctrine Most workers' compensation statutes require a showing that an employee's injury arose out of and in the course and scope of employment before the employer can be required to pay compensation. The relationship of the employee's injury to the employment is important if the injury occurs while the employee is traveling, particularly if the travel is based on motives that are both personal and employer-oriented. Under what is called the *dual purpose doctrine*, if the employee's work created the necessity for travel, he or she is in the course and scope of employment even though serving some personal purpose at the same time. In this way, courts have expressed the public policy that it is reasonable to place the risk of injury on the employer if it is established that the business mission was a concurrent cause of the employee's trip.

50:7   Employer's Liability for Employee's Torts

Under what is called the doctrine of *respondeat superior*, an employer is usually held liable for an employee's negligent acts or intentional torts committed during the course of employment. This liability is based on several theories. One is that because the employer can carry insurance as a cost of doing business, he must also assume the risk of his employees committing torts. Another theory is that the employee's acts can be regarded as the employer's acts (because the employee is engaged in the employer's work), so that the employer cannot, simply by delegating work, avoid the duty of due care to others.

An employer's liability under the respondeat superior doctrine is *vicarious*. That is, the liability is secondary and arises simply because the employment relationship exists. Depending on the circumstances, however, an employer can also be primarily liable in connection with an employee's tort. For example, the employer might have been negligent in training an employee or in entrusting the employee with a dangerous tool or machine. An employer can also be negligent in hiring or retaining an incompetent or unfit employee.

EXAMPLE: A hospital's hiring policy requires that it obtain from each applicant for employment at least four references and that it check at least two of them before hiring. Despite this policy, the hospital accepts Wilson's application, which lists only two references, and it hires Wilson as an orderly without checking either reference. On the job, Wilson assaults and robs a patient. Proper checking would have revealed that Wilson has a criminal record and that he was expelled from medical school due to a serious drug problem. The hospital is liable for the patient's loss and injury because it was negligent in hiring Wilson.

An employer who has been held liable for an employee's tort can, of course, sue the employee in an attempt to recover losses. As a practical matter, however, the lawsuit will usually be in vain. The employer will probably win a money judgment, but the chances of collecting that judgment are poor.

Course and Scope of Employment   A frequently disputed issue in respondeat superior cases is whether the employee was acting in the *course and scope of his employment* at the time of the incident in question. Relevant factors include (1) the employee's intent; (2) the nature, time, and place of his conduct; (3) his actual and implied authority; (4) the work he was hired to do; (5) incidental acts that the employer should reasonably have expected to be done; (6) the amount of freedom allowed the employee in performing his duties; and (7) the foreseeability of the employee's act. Note that an employer is not relieved of liability under the respondeat superior doctrine merely because the employee was combining his own business with that of the employer. This is similar to the rule under the dual purpose doctrine, discussed in 50:6. The following case illustrates how the courts usually hold the respondeat superior doctrine to apply so long as the employee's conduct was authorized, even if the specific activity was not required.

United States
v
Romitti
363 F2d 662 (1966)
United States Court of Appeals, Ninth Circuit

FACTS: Moore, a federal employee, was involved in a traffic accident while allegedly traveling on employment-related business. Plaintiff, injured in the accident, sued the federal government for its employee's negligence under the respondeat superior doctrine. Plaintiff was awarded judgment, and the government appealed.

ISSUE: Is the United States liable to a third party for the negligence of a Federal employee traveling on government-related business?

RESULT: Yes. The employee was acting in the course and scope of his employment.

REASONING:

*   *   *

To summarize, the trier of fact had before it evidence that Mr. Moore was traveling on direct orders of his employer and for the sole purpose of serving his employer's business; that he was transporting property of the employer and fellow employees (including his supervisor), both necessary to the performance of that business; that he was traveling on the most direct route between two of his employer's work locations; that he was using an expressly authorized means of transportation; that he was driving during regular working hours; and that he was being paid his regular salary plus per diem, plus costs of transportation. This was enough to support a finding that Moore's negligence occurred "in the transaction of the business of the agency," and therefore to justify the conclusion that a private employer would be liable. . . .

. . . As Chief Justice Traynor said in [a California case], "The principal justification for the application of the doctrine of respondeat superior in any case is the fact that the employer may spread the risk through insurance and carry the cost thereof as part of his costs of doing business." This purpose requires that the employer assume those risks which are attributable to the employer's business, rather than to purely personal pursuits of the employee. Since the trip involved in the present case was undertaken to serve the purposes of the United States, the United States should bear the risks incidental to it. This basic fact is not affected by the circumstance that Mr. Moore's normal duties were those of an electronics engineer rather than a chauffeur, and that he was authorized but not required to provide his own automobile for use in his employer's service. The . . . courts have imposed respondeat superior liability where the employee was not hired as a driver and the choice of means of conveyance was his. . . .

On the other hand, in some situations deviation from usual duties and use of other than required means may add support to an inference that the employee was not engaged in his employer's enterprise, but was on a "frolic of his own." . . .

Similarly, the failure of the employer to exercise control over the employee's driving is a factor of varying importance. Existence of the power to control the physical details of the service may be crucial when the question is whether the actor is an agent or an independent contractor, but may be relatively insignificant in determining whether an admitted agent is acting within the scope of his employment.

In this connection it is important to notice a distinction between a principal's liability for his own negligence and his liability for the negligence of his agent. If a principal negligently employs a person who is incapable of performing the task for which he is hired, or negligently fails to exercise proper control over the agent's performance, the principal is liable for injuries due to the principal's own negligence—without regard to the doctrine of respondeat superior. . . . But the liability imposed upon the principal by the doctrine of respondeat superior is vicarious and does not rest upon the principal's fault. The fault for which the principal is required to respond is not that of the principal but that of the agent, committed in the course of the principal's business. Thus, when respondeat superior liability is asserted, "we are not . . . looking for the master's fault but rather for risks that may fairly be regarded as typical of or broadly incidental to the enterprise he has undertaken." . . .

We assume that in exercising the election which the United States gave these employees to use a private vehicle in performing the employer's errand, the employees were motivated at least in part by considerations of personal comfort and convenience. Nevertheless, the choice also served the interests of the United States, and this is enough. . . .

Browning, Circuit Judge.

50:8   Termination of Employment Relationship

An employment contract can terminate by (1) expiration of the contractual term of employment, (2) the death or legal incapacity of either the employer or the employee, (3) the employer's discharge of the employee, or (4) the employee's resignation or retirement.

When an employment contract fixes no duration, the term of employment extends for the period that the parties have fixed for paying salary or wages. Hence, an employee paid a monthly salary is said to be hired on a month-to-month basis, while an employee paid weekly is hired on a week-to-week basis; an employee doing piecework is hired for no specified term. Some courts have held that a hiring at a yearly rate is presumed to be for one year, and that this presumption is not changed merely because salary is paid on a monthly basis. A person performing work at an agreed price and for a stated period of time can continue in the same employment after expiration of the term, without a new agreement. In this situation it is presumed that the terms of the original contract are continued.

If an employment contract is for a fixed period, the employer can legally discharge an employee prior to the contract's expiration only for "good cause." What constitutes a good cause is usually specified in the contract. Most business employers expressly reserve the right to discharge employees for such problems as habitual lateness to work, drinking on the job, or simply failure to perform their job satisfactorily.

Contract Requiring Employer's Satisfaction   Generally, where whim, taste, sensibility, or judgment is involved, a contract provision that the employee will perform to the employer's satisfaction makes the employer the sole judge of what this satisfaction is. The theory is that the relation of employer and employee is confidential and personal, and that such a satisfaction stipulation is equivalent to an agreement that the employee's performance depends on his service being agreeable to the employer. This is not to say, however, that the employer can act in bad faith. If the employee can show that the employer's actual reason for discharging the employee was other than dissatisfaction with the employee's services, then the employer has breached the contract, and the employee may be able to recover damages for wrongful discharge.[2]

---

[2] Discrimination against employees is discussed in Chapter 51.

Employee's Willful Breach of Duty   An employer can terminate the employment contract at any time for an employee's willful breach of duty in the course of employment. An example is disobedience of a reasonable order. A single act of disobedience can justify the employee's discharge, even if no injury results to the employer. If the employer's order is unreasonable or illegal, however, its disobedience does not justify the employee's discharge.

Employee's Remedies   An employee who is discharged without good cause prior to expiration of a fixed term of service can sue for breach of the employment contract (see Chapter 18). The employee also has the option of treating the contract as rescinded and suing the employer under the theory of *quantum meruit.* That is, the employee would seek the reasonable value of the service already performed, as if the original contract had never been made.

Employee's Breach of Contract   An employee who breaches an employment contract by unjustifiably refusing to perform the required services is liable to the employer for damages. Employment contracts are not usually subject to specific enforcement, meaning that a court will not compel the employee to perform. However, statutes in some jurisdictions provide that a valid contract to perform a service of unique, extraordinary, or intellectual character, the loss of which cannot be reasonably or adequately compensated in damages, can be enforced against the employee for a term of up to a particular number of years, frequently seven. At times, a contract for the exclusive services of an artist or performer can be enforced indirectly by means of a *negative injunction,* which is an injunction restraining the employee from rendering services to others. The rationale for this approach is that in contracts involving unique personal services of such persons as star performers and athletes, the employer has contracted for the exclusive right to display the celebrity for a given period; part of the right for which the employer had bargained and compensated the celebrity is that no other entrepreneur will have the right to display the celebrity during the contract period.

50:9   Termination of At-Will Contracts

The general rule is that an *at-will employment*—employment having no specified term—can be terminated at the will of either party on notice to the other. Historically, an at-will employment could be terminated by the employer with or without cause. The employer's motive in the termination was immaterial, and the employee was said to suffer no legal wrong even though the employer may have been capricious in discharging him. Today, however, the employer's right to discharge an employee under an at-will contract is often limited by statutes or public policy considerations. For example, an employer is not permitted to discharge an employee for a reason that amounts to discrimination (see Chapter 51).

Retaliatory Discharge   An important judicially created restriction on an employer's otherwise arbitrary right to discharge an at-will employee is the recognition of a civil cause of action for wrongful discharge when an employee is discharged in retaliation for actions that are protected by public policy. This public policy exception to the at-will doctrine has been applied to afford civil relief to an employee discharged under such circumstances as (1) refusing to commit perjury in testimony before a state legislative committee, (2) filing a workers' compensation claim against the employer, (3) designating an attorney to negotiate terms and conditions of employment, (4) participating in legal union activities, and (5) filing a complaint under the Fair Labor Standards Act (discussed in 50:11). The rationale is that a retaliatory discharge is done in bad faith and is not in the best interest of the economic system or the public good.

In the following case, the court permitted a group of employees fired for refusing to take a polygraph test to sue for wrongful discharge.

Cordle

v

General Hugh Mercer Corp.
325 SE2d 111 (1984)
Supreme Court of Appeals of West Virginia

FACTS: Mercer operated a Holiday Inn motel. The plaintiffs were hired by Mercer as cleaning maids whose employment was terminable at will. In mid January 1981 the plaintiffs signed agreements which provided that, when required by Mercer, they would take a polygraph test. Subsequently, by memorandum dated June 3, 1982, Mercer notified the plaintiffs and other employees that polygraph testing would begin. The plaintiffs, however, refused to take a polygraph test, and on October 12, 1982, their employment with Mercer was terminated.

ISSUE: Did Mercer's termination of plaintiffs' employment for their failure to undergo a polygraph test violate a substantial public policy of the state?

RESULT: Yes. The mandatory submission to polygraph testing violates the individual right to privacy, an important policy of the state.

REASONING:

*   *   *

First, we conclude that "at will" employees need not be distinguished from other employees in terms of whether the termination of employment for refusal to take a polygraph test violates public policy. At will employees, as well as other employees, have certain protections in circumstances involving public policy. In *Harless v. First National Bank in*

Fairmont, . . . (1978), the plaintiff, an at will employee at a bank, asserted that he was discharged from his employment for attempting to require his employer to comply with federal and state consumer credit and protection laws. This Court noted that the protection of consumers covered by consumer credit and protection laws is a matter of public policy in West Virginia and that such a policy should not be frustrated by denying to the plaintiff a remedy, under the facts alleged, against his employer relating to the discharge. This Court, in *Harless,* held in the syllabus as follows:

> The rule that an employer has an absolute right to discharge an at will employee must be tempered by the principle that where the employer's motivation for the discharge is to contravene some substantial public policy principle, then the employer may be liable to the employee for damages occasioned by this discharge. . . .

[T]he West Virginia Supreme Court of Appeals, as discussed below, has also recognized that certain areas of an individual's life are entitled to protection from unwarranted intrusion. Specifically, as the following cases indicate, in West Virginia, a legally protected interest in privacy is recognized.

A bag which the plaintiff carried into a grocery store was searched by a grocery store employee in [Sutherland]. . . . Noting that the plaintiff's cause of action against the store was based upon a trespass which involved an invasion of the plaintiff's right of privacy, the West Virginia Supreme Court of Appeals indicated that the plaintiff could seek recovery. . . . Specifically, this Court held in syllabus point 3 as follows: "An illegal search by a private individual is a trespass in violation of the right of privacy." In [Roach] . . . , the plaintiff asserted that her landlord, the defendant, installed a listening device in the plaintiff's apartment by way of which the defendant heard the plaintiff's confidential conversations. The West Virginia Supreme Court of Appeals concluded in *Roach* that the plaintiff had a right to maintain an action for "invasion of privacy." This Court stated that "the right to privacy is an individual right that should be held inviolate. To hold otherwise, under modern means of communication, hearing devices, photography, and other technological advancements, would effectively deny valuable rights and freedoms to the individual." . . . Syllabus point 1 of *Roach* states as follows: "The right of privacy, including the right of an individual to be let alone and to keep secret his private communications, conversations and affairs, is a right the unwarranted invasion or violation of which gives rise to a common law right of action for damages."

Finally, in [Golden] . . . , this Court discussed the right of privacy in the context of teacher employment. In *Golden,* a high school guidance counselor was dismissed from her employment for "immorality." This Court reversed the guidance counselor's dismissal and noted, *inter alia,* that unless the alleged immoral conduct had an impact upon a teacher's fitness to teach or upon the school community, such a dismissal would improperly intrude "upon the teacher's right of privacy." . . .

The teachings of *Sutherland, Roach* and *Golden* indicate a continuing concern for the protection of the privacy of the individual.

We hold that it is contrary to the public policy of West Virginia for an employer to require or request that an employee submit to a polygraph test or similar test as a condition of employment, and although the rights of employees under that public policy are not absolute, in that under certain circumstances, . . . such a polygraph test or similar test may be permitted, the public policy against such testing is grounded upon the recognition in this State of an individual's interest in privacy. . . .

McHugh, Chief Justice.

50:10 Occupational Safety and Health

Each year, many American workers are killed, suffer disabling injuries, or contract occupational diseases such as silicosis, asbestosis, pesticide and chemical poisoning, and lung and liver cancer. Technological advances and new processes in American industry have introduced hazards to the workplace. For example, carcinogenic chemicals, lasers, ultrasonic energy, beryllium metal, epoxy resin, and pesticides all have presented threats to the health of workers. Historically, employers were slow to protect employees from the dangers of industrialization, and the courts' conservatism resulted in a hesitation to extend the employer's common-law liability to fit changed conditions of industrial life. Due in large part to public pressure, states and the federal government began enacting legislation to help alleviate this problem.

OSHA Congress took a major step toward the protection of employees when it enacted the *Occupational Safety and Health Act of 1970* (OSHA) [29 USC §§ 651 et seq.]. The purpose of OSHA is to assure every worker safe and healthful working conditions and to preserve the nation's human resources. The legislation is administered by the Occupational Safety and Health Administration, under the Department of Labor. The Secretary of Labor issues mandatory occupational safety and health standards, derived from established federal standards, national consensus standards, and new standards developed under procedures explained in the act's standards-making provision.

OSHA is complex and far-reaching legislation. The core of the statute is the so-called "general duty clause," setting forth duties of employers and employees with respect to occupational health and safety and mandating that employers furnish employees a place of employment free from "recognized hazards" likely to cause death or serious physical harm. A hazard from which an employer must protect the employee is deemed a recognized hazard if it (1) is a condition of common knowledge or general recognition in the particular industry and detectable by means of the senses, or (2) is of such wide recognition as a hazard in the industry that even if it is not so detectable, there are generally known and accepted tests for its existence that should make its presence known to the employer. The act provides that each employee and employer must comply with occupational safety and health standards as well as all rules, regulations, and orders issued under the act applicable to his own actions and conduct.

Inspections   OSHA provides for inspections and investigations of workplaces by the Secretary of Labor and for the issuance of citations to employers who violate the act's provisions or regulations issued under it. A citation fixes a reasonable time for abatement of the violation; an employer who fails to abate a violation can face severe civil and criminal penalties. Any employer has the right to contest a citation, which is done in an administrative proceeding. Ultimately, the employer can file an appeal to the United States Court of Appeals from an adverse administrative decision.

Periodic Reports   Inadequacies in employers' reporting of occupational injuries or illnesses were recognized by Congress in enacting OSHA. As a result, the act sets forth a mandatory system of record-keeping and reporting. Among other things, employers are required to maintain a log of occupational injuries and illnesses, and to compile an annual summary of these injuries and illnesses based on information contained in the log. The shift from voluntary to mandatory compliance in the reporting of injuries and illnesses means that virtually all employers are now required to maintain records of work-related injuries and illnesses and to report their injury experience to the Bureau of Labor Statistics on request.

50:11   Fair Labor Standards Act

In 1938, Congress enacted the *Fair Labor Standards Act* (FLSA) [29 USC § 201 et seq.], which is also known as the Wage and Hour Law. The FLSA regulates hours and wages of employees engaged in commerce or involved in production of goods for commerce, and it prohibits oppressive child labor. It is administered by the Wage and Hour Division of the Department of Labor, which is empowered to establish and use local agencies to assist in carrying out the law. The act places a floor under wages and a ceiling over hours of employment. It also spreads employment among a greater number of workers by putting financial pressure on employers (by requiring extra pay for overtime work) and reinforces employee bargaining power concerning hourly wages (by prohibiting wage rates below certain levels).

The minimum wage provisions of the FLSA are read into and become part of every employment contract that is subject to the terms of the act. The effect of these provisions is to make an employee a creditor of his employer regardless of any actual attempted agreement as to compensation. Thus, the employer and employee are at liberty to contract with reference to hours and compensation in any manner they wish, *as long as the compensation to be paid is not less than the minimum fixed by the act.*

An employer should have its personnel director and legal counsel meet periodically for a review of how the minimum wage, overtime, equal pay, or hiring practices of the business are affected by recent legislation, amendments, or regulations. A good start is to contact the nearest Wage and Hour Division office for a copy of its latest amendments. Employees, either as individuals or as union members, are advised to do the same.

Key Concepts and Terms

- The relationship of employer and employee is contractual, and its creation is determined by principles governing formation of contracts generally. There is an implied provision of good faith and fair dealing in every employment contract.
- An employee has certain rights in the employment setting as to privacy. For example, there are statutory and judicial limits on the employer's right to administer lie detector tests and to conduct surveillance on employees.
- An employer is liable to an employee for injuries received in the course of employment that result from the employer's negligence. The employer may assert defenses ordinarily applicable in negligence cases.
- Under workers' compensation legislation, enacted in most jurisdictions, the theory of negligence is discarded, common-law defenses are eliminated, and the worker is given a right to compensation for all injuries arising from his or her employment.
- Under the doctrine of respondeat superior, even though an employer is personally innocent of wrongdoing, he may be vicariously liable for his employees' torts committed within the scope of employment.
- When an employment contract fixes no duration, the term of employment extends for the period that the parties have agreed on for payment of salary or wages. If the contract is for a fixed period, the employer can legally discharge an employee prior to its expiration only for "good cause."
- The general rule is that an at-will employment relationship—employment having no specified term—can be terminated at the will of either party on notice to the other. Historically, at-will employment could be terminated solely at the employer's discretion, but today the employer may be limited in this right by statute or public policy considerations.
- The Occupational Safety and Health Act of 1970 (OSHA) was enacted to give workers safer and healthier working conditions and to help preserve the nation's human resources.
- The Fair Labor Standards Act was enacted by Congress to set minimum wage levels for industries engaged in interstate commerce.

- At-Will Employment
- Course and Scope of Employment
- Dual Purpose Doctrine

- Fair Labor Standards Act
- Fellow Servant Doctrine
- Negative Injunction

- Occupational Safety and Health Act of 1970
- Polygraph Test
- Quantum Meruit
- Respondeat Superior
- Vicarious Liability
- Workers' Compensation

Questions and Case Problems

1. What is the difference between an employee and (a) an independent contractor and (b) an agent?

2. Gary operates a motor scooter supplied to him by the Rainbow Ice Cream Company for selling ice cream. He operates within an area designated by Rainbow, works whenever he pleases, pays his own expenses (including gas and oil), and sells the ice cream at prices fixed by Rainbow, later accounting to Rainbow for a percentage of the profits. While selling ice cream, Gary is injured when his scooter is struck by a hit-and-run driver. Gary sues Rainbow for his injuries. Should he recover?

3. The Thrush Paper Corporation sponsors an annual company picnic for its employees and their guests. During the course of a picnic, an employee playing in the traditional company baseball game hits a fly ball that leaves the park, strikes Larry, who is walking on the sidewalk adjacent to the park, and seriously injures him. Larry sues Thrush for his injuries. Will Larry win the case? Would it make any difference if Larry, too, were an employee of Thrush who was leaving the picnic at the time of the accident?

4. C & SRM, a consulting firm, employed Wildman as vice-president in charge of its technical team. Wildman was told from the beginning that it was his job to head up the "technical team" and not to make executive decisions. In early August the president of C & SRM called the technical team together and explained that the firm's income was down and that some expenses would be curtailed. As a result, Wildman and other officers of the firm became apprehensive and sought an outside buyer for the firm. Wildman went so far as to contact an investor and propose three alternative reorganization plans for the firm, with the idea that the firm would be acquired by the outside investor or that the technical team would leave C & SRM and form a separate firm. When the president of the firm learned of Wildman's actions, he fired Wildman, claiming a breach of the duty of loyalty and action exceeding his scope of authority. Wildman sues for breach of his contract of employment. Is the president correct?

5. Corey is employed by the Maser Electronics Company as its chief physicist. His employment contract specifies that his employment is "conditional on service and conduct being satisfactory to Maser Electronics, who shall be the sole judge in this regard." Later, Maser discharges Corey simply because it cannot afford to pay his high salary any longer. Corey sues Maser for breach of contract. How should the case be decided? Would it make any difference if Maser had discharged Corey so that it could hire a more qualified physicist?

6. Ralph is a salesman for the Reilly Shoe Company and is on the road, showing the new line of Reilly shoes to potential customers. On his way to see a customer, he stops at a local drive-in for lunch. While eating a hamburger, he has a "cafe coronary." That is, a portion of the hamburger becomes lodged in his throat, and he dies from suffocation. Is Ralph's death covered under workers' compensation

legislation? Would it make a difference if the incident had occurred after Ralph had seen the customer and was on his way home?

7. On October 22, 1974, Berkey Photo reported the theft of a case of cameras to the police. Two detectives went to the plant and met with Berkey's director of security, Ahern. It was established that during the preceding weekend the cameras had been stolen from a small area of the plant which had been accessible to only six employees. The police detectives found four of the six employees willing to take polygraph tests, and therefore recommended to Berkey that it ask all six employees to take the polygraphs. All six agreed. Berkey arranged for a private polygraph operator to conduct the test because use of state police operators would require a month's delay. One employee failed the test and was fired. Berkey is now being prosecuted under a state criminal statute that forbids employers to require polygraphs as a condition of employment. Berkey defends on the ground that the police initiated the polygraph investigation. Is this an adequate defense? Should it be an adequate defense?

8. Fred is employed by the Delcorte Hardware Company, which has, in the past few months, been subject to losses of items the company believes are being taken by a ring of employees in its main store. For this reason, and unknown to the employees in the main store, Delcorte installs closed-circuit television cameras which maintain continual surveillance on the employees from one-way windows in the ceiling. On discovering this surveillance procedure, Fred sues Delcorte for invasion of privacy, and he is immediately fired for "disloyalty" to the store. Fred sues again, this time for breach of contract. How should the case be decided? Why?

9. An employee of Careless Company has a demonstrated allergy to smoke from cigarettes. She sues to require the company to prohibit cigarette smoking in the vicinity of her work station. She alleges that Careless is subjecting her to work in "unsafe conditions" within the meaning of state occupational health and safety legislation. Should Careless be required to comply with the employee's demand?

10. Kopfman was employed by Freedom Drilling Company as a driller. Kopfman was required to provide his own transportation to drilling rigs, and he was not paid for the time spent traveling to and from rigs. Kopfman's supervisor Howard, however, was responsible for assembling a drilling crew and was paid by Freedom for his travel. Howard drove a 1979 Chevrolet Blazer which had been modified to run on propane fuel rather than gasoline. Howard routinely drove his crew members, including Kopfman, to the rig. One morning Kopfman was in Howard's Blazer when Howard stopped near an oil well site to fill his Blazer with propane. The propane exploded and severely injured Kopfman. Kopfman sues Freedom in respondeat superior for the actions of its employee Howard in the course and scope of his employment. Freedom defends on the ground that Kopfman's exclusive remedy lies with the Workers' Compensation Act and that his suit for negligence is barred. Kopfman argues that he was not acting within his scope and course of employment and therefore is neither covered by nor barred by the Workers' Compensation Act. What result?

51 Labor Relations and Job Discrimination

51:1 Introduction to Labor Relations

The Industrial Revolution brought sweeping changes to the workplace. Industrial empires hiring hundreds, thousands, then tens of thousands of employees spread across the land. This change created jobs for the common worker, but it created problems as well. Early labor unions and craft guilds were no match for employers whose interests were nearly always protected by the courts. At common law, for example, employees' collective activities, such as a strike for higher wages or safer working conditions, were frequently held to be criminal conspiracies and were enjoined under penalty of heavy fine or imprisonment. Finally, in 1914, Congress enacted the Clayton Antitrust Act [15 USC §§ 12–18]. The Act narrowed the availability of injunctions against labor organizations in cases involving employers and employees. It allows an injunction only if necessary to prevent irreparable harm to property, and only if no adequate legal remedy exists. However, far more by way of legislative action was required before employees were able to organize effectively to bargain for employment rights.

Modern American labor law is grounded on several federal statutes, which are discussed later in this chapter. Together, these statutes establish the right of workers to form unions and bargain with an employer. They prohibit unfair labor practices, recognize industrial arbitration, set forth labor's and management's rights and duties in the labor field, and establish individual employee rights as to employers and unions.

51:2 Right to Strike and Organize

A strike is a cessation of work by employees—or a refusal to work at their usual speed—to obtain more favorable terms from their employer. Before protective legislation was passed, courts frequently halted strikes by temporary injunction on employers' showings that the particular strike was "unjustified" or causing the employer "irreparable harm." Enactment of the Norris–LaGuardia Act of 1932 [29 USC §§ 101 et seq.] was a significant step toward the development of a national labor policy. It accorded full freedom to employees to organize and negotiate the terms and conditions of their employment through representatives of their choosing, and it limited the issuance of restraining orders and injunctions against unions by federal courts. The act expressly makes unenforceable a so-called *yellow-dog contract*, which is any agreement between employees and a company in which an employee promises either not to become or remain a member of any labor organization or to withdraw from the employment relationship if he joins any labor organization.

The Norris–LaGuardia Act did not place affirmative obligations on employers to negotiate with labor unions, but it assisted union organization and collective bargaining by modifying prior judicial decisions concerning the unions' role. In summary, the act (1) provides employees freedom of organization, association, and designation of representatives; (2) prevents federal courts from issuing injunctions in almost any case "involving or growing out of a labor dispute"; and (3) refuses injunctive relief to any person failing to make "every reasonable effort" to settle labor disputes by negotiation or mediation. In addition, the *National Labor Relations Act* (see 51:3), which expressly guarantees employees the right "to engage in other concerted activities for the purpose of collective bargaining or other mutual aid or protection," safeguards the right to strike for employees in commerce by preventing the states from regulating peaceful strikes in industries affecting commerce.

Picketing "Picketing" means walking or patrolling in the vicinity of a place of business involved in a labor dispute and, by word of mouth, banner, or placard, undertaking to inform the public about the dispute. Picketing may be intended to persuade workers to stay away from or quit their jobs, or to advise members of the public of the labor dispute and influence them to withhold patronage from the business being picketed. At common law, picketing was lawful in employer–employee controversies only when both its method and its object was legal.

State regulation of peaceful picketing is today subject to two principal limitations. The first is the free speech guaranty of the First Amendment to the Constitution. Although picketing has an element of communication, and this element is not lost simply because a labor dispute is involved. Peaceful picketing can, however, be restrained by the state when it is for an unlawful purpose, such as in support of an illegal strike. Picketing carried on with intimidation, threats, coercion, or force is illegal. Also unlawful is picketing conducted with vandalism or other overt criminal activity.

The second principal limitation on state regulation of peaceful picketing is *federal preemption* of the field, meaning that when the federal government has taken exclusive control over a given legal area, the states cannot act in that area. The National Labor Relations Act, discussed below, provides that a state cannot enjoin peaceful and legal picketing against an industry engaged in interstate commerce. Because so many businesses have been held to be "engaged in interstate commerce" as that phrase has been interpreted by the courts, the federal statute governs more often than not.

51:3 Expansion of Labor's Rights

During the New Deal Congress continued its movement toward encouraging unionism and collective bargaining. The National Labor Relations Act of 1935 (NLRA) [29 USC §§ 151 et seq.], also known as the Wagner Act, was the genesis of the present-day comprehensive federal legislation that regulates labor relations affecting interstate commerce. The NLRA's purposes are as follows:

- Removal of obstructions to the free flow of interstate commerce
- Promotion of industrial peace through fair, prompt, and just labor dispute settlements
- Balancing of labor's and management's competing interests
- Protection of employees' right of collective action in securing satisfactory wages, hours, and employment conditions
- Prevention of employers' unfair labor practices
- Establishment of national labor laws uniformly administered and enforced

The constitutionality of the NLRA was upheld by the United States Supreme Court.[1] The Court rejected contentions that the act was beyond congressional authority under the commerce clause, that it invaded Tenth Amendment rights of the states, and that it denied employers due process of law by restricting freedom of contract.

Sections 3 and 4 of the NLRA create the National Labor Relations Board (NLRB), which is given jurisdiction to administer the act and control over *unfair labor practices* and questions of union representation. The NLRB has power to issue and prosecute complaints under the act. Section 7, the heart of the act, guarantees that employees have the right to organize, form, join, or assist labor organizations; bargain collectively through representatives of their choosing; and engage in concerted activities for the purpose of collective bargaining. Section 8 of the act imposes on employers the duty to bargain collectively with the union designated as the exclusive representative for the employees. Section 8 also lists unfair labor practices on the part of employers. Examples are (1) interfering with, restraining, or coercing employees in the exercise of their right to form a union; (2) unlawfully assisting or sponsoring a labor union; (3) discriminating against employees because of union activity; (4) refusing to bargain collectively with a designated employee representative; and (5) discriminating against employees who file charges with the NLRB.

Notwithstanding its significance, the NLRA was not intended as "complete" labor legislation, and three factors particularly influenced subsequent changes and extensions in the law: (1) the act was concerned with the organizing phase of labor relations; (2) it dealt exclusively with restraining *employer* unfair labor practices, not union practices; and (3) it left substantive terms of employment entirely to private negotiation.

---

[1] *NLRB v Jones & Laughlin Steel Corp.,* 301 US 1 (1937).

51:4   The Swing Back Toward Management

As a result of favorable governmental policy toward unionism and sympathetic enforcement of the NLRA, union membership increased from 3 million to 15 million employees between 1935 and 1947. During this period, nationwide strikes occurred in entire industries, at times crippling national production of coal, textiles, lumber, oil, and both maritime and rail transportation. The public became alarmed in the years following, and the pendulum of public sentiment began swinging towards management. Congress responded to this movement in 1947 when it enacted the *Labor Management Relations Act* (LMRA) [29 USC §§ 141–144, 151–158], also known as the Taft–Hartley Act.

The LMRA was intended to lessen industrial disputes and place employers on an equal position with unions in bargaining and labor relations. It attempted to achieve a "balance of obligations" by recognizing that unions, too, could be guilty of unfair labor practices. Under the act, it is an unfair labor practice for a union to (1) refuse to bargain collectively with an employer; (2) coerce or restrain an employee in the exercise of his right to refrain from joining a union; (3) cause, or attempt to cause, an employer to discriminate against an employee who is not a union member; (4) impose excessive initiation fees to join a union; or (5) engage in *featherbedding* (forcing an employer to pay for unperformed work).

The LMRA provides that the President can intervene in industrywide disputes that would "imperil the national health or safety" if allowed to continue and, by invoking certain machinery under the law, ask a federal district court for an 80-day injunction against a strike or work stoppage imperiling national health or safety. The act also undertakes to regulate certain provisions in the collective bargaining agreement itself by, for example, outlawing the "closed shop" (in which employees have to be union members as a prerequisite to employment). Furthermore, the act provides for legal remedies both to enforce labor agreements and to recover damages for their breach.

51:5   Collective Bargaining

Section 8(d) of the NLRA imposes on both the union and the employer a mandatory duty "to meet at reasonable times and confer in good faith with respect to wages, hours and other terms and conditions of employment." Since the act does not define "wages, hours and other terms and conditions of employment," the NLRB and the courts determine what subjects are within the statutory requirements. An employer sometimes refuses to bargain collectively with a union as to a mandatory bargaining subject [a subject that the NLRB has ruled falls within the scope of § 8(d)]. In that event, the NLRB can petition a United States Court of Appeals for enforcement of its order against the employer to bargain with the union, as illustrated in the following case.

NLRB
v
Gulf Power Co.
384 F2d 822 (1967)
United States Court of Appeals, Fifth Circuit

FACTS: The NLRB petitioned the United States Court of Appeals for enforcement of its order requiring that an employer (Gulf Power Company) bargain collectively with a union as to safety rules and practices. The NLRB argued that safety rules and practices are "other terms and conditions of employment" within the meaning of NLRA § 8(d).

ISSUE: Are safety rules and practices included as "other terms and conditions of employment" within the meaning of the National Labor Relations Act and are they therefore mandatory subjects of collective bargaining.

RESULT: Yes. Safety rules are mandatory subjects of collective bargaining.

REASONING:

*   *   *

The issue we must decide is whether safety rules and safe work practices are mandatory subjects of collective bargaining under the provisions of Sections 8(d) of the Act relating to the mutual obligation of the employer and the employer and the Union "to meet at reasonable times and confer in good faith with respect to wages, hours and *other terms and conditions of employment. . . .* " [Court's emphasis.]

For more than twenty years the Union has been the exclusive bargaining agent for Gulf Power's employees in an appropriate unit. Gulf Power Company is a public utility engaged in the generation, transmission and sale of electric power, with principal offices at Pensacola, Florida, and is engaged in commerce within the meaning of the Act. A collective bargaining contract was entered into between the Company and the Union on December 27, 1962, effective until August 15, 1964, and from year to year thereafter unless either party should give notice of termination or revision. Article VI of said contract entitled "Safety" contained several provisions relative to safe employment practices. The Company also embodied other safety provisions in a 60-page "Safe Work Practices" handbook, prepared by it and issued to all employees, which provided also for discipline or discharge of employees who violated its provisions. . . . On April 30, 1963, the Company unilaterally revised its safety rules. On June 3, 1963, the Union wrote the Company that it protested the

Company's action in having on April 30, 1963 unilaterally placed a revised set of safety rules in operation without having bargained on this subject with the Union. The Company replied that it was required by law to provide reasonably safe and healthful places of employment for its employees, to provide compensation for workmen injured in the course of their employment; that this responsibility rested exclusively with it; and that it could not share its obligations with the Union and could not agree that the Union "take any part in the formulation of policy in respect to safety procedures or other matters for which it bears no responsibility under the law." The Union accordingly filed an unfair labor practice charge against the Company which it withdrew shortly thereafter. On June 15, 1964, the Company and the Union notified each other of intention to revise the contract between them. . . .

A number of bargaining sessions were held at which the Union stated that it was concerned about safety and wanted some type or program of cooperation with the Company on safety. The Company replied that it would be glad to discuss safety with the Union but was of the view that it could not delegate its responsibility for promulgating and regularly revising safety rules. After six bargaining sessions the Company steadfastly declined to bargain with reference to the promulgation and revision of safe work practice rules, maintaining that this was exclusively the legal and moral nondelegable responsibility of the Company. The present complaint of unfair labor practice was accordingly filed. The Board held a hearing after which it concluded that the Company's action in declining to bargain with the Union with respect to safe work practices and/or safety rules violated Section 8(a) (5) and (1) of the Act. We agree and accordingly order enforcement of the order. It is inescapable that in a public utility electric generating and transmission company the workers, through their chosen representative, should have the right to bargain with the Company in reference to safe work practices. This is not to say that there are not areas where the Company's obligations to the public are paramount and which may not properly be the subject of an agreement with the Union after a bargaining session is held. Nonetheless, the parties by their own actions in the past have clearly indicated that they consider safety rules and practices a bargainable issue by including several important provisions in Article VI of the contract already referred to. . . .

Ainsworth, Circuit Judge.

The end result of successful *collective bargaining* is a *collective bargaining agreement*, the labor contract that sets forth the rights and duties of the employer and the union. This contract is a generalized code to govern situations that those who drafted it could not wholly anticipate. Thus, it is not an ordinary contract governed by general contract principles. Indeed, central to an understanding of labor relations is the concept that the collective bargaining agreement is not a simple product of a consensual relationship, but rather covers the whole employment relationship and calls into being a new common law—the common law of a particular industry or shop.

Section 301 of the LMRA provides that suits to enforce terms of collective bargaining agreements between an employer and a union representing employees in an industry affecting commerce, or between two labor organizations, can be brought in any federal district court having jurisdiction. While § 301 expressly authorizes only "employers and unions" to sue one another for breach of the collective bargaining agreement, the United States Supreme Court has held that even individual employees can sue their employers to vindicate "uniquely personal rights" under the contract, such as special employment conditions or special rates of pay.[2]

51:6   Arbitration and Mediation

Virtually all collective bargaining agreements contain arbitration provisions. In the context of labor relations, *arbitration* is the process by which a dispute that cannot be settled voluntarily through an agreement's grievance procedure is referred to an impartial person–the arbitrator–for resolution. Both parties must agree in advance to accept the arbitrator's decision as final and binding. The decision itself is made on the basis of the evidence presented and arguments made at an arbitration hearing. Processing of an employee's grievance under a collective bargaining agreement usually consists of four steps: (1) presentation of the case to the employee's immediate supervisor; (2) if settlement is not obtained, presentation of the case in writing to the proper division superintendent; (3) if no agreement results, submission for determination by a company executive; and finally (4) if the executive's decision is not satisfactory, referral to the impartial arbitrator. The arbitrator acts according to the prevailing rules of arbitration law and the accepted practice and custom that has developed regarding industrial relations. Prior arbitration awards in similar cases are not binding or conclusive, although they have value as persuasive force. Generally, the "controlling law" is the collective bargaining agreement signed by the parties.

 As part of the consideration for an employer's agreement to arbitrate grievances or disputes arising under a collective bargaining agreement, the union usually will agree to a "no strike" clause. This means that the union will agree not to strike or cause work stoppages or slowdowns because of any dispute or grievance that is subject to arbitration.

Judicial Enforcement of Arbitration Agreement   The courts have made it clear that enforcement of arbitration clauses is crucial to industrial peace and that specific performance is the best means of assuring enforcement. Accordingly, when either an employer or a union refuses to arbitrate as provided in

---

[2] *Smith v Evening News Asso.*, 371 US 195 (1962).

the collective bargaining agreement, and the grievance procedure has been followed, as discussed above, the other party can sue in federal court to compel the nonbargaining party to arbitrate according to the terms of the agreement. Arbitration awards can also be enforced in federal court.

The question sometimes arises whether a particular grievance falls within the arbitration clause of a collective bargaining agreement. In such a case, the courts have ruled that all claims or grievances are to be resolved in favor of arbitration. Hence, if the claim of an employer or employee seeking arbitration *on its face* appears to fall within the scope of the arbitration clause, the court must order the opposing party to arbitrate that claim.

The substantive decision of the arbitrator can be reviewed by the courts in only a narrow and limited way. The judge's analysis in the following case represents the judicial attitude toward review of arbitration awards.

Ethyl Corp.

v

United Steelworkers of America
768 F2d 180 (1985)
United States Court of Appeals, Seventh Circuit

FACTS: Ethyl's collective bargaining agreement with Steelworkers provided that an employee with one or more years' service who had worked 1,040 hours during a calendar year and was "on the payroll" on December 31 was entitled to paid vacation the following year. It also provided that if a worker was laid off for any reason before December 31, the right to paid vacation would accrue in the following year if the worker was reemployed and worked 200 hours in the new year. In early December 1981 Ethyl closed a plant and discharged 33 workers who had worked more than 1,040 hours in 1981. The workers claimed a right to payment for 1982 vacation time, arguing that the 200-hour provision applied only where the worker had been laid off with a chance of recall, not to plant closings. An arbitrator agreed and awarded the workers vacation pay. Ethyl then sought to overturn the arbitrator's award.

ISSUE: Was the arbitrator's award beyond the terms of the collective bargaining agreement and therefore violative of the "essence of the agreement"?

RESULT: No. The arbitrator was merely interpreting the contract, not creating terms additional to the contract.

REASONING:

*   *   *

Ever since federal courts began enforcing arbitration awards, the scope of judicial review of the award has been extremely narrow. "Arbitrators are judges chosen by the parties to decide the matters submitted to them, finally and without appeal. As a mode of settling disputes it should receive every encouragement from courts of equity. If the award is within the submission, and contains the honest decision of the arbitrators, after a full and fair hearing of the parties, a court of equity will not set it aside for error either in law or fact. A contrary course would be a substitution of the judgment of the Chancellor in place of the judges chosen by the parties, and would make an award the commencement, not the end, of litigation." . . . To this we add that for judges to have taken upon themselves to determine the correctness of the arbitrator's award would inevitably have judicialized the arbitration process, in much the same way that judicial review, even of a deferential sort, tends to judicialize the administrative process. The administrative agency must (at least when its proceedings resemble adjudication) find facts like a court, and reason like a court, if it is to withstand correction by the court. And so it would be with arbitrators if their decisions were subject to the kind of review that courts give agencies. Yet the idea of arbitration, as of administrative decision-making but more strongly since there is no counterpart in arbitration to the Administrative Procedure Act, is to provide an alternative to judicial dispute resolution, not an echo of it. If the parties to an arbitration want appellate review of the merits of the arbitrator's decision, they can establish appellate arbitration panels, though they rarely do. But they cannot get such review from the federal courts—which would mean, first from the district court, and then, on appeal, from the court of appeals. This would make arbitration a three-tiered, rather than as in normal adjudication a two-tiered, process; it would make arbitration more judicial than adjudication. . . .

Whenever an arbitrator misreads a contract, it is possible to say that his award fails to draw its essence from the contract; that the ground of the award is not the contract but the arbitrator's misreading. But so long as the award is based on the arbitrator's interpretation—unsound though it may be—of the contract, it draws its essence from the contract. . . . It is only when the arbitrator *must* have based his award on some body of thought, or feeling, or policy, or law that is outside the contract (and not incorporated in it by reference, either, . . . that the award can be said not to "draw its essence from the collective bargaining agreement," as in our recent decisions. . . .

Now often it will be unclear whether the arbitrator has interpreted the contract or relied on some private notion of equity; and though any reasonable doubt must be resolved in favor of enforcing the award, . . . if the arbitrator here had said or implied that although the workers had not complied with a condition precedent to earning their paid vacations fairness required that they get vacations (or pay in lieu thereof), the district judge would have been right to set aside the award. But that would not be a proper characterization of what the arbitrator did. He applied what is after all a traditional principle of contract law: that you cannot prevent the other party to the contract from fulfilling a condition precedent to your own performance, and then use that failure to justify your nonperformance. . . . If Ethyl had laid off these workers without shutting down the plant, they would have had a chance to earn a paid vacation in 1982. For they might have been recalled in 1982, and if so they would have had to work only 200 hours in 1982 to be entitled to a paid vacation that year. The company eliminated that chance; it must bear the consequence. . . .

We have gone on at such length because we want to make clear that we take seriously the twin propositions that (1) the reviewing court's function (whether the district court's, or this court's) is at an end when it concludes that what the arbitrator did was interpretation of the contract, and (2) when in doubt the court must find that it was interpretation. We do not want to be plagued by cases in which companies or unions refuse to comply with arbitration awards merely because they think the arbitrator clearly misinterpreted the collective bargaining agreement. If parties to collective bargaining contracts are unhappy with arbitration awards they can bargain for a different method of selecting arbitrators, or for panels of arbitrators, trial or appellate. . . .

Posner, Circuit Judge.

Labor Mediation and Conciliation Services   Unlike arbitration, in which disputed issues are decided by a third person, *mediation and conciliation* is a process by which disputing parties are encouraged to reach an agreement on their own initiative. Typically, mediators do not propose settlements, and they never reach "decisions." Rather, they function as intermediaries between the parties, helping to create the proper "atmosphere for settlement." Toward this end, Congress created an independent agency known as the Federal Mediation and Conciliation Service, which has the duty of assisting parties to settle labor disputes through mediation and conciliation. During the course of any strike or protracted labor dispute, it is not unusual for one or both parties to decide that a point has been reached at which settlement must be had at all costs. At this time a labor mediator, whether federal, state, or local, might be able to serve as the catalyst to revive bogged-down negotiations, hastening the end of the strike or dispute.

51:7   Rights of Individuals

The NLRA, amended in 1947 by the LMRA, was further amended by Congress in 1959, when it enacted the *Labor Management Reporting and Disclosure Act* (LMRDA) [29 USC §§ 401, 402 et al.], also known as the Landrum–Griffin Act. The LMRDA is intended to eliminate certain improper practices of both unions and employers that had resulted in frequent deprivation of employees' rights. The act regulates the internal affairs of unions and establishes what has been termed a "bill of rights" for union members. Under the act, union members have (1) equal rights and privileges to nominate union officers and participate and vote in union membership meetings; (2) the right of free speech at union meetings; (3) procedural safeguards as to union dues, fees, and assessments; and (4) due process safeguards against improper union disciplinary actions. The act also gives union members the right to inspect union policy and financial statements, to be informed as to the provisions of the act, and to sue (when the union itself fails to do so) to recover misappropriated union assets.

Job Discrimination

51:8   Introduction to Job Discrimination

There may be no more fundamental right than the right to work and be treated fairly and equally by an employer. An interference with the right to fairness and equal treatment constitutes job discrimination, and numerous remedies are available to prevent it. For example, several states and municipalities have enacted fair employment practices laws, and an increasing number of collective bargaining agreements contain antidiscrimination provisions. In addition, there are several federal laws prohibiting discrimination in employment.

The most far-reaching federal statute in this regard is *Title VII of the Civil Rights Act of 1964* [42 USC §§ 2000e et seq.]. Title VII forbids discrimination in employment on the basis of race, color, religion, sex, or national origin. This prohibition is directed against most employers, employment agencies, and unions. It applies to any employer (1) engaged in an industry affecting commerce and (2) having 15 or more employees. Title VII does not, however, apply to other types of job discrimination, and it is intended neither to guarantee a job to every person regardless of his or her qualifications nor to command that any person be hired simply because he or she was formerly the subject of discrimination or a member of a minority group. Rather, Title VII forbids discriminatory job preferences for *any* group—minority or majority—by requiring the removal of artificial, arbitrary, and unnecessary barriers to employment when they operate invidiously to discriminate on the basis of impermissible classifications. Title VII is enforced through lawsuits both by private individuals and by the federal *Equal Employment Opportunity Commission* (EEOC), an administrative agency.

51:9 Racial Discrimination

Racial discrimination in employment can take a variety of forms and arise in many types of practices. For example, an employer's seniority system might operate to discriminate against persons of a particular race, as might a termination policy.

Courts have invalidated job requirements that have a disparate effect on the hiring of racial minorities and bear no clear relationship to job performance. For example, courts have held that requiring a high school diploma is impermissible if it effectively eliminates a racial minority and if there is no evidence that attainment of the diploma is related to job performance. The use of pre-employment tests is examined in the following case.

Gillespie

v

State of Wisconsin
771 F2d 1035 (1985)
United States Court of Appeals, Seventh Circuit

FACTS: Gillespie was one of 40 unsuccessful minority applicants for the position of Personnel Specialist I or Personnel Manager I with the State of Wisconsin. Gillespie allegedly was eliminated on the basis of an essay examination that the state had instituted because former tests used by the state had been held to have an inordinate adverse impact on minority applicants. The test was designed to test applicants' ability to use standard English and to analyze and organize information.

ISSUE: Did the state's use of the essay examination impermissibly discriminate against members of a racial minority?

RESULT: No. The examination was sufficiently related to job performance.

REASONING:

*   *   *

A test is job-related if it measures traits that are significantly related to the applicant's ability to perform the job. . . . The Uniform Guidelines on Employee Selections Procedures, 29 C.F.R. § 1607 *et seq.* (1978) ("Guidelines"), provide that an employer may conduct professional validation studies to determine whether its employment tests are job-related. The Uniform Guidelines draw upon current psychological literature on psychometrics as well as standards of test validation established by the American Psychological Association. . . . The Uniform Guidelines recognize three methods of validating employment tests: criterion—related, content, and construct validity. . . . The choice of validation strategy depends upon the type of inference the user wishes to draw from the test scores. . . .

A. Appropriateness of the Choice of a Content Validation Strategy.

1. The Uniform Guidelines do not favor criterion-related validity.

Gillespie points to two sections of the Uniform Guidelines and the APA Standards as support for his contention that the Uniform Guidelines prefer criterion-related validity. According to Gillespie, the APA Standards, incorporated by reference into the Uniform Guidelines, express a preference for criterion-related validity. . . . A review of the Uniform Guidelines and the relevant psychological literature reveals no preference for criterion-related validity. . . . [T]hose psychometricians who have studied employment tests have determined that criterion-related validation is often impracticable because of the limited numbers of employees available for test development and several measurement errors. . . . Thus, neither the Uniform Guidelines nor the psychological literature express a blanket preference for criterion-related validity. . . .

2. Whether the choice of a content validation strategy was appropriate for the characteristics to be measured.

Gillespie points to the district court's finding that one purpose of the test was to measure an applicant's ability to prepare written position descriptions and argues that the testing of this ability was inappropriate because writing a job description is a skill readily learned within the first few months of employment. The Uniform Guidelines caution that, "[i]n general, users should avoid making employment decisions on the basis of measures of knowledges, skills or abilities which are normally learned in a brief orientation period, and which have an adverse impact." . . . Use of tests which measure knowledge of factual information that will be acquired in a training program, "risks favoring applicants with prior exposure to that information, a course likely to discriminate against a disadvantaged minority." . . .

. . . [W]e reach the ultimate issue of whether the content validation strategy adopted by the DER was appropriate under the circumstances. Both Deborah Koyen and Daniel Wallock, a testing expert employed by the DER, testified that the purpose of the written examination was to screen out those persons who did not possess the fundamental skills necessary to perform as a Personnel Specialist/Personnel Manager I. A test that screens candidates for fundamental skills may be validated by the content validation procedure. . . . Furthermore, a review of the characteristics to be measured by the test and of the form of the test reveals that a content validation method was appropriate. The abilities to communicate in standard written English, to prepare a written job description, and to place the analysis of a recruiting problem in acceptable form are concrete, observable and quantifiable characteristics. Moreover, planning a recruiting trip and writing a job description and a memorandum closely simulate the actual work performed by a Personnel Specialist/Personnel Manager I. Because the test measured concrete characteristics in a form that simulated actual work behavior, we hold that the content validation procedure could be employed to validate the test.

B. Sufficiency of the Content Validation Study Conducted by the DER.

Gillespie argues that the job analysis performed by the DER as part of its content validation of the written test was inadequate, thus rendering the content validation study insufficient, because the job specialists were not trained in psychometrics and were unfamiliar with the job of Personnel Specialist/Personnel Managers I. An examination of the Uniform Guidelines and the APA Standards fails to reveal that job specialists must be trained psychometricians. The function of the job specialist is to provide the test developer with a detailed description of the position and to weigh and identify the knowledges, skills and abilities needed to perform the job. . . . The only qualification for being a job specialist is knowledge of the position to be analyzed. . . . Since the record amply demonstrates that the employees were knowledgeable about the positions, they were qualified to be job specialists. Because the position analysis was conducted by qualified job specialists who identified the necessary knowledges, skills and abilities required for the work and also ranked and weighted the elements as to the importance for the position, we hold that the plaintiff's contention that the position analysis was inadequate fails to find support in the record. . . .

C. Reliability and Use of the Test Scores.

According to the record, a pretest was conducted to determine whether the questions and instructions were clear. Gillespie claims that the DER should have graded the pretest responses and correlated them with some measure of the pretestees' job performance. Correlating test scores of present employees with a measure of their job performance is a form of criterion-related validity (concurrent validation), . . . and is not required in a proper content validation study. . . . Furthermore, the defendants' expert testified that the number of employees taking the pretest was so small that a correlation between the test scores and job performance would be statistically meaningless. The expert's opinion that the sample size was too small to support a statistically meaningful correlation between the pretest scores and present work performance is confirmed by the psychometric literature on sample size. . . .

Coffey, Circuit Judge.

 Employment testing raises serious problems for employers and employees if the test has a disparate impact on the members of a racial or sexual group. Before relying on any test as a screening mechanism or as a substitute for more precise information about a job candidate's abilities, the employer should consult an expert in personnel testing/industrial psychology.

Title VII is the major weapon against racial discrimination in employment. It provides for relief if the court finds that the alleged discriminator "has intentionally engaged in or is intentionally engaging in an unlawful employment practice" as described in the statute. The United States Supreme Court has held that proof that an employer adopted a discriminatory employment practice, *whether purposely discriminatory or not*, establishes a violation of Title VII.[3] Moreover, although Title VII was intended to have prospective application only, relief has been granted to remedy present and continuing effects of past discrimination.

51:10   Sex Discrimination

Women in American society hold more than two of every five jobs in the civilian labor force, yet the average pay for women who work full time is less than three-fifths of the average for men. Congress took one step to alleviate this situation when it enacted the Equal Pay Act of 1963 [29 USC § 206(d)]. This act prohibits discrimination between employees on the basis of sex in determining wages paid for equal work on jobs requiring equal skill, effort, and responsibility, when the jobs are performed under similar working conditions. Amounts due an employee that have been withheld in violation of the act are regarded to be unpaid minimum wages or unpaid overtime compensation, in violation of the Fair Labor Standards Act (discussed in Chapter 50). Accordingly, action to obtain payment of these wages can be brought by the Wage and Hour Administrator of the Department of Labor or by any affected employee.

Title VII of the Civil Rights Act of 1964 also addresses the problem of sex discrimination. Under Title VII, employment decisions cannot be predicted on mere stereotyped impressions about characteristics of males or females. Myth and purely habitual assumptions about the inability of women to perform certain kinds of work are not acceptable reasons for refusing to employ

---

[3] *Griggs v Duke Power Co.*, 401 US 424 (1971).

qualified individuals or for paying them less. Furthermore, an employer may not burden female employees in such manner as to deny them employment opportunities because of their gender. For example, an employer's denial of accumulated seniority to female employees who return to work following disability caused by childbirth violates Title VII if the employer permits employees on leave for other nonoccupational disabilities to retain seniority.

To find an unlawful sex bias, it is not necessary that the discriminatory practice focus on a characteristic peculiar to one of the genders or be directed at all members of a sex. It is only necessary that gender be a substantial factor in the determination; that is, for example, if a female plaintiff were male, she would have been treated differently. The following case illustrates the problem of sex discrimination in the employee-discipline context.

Wise
v
Mead Corp.
614 F Supp 1131 (1985)
United States District Court, Middle District of Georgia

FACTS: Wise, a woman, was fired by Mead after engaging in a fight in the lunchroom line with a male co-worker and using "abusive and uncivil" language in connection with the fight. At least four other fights had occurred at Mead under similar circumstances, all involving males. None of the males was fired for the first offense of fighting.

ISSUE: Was Wise discriminated against on account of sex?

RESULT: Yes. Mead's stated reasons for firing Wise were a pretext for sex discrimination.

REASONING:

*   *   *

The ultimate question in a disparate treatment case is whether the defendant intentionally discriminated against the plaintiff. . . . Intentional discrimination is an issue of fact. . . . It is difficult—if not impossible—for a plaintiff to produce direct evidence of discriminatory intent. Therefore, plaintiffs may rely upon circumstantial evidence to prove discrimination.

Circumstantial evidence should be analyzed under [a] three-step procedure. . . . First, the plaintiff must establish a prima facie case of sex discrimination. . . . By establishing a prima facie case, the plaintiff creates a presumption of discrimination. . . . A plaintiff fired for misconduct makes out a prima facie case of discriminatory discharge if she shows (1) that she is a member of a protected class, (2) that she was qualified for the job from which she was fired, and (3) that the misconduct for which she was discharged was nearly identical to that engaged in by an employee outside the protected class whom the employer retained. . . . The prima facie case of discrimination is established even if the plaintiff's replacement is also a member of the protected class. . . . Of course, women are protected by Title VII. . . . In addition, Mead does not dispute that plaintiff was qualified for her job. Therefore, in the present case, plaintiff can establish a prima facie case by establishing that she was fired but men were retained for nearly identical conduct. . . . Plaintiff has clearly established that the conduct of plaintiff and three male employees (Boyd, Thomas, and Butts) were nearly identical, and therefore has clearly met her burden of establishing a prima facie case.

Next, the defendant must "articulate some legitimate, nondiscriminatory reason for the employee's [discharge]." . . . The defendant can satisfy its intermediate burden if it introduces admissible evidence that clearly sets forth the reasons for the plaintiff's termination. . . . The burden of persuasion never shifts to the defendant. . . . "The defendant need not persuade the court that it was actually motivated by the proffered reasons." . . . The defendant's burden is merely one of production, not one of proof. . . . The Eleventh Circuit has described the defendant's burden as "exceedingly light." . . . In the present case, Mead has articulated two reasons for firing plaintiff: (1) she scratched and kicked Pruitt and (2) she used "abusive and uncivil" language. These reasons are sufficiently specific; therefore, Mead has met its burden of production.

The plaintiff may still prevail if she proves that the stated reasons were in fact a pretext for discrimination. . . . The Eleventh Circuit has observed that most disparate treatment cases turn on the plaintiff's ability to prove pretext. . . . The plaintiff may prove pretext "either directly by persuading the court that a discriminatory reason more likely motivated the employer or indirectly by showing that the employer's proffered explanation is unworthy of credence." . . . Stated another way, the plaintiff can prove that the defendant's reasons were "not the sole causes of the discharge but rather that discrimination made a difference in the decision." . . . The plaintiff can prove pretext by using comparative evidence. . . . In this case, a review of the facts proves beyond doubt that it is more likely that Mead was motivated by discrimination. Therefore, plaintiff has proved that Mead's proffered reasons for firing plaintiff are in fact pretext for discrimination. . . .

Owens, Chief Judge.

Sexual Harassment   An employer's policy of—or acquiescence in—compelling female employees to submit to sexual advances of male supervisors is unlawful under Title VII on the ground that it creates an artificial barrier to employment or advancement that is placed before one gender and not the other, despite the fact that both genders are similarly situated. Thus, for example, a Title VII violation occurs when (1) a supervisor makes sexual demands on a subordinate employee and conditions that employee's job status, in any manner, on a favorable response to those demands and (2) the employer does not take prompt remedial action after learning of the demands.

According to guidelines issued by the EEOC, *sexual harassment* exists if (1) submission to some "conduct" is either an explicit or implicit term or condition of employment; (2) submission or rejection serves as the basis for an employment decision; or (3) the "conduct" has the purpose or effect of substantially interfering with the individual's work performance or creating an intimidating, hostile, or offensive work environment.

Sexual harassment complaints can take the form of lawsuits filed in court or complaints filed with state, federal, or local administrative agencies. Judgments against employers and supervisors in sexual harassment cases have resulted in substantial monetary recoveries, as well as back wages, unemployment compensation, reinstatement and, in some cases, even payment of the employee's bills for psychiatric treatment.

 To minimize liability for employee sexual harassment, a business or other employer should (1) post a policy against such harassment, (2) include in the policy a workable mechanism for the prompt reporting of instances of harassment and for maintaining complainants' anonymity, (3) communicate a warning to supervisors against such conduct, and (4) promptly and fully investigate any complaints of harassment received and deal severely with supervisors found to have violated the policy.

51:11   Age Discrimination

The *Age Discrimination in Employment Act of 1967* (ADEA) [29 USC §§ 621 et seq.] prohibits an employer from refusing to hire, discharging, or otherwise discriminating against an individual with respect to compensation, terms, conditions, or privileges of employment, based on age.

The act, which applies to employers, employment agencies, and labor unions, prohibits discrimination against workers between the ages of 40 and 70. The act prohibits practices such as placing help wanted ads indicating preferences based on age. Nothing in the act affects the jurisdiction of state agencies performing similar functions with regard to discriminatory employment practices on account of age. Furthermore, a state statute that is broader in scope than the federal statute—such as one protecting persons of all ages—can be applied concurrently with the ADEA. To enforce the act, the Secretary of Labor can bring civil actions, and in those actions damages can be collected for the affected employees. However, before suing, the Secretary must attempt to eliminate the discriminatory practices and effect voluntary compliance with the act by conciliation, conference, and persuasion. The ADEA also specifically provides for lawsuits by individuals.

51:12   Religious Discrimination

Title VII makes it an unlawful employment practice for an employer to discriminate against an individual because of religion. "Religion" is defined as including all aspects of religious observance and practice, as well as belief. An obvious case of discrimination exists if an employer refuses to hire—or later discharges—a person because of religion. However, an employer is also required to make a reasonable attempt to accommodate an employee's religious beliefs. The touchstone of religious discrimination under Title VII is whether a "reasonable accommodation" can be reached between employer and employee without undue employer hardship. Although the precise limits of the employer's duty in this regard have not been established, the United States Supreme Court has held that to accommodate the needs of an employee whose religion required him or her to observe Saturday as the Sabbath, the employer was not required by Title VII to deny shift or job preferences to other employees, to take steps inconsistent with an otherwise valid collective bargaining agreement, or to bear more than a very small cost to effect an accommodation.[4]

 Title VII does not protect only those who are members of "recognized" religious societies. It also protects persons who express their religious views in an unorthodox fashion, as well as atheists and those who merely wish to be free from religious intimidation at work.

51:13   Discrimination Against the Handicapped

Several states have enacted legislation prohibiting job discrimination based on physical handicap. In some instances, this has been accomplished by amending existing antidiscrimination statutes to extend coverage to handicapped individuals. In other instances it has been done by enacting new statutes making nondiscrimination in employment a recognized right of the handicapped. The scope and application of this legislation depends on the language contained in its definitions with respect, for example, to who is to be considered "handicapped" or what constitutes a "physical handicap" under the statute. Availability of relief in each particular case rests on whether the handicap or disability was so related to job performance as to prevent the employee or applicant from actually fulfilling the requirements specified by the employer.

The Federal government has also acted in this area. Section 503(a) of the Rehabilitation Act of 1973 [29 USC § 793(a)] provides that any contract in excess of $2,500 entered into by any federal department or agency for pro-

---

[4] *Trans World Airlines, Inc. v Hardison*, 432 US 63 (1977).

curement of personal property and nonpersonal services (including construction) for the United States is required to contain a provision requiring that the party contracting with the government will take affirmative action to employ and advance qualified handicapped individuals. This provision also applies to subcontracts in excess of $2,500 entered into by the prime contractor.

51:14   Affirmative Action and Reverse Discrimination

An employer may have an obligation under Title VII to fashion and implement an affirmative action program, even if not ordered to do so by a court. According to the EEOC, *affirmative action* means those actions appropriate to overcome effects of past or present practices, policies, or other barriers to equal employment opportunity. It encompasses activities such as soliciting applicants from minority-group organizations, setting goals for hiring or promotion of minority-group persons, instituting sensitivity training for managers and supervisors, and selecting a minority-group person over other applicants where, at least theoretically, all applicants are equally qualified.

There is no separate concept of *reverse discrimination* under Title VII in the EEOC's view; discrimination against *all* individuals because of race, color, religion, sex, or national origin is illegal. Based on several judicial opinions, however, it may be said that reverse discrimination is a policy or practice that favors or prefers minorities over males or whites. Hence, claims of reverse discrimination often challenge the propriety of affirmative action policies.

In reverse discrimination cases involving outright prejudice against particular individuals, the courts have been as zealous in guarding the rights of these people as they have been in guarding the rights of members of minority groups. On the other hand, in cases in which affirmative relief has been sought by minorities in the form of preferential treatment or the imposition of quotas, some courts have granted the relief on the theory that it is usually temporary; is not directed against particular whites or males; and, though not desirable, is justified because it sometimes appears to be the only way in which the effects of discriminatory practices that have been directed against minority groups in the past can be corrected.

Key Concepts and Terms

- The National Labor Relations Act of 1935 gives employees the right of collective action in securing satisfactory wages, hours, and working conditions. It also lists employers' unfair labor practices and established the National Labor Relations Board to enforce the act.
- The Labor Management Relations Act (Taft–Hartley Act) attempted to place employers on an equal position with unions in bargaining and labor relations. It lists unfair labor practices on the part of unions and undertakes to regulate the collective bargaining process itself.
- The Labor Management Reporting and Disclosure Act (Landrum–Griffin Act) was intended to eliminate certain improper practices on the part of

labor unions and employers that had resulted in frequent deprivation of employees' rights. The act imposes what has become known as a "bill of rights" for union members.

- A collective bargaining agreement covers the whole employment relationship and calls into being a new common law—the common law of a particular industry or shop.

- Collective bargaining agreements contain a provision for arbitration, the process by which a labor dispute that cannot be settled voluntarily through the contract's grievance procedure is referred to an impartial person for resolution.

- Federal (as well as state and local) fair employment practices laws have been enacted to prevent job discrimination. The most far-reaching federal statute in this regard is Title VII of the Civil Rights Act of 1964, which forbids discrimination in employment on the basis of race, color, religion, sex, or national origin, by employers, employment agencies, and unions.

- The Federal Age Discrimination in Employment Act of 1967 prohibits an employer from discrimination against an individual with respect to compensation, terms, conditions, or privileges of employment, based on age.

- Under Title VII, an employer may have an obligation to create an affirmative action program, to overcome effects of past or present practices of policies that discriminate against minority groups. Some courts have held that reverse discrimination is also a form of prohibited conduct under Title VII.

- Affirmative Action
- Age Discrimination in Employment Act of 1967
- Arbitration
- Civil Rights Act of 1964
- Collective Bargaining
- Collective Bargaining Agreement
- Equal Employment Opportunity Commission
- Featherbedding
- Federal Mediation and Conciliation Service
- Federal Preemption
- Labor Management Relations Act (Taft–Hartley Act)
- Labor Management Reporting and Disclosure Act (Landrum–Griffin Act)
- Mediation and Conciliation
- National Labor Relations Act (Wagner Act)
- Norris–LaGuardia Act
- Picketing
- Reverse Discrimination
- Sexual Harassment
- Title VII
- Unfair Labor Practice
- Yellow-Dog Contract

Questions and Case Problems

1. What is collective bargaining? Discuss its significance in modern industrial relations.

2. What is an unfair labor practice? State examples of unfair labor practices by (a) an employer and (b) a union.

3. Discuss arbitration and the circumstances in which the need for it arises. How does it differ from mediation and conciliation?

4. Croller Power Company maintains a disability plan for employees. Under the plan, disabled employees are paid 65 percent of their normal wages. The plan excludes certain disabilities, including pregnancy. Barbara, who has been unable to work for eight weeks because of her pregnancy, sues Croller. She alleges that the failure of Croller's plan to cover pregnancy is unlawful sex discrimination under Title VII of the Civil Rights Act of 1964. How should the case be decided?

5. Harry, a white salesman for Rallam Carpet Company, has worked for Rallam for 15 years. At the age of 58 he is discharged, and he is told by Rallam that the "economic hard times being experienced by the company", are the sole reason for the discharge. Shortly before the discharge, however, Harry's manager had told him privately that "You might want to start looking around for a new position; I have word that upper management is seeking 'younger and newer' people." Three days after Harry's departure, Rallam hires a 27-year-old, highly qualified black woman to replace Harry. On what grounds might Harry sue Rallam? Would his lawsuit be successful?

6. Local 346 of an oil workers union operated under a three-year collective bargaining agreement with Jekko Oil Company. The contract expired on December 31, and negotiations for a new contract between Jekko and Local 346 had begun 35 days before that date. It is now 28 days into the new year, and no new agreement has been reached. Representatives of both sides have met every day. However, Local 346 has submitted none of Jekko's proposals to its members, has made no counteroffers, and has rejected all Jekko contract offers outright. The union's position is that "We've heard nothing from Jekko worth talking about." Has Local 346 refused to bargain in good faith?

7. The Salvation Army of Massachusetts operates a center to provide day-care services to 60 preschool-age children. The children are selected solely on the basis of need without regard to religious creed. The Center provides no religious instruction or activities for the children. The staff consists of nine teachers, a social worker, a janitor, and a cook. They, too, are selected without regard to religious creed, and no significant condition of their employment is of a religious nature. Only one of them is a member of the Salvation Army. The staff seeks to form a bargaining unit and negotiate a collective bargaining agreement under the National Labor Relations Act. The Salvation Army claims that as a religious institution it has a right under the First Amendment not to bargain collectively with its employees. What result?

8. Alice Jones, the chief flight instructor at Gaynor Airlines, a small intrastate carrier, applies to Arrow Airlines, a large interstate carrier, for a position as pilot. She meets all requirements for Arrow's position except its height requirement; Jones is five feet two inches tall, and Arrow requires that its pilots be between five feet seven inches and six feet two inches in height. Jones sues Arrow under Title VII, alleging sex discrimination. She argues that, statistically, Arrow's height requirement excludes 93 percent of all female pilots but only 26 percent of all male pilots. Arrow argues that any person who is not at least five feet seven inches tall cannot handle the controls of its planes safely because of visibility factors stemming from cockpit design. Has Arrow violated Title VII?

9. A union, in an attempt to organize the employees of Gallagher Iron Works, hands out union leaflets across the street from Gallagher's plant each day just as the employees are entering and leaving the plant during shift changes. Gallagher places large trash containers in front of its plant. Each container has on it a prominent label stating "PUT YOUR UNION TRASH HERE." Gallagher also has several management personnel on the street noting the names of all employees who accept union leaflets. Is Gallagher acting illegally? If so, how and why?

10. Bellow Motor Lines, an interstate trucking line, recruits its drivers primarily by word-of-mouth referrals. It neither publishes help-wanted ads nor recruits through job placement agencies. Statistically, 89 percent of Bellow's drivers are white males; only 11 percent are black, although blacks make up about 30 percent of the local population. Williams, a black male who is licensed to drive heavy trucks and is an experienced driver, applies for a job with Bellow. He is told that there are no openings for drivers. Later, Williams learns that Bellow hired Jackson, a white male, as a driver one week after refusing to hire Williams. Jackson is the second cousin of one of Bellow's current drivers, by whom he was advised about a job opening. Williams sues Bellow for violation of Title VII. How should the court decide the case?

52 Independent Contractors; The Accountant Relationship

52:1 Introduction

This chapter examines one of the most common employment relationships, that between an employer and an independent contractor. In addition, the chapter examines the relationship between the businessperson and the accountant. This second relationship, which is an independent contractor relationship, is particularly important to business and accounting students.

The chapter emphasizes the importance of anticipating problems and preventing disputes that could lead to legal liability. It treats the general principles governing the creation of the independent contractor relationship, the liability of the employer for injuries caused by his or her own negligence or by that of the independent contractor, and the liability of the contractor for injuries to others during the course of employment and after its completion.

52:2 The Independent Contractor Relationship

An *independent contractor* is a person who contracts to render services using personal means and methods to perform the work. He or she is accountable to the employer only for the final product of the work. In other words, the contractor is not under the *control* of the employer. If, on the other hand, the employer has the power to control not only the nature of the final product of the work but also the order, method, or plan of the work itself, the hired person is an ordinary employee.

A particular worker's status as an independent contractor is of considerable significance to the employer. One reason is that the employer of an independent contractor usually is not liable for the contractor's torts. This sets the employer apart from the principal in an agency relationship, who is liable for the agent's torts and from an ordinary employer, who is liable for his employee's torts. Independent contractor status is also important because independent contractors are not usually covered under workers' compensation and other labor legislation. This means that, for example, the employer will not be held accountable for injuries suffered by the contractor on the job.[1]

 An employer cannot always take advantage of the benefits that are available with an independent contractor relationship. For example, if an employer's words or conduct lead a third person to believe that a worker is an employee, the employer cannot later escape liability for the worker's tort by claiming that the worker was actually an independent contractor. The same is true if the employer has admitted personal liability for the worker's tort and the injured person has sued the employer in reliance on this admission.

52:3   Existence of the Relationship

No rigid rule determines whether a hired worker is an employee or an independent contractor. Each case is decided on its own facts. Over the years the courts have looked to the "realities of the relationship" between the employer and the worker to determine the worker's status. The basic determinative factor is the extent of the employer's control over the worker and the work.

Whether an employer has the right to control the work can sometimes be determined from the contract of employment. If the contract is silent about whether the employer has any right to control the contractor's work methods, the existence or nonexistence of control will be determined from all the circumstances. Some factors that indicate an *absence* of employer control—and therefore an independent contractor relationship—are (1) the existence of a contract for the performance of a certain type or piece of work at a fixed price; (2) the independent nature of the worker's business; (3) the worker's employment of assistants, with the right to supervise their activities; (4) the worker's obligation to furnish necessary tools, supplies, and materials; (5) the worker's right to control the progress of the work; (6) the time for which the worker is employed; (7) payment by job rather than by amount of time worked; and (8) the contracted work not being a part of the employer's regular business.

Factors that indicate the *presence* of employer control over the worker—and therefore an employer–employee relationship—include (1) the employer's right to discharge the worker or terminate the contract; (2) periodic payment rather than payment for either the completed job or completed phases of it; (3) the employer's furnishing or selecting the worker's assistants or equipment; and (4) the employer's possession and control of the premises on which the work is being performed.

In the following decision, the court discusses the factors it considered in determining whether a worker was an independent contractor. Note the court's emphasis on the extent of the employer's control over the worker.

---

[1] Workers' compensation is discussed in Chapter 50. Other labor legislation, such as the federal Fair Labor Standards Act, which sets minimum wages, is discussed in Chapters 50 and 51.

Massey

v

Tube Art Display, Inc.
551 P2d 1387 (1976)
Washington Court of Appeals

FACTS: Redford was hired by Tube Art Display Company to remove a sign. In so doing, he struck a gas pipeline, causing an explosion that injured people and damaged property. The injured persons sued Tube Art on the theory that, as an employer, Tube Art was liable for the negligence of its employee, Redford. Tube Art argued that it was not liable since Redford was only its independent contractor.

ISSUE: Was Redford an employee or an independent contractor?

RESULT: Redford was an employee of Tube Art Display Company.

REASONING:

*   *   *

Traditionally, servants . . . have been looked upon as persons employed to perform services in the affairs of others under an express or implied agreement, and who, with respect to physical conduct in the performance of those services, [are] subject to the other's control or right of control. . . .

An independent contractor, on the other hand, is generally defined as one who contracts to perform services for another, but who is not controlled by the other nor subject to the other's right to control with respect to his physical conduct in performing the services. . . .

In determining whether one acting for another is a servant or independent contractor, several factors must be taken into consideration. These are . . . as follows:

(a) the extent of control which, by the agreement, the master may exercise over the details of the work;

(b) whether or not the one employed is engaged in a distinct occupation or business;

(c) the kind of occupation, with reference to whether, in the locality, the work is usually done under the direction of the employer or by a specialist without supervision;

(d) the skill required in the particular occupation;

(e) whether the employer or the workman supplies the instrumentalities, tools, and the place of work for the person doing the work;

(f) the length of time for which the person is employed;

(g) the method of payment, whether by the time or by the job;

(h) whether or not the work is a part of the regular business of the employer;

(i) whether or not the parties believe they are creating the relation of master and servant; and

(j) whether the principal is or is not in business.

All of these factors are of varying importance in determining the type of relationship involved and, with the exception of the element of control, not all the elements need be present. . . . It is the right to control another's physical conduct that is the essential and oftentimes decisive factor in establishing . . . whether the person controlled is a servant. . . .

In discussing the actual extent to which the element of control must be exercised, we pointed out in [an earlier case] that the plaintiff need not show that the [employer] controlled or had the right to control every aspect of the [employee's] operation in order to incur vicarious liability. Rather,

> [i]t should be sufficient that plaintiff present substantial evidence of . . . control or right of control over those activities from whence the actionable negligence flowed. If the rule were otherwise, then a person wishing to accomplish a certain result through another could declare the other to be an independent contractor generally, and yet retain control over a particularly hazardous part of the undertaking without incurring liability for acts arising out of that part. Such a result would effectively thwart the purpose of the rules of vicarious liability. . . .

In making his ruling that Tube Art was responsible as a matter of law for Redford's actions the trial judge stated,

> I think that under the undisputed evidence in this case they not only had the right to control, but they did control. They controlled the location of the spot to dig. They controlled the dimensions. They controlled the excavation and they got the building permits. They did all of the discretionary work that was necessary before he started to operate. They knew that the method of excavation was going to be by use of a backhoe rather than a pick and shovel which might have made a little difference on the exposure in this situation. They in effect created the whole atmosphere in which he worked. And the fact that even though he did not work for them all of the time and they paid him on a piecework basis for the individual job didn't impress me particularly when they used him the number of times they did. Most of the time they used him for this type of work. . . .

Our review of the evidence supports the trial court's evaluation of both the right and exercise of control even though Redford had been essentially self-employed for about 5 years at the time of trial, was free to work for other contractors, selected the time of day to perform the work assigned, paid his own income and business taxes and did not participate in any of Tube Art's employee programs. The testimony advanced at trial, which we find determinative, established that during the previous 3 years Redford had worked exclusively for sign companies and 90 percent of his time for Tube Art. He had no employees, was not registered as a contractor or subcontractor, was not bonded, did not himself obtain permits or licenses for his jobs, and dug the holes at locations and in dimensions in exact accordance with the instructions of his employer. In fact, Redford was left no discretion with regard to the placement of the excavations that he dug. Rather, it was his skill in digging holes pursuant to the exact dimensions prescribed that caused him to be preferred over other backhoe operators. . . .

Swanson, Judge.

 An employer always has the right to see that the contractor's work is performed according to contract specifications. Thus, the employer's retention of the right to supervise or inspect work for this purpose as it progresses does not change the worker's status from independent contractor to employee.

52:4   Liability of Employer

The traditional rule is that an employer of an independent contractor is not liable for the contractor's torts committed in the performance of the work the contractor was hired to perform. The theory is that since the employer does not possess the power to control the details of the contractor's work, the employer should not have to answer for injuries resulting from the way the work is carried out. However, so many exceptions to the traditional rule have been created in recent years that the rule now serves primarily as a preamble to the list of its exceptions.

Exceptions to Employer's Nonliability   Exceptions to an employer's nonliability for the contractor's acts are based on the public policy that a person should not be relieved of the consequences of acts simply by delegating performance to another person. These exceptions arise when the employer is in some way at fault in bringing about or contributing to the contractor-caused injuries. Thus, for example, the employer can be liable for injuries sustained where (1) he interferes with the performance of the work and fails to exercise due care over whatever control he has assumed, (2) he has ratified the acts resulting in injury, (3) the work involved unlawful or tortious conduct, (4) he was negligent in selecting the independent contractor (this important exception is discussed further in 49:4), (5) he furnished the contractor with incompetent employees or defective tools, or (6) an employee of the contractor was injured as a result of defects existing on the employer's premises before the work began.

Another important exception to the employer's nonliability for the independent contractor's torts arises where the contractor fails to exercise due care in performing work that is *inherently dangerous.* The employer is liable on the theory that where danger is inherent in the nature of the work, it is only fair that the employer be responsible for injury resulting from it. "Inherently dangerous" work is work necessarily attended with danger no matter how skillfully or carefully it is performed. For example, the construction of a skyscraper in a populous city, the operation of certain types of machinery, and the use of pesticides could be considered inherently dangerous.

In the following case the court refused to impose liability on a principal, ruling that the activity of the agent was not ultrahazardous. After reading the case, are you surprised that the activity was not considered ultrahazardous?

Hawkins

v

Evans Cooperage Co.
766 F2d 904 (1985)
United States Court of Appeals, Fifth Circuit

FACTS: Olin Chemical Corporation, which produces toluene diisocyanate (TDI), contracted with Evans Cooperage, a common carrier, to transport TDI in steel drums. The drums were manufactured by Evans in accordance with instructions supplied by Olin and were labelled with a skull and crossbones using labels supplied by Olin. While Evans' truck driver, Hawkins, was rounding a curve in a truck loaded with TDI, two drums of the chemical fell off the truck. Hawkins' truck ran over one of the drums. Hawkins stopped his truck and crawled under it to check the damage. Hawkins did not notice the label on the leaking drums, and he inhaled the fumes of TDI and suffered injury. Hawkins sued Evans, Olin, and Evan's insurer. The insurer settled the claim and then sought to hold Olin liable as a principal for its share of the damages.

ISSUE: Is Olin liable for the negligence of its independent contractor, Evans?

RESULT: No.

REASONING:

* * *

Midland makes four arguments. . . . First, it argues that the transportation of TDI is an ultrahazardous activity, and Olin is therefore responsible for any injuries resulting from the activity. Second, it argues that Olin impliedly authorized the unsafe manner in which the drums of TDI were transported. Third, it argues that Olin had a duty to supply Evans with instructions concerning a safe manner of transport of the TDI, and its failure to supply such instructions makes it partly responsible for the accident. Finally, Midland argues that Olin was negligent in not supplying larger labels to Evans that would completely encircle the drums. . . .

A. Ultrahazardous Activity

. . . Louisiana law places in the ultrahazardous category activities that "can cause injury to others, even when conducted with the greatest prudence and care." . . . The activity, therefore, must present "a risk of harm that cannot be eliminated through the exercise of due care." . . . If the activity can be conducted without a high degree of risk of injury by exercising due care, it is not ultrahazardous. . . .

The record establishes that TDI can be safely transported with the exercise of due care. Robert Vaughn, an expert in safety engineering, testified that TDI can be safely transported in tank cars (a closed system) and on trucks in drums, if the drums are properly braced on the vehicle. Vaughn testified that proper bracing consists of strapping the drums onto pallets, then bracing or strapping the pallets to the floor of the vehicle. Moreover, if an unenclosed truck is used, there should be side rails on the vehicle. In the instant case, there was uncontroverted testimony that the trucks Evans used to transport the TDI did not have side rails, but rather had only a four inch "lip" around the bed. It was, therefore, Evans's negligence in using improper trucks and bracing that rendered the transportation of the TDI unsafe, rather than some particular feature of TDI that produces a risk of harm in its transportation that cannot be eliminated. We conclude that the transportation of TDI was not an ultrahazardous activity.

B. Exercise of Control

. . . There was overwhelming evidence that Olin never supplied instructions to Evans concerning the method of transport, nor was Olin aware of the method actually being used. Mildred Ordoyne, the office manager and treasurer of Evans, testified that Olin provided instructions to Evans on how the drums were to be manufactured and labelled, but not on how the drums were to be transported. She also testified that "when this accident happened, the feeling at Evans was that this was an Evans problem, not an Olin problem". Moreover, such written instructions as Olin did supply to Evans that were admitted into evidence contained no instructions concerning the method of transportation of the drums. . . .

. . . We therefore conclude that Midland offered no substantial evidence that Olin exercised control over, or impliedly authorized, the method of transportation of the TDI.

C. The Duty to Supply Instructions Concerning Shipment; the Size of the Labels

Midland's remaining two contentions require little discussion. Midland argues that, in view of the hazardous nature of TDI, Olin had a duty to supply instructions to Evans concerning its safe shipment. This contention has no merit. When the activity at issue is not ultrahazardous, the principal has no duty to ensure, through instructions or supervision, that the independent contractor performs its obligations in a reasonably safe manner. . . . Moreover, a principal who exercises no operational control has no duty to discover and remedy hazards created by acts of its independent contractors. . . . Olin was therefore under no duty either to provide advance written instructions to Evans concerning how the TDI should be transported or to check up on the method actually being used. Olin was entitled to rely on the expertise of its independent contractor, a common carrier with 20 years of experience in shipping hazardous substances of this nature.

Midland's final argument, that it was entitled to go to the jury on the issue whether the labels Olin provided to Evans were of sufficient size, is also of little merit. . . .

Because the transportation of TDI is not an ultrahazardous activity under Louisiana law, and because Olin neither exercised operational control over, nor impliedly authorized, the method of transportation used by Evans, Olin is not responsible for the negligent acts of its independent contractor. Olin had no duty to supply instructions for the safe shipment of the TDI to Evans, and Olin satisfied its duty to label its product with an adequate warning of its dangers. . . .

Wisdom, Circuit Judge.

 An employer hiring a contractor should make certain that the contract specifically provides that the contractor must assume liability for harm to a third person arising from the contractor's negligence and that the contractor must carry insurance to cover this obligation.

Employer's Nondelegable Duties   Some duties that an employer requests a contractor to assume are *nondelegable*. That is, an employer must retain responsibility for certain acts. For example, if a person is required to perform street repair work in conformance with an ordinance, he cannot relieve himself of that duty by contracting with another to do the work, nor can he escape responsibility on the theory that restoration of the street is under the independent contractor's control.

52:5   Lack of Care in Selecting Independent Contractor

An employer who failed to exercise reasonable care in selecting a competent independent contractor is liable for that contractor's negligence. A competent contractor is one who has the knowledge, skill, equipment, personal characteristics, and experience reasonably necessary to perform the required job without creating an unreasonable risk of harm to third persons.

Criteria of Care in Selection of Contractor In determining whether an employer has been negligent in checking the qualifications of an independent contractor, the courts have noted that the employer should pay particular attention to the contractor's age, experience, training for the work to be performed, and reputation. Courts have also looked to whether the contractor was licensed to do the work contracted for and was properly equipped to perform the work.

 To minimize legal liability for a contractor's negligence, an employer should, prior to hiring the contractor, make a careful inquiry about the contractor's qualifications. The extent of the necessary investigation is determined from the nature of the work to be performed. For example, if the contractor is to be hired for a job requiring special skills and involving potential danger to the public, such as driving a gasoline tank truck, a more thorough inquiry into the contractor's qualifications will be necessary than if the job is a routine or unskilled one.

Employer's Subsequent Knowledge of Contractor's Incompetence An employer can be liable for the contractor's negligence if, although the employer was originally unaware that the contractor was careless or incompetent, he or she acquired such knowledge after the contractor commenced the work. An employer who permits the contractor to continue working after learning of any such incompetence could be negligent for failure to terminate the relationship, even though there was no negligence in hiring the contractor.

52:6 Liability of Independent Contractor

An independent contractor who agrees to perform a job makes the implied promise to perform that job in a skillful, safe, and professional manner. Therefore, he is liable for negligent acts that he or his employees commit. This rule applies regardless of whether the person who hired him is also liable for the contractor's negligence. Furthermore, a contractor has the duty to make sure that the rights of other persons, be they persons on the premises, employees of the hiring party, or simply other contractors on the job, are not injured by his work.

Liability after Completion of Work The general rule is that the liability of an independent contractor ceases once his work has been completed, turned over to, and accepted by the employer. Under this rule, even though the contractor may have failed to perform the contract properly or with due care, the employer assumes responsibility for defects once the job is done. There are, however, exceptions to the general rule. For example, an independent contractor may remain liable after turning over defective work if (1) the defect was so concealed that the employer could not reasonably detect it; (2) the contractor fraudulently concealed the defect; or (3) the finished work constituted a nuisance, was inherently dangerous, or was so negligently defective that it was imminently dangerous to third persons.

52:7   Introduction to the Accountant Relationship

The accountant plays a major role in modern business because it is he or she who monitors a business's financial system. Clearly, the accountant is regarded as being an expert in money matters. When hired, the accountant gains access to a business' confidential financial information and can be called on to perform complicated or technical tasks. The accountant is responsible for, among other things, conducting audits—which entails the examination of business or financial records—preparing tax returns, and consulting with businesses and individuals about money management.

Usually an accountant is hired on a contract basis. The contract creates a relationship between the accountant and the employer, imposing on each person certain duties, rights, and liabilities, which are discussed here.

Unauthorized Practice of Law   Accountants are often asked to give advice on all phases of setting up and running a business. Because the accountant must interpret government rules and regulations in giving advice, he or she runs the risk of being guilty of practicing law without a license to do so. To a degree, an accountant cannot properly represent a client without giving some legal advice in connection with the practice of his ordinary work in keeping books and records and in preparing tax returns. At the same time, an accountant is generally barred from giving strictly legal advice or answering legal questions having no connection with his ordinary work.

52:8   Audits; Tax Return Preparation

Audits represent, by far, the bulk of accounting work and make up nearly 80 percent of most accounting firms' income. An audit consists of the examination of a business' financial records and the preparation of a report on its financial condition. The audit can be of several types, ranging from a complete audit, in which the total financial condition of a business is scrutinized, to a test audit, in which a company's financial position is merely sampled on a selective basis.

Most audits consist of four stages: (1) gathering information and data on which the audit will be based; (2) establishing the appropriate auditing procedures; (3) revising the audit program, if necessary, to comply with the work in progress; and (4) preparing the audit report based on the accumulated and analyzed data, detailing or summarizing the business' financial condition.

Tax Return Preparation   Many taxpayers have their income tax returns prepared by third persons for a fee, and these third persons are frequently accountants. Indeed, *tax return* preparation has become so large a business that it is now regulated to some extent by federal legislation, as discussed below. In addition, tax preparers may be subject to various state laws, the application of which is far from uniform.

The federal *Tax Reform Act of 1976* contains many rules that apply to income tax preparers. For example, any income tax preparer must furnish a completed copy of each return (the form on which the tax due is computed) to the taxpayer not later than the time the return is given to the taxpayer for his or her signature. Furthermore, any income tax return preparer must retain for three years after the close of the return period a completed copy of each return prepared, or retain a list of the names and taxpayer identification numbers of the taxpayers for whom returns were prepared. The preparer must make this copy or list available for inspection by the Internal Revenue Service. Penalties are prescribed for, among other things, failure to furnish a copy of a return to the taxpayer, failure to sign the return, failure to furnish an identifying number, failure to retain a copy or required list, and failure to file a correct information return.

 Various types of tax fraud are made crimes by the *Internal Revenue Code*. For example, any person, including an accountant, who willfully makes and signs a tax return containing a statement under oath that the tax return is correct when he or she does not believe it to be true, or who willfully assists another person in preparing a false return, is guilty of a felony that is punishable by fine and imprisonment.

52:9 Duty to Client

An accountant is subject to the same rules in his or her practice as any other professional engaged in rendering skilled professional services for compensation. The accountant must exercise the skill, care, knowledge, and judgment usually possessed by accountants in the community. He or she must conduct adequate investigations to discover embezzlement when performing an audit and other accounting services. The accountant must also follow standard accounting procedures and perform all the services for which he or she was hired.

An accountant is not an insurer against damage to a client and does not guarantee correct judgment. However, if he fails to exercise reasonable care according to normal professional standards, he may be held liable to the client for damages. For example, if an account uncovers suspicious circumstances, she must inform the client or fully investigate the matter. If she fails to do so, she can be held liable to the client for the resulting loss. In particular, an accountant may be held negligent for failing to pursue an inquiry into a company's finances where he knew or ought to have known of improper financial transactions.

52:10 Duty to Third Persons

Until recently, the recognized rule was that an accountant is not liable for negligence to a third person with whom he or she had not directly contracted. Under this view of limited liability, an accountant owes no duty to a "stranger"; the duty is only to the client. This practice is based on the notion that to expose an accountant to liability to third persons would constitute too great a burden on the accounting profession. In the words of one famous judge, "If liability for negligence exists, a thoughtless slip or blunder . . . may expose accountants to a liability in an indeterminate amount for an indeterminate time to an indeterminate class."[2]

In recent years, this policy of limited liability has been rejected in a number of states. In these states, an accountant can be held liable to a third person for negligence despite the absence of a direct contractual relationship with the third person. Thus, if an accountant knows that his or her work will be relied on by a particular person or group of persons and that it will be used for a particular purpose, a duty of reasonable care can arise. Breach of this duty of care subjects the accountant to liability to all persons who foreseeably may have relied on the work.

The following case illustrates the accountant's duty of care to third persons. Note how the court discusses public policy in support of its position. Consider the extent of liability and the class of persons in whose favor it can exist.

Credit Alliance Corp.

v

Arthur Andersen & Co.
483 NE2d 110 (1985)
Court of Appeals of New York

FACTS: Credit Alliance, a group of major financial service companies, provided capital to L. B. Smith, Inc. [Smith] on a regular basis. During 1978 Credit Alliance advised Smith that, as a condition to extending additional major financing, they would insist upon examining an audited financial statement. Accordingly, Smith provided Credit Alliance with two sets of consolidated financial statements covering itself and its subsidiaries. The statements contained an auditor's report prepared by Arthur Andersen stating that it had examined the statements in accordance with generally accepted auditing standards and found them to reflect fairly the financial position of Smith in conformity with generally accepted accounting principles. In reliance on these statements, Credit Alliance advanced funds to Smith, which eventually defaulted on the loans and declared bankruptcy in 1980. Credit Alliance alleged that the statements overstated Smith's assets, net worth, and general financial health, and that Andersen failed to conduct an investigation in accordance with proper auditing standards, thereby failing to discover Smith's precarious financial condition.

---

[2] Justice Benjamin Cardozo, in *Ultramares Corp. v Touche*, 255 NY 170 (New York Court of Appeals, 1931).

ISSUE: Is Arthur Andersen liable to Credit Alliance for negligent preparation of the audit report?

RESULT: No. The report was not prepared specifically for the Credit Alliance loan.

REASONING:

*   *   *

Upon examination of *Ultramares* and *Glanzer* and our recent affirmation of their holdings in *White*, certain criteria may be gleaned. Before accountants may be held liable in negligence to noncontractual parties who rely to their detriment on inaccurate financial reports, certain prerequisites must be satisfied: (1) the accountants must have been aware that the financial reports were to be used for a particular purpose or purposes; (2) in the furtherance of which a known party or parties was intended to rely; and (3) there must have been some conduct on the part of the accountants linking them to that party or parties, which evinces the accountants' understanding of that party or parties' reliance. While these criteria permit some flexibility in the application of the doctrine of privity to accountants' liability, they do not represent a departure from the principles articulated in *Ultramares*, . . . [and other cases] but, rather, they are intended to preserve the wisdom and policy set forth therein.

We are aware that the courts throughout this country are divided as to the continued validity of the holding in *Ultramares*. Some courts continue to insist that a strict application of the privity requirement governs the law of accountants' liability except, perhaps, where special circumstances compel a different result. . . . On the other hand, an increasing number of courts have adopted what they deem to be a more flexible approach than that permitted under this court's past decisions. A brief examination of some decisions of those courts is instructive.

In *Ryan v. Kanne*, . . . [Iowa], the court rejected the accountants' contention that a strict privity doctrine governed accountants' liability for negligence. Recovery was permitted where the audit report was used as the accountants had contemplated, by a known nonprivy party, to whom one of the accounting partners personally explained the report at meetings they both attended. In *Larsen v. United Fed. Sav. & Loan Assn.* . . . [Iowa], the same court permitted recovery by a nonprivy party who had actually paid for the accountant's appraisal, and was specifically designated on the appraisal itself as the one for whose benefit it was being prepared.

Likewise, in *Shatterproof Glass Corp. v. James* . . . [Tex.Civ.App.], where the court held that the accountants were under a duty to exercise due care toward the third party who had loaned money to the accountants' client in reliance on the financial statements, it was noted that the accountants knew that their reports would be issued to and relied upon by a particular creditor. Moreover, the accountants had furnished information directly to the third-party creditor as authorized by their client and, indeed, they had charged their client a separate and additional amount for rendering such services. Similarly, in *Coleco Indus. v. Berman*, . . . [E.D.Pa.], the nonprivy parties who relied upon the financial statements had, in fact, chosen the accountants, explained to those accountants the role they were to play in the ongoing transactions, and had direct dealings with them. The court concluded that the "lack of strict privity" should not preclude a negligence claim against the accountants. The relationship existing between the accountants and the nonprivy parties was found to be " 'so close as to approach that of privity, if not completely one with it.' " . . .

In all of the foregoing cases, the courts found the facts amenable to the imposition of accountants' liability under the principles of *Ultramares-Glanzer* or extended those principles to permit a more liberalized application. To the extent that the holdings in those cases are predicated upon certain criteria—to wit, a particular purpose for the accountants' report, a known relying party, and some conduct on the part of the accountants linking them to that party—they are consonant with the principles reaffirmed in this decision. To the extent, however, that those cases were decided upon the ground that *Ultramares* should not be followed and, instead, a rule permitting recovery by any foreseeable plaintiff should be adopted, the law in this State, as reiterated today, is clearly distinguishable.

In the appeals we decide today, application of the foregoing principles presents little difficulty. In *Credit Alliance*, the facts as alleged by plaintiffs fail to demonstrate the existence of a relationship between the parties sufficiently approaching privity. Though the complaint and supporting affidavit do allege that Andersen specifically knew, should have known or was on notice that plaintiffs were being shown the reports by Smith, Andersen's client, in order to induce their reliance thereon, nevertheless, there is no adequate allegation of either a particular purpose for the reports' preparation or the prerequisite conduct on the part of the accountants. While the allegations state that Smith sought to induce plaintiffs to extend credit, no claim is made that Andersen was being employed to prepare the reports with that particular purpose in mind. Moreover, there is no allegation that Andersen had any direct dealings with plaintiffs, had specifically agreed with Smith to prepare the report for plaintiffs' use or according to plaintiffs' requirements, or had specifically agreed with Smith to provide plaintiffs with a copy or actually did so. Indeed, there is simply no allegation of any word or action on the part of Andersen directed to plaintiffs, or anything contained in Andersen's retainer agreement with Smith which provided the necessary link between them. . . .

Jasen, Judge.

Note that, in *Credit Alliance*, the New York court considered it very important that Arthur Andersen had not prepared the report specifically for the Credit Alliance loan and had no knowledge of Credit Alliance's specific intended use of the report. In a companion case, decided the same day, the court held an accounting firm liable for a negligently prepared report where the accounting firm knew that the "end and aim" of auditing the client was to provide necessary financial information for a specific transaction.[3]

 Since "prevention is better than the best remedy," it is always advisable for an investor to have his own accountant explore any situation in which he intends to make a sizable investment. While the other party to the intended transaction may not always permit the investor to have his own accountant examine the other's books, the reception that the suggestion receives may in itself be a clue as to whether the investment should be made.

Unaudited Financial Statements   Although many states now hold accountants liable to third persons for negligence in the preparation of complete financial statements, as discussed above, they remain divided on the question of accountant liability in regard to working papers or *unaudited financial statements*. This question may arise when materials, supplied by a client to an accountant, are later shown to be false. In most circumstances, the accountant is not negligent—and hence is not liable to third persons—simply because he fails to discover that the materials with which he is supplied are incorrect. However, if he knows or has a reasonable basis for knowing that there are serious discrepancies or falsehoods in the materials supplied, he should make the appropriate inquiries and insist on some independent verification.

Key Concepts and Terms

- An independent contractor is a worker who contracts to do certain work according to personal methods, without being subject to the employer's control.
- Factors that indicate independent contractor status are (1) the existence of a contract for performance of a specified job at a fixed price; (2) the independent nature of the contractor's business; (3) the contractor's employment of assistants and retention of the right to supervise their activities; (4) the contractor's duty to furnish his or her own tools and supplies; and (5) the fact that the work is not part of the employer's regular business.
- An employer always has the right to see that the contract is performed according to specifications. The employer's retention of the right to check over the independent contractor's work as it progresses does not change the contractor's status to that of an employee.
- An independent contractor is liable for negligent acts that he or his employees commit.

---

[3] *European American Bank & Trust Co. v Strauhs & Kaye*, 483 NE2d 110 (1985).

- The general rule, subject to several exceptions, is that once a contractor's work has been completed and accepted by the employer, the employer is then liable for later injuries resulting from the work.

- An accountant's employment is based on a contract that sets forth the accountant's and employer's rights and duties.

- An accountant is permitted to apply legal knowledge in connection with his accounting work, but he cannot give legal advice or practice law (unless he is also a licensed attorney).

- An accountant is not an insurer of his advice. He is liable to his client only for failing to exercise the reasonable skill, care, knowledge, and judgment possessed by other accountants in the community.

- An accountant is liable for negligent acts and omissions in rendering tax services and in providing erroneous or untimely tax advice.

- An accountant can be liable for his negligence with respect to a third person, despite the absence of any contract between them. This liability can exist if, when preparing a report for a client, the accountant should reasonably have known that the report would be used by a particular third person for a particular purpose.

- Under the federal securities laws, an accountant can be liable for failing to properly prepare, to have prepared, or to supervise the preparation of a corporate client's materials issued in connection with an offering of securities.

• Audit	• Securities Exchange Act of 1934
• Control	• Tax Reform Act of 1976
• Independent Contractor	• Tax Return
• Inherently Dangerous	• Test Audit
• Internal Revenue Code	• Unaudited Financial Statement
• Nondelegable Duties	• Unauthorized Practice of Law
• Securities Act of 1933	

Questions and Case Problems

1. Hoosier Engineering, an independent contractor, contracts with CG&E, a power and gas company, for the replacement of some of CG&E's power poles, wires, and related equipment. The contract calls for transferring the power from the old circuitry to the new as soon as the work is completed. Tedesco is a Hoosier lineman, one of a crew of four. After completing his work on the last of the new poles being installed, he is about to descend when a short circuit occurs in front of him. The flash temporarily blinds him, and he loses his balance. Because he has failed to secure his safety belt, Tedesco falls and is seriously injured. The new circuitry should not have been "live" at the time of the accident, but another Hoosier employee had turned on the power prematurely. Tedesco sues CG&E for his injuries. How should the court decide the case?

2. Cole Department Store hires the Baker Security Service in an effort to reduce shoplifting. Baker assigns two uniformed and armed security guards to the store.

While on duty, one of the guards bends over to tie his shoe. He has forgotten to fasten his pistol in his holster, and the pistol falls to the floor and discharges, injuring Doris, a customer. Doris sues Cole Department Store for damages. Should she win the case? Why?

3. Roger owns a skyscraper in a large city. He hires a window-washing firm to maintain and clean the windows in his building. During the course of routine window cleaning, one of the workers drops a bucket, which injures a bystander in the street below. Is Roger liable for the injury? Discuss. Would Roger be liable if one of the workers fell while cleaning windows? Discuss.

4. Mark hires an independent contractor to sandblast the outside of a building and supplies him with sandblasting equipment to perform the work. While performing the job, the contractor is injured when the air hose on the sandblaster, which is in bad repair, ruptures. Is Mark liable for the contractor's injury? Discuss. Would it make any difference if the contractor had known before beginning the work that the equipment was defective? Would it make any difference if the hose was new and there was no indication that it was defective?

5. Brown needs a high retaining wall to be built on her land. The wall must be specially designed because of the steep slope of the land and the unstable condition of the soil. Brown accepts bids for the project from several general contractors, but she rejects all of them as being too high. She then contracts with her friend Peters to do the work for far less than what any of the contractors had quoted. Peters' only relevant experience is that he has built several low divider walls on level ground. Although he has no professional qualifications to do Brown's job, he states that he can do it satisfactorily. The wall designed and built by Peters gives way, damaging adjoining property. The neighbor sues Brown for damages. How should the case be decided? Why?

6. Eddy owns a dump truck. He contracts with Northpoint Gravel Co. for delivering gravel to various of Northpoint's customers. Each day Northpoint gives Eddy the necessary details about gravel orders to be filled that day. Eddy pays all his operating expenses, and he makes all decisions as to the size of each load he hauls, the number of loads hauled each day, and the routes he takes in making deliveries. While making a delivery to one of Northpoint's customers, Eddy negligently runs over and injuries Adams, one of the customer's employees. Adams sues Northpoint, claiming that Eddy is its employee. Is Adams correct? Discuss.

7. An amendment to the local fire code requires that an approved smoke detection and sprinkler system be installed in all apartment buildings containing five or more units. Warren owns a large apartment building. She hires Dooley, an independent contractor, to do all the work necessary to upgrade the building in compliance with the new fire code requirement. Without Warren's knowledge, Dooley installs a cheap, nonapproved smoke detection and sprinkler system. Before the work is even completed there is a fire, and one of the tenants is injured. It is established that the injury would not have occurred had the work already done by Dooley been in compliance with the fire code requirement. The tenant sues Warren, and Warren denies liability on the ground that Dooley is responsible. How should the court decide the case?

8. Carey owns and operates an apple orchard. He hires an independent contractor to spray the orchard with a pesticide. Carey's neighbor uses land adjoining the orchard for growing vegetables organically, that is, without the use of any chemicals. Organically-grown vegetables are worth twice as much as those grown by conventional methods. While the contractor is spraying Carey's orchard, the wind

starts blowing, and it carries some of the pesticide onto the vegetables growing on the adjacent land. Is Carey liable to his neighbor for the damage done to the organic crop? Is the contractor liable to the neighbor?

9. Wills prepares a financial report for Asher, who wants to buy all the assets of the Mondane Company. In preparing his report, Wills fails to follow standard accounting procedures, and his report is grossly misleading. Ultimately, the sale of the Mondane assets to Asher falls through for reasons not involving the financial report. However, Mondane's assets are bought by Wiggons, who somehow acquired Wills' misleading report and read and relied on it. After suffering severe financial losses, Wiggons sues Wills for damages. She alleges that Wills was negligent in the performance of his duties. Is Wills liable to Wiggons?

10. Sharon, a certified public accountant (CPA), is preparing Kenware Corporation's annual corporate tax returns. In so doing, she advises Kenware's president that she believes a particular IRS ruling is unconstitutional and will prepare the tax return ignoring the ruling. She further advises Kenware that, in the event of litigation, Kenware would probably win the case. After the forms are filed, the tax return is contested by the IRS, and Kenware is assessed a substantial penalty. Discuss the liability, if any, of Sharon to Kenware. Would it make any difference if Sharon happened to be an attorney as well as a CPA?

PART ELEVEN

Government Regulation of Business

Introductory Comments

Most of the material in this book has involved private law. While the introductory chapters focused on the legal environment of business in the broad sense, Parts Three through Nine explored the specific areas of private law particularly important to businesspeople. The materials in Part Ten on labor law and labor relations introduce federal regulation of an important business area. The materials in Part Eleven however, involve federal regulation of the conduct of business in the public interest.

Government regulation of business is not new. In the nineteenth century many states attempted, for various purposes and with varying degrees of success, to regulate industry. The federal government's first major incursion into business regulation occurred in 1887 with the creation of the Interstate Commerce Commission, empowered to enforce federal legislation regulating railroad rate discrimination. The 1890 Congress passed the Sherman Antitrust Act, inaugurating the comprehensive regulation of the competitive environment for American business. In 1933 and 1934, in the middle of the Great Depression, Congress initiated comprehensive regulation of the issuance and trading of securities. Then, with the growth of industrial urbanization in the post–World War II period, came increased environmental pollution and the legislation that has formed the complex web of environmental regulation.

Chapter 53 introduces you to the law of securities regulation. The chapter specially considers the liability of the professional accountant associated with securities law. Chapter 54 covers the law of unfair trade practices and the means by which government protects products and ideas. Chapter 55 examines the federal antitrust laws and the regulation of competition. And Chapter 56 explains the federal approach to environmental regulation.

53 Securities Regulation and Accountants' Liability

Since the time to which the memory of man runneth not to the contrary the human animal has been full of cunning and guile. Many of the schemes and artifices have been so sophisticated as almost to defy belief. But the ordinary run of those willing and able to take unfair advantage of others are mere apprentices in the art when compared with the manipulation thought up by those connected in one way or another with transactions in securities.

Green v Santa Fe Industries, Inc., 533 F2d 1283
(United States Court of Appeals, Second Circuit, 1976)

53:1 Introduction to Securities Regulation

The securities industry has long been regarded as particularly susceptible to sharp and fraudulent practices. To some extent, this reflects historical truth. To some extent, it reflects misunderstanding about the function of the capital markets in our economy. For many years American governments, at both the state and federal levels, have regulated the issuance and trading of securities in order to protect the investing public from unreasonable or concealed risk of loss. This chapter examines the basic framework of state and federal securities regulation. In addition, it examines the particular role of accountants in securities regulation and the very significant potential for liability associated with securities work.

53:2 State Regulation of Securities

Early in this century, there were many fraudulent sales of securities to unwary investors. In every state, the need to protect uninformed investors demanded legislation. As a consequence, state laws were first enacted to stop the sale of stock in fly-by-night companies, nonexistent oil wells and gold mines, and other fraudulent transactions. Because these laws were aimed at speculative schemes which had "no more basis than so many feet of blue sky," they were commonly referred to as *blue-sky laws*.

Generally, blue-sky laws are based on the premise that the investing public lacks knowledge and sophistication about securities investment. Many people are potentially easy prey for promoters of worthless securities or securities of doubtful value. The primary value of state blue-sky laws is therefore to protect the public from deceit and fraud in intrastate securities transactions. The laws regulate all investment schemes designed to lead investors into enterprises, the earnings and profits of which must come through the management, control, and operation of others. Blue-sky laws are obviously paternalistic in nature in that the states endeavor to shield their citizens from unscrupulous stock promoters and to protect innocent purchasers who may be induced to invest money in speculative enterprises over which they have little or no control.

Blue-sky laws differ widely from state to state. However, while statutory variations do exist, most states now incorporate one or more of three basic types of regulatory techniques: (1) antifraud provisions relating to securities transactions, (2) registration of securities, and (3) registration of brokers or dealers dealing with securities.

While the blue-sky laws are aimed primarily at the prevention of fraud in securities transactions, the controls imposed in some states are not limited to disclosure and antifraud provisions. In a few states, the selling price of securities is regulated. Likewise, maximum brokerage fees can be fixed by statute. In other states, blue-sky laws incorporate concepts embodied in the federal laws by regulating, for example, takeover bids or market manipulations.

Uniform Securities Act   Over half of the states and the District of Columbia have enacted all or part of the Uniform Securities Act. The Uniform Securities Act is divided into four parts. Each of the first three parts is devoted to the implementation of one of the three basic methods historically employed by the various states in the blue-sky laws to control the sale of and trading in securities. Recognizing that the various states have employed only one or two of the three basic methods of control, the Uniform Securities Act is thus constructed so that each of the first three parts may be enacted individually or in conjunction with one or both of the other two. The fourth part contains general provisions relating to the administration and enforcement of the act.

53:3   Federal Regulation of Securities

The federal regulation of equity and debt securities—and of the stock market—originated during the Great Depression. The stock market crash in 1929 and the subsequent depression prompted congressional investigations, which uncovered many undesirable, deceptive, and questionable practices in the marketing and sale of securities. As a consequence of these investigations various federal laws were enacted, beginning with the Securities Act of 1933 [15 USC §§ 77a et seq.], and followed by the Securities Exchange Act of 1934 [15 USC §§ 78a et seq.], the Investment Company Act of 1940 [15 USC §§ 80a-1 et seq.], the Investment Advisors Act of 1940 [15 USC §§ 80b-1 et seq.], and, more recently, the Securities Investor Protection Act of 1970 [15 USC §§ 78aaa et seq.].

The *Securities Act of 1933* and the *Securities Exchange Act of 1934* are the two principal federal statutes relating to the sale and distribution of securities. The former relates primarily to the initial issuance of securities; the latter regulates the trading of securities after their initial issuance.

Investment Company Act of 1940   The Investment Company Act requires registration of all investment companies that use the mail or other interstate facilities of communication. Investment companies must reveal through registration their intent with regard to specific subjects such as diversification, borrowing or lending money, issuing securities, and investing in real estate or commodities. In this manner, the act regulates the selling practices of investment companies, promotes honest and unbiased management, and ensures the availability of financial information to security holders.

Investment Advisors Act of 1940   The Investment Advisors Act requires all persons engaged in giving advice or issuing reports of any securities for compensation to register with the Securities and Exchange Commission (SEC). The act applies to all persons whose primary business enterprise is advising on investments. Fraudulent or deceptive practices by registered advisors are prohibited. The act also prohibits profit-sharing arrangements among advisors and the assignment to third parties of advisory contracts without client consent.

Securities Investor Protection Act of 1970   In 1970, a new federal securities act was adopted to protect securities investors against losses due to the financial failure of brokers or dealers. The act created the Securities Investment Protection Corporation (SIPC), which is composed of all brokers or dealers who are registered under the other federal securities laws. The SIPC is authorized to accumulate and manage an insurance fund to indemnify customers of brokers or dealers for losses suffered on the liquidation of a member broker or dealer. The basic means through which the act implements its purpose is the forced liquidation of any member who fails or is in danger of failing to meet his or her obligations to customers.

53:4   Securities Act of 1933

The Securities Act of 1933 (1933 Act) has two basic objectives. The first is to provide investors with full disclosure of all material investment information in connection with an original interstate issuance of securities from the issuer to the public. The second objective of the act is to prevent fraud and misrepresentation in the interstate sale of securities generally.

The provisions of the Securities Act of 1933 apply only to transactions in interstate commerce. However, the SEC and the federal courts have broadly interpreted the meaning of interstate commerce. Today, interstate commerce is involved whenever an individual uses some means of conducting interstate commerce, such as the telephone or mail, in any part of a securities transaction.

Issuers, Underwriters, and Dealers   With certain exceptions, the term "issuer" means any person who issues or proposes to issue any security. "Person" in this sense can refer to a natural person, but it also refers to a corporation, whether already formed or in the process of being formed.

The process of distributing securities from an original issuer to the investor or ultimate retail purchaser is called *underwriting*. Firms that contract with an issuer to market securities are known as underwriters. Firms that buy from underwriters and resell to the public are *dealers*.

Registration   The basic means by which the Securities Act of 1933 attempts to accomplish its purpose of protecting the investing public is advance disclosure. The act requires that before a security can be issued, the issuer must file with the SEC a registration statement containing information with respect to the security, the issuer, and the underwriters. This information must also be made available to the public, generally in the form of a *prospectus*. A prospectus is a digest of the most important information contained in the registration statement. The prospectus must be given to all investors before the sale or delivery of an issuer's security.

 The SEC does not have the authority to rule on what securities may or may not be distributed to the public. It has only the responsibility to see that the required disclosures are met before distribution. However, the SEC *is* empowered to prevent securities from being distributed if the disclosure requirements are not met. It does so by preventing or suspending the effectiveness of an issuer's registration statements. In addition, material misstatements or omissions pertaining to registration statements may subject an issuer to criminal or civil penalties.

Exempt Securities   Certain types of securities are exempt from registration. An exemption allows a sale or resale of the security without compliance with the registration or prospectus requirements of the Act. Securities issued or guaranteed by the government, by banks, or by nonprofit charitable organizations are exempt from the registration requirements. In addition, under SEC *Regulation A* an issuer may offer no more than $1.5 million of securities in any 12-month period without registration. Regulation A requires that such an issue be accompanied by a circular and that notification be filed with the SEC, but the full-scale registration process is not required.

In addition, sales of securities that are offered and sold only within one state by an issuer that is a resident doing business in that state are exempt as *intrastate sales* of securities. SEC Rule 147 provides a "safe-harbor" guide to the intrastate sales exemption. Compliance with the detailed requirements of the rule creates the presumption that the securities are exempt from registration. In order to preserve the intent of the exemption, intrastate securities may be resold, without registration, to nonresidents of the state only after they have been held for nine months by residents.

Finally, there is a variety of special types of securities that are exempt under the 1933 Act. For example, commercial paper having a maturity of no more than nine months is exempt as *short-term commercial paper*. Insurance policies and annuities regulated by state insurance commissions are exempt. Issuers regulated by the Interstate Commerce Commission are exempt. Securities issued by an issuer for exchange with its existing securities holders are exempt.

Exempt Transactions   Certain types of transactions in securities are exempt from the registration requirements of the 1933 Act. In general, transactions in stock by an investor on his or her own account, or between investors, are exempt. In addition, transactions by a dealer made more than 40 days after the date on which the security was offered to the public (or 90 days if the issue is the issuer's first public one) are exempt.

In 1982 the SEC promulgated *Regulation D,* which provides certain specific exemptions from registration. Regulation D has three major rules that establish these exemptions. *Rule 504* exempts issues of securities up to $500,000 sold in a 12-month period if there is no general offering or solicitation and if the securities are restricted as to resale. *Rule 505* exempts issues of up to $5,000,000 in a 12-month period if there is no general offering or solicitation and if the sale is made to no more than 35 "unaccredited" investors. An "accredited" investor is (1) an institutional investor (such as a bank) or (2) a person (a) whose net worth exceeds $1,000,000 or (b) who has an annual income of $200,000 for the past two years or (c) who buys more than $150,000 worth of the securities and that purchase does not exceed 20 percent of the investor's net worth at the time of the purchase. *Rule 506* allows private placement of unlimited value of securities under the same conditions as Rule 505. However, under Rule 506 the unaccredited investors must be sophisticated investors or be represented by an experienced and knowledgeable advisor.

 Even though a security is exempt from the registration and prospectus requirements of the 1933 Act there is no exemption from the antifraud provisions contained in Section 12 [15 USC § 77q]. Any person who offers or sells a security—whether exempt from registration or not—in interstate commerce and either makes an untrue statement of material fact or omits to state a material fact is liable to the purchaser of the security for all damages sustained.

What Is a Security?   As used in the federal securities laws, the word "security," or "securities," means more than merely stocks and bonds. The term has been applied to everything from annuities to cemetery lots, oil rights, orange groves, and even silver foxes. The 1933 Act defines "security" as any note; stock; treasury stock; bond; debenture; evidence of indebtedness; certificate of interest or participation in any profit-sharing agreement; transferable share; investment contract; voting-trust certificate; certificate of deposit for a security; fractional interest in oil, gas, or other mineral rights; or, in general, any interest commonly known as a security. Although a security ordinarily is a written document, oral agreements come within the scope of the Act as well.

"Investment contract" is a term that has been broadly interpreted by the SEC and the Supreme Court, thus bringing many transactions within the scope of federal securities regulation. An investment contract is deemed to be any contract, transaction, or scheme by which a person invests money in a common enterprise and expects profits to accrue solely from the efforts of the promoter or third parties. For example, a scheme in which an investor pays cash to be a distributor of cosmetics, but receives as well the right to recruit other investors as distributors and to receive a portion of the investment of such recruits, is an investment contract subject to the registration provisions of the 1933 Act.

Fraudulent Practices   The principal antifraud provision in the 1933 Act is contained in § 12. This section applies only to the sale of, or an offer to sell, securities, and not to their purchase. It makes it unlawful for any person, with respect to such a sale or offer in interstate commerce or through the use of the mail, to employ any device or scheme to defraud. Section 12 also prohibits any person from (1) obtaining money or property by means of any untrue statements of material facts or any omission to state material facts and (2) engaging in any transaction, practice, or course of business that operates or would operate as a fraud or deceit on a purchaser.

The following case illustrates the scope and coverage of the 1933 Act. Note that the stockbroker and brokerage firm were strictly liable for losses sustained by customers in the purchase of unregistered securities.

Lewis

v

Walston & Co.

487 F2d 617 (1973)

United States Court of Appeals, Fifth Circuit

FACTS: DeCasenave, a registered representative (stockbroker) of Walston, a brokerage firm, touted stock of Allied Automation to Lewis and McDonald by telephone and whenever they came into Walston's office on business. DeCasenave voiced optimistic opinions about the appreciation potential of Allied's stock and even went so far as to introduce Lewis and McDonald to an officer of the corporation. She arranged a meeting between Lewis and McDonald and officers of the corporation, and they either purchased or agreed to purchase Allied stock at that time. Walston knew about DeCasenave's efforts in touting Allied stock, but its office manager never asked the broker to halt her efforts in this regard. Allied stock was never registered with the SEC. After sustaining losses, Lewis and McDonald sued Walston and DeCasenave for damages under § 12 of the 1933 Act.

ISSUE: Is Walston & Co. liable for DeCasenave's sale of an unregistered security?

RESULT: Yes. DeCasenave was acting within the scope of her employment in advocating purchase of the unregistered stock.

REASONING:

*   *   *

Liability for the sale of unregistered securities is absolute under § 12(1) of the Securities Act of 1933. A purchaser may recover regardless of whether he can show any degree of fault, negligent or intentional, on the seller's part. Liability is established if the plaintiff proves three elements: (1) that no registration statement covering the securities involved was in effect; (2) that, in the language of the statutes, the defendants were "person[s] who [sold] or offer[ed] to sell" the securities; (3) that the mails, or facilities for interstate transportation or communications were used in making the sale. In this case, since the parties stipulated that the first and third elements were present, the only question for the jury to decide was whether Mrs. DeCasenave "sold" the Allied Automation stock, within the meaning of § 12(1).

Mrs. DeCasenave of course was not a "seller" in the most common sense of that word, that is, she was not the party who parted with the securities sold and received the consideration given in exchange. That, however, is not conclusive under § 12(1), for the courts have recognized that other parties who participate in the negotiations of or arrangements for the sale of unregistered securities "sell" those securities within the meaning of § 12(1). . . . Brokers have long been held liable as sellers under § 12(2), as have other parties responsible for bringing about sales of securities they themselves do not own. . . .

. . . Mrs. DeCasenave does not dispute the facts that she touted the Allied Automation stock heavily to the plaintiffs, arranged the January 3 meeting, and notified the plaintiffs that there was additional stock available before each of the plaintiffs' later purchases. The jury could permissibly infer from these facts that Mrs. DeCasenave's actions were a "substantial factor" in bringing about the plaintiffs' purchases, and thus the "proximate cause" of those purchases. . . .

. . . [W]e think it clear that there was an evidentiary basis for finding that Mrs. DeCasenave was acting within the scope of her employment in taking the actions the jury found constituted the proximate cause of the plaintiffs' purchases. Those actions included touting a stock, making recommendations, keeping customers informed of developments in a company whose securities the customers were considering buying, and arranging the mechanics of a purchase-and-sale transaction. These are "acts commonly done" by brokers. . . . at the very least, they would be "simila[r] in quality" to acts brokers are routinely authorized to perform. Mrs. DeCasenave used the Walston offices regularly in arranging the transaction; and she used her position as the representative who serviced McDonald's and Lewis's accounts to recruit them as purchasers of this new company's stock. Thus, to this extent, the "instrumentality by which the harm [was] done [was] furnished by the master to the servant". . . .

Walston argues that Mrs. DeCasenave was acting beyond the scope of her employment. For example, Walston did not deal in unregistered securities. Moreover, Mrs. DeCasenave and the brokerage house did not perform their usual roles as brokers; that is, the transaction did not involve the broker's placing an order through the house's New York office, which was then executed by the central office. In this regard, they note that Walston never stood to receive, and never did receive, any commission or other financial benefit from the direct and essentially private exchange Mrs. DeCasenave arranged. In addition, Walston points to Gaff's [Walston's office manager's] testimony that he advised Mrs. DeCasenave against dealing in the stock, and to Lewis's testimony that Gaff advised him to the same effect.

None of these superficially supportive bases for Walston's argument precludes the conclusion that Mrs. DeCasenave's actions were within the scope of her employment. That Walston did not deal in unregistered securities addresses only the question whether Mrs. DeCasenave's conduct was authorized; . . . however, conduct may be within the scope of employment even if it is unauthorized, if it is sufficiently similar to authorized conduct. That the transactions did not involve the execution of an order through the brokerage house also does not necessarily mean that Mrs. DeCasenave's acts were without the scope of her employment. Brokers may and do take many actions in the course of their dealings with customers that do not relate directly to transactions executed through the brokerage house; these actions are not for that reason necessarily beyond the scope of the brokers' employment. That Walston did not receive any financial benefit from the transaction is not of controlling importance. If a particular act is authorized, or sufficiently similar to an authorized act, finding that act to be within the scope of employment does not require that the act have conferred any particular benefit, financial or otherwise, on the employer. . . .

Thus . . . there was evidence to support the jury's conclusion that Mrs. DeCasenave was acting within the scope of her employment. . . .

Wisdon, Circuit Judge.

53:5   Securities Exchange Act of 1934

In contrast to the Securities Act of 1933, which was enacted to control the initial issuance of securities, the Securities Exchange Act of 1934 (1934 Act) was enacted to regulate securities after their initial issuance. The 1934 Act regulates both securities exchanges, such as the New York Stock Exchange, and the securities market. It is intended to make available to persons who buy and sell securities information relating to the issuers of the securities. The Act seeks to prevent (1) fraud in securities trading and the manipulation in stock markets and (2) abuses and fraudulent schemes by corporate owners, directors, or officers. It outlaws the use of *insider information* for the financial gain of privileged insiders or persons to whom such inside information is given ("tippees") to the detriment of uninformed security holders. The 1934 Act also promotes the self-regulation of business practices by the various stock exchanges and their members to achieve fair and honest markets available for those engaged in the purchase or sale of securities.

Securities and Exchange Commission   Among the most important aspects of the 1934 Act was the creation of the *Securities and Exchange Commission* (SEC). This federal agency consists of five commissioners appointed by the President with the advice and consent of the Senate. The SEC administers all the various federal securities laws. The SEC also has certain authority and responsibility over corporate reorganizations under the federal bankruptcy laws.[1]

Registration   The 1934 Act requires all stock exchanges, brokers, and dealers to register with the SEC unless exempted by the commission. The SEC has authority to expel or suspend member brokers or dealers from exchanges.

The 1934 Act also precludes securities from being listed on a stock exchange unless the issuer registers both with the exchange and with the SEC. An issuer must provide information that is substantially the same as that required for initial issues under the Securities Act of 1933. Registration requirements have been extended as well to securities traded in the over-the-counter market if an issuer has gross assets exceeding $1,000,000 and a minimum of 500 shareholders. Registrants are required to provide the SEC with current information by filing regular reports.

Annual 10-K Report   Every issuer of a security registered under the Securities Exchange Act of 1934 must file periodic reports with the SEC. These reports are intended to keep the information and documents required to be included in or filed with the registration statement reasonably current. Moreover, every issuer of securities must file an annual "10-K" form, which includes a description of the business of the company and its properties, a summary of operations for the last five fiscal years, and a list of parent corporations and subsidiaries. The 10-K reports must contain information concerning legal proceedings and the increase or decrease in outstanding securities and indebtedness, as well as other financial information. The reports must also contain the approximate number of security holders and information concerning compensation paid to executive officers and directors.

Annual Shareholder Report   To prompt greater disclosure of financial information to shareholders, the 1934 Act requires every corporation that has registered securities with the SEC to issue an annual shareholder report containing financial information for the last two fiscal years. Annual reports must reflect the financial position of the corporation and the results of oper-

---

[1] Bankruptcy is discussed in Chapter 32.

ations. They contain the same information, but in a briefer form, as that contained in the 10-K forms filed with the SEC. In addition, annual reports must contain a five-year summary of operations and an analysis of corporate operations by management. A brief description of the corporation's business and its various divisions or segments must also be included. Corporations must list corporate directors and executive officers, their principal occupations or businesses, and the name and business of any organization by which these people are employed. The annual reports must also include the annual range of trading prices for the corporate shares for each quarter during the past two fiscal years, the amount of dividends paid, and a statement offering to provide shareholders with a copy of the 10-K form filed with the SEC. Every reporting corporation must send the SEC a copy of its annual report.

Short-Swing Transactions   Because of their positions, corporate officers and employees can use inside information unknown to the general public profitably to personal advantage. Naturally, a person possessing inside information about how a corporation is doing—and hence what the corporation's stock is or will be worth—is at a great advantage over members of the general population who do not possess this information.

Section 16 of the 1934 Act [15 USC § 78p] was enacted in response to potential *insider* abuse. It is designed to prevent insiders—defined as any officer, director, or owner of more than ten percent of a corporation's stock—from using inside information to make profits on the sale or purchase of the corporation's securities. Section 16 applies to all corporations that have equity securities registered under § 12 of the Act. All insiders must report their beneficial interest of registered securities—stock owned by them or by members of their families—to the SEC. All purchases or sales of stock in the corporation must also be reported. Any profit made by an insider from either a purchase and sale or a sale and purchase of the corporation's stock within less than a six-month period belongs to the corporation.

 As a general rule, there are no defenses to an action based on § 16. If an insider purchased or sold a registered security within the specified time period, any profits so made must be turned over to the corporation. It makes no difference that an insider did not have actual access to inside information. Nor does it matter that a person did not use inside information. In short, any person coming within the terms of § 16 is liable for any profit made within the six-month period.

The following well-known case illustrates how § 16 was interpreted with respect to a two-step plan used to sell securities. Consider whether the reasoning of the majority is persuasive, and contrast it with the reasoning of the dissenting justices. It is interesting to note that Justice William O. Douglas, who wrote the dissenting opinion, was one of the early members of the Securities and Exchange Commission.

Reliance Electric Co.

v

Emerson Electric Co.
404 US 418 (1972)
United States Supreme Court

FACTS: In June 1967, in an unsuccessful takeover attempt, Emerson Electric acquired 13.2 percent of Dodge Manufacturing Company's stock. Later, Emerson decided to sell its shares when Dodge merged with Reliance Electric Company. Since Emerson owned over 10 percent of the stock and the sale was to take place within six months of purchase, it settled on a two-step plan to minimize the effect of the § 16 restriction on insider transactions. Emerson first sold 37,000 shares of Dodge to bring its holdings down to 9.96 percent. Two weeks later it sold the remainder. Reliance then demanded that Emerson's profits on both sales be turned over to it. Emerson sued in federal court for a declaration that it was not so liable. Emerson contended that at the time of the second sale it had not been a 10 percent shareholder in Dodge, so that § 16 did not apply.

ISSUE: Is Emerson liable for its trading profits under Section 16 of the 1934 Act?

RESULT: No, because the two sales were not interrelated parts of a single plan.

REASONING:

Stewart, Justice.

*   *   *

. . . In this case, the respondent, the owner of 13.2% of a corporation's shares, disposed of its entire holdings in two sales, both of them within six months of purchase. The first sale reduced the respondent's holdings to 9.96%, and the second disposed of the remainder. The question presented is whether the profits derived from the second sale are recoverable by the Corporation under § 16(b). We hold that they are not. . . .

The history and purpose of § 16(b) have been exhaustively reviewed by federal courts on several occasions since its enactment in 1934. . . . Those courts have recognized that the only method Congress deemed effective to curb the evils of insider trading was a flat rule taking the profits out of a class of transactions in which the possibility of abuse was believed to be intolerably great. As one court observed:

"In order to achieve its goals, Congress chose a relatively arbitrary rule capable of easy administration. The objective standard of Section 16(b) imposes strict liability upon substantially all transactions occurring within the statutory time period, regardless of the intent of the insider or the existence of actual speculation. This approach maximized the ability of the rule to eradicate speculative abuses by reducing difficulties in proof. Such arbitrary and sweeping coverage was deemed necessary to insure the optimum prophylactic effect." . . .

Thus Congress did not reach every transaction in which an investor actually relies on inside information. A person avoids liability if he does not meet the statutory definition of an "insider," or if he sells more than six months after purchase. Liability cannot be imposed simply because the investor structured his transaction with the intent of avoiding liability under § 16(b). The question is, rather, whether the method used to "avoid" liability is one permitted by the statute.

Among the "objective standards" contained in § 16(b) is the requirement that a 10% owner be such "both at the time of the purchase and sale . . . of the security involved." Read literally, this language clearly contemplates that a statutory insider might sell enough shares to bring his holdings below 10% and later—but still within six months—sell additional shares free from liability under the statute. Indeed, commentators on the securities laws have recommended this exact procedure for a 10% owner who, like Emerson, wishes to dispose of his holdings within six months of their purchase.

Under the approach urged by Reliance, and adopted by the District Court, the apparent immunity of profits derived from Emerson's second sale is lost where the two sales, though independent in every other respect, are "interrelated parts of a single plan." . . . But a "plan" to sell that is conceived within six months of purchase clearly would not fall within § 16(b) if the sale were made after the six months had expired, and we see no basis in the statute for a different result where the 10% requirement is involved rather than the six-month limitation. . . .

Justice Douglas, with whom Justice Brennan and Justice White concur, dissenting.

* * *

Section 16(b) is a "prophylactic" rule . . . whose wholesome purpose is to control the insiders whose access to confidential information gives them unfair advantage in the trading of their corporation's securities.

The congressional investigations which led to the enactment of the Securities Exchange Act unearthed convincing evidence that disregard by corporate insiders of their fiduciary positions was widespread and pervasive. Indeed, "the flagrant betrayal of their fiduciary duties by directors and officers of corporations who used their positions of trust and the confidential information which came to them in such positions, to aid them in their market activities," was reported by the Senate subcommittee charged with the investigation to be "[a]mong the most vicious practices unearthed at the hearings." . . . The subcommittee did not limit its attack to directors and officers. "Closely allied to this type of abuse was the unscrupulous employment of inside information by large stockholders who, while not directors and officers, exercised sufficient control over the destinies of their companies to enable them to acquire and profit by information not available to others." . . .

Section 16(b) was drafted to combat these "predatory operations," . . . by removing all possibility of profit from those short-swing insider trades occurring within the statutory period of six months. The statute is written broadly, and the liability it imposes is strict. Profits are forfeit without proof of an insider's intent to gain from inside information, and without proof that the insider was even privy to such information.

Today, however, in the guise of an "objective" approach, the Court undermines the statute. By the simple expedient of dividing what would ordinarily be a single transaction into two parts—both of which could be performed on the same day, so far as it appears from the Court's opinion—a more-than-10% owner may reap windfall profits on 10% of his corporation's outstanding stock. This result, " 'plainly at variance with the policy of the legislation as a whole,' " . . . is said to be required because Emerson, owning only 9.96%, was not a "beneficial owner" of more than 10% within the meaning of § 16(b) "at the time of" the disposition of this block of Dodge stock.

If § 16(b) is to have the "optimum prophylactic effect" which its architects intended, insiders must not be permitted so easily to circumvent its broad mandate. We should hold that there was only one sale—a plan of distribution conceived "at the time" Emerson owned 13.2% of the Dodge stock, and implemented within six months of a matching purchase. Moreover, in the spirit of the Act we should presume that *any* such "split-sale" by a more-than-10% owner was part of a single plan of disposition for purposes of § 16(b) liability. . . .

Antifraud Provisions The principal antifraud provision of the Securities Exchange Act is § 10(b). This section applies to both the sale and purchase of securities, but it is not self-implementing. Rather, it depends on implementing regulations by the SEC, which the SEC issued as *Rule 10b-5*. Section 10(b) makes it unlawful for any person to use, in connection with the purchase or sale of any security through interstate commerce, or the use of a national securities exchange, any manipulative or deceptive device or contrivance in contravention of any SEC rules or regulations. In turn, SEC Rule 10b-5 is the principal fraud control rule instituted under § 10(b). It is a broad rule outlining fraudulent practices in general, and specifying three general areas of proscribed activities: (1) using any device, scheme, or artifice to defraud; (2) making any untrue statement or omitting any statement of material fact; or (3) engaging in any act, practice, or course of business that does or would operate as a fraud or deceit. Section 10(b) and Rule 10b-5 do not apply exclusively to fraudulent acts or activities directed toward inducing the purchase or sale of securities. Each makes unlawful any such act or activity performed "in connection with the purchase or sale" of a security. In addition, the United States Supreme Court has held that these provisions are to be read flexibly, not technically or restrictively. Section 10(b) does not expressly authorize a civil remedy for damages, but courts have interpreted the act to permit private actions by those defrauded in securities transactions.

To recover under Rule 10b-5 there must be some fraudulent action or deception in connection with the purchase or sale of securities. A misrepresented or undisclosed fact must be a material one. Furthermore, for liability to exist, it must be shown that one person actually intended to deceive, manipulate, or defraud another.

In addition to its general prohibition of fraudulent activities by Rule 10b-5, the SEC has promulgated a number of other rules under § 10(b) which identify specific activities falling within the scope of the prohibitions of this section. Although these rules do not make any acts unlawful, they define certain activities as constituting "manipulative or deceptive devices or contrivances."

The following case examines the types of activities associated with the sale of a security that may create § 10(b) liability.

Angelastro

v

Prudential-Bache Securities, Inc.
764 F2d 939 (1985)
United States Court of Appeals, Third Circuit

FACTS: Angelastro maintained a margin account with Prudential-Bache's corporate predecessor, Bache Halsey. Angelastro claims that Bache Halsey misrepresented and failed to disclose material information regarding the interest rates applicable to its margin accounts, purportedly in violation of § 10(b) of the 1934 Act.

ISSUE: Is misrepresentation of the terms of a brokerage margin account an act sufficiently "in connection with" the sale of a security as to subject the broker to 10(b) liability?

RESULT: Yes. That act is within the scope of liability of § 10(b).

REASONING:

*　　*　　*

Section 10(b) and Rule 10b-5, the basic anti-fraud provision promulgated thereunder, interdict the misrepresentation or omission of material facts in connection with the purchase or sale of any securities. A Rule 10b-5 claim requires, *inter alia*, that the misrepresentation be made "in connection with" the purchase or sale of a security. . . . The purpose underlying section 10(b) and the rules adopted under it is to insure that investors obtain disclosure of material facts in connection with their investment decisions regarding the purchase or sale of securities. . . . Rule 10b–5 claims typically involve alleged misrepresentations with respect to the merits of a particular security. For example, nondisclosure of insider information concerning the value of securities states a claim under the rule. . . . Such a misrepresentation is obviously made "in connection with" the stock that is subsequently sold or purchased.

Rule 10b–5 also encompasses misrepresentations beyond those implicating the investment value of a particular security. The Supreme Court has declared that section 10(b) must be read "flexibly, not technically and restrictively." . . .

Like churning, concealment or misrepresentation of interest terms relating to a margin account does not affect the investment value of a particular security, but rather the course of dealing in securities. Accordingly, . . . Angelastro has pleaded a sufficient causal connection between the purported fraudulent concealment and her purchases of securities on margin to meet the "in connection with" requirement of section 10(b) of the Exchange Act. . . . The Supreme Court has emphasized that the federal securities laws were designed " "to achieve a high standard of business ethics . . . *in every facet of the securities industry.' '* . . . Holding that the concealment of credit terms of a margin account falls within the purview of Rule 10b–5 comports with this policy. . . .

Investors maintain margin accounts with brokerage firms for the very purpose of trading in securities. They need accurate information regarding the credit terms of their margin accounts in order that they may evaluate the desirability of purchasing securities on margin. The amount required to service the debt in a margin account may very well affect the profitability of such trading. Moreover, disclosure of the rate and method of calculation of interest payments is also critical in order that an investor will not become overextended, and then be forced to liquidate, possibly at substantial losses, all or part of his or her margin holdings to meet a margin call. We therefore reject Bache's assertion that, as a matter of law, plaintiff could prove no set of facts to demonstrate a connection between the credit terms of a margin account and her decision to purchase securities on margin. If Angelastro can establish what she sets forth in her complaint—that defendants' misstatements and nondisclosure of material terms induced her to purchase certain securities to her financial detriment—she may very well be entitled to some recovery. . . .

There is a danger in construing the "in connection with" requirement so broadly that virtually any type of misconduct related to a securities transaction even in the most tenuous or tangential way might be claimed to give rise to a federal securities law violation. The Supreme Court was aware of potential overextensions of section 10 when it established the scope of the "in connection with" requirement in *Bankers Life*. It observed that Congress "did not seek to regulate transactions which constitute no more than internal corporate mismanagement." . . . To avoid the pitfalls of such overreaching, we noted in *Ketchum*, 557 F.2d at 1027, that courts should adopt a case-by-case approach for determining the proper scope of the "in connection with" requirement. . . .

Thus the *in terrorem* argument advanced by defendants and accepted by the district court is not persuasive. Our holding that the misrepresentations alleged by Angelastro regarding her margin account are cognizable under Rule 10b–5 does not mean that every loan transaction in which a pledge of securities is involved or every bank loan for the purpose of purchasing securities is necessarily within the purview of section 10(b). We decide only the issue certified to us by the district court. . . .

Adams, Circuit Judge.

Corporate Tender Offers and Takeovers   A cash takeover bid is a public offer made by one corporation to the shareholders of another corporation to purchase a certain number, generally a controlling interest, of the second corporation's voting shares at a specific price. Cash tender offers generally provide hefty premiums to tendering shareholders, and the offer is usually open for a limited time. In 1968 Congress enacted the *Williams Act* [15 USC § 78n(d–f)], which specifically regulates tender offers and corporate takeovers. Under the act, an acquiring corporation making a cash takeover bid for the shares of another corporation must file certain reports with the SEC describing the acquirer's business plans and sources of financing. A minimum tender period is established, requiring that all offers remain open for at least ten days, thus precluding the speedy exchanges of control that occurred before the enactment of the act. The Williams Act also contains a broad proscription of fraud. Its basic purpose is to protect target shareholders by providing them with more information about an acquirer and by giving them more time to decide whether to tender shares for which a bid has been made. It is reasoned that disclosure provisions coupled with greater time for deliberation allow target shareholders to make better decisions. Largely as a consequence of the act, the sudden takeovers characteristic of earlier days are now almost extinct.

53:6   Liability Under Federal Securities Laws

Section 11 of the 1933 Act requires directors and officers to have significant legal, financial, and operational knowledge of a corporation whenever securities are registered with the SEC. If a registration statement contains material misstatements or omissions, officers or directors may be liable in damages to disappointed purchasers under § 11. Section 11 also contains the principal *defense* to a liability action against an officer or director. This defense is that the officer or director exercised *due diligence* in meeting federal registration requirements.

Violation of § 11 is not the only way an officer or director might incur liability under the 1933 Act. An officer or director could also be liable under § 12, which requires that a registration statement be filed with the SEC. Any officer or director who has taken an active role in offering or selling an unregistered security is subject to liability. Furthermore, directors may be held liable under § 17, which deals with fraud committed in the offer or sale of securities. Anyone who purchases an unregistered security is entitled to rescind the purchase or obtain damages against the seller.

An officer or director can also incur civil and criminal liability under the Securities Exchange Act of 1934. This liability can be incurred in connection with any of the following:

- Failure to file applications, reports, or documents
- Alteration, misrepresentation, or omission of information in statements as to stock ownership and transactions in such stock
- Manipulation of securities prices
- Use of manipulative and deceptive devices in the offer and sale of securities
- Improper solicitation of proxies
- Unlawful representations
- Concealment of material information

In addition to the Securities Act of 1933 and the Securities Exchange Act of 1934, there are other federal laws that impose responsibilities and liabilities on officers and directors. These laws specifically relate to an officer's or director's position as a controlling person in the corporation, as a conspirator, or as an aider or abettor of offenses committed by others.

 As a result of the federal securities laws, it is extremely important for officers and directors to take all reasonable steps to assure that corporate publicity and reports, for example, are accurate and complete. Complete and timely public disclosure of material developments affecting the corporation should be made when that information has been appropriately verified. All reports and documents filed with the SEC, the states, or other governmental entities should be accurate and free from omissions or misrepresentations.

The following case remains the dominant analysis of the due diligence defense under § 11 of the Securities Act of 1933. The case is reproduced in some detail in order to provide insight into the behavior of the defendants. What does the opinion indicate about the duty of a corporate officer or director?

Escott

v

BarChris Constr. Corp.

283 F Supp 643 (1968)

United States District Court, SD New York

FACTS: BarChris Construction Corporation built bowling alleys for resale. Needing funds to finance its operations, BarChris sold debt securities to the public. The company later defaulted on the securities and ultimately went bankrupt. The holders of the securities brought suit under § 11 of the Securities Act of 1933 against each officer and director of BarChris, alleging that the registration statement filed with the SEC contained material false statements and material omissions. Damages were sought from the corporate officers and from nine directors who signed the registration statement. After a trial, all the defendants moved to dismiss the complaint. In his opinion, the district court judge discussed the merits of the action against each officer and director separately. The court's discussion of the liability of several of these officers and directors is set forth below.

ISSUE: Is the due diligence defense available to these individual officers and directors?

RESULT: None of the officers and directors established an adequate due diligence defense.

REASONING:

*   *   *

Russo

Russo was, to all intents and purposes, the chief executive officer of BarChris. He was a member of the executive committee. He was familiar with all aspects of the business. . . . He acted on BarChris's behalf in making the financing statements. . . . He was thoroughly aware of BarChris's stringent financial condition. . . .

In short, Russo knew all the relevant facts. He could not have believed that there were no untrue statements or material omissions in the prospectus. Russo has no due diligence defenses.

Vitolo and Pugliese

They were the founders of the business who stuck with it to the end. Vitolo was president and Pugliese was vice president. Despite their titles, their field of responsibility in the administration of BarChris's affairs during the period in question seems to have been less all-embracing than Russo's. Pugliese in particular appears to have limited his activities to supervising the actual construction work.

Vitolo and Pugliese are each men of limited education. It is not hard to believe that for them the prospectus was difficult reading, if indeed they read it at all.

But whether it was or not is irrelevant. The liability of a director who signs a registration statement does not depend upon whether or not he read it or, if he did, whether or not he understood what he was reading.

And in any case, Vitolo and Pugliese were not as naive as they claim to be. They were members of BarChris's executive committee. At meetings of that committee BarChris's affairs were discussed at length. They must have known what was going on. Certainly they knew of the inadequacy of cash. . . . They knew of their own large advances to the company which remained unpaid. They knew that they had agreed not to deposit their checks until the financing proceeds were received. They knew and intended that part of the proceeds were to be used to pay their own loans.

All in all, the position of Vitolo and Pugliese is not significantly different, for present purposes, from Russo's. They could not have believed that the registration statement was wholly true and that no material facts had been omitted. And in any case, there is nothing to show that they made any investigation of anything which they may not have known about or understood. They have not proved their due diligence defenses.

Kircher

Kircher was treasurer of BarChris and its chief financial officer. He is a certified public accountant and an intelligent man. He was thoroughly familiar with BarChris's financial affairs. . . .

Moreover, as a member of the executive committee, Kircher was kept informed as to those branches of the business of which he did not have direct charge. He knew about the operation of alleys, present and prospective. . . . In brief, Kircher knew all the relevant facts.

Kircher worked on the preparation of the registration statement. . . . He supplied information . . . about the company's business. He read the prospectus and understood it. He knew what it said and what it did not say.

Kircher's contention is that he had never before dealt with a registration statement, that he did not know what it should contain, and that he relied wholly on [others] to guide him. He claims that it was their fault, not his, if there was anything wrong with it. He says that all the facts were recorded in BarChris's books where these "experts" could have seen them if they had looked. He says that he truthfully answered all their questions. In effect, he says that if they did not know enough to ask the right questions and to give him the proper instructions, that is not his responsibility.

There is an issue of credibility here. . . . Knowing the facts, Kircher had reason to believe that the expertised portion of the prospectus, i.e., the 1960 figures, was in part incorrect. He could not shut his eyes to the facts and rely on [the auditors] for that portion.

As to the rest of the prospectus, knowing the facts, he did not have a reasonable ground to believe it to be true. On the contrary, he must have known that in part it was untrue. Under these circumstances, he was not entitled to sit back and place the blame on the lawyers for not advising him about it.

Kircher has not proved his due diligence defenses.

Trilling

Trilling's position is somewhat different from Kircher's. He was BarChris's controller. He signed the registration statement in that capacity, although he was not a director.

Trilling entered BarChris's employ in October 1960. He was Kircher's subordinate. When Kircher asked him for information, he furnished it. On at least one occasion he got it wrong.

Trilling was not a member of the executive committee. He was a comparatively minor figure in BarChris. The description of BarChris's "management" on page 9 of the prospectus does not mention him. He was not considered to be an executive officer.

Trilling may well have been unaware of several of the inaccuracies in the prospectus. But he must have known of some of them. As a financial officer, he was familiar with BarChris's finances and with its books of account. . . . He should have known, although perhaps through carelessness he did not know at the time, that BarChris's contingent liability . . . was greater than the prospectus stated. In the light of these facts, I cannot find that Trilling believed the entire prospectus to be true.

But even if he did, he still did not establish his due diligence defenses. He did not prove that as to the [expertised] parts of the prospectus . . . he had no reasonable ground to believe that it was untrue. He also failed to prove, as to the [non-expertised] parts of the prospectus . . . that he made a reasonable investigation which afforded him a reasonable ground to believe that it was true. As far as appears, he made no investigation. He did what was asked of him and assumed that others would properly take care of supplying accurate data as to the other aspects of the company's business. This would have been well enough but for the fact that he signed the registration statement. As a signer, he could not avoid responsibility by leaving it up to others to make it accurate. Trilling did not sustain the burden of proving his due diligence defenses. . . .

Auslander

Auslander was an "outside" director, i.e., one who was not an officer of BarChris. He was chairman of the board of Valley Stream National

Bank in Valley Stream, Long Island. In February 1961 Vitolo asked him to become a director of BarChris. Vitolo gave him an enthusiastic account of BarChris's progress and prospects. As an inducement, Vitolo said that when BarChris received the proceeds of a forthcoming issue of securities, it would deposit $1,000,000 in Auslander's bank.

In February and early March 1961, before accepting Vitolo's invitation, Auslander made some investigation of BarChris. He obtained . . . reports which contained sales and earnings figures for periods earlier than December 31, 1960. He caused inquiry to be made of certain of BarChris's banks and was advised that they regarded BarChris favorably. . . .

On March 3, 1961, Auslander indicated his willingness to accept a place on the board. Shortly thereafter, on March 14, Kircher sent him a copy of BarChris's annual report for 1960. Auslander observed that BarChris's auditors were Peat, Marwick. They were also the auditors for the Valley Stream National Bank. He thought well of them.

Auslander was elected a director on April 17, 1961. The registration statement in its original form had already been filed, of course without his signature. On May 10, 1961, he signed a signature page for the first amendment to the registration statement which was filed [with the SEC] on May 11, 1961. This was a separate sheet without any document attached. Auslander did not know that it was a signature page for a registration statement. He vaguely understood that it was something "for the SEC."

Auslander attended a meeting of BarChris's directors on May 15, 1961. At that meeting he, along with the other directors, signed the signature sheet for the second amendment which constituted the registration statement in its final form. Again, this was only a separate sheet without any document attached. Auslander never saw a copy of the registration statement in its final form.

At the May 15 directors' meeting, however, Auslander did realize that what he was signing was a signature sheet to a registration statement. This was the first time that he had appreciated that fact. A copy of the registration statement in its earlier form as amended on May 11, 1961 was passed around at the meeting. Auslander glanced at it briefly. He did not read it thoroughly.

At the May 15 meeting, Russo and Vitolo stated that everything was in order and that the prospectus was correct. Auslander believed this statement. . . .

. . . Auslander made no investigation of the accuracy of the prospectus. He relied on the assurance of Vitolo and Russo, and upon the information he had received in answer to his inquiries back in February and early March. These inquiries were general ones, in the nature of a credit check. The information which he received in answer to them was also general, without specific reference to the statements in the prospectus, which was not prepared until some time thereafter.

It is true that Auslander became a director on the eve of the financing. He had little opportunity to familiarize himself with the company's affairs. The question is whether, under such circumstances, Auslander did enough to establish his due diligence defense with respect to the . . . prospectus.

Although there is a dearth of authority, . . . an English case . . . is of some value. In [that case] it was held that a director who knew nothing about the prospectus and did not even read it, but who relied on the statement of the company's managing director that it was "all right," was liable for its untrue statements. . . .

Section 11 [of the Securities Act of 1933] imposes liability in the first instance upon a director, no matter how new he is. He is presumed to know his responsibility when he becomes a director. He can escape liability only by using that reasonable care to investigate the facts which a prudent man would employ in the management of his own property. In my opinion, a prudent man would not act in an important matter without any knowledge of the relevant facts, in sole reliance upon representations of persons who are comparative strangers and upon general information which does not purport to cover the particular case. To say that such minimal conduct measures up to the statutory standard would, to all intents and purposes, absolve new directors from responsibility merely because they are new. This is not a sensible construction of Section 11, when one bears in mind its fundamental purpose of requiring full and truthful disclosure for the protection of investors.

I find and conclude that Auslander has not established his due diligence defense with respect to the misstatements and omissions in those portions of the prospectus. . . .

Grant

Grant became a director of BarChris in October 1960. His law firm was counsel to BarChris in matters pertaining to the registration of securities. Grant drafted the registration statement for the stock issue in 1959 and for the warrants in January 1961. He also drafted the registration statement for the debentures. In the preliminary division of work . . . , Grant took initial responsibility for preparing the registration statement. . . .

Grant is sued as a director and as a signer of the registration statement. This is not an action against him for malpractice in his capacity as a lawyer. Nevertheless, in considering Grant's due diligence defenses, the unique position which he occupied cannot be disregarded. As the director most directly concerned with writing the registration statement and assuring its accuracy, more was required of him in the way of reasonable investigation than could fairly be expected of a director who had no connection with this work.

There is no valid basis for plaintiffs' accusation that Grant knew that the prospectus was false in some respects and incomplete and misleading in others. Having seen him testify at length, I am satisfied as to his integrity. I find that Grant honestly believed that the registration statement was true and that no material facts had been omitted from it.

In this belief he was mistaken, and the fact is that for all his work, he never discovered any of the errors or omissions which have been recounted at length in this opinion. . . .

Grant contends that a finding that he did not make a reasonable investigation would be equivalent to a holding that a lawyer for an issuing company, in order to show due diligence, must make an independent audit of the figures supplied to him by his client. I do not consider this to be a realistic statement of the issue. There were errors and omissions here which could have been detected without an audit. The question is whether, despite his failure to detect them, Grant made a reasonable effort to that end.

Much of this registration statement is a scissors and paste-pot job. Grant lifted large portions from the earlier prospectuses, modifying them in some instances to the extent that he considered necessary. But BarChris's affairs had changed for the worse by May 1961. Statements that were accurate in January were no longer accurate in May. Grant never discovered this. He accepted the assurance of Kircher and Russo that any change which might have occurred had been for the better, rather than the contrary.

It is claimed that a lawyer is entitled to rely on the statements of his client and that to require him to verify their accuracy would set an unreasonably high standard. This is too broad a generalization. It is all a matter of degree. To require an audit would obviously be unreasonable. On the other hand, to require a check of matters easily verifiable is not unreasonable. Even honest clients can make mistakes. The statute imposes liability for untrue statements regardless of whether they are intentionally untrue. The way to prevent mistakes is to test oral information by examining the original written record.

There were things which Grant could readily have checked which he did not check. . . .

. . . After making all due allowances for the fact that BarChris's officers misled him, there are too many instances in which Grant failed to make an inquiry which he could easily have made which, if pursued, would have put him on his guard. In my opinion, this finding on the evidence in this case does not establish an unreasonably high standard in other cases for company counsel who are also directors. Each case must rest on its own facts. I conclude that Grant has not established his due diligence defenses except as to the audited 1960 figures. . . .

McLean, District Judge.

53:7 Obligations of Accountants Under the Federal Securities Laws

Accountants are particularly exposed to liability under the federal securities laws. Under the laws, an accountant who knowingly prepares, or assists in the preparation of, false materials in connection with an offering of corporate securities can be liable for failing to properly prepare or adequately supervise the preparation of a wide variety of materials that are routinely issued by corporations.

Like the defendants in the *Escott v BarChris* case above, accountants are subject to civil liability under § 11 of the 1933 Act if they include any untrue statement or omit to state a material fact in the financial statements of a securities registration. The "due diligence" defense is available, but the accountant is held to high professional standards.

The 1934 Act imposes liability on an accountant who knowingly makes a false or misleading statement in a document filed with the SEC. In addition, under § 10 and Rule 10b-5, accountants may be civilly liable as aiders or abettors of clients who engage in securities fraud under § 10. However, the accountant must either have known of the false or misleading statement or have been reckless or grossly negligent.

The following case examines the responsibility of an auditor under § 10.

In Re AM International, Inc. Securities Litigation
606 F Supp 600 (1985)
United States District Court, SD New York

FACTS: AMI stockholders brought suit against officers and directors of AMI and against its auditor, Price Waterhouse, alleging misrepresentations and omissions in AMI's fiscal 1979 and 1980 Annual Reports and Form 10-Ks, as to which Price Waterhouse gave its opinion, and in interim financial statements and Form 10-Qs for the first quarter of fiscal 1979 through the third quarter of fiscal 1981.

ISSUE: Is Price Waterhouse subject to liability for violating § 10 of the 1934 Act or for aiding and abetting a violation of the Act?

RESULT: No. The facts alleged are insufficient to impose such liability on the accounting firm.

REASONING:

*   *   *

Price Waterhouse was AMI's independent auditor, and issued its opinion as to both the 1979 and 1980 year-end reports. Plaintiffs therefore sue Price Waterhouse as a principal in connection with these reports. Since Price Waterhouse did not give any opinion with respect to the 1981 interim financials, plaintiffs sue Price Waterhouse as an aider and abettor with respect to those interim reports.

With respect to the 1980 report, the Court finds the complaint sufficient to state a claim against Price Waterhouse. The *Dubowski* complaint alleges with respect to 1980 that Price Waterhouse was aware of specific accounting and internal control problems at AMI, discussed those problems with management and the Audit Committee, and knew that the problems were not corrected. Plaintiffs also allege a pattern of compromise by Price Waterhouse on particular, necessary adjustments to the 1980 financials. . . . There is, therefore, an adequate, specific factual basis from which fraud may arguably be inferred.

The Court is mindful of the fact that an independent auditor's duty does not rise to the level of corporate insiders, and that one of the purposes of [Federal Rules of Civil Procedure] Rule 9(b) is to protect the reputation of professionals such as accountants from groundless allegations of fraud, . . . Nevertheless, the allegations regarding 1980 are sufficient.

However, a careful review of the claims against Price Waterhouse for the 1979 fiscal year demonstrates that those allegations fail to meet the requirements of Rule 9(b). For example, while plaintiffs allege specific compromises in required adjustments to the 1980 financials as noted above, no specific instance is pleaded regarding 1979. And . . . , it is not enough to merely allege "violation of generalized accounting principles requiring adequacy and fairness of disclosure, a conservative approach, [and] complete financial information. . . . " . . . Yet, with respect to 1979, there are no facts which would even arguably permit an inference of fraud. Indeed as has been noted, these allegations are at best marginally sufficient even with respect to the corporate insiders for that year. It follows that given the difference in status of an independent auditor, the Court finds that these allegations cannot be a sufficient predicate for imposing liability on Price Waterhouse for that year.

Plaintiffs also allege that Price Waterhouse aided and abetted fraud with respect to the uncertified 1981 interim financial reports. However, Price Waterhouse cannot be held liable for misrepresentations or omissions in reports as to which they did not issue an opinion, . . . unless there is a conscious or reckless violation of an independent duty to act, . . . or Price Waterhouse had a "conscious and specific motivation for not acting" and therefore "intended by its silence to forward completion of the fraudulent transactions in the expectation of benefiting from the success of the fraud." . . . There is no allegation which even remotely supports any such inference in this case. Certainly the fact that Price Waterhouse may have seen or reviewed some of the 1981 interims and that a "main objective" of Price Waterhouse was to retain AMI as a client, is not sufficient to justify that inference. . . . It follows that insofar as the complaint alleges aiding and abetting against Price Waterhouse in connection with the 1981 interim financial statements, these claims must be dismissed. . . .

Sprizzo, District Judge.

Key Concepts and Terms

- Almost every state has enacted a blue-sky law or adopted portions of the Uniform Securities Act, which regulates intrastate securities transactions. Most state laws contain (1) antifraud provisions, (2) requirements for the registration of securities, or (3) provisions requiring the registration of brokers or dealers.

- Federal regulation of securities is carried out primarily through the Securities Act of 1933 and the Securities Exchange Act of 1934. The Securities Act relates primarily to the initial issuance of securities, while the Exchange Act regulates the trading of securities after their initial issuance.

- The Securities and Exchange Commission is the federal agency that administers all of the various federal securities laws.

- The 1933 Act exempts certain types of securities and certain types of transactions from the registration requirements. The most significant exempt securities are those sold wholly intrastate, those placed with institutional investors, and short-term (nine month) commercial paper. The most significant exempt transactions are those subject to SEC Rules 504, 505, and 506 and those between private investors.

- Even if a security is exempt from registration, the antifraud provisions of the securities laws still apply to securities transactions.

- The 1934 Act regulates the securities markets. Section 10 of the 1934 Act, and SEC Rule 10b-5, prohibit fraud in either the sale or purchase of a security.

- Section 16 of the 1934 Act prevents a corporate insider from profiting in short-swing trading in the corporation's securities.

- Officers and directors can be held liable under § 11 of the Securities Act of 1933, which requires them to have a significant legal, financial, and operational knowledge of a corporation whenever securities are registered with the SEC before they are issued and sold to the public.

- Officers and directors can be held liable under the Securities Exchange Act of 1934 for misstatements, misrepresentations, half-truths, or the omission of material information in the offer or sale of any securities registered with the SEC. An officer or director can also incur civil and criminal liability under the 1934 act in connection with (1) applications, reports, or documents filed or required to be filed with the SEC; (2) statements as to stock ownership and transactions in such stock; (3) manipulation of securities prices; (4) use of manipulative and deceptive devices in the offer and sale of securities; and (5) concealing material information.

- Under the federal securities laws, an accountant can be liable for failing to properly prepare, to have prepared, or to supervise the preparation of a corporate client's materials issued in connection with an offering of securities.

- Accredited Investor
- Blue-Sky Laws
- Dealer
- Due Diligence
- Insider Information
- Intrastate Sales
- Investment Advisors Act of 1940
- Investment Company Act of 1940
- Issuer
- Prospectus
- Regulation A
- Rule 10b-5
- Securities Act of 1933

- Securities Exchange Act of 1934
- Securities and Exchange Commission (SEC)
- Securities Investor Protection Act of 1970
- Security
- Short-Swing Transaction
- Short-Term Commercial Paper
- 10-K Report
- Underwriting
- Uniform Securities Act
- Williams Act

Questions and Case Problems

1. Nu-Vo, a Florida corporation, issued 100,000 outstanding shares of common stock traded over the counter. Nu-Vo seeks additional capital through a public offering of 100,000 new shares of common stock. The new stock must be, but as yet has not been, registered under the Securities Act of 1933. Does Rich, Nu-Vo's president, violate any of the securities laws by offering a friend 10,000 shares when the two happen to meet on a fishing expedition?

2. Douglas, a leading aircraft manufacturer, informed a brokerage company of substantially reduced company earnings. This information was relayed the next day to other employees of the brokerage firm and then to selected companies with which the brokerage firm had dealings. These companies then sold virtually all of their Douglas holdings. When the company publicly announced disappointing earnings a few days later, the price of its stock fell dramatically. What laws, if any, were broken? Would the brokerage firm be liable to persons purchasing Douglas

stock after the firm knew of the unfavorable earnings but before they were made public? What remedies exist against those who profited from the inside information? Should Douglas be held liable for failing to disclose its earnings expectations as soon as they were known?

3. Texas Gulf Sulfur (TGS) was engaged in exploration and mining of minerals. In November 1963, it drilled a test hole on property in Canada which revealed significant deposits of copper, zinc, and silver. TGS then began to acquire rights to the surrounding property. The president of TGS instructed employees who knew of the discovery to keep it quiet. By April 1964, rumors of the find had reached New York newspapers. The president therefore had two TGS executives issue a news release on April 12 to discount the rumors and to indicate that insufficient information was available to evaluate a possible ore discovery. The release also stated that additional drilling would be required. On April 16, the company gave out two additional reports which indicated that a discovery had indeed been made. The stock of TGS went from $17.50 per share to over $58 in a few months. The SEC brought an action under Rule 10b-5 against TGS employees who purchased stock before full disclosure of the ore discovery had been made to the public. The SEC also sued TGS for the misleading press release, as well as employees who received options to purchase TGS stock prior to public disclosure of the information. The SEC also joined persons to whom the insiders had given information about the discovery. Did the officers, directors, and employees of TGS violate Rule 10b-5? Can those receiving inside information and purchasing securities based on this information also be held liable? Did TGS violate any of the securities laws by issuing a misleading press release that could have had a material effect on the price of its securities? Can the SEC request a judgment ordering restitution of illegal profits by an individual trading in TGS stock on the basis of undisclosed information?

4. Mr. Whiting, a director of Dow Chemical Company, bought 21,000 Dow shares. The money for this purchase was given to him by Mrs. Whiting, who sold 29,000 Dow shares in a separate transaction some weeks earlier. Mrs. Whiting maintained her own checking and brokerage accounts, and did not mingle her funds or assets with those of her husband. Although she controlled all transactions involving her property and did not discuss individual trades with Mr. Whiting, the two did discuss mutual financial goals. Must Mr. Whiting give up any profit made on his sale and purchase of Dow shares? Why?

5. Review the facts of the *Escott v BarChris* case (see page 1154). What standard of diligence is required of corporate directors and officers?

6. Yoder entered into an employment contract with Orthomolecular Nutrition Institute, Inc. (Ortho) whereby she agreed to work for Ortho and develop a computer diet program. She agreed to transfer, and did transfer, her diet-plan business, cookbooks, and other materials necessary to the development of the program. In return, Ortho agreed to issue to her shares of stock in Ortho, based on profits generated by the program. No stock was ever issued. Yoder alleges fraud in the contract and files a civil liability action against Ortho for securities fraud under the 1933 and 1934 Acts. Is the contract "in connection with" the issuance of a security?

7. Compare and contrast the antifraud provisions of the Securities Act of 1933 with those of the Securities Exchange Act of 1934.

8. The cost of registering a new issue of stock can easily exceed 10 percent of the issue price of the stock. What do the issuer and the investing public receive as a result of this increased cost?

54 Unfair Trade Practices and Wrongful Appropriation of Ideas

54:1 Wrongful Interference

Usually, a contract is made between two persons with both parties intending to perform exactly according to the agreement. Sometimes, however, a third person acts in such a manner as to prompt one of the contracting parties to breach the agreement. For example, a third person might persuade an independent contractor to terminate his employment with an employer. In other situations, the third person may substantially interfere with the performance of a contract short of causing its actual breach. In still other instances, a third person may dissuade a prospective contracting party from entering into a contract in the first place.

In each of these situations, wrongful *interference* with contract has occurred. The person interfering with the actual or prospective contractual relationship can be held liable to the injured party. Liability is imposed because the contracting parties have inviolable property rights to fulfill the contract or to have it fulfilled, to reap profits resulting from its performance, and to compel performance by the other party.

Although the existence of a valid contract usually must be shown before an injured party can recover for wrongful interference with contract, it is not necessary in all cases. If a contractual relation would have been created but for the third party's interference, liability may be imposed. Absolute certainty of an impending agreement with another is not required. Rather, reasonable assurance that a contract would have been formed but for the interference, in view of all the circumstances, is sufficient to establish liability.

The law is uncertain as to whether a contract must be legally enforceable before a third person can be held liable for interference. In some states, liability will be imposed even if the underlying contract is unenforceable against the other contracting party because of formal defects, oppressive provisions, or the like. In other states, liability will not be imposed if the contract itself is unenforceable. In view of the public policy to the effect that the basis of liability is the interference with an existing relationship—rather than interference with a contract—the first view appears to be the better approach. Indeed, a majority of states agree and have enacted statutes that impose liability despite the unenforceability of the underlying contract. The following case analyzes the elements of wrongful interference with contract.

Childress
v
Abeles
84 SE2d 176 (1954)
North Carolina Supreme Court

FACTS: Childress entered into a contract with the Trogdon Furniture Company to manufacture cabinets for Abeles. Under the contract, Childress was to be paid a commission for each cabinet Trogdon manufactured for Abeles. Subsequently, a dispute arose between Childress and Abeles. Abeles notified Trogdon that it was to cease paying commissions to Childress and that if it refused to cease, Abeles would not buy any more cabinets. As a result, Trogdon stopped paying commissions to Childress under the Childress–Trogdon contract.

ISSUE: Is Abeles liable to Childress for Trogdon's breach of its contract with Childress?

RESULT: Yes. Abeles willfully and wrongfully induced Trogdon to breach the contract.

REASONING:

*   *   *

"The right to make contracts is both a liberty and a property right." . . . In consequence, the overwhelming weight of authority in this nation is that an action in tort lies against an outsider who knowingly, intentionally and unjustifiably induces one party to a contract to breach it to the damage of the other party. . . .

To subject the outsider to liability for compensatory damages on account of this tort, the plaintiff must allege and prove these essential elements of the wrong: *First*, that a valid contract existed between the plaintiff and a third person, conferring upon the plaintiff some contractual right against the third person. . . . *Second*, that the outsider had knowledge of the plaintiff's contract with the third person. . . . *Third*, that the outsider intentionally induces the third person not to perform his contract with the plaintiff. . . . *Fourth*, that in so doing the outsider acted without justification. . . . *Fifth*, that the outsider's act caused the plaintiff actual damages. . . .

The outsider has knowledge of the contract within the meaning of the second element of the tort if he knows the facts which give rise to the plaintiff's contractual right against the third person. "If he knows those facts, he is subject to liability even though he is mistaken as to their legal significance and believes that there is no contract or that the contract means something other than what it is judicially held to mean." . . .

The complaint in substance alleges the existence of a valid contract between the plaintiff and the Trogdon Furniture Co., conferring on plaintiff contractual rights against the Trogdon Furniture Co.; that the defendants had knowledge of this contract; that plaintiff had fully performed and was entitled to the full commissions, and the defendants intentionally and without justification induced the Trogdon Furniture Company not to perform its contract with the plaintiff to the plaintiff's actual damage. The allegations of the complaint . . . contain all the essential allegations necessary to recover damages for wrongfully inducing a breach of contract. . . .

The evidence in the Record shows that the defendants had full knowledge of the facts which gave rise to the plaintiff's contractual right against the Trogdon Furniture Company, and full knowledge that the Trogdon Furniture Company was paying the plaintiff commissions on the goods manufactured and sold by it to them. Acting with this knowledge they knew that their acts in wrongfully inducing the Trogdon Furniture Company to breach its contract with plaintiff would be highly injurious to him. . . .

Parket, Justice.

Interference with Economic Advantage   By analogy to interference with contract, liability can also be imposed for intentional interference with economic advantage in the absence of contract. Under this theory, a party who has reasonable expectations of acquiring an economic advantage in a business transaction is protected from unjustified interference.

Permissible or Justifiable Interference   In certain situations, a third person is privileged to protect and further his or her own interests (or those of others) by interfering with another's contract or economic advantage. This privilege is called justification. Whether one is justified in interfering in any particular situation is not determined by precise standards. It is determined by balancing conflicting considerations. The importance of the objective advanced by the interference is weighed against the importance of the interest affected. The interfering party's conduct must be scrutinized, as must the relationship between the contracting parties and all other relevant matters. The line separating permissible behavior and unjustified interference reflects the ethical standards of the community. The question of justification often boils down to whether the third party transgressed generally accepted standards of common morality or merely played by the "rules of the game."

Competition is the most common basis of justifiable interference. This is so because a person has no right to be protected against reasonable competition. Thus, unless wrongful means are employed, or unless a restraint of trade is created, one who intentionally causes another not to enter into (or not to continue) a contractual relation with a competitor is usually not liable for interference. Competition justifies the conduct.

A person is also justified in interfering with a contract or economic advantage of another if he acts to protect a legitimate interest of his own and uses lawful and proper methods in doing so under the circumstances. Thus, a person who, having a financial interest in the business of a third person, intentionally causes that person not to enter into a prospective contractual relationship with another does not interfere improperly so long as he does not employ wrongful means. He is justified in acting in his own interest.

EXAMPLE: Caldwell loans money to Baker for a motion picture. Baker is on the verge of signing Claudine to play the lead role in the film. Caldwell objects to the casting of Claudine, and as a result Baker gives the part to Arcadia. Caldwell's interference with the prospective contract between Claudine and Baker is not improper, and Caldwell is not liable to Claudine. His financial interest in the film justifies his interest and participation in the choice of actresses.

Finally, a person who bears responsibility for another may be permitted to interfere in that person's contractual relations or business activities. So long as the person responsible acts to protect the other's welfare and does not employ wrongful measures, he is justified in interfering in the other person's business activities. This rule applies to situations in which, by ordinary standards of decent conduct, one person is charged with responsibility for protecting another's welfare. This situation may exist, for example, in the relationship of parent and child, minister and member of a congregation, teacher and pupil, attorney and client, and employer and employee.

54:2   Unfair Trade Practices; Trade Secrets

The economy of the United States is based on a compromise between the theory of laissez faire (a policy opposing governmental interference in business) and a policy advocating complete governmental control over business. During the past 80 years, American legislators and courts have adopted a so-called "regulated competition" under which private individuals have the maximum degree of discretion and control over their business activities so long as traditional notions of fairness and ethics are observed. In essence, the law acts as a reference to promote fairness in the marketplace.

The law of *unfair trade practices* originally focused on businesses that palmed off their own goods as being those of a rival business. Subsequently, the law was extended to proscribe parasitism under the theory that a business may not appropriate its competitor's skill, expenditures, or labor. Today, the law regulating unfair trade practices applies to a host of different business practices, including trade secrets, trade libel, unfair packaging and labeling, and false advertising.

Trade Secrets   The concept of *trade secret* is nebulous; the term has several definitions. Essentially, a trade secret can be any formula, pattern, device, or compilation of information used in business to obtain an advantage over competitors who do not know about it or who do not use it. A trade secret may also be a plan or process, tool, mechanism, or compound, known only to its owner and his or her key employees. A trade secret differs from other secret business information. Unlike business secrets in general, a trade secret is more than mere information about the conduct of a business, such as contract bids, salaries of key employees, or knowledge of new products. A trade secret is something actually used in a business to its advantage.

Misuse of a trade secret is an unfair business practice. Therefore, an employee who learns of a trade secret cannot use it after leaving his employment. The employee can take and use the general skill or knowledge acquired during the course of his employment but is not permitted to disclose the former employer's trade secrets. If the employee does so, the owner can obtain injunctive relief or even damages in appropriate cases.

Customer information and customer lists may constitute a trade secret. The following case discusses the factors used in determining whether a former employee can use such information acquired during prior employment.

Town & Country House & Homes Service, Inc.
v
Evans
189 A2d 390 (1963)
Connecticut Supreme Court

FACTS: The plaintiff, the owner of a housecleaning business, sued to enjoin a former employee from soliciting the plaintiff's customers, and for damages for having solicited his customers.

ISSUE: Does the personal business use of a customer list by an employee constitute appropriation of a trade secret?

RESULT: Yes. A well-developed customer list constitutes property of the employer which the employee may not appropriate to himself.

REASONING:

*   *   *

The plaintiff conducts a housecleaning business and provides men and machinery for that purpose. The defendant was employed by the plaintiff from May, 1957, to March, 1960. . . . He worked for the plaintiff at the homes of various customers . . . in this state and . . . in New York. During the latter part of his employment, he told a number of the plaintiff's customers that he was planning to enter the housecleaning business for himself, and he solicited business from them. Thereafter, the defendant terminated his employment and started his own housecleaning business. At the time of the trial he had fifteen regular customers, some of whom were former customers of the plaintiff.

The [trial] court found that the defendant solicited customers for his own business before his employment with the plaintiff was terminated. Such action was in direct competition with his employer and was contrary to the employer's interest. It was a betrayal of the employer's trust and confidence in the defendant. . . .

Trade secrets are the property of the employer and cannot be used by the employee for his own benefit. The lack of any express agreement on the part of the employee not to disclose a trade secret is not significant. The law will import into every contract of employment a prohibition against the use of a trade secret by the employee for his own benefit, to the detriment of his employer, if the secret was acquired by the employee in the course of his employment. . . . A list of customers, if their trade and patronage have been secured by years of business effort and advertising and the expenditure of time and money, constitutes an important part of a business and is in the nature of a trade secret. It is the property of the employer and may not be used by the employee as his own property or to his employer's prejudice. . . .

Shea, Associate Justice.

 The liability of third persons is quite different from liability imposed on employees for misuse of trade secrets. A third person will be held liable for misuse only if a trade secret has been wrongfully acquired. Therefore, if a competitor discovers another's trade secret by improper means, or has learned of it from a former employee, he or she may be enjoined from using the secret or held liable in damages to the secret's owner. If a competitor discovers a trade secret by fair means, such as through independent discovery, the owner will not be protected.

Covenants Not to Compete An employer frequently attempts to protect trade secrets by entering into a contract with employees under which the employees agree not to compete with the employer for a particular length of time within a specific geographical area, after leaving the employer's business. Such an agreement is known as a *covenant not to compete*. Although this kind of agreement was regarded as contrary to public policy and therefore void at common law, today a covenant not to compete is generally valid and enforceable if it is supported by consideration and is reasonable and consistent with the public interest.

A covenant not to compete can take any number of forms, including that of an agreement by the employee to forfeit benefits under a noncontributory retirement plan or profit-sharing trust in the event of postemployment competition. In most states, the restriction must be agreed on when employment first begins. There is no fixed formula for determining whether a particular covenant not to compete is reasonable; the question must be decided on a case-by-case basis. There are, however, certain elements the courts frequently consider in ascertaining reasonableness, including, for example, the consideration supporting the covenant, threatened danger to the employer in the absence of a restriction on competition, economic hardship imposed on the employee as a result of a limit on his ability to compete, and the effect of an anticompetitive covenant on the public interest. Usually, a covenant that is unlimited as to both time and area will be held invalid as being unreasonable.

Whether the employee will suffer an unreasonable economic hardship due to the restriction imposed on his or her ability to compete has been held to depend on such factors as the general business conditions then prevailing, the employee's ability to continue supporting a family, and the need for the employee to change occupation or residence.

EXAMPLE: Members of a medical partnership hire an obstetrician for their clinic for a three-year period. Under the contract, the obstetrician covenants that on separation from the clinic for any reason she will refrain from practicing medicine within a 25-mile radius of the city in which the clinic is located. Subsequently, she leaves the clinic and immediately establishes a new practice within the proscribed area. She has violated the anticompetition clause in the contract, and a court can issue an injunction against her because the anticompetitive covenant is reasonable.

 A businessperson should take steps to secure an understanding with and a legally binding commitment from all employees as to the confidential nature of information acquired by the employee during his or her employment. In this regard, the businessperson may set forth in the employment contract a provision under which the employee promises not to use or disclose any of the employer's trade secrets either during or subsequent to the employment relationship.

Abandonment of Trade Secret Once a trade secret has been abandoned it is no longer protectable, no longer a trade secret. Abandonment entails a general public disclosure, such as public sale of the article or its description in literature available to the public. Disclosure that destroys trade secret protection can also occur through the voluntary publication of the secret in, for example, technical or trade journals, or advertising material. The filing of a patent application does not constitute an abandonment of the trade secret. Nor is there an abandonment if the patent application is rejected. Actual issuance of a patent, however, is considered an abandonment.

54:3 Trade Libel

Trade libel, or disparagement as it is also called, arises when a person communicates false or disparaging statements about another's property, goods, or services, resulting in the actual loss of business. A trade libel need not be defamatory.[1] For example, a false statement made to a potential customer, such as "Smythe is out of business, so buy your goods from me" is a trade libel. It is not defamatory, because it does not say anything bad about Smythe.

A lawsuit based on trade libel is difficult to maintain successfully because of the well-recognized business privilege to promote one's own product at the expense of competitors. On the theory that one who offers goods or services in the marketplace opens himself to competitor criticism, the courts have allowed as "fair comment" a very broad scope of critical statements as to products or services without finding that trade libel has been committed. This privilege of fair comment, however, does not extend to the making of specific false claims about another's property, products, or business. For example, one business may claim that its product is "finer," of "higher quality," or performs "better" than another. At the same time, it may not state that another's goods are "seconds" or "prison-made" when in fact they are not.

The following case discusses the public policy considerations underpinning trade libel. Note the discussion of permissible product comparison and when comparisons are deemed unethical and unfair.

Testing Systems, Inc.

v

Magnaflux Corp.
251 F Supp 286 (1966)
United States District Court, ED Pennsylvania

FACTS: Testing Systems sued its business competitor, Magnaflux Corporation, alleging that Magnaflux had committed trade libel by falsely stating that the federal government had tested Testing Systems' product and found it to be only 40 percent as effective as its own. Magnaflux defended itself on the grounds that comparing products in such a manner was permissible and that no trade libel had occurred.

---

[1] Defamation is discussed in Chapter 5.

ISSUE: Is Magnaflux liable to Testing System for libel?

RESULT: Yes. The false assertion of a factual statement about a competitor's product is actionable trade libel.

REASONING:

*   *   *

The fine line that separates healthy competitive effort from underhanded business tactics is frequently difficult to determine. Apart from the tradesman's right of free speech, which must be vigorously safeguarded, the public has a genuine interest in learning the relative merits of particular products, however that may come about. To advance these interests the law of the market place gives the competitor a wide berth in the conduct of his business. As [was said in a 1932 case],

> "[H]e may send out circulars, or give information verbally, to customers of other men, knowing they are bound by contract for a definite term, although acting upon the expectation and with the purpose of getting the trade of such persons for himself.
> "[H]e may use any mode of persuasion with such a customer . . . which appeals to his self-interest, reason, or even his prejudices.
> "[H]e may descant upon the extent of his rival's facilities compared with his own, his rival's means, his insolvency, if it be a fact, and the benefits which will result to the customer in the future from coming to the solicitor rather than remaining where he is. . . . 'the law of competition' . . . takes little note of the ordinary rules of good neighborhood or abstract morality." . . .

Nonetheless, there is an outer perimeter to permissible conduct. The tradesman must be assured that his competitors will not be suffered to engage in conduct which falls below the minimum standard of fair dealing. "[I]t is no answer that they can defend themselves by also resorting to disparagement. A self-respecting business man will not voluntarily adopt, and should not be driven to adopt, a selling method which he regards as undignified, unfair, and repulsive. A competitor should not, by pursuing an unethical practice force his rival to choose between its adoption and the loss of his trade." . . .

The defendant's comments in the case presently before this Court do not entitle him to the protection accorded to "unfavorable comparison." There is a readily observable difference between saying that one's product is, in general, better than another's (though even this is subject to serious objection) . . . and asserting, as here, that such other's is only 40% as effective as one's own. The former, arguably, merely expresses an opinion, the truth or falsity of which is difficult or impossible of ascertainment. The latter, however, is an assertion of fact, not subject to the same frailties of proof, implying that the party making the statement is fortified with the substantive facts necessary to make it. This distinction has never been seriously questioned. . . . The defendant in this case admittedly circulated to plaintiff's present and prospective customers false statements to the effect that the government had tested both products and found the defendant's to be 60% more effective than plaintiff's. This is not the sort of "comparison" that courts will protect.

Apart from this, there is at least one additional factor which withdraws the defendant's comments from the category of unfavorable comparison. Not content with making the admittedly false statements and allowing them to be evaluated independently of any extraneous influence, the defendant here gave added authenticity to its assertions by invoking the reputation of a third party, the United States Government. It is unnecessary to speculate on the additional force the defendant's remarks must have had when coupled with the purported approval of so highly credible a source. This, of course, is to say nothing of the statements to the effect that the plaintiff had been "thrown out," which by no stretch of the imagination could be termed mere comparison. . . .

John W. Lord, Jr., District Judge.

54:4   Packaging and Labeling

Package design is vitally important to successful product marketing. It is often the sole difference between similar goods. Packaging is also a significant determinant of buying behavior. The term "trade dress" describes the appearance of a product. Trade dress consists of the peculiar visual appearance produced by a particular arrangement or combination of colors, symbols, words, and designs on a label, package, or product. The arrangement or combination is intended to make the source of one product distinguishable from another and to promote its sale. Trade dress is distinct from copyright, trademark, or trade name protection.

The underlying basis of unfair competition law as applied to *trade dress simulation* is the protection of consumers from confusion as to the source of goods. The law is also based on the goal of preventing one business from trading on the established goodwill of another by simulating the packaging or labeling of an existing product.

Many states have enacted legislation to protect business from trade dress simulation or from unfair packaging and labeling practices. The most important is the *Uniform Deceptive Trade Practices Act*. The act codifies the modern view of trade dress unfair competition by granting relief to businesses where there is a likelihood of confusion or misunderstanding as to the source of goods or services.

Confusion is especially likely to occur when a particular trade dress has acquired what is known as a *secondary meaning*. "Secondary meaning" in this context refers to consumer identification of the trade dress sought to be protected with the producer of the goods. A trade dress acquires a secondary meaning when its total image has become associated in the public mind with the source or origin of the goods (rather than with the goods themselves) and a particular manufacturer. In one case, for example, Clairol, Inc., a cosmetics manufacturer, was successful in convincing a court that the distinctive trade dress used for its hydrogen peroxide hair product had acquired a secondary meaning.[2]

54:5 False Advertising

False statements about a particular product constitute an unfair trade practice. The essence of *false advertising* is fraudulent misrepresentation, which results in injury to competitors or customers. Whether false advertising has occurred requires, in each case, a balancing of several interests: the interest of a business to advertise its goods and services as aggressively and effectively as possible, even to the point of issuing highly misleading overstatements (puffing); the interest of business competitors not to be unjustifiably maligned as to their products; and the interest of the consumer to be told the truth about the products and services offered.

A consumer damaged by false advertising can bring a common-law action against the false advertiser for fraud. The attorney general in some states is authorized to bring an action on behalf of all consumers who have been defrauded. In addition, many states have laws based on the Uniform Deceptive Trade Practices Act, which prohibits deceptive commercial conduct and, among other things, misleading advertising. The act permits "a person likely to be damaged by a deceptive trade practice of another" to sue for injunctive relief to prevent the practice. States that have not adopted the act have strong legislation against false advertising.

Lanham Act Because of the difficulties in establishing liability for common-law false advertising in state courts, and because the problems of false advertising are nationwide, Congress enacted § 43(a) of the *Lanham Act* [15 USC § 1125(a)] governing the sale of goods or services in interstate commerce. Section 43(a) prohibits competitors from transacting business in a manner that unnecessarily and unfairly harms another's business. It provides legal remedies to competitors who are injured by false advertising in interstate commerce.

EXAMPLE: A pharmaceutical company places advertising in magazines and on television. The ads compare pain relievers and claim that one of the company's drugs is superior to competitive drugs as an analgesic and inflammation reducer. On evidence that such claims are false, the advertising is enjoinable as a misrepresentation under § 43(a).

Liability under § 43(a) of the Lanham Act is not restricted solely to descriptions and representations that are literally false. Relief can also be granted if advertising simply creates a false impression by omission of relevant infor-

---

[2] *Clairol, Inc. v Andrea Dumon, Inc.*, 303 NE2d 177 (Illinois Appellate Court, 1973).

mation. For example, a distributor of foreign-made goods who omits placing the true country of origin of the imported goods on the packaging and uses the phrase "United States" on the package to create the impression of domestic origin creates a false impression; such advertising violates § 43(a).

Section 43(a) has been applied in many different circumstances. By way of illustration, the following acts have been held to constitute false advertising under § 43(a): selling goods by falsely representing that they are endorsed by a particular person or organization, falsely representing that a product was designed or authorized by a particular person, advertising an inferior product by using a picture of a competing product, selling goods from a catalog confusingly similar in format to another's catalog, advertising a product with a false representation of a consumer product testing organization's rating, and palming off an inferior product in response to orders for another product.

Federal Trade Commission   The *Federal Trade Commission Act* (FTCA) declares both "unfair methods of competition" and "unfair or deceptive acts or practices" in commerce to be unlawful [15 USC § 45(a)]. The *Federal Trade Commission* (FTC) has exclusive authority to enforce the FTCA. In determining whether a business practice is unfair, the FTC considers the following factors: (1) whether the practice offends public policy, as established by statutes, the common law, or otherwise; (2) whether it is immoral, unethical, oppressive, or unscrupulous; and (3) whether it causes substantial injury to consumers, competitors, or other businessmen. The FTC is specifically authorized to prevent false advertising of food, drugs, and cosmetics [15 USC § 52].

Several general principles applicable to determining whether particular business practices constitute false advertising under the FTCA have been recognized. Among these is that for an advertisement to be found deceptive, it need not be shown that the advertiser lacked good faith or intended to deceive. Nor need it be shown, if advertisements have a capacity to deceive, that actual deception resulted. Rather, advertisements are judged on the basis of the meaning they convey to an average or unsophisticated person, not an expert.

When the FTC, after a hearing, rules that a particular act, practice, or method of competition is prohibited by the FTCA, the FTC is required to make a written report of its findings. It may issue to the offending business a cease and desist order, which prohibits the method of competition in question. The party against whom a cease and desist order is issued may then appeal and seek judicial relief from the order.

If the FTC finds that a company has engaged in false and deceptive advertising with regard to a particular product, the FTC can also order the company to conduct corrective advertising. This could involve a specific proportion of the company's advertising print space or broadcast time or a specified proportion of the company's total advertising expenditures.

 Many states have so-called "little FTC" laws, which provide that the state attorney general, or a local prosecutor, can sue on behalf of defrauded buyers for injunctive relief or damages. Most state statutes of this sort also permit a consumer to sue a merchant who is engaged in unfair practices. Other states have enacted legislation under which private individuals or companies can sue other companies that have committed deceptive trade practices or false advertising.

Deceptive Television Commercials Television commercials represent a recurrent problem for the advertiser. The true colors of coffee, orange juice, and iced tea, for example, are lost in transmission on a television screen, and artificial substances must be substituted to obtain a "natural" look. The hot television lights require the use, for example, of mashed potatoes for ice cream, and shaving cream must be used to get the kind of head that is normal on a glass of beer. The use of such mock-ups or props in television commercials is not necessarily an unfair trade practice. However, it is an unfair trade practice to show a product experiment in a television commercial as objective proof of a product claim while conveying to viewers the false impression that they are seeing the experiment for themselves, when in fact they are seeing a mock-up.

54:6 Trademarks

A *trademark* is a word, name, symbol, or device used by a manufacturer to identify that manufacturer's goods and distinguish them from those made or sold by others. Symbols used to identify services, as opposed to goods, are usually called service marks. Since the legal requirements for trademarks and service marks are essentially the same, both are referred to as trademarks. The term "trade name" is used to distinguish partnerships, corporations, and other businesses. Specifically, a trade name is a term or symbol that identifies a business and its goodwill; trademarks and service marks identify and distinguish goods and services.

A trademark or service mark can be any identifying symbol. It may be a well-known word (such as "Jockey" with respect to underwear), a familiar design (such as that on the Kleenex tissue box), a distinctive container (such as the Coca Cola bottle), or a distinctive building design (such as McDonald's golden arches).

A word or symbol qualifies as a trademark if (1) there is a tangible symbol—a word, name, device, symbol, or any combination of these; (2) there is actual adoption and use of the symbol as a mark by a manufacturer or seller of goods or services, and (3) the function of the word or symbol is to identify and distinguish the seller's goods from goods made or sold by others. The symbol must be distinctive enough to identify and distinguish the goods that bear the symbol from other similar goods.

Trademark law serves a dual function: it protects the merchant in the use of his or her trademarks and it protects the people who rely on the trademarks in purchasing goods or services. The trademark has thus been likened to the "business autograph" of the owner; it is a representation that articles on which it is placed are made or prepared by a particular firm.

Lanham Act   While trademark protection is available under state law, the major source of trademark law is the Federal Trademark Act of 1946 [15 USC §§ 1051–1127], commonly known as the Lanham Act. Any person or business can register a trademark with the United States Patent and Trademark Office if the trademark has been used in interstate commerce. Once a trademark has been registered, the owner has the exclusive right to use it. Anyone who reproduces or copies the trademark in connection with the sale or advertising of goods or services when such use is likely to cause confusion or mistake, or to deceive, is liable in damages to the owner of the trademark.

There is no exact definition of the degree of resemblance that is necessary to constitute trademark *infringement.* However, a rule has been formulated that no merchant can adopt a trademark that so resembles another that ordinary purchasers, buying with ordinary care, are likely to be misled. The likelihood of purchaser confusion is determined by examining many factors. These factors include the type of trademark at issue, similarity of design, similarity of product, identity of retail outlets and purchasers, identity of advertising media utilized, the defendant's intent, and whether actual confusion resulted. These different factors are illustrated in the following decision.

Dallas Cowboys Cheerleaders, Inc.

v

Pussycat Cinema, Ltd.
604 F2d 200 (1979)
United States Court of Appeals, Second Circuit

FACTS: The Dallas Cowboys Cheerleaders, Inc. sued the owner and distributor of a motion picture for exhibiting a movie in which, without plaintiff's permission, the actresses wore uniforms essentially identical to uniforms in which plaintiff had a trademark. The suit alleged trademark infringement under the Lanham Act. At an early stage of the proceeding, the trial court gave plaintiff temporary relief by issuing a preliminary injunction. The injunction prevented defendants from exhibiting or distributing the movie until a final decision was reached in the lawsuit.

ISSUE: Does Cinema's depiction of a uniform almost identical to that of the Dallas Cowboy Cheerleaders violate the Lanham Act?

RESULT: Yes. The use of the uniform in the film may cause the audience to believe the Cheerleaders were connected in some way with the film, and that is sufficient "confusion" under the statute.

REASONING:

*   *   *

At all the football games and public events where plaintiff's cheer-leaders appear and on all commercial items depicting the cheerleaders, the women are clad in . . . distinctive uniform. The familiar outfit consists of white vinyl boots, white shorts, a white belt decorated with blue stars, a blue bolero blouse, and a white vest decorated with three blue stars on each side of the front and a white fringe around the bottom. In this action plaintiff asserts that it has a trademark in its uniform and that defendants have infringed . . . that trademark in advertising and exhibiting [the movie entitled] "Debbie Does Dallas."

Pussycat Cinema, Ltd., is a New York corporation which owns a movie theatre in New York City. . . . In November 1978 the Pussycat Cinema began to show "Debbie Does Dallas," . . . In the movie's final scene Debbie dons a uniform strikingly similar to that worn by the Dallas Cowboys Cheerleaders and for approximately twelve minutes of film footage engages in various sex acts while clad or partially clad in the uniform. Defendants advertised the movie with marquee posters depict-ing Debbie in the allegedly infringing uniform and containing such captions as "Starring Ex Dallas Cowgirl Cheerleader Bambi Woods" and "You'll do more than cheer for this X Dallas Cheerleader." Similar advertisements appeared in the newspapers. . . .

. . . In the instant case the combination of the white boots, white shorts, blue blouse, and white star-studded vest and belt is an arbitrary design which makes the otherwise functional uniform trademarkable. . . .

Having found that plaintiff has a trademark in its uniform, we must determine whether the depiction of the uniform in "Debbie Does Dallas" violates that trademark. The district court found that the uniform worn in the movie and shown on the marquee closely resembled plaintiff's uniform and that the public was likely to identify it as plaintiff's uniform. Our own comparison of the two uniforms convinces us that the district court was correct, and defendants do not seriously contend that the uniform shown in the movie is not almost identical with plaintiff's. Defendant's contention is that, despite the striking similarity of the two uniforms, the public is unlikely to be confused within the meaning of section 43(a) of the Lanham Act.

Defendants assert that the Lanham Act requires confusion as to the origin of the film, and they contend that no reasonable person would believe that the film originated with plaintiff. Appellants read the con-fusion requirement too narrowly. In order to be confused, a consumer need not believe that the owner of the mark actually produced the item and placed it on the market. . . . The public's belief that the mark's owner sponsored or otherwise approved the use of the trademark satisfies the confusion requirement. In the instant case, the uniform depicted in "Debbie Does Dallas" unquestionably brings to mind the Dallas Cowboys Cheerleaders. Indeed, it is hard to believe that anyone who had seen defendants' sexually depraved film could ever thereafter disassociate it from plaintiff's cheerleaders. . . .

Plaintiff expects to establish on trial that the public may associate it with defendants' movie and be confused into believing that plaintiff sponsored the movie, provided some of the actors, licensed defendants to use the uniform, or was in some other way connected with the production. The trademark laws are designed not only to prevent consumer confusion but also to protect "the synonymous right of a trademark owner to control his product's reputation." . . .

Van Graafeiland, Circuit Judge.

54:7 Copyright

A person has a common-law property right in the tangible expression of his creative works and can obtain redress against anyone who deprives him of that right or wrongfully copies his work. The common-law *copyright* protects such tangible forms of expression as writings, letters, prints, pictures, paintings, photographs, pictorial illustrations, statues, and other artistic productions, as well as musical, dramatic, and literary compositions, either written or printed. In short, common-law copyright protects virtually all original tangible expressions of a person's intellectual creativity.

The manner of presenting or interpreting a work is a recognized artistic expression and can also be protected by common-law copyright. For example, a news commentator has a common-law copyright in her voice and manner of presentation; an orchestra has an exclusive common-law right in its particular musical rendition of a musical composition, even though the composition is itself not copyrightable; and a broadcast of an athletic event is protected by common-law copyright. Copyright protection does not, however, extend to the *ideas* expressed in subject matter but only to the *form or mode of expression*. For example, the bare scheme or skeleton of a plot is an idea and therefore is not protected by common-law copyright.

Although ideas as such are not protected by copyright, they may be protected by the general principles of unfair competition where there has been a breach of some contractual or fiduciary relationship; for example, ideas can be protected by contract.

Federal Copyright Law Under the Constitution of the United States, Congress is empowered to grant to authors a limited monopoly (exclusive use) for their writings [Article 1, § 8]. This power covers not only literary work, but all works of artistic achievement. A work need not be fine art nor highly creative. It need only be an original creation.

The federal Copyright Act [17 USC §§ 101 et seq.], which was substantially revised in 1978, now provides statutory copyright protection in original works of authorship "fixed in any tangible medium of expression, now known or later developed, from which they can be perceived, reproduced, or otherwise communicated, either directly or with the aid of a machine or device." Such copyrightable works of authorship include literary, musical, or dramatic works, including any accompanying music; pantomimes and choreographic works; motion pictures and other audiovisual works; and sound recordings. The Act specifies, however, that in no case does copyright protection for an original work of authorship extend to any idea, procedure, process, system, method of operation, concept, principle, or discovery, regardless of the form in which it is described, explained, illustrated, or embodied in such work [17 USC § 102(b)].

Another section of the Act [17 USC § 106] gives the owner of a copyright the exclusive right to do (and to authorize others to do) the following: reproduce the copyrighted work; prepare derivative works based on the copyrighted work; distribute copies of the copyrighted work to the public by sale or other transfer of ownership, or by rental, lease, or lending; perform the copyrighted work publicly (in the case of literary, musical, dramatic, and choreographic works; pantomimes; and motion pictures and other audiovisual works); and display the copyrighted work publicly (in the case of literary, musical, dramatic, and choreographic, or sculptural works, including the individual images of a motion picture or other audiovisual work).

A copyright owner can transfer to another person his or her rights in a copyright. The transfer of *exclusive* rights to a federal copyright, however, is not valid unless the transfer is in writing and signed by the owner of the rights conveyed or the owner's authorized agent. The transfer of a statutory copyright on a nonexclusive basis does not require a writing.

It is illegal for anyone to infringe on any of the rights provided to the owner of a copyright by the Copyright Act. Infringement will be found if (1) the defendant's "work" is essentially identical to the plaintiff's and (2) the defendant is shown to have had access to the plaintiff's work. The owner of a statutory copyright has a wide choice of remedies in a copyright infringement suit. The Act provides for injunction against further infringement; damages against the infringer and recovery of profits made by him; seizure of all infringing copies during the pendency of the lawsuit; and destruction of infringing copies, plates, molds, and other devices necessary to make the infringing copies [17 USC §§ 501–504].

Securing a Statutory Copyright Under the Copyright Act, copyright is secured *automatically* for "original works of authorship" when the work is created. A work is "created" when it is fixed in a copy or phonorecord for the first time. In general, "copies" are material objects from which a work can be read or visually perceived either directly or with the aid of a machine or a device, such as books, manuscripts, sheet music, film, videotape, or microfilm. "Phonorecords" are material objects embodying fixations of sounds (excluding, by statutory definition, motion picture sound tracks), such as audiotapes and phonograph discs. Thus, for example, a song (the work) can be fixed in sheet music (copies) or in phonograph discs (phonorecords), or both. Prior to

1978, statutory copyright was secured under the Copyright Act by publication with notice of copyright, assuming compliance with other relevant statutory conditions. Under the copyright law that became effective on January 1, 1978, no publication, registration, or other action in the United States Copyright Office is required to secure copyright.

When a work is published under the authority of the copyright owner, a notice of copyright should be placed on all publicly distributed copies, even works published outside the United States. Failure to comply with the notice requirement can result in loss of certain rights otherwise available to the copyright owner. The notice for visually perceptible copies should contain the following three elements: (1) the symbol © (the letter c in a circle) or the word "copyright," (2) the year of first publication of the work, and (3) the name of the copyright owner.

 In general, copyright registration is a legal formality intended to make a public record of the basic facts of the particular copyright. Even though registration is not generally a requirement for protection, the copyright law provides several inducements to encourage copyright owners to register their copyright. Among these advantages are that the registration establishes a public record of the copyright claim, and registration is ordinarily necessary before an infringement suit can be filed in court. To register a work, the copyright owner sends to the United States Copyright Office, in the same envelope or package, a properly completed application form, a specified fee, and a deposit of the work being registered.

Fair Use Doctrine   In spite of a copyright owner's exclusive rights in copyrighted works, the Copyright Act provides that the "fair use" of a copyrighted work, including such use by reproduction in copies or phonorecords, for purposes such as criticism, comment, news reporting, teaching (including multiple copies for classroom use), scholarship, or research, is not an infringement of copyright. In determining whether the use made of a work in any particular case is a fair use, the factors to be considered include (1) the purpose and character of the use, including whether it is of a commercial nature or is for nonprofit educational purposes; (2) the nature of the copyrighted work; (3) the amount and substantiality of the portion used in relation to the copyrighted work as a whole; and (4) the effect of the use on the potential market for, or value of, the copyrighted work [17 USC § 107].

The *fair use doctrine*, as embodied in § 107, provides a means of balancing the exclusive rights of the copyright holder with the public's interest in the dissemination of information affecting areas of universal concern, such as art, science, history, or industry. Fair use cannot be determined by resort to arbitrary rules but requires examination of the facts in each case.

EXAMPLE: Jeannie is preparing a research paper for publication and, to support her thesis, quotes a paragraph from a copyrighted technical journal, properly crediting the source. Such limited quotation constitutes fair use of the copyrighted material within the meaning and spirit of

§ 107. Mark, another student, directly quotes more than 2,000 words of a copyrighted technical journal in his research paper. Mark properly cites the journal as the author, but he has probably infringed the copyright; such extensive use of another's work is not fair. If it is necessary for Mark to copy so extensively from copyrighted materials, he should obtain the express written permission of the author and publisher of the copyrighted work.

54:8   Patents

Just as copyright laws protect authors, *patent* laws protect inventors. The Constitution of the United States gives Congress the power to promote the progress of science by securing for limited times to inventors the exclusive right to their discoveries [Article 1, § 8]. Congress enacted the first patent law in 1790. The law has undergone many revisions, which have culminated in the Patent Act of 1952 [(35 USC §§ 1 et seq.]. The Act states that subject to the requirements of the statute, any person who invents or discovers any new and useful process, machine, manufacture, or composition of matter (or any new and useful improvements for one of them) can obtain a patent [35 USC § 101]. The Act established the federal Patent and Trademark Office for administering laws relating to patents.

The purposes of the federal patent system are (1) to foster and reward inventions; (2) to promote disclosure of inventions, to stimulate further innovation, and to permit the public to use the invention once the patent expires; and (3) to assure that ideas in the public domain remain there for the free use of the public.

A patent is personal property and can be sold, bequeathed by a will, or passed to the heirs of a deceased patent owner. The Patent Act provides for the transfer or sale of a patent, or of an application for a patent, by an instrument in writing. This instrument, called an "assignment," can transfer either the entire interest in the patent or only a partial interest. When the patent is assigned, the assignee becomes the owner of the patent and has the same rights as the original patentee.

 Applying for a patent requires knowledge of complex patent law and experience in dealing with the Patent and Trademark Office. Any business or individual inventor should employ a patent attorney to perform this service. The Patent and Trademark Office maintains a register of attorneys and other persons who have the appropriate legal and scientific qualifications to assist persons in obtaining patents.

Patents, Trademarks, and Copyrights Compared and Distinguished   The basic distinction between patentable and copyrightable subject matter is that a patent protects the *substance* or the *idea* embodied in a work, while a copyright protects the *mode of expression* of the work. Although patent and copyright protection are derived from the same section of the Constitution, there are different standards for obtaining and enforcing them. For example, a patent must comply with the statutory standards of novelty and lack of obviousness, while the only requirement for obtaining a copyright is that it be original. Trademark law is not concerned either with the content of words or the development of new technology, but rather simply with the protection of identifying symbols.

Although trademark, copyright, and patent are three separate and distinct areas of law, occasionally a single product is protectable by all three at the same time. For example, various features of a household lamp with a sculptured base are capable of protection by all three categories of law. The lamp base, if it qualifies as a "work of art" could be copyrightable. The electrical circuit or bulb might be protected by a patent. The label on the lamp could function as a trademark to identify and distinguish the manufacturer or seller.

Conditions for Obtaining Patent   For an invention to be patentable it must be "new" as defined in the Patent Act. Under the Act, if an invention has been described in a printed publication anywhere in the world, or if it has been in public use or on sale in this country before the date that the applicant *made his invention,* a patent cannot be obtained. In addition, if the invention has been described in a printed publication anywhere or has been in public use or on sale in this country more than one year before the date on which a *patent application is filed,* a valid patent cannot be obtained. In this connection, it is immaterial when the invention was made, or whether the printed publication or public use was by the inventor personally or by someone else.

The Patent Act also provides that a patent cannot be obtained if the differences between the subject matter sought to be patented and the prior art (the "state of the art") are such that the subject matter as a whole would have been obvious at the time the invention was made to a person having ordinary skill in the art to which the subject matter pertains [35 USC § 103]. In other words, the subject matter sought to be patented must be sufficiently different from what has been used or described before so that it may be said to amount to an invention. Small advances that would be obvious to a person having ordinary skill in the particular field are not inventions capable of being patented. For example, the substitution of one unimportant material for another, or mere changes in size, are ordinarily not patentable.

Under the Patent Act, it is generally only the inventor who can apply for a patent. If a person who is not the inventor applies for a patent, any patent obtained would be void. Joint inventors can apply for a patent jointly. It should be noted that a person who only makes a financial contribution is not a joint inventor and cannot be joined in the application as an inventor.

Infringement   A patent grants to the patentee the right to exclude others from making, using, or selling the invention throughout the United States for a term of 17 years. Accordingly, infringement of a patent is the unauthorized making, using, or selling of the patented invention during its term. If a patent is infringed, the patentee can sue for relief in federal court, seeking an injunction to prevent continuation of the infringement and also asking for damages. In an infringement suit, the defendant may question the validity of the patent.

A patentee who makes or sells patented articles is required to mark them with the word "patent" and the number of the patent. The penalty for failure to mark is that the patentee cannot recover damages from an infringer unless the infringer was notified of the infringement and continued to infringe after the notice. Some persons mark articles sold with the terms "patent applied for" or "patent pending." While these phrases have no legal significance, they do give information that an application for a patent has been filed. However, protection afforded by a patent does not start until the actual grant of the patent.

Key Concepts and Terms

- To encourage stability in business expectations, liability is imposed on a person who willfully interferes with another's contractual relations or prospective economic advantage.

- Misuse of a trade secret is actionable; it is based on an abuse of confidence. An employee who leaves a job can take and use skills and knowledge acquired during the employment. However, he cannot disclose his employer's trade secrets, such as processes, methods of doing business, trade routes, and secret customer lists.

- A covenant not to compete is generally valid and enforceable if it is reasonable as to time and place. State statutory provisions frequently regulate such covenants. Some statutes prohibit them.

- A person who communicates false disparaging statements as to the quality of another person's property, goods, or services, resulting in loss of business, is liable for trade libel, also known as trade disparagement. A business is privileged to make general claims about its own product, but the privilege does not extend to making specific false claims about another's property or business.

- The simulation by one business of the packaging or devices employed by another to identify its product or services is an actionable business tort.

- The manufacturer or supplier of goods or services who makes false statements about a product or service in advertisements commits an actionable unfair trade practice at common law. The federal Lanham Act creates liability for advertising misrepresentations as to goods or services in interstate commerce.

- The Federal Trade Commission Act makes "unfair methods of competition in commerce" and "unfair or deceptive acts or practices in commerce" unlawful. The act is administered by the Federal Trade Commission (FTC). The FTC is empowered to prevent deceptive sales approaches, product misrepresentations, and price misrepresentations.

- A copyright protects the mode of expression of a work. A patent protects the substance or idea embodied in the work. While a patent must comply with statutory standards of novelty and lack of obviousness to receive protection, the only requirement for obtaining a copyright is that the work be original. Trademark law is concerned with the protection of symbols that identify particular products or services.

- Under the fair use doctrine, a reasonable portion of a copyrighted work can be reproduced without the author's permission when necessary for a legitimate purpose that is not competitive with the copyright owner's market for his work.

- Copyright
- Covenant Not to Compete
- Fair Use Doctrine
- False Advertising
- Federal Trade Commission (FTC)
- Federal Trade Commission Act
- Infringement
- Interference
- Lanham Act

- Patent
- Secondary Meaning
- Trade Dress Simulation
- Trade Libel
- Trademark
- Trade Secret
- Unfair Trade Practice
- Uniform Deceptive Trade Practices Act

Questions and Case Problems

1. Darrow Company is a manufacturer of gumdrops sold under the trademark "Zest" in a red, white, and blue package bearing a picture of Uncle Sam and the slogan, "America's most American candy." Darrow's competitor, Fowler Company, begins to sell gumdrops under the trademark "Sest." Fowler adopts for its gumdrops red, white, and blue packaging bearing a picture of the American eagle and the slogan, "The best for red-blooded Americans." Can Darrow Company prevent Fowler Company from marketing its gumdrops in the manner it has employed? Why?

2. National Motors is negotiating with Sparko Batteries for the purchase of one million auto batteries. Sparko purchases its battery cases exclusively from Case. National Motors tells Sparko if it wants to do business with National, it will have to purchase all battery cases from another supplier. Can Case recover against National Motors for interference with its contractual relationship with Sparko?

3. What is the difference among a copyright, a trademark, and a patent?

4. Ethel Russell created what she considered to be original ideas for socks. In one design, there was a separate compartment for the big toe; another had a separate section for each toe. Because socks were gaining prominence in young women's casual fashion, the "mitten socks" and "glove socks" had wide appeal. Russell registered her two drawings on copyright forms entitled "registration of a claim to copyright in a work of art or model or design for a work of art." Trimfit, Inc., while acknowledging that the toe socks were Russell's idea, began to manufacture these socks under its own label. Russell sued for copyright infringement, claiming that she had the sole right to manufacture toe socks. How should the case be decided?

5. What is a covenant not to compete? How is it used in business?

6. William Trecker, a salesman at the Columbia Ribbon and Carbon Manufacturing Company, signed an agreement not to disclose to anyone the name, address, or requirements of any customer or prospective customer of Columbia, or to divulge

any other information acquired during his employment. The agreement also provided that for two years after leaving Columbia, Trecker would not sell any similar goods within any territory he had covered during the two years prior to leaving. Trecker's territory had been nationwide, and Trecker eventually quit to work for A-One Corporation, a Columbia competitor. Columbia sued to enjoin Trecker from competing with it in the United States for two years and to bar him permanently from soliciting Columbia customers. What relief, if any, should the court give Columbia?

7. What is the fair use doctrine?

8. The Crazy Cola Bottling Company employs Joe as a chemist. Joe subsequently leaves Crazy Cola and sets up his own business, manufacturing another soft drink. Crazy Cola asserts that Joe is using trade secrets he uncovered while employed by Crazy Cola and seeks to enjoin him from continuing the activity. Is Crazy Cola entitled to an injunction?

9. Pioneer Aviation and Aerospace Industries are competing to obtain a government contract. Pioneer's sales manager tells the government procurement officer, "Be careful about accepting any bids from Aerospace. They're in real hot water with their creditors. They could be in bankruptcy any day now." Has an unfair business practice been committed? If so, which type?

10. What is an FTC cease and desist order? How is it used?

55 Antitrust

55:1 Introduction

The federal and state antitrust laws were enacted to promote a competitive economy for the United States. The antitrust laws reflect a national commitment to the competitive market system as the principal means of producing and distributing goods and services in the society. In addition, the laws reflect a traditional American distrust of concentrated economic power.

The major federal antitrust statutes are the Sherman Act (1890); the Clayton Act (1914); the Federal Trade Commission Act (1914); and the Robinson–Patman Act (1936), which was made part of the Clayton Act. In addition, most states have enacted statutes patterned after the federal laws to give the states power to restrain anticompetitive practices. Both the federal and state statutes tend to be broad, general statements of public policy. The courts, however, have crafted legal concepts and theories in order to apply the statutes to the facts of particular cases. Often the resulting law is contradictory and the decisions controversial.

Even the fundamental goals of antitrust law are the source of much disagreement. One school of thought emphasizes the economic goals of *efficient resource allocation* and improved *consumer welfare*. Other schools of thought emphasize the political goals of discouraging aggregation of wealth and ensuring small businesses the opportunity to compete in the marketplace. The purpose of this chapter, however, is not to explain the complexities of the legal and economic theory of antitrust law—a subject to which some attorneys devote their entire practice. Instead, the chapter introduces the major federal antitrust statutes and remedies and discusses the more frequent types of antitrust violations.

 As a result of expanding judicial construction and application of the antitrust laws, potential antitrust liability is an important consideration in any business transaction or practice. Businesspersons who recognize a potential antitrust problem should seek the advice of an attorney with experience in antitrust. It is the antitrust lawyer's role to identify methods and procedures of operation that do not violate the antitrust laws.

55:2   The Sherman Act: Restraints of Trade

The Sherman Act was passed in 1890 in response to the abuses of the major industrial monopolies of the nineteenth century. Section 1 of the Act provides: "Every contract, combination in the form of trust or otherwise, or conspiracy, in restraint of trade or commerce among the several states, or with foreign nations, is hereby declared to be illegal. . . . "

The terms "combination," "restraint of trade or commerce," and "among the several states" were left to the courts for definition. The courts have interpreted the "combination" requirement to mean that there must be some agreement or common action by two or more persons or businesses to violate § 1. A single firm or individual cannot violate § 1.

The interstate commerce requirement ("commerce among the several states") originally was interpreted to mean that the mere manufacture or production of goods was not interstate commerce even if the goods were destined for shipment from one state to another. Today, however, the commerce requirement is satisfied simply by showing that the business or activity in question, even when purely intrastate, has a "substantial economic effect" on other states.

The Rule of Reason and the Per Se Doctrine   "Restraint of trade" has been interpreted to refer to restraints on competition rather than to all business practices that literally restrain trade. For example, every business contract restrains trade since it sets terms on which at least one commercial transaction will take place, thereby removing that transaction from the field of competition. Recognizing that Congress obviously did not intend to prohibit all contracts, the United States Supreme Court held that the Sherman Act was intended to forbid only "unreasonable" restraints of trade.

Under the "rule of reason" the trial court must examine the extent to which a particular business practice has both procompetitive and anticompetitive aspects and determine whether, in the light of that evidence, the practice should be forbidden. Certain types of business conduct, however, have been held to be "unreasonable per se." This means that the conduct virtually always has anticompetitive effects and few redeeming virtues. An extensive analysis of economic evidence in trial is unnecessary; proof that the conduct occurred is sufficient to establish a violation of the law. Price-fixing, for example, is a *per se* violation of § 1.

Horizontal and Vertical Restraints   In analyzing business practices, courts distinguish between agreements among competitors at the same level of commercial activity (horizontal agreements) and agreements among parties in successive levels of commercial activity (vertical agreements). In general, horizontal agreements tend to be regarded as suspect; they are more likely to be treated as *per se* violations than vertical agreements because horizontal competitors usually have few reasons, other than anticompetitive ones, to make agreements about business practices. Agreements among firms in a vertical relationship, however, may improve competition in the relevant market, and therefore are more likely to be analyzed under the rule of reason approach.

Horizontal Price Fixing and Horizontal Restraints   Horizontal price-fixing means any combination or agreement between or among competitors to raise, depress, fix, peg, or stabilize the price of goods in interstate commerce. For example, if several corporations form a trade association that fixes prices of the corporations' products and limits sales to a select list of jobbers, the corporations are guilty of illegal price-fixing. There is no defense or recognized justification for price-fixing. For example, it is no defense that the price fixed was reasonable, that the purpose of the price-fixing was to end "ruinous competition" in the marketplace, or that the price was fixed to eliminate unstable prices that plagued both producers and consumers.

The evil of price-fixing lies in the conspirators' ability to charge prices that the market would not otherwise bear. Usually, that results in higher prices to consumers. In any event, price-fixing reduces competition and produces a nonmarket allocation of resources. Courts have been expansive in determining what constitutes price-fixing. An agreement among competitors fixing either minimum or maximum prices constitutes illegal price-fixing. In addition, agreements among competitors on how much to produce, sell, or buy are illegal, even if no specific price is fixed. Agreements not to do business with a certain supplier or purchaser (*group boycotts*) are *per se* illegal if undertaken for anticompetitive purposes or if they are coercive in nature. Similarly, agreements among competitors not to compete in certain geographical or product markets, or not to solicit one another's customers, are *per se* violative of § 1. Such agreements reduce competition and give each firm the potential to charge higher prices than are competitive.

 Firms must be exceedingly cautious in their communications with competitors. Even within trade associations it is important not to engage in activity that could be regarded as anticompetitive or coercive. Many firms establish training programs for executives and sales representatives designed specifically to avoid antitrust liability.

Vertical Price-Fixing and Vertical Restraints   An agreement between a supplier and a dealer to fix the price at which the dealer resells the product is called vertical price-fixing, or *resale price maintenance*. From 1937 to 1976 such agreements were exempt from the antitrust laws. Since the repeal of the Miller–Tydings Act in 1976, however, resale price maintenance has fallen under the rule of *per se* illegality.

The law balances the government's interest in preventing resale price maintenance against the seller's traditional right to pick its customers. The seller and buyer may not *agree* on the price at which the buyer will resell goods. Nevertheless, the seller may try, in a noncoercive manner, to persuade the buyer to price the goods to maximize profits. The seller may print the suggested retail price on the goods and advertise a suggested price. Moreover, the seller may refuse to sell goods in the first instance to a buyer who is unlikely to follow the seller's suggested price. The *Monsanto* case upholds lower court decisions that a seller may even cut off a buyer whose pricing policy is not satisfactory, so long as the seller does not attempt to coerce the buyer into agreeing to a resale price.

Monsanto Co.
v
Spray-Rite Service Corp.
465 US 752 (1984)
United States Supreme Court

FACTS: From 1957 to 1968 Spray-Rite, a wholesale distributor of agricultural chemicals, sold agricultural herbicides manufactured by the Monsanto Company at discount prices. In 1968 Monsanto refused to renew Spray-Rite's one-year distributorship contract. Spray-Rite sued under § 1 of the Sherman Act, alleging that Monsanto and its other distributors conspired to fix the resale prices of Monsanto products and that Spray-Rite was terminated as a part of the conspiracy. Monsanto claimed that Spray-Rite was terminated because it failed to hire trained sales personnel and adequately promote sales to dealers. At trial, Spray-Rite presented evidence of complaints to Monsanto from numerous competing distributors about Spray-Rite's low prices.

ISSUE: What proof is sufficient for a jury to to find a vertical price-fixing conspiracy in violation of § 1 of the Sherman Act?

RESULT: A price-fixing agreement cannot be inferred from the existence of complaints by other distributors, or even from the fact that the termination came "in response to" complaints. There must be evidence that tends to exclude the possibility that the manufacturer and the nonterminated distributors were acting independently.

REASONING:

*   *   *

A manufacturer of course generally has a right to deal, or refuse to deal, with whomever it likes, as long as it does so independently, *United States v Colgate & Co.* . . . (1919). Under *Colgate*, the manufacturer can announce its resale prices in advance and refuse to deal with those who fail to comply. And a distributor is free to acquiesce in the manufacturer's demand in order to avoid termination. . . .

[T]he fact that a manufacturer and its distributors are in constant communication about prices and marketing strategy does not alone show that the distributors are not making independent pricing decisions. A manufacturer and its distributors have legitimate reasons to exchange information about the prices and the reception of their products in the market. Moreover, it is precisely in cases in which a manufacturer attempts to further a particular marketing strategy by means of agreements on often costly nonprice restrictions that it will have the most interest in the distributors' resale prices. The manufacturer often will want to ensure that its distributors earn sufficient profit to pay for programs such as hiring and training additional salesmen or demonstrating the technical features of the product, and will want to see that "free-riders" do not interfere. . . . Thus, the manufacturer's strongly felt concern about resale prices does not necessarily mean that it has done more than the *Colgate* doctrine allows. . . .

Permitting an agreement to be inferred merely from the existence of complaints, or even from the fact that termination came about "in response to" complaints, could deter or penalize perfectly legitimate conduct. As Monsanto points out, complaints about price-cutters "are natural—and, from the manufacturer's perspective, unavoidable—reactions by distributors to the activities of their rivals." Such complaints, particularly where the manufacturer has imposed a costly set of nonprice restrictions, "arise in the normal course of business and do not indicate illegal concerted action." . . . Moreover, distributors are an important source of information for manufacturers. In order to assure an efficient distribution system, manufacturers and distributors constantly must coordinate their activities to assure that their product will reach the consumer persuasively and efficiently. To bar a manufacturer from acting solely because the information upon which it acts originated as a price complaint would create an irrational dislocation in the market. . . .

Thus, something more than evidence of complaints is needed. There must be evidence that tends to exclude the possibility that the manufacturer and nonterminated distributors were acting independently. . . .

Powell, Justice.

Although resale price maintenance is *per se* illegal, most nonprice vertical restraints are analyzed under the rule of reason. For example, a manufacturer may grant a retailer the exclusive right to sell a product within a certain market territory, or grant the exclusive right to sell a particular product. This practice may encourage retailers to advertise and compete vigorously against other products in the territory. Similarly, a household appliance manufacturer may choose to compete with other manufacturers by marketing only through dealers who provide floor space for demonstration models and warranty service for the product. These types of vertical agreements may promote competition among different brands of a product even though they reduce competition among sellers of the same brand. Analysis under the rule of reason permits the manufacturer to demonstrate that the procompetitive effects outweigh any anticompetitive effects of the practice.

The following case established the United States Supreme Court's approach to vertical nonprice restraints.

Continental T.V., Inc.
v
GTE Sylvania, Inc.
433 US 36 (1977)
United States Supreme Court

FACTS: GTE Sylvania, Inc. sold televisions to retailers pursuant to franchise agreements that required the franchisee to sell his Sylvania products only from the location or locations at which he was franchised. Continental T.V., Inc., a franchisee, claimed that the franchise agreement restricting sales locations restrained trade in violation of § 1 of the Sherman Act. The jury assessed damages of $591,505, trebled to $1,774,515. The Ninth Circuit reversed the trial court's decision, ruling that a rule of reason analysis should have been used rather than a *per se* analysis. The plaintiff appealed to the United States Supreme Court.

ISSUE: Should nonprice vertical restrictions be analyzed using the rule of reason?

RESULT: The Supreme Court applied the rule of reason to vertical nonprice restrictions, overruling the Court's *Schwinn* decision applying the *per se* rule to nonprice vertical restrictions.

REASONING:

*   *   *

Section 1 prohibits "[e]very contract, combination . . . , or conspiracy, in restraint of trade or commerce." Since the early years of this century a judicial gloss on this statutory language has established the "rule of reason" as the prevailing standard of analysis. . . . Under this rule, the factfinder weighs all of the circumstances of a case in deciding whether a restrictive practice should be prohibited as imposing an unreasonable restraint on competition. *Per se* rules of illegality are appropriate only when they relate to conduct that is manifestly anticompetitive. . . .

The market impact of vertical restrictions is complex because of their potential for a simultaneous reduction of intrabrand competition and stimulation of interbrand competition.

Vertical restrictions reduce intrabrand competition by limiting the number of sellers of a particular product competing for the business of a given group of buyers. Location restrictions have this effect because of practical constraints on the effective marketing area of retail outlets. Although intrabrand competition may be reduced, the ability of retailers to exploit the resulting market may be limited both by the ability of consumers to travel to other franchised locations and, perhaps more importantly, to purchase the competing products of other manufacturers. None of these key variables, however, is affected by the form of the transaction by which a manufacturer conveys his products to the retailers.

Vertical restrictions promote interbrand competition by allowing the manufacturer to achieve certain efficiencies in the distribution of his products. These "redeeming virtues" are implicit in every decision sustaining vertical restrictions under the rule of reason. Economists have identified a number of ways in which manufacturers can use such restrictions to compete more effectively against other manufacturers. For example, new manufacturers and manufacturers entering new markets can use the restrictions in order to induce competent and aggressive retailers to make the kind of investment of capital and labor that is often required in the distribution of products unknown to the consumer. Established manufacturers can use them to induce retailers to engage in promotional activities or to provide service and repair facilities necessary to the efficient marketing of their products. Service and repair are vital to many products, such as automobiles and major household appliances. The availability and quality of such services affect a manufacturer's goodwill and competitiveness of his product.

Economists also have argued that manufacturers have an economic interest in maintaining as much intrabrand competition as is consistent with the efficient distribution of their products. . . .

Vertical restrictions, in varying forms, are widely used in our free market economy. . . . [T]here is substantial scholarly and judicial authority supporting their economic utility. There is relatively little authority to the contrary. . . .

Powell, Justice.

55:3   The Sherman Act: Monopolization

Section 2 of the Sherman Act [15 USC § 2] provides: "Every person who shall monopolize, or attempt to monopolize, or combine or conspire with any other person or persons, to monopolize any part of the trade or commerce among the several States, or with foreign nations, shall be deemed guilty of a felony. . . . "

To "monopolize" is to acquire or exercise the power to exclude competitors from a market or to control prices within a relevant market. The use of the term "monopolize" rather than "monopoly" indicates Congress' intent to punish action rather than merely status.

Violation of § 2 requires not only the acquisition of monopoly power but also a general intent to monopolize. A monopolist's general intent can be shown by proving participation in an agreement to restrain trade violative of § 1 or by proving that the firm engaged in predatory behavior. For example, pricing goods below the marginal cost of the goods in order to drive out competitors and establish a monopoly, and then raising prices, is predatory pricing behavior. Acquiring a monopoly through superior skill, foresight, or luck is not condemned under § 2.

The crime of "monopolization" requires the actual acquisition of monopoly power. The crime of "attempt to monopolize" requires that the defendant have acted overtly and thereby created a high probability of success in acquiring a monopoly. The crime of "conspiracy to monopolize" requires both a concerted action to restrain trade with the specific intent to create a monopoly and a high probability of doing so.

Relevant Market   The key to § 2 lies in the concept of "monopoly power." At some inexact point—the subject of much antitrust litigation—dominance of a market becomes "monopoly power," the power to control prices and to exclude competitors. To determine whether a firm has monopoly power it is necessary to define, at trial, the *relevant market* for the firm's product. Both the *geographic market* (for example, California, the West, or the nation) and the *product market* (for example, the market for cellophane wrapping material, or the market for *all* flexible wrapping material) must be identified through economic evidence. Naturally, an antitrust defendant will argue that it operates in a broad and large market, which will make its share of the market small, while the party alleging the violation will argue that the defendant's market is narrow and small, making the market share relatively large.

The geographic market is defined by the area in which the defendant and competing sellers effectively operate. If the product is sold nationwide, then the market is national. There may be regional submarkets where a number of local sellers compete with nationwide sellers; the market for beer is an example. In this case, the submarket might be found to be the relevant market. For many products, transportation cost is a principal factor limiting the size of a geographic market.

The product market is determined largely by consumer preferences and by the extent to which consumers will switch to physically similar products to meet their needs when prices increase. If close substitutes for a product exist and consumers switch readily to a substitute, even a high market share of a product may not confer the ability to raise prices and exclude competitors. In *United States v E. I. Dupont De Nemours & Co.*,[1] called the *Cellophane Case*, the United States Supreme Court announced the rule that goods reasonably interchangeable by consumers for the same purposes constitute the product market. In the *Cellophane* case, the relevant market was held to be *all* flexible wrapping material, not merely cellophane wrapping material. The Court stressed the functional interchangeability of those products. Under this rule, photocopiers, for example, are deemed to be interchangeable for antitrust purposes, even among brands using different mechanical processes.

Market Share   Frequently courts use the monopolist's share of the relevant market as a principal indicator of monopoly power. Depending on the circumstances, 90 percent, or even 75 percent, is sufficient to constitute "monopoly power." It has been argued that *market share* is an imperfect measure of monopoly power. Courts may also look to the structure of the industry and the probable development of the industry to assess the importance of market share. In addition, evidence of the actual use of monopoly power satisfies a court that such power exists.

55:4   The Clayton Act

The Clayton Act of 1914, as amended by the Robinson–Patman Act of 1936, specifically identifies and prohibits as restraints of trade certain business practices that *tend* to create monopolies. Section 2 of the Clayton Act forbids price discrimination that injures competition. Section 3 outlaws exclusive dealing and tying contracts that are anticompetitive. Section 7 prohibits anticompetitive corporate mergers. Finally, § 8 forbids members of corporate boards of directors from serving on the boards of competing firms.

Price Discrimination   Section 2 of the Clayton Act (as amended by the Robinson–Patman Act of 1936) makes it unlawful to discriminate, directly or indirectly, in price among different purchasers of goods of like grade and quality under certain conditions. Those conditions are that (1) any of the transactions is in commerce and (2) the effect of the discrimination may be substantially to (a) lessen competition; (b) tend to create a monopoly; or (c) injure, destroy, or prevent competition with any person who grants or knowingly receives the benefit of such a discrimination, or the customers of either. Both the seller who grants and the preferred buyer who knowingly receives discriminatory prices are guilty of violating the Act.

The purpose of the Robinson–Patman Act was to protect the small business firm from the purchasing power of the large chain stores and also from the power of chain stores to selectively lower prices in geographic markets where competition was high. The benefits to consumers of mass merchandising probably are better appreciated now than in 1936, and the Act is criticized for imposing costs on business with little benefit to small firms.

---

[1] 351 US 377 (1956).

Many types of conduct that amount to *price discrimination* have been held illegal under the Robinson–Patman Act. Selling of identical products to two or more competing wholesalers at different prices may violate the Act. Another type of price discrimination is a variation of predatory pricing.

EXAMPLE: Foran Corporation is a large national company with a milk-processing plant in Louisville. Foran sells milk in surrounding areas at lower prices than in Louisville, where it has a large market share. The surrounding areas are served by local companies, and Foran is trying to obtain a share of that market. Foran's policy is price discrimination and violates the Act.

Like Grade or Quality   Generally, physical differences in two products that affect their acceptability to buyers will preclude the products from being of "like grade or quality." However, differences in the brand name or label under which the product is sold are not alone sufficient to justify price discrimination. Only goods, and not services, are regulated under the Act.

Defenses   The Robinson–Patman Act expressly provides that nothing in it shall prevent price differentials that make only "due allowance for differences in the cost of manufacture, sale or delivery" resulting from the differing methods or quantities in which goods are sold or delivered. This defense rarely is relied on because it is expensive to compile the necessary evidence. In addition, the Federal Trade Commission (FTC) has interpreted the defense to mean that quantity discounts must be based on actual cost savings due to the quantity sold, not merely on an assumption that larger deliveries are more economical. A seller also can rebut a presumption of price discrimination by showing that his lower price was made in good faith to meet a competitor's equally low price, but this defense is hard to prove.

 The Robinson–Patman Act is an important legal constraint in marketing goods. Usually, however, procedures can be established to achieve marketing goals without violating the Act.

Tying and Exclusive Dealing Agreements   Section 3 of the Clayton Act addresses both the situation where a seller requires a buyer to purchase one good (tied product) as the condition for purchasing another good (tying product) and the situation where a seller forbids a buyer to buy from a competing seller as the condition for purchasing a product from the seller (exclusive dealing). Section 3 makes it illegal to sell or lease goods in interstate commerce on condition that the purchaser or lessee not use or deal in the goods of a competitor of the seller or lessor, if the effect may be substantially to lessen competition or to tend to create a monopoly in any line of commerce.

There are three basic requirements for an illegal tie. First, there must be separate tying and tied products. It is not always easy to distinguish the products. For example, are tires on a new automobile part of a single product or are they tied products? Second, the seller must have sufficient economic power to appreciably restrain competition in the tied product. Third, the tying arrangement must affect more than an "insubstantial" amount of commerce.

The tying product and the tied product can be related in a variety of ways. They can be products that normally are used in fixed proportions, such as nuts and bolts; the tied product might be designed to be used with the tying product, as software is used with a computer; or the tied and tying products might be usable together or separately, as are seed and fertilizer.

Franchise Tying and Exclusive Dealing Agreements The illegality of certain types of tying and exclusive dealing agreements has particular significance to the franchising industry. A major type of franchise is characterized by the franchisee's being granted the right to use, within a designated area, a franchisor's service mark; trade name; distinctive building, structure, or style of decor; and techniques of doing business. This type of franchising is essentially based on linking the distinctive image to a standardized operation with high quality control. Because the commercial success of the franchise usually depends on a nationwide uniform image, the courts tend to allow the franchisor to require the franchisee to use particular products to maintain high quality. However, if the franchisor insists that services, equipment, or supplies be obtained from the franchisor or a designated source as a condition of receiving and retaining the franchise, a potential tying problem exists. The *Chicken Delight* case is a classic franchising case.

Siegel
v
Chicken Delight, Inc.
448 F2d 43 (1971)
United States Court of Appeals, Ninth Circuit

FACTS: Siegel and other franchisees of defendant, Chicken Delight, sued for injuries allegedly resulting from illegal restraints imposed by Chicken Delight's standard form franchise agreements. The restraints consisted of Chicken Delight's contractual requirements that franchisees buy certain essential cooking equipment, dry-mix food items, and trademark-bearing packaging exclusively from Chicken Delight as a condition of obtaining a Chicken Delight trademark license. The trial court ruled that these requirements constituted a tying agreement that was unlawful under § 1 of the Sherman Act.

ISSUE: Is the trademark or license franchise an item distinct from necessary business equipment and inventory so as to constitute tying and tied products?

RESULT: Yes. The trademark is a separate and distinct item used to tie in the sale of equipment and inventory.

REASONING:

*   *   *

In determining whether an aggregation of separable items should be regarded as one or more items for tie-in purposes in the normal cases of sales of products the courts must look to the function of the aggregation. Consideration is given to such questions as whether the amalgamation of products resulted in cost savings apart from those reductions in sales expenses and the like normally attendant upon any tie-in, and whether the items are normally sold or used as a unit with fixed proportions.

Where one of the products sold as part of an aggregation is a trademark or franchise license, new questions are injected. In determining whether the license and the remaining ("tied") items in the aggregation are to be regarded as distinct items which can be traded in distinct markets consideration must be given to the function of trademarks.

. . . [T]he trademark simply reflects the goodwill and quality standards of the enterprise which it identifies. As long as the system of operation of the franchisees lives up to those quality standards and remains as represented by the mark so that the public is not misled, neither the protection afforded the trademark by law nor the value of the trademark to the licensee depends upon the source of the components.

This being so, it is apparent that the goodwill of the Chicken Delight trademark does not attach to the multitude of separate articles used in the operation of the licensed system or in the production of its end product. It is not what is used, but how it is used and what results, that have given the system and its end product their entitlement to trademark protection. It is to the system and the end product that the public looks with confidence that established goodwill has created.

Thus, sale of a franchise license, with the attendant rights to operate a business in the prescribed manner and to benefit from the goodwill of the trade name, in no way requires the forced sale by the franchisor of some or all of the component articles.

. . . One cannot immunize a tie-in from the antitrust laws by simply stamping a trademark symbol on the tied product—at least where the tied product is not itself the product represented by the mark. . . .

Merrill, Circuit Judge

Defenses   A defendant may legally justify a tie on either of two theories. Under the first—the new industry theory—some courts have permitted a tie instituted in launching a new business with a highly uncertain future; the theory is that the tied product is necessary to ensure proper functioning of the tying product, which might be, for example, electronic equipment. As the business becomes established and acceptable substitutes for the tied product enter the market, the tying loses its justification. The second defense theory is that of quality control for protection of a business' goodwill. This defense rarely succeeds. Indeed, it would succeed only if specifications for a substitute for the tied product were so detailed that they could not practicably be supplied.

Mergers   A merger is the acquisition by one firm of the stock or assets of another, with the result that the first firm achieves control over the second. A merger of two or more firms that compete at the same level of production or distribution in the same industry, such as two shoe manufacturers, is called a *horizontal merger*. A merger of firms at different levels of production or distribution in the same industry, such as a shoe manufacturer and a wholesale firm, is called a *vertical merger*. A merger of two firms in functionally separate industries is called a *conglomerate merger*.

Because mergers can result in concentration of economic power in an industry, they are regulated by the antitrust laws. Section 7 of the Clayton Act, as it was amended by the Cellar–Kefauver Act of 1950 [15 USC § 18], provides that a corporation cannot acquire stock or assets of another corporation engaged in interstate commerce if, in any line of commerce in any section of the country, the effect of the acquisition may be substantially to lessen competition or to create a monopoly.

The issues in merger cases usually relate to definitions of the product market (the "line of commerce") and the geographic market or submarket ("the section of the country") and to determination of the market shares of the corporations involved. As in Sherman Act § 2 cases, the defendant argues for a broad product market and a large geographic market; the party attacking the merger argues for a narrow definition of the product and a small geographic market or submarket. In addition, courts consider the status of the firms as actual or potential competitors in the market or submarket involved and the probable effect of the merger on competition. The concept of *potential competition*—the likelihood that a firm would enter a market other than by merger—is important not only in defining markets but also in assessing whether a conglomerate merger lessens competition. The major defense available in a merger case is that the merger does not substantially lessen competition in the relevant markets.

A merger that violates § 7 of the Clayton Act may also violate the Sherman Act. However, the showing of anticompetitive impact required for a successful prosecution is much less rigorous under § 7 than under the Sherman Act. Consequently, most merger cases are brought under Clayton Act § 7 rather than under the Sherman Act.

The U.S. Department of Justice and the Federal Trade Commission are the major public enforcers of § 7. Because of the difficulty of "unscrambling the eggs" when a merger is attacked after it has been consummated, Congress requires that certain types of mergers be reviewed in advance by the Justice Department and the FTC. The Justice Department has issued merger guidelines that indicate its approach to market definition, market power, and other problems of merger law. The guidelines do not have the force of law, but they are used by many courts in analyzing the legality of mergers.

Interlocking Directorates   Section 8 of the Clayton Act [15 USC § 19] prohibits a person from serving on the boards of directors of any two or more corporations if two conditions exist. The first condition is that any of the corporations has capital, surplus, and undivided profits aggregating more than $1 million. Certain regulated industries—banking and common carriers—are excluded from the Act. The second condition is that the corporations compete in such a way that eliminating competition by agreement between them would violate the antitrust laws. Section 8 has been construed to forbid corporations from having the same director if an agreement between the corporations to fix prices or divide territories would violate § 1 of the Sherman Act. By prohibiting interlocking directorates, § 8 seeks to remove the opportunity or temptation to enter into illegal arrangements, or to effect an arrangement through the actions of a board member.

55:5   The Federal Trade Commission Act

The Federal Trade Commission Act, enacted in 1914, gave the Federal Trade Commission jurisdiction to enforce §§ 2,3,7, and 8 of the Clayton Act. In addition, § 5 of the Federal Trade Commission Act prohibits "unfair methods of competition in commerce and unfair or deceptive acts or practices in commerce." This broad language has been interpreted to encompass anti-competitive business practices that the FTC regards as "unfair." Thus, the Commission can investigate, hear, and render orders in a broad range of cases involving business practices, even if the practice does not violate the Sherman or Clayton Acts.

55:6   Exemptions from the Antitrust Laws

Congress and the courts have carved out numerous exemptions from liability under the antitrust laws. Because antitrust remedies are often severe, the potential benefit of exemption great, and the law exceedingly complex and uncertain, antitrust exemption law is an important area of antitrust law.

Certain industries are statutorily exempt, to some extent, from the antitrust laws as a matter of public policy. For example, the Norris–LaGuardia Act of 1932 explicitly exempts most labor organization activity from antitrust liability. Similarly, the Capper–Volstead Act permits farmers to form agricultural cooperatives for processing, handling, and jointly marketing their products. Fisheries have a similar exemption. Other statutes grant some form of exemption for regulated industries such as banking, communications, insurance, ocean shipping, securities and commodities exchanges, and transportation. Activities such as research joint ventures, patents and copyrights, and foreign or export trade also have been granted partial statutory exemption from the antitrust laws.

The courts have recognized exemptions on several bases. For example, the sport of professional baseball is granted judicial immunity from the antitrust laws, although other professional sports are not exempt. Under the judicial doctrine of *state action* the federal and state governments are not subject to the antitrust laws; however, many activities of local governments are subject to the antitrust laws. Finally, the Supreme Court has held that First Amendment rights of free speech, freedom of assembly, and the right to petition government outweigh the governmental interest in enhancing competition. Thus, activities designed to influence legislative, judicial, or administrative decisions or actions are exempt from the antitrust laws, even if the effect of the action is to limit competition. This arrangement is known as the *Noerr–Pennington* doctrine.

55:7 Remedies and Enforcement

Antitrust legislation is enforced through a variety of types of lawsuits, each type having its own purpose and characteristics. The federal government can commence either a civil damages action or a criminal prosecution against a suspected violator. Under some circumstances state government officials can sue suspected antitrust violators on behalf of citizens injured by a violation. In addition, private individuals or firms can seek damages against an antitrust violator.

Criminal Actions Sections 1 and 2 of the Sherman Act are criminal statutes, the violation of which is a felony punishable by a fine of up to $1 million per violation for a corporation and up to $100,000 for an individual. In addition, individuals may receive up to three years in prison. The Robinson–Patman Act makes price discrimination for the purpose of eliminating a competitor a misdemeanor. Criminal investigation and prosecution of antitrust violators is the province of the U.S. Department of Justice. The Justice Department can commence a criminal prosecution if (1) a case involves a "per se violation" of the Sherman Act and (2) there is evidence of a knowing and willful violation of the law, such as a planned program of concealment. Most criminal antitrust prosecutions involve price-fixing. Antitrust criminal cases are investigated by grand jury proceedings, which are conducted through grand jury subpoenas commanding either the testimony of witnesses, the producing of documents, or both.

Government Civil Actions While the Justice Department has the responsibility to enforce the Sherman Act, both the Justice Department and the Federal Trade Commission may enforce the Clayton Act, including the Robinson–Patman Act. Either governmental enforcer may seek a *civil injunction* in court against a suspected violator. If a defendant is found guilty in such a proceeding of violating the antitrust laws, a decree is fashioned to stop the illegal activity and remedy the violation. Antitrust decrees can enjoin whole categories of conduct.

Consent Decrees Often the government and an antitrust defendant agree to settle a government antitrust case by a *consent decree*. This type of decree is based on a stipulation by both parties as to what remedy or relief the court should order, without the defendant acknowledging any guilt. The ultimate responsibility in fashioning an antitrust decree lies with the court, however. The court must determine what is or is not in the public interest, and it is not relieved of this responsibility simply because all parties to the proceeding, including the government, agree on or request a particular form of relief.

Federal Trade Commission Administrative Action   Section 11 of the Clayton Act gives the Federal Trade Commission power to take administrative action in an antitrust case. Administrative action by the FTC may be initiated by injured firms or by the Commission. If a formal complaint is rendered, the case is tried in an administrative hearing. Ultimately, a decision against a defendant may result in a cease-and-desist order or in an order to take corrective action, such as to divest assets or stock in another firm. Violation of an FTC cease and desist order may result in civil fines of $5,000 per day of violation.

The Private Treble Damage Action   Section 4 of the Clayton Act allows a private individual whose business or property has been or will be injured by reason of anything forbidden in the antitrust laws to sue in a federal district court. A plaintiff who proves the violation and the resulting injury can recover *treble damages* (three times the amount of the actual damages) plus the costs of the action, including reasonable attorney's fees. A plaintiff who shows only threatened injury is entitled to injunctive relief, such as the issuance of an injunction prohibiting the illegal conduct.

It is important to understand that a criminal conviction or a finding of guilt in a government civil action serves as proof of a violation of the law in a treble damage suit. Thus, the government suit—and any settlement of a government suit—takes place under the specter of private parties waiting in the wings while the government sustains the burden of proof of guilt. This is an important dynamic of antitrust law.

In recent years, private antitrust suits have increasingly been brought as *class actions*, meaning that all persons similarly injured by the antitrust defendant's conduct have been joined as plaintiffs in the same action. Sometimes, therefore, even very small actual damages attributed to each of many transactions (such as sales of a common but cheap consumer product), when multiplied by a large number of plaintiffs in the class and further multiplied by three under the treble damages provision of the Clayton Act, will become an extremely large sum.

The availability of treble damages is limited by the judicial requirement that a plaintiff have *standing* to sue under § 4 and that he or she have suffered an *antitrust injury*. Standing doctrine requires that the plaintiff have suffered directly from the antitrust violation. Antitrust injury doctrine requires that the plaintiff's injury be the type of injury that the antitrust laws were intended to prevent. Standing doctrine prevents a purchaser who has bought goods from someone who, in turn, had bought from a price-fixer—from suing the price-fixer: only the direct purchaser would have standing to sue. Antitrust injury doctrine would, for example, prevent a beer distributor from suing a beer maker for resale price maintenance when the basis of the damage claim is that the distributor would have been able to participate in a local horizontal price-fixing scheme but for the resale maintenance agreement; Congress did not intend to protect firms from being prevented from engaging in price-fixing.

The Parens Patriae Suit   The Hart–Scott–Rodino Antitrust Improvements Act of 1976 gave the state attorneys general the authority to sue under the Sherman Act on behalf of citizens of the state who have been injured by violation of the antitrust laws. The state attorneys general can bring such suits, called *parens patriae* suits, for treble damages. In addition, § 16 of the Clayton Act gives the attorney general of a state power to bring an action under the federal antitrust laws for injunctive relief to prevent injury to the state's economy from antitrust violations. Note that these federal powers are provided in addition to any state antitrust law.

Key Concepts and Terms

- The Sherman Antitrust Act (1890) is the foundation of antitrust law. Section 1 prohibits contracts, combinations, or conspiracies in restraint of trade. Only "unreasonable" restraints of trade are prohibited, but certain practices, such as price-fixing, are unreasonable per se. Other restraints, such as vertical division of territories, are judged under a "rule of reason."

- Section 2 of the Sherman Act makes illegal monopolizing, attempting to monopolize, or combining or conspiring to monopolize any part of interstate commerce. Monopoly power is the power to control prices or exclude competition in the relevant market.

- The Clayton Act (1914) seeks to stop monopolistic practices before they become monopolies. The Act prohibits certain specific business practices, including exclusive dealing and tying arrangements (§ 3), corporate mergers that injure competition (§ 7), and interlocking corporate boards of directors (§ 8).

- The Robinson–Patman Act (1936) prohibits price discrimination if the effect may be substantially to lessen competition or may tend to create a monopoly. Both the seller who offers and the preferred buyer who knowingly receives discriminatory prices are guilty of violating the Act.

- Section 5 of the Federal Trade Commission Act (1914) prohibits "unfair methods of competition . . . and unfair . . . acts or practices in commerce." The FTC can stop an anticompetitive business practice even if the practice does not violate the Sherman or Clayton Acts.

- Certain industries, particularly regulated industries, are partially exempt from antitrust liability by statute. In addition, certain activities are protected from liability by statute or by the federal Constitution.

- Antitrust violators may be prosecuted criminally or civilly by the United States Department of Justice for Sherman Act violations. Violators of the Clayton Act may be prosecuted civilly by the Justice Department or the Federal Trade Commission, and administratively by the Federal Trade Commission.

- Section 4 of the Clayton Act allows private persons whose business or property is injured by any violation of the Sherman or Clayton Acts to sue in federal court. A winning plaintiff can recover three times the damages sustained. In addition, state attorneys general can sue for treble damages on behalf of injured citizens of the state.

- Antitrust Injury
- Class Action
- Clayton Act
- Conglomerate Merger
- Consent Decree
- Consumer Welfare
- Efficient Resource Allocation
- Exclusive Dealing Arrangement
- Geographic Market
- Horizontal Competitors
- Interlocking Directorates
- Market Share
- Monopolization
- Monopoly
- Per Se Doctrine
- Potential Competition

- Price Discrimination
- Price Fixing
- Product Market
- Relevant Market
- Resale Price Maintenance
- Restraint of Trade
- Robinson–Patman Act
- Rule of Reason
- Sherman Act
- Standing
- State Action
- Treble Damages
- Tying Arrangements
- Unfair Methods of Competition
- Vertical Restraints

Questions and Case Problems

1. At a trade association meeting the manufacturers of corrugated cardboard boxes proposed an agreement whereby each manufacturer agreed to report the prices at which sales of boxes were made to specific customers. The purpose of the proposal was to stabilize prices and improve profits in the industry by providing better information for manufacturers to evaluate the truth of buyers claims about market prices. No specific prices were fixed, and compliance was made voluntary. Would such an agreement restrain competition? Would it violate § 1 of the Sherman Act?

2. The City of Gotham licenses taxicabs but does not regulate their fares. Gotham has 10,000 taxicabs, mostly independently owned. Taxicab fares are highly competitive. Two independent cab owners, each of whom owns one taxicab, agree to fix the fares of their cabs at a rate about 25 percent higher than the going rate per quarter-mile. Would such an agreement restrain competition? Would it violate § 1 of the Sherman Act?

3. Frizzy Company manufacturers hair dryers, which it sells through independent retail outlets. Can Frizzy place its dryers with retailers on consignment, setting the retail price and paying the dealer a percentage commission on each sale? Suppose Frizzy publishes suggested retail prices for its dryers and follows a policy of terminating dealers who refuse to adhere to the price list. Does this conduct violate § 1 of the Sherman Act?

4. In the *Monsanto* case, (see page 1194), what does Justice Powell mean by "a costly set of nonprice restrictions"? In what kinds of retail businesses would you expect to find such restrictions? Is the Court's test practical? If the seller can cut off the retailer for failing to establish retail prices sufficient to maintain the "costly non-price restrictions," and the retailer knows it, can the retailer make independent pricing decisions?

5. Daily Dairy sells vanilla ice cream under the "Daily" brand for $1.85 per quart and the same ice cream under the "Gourmet" label for $2.50 per quart. Is there a possible Robinson–Patman violation? Would the result be different if Daily's "Gourmet" brand contained pure vanilla extract, costing an extra two cents per quart, whereas the "Daily" brand used artificial flavoring?

6. Expando Corporation patents a new razor blade that costs much less and lasts much longer than any other blade on the market. Competitors try to persuade Expando to license the patent to them, but Expando refuses. Expando sues two competitors for patent infringement when they attempt to market blades that violate Expando's patent rights. If Expando subsequently acquires a monopoly of the razor blade market through sales of the new blade, is there a Sherman Act § 2 violation?

7. What is intrabrand competition? Would a manufacturer ever not want retailers competing with one another to sell the manufacturer's product? How do location restrictions retard intrabrand competition? What is interbrand competition? Which is more important—intrabrand or interbrand competition—in increasing market share? What is meant by the language about efficient product distribution in the second to the last paragraph in the *Sylvania* (see page 1196) case?

8. X Company sells flywheels to be used in the manufacture of electric motors. Y Motors, a customer, tells X that it can get a better price on flywheels from Z. Can X lower its price to Y without violating the Robinson–Patman Act? Would it make a difference if Z's flywheel were inferior in quality to X's? Can X call Z and ascertain the truth of Y's claim about Z's offer?

9. A computer printer manufacturer markets a brand of ink-jet printer that works only with a particular type of paper on which the firm holds a patent. Can the manufacturer refuse to permit computer paper firms to produce and sell the paper? What if the printer manufacturer acquires a dominant market share in ink-jet printers? Is this a tying problem or a Sherman Act § 2 problem?

10. Many economists argue that a seller can get no more for selling two distinct and separate products together than it could for selling the two products separately. If the "tie-in" package is inferior to, or more expensive than, what is available in the marketplace, the buyer will buy elsewhere. If the seller has market power in the tying product, because of a monopoly or a patent, for example, it can capture the full economic advantage of the monopoly in selling the tying product alone, without having to bother with the tied product. Discuss.

56 Environmental Law

56:1   Introduction

Human beings have been discharging waste into the air, water, and earth for centuries. Until relatively recently pollution was not regarded as a problem, except in densely developed areas. The advent of urban industrial society in the nineteenth and twentieth centuries, however, strained the environment's capacity to handle waste. The problem has become serious and continues to increase with population growth and the resulting demand for production of goods and services. Yet environmental pollution affects health, use of resources, and enjoyment of the natural environment.

The problem of balancing the need to use resources and the need to conserve and preserve resources challenges the legal system. The common law has served to adjudicate disputes between individuals in cases where one person's use of property diminishes the value of another's enjoyment of life and property. Since 1970, however, environmental law has become primarily statutory and administrative in nature. This chapter explores the problem of common-law adjudication of "environmental" problems and examines the major federal statutes protecting the environment.

56:2   The Common Law

Under the common law conflicts of an environmental nature can be adjudicated under *nuisance* law. The theory of nuisance is that the defendant has used his or her property in a manner that interferes unreasonably with the plaintiff's use of property. If the harm is to the public at large, the suit can be brought only by an appropriate public official on behalf of the public. Otherwise, the suit must be brought as a private nuisance suit.

The private nuisance suit, however, poses several problems. First, the plaintiff must have suffered a specific harm, not simply be a member of the public affected by the harmful activity. The plaintiff must have *standing*, a doctrine that limits the category of persons permitted to bring the lawsuit. Second, the plaintiff must show that the injury was caused by the harmful activity. Often causation is difficult to prove.

If the plaintiff satisfies the standing requirement and meets the burden of proving the unreasonableness of the activity, the cause of the injury, and the damage to the plaintiff, a court may award money damages for economic loss. If money damages are inadequate, the court may enjoin the harmful activity. It is difficult, however, to enjoin the conduct of a valuable business enterprise when adjoining landowners complain of injury. If the harm is substantial and ongoing, however, successive damage suits would be required to compensate the plaintiff for the harm. Some courts have resorted to forcing the business causing the nuisance to "buy" the landowner's right to sue for nuisance. The following case illustrates one court's struggle in fashioning an appropriate remedy in nuisance law. Note in particular the dissenting judge's view of the majority opinion.

Boomer

v

Atlantic Cement Co.
257 NE2d 870 (1970)
Court of Appeals of New York

FACTS: Atlantic operates a large cement plant, representing a $45,000,000 investment and employing more than 300 people. The surrounding landowners sought an injunction and damages for the injury to their property caused by dirt, smoke, and vibration emanating from the plant. The trial court awarded "temporary" damages to compensate plaintiffs for their loss to date. It refused to issue an injunction, but it did suggest that the parties could agree to a fixed amount of "permanent" damages in settlement of all present and future claims.

ISSUE: Are the surrounding landowners entitled to an injunction?

RESULT: Yes. However, the injunction will be vacated on Atlantic's payment of permanent damages to compensate the landowners for the present and future damage to their property.

REASONING:

Bergan, Judge.

*   *   *

The ground for the denial of injunction, notwithstanding the finding both that there is a nuisance and that plaintiffs have been damaged substantially, is the large disparity in economic consequences of the nuisance and of the injunction. This theory cannot, however, be sustained without overruling a doctrine which has been consistently reaffirmed in several leading cases in this court and which has never been disavowed here, namely that where a nuisance has been found and where there has been any substantial damage shown by the party complaining an injunction will be granted.

The rule in New York has been that such a nuisance will be enjoined although marked disparity be shown in economic consequence between the effect of the injunction and the effect of the nuisance. . . .

Although the [lower courts] held that injunction should be denied, it was found that plaintiffs had been damaged in various specific amounts up to the time of the trial and damages to the respective plaintiffs were awarded for those amounts. The effect of this was, injunction having been denied, plaintiffs could maintain successive actions at law for damages thereafter as further damage was incurred. . . .

The power of the court to condition on equitable grounds the continuance of an injunction on the payment of permanent damages seems undoubted. . . .

The damage base here suggested is consistent with the general rule in those nuisance cases where damages are allowed. "Where a nuisance is of such a permanent and unabatable character that a single recovery can be had, including the whole damage past and future resulting therefrom, there can be but one recovery." . . . It has been said that permanent damages are allowed where the loss recoverable would obviously be small as compared with the cost of removal of the nuisance. . . .

. . . [I]t seems fair to both sides to grant permanent damages to plaintiffs which will terminate this private litigation. . . .

Jasen, Judge, dissenting.

*   *   *

It has long been the rule in this State, as the majority acknowledges, that a nuisance which results in substantial continuing damage to neighbors must be enjoined. . . . To now change the rule to permit the cement company to continue polluting the air indefinitely upon the payment of permanent damages is, in my opinion, compounding the magnitude of a very serious problem in our State and Nation today. . . .

The harmful nature and widespread occurrence of air pollution have been extensively documented. Congressional hearings have revealed that air pollution causes substantial property damage, as well as being a contributing factor to a rising incidence of lung cancer, emphysema, bronchitis and asthma.

The specific problem faced here is known as particulate contamination because of the fine dust particles emanating from defendant's cement plant. The particular type of nuisance is not new, having appeared in many cases for at least the past 60 years. . . . It is interesting to note that cement production has recently been identified as a significant source of particulate contamination in the Hudson Valley. This type of pollution, wherein very small particles escape and stay in the atmosphere, has been denominated as the type of air pollution which produces the greatest hazard to human health. We have thus a nuisance which not only is damaging to the plaintiffs, but also is decidedly harmful to the general public. . . .

I see grave dangers in overruling our long-established rule of granting an injunction where a nuisance results in substantial continuing damage. In permitting the injunction to become inoperative upon the payment of permanent damages, the majority is, in effect, licensing a continuing wrong. It is the same as saying to the cement company, you may continue to do harm to your neighbors so long as you pay a fee for it. Furthermore, once such permanent damages are assessed and paid, the incentive to alleviate the wrong would be eliminated, thereby continuing air pollution of an area without abatement. . . .

I would enjoin the defendant cement company from continuing the discharge of dust particles upon its neighbors' properties unless, within 18 months, the cement company abated this nuisance. . . .

In a day when there is a growing concern for clean air, highly developed industry should not expect acquiescence by the courts, but should, instead, plan its operations to eliminate contamination of our air and damage to its neighbors. . . .

Nuisance law requires the court to balance the harm to the plaintiff against the value of the harmful enterprise, in order to determine the "unreasonableness" of the defendant's activity. Similarly, in negligence theory, the court must balance the cost of pollution control measures against the harm to the plaintiff of not using such measures, in order to determine whether the defendant had a duty to use a particular form of pollution control. In strict liability theory, the other available common-law tort theory, the court must make some assessment of the "ultrahazardous" nature of the activity in order to determine whether to impose strict liability. The difficulty of all of these common-law approaches is that only the interests of the parties are represented in the lawsuit. Even class action suits and public nuisance suits do not adequately address a problem of, for example, statewide air quality standards. For this reason, both the state and federal governments have enacted comprehensive regulation to address major environmental problems.

56:3   The National Environmental Policy Act

In 1970 the National Environmental Policy Act (NEPA) [42 USC §§ 4321 et seq.] went into effect. This Act imposes environmental responsibilities on all federal agencies. Section 101 of the NEPA creates a federal policy of using all practicable means to administer federal programs in such a way as to take environmental goals into account. The provision, in effect, gives all federal agencies the authority to consider environmental concerns in their decision-making.

Section 102 of the Act requires federal agencies to consider environmental effects of major decisions. Subsection c requires agencies to include in every recommendation or report on proposals for legislation and "other major Federal actions significantly affecting the quality of the human environment," a detailed statement on the environmental impact of the proposed action. The report, called the *environmental impact statement* (EIS), must be made available to all relevant decision-makers and to the public. This provision has been read strictly by the courts, which may reverse an agency action that was taken without an individualized consideration and balancing of environmental factors, made in good faith.

Because of the tremendous expense of time and money associated with a full environmental impact statement, and the possibility of having agency action overturned without such a statement, § 102 has generated several important legal issues. Consider in the following case the court's reasoning in determining whether the Nuclear Regulatory Commission had given sufficient consideration to environmental factors in permitting the reopening of a reactor at Three Mile Island.

Metropolitan Edison Co.
v
People Against Nuclear Energy
460 US 766 (1983)
United States Supreme Court

FACTS: Metropolitan Edison owned two nuclear power plants at Three Mile Island. One of them, TMI-2, suffered a serious accident that damaged the reactor, causing widespread public concern. The other, TMI-1, was shut down for refueling at the time of the accident. After the accident the Nuclear Regulatory Commission (NRC) ordered Metropolitan Edison to keep TMI-1 shut down until it had an opportunity to determine whether the plant could be operated safely. The NRC published a notice of hearing specifying certain safety-related issues for consideration. People Against Nuclear Energy (PANE) maintained that restarting TMI-1 would cause severe psychological health damage to persons living in the vicinity, and serious damage to the stability, cohesiveness, and well-being of the neighboring communities. When the NRC declined to consider these factors, PANE appealed.

ISSUE: Does the National Environmental Policy Act require that the NRC prepare an environmental impact statement considering the psychological health of the communities surrounding Three Mile Island before it may act on the decision to reopen the reactor?

RESULT: No, the NEPA does not impose such a requirement.

REASONING:

* * *

. . . [W]here an agency action significantly affects the quality of the human environment, the agency must evaluate the "environmental impact" and any unavoidable adverse environmental effects of its proposal. The theme of § 102 is sounded by the adjective "environmental": NEPA does not require the agency to assess *every* impact or effect of its proposed action, but only the impact or effect on the environment. If we were to seize the word "environmental" out of its context and give it the broadest possible definition, the words "adverse environmental effects" might embrace virtually any consequence of a governmental action that someone thought "adverse." But we think the context of the statute shows that Congress was talking about the physical environment—the world around us, so to speak. NEPA was designed to promote human welfare by alerting governmental actors to the effect of their proposed actions on the physical environment. . . .

To determine whether § 102 requires consideration of a particular effect, we must look at the relationship between that effect and the change in the physical environment caused by the major federal action at issue. For example, if the Department of Health and Human Services were to implement extremely stringent requirements for hospitals and nursing homes receiving federal funds, many perfectly adequate hospitals and homes might be forced out of existence. The remaining facilities might be so limited or so expensive that many ill people would be unable to afford medical care and would suffer severe health damage. Nonetheless, NEPA would not require the Department to prepare an EIS evaluating that health damage because it would not be proximately related to a change in the physical environment. . . .

Our understanding of the congressional concerns that led to the enactment of NEPA suggests that the terms "environmental effect" and "environmental impact" in § 102 be read to include a requirement of a reasonably close causal relationship between a change in the physical environment and the effect at issue. This requirement is like the familiar doctrine of proximate cause from tort law. . . . The issue before us, then, is how to give content to this requirement. This is a question of first impression in this Court. . . .

PANE argues that the psychological health damage it alleges "will flow directly from the risk of [a nuclear] accident." . . . But a *risk* of an accident is not an effect on the physical environment. A risk is, by definition, unrealized in the physical world. In a causal chain from renewed operation of TMI-1 to psychological health damage, the element of risk and its perception by PANE's members are necessary middle links. We believe that the element of risk lengthens the causal chain beyond the reach of NEPA.

Risk is a pervasive element of modern life; to say more would belabor the obvious. Many of the risks we face are generated by modern technology, which brings both the possibility of major accidents and opportunities for tremendous achievements. Medical experts apparently agree that risk can generate stress in human beings, which in turn may rise to the level of serious health damage. For this reason among many others, the question whether the gains from any technological advance are worth its attendant risks may be an important public policy issue. Nonetheless, it is quite different from the question whether the same gains are worth a given level of alteration of our physical environment or depletion of our natural resources. The latter question rather than the former is the central concern of NEPA. . . .

We do not mean to denigrate the fears of PANE's members, or to suggest that the psychological health damage they fear could not, in fact, occur. Nonetheless, it is difficult for us to see the differences between someone who dislikes a government decision so much that he suffers anxiety and stress, someone who fears the effects of that decision so much that he suffers similar anxiety and stress, and someone who suffers anxiety and stress that "flow directly," . . . from the risks associated with the same decision. It would be extraordinarily difficult for agencies to differentiate between "genuine" claims of psychological health damage and claims that are grounded solely in disagreement with a democratically adopted policy. Until Congress provides a more explicit statutory instruction than NEPA now contains, we do not think agencies are obliged to undertake the inquiry. . . .

Rehnquist, Justice.

56:4   The Environmental Protection Agency

The Environmental Protection Agency (EPA) was established in 1970 to centralize the environmental control functions of many different federal agencies into one agency. The EPA has become a major federal bureaucracy which conducts research, sponsors research, and advises on environmental issues. One of the EPA's major functions is to ensure compliance with the environmental impact statement requirements. In addition, the EPA serves as the administrative agency for many environmental protection acts, including those that regulate air, water, pesticides, and solid waste.

56:5   Air Pollution

Federal involvement in regulating air quality began in the mid-1950's, when Congress authorized the Surgeon General's office to study air pollution as a threat to human health. In 1963 and 1967 legislation was passed that increased research efforts, established emission controls for new vehicles, and provided limited authority to intervene in interstate pollution problems. Not until the 1970 amendments to the Clean Air Act [42 USC § 7521] was any real power or impact added to the federal interest in air quality.

The Clean Air Act   The Environmental Protection Agency was directed to establish national ambient air quality standards (*NAAQS*) for certain major pollutants. These standards were established with reference to health and welfare, without regard to feasibility. The standards were of two types: *"primary" standards* to protect human health and *"secondary" standards* to protect the public welfare. States were given nine months in which to submit a plan to the EPA for reducing air pollution to NAAQS levels. Thus, the basic structure of the law was that the EPA set standards for pollutants and the states bore responsibility for establishing a plan to implement the standards.

Section 111 of the 1970 Act provided for uniform national standards of performance for new sources of air pollution from *stationary sources*, such as factories, refineries, utility generators, and agriculture. Section 112 provided for uniform national emission standards for air pollutants emitted from *mobile sources*, such as airplanes and automobiles. In general, the states regulate pollution from stationary sources, such as utilities and industrial plants; the EPA regulates mobile sources, such as automobiles and airplanes, directly.

The 1977 Amendments   The 1977 Amendments to the Clean Air Act [42 USC §§ 7521–25, 7541–51] permitted the EPA to fine-tune its approach to NAAQS for stationary sources. The EPA identified "dirty" air areas, called *nonattainment areas*, and "clean" air areas. "Dirty" areas, in which air quality levels fell below NAAQS, were required to improve their compliance with improved pollution control devices and to impose preconstruction standards on new plants. To some extent, reduction of pollution in one area can offset failure to meet NAAQS in another area.

"Clean" air areas, in which air quality exceeds NAAQS, are required to take measures to "prevent the significant deterioration" of air quality. Clean air areas are classified by region, and maximum allowable increases are established for each pollutant. Many national parks and wilderness areas, for example, are Class I, and only very small increments in ambient concentration of air pollutants are permitted.

With respect to mobile sources of pollution, the EPA has established timetables for the reduction of emission from new automobile engines. Automobile manufacturers have varied in their capacity to meet these standards. The worth of the standards and the effectiveness of pollution control devices has been debated for many years. In general, the EPA and the industry have reduced automobile emission pollution; however, many timetables have been extended and forgiven in the process.

 Firms that engage in pollution-producing activities of any sort are subject to extensive state and federal regulation. Inevitably it will be necessary to hire an environmental engineer or other expert to assure compliance with the law and avoid incurring costs from delay, inspection, and enforcement proceedings.

Enforcement Public enforcement of air pollution law lies with the state governments that establish the implementation plans. In addition, the EPA has significant power to inspect plants for violation of the law and to seek injunctions or civil penalties for violations. In addition, private citizens may bring an action for a civil injunction against violators of the law and against administrators who do not enforce the law. Successful plaintiffs may recover costs and attorneys' fees.

56:6   Water Pollution

Water pollution may be caused by the introduction of heated water, toxic waste, organic waste, sediments, or other types of hazardous substances from industrial or agricultural sources into a waterway. The effect of water pollution may be very serious. Contact with or consumption of polluted water poses a threat to personal health and life, as does consumption of aquatic plants and fish. Heating water, and also polluting it with oxygen-consuming wastes, reduces its oxygen content. Such water will not sustain fish life and, eventually, turns dark and putrid. Dumping sediment and organic matter into lakes hastens the process of *eutrophication*, whereby lakes become swampy and marshy.

The 1972 Amendments to FWPCA The major federal measure to protect the nation's waterways from unwanted pollution was the Federal Water Pollution Control Act (FWPCA) Amendments of 1972 [33 USC §§ 1251 et seq.]. The 1972 Amendments established specific goals for water quality and adopted a system of standards and timetables for achieving the goals. The goals were ambitious: to make the nation's waterways safe for fishing and swimming and protect both aquatic and human life—and to eliminate all polluting discharge into the nation's navigable waterways by 1985.

In order to achieve these goals, all *point sources* of effluent pollution were required to adopt the "best practicable control technology currently available" (*BRT*) by 1977, and the "best available technology economically achievable" (*BAT*) by 1983. In addition, the EPA established separate standards for hazardous and toxic wastes; these standards were based on safety requirements, without regard to available technology.

A system of permits was established by the 1972 Amendments for discharging effluents into waterways. Discharge other than with a permit or in violation of the terms of a permit was declared unlawful, and criminal liability is available against company executives. The EPA then established industry-by-industry guidelines for permissible emission of specific pollutants and requirements for pollution control devices.

1977 Amendments; The Clean Water Act In 1977 Congress again amended the FWPCA and renamed the law the Clean Water Act. These amendments granted the EPA greater flexibility in compelling compliance with the law.

Specifically, the amendments established a technology-based standard for conventional, non-toxic pollutants. In subsequent amendments further deadline extensions were granted.

Enforcement   Both criminal penalties and civil fines are available remedies against a firm, or its officers, for violation of the Clean Water Act. Penalties for second violations include fines of up to $50,000 a day and up to two years' imprisonment for responsible officials. Injunctions are another available avenue of enforcement.

56:7   Toxic Substances

As chemical pollution of the soil and ground water becomes an increasingly serious environmental problem, toxic substance regulation has become a fast-growing area of environmental law. Federal regulation of toxic chemicals is piecemeal; no comprehensive legislation has been enacted. The Clean Air Act and the Clean Water Act regulate emission of toxic substances into the air and water. Nevertheless, toxic substances make their way into the water system through runoff from streets and agriculture. This section of Chapter 56 examines the major statutes that regulate different forms of chemical waste.

Pesticides   The Federal Insecticide, Fungicide and Rodenticide Act of 1972 [7 USC §§ 135 et seq.] regulates pesticides by requiring that they be registered with the EPA before being distributed in interstate commerce. The Act requires proper labeling of pesticides, including information on safe use of the substance. The EPA has the power to determine that a registered pesticide is an "unreasonable environmental risk" and ban its sale. Such a determination requires that the EPA weigh the risk of harm against the benefit of the product to agriculture.

Hazardous Waste   The Resource Conservation Recovery Act of 1976 [42 USC §§ 6901 et seq.] gives the EPA broad power to identify a list of hazardous substances and to prescribe such standards for their use "as may be required to protect human health and environment." In addition, the Act requires that records be kept of hazardous waste to ensure that generated waste is ultimately disposed of in accordance with the Act. The record-keeping requires that a *manifest* accompany all transport of the waste materials. A permit is required for disposal of waste, and safety standards must be met to obtain a permit. The EPA has broad powers to inspect, issue compliance orders, and seek civil remedies for violators. In addition, the EPA may seek injunctive relief.

Toxic Substance Control   The Toxic Substances Control Act of 1976 [15 USC § 2602] empowers the EPA to require a manufacturer to test toxic substances to determine their effect on the environment. In addition, it requires a manufacturer to notify the EPA before manufacturing a new chemical substance. Finally, the EPA has the power to issue restrictions on the use and distribution of new or old toxic substances. In issuing such restrictions, however, the EPA must find a "reasonable basis to conclude" that the substance poses an "unreasonable risk of injury to health or the environment." Then the EPA may restrict only "to the extent necessary to protect adequately against such risk using the least burdensome requirements."

56:8   Other Environmental Legislation

Both Congress and the states have passed many other statutes that regulate specific aspects of the environment. For example, the Noise Control Act of 1972 [42 USC § 1604] directs the EPA to establish limits for noise emitted by specific types of products, such as power mowers, trucks, industrial vehicles, and motorcycles. The statute was passed in response to evidence of the health effects of living in an oppressively noisy environment. In setting standards the EPA is required to take into account the benefit to the public health and welfare and the cost of compliance.

In addition, Congress has sought to protect wildlife directly from the disruptive effects of human industrialization and pollution. The Endangered Species Act of 1966 (as amended in 1973) permits the Secretary of the Interior to identify any species of wildlife that is threatened with extinction and promulgate regulations necessary to protect the species, and its habitat, from extinction. The statute is an excellent example of the difficulties presented by an environmental statute that is absolute in its tone, with little room for balancing interests. The following well-known case illustrates this point.

Tennessee Valley Authority

v

Hill

437 US 153 (1978)

United States Supreme Court

FACTS: While the Tellico Dam was under construction by the Tennessee Valley Authority, Congress passed the Endangered Species Act of 1973, which prohibited federal projects that jeopardized endangered species. The snail darter, a small fish, was regarded by the Secretary of the Interior as an endangered species. The snail darter made its habitat in an area of the Little Tennessee River that would be dammed in the project; the snail darter habitat would be destroyed, probably leading to extinction of the species. Environmental groups and others brought action under the Endangered Species Act of 1973 to enjoin the TVA from completing the dam.

ISSUE: Under the statute, may the court weigh the cost of complying with the literal language of the statute against the value of saving the endangered species.

RESULT: No. The statute does not permit such a balancing of values.

REASONING:

* * *

We begin with the premise that operation of the Tellico Dam will either eradicate the known population of snail darters or destroy their critical habitat. Petitioner does not now seriously dispute this fact. In any event, under § 4(a)(1) of the Act, . . . the Secretary of the Interior is vested with exclusive authority to determine whether a species such as the snail darter is "endangered" or "threatened" and to ascertain the factors which have led to such a precarious existence. By § 4(d) Congress has authorized—indeed commanded—the Secretary to "issue such regulations as he deems necessary and advisable to provide for the conservation of such species." . . .

As we have seen, the Secretary promulgated regulations which declared the snail darter an endangered species whose critical habitat would be destroyed by creation of the Tellico Dam. Doubtless petitioner would prefer not to have these regulations on the books, but there is no suggestion that the Secretary exceeded his authority or abused his discretion in issuing the regulations. Indeed, no judicial review of the Secretary's determinations has ever been sought and hence the validity of his actions are not open to review in this Court.

Starting from the above premise, two questions are presented: (a) Would TVA be in violation of the Act if it completed and operated the Tellico Dam as planned? (b) If TVA's actions would offend the Act, is an injunction the appropriate remedy for the violation? For the reasons stated hereinafter, we hold that both questions must be answered in the affirmative.

It may seem curious to some that the survival of a relatively small number of three-inch fish among all the countless millions of species extant would require the permanent halting of a virtually completed dam for which Congress has expended more than $100 million. The paradox is not minimized by the fact that Congress continued to appropriate large sums of public money for the project, even after congressional Appropriations Committees were apprised of its apparent impact upon the survival of the snail darter. We conclude, however, that the explicit provisions of the Endangered Species Act require precisely that result.

One would be hard pressed to find a statutory provision whose terms were any plainer than those in § 7 of the Endangered Species Act. Its very words affirmatively command all federal agencies "to *insure* that actions *authorized, funded,* or *carried out* by them do not *jeopardize* the continued existence" of an endangered species or "*result* in the destruction or modification of habitat of such species. . . . "

This language admits of no exception. Nonetheless, petitioner urges, as do the dissenters, that the Act cannot reasonably be interpreted as applying to a federal project which was well under way when Congress passed the Endangered Species Act of 1973. To sustain that position, however, we would be forced to ignore the ordinary meaning of plain language. It has not been shown, for example, how TVA can close the gates of the Tellico Dam without "carrying out" an action that has been "authorized" and "funded" by a federal agency. Nor can we understand how such action will *"insure"* that the snail darter's habitat is not disrupted. Accepting the Secretary's determinations, as we must, it is clear that TVA's proposed operation of the dam will have precisely the opposite effect, namely the *eradication* of an endangered species.

Concededly, this view of the Act will produce results requiring the sacrifice of the anticipated benefits of the project and of many millions of dollars in public funds. But examination of the language, history, and structure of the legislation under review here indicates beyond doubt that Congress intended endangered species to be afforded the highest of priorities. . . .

Here we are urged to view the Endangered Species Act "reasonably," and hence shape a remedy "that accords with some modicum of common sense and the public weal." . . . But is that our function? We have no expert knowledge on the subject of endangered species, much less do we have a mandate from the people to strike a balance of equities on the side of the Tellico Dam. Congress has spoken in the plainest of words, making it abundantly clear that the balance has been struck in favor of affording endangered species the highest of priorities, thereby adopting a policy which it described as "institutionalized caution."

Our individual appraisal of the wisdom or unwisdom of a particular course consciously selected by the Congress is to be put aside in the process of interpreting a statute. Once the meaning of an enactment is discerned and its constitutionality determined, the judicial process comes to an end. . . .

Berger, Chief Justice.

Energy Conservation and Regulation   Through a variety of statutes, Congress has regulated the conservation of energy resources and the damage to the environment caused by extraction of fossil fuels. For example, offshore drilling on the continental shelf is carried on through contract with the United States government. Such projects usually are governed by NEPA and require an environmental impact statement. In addition, they are governed directly by statutes controlling coastal zone management and the outer continental shelf. The Army Corps of Engineers has the power, under certain circumstances, to regulate construction of oil and gas pipelines.

The Surface Mining Control and Reclamation Act of 1977 [30 USC §§ 1201–1328] establishes minimum environmental standards for coal strip-mining operations. In general, strip mining may not be conducted without a permit. To obtain the permit the mining firm must disclose substantial information about the proposed operation and post a performance bond for all the requirements of the Act. In general, the mining firm must restore the surface to its original contours, preserve the topsoil, and restore the vegetation of the land.

56:9   The Limits of Environmental Regulation

In various contexts, environmental regulation has been attacked on constitutional grounds. The first line of attack is the claim that the federal government lacks the power to regulate wholly intrastate commerce. In general, however, the courts defer to Congress' finding that a regulated activity affects interstate commerce if there is any rational basis for the assertion. Usually it is not difficult to discern an effect on interstate commerce in the environmental regulatory area.

Another basis for attack is that many environmental regulations may violate the Tenth Amendment by directly regulating an activity of the state itself. The Tenth Amendment states:

> The powers not delegated to the United States by the Constitution, nor prohibited it by the States, are reserved to the States respectively, or to the people.

In the *Hodel* case (below) the Supreme Court clarified earlier case law on the Tenth Amendment and indicated that most regulatory statutes would not be struck down on Tenth Amendment grounds. Only if the statute directly regulated state officials in matters that are indisputably "attributes of state sovereignty," and in ways that impair the state's ability to conduct its traditional functions, would the statute be struck.

Finally, environmental legislation may be attacked on the ground that it deprives a property owner of the use of property so as to constitute a taking without just compensation. The following case examines this argument in the context of the Surface Mining Control and Reclamation Act of 1977. Note that the Court holds that the mere passage of the Act does not deprive the plaintiffs of their property; until they are deprived, the claim is not "ripe." What must a landowner prove to demonstrate deprivation of property under the Act?

Hodel

v

Virginia Surface Mining & Reclamation Asso.
452 US 264 (1981)
United States Supreme Court

FACTS: Steep-slope mining involves cutting back the mountainside above a
surface outcropping of coal on a slope. The surface is cut back so long as
it is economically feasible to do so. The Surface Mining Act requires that

surfaces so mined be restored to their original contours. The plaintiffs, an association of coal producers, claim that such a restoration requirement is so expensive that it effectively prohibits mining in certain locations, depriving a landowner or mineral-rights owner of the value of his property.

ISSUE: Does the regulation constitute a taking without just compensation under the Fifth Amendment of the federal Constitution?

RESULT: No. The plaintiffs have demonstrated no loss of property or use of property.

REASONING:

*   *   *

We conclude that the District Court's ruling on the "taking" issue suffers from a fatal deficiency: neither appellees nor the court identified any property in which appellees have an interest that has allegedly been taken by operation of the Act. By proceeding in this fashion, the court below ignored this Court's oft-repeated admonition that the constitutionality of statutes ought not be decided except in an actual factual setting that makes such a decision necessary. . . .

Because appellees' taking claim arose in the context of a facial challenge, it presented no concrete controversy concerning either application of the Act to particular surface mining operations or its effect on specific parcels of land. Thus, the only issue properly before the District Court and, in turn, this Court, is whether the "mere enactment" of the Surface Mining Act constitutes a taking. . . . The test to be applied in considering this facial challenge is fairly straightforward. A statute regulating the uses that can be made of property effects a taking if it "denies an owner economically viable use of his land. . . . " . . . The Surface Mining Act easily survives scrutiny under this test.

First, the Act does not, on its face, prevent beneficial use of coal-bearing lands. Except for the proscription of mining near certain locations by § 522(e), the Act does not categorically prohibit surface coal mining; it merely regulates the conditions under which such operations may be conducted. The Act does not purport to regulate alternative uses to which coal-bearing lands may be put. Thus, in the posture in which these cases comes before us, there is no reason to suppose that "mere enactment" of the Surface Mining Act has deprived appellees of economically viable use of their property.

Moreover, appellees cannot at this juncture legitimately raise complaints in this Court about the manner in which the challenged provisions of the Act have been or will be applied in specific circumstances, or about their effect on particular coal mining operations. There is no indication in the record that appellees have availed themselves of the opportunities provided by the Act to obtain administrative relief by requesting either a variance from the approximate-original-contour requirement of § 515(d) or a waiver from the surface mining restrictions in § 522(e). If appellees were to seek administrative relief under these procedures, a mutually acceptable solution might well be reached with regard to individual properties, thereby obviating any need to address the constitutional questions. The potential for such administrative solutions confirms the conclusion that the taking issue decided by the District Court simply is not ripe for judicial resolution. . . .

Marshall, Justice

Key Concepts and Terms

- Environmental law is primarily statutory and regulatory in nature.
- The theory of nuisance is that the defendant has used his or her property in such a way as to interfere unreasonably with the plaintiff's use and enjoyment of property.
- The doctrine of standing limits the category of persons permitted to bring a lawsuit.
- In a nuisance case the court must balance the harm to plaintiff against the benefit and value of the enterprise causing the harm.
- The National Environmental Policy Act of 1970 requires all federal agencies to consider the consequences which their major decisions will have on the environment.
- The Environmental Protection Agency (EPA) is the federal bureaucracy that administers most federal environmental protection law.
- Under the Clean Air Act the EPA established national air quality standards for each of several major air pollutants.
- The EPA has significant inspection and enforcement powers under the Clean Air Act.
- The Clean Water Act requires a permit for the introduction of polluted effluent into the nation's waterways.
- Under the Clean Water Act the EPA establishes industry-by-industry guidelines for permissible emission of specific pollutants.
- The EPA regulates pesticides by requiring a permit to sell a pesticide, by requiring disclosure of safety procedures, and by banning some pesticides.
- The EPA identifies hazardous waste products and requires that they be kept track of until disposal pursuant to a permit.

- BAT
- BRT
- Clean Air Act
- Clean Water Act
- Endangered Species Control Act
- Environmental Impact Statement
- Environmental Protection Agency
- Eutrophication
- Federal Insecticide, Fungicide and Rodenticide Act of 1972
- Federal Water Pollution Control Act
- Manifest
- Mobile Sources
- NAAQS
- National Environmental Policy Act of 1970
- Noise Control Act of 1972
- "Nonattainment Areas"
- Nuclear Regulatory Commission
- Nuisance
- Point Source
- Primary Standards
- Resource Conservation Recovery Act of 1976
- Secondary Standards
- Standing
- Stationary Sources
- Surface Mining Control and Reclamation Act of 1977
- Toxic Substances Control Act of 1976

Questions and Case Problems

1. Prah's solar-powered house was situated on his land in such a way as to take maximum advantage of the sun for his solar collectors. Prah's neighboring land-owner, Maretti, began building a house that interfered with Prah's unobstructed path of light. Maretti knew that his houseplans would interfere with Prah's access to unobstructed sunlight. Prah seeks an injunction based on nuisance against Maretti for the unreasonable use of his land. What result?

2. Dalsis is the owner of a small store. She seeks to enjoin the federal Department of Housing and Urban Development from continuing construction of a large shopping mall that has been under construction for over a year. The basis of her claim is that HUD did not prepare an environmental impact statement and that its determination that no adverse environmental effect would result from the mall's construction did not take into account the increased traffic congestion and possible urban decay and deterioration in the downtown area. Dalsis delayed filing the suit until well over a year after she knew of the proposed size of the project. Should the court enjoin construction and require an EIS?

3. The Department of Justice planned and began excavation for a nine-story federal jail in back of the United States Court House in Manhattan, just across the street from two large apartment buildings. Hanly, suing for himself and on behalf of a class of 50,000 "residents, merchants, businessmen, institutions, religious organizations and other members of the public living with the area," sought a preliminary injunction to halt the excavation. Hanly's theory is that the government failed to properly consider the effect of the construction on the surrounding neighborhood. The NEPA recognizes the "profound influences of . . . high-density urbanization," and declares it the responsibility of the federal government to assure for all Americans "safe, healthful, productive and esthetically and culturally pleasing surroundings." Is the government obligated to consider the effects on the

social and cultural environment of locating a nine-story jail across the street from a high-rise apartment building?

4. Review the *Boomer v Atlantic Cement Company* case (see page 1212). Explain why the court was not satisfied with the choice of enjoining the cement plant's operation or granting damages for the nuisance.

5. Review the facts of *Metropolitan Edison Co. v People Against Nuclear Energy* (see page 1215). What type of research would a federal agency have to include in an environmental impact statement if it were required to consider the psychological health of the community? Do you agree with the court's exclusion of that consideration? Explain fully.

6. Some states have experimented with state implementation plans under the Clean Air Act whereby reductions in emission levels can be used to offset the emissions effects of creating new sources of emissions. A firm that shut down a polluting plant could "bank" the offset and use it when a new plant opened or an old plant expanded. Offsets could also be transfered to other firms for their use. Thus a market is created in the right to emit pollutants. What do you think of this approach to air quality control?

7. In 1974 the President proposed to accelerate the program of granting oil exploration leases on the outer continental shelf along the east coast. The Secretary of the Interior proceeded to identify a prospective site for leasing and, among other things, prepared an EIS covering the possible risk of environmental pollution and damage from offshore oil exploration and drilling. The Natural Resources Defense Council, the State of New York, and a number of Long Island counties and towns sought an injunction on the ground that the EIS was inadequate. The EIS was written based on the assumption that a pipeline would be used to transport oil to the mainland, minimizing oil spills. The plaintiffs assert that the Department did not take into consideration the likelihood that surrounding states would bar the landing of pipelines on their shores, thereby necessitating the use of oil tankers, which are much more likely to spill oil. Should the government be enjoined from proceeding with the leasing in order to consider the effects of this possible political development? Discuss fully.

8. The Price–Anderson Act imposes a $560 million limit on liability for nuclear plant accidents. The Duke Power Co., which was building nuclear plants in North and South Carolina, and the Nuclear Regulatory Commission were sued by a group of individuals who lived near the proposed plant. The plaintiffs sought a declaratory judgment that the $560 million limitation violates the Fifth Amendment due process clause of the federal Constitution because it allows injuries to occur without assuring adequate compensation to the victim. The plaintiffs claim they have standing to sue because they are most likely to be victims of a nuclear accident and because the plant would not be built but for the limit on liability and, therefore, their risk of injury would be diminished. Should these plaintiffs have standing, as you understand that term?

9. Why is agricultural runoff exempt from the "point source" permit requirements of the Clean Water Act?

10. In the *Tennessee Valley Authority v Hill* case (see page 1221), what further measure could the TVA take to complete the dam? Does it surprise you that after the Supreme Court opinion Congress passed a statute exempting the Tellico dam project from the Endangered Species Act?

Appendix A

We the People of the United States, in Order to form a more perfect Union, establish Justice, insure domestic Tranquility, provide for the common defense, promote the general Welfare, and secure the Blessings of Liberty to ourselves and our Posterity, do ordain and establish this Constitution for the United States of America.

Article I

Section 1 All legislative Powers herein granted shall be vested in a Congress of the United States, which shall consist of a Senate and House of Representatives.

Section 2 [cl. 1] The House of Representatives shall be composed of Members chosen every second Year by the People of the several States, and the Electors in each State shall have the Qualifications requisite for Electors of the most numerous Branch of the State Legislature.

[cl. 2] No Person shall be a Representative who shall not have attained to the Age of twenty five Years, and been seven Years a Citizen of the United States, and who shall not, when elected, be an Inhabitant of that State in which he shall be chosen.

[cl. 3] Representatives and direct Taxes shall be apportioned among the several States which may be included within this Union, according to their respective Numbers, which shall be determined by adding to the whole Number of free Persons, including those bound to Service for a Term of Years, and excluding Indians not taxed, three fifths of all other Persons. The actual Enumeration shall be made within three Years after the first Meeting of the Congress of the United States, and within every subsequent Term of ten Years, in such Manner as they shall by Law direct. The Number of Representatives shall not exceed one for every thirty Thousand, but each State shall have at Least one Representative; and until such enumeration shall be made, the State of New Hampshire shall be entitled to chuse three, Massachusetts eight, Rhode-Island and Providence Plantations one, Connecticut five, New-York six, New Jersey four, Pennsylvania eight, Delaware one, Maryland six, Virginia ten, North Carolina five, South Carolina five, and Georgia three.

[cl. 4] When vacancies happen in the Representation from any State, the Executive Authority thereof shall issue Writs of Election to fill such Vacancies.

[cl. 5] The House of Representatives shall chuse their speaker and other Officers; and shall have the sole Power of Impeachment.

Section 3 [cl. 1] The Senate of the United States shall be composed of two Senators from each State, chosen by the Legislature thereof, for six Years; and each Senator shall have one Vote.

[cl. 2] Immediately after they shall be assembled in Consequence of the first Election, they shall be divided as equally as may be into three Classes. The Seats of the Senators of the first Class shall be vacated at the Expiration of the second Year, of the second Class at the Expiration of the fourth Year, and of the third Class at the Expiration of the sixth Year, so that one third may be chosen every second Year; and if Vacancies happen by Resignation, or otherwise, during the Recess of the Legislature of any State, the Executive thereof may make temporary Appointments until the next Meeting of the Legislature, which shall then fill such Vacancies.

[cl. 3] No Person shall be a Senator who shall not have attained to the Age of thirty years, and been nine Years a Citizen of the United States, and who shall not, when elected, be an Inhabitant of that State for which he shall be chosen.

[cl. 4] The Vice President of the United States shall be President of the Senate, but shall have no Vote, unless they be equally divided.

[cl. 5] The Senate shall chuse their other Officers, and also a President pro tempore, in the Absence of the Vice President, or when he shall exercise the Office of President of the United States.

[cl. 6] The Senate shall have the sole Power to try all Impeachments. When sitting for that Purpose, they shall be on Oath or Affirmation. When the President of the United States is tried, the Chief Justice shall preside: And no Person shall be convicted without the Concurrence of two thirds of the Members present.

[cl. 7] Judgment in Cases of Impeachment shall not extend further than to removal from Office, and disqualification to hold and enjoy any Office of honor, Trust or Profit under the United States: but the Party convicted shall nevertheless be liable and subject to Indictment, Trial, Judgment and Punishment, according to Law.

Section 4 [cl. 1] The Times, Places and Manner of holding Elections for Senators and Representatives, shall be prescribed in each State by the Legislature thereof; but the Congress may at any time by Law make or alter such Regulations, except as to the Places of chusing Senators.

[cl. 2] The Congress shall assemble at least once in every Year, and such Meeting shall be on the first Monday in December, unless they shall by Law appoint a different Day.

Section 5 [cl. 1] Each House shall be the Judge of the Elections, Returns and Qualifications of its own Members, and a Majority of each shall constitute a Quorum to do Business; but a smaller Number may adjourn from day to day, and may be authorized to compel the Attendance of absent Members, in such Manner, and under such Penalties as each House may provide.

[cl. 2] Each House may determine the Rules of its Proceedings, punish its Members for disorderly Behaviour, and, with the Concurrence of two thirds, expel a Member.

[cl. 3] Each House shall keep a Journal of its Proceedings, and from time to time publish the same, excepting such Parts as may in their Judgment require Secrecy; and the Yeas and Nays of the Members of either House on any question shall, at the Desire of one fifth of those Present, be entered on the Journal.

[cl. 4] Neither House, during the Session of Congress, shall, without the Consent of the other, adjourn for more than three days, nor to any other Place than that in which the two Houses shall be sitting.

Section 6 [cl. 1] The Senators and Representatives shall receive a Compensation for their Services, to be ascertained by Law, and paid out of the Treasury of the United States. They shall in all Cases, excep Treason, Felony and Breach of the Peace, be privileged from Arrest during their Attendance at the Session of their respective Houses, and in going to and returning from the same; and for any Speech or Debate in either House, they shall not be questioned in any other Place.

[cl. 2] No Senator or Representative shall, during the Time for which he was elected, be appointed to any civil Office under the Authority of the United States, which shall have been created, or the Emoluments whereof shall have been encreased during such time; and no Person holding any Office under the United States, shall be a Member of either House during his Continuance in Office.

Section 7 [cl. 1] All Bills for raising Revenue shall originate in the House of Representatives; but the Senate may propose or concur with Amendments as on other Bills.

[cl. 2] Every Bill which shall have passed the House of Representatives and the Senate, shall, before it become a Law, be presented to the President of the United States; If he approve he shall sign it, but if not he shall return it, with his Objections to that House in which it shall have originated, who shall enter the Objections at large on their Journal, and proceed to reconsider it. If after such Reconsideration two thirds of that House shall agree to pass the Bill, it shall be sent, together with the Objections, to the other House, by which it shall likewise be reconsidered, and if approved by two thirds of that House, it shall become a Law. But in all such Cases the Votes of both Houses shall be determined by yeas and Nays, and the Names of the Persons voting for and against the Bill shall be entered on the Journal of each House respectively. If any Bill shall not be returned by the President within ten Days (Sundays excepted) after it shall have been presented to him, the Same shall be a

Law, in like Manner as if he had signed it, unless the Congress by their Adjournment prevent its Return, in which Case it shall not be a Law.

[cl. 3] Every Order, Resolution, or Vote to which the Concurrence of the Senate and House of Representatives may be necessary (except on a question of Adjournment) shall be presented to the President of the United States; and before the Same shall take Effect, shall be approved by him, or being disapproved by him, shall be repassed by two thirds of the Senate and House of Representatives, according to the Rules and Limitations prescribed in the Case of a Bill.

Section 8   The Congress shall have Power
[cl. 1] To lay and collect Taxes, Duties, Imposts and Excises, to pay the Debts and provide for the common Defence and general Welfare of the United States; but all Duties, Imposts and Excises shall be uniform throughout the United States;

[cl. 2] To borrow Money on the Credit of the United States;

[cl. 3] To regulate Commerce with foreign Nations, and among the several States and with the Indian Tribes;

[cl. 4] To establish an uniform Rule of Naturalization, and uniform Laws on the subject of Bankruptcies throughout the United States;

[cl. 5] To coin Money, regulate the Value thereof, and of foreign Coin, and fix the Standard of Weights and Measures;

[cl. 6] To provide for the Punishment of counterfeiting the Securities and current Coin of the United States;

[cl. 7] To establish Post Offices and post Roads;

[cl. 8] To promote the Progress of Science and useful Arts, by securing for limited Times to Authors and Inventors the exclusive Right to their respective Writings and Discoveries;

[cl. 9] To constitute Tribunals inferior to the supreme Court;

[cl. 10] To define and punish Piracies and Felonies committed on the high Seas, and Offences against the Law of Nations;

[cl. 11] To declare War, grant Letters of Marque and Reprisal, and make Rules concerning Captures on Land and Water;

[cl. 12] To raise and support Armies, but no Appropriation of Money to that Use shall be for a longer Term than two Years;

[cl. 13] To provide and maintain a Navy;

[cl. 14] To make Rules for the Government and Regulation of the land and naval Forces;

[cl. 15] To provide for calling forth the Militia to execute the Laws of the Union, suppress Insurrections and repel Invasions;

[cl. 16] To provide for organizing arming, and disciplining, the Militia, and for governing such Part of them as may be employed in the Service of the United States, reserving to the States respectively, the Appointment of the Officers, and the Authority of training the Militia according to the discipline prescribed by Congress;

[cl. 17] To exercise exclusive Legislation in all Cases whatsoever, over such District (not exceeding ten Miles square) as may, by Cession of particular States, and the Acceptance of Congress become the Seat of the Government of the United States, and to exercise like Authority over all Places purchased by the Consent of the Legislature of the State in which the Same shall be for the Erection of Forts, Magazines, Arsenals, dock-Yards, and other needful Buildings;—And

[cl. 18] To make all Laws which shall be necessary and proper for carrying into Execution the foregoing Powers, and all other Powers vested by this Constitution in the Government of the United States, or in any Department or Officer thereof.

Section 9   [cl. 1] The Migration or Importation of such Persons as any of the States now existing shall think proper to admit, shall not be prohibited by the Congress prior to the Year one thousand eight hundred and eight, but a Tax or duty may be imposed on such Importation, not exceeding ten dollars for each Person.

[cl. 2] The Privilege of the Writ of Habeas Corpus shall not be suspended, unless when in Cases of Rebellion or Invasion the public Safety may require it.

[cl. 3] No Bill of Attainder or ex post facto Laws shall be passed.

[cl. 4] No Capitation, or other direct, Tax shall be laid, unless in Proportion to the Census or Enumeration herein before directed to be taken.

[cl. 5] No Tax or Duty shall be laid on Articles exported from any State.

[cl. 6] No Preference shall be given by any Regulation of Commerce or Revenue to the Ports of one State over those of another: nor shall Vessels bound to, or from, one State, be obliged to enter, clear, or pay Duties in another.

[cl. 7] No Money shall be drawn from the Treasury, but in Consequence of Appropriations made by Law; and a regular Statement and Account of the Receipts and Expenditures of all public Money shall be published from time to time.

[cl. 8] No Title of Nobility shall be granted by the United States; And no Person holding any Office of Profit or Trust under them, shall, without the Consent of the Congress, accept of any present, Emolument, Office, or Title, of any kind whatever, from any King, Prince, or foreign State.

Section 10 [cl. 1] No State shall enter into any Treaty, Alliance, or Confederation; grant Letters of Marque and Reprisal; coin Money; emit Bills of Credit; make any Thing but gold and silver Coin a Tender in Payment of Debts; pass any Bill of Attainder, ex post facto Law, or Law impairing the Obligation of Contracts, or grant any Title of Nobility.

[cl. 2] No State shall, without the Consent of the Congress, lay any Imposts or Duties on Imports or Exports, except what may be absolutely necessary for executing its inspection Laws: and the net Produce of all Duties and Imposts, laid by any State on Imports or Exports, shall be for the Use of the Treasury of the United States; and all such Laws shall be subject to the Revision and Control of the Congress.

[cl. 3] No State shall, without the Consent of Congress, lay any Duty of Tonnage, keep Troops, or Ships of War in time of Peace, enter into any Agreement or Compact with another State, or with a foreign Power, or engage in War, unless actually invaded, or in such imminent Danger as will not admit of delay.

Article II

Section 1 [cl. 1] the executive Power shall be vested in a President of the United States of America. He shall hold his Office during the Term of four Years, and, together with the Vice President, chosen for the same Term, be elected, as follows:

[cl. 2] Each State shall appoint, in such Manner as the Legislature thereof may direct, a Number of Electors, equal to the whole Number of Senators and Representatives to which the State may be entitled in the Congress: but no Senator or Representative, or Person holding an Office of Trust or Profit under the United States, shall be appointed an Elector.

[cl. 3] The Electors shall meet in their respective States, and vote by Ballot for two Persons, of whom one at least shall not be an Inhabitant of the same State with themselves. And they shall make a List of all the Persons voted for, and of the Number of Votes for each; which List they shall sign and certify, and transmit sealed to the Seat of the Government of the United States, directed to the President of the Senate. The President of the Senate shall in the Presence of the Senate and House of Representatives, open all the Certificates, and the Votes shall then be counted. The Person having the greatest Number of Votes shall be the President, if such Number be a Majority of the whole Number of Electors appointed; and if there be more than one who have such Majority, and have an equal Number of Votes, then the House of Representatives shall immediately chuse by Ballot one of them for President; and if no Person have a Majority, then from the five highest on the List the said House shall in like manner chuse the President. But in chusing the President, the Votes shall be taken by States, the Representation from each State having one vote; A quorum for this Purpose shall consist of a Member or Members from two thirds of the States, and a Majority of all the States shall be necessary to a Choice. In every Case, after the Choice of the President, the Person having the greatest Number of Votes of the Electors shall be the Vice President. But if there should remain two or more who have equal Votes, the Senate shall chuse from them by Ballot the Vice President.

[cl. 4] The Congress may determine the Time of chusing the Electors, and the Day on which they shall give their Votes; which Day shall be the same throughout the United States.

[cl. 5] No Person except a natural born Citizen, or a Citizen of the United States, at the time of the Adoption of this Constitution, shall be eligible to the Office of President; neither shall any Person be eligible to that Office who shall not have attained to the Age of thirty-five Years, and been fourteen Years a Resident within the United States.

[cl. 6] In Case of the Removal of the President from Office, or of his Death, Resignation, or Inability to discharge the Powers and Duties of the said Office, the Same shall devolve on the Vice President, and the Congress may by Law provide for the Case of Removal, Death, Resignation or Inability, both of the President and Vice President, declaring what Officer shall then act as President, and such

Officer shall act accordingly, until the Disability be removed, or a President shall be elected.

[cl. 7] The President shall, at stated Times, receive for his Services, a Compensation, which shall neither be encreased nor diminished during the Period for which he shall have been elected, and he shall not receive within that Period any other Emolument from the United States or any of them.

[cl. 8] Before he enter on the Execution of his Office, he shall take the following Oath or Affirmation:—"I do solemnly swear (or affirm) that I will faithfully execute the Office of President of the United States, and will to the best of my Ability, preserve, protect and defend the Constitution of the United States."

Section 2 [cl. 1] The President shall be Commander in Chief of the Army and Navy of the United States, and of the Militia of the several States, when called into the actual Service of the United States; he may require the Opinion, in writing, of the principal Officer in each of the executive Departments, upon any Subject relating to the Duties of their respective Offices, and he shall have Power to grant Reprieves and Pardons for Offences against the United States, except in Cases of Impeachment.

[cl. 2] He shall have Power, by and with the Advice and Consent of the Senate, to make Treaties, provided two thirds of the Senators present concur; and he shall nominate, and by and with the Advice and Consent of the Senate, shall appoint Ambassadors, other public Ministers and Consuls, Judges of the supreme Court, and all other Officers of the United States, whose Appointments are not herein otherwise provided for, and which shall be established by Law: but the Congress may by Law vest the Appointment of such inferior Officers, as they think proper, in the President alone, in the Courts of Law, or in the Heads of Departments.

[cl. 3] The President shall have Power to fill up all Vacancies that may happen during the Recess of the Senate, by granting Commissions which shall expire at the End of their next Session.

Section 3 He shall from time to time give to the Congress Information of the State of the Union, and recommend to their Consideration such Measures as he shall judge necessary and expedient; he may, on extraordinary Occasions, convene both Houses, or either of them, and in Case of Disagreement between them, with Respect to the Time of Adjourn-

ment, he may adjourn them to such Time as he shall think proper; he shall receive Ambassadors and other public Ministers; he shall take Care that the Laws be faithfully executed, and shall Commission all the Officers of the United States.

Section 4 The President, Vice President and all civil Officers of the United States, shall be removed from Office on Impeachment for, and Conviction of, Treason, Bribery, or other high Crimes and Misdemeanors.

Article III

Section 1 The judicial Power of the United States, shall be vested in one supreme Court, and in such inferior Courts as the Congress may from time to time ordain and establish. The Judges, both of the supreme and inferior Courts, shall hold their Offices during good Behaviour and shall, at stated Times, receive for their Services, a Compensation, which shall not be diminished during their Continuance in Office.

Section 2 [cl. 1] The judicial Power shall extend to all Cases, in Law and Equity, arising under this Constitution, the Laws of the United States, and Treaties made, or which shall be made, under their Authority;—to all Cases affecting Ambassadors, other public Ministers and Consuls;—to all Cases of admiralty and maritime Jurisdiction;—to Controversies to which the United States shall be a Party;—to Controversies between two or more States;—between a State and Citizens of another State; between Citizens of different States;—between Citizens of the same State claiming Lands under Grants of different States, and between a State, or the Citizens thereof, and foreign States, Citizens or Subjects.

[cl. 2] In all Cases affecting Ambassadors, other public Ministers and Consuls, and those in which a State shall be Party, the supreme Court shall have original Jurisdiction. In all the other Cases before mentioned, the supreme Court shall have appellate Jurisdiction, both as to Law and Fact, with such Exceptions, and under such Regulations as the Congress shall make.

[cl. 3] The Trial of all Crimes, except in Cases of Impeachment, shall be by Jury; and such Trial shall be held in the State where the said Crimes shall have been committed; but when not committed within any State the Trial shall be at such Place or Places as the Congress may by Law have directed.

Section 3 [cl. 1] Treason against the United States, shall consist only in levying War against them, or in adhering to their Enemies, giving them Aid and Comfort. No Person shall be convicted of Treason unless on the Testimony of two Witnesses to the same overt Act, or on Confession in open Court.

[cl. 2] The Congress shall have Power to declare the Punishment of Treason, but no Attainder of Treason shall work Corruption of Blood, or Forfeiture except during the Life of the Person attainted.

Article IV

Section 1 Full Faith and Credit shall be given in each State to the public Acts, Records, and judicial Proceedings of every other State. And the Congress may by general Laws prescribe the Manner in which such Acts, Records and Proceedings shall be proved, and the Effect thereof.

Section 2 [cl. 1] The Citizens of each State shall be entitled to all Privileges and Immunities of Citizens in the several States.

[cl. 2] A Person charged in any State with Treason, Felony, or other Crime, who shall flee from Justice, and be found in another State, shall on Demand of the executive Authority of the State from which he fled, be delivered up, to be removed to the State having Jurisdiction of the Crime.

[cl. 3] No Person held to Service or Labour in One State, under the Laws thereof, escaping into another, shall, in Consequence of any Law or Regulation therein, be discharged from such Service or Labour, but shall be delivered up on Claim of the Party to whom such Service or Labour may be due.

Section 3 [cl. 1] New States may be admitted by the Congress into this Union; but no new State shall be formed or erected within the Jurisdiction of any other State; nor any State be formed by the Junction of two or more States, or Parts of States, without the Consent of the Legislatures of the States concerned as well as of the Congress.

[cl. 2] The Congress shall have Power to dispose of and make all needful Rules and Regulations respecting the Territory or other Property belonging to the United States; and nothing in this Constitution shall be so construed as to Prejudice any Claims of the United States, or of any particular State.

Section 4 The United States shall guarantee to every State in this Union a Republican Form of Government, and shall protect each of them against Invasion; and on Application of the Legislature, or of the Executive (when the Legislature cannot be convened) against domestic Violence.

Article V

The Congress, whenever two thirds of both Houses shall deem it necessary, shall propose Amendments to this Constitution or, on the Application of the Legislatures of two thirds of the several States, shall call a Convention for proposing Amendments, which, in either Case, shall be valid to all Intents and Purposes, as Part of this Constitution, when ratified by the Legislatures of three fourths of the several States, or by Conventions in three fourths thereof, as the one or the other Mode of Ratification may be proposed by the Congress; Provided that no Amendment which may be made prior to the Year One thousand eight hundred and eight shall in any Manner affect the first and fourth Clauses in the Ninth Section of the first Article; and that no State, without its Consent, shall be deprived of its equal Suffrage in the Senate.

Article VI

[cl. 1] All Debts contracted and Engagements entered into, before the Adoption of this Constitution shall be as valid against the United States under this Constitution, as under the Confederation.

[cl. 2] This Constitution, and the Laws of the United States which shall be made in Pursuance thereof; and all Treaties made, or which shall be made, under the Authority of the United States, shall be the supreme Law of the Land; and the Judges in every State shall be bound thereby, any Thing in the Constitution or Laws of any State to the Contrary notwithstanding.

[cl. 3] The Senators and Representatives before mentioned, and the Members of the several State Legislatures, and all executive and judicial Officers, both of the United States and of the several States, shall be bound by Oath or Affirmation, to support this Constitution; but no religious Test shall ever be required as a Qualification to any Office or public Trust under the United States.

Article VII

The Ratification of the Conventions of nine States, shall be sufficient for the Establishment of this Constitution between the States so ratifying the Same.

AMENDMENTS

(The first 10 Amendments were adopted December 15, 1791.)

Amendment 1

Congress shall make no law respecting an establishment of religion, or prohibiting the free exercise thereof; or abridging the freedom of speech, or of the press; or the right of the people peaceably to assemble, and to petition the Government for a redress of grievances.

Amendment 2

A well regulated Militia, being necessary to the security of a free State, the right of the people to keep and bear Arms, shall not be infringed.

Amendment 3

No Soldier shall, in time of peace be quartered in any house, withouth the consent of the Owner, nor in time of war, but in a manner to be prescribed by law.

Amendment 4

The right of the people to be secure in their persons, houses, papers, and effects, against unreasonable searches and seizures, shall not be violated, and no Warrants shall issue, but upon probable cause, supported by Oath or affirmation, and particularly describing the place to be searched, and the persons or things to be seized.

Amendment 5

No person shall be held to answer for a capital, or otherwise infamous crime, unless on a presentment or indictment of a Grand Jury, except in cases arising in the land or naval forces, or in the Militia, when in actual service in time of War or public danger; nor shall any person be subject for the same offence to be twice put in jeopardy of life or limb; nor shall be compelled in any criminalcase to be a witness against himself, nor be deprived of life, liberty, or property, without due process of law; nor shall private property be taken for public use, without just compensation.

Amendment 6

In all criminal prosecutions, the accused shall enjoy the right to a speedy and public trial, by an impartial jury of the State and district wherein the crime shall have been committed, which district shall have been previously ascertained by law, and to be informed of the nature and cause of the accusation; to be confronted with the witnesses against him; to have compulsory process for obtaining witnesses in his favor, and to have the Assistance of Counsel for his defence.

Amendment 7

In Suits at common law, where the value in controversy shall exceed twenty dollars, the right of trial by jury shall be preserved, and no fact tried by a jury, shall be otherwise re-examined in any Court of the United States, than according to the rules of the common law.

Amendment 8

Excessive bail shall not be required, nor excessive fines imposed, nor cruel and unusual punishments inflicted.

Amendment 9

The enumeration in the Constitution, of certain rights, shall not be construed to deny or disparage others retained by the people.

Amendment 10

The powers not delegated to the United States by the Constitution, nor prohibited by it to the States, are reserved to the States respectively, or to the people.

Amendment 11
(Adopted January 8, 1798)

The Judicial power of the United States shall not be construed to extend to any suit in law or equity, commenced or prosecuted against one of the United States by Citizens of another State, or by Citizens or Subjects of any Foreign State.

Amendment 12
(Adopted September 25, 1804)

The Electors shall meet in their respective states and vote by ballot for President and Vice-President, one of whom, at least, shall not be an inhabitant of the same state with themselves; they shall name in their ballots the person voted for as President, and in distinct ballots the person voted for as Vice-President, and they shall make distinct lists of all persons voted for as President, and of all persons voted for as Vice-President, and of the number of votes for each, which lists they shall sign and certify, and transmit sealed to the seat of the government of the United States, directed to the President of the Senate;—The President of the Senate shall, in the presence of the Senate and House of Representatives, open all the certificates and the votes shall then be counted;—The person having the greatest number of votes for President, shall be the President, if such number be a majority of the whole number of Electors appointed; and if no person have such majority, then from the persons having the highest numbers not exceeding three on the list of those voted for as President, the House of Representatives shall choose immediately, by ballot, the President. But in choosing the President, the votes shall be taken by states, the representation from each state having one vote; a quorum for this purpose shall consist of a member or members from two-thirds of the states, and a majority of all the states shall be necessary to a choice. And if the House of Representatives shall not choose a President whenever the right of choice shall devolve upon them, before the fourth day of March next following, then the Vice-President shall act as President, as in the case of the death or other constitutional disability of the President.—The person having the greatest number of votes as Vice-President, shall be the Vice-President, if such number be a majority of the whole number of Electors appointed, and if no person have a majority, then from the two highest numbers on the list, the Senate shall choose the Vice-President; a quorum for the purpose shall consist of two-thirds of the whole number of Senators, and a majority of the whole number shall be necessary to a choice. But no person constitutionally ineligible to the office of President shall be eligible to that of Vice-President of the United States.

Amendment 13
(Adopted December 18, 1865)

Section 1   Neither slavery nor involuntary servitude, except as a punishment for crime whereof the party shall have been duly convicted, shall exist within the United States, or any place subject to their jurisdiction.

Section 2   Congress shall have power to enforce this article by appropriate legislation.

Amendment 14
(Adopted July 28, 1868)

Section 1   All persons born or naturalized in the United States, and subject to the jurisdiction thereof, are citizens of the United States and of the State wherein they reside. No State shall make or enforce any law which shall abridge the privileges or immunities of citizens of the United States; nor shall any State deprive any person of life, liberty, or property, without due process of law; nor deny to any person within its jurisdiction the equal protection of the laws.

Section 2   Representatives shall be apportioned among the several States according to their respective numbers, counting the whole number of persons in each State, excluding Indians not taxed. But when the right to vote at any election for the choice of electors for President and Vice President of the United States, Representatives in Congress, the Executive and Judicial officers of a State, or the members of the Legislature thereof, is denied to any of the male inhabitants of such State, being twenty-one years of age, and citizens of the United States, or in any way abridged, except for participation in rebellion, or other crime, the basis of representation therein shall be reduced in the proportion which the number of such male citizens shall bear to the whole number of male citizens twenty-one years of age in such State.

Section 3   No person shall be a Senator or Representative in Congress, or elector of President and Vice President, or hold any office, civil or military, under the United States, or under any State, who, having previously taken an oath, as a member of Congress, or as an officer of the United States, or as a member of any State legislature, or as an executive or judicial officer of any State, to support the Constitution of the United States, shall have engaged in insurrection or rebellion against the same, or given aid or comfort to the enemies thereof. But Congress may by a vote of two-thirds of each House, remove such disability.

Section 4   The validity of the public debt of the United States, authorized by law, including debts incurred for payment of pensions and bounties for services in suppressing insurrection or rebellion, shall not be questioned. But neither the United States nor any State shall assume or pay any debt or obligation incurred in aid of insurrection or rebellion against the United States, or any claim for the loss or emancipation of any slave; but all such debts, obligations and claims shall be held illegal and void.

Section 5 The Congress shall have power to enforce, by appropriate legislation, the provisions of this article.

Amendment 15
(Adopted March 30, 1870)

Section 1 The right of citizens of the United States to vote shall not be denied or abridged by the United States or by any State on account of race, color, or previous condition of servitude.

Section 2 The Congress shall have power to enforce this article by appropriate legislation.

Amendment 16
(Adopted February 25, 1913)

The Congress shall have power to lay and collect taxes on incomes, from whatever source derived, without apportionment among the several States, and without regard to any census or enumeration.

Amendment 17
(Adopted May 31, 1913)

The Senate of the United States shall be composed of two Senators from each State, elected by the people thereof, for six years; and each Senator shall have one vote. The electors in each State shall have the qualifications requisite for electors of the most numerous branch of the State legislatures.

When vacancies happen in the representation of any State in the Senate, the executive authority of such State shall issue writs of election to fill such vacancies: Provided, That the legislature of any State may empower the executive thereof to make temporary appointments until the people fill the vacancies by election as the legislature may direct.

This amendment shall not be so construed as to affect the election or term of any Senator chosen before it becomes valid as part of the Constitution.

Amendment 18
(Adopted January 29, 1919)

Section 1 After one year from the ratification of this article the manufacture, sale, or transportation of intoxicating liquors within, the importation thereof into, or the exportation thereof from the United States and all territory subject to the jurisdiction thereof for beverage purposes is hereby prohibited.

Section 2 The Congress and the several States shall have concurrent power to enforce this article by appropriate legislation.

Section 3 This article shall be inoperative unless it shall have been ratified, as an amendment to the Constitution by the legislatures of the several States, as provided in the Constitution, within seven years from the date of the submission hereof to the States by the Congress.

Amendment 19
(Adopted August 26, 1920)

The right of citizens of the United States to vote shall not be denied or abridged by the United States or by any State on account of sex.

Congress shall have power to enforce this article by appropriate legislation.

Amendment 20
(Adopted February 6, 1933)

Section 1 The terms of the President and Vice President shall end at noon on the 20th day of January, and the terms of Senators and Representatives at noon on the 3d of January, of the years in which such terms would have ended if this article had not been ratified; and the terms of their successors shall then begin.

Section 2 The Congress shall assemble at least once in every year, and such meeting shall begin at noon on the 3d day of January, unless they shall by law appoint a different day.

Section 3 If, at the time fixed for the beginning of the term of the President, the President elect shall have died, the Vice President elect shall become President. If a President shall not have been chosen before the time fixed for the beginning of his term, or if the President elect shall have failed to qualify, then the Vice President elect shall act as President until a President shall have qualified; and the Congress may by law provide for the case wherein neither a President elect nor a Vice-President elect shall have qualified, declaring who shall then act as President, or the manner in which one who is to act shall be selected, and such person shall act accordingly until a President or Vice President shall have qualified.

Section 4 The Congress may by law provide for the case of the death of any of the persons from whom the House of Representatives may choose a President whenever the right of choice shall have developed upon them, and for the case of the death of any of the persons from whom the Senate may choose a Vice President whenever the right of choice shall have devolved upon them.

Section 5 Sections 1 and 2 shall take effect on the 15th day of October following the ratification of this article.

Section 6 This article shall be inoperative unless it shall have been ratified as an amendment to the Constitution by the legislatures of three-fourths of the several States within seven years from the date of its submission.

Amendment 21
(Adopted December 5, 1933)

Section 1 The eighteenth article of amendment to the Constitution of the United States is hereby repealed.

Section 2 The transportation or importation into any State, Territory, or possession of the United States for delivery or use therein of intoxicating liquors, in violation of the laws thereof, is hereby prohibited.

Section 3 This article shall be inoperative unless it shall have been ratified as an amendment to the Constitution by conventions in the several States, as provided in the Constitution, within seven years from the date of submission hereof to the United States by the Congress.

Amendment 22
(Adopted February 26, 1951)

Section 1 No person shall be elected to the office of President more than twice, and no person who has held the office of President, or acted as President, for more than two years of a term to which some other person was elected President shall be elected to the office of the President more than once. But this article shall not apply to any person holding the office of President when this article was proposed by Congress, and shall not prevent any person who may be holding the office of President, or acting as President, during the term within which this article becomes operative from holding the

office of President or acting as President during the remainder of such term.

Section 2 This article shall be inoperative unless it shall have been ratified as an amendment to the Constitution by the legislatures of three fourths of the several states within seven years from the date of its submission to the states by the Congress.

Amendment 23
(Adopted April 3, 1961)

Section 1 The District constituting the seat of Government of the United States shall appoint in such manner as the Congress may direct.

A number of electors of President and Vice President equal to the whole number of Senators and Representatives in Congress to which the District would be entitled if it were a State, but in no event more than the least populous State; they shall be in addition to those appointed by the States, but they shall be considered, for the purposes of the election of President and Vice President, to be electors appointed by a State; and they shall meet in the District and perform such duties as provided by the twelfth article of amendment.

Section 2 The Congress shall have power to enforce this article by appropriate legislation.

Amendment 24
(Adopted January 23, 1964)

Section 1 The right of citizens of the United States to vote in any primary or other election for President or Vice President, for electors for President or Vice President, or for Senator or Representative in Congress, shall not be denied or abridged by the United States or any state by reason of failure to pay any poll tax or other tax.

Section 2 The Congress shall have the power to enforce this article by appropriate legislation.

Amendment 25
(Adopted February 10, 1967)

Section 1 In case of the removal of the President from office or of his death or resignation, the Vice President shall become President.

Section 2 Whenever there is a vacancy in the office of the Vice President, the President shall nominate a Vice President who shall take office upon confirmation by a majority vote of both Houses of Congress.

Section 3 Whenever the President transmits to the President pro tempore of the Senate and the Speaker of the House of Representatives his written declaration that he is unable to discharge the powers and duties of his office, and until he transmits to them a written declaration to the contrary, such powers and duties shall be discharged by the Vice President as Acting President.

Section 4 Whenever the Vice President and a majority of either the principal officers of the executive departments or of such other body as Congress may by law provide, transmit to the President pro tempore of the Senate and the Speaker of the House of Representatives their written declaration that the President is unable to discharge the powers and duties of his office, the Vice President shall immediately assume the powers and duties of the office as Acting President.

Thereafter, when the President transmits to the President pro tempore of the Senate and the Speaker of the House of Representatives his written declaration that no inability exists, he shall resume the powers and duties of his office unless the Vice President and a majority of either the principal officers of the executive department or of such other body as Congress may by law provide, transmit within four days to the President pro tempore of the Senate and the Speaker of the House of Representatives their written declaration that the President is unable to discharge the powers and duties of his office. Thereupon Congress shall decide the issue, assembling within forty-eight hours for that purpose if not in session. If the Congress, within twenty-one days after receipt of the latter written declaration, or, if Congress is not in session, within twenty-one days after Congress is required to assemble, determines by two-thirds vote of both Houses that the President is unable to discharge the powers and duties of his office, the Vice President shall continue to discharge the same as Acting President; otherwise, the President shall resume the powers and duties of his office.

Amendment 26
(Adopted July 5, 1971)

Section 1 The right of citizens of the United States, who are eighteen years of age or older, to vote shall not be denied or abridged by the United States or by any State on account of age.

Section 2 The Congress shall have power to enforce this article by appropriate legislation.

Appendix B

UNIFORM COMMERCIAL CODE

ARTICLE 1. GENERAL PROVISIONS

Part 1. Short Title, Construction, Application and Subject Matter of the Act

§ 1-101. Short Title. This Act shall be known and may be cited as Uniform Commercial Code.

§ 1-102. Purposes; Rules of Construction; Variation by Agreement.

(1) This Act shall be liberally construed and applied to promote its underlying purposes and policies.

(2) Underlying purposes and policies of this Act are

    (a)   to simplify, clarify and modernize the law governing commercial transactions;

    (b)   to permit the continued expansion of commercial practices through custom, usage and agreement of the parties;

    (c)   to make uniform the law among the various jurisdictions.

(3) The effect of provisions of this Act may be varied by agreement, except as otherwise provided in this Act and except that the obligations of good faith, diligence, reasonableness and care prescribed by this Act may not be disclaimed by agreement but the parties may by agreement determine the standards by which the performance of such obligations is to be measured if such standards are not manifestly unreasonable.

(4) The presence in certain provisions of this Act of the words "unless otherwise agreed" or words of similar import does not imply that the effect of other provisions may not be varied by agreement under subsection (3).

(5) In this Act unless the context otherwise requires

    (a)   words in the singular number include the plural, and in the plural include the singular;

    (b)   words of the masculine gender include the feminine and the neuter, and when the sense so indicates words of the neuter gender may refer to any gender.

§ 1-103. Supplementary General Principles of Law Applicable. Unless displaced by the particular provisions of this Act, the principles of law and equity, including the law merchant and the law relative to capacity to contract, principal and agent, estoppel, fraud, misrepresentation, duress, coercion, mistake, bankruptcy, or other validating or invalidating cause shall supplement its provisions.

§ 1-104. Construction Against Implicit Repeal. This Act being a general act intended as a unified coverage of its subject matter, no part of it shall be deemed to be impliedly repealed by subsequent legislation if such construction can reasonably be avoided.

§ 1-105. Territorial Application of the Act; Parties' Power to Choose Applicable Law.

(1) Except as provided hereafter in this section, when a transaction bears a reasonable relation to this state and also to another state or nation the parties may agree that the law either of this state or of such other state or nation shall govern their rights and duties. Failing such agreement this Act applies to transactions bearing an appropriate relation to this state.

(2) Where one of the following provisions of this Act specifies the applicable law, that provision governs and a contrary agreement is effective only to the extent permitted by the law (including the conflict of laws rules) so specified:

Rights of creditors against sold goods. Section 2-402.

Applicability of the Article on Bank Deposits and Collections. Section 4-102.

Bulk transfers subject to the Article on Bulk Transfers. Section 6-102.

Applicability of the Article on Investment Securities. Section 8-106.

Perfection provisions of the Article on Secured Transactions. Section 9-103.

§ 1-106. Remedies to Be Liberally Administered.

(1) The remedies provided by this Act shall be liberally administered to the end that the aggrieved party may be put in as good a position as if the other party had fully performed but neither consequential or special nor penal damages may be had except as specifically provided in this Act or by other rule of law.

(2) Any right or obligation declared by this Act is enforceable by action unless the provision declaring its specifies a different and limited effect.

§ 1-107. Waiver or Renunciation of Claim or Right After Breach.
Any claim or right arising out of an alleged breach can be discharged in whole or in part without consideration by a written waiver or renunciation signed and delivered by the aggrieved party.

§ 1-108. Severability.
If any provision or clause of this Act or application thereof to any person or circumstances is held invalid, such invalidity shall not affect other provisions or applications of the Act which can be given effect without the invalid provision or application, and to this end the provisions of this Act are declared to be severable.

§ 1-109. Section Captions.
Section captions are parts of this Act.

Part 2. General Definitions and Principles of Interpretation

§ 1-201. General Definitions.
Subject to additional definitions contained in the subsequent Articles of this Act which are applicable to specific Articles or Parts thereof, and unless the context otherwise requires, in this Act:

(1) "Action" in the sense of a judicial proceeding includes recoupment, counterclaim, set-off, suit in equity and any other proceedings in which rights are determined.

(2) "Aggrieved party" means a party entitled to resort to a remedy.

(3) "Agreement" means the bargain of the parties in fact as found in their language or by implication from other circumstances including course of dealing or usage of trade or course of performance as provided in this Act (Sections 1-205 and 2-208). Whether an agreement has legal consequences is determined by the provisions of this Act, if applicable; otherwise by the law of contracts (Section 1-103). (Compare "Contract.")

(4) "Bank" means any person engaged in the business of banking.

(5) "Bearer" means the person in possession of an instrument, document of title, or certificated security payable to bearer or indorsed in blank.

(6) "Bill of lading" means a document evidencing the receipt of goods for shipment issued by a person engaged in the business of transporting or forwarding goods, and includes an airbill. "Airbill" means a document serving for air transportation as a bill of lading does for marine or rail transportation, and includes an air consignment note or air waybill.

(7) "Branch" includes a separately incorporated foreign branch of a bank.

(8) "Burden of establishing" a fact means the burden of persuading the triers of fact that the existence of the fact is more probable than its non-existence.

(9) "Buyer in ordinary course of business" means a person who in good faith and without knowledge that the sale to him is in violation of the ownership rights or security interest of a third party in the goods buys in ordinary course from a person in the business of selling goods of that kind but does not include a pawnbroker. All persons who sell minerals or the like (including oil and gas) at wellhead or minehead shall be deemed to be persons in the business of selling goods of that kind. "Buying" may be for cash or by exchange of other property or on secured or unsecured credit and includes receiving goods or documents of title under a pre-existing contract for sale but does not include a transfer in bulk or as security for or in total or partial satisfaction of a money debt.

(10) "Conspicuous": A term or clause is conspicuous when it is so written that a reasonable person against whom it is to operate ought to have noticed it. A printed heading in capitals (as: NON-NEGOTIABLE BILL OF LADING is conspicuous. Language in the body of a form is "conspicuous" if it is in larger or other contrasting type or color. But in a telegram any stated term is "conspicuous." Whether

a term or clause is "conspicuous" or not is for decision by the court.

(11) "Contract" means the total legal obligation which results from the parties' agreement as affected by this Act and any other applicable rules of law. (Compare "Agreement.")

(12) "Creditor" includes a general creditor, a secured creditor, a lien creditor and any representative of creditors, including an assignee for the benefit of creditors, a trustee in bankruptcy, a receiver in equity and an executor or administrator of an insolvent debtor's or assignor's estate.

(13) "Defendant" includes a person in the position of defendant in a cross-action or counterclaim.

(14) "Delivery" with respect to instruments, documents of title, chattel paper, or certificated securities means voluntary transfer of possession.

(15) "Document of title" includes bill of lading, dock warrant, dock receipt, warehouse receipt or order for the delivery of goods, and also any other document which in the regular course of business or financing is treated as adequately evidencing that the person in possession of it is entitled to receive, hold and dispose of the document and the goods it covers. To be a document of title a document must purport to be issued by or addressed to a bailee and purport to cover goods in the bailee's possession which are either identified or are fungible portions of an identified mass.

(16) "Fault" means wrongful act, omission or breach.

(17) "Fungible" with respect to goods or securities means goods or securities of which any unit is, by nature or usage of trade, the equivalent of any other like unit. Goods which are not fungible shall be deemed fungible for the purposes of this Act to the extent that under a particular agreement or document unlike units are treated as equivalents.

(18) "Genuine" means free of forgery or counterfeiting.

(19) "Good faith" means honesty in fact in the conduct or transaction concerned.

(20) "Holder" means a person who is in possession of a document of title or an instrument or a certificated investment security drawn, issued, or indorsed to him or his order or to bearer or in blank.

(21) To "honor" is to pay or to accept and pay, or where a credit so engages to purchase or discount a draft complying with the terms of the credit.

(22) "Insolvency proceedings" includes any assignment for the benefit of creditors or other proceedings intended to liquidate or rehabilitate the estate of the person involved.

(23) A person is "insolvent" who either has ceased to pay his debts in the ordinary course of business or cannot pay his debts as they become due or is insolvent within the meaning of the federal bankruptcy law.

(24) "Money" means a medium of exchange authorized or adopted by a domestic or foreign government as a part of its currency.

(25) A person has "notice" of a fact when

   (a)   he has actual knowledge of it; or

   (b)   he has received a notice or notification of it; or

   (c)   from all the facts and circumstances known to him at the time in question he has reason to know that it exists.

A person "knows" or has "knowledge" of a fact when he has actual knowledge of it. "Discover" or "learn" or a word or phrase of similar import refers to knowledge rather than to reason to know. The time and circumstances under which a notice or notification may cease to be effective are not determined by this Act.

(26) A person "notifies" or "gives" a notice or notification to another by taking such steps as may be reasonably required to inform the other in ordinary course whether or not such other actually comes to know of it. A person "receives" a notice or notification when

   (a)   it comes to his attention; or

   (b)   it is duly delivered at the place of business through which the contract was made or at any other place held out by him as the place for receipt of such communications.

(27) Notice, knowledge or a notice or notification received by an organization is effective for a particular transaction from the time when it is brought to the attention of the individual conducting that transaction, and in any event from the time when it would have been brought to his attention if the organization had exercised due diligence. An organization exercises due diligence if it maintains reasonable routines for communicating significant information to the person conducting the transaction and there is reasonable compliance with the routines. Due diligence does not require an individual acting for the organization to communicate information unless such communication is part of his regular duties or unless he has reason to know

of the transaction and that the transaction would be materially affected by the information.

(28) "Organization" includes a corporation, government or governmental subdivision or agency, business trust, estate, trust, partnership or association, two or more persons having a joint or common interest, or any other legal or commercial entity.

(29) "Party," as distinct from "third party," means a person who has engaged in a transaction or made an agreement within this Act.

(30) "Person" includes an individual or an organization (See Section 1-102).

(31) "Presumption" or "presumed" means that the trier of fact must find the existence of the fact presumed unless and until evidence is introduced which would support a finding of its non-existence.

(32) "Purchase" includes taking by sale, discount, negotiation, mortgage, pledge, lien, issue or re-issue, gift or any other voluntary transaction creating an interest in property.

(33) "Purchaser" means a person who takes by purchase.

(34) "Remedy" means any remedial right to which an aggrieved party is entitled with or without resort to a tribunal.

(35) "Representative" includes an agent, an officer of a corporation or association, and a trustee, executor or administrator of an estate, or any other person empowered to act for another.

(36) "Rights" includes remedies.

(37) "Security interest" means an interest in personal property or fixtures which secures payment or performance of an obligation. The retention or reservation of title by a seller of goods notwithstanding shipment or delivery to the buyer (Section 2-401) is limited in effect to a reservation of a "security interest." The term also includes any interest of a buyer of accounts or chattel paper which is subject to Article 9. The special property interest of a buyer of goods on identification of such goods to a contract for sale under Section 2-401 is not a "security interest," but a buyer may also acquire a "security interest" by complying with Article 9. Unless a lease or consignment is intended as security, reservation of title thereunder is not a "security interest" but a consignment is in any event subject to the provisions on consignment sales (Section 2-326). Whether a lease is intended as security is to be determined by the facts of each case; however, (a) the inclusion of an option to purchase does not of itself make the lease one intended for security,

and (b) an agreement that upon compliance with the terms of the lease the lessee shall become or has the option to become the owner of the property for no additional consideration or for a nominal consideration does make the lease one intended for security.

(38) "Send" in connection with any writing or notice means to deposit in the mail or deliver for transmission by any other usual means of communication with postage or cost of transmission provided for and properly addressed and in the case of an instrument to an address specified thereon or otherwise agreed, or if there be none to any address reasonable under the circumstances. The receipt of any writing or notice within the time at which it would have arrived if properly sent has the effect of a proper sending.

(39) "Signed" includes any symbol executed or adopted by a party with present intention to authenticate a writing.

(40) "Surety" includes guarantor.

(41) "Telegram" includes a message transmitted by radio, teletype, cable, any mechanical method of transmission, or the like.

(42) "Term" means that portion of an agreement which relates to a particular matter.

(43) "Unauthorized" signature or indorsement means one made without actual, implied or apparent authority and includes a forgery.

(44) "Value." Except as otherwise provided with respect to negotiable instruments and bank collections (Section 3-303, 4-208 and 4-209) a person gives "value" for rights if he acquires them

   (a)   in return for a binding commitment to extend credit or for the extension of immediately available credit whether or not drawn upon and whether or not a chargeback is provided for in the event of difficulties in collection; or

   (b)   as security for or in total or partial satisfaction of a pre-existing claim; or

   (c)   by accepting delivery pursuant to a pre-existing contract for purchase; or

   (d)   generally, in return for any consideration sufficient to support a simple contract.

(45) "Warehouse receipt" means a receipt issued by a person engaged in the business of storing goods for hire.

(46) "Written" or "writing" includes printing, typewriting or any other intentional reduction to tangible form. Amended in 1962, 1972 and 1977.

§ 1-202. Prima Facie Evidence by Third Party Documents. A document in due form purporting to be a bill of lading, policy or certificate of insurance, official weigher's or inspector's certificate, consular invoice, or any other document authorized or required by the contract to be issued by a third party shall be prima facie evidence of its own authenticity and genuineness and of the facts stated in the document by the third party.

§ 1-203. Obligation of Good Faith. Every contract or duty within this Act imposes an obligation of good faith in its performance or enforcement.

§ 1-204. Time; Reasonable Time; "Seasonably."

(1) Whenever this Act requires any action to be taken within a reasonable time, any time which is not manifestly unreasonable may be fixed by agreement.

(2) What is a reasonable time for taking any action depends on the nature, purpose and circumstances of such action.

(3) An action is taken "seasonably" when it is taken at or within the time agreed or if no time is agreed at or within a reasonable time.

§ 1-205. Course of Dealing and Usage of Trade.

(1) A course of dealing is a sequence of previous conduct between the parties to a particular transaction which is fairly to be regarded as establishing a common basis of understanding for interpreting their expressions and other conduct.

(2) A usage of trade is any practice or method of dealing having such regularity of observance in a place, vocation or trade as to justify an expectation that it will be observed with respect to the transaction in question. The existence and scope of such a usage are to be proved as facts. If it is established that such a usage is embodied in a written trade code or similar writing the interpretation of the writing is for the court.

(3) A course of dealing between parties and any usage of trade in the vocation or trade in which they are engaged or of which they are or should be aware give particular meaning to and supplement or qualify terms of an agreement.

(4) The express terms of an agreement and an applicable course of dealing or usage of trade shall be construed wherever reasonable as consistent with each other; but when such construction is unreasonable express terms control both course of dealing and usage of trade and course of dealing controls usage of trade.

(5) An applicable usage of trade in the place where any part of performance is to occur shall be used in interpreting the agreement as to that part of the performance.

(6) Evidence of a relevant usage of trade offered by one party is not admissible unless and until he has given the other party such notice as the court finds sufficient to prevent unfair surprise to the latter.

§ 1-206. Statute of Frauds for Kinds of Personal Property Not Otherwise Covered.

(1) Except in the cases described in subsection (2) of this section a contract for the sale of personal property is not enforceable by way of action or defense beyond five thousand dollars in amount or value of remedy unless there is some writing which indicates that a contract for sale has been made between the parties at a defined or stated price, reasonably identifies the subject matter, and is signed by the party against whom enforcement is sought or by his authorized agent.

(2) Subsection (1) of this section does not apply to contracts for the sale of goods (Section 2-201) nor of securities (Section 8-319) nor to security agreements (Section 9-203).

§ 1-207. Performance or Acceptance Under Reservation of Rights. A party who with explicit reservation of rights performs or promises performance or assents to performance in a manner demanded or offered by the other party does not thereby prejudice the rights reserved. Such words as "without prejudice," "under protest" or the like are sufficient.

§ 1-208. Option to Accelerate at Will. A term providing that one party or his successor in interest may accelerate payment or performance or require collateral or additional collateral "at will" or "when he deems himself insecure" or in words of similar import shall be construed to mean that he shall have power to do so only if he in good faith believes that the prospect of payment or performance is impaired. The burden of establishing lack of good faith is on the party against whom the power has been exercised.

§ 1-209. Subordinated Obligations. An obligation may be issued as subordinated to payment of another obligation of the person obligated, or a creditor may subordinate his right to payment of an obligation by agreement with either the person obligated or another creditor of the person obligated. Such a subordination does not create a security interest as against either the common debtor or a subordinated creditor. This section shall be construed as declaring the law as it existed prior to the enactment of this section and not as modifying it. Added 1966.

Note: This new section is proposed as an optional provision to make it clear that a subordination agreement does not create a security interest unless so intended.

ARTICLE 2. SALES

Part 1. Short Title, General Construction and Subject Matter

§ 2-101. Short Title. This Article shall be known and may be cited as Uniform Commercial Code—Sales.

§ 2-102. Scope; Certain Security and Other Transactions Excluded From This Article. Unless the context otherwise requires, this Article applies to transactions in goods; it does not apply to any transaction which although in the form of an unconditional contract to sell or present sale is intended to operate only as a security transaction nor does this Article impair or repeal any statute regulating sales to consumers, farmers or other specified classes of buyers.

§ 2-103. Definitions and Index of Definitions.

(1) In this Article unless the context otherwise requires

    (a) "Buyer" means a person who buys or contracts to buy goods.

    (b) "Good faith" in the case of a merchant means honesty in fact and the observance of reasonable commercial standards of fair dealing in the trade.

    (c) "Receipt" of goods means taking physical possession of them.

    (d) "Seller" means a person who sells or contracts to sell goods.

(2) Other definitions applying to this Article or to specified Parts thereof, and the sections in which they appear are:

"Acceptance." Section 2-606.

"Banker's credit." Section 2-325.

"Between merchants." Section 2-104.

"Cancellation." Section 2-106(4).

"Commercial unit." Section 2-105.

"Confirmed credit." Section 2-325.

"Conforming to contract." Section 2-106.

"Contract for sale." Section 2-106.

"Cover." Section 2-712.

"Entrusting." Section 2-403.

"Financing agency." Section 2-104.

"Future goods." Section 2-105.

"Goods." Section 2-105.

"Identification." Section 2-501.

"Installment contract." Section 2-612.

"Letter of Credit." Section 2-325.

"Lot." Section 2-105.

"Merchant." Section 2-104.

"Overseas." Section 2-323.

"Person in position of seller." Section 2-707.

"Present sale." Section 2-106.

"Sale." Section 2-106.

"Sale on approval." Section 2-326.

"Sale or return." Section 2-326.

"Termination." Section 2-106.

(3) The following definitions in other Articles apply to this Article:

"Check." Section 3-104.

"Consignee." Section 7-102.

"Consignor." Section 7-102.

"Consumer goods." Section 9-109.

"Dishonor." Section 3-507.

"Draft." Section 3-104.

(4) In addition Article 1 contains general definitions and principles of construction and interpretation applicable throughout this Article.

§ 2-104. Definitions: "Merchant"; "Between Merchants"; "Financing Agency."

(1) "Merchant" means a person who deals in goods of the kind or otherwise by his occupation holds himself out as having knowledge or skill peculiar to the practices or goods involved in the transaction or to whom such knowledge or skill may be attributed by his employment of an agent or broker or other intermediary who by his occupation holds himself out as having such knowledge or skill.

(2) "Financing agency" means a bank, finance company or other person who in the ordinary course of business makes advances against goods or documents of title or who by arrangement with either the seller or the buyer intervenes in ordinary course

to make or collect payment due or claimed under the contract for sale, as by purchasing or paying the seller's draft or making advances against it or by merely taking it for collection whether or not documents of title accompany the draft. "Financing agency" includes also a bank or other person who similarly intervenes between persons who are in the position of seller and buyer in respect to the goods (Section 2-707).

(3) "Between merchants" means in any transaction with respect to which both parties are chargeable with the knowledge or skill of merchants.

§ 2-105. Definitions: Transferability; "Goods"; "Future" Goods; "Lot"; "Commercial Unit."

(1) "Goods" means all things (including specially manufactured goods) which are movable at the time of identification to the contract for sale other than the money in which the price is to be paid, investment securities (Article 8) and things in action. "Goods" also includes the unborn young of animals and growing crops and other identified things attached to realty as described in the section on goods to be severed from realty (Section 2-107).

(2) Goods must be both existing and identified before any interest in them can pass. Goods which are not both existing and identified are "future" goods. A purported present sale of future goods or of any interest therein operates as a contract to sell.

(3) There may be a sale of a part interest in existing identified goods.

(4) An undivided share in an identified bulk of fungible goods is sufficiently identified to be sold although the quantity of the bulk is not determined. Any agreed proportion of such a bulk or any quantity thereof agreed upon by number, weight or other measure may to the extent of the seller's interest in the bulk be sold to the buyer who then becomes an owner in common.

(5) "Lot" means a parcel or a single article which is the subject matter of a separate sale or delivery, whether or not it is sufficient to perform the contract.

(6) "Commercial unit" means such a unit of goods as by commercial usage is a single whole for purposes of sale and division of which materially impairs its character or value on the market or in use. A commercial unit may be a single article (as a machine) or a set of articles (as a suite of furniture or an assortment of sizes) or a quantity (as a bale,

gross, or carload) or any other unit treated in use or in the relevant market as a single whole.

§ 2-106. Definitions: "Contract"; "Agreement"; "Contract for Sale"; "Sale"; "Present Sale"; "Conforming" to Contract; "Termination"; "Cancellation."

(1) In this Article unless the context otherwise requires "contract" and "agreement" are limited to those relating to the present or future sale of goods. "Contract for sale" includes both a present sale of goods and a contract to sell goods at a future time. A "sale" consists in the passing of title from the seller to the buyer for a price (Section 2-401). A "present sale" means a sale which is accomplished by the making of the contract.

(2) Goods or conduct including any part of a performance are "conforming" or conform to the contract when they are in accordance with the obligations under the contract.

(3) "Termination" occurs when either party pursuant to a power created by agreement or law puts an end to the contract otherwise than for its breach. On "termination" all obligations which are still executory on both sides are discharged but any right based on prior breach or performance survives.

(4) "Cancellation" occurs when either party puts an end to the contract for breach by the other and its effect is the same as that of "termination" except that the cancelling party also retains any remedy for breach of the whole contract or any unperformed balance.

§ 2-107. Goods to Be Severed From Realty: Recording.

(1) A contract for the sale of minerals or the like (including oil and gas) or a structure or its materials to be removed from realty is a contract for the sale of goods within this Article if they are to be severed by the seller but until severance a purported present sale thereof which is not effective as a transfer of an interest in land is effective only as a contract to sell.

(2) A contract for the sale apart from the land of growing crops or other things attached to realty and capable of severance without material harm thereto but not described in subsection (1) or of timber to be cut is a contract for the sale of goods within this Article whether the subject matter is to be severed by the buyer or by the seller even though it forms part of the realty at the time of contracting, and the

parties can by identification effect a present sale before severance.

(3) The provisions of this section are subject to any third party rights provided by the law relating to realty records, and the contract for sale may be executed and recorded as a document transferring an interest in land and shall then constitute notice to third parties of the buyer's rights under the contract for sale.

Part 2. Form, Formation and Readjustment of Contract

§ 2-201. Formal Requirements; Statute of Frauds.

(1) Except as otherwise provided in this section a contract for the sale of goods for the price of $500 or more is not enforceable by way of action or defense unless there is some writing sufficient to indicate that a contract for sale has been made between the parties and signed by the party against whom enforcement is sought or by his authorized agent or broker. A writing is not insufficient because it omits or incorrectly states a term agreed upon but the contract is not enforceable under this paragraph beyond the quantity of goods shown in such writing.

(2) Between merchants if within a reasonable time a writing in confirmation of the contract and sufficient against the sender is received and the party receiving it has reason to know its contents, it satisfies the requirements of subsection (1) against such party unless written notice of objection to its contents is given within 10 days after it is received.

(3) A contract which does not satisfy the requirements of subsection (1) but which is valid in other respects is enforceable

    (a)   if the goods are to be specially manufactured for the buyer and are not suitable for sale to others in the ordinary course of the seller's business and the seller, before notice of repudiation is received and under circumstances which reasonably indicate that the goods are for the buyer, has made either a substantial beginning of their manufacture or commitments for their procurement; or

    (b)   if the party against whom enforcement is sought admits in his pleading, testimony or otherwise in court that a contract for sale was made, but the contract is not enforceable under this provision beyond the quantity of goods admitted; or

    (c)   with respect to goods for which payment has been made and accepted or which have been received and accepted (Section 2-606).

§ 2-202. Final Written Expression: Parol or Extrinsic Evidence.

Terms with respect to which the confirmatory memoranda of the parties agree or which are otherwise set forth in a writing intended by the parties as a final expression of their agreement with respect to such terms as are included therein may not be contradicted by evidence of any prior agreement or of a contemporaneous oral agreement but may be explained or supplemented

    (a)   by course of dealing or usage of trade (Section 1-205) or by course of performance (Section 2-208); and

    (b)   by evidence of consistent additional terms unless the court finds the writing to have been intended also as a complete and exclusive statement of the terms of the agreement.

§ 2-203. Seals Inoperative.

The affixing of a seal to a writing evidencing a contract for sale or an offer to buy or sell goods does not constitute the writing a sealed instrument and the law with respect to sealed instruments does not apply to such a contract or offer.

§ 2-204. Formation in General.

(1) A contract for sale of goods may be made in any manner sufficient to show agreement, including conduct by both parties which recognizes the existence of such a contract.

(2) An agreement sufficient to constitute a contract for sale may be found even though the moment of its making is undetermined.

(3) Even though one or more terms are left open a contract for sale does not fail for indefiniteness if the parties have intended to make a contract and there is a reasonably certain basis for giving an appropriate remedy.

§ 2-205. Firm Offers.

An offer by a merchant to buy or sell goods in a signed writing which by its terms gives assurance that it will be held open is not revocable, for lack of consideration, during the time stated or if no time is stated for a reasonable time, but in no event may such period of irrevocability exceed three months; but any such term of assurance on a form supplied by the offeree must be separately signed by the offeror.

§ 2-206. Offer and Acceptance in Formation of Contract.

(1) Unless otherwise unambiguously indicated by the language or circumstances

(a) an offer to make a contract shall be construed as inviting acceptance in any manner and by any medium reasonable in the circumstances;

(b) an order or other offer to buy goods for prompt or current shipment shall be construed as inviting acceptance either by a prompt promise to ship or by the prompt or current shipment of conforming or non-conforming goods, but such a shipment of non-conforming goods does not constitute an acceptance if the seller seasonably notifies the buyer that the shipment is offered only as an accommodation to the buyer.

(2) Where the beginning of a requested performance is a reasonable mode of acceptance an offeror who is not notified of acceptance within a reasonable time may treat the offer as having lapsed before acceptance.

§ 2-207. Additional Terms in Acceptance or Confirmation.

(1) A definite and seasonable expression of acceptance or a written confirmation which is sent within a reasonable time operates as an acceptance even though it states terms additional to or different from those offered or agreed upon, unless acceptance is expressly made conditional on assent to the additional or different terms.

(2) The additional terms are to be construed as proposals for addition to the contract. Between merchants such terms become part of the contract unless:

(a) the offer expressly limits acceptance to the terms of the offer;

(b) they materially alter it; or

(c) notification of objection to them has already been given or is given within a reasonable time after notice of them is received.

(3) Conduct by both parties which recognizes the existence of a contract is sufficient to establish a contract for sale although the writings of the parties do not otherwise establish a contract. In such case the terms of the particular contract consist of those terms on which the writings of the parties agree, together with any supplementary terms incorporated under any other provisions of this Act.

§ 2-208. Course of Performance or Practical Construction.

(1) Where the contract for sale involves repeated occasions for performance by either party with knowledge of the nature of the performance and opportunity for objection to it by the other, any course of performance accepted or acquiesced in without objection shall be relevant to determine the meaning of the agreement.

(2) The express terms of the agreement and any such course of performance, as well as any course of dealing and usage of trade, shall be construed whenever reasonable as consistent with each other; but when such construction is unreasonable, express terms shall control course of performance and course of performance shall control both course of dealing and usage of trade (Section 1-205).

(3) Subject to the provisions of the next section on modification and waiver, such course of performance shall be relevant to show a waiver or modification of any term inconsistent with such course of performance.

§ 2-209. Modification, Rescission and Waiver.

(1) An agreement modifying a contract within this Article needs no consideration to be binding.

(2) A signed agreement which excludes modification or rescission except by a signed writing cannot be otherwise modified or rescinded, but except as between merchants such a requirement on a form supplied by the merchant must be separately signed by the other party.

(3) The requirements of the statute of frauds section of this Article (Section 2-201) must be satisfied if the contract as modified is within its provisions.

(4) Although an attempt at modification or rescission does not satisfy the requirements of subsection (2) or (3) it can operate as a waiver.

(5) A party who has made a waiver affecting an executory portion of the contract may retract the waiver by reasonable notification received by the other party that strict performance will be required of any term waived, unless the retraction would be unjust in view of a material change of position in reliance on the waiver.

§ 2-210. Delegation of Performance; Assignment of Rights.

(1) A party may perform his duty through a delegate unless otherwise agreed or unless the other party has a substantial interest in having his original promisor perform or control the acts required by the contract. No delegation of performance relieves the party delegating of any duty to perform or any liability for breach.

(2) Unless otherwise agreed all rights of either seller or buyer can be assigned except where the assignment would materially change the duty of the other party, or increase materially the burden or risk imposed on him by his contract, or impair materially his chance of obtaining return performance. A right to damages for breach of the whole contract or a right arising out of the assignor's due performance of his entire obligation can be assigned despite agreement otherwise.

(3) Unless the circumstances indicate the contrary a prohibition of assignment of "the contract" is to be construed as barring only the delegation to the assignee of the assignor's performance.

(4) An assignment of "the contract" or of "all my rights under the contract" or an assignment in similar general terms is an assignment of rights and unless the language or the circumstances (as in an assignment for security) indicate the contrary, it is a delegation of performance of the duties of the assignor and its acceptance by the assignee constitutes a promise by him to perform those duties. This promise is enforceable by either the assignor or the other party to the original contract.

(5) The other party may treat any assignment which delegates performance as creating reasonable grounds for insecurity and may without prejudice to his rights against the assignor demand assurances from the assignee (Section 2-609).

Part 3. General Obligation and Construction of Contract

§ 2-301. General Obligations of Parties. The obligation of the seller is to transfer and deliver and that of the buyer is to accept and pay in accordance with the contract.

§ 2-302. Unconscionable Contract or Clause.

(1) If the court as a matter of law finds the contract or any clause of the contract to have been unconscionable at the time it was made the court may refuse to enforce the contract, or it may enforce the remainder of the contract without the unconscionable clause, or it may so limit the application of any unconscionable clause as to avoid any unconscionable result.

(2) When it is claimed or appears to the court that the contract or any clause thereof may be unconscionable the parties shall be afforded a reasonable opportunity to present evidence as to its commercial setting, purpose and effect to aid the court in making the determination.

§ 2-303. Allocation or Division of Risks. Where this Article allocates a risk or a burden as between the parties "unless otherwise agreed," the agreement may not only shift the allocation but may also divide the risk or burden.

§ 2-304. Price Payable in Money, Goods, Realty, or Otherwise.

(1) The price can be made payable in money or otherwise. If it is payable in whole or in part in goods each party is a seller of the goods which he is to transfer.

(2) Even though all or part of the price is payable in an interest in realty the transfer of the goods and the seller's obligations with reference to them are subject to this Article, but not the transfer of the interest in realty or the transferor's obligations in connection therewith.

§ 2-305. Open Price Term.

(1) The parties if they so intend can conclude a contract for sale even though the price is not settled. In such a case the price is a reasonable price at the time for delivery if

    (a)   nothing is said as to price; or

    (b)   the price is left to be agreed by the parties and they fail to agree; or

    (c)   the price is to be fixed in terms of some agreed market or other standard as set or recorded by a third person or agency and it is not so set or recorded.

(2) A price to be fixed by the seller or by the buyer means a price for him to fix in good faith.

(3) When a price left to be fixed otherwise than by agreement of the parties fails to be fixed through fault of one party the other may at his option treat the contract as cancelled or himself fix a reasonable price.

(4) Where, however, the parties intend not to be bound unless the price be fixed or agreed and it is not fixed or agreed there is no contract. In

such a case the buyer must return any goods already received or if unable so to do must pay their reasonable value at the time of delivery and the seller must return any portion of the price paid on account.

§ 2-306. Output, Requirements and Exclusive Dealings.

(1) A term which measures the quantity by the output of the seller or the requirements of the buyer means such actual output or requirements as may occur in good faith, except that no quantity unreasonably disproportionate to any stated estimate or in the absence of a stated estimate to any normal or otherwise comparable prior output or requirements may be tendered or demanded.

(2) A lawful agreement by either the seller or the buyer for exclusive dealing in the kind of goods concerned imposes unless otherwise agreed an obligation by the seller to use best efforts to supply the goods and by the buyer to use best efforts to promote their sale.

§ 2-307. Delivery in Single Lot or Several Lots.

Unless otherwise agreed all goods called for by a contract for sale must be tendered in a single delivery and payment is due only on such tender but where the circumstances give either party the right to make or demand delivery in lots the price if it can be apportioned may be demanded for each lot.

§ 2-308. Absence of Specified Place for Delivery.

Unless otherwise agreed
   (a) the place for delivery of goods is the seller's place of business or if he has none his residence; but
   (b) in a contract for sale of identified goods which to the knowledge of the parties at the time of contracting are in some other place, that place is the place for their delivery; and
   (c) documents of title may be delivered through customary banking channels.

§ 2-309. Absence of Specific Time Provisions; Notice of Termination.

(1) The time for shipment or delivery or any other action under a contract if not provided in this Article or agreed upon shall be a reasonable time.

(2) Where the contract provides for successive performances but is indefinite in duration it is valid for a reasonable time but unless otherwise agreed may be terminated at any time by either party.

(3) Termination of a contract by one party except on the happening of an agreed event requires that reasonable notification be received by the other party and an agreement dispensing with notification is invalid if its operation would be unconscionable.

§ 2-310. Open Time for Payment or Running of Credit; Authority to Ship Under Reservation.

Unless otherwise agreed
   (a) payment is due at the time and place at which the buyer is to receive the goods even though the place of shipment is the place of delivery; and
   (b) if the seller is authorized to send the goods he may ship them under reservation, and may tender the documents of title, but the buyer may inspect the goods after their arrival before payment is due unless such inspection is inconsistent with the terms of the contract (Section 2-513); and
   (c) if delivery is authorized and made by way of documents of title otherwise than by subsection (b) then payment is due at the time and place at which the buyer is to receive the documents regardless of where the goods are to be received; and
   (d) where the seller is required or authorized to ship the goods on credit the credit period runs from the time of shipment but post-dating the invoice or delaying its dispatch will correspondingly delay the starting of the credit period.

§ 2-311. Options and Cooperation Respecting Performance.

(1) An agreement for sale which is otherwise sufficiently definite (subsection (3) of Section 2-204) to be a contract is not made invalid by the fact that it leaves particulars of performance to be specified by one of the parties. Any such specification must be made in good faith and within the limits set by commercial reasonableness.

(2) Unless otherwise agreed specifications relating to assortment of the goods are at the buyer's option and except as otherwise provided in subsections (1) (c) and (3) of Section 2-319 specifications

or arrangements relating to shipment are at the seller's option.

(3) Where such specification would materially affect the other party's performance but is not seasonably made or where one party's cooperation is necessary to the agreed performance of the other but is not seasonably forthcoming, the other party in addition to all other remedies

(a)   is excused for any resulting delay in his own performance; and

(b)   may also either proceed to perform in any reasonable manner or after the time for a material part of his own performance treat the failure to specify or to cooperate as a breach by failure to deliver or accept the goods.

§ 2-312. Warranty of Title and Against Infringement; Buyer's Obligation Against Infringement.

(1) Subject to subsection (2) there is in a contract for sale a warranty by the seller that

(a)   the title conveyed shall be good, and its transfer rightful; and

(b)   the goods shall be delivered free from any security interest or other lien or encumbrance of which the buyer at the time of contracting has no knowledge.

(2) A warranty under subsection (1) will be excluded or modified only by specific language or by circumstances which give the buyer reason to know that the person selling does not claim title in himself or that he is purporting to sell only such right or title as he or a third person may have.

(3) Unless otherwise agreed a seller who is a merchant regularly dealing in goods of the kind warrants that the goods shall be delivered free of the rightful claim of any third person by way of infringement or the like but a buyer who furnishes specifications to the seller must hold the seller harmless against any such claim which arises out of compliance with the specifications.

§ 2-313. Express Warranties by Affirmation, Promise, Description, Sample.

(1) Express warranties by the seller are created as follows:

(a)   Any affirmation of fact or promise made by the seller to the buyer which relates to the goods and becomes part of the basis of the bargain creates an express warranty that the goods shall conform to the affirmation or promise.

(b)   Any description of the goods which is made part of the basis of the bargain creates an express warranty that the goods shall conform to the description.

(c)   Any sample or model which is made part of the basis of the bargain creates an express warranty that the whole of the goods shall conform to the sample or model.

(2) It is not necessary to the creation of an express warranty that the seller use formal words such as "warrant" or "guarantee" or that he have a specific intention to make a warranty, but an affirmation merely of the value of the goods or a statement purporting to be merely the seller's opinion or commendation of the goods does not create a warranty.

§ 2-314. Implied Warranty: Merchantability; Usage of Trade.

(1) Unless excluded or modified (Section 2-316), a warranty that the goods shall be merchantable is implied in a contract for their sale if the seller is a merchant with respect to goods of that kind. Under this section the serving for value of food or drink to be consumed either on the premises or elsewhere is a sale.

(2) Goods to be merchantable must be at least such as

(a)   pass without objection in the trade under the contract description; and

(b)   in the case of fungible goods, are of fair average quality within the description; and

(c)   are fit for the ordinary purposes for which such goods are used; and

(d)   run, within the variations permitted by the agreement, of even kind, quality and quantity within each unit and among all units involved; and

(e)   are adequately contained, packaged, and labeled as the agreement may require; and

(f)   conform to the promises or affirmations of fact made on the container or label if any.

(3) Unless excluded or modified (Section 2-316) other implied warranties may arise from course of dealing or usage of trade.

§ 2-315. Implied Warranty: Fitness for Particular Purpose. Where the seller at the time of contracting has reason to know any particular purpose for which the goods are required and that the buyer is relying on the seller's skill or judgment to select or furnish suitable goods, there is unless excluded or modified under the next section an implied warranty that the goods shall be fit for such purpose.

§ 2-316. Exclusion or Modification of Warranties.

(1) Words or conduct relevant to the creation of an express warranty and words or conduct tending to negate or limit warranty shall be construed wherever reasonable as consistent with each other; but subject to the provisions of this Article on parol or extrinsic evidence (Section 2-202) negation or limitation is inoperative to the extent that such construction is unreasonable.

(2) Subject to subsection (3), to exclude or modify the implied warranty of merchantability or any part of it the language must mention merchantability and in case of a writing must be conspicuous, and to exclude or modify any implied warranty of fitness the exclusion must be by a writing and conspicuous. Language to exclude all implied warranties of fitness is sufficient if it states, for example, that "There are no warranties which extend beyond the description on the face hereof."

(3) Notwithstanding subsection (2)

(a)   unless the circumstances indicate otherwise, all implied warranties are excluded by expressions like "as is," "with all faults" or other language which in common understanding calls the buyer's attention to the exclusion of warranties and makes plain that there is no implied warranty; and

(b)   when the buyer before entering into the contract has examined the goods or the sample or model as fully as he desired or has refused to examine the goods there is no implied warranty with regard to defects which an examination ought in the circumstances to have revealed to him; and

(c)   an implied warranty can also be excluded or modified by course of dealing or course of performance or usage of trade.

(4) Remedies for breach of warranty can be limited in accordance with the provisions of this Article on liquidation or limitation of damages and on contractual modification of remedy (Sections 2-718 and 2-719).

§ 2-317. Cumulation and Conflict of Warranties Express or Implied. Warranties whether express or implied shall be construed as consistent with each other and as cumulative, but if such construction is unreasonable the intention of the parties shall determine which warranty is dominant. In ascertaining that intention the following rules apply:

(a)   Exact or technical specifications displace an inconsistent sample or model or general language of description.

(b)   A sample from an existing bulk displaces inconsistent general language of description.

(c)   Express warranties displace inconsistent implied warranties other than an implied warranty of fitness for a particular purpose.

§ 2-318. Third Party Beneficiaries of Warranties Express or Implied.

Note: If this Act is introduced in the Congress of the United States this section should be omitted. (States to select one alternative.)

Alternative A   A seller's warranty whether express or implied extends to any natural person who is in the family or household of his buyer or who is a guest in his home if it is reasonable to expect that such person may use, consume or be affected by the goods and who is injured in person by breach of the warranty. A seller may not exclude or limit the operation of this section.

Alternative B   A seller's warranty whether express or implied extends to any natural person who may reasonably be expected to use, consume or be affected by the goods and who is injured in person by breach of the warranty. A seller may not exclude or limit the operation of this section.

Alternative C   A seller's warranty whether express or implied extends to any person who may reasonably be expected to use, consume or be affected by the goods and who is injured by breach of the warranty. A seller may not exclude or limit the operation of this section with respect to injury to the person of an individual to whom the warranty extends. As amended 1966.

§ 2-319. F.O.B. and F.A.S. Terms.

(1) Unless otherwise agreed the term F.O.B. (which means "free on board") at a named place, even though used only in connection with the stated price, is a delivery term under which

(a)   when the term is F.O.B. the place of shipment, the seller must at that place ship the goods in the manner provided in this Article (Section 2-504) and bear the expense and risk of putting them into the possession of the carrier; or

(b)   when the term is F.O.B. the place of destination, the seller must at his own expense and risk transport the goods to that place and there tender delivery of them in the manner provided in this Article (Section 2-503);

(c)   when under either (a) or (b) the term is also F.O.B. vessel, car or other vehicle, the seller must in addition at his own expense and risk load the goods on board. If the term is F.O.B. vessel the buyer must name the vessel and in an appropriate case the seller must comply with the provisions of this Article on the form of bill of lading (Section 2-323).

(2) Unless otherwise agreed the term F.A.S. vessel (which means "free alongside") at a named port, even though used only in connection with the stated price, is a delivery term under which the seller must

(a)   at his own expense and risk deliver the goods alongside the vessel in the manner usual in that port or on a dock designated and provided by the buyer; and

(b)   obtain and tender a receipt for the goods in exchange for which the carrier is under a duty to issue a bill of lading.

(3) Unless otherwise agreed in any case falling within subsection (1) (a) or (c) or subsection (2) the buyer must seasonably give any needed instructions for making delivery, including when the term is F.A.S. or F.O.B. the loading berth of the vessel and in an appropriate case its name and sailing date. The seller may treat the failure of needed instructions as a failure of cooperation under this Article (Section 2-311). He may also at his option move the goods in any reasonable manner preparatory to delivery or shipment.

(4) Under the term F.O.B. vessel or F.A.S. unless otherwise agreed the buyer must make payment against tender of the required documents and the seller may not tender nor the buyer demand delivery of the goods in substitution for the documents.

§ 2-320. C.I.F. and C. & F. Terms.

(1) The term C.I.F. means that the price includes in a lump sum the cost of the goods and the insurance and freight to the named destination. The term C. & F. or C.F. means that the price so includes cost and freight to the named destination.

(2) Unless otherwise agreed and even though used only in connection with the stated price and destination, the term C.I.F. destination or its equivalent requires the seller at his own expense and risk to

(a)   put the goods into the possession of a carrier at the port for shipment and obtain a negotiable bill or bills of lading covering the entire transportation to the named destination; and

(b)   load the goods and obtain a receipt from the carrier (which may be contained in the bill of lading) showing that the freight has been paid or provided for; and

(c)   obtain a policy or certificate of insurance, including any war risk insurance, of a kind and on terms then current at the port of shipment in the usual amount, in the currency of the contract, shown to cover the same goods covered by the bill of lading and providing for payment of loss to the order of the buyer or for the account of whom it may concern; but the seller may add to the price the amount of the premium for any such war risk insurance; and

(d)   prepare an invoice of the goods and procure any other documents required to effect shipment or to comply with the contract; and

(e)   forward and tender with commercial promptness all the documents in due form and with any indorsement necessary to perfect the buyer's rights.

(3) Unless otherwise agreed the term C. & F. or its equivalent has the same effect and imposes upon the seller the same obligations and risks as a C.I.F. term except the obligation as to insurance.

(4) Under the term C.I.F. or C. & F. unless otherwise agreed the buyer must make payment against

tender of the required documents and the seller may not tender nor the buyer demand delivery of the goods in substitution for the documents.

§ 2-321. C.I.F. or C. & F.: "Net Landed Weights"; "Payment on Arrival"; Warranty of Condition on Arrival.
Under a contract containing a term C.I.F. or C. & F.

(1) Where the price is based on or is to be adjusted according to "net landed weights," "delivered weights," "out turn" quantity or quality or the like, unless otherwise agreed the seller must reasonably estimate the price. The payment due on tender of the documents called for by the contract is the amount so estimated, but after final adjustment of the price a settlement must be made with commercial promptness.

(2) An agreement described in subsection (1) or any warranty of quality or condition of the goods on arrival places upon the seller the risk of ordinary deterioration, shrinkage and the like in transportation but has no effect on the place or time of identification to the contract for sale or delivery or on the passing of the risk of loss.

(3) Unless otherwise agreed where the contract provides for payment on or after arrival of the goods the seller must before payment allow such preliminary inspection as is feasible; but if the goods are lost delivery of the documents and payment are due when the goods should have arrived.

§ 2-322. Delivery "Ex-Ship."

(1) Unless otherwise agreed a term for delivery of goods "ex-ship" (which means from the carrying vessel) or in equivalent language is not restricted to a particular ship and requires delivery from a ship which has reached a place at the named port of destination where goods of the kind are usually discharged.

(2) Under such a term unless otherwise agreed
  (a)   the seller must discharge all liens arising out of the carriage and furnish the buyer with a direction which puts the carrier under a duty to deliver the goods; and
  (b)   the risk of loss does not pass to the buyer until the goods leave the ship's tackle or are otherwise properly unloaded.

§ 2-323. Form of Bill of Lading Required in Overseas Shipment; "Overseas."

(1) Where the contract contemplates overseas shipment and contains a term C.I.F. or C. & F. or

F.O.B. vessel, the seller unless otherwise agreed must obtain a negotiable bill of lading stating that the goods have been loaded on board or, in the case of a term C.I.F. or C. & F., received for shipment.

(2) Where in a case within subsection (1) a bill of lading has been issued in a set of parts, unless otherwise agreed if the documents are not to be sent from abroad the buyer may demand tender of the full set; otherwise only one part of the bill of lading need be tendered. Even if the agreement expressly requires a full set
  (a)   due tender of a single part is acceptable within the provisions of this Article on cure of improper delivery (subsection (1) of Section 2-508); and
  (b)   even though the full set is demanded, if the documents are sent from abroad the person tendering an incomplete set may nevertheless require payment upon furnishing an indemnity which the buyer in good faith deems adequate.

(3) A shipment by water or by air or a contract contemplating such shipment is "overseas" insofar as by usage of trade or agreement it is subject to the commercial, financing or shipping practices characteristic of international deep water commerce.

§ 2-324. "No Arrival, No Sale" Term.
Under a term "no arrival, no sale" or terms of like meaning, unless otherwise agreed,
  (a)   the seller must properly ship conforming goods and if they arrive by any means he must tender them on arrival but he assumes no obligation that the goods will arrive unless he has caused the non-arrival; and
  (b)   where without fault of the seller the goods are in part lost or have so deteriorated as no longer to conform to the contract or arrive after the contract time, the buyer may proceed as if there had been casualty to identified goods (Section 2-613).

§ 2-325. "Letter of Credit" Term; "Confirmed Credit."

(1) Failure of the buyer seasonably to furnish an agreed letter of credit is a breach of the contract for sale.

(2) The delivery to seller of a proper letter of credit suspends the buyer's obligation to pay. If the letter of credit is dishonored, the seller may on

seasonable notification to the buyer require payment directly from him.

(3) Unless otherwise agreed the term "letter of credit" or "banker's credit" in a contract for sale means an irrevocable credit issued by a financing agency of good repute and, where the shipment is overseas, of good international repute. The term "confirmed credit" means that the credit must also carry the direct obligation of such an agency which does business in the seller's financial market.

§ 2-326. Sale on Approval and Sale or Return; Consignment Sales and Rights of Creditors.

(1) Unless otherwise agreed, if delivered goods may be returned by the buyer even though they conform to the contract, the transaction is

    (a)   a "sale on approval" if the goods are delivered primarily for use, and

    (b)   a "sale or return" if the goods are delivered primarily for resale.

(2) Except as provided in subsection (3), goods held on approval are not subject to the claims of the buyer's creditors until acceptance; goods held on sale or return are subject to such claims while in the buyer's possession.

(3) Where goods are delivered to a person for sale and such person maintains a place of business at which he deals in goods of the kind involved, under a name other than the name of the person making delivery, then with respect to claims of creditors of the person conducting the business the goods are deemed to be on sale or return. The provisions of this subsection are applicable even though an agreement purports to reserve title to the person making delivery until payment or resale or uses such words as "on consignment" or "on memorandum." However, this subsection is not applicable if the person making delivery

    (a)   complies with an applicable law providing for a consignor's interest or the like to be evidenced by a sign, or

    (b)   establishes that the person conducting the business is generally known by his creditors to be substantially engaged in selling the goods of others, or

    (c)   complies with the filing provisions of the Article on Secured Transactions (Article 9).

(4) Any "or return" term of a contract for sale is to be treated as a separate contract for sale within the statute of frauds section of this Article (Section 2-201) and as contradicting the sale aspect of the contract within the provisions of this Article on parol or extrinsic evidence (Section 2-202).

§ 2-327. Special Incidents of Sale on Approval and Sale or Return.

(1) Under a sale on approval unless otherwise agreed

    (a)   although the goods are identified to the contract the risk of loss and the title do not pass to the buyer until acceptance; and

    (b)   use of the goods consistent with the purpose of trial is not acceptance but failure seasonably to notify the seller of election to return the goods is acceptance, and if the goods conform to the contract acceptance of any part is acceptance of the whole; and

    (c)   after due notification of election to return, the return is at the seller's risk and expense but a merchant buyer must follow any reasonable instructions.

(2) Under a sale or return unless otherwise agreed

    (a)   the option to return extends to the whole or any commercial unit of the goods while in substantially their original condition, but must be exercised seasonably; and

    (b)   the return is at the buyer's risk and expense.

§ 2-328. Sale by Auction.

(1) In a sale by auction if goods are put up in lots each lot is the subject of a separate sale.

(2) A sale by auction is complete when the auctioneer so announces by the fall of the hammer or in other customary manner. Where a bid is made while the hammer is falling in acceptance of a prior bid the auctioneer may in his discretion reopen the bidding or declare the goods sold under the bid on which the hammer was falling.

(3) Such a sale is with reserve unless the goods are in explicit terms put up without reserve. In an auction with reserve the auctioneer may withdraw the goods at any time until he announces completion of the sale. In an auction without reserve, after the auctioneer calls for bids on an article or lot, that article or lot cannot be withdrawn unless no bid is made within a reasonable time. In either case a bidder may retract his bid until the auctioneer's announcement of completion of the sale, but a bidder's retraction does not revive any previous bid.

(4) If the auctioneer knowingly receives a bid on the seller's behalf or the seller makes or procures such a bid, and notice has not been given that liberty for such bidding is reserved, the buyer may at his option avoid the sale or take the goods at the price of the last good faith bid prior to the completion of the sale. This subsection shall not apply to any bid at a forced sale.

Part 4. Title, Creditors and Good Faith Purchasers

§ 2-401. Passing of Title; Reservation for Security; Limited Application of This Section. Each provision of this Article with regard to the rights, obligations and remedies of the seller, the buyer, purchasers or other third parties applies irrespective of title to the goods except where the provision refers to such title. Insofar as situations are not covered by the other provisions of this Article and matters concerning title become material the following rules apply:

(1) Title to goods cannot pass under a contract for sale prior to their identification to the contract (Section 2-501), and unless otherwise explicitly agreed the buyer acquires by their identification a special property as limited by this Act. Any retention or reservation by the seller of the title (property) in goods shipped or delivered to the buyer is limited in effect to a reservation of a security interest. Subject to these provisions and to the provisions of the Article on Secured Transactions (Article 9), title to goods passes from the seller to the buyer in any manner and on any conditions explicitly agreed on by the parties.

(2) Unless otherwise explicitly agreed title passes to the buyer at the time and place at which the seller completes his performance with reference to the physical delivery of the goods, despite any reservation of a security interest and even though a document of title is to be delivered at a different time or place; and in particular and despite any reservation of a security interest in the bill of lading

    (a)   if the contract requires or authorizes the seller to send the goods to the buyer but does not require him to deliver them at destination, title passes to the buyer at the time and place of shipment; and

    (b)   if the contract requires delivery at destination, title passes on tender there.

(3) Unless otherwise explicitly agreed where delivery is to be made without moving the goods,

    (a)   if the seller is to deliver a document of title, title passes at the time when and the place where he delivers such documents; or

    (b)   if the goods are at the time of contracting already identified and no documents are to be delivered, title passes at the time and place of contracting.

(4) A rejection or other refusal by the buyer to receive or retain the goods, whether or not justified, or a justified revocation of acceptance revests title to the goods in the seller. Such revesting occurs by operation of law and is not a "sale."

§ 2-402. Rights of Seller's Creditors Against Sold Goods.

(1) Except as provided in subsections (2) and (3), rights of unsecured creditors of the seller with respect to goods which have been identified to a contract for sale are subject to the buyer's rights to recover the goods under this Article (Sections 2-502 and 2-716).

(2) A creditor of the seller may treat a sale or an identification of goods to a contract for sale as void if as against him a retention of possession by the seller is fraudulent under any rule of law of the state where the goods are situated, except that retention of possession in good faith and current course of trade by a merchant-seller for a commercially reasonable time after a sale or identification is not fraudulent.

(3) Nothing in this Article shall be deemed to impair the rights of creditors of the seller

    (a)   under the provisions of the Article on Secured Transactions (Article 9); or

    (b)   where identification to the contract or delivery is made not in current course of trade but in satisfaction of or as security for a pre-existing claim for money, security or the like and is made under circumstances which under any rule of law of the state where the goods are situated would apart from this Article constitute the transaction a fraudulent transfer or voidable preference.

§ 2-403. Power to Transfer; Good Faith Purchase of Goods; "Entrusting."

(1) A purchaser of goods acquires all title which his transferor had or had power to transfer except that a purchaser of a limited interest acquires rights only to the extent of the interest purchased. A

person with voidable title has power to transfer a good title to a good faith purchaser for value. When goods have been delivered under a transaction of purchase the purchaser has such power even though

- (a) the transferor was deceived as to the identity of the purchaser, or
- (b) the delivery was in exchange for a check which is later dishonored, or
- (c) it was agreed that the transaction was to be a "cash sale," or
- (d) the delivery was procured through fraud punishable as larcenous under the criminal law.

(2) Any entrusting of possession of goods to a merchant who deals in goods of that kind gives him power to transfer all rights of the entruster to a buyer in ordinary course of business.

(3) "Entrusting" includes any delivery and any acquiescence in retention of possession regardless of any condition expressed between the parties to the delivery or acquiescence and regardless of whether the procurement of the entrusting or the possessor's disposition of the goods have been such as to be larcenous under the criminal law.

(4) The rights of other purchasers of goods and of lien creditors are governed by the Articles on Secured Transactions (Article 9), Bulk Transfers (Article 6) and Documents of Title (Article 7).

Part 5. Performance

§ 2-501. Insurable Interest in Goods; Manner of Identification of Goods.

(1) The buyer obtains a special property and an insurable interest in goods by identification of existing goods as goods to which the contract refers even though the goods so identified are non-conforming and he has an option to return or reject them. Such identification can be made at any time and in any manner explicitly agreed to by the parties. In the absence of explicit agreement identification occurs

- (a) when the contract is made if it is for the sale of goods already existing and identified;
- (b) if the contract is for the sale of future goods other than those described in paragraph (c), when goods are shipped, marked or otherwise designated by the seller as goods to which the contract refers;
- (c) when the crops are planted or otherwise become growing crops or the young are conceived if the contract is for the sale of

unborn young to be born within twelve months after contracting or for the sale of crops to be harvested within twelve months or the next normal harvest season after contracting whichever is longer.

(2) The seller retains an insurable interest in goods so long as title to or any security interest in the goods remains in him and where the identification is by the seller alone he may until default or insolvency or notification to the buyer that the identification is final substitute other goods for those identified.

(3) Nothing in this section impairs any insurable interest recognized under any other statute or rule of law.

§ 2-502. Buyer's Right to Goods on Seller's Insolvency.

(1) Subject to subsection (2) and even though the goods have not been shipped a buyer who has paid a part or all of the price of goods in which he has a special property under the provisions of the immediately preceding section may on making and keeping good a tender of any unpaid portion of their price recover them from the seller if the seller becomes insolvent within ten days after receipt of the first installment on their price.

(2) If the identification creating his special property has been made by the buyer he acquires the right to recover the goods only if they conform to the contract for sale.

§ 2-503. Manner of Seller's Tender of Delivery.

(1) Tender of delivery requires that the seller put and hold conforming goods at the buyer's disposition and give the buyer any notification reasonably necessary to enable him to take delivery. The manner, time and place for tender are determined by the agreement and this Article, and in particular

- (a) tender must be at a reasonable hour, and if it is of goods they must be kept available for the period reasonably necessary to enable the buyer to take possession; but
- (b) unless otherwise agreed the buyer must furnish facilities reasonably suited to the receipt of the goods.

(2) Where the case is within the next section respecting shipment tender requires that the seller comply with its provisions.

(3) Where the seller is required to deliver at a particular destination tender requires that he com-

ply with subsection (2) and also in any appropriate case tender documents as described in subsections (4) and (5) of this section.

(4) Where goods are in the possession of a bailee and are to be delivered without being moved

(a) tender requires that the seller either tender a negotiable document of title covering such goods or procure acknowledgment by the bailee of the buyer's right to possession of the goods; but

(b) tender to the buyer of a non-negotiable document of title or of a written direction to the bailee to deliver is sufficient tender unless the buyer seasonably objects, and receipt by the bailee of notification of the buyer's rights fixes those rights as against the bailee and all third persons; but risk of loss of the goods and of any failure by the bailee to honor the non-negotiable document of title or to obey the direction remains on the seller until the buyer has had a reasonable time to present the document or direction, and a refusal by the bailee to honor the document or to obey the direction defeats the tender.

(5) Where the contract requires the seller to deliver documents

(a) he must tender all such documents in correct form, except as provided in this Article with respect to bills of lading in a set (subsection (2) of Section 2-323); and

(b) tender through customary banking channels is sufficient and dishonor of a draft accompanying the documents constitutes non-acceptance or rejection.

§ 2-504. Shipment by Seller.
Where the seller is required or authorized to send the goods to the buyer and the contract does not require him to deliver them at a particular destination, then unless otherwise agreed he must

(a) put the goods in the possession of such a carrier and make sure a contract for their transportation as may be reasonable having regard to the nature of the goods and other circumstances of the case; and

(b) obtain and promptly deliver or tender in due form any document necessary to enable the buyer to obtain possession of the goods or otherwise required by the agreement or by usage of trade; and

(c) promptly notify the buyer of the shipment.

Failure to notify the buyer under paragraph (c) or to make a proper contract under paragraph (a) is a ground for rejection only if material delay or loss ensues.

§ 2-505. Seller's Shipment Under Reservation.
(1) Where the seller has identified goods to the contract by or before shipment:

(a) his procurement of a negotiable bill of lading to his own order or otherwise reserves in him a security interest in the goods. His procurement of the bill to the order of a financing agency or of the buyer indicates in addition only the seller's expectation of transferring that interest to the person named.

(b) a non-negotiable bill of lading to himself or his nominee reserves possession of the goods as security but except in a case of conditional delivery (subsection (2) of Section 2-507) a non-negotiable bill of lading naming the buyer as consignee reserves no security interest even though the seller retains possession of the bill of lading.

(2) When shipment by the seller with reservation of a security interest is in violation of the contract for sale it constitutes an improper contract for transportation within the preceding section but impairs neither the rights given to the buyer by shipment and identification of the goods to the contract nor the seller's powers as a holder of a negotiable document.

§ 2-506. Rights of Financing Agency.
(1) A financing agency by paying or purchasing for value a draft which relates to a shipment of goods acquires to the extent of the payment or purchase and in addition to its own rights under the draft and any document of title securing it any rights of the shipper in the goods including the right to stop delivery and the shipper's right to have the draft honored by the buyer.

(2) The right to reimbursement of a financing agency which has in good faith honored or purchased the draft under commitment to or authority from the buyer is not impaired by subsequent dis-

covery of defects with reference to any relevant document which was apparently regular on its face.

§ 2-507. Effect of Seller's Tender; Delivery on Condition.

(1) Tender of delivery is a condition to the buyer's duty to accept the goods and, unless otherwise agreed, to his duty to pay for them. Tender entitles the seller to acceptance of the goods and to payment according to the contract.

(2) Where payment is due and demanded on the delivery to the buyer of goods or documents of title, his right as against the seller to retain or dispose of them is conditional upon his making the payment due.

§ 2-508. Cure by Seller of Improper Tender or Delivery; Replacement.

(1) Where any tender or delivery by the seller is rejected because non-conforming and the time for performance has not yet expired, the seller may seasonably notify the buyer of his intention to cure and may then within the contract time make a conforming delivery.

(2) Where the buyer rejects a non-conforming tender which the seller had reasonable grounds to believe would be acceptable with or without money allowance the seller may if he seasonably notifies the buyer have a further reasonable time to substitute a conforming tender.

§ 2-509. Risk of Loss in the Absence of Breach.

(1) Where the contract requires or authorizes the seller to ship the goods by carrier
- (a) if it does not require him to deliver them at a particular destination, the risk of loss passes to the buyer when the goods are duly delivered to the carrier even though the shipment is under reservation (Section 2-505); but
- (b) if it does require him to deliver them at a particular destination and the goods are there duly tendered while in the possession of the carrier, the risk of loss passes to the buyer when the goods are there duly so tendered as to enable the buyer to take delivery.

(2) Where the goods are held by a bailee to be delivered without being moved, the risk of loss passes to the buyer
- (a) on his receipt of a negotiable document of title covering the goods; or

- (b) on acknowledgment by the bailee of the buyer's right to possession of the goods; or
- (c) after his receipt of a non-negotiable document of title or other written direction to deliver, as provided in subsection (4)(b) of Section 2-503.

(3) In any case not within subsection (1) or (2), the risk of loss passes to the buyer on his receipt of the goods if the seller is a merchant; otherwise the risk passes to the buyer on tender of delivery.

(4) The provisions of this section are subject to contrary agreement of the parties and to the provisions of this Article on sale on approval (Section 2-327) and on effect of breach on risk of loss (Section 2-510).

§ 2-510. Effect of Breach on Risk of Loss.

(1) Where a tender or delivery of goods so fails to conform to the contract as to give a right of rejection the risk of their loss remains on the seller until cure or acceptance.

(2) Where the buyer rightfully revokes acceptance he may to the extent of any deificiency in his effective insurance coverage treat the risk of loss as having rested on the seller from the beginning.

(3) Where the buyer as to conforming goods already identified to the contract for sale repudiates or is otherwise in breach before risk of their loss has passed to him, the seller may to the extent of any deficiency in his effective insurance coverage treat the risk of loss as resting on the buyer for a commercially reasonable time.

§ 2-511. Tender of Payment by Buyer; Payment by Check.

(1) Unless otherwise agreed tender of payment is a condition to the seller's duty to tender and complete any delivery.

(2) Tender of payment is sufficient when made by any means or in any manner current in the ordinary course of business unless the seller demands payment in legal tender and gives any extension of time reasonably necessary to procure it.

(3) Subject to the provisions of this Act on the effect of an instrument on an obligation (Section 3-802), payment by check is conditional and is defeated as between the parties by dishonor of the check on due presentment.

§ 2-512. Payment by Buyer Before Inspection.

(1) Where the contract requires payment before inspection non-conformity of the goods does not excuse the buyer from so making payment unless

(a)   the non-conformity appears without inspection; or

(b)   despite tender of the required documents the circumstances would justify injunction against honor under the provisions of this Act (Section 5-114).

(2) Payment pursuant to subsection (1) does not constitute an acceptance of goods or impair the buyer's right to inspect or any of his remedies.

§ 2-513. Buyer's Right to Inspection of Goods.

(1) Unless otherwise agreed and subject to subsection (3), where goods are tendered or delivered or identified to the contract for sale, the buyer has a right before shipment or acceptance to inspect them at any reasonable place and time and in any reasonable manner. When the seller is required or authorized to send the goods to the buyer, the inspection may be after their arrival.

(2) Expenses of inspection must be borne by the buyer but may be recovered from the seller if the goods do not conform and are rejected.

(3) Unless otherwise agreed and subject to the provisions of this Article on C.I.F. contracts (subsection (3) of Section 2-321), the buyer is not entitled to inspect the goods before payment of the price when the contract provides

(a)   for delivery "C.O.D." or on other like terms; or

(b)   for payment against documents of title, except where such payment is due only after the goods are to become available for inspection.

(4) A place or method of inspection fixed by the parties is presumed to be exclusive but unless otherwise expressly agreed it does not postpone identification or shift the place for delivery or for passing the risk of loss. If compliance becomes impossible, inspection shall be as provided in this section unless the place or method fixed was clearly intended as an indispensable condition failure of which avoids the contract.

§ 2-514. When Documents Deliverable on Acceptance; When on Payment.   Unless otherwise agreed documents against which a draft is drawn are to be delivered to the drawee on acceptance of the draft if

it is payable more than three days after presentment; otherwise, only on payment.

§ 2-515. Preserving Evidence of Goods in Dispute.

In furtherance of the adjustment of any claim or dispute

(a)   either party on reasonable notification to the other and for the purpose of ascertaining the facts and preserving evidence has the right to inspect, test and sample the goods including such of them as may be in the possession or control of the other; and

(b)   the parties may agree to a third party inspection or survey to determine the conformity or condition of the goods and may agree that the findings shall be binding upon them in any subsequent litigation or adjustment.

Part 6. Breach, Repudiation and Excuse

§ 2-601. Buyer's Rights on Improper Delivery.

Subject to the provisions of this Article on breach in installment contracts (Section 2-612) and unless otherwise agreed under the sections on contractual limitations of remedy (Sections 2-718 and 2-719), if the goods or the tender of delivery fail in any respect to conform to the contract, the buyer may

(a)   reject the whole; or

(b)   accept the whole; or

(c)   accept any commercial unit or units and reject the rest.

§ 2-602. Manner and Effect of Rightful Rejection.

(1) Rejection of goods must be within a reasonable time after their delivery or tender. It is ineffective unless the buyer seasonably notifies the seller.

(2) Subject to the provisions of the two following sections on rejected goods (Sections 2-603 and 2-604),

(a)   after rejection any exercise of ownership by the buyer with respect to any commercial unit is wrongful as against the seller; and

(b)   if the buyer has before rejection taken physical possession of goods in which he does not have a security interest under the provisions of this Article (subsection (3) of Section 2-711), he is under a duty after rejection to hold them with reasonable care at the seller's disposition for a time sufficient to permit the seller to remove them; but

(c)   the buyer has no further obligations with regard to goods rightfully rejected.

(3) The seller's rights with respect to goods wrongfully rejected are governed by the provisions of this Article on Seller's remedies in general (Section 2-703).

§ 2-603. Merchant Buyer's Duties as to Rightfully Rejected Goods.

(1) Subject to any security interest in the buyer (subsection (3) of Section 2-711), when the seller has no agent or place of business at the market of rejection a merchant buyer is under a duty after rejection of goods in his possession or control to follow any reasonable instructions received from the seller with respect to the goods and in the absence of such instructions to make reasonable efforts to sell them for the seller's account if they are perishable or threaten to decline in value speedily. Instructions are not reasonable if on demand indemnity for expenses is not forthcoming.

(2) When the buyer sells goods under subsection (1), he is entitled to reimbursement from the seller or out of the proceeds for reasonable expenses of caring for and selling them, and if the expenses include no selling commission then to such commission as is usual in the trade or if there is none to a reasonable sum not exceeding ten per cent on the gross proceeds.

(3) In complying with this section the buyer is held only to good faith and good faith conduct hereunder is neither acceptance nor conversion nor the basis of an action for damages.

§ 2-604. Buyer's Options as to Salvage of Rightfully Rejected Goods.
Subject to the provisions of the immediately preceding section on perishables if the seller gives no instructions within a reasonable time after notification of rejection the buyer may store the rejected goods for the seller's account or reship them to him or resell them for the seller's account with reimbursement as provided in the preceding section. Such action is not acceptance or conversion.

§ 2-605. Waiver of Buyer's Objections by Failure to Particularize.

(1) The buyer's failure to state in connection with rejection a particular defect which is ascertainable by reasonable inspection precludes him from relying on the unstated defect to justify rejection or to establish breach

(a)   where the seller could have cured it if stated seasonably; or

(b)   between merchants when the seller has after rejection made a request in writing for a full and final written statement of all defects on which the buyer proposes to rely.

(2) Payment against documents made without reservation of rights precludes recovery of the payment for defects apparent on the face of the documents.

§ 2-606. What Constitutes Acceptance of Goods.

(1) Acceptance of goods occurs when the buyer

(a)   after a reasonable opportunity to inspect the goods signifies to the seller that the goods are conforming or that he will take or retain them in spite of their non-conformity; or

(b)   fails to make an effective rejection (subsection (1) of Section 2-602), but such acceptance does not occur until the buyer has had a reasonable opportunity to inspect them; or

(c)   does not act inconsistent with the seller's ownership; but if such act is wrongful as against the seller it is an acceptance only if ratified by him.

(2) Acceptance of a part of any commercial unit is acceptance of that entire unit.

§ 2-607. Effect of Acceptance; Notice of Breach; Burden of Establishing Breach After Acceptance; Notice of Claim or Litigation to Person Answerable Over.

(1) The buyer must pay at the contract rate for any goods accepted.

(2) Acceptance of goods by the buyer precludes rejection of the goods accepted and if made with knowledge of a non-conformity cannot be revoked because of it unless the acceptance was on the reasonable assumption that the non-conformity would be seasonably cured but acceptance does not of itself impair any other remedy provided by this Article for non-conformity.

(3) Where a tender has been accepted

(a)   the buyer must within a reasonable time after he discovers or should have discovered any breach notify the seller of breach or be barred from any remedy; and

(b) if the claim is one for infringement or the like (subsection (3) of Section 2-312) and the buyer is sued as a result of such a breach he must so notify the seller within a reasonable time after he receives notice of the litigation or be barred from any remedy over for liability established by the litigation.

(4) The burden is on the buyer to establish any breach with respect to the goods accepted.

(5) Where the buyer is sued for breach of a warranty or other obligation for which his seller is answerable over

(a) he may give his seller written notice of the litigation. If the notice states that the seller may come in and defend and that if the seller does not do so he will be bound in any action against him by his buyer by any determination of fact common to the two litigations, then unless the seller after seasonable receipt of the notice does come in and defend he is so bound.

(b) if the claim is one for infringement or the like (subsection (3) of Section 2-312) the original seller may demand in writing that his buyer turn over to him control of the litigation including settlement or else be barred from any remedy over and if he also agrees to bear all expense and to satisfy any adverse judgment, then unless the buyer after seasonable receipt of the demand does turn over control the buyer is so barred.

(6) The provisions of subsections (3), (4) and (5) apply to any obligation of a buyer to hold the seller harmless against infringement or the like (subsection (3) of Section 2-312).

§ 2-608. Revocation of Acceptance in Whole or in Part.

(1) The buyer may revoke his acceptance of a lot or commercial unit whose non-conformity substantially impairs its value to him if he has accepted it

(a) on the reasonable assumption that its non-conformity would be cured and it has not been seasonably cured; or

(b) without discovery of such non-conformity if his acceptance was reasonably induced either by the difficulty of discovery

before acceptance or by the seller's assurances.

(2) Revocation of acceptance must occur within a reasonable time after the buyer discovers or should have discovered the ground for it and before any substantial change in condition of the goods which is not caused by their own defects. It is not effective until the buyer notifies the seller of it.

(3) A buyer who so revokes has the same rights and duties with regard to the goods involved as if he had rejected them.

§ 2-609. Right to Adequate Assurance of Performance.

(1) A contract for sale imposes an obligation on each party that the other's expectation of receiving due performance will not be impaired. When reasonable grounds for insecurity arise with respect to the performance of either party the other may in writing demand adequate assurance of due performance and until he receives such assurance may if commercially reasonable suspend any performance for which he has not already received the agreed return.

(2) Between merchants the reasonableness of grounds for insecurity and the adequacy of any assurance offered shall be determined according to commercial standards.

(3) Acceptance of any improper delivery or payment does not prejudice the aggrieved party's right to demand adequate assurance of future performance.

(4) After receipt of a justified demand failure to provide within a reasonable time not exceeding thirty days such assurance of due performance as is adequate under the circumstances of the particular case is a repudiation of the contract.

§ 2-610. Anticipatory Repudiation.

When either party repudiates the contract with respect to a performance not yet due the loss of which will substantially impair the value of the contract to the other, the aggrieved party may

(a) for a commercially reasonable time await performance by the repudiating party; or

(b) resort to any remedy for breach (Section 2-703 or Section 2-711), even though he has notified the repudiating party that he would await the latter's performance and has urged retraction; and

(c) in either case suspend his own performance or proceed in accordance with the provisions of this Article on the seller's right to identify goods to the contract notwithstanding breach or to salvage unfinished goods (Section 2-704).

§ 2-611. Retraction of Anticipatory Repudiation.

(1) Until the repudiating party's next performance is due he can retract his repudiation unless the aggrieved party has since the repudiation cancelled or materially changed his position or otherwise indicated that he considers the repudiation final.

(2) Retraction may be by any method which clearly indicates to the aggrieved party that the repudiating party intends to perform, but must include any assurance justifiably demanded under the provisions of this Article (Section 2-609).

(3) Retraction reinstates the repudiating party's rights under the contract with due excuse and allowance to the aggrieved party for any delay occasioned by the repudiation.

§ 2-612. "Installment Contract"; Breach.

(1) An "installment contract" is one which requires or authorizes the delivery of goods in separate lots to be separately accepted, even though the contract contains a clause "each delivery is a separate contract" or its equivalent.

(2) The buyer may reject any installment which is non-conforming if the non-conformity substantially impairs the value of that installment and cannot be cured or if the non-conformity is a defect in the required documents; but if the non-conformity does not fall within subsection (3) and the seller gives adequate assurance of its cure the buyer must accept that installment.

(3) Whenever non-conformity or default with respect to one or more installments substantially impairs the value of the whole contract there is a breach of the whole. But the aggrieved party reinstates the contract if he accepts a non-conforming installment without seasonably notifying of cancellation or if he brings an action with respect only to past installments or demands performance as to future installments.

§ 2-613. Casualty to Identified Goods.

Where the contract requires for its performance goods identified when the contract is made, and the goods suffer casualty without fault of either party before the rise of loss passes to the buyer, or in a proper case under a "no arrival, no sale" term (Section 2-324) then

(a) if the loss is total the contract is avoided; and

(b) if the loss is partial or the goods have so deteriorated as no longer to conform to the contract the buyer may nevertheless demand inspection and at his option either treat the contract as avoided or accept the goods with due allowance from the contract price for the deterioration or the deficiency in quantity but without further right against the seller.

§ 2-614. Substituted Performance.

(1) Where without fault of either party the agreed berthing, loading, or unloading facilities fail or an agreed type of carrier becomes unavailable or the agreed manner of delivery otherwise becomes commercially impracticable but a commercially reasonable substitute is available, such substitute performance must be tendered and accepted.

(2) If the agreed means or manner of payment fails because of domestic or foreign governmental regulation, the seller may withhold or stop delivery unless the buyer provides a means or manner of payment which is commercially a substantial equivalent. If delivery has already been taken, payment by the means or in the manner provided by the regulation discharges the buyer's obligation unless the regulation is discriminatory, oppressive or predatory.

§ 2-615. Excuse by Failure of Presupposed Conditions.

Except so far as a seller may have assumed a greater obligation and subject to the preceding section on substituted performance:

(a) Delay in delivery or non-delivery in whole or in part by a seller who complies with paragraphs (b) and (c) is not a breach of his duty under a contract for sale if performance as agreed has been made impracticable by the occurrence of a contingency the non-occurrence of which was a basic assumption on which the contract was made or by compliance in good faith with any applicable foreign or domestic governmental regulation or order whether or not it later proves to be invalid.

(b) Where the causes mentioned in paragraph (a) affect only a part of the seller's capacity to perform, he must allocate production and deliveries among his customers but may at his option include regular customers not then under contract as well as his own requirements for further manufacture. He may so allocate in any manner which is fair and reasonable.

(c) The seller must notify the buyer seasonably that there will be delay or nondelivery and, when allocation is required under paragraph (b), of the estimated quota thus made available for the buyer.

§ 2-616. Procedure on Notice Claiming Excuse.

(1) Where the buyer receives notification of a material or indefinite delay or an allocation justified under the preceding section he may by written notification to the seller as to any delivery concerned, and where the prospective deficiency substantially impairs the value of the whole contract under the provisions of this Article relating to breach of installment contracts (Section 2-612), then also as to the whole,

(a) terminate and thereby discharge any unexecuted portion of the contract; or

(b) modify the contract by agreeing to take his available quota in substitution.

(2) If after receipt of such notification from the seller the buyer fails so to modify the contract within a reasonable time not exceeding thirty days the contract lapses with respect to any deliveries affected.

(3) The provisions of this section may not be negated by agreement except in so far as the seller has assumed a greater obligation under the preceding section.

Part 7. Remedies

§ 2-701. Remedies for Breach of Collateral Contracts Not Impaired.
Remedies for breach of any obligation or promise collateral or ancillary to a contract for sale are not impaired by the provisions of this Article.

§ 2-702. Seller's Remedies on Discovery of Buyer's Insolvency.

(1) Where the seller discovers the buyer to be insolvent he may refuse delivery except for cash including payment for all goods theretofore delivered under the contract, and stop delivery under this Article (Section 2-705).

(2) Where the seller discovers that the buyer has received goods on credit while insolvent he may reclaim the goods upon demand made within ten days after the receipt, but if misrepresentation of

solvency has been made to the particular seller in writing within three months before delivery the ten day limitation does not apply. Except as provided in this subsection the seller may not base a right to reclaim goods on the buyer's fraudulent or innocent misrepresentation of solvency or of intent to pay.

(3) The seller's right to reclaim under subsection (2) is subject to the rights of a buyer in ordinary course or other good faith purchaser under this Article (Section 2-403). Successful reclamation of goods excludes all other remedies with respect to them.

§ 2-703. Seller's Remedies in General.
Where the buyer wrongfully rejects or revokes acceptance of goods or fails to make a payment due on or before delivery or repudiates with respect to a part or the whole, then with respect to any goods directly affected and, if the breach is of the whole contract (Section 2-612), then also with respect to the whole undelivered balance, the aggrieved seller may

(a) withhold delivery of such goods;

(b) stop delivery by any bailee as hereafter provided (Section 2-705);

(c) proceed under the next section respecting goods still unidentified to the contract;

(d) resell and recover damages as hereafter provided (Section 2-706);

(e) recover damages for non-acceptance (Section 2-708) or in a proper case the price (Section 2-709);

(f) cancel.

§ 2-704. Seller's Right to Identify Goods to the Contract Notwithstanding Breach or to Salvage Unfinished Goods.

(1) An aggrieved seller under the preceding section may

(a) identify to the contract conforming goods not already identified if at the time he learned of the breach they are in his possession or control;

(b) treat as the subject of resale goods which have demonstrably been intended for the particular contract even though those goods are unfinished.

(2) Where the goods are unfinished an aggrieved seller may in the exercise of reasonable commercial judgment for the purposes of avoiding loss and of effective realization either complete the manufacture and wholly identify the goods to the

contract or cease manufacture and resell for scrap or salvage value or proceed in any other reasonable manner.

§ 2-705. Seller's Stoppage of Delivery in Transit or Otherwise.

(1) The seller may stop delivery of goods in the possession of a carrier or other bailee when he discovers the buyer to be insolvent (Section 2-702) and may stop delivery of carload, truckload, planeload or larger shipments of express or freight when the buyer repudiates or fails to make a payment due before delivery or if for any other reason the seller has a right to withhold or reclaim the goods.

(2) As against such buyer the seller may stop delivery until

    (a) receipt of the goods by the buyer; or

    (b) acknowledgment to the buyer by any bailee of the goods except a carrier that the bailee holds the goods for the buyer; or

    (c) such acknowledgment to the buyer by a carrier by reshipment or as warehouseman; or

    (d) negotiation to the buyer of any negotiable document of title covering the goods.

(3)

    (a) To stop delivery the seller must so notify as to enable the bailee by reasonable diligence to prevent delivery of the goods.

    (b) After such notification the bailee must hold and deliver the goods according to the directions of the seller but the seller is liable to the bailee for any ensuing charges or damages.

    (c) If a negotiable document of title has been issued for goods the bailee is not obliged to obey a notification to stop until surrender of the document.

    (d) A carrier who has issued a non-negotiable bill of lading is not obliged to obey a notification to stop received from a person other than the consignor.

§ 2-706. Seller's Resale Including Contract for Resale.

(1) Under the conditions stated in Section 2-703 on seller's remedies, the seller may resell the goods concerned or the undelivered balance thereof. Where the resale is made in good faith and in a commercially reasonable manner the seller may recover the difference between the resale price and the contract price together with any incidental damages allowed under the provisions of this Article (Section 2-710), but less expenses saved in consequence of the buyer's breach.

(2) Except as otherwise provided in subsection (3) or unless otherwise agreed resale may be at public or private sale including sale by way of one or more contracts to sell or of identification to an existing contract of the seller. Sale may be as a unit or in parcels and at any time and place and on any terms but every aspect of the sale including the method, manner, time, place and terms must be commercially reasonable. The resale must be reasonably identified as referring to the broken contract, but it is not necessary that the goods be in existence or that any or all of them have been identified to the contract before the breach.

(3) Where the resale is at private sale the seller must give the buyer reasonable notification of his intention to resell.

(4) Where the resale is at public sale

    (a) only identified goods can be sold except where there is a recognized market for a public sale of futures in goods of the kind; and

    (b) it must be made at a usual place or market for public sale if one is reasonably available and except in the case of goods which are perishable or threaten to decline in value speedily the seller must give the buyer reasonable notice of the time and place of the resale; and

    (c) if the goods are not to be within the view of those attending the sale the notification of sale must state the place where the goods are located and provide for their reasonable inspection by prospective bidders; and

    (d) the seller may buy.

(5) A purchaser who buys in good faith at a resale takes the goods free of any rights of the original buyer even though the seller fails to comply with one or more of the requirements of this section.

(6) The seller is not accountable to the buyer for any profit made on any resale. A person in the position of a seller (Section 2-707) or a buyer who has rightfully rejected or justifiably revoked acceptance must account for any excess over the amount of his security interest, as hereinafter defined (subsection (3) of Section 2-711).

§ 2-707. "Person in the Position of a Seller."

(1) A "person in the position of a seller" includes as against a principal an agent who has paid or become responsible for the price of goods on behalf of his principal or anyone who otherwise holds a security interest or other right in goods similar to that of a seller.

(2) A person in the position of a seller may as provided in this Article withhold or stop delivery (Section 2-705) and resell (Section 2-706) and recover incidental damages (Section 2-710).

§ 2-708. Seller's Damages for Non-acceptance or Repudiation.

(1) Subject to subsection (2) and to the provisions of this Article with respect to proof of market price (Section 2-723), the measure of damages for non-acceptance or repudiation by the buyer is the difference between the market price at the time and place for tender and the unpaid contract price together with any incidental damages provided in this Article (Section 2-710), but less expenses saved in consequence of the buyer's breach.

(2) If the measure of damages provided in subsection (1) is inadequate to put the seller in as good a position as performance would have done then the measure of damages is the profit (including reasonable overhead) which the seller would have made from full performance by the buyer, together with any incidental damages provided in this Article (Section 2-710), due allowance for costs reasonably incurred and due credit for payments or proceeds of resale.

§ 2-709. Action for the Price.

(1) When the buyer fails to pay the price as it becomes due the seller may recover, together with any incidental damages under the next section, the price

    (a)   of goods accepted or of conforming goods lost or damaged within a commercially reasonable time after risk of their loss has passed to the buyer; and

    (b)   of goods identified to the contract if the seller is unable after reasonable effort to resell them at a reasonable price or the circumstances reasonably indicate that such effort will be unavailing.

(2) Where the seller sues for the price he must hold for the buyer any goods which have been identified to the contract and are still in his control except that if resale becomes possible he may resell them at any time prior to the collection of the judgment. The net proceeds of any such resale must be credited to the buyer and payment of the judgment entitles him to any goods not resold.

(3) After the buyer has wrongfully rejected or revoked acceptance of the goods or has failed to make a payment due or has repudiated (Section 2-610), a seller who is held not entitled to the price under this section shall nevertheless be awarded damages for non-acceptance under the preceding section.

§ 2-710. Seller's Incidental Damages.
Incidental damages to an aggrieved seller include any commercially reasonable charges, expenses or commissions incurred in stopping delivery, in the transportation, care and custody of goods after the buyer's breach, in connection with return or resale of the goods or otherwise resulting from the breach.

§ 2-711. Buyer's Remedies in General; Buyer's Security Interest in Rejected Goods.

(1) Where the seller fails to make delivery or repudiates or the buyer rightfully rejects or justifiably revokes acceptance then with respect to any goods involved, and with respect to the whole if the breach goes to the whole contract (Section 2-612), the buyer may cancel and whether or not he has done so may in addition to recovering so much of the price as has been paid

    (a)   "cover" and have damages under the next section as to all the goods affected whether or not they have been identified to the contract; or

    (b)   recover damages for non-delivery as provided in this Article (Section 2-713).

(2) Where the seller fails to deliver or repudiates the buyer may also

    (a)   if the goods have been identified recover them as provided in this Article (Section 2-502); or

    (b)   in a proper case obtain specific performance or replevy the goods as provided in this Article (Section 2-716).

(3) On rightful rejection or justifiable revocation of acceptance a buyer has a security interest in goods in his possession or control for any payments made on their price and any expenses reasonably incurred in their inspection, receipt, transportation, care and custody and may hold such goods and resell them in like manner as an aggrieved seller (Section 2-706).

§ 2-712. "Cover"; Buyer's Procurement of Substitute Goods.

(1) After a breach within the preceding section the buyer may "cover" by making in good faith and without unreasonable delay any reasonable purchase of or contract to purchase goods in substitution for those due from the seller.

(2) The buyer may recover from the seller as damages the difference between the cost of cover and the contract price together with any incidental or consequential damages as hereinafter defined (Section 2-715), but less expenses saved in consequence of the seller's breach.

(3) Failure of the buyer to effect cover within this section does not bar him from any other remedy.

§ 2-713. Buyer's Damages for Non-Delivery or Repudiation.

(1) Subject to the provisions of this Article with respect to proof of market price (Section 2-723), the measure of damages for non-delivery or repudiation by the seller is the difference between the market price at the time when the buyer learned of the breach and the contract price together with any incidental and consequential damages provided in this Article (Section 2-715), but less expenses saved in consequence of the seller's breach.

(2) Market price is to be determined as of the place for tender or, in cases of rejection after arrival or revocation of acceptance, as of the place of arrival.

§ 2-714. Buyer's Damages for Breach in Regard to Accepted Goods.

(1) Where the buyer has accepted goods and given notification (subsection (3) of Section 2-607) he may recover as damages for any non-conformity of tender the loss resulting in the ordinary course of events from the seller's breach as determined in any manner which is reasonable.

(2) The measure of damages for breach of warranty is the difference at the time and place of acceptance between the value of the goods accepted and the value they would have had if they had been warranted, unless special circumstances show proximate damages of a different amount.

(3) In a proper case any incidental and consequential damages under the next section may also be recovered.

§ 2-715. Buyer's Incidental and Consequential Damages.

(1) Incidental damages resulting from the seller's breach include expenses reasonably incurred in inspection, receipt, transportation and care and custody of goods rightfully rejected, any commercially reasonable charges, expenses or commissions in connection with effecting cover and any other reasonable expense incident to the delay or other breach.

(2) Consequential damages resulting from the seller's breach include

   (a)   any loss resulting from general or particular requirements and needs of which the seller at the time of contracting had reason to know and which could not reasonably be prevented by cover or otherwise; and

   (b)   injury to person or property proximately resulting from any breach of warranty.

§ 2-716. Buyer's Right to Specific Performance or Replevin.

(1) Specific performance may be decreed where the goods are unique or in other proper circumstances.

(2) The decree for specific performance may include such terms and conditions as to payment of the price, damages, or other relief as the court may deem just.

(3) The buyer has a right of replevin for goods identified to the contract if after reasonable effort he is unable to effect cover for such goods or the circumstances reasonably indicate that such effort will be unavailing or if the goods have been shipped under reservation and satisfaction of the security interest in them has been made or tendered.

§ 2-717. Deduction of Damages From the Price.
The buyer on notifying the seller of his intention to do so may deduct all or part of the damages resulting from any breach of the contract from any part of the price still due under the same contract.

§ 2-718. Liquidation or Limitation of Damages; Deposits.

(1) Damages for breach by either party may be liquidated in the agreement but only at an amount which is reasonable in the light of the anticipated or actual harm caused by the breach, the difficulties of proof of loss, and the inconvenience or nonfeasibility of otherwise obtaining an adequate rem-

edy. A term fixing unreasonably large liquidated damages is void as a penalty.

(2) Where the seller justifiably withholds delivery of goods because of the buyer's breach, the buyer is entitled to restitution of any amount by which the sum of his payments exceeds

    (a) the amount to which the seller is entitled by virtue of terms liquidating the seller's damages in accordance with subsection (1), or

    (b) in the absence of such terms, twenty per cent of the value of the total performance for which the buyer is obligated under the contract or $500, whichever is smaller.

(3) The buyer's right to restitution under subsection (2) is subject to offset to the extent that the seller establishes

    (a) a right to recover damages under the provisions of this Article other than subsection (1), and

    (b) the amount or value of any benefits received by the buyer directly or indirectly by reason of the contract.

(4) Where a seller has received payment in goods their reasonable value or the proceeds of their resale shall be treated as payments for the purposes of subsection (2); but if the seller has notice of the buyer's breach before reselling goods received in part performance, his resale is subject to the conditions laid down in this Article on resale by an aggrieved seller (Section 2-706).

§ 2-719. Contractual Modification or Limitation of Remedy.

(1) Subject to the provisions of subsections (2) and (3) of this section and of the preceding section on liquidation and limitation of damages,

    (a) the agreement may provide for remedies in addition to or in substitution for those provided in this Article and may limit or alter the measure of damages recoverable under this Article, as by limiting the buyer's remedies to return of the goods and repayment of the price or to repair and replacement of non-conforming goods or parts; and

    (b) resort to a remedy as provided is optional unless the remedy is expressly agreed to be exclusive, in which case it is the sole remedy.

(2) Where circumstances cause an exclusive or limited remedy to fail of its essential purpose, remedy may be had as provided in this Act.

(3) Consequential damages may be limited or excluded unless the limitation or exclusion is unconscionable. Limitation of consequential damages for injury to the person in the case of consumer goods is prima facie unconscionable but limitation of damages where the loss is commercial is not.

§ 2-720. Effect of "Cancellation" or "Rescission" on Claims for Antecedent Breach.

Unless the contrary intention clearly appears, expressions of "cancellation" or "rescission" of the contract or the like shall not be construed as a renunciation or discharge of any claim in damages for an antecedent breach.

§ 2-721. Remedies for Fraud.

Remedies for material misrepresentation or fraud include all remedies available under this Article for non-fraudulent breach. Neither rescission or a claim for rescission of the contract for sale nor rejection or return of the goods shall bar or be deemed inconsistent with a claim for damages or other remedy.

§ 2-722. Who Can Sue Third Parties for Injury to Goods.

Where a third party so deals with goods which have been identified to a contract for sale as to cause actionable injury to a party to that contract.

    (a) a right of action against the third party is in either party to the contract for sale who has title to or a security interest or a special property or an insurable interest in the goods; and if the goods have been destroyed or converted a right of action is also in the party who either bore the risk of loss under the contract for sale or has since the injury assumed that risk as against the other;

    (b) if at the time of the injury the party plaintiff did not bear the risk of loss as against the other party to the contract for sale and there is no arrangement between them for disposition of the recovery, his suit or settlement is, subject to his own interest, as a fiduciary for the other party to the contract;

    (c) either party may with the consent of the other sue for the benefit of whom it may concern.

§ 2-723. Proof of Market Price: Time and Place.

(1) If an action based on anticipatory repudiation comes to trial before the time for performance with respect to some or all of the goods, any damages based on market price (Section 2-708 or Section 2-713) shall be determined according to the price of such goods prevailing at the time when the aggrieved party learned of the repudiation.

(2) If evidence of a price prevailing at the times or places described in this Article is not readily available the price prevailing within any reasonable time before or after the time described or at any other place which in commercial judgment or under usage of trade would serve as a reasonable substitute for the one described may be used, making any proper allowance for the cost of transporting the goods to or from such other place.

(3) Evidence of a relevant price prevailing at a time or place other than the one described in this Article offered by one party is not admissible unless and until he has given the other party such notice as the court finds sufficient to prevent unfair surprise.

§ 2-724. Admissibility of Market Quotations.

Whenever the prevailing price or value of any goods regularly bought and sold in any established commodity market is in issue, reports in official publications or trade journals or in newspapers or periodicals of general circulation published as the reports of such market shall be admissible in evidence. The circumstances of the preparation of such a report may be shown to affect its weight but not its admissibility.

§ 2-725. Statute of Limitations in Contracts for Sale.

(1) An action for breach of any contract for sale must be commenced within four years after the cause of action has accrued. By the original agreement the parties may reduce the period of limitation to not less than one year but may not extend it.

(2) A cause of action accrues when the breach occurs, regardless of the aggrieved party's lack of knowledge of the breach. A breach of warranty occurs when tender of delivery is made, except that where a warranty explicitly extends to future performance of the goods and discovery of the breach must await the time of such performance the cause of action accrues when the breach is or should have been discovered.

(3) Where an action commenced within the time limited by subsection (1) is so terminated as to leave available a remedy by another action for the same breach such other action may be commenced after the expiration of the time limited and within six months after the termination of the first action unless the termination resulted from voluntary discontinuance or from dismissal for failure or neglect to prosecute.

(4) This section does not alter the law on tolling of the statute of limitations nor does it apply to causes of action which have accrued before this Act becomes effective.

ARTICLE 3. COMMERCIAL PAPER

Part 1. Short Title, Form and Interpretation

§ 3-101. Short Title.   This Article shall be known and may be cited as Uniform Commercial Code—Commercial Paper.

§ 3-102. Definitions and Index of Definitions.

(1) In this Article unless the context otherwise requires

   (a)   "Issue" means the first delivery of an instrument to a holder or a remitter.

   (b)   An "order" is a direction to pay and must be more than an authorization or request. It must identify the person to pay with reasonable certainty. It may be addressed to one or more such persons jointly or in the alternative but not in succession.

   (c)   A "promise" is an undertaking to pay and must be more than an acknowledgment of an obligation.

   (d)   "Secondary party" means a drawer or endorser.

   (e)   "Instrument" means a negotiable instrument.

(2) Other definitions applying to this Article and the sections in which they appear are:

"Acceptance." Section 3-410.
"Accommodation party." Section 3-415.
"Alteration." Section 3-407.
"Certificate of deposit." Section 3-104.
"Certification." Section 3-411.
"Check." Section 3-104.
"Definite time." Section 3-109.
"Dishonor." Section 3-507.
"Draft." Section 3-104.
"Holder in due course." Section 3-302.

"Negotiation." Section 3-202.

"Note." Section 3-104.

"Notice of dishonor." Section 3-508.

"On demand." Section 3-108.

"Presentment." Section 3-504.

"Protest." Section 3-509.

"Restrictive Indorsement." Section 3-205.

"Signature." Section 3-401.

(3) The following definitions in other Articles apply to this Article:

"Account." Section 4-104.

"Banking Day." Section 4-104.

"Clearing house." Section 4-104.

"Collecting bank." Section 4-105.

"Customer." Section 4-104.

"Depositary Bank." Section 4-105.

"Documentary Draft." Section 4-104.

"Intermediary Bank." Section 4-105.

"Item." Section 4-104.

"Midnight deadline." Section 4-104.

"Payor bank." Section 4-105.

(4) In addition Article 1 contains general definitions and principles of construction and interpretation applicable throughout this Article.

§ 3-103. Limitations on Scope of Article.

(1) This Article does not apply to money, documents of title or investment securities.

(2) The provisions of this Article are subject to the provisions of the Article on Bank Deposits and Collections (Article 4) and Secured Transactions (Article 9).

§ 3-104. Form of Negotiable Instruments; "Draft"; "Check"; "Certificate of Deposit"; "Note."

(1) Any writing to be a negotiable instrument within this Article must

(a)   be signed by the maker or drawer; and

(b)   contain an unconditional promise or order to pay a sum certain in money and no other promise, order, obligation or power given by the maker or drawer except as authorized by this Article; and

(c)   be payable on demand or at a definite time; and

(d)   be payable to order or to bearer.

(2) A writing which complies with the requirements of this section is

(a)   a "draft" ("bill of exchange") if it is an order;

(b)   a "check" if it is a draft drawn on a bank and payable on demand;

(c)   a "certificate of deposit" if it is an acknowledgment by a bank of receipt of money with an engagement to repay it;

(d)   a "note" if it is a promise other than a certificate of deposit.

(3) As used in other Articles of this Act, and as the context may require, the terms "draft," "check," "certificate of deposit" and "note" may refer to instruments which are not negotiable within this Article as well as to instruments which are so negotiable.

§ 3-105. When Promise or Order Unconditional.

(1) A promise or order otherwise unconditional is not made conditional by the fact that the instrument

(a)   is subject to implied or constructive conditions; or

(b)   states its consideration, whether performed or promised, or the transaction which gave rise to the instrument, or that the promise or order is made or the instrument matures in accordance with or "as per" such transaction; or

(c)   refers to or states that it arises out of a separate agreement or refers to a separate agreement for rights as to prepayment or acceleration; or

(d)   states that it is drawn under a letter of credit; or

(e)   states that it is secured, whether by mortgage, reservation of title or otherwise; or

(f)   indicates a particular account to be debited or any other fund or source from which reimbursement is expected; or

(g)   is limited to payment out of a particular fund or the proceeds of a particular source, if the instrument is issued by a government or governmental agency or unit; or

(h)   is limited to payment out of the entire assets of a partnership, unincorporated association, trust or estate by or on behalf of which the instrument is issued.

(2) A promise or order is not unconditional if the instrument

(a)   states that it is subject to or governed by any other agreement; or

(b)   states that it is to be paid only out of a particular fund or source except as provided in this section.

§ 3-106. Sum Certain.

(1) The sum payable is a sum certain even though it is to be paid

    (a)   with stated interest or by stated installments; or

    (b)   with stated different rates of interest before and after default or a specified date; or

    (c)   with a stated discount or addition if paid before or after the date fixed for payment; or

    (d)   with exchange or less exchange, whether at a fixed rate or at the current rate; or

    (e)   with costs of collection or an attorney's fee or both upon default.

(2) Nothing in this section shall validate any term which is otherwise illegal.

§ 3-107. Money.

(1) An instrument is payable in money if the medium of exchange in which it is payable is money at the time the instrument is made. An instrument payable in "currency" or "current funds" is payable in money.

(2) A promise or order to pay a sum stated in a foreign currency is for a sum certain in money and, unless a different medium of payment is specified in the instrument, may be satisfied by payment of that number of dollars which the stated foreign currency will purchase at the buying sight rate for that currency on the day on which the instrument is payable or, if payable on demand, on the day of demand. If such an instrument specifies a foreign currency as the medium of payment the instrument is payable in that currency.

§ 3-108. Payable on Demand. Instruments payable on demand include those payable at sight or on presentation and those in which no time for payment is stated.

§ 3-109. Definite Time.

(1) An instrument is payable at a definite time if by its terms it is payable

    (a)   on or before a stated date or at a fixed period after a stated date; or

    (b)   at a fixed period after sight; or

    (c)   at a definite time subject to any acceleration; or

    (d)   at a definite time subject to extension at the option of the holder, or to extension to a further definite time at the option of the maker or acceptor or automatically upon or after a specified act or event.

(2) An instrument which by its terms is otherwise payable only upon an act or event uncertain as to time of occurrence is not payable at a definite time even though the act or event has occurred.

§ 3-110. Payable to Order.

(1) An instrument is payable to order when by its terms it is payable to the order or assigns of any person therein specified with reasonable certainty, or to him or his order, or when it is conspicuously designated on its face as "exchange" or the like and names a payee. It may be payable to the order of

    (a)   the maker or drawer; or

    (b)   the drawee; or

    (c)   a payee who is not maker, drawer or drawee; or

    (d)   two or more payees together or in the alternative; or

    (e)   an estate, trust or fund, in which case it is payable to the order of the representative of such estate, trust or fund or his successors; or

    (f)   an office, or an officer by his title as such in which case it is payable to the principal but the incumbent of the office or his successors may act as if he or they were the holder; or

    (g)   a partnership or unincorporated association, in which case it is payable to the partnership or association and may be indorsed or transferred by any person thereto authorized.

(2) An instrument not payable to order is not made so payable by such words as "payable upon return of this instrument properly indorsed."

(3) An instrument made payable both to order and to bearer is payable to order unless the bearer words are handwritten or typewritten.

§ 3-111. Payable to Bearer. An instrument is payable to bearer when by its terms it is payable to

    (a)   bearer or the order of bearer; or

    (b)   a specified person or bearer; or

    (c)   "cash" or the order of "cash," or any other indication which does not purport to designate a specific payee.

§ 3-112. Terms and Omissions Not Affecting Negotiability.

(1) The negotiability of an instrument is not affected by

(a) the omission of a statement of any consideration or of the place where the instrument is drawn or payable; or

(b) a statement that collateral has been given to secure obligations either on the instrument or otherwise of an obligor on the instrument or that in case of default on those obligations the holder may realize on or dispose of the collateral; or

(c) a promise or power to maintain or protect collateral or to give additional collateral; or

(d) a term authorizing a confession of judgment on the instrument if it is not paid when due; or

(e) a term purporting to waive the benefit of any law intended for the advantage or protection of any obligor; or

(f) a term in a draft providing that the payee by indorsing or cashing it acknowledges full satisfaction of an obligation of the drawer; or

(g) A statement in a draft drawn in a set of parts (Section 3-801) to the effect that the order is effective only if no other part has been honored.

(2) Nothing in this section shall validate any term which is otherwise illegal.

§ 3-113. Seal.

An instrument otherwise negotiable is within this Article even though it is under a seal.

§ 3-114. Date, Antedating, Postdating.

(1) The negotiability of an instrument is not affected by the fact that it is undated, antedated or postdated.

(2) Where an instrument is antedated or postdated the time when it is payable is determined by the stated date if the instrument is payable on demand or at a fixed period after date.

(3) Where the instrument or any signature thereon is dated, the date is presumed to be correct.

§ 3-115. Incomplete Instruments.

(1) When a paper whose contents at the time of signing show that it is intended to become an instrument is signed while still incomplete in any necessary respect it cannot be enforced until completed, but when it is completed in accordance with authority given it is effective as completed.

(2) If the completion is unauthorized the rules as to material alteration apply (Section 3-407), even though the paper was not delivered by the maker or drawer; but the burden of establishing that any completion is unauthorized is on the party so asserting.

§ 3-116. Instruments Payable to Two or More Persons.

An instrument payable to the order of two or more persons

(a) if in the alternative is payable to any one of them and may be negotiated, discharged or enforced by any of them who has possession of it;

(b) if not in the alternative is payable to all of them and may be negotiated, discharged or enforced only by all of them.

§ 3-117. Instruments Payable With Words of Description.

An instrument made payable to a named person with the addition of words describing him

(a) as agent or officer of a specified person is payable to his principal but the agent or officer may act as if he were the holder;

(b) as any other fiduciary for a specified person or purpose is payable to the payee and may be negotiated, discharged or enforced by him;

(c) in any other manner is payable to the payee unconditionally and the additional words are without effect on subsequent parties.

§ 3-118. Ambiguous Terms and Rules of Construction.

The following rules apply to every instrument:

(a) Where there is doubt whether the instrument is a draft or a note the holder may treat it as either. A draft drawn on the drawer is effective as a note.

(b) Handwritten terms control typewritten and printed terms, and typewritten control printed.

(c) Words control figures except that if the words are ambiguous figures control.

(d) Unless otherwise specified a provision for interest means interest at the judgment rate at the place of payment from the date of the instrument, or if it is undated from the date of issue.

(e)   Unless the instrument otherwise specifies two or more persons who sign as maker, acceptor or drawer or indorser and as a part of the same transaction are jointly and severally liable even though the instrument contains such words as "I promise to pay."

(f)   Unless otherwise specified consent to extension authorizes a single extension for not longer than the original period. A consent to extension, expressed in the instrument, is binding on secondary parties and accommodation makers. A holder may not exercise his option to extend an instrument over the objection of a maker or acceptor or other party who in accordance with Section 3-604 tenders full payment when the instrument is due.

§ 3-119. Other Writings Affecting Instrument.

(1) As between the obligor and his immediate obligee or any transferee the terms of an instrument may be modified or affected by any other written agreement executed as a part of the same transaction, except that a holder in due course is not affected by any limitation of his rights arising out of the separate written agreement if he had no notice of the limitation when he took the instrument.

(2) A separate agreement does not affect the negotiability of an instrument.

§ 3-120. Instruments "Payable Through" Bank.

An instrument which states that it is "payable through" a bank or the like designates that bank as a collecting bank to make presentment but does not of itself authorize the bank to pay the instrument.

§ 3-121. Instruments payable at Bank.

Note: If this Act is introduced in the Congress of the United States this section should be omitted. (States to select either alternative.)

Alternative A   A note or acceptance which states that it is payable at a bank is the equivalent of a draft drawn on the bank payable when it falls due out of any funds of the maker or acceptor in current account or otherwise available for such payment.

Alternative B   A note or acceptance which states that it is payable at a bank is not of itself an order or authorization to the bank to pay it.

§ 3-122. Accrual of Cause of Action.

(1) A cause of action against a maker or an acceptor accrues

(a)   in the case of a time instrument on the day after maturity;

(b)   in the case of a demand instrument upon its date or, if no date is stated, on the date of issue.

(2) A cause of action against the obligor of a demand or time certificate of deposit accrues upon demand, but demand on a time certificate may not be made until on or after the date of maturity.

(3) A cause of action against a drawer of a draft or an indorser of any instrument accrues upon demand following dishonor of the instrument. Notice of dishonor is a demand.

(4) Unless an instrument provides otherwise, interest runs at the rate provided by law for a judgment

(a)   in the case of a maker, acceptor or other primary obligor of a demand instrument, from the date of demand;

(b)   in all other cases from the date of accrual of the cause of action.

Part 2. Transfer and Negotiation

§ 3-201. Transfer: Right to Indorsement.

(1) Transfer of an instrument vests in the transferee such rights as the transferor has therein, except that a transferee who has himself been a party to any fraud or illegality affecting the instrument or who as a prior holder had notice of a defense or claim against it cannot improve his position by taking from a later holder in due course.

(2) A transfer of a security interest in an instrument vests the foregoing rights in the transferee to the extent of the interest transferred.

(3) Unless otherwise agreed any transfer for value of an instrument not then payable to bearer gives the transferee the specifically enforceable right to have the unqualified indorsement of the transferor. Negotiation takes effect only when the indorsement is made and until that time there is no presumption that the transferee is the owner.

§ 3-202. Negotiation.

(1) Negotiation is the transfer of an instrument in such form that the transferee becomes a holder. If the instrument is payable to order it is negotiated by delivery with any necessary indorsement; if payable to bearer it is negotiated by delivery.

(2) An indorsement must be written by or on behalf of the holder and on the instrument or on a paper so firmly affixed thereto as to become a part thereof.

(3) An indorsement is effective for negotiation only when it conveys the entire instrument or any unpaid residue. If it purports to be of less it operates only as a partial assignment.

(4) Words of assignment, condition, waiver, guaranty, limitation or disclaimer of liability and the like accompanying an indorsement do not affect its character as an indorsement.

§ 3-203. Wrong or Misspelled Name. Where an instrument is made payable to a person under a misspelled name or one other than his own he may indorse in that name or his own or both; but signature in both names may be required by a person paying or giving value for the instrument.

§ 3-204. Special Indorsement; Blank Indorsement.

(1) A special indorsement specifies the person to whom or to whose order it makes the instrument payable. Any instrument specially indorsed becomes payable to the order of the special indorsee and may be further negotiated only by his indorsement.

(2) An indorsement in blank specifies no particular indorsee and may consist of a mere signature. An instrument payable to order and indorsed in blank becomes payable to bearer and may be negotiated by delivery alone until specially indorsed.

(3) The holder may convert a blank indorsement into a special indorsement by writing over the signature of the indorser in blank any contract consistent with the character of the indorsement.

§ 3-205. Restrictive Indorsement. An indorsement is restrictive which either

    (a)   is conditional; or

    (b)   purports to prohibit further transfer of the instrument; or

    (c)   includes the words "for collection," "for deposit," "pay any bank," or like terms signifying a purpose of deposit or collection; or

    (d)   otherwise states that it is for the benefit or use of the indorser or of another person.

§ 3-206. Effect of Restrictive Indorsement.

(1) No restrictive indorsement prevents further transfer or negotiation of the instrument.

(2) An intermediary bank, or a payor bank which is not the depositary bank, is neither given notice nor otherwise affected by a restrictive indorsement of any person except the bank's immediate transferor or the person presenting for payment.

(3) Except for an intermediary bank, any transferee under an indorsement which is conditional or includes the words "for collection," "for deposit," "pay any bank," or like terms (subparagraphs (a) and (c) of Section 3-205) must pay or apply any value given by him for or on the security of the instrument consistently with the indorsement and to the extent that he does so he becomes a holder for value. In addition such transferee is a holder in due course if he otherwise complies with the requirements of Section 3-302 on what constitutes a holder in due course.

(4) The first taker under an indorsement for the benefit of the indorser or another person (subparagraph (d) of Section 3-205) must pay or apply any value given by him for or on the security of the instrument consistently with the indorsement and to the extent that he does so he becomes a holder for value. In addition such taker is a holder in due course if he otherwise complies with the requirements of Section 3-302 on what constitutes a holder in due course. A later holder for value is neither given notice nor otherwise affected by such restrictive indorsement unless he has knowledge that a fiduciary or other person has negotiated the instrument in any transaction for his own benefit or otherwise in breach of duty (subsection (2) of Section 3-304).

§ 3-207. Negotiation Effective Although It May Be Rescinded.

(1) Negotiation is effective to transfer the instrument although the negotiation is

    (a)   made by an infant, a corporation exceeding its powers, or any other person without capacity; or

    (b)   obtained by fraud, duress or mistake of any kind; or

    (c)   part of an illegal transaction; or

    (d)   made in breach of duty.

(2) Except as against a subsequent holder in due course such negotiation is in an appropriate case subject to rescission, the declaration of a constructive trust or any other remedy permitted by law.

§ 3-208. Reacquisition. Where an instrument is returned to or reacquired by a prior party he may cancel any indorsement which is not necessary to his title and reissue or further negotiate the instrument, but any intervening party is discharged as against the reacquiring party and subsequent holders not in due course and if his indorsement has been cancelled is discharged as against subsequent holders in due course as well.

Part 3. Rights of a Holder

§ 3-301. Rights of a Holder. The holder of an instrument whether or not he is the owner may transfer or negotiate it and, except as otherwise provided in Section 3-603 on payment or satisfaction, discharge it or enforce payment in his own name.

§ 3-302. Holder in Due Course.

(1) A holder in due course is a holder who takes the instrument

   (a)   for value; and
   (b)   in good faith; and
   (c)   without notice that it is overdue or has been dishonored or of any defense against or claim to it on the part of any person.

(2) A payee may be a holder in due course.

(3) A holder does not become a holder in due course of an instrument:

   (a)   by purchase of it at judicial sale or by taking it under legal process; or
   (b)   by acquiring it in taking over an estate; or
   (c)   by purchasing it as part of a bulk transaction not in regular course of business of the transferor.

(4) A purchaser of a limited interest can be a holder in due course only to the extent of the interest purchased.

§ 3-303. Taking for Value. A holder takes the instrument for value

   (a)   To the extent that the agreed consideration has been performed or that he acquires a security interest in or a lien on the instrument otherwise than by legal process; or
   (b)   when he takes the instrument in payment of or as security for an antecedent claim against any person whether or not the claim is due; or
   (c)   when he gives a negotiable instrument for it or makes an irrevocable commitment to a third person.

§ 3-304. Notice to Purchaser.

(1) The purchaser has notice of a claim or defense if

   (a)   the instrument is so incomplete, bears such visible evidence of forgery or alteration, or is otherwise so irregular as to call into question its validity, terms or ownership or to create an ambiguity as to the party to pay; or
   (b)   the purchaser has notice that the obligation of any party is voidable in whole or in part, or that all parties have been discharged.

(2) The purchaser has notice of a claim against the instrument when he has knowledge that a fiduciary has negotiated the instrument in payment of or as security for his own debt or in any transaction for his own benefit or otherwise in breach of duty.

(3) The purchaser has notice that an instrument is overdue if he has reason to know

   (a)   that any part of the principal amount is overdue or that there is an uncured default in payment of another instrument of the same series; or
   (b)   that acceleration of the instrument has been made; or
   (c)   that he is taking a demand instrument after demand has been made or more than a reasonable length of time after its issue. A reasonable time for a check drawn and payable within the states and territories of the United States and the District of Columbia is presumed to be thirty days.

(4) Knowledge of the following facts does not of itself give the purchaser notice of a defense or claim

   (a)   that the instrument is antedated or postdated;
   (b)   that it was issued or negotiated in return for an executory promise or accompanied by a separate agreement, unless the purchaser has notice that a defense or claim has arisen from the terms thereof;
   (c)   that any party has signed for accommodation;
   (d)   that an incomplete instrument has been completed, unless the purchaser has notice of any improper completion;
   (e)   that any person negotiating the instrument is or was a fiduciary;
   (f)   that there has been default in payment of interest on the instrument or in payment of any other instrument, except one of the same series.

(5) The filing or recording of a document does not of itself constitute notice within the provisions of this Article to a person who would otherwise be a holder in due course.

(6) To be effective notice must be received at such time and in such manner as to give a reasonable opportunity to act on it.

§ 3-305. Rights of a Holder in Due Course.
To the extent that a holder is a holder in due course he takes the instrument free from

(1) all claims to it on the part of any person; and

(2) all defenses of any party to the instrument with whom the holder has not dealt except

    (a)   infancy, to the extent that it is a defense to a simple contract; and

    (b)   such other incapacity, or duress, or illegality of the transaction, as renders the obligation of the party a nullity; and

    (c)   such misrepresentation as has induced the party to sign the instrument with neither knowledge nor reasonable opportunity to obtain knowledge of its character or its essential terms; and

    (d)   discharge in insolvency proceedings; and

    (e)   any other discharge of which the holder has notice when he takes the instrument.

§ 3-306. Rights of One Not Holder in Due Course.
Unless he has the rights of a holder in due course any person takes the instrument subject to

    (a)   all valid claims to it on the part of any person; and

    (b)   all defenses of any party which would be available in an action on a simple contract; and

    (c)   the defenses of want or failure of consideration, non-performance of any condition precedent, non-delivery, or delivery for a special purpose (Section 3-408); and

    (d)   the defense that he or a person through whom he holds the instrument acquired it by theft, or that payment or satisfaction to such holder would be inconsistent with the terms of a restrictive indorsement. The claim of any third person to the instrument is not otherwise available as a defense to any party liable thereon unless the third person himself defends the action for such party.

§ 3-307. Burden of Establishing Signatures, Defenses and Due Course.
(1) Unless specifically denied in the pleadings each signature on an instrument is admitted. When the effectiveness of a signature is put in issue

    (a)   the burden of establishing it is on the party claiming under the signature; but

    (b)   the signature is presumed to be genuine or authorized except where the action is to enforce the obligation of a purported signer who has died or become incompetent before proof is required.

(2) When signatures are admitted or established, production of the instrument entitles a holder to recover on it unless the defendant establishes a defense.

(3) After it is shown that a defense exists a person claiming the rights of a holder in due course has the burden of establishing that he or some person under whom he claims is in all respects a holder in due course.

Part 4. Liability of Parties

§ 3-401. Signature.
(1) No person is liable on an instrument unless his signature appears thereon.

(2) A signature is made by use of any name, including any trade or assumed name, upon an instrument, or by any word or mark used in lieu of a written signature.

§ 3-402. Signature in Ambiguous Capacity.
Unless the instrument clearly indicates that a signature is made in some other capacity it is an indorsement.

§ 3-403. Signature by Authorized Representative.
(1) A signature may be made by an agent or other representative, and his authority to make it may be established as in other cases of representation. No particular form of appointment is necessary to establish such authority.

(2) An authorized representative who signs his own name to an instrument

    (a)   is personally obligated if the instrument neither names the person represented nor shows that the representative signed in a representative capacity;

    (b)   except as otherwise established between the immediate parties, is personally obligated if the instrument names the person represented but does not show that the representative signed in a representative capacity, or if the instrument does not name the person represented but does show that the representative signed in a representative capacity.

(3) Except as otherwise established the name of an organization preceded or followed by the name and office of an authorized individual is a signature made in a representative capacity.

§ 3-404. Unauthorized Signatures.

(1) Any unauthorized signature is wholly inoperative as that of the person whose name is signed unless he ratifies it or is precluded from denying it; but it operates as the signature of the unauthorized signer in favor of any person who in good faith pays the instrument or takes it for value.

(2) Any unauthorized signature may be ratified for all purposes of this Article. Such ratification does not of itself affect any rights of the person ratifying against the actual signer.

§ 3-405. Impostors; Signature in Name of Payee.

(1) An indorsement by any person in the name of a named payee is effective if

(a) an impostor by use of the mails or otherwise has induced the maker or drawer to issue the instrument to him or his confederate in the name of the payee; or

(b) a person signing as or on behalf of a maker or drawer intends the payee to have no interest in the instrument; or

(c) an agent or employee of the maker or drawer has supplied him with the name of the payee intending the latter to have no such interest.

(2) Nothing in this section shall affect the criminal or civil liability of the person so indorsing.

§ 3-406. Negligence Contributing to Alteration or Unauthorized Signature.

Any person who by his negligence substantially contributes to a material alteration of the instrument or to the making of an unauthorized signature is precluded from asserting the alteration or lack of authority against a holder in due course or against a drawee or other payor who pays the instrument in good faith and in accordance with the reasonable commercial standards of the drawee's or payor's business.

§ 3-407. Alteration.

(1) Any alteration of an instrument is material which changes the contract of any party thereto in any respect, including any such change in

(a) the number of relations of the parties; or

(b) an incomplete instrument, by completing it otherwise than as authorized; or

(c) the writing as signed, by adding to it or by removing any part of it.

(2) As against any person other than a subsequent holder in due course.

(a) alteration by the holder which is both fraudulent and material discharges any party whose contract is thereby changed unless that party assents or is precluded from asserting the defense;

(b) no other alteration discharges any party and the instrument may be enforced according to its original tenor, or as to incomplete instruments according to the authority given.

(3) A subsequent holder in due course may in all cases enforce the instrument according to its original tenor, and when an incomplete instrument has been completed, he may enforce it as completed.

§ 3-408. Consideration.

Want or failure of consideration is a defense as against any person not having the rights of a holder in due course (Section 3-305), except that no consideration is necessary for an instrument or obligation thereon given in payment of or as security for an antecedent obligation of any kind. Nothing in this section shall be taken to displace any statute outside this Act under which a promise is enforceable notwithstanding lack or failure of consideration. Partial failure of consideration is a defense pro tanto whether or not the failure is in an ascertained or liquidated amount.

§ 3-409. Draft Not an Assignment.

(1) A check or other draft does not of itself operate as an assignment of any funds in the hands of the drawee available for its payment, and the drawee is not liable on the instrument until he accepts it.

(2) Nothing in this section shall affect any liability in contract, tort or otherwise arising from any letter of credit or other obligation or representation which is not an acceptance.

§ 3-410. Definition and Operation of Acceptance.

(1) Acceptance is the drawee's signed engagement to honor the draft as presented. It must be written on the draft, and may consist of his signature alone. It becomes operative when completed by delivery or notification.

(2) A draft may be accepted although it has not been signed by the drawer or is otherwise incomplete or is overdue or has been dishonored.

(3) Where the draft is payable at a fixed period after sight and the acceptor fails to date his acceptance the holder may complete it by supplying a date in good faith.

§ 3-411. Certification of a Check.

(1) Certification of a check is acceptance. Where a holder procures certification the drawer and all prior indorsers are discharged.

(2) Unless otherwise agreed a bank has no obligation to certify a check.

(3) A bank may certify a check before returning it for lack of proper indorsement. If it does so the drawer is discharged.

§ 3-412. Acceptance Varying Draft.

(1) Where the drawee's proffered acceptance in any manner varies the draft as presented the holder may refuse the acceptance and treat the draft as dishonored in which case the drawee is entitled to have his acceptance cancelled.

(2) The terms of the draft are not varied by an acceptance to pay at any particular bank or place in the United States, unless the acceptance states that the draft is to be paid only at such bank or place.

(3) Where the holder assents to an acceptance varying the terms of the draft each drawer and indorser who does not affirmatively assent is discharged.

§ 3-413. Contract of Maker, Drawer and Acceptor.

(1) The maker or acceptor engages that he will pay the instrument according to its tenor at the time of his engagement or as completed pursuant to Section 3-115 or incomplete instruments.

(2) The drawer engages that upon dishonor of the draft and any necessary notice of dishonor or protest he will pay the amount of the draft to the holder or to any indorser who takes it up. The drawer may disclaim this liability by drawing without recourse.

(3) By making, drawing or accepting the party admits as against all subsequent parties including the drawee the existence of the payee and his then capacity to indorse.

§ 3-414. Contract of Indorser; Order of Liability.

(1) Unless the indorsement otherwise specifies (as by such words as "without recourse") every indorser engages that upon dishonor and any necessary notice of dishonor and protest he will pay the instrument according to its tenor at the time of his indorsement to the holder or to any subsequent indorser who takes it up, even though the indorser who takes it up was not obligated to do so.

(2) Unless they otherwise agree indorsers are liable to one another in the order in which they indorse, which is presumed to be the order in which their signatures appear on the instrument.

§ 3-415. Contract of Accommodation Party.

(1) An accommodation party is one who signs the instrument in any capacity for the purpose of lending his name to another party to it.

(2) When the instrument has been taken for value before it is due the accommodation party is liable in the capacity in which he has signed even though the taker knows of the accommodation.

(3) As against a holder in due course and without notice of the accommodation oral proof of the accommodation is not admissible to give the accommodation party the benefit of discharges dependent on his character as such. In other cases the accommodation character may be shown by oral proof.

(4) An indorsement which shows that it is not in the chain of title is notice of its accommodation character.

(5) An accommodation party is not liable to the party accommodated, and if he pays the instrument has a right of recourse on the instrument against such party.

§ 3-416. Contract of Guarantor.

(1) "Payment guaranteed" or equivalent words added to a signature mean that the signer engages that if the instrument is not paid when due he will pay it according to its tenor without resort by the holder to any other party.

(2) "Collection guaranteed" or equivalent words added to a signature mean that the signer engages that if the instrument is not paid when due he will pay it according to its tenor, but only after the holder has reduced his claim against the maker or acceptor to judgment and execution has been returned unsatisfied, or after the maker or acceptor has become insolvent or it is otherwise apparent that it is useless to proceed against him.

(3) Words of guaranty which do not otherwise specify guarantee payment.

(4) No words of guaranty added to the signature of a sole maker or acceptor affect his liability on the instrument. Such words added to the signature of one of two or more makers or acceptors create a

presumption that the signature is for the accommodation of the others.

(5) When words of guaranty are used presentment, notice of dishonor and protest are not necessary to charge the user.

(6) Any guaranty written on the instrument is enforcible notwithstanding any statute of frauds.

§ 3-417. Warranties on Presentment and Transfer.

(1) Any person who obtains payment or acceptance and any prior transferor warrants to a person who in good faith pays or accepts that

    (a)   he has a good title to the instrument or is authorized to obtain payment or acceptance on behalf of one who has a good title; and

    (b)   he has no knowledge that the signature of the maker or drawer is unauthorized, except that this warranty is not given by a holder in due course acting in good faith

        (i)   to a maker with respect to the maker's own signature; or

        (ii)   to a drawer with respect to the drawer's own signature, whether or not the drawer is also the drawee; or

        (iii)   to an acceptor of a draft if the holder in due course took the draft after the acceptance or obtained the acceptance without knowledge and the drawer's signature was unauthorized; and

    (c)   the instrument has not been materially altered, except that this warranty is not given by a holder in due course acting in good faith

        (i)   to the maker of a note; or

        (ii)   to the drawer of a draft whether or not the drawer is also the drawee; or

        (iii)   to the acceptor of a draft with respect to an alteration made prior to the acceptance if the holder in due course took the draft after the acceptance, even though the acceptance provided "payable as originally drawn" or equivalent terms; or

        (iv)   to the acceptor of a draft with respect to an alteration made after the acceptance.

(2) Any person who transfers an instrument and receives consideration warrants to his transferee and if the transfer is by indorsement to any subsequent holder who takes the instrument in good faith that

    (a)   he has a good title to the instrument or is authorized to obtain payment or acceptance on behalf of one who has a good title and the transfer is otherwise rightful; and

    (b)   all signatures are genuine or authorized; and

    (c)   the instrument has not been materially altered; and

    (d)   no defense of any party is good against him; and

    (e)   he has no knowledge of any insolvency proceeding instituted with respect to the maker or acceptor or the drawer of an unaccepted instrument.

(3) By transferring "without recourse" the transferor limits the obligation stated in subsection (2)(d) to a warranty that he has no knowledge of such a defense.

(4) A selling agent or broker who does not disclose the fact that he is acting only as such gives the warranties provided in this section, but if he makes such disclosure warrants only his good faith and authority.

§ 3-418. Finality of Payment or Acceptance.

Except for recovery of bank payments as provided in the Article on Bank Deposits and Collections (Article 4) and except for liability for breach of warranty on presentment under the preceding section, payment or acceptance of any instrument is final in favor of a holder in due course, or a person who has in good faith changed his position in reliance on the payment.

§ 3-419. Conversion of Instrument; Innocent Representative.

(1) An instrument is converted when

    (a)   a drawee to whom it is delivered for acceptance refuses to return it on demand; or

    (b)   any person to whom it is delivered for payment refuses on demand either to pay or to return it; or

    (c)   it is paid on a forged indorsement.

(2) In an action against a drawee under subsection (1) the measure of the drawee's liability is the face amount of the instrument. In any other action under subsection (1) the measure of liability is presumed to be the face amount of the instrument.

(3) Subject to the provisions of this Act concerning restrictive indorsements a representative, including a depositary or collecting bank, who has in good faith and in accordance with the reasonable commercial standards applicable to the business of such representative dealt with an instrument or its proceeds on behalf of one who was not the true owner is not liable in conversion or otherwise to the true owner beyond the amount of any proceeds remaining in his hands.

(4) An intermediary bank or payor bank which is not a depositary bank is not liable in conversion solely by reason of the fact that proceeds of an item indorsed restrictively (Sections 3-205 and 3-206) are not paid or applied consistently with the restrictive indorsement of an indorser other than its immediate transferor.

Part 5. Presentment, Notice of Dishonor and Protest

§ 3-501. When Presentment, Notice of Dishonor, and Protest Necessary or Permissible.

(1) Unless excused (Section 3-511) presentment is necessary to charge secondary parties as follows:

(a)　presentment for acceptance is necessary to charge the drawer and indorsers of a draft where the draft so provides, or is payable elsewhere than at the residence or place of business of the drawee, or its date of payment depends upon such presentment. The holder may at his option present for acceptance any other draft payable at a stated date;

(b)　presentment for payment is necessary to charge any indorser;

(c)　in the case of any drawer, the acceptor of a draft payable at a bank or the maker of a note payable at a bank, presentment for payment is necessary, but failure to make presentment discharges such drawer, acceptor or maker only as stated in Section 3-502(1) (b).

(2) Unless excused (Section 3-511),

(a)　notice of any dishonor is necessary to charge any indorser;

(b)　in the case of any drawer, the acceptor of a draft payable at a bank or the maker of a note payable at a bank, notice of any dishonor is necessary, but failure to give such notice discharges such drawer, acceptor or maker only as stated in Section 3-502(1) (b).

(3) Unless excused (Section 3-511), protest of any dishonor is necessary to charge the drawer and indorsers of any draft which on its face appears to be drawn or payable outside of the states, territories, dependencies and possessions of the United States, the District of Columbia and the Commonwealth of Puerto Rico. The holder may at his option make protest of any dishonor of any other instrument and in the case of a foreign draft may on insolvency of the acceptor before maturity make protest for better security.

(4) Notwithstanding any provision of this section, neither presentment nor notice of dishonor nor protest is necessary to charge an indorser who has indorsed an instrument after maturity.

§ 3-502. Unexcused Delay; Discharge.

(1) Where without excuse any necessary presentment or notice of dishonor is delayed beyond the time when it is due

(a)　any indorser is discharged; and

(b)　any drawer or the acceptor of a draft payable at a bank or the maker of a note payable at a bank who because the drawee or payor bank becomes insolvent during the delay is deprived of funds maintained with the drawee or payor bank to cover the instrument may discharge his liability by written assignment to the holder of his rights against the drawee or payor bank in respect of such funds, but such drawer, acceptor or maker is not otherwise discharged.

(2) Where without excuse a necessary protest is delayed beyond the time when it is due any drawer or indorser is discharged.

§ 3-503. Time of Presentment.

(1) Unless a different time is expressed in the instrument the time for any presentment is determined as follows:

(a)　where an instrument is payable at or a fixed period after a stated date any presentment for acceptance must be made on or before the date it is payable;

(b)　where an instrument is payable after sight it must either be presented for acceptance or negotiated within a reasonable time after date or issue whichever is later;

(c)　where an instrument shows the date on which it is payable presentment for payment is due on that date;

(d)   where an instrument is accelerated presentment for payment is due within a reasonable time after the acceleration;

(e)   with respect to the liability of any secondary party presentment for acceptance or payment of any other instrument is due within a reasonable time after such party becomes liable thereon.

(2) A reasonable time for presentment is determined by the nature of the instrument, any usage of banking or trade and the facts of the particular case. In the case of an uncertified check which is drawn and payable within the United States and which is not a draft drawn by a bank the following are presumed to be reasonable periods within which to present for payment or to initiate bank collection:

(a)   with respect to the liability of the drawer, thirty days after date or issue whichever is later; and

(b)   with respect to the liability of an indorser, seven days after his indorsement.

(3) Where any presentment is due on a day which is not a full business day for either the person making presentment or the party to pay or accept, presentment is due on the next following day which is a full business day for both parties.

(4) Presentment to be sufficient must be made at a reasonable hour, and if at a bank during its banking day.

§ 3-504. How Presentment Made.

(1) Presentment is a demand for acceptance or payment made upon the maker, acceptor, drawee or other payor by or on behalf of the holder.

(2) Presentment may be made

(a)   by mail, in which event the time of presentment is determined by the time of receipt of the mail; or

(b)   through a clearing house; or

(c)   at the place of acceptance or payment specified in the instrument or if there be none at the place of business or residence of the party to accept or pay. If neither the party to accept or pay nor anyone authorized to act for him is present or accessible at such place presentment is excused.

(3) It may be made

(a)   to any one of two or more makers, acceptors, drawees or other payors; or

(b)   to any person who has authority to make or refuse the acceptance or payment.

(4) A draft accepted or a note made payable at a bank in the United States must be presented at such bank.

(5) In the cases described in Section 4-210 presentment may be made in the manner and with the result stated in that section.

§ 3-505. Rights of Party to Whom Presentment Is Made.

(1) The party to whom presentment is made may without dishonor require

(a)   exhibition of the instrument; and

(b)   reasonable identification of the person making presentment and evidence of his authority to make it if made for another; and

(c)   that the instrument be produced for acceptance or payment at a place specified in it, or if there be none at any place reasonable in the circumstances; and

(d)   a signed receipt on the instrument for any partial or full payment and its surrender upon full payment.

(2) Failure to comply with any such requirement invalidates the presentment but the person presenting has a reasonable time in which to comply and the time for acceptance or payment runs from the time of compliance.

§ 3-506. Time Allowed for Acceptance or Payment.

(1) Acceptance may be deferred without dishonor until the close of the next business day following presentment. The holder may also in a good faith effort to obtain acceptance and without either dishonor of the instrument or discharge of secondary parties allow postponement of acceptance for an additional business day.

(2) Except as a longer time is allowed in the case of documentary drafts drawn under a letter of credit, and unless an earlier time is agreed to by the party to pay, payment of an instrument may be deferred without dishonor pending reasonable examination to determine whether it is properly payable, but payment must be made in any event before the close of business on the day of presentment.

§ 3-507. Dishonor; Holder's Right of Recourse; Term Allowing Re-Presentment.

(1) An instrument is dishonored when

(a)   a necessary or optional presentment is duly made and due acceptance or payment is refused or cannot be obtained within the prescribed time or in case of bank collections the instrument is seasonably returned by the midnight deadline (Section 4-301); or

(b) presentment is excused and the instrument is not duly accepted or paid.

(2) Subject to any necessary notice of dishonor and protest, the holder has upon dishonor an immediate right of recourse against the drawers and indorsers.

(3) Return of an instrument for lack of proper indorsement is not dishonor.

(4) A term in a draft or an indorsement thereof allowing a stated time for re-presentment in the event of any dishonor of the draft by nonacceptance of a time draft or by nonpayment if a sight draft gives the holder as against any secondary party bound by the term an option to waive the dishonor without affecting the liability of the secondary party and he may present again up to the end of the stated time.

§ 3-508. Notice of Dishonor.

(1) Notice of dishonor may be given to any person who may be liable on the instrument by or on behalf of the holder or any party who has himself received notice, or any other party who can be compelled to pay the instrument. In addition an agent or bank in whose hands the instrument is dishonored may give notice to his principal or customer or to another agent or bank from which the instrument was received.

(2) Any necessary notice must be given by a bank before its midnight deadline and by any other person before midnight of the third business day after dishonor or receipt of notice of dishonor.

(3) Notice may be given in any reasonable manner. It may be oral or written and in any terms which identify the instrument and state that it has been dishonored. A misdescription which does not mislead the party notified does not vitiate the notice. Sending the instrument bearing a stamp, ticket or writing stating that acceptance or payment has been refused or sending a notice of debit with respect to the instrument is sufficient.

(4) Written notice is given when sent although it is not received.

(5) Notice to one partner is notice to each although the firm has been dissolved.

(6) When any party is in insolvency proceedings instituted after the issue of the instrument notice may be given either to the party or to the representative of his estate.

(7) When any party is dead or incompetent notice may be sent to his last known address or given to his personal representative.

(8) Notice operates for the benefit of all parties who have rights on the instrument against the party notified.

§ 3-509. Protest; Noting for Protest.

(1) A protest is a certificate of dishonor made under the hand and seal of a United States consul or vice consul or a notary public or other person authorized to certify dishonor by the law of the place where dishonor occurs. It may be made upon information satisfactory to such person.

(2) The protest must identify the instrument and certify either that due presentment has been made or the reason why it is excused and that the instrument has been dishonored by nonacceptance or nonpayment.

(3) The protest may also certify that notice of dishonor has been given to all parties or to specified parties.

(4) Subject to subsection (5) any necessary protest is due by the time that notice of dishonor is due.

(5) If, before protest is due, an instrument has been noted for protest by the officer to make protest, the protest may be made at any time thereafter as of the date of the noting.

§ 3-510. Evidence of Dishonor and Notice of Dishonor. The following are admissible as evidence and create a presumption of dishonor and of any notice of dishonor therein shown:

(a) a document regular in form as provided in the preceding section which purports to be a protest;

(b) the purported stamp or writing of the drawee, payor bank or presenting bank on the instrument or accompanying it stating that acceptance or payment has been refused for reasons consistent with dishonor;

(c) any book or record of the drawee, payor bank, or any collecting bank kept in the usual course of business which shows dishonor, even though there is no evidence of who made the entry.

§ 3-511. Waived or Excused Presentment, Protest or Notice of Dishonor or Delay Therein.

(1) Delay in presentment, protest or notice of dishonor is excused when the party is without notice that it is due or when the delay is caused by circumstances beyond his control and he exercises reasonable diligence after the cause of the delay ceases to operate.

(2) Presentment or notice or protest as the case may be is entirely excused when

    (a)   the party to be charged has waived it expressly or by implication either before or after it is due; or

    (b)   such party has himself dishonored the instrument or has countermanded payment or otherwise has no reason to expect or right to require that the instrument be accepted or paid; or

    (c)   by reasonable diligence the presentment or protest cannot be made or the notice given.

(3) Presentment is also entirely excused when

    (a)   the maker, acceptor or drawee of any instrument except a documentary draft is dead or in insolvency proceedings instituted after the issue of the instrument; or

    (b)   acceptance or payment is refused but not for want of proper presentment.

(4) Where a draft has been dishonored by nonacceptance a later presentment for payment and any notice of dishonor and protest for nonpayment are excused unless in the meantime the instrument has been accepted.

(5) A waiver of protest is also a waiver of presentment and of notice of dishonor even though protest is not required.

(6) Where a waiver of presentment or notice or protest is embodied in the instrument itself it is binding upon all parties; but where it is written above the signature of an indorser it binds him only.

Part 6. Discharge

§ 3-601. Discharge of Parties.

(1) The extent of the discharge of any party from liability on an instrument is governed by the sections on

    (a)   payment or satisfaction (Section 3-603); or

    (b)   tender of payment (Section 3-604); or

    (c)   cancellation or renunciation (Section 3-605); or

    (d)   impairment of right of recourse or of collateral (Section 3-606); or

    (e)   reacquisition of the instrument by a prior party (Section 3-208); or

    (f)   fraudulent and material alteration (Section 3-407); or

    (g)   certification of a check (Section 3-411); or

    (h)   acceptance varying a draft (Section 3-412); or

    (i)   unexcused delay in presentment or notice of dishonor or protest (Section 3-502).

(2) Any party is also discharged from his liability on an instrument to another party by any other act or agreement with such party which would discharge his simple contract for the payment of money.

(3) The liability of all parties is discharged when any party who has himself no right of action or recourse on the instrument

    (a)   reacquires the instrument in his own right; or

    (b)   is discharged under any provision of this Article, except as otherwise provided with respect to discharge for impairment of recourse or of collateral (Section 3-606).

§ 3-602. Effect of Discharge Against Holder in Due Course.

No discharge of any party provided by this Article is effective against a subsequent holder in due course unless he has notice thereof when he takes the instrument.

§ 3-603. Payment or Satisfaction.

(1) The liability of any party is discharged to the extent of his payment or satisfaction to the holder even though it is made with knowledge of a claim of another person to the instrument unless prior to such payment or satisfaction the person making the claim either supplies indemnity deemed adequate by the party seeking the discharge or enjoins payment or satisfaction by order of a court of competent jurisdiction in an action in which the adverse claimant and the holder are parties. This subsection does not, however, result in the discharge of the liability

    (a)   of a party who in bad faith pays or satisfies a holder who acquired the instrument by theft or who (unless having the rights of a holder in due course) holds through one who so acquired it; or

(b) of a party (other than an intermediary bank or a payor bank which is not a depositary bank) who pays or satisfies the holder of an instrument which has been restrictively indorsed in a manner not consistent with the terms of such restrictive indorsement.

(2) Payment or satisfaction may be made with the consent of the holder by any person including a stranger to the instrument. Surrender of the instrument to such a person gives him the rights of a transferee (Section 3-201).

§ 3-604. Tender of Payment.

(1) Any party making tender of full payment to a holder when or after it is due is discharged to the extent of all subsequent liability for interest, costs and attorney's fees.

(2) The holder's refusal of such tender wholly discharges any party who has a right of recourse against the party making the tender.

(3) Where the maker or acceptor of an instrument payable otherwise than on demand is able and ready to pay at every place of payment specified in the instrument when it is due, it is equivalent to tender.

§ 3-605. Cancellation and Renunciation.

(1) The holder of an instrument may even without consideration discharge any party

(a) in any manner apparent on the face of the instrument or the indorsement, as by intentionally cancelling the instrument or the party's signature by destruction or mutilation, or by striking out the party's signature; or

(b) by renouncing his rights by a writing signed and delivered or by surrender of the instrument to the party to be discharged.

(2) Neither cancellation nor renunciation without surrender of the instrument affects the title thereto.

§ 3-606. Impairment of Recourse or of Collateral.

(1) The holder discharges any party to the instrument to the extent that without such party's consent the holder

(a) without express reservation of rights releases or agrees not to sue any person against whom the party has to the knowledge of the holder a right of recourse or agrees to suspend the right to enforce

against such person the instrument or collateral or otherwise discharges such person, except that failure or delay in effecting any required presentment, protest or notice of dishonor with respect to any such person does not discharge any party as to whom presentment, protest or notice of dishonor is effective or unnecessary; or

(b) unjustifiably impairs any collateral for the instrument given by or on behalf of the party or any person against whom he has a right of recourse.

(2) By express reservation of rights against a party with a right of recourse the holder preserves

(a) all his rights against such party as of the time when the instrument was originally due; and

(b) the right of the party to pay the instrument as of that time; and

(c) all rights of such party to recourse against others.

Part 7. Advice of International Sight Draft

§ 3-701. Letter of Advice of International Sight Draft.

(1) A "letter of advice" is a drawer's communication to the drawee that a described draft has been drawn.

(2) Unless otherwise agreed when a bank receives from another bank a letter of advice of an international sight draft that drawee bank may immediately debit the drawer's account and stop the running of interest pro tanto. Such a debit and any resulting credit to any account covering outstanding drafts leaves in the drawer full power to stop payment or otherwise dispose of the amount and creates no trust or interest in favor of the holder.

(3) Unless otherwise agreed and except where a draft is drawn under a credit issued by the drawee, the drawee of an international sight draft owes the drawer no duty to pay an unadvised draft but if it does so and the draft is genuine, may appropriately debit the drawer's account.

Part 8. Miscellaneous

§ 3-801. Drafts in a Set.

(1) Where a draft is drawn in a set of parts, each of which is numbered and expressed to be an order only if no other part has been honored, the whole

of the parts constitutes one draft but a taker of any part may become a holder in due course of the draft.

(2) Any person who negotiates, indorses or accepts a single part of a draft drawn in a set thereby becomes liable to any holder in due course of that part as if it were the whole set, but as between different holders in due course to whom different parts have been negotiated the holder whose title first accrues has all rights to the draft and its proceeds.

(3) As against the drawee the first presented part of a draft drawn in a set is the part entitled to payment, or if a time draft to acceptance and payment. Acceptance of any subsequently presented part renders the drawee liable thereon under subsection (2). With respect both to a holder and to the drawer payment of a subsequently presented part of a draft payable at sight has the same effect as payment of a check notwithstanding an effective stop order (Section 4-407).

(4) Except as otherwise provided in this section, where any part of a draft in a set is discharged by payment or otherwise the whole draft is discharged.

§ 3-802. Effect of Instrument on Obligation for Which It Is Given.

(1) Unless otherwise agreed where an instrument is taken for an underlying obligation

    (a)   the obligation is pro tanto discharged if a bank is drawer, maker or acceptor of the instrument and there is no recourse on the instrument against the underlying obligor; and

    (b)   in any other case the obligation is suspended pro tanto until the instrument is due or if it is payable on demand until its presentment. If the instrument is dishonored action may be maintained on either the instrument or the obligation; discharge of the underlying obligor on the instrument also discharges him on the obligation.

(2) The taking in good faith of a check which is not postdated does not of itself so extend the time on the original obligation as to discharge a surety.

§ 3-803. Notice to Third Party.

Where a defendant is sued for breach of an obligation for which a third person is answerable over under this Article he may give the third person written notice of the litigation, and the person notified may then give similar notice to any other person who is answerable over to him under this Article. If the notice states that the person notified may come in and defend and that if the person notified does not do so he will in any action against him by the person giving the notice be bound by any determination of fact common to the two litigations, then unless after seasonable receipt of the notice the person notified does come in and defend he is so bound.

§ 3-804. Lost, Destroyed or Stolen Instruments.

The owner of an instrument which is lost, whether by destruction, theft or otherwise, may maintain an action in his own name and recover from any party liable thereon upon due proof of his ownership, the facts which prevent his production of the instrument and its terms. The court may require security indemnifying the defendant against loss by reason of further claims on the instrument.

§ 3-805. Instruments Not Payable to Order or to Bearer.

This Article applies to any instrument whose terms do not preclude transfer and which is otherwise negotiable within this Article but which is not payable to order or to bearer, except that there can be no holder in due course of such an instrument.

ARTICLE 4. BANK DEPOSITS AND COLLECTIONS

Part 1. General Provisions and Definitions

§ 4-101. Short Title.

This Article shall be known and may be cited as Uniform Commercial Code—Bank Deposits and Collections.

§ 4-102. Applicability.

(1) To the extent that items within this Article are also within the scope of Articles 3 and 8, they are subject to the provisions of those Articles. In the event of conflict the provisions of this Article govern those of Article 3 but the provisions of Article 8 govern those of this Article.

(2) The liability of a bank for action or non-action with respect to any item handled by it for purposes of presentment, payment or collection is governed by the law of the place where the bank is located. In the case of action or non-action by or at a branch or separate office of a bank, its liability is governed by the law of the place where the branch or separate office is located.

§ 4-103. Variation by Agreement; Measure of Damages; Certain Action Constituting Ordinary Care.

(1) The effect of the provisions of this Article may be varied by agreement except that no agreement can disclaim a bank's responsibility for its own lack of good faith or failure to exercise ordinary care or can limit the measure of damages for such lack or failure; but the parties may by agreement determine the standards by which such responsibility is to be measured if such standards are not manifestly unreasonable.

(2) Federal Reserve regulations and operating letters, clearing house rules, and the like, have the effect of agreements under subsection (1), whether or not specifically assented to by all parties interested in items handled.

(3) Action or non-action approved by this Article or pursuant to Federal Reserve regulations or operating letters constitutes the exercise of ordinary care and, in the absence of special instructions, action or non-action consistent with clearing house rules and the like or with a general banking usage not disapproved by this Article, prima facie constitutes the exercise of ordinary care.

(4) The specification or approval of certain procedures by this Article does not constitute disapproval of other procedures which may be reasonable under the circumstances.

(5) The measure of damages for failure to exercise ordinary care in handling an item is the amount of the item reduced by an amount which could not have been realized by the use of ordinary care, and where there is bad faith it includes other damages, if any, suffered by the party as a proximate consequence.

§ 4-104. Definitions and Index of Definitions.

(1) In this Article unless the context otherwise requires

(a) "Account" means any account with a bank and includes a checking, time, interest or savings account;

(b) "Afternoon" means the period of a day between noon and midnight;

(c) "Banking day" means that part of any day on which a bank is open to the public for carrying on substantially all of its banking functions;

(d) "Clearing house" means any association of banks or other payors regularly clearing items;

(e) "Customer" means any person having an account with a bank or for whom a bank has agreed to collect items and includes a bank carrying an account with another bank;

(f) "Documentary draft" means any negotiable or non-negotiable draft with accompanying documents, securities or other papers to be delivered against honor of the draft;

(g) "Item" means any instrument for the payment of money even though it is not negotiable but does not include money;

(h) "Midnight deadline" with respect to a bank is midnight on its next banking day following the banking day on which it receives the relevant item or notice or from which the time for taking action commences to run, whichever is later;

(i) "Properly payable" includes the availability of funds for payment at the time of decision to pay or dishonor;

(j) "Settle" means to pay in cash, by clearing house settlement, in a charge or credit or by remittance, or otherwise as instructed. A settlement may be either provisional or final;

(k) "Suspends payments" with respect to a bank means that it has been closed by order of the supervisory authorities, that a public officer has been appointed to take it over or that it ceases or refuses to make payments in the ordinary course of business.

(2) Other definitions applying to this Article and the sections in which they appear are:

"Collecting bank." Section 4-105.

"Depositary bank." Section 4-105.

"Intermediary bank." Section 4-105.

"Payor bank." Section 4-105.

"Presenting bank." Section 4-105.

"Remitting bank." Section 4-105.

(3) The following definitions in other Articles apply to this Article:

"Acceptance." Section 3-410.

"Certificate of deposit." Section 3-104.

"Certification." Section 3-411.

"Check." Section 3-104.

"Draft." Section 3-104.

"Holder in due course." Section 3-302.

"Notice of dishonor." Section 3-508.

"Presentment." Section 3-504.

"Protest." Section 3-509.

"Secondary party." Section 3-102.

(4) In addition Article 1 contains general definitions and principles of construction and interpretation applicable throughout this Article.

§ 4-105. "Depositary Bank"; "Intermediary Bank"; "Collecting Bank"; "Payor Bank"; "Presenting Bank"; "Remitting Bank." In this Article unless the context otherwise requires:

(a) "Depositary bank" means the first bank to which an item is transferred for collection even though it is also the payor bank;

(b) "Payor bank" means a bank by which an item is payable as drawn or accepted;

(c) "Intermediary bank" means any bank to which an item is transferred in course of collection except the depositary or payor bank;

(d) "Collecting bank" means any bank handling the item for collection except the payor bank;

(e) "Presenting bank" means any bank presenting an item except a payor bank;

(f) "Remitting bank" means any payor or intermediary bank remitting for an item.

§ 4-106. Separate Office of a Bank. A branch or separate office of a bank [maintaining its own deposit ledgers] is a separate bank for the purpose of computing the time within which and determining the place at or to which action may be taken or notices or orders shall be given under this Article and under Article 3.

Note: The brackets are to make it optional with the several states whether to require a branch to maintain its own deposit ledgers in order to be considered to be a separate bank for certain purposes under Article 4. In some states "maintaining its own deposit ledgers" is a satisfactory test. In others branch banking practices are such that this test would not be suitable.

§ 4-107. Time of Receipt of Items.

(1) For the purpose of allowing time to process items, prove balances and make the necessary entries on its books to determine its position for the day, a bank may fix an afternoon hour of 2 p.m. or later as a cut-off hour for the handling of money and items and the making of entries on its books.

(2) Any item or deposit of money received on any day after a cut-off hour so fixed or after the close of the banking day may be treated as being received at the opening of the next banking day.

§ 4-108. Delays.

(1) Unless otherwise instructed, a collecting bank in a good faith effort to secure payment may, in the case of specific items and with or without the approval of any person involved, waive, modify or extend time limits imposed or permitted by this Act for a period not in excess of an additional banking day without discharge of secondary parties and without liability to its transferor or any prior party.

(2) Delay by a collecting bank or payor bank beyond time limits prescribed or permitted by this Act or by instructions excused if caused by interruption of communication facilities, suspension of payments by another bank, war, emergency conditions or other circumstances beyond the control of the bank provided it exercises such diligence as the circumstances require.

§ 4-109. Process of Posting. The "process of posting" means the usual procedure followed by a payor bank in determining to pay an item and in recording the payment including one or more of the following or other steps as determined by the bank.

(a) verification of any signature;

(b) ascertaining that sufficient funds are available;

(c) affixing a "paid" or other stamp;

(d) entering a charge or entry to a customer's account;

(e) correcting or reversing an entry or erroneous action with respect to the item.

Part 2. Collection of Items: Depositary and Collecting Banks

§ 4-201. Presumption and Duration of Agency Status of Collecting Banks and Provisional Status of Credits; Applicability of Article; Item Indorsed "Pay Any Bank."

(1) Unless a contrary intent clearly appears and prior to the time that a settlement given by a col-

lecting bank for an item is or becomes final (subsection (3) of Section 4-211 and Sections 4-212 and 4-213) the bank is an agent or sub-agent of the owner of the item and any settlement given for the item is provisional. This provision applies regardless of the form of indorsement or lack of indorsement and even though credit given for the item is subject to immediate withdrawal as of right or is in fact withdrawn; but the continuance of ownership of an item by its owner and any rights of the owner to proceeds of the item are subject to rights of a collecting bank such as those resulting from outstanding advances on the item and valid rights of setoff. When an item is handled by banks for purposes of presentment, payment and collection, the relevant provisions of this Article apply even though action of parties clearly establishes that a particular bank has purchased the item and is the owner of it.

(2) After an item has been indorsed with the words "pay any bank" or the like, only a bank may acquire the rights of a holder

   (a)   until the item has been returned to the customer initiating collection; or

   (b)   until the item has been specially indorsed by a bank to a person who is not a bank.

§ 4-202. Responsibility for Collection; When Action Seasonable.

(1) A collecting bank must use ordinary care in

   (a)   presenting an item or sending it for presentment; and

   (b)   sending notice of dishonor or non-payment or returning an item other than a documentary draft to the bank's transferor [or directly to the depositary bank under subsection (2) of Section 4-212] (see note to Section 4-212) after learning that the item has not been paid or accepted, as the case may be; and

   (c)   settling for an item when the bank receives final settlement; and

   (d)   making or providing for any necessary protest; and

   (e)   notifying its transferor of any loss or delay in transit within a reasonable time after discovery thereof.

(2) A collecting bank taking proper action before its midnight deadline following receipt of an item, notice or payment acts seasonably; taking proper action within a reasonably longer time may be seasonable but the bank has the burden of so establishing.

(3) Subject to subsection (1)(a), a bank is not liable for the insolvency, neglect, misconduct, mistake or default of another bank or person or for loss or destruction of an item in transit or in the possession of others.

§ 4-203. Effect of Instructions.
Subject to the provisions of Article 3 concerning conversion of instruments (Section 3-419) and the provisions of both Article 3 and this Article concerning restrictive indorsements only a collecting bank's transferor can give instructions which affect the bank or constitute notice to it and a collecting bank is not liable to prior parties for any action taken pursuant to such instructions or in accordance with any agreement with its transferor.

§ 4-204. Methods of Sending and Presenting; Sending Direct to Payor Bank.

(1) A collecting bank must send items by reasonably prompt method taking into consideration any relevant instructions, the nature of the item, the number of such items on hand, and the cost of collection involved and the method generally used by it or others to present such items.

(2) A collecting bank may send

   (a)   any item direct to the payor bank;

   (b)   any item to any non-bank payor if authorized by its transferor; and

   (c)   any item other than documentary drafts to any non-bank payor, if authorized by Federal Reserve regulation or operating letter, clearing house rule or the like.

(3) Presentment may be made by a presenting bank at a place where the payor bank has requested that presentment be made.

§ 4-205. Supplying Missing Indorsement; No Notice from Prior Indorsement.

(1) A depositary bank which has taken an item for collection may supply any indorsement of the customer which is necessary to title unless the item contains the words "payee's indorsement required" or the like. In the absence of such a requirement a statement placed on the item by the depositary bank to the effect that the item was deposited by a customer or credited to his account is effective as the customer's indorsement.

(2) An intermediary bank, or payor bank which is not a depositary bank, is neither given notice nor otherwise affected by a restrictive indorsement of any person except the bank's immediate transferor.

§ 4-206. Transfer Between Banks. Any agreed method which identifies the transferor bank is sufficient for the item's further transfer to another bank.

§ 4-207. Warranties of Customer and Collecting Bank on Transfer or Presentment of Items; Time for Claims.

(1) Each customer or collecting bank who obtains payment or acceptance of an item and each prior customer and collecting bank warrants to the payor bank or other payor who in good faith pays or accepts the item that

(a) he has a good title to the item or is authorized to obtain payment or acceptance on behalf of one who has a good title; and

(b) he has no knowledge that the signature of the maker or drawer is unauthorized, except that this warranty is not given by any customer or collecting bank that is a holder in due course and acts in good faith

(i) to a maker with respect to the maker's own signature; or

(ii) to a drawer with respect to the drawer's own signature, whether or not the drawer is also the drawee; or

(iii) to an acceptor of an item if the holder in due course took the item after the acceptance or obtained the acceptance without knowledge that the drawer's signature was unauthorized; and

(c) the item has not been materially altered, except that this warranty is not given by any customer or collecting bank that is a holder in due course and acts in good faith

(i) to the maker of a note; or

(ii) to the drawer of a draft whether or not the drawer is also the drawee; or

(iii) to the acceptor of an item with respect to an alteration made prior to the acceptance if the holder in due course took the item after the acceptance, even though the acceptance provided "payable as originally drawn" or equivalent terms; or

(iv) to the acceptor of an item with respect to an alteration made after the acceptance.

(2) Each customer and collecting bank who transfers an item and receives a settlement or other consideration for it warrants to his transferee and to any subsequent collecting bank who takes the item in good faith that

(a) he has a good title to the item or is authorized to obtain payment or acceptance on behalf of one who has a good title and the transfer is otherwise rightful; and

(b) all signatures are genuine or authorized; and

(c) the item has not been materially altered; and

(d) no defense of any party is good against him; and

(e) he has no knowledge of any insolvency proceeding instituted with respect to the maker or acceptor or the drawer of an unaccepted item.

In addition each customer and collecting bank so transferring an item and receiving a settlement or other consideration engages that upon dishonor and any necessary notice of dishonor and protest he will take up the item.

(3) The warranties and the engagement to honor set forth in the two preceding subsections arise notwithstanding the absence of indorsement or words of guaranty or warranty in the transfer or presentment and a collecting bank remains liable for their breach despite remittance to its transferor. Damages for breach of such warranties or engagement to honor shall not exceed the consideration received by the customer or collecting bank responsible plus finance charges and expenses related to the item, if any.

(4) Unless a claim for breach of warranty under this section is made within a reasonable time after the person claiming learns of the breach, the person liable is discharged to the extent of any loss caused by the delay in making claim.

§ 4-208. Security Interest of Collecting Bank in Items, Accompanying Documents and Proceeds.

(1) A bank has a security interest in an item and any accompanying documents or the proceeds of either

(a) in case of an item deposited in an account to the extent to which credit given for the item has been withdrawn or applied;

(b) in case of an item for which it has given credit available for withdrawal as of right, to the extent of the credit given whether or not the credit is drawn upon and whether or not there is a right of charge-back; or

(c) if it makes an advance on or against the item.

(2) When credit which has been given for several items received at one time or pursuant to a single agreement is withdrawn or applied in part the security interest remains upon all the items, any accompanying documents or the proceeds of either. For the purpose of this section, credits first given are first withdrawn.

(3) Receipt by a collecting bank of a final settlement for an item is a realization on its security interest in the item, accompanying documents and proceeds. To the extent and so long as the bank does not receive final settlement for the item or give up possession of the item or accompanying documents for purposes other than collection, the security interest continues and is subject to the provisions of Article 9 except that

(a) no security agreement is necessary to make the security interest enforceable (subsection (1)(a) of Section 9-203); and

(b) no filing is required to perfect the security interest; and

(c) the security interest has priority over conflicting perfected security interests in the item, accompanying documents or proceeds.

§ 4-209. When Bank Gives Value for Purposes of Holder in Due Course.
For purposes of determining its status as a holder in due course, the bank has given value to the extent that it has a security interest in an item provided that the bank otherwise complies with the requirements of Section 3-302 on what constitutes a holder in due course.

§ 4-210. Presentment by Notice of Item Not Payable by, Through or at a Bank; Liability of Secondary Parties.
(1) Unless otherwise instructed, a collecting bank may present an item not payable by, through or at a bank by sending to the party to accept or pay a written notice that the bank holds the item for acceptance or payment. The notice must be sent in time to be received on or before the day when presentment is due and the bank must meet any requirement of the party to accept or pay under Section 3-505 by the close of the bank's next banking day after it knows of the requirement.

(2) Where presentment is made by notice and neither honor nor request for compliance with a requirement under Section 3-505 is received by the close of business on the day after maturity or in the case of demand items by the close of business on the third banking day after notice was sent, the presenting bank may treat the item as dishonored and charge any secondary party by sending him notice of the facts.

§ 4-211. Media of Remittance; Provisional and Final Settlement in Remittance Cases.
(1) A collecting bank may take in settlement of an item

(a) a check of the remitting bank or of another bank on any bank except the remitting bank; or

(b) a cashier's check or similar primary obligation of a remitting bank which is a member of or clears through a member of the same clearing house or group as the collecting bank; or

(c) appropriate authority to charge an account of the remitting bank or of another bank with the collecting bank; or

(d) if the item is drawn upon or payable by a person other than a bank, a cashier's check, certified check or other bank check or obligation.

(2) If before its midnight deadline the collecting bank properly dishonors a remittance check or authorization to charge on itself or presents or forwards for collection a remittance instrument of or on another bank which is of a kind approved by subsection (1) or has not been authorized by it, the collecting bank is not liable to prior parties in the event of the dishonor of such check, instrument or authorization.

(3) A settlement for an item by means of a remittance instrument or authorization to charge is or becomes a final settlement as to both the person making and the person receiving the settlement

(a) if the remittance instrument or authorization to charge is of a kind approved by subsection (1) or has not been authorized by the person receiving the settlement and in either case the person receiving the settlement acts seasonably before its midnight deadline in presenting, forwarding for collection or paying the instrument or authorization—at the time the remittance instrument or authorization is finally paid by the payor by which it is payable;

(b) if the person receiving the settlement has authorized remittance by a non-bank check or obligation or by a cashier's check or similar primary obligation of or a check upon the payor or other remitting bank which is not of a kind approved by subsection (1) (b),—at the time of the receipt of such remittance check or obligation; or

(c) if in a case not covered by sub-paragraphs (a) or (b) the person receiving the settlement fails to seasonably present, forward for collection, pay or return a remittance instrument or authorization to it to charge before its midnight deadline,—at such midnight deadline.

§ 4-212. Right of Charge-Back or Refund.

(1) If a collecting bank has made provisional settlement with its customer for an item and itself fails by reason of dishonor, suspension of payments by a bank or otherwise to receive a settlement for the item which is or becomes final, the bank may revoke the settlement given by it, charge back the amount of any credit given for the item to its customer's account or obtain refund from its customer whether or not it is able to return the items if by its midnight deadline or within a longer reasonable time after it learns the facts it returns the item or sends notification of the facts. These rights to revoke, charge-back and obtain refund terminate if and when a settlement for the item received by the bank is or becomes final (subsection (3) of Section 4-211 and subsections (2) and (3) of Section 4-213).

[(2) Within the time and manner prescribed by this section and Section 4-301, an intermediary or payor bank, as the case may be, may return an unpaid item directly to the depositary bank and may send for collection a draft on the depositary bank and obtain reimbursement. In such case, if the depositary bank has received provisional settlement for the item, it must reimburse the bank drawing the draft and any provisional credits for the item between banks shall become and remain final]

Note: Direct returns is recognized as an innovation that is not yet established bank practice, and therefore, Paragraph 2 has been bracketed. Some lawyers have doubts whether it should be included in legislation or left to development by agreement.

(3) A depositary bank which is also the payor may charge-back the amount of an item to its customer's account or obtain refund in accordance with the section governing return of an item received by a payor bank for credit on its books (Section 4-301).

(4) The right to charge-back is not affected by

(a) prior use of the credit given for the item; or

(b) failure by any bank to exercise ordinary care with respect to the item but any bank so failing remains liable.

(5) A failure to charge-back or claim refund does not affect other rights of the bank against the customer or any other party.

(6) If credit is given in dollars as the equivalent of the value of an item payable in a foreign currency the dollar amount of any charge-back or refund shall be calculated on the basis of the buying sight rate for the foreign currency prevailing on the day when the person entitled to the charge-back or refund learns that it will not receive payment in ordinary course.

§ 4-213. Final Payment of Item by Payor Bank; When Provisional Debits and Credits Become Final; When Certain Credits Become Available for Withdrawal.

(1) An item is finally paid by a payor bank when the bank has done any of the following, whichever happens first:

(a) paid the item in cash; or

(b) settled for the item without reserving a right to revoke the settlement and without having such right under statute, clearing house rule or agreement; or

(c) completed the process of posting the item to the indicated account of the drawer, maker or other person to be charged therewith; or

(d) made a provisional settlement for the item and failed to revoke the settlement in the time and manner permitted by statute, clearing house rule or agreement.

Upon a final payment under subparagraphs (b), (c) or (d) the payor bank shall be accountable for the amount of the item.

(2) If provisional settlement for an item between the presenting and payor banks is made through a clearing house or by debits or credits in an account between them, then to the extent that provisional debits or credits for the item are entered in accounts

between the presenting and payor banks or between the presenting and successive prior collecting banks seriatim, they become final upon final payment of the item by the payor bank.

(3) If a collecting bank receives a settlement for an item which is or becomes final (subsection (3) of Section 4-211, subsection (2) of Section 4-213) the bank is accountable to its customer for the amount of the item and any provisional credit given for the item in an account with its customer becomes final.

(4) Subject to any right of the bank to apply the credit to an obligation of the customer, credit given by a bank for an item in an account with its customer becomes available for withdrawal as of right

   (a) in any case where the bank has received a provisional settlement for the item,—when such settlement becomes final and the bank has had a reasonable time to learn that the settlement is final;

   (b) in any case where the bank is both a depositary bank and a payor bank and the item is finally paid,—at the opening of the bank's second banking day following receipt of the item.

(5) A deposit of money in a bank is final when made but, subject to any right of the bank to apply the deposit to an obligation of the customer, the deposit becomes available for withdrawal as of right at the opening of the bank's next banking day following receipt of the deposit.

§ 4-214. Insolvency and Preference.

(1) Any item in or coming into the possession of a payor or collecting bank which suspends payment and which item is not finally paid shall be returned by the receiver, trustee or agent in charge of the closed bank to the presenting bank or the closed bank's customer.

(2) If a payor bank finally pays an item and suspends payments without making a settlement for the item with its customer or the presenting bank which settlement is or becomes final, the owner of the item has a preferred claim against the payor bank.

(3) If a payor bank gives or a collecting bank gives or receives a provisional settlement for an item and thereafter suspends payments, the suspension does not prevent or interfere with the settlement becoming final if such finality occurs automatically upon the lapse of certain time or the happening of certain events (subsection (3) of Section 4-211, subsections (1) (d), (2) and (3) of Section 4-213).

(4) If a collecting bank receives from subsequent parties settlement for an item which settlement is or becomes final and suspends payments without making a settlement for the item with its customer which is or becomes final, the owner of the item has a preferred claim against such collecting bank.

Part 3. Collection of Items: Payor Banks

§ 4-301. Deferred Posting; Recovery of Payment by Return of Items; Time of Dishonor.

(1) Where an authorized settlement for a demand item (other than a documentary draft) received by a payor bank otherwise than for immediate payment over the counter has been made before midnight of the banking day of receipt the payor bank may revoke the settlement and recover any payment if before it has made final payment (subsection (1) of Section 4-213) and before its midnight deadline it

   (a) returns the item; or

   (b) sends written notice of dishonor or non-payment if the item is held for protest or is otherwise unavailable for return.

(2) If a demand item is received by a payor bank for credit on its books it may return such item or send notice of dishonor and may revoke any credit given or recover the amount thereof withdrawn by its customer, if it acts within the time limit and in the manner specified in the preceding subsection.

(3) Unless previous notice of dishonor has been sent an item is dishonored at the time when for purposes of dishonor it is returned or notice sent in accordance with this section.

(4) An item is returned:

   (a) as to an item received through a clearing house, when it is delivered to the presenting or last collecting bank or to the clearing house or is sent or delivered in accordance with its rules; or

   (b) in all other cases, when it is sent or delivered to the bank's customer or transferor or pursuant to his instructions.

§ 4-302. Payor Bank's Responsibility for Late Return of Item.
In the absence of a valid defense such as breach of a presentment warranty (subsection (1) of Section 4-207), settlement effected or the like, if an item is presented on and received by a payor bank the bank is accountable for the amount of

(a) a demand item other than a documentary draft whether properly payable or not if the bank, in any case where it is not also the depositary bank, retains the item beyond midnight of the banking day of receipt without settling for it or, regardless of whether it is also the depositary bank, does not pay or return the item or send notice of dishonor until after its midnight deadline; or

(b) any other properly payable item unless within the time allowed for acceptance or payment of that item the bank either accepts or pays the item or returns it and accompanying documents.

§ 4-303. When Items Subject to Notice, Stop-Order, Legal Process or Setoff; Order in Which Items May Be Charged or Certified.

(1) Any knowledge, notice or stop-order received by, legal process served upon or setoff exercised by a payor bank, whether or not effective under other rules of law to terminate, suspend or modify the bank's right or duty to pay an item or to charge its customer's account for the item, comes too late to so terminate, suspend or modify such right or duty if the knowledge, notice, stop-order or legal process is received or served and a reasonable time for the bank to act thereon expires or the setoff is exercised after the bank has done any of the following:

(a) accepted or certified the item;

(b) paid the item in cash;

(c) settled for the item without reserving a right to revoke the settlement and without having such right under statute, clearing house rule or agreement;

(d) completed the process of posting the item to the indicated account of the drawer, maker or other person to be charged therewith or otherwise has evidenced by examination of such indicated account and by action its decision to pay the item; or

(e) become accountable for the amount of the item under subsection (1)(d) of Section 4-213 and Section 4-302 dealing with the payor bank's responsibility for late return of items.

(2) Subject to the provisions of subsection (1) items may be accepted, paid, certified or charged to the indicated account of its customer in any order convenient to the bank.

Part 4. Relationship Between Payor Bank and Its Customers

§ 4-401. When Bank May Charge Customer's Account.

(1) As against its customer, a bank may charge against his account any item which is otherwise properly payable from that account even though the charge creates an overdraft.

(2) A bank which in good faith makes payment to a holder may charge the indicated account of its customer according to

(a) the original tenor of his altered item; or

(b) the tenor of his completed item, even though the bank knows the item has been completed unless the bank has notice that the completion was improper.

§ 4-402. Bank's Liability to Customer for Wrongful Dishonor.
A payor bank is liable to its customer for damages proximately caused by the wrongful dishonor of an item. When the dishonor occurs through mistake liability is limited to actual damages proved. If so proximately caused and proved damages may include damages for an arrest or prosecution of the customer or other consequential damages. Whether any consequential damages are proximately caused by the wrongful dishonor is a question of fact to be determined in each case.

§ 4-403. Customer's Right to Stop Payment; Burden of Proof of Loss.

(1) A customer may by order to his bank stop payment of any item payable for his account but the order must be received at such time and in such manner as to afford the bank a reasonable opportunity to act on it prior to any action by the bank with respect to the item described in Section 4-303.

(2) An oral order is binding upon the bank only for fourteen calendar days unless confirmed in writing within that period. A written order is effective for only six months unless renewed in writing.

(3) The burden of establishing the fact and amount of loss resulting from the payment of an item contrary to a binding stop payment order is on the customer.

§ 4-404. Bank Not Obligated to Pay Check More Than Six Months Old. A bank is under no obligation to a customer having a checking account to pay a check, other than a certified check, which is presented more than six months after its date, but it may charge its customer's account for a payment made thereafter in good faith.

§ 4-405. Death or Incompetence of Customer.

(1) A payor or collecting bank's authority to accept, pay or collect an item or to account for proceeds of its collection if otherwise effective is not rendered ineffective by incompetence of a customer of either bank existing at the time the item is issued or its collection is undertaken if the bank does not know of an adjudication of incompetence. Neither death nor incompetence of a customer revokes such authority to accept, pay, collect or account until the bank knows of the fact of death or of an adjudication of incompetence and has reasonable opportunity to act on it.

(2) Even with knowledge a bank may for 10 days after the date of death pay or certify checks drawn on or prior to that date unless ordered to stop payment by a person claiming an interest in the account.

§ 4-406. Customer's Duty to Discover and Report Unauthorized Signature or Alteration.

(1) When a bank sends to its customer a statement of account accompanied by items paid in good faith in support of the debit entries or holds the statement and items pursuant to a request for instructions of its customer or otherwise in a reasonable manner makes the statement and items available to the customer, the customer must exercise reasonable care and promptness to examine the statement and items to discover his unauthorized signature or any alteration on an item and must notify the bank promptly after discovery thereof.

(2) If the bank establishes that the customer failed with respect to an item to comply with the duties imposed on the customer by subsection (1) the customer is precluded from asserting against the bank.

    (a)   his unauthorized signature or any alteration on the item if the bank also establishes that it suffered a loss by reason of such failure; and

    (b)   an unauthorized signature or alteration by the same wrongdoer on any other item paid in good faith by the bank after the first item and statement was available to the customer for a reasonable period not exceeding fourteen calendar days and before the bank receives notification from the customer of any such unauthorized signature or alteration.

(3) The preclusion under subsection (2) does not apply if the customer establishes lack of ordinary care on the part of the bank in paying the item(s).

(4) Without regard to care or lack of care of either the customer or the bank a customer who does not within one year from the time the statement and items are made available to the customer (subsection (1) discover and report his unauthorized signature or any alteration on the face or back of the item or does not within 3 years from that time discover and report any unauthorized indorsement is precluded from asserting against the bank such unauthorized signature or indorsement or such alteration.

(5) If under this section a payor bank has a valid defense against a claim of a customer upon or resulting from payment of an item and waives or fails upon request to assert the defense the bank may not assert against any collecting bank or other prior party presenting or transferring the item a claim based upon the unauthorized signature or alteration giving rise to the customer's claim.

§ 4-407. Payor Bank's Right to Subrogation on Improper Payment. If a payor bank has paid an item over the stop payment order of the drawer or maker or otherwise under circumstances giving a basis for objection by the drawer or maker, to prevent unjust enrichment and only to the extent necessary to prevent loss to the bank by reason of its payment of the item, the payor bank shall be subrogated to the rights

    (a)   of any holder in due course on the item against the drawer or maker; and

    (b)   of the payee or any other holder of the item against the drawer or maker either on the item or under the transaction out of which the item arose; and

    (c)   of the drawer or maker against the payee or any other holder of the item with respect to the transaction out of which the item arose.

Part 5. Collection of Documentary Drafts

§ 4-501. Handling of Documentary Drafts; Duty to Send for Presentment and to Notify Customer of Dishonor.

A bank which takes a documentary draft for collection must present or send the draft and accompanying documents for presentment and upon learning that the draft has not been paid or accepted in due course must seasonably notify its customer of such fact even though it may have discounted or bought the draft or extended credit available for withdrawal as of right.

§ 4-502. Presentment of "On Arrival" Drafts.

When a draft or the relevant instructions require presentment "on arrival," "When goods arrive" or the like, the collecting bank need not present until in its judgment a reasonable time for arrival of the goods has expired. Refusal to pay or accept because the goods have not arrived is not dishonor; the bank must notify its transferor of such refusal but need not present the draft again until it is instructed to do so or learns of the arrival of the goods.

§ 4-503. Responsibility of Presenting Bank for Documents and Goods; Report of Reasons for Dishonor; Referee in Case of Need.

Unless otherwise instructed and except as provided in Article 5 a bank presenting a documentary draft

(a) must deliver the documents to the drawee on acceptance of the draft if it is payable more than three days after presentment; otherwise, only on payment; and

(b) upon dishonor, either in the case of presentment for acceptance or presentment for payment, may seek and follow instructions from any referee in case of need designated in the draft or if the presenting bank does not choose to utilize his services it must use diligence and good faith to ascertain the reason for dishonor, must notify its transferor of the dishonor and of the results of its effort to ascertain the reasons therefor and must request instructions.

But the presenting bank is under no obligation with respect to goods represented by the documents except to follow any reasonable instructions seasonably received; it has a right to reimbursement for any expense incurred in following instructions and to prepayment of or indemnity for such expenses.

§ 4-504. Privilege of Presenting Bank to Deal With Goods; Security Interest for Expenses.

(1) A presenting bank which, following the dishonor of a documentary draft, has seasonably requested instructions but does not receive them within a reasonable time may store, sell, or otherwise deal with the goods in any reasonable manner.

(2) For its reasonable expenses incurred by action under subsection (1) the presenting bank has a lien upon the goods or their proceeds, which may be foreclosed in the same manner as an unpaid seller's lien.

ARTICLE 5. LETTERS OF CREDIT

§ 5-101. Short Title.

This Article shall be known and may be cited as Uniform Commercial Code—Letters of Credit.

§ 5-102. Scope.

(1) This Article applies

(a) to a credit issued by a bank if the credit requires a documentary draft or a documentary demand for payment; and

(b) to a credit issued by a person other than a bank if the credit requires that the draft or demand for payment be accompanied by a document of title; and

(c) to a credit issued by a bank or other person if the credit is not within subparagraphs (a) or (b) but conspicuously states that it is a letter of credit or is conspicuously so entitled.

(2) Unless the engagement meets the requirements of subsection (1), this Article does not apply to engagements to make advances or to honor drafts or demands for payment, to authorities to pay or purchase, to guarantees or to general agreements.

(3) This Article deals with some but not all of the rules and concepts of letters of credit as such rules or concepts have developed prior to this act or may hereafter develop. The fact that this Article states a rule does not by itself require, imply or negate application of the same or a converse rule to a situation not provided for or to a person not specified by this Article.

§ 5-103. Definitions.

(1) In this Article unless the context otherwise requires

(a) "Credit" or "letter of credit" means an engagement by a bank or other person made at the request of a customer and of a kind within the scope of this Article (Section 5-102) that the issuer will honor drafts or other demands for payment upon compliance with the conditions specified in the credit. A credit may be either revocable or irrevocable. The engagement may be either an agreement to honor or a statement that the bank or other person is authorized to honor.

(b) A "documentary draft" or a "documentary demand for payment" is one honor of which is conditioned upon the presentation of a document or documents. "Document" means any paper including document of title, security, invoice, certificate, notice of default and the like.

(c) An "issuer" is a bank or other person issuing a credit.

(d) A "beneficiary" of a credit is a person who is entitled under its terms to draw or demand payment.

(e) An "advising bank" is a bank which gives notification of the issuance of a credit by another bank.

(f) A "confirming bank" is a bank which engages either that it will itself honor a credit already issued by another bank or that such credit will be honored by the issuer or a third bank.

(g) A "customer" is a buyer or other person who causes an issuer to issue a credit. The term also includes a bank which procures issuance or confirmation on behalf of that bank's customer.

(2) Other definitions applying to this Article and the sections in which they appear are:
"Notation of Credit." Section 5-108.
"Presenter." Section 5-112(3).
(3) Definitions in other Articles applying to this Article and the sections in which they appear are:
"Accept" or "Acceptance." Section 3-410.
"Contract for sale." Section 2-106.
"Draft." Section 3-104.
"Holder in due course." Section 3-302.
"Midnight deadline." Section 4-104.
"Security." Section 8-102.

(4) In addition, Article 1 contains general definitions and principles of construction and interpretation applicable throughout this Article.

§ 5-104. Formal Requirements; Signing.

(1) Except as otherwise required in subsection (1) (c) of Section 5-102 on scope, no particular form of phrasing is required for a credit. A credit must be in writing and signed by the issuer and a confirmation must be in writing and signed by the confirming bank. A modification of the terms of a credit or confirmation must be signed by the issuer or confirming bank.

(2) A telegram may be a sufficient signed writing if it identifies its sender by an authorized authentication. The authentication may be in code and the authorized naming of the issuer in an advice of credit is a sufficient signing.

§ 5-105. Consideration.
No consideration is necessary to establish a credit or to enlarge or otherwise modify its terms.

§ 5-106. Time and Effect of Establishment of Credit.

(1) Unless otherwise agreed a credit is established

(a) as regards the customer as soon as a letter of credit is sent to him or the letter of credit or an authorized written advice of its issuance is sent to the beneficiary; and

(b) as regards the beneficiary when he receives a letter of credit or an authorized written advice of its issuance.

(2) Unless otherwise agreed once an irrevocable credit is established as regards the customer it can be modified or revoked only with the consent of the customer and once it is established as regards the beneficiary it can be modified or revoked only with his consent.

(3) Unless otherwise agreed after a revocable credit is established it may be modified or revoked by the issuer without notice to or consent from the customer or beneficiary.

(4) Notwithstanding any modification or revocation of a revocable credit any person authorized to honor or negotiate under the terms of the original credit is entitled to reimbursement for or honor of any draft or demand for payment duly honored or negotiated before receipt of notice of the modifica-

tion or revocation and the issuer in turn is entitled to reimbursement from its customer.

§ 5-107. Advice of Credit; Confirmation; Error in Statement of Terms.

(1) Unless otherwise specified an advising bank by advising a credit issued by another bank does not assume any obligation to honor drafts drawn or demands for payment made under the credit but it does assume obligation for the accuracy of its own statement.

(2) A confirming bank by confirming a credit becomes directly obligated on the credit to the extent of its confirmation as though it were its issuer and acquires the rights of an issuer.

(3) Even though an advising bank incorrectly advises the terms of a credit it has been authorized to advise the credit is established as against the issuer to the extent of its original terms.

(4) Unless otherwise specified the customer bears as against the issuer all risks of transmission and reasonable translation or interpretation of any message relating to a credit.

§ 5-108. "Notation Credit," Exhaustion of Credit.

(1) A credit which specifies that any person purchasing or paying drafts drawn or demands for payment made under it must note the amount of the draft or demand on the letter or advice of credit is a "notation credit."

(2) Under a notation credit

(a) a person paying the beneficiary or purchasing a draft or demand for payment from him acquires a right to honor only if the appropriate notation is made and by transferring or forwarding for honor the documents under the credit such a person warrants to the issuer that the notation has been made; and

(b) unless the credit or a signed statement that an appropriate notation has been made accompanies the draft or demand for payment the issuer may delay honor until evidence of notation has been procured which is satisfactory to it but its obligation and that of its customer continue for a reasonable time not exceeding thirty days to obtain such evidence.

(3) If the credit is not a notation credit

(a) the issuer may honor complying drafts or demands for payment presented to it in the order in which they are presented

and is discharged pro tanto by honor of any such draft or demand;

(b) as between competing good faith purchasers of complying drafts or demands the person first purchasing has priority over a subsequent purchaser even though the later purchased draft or demand has been first honored.

§ 5-109. Issuer's Obligation to Its Customer.

(1) An issuer's obligation to its customer includes good faith and observance of any general banking usage but unless otherwise agreed does not include liability or responsibility

(a) for performance of the underlying contract for sale or other transaction between the customer and the beneficiary; or

(b) for any act or omission of any person other than itself or its own branch or for loss or destruction of a draft, demand or document in transit or in the possession of others; or

(c) based on knowledge or lack of knowledge of any usage of any particular trade.

(2) An issuer must examine documents with care so as to ascertain that on their face they appear to comply with the terms of the credit but unless otherwise agreed assumes no liability or responsibility for the genuineness, falsification or effect of any document which appears on such examination to be regular on its face.

(3) A non-bank issuer is not bound by any banking usage of which it has no knowledge.

§ 5-110. Availability of Credit in Portions; Presenter's Reservation of Lien or Claim.

(1) Unless otherwise specified a credit may be used in portions in the discretion of the beneficiary.

(2) Unless otherwise specified a person by presenting a documentary draft or demand for payment under a credit relinquishes upon its honor all claims to the documents and a person by transferring such draft or demand or causing such presentment authorizes such relinquishment. An explicit reservation of claim makes the draft or demand non-complying.

§ 5-111. Warranties on Transfer and Presentment.

(1) Unless otherwise agreed the beneficiary by transferring or presenting a documentary draft or demand for payment warrants to all interested parties that the necessary conditions of the credit have

been complied with. This is in addition to any warranties arising under Articles 3, 4, 7 and 8.

(2) Unless otherwise agreed a negotiating, advising, confirming, collecting or issuing bank presenting or transferring a draft or demand for payment under a credit warrants only the matters warranted by a collecting bank under Article 4 and any such bank transferring a document warrants only the matters warranted by an intermediary under Articles 7 and 8.

§ 5-112. Time Allowed for Honor or Rejection; Withholding Honor or Rejection by Consent; "Presenter."

(1) A bank to which a documentary draft or demand for payment is presented under a credit may without dishonor of the draft, demand or credit

    (a)   defer honor until the close of the third banking day following receipt of the documents; and

    (b)   further defer honor if the presenter has expressly or impliedly consented thereto.

Failure to honor within the time here specified constitutes dishonor of the draft or demand and of the credit [except as otherwise provided in subsection (4) of Section 5-114 on conditional payment].

Note: The bracketed language in the last sentence of subsection (1) should be included only if the optional provisions of Section 5-114(4) and (5) are included.

(2) Upon dishonor the bank may unless otherwise instructed fulfill its duty to return the draft or demand and the documents by holding them at the disposal of the presenter and sending him an advice to that effect.

(3) "Presenter" means any person presenting a draft or demand for payment for honor under a credit even though that person is a confirming bank or other correspondent which is acting under an issuer's authorization.

§ 5-113. Indemnities.

(1) A bank seeking to obtain (whether for itself or another) honor, negotiation or reimbursement under a credit may give an indemnity to induce such honor, negotiation or reimbursement.

(2) An indemnity agreement inducing honor, negotiation or reinbursement

    (a)   unless otherwise explicitly agreed applies to defects in the documents but not in the goods; and

    (b)   unless a longer time is explicitly agreed expires at the end of ten business days

following receipt of the documents by the ultimate customer unless notice of objection is sent before such expiration date. The ultimate customer may send notice of objection to the person from whom he received the documents and any bank receiving such notice is under a duty to send notice to its transferor before its midnight deadline.

§ 5-114. Issuer's Duty and Privilege to Honor; Right to Reimbursement.

(1) An issuer must honor a draft or demand for payment which complies with the terms of the relevant credit regardless of whether the goods or documents conform to the underlying contract for sale or other contract between the customer and the beneficiary. The issuer is not excused from honor of such a draft or demand by reason of an additional general term that all documents must be satisfactory to the issuer, but an issuer may require that specified documents must be satisfactory to it.

(2) Unless otherwise agreed when documents appear on their face to comply with the terms of a credit but a required document does not in fact conform to the warranties made on negotiation or transfer of a document of title (Section 7-507) or of a certificated security (Section 8-306) or is forged or fraudulent or there is fraud in the transaction:

    (a)   the issuer must honor the draft or demand for payment if honor is demanded by a negotiating bank or other holder of the draft or demand which has taken the draft or demand under the credit and under circumstances which would make it a holder in due course (Section 3-302) and in an appropriate case would make it a person to whom a document of title has been duly negotiated (Section 7-502) or a bona fide purchaser of a certificated security (Section 8-302); and

    (b)   in all other cases as against its customer, an issuer acting in good faith may honor the draft or demand for payment despite notification from the customer of fraud, forgery or other defect not apparent on the face of the documents but a court of appropriate jurisdiction may enjoin such honor.

(3) Unless otherwise agreed an issuer which has duly honored a draft or demand for payment is

entitled to immediate reimbursement of any payment made under the credit and to be put in effectively available funds not later than the day before maturity of any acceptance made under the credit.

[(4) When a credit provides for payment by the issuer on receipt of notice that the required documents are in the possession of a correspondent or other agent of the issuer

    (a)   any payment made on receipt of such notice is conditional; and

    (b)   the issuer may reject documents which do not comply with the credit if it does so within three banking days following its receipt of the documents; and

    (c)   in the event of such rejection, the issuer is entitled by charge back or otherwise to return of the payment made.]

[(5) In the case covered by subsection (4) failure to reject documents within the time specified in subparagraph (b) constitutes acceptance of the documents and makes the payment final in favor of the beneficiary.]

Amended in 1977.

Note: Subsections (4) and (5) are bracketed as optional. If they are included the bracketed language in the last sentence of Section 5-112(1) should also be included.

§ 5-115. Remedy for Improper Dishonor or Anticipatory Repudiation.

(1) When an issuer wrongfully dishonors a draft or demand for payment presented under a credit the person entitled to honor has with respect to any documents the rights of a person in the position of a seller (Section 2-707) and may recover from the issuer the face amount of the draft or demand together with incidental damages under Section 2-710 on seller's incidental damages and interest but less any amount realized by resale or other use or disposition of the subject matter of the transaction. In the event no resale or other utilization is made the documents, goods or other subject matter involved in the transaction must be turned over to the issuer on payment of judgment.

(2) When an issuer wrongfully cancels or otherwise repudiates a credit before presentment of a draft or demand for payment drawn under it the beneficiary has the rights of a seller after anticipatory repudiation by the buyer under Section 2-610 if he learns of the repudiation in time reasonably to avoid procurement of the required documents. Oth-

erwise the beneficiary has an immediate right of action for wrongful dishonor.

§ 5-116. Transfer and Assignment.

(1) The right to draw under a credit can be transferred or assigned only when the credit is expressly designated as transferable or assignable.

(2) Even though the credit specifically states that it is non-transferable or non-assignable the beneficiary may before performance of the conditions of the credit assign his right to proceeds. Such an assignment is an assignment of an account under Article 9 on Secured Transactions and is governed by that Article except that

    (a)   the assignment is ineffective until the letter of credit or advice of credit is delivered to the assignee which delivery constitutes perfection of the security interest under Article 9; and

    (b)   the issuer may honor drafts or demands for payment drawn under the credit until it receives a notification of the assignment signed by the beneficiary which reasonably identifies the credit involved in the assignment and contains a request to pay the assignee; and

    (c)   after what reasonably appears to be such a notification has been received the issuer may without dishonor refuse to accept or pay even to a person otherwise entitled to honor until the letter of credit or advice of credit is exhibited to the issuer.

(3) Except where the beneficiary has effectively assigned his right to draw or his right to proceeds, nothing in this section limits his right to transfer or negotiate drafts or demands drawn under the credit.

§ 5-117. Insolvency of Bank Holding Funds for Documentary Credit.

(1) Where an issuer or an advising or confirming bank or a bank which has for a customer procured issuance of a credit by another bank becomes insolvent before final payment under the credit and the credit is one to which this Article is made applicable by paragraphs (a) or (b) of Section 5-102(1) on scope, the receipt or allocation of funds or collateral to secure or meet obligations under the credit shall have the following results:

    (a)   to the extent of any funds or collateral turned over after or before the insolvency as indemnity against or specifically for the purpose of payment of drafts or demands for payment drawn under the designated credit, the drafts or demands are entitled to payment in preference over deposits or other general creditors of the issuer or bank; and

(b) on expiration of the credit or surrender of the beneficiary's rights under it unused any person who has given such funds or collateral is similarly entitled to return thereof; and

(c) a charge to a general or current account with a bank if specifically consented to for the purpose of indemnity against or payment of drafts or demands for payment drawn under the designated credit falls under the same rules as if the funds had been drawn out in cash and then turned over with specific instructions.

(2) After honor or reimbursement under this section the customer or other person for whose account the insolvent bank has acted is entitled to receive the documents involved.

ARTICLE 6. BULK TRANSFERS

§ 6-101. Short Title. This Article shall be known and may be cited as Uniform Commercial Code—Bulk Transfers.

§ 6-102. "Bulk Transfers"; Transfers of Equipment; Enterprises Subject to This Article; Bulk Transfers Subject to This Article.

(1) A "bulk transfer" is any transfer in bulk and not in the ordinary course of the transferor's business of a major part of the materials, supplies, merchandise or other inventory (Section 9-109) of an enterprise subject to this Article.

(2) A transfer of a substantial part of the equipment (Section 9-109) of such an enterprise is a bulk transfer if it is made in connection with a bulk transfer of inventory, but not otherwise.

(3) The enterprises subject to this Article are all those whose principal business is the sale of merchandise from stock, including those who manufacture what they sell.

(4) Except as limited by the following section all bulk transfers of goods located within this state are subject to this Article.

§ 6-103. Transfers Excepted From This Article.
The following transfers are not subject to this Article:

(1) Those made to give security for the performance of an obligation;

(2) General assignments for the benefit of all the creditors of the transferor, and subsequent transfers by the assignee thereunder;

(3) Transfers in settlement or realization of a lien or other security interests;

(4) Sales by executors, administrators, receivers, trustees in bankruptcy, or any public officer under judicial process;

(5) Sales made in the course of judicial or administrative proceedings for the dissolution or reorganization of a corporation and of which notice is sent to the creditors of the corporation pursuant to order of the court or administrative agency;

(6) Transfers to a person maintaining a known place of business in this State who becomes bound to pay the debts of the transferor in full and gives public notice of that fact, and who is solvent after becoming so bound;

(7) A transfer to a new business enterprise organized to take over and continue the business, if public notice of the transaction is given and the new enterprise assumes the debts of the transferor and he receives nothing from the transaction except an interest in the new enterprise junior to the claims of creditors;

(8) Transfers of property which is exempt from execution.

Public notice under subsection (6) or subsection (7) may be given by publishing once a week for two consecutive weeks in a newspaper of general circulation where the transferor had its principal place of business in this state an advertisement including the names and addresses of the transferor and transferee and the effective date of the transfer.

§ 6-104. Schedule of Property, List of Creditors.

(1) Except as provided with respect to auction sales (Section 6-108), a bulk transfer subject to this Article is ineffective against any creditor of the transferor unless:

(a) The transferee requires the transferor to furnish a list of his existing creditors prepared as stated in this section; and

(b) The parties prepare a schedule of the property transferred sufficient to identify it; and

(c) The transferee preserves the list and schedule for six months next following the transfer and permits inspection of either or both and copying therefrom at all reasonable hours by any creditor of the transferor, or files the list and schedule in (a public office to be here identified).

(2) The list of creditors must be signed and sworn to or affirmed by the transferor or his agent. It must contain the names and business addresses of all creditors of the transferor, with the amounts when known, and also the names of all persons who are known to the transferor to assert claims against him even though such claims are disputed. If the transferor is the obligor of an outstanding issue of bonds, debentures or the like as to which there is an indenture trustee, the list of creditors need include only the name and address of the indenture trustee and the aggregate outstanding principal amount of the issue.

(3) Responsibility for the completeness and accuracy of the list of creditors rests on the transferor, and the transfer is not rendered ineffective by errors or omissions therein unless the transferee is shown to have had knowledge.

§ 6-105. Notice to Creditors. In addition to the requirements of the preceding section, any bulk transfer subject to this Article except one made by auction sale (Section 6-108) is ineffective against any creditor of the transferor unless at least ten days before he takes possession of the goods or pays for them, whichever happens first, the transferee gives notice of the transfer in the manner and to the persons hereafter provided (Section 6-107).

[§ 6-106. Applications of the Proceeds. In addition to the requirements of the two preceding sections:

(1) Upon every bulk transfer subject to this Article for which new consideration becomes payable except those made by sale at auction it is the duty of the transferee to assure that such consideration is applied so far as necessary to pay those debts of the transferor which are either shown on the list furnished by the transferor (Section 6-104) or filed in writing in the place stated in the notice (Section 6-107) within thirty days after the mailing of such notice. This duty of the transferee runs to all the holders of such debts, and may be enforced by any of them for the benefit of all.

(2) If any of said debts are in dispute the necessary sum may be withheld from distribution until the dispute is settled or adjudicated.

(3) If the consideration payable is not enough to pay all of the said debts in full distribution shall be made pro rata.]

Note: This section is bracketed to indicate division of opinion as to whether or not it is a wise provision, and to suggest that this is a point on which State enactments may differ without serious damage to the principle of uniformity.

In any State where this section is omitted, the following parts of sections, also bracketed in the text, should also be omitted, namely:

Section 6-107(2)(e).

6-108(3)(c).

6-109(2).

In any State where this section is enacted, these other provisions should be also.

Optional Subsection (4)

[(4) The transferee may within ten days after he takes possession of the goods pay the consideration into the (specify court) in the county where the transferor had its principal place of business in this state and thereafter may discharge his duty under this section by giving notice by registered or certified mail to all the persons to whom the duty runs that the consideration has been paid into that court and that they should file their claims there. On motion of any interested party, the court may order the distribution of the consideration to the persons entitled to it.]

Note: Optional subsection (4) is recommended for those states which do not have a general statute providing for payment of money into court.

§ 6-107. The Notice.

(1) The notice to creditors (Section 6-105) shall state:

(a) that a bulk transfer is about to be made; and

(b) the names and business addresses of the transferor and transferee, and all other business names and addresses used by the transferor within three years last past so far as known to the transferee; and

(c) whether or not all the debts of the transferor are to be paid in full as they fall due as a result of the transaction, and if so, the address to which creditors should send their bills.

(2) If the debts of the transferor are not to be paid in full as they fall due or if the transferee is in doubt on that point then the notice shall state further:

    (a)   the location and general description of the property to be transferred and the estimated total of the transferor's debts;

    (b)   the address where the schedule of property and list of creditors (Section 6-104) may be inspected;

    (c)   whether the transfer is to pay existing debts and if so the amount of such debts and to whom owing;

    (d)   whether the transfer is for new consideration and if so the amount of such consideration and the time and place of payment; [and]

    [(e)   if for new consideration the time and place where creditors of the transferor are to file their claims.]

(3) The notice in any case shall be delivered personally or sent by registered or certified mail to all the persons shown on the list of creditors furnished by the transferor (Section 6-104) and to all other persons who are known to the transferee to hold or assert claims against the transforer. As amended 1962.

Note: The words in brackets are optional. See Note under § 6-106.

§ 6-108. Auction Sales; "Auctioneer."

(1) A bulk transfer is subject to this Article even though it is by sale at auction, but only in the manner and with the results stated in this section.

(2) The transferor shall furnish a list of his creditors and assist in the preparation of a schedule of the property to be sold, both prepared as before stated (Section 6-104).

(3) The person or persons other than the transferor who direct, control or are responsible for the auction are collectively called the "auctioneer." The auctioneer shall:

    (a)   receive and retain the list of creditors and prepare and retain the schedule of property for the period stated in this Article (Section 6-104);

    (b)   give notice of the auction personally or by registered or certified mail at least ten days before it occurs to all persons shown on the list of creditors and to all other persons who are known to him to hold

or assert claims against the transferor; [and]

    (c)   [assure that the net proceeds of the auction are applied as provided in this Article (Section 6-106).]

(4) Failure of the auctioneer to perform any of these duties does not affect the validity of the sale or the title of the purchasers, but if the auctioneer knows that the auction constitutes a bulk transfer such failure renders the auctioneer liable to the creditors of the transferor as a class for the sums owing to them from the transferor up to but not exceeding the net proceeds of the auction. If the auctioneer consists of several persons their liability is joint and several.

Note: The words in brackets are optional. See Note under § 6-106.

§ 6-109. What Creditors Protected; [Credit for Payment to Particular Creditors].

(1) The creditors of the transferor mentioned in this Article are those holding claims based on transactions or events occurring before the bulk transfer, but creditors who become such after notice to creditors is given (Sections 6-105 and 6-107) are not entitled to notice.

[(2) Against the aggregate obligation imposed by the provisions of this Article concerning the application of the proceeds (Section 6-106 and subsection (3) (c) of 6-108) the transferee or auctioneer is entitled to credit for sums paid to particular creditors of the transferor, not exceeding the sums believed in good faith at the time of the payment to be properly payable to such creditors.]

Note: The words in brackets are optional. See Note under § 6-106.

§ 6-110. Subsequent Transfers.
When the title of a transferee to property is subject to a defect by reason of his non-compliance with the requirements of this Article, then:

(1) a purchaser of any of such property from such transferee who pays no value or who takes with notice of such non-compliance takes subject to such defect, but

(2) a purchaser for value in good faith and without such notice takes free of such defect.

§ 6-111. Limitation of Actions and Levies.
No action under this Article shall be brought nor levy made more than six months after the date on which

the transferee took possession of the goods unless the transfer has been concealed. If the transfer has been concealed, actions may be brought or levies made within six months after its discovery.

Note to Article 6:   Section 6-106 is bracketed to indicate division of opinion as to whether or not it is a wise provision, and to suggest that this is a point on which State enactments may differ without serious damage to the principle of uniformity.

In any State where Section 6-106 is not enacted, the following parts of sections, also bracketed in the text, should also be omitted, namely:

   Sec. 6-107(2) (e).

      6-108(3) (c).

      6-109(2).

In any State where Section 6-106 is enacted, these other provisions should be also.

ARTICLE 7. WAREHOUSE RECEIPTS, BILLS OF LADING AND OTHER DOCUMENTS OF TITLE

Part 1. General

§ 7-101. Short Title.   This Article shall be known and may be cited as Uniform Commercial Code—Documents of Title.

§ 7-102. Definitions and Index of Definitions.

(1) In this Article, unless the context otherwise requires:

   (a)   "Bailee" means the person who by a warehouse receipt, bill of lading or other document of title acknowledges possession of goods and contracts to deliver them.

   (b)   "Consignee" means the person named in a bill to whom or to whose order the bill promises delivery.

   (c)   "Consignor" means the person named in a bill as the person from whom the goods have been received for shipment.

   (d)   "Delivery order" means a written order to deliver goods directed to a warehouseman, carrier or other person who in the ordinary course of business issues warehouse receipts or bills of lading.

   (e)   "Document" means document of title as defined in the general definitions in Article 1 (Section 1-201).

   (f)   "Goods" means all things which are

treated as movable for the purposes of a contract of storage or transportation.

   (g)   "Issuer" means a bailee who issues a document except that in relation to an unaccepted delivery order it means the person who orders the possessor of goods to deliver. Issuer includes any person for whom an agent or employee purports to act in issuing a document if the agent or employee has real or apparent authority to issue documents, notwithstanding that the issuer received no goods or that the goods were misdescribed or that in any other respect the agent or employee violated his instructions.

   (h)   "Warehouseman" is a person engaged in the business of storing goods for hire.

(2) Other definitions applying to this Article or to specified Parts thereof, and the sections in which they appear are:

   "Duly negotiate." Section 7-501.

   "Person entitled under the document." Section 7-403(4).

(3) Definitions in other Articles applying to this Article and the sections in which they appear are:

   "Contract for sale." Section 2-106.

   "Overseas." Section 2-323.

   "Receipt" of goods. Section 2-103.

(4) In addition Article 1 contains general definitions and principles of construction and interpretation applicable throughout this Article.

§ 7-103. Relation of Article to Treaty, Statute, Tariff, Classification or Regulation.   To the extent that any treaty or statute of the United States, regulatory statute of this State or tariff, classification or regulation filed or issued pursuant thereto is applicable, the provisions of this Article are subject thereto.

§ 7-104. Negotiable and Non-Negotiable Warehouse Receipt, Bill of Lading or Other Document of Title.

(1) A warehouse receipt, bill of lading or other document of title is negotiable

   (a)   if by its terms the goods are to be delivered to bearer or to the order of a named person; or

   (b)   where recognized in overseas trade, if it runs to a named person or assigns.

(2) Any other document is non-negotiable. A bill of lading in which it is stated that the goods are

consigned to a named person is not made negotiable by a provision that the goods are to be delivered only against a written order signed by the same or another named person.

§ 7-105. Construction Against Negative Implication. The omission from either Part 2 or Part 3 of this Article of a provision corresponding to a provision made in the other Part does not imply that a corresponding rule of law is not applicable.

Part 2. Warehouse Receipts: Special Provisions

§ 7-201. Who May Issue a Warehouse Receipt; Storage Under Government Bond.

(1) A warehouse receipt may be issued by any warehouseman.

(2) Where goods including distilled spirits and agricultural commodities are stored under a statute requiring a bond against withdrawal or a license for the issuance of receipts in the nature of warehouse receipts, a receipt issued for the goods has like effect as a warehouse receipt even though issued by a person who is the owner of the goods and is not a warehouseman.

§ 7-202. Form of Warehouse Receipt; Essential Terms; Optional Terms.

(1) A warehouse receipt need not be in any particular form.

(2) Unless a warehouse receipt embodies within its written or printed terms each of the following, the warehouseman is liable for damages caused by the omission to a person injured thereby:

  (a) the location of the warehouse where the goods are stored;

  (b) the date of issue of the receipt;

  (c) the consecutive number of the receipt;

  (d) a statement whether the goods received will be delivered to the bearer, to a specified person, or to a specified person or his order;

  (e) the rate of storage and handling charges, except that where goods are stored under a field warehousing arrangement a statement of that fact is sufficient on a nonnegotiable receipt;

  (f) a description of the goods or of the packages containing them;

  (g) the signature of the warehouseman, which may be made by his authorized agent;

  (h) if the receipt is issued for goods of which the warehouseman is owner, either solely or jointly or in common with others, the fact of such ownership; and

  (i) a statement of the amount of advances made and of liabilities incurred for which the warehouseman claims a lien or security interest (Section 7-209). If the precise amount of such advances made or of such liabilities incurred is, at the time of the issue of the receipt, unknown to the warehouseman or to his agent who issues it, a statement of the fact that advances have been made or liabilities incurred and the purpose thereof is sufficient.

(3) A warehouseman may insert in his receipt any other terms which are not contrary to the provisions of this Act and do not impair his obligation of delivery (Section 7-403) or his duty of care (Section 7-204). Any contrary provisions shall be ineffective.

§ 7-203. Liability for Non-Receipt or Misdescription. A party to or purchaser for value in good faith of a document of title other than a bill of lading relying in either case upon the description therein of the goods may recover from the issuer damages caused by the non-receipt or misdescription of the goods, except to the extent that the document conspicuously indicates that the issuer does not know whether any part or all of the goods in fact were received or conform to the description, as where the description is in terms of marks or labels or kind, quantity or condition, or the receipt or description is qualified by "contents, condition and quality unknown," "said to contain" or the like, if such indication be true, or the party or purchaser otherwise has notice.

§ 7-204. Duty of Care; Contractual Limitation of Warehouseman's Liability.

(1) A warehouseman is liable for damages for loss of or injury to the goods caused by his failure to exercise such care in regard to them as a reasonably careful man would exercise under like circumstances but unless otherwise agreed he is not liable for damages which could not have been avoided by the exercise of such care.

(2) Damages may be limited by a term in the warehouse receipt or storage agreement limiting the amount of liability in case of loss or damage, and setting forth a specific liability per article or item, or value per unit of weight, beyond which the ware-

houseman shall not be liable; provided, however, that such liability may on written request of the bailor at the time of signing such storage agreement or within a reasonable time after receipt of the warehouse receipt be increased on part or all of the goods thereunder, in which event increased rates may be charged based on such increased valuation, but that no such increase shall be permitted contrary to a lawful limitation of liability contained in the warehouseman's tariff, if any. No such limitation is effective with respect to the warehouseman's liability for conversion to his own use.

(3) Reasonable provisions as to the time and manner of presenting claims and instituting actions based on the bailment may be included in the warehouse receipt or tariff.

(4) This section does not impair or repeal . . .

Note: Insert in subsection (4) a reference to any statute which imposes a higher responsibility upon the warehouseman or invalidates contractual limitations which would be permissible under this Article.

§ 7-205. Title Under Warehouse Receipt Defeated in Certain Cases.
A buyer in the ordinary course of business of fungible goods sold and delivered by a warehouseman who is also in the business of buying and selling such goods takes free of any claim under a warehouse receipt even though it has been duly negotiated.

§ 7-206. Termination of Storage at Warehouseman's Option.

(1) A warehouseman may on notifying the person on whose account the goods are held and any other person known to claim an interest in the goods require payment of any charges and removal of the goods from the warehouse at the termination of the period of storage fixed by the document, or, if no period is fixed, within a stated period not less than thirty days after the notification. If the goods are not removed before the date specified in the notification, the warehouseman may sell them in accordance with the provisions of the section on enforcement of a warehouseman's lien (Section 7-210).

(2) If a warehouseman in good faith believes that the goods are about to deteriorate or decline in value to less than the amount of his lien within the time prescribed in subsection (1) for notification, advertisement and sale, the warehouseman may specify in the notification any reasonable shorter time for removal of the goods and in case the goods are not removed, may sell them at public sale held not less than one week after a single advertisement or posting.

(3) If as a result of a quality or condition of the goods of which the warehouseman had no notice at the time of deposit the goods are a hazard to other property or to the warehouse or to persons, the warehouseman may sell the goods at public or private sale without advertisement on reasonable notification to all persons known to claim an interest in the goods. If the warehouseman after a reasonable effort is unable to sell the goods he may dispose of them in any lawful manner and shall incur no liability by reason of such disposition.

(4) The warehouseman must deliver the goods to any person entitled to them under this Article upon due demand made at any time prior to sale or other disposition under this section.

(5) The warehouseman may satisfy his lien from the proceeds of any sale or disposition under this section but must hold the balance for delivery on the demand of any person to whom he would have been bound to deliver the goods.

§ 7-207. Goods Must Be Kept Separate; Fungible Goods.

(1) Unless the warehouse receipt otherwise provides, a warehouseman must keep separate the goods covered by each receipt so as to permit at all times identification and delivery of those goods except that different lots of fungible goods may be comingled.

(2) Fungible goods so commingled are owned in common by the persons entitled thereto and the warehouseman is severally liable to each owner for that owner's share. Where because of overissue a mass of fungible goods is insufficient to meet all the receipts which the warehouseman has issued against it, the persons entitled include all holders to whom overissued receipts have been duly negotiated.

§ 7-208. Altered Warehouse Receipts.
Where a blank in a negotiable warehouse receipt has been filled in without authority, a purchaser for value and without notice of the want of authority may treat the insertion as authorized. Any other unauthorized alteration leaves any receipt enforceable against the issuer according to its original tenor.

§ 7-209. Lien of Warehouseman.

(1) A warehouseman has a lien against the bailor on the goods covered by a warehouse receipt or on

the proceeds thereof in his possession for charges for storage or transportation (including demurrage and terminal charges), insurance, labor, or charges present or future in relation to the goods, and for expenses necessary for preservation of the goods or reasonably incurred in their sale pursuant to law. If the person on whose account the goods are held is liable for like charges or expenses in relation to other goods whenever deposited and it is stated in the receipt that a lien is claimed for charges and expenses in relation to other goods, the warehouseman also has a lien against him for such charges and expenses whether or not the other goods have been delivered by the warehouseman. But against a person to whom a negotiable warehouse receipt is duly negotiated a warehouseman's lien is limited to charges in an amount or at a rate specified on the receipt or if no charges are so specified then to a reasonable charge for storage of the goods covered by the receipt subsequent to the date of the receipt.

(2) The warehouseman may also reserve a security interest against the bailor for a maximum amount specified on the receipt for charges other than those specified in subsection (1), such as for money advanced and interest. Such a security interest is governed by the Article on Secured Transactions (Article 9).

    (3)(a) A warehouseman's lien for charges and expenses under subsection (1) or a security interest under subsection (2) is also effective against any person who so entrusted the bailor with possession of the goods that a pledge of them by him to a good faith purchaser for value would have been valid but is not effective against a person as to whom the document confers no right in the goods covered by it under Section 7-503.

    (b) A warehouseman's lien on household goods for charges and expenses in relation to the goods under subsection (1) is also effective against all persons if the depositor was the legal possessor of the goods at the time of deposit. "Household goods" means furniture, furnishings and personal effects used by the depositor in a dwelling.

(4) A warehouseman loses his lien on any goods which he voluntarily delivers or which he unjustifiably refuses to deliver.

§ 7-210. Enforcement of Warehouseman's Lien.

(1) Except as provided in subsection (2), a warehouseman's lien may be enforced by public or private sale of the goods in block or in parcels, at any time or place and on any terms which are commercially reasonable, after notifying all persons known to claim an interest in the goods. Such notification must include a statement of the amount due, the nature of the proposed sale and the time and place of any public sale. The fact that a better price could have been obtained by a sale at a different time or in a different method from that selected by the warehouseman is not of itself sufficient to establish that the sale was not made in a commercially reasonable manner. If the warehouseman either sells the goods in the usual manner in any recognized market therefor, or if he sells at the price current in such market at the time of his sale, or if he has otherwise sold in conformity with commercially reasonable practices among dealers in the type of goods sold, he has sold in a commercially reasonable manner. A sale of more goods than apparently necessary to be offered to insure satisfaction of the obligation is not commercially reasonable except in cases covered by the preceding sentence.

(2) A warehouseman's lien on goods other than goods stored by a merchant in the course of his business may be enforced only as follows:

    (a) All persons known to claim an interest in the goods must be notified.

    (b) The notification must be delivered in person or sent by registered or certified letter to the last known address of any person to be notified.

    (c) The notification must include an itemized statement of the claim, a description of the goods subject to the lien, a demand for payment within a specified time not less than ten days after receipt of the notification, and a conspicuous statement that unless the claim is paid within that time the goods will be advertised for sale and sold by auction at a specified time and place.

    (d) The sale must conform to the terms of the notification.

    (e) The sale must be held at the nearest suitable place to that where the goods are held or stored.

    (f) After the expiration of the time given in the notification, an advertisement of the sale must be published once a week for two weeks consecutively in a newspaper of general circulation where the sale is to be held. The advertisement must include a description of the goods, the name of the person on whose account they are being held, and the time and place of the sale. The sale must take place at least fifteen days after the first publication. If there is no newspaper of general circulation where the sale is to be held, the advertisement must be posted at least ten days before the sale in not less than six conspicuous places in the neighborhood of the proposed sale.

(3) Before any sale pursuant to this section any person claiming a right in the goods may pay the amount necessary to satisfy the lien and the reasonable expenses incurred under this section. In that event the goods must not be sold, but must be retained by the warehouseman subject to the terms of the receipt and this Article.

(4) The warehouseman may buy at any public sale pursuant to this section.

(5) A purchaser in good faith of goods sold to enforce a warehouseman's lien takes the goods free of any rights of persons against whom the lien was valid, despite noncompliance by the warehouseman with the requirements of this section.

(6) The warehouseman may satisfy his lien from the proceeds of any sale pursuant to this section but most hold the balance, if any, for delivery on demand to any person to whom he would have been bound to deliver the goods.

(7) The rights provided by this section shall be in addition to all other rights allowed by law to a creditor against his debtor.

(8) Where a lien is on goods stored by a merchant in the course of his business the lien may be enforced in accordance with either subsection (1) or (2).

(9) The warehouseman is liable for damages caused by failure to comply with the requirements for sale under this section and in case of willful violation is liable for conversion.

Part 3. Bills of Lading: Special Provisions

§ 7-301. Liability for Non-Receipt or Misdescription; "Said to Contain"; "Shipper's Load and Count"; Improper Handling.

(1) A consignee of a non-negotiable bill who has given value in good faith or a holder to whom a negotiable bill has been duly negotiated relying in either case upon the description therein of the goods, or upon the date therein shown, may recover from the issuer damages caused by the misdating of the bill or the non-receipt or misdescription of the goods, except to the extent that the document indicates that the issuer does not know whether any part or all of the goods in fact were received or conform to the description, as where the description is in terms of marks or labels or kind, quantity, or condition or the receipt or description is qualified by "contents or condition of contents of packages unknown," "said to contain," "shipper's weight, load and count" or the like, if such indication be true.

(2) When goods are loaded by an issuer who is a common carrier, the issuer must count the packages of goods if package freight and ascertain the kind and quantity if bulk freight. In such cases "shipper's weight, load and count" or other words indicating that the description was made by the shipper are ineffective except as to freight concealed by packages.

(3) When bulk freight is loaded by a shipper who makes available to the issuer adequate facilities for weighing such freight, an issuer who is a common carrier must ascertain the kind and quantity within a reasonable time after receiving the written request of the shipper to do so. In such cases "shipper's weight" or other words of like purport are ineffective.

(4) The issuer may be inserting in the bill the words "shipper's weight, load and count" or other words of like purport indicate that the goods were loaded by the shipper; and if such statement be true the issuer shall not be liable for damages caused by the improper loading. But their omission does not imply liability for such damages.

(5) The shipper shall be deemed to have guaranteed to the issuer the accuracy at the time of shipment of the description, marks, labels, number, kind, quantity, condition and weight, as furnished by him; and the shipper shall indemnify the issuer against damage caused by inaccuracies in such particulars. The right of the issuer to such indemnity shall in no way limit his responsibility and liability under the contract of carriage to any person other than the shipper.

§ 7-302. Through Bills of Lading and Similar Documents.

(1) The issuer of a through bill of lading or other document embodying an undertaking to be performed in part by persons acting as its agents or by connecting carriers is liable to anyone entitled to recover on the document for any breach by such other persons or by a connecting carrier of its obligation under the document but to the extent that the bill covers an undertaking to be performed overseas or in territory not contiguous to the continental United States or an undertaking including matters other than transportation this liability may be varied by agreement of the parties.

(2) Where goods covered by a through bill of lading or other document embodying an undertaking to be performed in part by persons other than the issuer are received by any such person, he is subject with respect to his own performance while the goods are in his possession to the obligation of the issuer. His obligation is discharged by delivery of the goods to another such person pursuant to the document, and does not include liability for breach by any other such persons or by the issuer.

(3) The issuer of such through bill of lading or other document shall be entitled to recover from the connecting carrier or such other person in possession of the goods when the breach of the obligation under the document occurred, the amount it may be required to pay to anyone entitled to recover on the document therefor, as may be evidenced by any receipt, judgment, or transcript thereof, and the amount of any expense reasonably incurred by it in defending any action brought by anyone entitled to recover on the document therefor.

§ 7-303. Diversion; Reconsignment; Change of Instructions.

(1) Unless the bill of lading otherwise provides, the carrier may deliver the goods to a person or destination other than that stated in the bill or may otherwise dispose of the goods on instruction from

    (a) the holder of a negotiable bill; or

    (b) the consignor on a non-negotiable bill notwithstanding contrary instructions from the consignee; or

    (c) the consignee on a non-negotiable bill in the absence of contrary instructions from the consignor, if the goods have

arrived at the billed destination or if the consignee is in possession of the bill; or

    (d) the consignee on a non-negotiable bill if he is entitled as against the consignor to dispose of them.

(2) Unless such instructions are noted on a negotiable bill of lading, a person to whom the bill is duly negotiated can hold the bailee according to the original terms.

§ 7-304. Bills of Lading in a Set.

(1) Except where customary in overseas transportation, a bill of lading must not be issued in a set of parts. The issuer is liable for damages caused by violation of this subsection.

(2) Where a bill of lading is lawfully drawn in a set of parts, each of which is numbered and expressed to be valid only if the goods have not been delivered against any other part, the whole of the parts constitute one bill.

(3) Where a bill of lading is lawfully issued in a set of parts and different parts are negotiated to different persons, the title of the holder to whom the first due negotiation is made prevails as to both the document and the goods even though any later holder may have received the goods from the carrier in good faith and discharged the carrier's obligation by surrender of his part.

(4) Any person who negotiates or transfers a single part of a bill of lading drawn in a set is liable to holders of that part as if it were the whole set.

(5) The bailee is obliged to deliver in accordance with Part 4 of this Article against the first presented part of a bill of lading lawfully drawn in a set. Such delivery discharges the bailee's obligation on the whole bill.

§ 7-305. Destination Bills.

(1) Instead of issuing a bill of lading to the consignor at the place of shipment a carrier may at the request of the consignor procure the bill to be issued at destination or at any other place designated in the request.

(2) Upon request of anyone entitled as against the carrier to control the goods while in transit and on surrender of any outstanding bill of lading or other receipt covering such goods, the issuer may procure a substitute bill to be issued at any place designated in the request.

§ 7-306. **Altered Bills of Lading.** An unauthorized alteration or filling in of a blank in a bill of lading leaves the bill enforceable according to its original tenor.

§ 7-307. **Lien of Carrier.**

(1) A carrier has a lien on the goods covered by a bill of lading for charges subsequent to the date of its receipt of the goods for storage or transportation (including demurrage and terminal charges) and for expenses necessary for preservation of the goods incident to their transportation or reasonably incurred in their sale pursuant to law. But against a purchaser for value of a negotiable bill of lading a carrier's lien is limited to charges stated in the bill or the applicable tariffs, or if no charges are stated then to a reasonable charge.

(2) A lien for charges and expenses under subsection (1) on goods which the carrier was required by law to receive for transportation is effective against the consignor or any person entitled to the goods unless the carrier had notice that the consignor lacked authority to subject the goods to such charges and expenses. Any other lien under subsection (1) is effective against the consignor and any person who permitted the bailor to have control or possession of the goods unless the carrier had notice that the bailor lacked such authority.

(3) A carrier loses his lien on any goods which he voluntarily delivers or which he unjustifiably refuses to deliver.

§ 7-308. **Enforcement of Carrier's Lien.**

(1) A carrier's lien may be enforced by public or private sale of the goods, in block or in parcels, at any time or place and on any terms which are commercially reasonable, after notifying all persons known to claim an interest in the goods. Such notification must include a statement of the amount due, the nature of the proposed sale and the time and place of any public sale. The fact that a better price could have been obtained by a sale at a different time or in a different method from that selected by the carrier is not of itself sufficient to establish that the sale was not made in a commercially reasonable manner. If the carrier either sells the goods in the usual manner in any recognized market therefor or if he sells at the price current in such market at the time of his sale or if he has otherwise sold in conformity with commercially reasonable practices among dealers in the type of goods sold he has sold in a commercially reasonable manner. A sale of more goods than apparently

necessary to be offered to ensure satisfaction of the obligation is not commercially reasonable except in cases covered by the preceding sentence.

(2) Before any sale pursuant to this section any person claiming a right in the goods may pay the amount necessary to satisfy the lien and the reasonable expenses incurred under this section. In that event the goods must not be sold, but must be retained by the carrier subject to the terms of the bill and this Article.

(3) The carrier may buy at any public sale pursuant to this section.

(4) A purchaser in good faith of goods sold to enforce a carrier's lien takes the goods free of any rights of persons against whom the lien was valid, despite noncompliance by the carrier with the requirements of this section.

(5) The carrier may satisfy his lien from the proceeds of any sale pursuant to this section but must hold the balance, if any, for delivery on demand to any person to whom he would have been bound to deliver the goods.

(6) The rights provided by this section shall be in addition to all other rights allowed by law to a creditor against his debtor.

(7) A carrier's lien may be enforced in accordance with either subsection (1) or the procedure set forth in subsection (2) of Section 7-210.

(8) The carrier is liable for damages caused by failure to comply with the requirements for sale under this section and in case of willful violation is liable for conversion.

§ 7-309. **Duty of Care; Contractual Limitation of Carrier's Liability.**

(1) A carrier who issues a bill of lading whether negotiable or non-negotiable must exercise the degree of care in relation to the goods which a reasonably careful man would exercise under like circumstances. This subsection does not repeal or change any law or rule of law which imposes liability upon a common carrier for damages not caused by its negligence.

(2) Damages may be limited by a provision that the carrier's liability shall not exceed a value stated in the document if the carrier's rates are dependent upon value and the consignor by the carrier's tariff is afforded an opportunity to declare a higher value or a value as lawfully provided in the tariff, or where no tariff is filed he is otherwise advised of such opportunity; but no such limitation is effective

with respect to the carrier's liability for conversion to its own use.

(3) Reasonable provisions as to the time and manner of presenting claims and instituting actions based on the shipment may be included in a bill of lading or tariff.

Part 4. Warehouse Receipts and Bills of Lading: General Obligations

§ 7-401. Irregularities in Issue of Receipt or Bill or Conduct of Issuer. The obligations imposed by this Article on an issuer apply to a document of title regardless of the fact that

(a)   the document may not comply with the requirements of this Article or of any other law or regulation regarding its issue, form or content; or

(b)   the issuer may have violated laws regulating the conduct of his business; or

(c)   the goods covered by the document were owned by the bailee at the time the document was issued; or

(d)   the person issuing the document does not come within the definition of warehouseman if it purports to be a warehouse receipt.

§ 7-402. Duplicate Receipt or Bill; Overissue. Neither a duplicate nor any other document of title purporting to cover goods already represented to an outstanding document of the same issuer confers any right in the goods, except as provided in the case of bills in a set, overissue of documents for fungible goods and substitutes for lost, stolen or destroyed documents. But the issuer is liable for damages caused by his overissue or failure to identify a duplicate document as such by conspicuous notation on its face.

§ 7-403. Obligation of Warehouseman or Carrier to Deliver; Excuse.

(1) The bailee must deliver the goods to a person entitled under the document who complies with subsections (2) and (3), unless and to the extent that the bailee establishes any of the following:

(a)   delivery of the goods to a person whose receipt was rightful as against the claimant;

(b)   damage to or delay, loss or destruction of the goods for which the bailee is not liable [, but the burden of establishing

negligence in such cases is on the person, entitled under the document];

Note: The brackets in (1)(b) indicate that State enactments may differ on this point without serious damage to the principle of uniformity.

(c)   previous sale or other disposition of the goods in lawful enforcement of a lien or on warehouseman's lawful termination of storage;

(d)   the exercise by a seller of his right to stop delivery pursuant to the provisions of the Article on Sales (Section 2-705);

(e)   a diversion, reconsignment or other disposition pursuant to the provisions of this Article (Section 7-303) or tariff regulating such right;

(f)   release, satisfaction or any other fact affording a personal defense against the claimant;

(g)   any other lawful excuse.

(2) A person claiming goods covered by a document of title must satisfy the bailee's lien where the bailee so requests or where the bailee is prohibited by law from delivering the goods until the charges are paid.

(3) Unless the person claiming is one against whom the document confers no right under Section 7-503(1), he must surrender for cancellation or notation of partial deliveries any outstanding negotiable document covering the goods, and the bailee must cancel the document or conspicuously note the partial delivery thereon or be liable to any person to whom the document is duly negotiated.

(4) "Person entitled under the document" means holder in the case of a negotiable document, or the person to whom delivery is to be made by the terms of or pursuant to written instructions under a nonnegotiable document.

§ 7-404. No Liability for Good Faith Delivery Pursuant to Receipt or Bill. A bailee who in good faith including observance of reasonable commercial standards has received goods and delivered or otherwise disposed of them according to the terms of the document of title or pursuant to this Article is not liable therefor. This rule applies even though the person from whom he received the goods had no authority to procure the document or to dispose of the goods and even though the person to whom he delivered the goods had no authority to receive them.

Part 5. Warehouse Receipts and Bills of Lading: Negotiation and Transfer

§ 7-501. Form of Negotiation and Requirements of "Due Negotiation."

(1) A negotiable document of title running to the order of a named person is negotiated by his indorsement and delivery. After his indorsement in blank or to bearer any person can negotiate it by delivery alone.

(2)
  (a) A negotiable document of title is also negotiated by delivery alone when by its original terms it runs to bearer.
  (b) When a document running to the order of a named person is delivered to him the effect is the same as if the document has been negotiated.

(3) Negotiation of a negotiable document of title after it has been indorsed to a specified person requires indorsement by the special indorsee as well as delivery.

(4) A negotiable document of title is "duly negotiated" when it is negotiated in the manner stated in this section to a holder who purchases it in good faith without notice of any defense against or claim to it on the part of any person and for value, unless it is established that the negotiation is not in the regular course of business or financing or involves receiving the document in settlement or payment of a money obligation.

(5) Indorsement of a non-negotiable document neither makes it negotiable nor adds to the transferee's rights.

(6) The naming in a negotiable bill of a person to be notified of the arrival of the goods does not limit the negotiability of the bill nor constitute notice to a purchaser thereof of any interest of such person in the goods.

§ 7-502. Rights Acquired by Due Negotiation.

(1) Subject to the following section and to the provisions of Section 7-205 on fungible goods, a holder to whom a negotiable document of title has been duly negotiated acquires thereby:
  (a) title to the document;
  (b) title to the goods;
  (c) all rights accruing under the law of agency or estoppel, including rights to goods delivered to the bailee after the document was issued; and
  (d) the direct obligation of the issuer to hold or deliver the goods according to the terms of the document free of any defense or claim by him except those arising under the terms of the document or under this Article. In the case of a delivery order the bailee's obligation accrues only upon acceptance and the obligation acquired by the holder in that the issuer and any indorser will procure the acceptance of the bailee.

(2) Subject to the following section, title and rights so acquired are not defeated by any stoppage of the goods represented by the document or by surrender of such goods by the bailee, and are not impaired even though the negotiation or any prior negotiation constituted a breach of duty or even though any person has been deprived of possession of the document by misrepresentation, fraud, accident, mistake, duress, loss, theft or conversion, or even though a previous sale or other transfer of the goods or document has been made to a third person.

§ 7-503. Document of Title to Goods Defeated in Certain Cases.

(1) A document of title confers no right in goods against a person who before issuance of the document had a legal interest or a perfected security interest in them and who neither
  (a) delivered or entrusted them or any document of title covering them to the bailor or his nominee with actual or apparent authority to ship, store or sell or with power to obtain delivery under this Article (Section 7-403) or with power of disposition under this Act (Sections 2-403 and 9-307) or other statute or rule of law; nor
  (b) acquiesced in the procurement by the bailor or his nominee of any document of title.

(2) Title to goods based upon an unaccepted delivery order is subject to the rights of anyone to whom a negotiable warehouse receipt or bill of lading covering the goods has been duly negotiated. Such a title may be defeated under the next section to the same extent as the rights of the issuer or a transferee from the issuer.

(3) Title to goods based upon a bill of lading issued to a freight forwarder is subject to the rights of anyone to whom a bill issued by the freight

forwarder is duly negotiated; but delivery by the carrier in accordance with Part 4 of this Article pursuant to its own bill of lading discharges the carrier's obligation to deliver.

§ 7-504. Rights Acquired in the Absence of Due Negotiation; Effect of Diversion; Seller's Stoppage of Delivery.

(1) A transferee of a document, whether negotiable or non-negotiable, to whom the document has been delivered but not duly negotiated, acquires the title and rights which his transferor had or had actual authority to convey.

(2) In the case of a non-negotiable document, until but not after the bailee receives notification of the transfer, the rights of the transferee may be defeated

   (a)   by those creditors of the transferor who could treat the sale as void under Section 2-402; or

   (b)   by a buyer from the transferor in ordinary course of business if the bailee has delivered the goods to the buyer or received notification of his rights; or

   (c)   as against the bailee by good faith dealings of the bailee with the transferor.

(3) A diversion or other change of shipping instructions by the consignor in a non-negotiable bill of lading which causes the bailee not to deliver to the consignee defeats the consignee's title to the goods if they have been delivered to a buyer in ordinary course of business and in any event defeats the consignee's rights against the bailee.

(4) Delivery pursuant to a non-negotiable document may be stopped by a seller under Section 2-705, and subject to the requirement of due notification there provided. A bailee honoring the seller's instructions is entitled to be indemnified by the seller against any resulting loss or expense.

§ 7-505. Indorser Not a Guarantor for Other Parties.
The indorsement of a document of title issued by a bailee does not make the indorser liable for any default by the bailee or by previous indorsers.

§ 7-506. Delivery Without Indorsement: Right to Compel Indorsement.
The transferee of a negotiable document of title has a specifically enforceable right to have his transferor supply any necessary indorsement but the transfer becomes a negotiation only as of the time the indorsement is supplied.

§ 7-507. Warranties on Negotiation or Transfer of Receipt or Bill.
Where a person negotiates or transfers a document of title for value otherwise than as a mere intermediary under the next following section, then unless otherwise agreed he warrants to his immediate purchaser only in addition to any warranty made in selling the goods

   (a)   that the document is genuine; and

   (b)   that he has no knowledge of any fact which would impair its validity or worth; and

   (c)   that his negotiation or transfer is rightful and fully effective with respect to the title to the document and the goods it represents.

§ 7-508. Warranties of Collecting Bank as to Documents.
A collecting bank or other intermediary known to be entrusted with documents on behalf of another or with collection of a draft or other claim against delivery of documents warrants by such delivery of the documents only its own good faith and authority. This rule applies even though the intermediary has purchased or made advances against the claim or draft to be collected.

§ 7-509. Receipt or Bill: When Adequate Compliance With Commercial Contract.
The question whether a document is adequate to fulfill the obligations of a contract for sale or the conditions of a credit is governed by the Articles on Sales (Article 2) and on Letters of Credit (Article 5).

Part 6. Warehouse Receipts and Bills of Lading: Miscellaneous Provisions

§ 7-601. Lost and Missing Documents.

(1) If a document has been lost, stolen or destroyed, a court may order delivery of the goods or issuance of a substitute document and the bailee may without liability to any person comply with such order. If the document was negotiable the claimant must post security approved by the court to indemnify any person who may suffer loss as a result of non-surrender of the document. If the document was not negotiable, such security may be required at the discretion of the court. The court may also in its discretion order payment of the bailee's reasonable costs and counsel fees.

(2) A bailee who without court order delivers goods to a person claiming under a missing negotiable document is liable to any person injured

thereby, and if the delivery is not in good faith becomes liable for conversion. Delivery in good faith is not conversion if made in accordance with a filed classification or tariff or, where no classification or tariff is filed, if the claimant posts security with the bailee in an amount at least double the value of the goods at the time of posting to indemnify any person injured by the delivery who files a notice of claim within one year after the delivery.

§ 7-602 Attachment of Goods Covered by a Negotiable Document. Except where the document was originally issued upon delivery of the goods by a person who had no power to dispose of them, no lien attaches by virtue of any judicial process to goods in the possession of a bailee for which a negotiable document of title is outstanding unless the document be first surrendered to the bailee or its negotiation enjoined, and the bailee shall not be compelled to deliver the goods pursuant to process until the document is surrendered to him or impounded by the court. One who purchases the document for value without notice of the process or injunction takes free of the lien imposed by judicial process.

§ 7-603. Conflicting Claims; Interpleader. If more than one person claims title or possession of the goods, the bailee is excused from delivery until he has had a reasonable time to ascertain the validity of the adverse claims or to bring an action to compel all claimants to interplead and may compel such interpleader, either in defending an action for nondelivery of the goods, or by original action, whichever is appropriate.

ARTICLE 8. INVESTMENT SECURITIES

Part 1. Short Title and General Matters

§ 8-101. Short Title. This Article shall be known and may be cited as Uniform Commercial Code—Investment Securities.

§ 8-102. Definitions and Index of Definitions.

(1) In this Article, unless the context otherwise requires:

  (a) A "certified security" is a share, participation, or other interest in property of or an enterprise of the issuer or an obligation of the issuer which is

    (i) represented by an instrument issued in bearer or registered form;

    (ii) of a type commonly dealt in on securities exchanges or markets or commonly recognized in any area in which it is issued or dealt in as a medium for investment; and

    (iii) either one of a class or series or by its terms divisible into a class or series of shares, participations, interests, or obligations.

  (b) An "uncertificated security" is a share, participation, or other interest in property or an enterprise of the issuer or an obligation of the issuer which is

    (i) not represented by an instrument and the transfer of which is registered upon books maintained for that purpose by or on behalf of the issuer;

    (ii) of a type commonly dealt in on securities exchanges or markets; and

    (iii) either one of a class or series or by its terms divisible into a class or series of shares, participations, interests, or obligations.

  (c) A "security" is either a certificated or an uncertificated security. If a security is certificated, the terms "security" and "certificated security" may mean either the intangible interest, the instrument representing that interest, or both, as the context requires. A writing that is a certificated security is governed by this Article and not by Article 3, even though it also meets the requirements of that Article. This Article does not apply to money. If a certificated security has been retained by or surrendered to the issuer or its transfer agent for reasons other than registration of transfer, other temporary purpose, payment, exchange, or acquisition by the issuer, that security shall be treated as an uncertificated security for purposes of this Article.

  (d) A certificated security is in "registered form" if

    (i) it specifies a person entitled to the security or the rights it represents; and

    (ii) its transfer may be registered upon books maintained for that purpose by or on behalf of the issuer, or the security so states.

(e) A certificated security is in "bearer form" if it runs to bearer according to its terms and not by reason of any indorsement.

(2) A "subsequent purchaser" is a person who takes other than by original issue.

(3) A "clearing corporation" is a corporation registered as a "clearing agency" under the federal securities laws or a corporation:

    (a) at least 90 percent of whose capital stock is held by or for one or more organizations, none of which, other than a national securities exchange or association, holds in excess of 20 percent of the capital stock of the corporation, and each of which is

        (i) subject to supervision or regulation pursuant to the provisions of federal or state banking laws or state insurance laws,

        (ii) a broker or dealer or investment company registered under the federal securities laws, or

        (iii) a national securities exchange or association registered under the federal securities laws; and

    (b) any remaining capital stock of which is held by individuals who have purchased it at or prior to the time of their taking office as directors of the corporation and who have purchased only so much of the capital stock as is necessary to permit them to qualify as directors.

(4) A "custodian bank" is a bank or trust company that is supervised and examined by state or federal authority having supervision over banks and is acting as custodian for a clearing corporation.

(5) Other definitions applying to this Article or to specified Parts thereof and the sections in which they appear are:

"Adverse claim." Section 8-302.
"Bona fide purchaser." Section 8-302.
"Broker." Section 8-303.
"Debtor." Section 9-105.
"Financial intermediary." Section 8-313.
"Guarantee of the signature." Section 8-402.
"Initial transaction statement." Section 8-408.
"Instruction." Section 8-308.
"Intermediary bank." Section 4-105.
"Issuer." Section 8-201.
"Overissue." Section 8-104.
"Secured Party." Section 9-105.

"Security Agreement." Section 9-105.

(6) In addition, Article 1 contains general definitions and principles of construction and interpretation applicable throughout this Article.

§ 8-103. Issuer's Lien. A lien upon a security in favor of an issuer thereof is valid against a purchaser only if:

    (a) the security is certificated and the right of the issuer to the lien is noted conspicuously thereon; or

    (b) the security is uncertificated and a notation of the right of the issuer to the lien is contained in the initial transaction statement sent to the purchaser or, if his interest is transferred to him other than by registration of transfer, pledge, or release, the initial transaction statement sent to the registered owner or the registered pledgee.

§ 8-104. Effect of Overissue; "Overissue."

(1) The provisions of this Article which validate a security or compel its issue or reissue do not apply to the extent that validation, issue, or reissue would result in overissue; but if:

    (a) an identical security which does not constitute an overissue is reasonably available for purchase, the person entitled to issue or validation may compel the issuer to purchase the security for him and either to deliver a certificated security or to register the transfer of an uncertificated security to him, against surrender of any certificated security he holds; or

    (b) a security is not so available for purchase, the person entitled to issue or validation may recover from the issuer the price he or the last purchaser for value paid for it with interest from the date of his demand.

(2) "Overissue" means the issue of securities in excess of the amount the issuer has corporate power to issue.

§ 8-105. Certificated Securities Negotiable; Statements and Instructions Not Negotiable; Presumptions.

(1) Certificated securities governed by this Article are negotiable instruments.

(2) Statements (Section 8-408), notices, or the like, sent by the issuer of uncertificated securities

and instructions (Section 8-308) are neither negotiable instruments nor certificated securities.

(3) In any action on a security:

(a) unless specifically denied in the pleadings, each signature on a certificated security, in a necessary indorsement, on an initial transaction statement, or on an instruction, is admitted;

(b) if the effectiveness of a signature is put in issue, the burden of establishing it is on the party claiming under the signature, but the signature is presumed to be genuine or authorized;

(c) if signatures on a certificated security are admitted or established, production of the security entitles a holder to recover on it unless the defendant establishes a defense or a defect going to the validity of the security;

(d) if signatures on an initial transaction statement are admitted or established, the facts stated in the statement are presumed to be true as of the time of its issuance; and

(e) after it is shown that a defense or defect exists, the plaintiff has the burden of establishing that he or some person under whom he claims is a person against whom the defense or defect is ineffective (Section 8-202).

§ 8-106. Applicability. The law (including the conflict of laws rules) of the jurisdiction of organization of the issuer governs the validity of a security, the effectiveness of registration by the issuer, and the rights and duties of the issuer with respect to:

(a) registration of transfer of a certificated security;

(b) registration of transfer, pledge, or release of an uncertificated security; and

(c) sending of statements of uncertificated securities.

§ 8-107. Securities Transferable; Action for Price.

(1) Unless otherwise agreed and subject to any applicable law or regulation respecting short sales, a person obligated to transfer securities may transfer any certificated security of the specified issue in bearer form or registered in the name of the transferee, or indorsed to him or in blank, or he may transfer an equivalent uncertificated security to the transferee or a person designated by the transferee.

(2) If the buyer fails to pay the price as it comes due under a contract of sale, the seller may recover the price of:

(a) certificated securities accepted by the buyer;

(b) uncertificated securities that have been transferred to the buyer or a person designated by the buyer; and

(c) other securities if efforts at their resale would be unduly burdensome or if there is no readily available market for their resale.

§ 8-108. Registration of Pledge and Release of Uncertificated Securities. A security interest in an uncertificated security may be evidenced by the registration of pledge to the secured party or a person designated by him. There can be no more than one registered pledge of an uncertificated security at any time. The registered owner of an uncertificated security is the person in whose name the security is registered, even if the security is subject to a registered pledge. The rights of a registered pledgee of an uncertificated security under this Article are terminated by the registration of release.

Part 2. Issue–Issuer

§ 8-201. "Issuer."

(1) With respect to obligations on or defenses to a security, "issuer" includes a person who:

(a) places or authorizes the placing of his name on a certificated security (otherwise than as authenticating trustee, registrar, transfer agent, or the like) to evidence that it represents a share, participation, or other interest in his property or in an enterprise, or to evidence his duty to perform an obligation represented by the certificated security;

(b) creates shares, participations, or other interests in his property or in an enterprise or undertakes obligations, which shares, participations, interests, or obligations are uncertificated securities;

(c) directly or indirectly creates fractional interests in his rights or property, which fractional interests are represented by certificated securities; or

(d) becomes responsible for or in place of any other person described as an issuer in this section.

(2) With respect to obligations on or defenses to a security, a guarantor is an issuer to the extent of his guaranty, whether or not his obligation is noted on a certificated security or on statements of uncertificated securities sent pursuant to Section 8-408.

(3) With respect to registration of transfer, pledge, or release (Part 4 of this Article), "issuer" means a person on whose behalf transfer books are maintained.

§ 8-202. Issuer's Responsibility and Defenses; Notice of Defect or Defense.

(1) Even against a purchaser for value and without notice, the terms of a security include:

(a) if the security is certificated, those stated on the security;

(b) if the security is uncertificated, those contained in the initial transaction statement sent to such purchaser or, if his interest is transferred to him other than by registration of transfer, pledge, or release, the initial transaction statement sent to the registered owner or registered pledgee; and

(c) those made part of the security by reference, on the certificated security or in the initial transaction statement, to another instrument, indenture, or document or to a constitution, statute, ordinance, rule, regulation, order or the like, to the extent that the terms referred to do not conflict with the terms stated on the certificated security or contained in the statement. A reference under this paragraph does not of itself charge a purchaser for value with notice of a defect going to the validity of the security, even though the certificated security or statement expressly states that a person accepting it admits notice.

(2) A certificated security in the hands of a purchaser for value or an uncertificated security as to which an initial transaction statement has been sent to a purchaser for value, other than a security issued by a government or governmental agency or unit, even though issued with a defect going to its valid-

ity, is valid with respect to the purchaser if he is without notice of the particular defect unless the defect involves a violation of constitutional provisions, in which case the security is valid with respect to a subsequent purchaser for value and without notice of the defect. This subsection applies to an issuer that is a government or governmental agency or unit only if either there has been substantial compliance with the legal requirements governing the issue or the issuer has received a substantial consideration for the issue as a whole or for the particular security and a stated purpose of the issue is one for which the issuer has power to borrow money or issue the security.

(3) Except as provided in the case of certain unauthorized signatures (Section 8-205), lack of genuineness of a certificated security or an initial transaction statement is a complete defense, even against a purchaser for value and without notice.

(4) All other defenses of the issuer of a certificated or uncertificated security, including nondelivery and conditional delivery of a certificated security, are ineffective against a purchaser for value who has taken without notice of the particular defense.

(5) Nothing in this section shall be construed to affect the right of a party to a "when, as and if issued" or a "when distributed" contract to cancel the contract in the event of a material change in the character of the security that is the subject of the contract or in the plan or arrangement pursuant to which the security is to be issued or distributed.

§ 8-203. Staleness as Notice of Defects or Defenses.

(1) After an act or event creating a right to immediate performance of the principal obligation represented by a certificated security or that sets a date on or after which the security is to be presented or surrendered for redemption or exchange, a purchaser is charged with notice of any defect in its issue or defense of the issuer if:

(a) the act or event is one requiring the payment of money, the delivery of certificated securities, the registration of transfer of uncertificated securities, or any of these on presentation or surrender of the certificated security, the funds or securities are available on the date set for payment or exchange, and he takes the security more than one year after that date; and

(b) the act or event is not covered by paragraph (a) and he takes the security more than 2 years after the date set for surrender or presentation or the date on which performance became due.

(2) A call that has been revoked is not within subsection (1).

§ 8-204. Effect of Issuer's Restrictions on Transfer. A restriction on transfer of a security imposed by the issuer, even if otherwise lawful, is ineffective against any person without actual knowledge of it unless:

(a) the security is certificated and the restriction is noted conspicuously thereon; or

(b) the security is uncertificated and a notation of the restriction is contained in the initial transaction statement sent to the person or, if his interest is transferred to him other than by registration of transfer, pledge, or release, the initial transaction statement sent to the registered owner or the registered pledgee.

§ 8-205. Effect of Unauthorized Signature on Certificated Security or Initial Transaction Statement. An unauthorized signature placed on a certificated security prior to or in the course of issue or placed on an initial transaction statement is ineffective, but the signature is effective in favor of a purchaser for value of the certificated security or a purchaser for value of an uncertificated security to whom the initial transaction statement has been sent, if the purchaser is without notice of the lack of authority and the signing has been done by:

(a) an authenticating trustee, registrar, transfer agent, or other person entrusted by the issuer with the signing of the security, of similar securities, or of initial transaction statements or the immediate preparation for signing of any of them; or

(b) an employee of the issuer, or of any of the foregoing, entrusted with responsible handling of the security or initial transaction statement.

§ 8-206. Completion or Alteration of Certificated Security or Initial Transaction Statement.

(1) If a certificated security contains the signatures necessary to its issue or transfer but is incomplete in any other respect:

(a) any person may complete it by filling in the blanks as authorized; and

(b) even though the blanks are incorrectly filled in, the security as completed is enforceable by a purchaser who took it for value and without notice of the incorrectness.

(2) A complete certificated security that has been improperly altered, even though fraudulently, remains enforceable, but only according to its original terms.

(3) If an initial transaction statement contains the signatures necessary to its validity, but is incomplete in any other respect:

(a) any person may complete it by filling in the blanks as authorized; and

(b) even though the blanks are incorrectly filled in, the statement as completed is effective in favor of the person to whom it is sent if he purchased the security referred to therein for value and without notice of the incorrectness.

(4) A complete initial transaction statement that has been improperly altered, even though fraudulently, is effective in favor of a purchaser to whom it has been sent, but only according to its original terms.

§ 8-207. Rights and Duties of Issuer With Respect to Registered Owners and Registered Pledgees.

(1) Prior to due presentment for registration of transfer of a certificated security in registered form, the issuer or indenture trustee may treat the registered owner as the person exclusively entitled to vote, to receive notifications, and otherwise to exercise all the rights and powers of an owner.

(2) Subject to the provisions of subsections (3), (4), and (6), the issuer or indenture trustee may treat the registered owner of an uncertificated security as the person exclusively entitled to vote, to receive notifications, and otherwise to exercise all the rights and powers of an owner.

(3) The registered owner of an uncertificated security that is subject to a registered pledge is not entitled to registration of transfer prior to the due presentment to the issuer of a release instruction. The exercise of conversion rights with respect to a convertible uncertificated security is a transfer within the meaning of this section.

(4) Upon due presentment of a transfer instruction from the registered pledgee of an uncertificated security, the issuer shall:

(a) register the transfer of the security to the

new owner free of pledge, if the instruction specifies a new owner (who may be the registered pledgee) and does not specify a pledgee;

(b) register the transfer of the security to the new owner subject to the interest of the existing pledgee, if the instruction specifies a new owner and the existing pledgee; or

(c) register the release of the security from the existing pledge and register the pledge of the security to the other pledgee, if the instruction specifies the existing owner and another pledgee.

(5) Continuity of perfection of a security interest is not broken by registration of transfer under subsection (4)(b) or by registration of release and pledge under subsection (4)(c), if the security interest is assigned.

(6) If an uncertificated security is subject to a registered pledge:

(a) any uncertificated securities issued in exchange for or distributed with respect to the pledged security shall be registered subject to the pledge;

(b) any certificated securities issued in exchange for or distributed with respect to the pledge security shall be delivered to the registered pledgee; and

(c) any money paid in exchange for or in redemption of part or all of the security shall be paid to the registered pledgee.

(7) Nothing in this Article shall be construed to affect the liability of the registered owner of a security for calls, assessments, or the like.

§ 8-208. Effect of Signature of Authenticating Trustee, Registrar, or Transfer Agent.

(1) A person placing his signature upon a certificated security or an initial transaction statement as authenticating trustee, registrar, transfer agent, or the like, warrants to a purchaser for value of the certificated security or a purchaser for value of an uncertificated security to whom the initial transaction statement has been sent, if the purchaser is without notice of the particular defect, that:

(a) the certificated security or initial transaction statement is genuine;

(b) his own participation in the issue or registration of the transfer, pledge, or release of the security is within his capacity and within the scope of the authority received by him from the issuer; and

(c) he has reasonable grounds to believe the security is in the form and within the amount the issuer is authorized to issue.

(2) Unless otherwise agreed, a person by so placing his signature does not assume responsibility for the validity of the security in other respects.

Part 3. Transfer

§ 8-301. Rights Acquired by Purchaser.

(1) Upon transfer of a security to a purchaser (Section 8-313), the purchaser acquires the rights in the security which his transferor had or had actual authority to convey unless the purchaser's rights are limited by Section 8-302(4).

(2) A transferee of a limited interest acquires rights only to the extent of the interest transferred. The creation or release of a security interest in a security is the transfer of a limited interest in that security.

§ 8-302. "Bona Fide Purchaser"; "Adverse Claim"; Title Acquired by Bona Fide Purchaser.

(1) A "bona fide purchaser" is a purchaser for value in good faith and without notice of any adverse claim:

(a) who takes delivery of a certificated security in bearer form or in registered form, issued or indorsed to him or in blank;

(b) to whom the transfer, pledge, or release of an uncertificated security is registered on the books of the issuer; or

(c) to whom a security is transferred under the provisions of paragraph (c), (d)(i), or (g) of Section 8-313(1).

(2) "Adverse claim" includes a claim that a transfer was or would be wrongful or that a particular adverse person is the owner of or has an interest in the security.

(3) A bona fide purchaser in addition to acquiring the rights of a purchaser (Section 8-301) also acquires his interest in the security free of any adverse claim.

(4) Notwithstanding Section 8-301(1), the transferee of a particular certificated security who has been a party to any fraud or illegality affecting the security, or who as a prior holder of that certificated security had notice of an adverse claim, cannot improve his position by taking from a bona fide purchaser.

§ 8-303. "Broker." "Broker" means a person engaged for all or part of his time in the business of buying and selling securities, who in the transaction concerned acts for, buys a security from, or sells a security to, a customer. Nothing in this Article determines the capacity in which a person acts for purposes of any other statute or rule to which the person is subject.

§ 8-304. Notice to Purchaser of Adverse Claims.

(1) A purchaser (including a broker for the seller or buyer, but excluding an intermediary bank) of a certificated security is charged with notice of adverse claims if:

> (a)   the security, whether in bearer or registered form, has been indorsed "for collection" or "for surrender" or for some other purpose not involving transfer; or
>
> (b)   the security is in bearer form and has on it an unambiguous statement that it is the property of a person other than the transferor. The mere writing of a name on a security is not such a statement.

(2) A purchaser (including a broker for the seller or buyer, but excluding an intermediary bank) to whom the transfer, pledge, or release of an uncertificated security is registered is charged with notice of adverse claims as to which the issuer has a duty under Section 8-403(4) at the time of registration and which are noted in the initial transaction statement sent to the purchaser or, if his interest is transferred to him other than by registration of transfer, pledge, or release, the initial transaction statement sent to the registered owner or the registered pledgee.

(3) The fact that the purchaser (including a broker for the seller or buyer) of a certificated or uncertificated security has notice that the security is held for a third person or is registered in the name of or indorsed by a fiduciary does not create a duty of inquiry into the rightfulness of the transfer or constitute constructive notice of adverse claims. However, if the purchaser (excluding an intermediary bank) has knowledge that the proceeds are being used or that the transaction is for the individual benefit of the fiduciary or otherwise in breach of duty, the purchaser is charged with notice of adverse claims.

§ 8-305. Staleness as Notice of Adverse Claims.

An act or event that creates a right to immediate performance of the principal obligation represented by a certificated security or sets a date on or after which a certificated security is to be presented or surrendered for redemption or exchange does not itself constitute any notice of adverse claims except in the case of a transfer:

> (a)   after one year from any date set for presentment or surrender for redemption or exchange; or
>
> (b)   after 6 months from any date set for payment of money against presentation or surrender of the security if funds are available for payment on that date.

§ 8-306. Warranties on Presentment and Transfer of Certificated Securities; Warranties of Originators of Instructions.

(1) A person who presents a certificated security for registration of transfer or for payment or exchange warrants to the issuer that he is entitled to the registration, payment, or exchange. But, a purchaser for value and without notice of adverse claims who receives a new, reissued, or re-registered certificated security on registration of transfer or receives an initial transaction statement confirming the registration of transfer of an equivalent uncertificated security to him warrants only that he has no knowledge of any unauthorized signature (Section 8-311) in a necessary indorsement.

(2) A person by transferring a certificated security to a purchaser for value warrants only that:

> (a)   his transfer is effective and rightful;
>
> (b)   the security is genuine and has not been materially altered; and
>
> (c)   he knows of no fact which might impair the validity of the security.

(3) If a certificated security is delivered by an intermediary known to be entrusted with delivery of the security on behalf of another or with collection of a draft or other claim against delivery, the intermediary by delivery warrants only his own good faith and authority, even though he has purchased or made advances against the claim to be collected against the delivery.

(4) A pledgee or other holder for security who redelivers a certificated security received, or after payment and on order of the debtor delivers that security to a third person, makes only the warranties of an intermediary under subsection (3).

(5) A person who originates an instruction warrants to the issuer that:

> (a)   he is an appropriate person to originate the instruction; and
>
> (b)   at the time the instruction is presented to

the issuer he will be entitled to the registration of transfer, pledge, or release.

(6) A person who originates an instruction warrants to any person specially guaranteeing his signature (subsection 8-312(3)) that:

(a) he is an appropriate person to originate the instruction; and

(b) at the time the instruction is presented to the issuer

(i) he will be entitled to the registration of transfer, pledge, or release; and

(ii) the transfer, pledge, or release requested in the instruction will be registered by the issuer free from all liens, security interests, restrictions, and claims other than those specified in the instruction.

(7) A person who originates an instruction warrants to a purchaser for value and to any person guaranteeing the instruction (Section 8-312(6)) that:

(a) he is an appropriate person to originate the instruction;

(b) the uncertificated security referred to therein is valid; and

(c) at the time the instruction is presented to the issuer

(i) the transferor will be entitled to the registration of transfer, pledge, or release;

(ii) the transfer, pledge, or release requested in the instruction will be registered by the issuer free from all liens, security interests, restrictions, and claims other than those specified in the instruction; and

(iii) the requested transfer, pledge, or release will be rightful.

(8) If a secured party is the registered pledgee or the registered owner of an uncertificated security, a person who originates an instruction of release or transfer to the debtor or, after payment and on order of the debtor, a transfer instruction to a third person, warrants to the debtor or the third person only that he is an appropriate person to originate the instruction and, at the time the instruction is presented to the issuer, the transferor will be entitled to the registration of release or transfer. If a transfer instruction to a third person who is a purchaser for value is originated on order of the debtor, the debtor makes to the purchaser the warranties of paragraphs (b), (c)(ii) and (c)(iii) of subsection (7).

(9) A person who transfers an uncertificated security to a purchaser for value and does not originate an instruction in connection with the transfer warrants only that:

(a) his transfer is effective and rightful; and

(b) the uncertificated security is valid.

(10) A broker gives to his customer and to the issuer and a purchaser the applicable warranties provided in this section and has the rights and privileges of a purchaser under this section. The warranties of and in favor of the broker, acting as an agent are in addition to applicable warranties given by and in favor of his customer.

§ 8-307. Effect of Delivery Without Indorsement; Right to Compel Indorsement. If a certificated security in registered form has been delivered to a purchaser without a necessary indorsement he may become a bona fide purchaser only as of the time the indorsement is supplied; but against the transferor, the transfer is complete upon delivery and the purchaser has a specifically enforceable right to have any necessary indorsement supplied.

§ 8-308. Indorsement; Instructions.

(1) An indorsement of a certificated security in registered form is made when an appropriate person signs on it or on a separate document an assignment or transfer of the security or a power to assign or transfer it or his signature is written without more upon the back of the security.

(2) An endorsement may be in blank or special. An indorsement in blank includes an indorsement to bearer. A special indorsement specifies to whom the security is to be transferred, or who has power to transfer it. A holder may convert a blank indorsement into a special indorsement.

(3) An indorsement purporting to be only of part of a certificated security representing units intended by the issuer to be separately transferable is effective to the extent of the indorsement.

(4) An ''instruction'' is an order to the issuer of an uncertificated security requesting that the transfer, pledge, or release from pledge of the uncertificated security specified therein be registered.

(5) An instruction originated by an appropriate person is:

(a) a writing signed by an appropriate person; or

(b) a communication to the issuer in any form agreed upon in a writing signed by the issuer and an appropriate person.

If an instruction has been originated by an appropriate person but is incomplete in any other respect, any person may complete it as authorized and the issuer may rely on it as completed even though it has been completed incorrectly.

(6) "An appropriate person" in subsection (1) means the person specified by the certificated security or by special indorsement to be entitled to the security.

(7) "An appropriate person" in subsection (5) means:

    (a)   for an instruction to transfer or pledge an uncertificated security which is then not subject to a registered pledge, the registered owner; or

    (b)   for an instruction to transfer or release an uncertificated security which is then subject to a registered pledge, the registered pledgee.

(8) In addition to the persons designated in subsections (6) and (7), "an appropriate person" in subsections (1) and (5) includes:

    (a)   if the person designated is described as a fiduciary but is no longer serving in the described capacity, either that person or his successor;

    (b)   if the persons designated are described as more than one person as fiduciaries and one or more are no longer serving in the described capacity, the remaining fiduciary or fiduciaries, whether or not a successor has been appointed or qualified;

    (c)   if the person designated is an individual and is without capacity to act by virtue of death, incompetence, infancy, or otherwise, his executor, administrator, guardian, or like fiduciary;

    (d)   if the persons designated are described as more than one person as tenants by the entirety or with right of survivorship and by reason of death all cannot sign, the survivor or survivors;

    (e)   a person having power to sign under applicable law or controlling instrument; and

    (f)   to the extent that the person designated or any of the foregoing persons may act through an agent, his authorized agent.

(9) Unless otherwise agreed, the indorser of a certificated security by his indorsement or the originator of an instruction by his origination assumes no obligation that the security will be honored by the issuer but only the obligations provided in Section 8-306.

(10) Whether the person signing is appropriate is determined as of the date of signing and an indorsement made by or an instruction originated by him does not become unauthorized for the purposes of this Article by virtue of any subsequent change of circumstances.

(11) Failure of a fiduciary to comply with a controlling instrument or with the law of the state having jurisdiction of the fiduciary relationship, including any law requiring the fiduciary to obtain court approval of the transfer, pledge, or release, does not render his indorsement or an instruction originated by him unauthorized for the purposes of this Article.

§ 8-309. Effect of Indorsement Without Delivery. An indorsement of a certificated security, whether special or in blank, does not constitute a transfer until delivery of the certificated security on which it appears or, if the indorsement is on a separate document, until delivery of both the document and the certificated security.

§ 8-310. Indorsement of Certificated Security in Bearer Form. An indorsement of a certificated security in bearer form may give notice of adverse claims (Section 8-304) but does not otherwise affect any right to registration the holder possesses.

§ 8-311. Effect of Unauthorized Indorsement or Instruction. Unless the owner or pledgee has ratified an unauthorized indorsement or instruction or is otherwise precluded from asserting its ineffectiveness:

    (a)   he may assert its ineffectiveness against the issuer or any purchaser, other than a purchaser for value and without notice of adverse claims, who has in good faith received a new, reissued, or re-registered certificated security on registration of transfer or received an initial transaction statement confirming the registration of transfer, pledge, or release of an equivalent uncertificated security to him; and

    (b)   an issuer who registers the transfer of a certificated security upon the unauthorized indorsement or who registers the transfer, pledge, or release of an uncertificated security upon the unauthorized instruction is subject to liability for improper registration (Section 8-404).

§ 8-312. Effect of Guaranteeing Signature, Indorsement or Instruction.

(1) Any person guaranteeing a signature of an indorser of a certificated security warrants that at the time of signing:

   (a)   the signature was genuine;
   (b)   the signer was an appropriate person to indorse (Section 8-308); and
   (c)   the signer had legal capacity to sign.

(2) Any person guaranteeing a signature of the originator of an instruction warrants that at the time of signing:

   (a)   the signature was genuine;
   (b)   the signer was an appropriate person to originate the instruction (Section 8-308) if the person specified in the instruction as the registered owner or registered pledgee of the uncertificated security was, in fact, the registered owner or registered pledgee of the security, as to which fact the signature guarantor makes no warranty;
   (c)   the signer had legal capacity to sign; and
   (d)   the taxpayer identification number, if any, appearing on the instruction as that of the registered owner or registered pledgee was the taxpayer identification number of the signer or of the owner or pledgee for whom the signer was acting.

(3) Any person specially guaranteeing the signature of the originator of an instruction makes not only the warranties of a signature guarantor (subsection (2) but also warrants that at the time the instruction is presented to the issuer:

   (a)   the person specified in the instruction as the registered owner or registered pledgee of the uncertificated security will be the registered owner or registered pledgee; and
   (b)   the transfer, pledge, or release of the uncertificated security requested in the instruction will be registered by the issuer free from all liens, security interests, restrictions, and claims other than those specified in the instruction.

(4) The guarantor under subsections (1) and (2) or the special guarantor under subsection (3) does not otherwise warrant the rightfulness of the particular transfer, pledge, or release.

(5) Any person guaranteeing an indorsement of a certificated security makes not only the warranties of a signature guarantor under subsection (1) but also warrants the rightfulness of the particular transfer in all respects.

(6) Any person guaranteeing an instruction requesting the transfer, pledge, or release of an uncertificated security makes not only the warranties of a special signature guarantor under subsection (3) but also warrants the rightfulness of the particular transfer, pledge, or release in all respects.

(7) No issuer may require a special guarantee of signature (subsection (3)), a guarantee of indorsement (subsection (5)), or a guarantee of instruction (subsection (6)) as a condition to registration of transfer, pledge, or release.

(8) The foregoing warranties are made to any person taking or dealing with the security in reliance on the guarantee, and the guarantor is liable to the person for any loss resulting from breach of the warranties.

§ 8-313. When Transfer to Purchaser Occurs; Financial Intermediary as Bona Fide Purchaser; "Financial Intermediary."

(1) Transfer of a security or a limited interest (including a security interest) therein to a purchaser occurs only:

   (a)   at the time he or a person designated by him acquires possession of a certificated security;
   (b)   at the time the transfer, pledge, or release of an uncertificated security is registered to him or a person designated by him;
   (c)   at the time his financial intermediary acquires possession of a certificated security specially indorsed to or issued in the name of the purchaser;
   (d)   at the time a financial intermediary, not a clearing corporation, sends him confirmation of the purchase and also by book entry or otherwise identifies as belonging to the purchaser.
      (i)   a specific certificated security in the financial intermediary's possession;
      (ii)   a quantity of securities that constitute or are part of a fungible bulk

of certificated securities in the financial intermediary's possession or of uncertificated securities registered in the name of the financial intermediary; or

(iii) a quantity of securities that constitute or are part of a fungible bulk of securities shown on the account of the financial intermediary on the books of another financial intermediary;

(e) with respect to an identified certificated security to be delivered while still in the possession of a third person, not a financial intermediary, at the time that person acknowledges that he holds for the purchaser;

(f) with respect to a specific uncertificated security the pledge or transfer of which has been registered to a third person, not a financial intermediary, at the time that person acknowledges that he holds for the purchaser;

(g) at the time appropriate entries to the account of the purchaser or a person designated by him on the books of a clearing corporation are made under Section 8-320;

(h) with respect to the transfer of a security interest where the debtor has signed a security agreement containing a description of the security, at the time a written notification, which, in the case of the creation of the security interest, is signed by the debtor (which may be a copy of the security agreement) or which, in the case of the release or assignment of the security interest created pursuant to this paragraph, is signed by the secured party, is received by

(i) a financial intermediary on whose books the interest of the transferor in the security appears;

(ii) a third person, not a financial intermediary, in possession of the security, if it is certificated;

(iii) a third person, not a financial intermediary, who is the registered owner of the security, if it is uncertificated and not subject to a registered pledge; or

(iv) a third person, not a financial intermediary, who is the registered pledgee of the security, if it is

uncertificated and subject to a registered pledge;

(i) with respect to the transfer of a security interest where the transferor has signed a security agreement containing a description of the security, at the time new value is given by the secured party; or

(j) with respect to the transfer of a security interest where the secured party is a financial intermediary and the security has already been transferred to the financial intermediary under paragraphs (a), (b), (c), (d), or (g), at the time the transferor has signed a security agreement containing a description of the security and value is given by the secured party.

(2) The purchaser is the owner of a security held for him by a financial intermediary, but cannot be a bona fide purchaser of a security so held except in the circumstances specified in paragraphs (c), (d)(i), and (g) of subsection (1). If a security so held is part of a fungible bulk, as in the circumstances specified in paragraphs (d)(ii) and (d)(iii) of subsection (1), the purchaser is the owner of a proportionate property interest in the fungible bulk.

(3) Notice of an adverse claim received by the financial intermediary or by the purchaser after the financial intermediary takes delivery of a certificated security as a holder for value or after the transfer, pledge, or release of an uncertificated security has been registered free of the claim to a financial intermediary who has given value is not effective either as to the financial intermediary or as to the purchaser. However, as between the financial intermediary and the purchaser the purchaser may demand transfer of an equivalent security as to which no notice of adverse claim has been received.

(4) A "financial intermediary" is a bank, broker, clearing corporation, or other person (or the nominee of any of them) which in the ordinary course of its business maintains security accounts for its customers and is acting in that capacity. A financial intermediary may have a security interest in securities held in account for its customer.

§ 8-314. Duty to Transfer, When Completed.

(1) Unless otherwise agreed, if a sale of a security is made on an exchange or otherwise through brokers:

(a) the selling customer fulfills his duty to transfer at the time he:

(i) places a certificated security in the possession of the selling broker or a person designated by the broker;

(ii) causes an uncertificated security to be registered in the name of the selling broker or a person designated by the broker;

(iii) if requested, causes an acknowledgment to be made to the selling broker that a certificated or uncertificated security is held for the broker; or

(iv) places in the possession of the selling broker or of a person designated by the broker a transfer instruction for an uncertificated security, providing the issuer does not refuse to register the requested transfer if the instruction is presented to the issuer for registration within 30 days thereafter; and

(b) the selling broker, including a correspondent broker acting for a selling customer, fulfills his duty to transfer at the time he:

(i) places a certificated security in the possession of the buying broker or a person designated by the buying broker;

(ii) causes an uncertificated security to be registered in the name of the buying broker or a person designated by the buying broker;

(iii) places in the possession of the buying broker or of a person designated by the buying broker a transfer instruction for an uncertificated security, providing the issuer does not refuse to register the requested transfer if the instruction is presented to the issuer for registration within 30 days thereafter; or

(iv) effects clearance of the sale in accordance with the rules of the exchange on which the transaction took place.

(2) Except as provided in this section or unless otherwise agreed, a transferor's duty to transfer a security under a contract of purchase is not fulfilled until he:

(a) places a certificated security in form to be negotiated by the purchaser in the possession of the purchaser or of a person designated by the purchaser;

(b) causes an uncertificated security to be registered in the name of the purchaser or a person designated by the purchaser; or

(c) if the purchaser requests, causes an acknowledgment to be made to the purchaser that a certificated or uncertificated security is held for the purchaser.

(3) Unless made on an exchange, a sale to a broker purchasing for his own account is within subsection (2) and not within subsection (1).

§ 8-315. Action Against Transferee Based Upon Wrongful Transfer.

(1) Any person against whom the transfer of a security is wrongful for any reason, including his incapacity, as against anyone except a bona fide purchaser, may:

(a) reclaim possession of the certificated security wrongfully transferred;

(b) obtain possession of any new certificated security representing all or part of the same rights;

(c) compel the origination of an instruction to transfer to him or a person designated by him an uncertificated security constituting all or part of the same rights; or

(d) have damages.

(2) If the transfer is wrongful because of an unauthorized indorsement of a certificated security, the owner may also reclaim or obtain possession of the security or a new certificated security, even from a bona fide purchaser, if the ineffectiveness of the purported indorsement can be asserted against him under the provisions of this Article on unauthorized indorsements (Section 8-311).

(3) The right to obtain or reclaim possession of a certificated security or to compel the origination of a transfer instruction may be specifically enforced and the transfer of a certificated or uncertificated security enjoined and a certificated security impounded pending the litigation.

§ 8-316. Purchaser's Right to Requisites for Registration of Transfer, Pledge, or Release on Books.

Unless otherwise agreed, the transferor of a certificated security or the transferor, pledgor, or pledgee of an uncertificated security on due demand must supply his purchaser with any proof of his authority to transfer, pledge, or release or with any other requisite necessary to obtain registration of the transfer, pledge, or release of the security; but if the transfer, pledge, or release is not for value, a transferor, pledgor, or pledgee need not do so unless the purchaser furnishes the necessary expenses. Failure within a reasonable time to comply with a demand made gives the purchaser the right to reject or rescind the transfer, pledge, or release.

§ 8-317. Creditors' Rights.

(1) Subject to the exceptions in subsections (3) and (4), no attachment or levy upon a certificated security or any share or other interest represented thereby which is outstanding is valid until the security is actually seized by the officer making the attachment or levy, but a certificated security which has been surrendered to the issuer may be reached by a creditor by legal process at the issuer's chief executive office in the United States.

(2) An uncertificated security registered in the name of the debtor may not be reached by a creditor except by legal process at the issuer's chief executive office in the United States.

(3) The interest of a debtor in a certificated security that is in the possession of a secured party not a financial intermediary or in an uncertificated security registered in the name of a secured party not a financial intermediary (or in the name of a nominee of the secured party) may be reached by a creditor by legal process upon the secured party.

(4) The interest of a debtor in a certificated security that is in the possession of or registered in the name of a financial intermediary or in an uncertificated security registered in the name of a financial intermediary may be reached by a creditor by legal process upon the financial intermediary on whose books the interest of the debtor appears.

(5) Unless otherwise provided by law, a creditor's lien upon the interest of a debtor in a security obtained pursuant to subsection (3) or (4) is not a restraint on the transfer of the security, free of the lien, to a third party for new value; but in the event of a transfer, the lien applies to the proceeds of the transfer in the hands of the secured party or financial intermediary, subject to any claims having priority.

(6) A creditor whose debtor is the owner of a security is entitled to aid from courts of appropriate jurisdiction, by injunction or otherwise, in reaching the security or in satisfying the claim by means allowed at law or in equity in regard to property that cannot readily be reached by ordinary legal process.

§ 8-318. No Conversion by Good Faith Conduct.
An agent or bailee who in good faith (including observance of reasonable commercial standards if he is in the business of buying, selling, or otherwise

dealing with securities) has received certificated securities and sold, pledged, or delivered them or has sold or caused the transfer or pledge of uncertificated securities over which he had control according to the instructions of his principal, is not liable for conversion or for participation in breach of fiduciary duty although the principal had no right so to deal with the securities.

§ 8-319. Statute of Frauds.
A contract for the sale of securities is not enforceable by way of action or defense unless:

(a) there is some writing signed by the party against whom enforcement is sought or by his authorized agent or broker, sufficient to indicate that a contract has been made for sale of a stated quantity of described securities at a defined or stated price;

(b) delivery of a certificated security or transfer instruction has been accepted, or transfer of an uncertificated security has been registered and the transferee has failed to send written objection to the issuer within 10 days after receipt of the initial transaction statement confirming the registration, or payment has been made, but the contract is enforceable under this provision only to the extent of the delivery, registration, or payment;

(c) within a reasonable time a writing in confirmation of the sale or purchase and sufficient against the sender under paragraph (a) has been received by the party against whom enforcement is sought and he has failed to send written objection to its contents within 10 days after its receipt; or

(d) the party against whom enforcement is sought admits in his pleading, testimony, or otherwise in court that a contract was made for the sale of a stated quantity of described securities at a defined or stated price.

§ 8-320. Transfer or Pledge Within Central Depository System.

(1) In addition to other methods, a transfer, pledge, or release of a security or any interest therein may be effected by the making of appropriate entries on the books of a clearing corporation reducing the account of the transferor, pledgor, or

pledgee and increasing the account of the transferee, pledgee, or pledgor by the amount of the obligation or the number of shares or rights transferred, pledge, or released, if the security is shown on the account of a transferor, pledgor, or pledgee on the books of the clearing corporation; is subject to the control of the clearing corporation; and

    (a)   if certificated,

        (i)   is in the custody of the clearing corporation, another clearing corporation, a custodian bank, or a nominee of any of them; and

        (ii)   is in bearer form or indorsed in blank by an appropriate person or registered in the name of the clearing corporation, a custodian bank, or a nominee of any of them; or

    (b)   if uncertificated, is registered in the name of the clearing corporation, another clearing corporation, a custodian bank, or a nominee of any of them.

(2) Under this section entries may be made with respect to like securities or interests therein as a part of a fungible bulk and may refer merely to a quantity of a particular security without reference to the name of the registered owner, certificate or bond number, or the like, and, in appropriate cases, may be on a net basis taking into account other transfers, pledges, or releases of the same security.

(3) A transfer under this section is effective (Section 8-313) and the purchaser acquires the rights of the transferor (Section 8-301). A pledge or release under this section is the transfer of a limited interest. If a pledge or the creation of a security interest is intended, the security interest is perfected at the time when both value is given by the pledgee and the appropriate entries are made (Section 8-321). A transferee or pledgee under this section may be a bona fide purchaser (Section 8-302).

(4) A transfer or pledge under this section is not a registration of transfer under Part 4.

(5) That entries made on the books of the clearing corporation as provided in subsection (1) are not appropriate does not affect the validity or effect of the entries or the liabilities or obligations of the clearing corporation to any person adversely affected thereby.

§ 8-321. Enforceability, Attachment, Perfection and Termination of Security Interests.

(1) A security interest in a security is enforceable and can attach only if it is transferred to the secured party or a person designated by him pursuant to a provision of Section 8-313(1).

(2) A security interest so transferred pursuant to agreement by a transferor who has rights in the security to a transferee who has given value is a perfected security interest, but a security interest that has been transferred solely under paragraph (i) of Section 8-313(1) becomes unperfected after 21 days unless, within that time, the requirements for transfer under any other provision of Section 8-313(1) are satisfied.

(3) A security interest in a security is subject to the provisions of Article 9, but:

    (a)   no filing is required to perfect the security interest; and

    (b)   no written security agreement signed by the debtor is necessary to make the security interest enforceable, except as provided in paragraph (h), (i), or (j) of Section 8-313(1). The secured party has the rights and duties provided under Section 9-207, to the extent they are applicable, whether or not the security is certificated, and, if certificated, whether or not it is in his possession.

(4) Unless otherwise agreed, a security interest in a security is terminated by transfer to the debtor or a person designated by him pursuant to a provision of Section 8-313(1). If a security is thus transferred, the security interest, if not terminated, becomes unperfected unless the security is certificated and is delivered to the debtor for the purpose of ultimate sale or exchange or presentation, collection, renewal, or registration of transfer. In that case, the security interest becomes unperfected after 21 days unless, within that time, the security (or securities for which it has been exchanged) is transferred to the secured party or a person designated by him pursuant to a provision of Section 8-313(1).

Part 4. Registration

§ 8-401. Duty of Issuer to Register Transfer, Pledge, or Release.

(1) If a certificated security in registered form is presented to the issuer with a request to register transfer or an instruction is presented to the issuer with a request to register transfer, pledge, or release, the issuer shall register the transfer, pledge, or release as requested if:

    (a)   the security is indorsed or the instruction was originated by the appropriate person or persons (Section 8-308);

(b)   reasonable assurance is given that those indorsements or instructions are genuine and effective (Section 8-402);

(c)   the issuer has no duty as to adverse claims or has discharged the duty (Section 8-403);

(d)   any applicable law relating to the collection of taxes has been complied with; and

(e)   the transfer, pledge, or release is in fact rightful or is to a bona fide purchaser.

(2) If an issuer is under a duty to register a transfer, pledge, or release of a security, the issuer is also liable to the person presenting a certificated security or an instruction for registration or his principal for loss resulting from any unreasonable delay in registration or from failure or refusal to register the transfer, pledge, or release.

§ 8-402. Assurance that Indorsements and Instructions Are Effective.

(1) The issuer may require the following assurance that each necessary indorsement of a certificated security or each instruction (Section 8-308) is genuine and effective:

(a)   in all cases, a guarantee of the signature (Section 8-312(1) or (2)) of the person indorsing a certificated security or originating an instruction including, in the case of an instruction, a warranty of the taxpayer identification number or, in the absence thereof, other reasonable assurance of identity;

(b)   if the indorsement is made or the instruction is originated by an agent, appropriate assurance of authority to sign;

(c)   if the indorsement is made or the instruction is originated by a fiduciary, appropriate evidence of appointment or incumbency;

(d)   if there is more than one fiduciary, reasonable assurance that all who are required to sign have done so; and

(e)   if the indorsement is made or the instruction is originated by a person not covered by any of the foregoing, assurance appropriate to the case corresponding as nearly as may be to the foregoing.

(2) A "guarantee of the signature" in subsection (1) means a guarantee signed by or on behalf of a person reasonably believed by the issuer to be responsible. The issuer may adopt standards with respect to responsibility if they are not manifestly unreasonable.

(3) "Appropriate evidence of appointment or incumbency" in subsection (1) means:

(a)   in the case of a fiduciary appointed or qualified by a court, a certificate issued by or under the direction or supervision of that court or an officer thereof and dated within 60 days before the date of presentation for transfer, pledge, or release; or

(b)   in any other case, a copy of a document showing the appointment or a certificate issued by or on behalf of a person reasonably believed by the issuer to be responsible or, in the absence of that document or certificate, other evidence reasonably deemed by the issuer to be appropriate. The issuer may adopt standards with respect to the evidence if they are not manifestly unreasonable. The issuer is not charged with notice of the contents of any document obtained pursuant to this paragraph (b) except to the extent that the contents relate directly to the appointment or incumbency.

(4) The issuer may elect to require reasonable assurance beyond that specified in this section, but if it does so and, for a purpose other than that specified in subsection (3)(b), both requires and obtains a copy of a will, trust, indenture, articles of co-partnership, by-laws, or other controlling instrument, it is charged with notice of all matters contained therein affecting the transfer, pledge, or release.

§ 8-403. Issuer's Duty as to Adverse Claims.

(1) An issuer to whom a certificated security is presented for registration shall inquire into adverse claims if:

(a)   a written notification of an adverse claim is received at a time and in a manner affording the issuer a reasonable opportunity to act on it prior to the issuance of a new, reissued, or re-registered certificated security and the notification identifies the claimant, the registered owner, and the issue of which the security is a part, and provides an address for communications directed to the claimant; or

(b) the issuer is charged with notice of an adverse claim from a controlling instrument it has elected to require under Section 8-402(4).

(2) The issuer may discharge any duty of inquiry by any reasonable means, including notifying an adverse claimant by registered or certified mail at the address furnished by him or, if there be no such address, at his residence or regular place of business that the certificated security has been presented for registration of transfer by a named person, and that the transfer will be registered unless within 30 days from the date of mailing the notification, either:

(a) an appropriate restraining order, injunction, or other process issues from a court of competent jurisdiction; or

(b) there is filed with the issuer an indemnity bond, sufficient in the issuer's judgment to protect the issuer and any transfer agent, registrar, or other agent of the issuer involved from any loss it or they may suffer by complying with the adverse claim.

(3) Unless an issuer is charged with notice of an adverse claim from a controlling instrument which it has elected to require under Section 8-402(4) or receives notification of an adverse claim under subsection (1), if a certificated security presented for registration is indorsed by the appropriate person or persons the issuer is under no duty to inquire into adverse claims. In particular:

(a) an issuer registering a certificated security in the name of a person who is a fiduciary or who is described as a fiduciary is not bound to inquire into the existence, extent, or correct description of the fiduciary relationship; and thereafter the issuer may assume without inquiry that the newly registered owner continues to be the fiduciary until the issuer receives written notice that the fiduciary is no longer acting as such with respect to the particular security;

(b) an issuer registering transfer on an indorsement by a fiduciary is not bound to inquire whether the transfer is made in compliance with a controlling instrument or with the law of the state having jurisdiction of the fiduciary relationship, including any law requiring the fiduciary

to obtain court approval of the transfer; and

(c) the issuer is not charged with notice of the contents of any court record or file or other recorded or unrecorded document even though the document is in its possession and even though the transfer is made on the indorsement of a fiduciary to the fiduciary himself or to his nominee.

(4) An issuer is under no duty as to adverse claims with respect to an uncertificated security except:

(a) claims embodied in a restraining order, injunction, or other legal process served upon the issuer if the process was served at a time and in a manner affording the issuer a reasonable opportunity to act on it in accordance with the requirements of subsection (5);

(b) claims of which the issuer has received a written notification from the registered owner or the registered pledgee if the notification was received at a time and in a manner affording the issuer a reasonable opportunity to act on it in accordance with the requirements of subsection (5);

(c) claims (including restrictions on transfer not imposed by the issuer) to which the registration of transfer to the present registered owner was subject and were so noted in the initial transaction statement sent to him; and

(d) claims as to which an issuer is charged with notice from a controlling instrument it has elected to require under Section 8-402(4).

(5) If the issuer of an uncertificated security is under a duty as to an adverse claim, he discharges that duty by:

(a) including a notation of the claim in any statements sent with respect to the security under Section 8-408(3), (6), and (7); and

(b) refusing to register the transfer or pledge of the security unless the nature of the claim does not preclude transfer or pledge subject thereto.

(6) If the transfer or pledge of the security is registered subject to an adverse claim, a notation

of the claim must be included in the initial transaction statement and all subsequent statements sent to the transferee and pledgee under Section 8-408.

(7) Notwithstanding subsections (4) and (5), if an uncertificated security was subject to a registered pledge at the time the issuer first came under a duty as to a particular adverse claim, the issuer has no duty as to that claim if transfer of the security is requested by the registered pledgee or an appropriate person acting for the registered pledgee unless:

(a) the claim was embodied in legal process which expressly provides otherwise;

(b) the claim was asserted in a written notification from the registered pledgee;

(c) the claim was one as to which the issuer was charged with notice from a controlling instrument it required under Section 8-402(4) in connection with the pledgee's request for transfer; or

(d) the transfer requested is to the registered owner.

§ 8-404. Liability and Non-Liability for Registration.

(1) Except as provided in any law relating to the collection of taxes, the issuer is not liable to the owner, pledgee, or any other person suffering loss as a result of the registration of a transfer, pledge, or release of a security if:

(a) there were on or with a certificated security the necessary indorsements or the issuer had received an instruction originated by an appropriate person (Section 8-308); and

(b) the issuer had no duty as to adverse claims or has discharged the duty (Section 8-403).

(2) If an issuer has registered a transfer of a certificated security to a person not entitled to it, the issuer on demand shall deliver a like security to the true owner unless:

(a) the registration was pursuant to subsection (1);

(b) the owner is precluded from asserting any claim for registering the transfer under Section 8-405(1); or

(c) the delivery would result in overissue, in which case the issuer's liability is governed by Section 8-104.

(3) If an issuer has improperly registered a transfer, pledge, or release of an uncertificated security, the issuer on demand from the injured party shall restore the records as to the injured party to the condition that would have obtained if the improper registration had not been made unless:

(a) the registration was pursuant to subsection (1); or

(b) the registration would result in overissue, in which case the issuer's liability is governed by Section 8-104.

§ 8-405. Lost, Destroyed, and Stolen Certificated Securities.

(1) If a certificated security has been lost, apparently destroyed, or wrongfully taken, and the owner fails to notify the issuer of that fact within a reasonable time after he has notice of it and the issuer registers a transfer of the security before receiving notification, the owner is precluded from asserting against the the issuer any claim for registering the transfer under Section 8-404 or any claim to a new security under this section.

(2) If the owner of a certificated security claims that the security has been lost, destroyed, or wrongfully taken, the issuer shall issue a new certificated security or, at the option of the issuer, an equivalent uncertificated security in place of the original security if the owner:

(a) so requests before the issuer has notice that the security has been acquired by a bona fide purchaser;

(b) files with the issuer a sufficient indemnity bond; and

(c) satisfies any other reasonable requirements imposed by the issuer.

(3) If, after the issue of a new certificated or uncertificated security, a bona fide purchaser of the original certificated security presents it for registration of transfer, the issuer shall register the transfer unless registration would result in overissue, in which event the issuer's liability is governed by Section 8-104. In addition to any rights on the indemnity bond, the issuer may recover the new certificated security from the person to whom it was issued or any person taking under him except a bona fide purchaser or may cancel the uncertificated security unless a bona fide purchaser or any person taking under a bona fide purchaser is then the registered owner or registered pledgee thereof.

§ 8-406. Duty of Authenticating Trustee, Transfer Agent, or Registrar.

(1) If a person acts as authenticating trustee, transfer agent, registrar, or other agent for an issuer in the registration of transfers of its certificated securities or in the registration of transfers, pledges, and releases of its uncertificated securities, in the issue of new securities, or in the cancellation of surrendered securities:

    (a)   he is under a duty to the issuer to exercise good faith and due diligence in performing his functions; and

    (b)   with regard to the particular functions he performs, he has the same obligation to the holder or owner of a certificated security or to the owner or pledgee of an uncertificated security and has the same rights and privileges as the issuer has in regard to those functions.

(2) Notice to an authenticating trustee, transfer agent, registrar or other agent is notice to the issuer with respect to the functions performed by the agent.

§ 8-407. Exchangeability of Securities.

(1) No issuer is subject to the requirements of this section unless it regularly maintains a system for issuing the class of securities involved under which both certificated and uncertificated securities are regularly issued to the category of owners, which includes the person in whose name the new security is to be registered.

(2) Upon surrender of a certificated security with all necessary indorsements and presentation of a written request by the person surrendering the security, the issuer, if he has no duty as to adverse claims or has discharged the duty (Section 8-403), shall issue to the person or a person designated by him an equivalent uncertificated security subject to all liens, restrictions, and claims that were noted on the certificated security.

(3) Upon receipt of a transfer instruction originated by an appropriate person who so requests, the issuer of an uncertificated security shall cancel the uncertificated security and issue an equivalent certificated security on which must be noted conspicuously any liens and restrictions of the issuer and any adverse claims (as to which the issuer has a duty under Section 8-403(4)) to which the uncertificated security was subject. The certificated security shall be registered in the name of and delivered to:

    (a)   the registered owner, if the uncertificated security was not subject to a registered pledge; or

    (b)   the registered pledgee, if the uncertificated security was subject to a registered pledge.

§ 8-408. Statements of Uncertificated Securities.

(1) Within 2 business days after the transfer of an uncertificated security has been registered, the issuer shall send to the new registered owner and, if the security has been transferred subject to a registered pledge, to the registered pledgee a written statement containing:

    (a)   a description of the issue of which the uncertificated security is a part;

    (b)   the number of shares or units transferred;

    (c)   the name and address and any taxpayer identification number of the new registered owner and, if the security has been transferred subject to a registered pledge, the name and address and any taxpayer identification number of the registered pledgee;

    (d)   a notation of any liens and restrictions of the issuer and any adverse claims (as to which the issuer has a duty under Section 8-403(4)) to which the uncertificated security is or may be subject at the time of registration or a statement that there are none of those liens, restrictions, or adverse claims; and

    (e)   the date the transfer was registered.

(2) Within 2 business days after the pledge of an uncertificated security has been registered, the issuer shall send to the registered owner and the registered pledgee a written statement containing:

    (a)   a description of the issue of which the uncertificated security is a part;

    (b)   the number of shares or units pledged;

    (c)   the name and address and any taxpayer identification number of the registered owner and the registered pledgee;

    (d)   a notation of any liens and restrictions of the issuer and any adverse claims (as to which the issuer has a duty under Section 8-403(4)) to which the uncertificated security is or may be subject at the time of registration or a statement that there are none of those liens, restrictions, or adverse claims; and

    (e)   the date the pledge was registered.

(3) Within 2 business days after the release from pledge of an uncertificated security has been registered, the issuer shall send to the registered owner and the pledgee whose interest was released a written statement containing:

    (a)   a description of the issue of which the uncertificated security is a part;

    (b)   the number of shares or units released from pledge;

    (c)   the name and address and any taxpayer identification number of the registered owner and the pledge whose interest was released;

    (d)   a notation of any liens and restrictions of the issuer and any adverse claims (as to which the issuer has a duty under Section 8-403(4)) to which the uncertificated security is or may be subject at the time of registration or a statement that there are none of those liens, restrictions, or adverse claims; and

    (e)   the date the release was registered.

(4) An "initial transaction statement" is the statement sent to:

    (a)   the new registered owner and, if applicable, to the registered pledgee pursuant to subsection (1);

    (b)   the registered pledgee pursuant to subsection (2); or

    (c)   the registered owner pursuant to subsection (3).

Each initial transaction statement shall be signed by or on behalf of the issuer and must be identified as "Initial Transaction Statement."

(5) Within 2 business days after the transfer of an uncertificated security has been registered, the issuer shall send to the former registered owner and the former registered pledgee, if any, a written statement containing:

    (a)   a description of the issue of which the uncertificated security is a part;

    (b)   the number of shares or units transferred;

    (c)   the name and address and any taxpayer identification number of the former registered owner and of any former registered pledgee; and

    (d)   the date the transfer was registered.

(6) At periodic intervals no less frequent than annually and at any time upon the reasonable written request of the registered owner, the issuer shall send to the registered owner of each uncertificated security a dated written statement containing:

    (a)   a description of the issue of which the uncertificated security is a part;

    (b)   the name and address and any taxpayer identification number of the registered owner;

    (c)   the number of shares or units of the uncertificated security registered in the name of the registered owner on the date of the statement;

    (d)   the name and address and any taxpayer identification number of any registered pledgee and the number of shares or units subject to the pledge; and

    (e)   a notation of any liens and restrictions of the issuer and any adverse claims (as to which the issuer has a duty under Section 8-403(4)) to which the uncertificated security is or may be subject or a statement that there are none of those liens, restrictions, or adverse claims.

(7) At periodic intervals no less frequent than annually and at any time upon the reasonable written request of the registered pledgee, the issuer shall send to the registered pledgee of each uncertificated security a dated written statement containing:

    (a)   a description of the issue of which the uncertificated security is a part;

    (b)   the name and address and any taxpayer identification number of the registered owner;

    (c)   the name and address and any taxpayer identification number of the registered pledgee;

    (d)   the number of shares or units subject to the pledge; and

    (e)   a notation of any liens and restrictions of the issuer and any adverse claims (as to which the issuer has a duty under Section 8-403(4)) to which the uncertificated security is or may be subject or a statement that there are none of those liens, restrictions, or adverse claims.

(8) If the issuer sends the statements described in subsections (6) and (7) at periodic intervals no less frequent than quarterly, the issuer is not obliged to

send additional statements upon request unless the owner or pledgee requesting them pays to the issuer the reasonable cost of furnishing them.

(9) Each statement sent pursuant to this section must bear a conspicuous legend reading substantially as follows: "This statement is merely a record of the rights of the addressee as of the time of its issuance. Delivery of this statement, of itself, confers no rights on the recipient. This statement is neither a negotiable instrument nor a security."

ARTICLE 9. SECURED TRANSACTIONS; SALES OF ACCOUNTS AND CHATTEL PAPER

Part 1. Short Title, Applicability and Definitions

§ 9-101. Short Title. This Article shall be known and may be cited as Uniform Commercial Code—Secured Transactions.

§ 9-102. Policy and Subject Matter of Article.

(1) Except as otherwise provided in Section 9-104 on excluded transactions, this Article applies

    (a)   to any transaction (regardless of its form) which is intended to create a security interest in personal property or fixtures including goods, documents, instruments, general intangibles, chattel paper or accounts; and also

    (b)   to any sale of accounts or chattel paper.

(2) This Article applies to security interests created by contract including pledge, assignment, chattel mortgage, chattel trust, trust deed, factor's lien, equipment trust, conditional sale, trust receipt, other lien or title retention contract and lease or consignment intended as security. This Article does not apply to statutory liens except as provided in Section 9-310.

(3) The application of this Article to a security interest in a secured obligation is not affected by the fact that the obligation is itself secured by a transaction or interest to which this Article does not apply. Amended in 1972.

Note: The adoption of this Article should be accompanied by the repeal of existing statutes dealing with conditional sales, trust receipts, factor's liens where the factor is given a non-possessory lien, chattel mortgages, crop mortgages, mortgages on railroad equipment, assignment of accounts and generally statutes regulating security interests in personal property.

Where the state has a retail installment selling act or small loan act, that legislation should be carefully examined to determine what changes in those acts are needed to conform them to this Article. This Article primarily sets out rules defining rights of a secured party against persons dealing with the debtor; it does not prescribe regulations and controls which may be necessary to curb abuses arising in the small loan business or in the financing of consumer purchases on credit. Accordingly there is no intention to repeal existing regulatory acts in those fields by enactment or re-enactment of Article 9. See Section 9-203(4) and the Note thereto.

§ 9-103. Perfection of Security Interest in Multiple State Transactions.

(1) Documents, instruments and ordinary goods.

    (a)   This subsection applies to documents and instruments and to goods other than those covered by a certificate of title described in subsection (2), mobile goods described in subsection (3), and minerals described in subsection (5).

    (b)   Except as otherwise provided in this subsection, perfection and the effect of perfection or non-perfection of a security interest in collateral are governed by the law of the jurisdiction where the collateral is when the last event occurs on which is based the assertion that the security interest is perfected or unperfected.

    (c)   If the parties to a transaction creating a purchase money security interest in goods in one jurisdiction understand at the time that the security interest attaches that the goods will be kept in another jurisdiction, then the law of the other jurisdiction governs the perfection and the effect of perfection or non-perfection of the security interest from the time it attaches until thirty days after the debtor receives possession of the goods and thereafter if the goods are taken to the other jurisdiction before the end of the thirty-day period.

    (d)   When collateral is brought into and kept in this state while subject to a security interest perfected under the law of the jurisdiction from which the collateral was removed, the security interest remains perfected, but if action is required by Part 3 of this Article to perfect the security interest,

(i) if the action is not taken before the expiration of the period of perfection in the other jurisdiction or the end of four months after the collateral is brought into this state, whichever period first expires, the security interest becomes unperfected at the end of that period and is thereafter deemed to have been unperfected as against a person who became a purchaser after removal;

(ii) if the action is taken before the expiration of the period specified in subparagraph (i), the security interest continues perfected thereafter;

(iii) for the purpose of priority over a buyer of consumer goods (subsection (2) of Section 9-307), the period of the effectiveness of a filing in the jurisdiction from which the collateral is removed is governed by the rules with respect to perfection in subparagraphs (i) and (ii).

(2) Certificate of title.

(a) This subsection applies to goods covered by a certificate of title issued under a statute of this state or of another jurisdiction under the law of which indication of a security interest on the certificate is required as a condition of perfection.

(b) Except as otherwise provided in this subsection, perfection and the effect of perfection or non-perfection of the security interest are governed by the law (including the conflict of laws rules) of the jurisdiction issuing the certificate until four months after the goods are removed from that jurisdiction and thereafter until the goods are registered in another jurisdiction, but in any event not beyond surrender of the certificate. After the expiration of that period, the goods are not covered by the certificate of title within the meaning of this section.

(c) Except with respect to the rights of a buyer described in the next paragraph, a security interest, perfected in another jurisdiction otherwise than by notation on a certificate of title, in goods brought into this state and thereafter covered by a certificate of title issued by this state is subject to the rules stated in paragraph (d) of subsection (1).

(d) If goods are brought into this state while a security interest therein is perfected in any manner under the law of the jurisdiction from which the goods are removed and a certificate of title is issued by this state and the certificate does not show that the goods are subject to the security interest or that they may be subject to security interests not shown on the certificate, the security interest is subordinate to the rights of a buyer of the goods who is not in the business of selling goods of that kind to the extent that he gives value and receives delivery of the goods after issuance of the certificate and without knowledge of the security interest.

(3) Accounts, general intangibles and mobile goods.

(a) This subsection applies to accounts (other than an account described in subsection (5) on minerals) and general intangibles (other than uncertificated securities) and to goods which are mobile and which are of a type normally used in more than one jurisdiction, such as motor vehicles, trailers, rolling stock, airplanes, shipping containers, road building and construction machinery and commercial harvesting machinery and the like, if the goods are equipment or are inventory leased or held for lease by the debtor to others, and are not covered by a certificate of title described in subsection (2).

(b) The law (including the conflict of laws rules) of the jurisdiction in which the debtor is located governs the perfection and the effect of perfection or non-perfection of the security interest.

(c) If, however, the debtor is located in jurisdiction which is not a part of the United States, and which does not provide for perfection of the security interest by filing or recording in that jurisdiction, the law of the jurisdiction in the United States in which the debtor has its major executive office in the United States governs the perfection and the effect of perfection or non-perfection of the security interest through filing. In the alternative, if the debtor is located in a jurisdiction which is not a part of the United States or Canada and the collateral is accounts or general intangibles for money due or to become due, the security interest may be perfected by notification to the account debtor. As used in this paragraph, "United States" includes its territories and possessions and the Commonwealth of Puerto Rico.

(d)   A debtor shall be deemed located at his place of business if he has one, at his chief executive office if he has more than one place of business, otherwise at his residence. If, however, the debtor is a foreign air carrier under the Federal Aviation Act of 1958, as amended, it shall be deemed located at the designated office of the agent upon whom service of process may be made on behalf of the foreign air carrier.

(e)   A security interest perfected under the law of the jurisdiction of the location of the debtor is perfected until the expiration of four months after a change of the debtor's location to another jurisdiction, or until perfection would have ceased by the law of the first jurisdiction, whichever period first expires. Unless perfected in the new jurisdiction before the end of that period, it becomes unperfected thereafter and is deemed to have been unperfected as against a person who became a purchaser after the change.

(4) Chattel paper.

The rules stated for goods in subsection (1) apply to a possessory security interest in chattel paper. The rules stated for accounts in subsection (3) apply to a non-possessory security interest in chattel paper, but the security interest may not be perfected by notification to the account debtor.

(5) Minerals.

Perfection and the effect of perfection or non-perfection of a security interest which is created by a debtor who has an interest in minerals or the like (including oil and gas) before extraction and which attaches thereto as extracted, or which attaches to an account resulting from the sale thereof at the wellhead or minehead are governed by the law (including the conflict of laws rules) of the jurisdiction wherein the wellhead or minehead is located.

(6) Uncertificated securities.

The law (including the conflict of laws rules) of the jurisdiction of organization of the issuer governs the perfection and the effect of perfection or non-perfection of a security interest in uncertificated securities.

§ 9-104. Transactions Excluded From Article.

This Article does not apply

(a)   to a security interest subject to any statute of the United States, to the extent that such statute governs the rights of parties to and third parties affected by transactions in particular types of property; or

(b)   to a landlord's lien; or

(c)   to a lien given by statute or other rule of law for services or materials except as provided in Section 9-310 on priority of such liens; or

(d)   to a transfer of a claim for wages, salary or other compensation of an employee; or

(e)   to a transfer by a government or governmental subdivision or agency; or

(f)   to a sale of accounts or chattel paper as part of a sale of the business out of which they arose, or an assignment of accounts or chattel paper which is for the purpose of collection only, or a transfer of a right to payment under a contract to an assignee who is also to do the performance under the contract or a transfer of a single account to an assignee in whole or partial satisfaction of a preexisting indebtedness; or

(g)   to a transfer of an interest in or claim in or under any policy of insurance, except as provided with respect to proceeds (Section 9-306) and priorities in proceeds (Section 9-312); or

(h)   to a right represented by a judgment (other than a judgment taken on a right to payment which was collateral); or

(i)   to any right of set-off; or

(j)   except to the extent that provision is made for fixtures in Section 9-313, to the creation or transfer of an interest in or lien on real estate, including a lease or rents thereunder; or

(k) to a transfer in whole or in part of any claim arising out of tort; or

(l) to a transfer of an interest in any deposit account (subsection (1) of Section 9-105), except as provided with respect to proceeds (Section 9-306) and priorities in proceeds (Section 9-312).

§ 9-105. Definitions and Index of Definitions.

(1) In this Article unless the context otherwise requires:

(a) "Account debtor" means the person who is obligated on an account, chattel paper or general intangible;

(b) "Chattel paper" means a writing or writings which evidence both a monetary obligation and a security interest in or a lease of specific goods, but a charter or other contract involving the use or hire of a vessel is not chattel paper. When a transaction is evidenced both by such a security agreement or a lease and by an instrument or a series of instruments, the group of writings taken together constitutes chattel paper;

(c) "Collateral" means the property subject to a security interest, and includes accounts and chattel paper which have been sold;

(d) "Debtor" means the person who owes payment or other performance of the obligation secured, whether or not he owns or has rights in the collateral, and includes the seller of accounts or chattel paper. Where the debtor and the owner of the collateral are not the same person, the term "debtor" means the owner of the collateral in any provision of the Article dealing with the collateral, the obligor in any provision dealing with the obligation, and may include both where the context so requires;

(e) "Deposit account" means a demand, time, savings, passbook or like account maintained with a bank, savings and loan association, credit union or like organization, other than an account evidenced by a certificate of deposit;

(f) "Document" means document of title as defined in the general definitions of Article 1 (Section 1-201), and a receipt of the kind described in subsection (2) of Section 7-201;

(g) "Encumbrance" includes real estate mortgages and other liens on real estate and all other rights in real estate that are not ownership interests;

(h) "Goods" includes all things which are movable at the time the security interest attaches or which are fixtures (Section 9-313), but does not include money, documents, instruments, accounts, chattel paper, general intangibles, or minerals or the like (including oil and gas) before extraction. "Goods" also includes standing timber which is to be cut and removed under a conveyance or contract for sale, and unborn young of animals, and growing crops;

(i) "Instrument" means a negotiable instrument (defined in Section 3-104), or a certificated security (defined in Section 8-102) or any other writing which evidences a right to the payment of money and is not itself a security agreement or lease and is of a type which is in ordinary course of business transferred by delivery with any necessary indorsement or assignment;

(j) "Mortgage" means a consensual interest created by a real estate mortgage, a trust deed on real estate, or the like;

(k) An advance is made "pursuant to commitment" if the secured party has bound himself to make it, whether or not a subsequent event of default or other event not within his control has relieved or may relieve him from his obligation;

(l) "Security agreement" means an agreement which creates or provides for a security interest;

(m) "Secured party" means a lender, seller or other person in whose favor there is a security interest, including a person to whom accounts or chattel paper have been sold. When the holders of obligations issued under an indenture of trust, equipment trust agreement or the like are represented by a trustee or other person, the representative is the secured party;

(n) "Transmitting utility" means any person primarily engaged in the railroad, street railway or trolley bus business, the electric or electronics communications transmission business, the transmission of goods by pipeline, or the transmission or the production and transmission of electricity, steam, gas or water, or the provision of sewer service.

(2) Other definitions applying to this Article and the sections in which they appear are:

"Account." Section 9-106.

"Attach." Section 9-203.

"Construction mortgage." Section 9-313(1).

"Consumer goods." Section 9-109(1).

"Equipment." Section 9-109(2).

"Farm products." Section 9-109(3).

"Fixture." Section 9-313(1).

"Fixture filing." Section 9-313(1).

"General intangibles." Section 9-106.

"Inventory." Section 9-109(4).

"Lien creditor." Section 9-301(3).

"Proceeds." Section 9-306(1).

"Purchase money security interest." Section 9-107.

"United States." Section 9-103.

(3) The following definitions in other Articles apply to this Article:

"Check." Section 3-104.

"Contract for sale." Section 2-106.

"Holder in due course." Section 3-302.

"Note." Section 3-104.

"Sale." Section 2-106.

(4) In addition Article 1 contains general definitions and principles of construction and interpretation applicable throughout this Article.

§ 9-106. Definitions: "Account"; "General Intangibles." "Account" means any right to payment for goods sold or leased or for services rendered which is not evidenced by an instrument or chattel paper, whether or not it has been earned by performance. "General intangibles" means any personal property (including things in action) other than goods, accounts, chattel paper, documents, instruments, and money. All rights to payment earned or unearned under a charter or other contract involving the use or hire of a vessel and all rights incident to the charter or contract are accounts.

§ 9-107. Definitions: "Purchase Money Security Interest." A security interest is a "purchase money security interest" to the extent that it is

(a) taken or retained by the seller of the collateral to secure all or part of its price; or

(b) taken by a person who by making advances or incurring an obligation gives value to enable the debtor to acquire rights in or the use of collateral if such value is in fact so used.

§ 9-108. When After-Acquired Collateral Not Security for Antecedent Debt. Where a secured party makes an advance, incurs an obligation, releases a perfected security interest, or otherwise gives new value which is to be secured in whole or in part by after-acquired property his security interest in the after-acquired collateral shall be deemed to be taken for new value and not as security for an antecedent debt if the debtor acquires his rights in such collateral either in the ordinary course of his business or under a contract of purchase made pursuant to the security agreement within a reasonable time after new value is given.

§ 9-109. Classification of Goods; "Consumer Goods"; "Equipment"; "Farm Products"; "Inventory." Goods are

(1) "consumer goods" if they are used or bought for use primarily for personal, family or household purposes;

(2) "equipment" if they are used or bought for use primarily in business (including farming or a profession) or by a debtor who is a non-profit organization or a governmental subdivision or agency or if the goods are not included in the definitions of inventory, farm products or consumer goods;

(3) "farm products" if they are crops or livestock or supplies used or produced in farming operations or if they are products of crops or livestock in their unmanufactured states (such as ginned cotton, woolclip, maple syrup, milk and eggs), and if they are in the possession of a debtor engaged in raising, fattening, grazing or other farming operations. If goods are farm products they are neither equipment nor inventory;

(4) "inventory" if they are held by a person who holds them for sale or lease or to be furnished under contracts of service or if he has so furnished them, or if they are raw materials, work in process or materials used or consumed in a business. Inventory of a person is not to be classified as his equipment.

§ 9-110. Sufficiency of Description. For the purposes of this Article any description of personal property or real estate is sufficient whether or not it is specific if it reasonably identifies what is described.

§ 9-111. Applicability of Bulk Transfer Laws. The creation of a security interest is not a bulk transfer under Article 6 (see Section 6-103).

§ 9-112. Where Collateral Is Not Owned by Debtor. Unless otherwise agreed, when a secured party knows that collateral is owned by a person who is not the debtor, the owner of the collateral is entitled to receive from the secured party any surplus under Section 9-502(2) or under Section 9-504(1), and is not liable for the debt or for any deficiency after resale, and he has the same right as the debtor

   (a)   to receive statements under Section 9-208;

   (b)   to receive notice of and to object to a secured party's proposal to retain the collateral in satisfaction of the indebtedness under Section 9-505;

   (c)   to redeem the collateral under Section 9-506;

   (d)   to obtain injunctive or other relief under Section 9-507(1); and

   (e)   to recover losses caused to him under Section 9-208(2).

§ 9-113. Security Interests Arising Under Article on Sales. A security interest arising solely under the Article on Sales (Article 2) is subject to the provisions of this Article except that to the extent that and so long as the debtor does not have or does not lawfully obtain possession of the goods

   (a)   no security agreement is necessary to make the security interest enforceable; and

   (b)   no filing is required to perfect the security interest; and

   (c)   the rights of the secured party on default by the debtor are governed by the Article on Sales (Article 2).

§ 9-114. Consignment.

(1) A person who delivers goods under a consignment which is not a security interest and who would be required to file under this Article by paragraph (3)(c) of Section 2-326 has priority over a secured party who is or becomes a creditor of the consignee and who would have a perfected security interest in the goods if they were the property of the consignee, and also has priority with respect to identi-fiable cash proceeds received on or before delivery of the goods to a buyer, if

   (a)   the consignor complies with the filing provision of the Article on Sales with respect to consignments (paragraph (3)(c) of Section 2-326) before the consignee receives possession of the goods; and

   (b)   the consignor gives notification in writing to the holder of the security interest if the holder has filed a financing statement covering the same types of goods before the date of the filing made by the consignor; and

   (c)   the holder of the security interest receives the notification within five years before the consignee receives possession of the goods; and

   (d)   the notification states that the consignor expects to deliver goods on consignment to the consignee, describing the goods by item or type.

(2) In the case of a consignment which is not a security interest and in which the requirements of the preceding subsection have not been met, a person who delivers goods to another is subordinate to a person who would have a perfected security interest in the goods if they were the property of the debtor.

Part 2. Validity of Security Agreement and Rights of Parties Thereto

§ 9-201. General Validity of Security Agreement. Except as otherwise provided by this Act a security agreement is effective according to its terms between the parties, against purchasers of the collateral and against creditors. Nothing in this Article validates any charge or practice illegal under any statute or regulation thereunder governing usury, small loans, retail installment sales, or the like, or extends the application of any such statute or regulation to any transaction not otherwise subject thereto.

§ 9-202. Title to Collateral Immaterial. Each provision of this Article with regard to rights, obligations and remedies applies whether title to collateral is in the secured party or in the debtor.

§ 9-203. Attachment and Enforceability of Security Interest; Proceeds; Formal Requisites.

(1) Subject to the provisions of Section 4-208 on the security interest of a collecting bank, Section

8-321 on security interests in securities and Section 9-113 on a security interest arising under the Article on Sales, a security interest is not enforceable against the debtor or third parties with respect to the collateral and does not attach unless:

    (a)   the collateral is in the possession of the secured party pursuant to agreement, or the debtor has signed a security agreement which contains a description of the collateral and in addition, when the security interest covers crops growing or to be grown or timber to be cut, a description of the land concerned;

    (b)   value has been given; and

    (c)   the debtor has rights in the collateral

(2) A security interest attaches when it becomes enforceable against the debtor with respect to the collateral. Attachment occurs as soon as all of the events specified in subsection (1) have taken place unless explicit agreement postpones the time of attaching.

(3) Unless otherwise agreed a security agreement gives the secured party the rights to proceeds provided by Section 9-306.

(4) A transaction, although subject to this Article, is also subject to ....*, and in the case of conflict between the provisions of this Article and any such statute, the provisions of such statute control. Failure to comply with any applicable statute has only the effect which is specified therein.

Note: *At * in subsection (4) insert reference to any local statue regulating small loans, retail installment sales and the like.*

The foregoing subsection (4) is designed to make it clear that certain transactions, although subject to this Article, must also comply with other applicable legislation.

This Article is designed to regulate all the "security" aspects of transactions within its scope. There is, however, much regulatory legislation, particularly in the consumer field, which supplements this Article and should not be repealed by its enactment. Examples are small loan acts, retail installment selling acts and the like. Such acts may provide for licensing and rate regulation and may prescribe particular forms of contract. Such provisions should remain in force despite the enactment of this Article. On the other hand if a retail installment selling act contains provisions on filing, rights on default, etc., such provisions should be repealed as inconsistent

with this Article except that inconsistent provisions as to deficiencies, penalties, etc., in the Uniform Consumer Credit Code and other recent related legislation should remain because those statutes were drafted after the substantial enactment of the Article and with the intention of modifying certain provisions of this Article as to consumer credit.

§ 9-204. After-Acquired Property; Future Advances.

(1) Except as provided in subsection (2), a security agreement may provide that any or all obligations covered by the security agreement are to be secured by after-acquired collateral.

(2) No security interest attaches under an after-acquired property clause to consumer goods other than accessions (Section 9-314) when given as additional security unless the debtor acquires rights in them within ten days after the secured party gives value.

(3) Obligations covered by a security agreement may include future advances or other value whether or not the advances or value are given pursuant to commitment (subsection (1) of Section 9-105).

§ 9-205. Use or Disposition of Collateral Without Accounting Permissible.   A security interest is not invalid or fraudulent against creditors by reason of liberty in the debtor to use, commingle or dispose of all or part of the collateral (including returned or repossessed goods) or to collect or compromise accounts or chattel paper, or to accept the return of goods or make repossessions, or to use, commingle or dispose of proceeds, or by reason of the failure of the secured party to require the debtor to account for proceeds or replace collateral. This section does not relax the requirements of possession where perfection of a security interest depends upon possession of the collateral by the secured party or by a bailee.

§ 9-206. Agreement Not to Assert Defenses Against Assignee; Modification of Sales Warranties Where Security Agreement Exists.

(1) Subject to any statute or decision which establishes a different rule for buyers or lessees of consumer goods, an agreement by a buyer or lessee that he will not assert against an assignee any claim or defense which he may have against the seller or lessor is enforceable by an assignee who takes his assignment for value, in good faith and without notice of a claim or defense, except as to defenses

of a type which may be asserted against a holder in due course of a negotiable instrument under the Article on Commercial Paper (Article 3). A buyer who as part of one transaction signs both a negotiable instrument and a security agreement makes such an agreement.

(2) When a seller retains a purchase money security interest in goods the Article on Sales (Article 2) governs the sale and any disclaimer, limitation or modification of the seller's warranties.

§ 9-207. Rights and Duties When Collateral is in Secured Party's Possession.

(1) A secured party must use reasonable care in the custody and preservation of collateral in his possession. In the case of an instrument or chattel paper reasonable care includes taking necessary steps to preserve rights against prior parties unless otherwise agreed.

(2) Unless otherwise agreed, when collateral is in the secured party's possession

    (a)   reasonable expenses (including the cost of any insurance and payment of taxes or other changes) incurred in the custody, preservation, use or operation of the collateral are chargeable to the debtor and are secured by the collateral;

    (b)   the risk of accidental loss or damage is on the debtor to the extent of any deficiency in any effective insurance coverage;

    (c)   the secured party may hold as additional security any increase or profits (except money) received from the collateral, but money so received, unless remitted to the debtor, shall be applied in reduction of the secured obligation;

    (d)   the secured party must keep the collateral identifiable but fungible collateral may be commingled;

    (e)   the secured party may repledge the collateral upon terms which do not impair the debtor's right to redeem it.

(3) A secured party is liable for any loss caused by his failure to meet any obligation imposed by the preceding subsections but does not lose his security interest.

(4) A secured party may use or operate the collateral for the purpose of preserving the collateral or its value or pursuant to the order of a court of appropriate jurisdiction or, except in the case of consumer goods, in the manner and to the extent provided in the security agreement.

§ 9-208. Request for Statement of Account or List of Collateral.

(1) A debtor may sign a statement indicating what he believes to be the aggregate amount of unpaid indebtedness as of a specified date and may send it to the secured party with a request that the statement be approved or corrected and returned to the debtor. When the security agreement or any other record kept by the secured party identifies the collateral a debtor may similarly request the secured party to approve or correct a list of the collateral.

(2) The secured party must comply with such a request within two weeks after receipt by sending a written correction or approval. If the secured party claims a security interest in all of a particular type of collateral owned by the debtor he may indicate that fact in his reply and need not approve or correct an itemized list of such collateral. If the secured party without reasonable excuse fails to comply he is liable for any loss caused to the debtor thereby; and if the debtor has properly included in his request a good faith statement of the obligation or a list of the collateral or both the secured party may claim a security interest only as shown in the statement against persons misled by his failure to comply. If he no longer has an interest in the obligation or collateral at the time the request is received he must disclose the name and address of any successor in interest known to him and he is liable for any loss caused to the debtor as a result of failure to disclose. A successor in interest is not subject to this section until a request is received by him.

(3) A debtor is entitled to such a statement once every six months without charge. The secured party may require payment of a charge not exceeding $10 for each additional statement furnished.

Part 3. Rights of Third Parties; Perfected and Unperfected Security Interests; Rules of Priority

§ 9-301. Persons Who Take Priority Over Unperfected Security Interests; Rights of "Lien Creditor"

(1) Except as otherwise provided in subsection (2), an unperfected security interest is subordinate to the rights of

    (a)   persons entitled to priority under Section 9-312;

(b) a person who becomes a lien creditor before the security interest is perfected;

(c) in the case of goods, instruments, documents, and chattel paper, a person who is not a secured party and who is a transferee in bulk or other buyer not in ordinary course of business or is a buyer of farm products in ordinary course of business, to the extent that he gives value and receives delivery of the collateral without knowledge of the security interest and before it is perfected;

(d) in the case of accounts and general intangibles, a person who is not a secured party and who is a transferee to the extent that he gives value without knowledge of the security interest and before it is perfected.

(2) If the secured party files with respect to a purchase money security interest before or within ten days after the debtor receives possession of the collateral, he takes priority over the rights of a transferee in bulk or of a lien creditor which arise between the time the security interest attaches and the time of filing.

(3) A "lien creditor" means a creditor who has acquired a lien on the property involved by attachment, levy or the like and includes an assignee for benefit of creditors from the time of assignment, and a trustee in bankruptcy from the date of the filing of the petition or a receiver in equity from the time of appointment.

(4) A person who becomes a lien creditor while a security interest is perfected takes subject to the security interest only to the extent that it secures advances made before he becomes a lien creditor or within 45 days thereafter or made without knowledge of the lien or pursuant to a commitment entered into without knowledge of the lien.

§ 9-302. When Filing Is Required to Perfect Security Interest; Security Interests to Which Filing Provisions of This Article Do Not Apply.

(1) A financing statement must be filed to perfect all security interests except the following:

(a) a security interest in collateral in possession of the secured party under Section 9-305;

(b) a security interest temporarily perfected in instruments or documents without delivery under Section 9-304 or in proceeds for a 10 day period under Section 9-306;

(c) a security interest created by an assignment of a beneficial interest in a trust or a decedent's estate;

(d) a purchase money security interest in consumer goods; but filing is required for a motor vehicle required to be registered; and fixture filing is required for priority over conflicting interests in fixtures to the extent provided in Section 9-313;

(e) an assignment of accounts which does not alone or in conjunction with other assignments to the same assignee transfer a significant part of the outstanding accounts of the assignor;

(f) a security interest of a collecting bank (Section 4-208) or in securities (Section 8-321) or arising under the Article on Sales (see Section 9-113) or covered in subsection (3) of this section;

(g) an assignment for the benefit of all the creditors of the transferor, and subsequent transfers by the assignee thereunder.

(2) If a secured party assigns a perfected security interest, no filing under this Article is required in order to continue the perfected status of the security interest against creditors of and transferees from the original debtor.

(3) The filing of a financing statement otherwise required by this Article is not necessary or effective to perfect a security interest in property subject to

(a) a statute or treaty of the United States which provides for a national or international registration or a national or international certificate of title or which specifies a place of filing different from that specified in this Article for filing of the security interest; or

(b) the following statutes of this state; [list any certificate of title statute covering automobiles, trailers, mobile homes, boats, farm tractors, or the like and any central filing statute.*]; but during any period in which collateral is inventory held for sale by a person who is in the business of selling goods of that kind, the filing provisions of this Article (Part 4) apply to a security interest in that collateral created by him as debtor; or

(c) a certificate of title statute of another

jurisdiction under the law of which indication of a security interest on the certificate is required as a condition of perfection (subsection (2) of Section 9-103).

(4) Compliance with a statute or treaty described in subsection (3) is equivalent to the filing of a financing statement under this Article, and a security interest in property subject to the statute or treaty can be perfected only by compliance therewith except as provided in Section 9-103 on multiple state transactions. Duration and renewal of perfection of a security interest perfected by compliance with the statute or treaty are governed by the provisions of the statute or treaty; in other respects the security interest is subject to this Article.

Note: It is recommended that the provisions of certificate of title acts for perfection of security interests by notation on the certificates should be amended to exclude coverage of inventory held for sale.

§ 9-303. When Security Interest Is Perfected; Continuity of Perfection.

(1) A security interest is perfected when it has attached and when all of the applicable steps required for perfection have been taken. Such steps are specified in Sections 9-302, 9-304, 9-305 and 9-306. If such steps are taken before the security interest attaches, it is perfected at the time when it attaches.

(2) If a security interest is originally perfected in any way permitted under this Article and is subsequently perfected in some other way under this Article, without an intermediate period when it was unperfected, the security interest shall be deemed to be perfected continuously for the purposes of this Article.

§ 9-304. Perfection of Security Interest in Instruments, Documents, and Goods Covered by Documents; Perfection by Permissive Filing; Temporary Perfection Without Filing or Transfer of Possession.

(1) A security interest in chattel paper or negotiable documents may be perfected by filing. A security interest in money or instruments (other than certificated securities or instruments which constitute part of chattel paper) can be perfected only by the secured party's taking possession, except as provided in subsections (4) and (5) of this section

and subsections (2) and (3) of Section 9-306 on proceeds.

(2) During the period that goods are in the possession of the issuer of a negotiable document therefor, a security interest in the goods is perfected by perfecting a security interest in the document, and any security interest in the goods otherwise perfected during such period is subject thereto.

(3) A security interest in goods in the possession of a bailee other than one who has issued a negotiable document therefor is perfected by issuance of a document in the name of the secured party or by the bailee's receipt of notification of the secured party's interest or by filing as to the goods.

(4) A security interest in instruments (other than certificated securities) or negotiable documents is perfected without filing or the taking of possession for a period of 21 days from the time it attaches to the extent that it arises for new value given under a written security agreement.

(5) A security interest remains perfected for a period of 21 days without filing where a secured party having a perfected security interest in an instrument (other than a certificated security), a negotiable document or goods in possession of a bailee other than one who has issued a negotiable document therefor

> (a)   makes available to the debtor the goods or documents representing the goods for the purpose of ultimate sale or exchange or for the purpose of loading, unloading, storing, shipping, transshipping, manufacturing, processing or otherwise dealing with them in a manner preliminary to their sale or exchange, but priority between conflicting security interests in the goods is subject to subsection (3) of Section 9-312; or

> (b)   delivers the instrument to the debtor for the purpose of ultimate sale or exchange or of presentation, collection, renewal or registration of transfer.

(6) After the 21 day period in subsections (4) and (5) perfection depends upon compliance with applicable provisions of this Article.

§ 9-305. When Possession by Secured Party Perfects Security Interest Without Filing.   A security interest in letters of credit and advices of credit (subsection (2)(a) of Section 5-116), goods, instru-

ments (other than certificated securities), money, negotiable documents, or chattel paper may be perfected by the secured party's taking possession of the collateral. If such collateral other than goods covered by a negotiable document is held by a bailee, the secured party is deemed to have possession from the time the bailee receives notification of the secured party's interest. A security interest is perfected by possession from the time possession is taken without a relation back and continues only so long as possession is retained, unless otherwise specified in this Article. The security interest may be otherwise perfected as provided in this Article before or after the period of possession by the secured party.

§ 9-306. "Proceeds"; Secured Party's Rights on Disposition of Collateral.

(1) "Proceeds" includes whatever is received upon the sale, exchange, collection or other disposition of collateral or proceeds. Insurance payable by reason of loss or damage to the collateral is proceeds, except to the extent that it is payable to a person other than a party to the security agreement. Money, checks, deposit accounts, and the like are "cash proceeds." All other proceeds are "non-cash proceeds."

(2) Except where this Article otherwise provides, a security interest continues in collateral notwithstanding sale, exchange or other disposition thereof unless the disposition was authorized by the secured party in the security agreement or otherwise, and also continues in any identifiable proceeds including collections received by the debtor.

(3) The security interest in proceeds is a continuously perfected security interest if the interest in the original collateral was perfected but it ceases to be a perfected security interest and becomes unperfected ten days after receipt of the proceeds by the debtor unless

(a)   a filed financing statement covers the original collateral and the proceeds are collateral in which a security interest may be perfected by filing in the office or offices where the financing statement has been filed and, if the proceeds are acquired with cash proceeds, the description of collateral in the financing statement indicates the types of property constituting the proceeds; or

(b)   a filed financing statement covers the original collateral and the proceeds are identifiable cash proceeds; or

(c)   the security interest in the proceeds is perfected before the expiration of the ten day period.

Except as provided in this section, a security interest in proceeds can be perfected only by the methods or under the circumstances permitted in this Article for original collateral of the same type.

(4) In the event of insolvency proceedings instituted by or against a debtor, a secured party with a perfected security interest in proceeds has a perfected security interest only in the following proceeds:

(a)   in identifiable non-cash proceeds and in separate deposit accounts containing only proceeds;

(b)   in identifiable cash proceeds in the form of money which is neither commingled with other money nor deposited in a deposit account prior to the insolvency proceedings;

(c)   in identifiable cash proceeds in the form of checks and the like which are not deposited in a deposit account prior to the insolvency proceedings; and

(d)   in all cash and deposit accounts of the debtor in which proceeds have been commingled with other funds, but the perfected security interest under this paragraph (d) is

(i)   subject to any right to set-off; and

(ii) limited to an amount not greater than the amount of any cash proceeds received by the debtor within ten days before the institution of the insolvency proceedings less the sum of (I) the payments to the secured party on account of cash proceeds received by the debtor during such period and (II) the cash proceeds received by the debtor during such period to which the secured party is entitled under paragraphs (a) through (c) of this subsection (4).

(5) If a sale of goods results in an account or chattel paper which is transferred by the seller to a secured party, and if the goods are returned to or are repossessed by the seller or the secured party, the following rules determine priorities:

(a)   If the goods were collateral at the time of sale, for an indebtedness of the seller which is still unpaid, the original security interest attaches again to the goods and continues as a perfected security interest if it was perfected at the time when the goods were sold. If the security interest was originally perfected by a filing which is still effective, nothing further is required to continue the perfected status; in any other case, the secured party must take possession of the returned or repossessed goods or must file.

(b) An unpaid transferee of the chattel paper has a security interest in the goods against the transferor. Such security interest is prior to a security interest asserted under paragraph (a) to the extent that the transferee of the chattel paper was entitled to priority under Section 9-308.

(c) An unpaid transferee of the account has a security interest in the goods against the transferor. Such security interest is subordinate to a security interest asserted under paragraph (a).

(d) A security interest of an unpaid transferee asserted under paragraph (b) or (c) must be perfected for protection against creditors of the transferor and purchasers of the returned or repossessed goods.

§ 9-307. Protection of Buyers of Goods.

(1) A buyer in ordinary course of business (subsection (9) of Section 1-201) other than a person buying farm products from a person engaged in farming operations takes free of a security interest created by his seller even though the security interest is perfected and even though the buyer knows of its existence.

(2) In the case of consumer goods, a buyer takes free of a security interest even though perfected if he buys without knowledge of the security interest, for value and for his own personal, family or household purposes unless prior to the purchase the secured party has filed a financing statement covering such goods.

(3) A buyer other than a buyer in ordinary course of business (subsection (1) of this section) takes free of a security interest to the extent that it secures future advances made after the secured party acquires knowledge of the purchase, or more than 45 days after the purchase, whichever first occurs, unless made pursuant to a commitment entered into without knowledge of the purchase and before the expiration of the 45-day period.

§ 9-308. Purchase of Chattel Paper and Instruments.

A purchaser of chattel paper or an instrument who gives new value and takes possession of it in the ordinary course of his business has priority over a security interest in the chattel paper or instrument

(a) which is perfected under Section 9-304 (permissive filing and temporary perfection) or under Section 9-306 (perfection as to proceeds) if he acts without knowledge that the specific paper or instrument is subject to a security interest; or

(b) which is claimed merely as proceeds of inventory subject to a security interest (Section 9-306) even though he knows that the specific paper or instrument is subject to the security interest.

§ 9-309. Protection of Purchasers of Instruments, Documents and Securities.

Nothing in this Article limits the rights of a holder in due course of a negotiable instrument (Section 3-302) or a holder to whom a negotiable document of title has been duly negotiated (Section 7-501) or a bona fide purchaser of a security (Section 8-302) and the holders or purchasers take priority over an earlier security interest even though perfected. Filing under this Article does not constitute notice of the security interest to such holders or purchasers.

§ 9-310. Priority of Certain Liens Arising by Operation of Law.

When a person in the ordinary course of his business furnishes services or materials with respect to goods subject to a security interest, a lien upon goods in the possession of such person given by statute or rule of law for such materials or services takes priority over a perfected security interest unless the lien is statutory and the statute expressly provides otherwise.

§ 9-311. Alienability of Debtor's Rights: Judicial Process.

The debtor's rights in collateral may be voluntarily or involuntarily transferred (by way of sale, creation of a security interest, attachment, levy, garnishment or other judicial process) notwithstanding a provision in the security agreement prohibiting any transfer or making the transfer constitute a default.

§ 9-312. Priorities Among Conflicting Security Interests in the Same Collateral.

(1) The rules of priority stated in other sections of this Part and in the following sections shall govern when applicable: Section 4-208 with respect to the security interests of collecting banks in items being collected, accompanying documents and proceeds; Section 9-103 on security interests related to other jurisdictions; Section 9-114 on consignments.

(2) A perfected security interest in crops for new value given to enable the debtor to produce the crops during the production season and given not more than three months before the crops become growing crops by planting or otherwise takes priority over an earlier perfected security interest to the extent that such earlier interest secures obligations due more than six months before the crops become growing crops by planting or otherwise, even though the person giving new value had knowledge of the earlier security interest.

(3) A perfected purchase money security interest in inventory has priority over a conflicting security interest in the same inventory and also has priority in identifiable cash proceeds received on or before the delivery of the inventory to a buyer if

(a) the purchase money security interest is perfected at the time the debtor receives possession of the inventory; and

(b) the purchase money secured party gives notification in writing to the holder of the conflicting security interest if the holder had filed a financing statement covering the same types of inventory (i) before the date of the filing made by the purchase money secured party, or (ii) before the beginning of the 21 day period where the purchase money security interest is temporarily perfected without filing or possession (subsection (5) of Section 9-304); and

(c) the holder of the conflicting security interest receives the notification within five years before the debtor receives possession of the inventory; and

(d) the notification states that the person giving the notice has or expects to acquire a purchase money security interest in inventory of the debtor, describing such inventory by item or type.

(4) A purchase money security interest in collateral other than inventory has priority over a conflicting security interest in the same collateral or its proceeds if the purchase money security interest is perfected at the time the debtor receives possession of the collateral or within ten days thereafter.

(5) In all cases not governed by other rules stated in this section (including cases of purchase money security interests which do not qualify for the special priorities set forth in subsections (3) and (4) of this section), priority between conflicting security interests in the same collateral shall be determined according to the following rules:

(a) Conflicting security interests rank according to priority in time of filing or perfection. Priority dates from the time a filing is first made covering the collateral or the time the security interest is first perfected, whichever is earlier, provided that there is no period thereafter when there is neither filing nor perfection.

(b) So long as conflicting security interests are unperfected, the first to attach has priority.

(6) For the purposes of subsection (5) a date of filing or perfection as to collateral is also a date of filing or perfection as to proceeds.

(7) If future advances are made while a security interest is perfected by filing, the taking of possession, or under Section 8-321 on securities, the security interest has the same priority for the purposes of subsection (5) with respect to the future advances as it does with respect to the first advance. If a commitment is made before or while the security interest is so perfected, the security interest has the same priority with respect to advances made pursuant thereto. In other cases a perfected security interest has priority from the date the advance is made.

§ 9-313. Priority of Security Interests in Fixtures.

(1) In this section and in the provisions of Part 4 of this Article referring to fixture filing, unless the context otherwise requires,

(a) goods are "fixtures" when they become so related to particular real estate that an interest in them arises under real estate law;

(b) a "fixture filing" is the filing in the office where a mortgage on the real estate would be filed or recorded of a financing statement covering goods which are or are to become fixtures and conforming to the requirements of subsection (5) of Section 9-402;

(c)   a mortgage is a "construction mortgage" to the extent that it secures an obligation incurred for the construction of an improvement on land including the acquisition cost of the land, if the recorded writing so indicates.

(2) A security interest under this Article may be created in goods which are fixtures or may continue in goods which become fixtures, but no security interest exists under this Article in ordinary building materials incorporated into an improvement on land.

(3) This Article does not prevent creation of an encumbrance upon fixtures pursuant to real estate law.

(4) A perfected security interest in fixtures has priority over the conflicting interest of an encumbrancer or owner of the real estate where

(a)   the security interest is a purchase money security interest, the interest of the encumbrancer or owner arises before the goods become fixtures, the security interest is perfected by a fixture filing before the goods become fixtures or within ten days thereafter, and the debtor has an interest of record in the real estate or is in possession of the real estate; or

(b)   the security interest is perfected by a fixture filing before the interest of the encumbrancer or owner is of record, the security interest has priority over any conflicting interest of a predecessor in title of the encumbrancer or owner, and the debtor has an interest of record in the real estate or is in possession of the real estate; or

(c)   the fixtures are readily removable factory or office machines or readily removable replacements of domestic appliances which are consumer goods, and before the goods become fixtures the security interest is perfected by any method permitted by this Article; or

(d)   the conflicting interest is a lien on the real estate obtained by legal or equitable proceedings after the security interest was perfected by any method permitted by this Article.

(5) A security interest in fixtures, whether or not perfected, has priority over the conflicting interest of an encumbrancer or owner of the real estate where

(a)   the encumbrancer or owner has consented in writing to the security interest or has disclaimed an interest in the goods as fixtures; or

(b)   the debtor has a right to remove the goods as against the encumbrancer or owner. If the debtor's right terminates, the priority of the security interest continues for a reasonable time.

(6) Notwithstanding paragraph (a) of subsection (4) but otherwise subject to subsections (4) and (5), a security interest in fixtures is subordinate to a construction mortgage recorded before the goods become fixtures if the goods become fixtures before the completion of the construction. To the extent that it is given to refinance a construction mortgage, a mortgage has this priority to the same extent as the construction mortgage.

(7) In cases not within the preceding subsections, a security interest in fixtures is subordinate to the conflicting interest of an encumbrancer or owner of the related real estate who is not the debtor.

(8) When the secured party has priority over all owners and encumbrancers of the real estate, he may, on default, subject to the provisions of Part 5, remove his collateral from the real estate but he must reimburse any encumbrancer or owner of the real estate who is not the debtor and who has not otherwise agreed for the cost of repair of any physical injury, but not for any diminution in value of the real estate caused by the absence of the goods removed or by any necessity of replacing them. A person entitled to reimbursement may refuse permission to remove until the secured party gives adequate security for the performance of this obligation.

§ 9-314. Accessions.

(1) A security interest in goods which attaches before they are installed in or affixed to other goods takes priority as to the goods installed or affixed (called in this section "accessions") over the claims of all persons to the whole except as stated in subsection (3) and subject to Section 9-315(1).

(2) A security interest which attaches to goods after they become part of a whole is valid against all persons subsequently acquiring interests in the whole except as stated in subsection (3) but is invalid against any person with an interest in the

whole at the time the security interest attaches to the goods who has not in writing consented to the security interest or disclaimed an interest in the goods as part of the whole.

(3) The security interests described in subsections (1) and (2) do not take priority over

(a) a subsequent purchaser for value of any interest in the whole; or

(b) a creditor with a lien on the whole subsequently obtained by judicial proceedings; or

(c) a creditor with a prior perfected security interest in the whole to the extent that he makes subsequent advances

if the subsequent purchase is made, the lien by judicial proceedings obtained or the subsequent advance under the prior perfected security interest is made or contracted for without knowledge of the security interest and before it is perfected. A purchaser of the whole at a foreclosure sale other than the holder of a perfected security interest purchasing at his own foreclosure sale is a subsequent purchaser within this section.

(4) When under subsections (1) or (2) and (3) a secured party has an interest in accessions which has priority over the claims of all persons who have interests in the whole, he may on default subject to the provisions of Part 5 remove his collateral from the whole but he must reimburse any encumbrancer or owner of the whole who is not the debtor and who has not otherwise agreed for the cost of repair of any physical injury but not for any diminution in value of the whole caused by the absence of the goods removed or by any necessity for replacing them. A person entitled to reimbursement may refuse permission to remove until the secured party gives adequate security for the performance of this obligation.

§ 9-315. Priority When Goods Are Commingled or Processed.

(1) If a security interest in goods was perfected and subsequently the goods or a part thereof have become part of a product or mass, the security interest continues in the product or mass if

(a) the goods are so manufactured, processed, assembled or commingled that their identity is lost in the product or mass; or

(b) a financing statement covering the original goods also covers the product into which the goods have been manufactured, processed or assembled.

In a case to which paragraph (b) applies, no separate security interest in that part of the original goods which has been manufactured, processed or assembled into the product may be claimed under Section 9-314.

(2) When under subsection (1) more than one security interest attaches to the product or mass, they rank equally according to the ratio that the cost of the goods to which each interest originally attached bears to the cost of the total product or mass.

§ 9-316. Priority Subject to Subordination.

Nothing in this Article prevents subordination by agreement by any person entitled to priority.

§ 9-317. Secured Party Not Obligated on Contract of Debtor. The mere existence of a security interest or authority given to the debtor to dispose of or use collateral does not impose contract or tort liability upon the secured party for the debtor's acts or omissions.

§ 9-318. Defenses Against Assignee; Modification of Contract After Notification of Assignment; Term Prohibiting Assignment Ineffective; Identification and Proof of Assignment.

(1) Unless an account debtor has made an enforceable agreement not to assert defenses or claims arising out of a sale as provided in Section 9-206 the rights of an assignee are subject to

(a) all the terms of the contract between the account debtor and assignor and any defense or claim arising therefrom; and

(b) any other defense or claim of the account debtor against the assignor which accrues before the account debtor receives notification of the assignment.

(2) So far as the right to payment or a part thereof under an assigned contract has not been fully earned by performance, and notwithstanding notification of the assignment, any modification of or substitution for the contract made in good faith and in accordance with reasonable commercial standards is effective against an assignee unless the account debtor has otherwise agreed but the assignee acquires corresponding rights under the modified or substituted contract. The assignment may provide that such modification or substitution is a breach by the assignor.

(3) The account debtor is authorized to pay the assignor until the account debtor receives notification that the amount due or to become due has been assigned and that payment is to be made to the assignee. A notification which does not reasonably identify the rights assigned is ineffective. If requested by the account debtor, the assignee must seasonably furnish reasonable proof that the assignment has been made and unless he does so the account debtor may pay the assignor.

(4) A term in any contract between an account debtor and an assignor is ineffective if it prohibits assignment of an account or prohibits creation of a security interest in a general intangible for money due or to become due or requires the account debtor's consent to such assignment or security interest.

Part 4. Filing

§ 9-401. Place of Filing; Erroneous Filing; Removal of Collateral.

First Alternative Subsection (1)

(1) The proper place to file in order to perfect a security interest is as follows:

    (a)   when the collateral is timber to be cut or is minerals or the like (including oil and gas) or accounts subject to subsection (5) of Section 9-103, or when the financing statement is filed as a fixture filing (Section 9-313) and the collateral is goods which are or are to become fixtures, then in the office where a mortgage on the real estate would be filed or recorded;

    (b)   in all other cases, in the office of the [Secretary of State]

Second Alternative Subsection (1)

(1) The proper place to file in order to perfect a security interest is as follows:

    (a)   when the collateral is equipment used in farming operations, or farm products, or accounts or general intangibles arising from or relating to the sale of farm products by a farmer, or consumer goods, then in the office of the .... in the county of the debtor's residence or if the debtor is not a resident of this state then in the office of the .... in the county where the goods are kept, and in addition when the collateral is crops growing

or to be grown in the office of the .... in the county where the land is located;

    (b)   when the collateral is timber to be cut or is minerals or the like (including oil and gas) or accounts subject to subsection (5) of Section 9-103, or when the financing statement is filed as a fixture filing (Section 9-313) and the collateral is goods which are or are to become fixtures, then in the office where a mortgage on the real estate would be filed or recorded;

    (c)   in all other cases, in the office of the [Secretary of State].

Third Alternative Subsection (1)

(1) The proper place to file in order to perfect a security interest is as follows:

    (a)   when the collateral is equipment used in farming operations, or farm products, or accounts or general intangibles arising from or relating to the sale of farm products by a farmer, or consumer goods, then in the office of the .... in the county of the debtor's residence or if the debtor is not a resident of this state then in the office of the .... in the county where the goods are kept, and in addition when the collateral is crops growing or to be grown in the office of the .... in the county where the land is located;

    (b)   when the collateral is timber to be cut or is minerals or the like (including oil and gas) or accounts subject to subsection (5) of Section 9-103, or when the financing statement is filed as a fixture filing (Section 9-313) and the collateral is goods which are or are to become fixtures, then in the office where a mortgage on the real estate would be filed or recorded;

    (c)   (c) in all other cases, in the office of the [Secretary of State] and in addition, if the debtor has a place of business in only one county of this state, also in the office of .... of such county, or, if the debtor has no place of business in this state, but resides in the state, also in the office of .... of the county in which he resides.

Note: One of the three alternatives should be selected as subsection (1).

(2) A filing which is made in good faith in an improper place or not in all of the places required by this section is nevertheless effective with regard to any collateral as to which the filing complied with the requirements of this Article and is also effective with regard to collateral covered by the financing statement against any person who has knowledge of the contents of such financing statement.

(3) A filing which is made in the proper place in this state continues effective even though the debtor's residence or place of business or the location of the collateral or its use, whichever controlled the original filing, is thereafter changed.

Alternative Subsection (3)

[(3) A filing which is made in the proper county continues effective for four months after a change to another county of the debtor's residence or place of business or the location of the collateral, whichever controlled the original filing. It becomes ineffective thereafter unless a copy of the financing statement signed by the secured party is filed in the new county within said period. The security interest may also be perfected in the new county after the expiration of the four-month period; in such case perfection dates from the time of perfection in the new county. A change in the use of the collateral does not impair the effectiveness of the original filing.]

(4) The rules stated in Section 9-103 determine whether filing is necessary in this state.

(5) Notwithstanding the preceding subsections, and subject to subsection (3) of Section 9-302, the proper place to file in order to perfect a security interest in collateral, including fixtures, of a transmitting utility is the office of the [Secretary of State]. This filing constitutes a fixture filing (Section 9-313) as to the collateral described therein which is or is to become fixtures.

(6) For the purposes of this section, the residence of an organization is its place of business if it has one or its chief executive office if it has more than one place of business.

Note: *Subsection (6) should be used only if the state chooses the Second or Third Alternative Subsection (1).*

§ 9-402. Formal Requisites of Financing Statement; Amendments; Mortgage as Financing Statement.

(1) A financing statement is sufficient if it gives the names of the debtor and the secured party, is signed by the debtor, gives an address of the secured party from which information concerning the security interest may be obtained, gives a mailing address of the debtor and contains a statement indicating the types, or describing the items, of collateral. A financing statement may be filed before a security agreement is made or a security interest otherwise attaches. When the financing statement covers crops growing or to be grown, the statement must also contain a description of the real estate concerned. When the financing statement covers timber to be cut or covers minerals or the like (including oil and gas) or accounts subject to subsection (5) of Section 9-103, or when the financing statement is filed as a fixture filing (Section 9-313) and the collateral is goods which are or are to become fixtures, the statement must also comply with subsection (5). A copy of the security agreement is sufficient as a financing statement if it contains the above information and is signed by the debtor. A carbon, photographic or other reproduction of a security agreement or a financing statement is sufficient as a financing statement if the security agreement so provides or if the original has been filed in this state.

(2) A financing statement which otherwise complies with subsection (1) is sufficient when it is signed by the secured party instead of the debtor if it is filed to perfect a security interest in

(a) collateral already subject to a security interest in another jurisdiction when it is brought into this state, or when the debtor's location is changed to this state. Such a financing statement must state that the collateral was brought into this state or that the debtor's location was changed to this state under such circumstances; or

(b) proceeds under Section 9-306 if the security interest in the original collateral was perfected. Such a financing statement must describe the original collateral; or

(c) collateral as to which the filing has lapsed; or

(d) collateral acquired after a change of name, identity or corporate structure of the debtor (subsection (7)).

(3) A form substantially as follows is sufficient to comply with subsection (1):

Name of debtor (or assignor) ....

Address ....

Name of secured party (or assignee) ....

Address ....

1. This financing statement covers the following types (or items) of property:
   (Describe) ....

2. (If collateral is crops) The above described crops are growing or are to be grown on:
   (Describe Real Estate) ....

3. (If applicable) The above goods are to become fixtures on [where appropriate substitute either "The above timber is standing on _____" or "The above minerals or the like (including oil and gas) or accounts will be financed at the wellhead of the well or mine located on _____."

   (Describe Real Estate) ....
   and this financing statement is to be filed [for record] in the real estate records. (If the debtor does not have an interest of record) The name of a record owner is

   ....

4. (If products of collateral are claimed) Products of the collateral are also covered.

(use whichever is applicable)

....
Signature of Debtor (or Assignor)

....
Signature of Secured Party (or Assignee)

(4) A financing statement may be amended by filing a writing signed by both the debtor and the secured party. An amendment does not extend the period of effectiveness of a financing statement. If any amendment adds collateral, it is effective as to the added collateral only from the filing date of the amendment. In this Article, unless the context otherwise requires, the term "financing statement" means the original financing statement and any amendments.

(5) A financing statement covering timber to be cut or covering minerals or the like (including oil and gas) or accounts subject to subsection (5) of Section 9-103, or a financing statement filed as a fixture filing (Section 9-313) where the debtor is not a transmitting utility, must show that it covers this type of collateral, must recite that it is to be filed [for record] in the real estate records, and the financ-

ing statement must contain a description of the real estate [sufficient if it were contained in a mortgage of the real estate to give constructive notice of the mortgage under the law of this state]. If the debtor does not have an interest of record in the real estate, the financing statement must show the name of a record owner.

(6) A mortgage is effective as a financing statement filed as a fixture filing from the date of its recording if

(a) the goods are described in the mortgage by item or type; and

(b) the goods are or are to become fixtures related to the real estate described in the mortgage; and

(c) the mortgage complies with the requirements for a financing statement in this section other than a recital that it is to be filed in the real estate records; and

(d) the mortgage is duly recorded.

No fee with reference to the financing statement is required other than the regular recording and satisfaction fees with respect to the mortgage.

(7) A financing statement sufficiently shows the name of the debtor if it gives the individual, partnership or corporate name of the debtor, whether or not it adds other trade names or names of partners. Where the debtor so changes his name or in the case of an organization its name, identity or corporate structure that a filed financing statement becomes seriously misleading, the filing is not effective to perfect a security interest in collateral acquired by the debtor more than four months after the change, unless a new appropriate financing statement is filed before the expiration of that time. A filed financing statement remains effective with respect to collateral transferred by the debtor even though the secured party knows of or consents to the transfer.

(8) A financing statement substantially complying with the requirements of this section is effective even though it contains minor errors which are not seriously misleading.

Note: Language in brackets is optional.

Note: Where the state has any special recording system for real estate other than the usual grantor–grantee index (as, for instance, a tract system or a title registration or Torrens system) local adaptations of subsection (5) and Section 9-403(7) may be necessary. See Mass. Gen. Laws Chapter 106, Section 9-409.

§ 9-403. What Constitutes Filing; Duration of Filing; Effect of Lapsed Filing; Duties of Filing Officer.

(1) Presentation for filing of a financing statement and tender of the filing fee or acceptance of the statement by the filing officer constitutes filing under this Article.

(2) Except as provided in subsection (6) a filed financing statement is effective for a period of five years from the date of filing. The effectiveness of a filed financing statement lapses on the expiration of the five year period unless a continuation statement is filed prior to the lapse. If a security interest perfected by filing exists at the time insolvency proceedings are commenced by or against the debtor, the security interest remains perfected until termination of the insolvency proceedings and thereafter for a period of sixty days or until expiration of the five year period, whichever occurs later. Upon lapse the security interest becomes unperfected, unless it is perfected without filing. If the security interest becomes unperfected upon lapse, it is deemed to have been unperfected as against a person who became a purchaser or lien creditor before lapse.

(3) A continuation statement may be filed by the secured party within six months prior to the expiration of the five year period specified in subsection (2). Any such continuation statement must be signed by the secured party, identify the original statement by file number and state that the original statement is still effective. A continuation statement signed by a person other than the secured party of record must be accompanied by a separate written statement of assignment signed by the secured party of record and complying with subsection (2) of Section 9-405, including payment of the required fee. Upon timely filing of the continuation statement, the effectiveness of the original statement is continued for five years after the last date to which the filing was effective whereupon it lapses in the same manner as provided in subsection (2) unless another continuation statement is filed prior to such lapse. Succeeding continuation statements may be filed in the same manner to continue the effectiveness of the original statement. Unless a statute on disposition of public records provides otherwise, the filing officer may remove a lapsed statement from the files and destroy it immediately if he has retained a microfilm or other photographic record, or in other cases after one year after the lapse. The filing officer shall so arrange matters by physical annexation of financing statements to continuation statements or other related filings, or by other means, that if he physically destroys the financing statements of a period more than five years past, those which have been continued by a continuation statement or which are still effective under subsection (6) shall be retained.

(4) Except as provided in subsection (7) a filing officer shall mark each statement with a file number and with the date and hour of filing and shall hold the statement or a microfilm or other photographic copy thereof for public inspection. In addition the filing officer shall index the statement according to the name of the debtor and shall note in the index the file number and the address of the debtor given in the statement.

(5) The uniform fee for filing and indexing and for stamping a copy furnished by the secured party to show the date and place of filing for an original financing statement or for a continuation statement shall be $........ if the statement is in the standard form prescribed by the [Secretary of State] and otherwise shall be $........, plus in each case, if the financing statement is subject to subsection (5) of Section 9-402, $........ The uniform fee for each name more than one required to be indexed shall be $........ The secured party may at his option show a trade name for any person and an extra uniform indexing fee of $........ shall be paid with respect thereto.

(6) If the debtor is a transmitting utility (subsection (5) of Section 9-401) and a filed financing statement so states, it is effective until a termination statement is filed. A real estate mortgage which is effective as a fixture filing under subsection (6) of Section 9-402 remains effective as a fixture filing until the mortgage is released or satisfied of record or its effectiveness otherwise terminates as to the real estate.

(7) When a financing statement covers timber to be cut or covers minerals or the like (including oil and gas) or accounts subject to subsection (5) of Section 9-103, or is filed as a fixture filing, [it shall be filed for record and] the filing officer shall index it under the names of the debtor and any owner of record shown on the financing statement in the same fashion as if they were the mortgagors in a mortgage of the real estate described, and, to the extent that the law of this state provides for indexing of mortgages under the name of the mortgagee, under the name of the secured party as if he were

the mortgagee thereunder, or where indexing is by description in the same fashion as if the financing statement were a mortgage of the real estate described.

Note: In states in which writings will not appear in the real estate records and indices unless actually recorded the bracketed language in subsection (7) should be used.

§ 9-404. Termination Statement.

(1) If a financing statement covering consumer goods is filed on or after ...., then within one month or within ten days following written demand by the debtor after there is no outstanding secured obligation and no commitment to make advances, incur obligations or otherwise give value, the secured party must file with each filing officer with whom the financing statement was filed, a termination statement to the effect that he no longer claims a security interest under the financing statement, which shall be identified by file number. In other cases whenever there is no outstanding secured obligation and no commitment to make advances, incur obligations or otherwise give value, the secured party must on written demand by the debtor send the debtor, for each filing officer with whom the financing statement was filed, a termination statement to the effect that he no longer claims a security interest under the financing statement, which shall be identified by file number. A termination statement signed by a person other than the secured party of record must be accompanied by a separate written statement of assignment signed by the secured party of record complying with subsection (2) of Section 9-405, including payment of the required fee. If the affected secured party fails to file such a termination statement as required by this subsection, or to send such a termination statement within ten days after proper demand therefor, he shall be liable to the debtor for one hundred dollars, and in addition for any loss caused to the debtor by such failure.

(2) On presentation to the filing officer of such a termination statement he must note it in the index. If he has received the termination statement in duplicate, he shall return one copy of the termination statement to the secured party stamped to show the time of receipt thereof. If the filing officer has a microfilm or other photographic record of the financing statement, and of any related continuation statement, statement of assignment and state-

ment of release, he may remove the originals from the files at any time after receipt of the termination statement, or if he has no such record, he may remove them from the files at any time after one year after receipt of the termination statement.

(3) If the termination statement is in the standard form prescribed by the [Secretary of State] the uniform fee for filing and indexing the termination statement shall be $........, and otherwise shall be $........, plus in each case an additional fee of $........ for each name more than one against which the termination statement is required to be indexed.

Note: The date to be inserted should be the effective date of the revised Article 9.

§ 9-405. Assignment of Security Interest; Duties of Filing Officer; Fees.

(1) A financing statement may disclose an assignment of a security interest in the collateral described in the financing statement by indication in the financing statement of the name and address of the assignee or by an assignment itself or a copy thereof on the face or back of the statement. On presentation to the filing officer of such a financing statement the filing officer shall mark the same as provided in Section 9-403(4). The uniform fee for filing, indexing and furnishing filing data for a financing statement so indicating an assignment shall be $........ if the statement is in the standard form prescribed by the [Secretary of State] and other wise shall be $........, plus in each case an additional fee of $........ for each name more than one against which the financing statement is required to be indexed.

(2) A secured party may assign of record all or part of his rights under a financing statement by the filing in the place where the original financing statement was filed of a separate written statement of assignment signed by the secured party of record and setting forth the name of the secured party of record and the debtor, the file number and the date of filing of the financing statement and the name and address of the assignee and containing a description of the collateral assigned. A copy of the assignment is sufficient as a separate statement if it complies with the preceding sentence. On presentation to the filing officer of such a separate statement, the filing officer shall mark such separate statement with the date and hour of the filing. He shall note the assignment on the index of the financing statement, or in the case of a fixture filing, or a

filing covering timber to be cut, or covering minerals or the like (including oil and gas) or accounts subject to subsection (5) of Section 9-103, he shall index the assignment under the name of the assignor as grantor and, to the extent that the law of this state provides for indexing the assignment of a mortgage under the name of the assignee, he shall index the assignment of the financing statement under the name of the assignee. The uniform fee for filing, indexing and furnishing filing data about such a separate statment of assignment shall be $........ if the statement is in the standard form prescribed by the [Secretary of State] and otherwise shall be $........, plus in each case an additional fee of $........ for each name more than one against which the statement of assignment is required to be indexed. Notwithstanding the provisions of this subsection, an assignment of record of a security interest in a fixture contained in a mortgage effective as a fixture filing (subsection (6) of Section 9-402) may be made only by an assignment of the mortgage in the manner provided by the law of this state other than this Act.

(3) After the disclosure or filing of an assignment under this section, the assignee is the secured party of record.

§ 9-406. Release of Collateral; Duties of Filing Officer; Fees.   A secured party of record may by his signed statement release all or a part of any collateral described in a filed financing statement. The statement of release is sufficient if it contains a description of the collateral being released, the name and address of the debtor, the name and address of the secured party, and the file number of the financing statement. A statement of release signed by a person other than the secured party of record must be accompanied by a separate written statement of assignment signed by the secured party of record and complying with subsection (2) of Section 9-405, including payment of the required fee. Upon presentation of such a statement of release to the filing officer he shall mark the statement with the hour and date of filing and shall note the same upon the margin of the index of the filing of the financing statement. The uniform fee for filing and noting such a statement of release shall be $........ if the statement is in the standard form prescribed by the [Secretary of State] and otherwise shall be $........, plus in each case an additional fee of $........ for each

name more than one against which the statement of release is required to be indexed.

[§ 9-407. Information From Filing Officer.]

[(1) If the person filing any financing statement, termination statement, statement of assignment, or statement of release, furnishes the filing officer a copy thereof, the filing officer shall upon request note upon the copy the file number and date and hour of the filing of the original and deliver or send the copy to such person.]

[(2) Upon request of any person, the filing officer shall issue his certificate showing whether there is on file on the date and hour stated therein, any presently effective financing statement naming a particular debtor and any statement of assignment thereof and if there is, giving the date and hour of filing of each such statement and the names and addresses of each secured party therein. The uniform fee for such a certificate shall be $........ if the request for the certificate is in the standard form prescribed by the [Secretary of State] and otherwise shall be $........ Upon request the filing officer shall furnish a copy of any filed financing statement or statement of assignment for a uniform fee of $........ per page.]

Note: This section is proposed as an optional provision to require filing officers to furnish certificates. Local law and practices should be consulted with regard to the advisability of adoption.

§ 9-408. Financing Statements Covering Consigned or Leased Goods.   A consignor or lessor of goods may file a financing statement using the terms "consignor," "consignee," "lessor," "lessee" or the like instead of the terms specified in Section 9-402. The provisions of this Part shall apply as appropriate to such a financing statement but its filing shall not of itself be a factor in determining whether or not the consignment of lease is intended as security (Section 1-201(37)). However, if it is determined for other reasons that the consignment or lease is so intended, a security interest of the consignor or lessor which attaches to the consigned or leased goods is perfected by such filing.

Part 5. Default

§ 9-501. Default; Procedure When Security Agreement Covers Both Real and Personal Property.

(1) When a debtor is in default under a security agreement, a secured party has the rights and rem-

edies provided in this Part and except as limited by subsection (3) those provided in the security agreement. He may reduce his claim to judgment, foreclose or otherwise enforce the security interest by any available judicial procedure. If the collateral is documents the secured party may proceed either as to the documents or as to the goods covered thereby. A secured party in possession has the rights, remedies and duties provided in Section 9-207. The rights and remedies referred to in this subsection are cumulative.

(2) After default, the debtor has the rights and remedies provided in this Part, those provided in the security agreement and those provided in Section 9-207.

(3) To the extent that they give rights to the debtor and impose duties on the secured party, the rules stated in the subsections referred to below may not be waived or varied except as provided with respect to compulsory disposition of collateral (subsection (3) of Section 9-504 and Section 9-505) and with respect to redemption of collateral (Section 9-506) but the parties may by agreement determine the standards by which the fulfillment of these rights and duties is to be measured if such standards are not manifestly unreasonable:

    (a)   subsection (2) of Section 9-502 and subsection (2) of Section 9-504 insofar as they require accounting for surplus proceeds of collateral;

    (b)   subsection (3) of Section 9-504 and subsection (1) of Section 9-505 which deal with disposition of collateral;

    (c)   subsection (2) of Section 9-505 which deals with acceptance of collateral as discharge of obligation;

    (d)   Section 9-506 which deals with redemption of collateral; and

    (e)   subsection (1) of Section 9-507 which deals with the secured party's liability for failure to comply with this Part.

(4) If the security agreement covers both real and personal property, the secured party may proceed under this Part as to the personal property or he may proceed as to both the real and the personal property in accordance with his rights and remedies in respect of the real property in which case the provisions of this Part do not apply.

(5) When a secured party has reduced his claim to judgment the lien of any levy which may be made upon his collateral by virtue of any execution based upon the judgment shall relate back to the date of the perfection of the security interest in such collateral. A judicial sale, pursuant to such execution, is a foreclosure of the security interest by judicial procedure within the meaning of this section, and the secured party may purchase at the sale and thereafter hold the collateral free of any other requirements of this Article.

§ 9-502. Collection Rights of Secured Party.

(1) When so agreed and in any event on default the secured party is entitled to notify an account debtor or the obligor on an instrument to make payment to him whether or not the assignor was theretofore making collections on the collateral, and also to take control of any proceeds to which he is entitled under Section 9-306.

(2) A secured party who by agreement is entitled to charge back uncollected collateral or otherwise to full or limited recourse against the debtor and who undertakes to collect from the account debtors or obligors must proceed in a commercially reasonable manner and may deduct his reasonable expenses of realization from the collections. If the security agreement secures an indebtedness, the secured party must account to the debtor for any surplus, and unless otherwise agreed, the debtor is liable for any deficiency. But, if the underlying transaction was a sale of accounts or chattel paper, the debtor is entitled to any surplus or is liable for any deficiency only if the security agreement so provides.

§ 9-503. Secured Party's Right to Take Possession After Default.   Unless otherwise agreed a secured party has on default the right to take possession of the collateral. In taking possession a secured party may proceed without judicial process if this can be done without breach of the peace or may proceed by action. If the security agreement so provides the secured party may require the debtor to assemble the collateral and make it available to the secured party at a place to be designated by the secured party which is reasonably convenient to both parties. Without removal a secured party may render equipment unusable, and may dispose of collateral on the debtor's premises under Section 9-504.

§ 9-504. Secured Party's Right to Dispose of Collateral After Default; Effect of Disposition.

(1) A secured party after default may sell, lease or otherwise dispose of any or all of the collateral

in its then condition or following any commercially reasonable preparation or processing. Any sale of goods is subject to the Article on Sales (Article 2). The proceeds of disposition shall be applied in the order following to

(a) the reasonable expenses of retaking, holding, preparing for sale or lease, selling, leasing and the like and, to the extent provided for in the agreement and not prohibited by law, the reasonable attorneys' fees and legal expenses incurred by the secured party;

(b) the satisfaction of indebtedness secured by the security interest under which the disposition is made;

(c) the satisfaction of indebtedness secured by any subordinate security interest in the collateral if written notification of demand therefor is received before distribution of the proceeds is completed. If requested by the secured party, the holder of a subordinate security interest must seasonably furnish reasonable proof of his interest, and unless he does so, the secured party need not comply with his demand.

(2) If the security interest secures an indebtedness, the secured party must account to the debtor for any surplus, and, unless otherwise agreed, the debtor is liable for any deficiency. But if the underlying transaction was a sale of accounts or chattel paper, the debtor is entitled to any surplus or is liable for any deficiency only if the security agreement so provides.

(3) Disposition of the collateral may be by public or private proceedings and may be made by way of one or more contracts. Sale or other disposition may be as a unit or in parcels and at any time and place and on any terms but every aspect of the disposition including the method, manner, time, place and terms must be commercially reasonable. Unless collateral is perishable or threatens to decline speedily in value or is of a type customarily sold on a recognized market, reasonable notification of the time and place of any public sale or reasonable notification of the time after which any private sale or other intended disposition is to be made shall be sent by the secured party to the debtor, if he has not signed after default a statement renouncing or modifying his right to notification of sale. In the case of consumer goods no other notification need be sent. In other cases notification shall be sent to any other secured party from whom the secured party has received (before sending his notification to the debtor or before the debtor's renunciation of his rights) written notice of a claim of an interest in the collateral. The secured party may buy at any public sale and if the collateral is of a type customarily sold in a recognized market or is of a type which is the subject of widely distributed standard price quotations he may buy at private sale.

(4) When collateral is disposed of by a secured party after default, the disposition transfers to a purchaser for value all of the debtor's rights therein, discharges the security interest under which it is made and any security interest or lien subordinate thereto. The purchaser takes free of all such rights and interests even though the secured party fails to comply with the requirements of this Part or of any judicial proceedings

(a) in the case of a public sale, if the purchaser has no knowledge of any defects in the sale and if he does not buy in collusion with the secured party, other bidders or the person conducting the sale; or

(b) in any other case, if the purchaser acts in good faith.

(5) A person who is liable to a secured party under a guaranty, indorsement, repurchase agreement or the like and who receives a transfer of collateral from the secured party or is subrogated to his rights has thereafter the rights and duties of the secured party. Such a transfer of collateral is not a sale or disposition of the collateral under this Article.

§ 9-505. Compulsory Disposition of Collateral; Acceptance of the Collateral as Discharge of Obligation.

(1) If the debtor has paid sixty per cent of the cash price in the case of a purchase money security interest in consumer goods or sixty per cent of the loan in the case of another security interest in consumer goods, and has not signed after default a statement renouncing or modifying his rights under this Part a secured party who has taken possession of collateral must dispose of it under Section 9-504 and if he fails to do so within ninety days after he takes possession the debtor at his option may recover in conversion or under Section 9-507(1) on secured party's liability.

(2) In any other case involving consumer goods or any other collateral secured party in possession may, after default, propose to retain the collateral in satisfaction of the obligation. Written notice of such proposal shall be sent to the debtor if he has not signed after default a statement renouncing or modifying his rights under this subsection. In the case of consumer goods no other notice need be given. In other case notice shall be sent to any other secured party from whom the secured party has received (before sending his notice to the debtor or before the debtor's renunciation of his rights) written notice of a claim of an interest in the collateral. If the secured party receives objection in writing from a person entitled to receive notification within twenty-one days after the notice was sent, the secured party must dispose of the collateral under Section 9-504. In the absence of such written objection the secured party may retain the collateral in satisfaction of the debtor's obligation

§ 9-506. Debtor's Right to Redeem Collateral. At any time before the secured party has disposed of collateral or entered into a contract for its disposition under Section 9-504 or before the obligation has been discharged under Section 9-505(2) the debtor or any other secured party may unless otherwise agreed in writing after default redeem the collateral by tendering fulfillment of all obligation secured by the collateral as well as the expenses reasonable incurred by the secured party in retaking, holding and preparing the collateral for disposition, in arranging for the sale, and to the extent provided in the agreement and not prohibited by law, his reasonable attorney's fees and legal expenses.

§ 9-507. Secured Party's Liability for Failure to Comply With This Part.
(1) If it is established that the secured party is not proceeding in accordance with the provisions of this Part disposition may be ordered or restrained on appropriate terms and conditions. If the disposition has occurred the debtor or any person entitled to notification or whose security interest has been made known to the secured party prior to the disposition has a right to recover from the secured party any loss caused by a failure to comply with the provisions of this Part. If the collateral is consumer goods, the debtor has a right to recover in any event an amount not less than the credit service charge plus ten per cent of the principal amount of the debt or the time price differential plus 10 per cent of the cash price.

(2) The fact that a better price could have been obtained by a sale at a different time or in a different method from that selected by the secured party is not of itself sufficient to establish that the sale was not made in a commercially reasonable manner. If the secured party either sells the collateral in the usual manner in any recognized market therefor or if he sells at the price current in such market at the time of his sale or if he has otherwise sold in conformity with reasonable commercial practices among dealers in the type of property sold he has sold in a commercially reasonable manner. The principles stated in the two preceding sentences with respect to sales also apply as may be appropriate to other types of disposition. A disposition which has been approved in any judicial proceeding or by any bona fide creditors' committee or representative of creditors shall conclusively be deemed to be commercially reasonable, but this sentence does not indicate that any such approval must be obtained in any case nor does it indicate that any disposition not so approved is not commercially reasonable.

ARTICLE 10. EFFECTIVE DATE AND REPEALER

§ 10-101. Effective Date. This Act shall become effective at midnight on December 31st following its enactment. It applies to transactions entered into and events occurring after that date.

§ 10-102. Specific Repealer; Provision for Transition.
(1) The following acts and all other acts and parts of acts inconsistent herewith are hereby repealed:
(Here should follow the acts to be specifically repealed including the following:
Uniform Negotiable Instruments Act
Uniform Warehouse Receipts Act
Uniform Sales Act
Uniform Bills of Lading Act
Uniform Stock Transfer Act
Uniform Conditional Sales Act
Uniform Trust Receipts Act
Also any acts regulating:
Bank collections
Bulk sales
Chattel mortgages
Conditional sales
Factor's lien acts

Farm storage of grain and similar acts
Assignment of accounts receivable)

(2) Transactions validly entered into before the effective date specified in Section 10-101 and the rights, duties and interests flowing from them remain valid thereafter and may be terminated, completed, consummated or enforced as required or permitted by any statute or other law amended or repealed by this Act as though such repeal or amendment had not occurred.

Note: *Subsection (1) should be separately prepared for each state. The foregoing is a list of statutes to be checked.*

§ 10-103. **General Repealer.** Except as provided in the following section, all acts and parts of acts inconsistent with this Act are hereby repealed.

§ 10-104. **Laws Not Repealed.**

[(1)] The Article on Documents of Title (Article 7) does not repeal or modify any laws prescribing the form or contents of documents of title or the services or facilities to be afforded by bailees, or otherwise regulating bailees' businesses in respects not specifically dealt with herein; but the fact that such laws are violated does not affect the status of a document of title which otherwise complies with the definition of a document of title (Section 1-201).

[(2) This Act does not repeal ....
....,

cited as the Uniform Act for the Simplification of Fiduciary Security Transfers, and if in any respect there is any inconsistency between that Act and the Article of this Act on investment securities (Article 8) the provisions of the former Act shall control.]

Appendix C

§ 1. Short Title. This Act shall be known and may be cited as the "_____ [insert name of state] Business Corporation Act."

§ 2. Definitions. As used in this Act, unless the context otherwise requires, the term:

(a) "Corporation" or "domestic corporation" means a corporation for profit subject to the provisions of this Act, except a foreign corporation.

(b) "Foreign corporation" means a corporation for profit organized under laws other than the laws of this State for a purpose or purposes for which a corporation may be organized under this Act.

(c) "Articles of incorporation" means the original or restated articles of incorporation or articles of consolidation and all amendments thereto including articles of merger.

(d) "Shares" means the units into which the proprietary interests in a corporation are divided.

(e) "Subscriber" means one who subscribes for shares in a corporation, whether before or after incorporation.

(f) "Shareholder" means one who is a holder of record of shares in a corporation. If the articles of incorporation or the by-laws so provide, the board of directors may adopt by resolution a procedure whereby a shareholder of the corporation may certify in writing to the corporation that all or a portion of the shares registered in the name of such shareholder are held for the account of a specified person or persons. The resolution shall set forth (1) the classification of shareholder who may certify, (2) the purpose or purposes for which the certification may be made, (3) the form of certification and information to be contained therein, (4) if the certification is with respect to a record date or closing of the stock transfer books within which the certi-

fication must be received by the corporation and (5) such other provisions with respect to the procedure as are deemed necessary or desirable. Upon receipt by the corporation of a certification complying with the procedure, the persons specified in the certification shall be deemed, for the purpose or purposes set forth in the certification, to be the holders of record of the number of shares specified in place of the shareholder making the certification.

(g) "Authorized shares" means the shares of all classes which the corporation is authorized to issue.

(h) "Employee" includes officers but not directors. A director may accept duties which make him also an employee.

(i) "Distribution" means a direct or indirect transfer of money or other property (except its own shares) or incurrence of indebtedness, by a corporation to or for the benefit of any of its shareholders in respect of any of its shares, whether by dividend or by purchase, redemption or other acquisition of its shares, or otherwise.

§ 3. Purposes. Corporations may be organized under this Act for any lawful purpose or purposes, except for the purpose of banking or insurance.

§ 4. General Powers. Each corporation shall have power:

(a) To have perpetual succession by its corporate name unless a limited period of duration is stated in its articles of incorporation.

(b) To sue and be sued, complain and defend, in its corporate name.

(c) To have a corporate seal which may be altered at pleasure, and to use the same by causing it, or a facsimile thereof, to be impressed or affixed or in any other manner reproduced.

(d) To purchase, take, receive, lease, or otherwise acquire, own, hold, improve, use and otherwise deal in and with, real or personal property, or any interest therein, wherever situated.

(e) To sell, convey, mortgage, pledge, lease, exchange, transfer and otherwise dispose of all or any part of its property and assets.

(f) To lend money and use its credit to assist its employees.

(g) To purchase, take, receive, subscribe for, or otherwise acquire, own, hold, vote, use, employ, sell, mortgage, lend, pledge, or otherwise dispose of, and otherwise use and deal in and with, shares or other interests in, or obligations of, other domestic or foreign corporations, associations, partnerships or individuals, or direct or indirect obligations of the United States or of any other government, state, territory, governmental district or municipality or of any instrumentality thereof.

(h) To make contracts and guarantees and incur liabilities, borrow money at such rates of interest as the corporation may determine, issue its notes, bonds, and other obligations, and secure any of its obligations by mortgage or pledge of all or any of its property, franchises and income.

(i) To lend money for its corporate purposes, invest and reinvest its funds, and take and hold real and personal property as security for the payment of funds so loaned or invested.

(j) To conduct its business, carry on its operations and have offices and exercise the powers granted by this Act, within or without this State.

(k) To elect or appoint officers and agents of the corporation, and define their duties and fix their compensation.

(l) To make and alter by-laws, not inconsistent with its articles of incorporation or with the laws of this State, for the administration and regulation of the affairs of the corporation.

(m) To make donations for the public welfare or for charitable, scientific or educational purposes.

(n) To transact any lawful business which the board of directors shall find will be in aid of governmental policy.

(o) To pay pensions and establish pension plans, pension trusts, profit sharing plans, stock bonus plans, stock option plans and other incentive plans for any or all of its directors, officers and employees.

(p) To be a promoter, partner, member, associate, or manager of any partnership, joint venture, trust or other enterprise.

(q) To have and exercise all powers necessary or convenient to effect its purposes.

§ 5. Indemnification of Directors and Officers.

(a) As used in this section:

(1) *Director* means any person who is or was a director of the corporation and any person who, while a director of the corporation, is or was serving at the request of the corporation as a director, officer, partner, trustee, employee or agent of another foreign or domestic corporation, partnership, joint venture, trust, other enterprise or employee benefit plan.

(2) *Corporation* includes any domestic or foreign predecessor entity of the corporation in a merger, consolidation or other transaction in which the predecessor's existence ceased upon consummation of such transaction.

(3) *Expenses* include attorneys' fees.

(4) *Official capacity* means

(A) when used with respect to a director, the office of director in the corporation, and

(B) when used with respect to a person other than a director, as contemplated in subsection (i), the elective or appointive office in the corporation held by the officer or the employment or agency relationship undertaken by the employee or agent in behalf of the corporation,

but in each case does not include service for any other foreign or domestic corporation or any partnership, joint venture, trust, other enterprise, or employee benefit plan.

(5) *Party* includes a person who was, is, or is threatened to be made, a named defendant or respondent in a proceeding.

(6) *Proceeding* means any threatened, pending or completed action, suit or proceeding, whether civil, criminal, administrative or investigative.

(b) A corporation shall have power to indemnify any person made a party to any proceeding by reason of the fact that he is or was a director if

(1) he conducted himself in good faith; and

(2) he reasonably believed

(A) in the case of conduct in his official capacity with the corporation, that his conduct was in its best interests, and

(B) in all other cases, that his conduct was at least not opposed to its best interests; and

(3) in the case of any criminal proceeding, he had no reasonable cause to believe his conduct was unlawful.

Indemnification may be made against judgments, penalties, fines, settlements and reasonable expenses, actually incurred by the person in connection with the proceeding; except that if the proceeding was by or in the right of the corporation, indemnification may be made only against such reasonable expenses and shall not be made in respect of any proceeding in which the person shall have been adjudged to be liable to the corporation. The termination of any proceeding by judgment, order, settlement, conviction, or upon a plea of nolo contendere or its equivalent, shall not, of itself, be determinative that the person did not meet the requisite standard of conduct set forth in this subsection (b).

(c) A director shall not be indemnified under subsection (b) in respect of any proceeding charging improper personal benefit to him, whether or not involving action in his official capacity, in which he shall have been adjudged to be liable on the basis that personal benefit was improperly received by him.

(d) Unless limited by the articles of incorporation,

(1) a director who has been wholly successful, on the merits or otherwise, in the defense of any proceeding referred to in subsection (b) shall be indemnified against reasonable expenses incurred by him in connection with the proceeding; and

(2) a court of appropriate jurisdiction, upon application of a director and such notice as the court shall require, shall have authority to order indemnification in the following circumstances:

(A) if it determines a director is entitled to reimbursement under clause (1), the court shall order indemnification, in which case the director shall also be entitled to recover the expenses securing such reimbursement; or

(B) if it determines that the director is fairly and reasonably entitled to indemnification in view of all the relevant circumstances, whether or not he has met the standard of conduct set forth in subsection (b) or has been adjudged liable in the circumstances described in subsection (c), the court may order such indemnification with respect to any proceeding by or in the right of the corporation or in which liability shall have been adjudged in the circumstances described in subsection (c) shall be limited to expenses.

A court of appropriate jurisdiction may be the same court in which the proceeding involving the director's liability took place.

(e) No indemnification under subsection (b) shall be made by the corporation unless authorized in the specific case after a determination has been made that indemnification of the director is permissible in the circumstances because he has met the standard of conduct set forth in subsection (b). Such determination shall be made:

(1) by the board of directors by a majority vote of a quorum consisting of directors not at the time parties to the proceeding; or

(2) If such a quorum cannot be obtained, then by a majority vote of a committee of the board, duly designated to act in the matter by a majority vote of the full board (in which designation directors who are parties may participate), consisting solely of two or more directors not at the time parties to the proceeding; or

(3) by special legal counsel, selected by the board of directors or a committee thereof by vote as set forth in clauses (1) or (2) of this subsection (e), or, if the requisite quorum of the full board cannot be obtained therefor and such committee cannot be established, by a majority vote of the full board (in which selection directors who are parties may participate); or

(4) by the shareholders.

Authorization of indemnification and determination as to reasonableness of expenses shall be made in the same manner as the determination that indemnification is permissible, except that if the determination that indemnification is permissible is made by special legal counsel, authorization of indemnification and determination as to reasonableness of expenses shall be made in a manner specified in clause (3) in the preceding sentence for the selection of such counsel. Shares held by directors who are parties to the proceeding shall not be voted on the subject matter under this subsection (e).

(f) Reasonable expenses incurred by a director who is a party to a proceeding may be paid or reimbursed by the corporation in advance of the final disposition of such proceeding upon receipt by the corporation of

(1) a written affirmation by the director of his good faith belief that he has met the standard of conduct necessary for indemnification by the corporation as authorized in this section, and

(2) a written undertaking by or on behalf of the director to repay such amount if it shall ultimately be determined that he has not met such standard of conduct, and after a determination that the facts then known to those making the determination would not preclude indemnification under this

section. The undertaking required by clause (2) shall be an unlimited general obligation of the director but need not be secured and may be accepted without reference to financial ability to make repayment. Determinations and authorizations of payments under this subsection (f) shall be made in the manner specified in subsection (e).

(g) No provision for the corporation to indemnify or to advance expenses to a director who is made a party to a proceeding, whether contained in the articles of incorporation, the by-laws, a resolution of shareholders or directors, an agreement or otherwise (except as contemplated by subsection (j)), shall be valid unless consistent with this section or, to the extent that indemnity hereunder is limited by the articles of incorporation, consistent therewith. Nothing contained in this section shall limit the corporation's power to pay or reimburse expenses incurred by a director in connection with his appearance as a witness in a proceeding at a time when he has not been made a named defendant or respondent in the proceeding.

(h) For purposes of this section, the corporation shall be deemed to have requested a director to serve an employee benefit plan whenever the performance by him of his duties to the corporation also imposes duties on, or otherwise involves services by, him to the plan or participants or beneficiaries of the plan; excise taxes assessed on a director with respect to an employee benefit plan pursuant to applicable law shall be deemed "fines"; and action taken or omitted by him with respect to an employee benefit plan in the performance of his duties for a purpose reasonably believed by him to be in the interest of the participants and beneficiaries of the plan shall be deemed to be for a purpose which is not opposed to the best interest of the corporation.

(i) Unless limited by the articles of incorporation,

(1) an officer of the corporation shall be indemnified as and to the same extent provided in subsection (d) for a director and shall be entitled to the same extent as a director to seek indemnification pursuant to the provisions of subsection (d);

(2) a corporation shall have the power to indemnify and to advance expenses to an officer, employee or agent of the corporation to the same extent that it may indemnify and advance expenses to directors pursuant to this section; and

(3) a corporation, in addition, shall have the power to indemnify and to advance expenses to an officer, employee or agent who is not a director to such further extent, consistent with law, as may be provided by its articles of incorporation, by-laws, general or specific action of its board of directors, or contract.

(j) A corporation shall have power to purchase and maintain insurance on behalf of any person who is or was a director, officer, employee or agent of the corporation, or who, while a director, officer, employee or agent of the corporation, is or was serving at the request of the corporation as a director, officer, partner, trustee, employee or agent of another foreign or domestic corporation, partnership, joint venture, trust, other enterprise or employee benefit plan, against any liability asserted against him and incurred by him in any such capacity or arising out of his status as such, whether or not the corporation would have the power to indemnify him against such liability under the provisions of this section.

(k) Any indemnification of, or advance of expenses to, a director in accordance with this section, if arising out of a proceeding by or in the right of the corporation, shall be reported in writing to the shareholders with or before the notice of the next shareholders' meeting.

§ 6. Power of Corporation to Acquire its Own Shares.

A corporation shall have the power to acquire its own shares. All of its own shares acquired by a corporation shall, upon acquisition, constitute authorized but unissued shares, unless the articles of incorporation provide that they shall not be reissued, in which case the authorized shares shall be reduced by the number of shares acquired.

If the number of authorized shares is reduced by an acquisition, the corporation shall, not later than the time it files its next annual report under this Act with the Secretary of State, file a statement of cancellation showing the reduction in the authorized shares. The statement of cancellation shall be executed in duplicate by the corporation by its president or a vice president and by its secretary or an assistant secretary, and verified by one of the officers signing such statement, and shall set forth:

(a) The name of the corporation.

(b) The number of acquired shares cancelled, itemized by the classes and series.

(c) The aggregate number of authorized shares, itemized by classes and series, after giving effect to such cancellation.

Duplicate originals of such statements shall be delivered to the Secretary of State. If the Secretary of State finds that such statement conforms to law, he shall, when all fees and franchise taxes have been paid as in this Act prescribed:

(1) Endorse on each of such duplicate originals the word "filed," and the month, day and year of the filing thereof.

(2) File one of such duplicate originals in his office.

(3) Return the other duplicate original to the corporation or its representative.

§ 7. **Defense of Ultra Vires.**   No act of corporation and no conveyance or transfer of real or personal property to or by a corporation shall be invalid by reason of the fact that the corporation was without capacity or power to do such act or to make or receive such conveyance or transfer, but such lack of capacity or power may be asserted:

(a) In a proceeding by a shareholder against the corporation to enjoin the doing of any act or the transfer of real or personal property by or to the corporation. If the unauthorized act or transfer sought to be enjoined is being, or is to be, performed or made pursuant to a contract to which the corporation is a party, the court may, if all of the parties to the contract are parties to the proceeding and if it deems the same to be equitable, set aside and enjoin the performance of such contract, and in so doing may allow to the corporation or to the other parties to the contract, as the case may be, compensation for the loss or damage sustained by either of them which may result from the action of the court in setting aside and enjoining the performance of such contract, but anticipated profits to be derived from the performance of the contract shall not be awarded by the court as a loss or damage sustained.

(b) In a proceeding by the corporation, whether acting directly or through a receiver, trustee, or other legal representative, or through shareholders in a representative unit, against the incumbent or former officers or directors of the corporation.

(c) In a proceeding by the Attorney General, as provided in this Act, to dissolve the corporation, or in a proceeding by the Attorney General to enjoin the corporation from the transaction of unauthorized business.

§ 8. **Corporate Name.**   The corporate name:

(a) Shall contain the word "corporation," "company," "incorporated" or "limited," or shall contain an abbreviation of one of such words.

(b) Shall not contain any word or phrase which indicates or implies that it is organized for any purpose other than one or more of the purposes contained in its articles of incorporation.

(c) Shall not be the same as, or deceptively similar to, the name of any domestic corporation existing under the laws of this State or any foreign corporation authorized to transact business in this State, or a name the exclusive right to which is, at the time, reserved in the manner provided in this Act, or the name of a corporation which has in effect a registration of its corporate name as provided in this Act, except that this provision shall not apply if the applicant files with the Secretary of State either of the following: (1) the written consent of such other corporation or holder of a reserved or registered name to use the same or deceptively similar name and one or more words are added to make such name distinguishable from such other name, or (2) a certified copy of a final decree of a court of competent jurisdiction establishing the prior right of the applicant to the use of such name in this State.

A corporation with which another corporation, domestic or foreign, is merged, or which is formed by the reorganization or consolidation of one or more domestic or foreign corporations or upon a sale, lease or other disposition to or exchange with, a domestic corporation of all or substantially all the assets of another corporation, domestic or foreign, including its name, may have the same name as that used in this State by any of such corporations if such other corporation was organized under the laws of, or is authorized to transact business in, this State.

§ 9. **Reserved Name.**   The exclusive right to the use of a corporate name may be reserved by:

(a) Any person intending to organize a corporation under this Act.

(b) Any domestic corporation intending to change its name.

(c) Any foreign corporation intending to make application for a certificate of authority to transact business in this State.

(d) Any foreign corporation authorized to transact business in this state and intending to change its name.

(e) Any person intending to organize a foreign corporation and intending to have such corporation make application for a certificate of authority to transact business in this State.

The reservation shall be made by filing with the Secretary of State an application to reserve a specified corporate name, executed by the applicant. If the Secretary of State finds that the name is available for corporate use, he shall reserve the same for the exclusive use of the applicant for a period of one hundred and twenty days.

The right to the exclusive use of a specified corporate name so reserved may be transferred to any other person or corporation by filing in the office of the Secretary of State a notice of such transfer, executed by the applicant for whom the name was reserved, and specifying the name and address of the transferee.

§ 10. Registered Name. Any corporation organized and existing under the laws of any state or territory of the United States may register its corporate name under this Act, provided its corporate name is not the same as, or deceptively similar to, the name of any domestic corporation existing under the laws of this State, or the name of any foreign corporation authorized to transact business in this State, or any corporate name reserved or registered under this Act.

Such registration shall be made by:

(a) Filing with the Secretary of State (1) an application for registration executed by the corporation by an officer thereof, setting forth the name of the corporation, the state or territory under the laws of which it is incorporated, the date of its incorporation, a statement that it is carrying on or doing business, and a brief statement of the business in which it is engaged, and (2) a certificate setting forth that such corporation is in good standing under the laws of the state or territory wherein it is organized, executed by the Secretary of State of such state or territory or by such other official as may have custody of the records pertaining to corporations, and

(b) Paying to the Secretary of State a registration fee in the amount of _____ for each month, or fraction thereof, between the date of filing such application and December 31st of the calendar year in which such application is filed.

Such registration shall be effective until the close of the calendar year in which the application for registration is filed.

§ 11. Renewal of Registered Name. A corporation which has in effect a registration of its corporate name, may renew such registration from year to year by annually filing an application for renewal setting forth the facts required to be set forth in an original application for registration and a certificate of good standing as required for the original registration and by paying a fee of _____ . A renewal application may be filed between the first day of October and the thirty-first day of December in each year, and shall extend the registration for the following calendar year.

§ 12. Registered Office and Registered Agent. Each corporation shall have and continuously maintain in this state:

(a) A registered office which may be, but need not be, the same as its place of business.

(b) A registered agent, which agent may be either an individual resident in this State whose business office is identical with such registered office, or a domestic corporation, or a foreign corporation authorized to transact business in this State, having a business office identical with such registered office.

§ 13. Change of Registered Office or Registered Agent. A corporation may change its registered office or change its registered agent, or both, upon filing in the office of the Secretary of State a statement setting forth:

(a) The name of the corporation.

(b) The address of its then registered office.

(c) If the address of its registered office is to be changed, the address to which the registered office is to be changed.

(d) The name of its then registered agent.

(e) If its registered agent is to be changed, the name of its successor registered agent.

(f) That the address of its registered office and the address of the business office of its registered agent, as changed, will be identical.

(g) That such change was authorized by resolution duly adopted by its board of directors.

Such statement shall be executed by the corporation by its president, or a vice president, and verified by him, and delivered to the Secretary of State. If the Secretary of State finds that such statement conforms to the provisions of this Act, he shall file such statement in his office, and upon such filing the change of address of the registered office, or the appointment of a new registered agent, or both, as the case may be, shall become effective.

Any registered agent of a corporation may resign as such agent upon filing a written notice thereof, executed in duplicate, with the Secretary of State, who shall forthwith mail a copy thereof to the corporation at its registered office. The appointment of such agent shall terminate upon the expiration of thirty days after receipt of such notice by the Secretary of State.

If a registered agent changes his or its business address to another place within the same _____ [supply designation of jurisdiction, such as county, etc., in accordance with local practice], he or it may change such address and the address of the registered office of any corporation of which he or it is registered agent by filing a statement as required above except that it need be signed only by the registered agent and need not be responsive to (e) or (g) and must recite that a copy of the statement has been mailed to the corporation.

§ 14. Service of Process on Corporation. The registered agent so appointed by a corporation shall be an agent of such corporation upon whom any process, notice or demand required or permitted by law to be served upon the corporation may be served.

Whenever a corporation shall fail to appoint or maintain a registered agent in this State, or whenever its registered agent cannot with reasonable diligence be found at the registered office, then the Secretary of State shall be an agent of such corporation upon whom any such process, notice or demand may be served. Service on the Secretary of State of any such process, notice, or demand shall be made by delivering to and leaving with him, or with any clerk having charge of the corporation department of his office, duplicate copies of such process, notice or demand. In the event any such process, notice or demand is served on the Secretary of State, he shall immediately cause one of the copies thereof to be forwarded by registered mail, addressed to the corporation at its registered office. Any service so had on the Secretary of State shall be returnable in not less than thirty days.

The Secretary of State shall keep a record of all processes, notices and demands served upon him under this section, and shall record therein the time of such service and his action with reference thereto.

Nothing herein contained shall limit or affect the right to serve any process, notice or demand required or permitted by law to be served upon a corporation in any other manner now or hereafter permitted by law.

§ 15. Authorized Shares. Each corporation shall have power to create and issue the number of shares stated in its articles of incorporation. Such shares may be divided into one or more classes with such designations, preferences, limitations, and relative rights as shall be stated in the articles of incorporation. The articles of incorporation may limit or deny the voting rights of or provide special voting rights for the shares of any class to the extent not inconsistent with the provisions of this Act.

Without limiting the authority herein contained, a corporation, when so provided in its articles of incorporation, may issue shares of preferred or special classes:

(a)   Subject to the right of the corporation to redeem any of such shares at the price fixed by the articles of incorporation for the redemption thereof.

(b)   Entitling the holders thereof to cumulative, noncumulative or partially cumulative dividends.

(c)   Having preference over any other class or classes of shares as to the payment of dividends.

(d)   Having preference in the assets of the corporation over any other class or classes of shares upon the voluntary or involuntary liquidation of the corporation.

(e)   Convertible into shares of any other class or into shares of any series of the same or any other class, except a class having prior or superior rights and preferences as to dividends or distribution of assets upon liquidation.

§ 16. Issuance of Shares of Preferred or Special Classes in Series. If the articles of incorporation so provide, the shares of any preferred or special class may be divided into and issued in series. If the shares of any such class are to be issued in series, then each series shall be so designated as to distinguish the shares thereof from the shares of all other series and classes. Any or all of the series of any such class and the variations in the relative rights and preferences as between different series may be fixed and determined by the articles or incorporation, but all shares of the same class shall be identical except as to the following relative rights and preferences, as to which there may be variations between different series:

    (A) The rate of dividend.

    (B) Whether shares may be redeemed and, if so, the redemption price and the terms and conditions of redemption.

    (C) The amount payable upon shares in event of voluntary and involuntary liquidation.

    (D) Sinking fund provisions, if any, for the redemption or purchase of shares.

    (E) The terms and conditions, if any, on which shares may be converted.

    (F) Voting rights, if any.

If the articles of incorporation shall expressly vest authority in the board of directors, then, to the extent that the articles of incorporation shall not have established series and fixed and determined the variations in the relative rights and preferences as between series, the board of directors shall have authority to divide any or all of such classes into series and, within the limitations set forth in this section and in the articles of incorporation, fix and determine the relative rights and preferences of the shares of any series so established.

In order for the board of directors to establish a series, where authority so to do is contained in the articles of incorporation, the board of directors shall adopt a resolution setting forth the designation of the series and fixing and determining the relative rights and preferences thereof, or so much thereof as shall not be fixed and determined by the articles of incorporation.

Prior to the issue of any shares of a series established by resolution adopted by the board of directors, the corporation shall file in the office of the Secretary of State a statement setting forth:

    (a)   The name of the corporation.

    (b)   A copy of the resolution establishing and designating the series, and fixing and determining the relative rights and preferences thereof.

    (c)   The date of adoption of such resolution.

    (d)   That such resolution was duly adopted by the board of directors.

Such statement shall be executed in duplicate by the corporation by its president or a vice president and by its secretary or an assistant secretary, and verified by one of the officers signing such statement, and shall be delivered to the Secretary of State. If the Secretary of State finds that such statement conforms to law, he shall, when all franchise taxes and fees have been paid as in this Act prescribed:

    (1) Endorse on each of such duplicate originals the word "Filed," and the month, day, and year of the filing thereof.

    (2) File one of such duplicate originals in his office.

    (3) Return the other duplicate original to the corporation or its representative.

Upon the filing of such statement by the Secretary of State, the resolution establishing and designating the series and fixing and determining the relative rights and preferences thereof shall become effective and shall constitute an amendment of the articles of incorporation.

§ 17. Subscriptions for Shares. A subscription for shares of a corporation to be organized shall be irrevocable for a period of six months, unless otherwise provided by the terms of the subscription agreement or unless all of the subscribers consent to the revocation of such subscription.

Unless otherwise provided in the subscription agreement, subscriptions for shares, whether made before or after the organization of a corporation, shall be paid in full at such time, or in such installments and at such times, as shall be determined by the board of directors. Any call made by the board of directors for payment on subscriptions shall be uniform as to all shares of the same class or as to all shares of the same series, as the case may be. In case of default in the payment of any installment or call when such payment is due, the corporation may proceed to collect the amount due in the same manner as any debt due the corporation. The by-laws may prescribe other penalties for failure to pay installments or calls that may become due, but no penalty working a forfeiture of a subscription, or of the amounts paid thereon, shall be declared as against any subscriber unless the amount due thereon shall remain unpaid for a period of twenty days after written demand has been made therefor. If mailed, such written demand shall be deemed to be made when deposited in the United States mail in a sealed envelope addressed to the subscriber at his last post-office address known to the corporation, with postage thereon prepaid. In the event of the sale of any shares by reason of any forfeiture, the excess of proceeds realized over the amount due and unpaid on such shares shall be paid to the delinquent subscriber or to his legal representative.

§ 18. Issuance of Shares. Subject to any restrictions in the articles of incorporation:

  (a)   Shares may be issued for such consideration as shall be authorized by the board of directors establishing a price (in money or other consideration) or a minimum price or general formula or method by which the price will be determined; and

  (b)   Upon authorization by the board of directors, the corporation may issue its own shares in exchange for or in conversion of its outstanding shares, or distribute its own shares, pro rata to its shareholders or the shareholders of one or more classes or series, to effectuate stock dividends or splits, and any such transaction shall not require consideration; provided, that no such issuance of shares of any class or series shall be made to the holders of shares of any other class or series unless it is either expressly provided for in the articles of incorporation, or is authorized by an affirmative vote or the written consent of the holders of at least a majority of the outstanding shares of the class or series in which the distribution is to be made.

§ 19. Payment for Shares. The consideration for the issuance of shares may be paid, in whole or in part, in money, in other property, tangible or intangible, or in labor or services actually performed for the corporation. When payment of the consideration for which shares are to be issued shall have been received by the corporation, such shares shall be nonassessable.

Neither promissory notes nor future services shall constitute payment or part payment for the issuance of shares of a corporation.

In the absence of fraud in the transaction, the judgment of the board of directors or the shareholders, as the case may be, as to the value of the consideration received for shares shall be conclusive.

§ 20. Stock Rights and Options. Subject to any provisions in respect thereof set forth in its articles of incorporation, a corporation may create and issue, whether or not in connection with the issuance and sale of any of its shares or other securities, rights or options entitling the holders thereof to purchase from the corporation shares of any class or classes.

Such rights or options shall be evidenced in such manner as the board of directors shall approve and, subject to the provisions of the articles of incorporation, shall set forth the terms upon which, the time or times within which and the price or prices at which such shares may be purchased from the corporation upon the exercise of any such right or option. If such rights or options are to issued to directors, officers or employees as such of the corporation or of any subsidiary thereof, and not to the shareholders generally, their issuance shall be approved by the affirmative vote of the holders of a majority of the shares entitled to vote thereon or shall be authorized by and consistent with a plan approved or ratified by such a vote of shareholders. In the absence of fraud in the transaction, the judgment of the board of directors as to the adequacy of the consideration received for such rights or options shall be conclusive.

§ 21. Determination of Amount of Stated Capital. [This section was repealed in 1979.]

§ 22. Expenses of Organization, Reorganization and Financing. The reasonable charges and expenses of organization or reorganization of a corporation, and the reasonable expenses of and compensation for the sale or underwriting of its shares, may be paid or allowed by such corporation out of the consideration received by it in payment for its shares without thereby rendering such shares non-assessable.

§ 23. Shares Represented by Certificates and Uncertificated Shares. The shares of a corporation shall be represented by certificates or shall be uncertificated shares. Certificates shall be signed by the chairman or vice-chairman of the board of directors or a vice president and by the treasurer or an assistant treasurer or the secretary or an assistant secretary of the corporation, and may be sealed with the seal of the corporation or a facsimile therof. Any of or all the signatures upon a certificate may be a facsimile. In case any officer, transfer agent or registrar who has signed or whose facsimile signature has been placed upon such certificate shall have ceased to be such officer, transfer agent or registrar before such certificate is issued, it may be issued by the corporation with the same effect as if he were such officer, transfer agent or registrar at the date of its issue.

Every certificate representing shares issued by a corporation which is authorized to issue shares of more than one class shall set forth upon the face or back of the certificate, or shall state that the corporation will furnish to any shareholder upon request and without charge, a full statement of the designations, preferences, limitations, and relative rights of the shares of each class authorized to be issued, and if the corporation is authorized to issue any preferred or special class in series, the variations in the relative rights and preferences between the shares of each such series so far as the same have been fixed and determined and the authority of the board of directors to fix and determine the relative rights and preferences of subsequent series.

Each certificate representing shares shall state upon the face thereof:

(a) That the corporation is organized under the laws of this State.

(b) The name of the person to whom issued.

(c) The number and class of shares, and the designation of the series, if any, which such certificate represents.

No certificate shall be issued for any share until the consideration established for its issuance shall have been paid.

Unless otherwise provided by the articles of incorporation or by-laws, the board of directors of a corporation may provide by resolution that some or all of any or all classes and series of its shares shall be uncertificated shares, provided that such resolution shall not apply to shares represented by a certificate until such certificate is surrendered to the corporation. Within a reasonable time after the issuance or transfer of uncertificated shares, the corporation shall send to the registered owner thereof a written notice containing the information required to be set forth or stated on certificates pursuant to the second and third paragraphs of this section. Except as otherwise expressly provided by law, the rights and obligations of the holders of uncertificated shares and the rights and obligations of the holders of certificates representing shares of the same class and series shall be identical.

§ 24. Fractional Shares. A corporation may (1) issue fractions of a share, either represented by a certificate or uncertificated, (2) arrange for the disposition of fractional interests by those entitled thereto, (3) pay in money the fair value of fractions of a share as of a time when those entitled

to receive such fractions are determined, or (4) issue scrip in registered or bearer form which shall entitle the holder to receive a certificate for a full share or an uncertificated full share upon the surrender of such scrip aggregating a full share. A certificate for a fractional share or an uncertificated fractional share shall, but scrip shall not unless otherwise provided therein, entitle the holder to exercise voting rights, to receive dividends thereon, and to participate in any of the assets of the corporation in the event of liquidation. The board of directors may cause scrip to be issued subject to the condition that it shall become void if not exchanged for certificates representing full shares or uncertificated full shares before a specified date, or subject to the condition that the shares for which scrip is exchangeable may be sold by the corporation and the proceeds thereof distributed to the holders of scrip, or subject to any other conditions which the board of directors may deem advisable.

§ 25. Liability of Subscribers and Shareholders. A holder of or subscriber to shares of a corporation shall be under no obligation to the corporation or its creditors with respect to such shares other than the obligation to pay to the corporation the full consideration for which such shares were issued or to be issued.

Any person becoming an assignee or transferee of shares or of a subscription for shares in good faith and without knowledge or notice that the full consideration therefor has not been paid shall not be personally liable to the corporation or its creditors for any unpaid portion of such consideration.

An executor, administrator, conservator, guardian, trustee, assignee for the benefit of creditors, or receiver shall not be personally liable to the corporation as a holder of or subscriber to shares of a corporation but the estate and funds in his hands shall be so liable.

No pledgee or other holder of shares as collateral security shall be personally liable as a shareholder.

§ 26. Shareholders' Preemptive Rights. The shareholders of a corporation shall have no preemptive right to acquire unissued shares of the corporation, or securities of the corporation convertible into or carrying a right to subscribe to or acquire shares, except to the extent, if any, that such right is provided in the articles of incorporation.

§ 26A. Shareholders' Preemptive Rights [Alternative].

Except to the extent limited or denied by this section or by the articles of incorporation, shareholders shall have a preemptive right to acquire unissued shares or securities convertible into such shares or carrying a right to subscribe to or acquire shares.

Unless otherwise provided in the articles of incorporation,

(a) No preemptive right shall exist

(1) to acquire any shares issued to directors, officers or employees pursuant to approval by the affirmative vote of the holders of a majority of the shares entitled to vote thereon or when authorized by and consistent with a plan theretofore approved by such a vote of shareholders; or

(2) to acquire any shares sold otherwise than for money.

(b) Holders of shares of any class that is preferred or limited as to dividends or assets shall not be entitled to any preemptive right.

(c) Holders of shares of common stock shall not be entitled to any preemptive right to shares of any class that is preferred or limited as to dividends or assets or to any obligations, unless convertible into shares of common stock or carrying a right to subscribe to or acquire shares of common stock.

(d) Holders of common stock without voting power shall have no preemptive right to shares of common stock with voting power.

(e) The preemptive right shall be only an opportunity to acquire shares or other securities under such terms and conditions as the board of directors may fix for the purpose of providing a fair and reasonable opportunity for the exercise of such right.

§ 27. By-Laws.

The initial by-laws of a corporation shall be adopted by its board of directors. The power to alter, amend or repeal the by-laws or adopt new by-laws, subject to repeal or change by action of the shareholders, shall be vested in the board of directors unless reserved to the shareholders by the articles of incorporation. The by-laws may contain any provisions for the regulation and management of the affairs of the corporation not inconsistent with law or the articles of incorporation.

§ 27A. By-Laws and Other Powers in Emergency [Optional].

The board of directors of any corporation may adopt emergency by-laws, subject to repeal or change by action of the shareholders, which shall, notwithstanding any different provision elsewhere in this Act or in the articles of incorporation or by-laws, be operative during any emergency in the conduct of the business of the corporation resulting from an attack on the United States or any nuclear or atomic disaster. The emergency by-laws may make any provision that may be practical and necessary for the circumstances of the emergency, including provisions that:

(a) A meeting of the board of directors may be called by any officer or director in such manner and under such conditions as shall be prescribed in the emergency by-laws;

(b) The director or directors in attendance at the meeting, or any greater number fixed by the emergency by-laws, shall constitute a quorum; and

(c) The officers or other persons designated on a list approved by the board of directors before the emergency, all in such order of priority and subject to such conditions, and for such period of time (not longer than reasonably necessary after the termination of the emergency) as may be provided in the emergency by-laws or in the resolution approving the list shall, to the extent required to provide a quorum at any meeting of the board of directors, be deemed directors for such meeting.

The board of directors, either before or during any such emergency, may provide, and from time to time modify, lines of succession in the event that during such an emergency any or all officers or agents of the corporation shall for any reason be rendered incapable of discharging their duties.

The board of directors, either before or during any such emergency, may, effective in the emergency, change the head office or designate several alternative head offices or regional offices, or authorize the officers so to do.

To the extent not inconsistent with any emergency by-laws so adopted, the by-laws of the corporation shall remain in effect during any such emergency and upon its termination the emergency by-laws shall cease to be operative.

Unless otherwise provided in emergency by-laws, notice of any meeting of the board of directors during any such emergency may be given only to such of the directors as it may be feasible to reach at the time and by such means as may be feasible at the time, including publication or radio.

To the extent required to constitute a quorum at any meeting of the board of directors during any such emergency, the officers of the corporation who are present shall, unless otherwise provided in emergency by-laws, be deemed, in order of rank and within the same rank in order of seniority, directors for such meeting.

No officer, director or employee acting in accordance with any emergency by-laws shall be liable except for willful misconduct. No officer, director or employee shall be liable for any action taken by him in good faith in such an emergency in furtherance of the ordinary business affairs of the corporation even though not authorized by the by-laws then in effect.

§ 28. Meetings of Shareholders. Meetings of shareholders may be held at such place within or without this State as may be stated in or fixed in accordance with the by-laws. If no other place is stated or so fixed, meetings shall be held at the registered office of the corporation.

An annual meeting of the shareholders shall be held at such time as may be stated in or fixed in accordance with the by-laws. If the annual meeting is not held within any thirteen-month period the Court of _____ may, on the application of any shareholder, summarily order a meeting to be held.

Special meetings of the shareholders may be called by the board of directors, the holders of not less than one-tenth of all the shares entitled to vote at the meeting, or such other persons as may be authorized in the articles of incorporation or the by-laws.

§ 29. Notice of Shareholders' Meetings. Written notice stating the place, day and hour of the meeting and, in case of a special meeting, the purpose or purposes for which the meeting is called, shall be delivered not less than ten nor more than fifty days before the date of the meeting, either personally or by mail, by or at the direction of the president, the secretary, or the officer or persons calling the meeting, to each shareholder of record entitled to vote at such meeting. If mailed, such notice shall be deemed to be delivered when deposited in the United States mail addressed to the shareholder at his address as it appears on the stock transfer books of the corporation, with postage thereon prepaid.

§ 30. Closing of Transfer Books and Fixing Record Date. For the purpose of determining shareholders entitled to notice of or to vote at any meeting of shareholders or any adjournment thereof, or entitled to receive payment of any dividend, or in order to make a determination of shareholders for any other proper purpose, the board of directors of a corporation may provide that the stock transfer books shall be closed for a stated period but not to exceed, in any case, fifty days. If the stock transfer books shall be closed for the purpose of determining shareholders entitled to notice of or to vote at a meeting of shareholders, such books shall be closed for at least ten days immediately preceding such meeting. In lieu of closing the stock transfer books, the by-laws, or in the absence of an applicable by-law the board of directors, may fix in advance a date as the record date for any such determination of shareholders, such date in any case to be not more than fifty days and, in case of a meeting of shareholders, not less than ten days prior to the date on which the particular action, requiring such determination of shareholders, is to be taken. If the stock transfer books are not closed and no record date is fixed for the determination of shareholders entitled to notice of or to vote at a meeting of shareholders, or shareholders entitled to receive payment of a dividend, the date on which notice of the meeting is mailed or the date on which the resolution of the board of directors declaring such dividend is adopted, as the case may be, shall be the record date for such determination of shareholders. When a determination of shareholders entitled to vote at any meeting of shareholders has been made as provided in this section, such determination shall apply to any adjournment thereof.

§ 31. Voting Record. The officer or agent having charge of the stock transfer books for shares of a corporation shall make a complete record of the shareholders entitled to vote at such meeting or any adjournment thereof, arranged in alphabetical order, with the address of and the number of shares held by each. Such record shall be produced and kept open at the time and place of the meeting and shall be subject to the inspection of any shareholder during the whole time of the meeting for the purposes thereof. Failure to comply with the requirements of this section shall not affect the validity of any action taken at such meeting.

An officer or agent having charge of the stock transfer books who shall fail to prepare the record of shareholders, or produce and keep it open for inspection at the meeting, as provided in this section, shall be liable to any shareholder suffering damage on account of such failure, to the extent of such damage.

§ 32. Quorum of Shareholders.   Unless otherwise provided in the articles of incorporation, a majority of the shares entitled to vote, represented in person or by proxy, shall constitute a quorum at a meeting of shareholders, but in no event shall a quorum consist of less than one-third of the shares entitled to vote at the meeting. If a quorum is present, the affirmative vote of the majority of the shares represented at the meeting and entitled to vote on the subject matter shall be the act of the shareholders, unless the vote of a greater number or voting by classes is required by this Act or the articles of incorporation or by-laws.

§ 33. Voting of Shares.   Each outstanding share, regardless of class, shall be entitled to one vote on each matter submitted to a vote at a meeting of shareholders, except as may be otherwise provided in the articles of incorporation. If the articles of incorporation provide for more or less than one vote for any share, on any matter, every reference in this Act to a majority or other proportion of shares shall refer to such a majority or other proportion of votes entitled to be cast.

Shares held by another corporation if a majority or the shares entitled to vote for the election of directors of such other corporation is held by the corporation, shall not be voted at any meeting or counted in determining the total number of outstanding shares at any given time.

A shareholder may vote either in person or by proxy executed in writing by the shareholder or by his duly authorized attorney-in-fact. No proxy shall be valid after eleven months from the date of its execution, unless otherwise provided in the proxy.

[Either of the following prefatory phrases may be inserted here: "The articles of incorporation may provide that" or "Unless the articles of incorporation otherwise provide"] . . . at each election for directors every shareholder entitled to vote at such election shall have the right to vote, in person or by proxy, the number of shares owned by him for as

many persons as there are directors to be elected and for whose election he has a right to vote, or to cumulate his votes by giving one candidate as many votes as the number of such directors multiplied by the number of his shares shall equal, or by distributing such votes on the same principle among any number of such candidates.

Shares standing in the name of another corporation, domestic or foreign, may be voted by such officer, agent or proxy as the by-laws of such other corporation may prescribe, or, in the absence of such provision, as the board of directors of such other corporation may determine.

Shares held by an administrator, executor, guardian or conservator may be voted by him, either in person or by proxy, without a transfer of such shares into his name. Shares standing in the name of a trustee may be voted by him, either in person or by proxy, but no trustee shall be entitled to vote shares held by him without a transfer of such shares into his name.

Shares standing in the name of a receiver may be voted by such receiver, and shares held by or under the control of a receiver may be voted by such receiver without the transfer thereof into his name if authority so to do be contained in an appropriate order of the court by which such receiver was appointed.

A shareholder whose shares are pledged shall be entitled to vote such shares until the shares have been transferred into the name of the pledgee, and thereafter the pledge shall be entitled to vote the shares so transferred.

On and after the date on which written notice of redemption of redeemable shares has been mailed to the holders thereof and a sum sufficient to redeem such shares has been deposited with a bank or trust company with irrevocable instruction and authority to pay the redemption price to the holders thereof upon surrender of certificates therefor, such shares shall not be entitled to vote on any matter and shall not be deemed to be outstanding shares.

§ 34. Voting Trusts and Agreements Among Shareholders.   Any number of shareholders of a corporation may create a voting trust for the purpose of conferring upon a trustee or trustees the right to vote or otherwise represent their shares, for a period of not to exceed ten years, by entering into a written voting trust agreement specifying the terms and conditions of the voting trust, by depositing a counterpart of the agreement with the corporation at its registered office, and by transferring their shares to such trustee or trustees for the purposes of the agreement. Such trustee or trustees shall keep a record of the holders of voting trust certificates evidencing a beneficial interest in the voting trust, giving the names and addresses of all such holders and the number and class of the shares in respect of which the voting trust certificates held by each are issued, and shall deposit a copy of such record with the corporation at its registered office. The counterpart of the voting trust agreement and the copy of such record so deposited with the corporation shall be subject to the same right of examination by a shareholder of the corporation, in person or by agent or attorney, as are the books and records of the corporation, and such counterpart and such copy of such record shall be subject to examination by any holder of record of voting trust certificates, either in person or by agent or attorney, at any reasonable time for any proper purpose.

Agreements among shareholders regarding the voting of their shares shall be valid and enforceable in accordance with their terms. Such agreements shall not be subject to the provisions of this section regarding voting trusts.

§ 35. Board of Directors.   All corporate powers shall be exercised by or under authority of, and the business and affairs of a corporation shall be managed under the direction of, a board of directors except as may be otherwise provided in this Act or the articles of incorporation, the powers and duties conferred or imposed upon the board of directors by this Act shall be exercised or performed to such extent and by such person or persons as shall be provided in the articles of incorporation. Directors need not be residents of this State or shareholders of the corporation unless the articles of incorporation or by-laws so require. The articles of incorporation or by-laws may prescribe other qualifications for directors. The board of directors shall have authority to fix the compensation of directors unless otherwise provided in the articles of incorporation.

A director shall perform his duties as a director, including his duties as a member of any committee of the board upon which he may serve, in good faith, in a manner he reasonably believes to be in the best interests of the corporation, and with such care as an ordinarily prudent person in a like position would use under similar circumstances. In per-

forming his duties, a director shall be entitled to rely on information, opinions, reports or statements, including financial statements and other financial data, in each case prepared or presented by:

(a)   one or more officers or employees of the corporation whom the director reasonably believes to be reliable and competent in the matters presented,

(b)   counsel, public accountants or other persons as to matters which the director reasonably believes to be within such person's professional or expert competence, or

(c)   a committee of the board upon which he does not serve, duly designated in accordance with a provision of the articles of incorporation or the by-laws, as to matters within its designated authority, which committee the director reasonably believes to merit confidence,

but he shall not be considered to be acting in good faith if he has knowledge concerning the matter in question that would cause such reliance to be unwarranted. A person who so performs his duties shall have no liability by reason of being or having been a director of the corporation.

A director of a corporation who is present at a meeting of its board of directors at which action on any corporate matter is taken shall be presumed to have assented to the action taken unless his dissent shall be entered in the minutes of the meeting or unless he shall file his written dissent to such action with the secretary of the meeting before the adjournment thereof or shall forward such dissent by registered mail to the secretary of the corporation immediately after the adjournment of the meeting. Such right to dissent shall not apply to a director who voted in favor of such action.

§ 36. Number and Election of Directors.   The board of directors of a corporation shall consist of one or more members. The number of directors shall be fixed by, or in the manner provided in, the articles of incorporation or the by-laws, except as to the number constituting the initial board of directors, which number shall be fixed by the articles of incorporation. The number of directors may be increased or decreased from time to time by amendment to, or in the manner provided in, the articles of incorporation or the by-laws, but no decrease shall have the effect of shortening the term of any incumbent director. In the absence of a by-law providing for the number of directors, the number shall be the same as that provided for in the articles of incorporation. The names and addresses of the members of the first board of directors shall be stated in the articles of incorporation. Such persons shall hold office until the first annual meeting of shareholders, and until their successors shall have been elected and qualified. At the first annual meeting of shareholders and at each annual meeting thereafter the shareholders shall elect directors to hold office until the next succeeding annual meeting, except in case of the classification of directors as permitted by this Act. Each director shall hold office for the term for which he is elected and until his successor shall have been elected and qualified.

§ 37. Classification of Directors.
When the board of directors shall consist of nine or more members, in lieu of electing the whole number of directors annually, the articles of incorporation may provide that the directors be divided into either two or three classes, each class to be as nearly equal in number as possible, the term of office of directors of the first class to expire at the first annual meeting of shareholders after their election, that of the second class to expire at the second annual meeting after their election, and that of the third class, if any, to expire at the third annual meeting after their election. At each annual meeting after such classification the number of directors equal to the number of the class whose term expires at the time of such meeting shall be elected to hold office until the second succeeding annual meeting, if there be two classes, or until the third succeeding annual meeting, if there be three classes. No classification of directors shall be effective prior to the first annual meeting of shareholders.

§ 38. Vacancies.
Any vacancy occurring in the board of directors may be filled by the affirmative vote of a majority of the remaining directors though less than a quorum of the board of directors. A director elected to fill a vacancy shall be elected for the unexpired term of his predecessor in office. Any directorship to be filled by reason of an increase in the number of directors may be filled by the board of directors for a term of office continuing only until the next election of directors by the shareholders.

§ 39. Removal of Directors.
At a meeting of shareholders called expressly for that purpose, directors may be removed in the manner provided in this section. Any director or the entire board of directors may be removed, with or without cause, by a vote of the holders of a majority of the shares then entitled to vote at an election of directors.

In the case of a corporation having cumulative voting, if less than the entire board is to be removed, no one of the directors may be removed if the votes cast against his removal would be sufficient to elect him if then cumulatively voted at an election of the entire board of directors, or, if there be classes of directors, at an election of the class of directors of which he is a part.

Whenever the holders of the shares of any class are entitled to elect one or more directors by the provisions of the articles of incorporation, the provisions of this section shall apply, in respect to the removal of a director or directors so elected, to the vote of the holders of the outstanding shares of that class and not to the vote of the outstanding shares as a whole.

§ 40. Quorum of Directors.
A majority of the number of directors fixed by or in the manner provided in the by-laws or in the absence of a by-law fixing or providing for the number of directors, then of the number stated in the articles of incorporation, shall constitute a quorum for the transaction of business unless a greater number is required by the articles of incorporation or the by-laws. The act of the majority of the directors present at a meeting at which a quorum is present shall be the act of the board of directors, unless the act of a greater number is required by the articles of incorporation or the by-laws.

§ 41. Director Conflicts of Interest.
No contract or other transaction between a corporation and one or more of its directors or any other corporation, firm, association or entity in which one or more of its directors are directors or officers or are financially interested, shall be either void or voidable because of such relationship or interest or because such director or directors are present at the meeting of the board of directors or a committee thereof which authorized, approves or ratifies such contract or transaction or because his or their votes are counted for such purpose, if:

    (a)   the fact of such relationship or interest is disclosed or known to the board of directors or committee which authorizes, approves or ratifies the contract or transaction by a vote or consent sufficient for the purpose without counting the votes or consents of such interested directors; or

(b) the fact of such relationship or interest is disclosed or known to the shareholders entitled to vote and they authorize, approve or ratify such contract or transaction by vote or written consent; or

(c) the contract or transaction is fair and reasonable to the corporation.

Common or interested directors may be counted in determining the presence of a quorum at a meeting of the board of directors or a committee thereof which authorizes, approves or ratifies such a contract or transaction.

§ 42. Executive and Other Committees.

If the articles of incorporation or the by-laws so provide, the board of directors, by resolution adopted by a majority of the full board of directors, may designate from among its members an executive committee and one or more other committees each of which, to the extent provided in such resolution or in the articles of incorporation or the by-laws of the corporation, shall have and may exercise all the authority of the board of directors, except that no such committee shall have authority to (i) authorize distributions, (ii) approve or recommend to shareholders actions or proposals required by this Act to be approved by shareholders, (iii) designate candidates for the office of director, for purposes of proxy solicitation or otherwise, or fill vacancies on the board of directors or any committee thereof, (iv) amend the by-laws, (v) approve a plan of merger not requiring shareholder approval, (vi) authorize or approve the reacquisition of shares unless pursuant to a general formula or method specified by the board of directors, or (vii) authorize or approve the issuance or sale of, or any contract to issue or sell, shares or designate the terms of a series of a class of shares, provided that the board of directors, having acted regarding general authorization for the issuance or sale of shares, or any contract therefor, and, in the case of a series, the designation thereof, may, purboard by resolution or by adoption of a stock option or other plan, authorize a committee to fix the terms of any contract for the sale of the shares and to fix the terms upon which such shares may be issued or sold, including, without limitation, the price, the dividend rate, provisions for redemption, sinking fund, conversion, voting or preferential rights, and provisions for other features of a class of shares, or a series of a class of shares, with full power in such committee to adopt any final resolution setting forth all terms thereof and to authorize the statement of the terms of a series for filing with the Secretary of State under this Act.

Neither the designation of any such committee, the delegation thereto of authority, nor action by such committee pursuant to such authority shall alone constitute compliance by any member of the board of directors, not a member of the committee in question, with his responsibility to act in good faith, in a manner he reasonably believes to be in the best interests of the corporation, and with such care as an ordinarily prudent person in a like position would use under similar circumstances.

§ 43. Place and Notice of Directors' Meetings; Committee Meetings.

Meetings of the board of directors, regular or special, may be held either within or without this State.

Regular meetings of the board of directors or any committee designated thereby may be held with or without notice as prescribed in the by-laws. Special meetings of the board of directors or any committee designated thereby shall be held upon such notice as is prescribed in the by-laws. Attendance of a director at a meeting shall constitute a waiver of notice of such meeting, except where a director attends a meeting for the express purpose of objecting to the transaction of any business because the meeting is not lawfully called or convened. Neither the business to be transacted at, nor the purpose of, any regular or special meeting of the board of directors or any committee designated thereby need be specified in the notice or waiver of notice of such meeting unless required by the by-laws.

Except as may be otherwise restricted by the articles of incorporation or by-laws, members of the board of directors or any committee designated thereby may participate in a meeting of such board or committee by means of a conference telephone or similar communications equipment by means of which all persons participating in the meeting can hear each other at the same time and participation by such means shall constitute presence in person at a meeting.

§ 44. Action by Directors Without a Meeting.
Unless otherwise provided by the articles of incorporation or by-laws, any action required by this Act to be taken at a meeting of the directors of a corporation, or any action which may be taken at a meeting of the directors or of a committee, may be taken without a meeting if a consent in writing, setting forth the action so taken, shall be signed by all of the directors, or all of the members of the committee, as the case may be. Such consent shall have the same effect as a unanimous vote.

§ 45. Distributions to Shareholders. Subject to any restrictions in the articles of incorporation, the board of directors may authorize and the corporation may make distributions, except that no distribution may be made if, after giving effect thereto, either:

(a) the corporation would be unable to pay its debts as they become due in the usual course of its business; or

(b) the corporation's total assets would be less than the sum of its total liabilities and (unless the articles of incorporation otherwise permit) the maximum amount that then would be payable, in any liquidation, in respect of all outstanding shares having preferential rights in liquidation.

Determinations under subparagraph (b) may be based upon (i) financial statements prepared on the basis of accounting practices and principles that are reasonable in the circumstances, or (ii) a fair valuation or other method that is reasonable in the circumstances.

In the case of a purchase, redemption or other acquisition of a corporation's shares, the effect of a distribution shall be measured as of the date money or other property is transferred or debt is incurred by the corporation, or as of the date the shareholder ceases to be a shareholder of the corporation with respect to such shares, whichever is earlier. In all other cases, the effect of a distribution shall be measured as of the date of its authorization if payment occurs 120 days or less following the date of authorization, or as of the date of payment if payment occurs more than 120 days following the date of authorization.

Indebtedness of a corporation incurred or issued to a shareholder in a distribution in accordance with this Section shall be on a parity with the indebtedness of the corporation to its general unsecured creditors except to the extent subordinated by agreement.

§ 46. Distribution From Capital Surplus. [This section was repealed in 1979.]

§ 47. Loans to Employees and Directors. A corporation shall not lend money to or use its credit to assist its directors without authorization in the particular case by its shareholders, but may lend money to and use its credit to assist any employee of the corporation or of a subsidiary, including any such employee who is a director of the corporation, if the board of directors decides that such loan or assistance may benefit the corporation.

§ 48. Liabilities of Directors in Certain Cases.
In addition to any other liabilities, a director who votes for or assents to any distribution contrary to the provisions of this Act or contrary to any restrictions contained in the articles of incorporation, shall, unless he complies with the standard provided in this Act for the performance of the duties of directors, be liable to the corporation, jointly and severally with all other directors so voting or assenting, for the amount of such dividend which is paid or the value of such distribution in excess of the amount of such distribution which could have been made without a violation of the provisions of this Act or the restrictions in the articles of incorporation.

Any director against whom a claim shall be asserted under or pursuant to this section for the making of a distribution and who shall be held liable thereon, shall be entitled to contribution from the shareholders who accepted or received any such distribution, knowing such distribution to have been made in violation of this Act, in proportion to the amounts received by them.

Any director against whom a claim shall be asserted under or pursuant to this section shall be entitled to contribution from any other director who voted for or assented to the action upon which the claim is asserted and who did not comply with the standard provided in this Act for the performance of the duties of directors.

§ 49. Provisions Relating to Actions by Shareholders. No action shall be brought in this State by a shareholder in the right of a domestic or foreign corporation unless the plaintiff was a holder of record of shares or of voting trust certificates therefor at the time of the transaction of which he complains, or his shares or voting trust certificates thereafter devolved upon him by operation of law from a person who was a holder of record at such time.

In any action hereafter instituted in the right of any domestic or foreign corporation by the holder or holders of record of shares of such corporation or of voting trust certificates therefor, the court having jurisdiction, upon final judgment and a finding that the action was brought without reasonable cause, may require the plaintiff or plaintiffs to pay to the parties named as defendant the reasonable expenses, including fees of attorneys, incurred by them in the defense of such action.

In any action now pending or hereafter instituted or maintained in the right of any domestic or foreign corporation by the holder or holders of record of less than five per cent of the outstanding shares of any class of such corporation or of voting trust certificates therefor, unless the shares or voting trust certificates so held have a market value in excess of twenty-five thousand dollars, the corporation in whose right such action is brought shall be entitled at any time before final judgment to require the plaintiff or plaintiffs to give security for the reasonable expenses, including fees of attorneys, that may be incurred by it in connection with such action or may be incurred by other parties named as defendant for which it may become legally liable. Market value shall be determined as of the date that the plaintiff institutes the action or, in the case of an intervenor, as of the date that he becomes a party to the action. The amount of such security may from time to time be increased or decreased in the discretion of the court, upon showing that the security provided has or may become inadequate or is excessive. The corporation shall have recourse to such security in such amount as the court having jurisdiction shall determine upon the termination of such action, whether or not the court finds the action was brought without reasonable cause.

§ 50. Officers. The officers of a corporation shall consist of a president, one or more vice presidents as may be prescribed by the by-laws, a secretary, and a treasurer, each of whom shall be elected by the board of directors at such time and in such manner as may be prescribed by the by-laws. Such other officers and assistant officers and agents as may be deemed necessary may be elected or appointed by the board of directors or chosen in such other manner as may be prescribed by the by-laws. Any two or more officers may be held by the same person, except the offices of president and secretary.

All officers and agents of the corporation, as between themselves and the corporation, shall have such authority and perform such duties in the management of the corporation as may be provided in the by-laws, or as may be determined by resolution of the board of directors not inconsistent with the by-laws.

§ 51. Removal of Officers. Any officer or agent may be removed by the board of directors whenever in its judgment the best interests of the corporation will be served thereby, but such removal shall be without prejudice to the contract rights, if any, of the person so removed. Election or appointment of an officer or agent shall not of itself create contract rights.

§ 52. Books and Records: Financial Reports to Shareholders; Examination of Records. Each corporation shall keep correct and complete books and records of account and shall keep minutes of the proceedings of its shareholders and board of directors and shall keep at its registered office or principal place of business, or at the office of its transfer agent or registrar, a record of its shareholders, giving the names and addresses of all shareholders and the number and class of the shares held by each. Any books, records and minutes may be in written form or in any other form capable of being converted into written form within a reasonable time.

Any person who shall have been a holder of record of shares or of voting trust certificates therefor at least six months immediately preceding his demand or shall be the holder of record of, or the holder of record of voting trust certificates for, at least five per cent of all the outstanding shares of the corporation, upon written demand stating the purpose thereof, shall have the right to examine, in person, or by agent or attorney, at any reasonable time or times, for any proper purpose its relevant books and records of accounts, minutes, and record of shareholders and to make extracts therefrom.

Any officer or agent who, or a corporation which, shall refuse to allow any such shareholder or holder of voting trust certificates, or his agent or attorney, so to examine and make extracts from its books and records of account, minutes, and record of shareholders, for any purpose, shall be liable to such shareholder or holder of voting trust certificates in a penalty of ten per cent of the value of the shares owned by such shareholder, or in respect of which such voting trust certificates are issued, in addition to any other damages or remedy afforded him by law. It shall be a defense to any action for penalties under this section that the person suing therefor has within two years sold or offered for sale any list of shareholders or of holders of voting trust certificates for shares of such corporation or any other corporation or has aided or abetted any person in procuring any list of shareholders or of holders of voting trust certificates for any such purpose, or has improperly used any information secured through any prior examination of the books and records of account, or minutes, or record of shareholders or of holders of voting trust certificates for shares of such corporation or any other corporation, or was not acting in good faith or for a proper purpose in making his demand.

Nothing herein contained shall impair the power of any court of competent jurisdiction, upon proof by a shareholder or holder of voting trust certificates of proper purpose, irrespective of the period of time during which such shareholder or holder of voting trust certificates shall have been a shareholder of record or a holder of record of voting trust certificates, and irrespective of the number of shares held by him or represented by voting trust certificates held by him, to compel the production for examination by such shareholder or holder of voting trust certificates of the books and records of account, minutes and record of shareholders of a corporation.

Each corporation shall furnish to its shareholders annual financial statements, including at least a balance sheet as of the end of each fiscal year and a statement of income for such fiscal year, which shall be prepared on the basis of generally accepted accounting principles, if the corporation prepares financial statements for such fiscal year on that basis for any purpose, and may be consolidated statements of the corporation and one or more of its subsidiaries. The financial statements shall be mailed by the corporation to each of its shareholders within 120 days after the close of each fiscal year and, after such mailing and upon written request, shall be mailed by the corporation to any shareholder (or holder of a voting trust certificate for its shares) to whom a copy of the most recent annual financial statements has not previously been mailed.

In the case of statements audited by a public accountant, each copy shall be accompanied by a report setting forth his opinion thereon; in other cases, each copy shall be accompanied by a statement of the president or the person in charge of the corporation's financial accounting records (1) stating his reasonable belief as to whether or not the financial statements were prepared in accordance with generally accepted accounting principles and, if not, describing the basis of presentation, and (2) describing any respects in which the financial statements were not prepared on a basis consistent with those prepared for the previous year.

§ 53. Incorporators. One or more persons, or a domestic or foreign corporation, may act as incorporator or incorporators of a corporation by signing and delivering in duplicate to the Secretary of State articles of incorporation for such corporation.

§ 54. Articles of Incorporation. The articles of incorporation shall set forth:

(a)   The name of the corporation.

(b)   The period of duration, which may be perpetual.

(c)   The purpose or purposes for which the corporation is organized which may be stated to be, or to include, the transaction of any or all lawful business for which corporations may be incorporated under this Act.

(d)   The aggregate number of shares which the corporation shall have authority to issue and, if such shares are to be divided into classes, the number of shares of each class.

(e)   If the shares are to be divided into classes, the designation of each class and a statement of the preferences, limitations and relative rights in respect of the shares of each class.

(f)   If the corporation is to issue the shares of any preferred or special class in series, then the designation of each series and a statement of the variations in the relative rights and preferences as between series insofar as the same are to be fixed in the articles of incorporation, and a statement of any authority to be vested in the board of directors to establish series and fix and determine the variations in the relative rights and preferences as between series.

(g)   If any preemptive right is to be granted to shareholders, the provisions therefor.

(h)   The address of its initial registered office, and the name of its initial registered agent at such address.

(i)   The number of directors constituting the initial board of directors and the names and addresses of the persons who are to serve as directors until the first annual meeting of shareholders or until their successors be elected and qualify.

(j)   The name and address of each incorporator.

In addition to provisions required therein, the articles of incorporation may also contain provisions not inconsistent with law regarding:

(1) the direction of the management of the business and the regulation of the affairs of the corporation;

(2) the definition, limitation and regulation of the powers of the corporation, the directors, and the shareholders, or any class of the shareholders, including restrictions on the transfer of shares;

(3) the par value of any authorized shares or class of shares;

(4) any provision which under this Act is required or permitted to be set forth in the by-laws.

It shall not be necessary to set forth in the articles of incorporation any of the corporate powers enumerated in this Act.

§ 55. Filing of Articles of Incorporation. Duplicate originals of the articles of incorporation shall be delivered to the Secretary of State. If the Secretary of State finds that the articles of incorporation conform to law, he shall, when all fees have been paid as in this Act prescribed:

(a)   Endorse on each of such duplicate originals the word "Filed," and the month, day and year of the filing thereof.

(b)   File one of such duplicate originals in his office.

(c)   Issue a certificate of incorporation to which he shall fix the other duplicate original.

The certificate of incorporation, together with the duplicate original of the articles of incorporation affixed thereto by the Secretary of State, shall be returned to the incorporators or their representative.

§ 56. Effect of Issuance of Certificate of Incorporation. Upon the issuance of the certificate of incorporation, the corporate existence shall begin, and such certificate of incorporation shall be conclusive evidence that all conditions precedent required to be performed by the incorporators have been complied with and that the corporation has been incorporated under this Act, except as against this State in a proceeding to cancel or revoke the certificate of incorporation or for involuntary dissolution of the corporation.

§ 57. Organization Meeting of Directors. After the issuance of the certificate of incorporation an organization meeting of the board of directors named in the articles of incorporation shall be held, either within or without this State, at the call of a majority of the directors named in the articles of incorporation, for the purpose of adopting by-laws, electing officers and transacting such other business as may come before the meeting. The directors calling the meeting shall give at least three days' notice thereof by mail to each director so named, stating the time and place of the meeting.

§ 58. Right to Amend Articles of Incorporation. A corporation may amend its articles of incorporation, from time to time, in any and as many respects as may be desired, so long as its articles of incorporation as amended contain only such provisions as might be lawfully contained in original articles of incorporation at the time of making such amendment, and, if a change in shares or the rights of shareholders, or an exchange, reclassification or cancellation of shares or rights of shareholders is to be made, such provisions as may be necessary to effect such change, exchange, reclassification or cancellation.

In particular, and without limitation upon such general power of amendment, a corporation may amend its articles of incorporation, from time to time, so as:

(a)   To change its corporate name.

(b)   To change its period of duration.

(c)   To change, enlarge or diminish its corporate purposes.

(d)   To increase or decrease the aggregate number of shares, or shares of any class, which the corporation has authority to issue.

(e) To provide, change or eliminate any provision with respect to the par value of any shares or class of shares.

(f) To exchange, classify, reclassify or cancel all or any part of its shares, whether issued or unissued.

(g) To change the designation of all or any part of its shares, whether issued or unissued, and to change the preferences, limitations, and the relative rights in respect of all or any part of its shares, whether issued or unissued.

(h) To change the shares of any class, whether issued or unissued into a different number of shares of the same class or into the same or a different number of shares of other classes.

(i) To create new classes of shares having rights and preferences either prior and superior or subordinate and inferior to the shares of any class then authorized, whether issued or unissued.

(j) To cancel or otherwise affect the right of the holders of the shares of any class to receive dividends which have accrued but have not been declared.

(k) To divide any preferred or special class of shares, whether issued or unissued, into series and fix and determine the designations of such series and the variations in the relative rights and preferences as between the shares of such series.

(l) To authorize the board of directors to establish, out of authorized but unissued shares, series of any preferred or special class of shares and fix and determine the relative rights and preferences of the shares of any series so established.

(m) To authorize the board of directors to fix and determine the relative rights and preferences of the authorized but unissued shares of series theretofore established in respect of which either the relative rights and preferences have not been fixed and determined or the relative rights and preferences theretofore fixed and determined are to be changed.

(n) To revoke, diminish, or enlarge the authority of the board of directors to establish series out of authorized but unissued shares of any preferred or special class

and fix and determine the relative rights and preferences of the shares of any series so established.

(o) To limit, deny or grant to shareholders of any class the preemptive right to acquire additional shares of the corporation, whether then or thereafter authorized.

§ 59. Procedure to Amend Articles of Incorporation. Amendments to the articles of incorporation shall be made the following manner:

(a) The board of directors shall adopt a resolution setting forth the proposed amendment and, if shares have been issued, directing that it be submitted to a vote at a meeting of shareholders, which may be either the annual or a special meeting. If no shares have been issued, the amendment shall be adopted by resolution of the board of directors and the provisions for adoption by shareholders shall not apply. If the corporation has only one of shares outstanding, an amendment solely to change the number of authorized shares to effectuate a split of, or stock dividend in, the corporation's own shares, or solely to do so and to change the number of authorized shares in proportion thereto, may be adopted by the board of directors, and the provisions for adoption by shareholders shall not apply, unless otherwise provided by the articles of incorporation. The resolution may incorporate the proposed amendment in restated articles of incorporation which contain a statement that except for the designated amendment the restated articles of incorporation correctly set forth without change the corresponding provisions of the articles of incorporation as theretofore amended, and that the restated articles of incorporation together with the designated amendment supersede the original articles of incorporation and all amendments thereto.

(b) Written notice setting forth the proposed amendment or a summary of the changes to be affected thereby shall be given to each shareholder of record entitled to vote thereon within the time and in the manner provided in the Act for the giving of notice of meetings of shareholders.

If the meeting be an annual meeting, the proposed amendment of each summary may be included in the notice of such annual meeting.

§ 60. Class Voting on Amendments.   The holders of the outstanding shares of a class shall be entitled to vote as a class upon a proposed amendment, whether or not entitled to vote thereon by the provisions of the articles of incorporation, if the amendment would:

(a)   Increase or decrease the aggregate number of authorized shares of such class.

(b)   Effect an exchange, reclassification or cancellation of all or part of the shares of such class.

(c)   Effect an exchange, or create a right of exchange, of all or any part of the shares of another class into the shares of such class.

(d)   Change the designations, preferences, limitations or relative rights of the shares of such class.

(e)   Change the shares of such class into the same or a different number of shares of the same class or another class or classes.

(f)   Create a new class of shares having rights and preferences prior and superior to the shares of such class, or increase the rights and preferences or the number of authorized shares, of any class having rights and preferences prior or superior to the shares of such class.

(g)   In the case of a preferred or special class of shares, divide the shares of such class into series and fix and determine the designation of such series and the variations in the relative rights and preferences between the shares of such series, or authorize the board of directors to do so.

(h)   Limit or deny any existing preemptive rights of the shares of such class.

(i)   Cancel or otherwise affect dividends on the shares of such class which have accrued but have not been declared.

§ 61. Articles of Amendment.   The articles of amendment shall be executed in duplicate by the corporation by its president or a vice president and by its secretary or an assistant secretary, and verified by one of the officers signing such articles, and shall set forth:

(a)   The name of the corporation.

(b)   The amendments so adopted.

(c)   The date of the adoption of the amendment by the shareholders, or by the board of directors where no shares have been issued.

(d)   The number of shares outstanding, and the number of shares entitled to vote thereon, and if the shares of any class are entitled to vote thereon as a class, the designation and number of outstanding shares entitled to vote thereon of each such class.

(e)   The number of shares voted for and against such amendment, respectively, and, if the shares of any class are entitled to vote thereon as a class, the number of shares of each such class voted for and against such amendment, respectively, or if no shares have been issued, a statement to that effect.

(f)   If such amendment provides for an exchange, reclassification or cancellation of issued shares, and if the manner in which the same shall be effected is not set forth in the amendment, then a statement of the manner in which the same shall be effected.

§ 62. Filing of Articles of Amendment.   Duplicate originals of the articles of amendment shall be delivered to the Secretary of State. If the Secretary of State finds that the articles of amendment conform to law, he shall, when all fees and franchise taxes have been paid as in this Act prescribed:

(a)   Endorse on each of such duplicate originals the word "Filed," and the month, day and year of the filing thereof.

(b)   File one of such duplicate originals in his office.

(c)   Issue a certificate of amendment to which he shall affix the other duplicate original.

The certificate of amendment, together with the duplicate original of the articles of amendment affixed thereto by the Secretary of State, shall be returned to the corporation or its representative.

§ 63. Effect of Certificate of Amendment.   The amendment shall become effective upon the issuance of the certificate of amendment by the Secretary of State, or on such later date, not more than thirty days subsequent to the filing thereof with the

Secretary of State, as shall be provided for in the articles of amendment.

No amendment shall affect any existing cause of action in favor of or against such corporation, or any pending suit to which such corporation shall be a party, or the existing rights of persons other than shareholders; and, in the event the corporate name shall be changed by amendment, no suit brought by or against such corporation under its former name shall abate for that reason.

§ 64. Restated Articles of Incorporation. A domestic corporation may at any time restate its articles of incorporation as theretofore amended, by a resolution adopted by the board of directors.

Upon the adoption of such resolution, restated articles of incorporation shall be executed in duplicate by the corporation by its president or a vice president and by its secretary or assistant secretary and verified by one of the officers signing such articles and shall set forth all of the operative provisions of the articles of incorporation as theretofore amended together with a statement that the restated articles of incorporation correctly set forth without change the corresponding provisions of the articles of incorporation as theretofore amended and that the restated articles of incorporation supersede the original articles of incorporation and all amendments thereto.

Duplicate originals of the restated articles of incorporation shall be delivered to the Secretary of State. If the Secretary of State finds that such restated articles of incorporation conform to law, he shall, when all fees and franchise taxes have been paid as in this Act prescribed:

(1) Endorse on each of such duplicate originals the word "Filed," and the month, day and year of the filing thereof.

(2) File one of such duplicate originals in his office.

(3) Issue a restated certificate of incorporation, to which he shall affix the other duplicate original.

The restated certificate of incorporation, together with the duplicate original of the restated articles of incorporation affixed thereto by the Secretary of State, shall be returned to the corporation or its representative.

Upon the issuance of the restated certificate of incorporation by the Secretary of State, the restated articles of incorporation shall become effective and shall supersede the original articles of incorporation and all amendments thereto.

§ 65. Amendment of Articles of Incorporation in Reorganization Proceedings. When a plan of reorganization of a corporation has been confirmed by decree or order of a court of competent jurisdiction in proceedings for the reorganization of such corporation, pursuant to the provisions of any applicable statute of the United States relating to reorganizations of corporations, the articles of incorporation of the corporation may be amended, in the manner provided in this section, in as many respects as may be necessary to carry out the plan and put it into effect, so long as the articles of incorporation as amended contain only such provisions as might be lawfully contained in original articles of incorporation at the time of making such amendment.

In particular and without limitation upon such general power of amendment, the articles of incorporation may be amended for such purpose so as to:

(A) Change the corporate name, period of duration or corporate purposes of the corporation;

(B) Repeal, alter or amend the by-laws of the corporation;

(C) Change the aggregate number of shares or shares of any class, which the corporation has authority to issue;

(D) Change the preferences, limitations and relative rights in respect of all or any part of the shares of the corporation, and classify, reclassify or cancel all or any part thereof, whether issued or unissued;

(E) Authorize the issuance of bonds, debentures or other obligations of the corporation, whether or not convertible into shares of any class or bearing warrants or other evidences of optional rights to purchase or subscribe for shares of any class, and fix the terms and conditions thereof; and

(F) Constitute or reconstitute and classify or reclassify the board of directors of the corporation, and appoint directors and officers in place of or in addition to all or any of the directors or officers then in office.

Amendments to the articles of incorporation pursuant to this section shall be made in the following manner:

(a) Articles of amendment approved by decree or order of such court shall be executed and verified in duplicate by such person or persons as the court shall designate or appoint for the purpose, and shall set forth the name of the corporation, the amendments of the articles of incorporation approved by the court, the date of the decree or order approving the articles of amendment, the title of the proceedings in which the decree or order was entered, and a statement that such decree or order was entered by a court having jurisdiction of the proceedings for the reorganization of the corporation pursuant to the provisions of an applicable statute of the United States.

(b) Duplicate originals of the articles of amendment shall be delivered to the Secretary of State. If the Secretary of State finds that the articles of amendment conform to law, he shall, when all fees and franchise taxes have been paid as in this Act prescribed:

(1) Endorse on each of such duplicate originals the word "Filed," and the month, day and year of the filing thereof.

(2) File one of such duplicate originals in his office.

(3) Issue a certificate of amendment to which he shall affix the other duplicate original.

The certificate of amendment, together with the duplicate original of the articles of amendment affixed thereto by the Secretary of State, shall be returned to the corporation or its representative.

The amendment shall become effective upon the issuance of the certificate of amendment by the Secretary of State, or on such later date, not more than thirty days subsequent to the filing thereof with the Secretary of State, as shall be provided for in the articles of amendment without any action thereon by the directors or shareholders of the corporation and with the same effect as if the amendments had been adopted by unanimous action of the directors and shareholders of the corporation.

§ 66. Restriction on Redemption or Purchase of Redeemable Shares. [This section was repealed in 1979.]

§ 67. Cancellation of Redeemable Shares by Redemption or Purchase. [This section was repealed in 1979.]

§ 68. Cancellation of Other Reacquired Shares. [This section was repealed in 1979.]

§ 69. Reduction of Stated Capital in Certain Cases.]This section was repealed in 1979.]

§ 70. Special Provisions Relating to Surplus and Reserves. [This section was repealed in 1979.]

§ 71. Procedure for Merger. Any two or more domestic corporations may merge into one of such corporations pursuant to a plan of merger approved in the manner provided in this Act.

The board of directors of each corporation shall, by resolution adopted by each such board, approve a plan of merger setting forth:

(a) The names of the corporations proposing to merge, and the name of the corporation into which they propose to merge, which is hereafter designated as the surviving corporation.

(b) The terms and conditions of the proposed merger.

(c) The manner and basis of converting the shares of each corporation into shares, obligations or other securities of the surviving corporation or of any other corporation or, in whole or in part, into cash or other property.

(d) A statement of any changes in the articles of incorporation of the surviving corporation to be effected by such merger.

(e) Such other provisions with respect to the proposed merger as are deemed necessary or desirable.

§ 72. Procedure for Consolidation. Any two or more domestic corporations may consolidate into a new corporation pursuant to a plan of consolidation approved in the manner provided in this Act.

The board of directors of each corporation shall, by a resolution adopted by each such board, approve a plan of consolidation setting forth:

(a) The names of the corporations proposing to consolidate, and the name of the new corporation into which they propose to consolidate, which is hereinafter designated as the new corporation.

(b) The terms and conditions of the proposed consolidation.

(c) The terms and conditions of the proposed consolidation.

(d) The manner and basis of converting the shares of each corporation into shares, obligations or other securities of the new corporation or of any other corporation or, in whole or in part, into cash or other property.

(e) With respect to the new corporation, all of the statements required to be set forth in articles of incorporation for corporations organized under this Act.

(f) Such other provisions with respect to the proposed consolidation as are deemed necessary or desirable.

§ 72A. Procedure for Share Exchange. All the issued or all the outstanding shares of one or more classes of any domestic corporation may be acquired through the exchange of all such shares of such class or classes by another domestic or foreign corporation pursuant to a plan of exchange approved in the manner provided in this Act.

The board of directors of each corporation shall, by resolution adopted by each such board, approve a plan of exchange setting forth:

(a) The name of the corporation the shares of which are proposed to be acquired by exchange and the name of the corporation to acquire the shares of such corporation in the exchange, which is hereinafter designated as the acquiring corporation.

(b) The terms and conditions of the proposed exchange.

(c) The manner and basis of exchanging the shares to be acquired for shares, obligations or other securities of the acquiring corporation or any other corporation, or, in whole or in part, for cash or other property.

(d) Such other provisions with respect to the proposed exchange as are deemed necessary or desirable.

The procedure authorized by this section shall not be deemed to limit the power of a corporation to acquire all or part of the shares of any class or classes of a corporation through a voluntary exchange or otherwise by agreement with the shareholders.

§ 73. Approval by Shareholders.

(a) The board of directors of each corporation in the case of a merger or consolidation, and the board of directors of the corporation the shares of which are to be acquired in the case of an exchange, upon approving such plan of merger,

consolidation or exchange, shall, by resolution, direct that the plan be submitted to a vote at a meeting of its shareholders, which may be either an annual or a special meeting. Written notice shall be given to each shareholder of record, whether or not entitled to vote at such meeting, not less than twenty days before such meeting, in the manner provided in this Act for the giving of notice of meetings of shareholders, and, whether the meeting be an annual or a special meeting, shall state that the purpose or one of the purposes is to consider the proposed plan of merger, consolidation or exchange. A copy or a summary of the plan of merger, consolidation or exchange, as the case may be, shall be included in or enclosed with such notice.

(b) At each such meeting, a vote of the shareholders shall be taken on the proposed plan. The plan shall be approved upon receiving the affirmative vote of the holders of a majority of the shares entitled to vote thereon of each such corporation, unless any class of shares of any such corporation is entitled to vote thereon as a class, in which event, as to such corporation, the plan shall be approved upon receiving the affirmative vote of the holders of a majority of the shares of each class of shares entitled to vote thereon as a class and of the total shares entitled to vote thereon. Any class of shares of any such corporation shall be entitled to vote as a class if any such plan contains any provision which, if contained in a proposed amendment to articles of incorporation, would entitle such class of shares to vote as a class and, in the case of an exchange, if the class is included in the exchange.

(c) After such approval by a vote of the shareholders of each such corporation, and at any time prior to the filing of the articles of merger, consolidation or exchange, the merger, consolidation or exchange may be abandoned pursuant to provisions therefor, if any, set forth in the plan.

(d)(1) Notwithstanding the provisions of subsections (a) and (b), submission of a plan of merger to a vote at a meeting of shareholders of a surviving corporation shall not be required if:

(i) the articles of incorporation of the surviving corporation do not differ except in name from those of the corporation before the merger,

(ii) each holder of shares of the surviving corporation which were outstanding immediately before the effective date of the merger is to hold the same number of shares with identical rights immediately after,

(iii) the number of voting shares outstanding immediately after the merger, plus the number of voting shares issuable on conversion of other securities issued by virtue of the terms of the merger and on exercise of rights and warrants so issued, will not exceed by more than 20 per cent the number of voting shares outstanding immediately before the merger, and

(iv) the number of participating shares outstanding immediately after the merger, plus the number of participating shares issuable on conversion of other securities issued by virtue of the terms of the merger and on exercise of rights and warrants so issued, will not exceed by more than 20 per cent the number of participating shares outstanding immediately before the merger.

(2) As used in this subsection:

(i) "voting shares" means shares which entitle their holders to vote unconditionally in elections of directors;

(ii) "participating shares" means shares which entitle their holders to participate without limitation in distribution of earnings or surplus.

§ 74. Articles of Merger, Consolidation or Exchange.

(a) Upon receiving the approvals required by Sections 71, 72 and 73, articles of merger or articles of consolidation shall be executed in duplicate by each corporation by its president or a vice president and by its secretary or an assistant secretary, and verified by one of the officers of each corporation signing such articles, and shall set forth:

(1) The plan of merger or the plan of consolidation;

(2) As to each corporation, either (i) the number of shares outstanding, and, if the shares of any class are entitled to vote as a class, the designation and number of outstanding shares of each such class, or (ii) a statement that the vote of shareholders is not required by virtue of subsection 73(d);

(3) As to each corporation the approval of whose shareholders is required, the number of shares voted for and against such plan, respectively, and, if the shares of any class are entitled to vote as a class, the number of shares of each such class voted for and against such plan, respectively.

(b) Duplicate originals of the articles of merger, consolidation or exchange shall be delivered to the Secretary of State. If the Secretary of State finds that such articles conform to law, he shall, when all fees and franchise taxes have been paid as in this Act prescribed:

(1) Endorse on each of such duplicate originals the word "Filed," and the month, day and year of the filing thereof.

(2) File one of such duplicate originals in his office.

(3) Issue a certificate of merger, consolidation or exchange to which he shall affix the other duplicate original.

(c) The certificate of merger, consolidation or exchange together with the duplicate original of the articles affixed thereto by the Secretary of State, shall be returned to the surviving, new or acquiring corporation, as the case may be, or its representative.

§ 75. Merger of Subsidiary Corporation. Any corporation owning at least ninety per cent of the outstanding shares of each class of another corporation may merge such other corporation into itself without approval by a vote of the shareholders of either corporation. Its board of directors shall, by resolution, approve a plan of merger setting forth:

(A) The name of the subsidiary corporation and the name of the corporation owning at least ninety per cent of its shares, which is hereinafter designated as the surviving corporation.

(B) The manner and basis of converting the shares of the subsidiary corporation into shares, obligations or other securities of the surviving corporation or of any other corporation or, in whole or in part, into cash or other property.

A copy of such plan of merger shall be mailed to each shareholder of record of the subsidiary corporation.

Articles of merger shall be executed in duplicate by the surviving corporation by its president or a vice president and by its secretary or an assistant secretary, and verified by one of its officers signing such articles, and shall set forth:

(a) The plan of merger;

(b) The number of outstanding shares of each class of the subsidiary corporation and the number of such shares of each class owned by the surving corporation; and

(c) The date of the mailing to shareholders of the subsidiary corporation of a copy of the plan of merger.

On and after the thirtieth day after the mailing of a copy of the plan of merger to shareholders of the subsidiary corporation or upon the waiver thereof by the holders of all outstanding shares duplicate originals of the articles of merger shall be delivered to the Secretary of State. If the Secretary of State finds that such articles conform to law, he shall, when all fees and franchise taxes have been paid as in this Act prescribed:

(1) Endorse on each of such duplicate originals the word "Filed," and the month, day and year of the filing thereof,

(2) File one of such duplicate originals in his office, and

(3) Issue a certificate of merger to which he shall affix the other duplicate original.

The certificate of merger, together with the duplicate original of the articles of merger affixed thereto by the Secretary of State, shall be returned to the surviving corporation or its representative.

§ 76. Effect of Merger, Consolidation or Exchange.

A merger, consolidation or exchange shall become effective upon the issuance of a certificate of merger, consolidation or exchange by the Secretary of State, or on such later date, not more than thirty days subsequent to the filing thereof with the Secretary of State, as shall be provided for in the plan.

When a merger or consolidation has become effective:

(a) The several corporations parties to the plan of merger or consolidation shall be a single corporation, which, in the case of a merger, shall be that corporation designated in the plan of merger as the surviving corporation, and, in the case of a consolidation, shall be the new corporation provided for in the plan of consolidation.

(b) The separate existence of all corporations parties to the plan of merger or consolidation, except the surviving or new corporation, shall cease.

(c) Such surviving or new corporation shall have all the rights, privileges, immunities and powers and shall be subject to all the duties and liabilities of a corporation organized under this Act.

(d) Such surviving or new corporation shall thereupon and thereafter possess all the rights, privileges, immunities, and franchises, of a public as well as of a private nature, of each of the merging or consolidating corporations; and all property, real, personal and mixed, and all debts due on whatever account, including subscriptions to shares, and all other choices in action, and all and every other interest of or belonging to or due to each of the corporations so merged or consolidated, shall be taken and deemed to be transferred to and vested in such single corporation without further act or deed; and the title to any real estate, or any interest therein, vested in any of such corporations shall not revert or be in any way impaired by reason of such merger or consolidation.

(e) Such surviving or new corporation shall thenceforth be responsible and liable for all the liabilities and obligations of each of the corporations so merged or consolidated; and any claim existing or action or proceeding pending by or against any of such corporations may be prosecuted as if such merger or consolidation had not taken place, or such surviving or new corporation may be substituted in its place. Neither the rights of creditors nor any liens upon the property of any such corporation shall be impaired by such merger or consolidation.

(f) In the case of a merger, the articles of incorporation of the surviving corporation shall be deemed to be amended to the extent, if any, that changes in its articles of incorporation are stated in the plan of merger; and, in the case of a consolidation, the statements set forth in the articles of consolidation and which are required or permitted to be set forth in the articles of incorporation of corporations organized under this Act shall be deemed to be the original articles of incorporation of the new corporation.

When a merger, consolidation or exchange has become effective, the shares of the corporation or corporations party to the plan that are, under the terms of the plan, to be converted or exchanged, shall cease to exist, in the case of a merger or consolidation, or be deemed to be exchanged in the case of an exchange, and the holders of such shares shall thereafter be entitled only to the shares, obligations, other securities, cash or other property into which they shall have been converted or for which they shall have been exchanged, in accordance with the plan, subject to any rights under Section 80 of this Act.

§ 77. Merger, Consolidation or Exchange of Shares Between Domestic and Foreign Corporations.

One or more foreign corporations and one or more domestic corporations may be merged or consolidated, or participate in an exchange, in the following manner, if such merger, consolidation or exchange is permitted by the laws of the state under which each such foreign corporation is organized:

(a) Each domestic corporation shall comply with the provisions of this Act with respect to the merger, consolidation or exchange, as the case may be, of domestic corporations and each foreign corporation shall comply with the applicable provisions of the laws of the state under which it is organized.

(b) If the surviving or new corporation in a merger or consolidation is to be governed by the laws of any state other than this State, it shall comply with the provisions of this Act with respect to foreign corporations if it is to transact business in this State, and in every case it shall file with the Secretary of State of this State:

(1) An agreement that it may be served with process in this State in any proceeding for the enforcement of any obligation of any domestic corporation which is a party to such merger or consolidation and in any proceeding for the enforcement of the rights of a dissenting shareholder of any such domestic corporation against the surviving or new corporation;

(2) An irrevocable appointment of the Secretary of State of this State as its agent to accept service of process in any such proceeding; and

(3) An agreement that it will promptly pay to the dissenting shareholders of any such domestic corporation, the amount, if any, to which they shall be entitled under provisions of this Act with respect to the rights of dissenting shareholders.

§ 78. Sale of Assets in Regular Course of Business and Mortgage or Pledge of Assets.

The sale, lease, exchange, or other disposition of all, or substantially all, the property and assets of a corporation in the usual and regular course of its business and the mortgage or pledge of any or all property and assets of a corporation whether or not in the usual and regular course of business may be made upon such terms and conditions and for such consideration, which may consist in whole or in part of cash or other property, including shares, obligations or other securities of any other corporation, domestic or foreign, as shall be authorized by its board of directors; and in any such case no authorization or consent of the shareholders shall be required.

§ 79. Sale of Assets Other Than in Regular Course of Business.

A sale, lease, exchange, or other disposition of all, or substantially all, the property and assets, with or without the good will, of a corporation, if not in the usual and regular course of its business, may be made upon such terms and conditions and for such consideration, which may consist in whole or in part of cash or other property, including shares, obligations or other securities of any other corporation, domestic or foreign, as may be authorized in the following manner:

(a) The board of directors shall adopt a resolution recommending such sale, lease, exchange, or other disposition and directing the submission thereof to a vote at a meeting of shareholders, which may be either an annual or a special meeting.

(b) Written notice shall be given to each shareholder of record, whether or not entitled to vote at such meeting, not less than twenty days before such meeting, in the manner provided in this Act for the giving of notice of meetings of shareholders, and, whether the meeting be an annual or a special meeting, shall state that the purpose, or one of the purposes is to consider the proposed sale, lease, exchange, or other disposition.

(c)   At such meeting the shareholders may authorize such sale, lease, exchange, or other disposition and may fix, or may authorize the board of directors to fix, any or all of the terms and conditions thereof and the consideration to be received by the corporation therefor. Such authorization shall require the affirmative vote of the holders of a majority of the shares of the corporation entitled to vote thereon, unless any class of shares is entitled to vote thereon as a class, in which event such authorization shall require the affirmative vote of the holders of a majority of the shares of each class of shares entitled to vote as a class thereon and of the total shares entitled to vote thereon.

(d)   After such authorization by a vote of shareholders, the board of directors nevertheless, in its discretion, may abandon such sale, lease, exchange, or other disposition of assets, subject to the rights of third parties under any contracts relating thereto, without further action or approval by shareholders.

§ 80. Right of Shareholders to Dissent and Obtain Payment For Shares.

(a) Any shareholder of a corporation shall have the right to dissent from, and to obtain payment for his shares in the event of, any of the following corporate actions:

(1) Any plan of merger or consolidation to which the corporation is a party, except as provided in subsection (c):

(2) Any sale or exchange of all or substantially all of the property and assets of the corporation not made in the usual or regular course of its business, including a sale in dissolution, but not including a sale pursuant to an order of a court having jurisdiction in the premises or a sale for cash on terms requiring that all or substantially all of the net proceeds of sale be distributed to the shareholders

in accordance with their respective interests within one year after the date of sale;

(3) Any plan of exchange to which the corporation is a party as the corporation the shares of which are to be acquired;

(4) Any amendment of the articles of incorporation which materially and adversely affects the rights appurtenant to the shares of the dissenting shareholders in that it:

(i)   alters or abolishes a preferential right of such shares;

(ii)   creates, alters or abolishes a right in respect of the redemption of such shares, including a provision respecting a sinking fund for the redemption or repurchase of such shares;

(iii)   alters or abolishes a preemptive right of the holder of such shares to acquire shares or other securities;

(iv)   excludes or limits the right of the holder of such shares to vote on any matter, or to cumulate his votes, except as such right may be limited by dilution through the issuance of shares or other securities with similar voting rights; or

(5) Any other corporate action taken pursuant to a shareholder vote with respect to which the articles of incorporation, the by-laws, or a resolution of the board of directors directs that dissenting shareholders shall have a right to obtain payment for their shares.

(b)(1) A record holder of shares may assert dissenters' rights as to less than all of the shares registered in his name only if he dissents with respect to all the shares beneficially owned by any one person, and discloses the name and address of the person or persons on whose behalf he dissents. In that event, his rights shall be determined as if the shares as to which he has dissented and his other shares were registered in the names of different shareholders.

(2) A beneficial owner of shares who is not the record holder may assert dissenters' rights with respect to shares held on his behalf, and shall be treated as a dissenting shareholder under the terms of this section and Section 31 if he submits to the corporation at the time of or before the assertion of these rights a written consent of the record holder.

(c) The right to obtain payment under this section shall not apply to the shareholders of the surviving corporation in a merger if a vote of the shareholders of such corporation is not necessary to authorize such merger.

(d) A shareholder of a corporation who has a right under this section to obtain payment for his shares shall have no right at law or in equity to attack the validity of the corporate action that gives rise to his right to obtain payment, nor to have the action set aside or rescinded, except when the corporate action is unlawful or fraudulent with regard to the complaining shareholder or to the corporation.

§ 81. Procedures for Protection of Dissenters' Rights.

(a) As used in this section:

(1) "Dissenter" means a shareholder or beneficial owner who is entitled to and does assert dissenters' rights under Section 80, and who has performed every act required up to the time involved for the assertion of such rights.

(2) "Corporation" means the issuer of the shares held by the dissenter before the corporate action, or the successor by merger or consolidation of that issuer.

(3) "Fair value" of shares means their value immediately before the effectuation of the corporate action to which the dissenter objects, excluding any appreciation or depreciation in anticipation of such corporate action unless such exclusion would be inequitable.

(4) "Interest" means interest from the effective date of the corporate action until the date of payment, at the average rate currently paid by the corporation on its principal bank loans, or, if none, at such rate as is fair and equitable under all the circumstances.

(b) If a proposed corporate action which would give rise to dissenters' rights under Section 80(a) is submitted to a vote at a meeting of shareholders, the notice of meeting shall notify all shareholders that they have or may have a right to dissent and obtain payment for their shares by complying with the terms of this section, and shall be accompanied by a copy of Sections 80 and 81 of this Act.

(c) If the proposed corporate action is submitted to a vote at a meeting of shareholders, any shareholder who wishes to dissent and obtain payment for his shares must file with the corporation, prior to the vote, a written notice of intention to demand that he be paid fair compensation for his shares if the proposed action is effectuated, and shall refrain from voting his shares in approval of such action. A shareholder who fails in either respect shall acquire no right to payment for his shares under this section or Section 80.

(d) If the proposed corporate action is approved by the required vote at a meeting of shareholders, the corporation shall mail a further notice to all shareholders who gave due notice of intention to demand payment and who refrained from voting in favor of the proposed action. If the proposed corporate action is to be taken without a vote of shareholders, the corporation shall send to all shareholders who are entitled to dissent and demand payment for their shares a notice of the adoption of the plan of corporate action. The notice shall (1) state where and when a demand for payment must be sent and certificates of certificated shares must be deposited in order to obtain payment, (2) inform holders of uncertificated shares to what extent transfer of shares will be restricted from the time that demand for payment is received, (3) supply a form for demanding payment which includes a request for certification of the date on which the shareholder, or the person on whose behalf the shareholder dissents, acquired beneficial ownership of the shares, and (4) be accompanied by a copy of Section 80 and 81 of this Act. The time set for the demand and deposit shall be not less than 30 days from the mailing of the notice.

(e) A shareholder who fails to demand payment, or fails (in the case of certificated shares) to deposit certificates, as required by a notice pursuant to subsection (d) shall have no right under this section or Section 80 to receive payment for his shares. If the shares are not represented by certificates, the corporation may restrict their transfer from the time of receipt of demand for payment until effectuation of the proposed corporate action, or the release of restrictions under the terms of subsection (f). The dissenter shall retain all other rights of a shareholder until these rights are modified by effectuation of the proposed corporate action.

(f)(1) Within 60 days after the date set for demanding payment and depositing certificates, if the corporation has not effectuated the proposed corporate action and remitted payment for shares pursuant to paragraph (3), it shall return any certificates that have been deposited, and release uncertificated shares from any transfer restrictions imposed by reason of the demand for payment.

(2) When uncertificated shares have been released from transfer restrictions, and deposited certificates have been returned, the corporation may at any later time send a new notice conforming to the requirements of subsection (d), with like effect.

(3) Immediately upon effectuation of the proposed corporate action, or upon receipt of demand for payment if the corporate action has already been effectuated, the corporation shall remit to dissenters who have made demand and (if their shares are certificated) have deposited their certificates the amount which the corporation estimates to be the fair value of the shares, with interest if any has accrued. The remittance shall be accompanied by:

    (i)   the corporation's closing balance sheet and statement of income for a fiscal year ending not more than 16 months before the date of remittance, together with the latest available interim financial statements;

    (ii) a statement of the corporation's estimate of fair value of the shares; and

    (iii) a notice of the dissenter's right to demand supplemental payment, accompanied by a copy of Sections 80 and 81 of this Act.

(g)(1) If the corporation fails to remit as required by subsection (f), or if the dissenter believes that the amount remitted is less than the fair value of his shares, or that the interest is not correctly determined, he may send the corporation his own estimate of the value of the shares or of the interest, and demand payment of the deficiency.

(2) If the dissenter does not file such an estimate within 30 days after the corporation's mailing of its remittance, he shall be entitled to no more than the amount remitted.

(h)(1) Within 60 days after receiving a demand for payment pursuant to subsection (g), if any such demands for payment remain unsettled, the corporation shall file in an appropriate court a petition requesting that the fair value of the shares and interest thereon be determined by the court.

(2) An appropriate court shall be a court of competent jurisdiction in the county of this state where the registered office of the corporation is located. If, in the case of a merger or consolidation or exchange of shares, the corporation is a foreign corporation without a registered office in this state, the petition shall be filed in the county where the registered office of the domestic corporation was last located.

(3) All dissenters, wherever residing, whose demands have not been settled shall be made parties to the proceeding as in an action against their shares. A copy of the petition shall be served on each such dissenter; if a dissenter is a nonresident, the copy may be served on him by registered or certified mail or by publication as provided by law.

(4) The jurisdiction of the court shall be plenary and exclusive. The court may appoint one or more persons as appraisers to receive evidence and recommend a decision on the question of fair value. The appraisers shall have such power and authority as shall be specified in the order of their appointment or in any amendment thereof. The dissenters shall be entitled to discovery in the same manner as parties in other civil suits.

(5) All dissenters who are made parties shall be entitled to judgment for the amount by which the fair value of their shares is found to exceed the amount previously remitted, with interest.

(6) If the corporation fails to file a petition as provided in paragraph (1) of this subsection, each dissenter who made a demand and who has not already settled his claim against the corporation shall be paid by the corporation the amount demanded by him, with interest, and may sue therefore in an appropriate court.

(i)(1) The costs and expenses of any proceeding under subsection (h), including the reasonable compensation and expenses of appraisers appointed by the court, shall be determined by the court and assessed against the corporation, except that any part of the costs and expenses may be apportioned and assessed as the court may deem equitable against all or some of the dissenters who are parties and whose action in demanding supplemental payment the court finds to be arbitrary, vexatious, or not in good faith.

(2) Fees and expenses of counsel and of experts for the respective parties may be assessed as the court may deem equitable against the corporation and in favor of any or all dissenters if the corporation failed to comply substantially with the requirements of this section, and may be assessed against either the corporation or a dissenter, in favor of any other party, if the court finds that the party against whom the fees and expenses are assessed acted arbitrarily, vexatiously, or not in good faith in respect to the rights provided by this section and Section 80.

(3) If the court finds that the services of counsel for any dissenter were of substantial benefit to other dissenters similarly situated, and should not be assessed against the corporation, it may award to these counsel reasonable fees to be paid out of the amounts awarded to the dissenters who were benefited.

(j)(1) Notwithstanding the foregoing provisions of this section, the corporation may elect to withhold the remittance required by subsection (f) from any dissenter with respect to shares of which the dissenter (or the person on whose behalf the dissenter acts) was not the beneficial owner on the date of the first announcement to news media or to shareholders of the terms of the proposed corporate action. With respect to such shares, the corporation shall, upon effectuating the corporate action, state to each dissenter its estimate of the fair value of the shares, state the rate of interest to be used (explaining the basis thereof), and offer to pay the resulting amounts on receiving the dissenter's agreement to accept them in full satisfaction.

(2) If the dissenter believes that the amount offered is less than the fair value of the shares and interest determined according to this section, he may within 30 days after the date of mailing of the corporation's offer, mail the corporation his own estimate of fair value and interest, and demand their payment. If the dissenter fails to do so, he shall be entitled to no more than the corporation's offer.

(3) If the dissenter makes a demand as provided in paragraph (2), the provisions of subsections (h) and (i) shall apply to further proceedings on the dissenter's demand.

§ 82. Voluntary Dissolution by Incorporators.

A corporation which has not commenced business and which has not issued any shares, may be voluntarily dissolved by its incorporators at any time in the following manner:

(a) Articles of dissolution shall be executed in duplicate by a majority of the incorporators, and verified by them, and shall set forth:

(1) The name of the corporation.

(2) The date of issuance of its certificate of incorporation.

(3) That none of its shares has been issued.

(4) That the corporation has not commenced business.

(5) That the amount, if any, actually paid in on subscriptions for its shares, less any part thereof disbursed for necessary expenses, has been returned to those entitled thereto.

(6) That no debts of the corporation remain unpaid.

(7) That a majority of the incorporators elect that the corporation be dissolved.

(b) Duplicate originals of the articles of dissolution shall be delivered to the Secretary of State. If the Secretary of State finds that the articles of dissolution conform to law, he shall, when all fees and franchise taxes have been paid as in this Act prescribed:

(1) Endorse on each of such duplicate originals the word "Filed," and the month, day and year of the filing thereof.

(2) File one of such duplicate originals in his office.

(3) Issue a certificate of dissolution to which he shall affix the other duplicate original.

The certificate of dissolution, together with the duplicate original of the articles of dissolution affixed thereto by the Secretary of State, shall be returned to the incorporators or their representative. Upon the issuance of such certificate of dissolution by the Secretary of State, the existence of the corporation shall cease.

§ 83. Voluntary Dissolution By Consent of Shareholders.

A corporation may be voluntarily dissolved by the written consent of all of its shareholders.

Upon the execution of such written consent, a statement of intent to dissolve shall be executed in duplicate by the corporation by its president or a vice president and by its secretary or an assistant secretary, and verified by one of the officers signing such statement, which statement shall set forth:

(a) The name of the corporation.

(b) The names and respective addresses of its officers.

(c) The names and respective addresses of its directors.

(d) A copy of the written consent signed by all shareholders of the corporation.

(e) A statement that such written consent has been signed by all shareholders of the corporation or signed in their names by their attorneys thereunto duly authorized.

§84. Voluntary Dissolution By Act of Corporation.

A corporation may be dissolved by the act of the corporation, when authorized in the following manner:

(a) The board of directors shall adopt a resolution recommending that the corporation be dissolved, and directing that the question of such dissolution be submitted to a vote at a meeting of shareholders, which may be either an annual or a special meeting.

(b) Written notice shall be given to each shareholder of record entitled to vote at such meeting within the time and in the manner provided in this Act for the giving of notice of meetings of shareholders, and, whether the meeting be an annual or special meeting shall state that the purpose, or one of the purposes, of such meeting is to consider the advisability of dissolving the corporation.

(c) At such meeting a vote of shareholders entitled to vote thereat shall be taken on a resolution to dissolve the corporation. Such resolution shall be adopted upon receiving the affirmative vote of the holders of a majority of the shares of the corporation entitled to vote thereon, unless any class of shares is entitled to vote thereon as a class, in which event the resolution shall be adopted upon receiving the affirmative vote of the holders of a majority of the shares of each class of shares entitled to vote thereon as a class and of the total shares entitled to vote thereon.

(d) Upon the adoption of such resolution, a statement of intent to dissolve shall be executed in duplicate by the corporation by its president or a vice president and by its secretary or an assistant secretary, and verified by one of the officers signing such statement, which statement shall set forth:

(1) The name of the corporation.

(2) The names and respective addresses of its officers.

(3) The names and respective addresses of its directors.

(4) A copy of the resolution adopted by the shareholders authorizing the dissolution of the corporation.

(5) The number of shares outstanding, and, if the shares of any class are entitled to vote as a class, the designation and number of outstanding shares of each such class.

(6) The number of shares voted for and against the resolution, respectively, and, if the shares of any class are entitled to vote as a class, the number of shares of each such class voted for and against the resolution, respectively.

§ 85. Filing of Statement of Intent to Dissolve.

Duplicate originals of the statement of intent to dissolve, whether by consent of shareholders or by act of the corporation, shall be delivered to the Secretary of State. If the Secretary of State finds that such statement conforms to law, he shall, when all fees and franchise taxes have been paid as in this Act prescribed:

(a) Endorse on each of such duplicate originals the word "Filed," and the month, day and year of the filing thereof.

(b) File one of such duplicate originals in his office.

(c) Return the other duplicate original to the corporation or its representative.

§ 86. Effect of Statement of Intent to Dissolve.

Upon the filing by the Secretary of State of a statement of intent to dissolve, whether by consent of shareholders or by act of the corporation, the corporation shall cease to carry on its business, except insofar as may be necessary for the winding up thereof, but its corporate existence shall continue until a certificate of dissolution has been issued by the Secretary of State or until a decree dissolving the corporation has been entered by a court of competent jurisdiction as in this Act provided.

§ 87. Procedure After Filing of Statement of Intent to Dissolve.

After the filing by the Secretary of State of a statement of intent to dissolve:

(a) The corporation shall immediately cause notice thereof to be mailed to each known creditor of the corporation.

(b) The corporation shall proceed to collect its assets, convey and dispose of such of its properties as are not to be distributed in kind to its shareholders, pay, satisfy and discharge its liabilities and obligations and do all other acts required to liquidate its business and affairs, and, after paying or adequately providing for the payment of all its obligations, distribute the remainder of its assets, either in cash or in kind, among its shareholders according to their respective rights and interests.

(c) The corporation, at any time during the liquidation of its business and affairs, may make application to a court of competent jurisdiction within the state and judicial subdivision in which the registered office or principal place of business of the corporation is situated, to have the liquidation continued under the supervision of the court as provided in this Act.

§ 88. Revocation of Voluntary Dissolution Proceedings By Consent of Shareholders. By the written consent of all of its shareholders, a corporation may, at any time prior to the issuance of a certificate of dissolution by the Secretary of State, revoke voluntary dissolution proceedings theretofore taken, in the following manner:

Upon the execution of such written consent, a statement of revocation of voluntary dissolution proceedings shall be executed in duplicate by the corporation by its president or a vice president and by its secretary or an assistant secretary, and verified by one of the officers signing such statement, which statement shall set forth:

(a) The name of the corporation.

(b) The names and respective addresses of its officers.

(c) The names and respective addresses of its directors.

(d) A copy of the written consent signed by all shareholders of the corporation revoking such voluntary dissolution proceedings.

(e) That such written consent has been signed by all shareholders of the corporation or signed in their names by their attorneys thereunto duly authorized.

§ 89. Revocation of Voluntary Dissolution Proceedings By Act of Corporation. By the act of the corporation, a corporation may, at any time prior to the issuance of a certificate of dissolution by the

Secretary of State, revoke voluntary dissolution proceedings theretofore taken, in the following manner:

(a) The board of directors shall adopt a resolution recommending that the voluntary dissolution proceedings be revoked, and directing that the question of such revocation be submitted to a vote at a special meeting of shareholders.

(b) Written notice, stating that the purpose or one of the purposes of such meeting is to consider the advisability of revoking the voluntary dissolution proceedings, shall be given to each shareholder of record entitled to vote at such meeting within the time and in the manner provided in this Act for the giving of notice of special meetings of shareholders.

(c) At such meeting a vote of the shareholders entitled to vote thereat shall be taken on a resolution to revoke the voluntary dissolution proceedings, which shall require for its adoption the affirmative vote of the holders of a majority of the shares entitled to vote thereon.

(d) Upon the adoption of such resolution, a statement of revocation of voluntary disolution proceedings shall be executed in duplicate by the corporation by its president or a vice president and by its secretary or an assistant secretary, and verified by one of the officers signing such statement, which statement shall set forth:

(1) The name of the corporation.

(2) The names and respective addresses of its officers.

(3) The names and respective addresses of its directors.

(4) A copy of the resolution adopted by the shareholders revoking the voluntary dissolution proceedings.

(5) The number of shares outstanding.

(6) The number of shares voted for and against the resolution, respectively.

§ 90. Filing of Statement of Revocation of Voluntary Dissolution Proceedings. Duplicate originals of the statement of revocation of voluntary dissolution proceedings, whether by consent of shareholders or by act of the corporation, shall be delivered to the Secretary of State. If the Secretary of State finds that such statement conforms to law, he shall, when all fees and franchise taxes have been paid as in this Act prescribed:

(a) Endorse on each of such duplicate originals the word "Filed," and the month, day and year of the filing thereof.

(b) File one of such duplicate originals in his office.

(c) Return the other duplicate original to the corporation or its representative.

§ 91. Effect of Statement of Revocation of Voluntary Dissolution Proceedings.   Upon the filing by the Secretary of State of a statement of revocation of voluntary dissolution proceedings, whether by consent of shareholders or by act of the corporation, the revocation of the voluntary dissolution proceedings shall become effective and the corporation may again carry on its business.

§ 92. Articles of Dissolution.   If voluntary dissolution proceedings have not been revoked, then when all debts, liabilities and obligations of the corporation have been paid and discharged, or adequate provision has been made therefor, and all of the remaining property and assets of the corporation have been distributed to its shareholders, articles of dissolution shall be executed in duplicate by the corporation by its president or a vice president and by its secretary or an assistant secretary, and verified by one of the officers signing such statement, which statement shall set forth:

(a) The name of the corporation.

(b) That the Secretary of State has theretofore filed a statement of intent to dissolve the corporation, and the date on which such statement was filed.

(c) That all debts, obligations and liabilities of the corporation have been paid and discharged or that adequate provision has been made therefor.

(d) That all the remaining property and assets of the corporation have been distributed among its shareholders in accordance with their respective rights and interests.

(e) That there are no suits pending against the corporation in any court, or that adequate provision has been made for the satisfaction of any judgment, order or decree which may be entered against it in any pending suit.

§ 93. Filing of Articles of Dissolution.   Duplicate originals of such articles of dissolution shall be delivered to the Secretary of State. If the Secretary of State finds that such articles of dissolution conform to law, he shall, when all fees and franchise taxes have been paid as in this Act prescribed:

(a) Endorse on each of such duplicate originals the word "Filed," and the month, day and year of the filing thereof.

(b) File one of such duplicate originals in his office.

(c) Issue a certificate of dissolution to which he shall affix the other duplicate original.

The certificate of dissolution, together with the duplicate original of the articles of dissolution affixed thereto by the Secretary of State, shall be returned to the representative of the dissolved corporation. Upon the issuance of such certificate of dissolution the existence of the corporation shall cease, except for the purpose of suits, other proceedings and appropriate corporate action by shareholders, directors and officers as provided in this Act.

§ 94. Involuntary Dissolution.   A corporation may be dissolved involuntarily by a decree of the _____ court in an action filed by the Attorney General when it is established that:

(a) The corporation has failed to file its annual report within the time required by this Act, or has failed to pay its franchise tax on or before the first day of August of the year in which such franchise tax becomes due and payable; or

(b) The corporation procured its articles of incorporation through fraud; or

(c) The corporation has continued to exceed or abuse the authority conferred upon it by law; or

(d) The corporation has failed for thirty days to appoint and maintain a registered agent in this State; or

(e) The corporation has failed for thirty days after change of its registered office or registered agent to file in the office of the Secretary of State a statement of such change.

§ 95. Notification to Attorney General.   The Secretary of State, on or before the last day of December of each year, shall certify to the Attorney General the names of all corporations which have failed to file their annual reports or to pay franchise taxes in accordance with the provisions of this Act, together with the facts pertinent thereto. He shall also certify, from time to time, the names of all corporations which have given other cause for dissolution as provided in this Act, together with the facts pertinent thereto. Whenever the Secretary of State shall certify the name of a corporation to the Attorney General as having given any cause for dissolution, the Secretary of State shall concurrently mail to the corporation at its registered office a notice that such certification has been made. Upon the receipt of such certification, the Attorney General shall file an action in the name of the State against such corporation for its dissolution. Every such certificate from the Secretary of State to the Attorney General pertaining to the failure of a corporation to file an annual report or pay a franchise tax shall be taken and received in all courts as prima facie evidence of the facts therein stated. If, before action is filed, the corporation shall file its annual report or pay its franchise tax, together with all penalties thereon, or shall appoint or maintain a registered agent as provided in this Act, or shall file with the Secretary of State the required statement of change of registered office or registered agent, such fact shall be forthwith certified by the Secretary of State to the Attorney General and he shall not file an action against such corporation for such cause. If, after action is filed, the corporation shall file its annual report or pay its franchise tax, together with all penalties thereon, or shall appoint or maintain a registered agent as provided in this Act, or shall file with the Secretary of State the required statement of change of registered office or registered agent, and shall pay the costs of such action, the action for such cause shall abate.

§ 96. Venue and Process. Every action for the involuntary dissolution of a corporation shall be commenced by the Attorney General either in the _____ court of the county in which the registered office of the corporation is situated, or in the _____ court of _____ county. Summons shall issue and be served as in other civil actions. If process is returned not found, the Attorney General shall cause publication to be made as in other civil cases in some newspaper published in the county where the registered office of the corporation is situated, containing a notice of the pendency of such action, the title of the court, the title of the action, and the date on or after which default may

be entered. The Attorney General may include in one notice the names of any number of corporations against which actions are then pending in the same court. The Attorney General shall cause a copy of such notice to be mailed to the corporation at its registered office within ten days after the first publication thereof. The certificate of the Attorney General of the mailing of such notice shall be prima facie evidence thereof. Such notice shall be published at least once each week for two successive weeks, and the first publication thereof may begin at any time after the summons has been returned. Unless a corporation shall have been served with summons, no default shall be taken against it earlier than thirty days after the first publication of such notice.

§ 97. Jurisdiction of Court to Liquidate Assets and Business of Corporation. The _____ courts shall have full power to liquidate the assets and business of a corporation:

(a) In an action by a shareholder when it is established:

(1) That the directors are deadlocked in the management of the corporate affairs and the shareholders are unable to break the deadlock, and that irreparable injury to the corporation is being suffered or is threatened by reason thereof; or

(2) That the acts of the directors or those in control of the corporation are illegal, oppressive or fraudulent; or

(3) That the shareholders are deadlocked in voting power, and have failed, for a period which includes at least two consecutive annual meeting dates, to elect successors to directors whose terms have expired or would have expired upon the election of their successors; or

(4) That the corporate assets are being misapplied or wasted.

(b) In an action by a creditor:

(1) When the claim of the creditor has been reduced to judgment and an execution thereon returned unsatisfied and it is established that the corporation is insolvent; or

(2) When the corporation has admitted in writing that the claim of the creditor is due and owing and it is established that the corporation is insolvent.

(c) Upon application by a corporation which has filed a statement of intent to dissolve, as provided in this Act, to have its liquidation continued under the supervision of the court.

(d) When an action has been filed by the Attorney General to dissolve a corporation and it is established that liquidation of its business and affairs should precede the entry of a decree of dissolution.

Proceedings under clause (a), (b) or (c) of this section shall be brought in the county in which the registered office or the principal office of the corporation is situated.

It shall not be necessary to make shareholders parties to any such action or proceeding unless relief is sought against them personally.

§ 98. Procedure in Liquidation of Corporation by Court.   In proceedings to liquidate the assets and business of a corporation the court shall have power to issue injunctions, to appoint a receiver or receivers pendente lite, with such powers and duties as the court, from time to time, may direct, and to take such other proceedings as may be requisite to preserve the corporate assets wherever situated, and carry on the business of the corporation until a full hearing can be had.

After a hearing had upon such notice as the court may direct to be given to all parties to the proceedings and to any other parties in interest designated by the court, the court may appoint a liquidating receiver or receivers with authority to collect the assets of the corporation, including all amounts owing to the corporation by subscribers on account of any unpaid portion of the consideration for the issuance of shares. Such liquidating receiver or receivers shall sell, convey and dispose of all or any part of the assets of the corporation wherever situated, either at public or private sale. The assets of the corporation or the proceeds resulting from a sale, conveyance or other disposition thereof shall be applied to the expenses of such liquidation and to the payment of the liabilities and obligations of the corporation, and any remaining assets or proceeds shall be distributed among its shareholders according to their respective rights and interests. The order appointing such liquidating receiver or receivers shall state their powers and duties. Such powers and duties may be increased or diminished at any time during the proceedings.

The court shall have power to allow from time to time as expenses of the liquidation compensation to the receiver or receivers and to attorneys in the proceeding, and to direct the payment thereof out of the assets of the corporation or the proceeds of any sale or disposition of such assets.

A receiver of a corporation appointed under the provisions of this section shall have authority to sue and defend in all courts in his own name as receiver of such corporation. The court appointing such receiver shall have exclusive jurisdiction of the corporation and its property, wherever situated.

§ 99. Qualifications of Receivers.   A receiver shall in all cases be a natural person or a corporation authorized to act as receiver, which corporation may be a domestic corporation or a foreign corporation authorized to transact business in this State, and shall in all cases give such bond as the court may direct with such sureties as the court may require.

§ 100. Filing of Claims in Liquidation Proceedings. In proceedings to liquidate the assets and business of a corporation the court may require all creditors of the corporation to file with the clerk of the court or with the receiver, in such form as the court may prescribe, proofs under oath of their respective claims. If the court requires the filing of claims it shall fix a date, which shall be not less than four months from the date of the order, as the last day for the filing of claims, and shall prescribe the notice that shall be given to creditors and claimants of the date so fixed. Prior to the date so fixed, the court may extend the time for the filing of claims. Creditors and claimants failing to file proofs of claim on or before the date so fixed may be barred, by order of court, from participating in the distribution of the assets of the corporation.

§ 101. Discontinuance of Liquidation Proceedings. The liquidation of the assets and business of a corporation may be discontinued at any time during the liquidation proceedings when it is established that cause for liquidation no longer exists. In such event the court shall dismiss the proceedings and direct the receiver to redeliver to the corporation all its remaining property and assets.

§ 102. Decree of Involuntary Dissolution.   In proceedings to liquidate the assets and business of a corporation, when the costs and expenses of such proceedings and all debts, obligations and liabilities of the corporation shall have been paid and discharged and all of its remaining property and assets distributed to its shareholders, or in case its property and assets are not sufficient to satisfy and discharge such costs, expenses, debts and obligations, all the property and assets have been applied so far as they will go to their payment, the court shall enter a decree dissolving the corporation, whereupon the existence of the corporation shall cease.

§ 103. Filing of Decree of Dissolution. In case the court shall enter a decree dissolving a corporation, it shall be the duty of the clerk of such court to cause a certified copy of the decree to be filed with the Secretary of State. No fee shall be charged by the Secretary of State for the filing thereof.

§ 104. Deposit With State Treasurer of Amount Due Certain Shareholders. Upon the voluntary or involuntary dissolution of a corporation, the portion of the assets distributable to a creditor or shareholder who is unknown or cannot be found, or who is under disability and there is no person legally competent to receive such distributive portion, shall be reduced to cash and deposited with the State Treasurer and shall be paid over to such creditor or shareholder or to his legal representative upon proof satisfactory to the State Treasurer of his right thereto.

§ 105. Survival of Remedy After Dissolution. The dissolution of a corporation either (1) by the issuance of a certificate of dissolution by the Secretary of State, or (2) by a decree of court when the court has not liquidated the assets and business of the corporation as provided in this Act, or (3) by expiration of its period of duration, shall not take away or impair any remedy available to or against such corporation, its directors, officers, or shareholders, for any right or claim existing, or any liability incurred, prior to such dissolution if action or other proceeding thereon is commenced within two years after the date of such dissolution. Any such action or proceeding by or against the corporation may be prosecuted or defended by the corporation in its corporate name. The shareholders, directors and officers shall have power to take such corporate or other action as shall be appropriate to protect such remedy, right or claim. If such corporation was dissolved by the expiration of its period of duration, such corporation may amend its articles of incorporation at any time during such period of two years so as to extend its period of duration.

§ 106. Admission of Foreign Corporation. No foreign corporation shall have the right to transact business in this State until it shall have procured a certificate of authority so to do from the Secretary of State. No foreign corporation shall be entitled to procure a certificate of authority under this Act to transact in this State any business which a corporation organized under this Act is not permitted to transact. A foreign corporation shall not be denied a certificate of authority by reason of the fact that the laws of the state or country under which such corporation is organized governing its organization and internal affairs differ from the laws of this State, and nothing in this Act contained shall be construed to authorize this State to regulate the organization or the internal affairs of such corporation.

Without excluding other activities which may not constitute transacting business in this State, a foreign corporation shall not be considered to be transacting business in the State, for the purposes of this Act, by reason of carrying on in this State any one or more of the following activities:

(a)   Maintaining or defending any action or suit or any administrative or arbitration proceeding, or effecting the settlement thereof or the settlement of claims or disputes.

(b)   Holding meetings of its directors or shareholders or carrying on other activities concerning its internal affairs.

(c)   Maintaining bank accounts.

(d)   Maintaining offices or agencies for the transfer, exchange and registration of its securities, or appointing and maintaining trustees or depositaries with relation to its securities.

(e)   Effecting sales through independent contractors.

(f)   Soliciting or procuring orders, whether by mail or through employees or agents or otherwise, where such orders require acceptance without this State before becoming binding contracts.

(g)   Creating as borrower or lender, or acquiring, indebtedness or mortgages or other security interests in real or personal property.

(h)   Securing or collecting debts or enforcing any rights in property securing the same.

(i)   Transacting any business in interstate commerce.

(j)   Conducting an isolated transaction completed within a period of thirty days and not in the course of a number of repeated transactions of like nature.

§ 107. Powers of Foreign Corporation. A foreign corporation which shall have received a certificate of authority under this Act shall, until a certificate of revocation or of withdrawal shall have been issued as provided in this Act, enjoy the same, but no greater, rights and privileges as a domestic corporation organized for the purposes set forth in the application pursuant to which such certificate of authority is issued; and, except as in this Act otherwise provided, shall be subject to the same duties, restrictions, penalties and liabilities now or hereafter imposed upon a domestic corporation of like character.

§ 108. Corporate Name of Foreign Corporation. No certificate of authority shall be issued to a foreign corporation unless the corporate name of such corporation:

(a) Shall contain the word "corporation," "company," "incorporated," or "limited," or shall contain an abbreviation of one of such words, or such corporation shall, for use in this State, add at the end of its name one of such words or an abbreviation thereof.

(b) Shall not contain any word or phrase which indicates or implies that it is organized for any purpose other than one or more of the purposes contained in its articles of incorporation or that it is authorized or empowered to conduct the business of banking or insurance.

(c) Shall not be the same as, or deceptively similar to, the name of any domestic corporation existing under the laws of this State or any other foreign corporation authorized to transact business in this State, or a name the exclusive right to which is, at the time, reserved in the manner provided in this Act, or the name of a corporation which has in effect a registration of its name as provided in this Act except that this provision shall not apply if the foreign corporation applying for a certificate of authority files with the Secretary of State any one of the following:

(1) a resolution of its board of directors adopting a fictitious name for use in transacting business in this State which fictitious name is not deceptively similar to the name of any domestic corporation or of any foreign corporation authorized to transact business in this State or to any name reserved or registered as provided in this Act, or

(2) the written consent of such other corporation or holder of a reserved or registered name to use the same or deceptively similar name and one or more words are added to make such name distinguishable from such other name, or

(3) a certified copy of a final decree of a court of competent jurisdiction establishing the prior right of such foreign corporation to the use of such name in this State.

§ 109. Change of Name by Foreign Corporation. Whenever a foreign corporation which is authorized to transact business in this State shall change its name to one under which a certificate of authority would not be granted to it on application therefor, the certificate of authority of such corporation shall be suspended and it shall not thereafter transact any business in this State until it has changed its name to a name which is available to it under the laws of this State or has otherwise complied with the provisions of this Act.

§ 110. Application for Certificate of Authority. A foreign corporation, in order to procure a certificate of authority to transact business in this State, shall make application therefor to the Secretary of State, which application shall set forth:

(a) The name of the corporation and the state or country under the laws of which it is incorporated.

(b) If the name of the corporation does not contain the word "corporation," "company," "incorporated," or "limited," or does not contain an abbreviation of one of such words, then the name of the corporation with the word or abbreviation which it elects to add thereto for use in this state.

(c) The date of incorporation and the period of duration of the corporation.

(d) The address of the principal office of the corporation in the state or country under the laws of which it is incorporated.

(e) The address of the proposed registered office of the corporation in this State, and the name of its proposed registered agent in this State at such address.

(f)   The purpose or purposes of the corporation which it proposes to pursue in the transaction of business in this State.

(g)   The names and respective addresses of the directors and officers of the corporation.

(h)   A statement of the aggregate number of shares which the corporation has authority to issue, itemized by classes and series, if any, within a class.

(i)   A statement of the aggregate number of issued shares itemized by class and by series, if any, within each class.

(j)   An estimate, expressed in dollars, of the value of all property to be owned by the corporation for the following year, wherever located, and an estimate of the value of the property of the corporation to be located within this State during such year, and an estimate, expressed in dollars, of the gross amount of business which will be transacted by the corporation during such year, and an estimate of the gross amount thereof which will be transacted by the corporation at or from places of business in this State during such year.

(k)   Such additional information as may be necessary or appropriate in order to enable the Secretary of State to determine whether such corporation is entitled to a certificate of authority to transact business in this State and to determine and assess the fees and franchise taxes payable as in this Act prescribed.

Such application shall be made on forms prescribed and furnished by the Secretary of State and shall be executed in duplicate by the corporation by its president or a vice president and by its secretary or an assistant secretary, and verified by one of the officers signing such application.

§ 111. Filing of Application for Certificate of Authority.   Duplicate originals of the application of the corporation for a certificate of authority shall be delivered to the Secretary of State, together with a copy of its articles of incorporation and all amendments thereto, duly authenticated by the proper officer of the state or country under the laws of which it is incorporated.

If the Secretary of State finds that such application conforms to law, he shall, when all fees and franchise taxes have been paid as in this Act prescribed:

(a)   Endorse on each of such documents the word "Filed," and the month, day and year of the filing thereof.

(b)   File in his office one of such duplicate originals of the application and the copy of the articles of incorporation and amendments thereto.

(c)   Issue a certificate of authority to transact business in this State to which he shall affix the other duplicate original application.

The certificate of authority, together with the duplicate original of the application affixed thereto by the Secretary of State, shall be returned to the corporation or its representative.

§ 112. Effect of Certificate of Authority.   Upon the issuance of a certificate of authority by the Secretary of State, the corporation shall be authorized to transact business in this State for those purposes set forth in its application, subject, however, to the right of this State to suspend or to revoke such authority as provided in this Act.

§ 113. Registered Office and Registered Agent of Foreign Corporation.   Each foreign corporation authorized to transact business in this State shall have and continuously maintain in this State:

(a)   A registered office which may be, but need not be, the same as its place of business in this State.

(b)   A registered agent, which agent may be either an individual resident in this State whose business office is identical with such registered office, or a domestic corporation, or a foreign corporation authorized to transact business in this State, having a business office identical with such registered office.

§ 114. Change of Registered Office or Registered Agent of Foreign Corporation.   A foreign corporation authorized to transact business in this State may change its registered office or change its registered agent, or both, upon filing in the office of the Secretary of State a statement setting forth:

(a)   The name of the corporation.

(b)   The address of its then registered office.

(c) If the address of its registered office be changed, the address to which the registered office is to be changed.

(d) The name of its then registered agent.

(e) If its registered agent be changed, the name of its successor registered agent.

(f) That the address of its registered office and the address of the business office of its registered agent, as changed, will be identical.

(g) That such change was authorized by resolution duly adopted by its board of directors.

Such statement shall be executed by the corporation by its president or a vice president, and verified by him, and delivered to the Secretary of State. If the Secretary of State finds that such statement conforms to the provisions of this Act, he shall file such statement in his office, and upon such filing the change of address of the registered office, or the appointment of a new registered agent, or both, as the case may be, shall become effective.

Any registered agent of a foreign corporation may resign as such agent upon filing a written notice thereof, executed in duplicate, with the Secretary of State, who shall forthwith mail a copy thereof to the corporation at its principal office in the state or country under the laws of which it is incorporated. The appointment of such agent shall terminate upon the expiration of thirty days after receipt of such notice by the Secretary of State.

If a registered agent changes his or its business address to another place within the same _____ [supply designation of jurisdiction, such as county, etc., in accordance with local practice], he or it may change such address and the address of the registered office of any corporation of which he or it is registered agent by filing a statement as required above except that it need be signed only by the registered agent and need not be responsive to (e) or (g) and must recite that a copy of the statement has been mailed to the corporation.

§ 115. Service of Process on Foreign Corporation.
The registered agent so appointed by a foreign corporation authorized to transact business in this State shall be an agent of such corporation upon whom any process, notice or demand required or permitted by law to be served upon the corporation may be served.

Whenever a foreign corporation authorized to transact business in this State shall fail to appoint or maintain a registered agent in this State, or whenever any such registered agent cannot with reasonable diligence be found at the registered office, or whenever the certificate of authority of a foreign corporation shall be suspended or revoked, then the Secretary of State shall be an agent of such corporation upon whom any such process, notice, or demand may be served. Service on the Secretary of State of any such process, notice or demand shall be made by delivering to and leaving with him, or with any clerk having charge of the corporation department of his office, duplicate copies of such process, notice or demand. In the event any such process, notice or demand is served on the Secretary of State, he shall immediately cause one of such copies thereof to be forwarded by registered mail, addressed to the corporation at its principal office in the state or country under the laws of which it is incorporated. Any service so had on the Secretary of State shall be returnable in not less than thirty days.

The Secretary of State shall keep a record of all processes, notices and demands served upon him under this section, and shall record therein the time of such service and his action with reference thereto.

Nothing herein contained shall limit or affect the right to serve any process, notice or demand, required or permitted by law to be served upon a foreign corporation in any other manner now or hereafter permitted by law.

§ 116. Amendment to Articles of Incorporation of Foreign Corporation.
Whenever the articles of incorporation of a foreign corporation authorized to transact business in this State are amended, such foreign corporation shall, within thirty days after such amendment become effective, file in the office of the Secretary of State a copy of such amendment duly authenticated by the proper officer of the state or country under the laws of which it is incorporated; but the filing thereof shall not of itself enlarge or alter the purpose or purposes which such corporation is authorized to pursue in the transaction of business in this State, nor authorize such corporation to transact business in this State under any other name than the name set forth in its certificate of authority.

§ 117. Merger of Foreign Corporation Authorized to Transact Business in This State.
Whenever a foreign corporation authorized to transact business in this State shall be a party to a statutory merger

permitted by the laws of the state or country under the laws of which it is incorporated, and such corporation shall be the surviving corporation, it shall, within thirty days after such merger becomes effective, file with the Secretary of State a copy of the articles of merger duly authenticated by the proper officer of the state or country under the laws of which such statutory merger was effected; and it shall not be necessary for such corporation to procure either a new or amended certificate of authority to transact business in this State unless the name of such corporation be changed thereby or unless the corporation desires to pursue in this State other or additional purposes than those which it is then authorized to transact in this State.

§ 118. Amended Certificate of Authority. A foreign corporation authorized to transact business in this State shall procure an amended certificate of authority in the event it changes its corporate name, or desires to pursue in this State other or additional purposes than those set forth in its prior application for a certificate of authority, by making application therefor to the Secretary of State.

The requirements in respect to the form and contents of such application, the manner of its execution, the filing of duplicate originals thereof with the Secretary of State, the issuance of an amended certificate of authority and the effect thereof, shall be the same as in the case of an original application for a certificate of authority.

§ 119. Withdrawal of Foreign Corporation. A foreign corporation authorized to transact business in this State may withdraw from this State upon procuring from the Secretary of State a certificate of withdrawal. In order to procure such certificate of withdrawal, such foreign corporation shall deliver to the Secretary of State an application for withdrawal, which shall set forth:

   (a)   The name of the corporation and the state or country under the laws of which it is incorporated.

   (b)   That the corporation is not transacting business in this State.

   (c)   That the corporation surrenders its authority to transact business in this State.

   (d)   That the corporation revokes the authority of its registered agent in this State to accept service of process and consents that service of process in any action, suit or proceeding based upon any cause of

action arising in this State during the time the corporation was authorized to transact business in this State may thereafter be made on such corporation by service thereof on the Secretary of State.

   (e)   A post-office address to which the Secretary of State may mail a copy of any process against the corporation that may be served on him.

   (f)   A statement of the aggregate number of shares which the corporation has authority to issue, itemized by class and series, if any, within each class, as of the date of such application.

   (g)   A statement of the aggregate number of issued shares, itemized by class and series, if any, within each class, as of the date of such application.

   (h)   Such additional information as may be necessary or appropriate in order to enable the Secretary of State to determine and assess any unpaid fees or franchise taxes payable by such foreign corporation as in this Act prescribed.

The application for withdrawal shall be made on forms prescribed and furnished by the Secretary of State and shall be executed by the corporation by its president or a vice president and by its secretary or an assistant secretary, and verified by one of the officers signing the application, or, if the corporation is in the hands of a receiver or trustee, shall be executed on behalf of the corporation by such receiver or trustee and verified by him.

§ 120. Filing of Application for Withdrawal. Duplicate originals of such application for withdrawal shall be delivered to the Secretary of State. If the Secretary of State finds that such application conforms to the provisions of this Act, he shall, when all fees and franchise taxes have been paid as in this Act prescribed:

   (a)   Endorse on each of such duplicate originals the word "Filed," and the month, day and year of the filing thereof.

   (b)   File one of such duplicate originals in his office.

   (c)   Issue a certificate of withdrawal to which he shall affix the other duplicate original.

The certificate of withdrawal, together with the duplicate original of the application for withdrawal affixed thereto by the Secretary of State, shall be returned to the corporation or its representative. Upon the issuance of such certificate of withdrawal, the authority of the corporation to transact business in this State shall cease.

§ 121. Revocation of Certificate of Authority.
The certificate of authority of a foreign corporation to transact business in this State may be revoked by the Secretary of State upon the conditions prescribed in this section when:

(a) The corporation has failed to file its annual report within the time required by this Act, or has failed to pay any fees, franchise taxes or penalties prescribed by this Act when they have become due and payable; or

(b) The corporation has failed to appoint and maintain a registered agent in this State as required by this Act; or

(c) The corporation has failed, after change of its registered office or registered agent, to file in the office of the Secretary of State a statement of such change as required by this Act; or

(d) The corporation has failed to file in the office of the Secretary of State any amendment to its articles of incorporation or any articles of merger within the time prescribed by this Act; or

(e) A misrepresentation has been made of any material matter in any application, report, affidavit, or other document submitted by such corporation pursuant to this Act.

No certificate of authority of a foreign corporation shall be revoked by the Secretary of State unless (1) he shall have given the corporation not less than sixty days' notice thereof by mail addressed to its registered office in this State, and (2) the corporation shall fail prior to revocation to file such annual report, or pay such fees, franchise taxes or penalties, or file the required statement of change of registered agent or registered office, or file such articles of amendment or articles of merger, or correct such misrepresentation.

§ 122. Issuance of Certificate of Revocation.
Upon revoking any such certificate of authority, the Secretary of State shall:

(a) Issue a certificate of revocation in duplicate.

(b) File one of such certificates in his office.

(c) Mail to such corporation at its registered office in this State a notice of such revocation accompanied by one of such certificates.

Upon the issuance of such certificate of revocation, the authority of the corporation to transact business in this State shall cease.

§ 123. Application to Corporations Heretofore Authorized to Transact Business in This State.
Foreign corporations which are duly authorized to transact business in this State at the time this Act takes effect, for a purpose or purposes for which a corporation might secure such authority under this Act, shall, subject to the limitations set forth in their respective certificates of authority, be entitled to all the rights and privileges applicable to foreign corporations procuring certificates of authority to transact business in this State under this Act, and from the time this Act takes effect such corporations shall be subject to all the limitations, restrictions, liabilities, and duties prescribed herein for foreign corporations procuring certificates of authority to transact business in this State under this Act.

§ 124. Transacting Business Without Certificate of Authority.
No foreign corporation transacting business in this State without a certificate of authority shall be permitted to maintain any action, suit or proceeding in any court of this State, until such corporation shall have obtained a certificate of authority. Nor shall any action, suit or proceeding be maintained in any court of this State by any successor or assignee of such corporation on any right, claim or demand arising out of the transaction of business by such corporation in this State, until a certificate of authority shall have been obtained by such corporation or by a corporation which has acquired all or substantially all of its assets.

The failure of a foreign corporation to obtain a certificate of authority to transact business in this State shall not impair the validity of any contract or act of such corporation, and shall not prevent such corporation from defending any action, suit or proceeding in any court of this State.

A foreign corporation which transacts business in this State without a certificate of authority shall be liable to this State, for the years or parts thereof during which it transacted business in this State without a certificate of authority, in an amount equal to all fees and franchise taxes which would have been imposed by this Act upon such corporation had it duly applied for and received a certificate of authority to transact business in this State as required by this Act and thereafter filed all reports required by this Act, plus all penalties imposed by this Act for failure to pay such fees and franchise taxes. The Attorney General shall bring proceedings to recover all amounts due this State under the provisions of this Section.

§ 125. Annual Report of Domestic and Foreign Corporations. Each domestic corporation, and each foreign corporation authorized to transact business in this State, shall file, within the time prescribed by this Act, an annual report setting forth:

(a)   The name of the corporation and the state or country under the laws of which it is incorporated.

(b)   The address of the registered office of the corporation in this State, and the name of its registered agent in this State at such address, and, in case of a foreign corporation, the address of its principal office in the state or country under the laws of which it is incorporated.

(c)   A brief statement of the character of the business in which the corporation is actually engaged in this State.

(d)   The names and respective addresses of the directors and officers of the corporation.

(e)   A statement of the aggregate number of shares which the corporation has authorized to issue, itemized by class and series, if any, within each class.

(f)   A statement of the aggregate number of issued shares, itemized by class and series, if any, within each class.

(g)   A statement, expressed in dollars, of the value of all the property owned by the corporation, wherever located, and the value of the property of the corporation located within this State, and a statement, expressed in dollars, of the gross amount of business transacted by the corporation for the twelve months ended on the thirty-first day of December preceding the date herein provided for the filing of such report and the gross amount thereof transacted by the corporation at or from places of busi-

ness in this State. If, on the thirty-first day of December preceding the time herein provided for the filing of such report, the corporation had not been in existence for a period of twelve months, or in the case of a foreign corporation had not been authorized to transact business in this State for a period of twelve months, the statement with respect to business transacted shall be furnished for the period between the date of incorporation or the date of its authorization to transact business in this State, as the case may be, and such thirty-first day of December. If all the property of the corporation is located in this State and all of its business in this State, then the information required by this subparagraph need not be set forth in such report.

(h)   Such additional information as may be necessary or appropriate in order to enable the Secretary of State to determine and assess the proper amount of franchise taxes payable by such corporation.

Such annual report shall be made on forms prescribed and furnished by the Secretary of State, and the information therein contained shall be given as of the date of the execution of the report, except as to the information required by subparagraphs (g) and (h) which shall be given as of the close of business on the thirty-first day of December next preceding the date herein provided for the filing of such report. It shall be executed by the corporation by its president, a vice president, secretary, an assistant secretary, or treasurer, and verified by the officer executing the report, or, if the corporation is in the hands of a receiver or trustee, it shall be executed on behalf of the corporation and verified by such receiver or trustee.

§ 126. Filing of Annual Report of Domestic and Foreign Corporations. Such annual report of a domestic or foreign corporation shall be delivered to the Secretary of State between the first day of January and the first day of March of each year, except that the first annual report of a domestic or foreign corporation shall be filed between the first day of January and the first day of March of the year next succeeding the calendar year in which its certificate of incorporation or its certificate of authority, as the case may be, was issued by the Secretary of State. Proof to the satisfaction of the Secretary of State that prior to the first day of March such report was deposited in the United States mail in a sealed envelope, properly addressed, with postage prepaid, shall be deemed a compliance with this requirement. If the Secretary of State finds that such report conforms to the requirements of this Act, he shall file the same. If he finds that it does not so conform, he shall promptly return the same to the corporation for any necessary corrections, in which event the penalties hereinafter prescribed for failure to file such report within the time hereinabove provided shall not apply, if such report is corrected to conform to the requirements of this Act and returned to the Secretary of State within thirty days from the date on which it was mailed to the corporation by the Secretary of State.

§ 127. Fees, Franchise Taxes and Charges to be Collected by Secretary of State. [Text omitted.]

§ 128. Fees for Filing Documents and Issuing Certificates. [Text omitted.]

§ 129. Miscellaneous Charges. [Text omitted.]

§ 130. License Fees Payable by Domestic Corporations. [Text omitted.]

§ 131. License Fees Payable by Foreign Corporations. [Text omitted.]

§ 132. Franchise Taxes Payable by Domestic Corporations. [Text omitted.]

§ 133. Franchise Taxes Payable by Foreign Corporations. [Text omitted.]

§ 134. Assessment and Collection of Annual Franchise Taxes. It shall be the duty of the Secretary of State to collect all annual franchise taxes and penalties imposed by, or assessed in accordance with, this Act.

Between the first day of March and the first day of June of each year, the Secretary of State shall assess against each corporation, domestic and foreign, required to file an annual report in such year, the franchise tax payable by it for the period from July 1 of such year to July 1 of the succeeding year in accordance with the provisions of this Act, and, if it has failed to file its annual report within the

time prescribed by this Act, the penalty imposed by this Act upon such corporation for its failure so to do; and shall mail a written notice to each corporation against which such tax is assessed, addressed to such corporation at its registered office in this State, notifying the corporation (1) of the amount of franchise tax assessed against it for the ensuring year and the amount of penalty, if any, assessed against it for failure to file its annual report; (2) that objections, if any, to such assessment will be heard by the officer making the assessment on or before the fifteenth day of June of such year, upon receipt of a request from the corporation; and (3) that such tax and penalty shall be payable to the Secretary of State on the first day of July next succeeding the date of the notice. Failure to receive such notice shall not relieve the corporation of its obligation to pay the tax and any penalty assessed, or invalidate the assessment thereof.

The Secretary of State shall have power to hear and determine objections to any assessment of franchise tax at any time after such assessment and, after hearing, to change or modify any such assessment. In the event of any adjustment of franchise tax with respect to which a penalty has been assessed for failure to file an annual report, the penalty shall be adjusted in accordance with the provisions of this Act imposing such penalty.

All annual franchise taxes and all penalties for failure to file annual reports shall be due and payable on the first day of July of each year. If the annual franchise tax assessed against any corporation subject to the provisions of this Act, together with all penalties assessed thereon, shall not be paid to the Secretary of State on or before the thirty-first day of July of the year in which such tax is due and payable, the Secretary of State shall certify such fact to the Attorney General on or before the fifteenth day of November of such year, whereupon the Attorney General may institute an action against such corporation in the name of this State, in any court of competent jurisdiction, for the recovery of the amount of such franchise tax and penalties, together with the cost of suit, and prosecute the same to final judgment.

For the purpose of enforcing collection, all annual franchise taxes assessed in accordance with this Act, and all penalties assessed thereon and all interest and costs that shall accrue in connection with the collection thereof, shall be a prior and first lien on the real and personal property of the corporation from and including the first day of July of the year when such franchise taxes become due and payable until such taxes, penalties, interest, and costs shall have been paid.

§ 135. Penalties Imposed Upon Corporations.

Each corporation, domestic or foreign, that fails or refuses to file its annual report for any year within the time prescribed by this Act shall be subject to a penalty of ten per cent of the amount of the franchise tax assessed against it for the period beginning July 1 of the year in which such report should have been filed. Such penalty shall be assessed by the Secretary of State at the time of the assessment of the franchise tax. If the amount of the franchise tax as originally assessed against such corporation be thereafter adjusted in accordance with the provisions of this Act, the amount of the penalty shall be likewise adjusted to ten per cent of the amount of the adjusted franchise tax. The amount of the franchise tax and the amount of the penalty shall be separately stated in any notice to the corporation with respect thereto.

If the franchise tax assessed in accordance with the provisions of this Act shall not be paid on or before the thirty-first day of July, it shall be deemed to be delinquent, and there shall be added a penalty of one per cent for each month or part of month that the same is delinquent, commencing with the month of August.

Each corporation, domestic or foreign, that fails or refuses to answer truthfully and fully within the time prescribed by this Act interrogatories propounded by the Secretary of State in accordance with the provisions of this Act, shall be deemed to be guilty of a misdemeanor and upon conviction thereof may be fined in any amount not exceeding five hundred dollars.

§ 136. Penalties Imposed Upon Officers and Directors.

Each officer and director of a corporation, domestic or foreign, who fails or refuses within the time prescribed by this Act to answer truthfully and fully interrogatories propounded to him by the Secretary of State in accordance with the provisions of this Act, or who signs any articles, statement, report, application or other document filed with the Secretary of State which is known to such officer or director to be false in any material respect, shall be deemed to be guilty of a misdemeanor, and upon conviction thereof may be fined in any amount not exceeding _____ dollars.

§ 137. Interrogatories by Secretary of State.

The Secretary of State may propound to any corporation, domestic or foreign, subject to the provisions of this Act, and to any officer or director thereof, such interrogatories as may be reasonably necessary and proper to enable him to ascertain whether such corporation has complied with all the provisions of this Act applicable to such corporation. Such interrogatories shall be answered within thirty days after the mailing thereof, or within such additional time as shall be fixed by the Secretary of State, and the answers thereto shall be full and complete and shall be made in writing and under oath. If such interrogatories be directed to an individual they shall be answered by him, and if directed to a corporation they shall be answered by the president, vice president, secretary or assistant secretary thereof. The Secretary of State need not file any document to which such interrogatories relate until such interrogatories be answered as herein provided, and not then if the answers thereto disclose that such document is not in conformity with the provisions of this Act. The Secretary of State shall certify to the Attorney General, for such action as the Attorney General may deem appropriate, all interrogatories and answers thereto which disclose a violation of any of the provisions of this Act.

§ 138. Information Disclosed by Interrogatories.

Interrogatories propounded by the Secretary of State and the answers thereto shall not be open to public inspection nor shall the Secretary of State disclose any facts or information obtained therefrom except insofar as his official duty may require the same to be made public or in the event such interrogatories or the answers thereto are required for evidence in any criminal proceedings or in any other action by this State.

§ 139. Powers of Secretary of State.

The Secretary of State shall have the power and authority reasonably necessary to enable him to administer this Act efficiently and to perform the duties therein imposed upon him.

§ 140. Appeal From Secretary of State.

If the Secretary of State shall fail to approve any articles of incorporation, amendment, merger, consolidation or dissolution, or any other document required by this Act to be approved by the Secretary of State before the same shall be filed in his office, he shall, within ten days after the delivery thereof to him, give written notice of his disapproval to the person or corporation, domestic or foreign, delivering the same, specifying the reasons therefor. From such disapproval such person or corporation may appeal to the _____ court of the county in which the registered office of such corporation is, or is proposed to be situated by filing with the clerk of such court a petition setting forth a copy of the articles or other documents sought to be filed and a copy of the written disapproval thereof by the Secretary of State; where-upon the matter shall be tried de novo by the court, and the court shall either sustain the action of the Secretary of State or direct him to take such action as the court may deem proper.

If the Secretary of State shall revoke the certificate of authority to transact business in this State of any foreign corporation, pursuant to the provisions of this Act, such foreign corporation may likewise appeal to the _____ court of the county where the registered office of such corporation in this State is situated, by filing with the clerk of such court a petition setting forth a copy of its certificate of authority to transact business in this State and a copy of the notice of revocation given by the Secretary of State; whereupon the matter shall be tried de novo by the court, and the court shall either sustain the action of the Secretary of State or direct him to take such action as the court may deem proper.

Appeals from all final orders and judgments entered by the _____ court under this section in review of any ruling or decision of the Secretary of State may be taken as in other civil actions.

§ 141. Certificates and Certified Copies to be Received in Evidence.   All certificates issued by the Secretary of State in accordance with the provisions of this Act, and all copies of documents filed in his office in accordance with the provisions of this Act when certified by him, shall be taken and received in all courts, public offices, and official bodies as prima facie evidence of the facts therein stated. A certificate by the Secretary of State under the great seal of this State, as to the existence or non-existence of the facts relating to corporations shall be taken and received in all courts, public offices, and official bodies as prima facie evidence of the existence or non-existence of the facts therein stated.

§ 142. Forms to be Furnished by Secretary of State.   All reports required by this Act to be filed in the office of the Secretary of State shall be made on forms which shall be prescribed and furnished by the Secretary of State. Forms for all other documents to be filed in the office of the Secretary of State shall be furnished by the Secretary of State on request therefor, but the use thereof, unless otherwise specifically prescribed in this Act, shall not be mandatory.

§ 143. Greater Voting Requirements.   Whenever, with respect to any action to be taken by the shareholders of a corporation, the articles of incorporation, require the vote or concurrence of the holders of a greater proportion of the shares, or of any class or series thereof, than required by this Act with respect to such action, the provisions of the articles of incorporation shall control.

§ 144. Waiver of Notice.   Whenever any notice is required to be given to any shareholder or director of a corporation under the provisions of this Act or under the provisions of the articles of incorporation or by-laws of the corporation, a waiver thereof in writing signed by the person or persons entitled to such notice, whether before or after the time stated therein, shall be equivalent to the giving of such notice.

§ 145. Action by Shareholders Without a Meeting.   Any action required by this Act to be taken at a meeting of the shareholders of a corporation, or any action which may be taken at a meeting of the shareholders, may be taken without a meeting if a consent in writing, setting forth the action so taken shall be signed by all of the shareholders entitled to vote with respect to the subject matter thereof.

Such consent shall have the same effect as a unanimous vote of shareholders, and may be stated as such in any articles or document filed with the Secretary of State under this Act.

§ 146. Unauthorized Assumption of Corporate Powers.   All persons who assume to act as a corporation without authority so to do shall be jointly and severally liable for all debts and liabilities incurred or arising as a result thereof.

§ 147. Application to Existing Corporations.   The provisions of this Act shall apply to all existing corporations organized under any general act of this State providing for the organization of corporations for a purpose or purposes for which a corporation might be organized under this Act, where the power has been reserved to amend, repeal or modify the act under which such corporation was organized and where such act is repealed by this Act.

§ 148. Application to Foreign and Interstate Commerce.   The provisions of this Act shall apply to commerce with foreign nations and among the several states only insofar as the same may be permitted under the provisions of the Constitution of the United States.

§ 149. Reservation of Power.   The _____ [insert name of legislative body] shall at all times have power to prescribe such regulations, provisions and limitations as it may deem advisable, which regulations, provisions and limitations shall be binding upon any and all corporations subject to the provisions of this Act, and the _____ [insert name of legislative body] shall have power to amend, repeal or modify this Act at pleasure.

§ 150. Effect of Repeal of Prior Acts.   The repeal of a prior act by this Act shall not affect any right accrued or established, or any liability or penalty incurred, under the provisions of such act, prior to the repeal thereof.

§ 151. Effect of Invalidity of Part of This Act.   If a court of competent jurisdiction shall adjudge to be invalid or unconstitutional any clause, sentence, paragraph, section or part of this Act, such judgment or decree shall not affect, impair, invalidate or nullify the remainder of this Act, but the effect thereof shall be confined to the clause, sentence, paragraph, section or part of this Act so adjudged to be invalid or unconstitutional.

§ 152. Exclusivity of Certain Provisions. [Optional Provision.]   In circumstances to which section 45 and related sections of this Act are applicable, such provisions supersede the applicability of any other statutes of this state with respect to the legality of distributions.

§ 153. Repeal of Prior Acts.   _____ [Insert appropriate provisions.]

Appendix D

Part 1. Preliminary Provisions

§ 1. Name of Act. This act may be cited as Uniform Partnership Act.

§ 2. Definition of Terms. In this act, "Court" includes every court and judge having jurisdiction in the case.

"Business" includes every trade, occupation, or profession.

"Person" includes individuals, partnerships, corporations, and other associations.

"Bankrupt" includes bankrupt under the Federal Bankruptcy Act or insolvent under any state insolvent act.

"Conveyance" includes every assignment, lease, mortgage, or encumbrance.

"Real property" includes land and any interest or estate in land.

§ 3. Interpretation of Knowledge and Notice. (1) A person has "knowledge" of a fact within the meaning of this act not only when he has actual knowledge thereof, but also when he has knowledge of such other facts as in the circumstances shows bad faith.

(2) A person has "notice" of a fact within the meaning of this act when the person who claims the benefit of the notice:

    (a)   States the fact to such person, or

    (b)   Delivers through the mail, or by other means of communication, a written statement of the fact to such person or to a proper person at his place of business or residence.

§ 4. Rules of Construction.

(1) The rule that statutes in derogation of the common law are to be strictly construed shall have no application to this act.

(2) The law of estoppel shall apply under this act.

(3) The law of agency shall apply under this act.

(4) This act shall be so interpreted and construed as to effect its general purpose to make uniform the law of those states which enact it.

(5) This act shall not be construed so as to impair the obligations of any contract existing when the act goes into effect, nor to affect any action or proceedings begun or right accrued before this act takes effect.

§ 5. Rules for Cases Not Provided for in This Act.

In any case not provided for in this act the rules of law and equity, including the law merchant, shall govern.

Part 2. Nature of Partnership

§ 6. Partnership Defined.

(1) A partnership is an association of two or more persons to carry on as co-owners a business for profit.

(2) But any association formed under any other statute of this state, or any statute adopted by authority, other than the authority of this state, is not a partnership under this act, unless such association would have been a partnership in this state prior to the adoption of this act; but this act shall apply to limited partnerships except in so far as the statutes relating to such partnerships are inconsistent herewith.

§ 7. Rules for Determining the Existence of a Partnership. In determining whether a partnership exists, these rules shall apply:

(1) Except as provided by section 16 persons who are not partners as to each other are not partners as to third persons.

(2) Joint tenancy, tenancy in common, tenancy by the entireties, joint property, common property, or part ownership does not of itself establish a partnership, whether such co-owners do or do not share any profits made by the use of the property.

(3) The sharing of gross returns does not of itself establish a partnership, whether or not the persons sharing them have a joint or common right or interest in any property from which the returns are derived.

(4) The receipt by a person of a share of the profits of a business is prima facie evidence that he is a partner in the business, but no such inference shall be drawn if such profits were received in payment:

(a)   As a debt by installments or otherwise,

(b)   As wages of an employee or rent to a landlord,

(c)   As an annuity to a widow or representative of a deceased partner,

(d)   As interest on a loan, though the amount of payment vary with the profits of the business,

(e)   As the consideration for the sale of a good-will of a business or other property by installments or otherwise.

§ 8. Partnership Property.

(1) All property originally brought into the partnership stock or subsequently acquired by purchase or otherwise, on account of the partnership, is partnership property.

(2) Unless the contrary intention appears, property acquired with partnership funds is partnership property.

(3) Any estate in real property may be acquired in the partnership name. Title so acquired can be conveyed only in the partnership name.

(4) A conveyance to a partnership in the partnership name, though without words of inheritance, passes the entire estate of the grantor unless a contrary intent appears.

Part 3. Relations of Partners to Persons Dealing with the Partnership

§ 9. Partner Agent of Partnership as to Partnership Business.

(1) Every partner is an agent of the partnership for the purpose of its business, and the act of every partner, including the execution in the partnership name of any instrument, for apparently carrying on in the usual way the business of the partnership of which he is a member binds the partnership, unless the partner so acting has in fact no authority to act for the partnership in the particular matter, and the person with whom he is dealing has knowledge of the fact that he has no such authority.

(2) An act of a partner which is not apparently for the carrying on of the business of the partnership in the usual way does not bind the partnership unless authorized by the other partners.

(3) Unless authorized by the other partners or unless they have abandoned the business, one or more but less than all the partners have no authority to:

(a)   Assign the partnership property in trust for creditors or on the assignee's promise to pay the debts of the partnership.

(b)   Dispose of the good-will of the business,

(c)   Do any other act which would make it impossible to carry on the ordinary business of a partnership,

(d)   Confess a judgment,

(e)   Submit a partnership claim or liability to arbitration or reference.

(4) No act of a partner in contravention of a restriction on authority shall bind the partnership to persons having knowledge of the restriction.

§ 10. Conveyance of Real Property of the Partnership.

(1) Where title to real property is in the partnership name, any partner may convey title to such property by a conveyance executed in the partnership name; but the partnership may recover such property unless the partner's act binds the partnership under the provisions of paragraph (1) of section 9, or unless such property has been conveyed by the grantee or a person claiming through such grantee to a holder for value without knowledge that the partner, in making the conveyance, has exceeded his authority.

(2) Where title to real property is in the name of the partnership, a conveyance executed by a partner, in his own name, passes the equitable interest of the partnership, provided the act is one within the authority of the partner under the provisions of paragraph (1) of section 9.

(3) Where title to real property is in the name of one or more but not all the partners, and the record

does not disclose the right of the partnership, the partners in whose name the title stands may convey title to such property, but the partnership may recover such property if the partners' act does not bind the partnership under the provisions of paragraph (1) of section 9, unless the purchaser or his assignee, is a holder for value, without knowledge.

(4) Where the title to real property is in the name of one or more of all the partners, or in a third person in trust for the partnership, a conveyance executed by a partner in the partnership name, or in his own name, passes the equitable interest of the partnership, provided the act is one within the authority of the partner under the provisions of paragraph (1) of section 9.

(5) Where the title to real property is in the names of all the partners a conveyance executed by all the partners passes all their rights in such property.

§ 11. Partnership Bound by Admission of Partner.
An admission or representation made by any partner concerning partnership affairs within the scope of his authority as conferred by this act is evidence against the partnership.

§ 12. Partnership Charged with Knowledge of or Notice to Partner.
Notice to any partner of any matter relating to partnership affairs, and the knowledge of the partner acting in the particular matter, acquired while a partner or then present to his mind, and the knowledge of any other partner who reasonably could and should have communicated it to the acting partner, operate as notice to or knowledge of the partnership, except in the case of a fraud on the partnership committed by or with the consent of that partner.

§ 13. Partnership Bound by Partner's Wrongful Act.
Where, by any wrongful act or omission of any partner acting in the ordinary course of the business of the partnership or with the authority of his copartners, loss or injury is caused to any person, not being a partner in the partnership, or any penalty is incurred, the partnership is liable therefor to the same extent as the partner so acting or omitting to act.

§ 14. Partnership Bound by Partner's Breach of Trust.
The partnership is bound to make good the loss:

(a) Where one partner acting within the scope of his apparent authority receives money or property of a third person and misapplies it; and

(b) Where the partnership in the course of its business receives money or property of a third person and the money or property so received is misapplied by any partner while it is in the custody of the partnership.

§ 15. Nature of Partner's Liability.
All partners are liable.

(a) Jointly and severally for everything chargeable to the partnership under sections 13 and 14.

(b) Jointly for all other debts and obligations of the partnership; but any partner may enter into a separate obligation to perform a partnership contract.

§ 16. Partner by Estoppel.
(1) When a person, by words spoken or written or by conduct, represents himself, or consents to another representing him to any one, as a partner in an existing partnership or with one or more persons not actual partners, he is liable to any such person to whom such representation has been made, who has, on the faith of such representation, given credit to the actual or apparent partnership, and if he has made such representation or consented to its being made in a public manner he is liable to such person, whether the representation has or has not been made or communicated to such person so giving credit by or with the knowledge of the apparent partner making the representation or consenting to its being made.

(a) When a partnership liability results, he is liable as though he were an actual member of the partnership.

(b) When no partnership liability results, he is liable jointly with the other persons, if any, so consenting to the contract or representation as to incur liability, otherwise separately.

(2) When a person has been thus represented to be a partner in an existing partnership, or with one or more persons not actual partners, he is an agent of the persons consenting to such representation to bind them to the same extent and in the same manner as though he were a partner in fact, with respect to persons who rely upon the representation. Where all the members of the existing partnership consent to the representation, a partnership

act or obligation results; but in all other cases it is the joint act or obligation of the person acting and the persons consenting to the representation.

§ 17. Liability of Incoming Partner. A person admitted as a partner into an existing partnership is liable for all the obligations of the partnership arising before his admission as though he had been a partner when such obligations were incurred, except that this liability shall be satisfied only out of partnership property.

Part 4. Relations of Partners to One Another

§ 18. Rules Determining Rights and Duties of Partners. The rights and duties of the partners in relation to the partnership shall be determined, subject to any agreement between them, by the following rules:

   (a)   Each partner shall be repaid his contributions, whether by way of capital or advances to the partnership property and share equally in the profits and surplus remaining after all liabilities, including those to partners, are satisfied; and must contribute towards the losses, whether of capital or otherwise, sustained by the partnership according to his share in the profits.

   (b)   The partnership must indemnify every partner in respect of payments made and personal liabilities reasonably incurred by him in the ordinary and proper conduct of its business, or for the preservation of its business or property.

   (c)   A partner, who in aid of the partnership makes any payment or advance beyond the amount of capital which he agreed to contribute, shall be paid interest from the date of the payment or advance.

   (d)   A partner shall receive interest on the capital contributed by him only from the date when repayment should be made.

   (e)   All partners have equal rights in the management and conduct of the partnership business.

   (f)   No partner is entitled to remuneration for acting in the partnership business, except that a surviving partner is entitled to reasonable compensation for his services in winding up the partnership affairs.

   (g)   No person can become a member of a partnership without the consent of all the partners.

   (h)   Any difference arising as to ordinary matters connected with the partnership business may be decided by a majority of the partners; but no act in contravention of any agreement between the partners may be done rightfully without the consent of all the partners.

§ 19. Partnership Books. The partnership books shall be kept, subject to any agreement between the partners, at the principal place of business of the partnership, and every partner shall at all times have access to and may inspect and copy any of them.

§ 20. Duty of Partners to Render Information. Partners shall render on demand true and full information of all things affecting the partnership to any partner or the legal representative of any deceased partner or partner under legal disability.

§ 21. Partner Accountable as a Fiduciary.

(1) Every partner must account to the partnership for any benefit, and hold as trustee for it any profits derived by him without the consent of the other partners from any transaction connected with the formation, conduct, or liquidation of the partnership or from any use by him of its property.

(2) This section applies also to the representatives of a deceased partner engaged in the liquidation of the affairs of the partnership as the personal representatives of the last surviving partner.

§ 22. Right to an Account. Any partner shall have the right to a formal account as to partnership affairs:

   (a)   If he is wrongfully excluded from the partnership business or possession of its property by his co-partners,

   (b)   If the right exists under the terms of any agreement,

   (c)   As provided by section 21,

   (d)   Whenever other circumstances render it just and reasonable.

§ 23. Continuation of Partnership Beyond Fixed Term.

(1) When a partnership for a fixed term or particular undertaking is continued after the termination of such term or particular undertaking without any

express agreement, the rights and duties of the partners remain the same as they were at such termination, so far as is consistent with a partnership at will.

(2) A continuation of the business by the partners or such of them as habitually acted therein during the term, without any settlement or liquidation of the partnership affairs, is prima facie evidence of a continuation of the partnership.

Part 5. Property Rights of a Partner

§ 24. Extent of Property Rights of a Partner. The property rights of a partner are (1) his rights in specific partnership property, (2) his interest in the partnership, and (3) his right to participate in the management.

§ 25. Nature of a Partner's Right in Specific Partnership Property.

(1) A partner is co-owner with his partners of specific partnership property holding as a tenant in partnership.

(2) The incidents of this tenancy are such that:

(a)   A partner, subject to the provisions of this act and to any agreement between the partners, has an equal right with his partners to possess specific partnership property for partnership purposes; but he has no right to possess such property for any other purpose without the consent of his partners.

(b)   A partner's right in specific partnership property is not assignable except in connection with the assignment of rights of all the partners in the same property.

(c)   A partner's right in specific partnership property is not subject to attachment or execution, except on a claim against the partnership. When partnership property is attached for a partnership debt the partners, or any of them, or the representatives of a deceased partner, cannot claim any right under the homestead or exemption laws.

(d)   On the death of a partner his right in specific partnership property vests in the surviving partner or partners, except where the deceased was the last surviving partner, when his right in such property vests in his legal representative. Such surviving partner or partners, or the legal representative of the last surviving partner, has no right to possess the partnership property for any but a partnership purpose.

(e)   A partner's right in specific partnership property is not subject to dower, curtesy, or allowances to widows, heirs, or next of kin.

§ 26. Nature of Partner's Interest in the Partnership. A partner's interest in the partnership is his share of the profits and surplus, and the same is personal property.

§ 27. Assignment of Partner's Interest.

(1) A conveyance by a partner of his interest in the partnership does not of itself dissolve the partnership, nor, as against the other partners in the absence of agreement, entitle the assignee, during the continuance of the partnership, to interfere in the management or administration of the partnership business or affairs, or to require any information or account of partnership transactions, or to inspect the partnership books; but it merely entitles the assignee to receive in accordance with his contract the profits to which the assigning partner would otherwise be entitled.

(2) In case of a dissolution of the partnership, the assignee is entitled to receive his assignor's interest and may require an account from the date only of the last account agreed to by all the partners.

§ 28. Partner's Interest Subject to Changing Order.

(1) On due application to a competent court by any judgment creditor of a partner, the court which entered the judgment, order, or decree, or any other court, may charge the interest of the debtor partner with payment of the unsatisfied amount of such judgment debt with interest thereon; and may then or later appoint a receiver of his share of the profits, and of any other money due or to fall due to him in respect of the partnership, and make all other orders, directions, accounts and inquiries which the debtor partner might have made, or which the circumstances of the case may require.

(2) The interest charged may be redeemed at any time before foreclosure, on in case of a sale being directed by the court may be purchased without thereby causing a dissolution:

(a)   With separate property, by any one or more of the partners, or

(b)   With partnership property, by any one or more of the partners with the consent of all the partners whose interests are not so charged or sold.

(3) Nothing in this act shall be held to deprive a partner of his right, if any, under the exemption laws, as regards his interest in the partnership.

Part 6. Dissolution and Winding Up

§ 29. Dissolution Defined.   The dissolution of a partnership is the change in the relation of the partners caused by any partner ceasing to be associated in the carrying on as distinguished from the winding up of the business.

§ 30. Partnership not Terminated by Dissolution. On dissolution the partnership is not terminated, but continues until the winding up of partnership affairs is completed.

§ 31. Causes of Dissolution.   Dissolution is caused:

(1) Without violation of the agreement between the partners,

(a)   By the termination of the definite term or particular undertaking specified in the agreement,

(b)   By the express will of any partner when no definite term or particular undertaking is specified,

(c)   By the express will of all the partners who have not assigned their interests or suffered them to be charged for their separate debts, either before or after the termination of any specified term or particular undertaking,

(d)   By the expulsion of any partner from the business bona fide in accordance with such a power conferred by the agreement between the partners;

(2) In contravention of the agreement between the partners, where the circumstances do not permit a dissolution under any other provision of this section, by the express will of any partner at any time;

(3) By any event which makes it unlawful for the business of the partnership to be carried on or for the members to carry it on in partnership;

(4) By the death of any partner;

(5) By the bankruptcy of any partner or the partnership;

(6) By decree of court under section 32.

§ 32. Dissolution by Decree of Court.

(1) On application by or for a partner the court shall decree a dissolution whenever:

(a)   A partner has been declared a lunatic in any judicial proceeding or is shown to be of unsound mind,

(b)   A partner becomes in any other way incapable of performing his part of the partnership contract,

(c)   A partner has been guilty of such conduct as tends to affect prejudicially the carrying on of the business,

(d)   A partner wilfully or persistently commits a breach of the partnership agreement, or otherwise so conducts himself in matters relating to the partnership business that it is not reasonably practicable to carry on the business in partnership with him,

(e)   The business of the partnership can only be carried on at a loss,

(f)   Other circumstances render a dissolution equitable.

(2) On the application of the purchaser of a partner's interest under sections 27 or 28:

(a)   After the termination of the specified term or particular undertaking,

(b)   At any time if the partnership was a partnership at will when the interest was assigned or when the charging order was issued.

§ 33. General Effect of Dissolution on Authority of Partner.   Except so far as may be necessary to wind up partnership affairs or to complete transactions begun but not then finished, dissolution terminates all authority of any partner to act for the partnership.

(1) With respect to the partners,

(a)   When the dissolution is not by the act, bankruptcy or death of a partner; or

(b)   When the dissolution is by such act, bankruptcy or death or a partner, in cases where section 34 so requires.

(2) With respect to persons not partners, as declared in section 35.

§ 34. Right of Partner to Contribution from Co-partners after Dissolution.   Where the dissolution is caused by the act, death or bankruptcy of a partner, each partner is liable to his co-partners for his share of any liability created by any partner acting for the partnership as if the partnership had not been dissolved unless

- (a) The dissolution being by act of any partner, the partner acting for the partnership had knowledge of the dissolution, or
- (b) The dissolution being by the death or bankruptcy of a partner, the partner acting for the partnership had knowledge or notice of the death or bankruptcy.

§ 35. Power of Partner to Bind Partnership to Third Persons after Dissolution.

(1) After dissolution a partner can bind the partnership except as provided in paragraph (3).

- (a) By any act appropriate for winding up partnership affairs or completing transactions unfinished at dissolution;
- (b) By any transaction which would bind the partnership if dissolution had not taken place, provided the other party to the transaction
- (I) Had extended credit to the partnership prior to dissolution and had no knowledge or notice of the dissolution; or
- (II) Though he had not so extended credit, had nevertheless known of the partnership prior to dissolution, and, having no knowledge or notice of dissolution, the fact of dissolution had not been advertised in a newspaper of general circulation in the place (or in each place if more than one) at which the partnership business was regularly carried on.

(2) The liability of a partner under paragraph (1b) shall be satisfied out of partnership assets alone when such partner had been prior to dissolution

- (a) Unknown as a partner to the person with whom the contract is made; and
- (b) So far unknown and inactive in partnership affairs that the business reputation of the partnership could not be said to have been in any degree due to his connection with it.

(3) The partnership is in no case bound by any act of a partner after dissolution

- (a) Where the partnership is dissolved because it is unlawful to carry on the business, unless the act is appropriate for winding up partnership affairs; or
- (b) Where the partner has become bankrupt; or

- (c) Where the partner has no authority to wind up partnership affairs; except by a transaction with one who
- (I) Had extended credit to the partnership prior to dissolution and had no knowledge or notice of his want of authority; or
- (II) Had not extended credit to the partnership prior to dissolution, and, having no knowledge or notice of his want of authority, the fact of his want or authority has not been advertised in the manner provided for advertising the fact of dissolution in paragraph 1bII).

(4) Nothing in this section shall affect the liability under section 16 of any person who after dissolution represents himself or consents to another representing him as a partner in a partnership engaged in carrying on a business.

§ 36. Effect of Dissolution on Partner's Existing Liability.

(1) The dissolution of the partnership does not of itself discharge the existing liability of any partner.

(2) A partner is discharged from any existing liability upon dissolution of the partnership by an agreement to that effect between himself, the partnership creditor and the person or partnership continuing the business; and such agreement may be inferred from the course of dealing between the creditor having knowledge of the dissolution and the person or partnership continuing the business.

(3) Where a person agrees to assume the existing obligations of a dissolved partnership, the partners whose obligations have been assumed shall be discharged from any liability to any creditor of the partnership who, knowing of the agreement, consents to a material alteration in the nature or time of payment of such obligations.

(4) The individual property of a deceased partner shall be liable for all obligations of the partnership incurred while he was a partner but subject to the prior payment of his separate debts.

§ 37. Right to Wind Up.
Unless otherwise agreed the partners who have not wrongfully dissolved the partnership or the legal representative of the last surviving partner, not bankrupt, has the right to wind up the partnership affairs; provided, however, that any partner, his legal representative or his assignee, upon cause shown, may obtain winding up by the court.

§ 38. Rights of Partners to Application of Partnership Property.

(1) When dissolution is caused in any way, except in contravention of the partnership agreement, each partner, as against his co-partners and all persons claiming through them in respect of their interests in the partnership, unless otherwise agreed, may have the partnership property applied to discharge its liabilities, and the surplus applied to pay in cash the net amount owing to the respective partners. But if dissolution is caused by expulsion of a partner, bona fide under the partnership agreement and if the expelled partner is discharged from all partnership liabilities, either by payment or agreement under section 36(2), he shall receive in cash only the net amount due him from the partnership.

(2) When dissolution is caused in contravention of the partnership agreement the rights of the partners shall be as follows:

(a) Each partner who has not caused dissolution wrongfully shall have,

(I) All the rights specified in paragraph (1) of this section, and

(II) The right, as against each partner who has caused the dissolution wrongfully, to damages for breach of the agreement.

(b) The partners who have not caused the dissolution wrongfully, if they all desire to continue the business in the same name, either by themselves or jointly with others, may do so, during the agreed term for the partnership and for that purpose may possess the partnership property, provided they secure the payment by bond approved by the court, or pay to any partner who has caused the dissolution wrongfully, the value of his interest in the partnership at the dissolution, less any damages recoverable under clause (2aII) of this section, and in like manner indemnify him against all present or future partnership liabilities.

(c) A partner who has caused the dissolution wrongfully shall have

(I) If the business is not continued under the provisions of paragraph (2b) all the rights of a partner under paragraph (1), subject to clause (2aII), of this section,

(II) If the business is continued under paragraph (2b) of this section the right as

against his co-partners and all claiming through them in respect of their interests in the partnership, to have the value of his interest in the partnership, less any damages caused to his co-partners by the dissolution, ascertained and paid to him in cash, or the payment secured by bond approved by the court, and to be released from all existing liabilities of the partnership; but in ascertaining the value of the partner's interest the value of the goodwill of the business shall not be considered.

§ 39. Rights Where Partnership is Dissolved for Fraud or Misrepresentation.

Where a partnership contract is rescinded on the ground of the fraud or misrepresentation of one of the parties thereto, the party entitled to rescind is, without prejudice to any other right, entitled,

(a) To a lien on, or a right of retention of, the surplus of the partnership property after satisfying the partnership liabilities to third persons for any sum of money paid by him for the purchase of an interest in the partnership and for any capital or advances contributed by him; and

(b) To stand, after all liabilities to third persons have been satisfied, in the place of the creditors or the partnership for any payments made by him in respect of the partnership liabilities; and

(c) To be indemnified by the person guilty of the fraud or making the representation against all debts and liabilities of the partnership.

§ 40. Rules for Distribution.

In settling accounts between the partners after dissolution, the following rules shall be observed, subject to any agreement to the contrary:

(a) The assets of the partnership are:

(I) The partnership property,

(II) The contributions of the partners necessary for the payment of all the liabilities specified in clause (b) of this paragraph.

(b) The liabilities of the partnership shall rank in order of payment, as follows:

(I) Those owing to creditors other than partners,

(II) Those owing to partners other than for capital and profits,

(III) Those owing to partners in respect of capital,

(IV) Those owing to partners in respect of profits.

(c) The assets shall be applied in order of their declaration in clause (a) of this paragraph to the satisfaction of the liabilities.

(d) The partners shall contribute, as provided by section 18(a) the amount necessary to satisfy the liabilities; but if any, but not all, of the partners are insolvent, or, not being subject to process, refuse to contribute, the other partners shall contribute their share of the liabilities, and, in the relative proportions in which they share the profits, the additional amount necessary to pay the liabilities.

(e) An assignee for the benefit of creditors or any person appointed by the court shall have the right to enforce the contributions specified in clause (d) of this paragraph.

(f) Any partner or his legal representative shall have the right to enforce the contributions specified in clause (d) of this paragraph, to the extent of the amount which he has paid in excess of his share of the liability.

(g) The individual property of a deceased partner shall be liable for the contributions specified in clause (d) of this paragraph.

(h) When partnership property and the individual properties of the partners are in possession of a court for distribution, partnership creditors shall have priority on partnership property and separate creditors on individual property, saving the rights of lien or secured creditors as heretofore.

(i) Where a partner has become bankrupt or his estate is insolvent the claims against his separate property shall rank in the following order:

(I) Those owing to separate creditors,

(II) Those owing to partnership creditors,

(III) Those owing to partners by way of contribution.

§ 41. Liability of Persons Continuing the Business in Certain Cases.

(1) When any new partner is admitted into an existing partnership, or when any partner retires and assigns (or the representative of the deceased partner assigns) his rights in partnership property to two or more of the partners, or to one or more of the partners and one or more third persons, if the business is continued without liquidation of the partnership affairs, creditors of the first or dissolved partnership are also creditors of the partnership so continuing the business.

(2) When all but one partner retire and assign (or the representative of a deceased partner assigns) their rights in partnership property to the remaining partner, who continues the business without liquidation of partnership affairs, either alone or with others, creditors of the dissolved partnership are also creditors of the person or partnership so continuing the business.

(3) When any partner retires or dies and the business of the dissolved partnership is continued as set forth in paragraphs (1) and (2) of this section, with the consent of the retired partners or the representative of the deceased partner, but without any assignment of his right in partnership property, rights of creditors of the dissolved partnership and of the creditors of the person or partnership continuing the business shall be as if such assignment had been made.

(4) When all the partners or their representatives assign their rights in partnership property to one or more third persons who promise to pay the debts and who continue the business of the dissolved partnership, creditors of the dissolved partnership are also creditors of the person or partnership continuing the business.

(5) When any partner wrongfully causes a dissolution and the remaining partners continue the business under the provisions of section 38(2b), either alone or with others, and without liquidation of the partnership affairs, creditors of the dissolved partnership are also creditors of the person or partnership continuing the business.

(6) When a partner is expelled and the remaining partners continue the business either alone or with others, without liquidation of the partnership affairs, creditors of the dissolved partnership are also creditors of the person or partnership continuing the business.

(7) The liability of a third person becoming a partner in the partnership continuing the business, under this section, to the creditors of the dissolved partnership shall be satisfied out of partnership property only.

(8) When the business of a partnership after dissolution is continued under any conditions set forth in this section the creditors of the dissolved partnership, as against the separate creditors of the retiring or deceased partner or the representative of the deceased partner, have a prior right to any claim of the retired partner or the representative of the deceased partner against the person or partnership continuing the business, on account of the retired or deceased partner's interest in the dissolved partnership or on account of any consideration promised for such interest or for his right in partnership property.

(9) Nothing in this section shall be held to modify any right of creditors to set aside any assignment on the ground of fraud.

(10) The use by the person or partnership continuing the business of the partnership name, or the name of a deceased partner as part thereof, shall not of itself make the individual property of the deceased partner liable for any debts contracted by such person or partnership.

§ 42. Rights of Retiring or Estate of Deceased Partner When the Business is Continued.   When any partner retires or dies, and the business is continued under any of the conditions set forth in section 41(1, 2, 3, 5, 6), or section 38(2b) without

any settlement of accounts as between him or his estate and the person or partnership continuing the business, unless otherwise agreed, he or his legal representative as against such persons or partnership may have the value of his interest at the date of dissolution ascertained, and shall receive as an ordinary creditor an amount equal to the value of his interest in the dissolved partnership with interest, or, at his option or at the option of his legal representative, in lieu of interest, the profits attributable to the use of his right in the property of the dissolved partnership; provided that the creditors of the dissolved partnership as against the separate creditors, or the representative of the retired or deceased partner, shall have priority on any claim arising under this section, as provided by section 41(8) of this act.

§ 43. Accural of Actions.   The right to an account of his interest shall accrue to any partner, or his legal representative, as against the winding up partners or the surviving partners or the person or partnership continuing the business, at the date of dissolution, in the absence of any agreement to the contrary.

Part 7. Miscellaneous Provisions

§ 44. When Act Takes Effect.   This act shall take effect on the _____ day of _____ one thousand nine hundred and _____ .

§ 45. Legislation Repealed.   All acts or parts of acts inconsistent with this act are hereby repealed.

Appendix E

UNIFORM LIMITED PARTNERSHIP ACT*

§ 1. Limited Partnership Defined. A limited partnership is a partnership formed by two or more persons under the provisions of Section 2, having as members one or more general partners and one or more limited partners. The limited partners as such shall not be bound by the obligations of the partnership.

§ 2. Formation.

(1) Two or more persons desiring to form a limited partnership shall

(a) Sign and swear to a certificate, which shall state

I. The name of the partnership,

II. The character of the business,

III. The location of the principal place of business,

IV. The name and place of residence of each member; general and limited partners being respectively designated,

V. The term for which the partnership is to exist,

VI. The amount of cash and a description of and the agreed value of the other property contributed by each limited partner,

VII. The additional contributions, if any, agreed to be made by each limited partner and the times at which or events on the happening of which they shall be made,

VIII. The time, if agreed upon, when the contribution of each limited partner is to be returned,

IX. The share of the profits or the other compensation by way of income which each limited partner shall receive by reason of his contribution,

X. The right, if given, of a limited partner to substitute an assignee as contributor in his place, and the terms and conditions of the substitution,

XI. The right, if given, of the partners to admit additional limited partners,

XII. The right, if given, of one or more of the limited partners to priority over other limited partners, as to contributions or as to compensation by way of income, and the nature of such priority.

XIII. The right, if given, of the remaining general partner or partners to continue the business on the death, retirement or insanity of a general partner, and

XIV. The right, if given, of a limited partner to demand and receive property other than cash in return for his contribution.

(b) File for record the certificate in the office of [here designate the proper office].

(2) A limited partnership is formed if there has been substantial compliance in good faith with the requirements of paragraph (1).

§ 3. Business Which May Be Carried On. A limited partnership may carry on any business which a partnership without limited partners may carry on, except [here designate the business to be prohibited].

§ 4. Character of Limited Partner's Contribution. The contributions of a limited partner may be cash or other property, but not services.

§ 5. A Name Not to Contain Surname of Limited Partner; Exceptions.

(1) The surname of a limited partner shall not appear in the partnership name, unless

(a) It is also the surname of a general partner, or

---

* The text of this act was obtained from the National Conference of Commissioners on Uniform State Laws, and is reprinted with the Commission's consent.

(b) Prior to the time when the limited partner became such the business had been carried on under a name in which his surname appeared.

(2) A limited partner whose name appears in a partnership name contrary to the provisions of paragraph (1) is liable as a general partner to partnership creditors who extend credit to the partnership without actual knowledge that he is not a general partner.

§ 6. Liability For False Statements in Certificate.
If the certificate contains a false statement, one who suffers loss by reliance on such statement may hold liable any party to the certificate who knew the statement to be false.

(a) At the time he signed the certificate, or

(b) Subsequently, but within a sufficient time before the statement was relied upon to enable him to cancel or amend the certificate, or to file a petition for its cancellation or amendment as provided in Section 25(3).

§ 7. Limited Partner Not Liable to Creditors.
A limited partner shall not become liable as a general partner unless, in addition to the exercise of his rights and powers as a limited partner, he takes part in the control of the business.

§ 8. Admission of Additional Limited Partners.
After the formation of a limited partnership, additional limited partners may be admitted upon filing an amendment to the original certificate in accordance with the requirements of Section 25.

§ 9. Rights, Powers and Liabilities of a General Partner.
(1) A general partner shall have all the rights and powers and be subject to all the restrictions and liabilities of a partner in a partnership without limited partners, except that without the written consent or ratification of the specific act by all the limited partners, a general partner or all of the general partners have no authority to

(a) Do any act in contravention of the certificate,

(b) Do any act which would make it impossible to carry on the ordinary business of the partnership,

(c) Confess a judgment against the partnership,

(d) Possess partnership property, or assign their rights in specific partnership prop-

erty, for other than a partnership purpose,

(e) Admit a person as a general partner,

(f) Admit a person as a limited partner, unless the right so to do is given in the certificate,

(g) Continue the business with partnership property on the death, retirement or insanity of a general partner, unless the right so to do is given in the certificate.

§ 10. Rights of a Limited Partner.
A limited partner shall have the same rights as a general partner to

(a) Have the partnership books kept at the principal place of business of the partnership, and at all times to inspect and copy any of them.

(b) Have on demand true and full information of all things affecting the partnership, and a formal account of partnership affairs whenever circumstances render it just and reasonable, and

(c) Have dissolution and winding up by decree of court.

(2) A limited partner shall have the right to receive a share of the profits or other compensation by way of income, and to the return of his contribution as provided in Sections 15 and 16.

§ 11. Status of Person Erroneously Believing Himself a Limited Partner.
A person who has contributed to the capital of a business conducted by a person or partnership erroneously believing that he has become a limited partner in a limited partnership, is not, by reason of his exercise of the rights of a limited partner, a general partner with the person or in the partnership carrying on the business, or bound by the obligations of such person or partnership; provided that on ascertaining the mistake he promptly renounces his interest in the profits of the business, or other compensation by way of income.

§ 12. One Person Both General and Limited Partner.
(1) A person may be a general partner and a limited partner in the same partnership at the same time.

(2) A person who is a general, and also at the same time a limited partner, shall have all the rights and powers and be subject to all the restrictions of

a general partner; except that, in respect to his contribution, he shall have the rights against the other members which he would have had if he were not also a general partner.

§ 13. Loans and Other Business Transactions With Limited Partner.

(1) A limited partner also may loan money to and transact other business with the partnership, and, unless he is also a general partner, receive on account of resulting claims against the partnership, with general creditors, a pro rata share of the assets. No limited partner shall in respect to any such claim

  (a) Receive or hold as collateral security any partnership property, or

  (b) Receive from a general partner or the partnership any payment, conveyance, or release from liability, if at the time the assets of the partnership are not sufficient to discharge partnership liabilities to persons not claiming as general or limited partners,

(2) The receiving of collateral security, or a payment, conveyance, or release in violation of the provisions of paragraph (1) is a fraud on the creditors of the partnership.

§ 14. Relation of Limited Partners Inter Se.
Where there are several limited partners the members may agree that one or more of the limited partners shall have a priority over other limited partners as to the return of their contributions, as to their compensation by way of income, or as to any other matter. If such an agreement is made it shall be stated in the certificate, and in the absence of such a statement all the limited partners shall stand upon equal footing.

§ 15. Compensation of Limited Partner.
A limited partner may receive from the partnership the share of the profits or the compensation by way of income stipulated for in the certificate; provided, that after such payment is made, whether from the property of the partnership or that of a general partner, the partnership assets are in excess of all liabilities of the partnership except liabilities to limited partners on account of their contributions and to general partners.

§ 16. Withdrawal or Reduction of Limited Partner's Contribution.

(1) A limited partner shall not receive from a general partner or out of partnership property any part of his contribution until

  (a) All liabilities of the partnership, except liabilities to general partners and to limited partners on account of their contributions, have been paid or there remains property of the partnership sufficient to pay them,

  (b) The consent of all members is had, unless the return of the contribution may be rightfully demanded under the provisions of paragraph (2), and

  (c) The certificate is cancelled or so amended as to set forth the withdrawal or reduction.

(2) Subject to the provisions of paragraph (1) a limited partner may rightfully demand the return of his contribution

  (a) On the dissolution of a partnership, or

  (b) When the date specified in the certificate for its return has arrived, or

  (c) After he has given six months' notice in writing to all other members, if no time is specified in the certificate either for the return of the contribution or for the dissolution of the partnership,

(3) In the absence of any statement in the certificate to the contrary or the consent of all members, a limited partner, irrespective of the nature of his contribution, has only the right to demand and receive cash in return for his contribution.

(4) A limited partner may have the partnership dissolved and its affairs wound up when

  (a) He rightfully but unsuccessfully demands the return of his contribution, or

  (b) The other liabilities of the partnership have not been paid, or the partnership property is insufficient for their payment as required by paragraph (1a) and the limited partner would otherwise be entitled to the return of his contribution.

§ 17. Liability of Limited Partner to Partnership.
(1) A limited partner is liable to the partnership

  (a) For the difference between his contribution as actually made and that stated in the certificate as having been made, and

(b)   For any unpaid contribution which he agreed in the certificate to make in the future at the time and on the conditions stated in the certificate.

(2) A limited partner holds as trustee for the partnership

(a)   Specific property stated in the certificate as contributed by him, but which was not contributed or which has been wrongfully returned, and

(b)   Money or other property wrongfully paid or conveyed to him on account of his contribution.

(3) The liabilities of a limited partner as set forth in this section can be waived or compromised only by the consent of all members; but a waiver or compromise shall not affect the right of a creditor of a partnership who extended credit or whose claim arose after the filing and before a cancellation or amendment of the certificate, to enforce such liabilities.

(4) When a contributor has rightfully received the return in whole or in part of the capital of his contribution, he is nevertheless liable to the partnership for any sum, not in excess of such return with interest, necessary to discharge its liabilities to all creditors who extended credit or whose claims arose before such return.

§ 18. Nature of Limited Partner's Interest in Partnership.

A limited partner's interest in the partnership is personal property.

§ 19. Assignment of Limited Partner's Interest.

(1) A limited partner's interest is assignable.

(2) A substituted limited partner is a person admitted to all the rights of a limited partner who has died or has assigned his interest in a partnership.

(3) An assignee, who does not become a substituted limited partner, has no right to require any information or account of the partnership transactions or to inspect the partnership books; he is only entitled to receive the share of the profits or other compensation by way of income, or the return of his contribution, to which his assignor would otherwise be entitled.

(4) An assignee shall have the right to become a substituted limited partner if all the members (except the assignor) consent thereto or if the assignor, being thereunto empowered by the certificate, gives the assignee that right.

(5) An assignee becomes a substituted limited partner when the certificate is appropriately amended in accordance with Section 25.

(6) The substituted limited partner has all the rights and powers, and is subject to all the restrictions and liabilities of his assignor, except those liabilities of which he was ignorant at the time he became a limited partner and which could not be ascertained from the certificate.

(7) The substitution of the assignee as a limited partner does not release the assignor from liability to the partnership under Sections 6 and 17.

§ 20. Effect of Retirement, Death or Insanity of a General Partner.

The retirement, death or insanity of a general partner dissolves the partnership, unless the business is continued by the remaining general partners

(a) Under a right so to do stated in the certificate, or

(b) With the consent of all members.

§ 21. Death of Limited Partner.

(1) On the death of a limited partner his executor or administrator shall have all the rights of a limited partner for the purpose of settling his estate, and such power as the deceased had to constitute his assignee a substituted limited partner.

(2) The estate of a deceased limited partner shall be liable for all his liabilities as a limited partner.

§ 22. Rights of Creditors of Limited Partner.

(1) On due application to a court of competent jurisdiction by any judgment creditor of a limited partner, the court may charge the interest of the indebted limited partner with payment of the unsatisfied amount of the judgment debt; and may appoint a receiver, and make all other orders, directions, and inquires which the circumstances of the case may require.

(2) The interest may be redeemed with the separate property of any general partner, but may not be redeemed with partnership property.

(3) The remedies conferred by paragraph (1) shall not be deemed exclusive of others which may exist.

(4) Nothing in this act shall be held to deprive a limited partner of his statutory exemption.

§ 23. Distribution of Assets.

(1) In settling accounts after dissolution of liabilities, the partnership shall be entitled to payment in the following order:

(a) Those to creditors, in the order of priority as provided by law, except those to limited partners on account of their contributions, and to general partners,

(b) Those to limited partners in respect to their share of the profits and other compensation by way of income on their contributions,

(c) Those to limited partners in respect to the capital of their contributions,

(d) Those to general partners other than for capital and profits,

(e) Those to general partners in respect to profits,

(f) Those to general partners in respect to capital.

(2) Subject to any statement in the certificate or to subsequent agreement, limited partners share in the partnership assets in respect to their claims for capital, and in respect to their claims for profits or for compensation by way of income on their contributions respectively, in proportion to the respective amounts of such claims.

§ 24. When Certificate Shall be Cancelled or Amended.

(1) The certificate shall be cancelled when the partnership is dissolved or all limited partners cease to be such.

(2) A certificate shall be amended when

(a) There is a change in the name of the partnership or in the amount or character of the contribution of any limited partner,

(b) A person is substituted as a limited partner,

(c) An additional limited partner is admitted,

(d) A person is admitted as a general partner,

(e) A general partner retires, dies or becomes insane, and the business is continued under Section 20,

(f) There is a change in the character of the business of the partnership,

(g) There is a false or erroneous statement in the certificate,

(h) There is a change in the time as stated in the certificate for the dissolution of the partnership or for the return of a contribution,

(i) A time is fixed for the dissolution of the partnership, or the return of a contribution, no time having been specified in the certificate, or

(j) The members desire to make a change in any other statement in the certificate in order that it shall accurately represent the agreement between them.

§ 25. Requirements for Amendment and for Cancellation of Certificate.

(1) The writing to amend a certificate shall

(a) Conform to the requirements of Section 2(1a) as far as necessary to set forth clearly the change in the certificate which it is desired to make, and

(b) Be signed and sworn to by all members, and an amendment substituting a limited partner or adding a limited or general partner shall be signed also by the member to be substituted or added, and when a limited partner is to be substituted, the amendment shall also be signed by the assigning limited partner.

(2) The writing to cancel a certificate shall be signed by all members.

(3) A person desiring the cancellation or amendment of a certificate, if any person designated in paragraphs (1) and (2) as a person who must execute the writing refuses to do so, may petition the [here designate the proper court] to direct a cancellation or amendment thereof.

(4) If the court finds that the petitioner has a right to have the writing executed by a person who refuses to do so, it shall order the [here designate the responsible official in the office designated in Section 2] in the office where the certificate is recorded to record the cancellation or amendment of the certificate; and where the certificate is to be amended, the court shall also cause to be filed for record in said office a certified copy of its decree setting forth the amendment.

(5) A certificate is amended or cancelled when there is filed for record in the office [here designate the office designated in Section 2] where the certificate is recorded.

(a) A writing in accordance with the provisions of paragraph (1), or (2) or

(b) A certified copy of the order of court in accordance with the provisions of paragraph (4).

(6) After the certificate is duly amended in accordance with this section, the amended certificate shall thereafter be for all purposes the certificate provided for by this act.

§ 26. Parties to Actions.
A contributor, unless he is a general partner, is not a proper party to proceedings by or against a partnership, except where the object is to enforce a limited partner's right against or liability to the partnership.

§ 27. Name of Act.
This act may be cited as The Uniform Limited Partnership Act.

§ 28. Rules of Construction.
(1) The rule that statutes in derogation of the common law are to be strictly construed shall have no application to this act.

(2) This act shall be so interpreted and construed as to effect its general purpose to make uniform the law of those states which enact it.

(3) This act shall not be so construed as to impair the obligations of any contract existing when the act goes into effect, nor to affect any action or proceedings begun or right accrued before this act takes effect.

§ 29. Rules for Cases Not Provided For in This Act.
In any case not provided for in this act the rules of law and equity, including the law merchant, shall govern.

§ 30. Provisions for Existing Limited Partnerships.
(1) A limited partnership formed under any statute of this state prior to the adoption of this act, may become a limited partnership under this act by complying with the provisions of Section 2; provided the certificate set forth

(a) The amount of the original contribution of each limited partner, and the time when the contribution was made, and

(b) That the property of the partnership exceeds the amount sufficient to discharge its liabilities to persons not claiming as general or limited partners by an amount greater than the sum of the contributions of its limited partners.

(2) A limited partnership formed under any statute of this state prior to the adoption of this act, until or unless it becomes a limited partnership under this act, shall continue to be governed by the provisions of [here insert proper reference to the existing limited partnership act or acts], except that such partnership shall not be renewed unless so provided in the original agreement.

§ 31. Act (Acts) Repealed.
Except as affecting existing limited partnerships to the extent set forth in Section 30, the act (acts) of [here designate the existing limited partnership act or acts] is (are) hereby repealed.

Appendix F

REVISED UNIFORM LIMITED PARTNERSHIP ACT (1976)*

Article 1. General Provisions

§ 101. Definitions. As used in this Act, unless the context otherwise requires:

(1) "Certificate of limited partnership" means the certificate referred to in Section 201, and the certificate as amended.

(2) "Contribution" means any cash, property, services rendered, or a promissory note or other binding obligation to contribute cash or property or to perform services, which a partner contributes to a limited partnership in his capacity as a partner.

(3) "Event of withdrawal of a general partner" means an event that causes a person to cease to be a general partner as provided in Section 402.

(4) "Foreign limited partnership" means a partnership formed under the laws of any State other than this State and having as partners one or more general partners and one or more limited partners.

(5) "General partner" means a person who has been admitted to a limited partnership as a general partner in accordance with the partnership agreement and named in the certificate of limited partnership as a general partner.

(6) "Limited partner" means a person who has been admitted to a limited partnership as a limited partner in accordance with the partnership agreement and named in the certificate of limited partnership as a limited partner.

(7) "Limited partnership" and "domestic limited partnership" mean a partnership formed by 2 or more persons under the laws of this State and having one or more general partners and one or more limited partners.

(8) "Partner" means a limited or general partner.

(9) "Partnership agreement" means any valid agreement, written or oral, of the partners as to the affairs of a limited partnership and the conduct of its business.

(10) "Partnership interest" means a partner's share of the profits and losses of a limited partnership and the right to receive distributions of partnership assets.

(11) "Person" means a natural person, partnership, limited partnership (domestic or foreign), trust, estate, association, or corporation.

(12) "State" means a state, territory, or possession of the United States, the District of Columbia, or the Commonwealth of Puerto Rico.

§ 102. Name. The name of each limited partnership as set forth in its certificate of limited partnership:

(1) shall contain without abbreviation the words "limited partnership";

(2) may not contain the name of a limited partner unless (i) it is also the name of a general partner or the corporate name of a corporate general partner, or (ii) the business of the limited partnership had been carried on under that name before the admission of that limited partner;

(3) may not contain any word or phrase indicating or implying that it is organized other than for a purpose stated in its certificate of limited partnership;

(4) may not be the same as, or deceptively similar to, the name of any corporation or limited partner-

* The text of this act was obtained from the National Conference of Commissioners on Uniform State Laws, and is reprinted with the Commission's consent.

ship organized under the laws of this State or licensed or registered as a foreign corporation or limited partnership in this State; and

(5) may not contain the following words [here insert prohibited words].

§ 103. Reservation of Name.

(a) The exclusive right to the use of a name may be reserved by:

(1) any person intending to organize a limited partnership under this Act and to adopt that name;

(2) any domestic limited partnership or any foreign limited partnership registered in this State which, in either case, intends to adopt that name;

(3) any foreign limited partnership intending to register in this State and adopt that name; and

(4) any person intending to organize a foreign limited partnership and intending to have it register in this State and adopt that name.

(b) The reservation shall be made by filing with the Secretary of State an application, executed by the applicant, to reserve a specified name. If the Secretary of State finds that the name is available for use by a domestic or foreign limited partnership, he shall reserve the name for the exclusive use of the applicant for a period of 120 days. Once having so reserved a name, the same applicant may not again reserve the same name until more than 60 days after the expiration of the last 120-day period for which that applicant reserved that name. The right to the exclusive use of a reserved name may be transferred to any other person by filing in the office of the Secretary of State a notice of the transfer, executed by the applicant for whom the name was reserved and specifying the name and address of the transferee.

§ 104. Specified Office and Agent.   Each limited partnership shall continuously maintain in this State:

(1) an office, which may but need not be a place of its business in this State, at which shall be kept the records required by Section 105 to be maintained; and

(2) an agent for service of process on the limited partnership, which agent must be an individual resident of this State, a domestic corporation, or a foreign corporation authorized to do business in this State.

§ 105. Records to Be Kept   Each limited partnership shall keep at the office referred to in Section 104(1) the following: (1) a current list of the full name and last known business address of each partner set forth in alphabetical order, (2) a copy of the certificate of limited partnership and all certificates of amendment thereto, together with executed copies of any powers of attorney pursuant to which any certificate has been executed, (3) copies of the limited partnership's federal, state, and local income tax returns and reports, if any, for the 3 most recent years, and (4) copies of any then effective written partnership agreements and of any financial statements of the limited partnership for the 3 most recent years. Those records are subject to inspection and copying at the reasonable request, and at the expense, of any partner during ordinary business hours.

§ 106. Nature of Business.   A limited partnership may carry on any business that a partnership without limited partners may carry on except [here designate prohibited activities].

§ 107. Business Transactions of Partner With the Partnership.   Except as provided in the partnership agreement, a partner may lend money to and transact other business with the limited partnership and, subject to other applicable law, has the same rights and obligations with respect thereto as a person who is not a partner.

Article 2. Formation; Certificate of Limited Partnership.

§ 201. Certificate of Limited Partnership.

(a) In order to form a limited partnership two or more persons must execute a certificate of limited partnership. The certificate shall be filed in the office of the Secretary of State and set forth:

(1) the name of the limited partnership;

(2) the general character of its business;

(3) the address of the office and the name and address of the agent for service of process required to be maintained by Section 104;

(4) the name and the business address of each partner (specifying separately the general partners and limited partners);

(5) the amount of cash and a description and statement of the agreed value of the other property or services contributed by each partner and which each partner has agreed to contribute in the future;

(6) the times at which or events on the happening of which any additional contributions agreed to be made by each partner are to be made;

(7) any power of a limited partner to grant the right to become a limited partner to an assignee of any part of his partnership interest, and the terms and conditions of the power;

(8) if agreed upon, the time at which or the events on the happening of which a partner may terminate his membership in the limited partnership and the amount of, or the method of determining, the distribution to which he may be entitled respecting his partnership interest, and the terms and conditions of the termination and distribution;

(9) any right of a partner to receive distributions of property, including cash from the limited partnership;

(10) any right of a partner to receive, or of a general partner to make, distributions to a partner which include a return of all or any part of the partner's contribution;

(11) any time at which or events upon the happening of which the limited partnership is to be dissolved and its affairs wound up;

(12) any right of the remaining general partners to continue the business on the happening of an event of withdrawal of a general partner; and

(13) any other matters the partners determine to include therein.

(b) A limited partnership is formed at the time of the filing of the certificate of limited partnership in the office of the Secretary of State or at any later time specified in the certificate of limited partnership if, in either case, there has been substantial compliance with the requirements of this section.

§ 202. Amendment to Certificate.

(a) A certificate of limited partnership is amended by filing a certificate of amendment thereto in the office of the Secretary of State. The certificate shall set forth:

(1) the name of the limited partnership;

(2) the date of filing of the certificate; and

(3) the amendment to the certificate.

(b) Within 30 days after the happening of any of the following events an amendment to a certificate of limited partnership reflecting the occurrence of the event or events shall be filed:

(1) a change in the amount or character of the contribution of any partner, or in any partner's obligation to make a contribution;

(2) the admission of a new partner;

(3) the withdrawal of a partner; or

(4) the continuation of the business under Section 801 after an event of withdrawal of a general partner.

(c) A general partner who becomes aware that any statement in a certificate of limited partnership was false when made or that any arrangements or other facts described have changed, making the certificate inaccurate in any respect, shall promptly amend the certificate, but an amendment to show a change of address of a limited partner need be filed only once every 12 months.

(d) A certificate of limited partnership may be amended at any time for any other proper purpose the general partners may determine.

(e) No person has any liability because an amendment to a certificate of limited partnership has not been filed to reflect the occurrence of any event referred to in subsection (b) of this Section if the amendment is filed within the 30-day period specified in subsection (b).

§ 203. Cancellation of Certificate.

A certificate of limited partnership shall be cancelled upon the dissolution and the commencement of winding up of the partnership or at any other time there are no limited partners. A certificate of cancellation shall be filed in the office of the Secretary of State and set forth:

(1) the name of the limited partnership;

(2) the date of filing of its certificate of limited partnership;

(3) the reason for filing the certificate of cancellation;

(4) the effective date (which shall be a date certain) of cancellation if it is not to be effective upon the filing of the certificate; and

(5) any other information the general partners filing the certificate determine.

§ 204. Execution of Certificates.

(a) Each certificate required by this Article to be filed in the office of the Secretary of State shall be executed in the following manner:

(1) an original certificate of limited partnership must be signed by all partners named therein;

(2) a certificate of amendment must be signed by at least one general partner and by each other partner designated in the certificate as a new part-

ner or whose contribution is described as having been increased; and

(3) a certificate of cancellation must be signed by all general partners;

(b) Any person may sign a certificate by an attorney-in-fact, but a power of attorney to sign a certificate relating to the admission, or increased contribution, of a partner must specifically describe the admission or increase.

(c) The execution of a certificate by a general partner constitutes an affirmation under the penalties of perjury that the facts stated therein are true.

§ 205. Amendment or Cancellation by Judicial Act.   If a person required by Section 204 to execute a certificate of amendment or cancellation fails or refuses to do so, any other partner, and any assignee of a partnership interest, who is adversely affected by the failure or refusal, may petition the [here designate the proper court] to direct the amendment or cancellation. If the court finds that the amendment or cancellation is proper and that any person so designated has failed or refused to execute the certificate, it shall order the Secretary of State to record an appropriate certificate of amendment or cancellation.

§ 206. Filing in Office of Secretary of State.

(a) Two signed copies of the certificate of limited partnership and of any certificates of amendment or cancellation (or of any judicial decree of amendment or cancellation) shall be delivered to the Secretary of State. A person who executes a certificate as an agent or fiduciary need not exhibit evidence of his authority as a prerequisite to filing. Unless the Secretary of State finds that any certificate does not conform to law, upon receipt of all filing fees required by law he shall:

(1) endorse on each duplicate original the word "Filed" and the day, month, and year of the filing thereof;

(2) file one duplicate original in his office; and

(3) return the other duplicate original to the person who filed it or his representative.

(b) Upon the filing of a certificate or amendment (or judicial decree of amendment) in the office of the Secretary of State, the certificate of limited partnership shall be amended as set forth herein, and upon the effective date of a certificate of cancellation (or a judicial decree thereof), the certificate of limited partnership is cancelled.

§ 207. Liability for False Statement in Certificate. If any certificate or limited partnership or certificate of amendment or cancellation contains a false statement, one who suffers loss by reliance on the statement may recover damages for the loss from:

(1) any person who executes the certificate, or causes another to execute it on his behalf, and knew, and any general partner who knew or should have known, the statement to be false at the time the certificate was executed; and

(2) any general partner who thereafter knows or should have known that any arrangement or other fact described in the certificate has changed, making the statement inaccurate in any respect within a sufficient time before the statement was relied upon reasonably to have enabled that general partner to cancel or amend the certificate, or to file a petition for its cancellation or amendment under Section 205.

§ 208. Notice.   The fact that a certificate of limited partnership is on file in the office of the Secretary of State is notice that the partnership is a limited partnership and the persons designated therein as limited partners are limited partners, but it is not notice of any other fact.

§ 209. Delivery of Certificates to Limited Partners. Upon the return by the Secretary of State pursuant to Section 206 of a certificate marked "Filed," the general partners shall promptly deliver or mail a copy of the certificate of limited partnership and each certificate to each limited partner unless the partnership agreement provides otherwise.

Article 3. Limited Partners

§ 301. Admission of Additional Limited Partners.

(a) After the filing of a limited partnership's original certificate of limited partnership, a person may be admitted as an additional limited partner:

(1) in the case of a person acquiring a partnership interest directly from the limited partnership, upon the compliance with the partnership agreement or, if the partnership agreement does not so provide, upon the written consent of all partners; and

(2) in the case of an assignee of a partnership interest of a partner who has the power, as provided in Section 704, to grant the assignee the right to become a limited partner, upon the exercise of that power and compliance with any conditions limiting the grant or exercise of the power.

(b) In each case under subsection (a), the person acquiring the partnership interest becomes a limited partner only upon amendment of the certificate of limited partnership reflecting that fact.

§ 302. Voting.   Subject to Section 303, the partnership agreement may grant to all or a specified group of the limited partners the right to vote (on a per capita or other basis) upon any matter.

§ 303. Liability to Third Parties.

(a) Except as provided in subsection (d), a limited partner is not liable for the obligations of a limited partnership unless he is also a general partner or, in addition to the exercise of his rights and powers as a limited partner, he takes part in the control of the business. However, if the limited partner's participation in the control of the business is not substantially the same as the exercise of the powers of a general partner, he is liable only to persons who transact business with the limited partnership with actual knowledge of his participation in control.

(b) A limited partner does not participate in the control of the business within the meaning of subsection (a) solely by doing one or more of the following:

(1) being a contractor for or an agent or employee of the limited partnership or of a general partner;

(2) consulting with and advising a general partner with respect to the business of the limited partnership;

(3) acting as surety for the limited partnership;

(4) approving or disapproving an amendment to the partnership agreement; or

(5) voting on one or more of the following matters:

(i)   the dissolution and winding up of the limited partnership;

(ii) the sale, exchange, lease, mortgage, pledge, or other transfer of all or substantially all of the assets of the limited partnership other than in the ordinary course of its business;

(iii) the incurrence of indebtedness by the limited partnership other than in the ordinary course of its business;

(iv) a change in the nature of the business; or

(v)   the removal of a general partner.

(c) The enumeration in subsection (b) does not mean that the possession or exercise of any other powers by a limited partner constitutes participation by him in the business of the limited partnership.

(d) A limited partner who knowingly permits his name to be used in the name of the limited partnership, except under circumstances permitted by Section 102(2)(i), is liable to creditors who extend credit to the limited partnership without actual knowledge that the limited partner is not a general partner.

§ 304. Person Erroneously Believing Himself Limited Partner.

(a)   Except as provided in subsection (b), a person who makes a contribution to a business enterprise and erroneously but in good faith believes that he has become a limited partner in the enterprise is not a general partner in the enterprise and is not bound by its obligations by reason of making the contribution, receiving distributions from the enterprise, or exercising any rights of a limited partner, if, on ascertaining the mistake, he:

(1) causes an appropriate certificate of limited partnership or a certificate of amendment to be executed and filed; or

(2) withdraws from future equity participation in the enterprise.

(b)   A person who makes a contribution of the kind described in subsection (a) is liable as a general partner to any third party who transacts business with the enterprise (i) before the person withdraws and an appropriate certificate is filed to show withdrawal, or (ii) before an appropriate certificate is filed to show his status as a limited partner and, in the case of an amendment, after expiration of the 30-day period for filing an amendment relating to the person as a limited partner under Section 202, but in either case only if the third party actually believed in good faith that the person was a general partner at the time of the transaction.

§ 305. Information.   Each limited partner has the right to:

(1) inspect and copy any of the partnership records required to be maintained by Section 105; and

(2) obtain from the general partners from time to time upon reasonable demand (i) true and full information regarding the state of the business and financial condition of the limited partnership, (ii) promptly

after becoming available, a copy of the limited partnership's federal, state, and local income tax returns for each year, and (iii) other information regarding the affairs of the limited partnership as is just and reasonable.

Article 4. General Partners

§ 401. Admission of Additional General Partners. After the filing of a limited partnership's original certificate of limited partnership, additional general partners may be admitted only with the specific written consent of each partner.

§ 402. Events of Withdrawal. Except as approved by the specific written consent of all partners at the time, a person ceases to be a general partner of a limited partnership upon the happening of any of the following events:

(1) the general partner withdraws from the limited partnership as provided in Section 602;

(2) the general partner ceases to be a member of the limited partnership as provided in Section 702;

(3) the general partner is removed as a general partner in accordance with the partnership agreement;

(4) unless otherwise provided in the certificate of limited partnership, the general partner; (i) makes an assignment for the benefit of creditors; (ii) files a voluntary petition in bankruptcy; (iii) is adjudicated a bankrupt or insolvent; (iv) files a petition or answer seeking for himself any reorganization, arrangement, composition, readjustment, liquidation, dissolution, or similar relief under any statute, law, or regulation; (v) files an answer or other pleading admitting or failing to contest the material allegations of a petition filed against him in any proceeding of this nature; or (vi) seeks, consents to, or acquiesces in the appointment of a trustee, receiver, or liquidator of the general partner or of all or any substantial part of his properties;

(5) unless otherwise provided in the certificate of limited partnership, [120] days after the commencement of any proceeding against the general partner seeking reorganization, arrangement, composition, readjustment, liquidation, dissolution, or similar relief under any statute, law, or regulation, the proceeding has not been dismissed, or if within [90] days after the appointment without his consent or acquiescence of a trustee, receiver, or liquidator of the general partner or of all or any substantial part

of his properties the appointment is not vacated or stayed, or within [90] days after the expiration of any such

(6) in the case of a general partner who is a natural person,

(i)   his death; or

(ii)   the entry by a court of competent jurisdiction adjudicating him incompetent to manage his person or his estate;

(7) in the case of a general partner who is acting as a general partner by virtue of being a trustee of a trust, the termination of the trust (but not merely the substitution of a new trustee);

(8) in the case of a general partner that is a separate partnership, the dissolution and commencement of winding up of the separate partnership;

(9) in the case of a general partner that is a corporation, the filing of a certificate of dissolution, or its equivalent, for the corporation or the revocation of its charter; or

(10) in the case of an estate, the distribution by the fiduciary of the estate's entire interest in the partnership.

§ 403. General Powers and Liabilities. Except as provided in this Act or in the partnership agreement, a general partner of a limited partnership has the rights and powers and is subject to the restrictions and liabilities of a partner in a partnership without limited partners.

§ 404. Contributions by a General Partner. A general partner of a limited partnership may make contributions to the partnership and share in the profits and losses of, and in distributions from, the limited partnership as a general partner. A general partner also may make contributions to and share in profits, losses, and distributions as a limited partner. A person who is both a general partner and a limited partner has the rights and powers, and is subject to the restrictions and liabilities, of a general partner and, except as provided in the partnership agreement, also has the powers, and is subject to the restrictions, of a limited partner to the extent of his participation in the partnership as a limited partner.

§ 405. Voting. The partnership agreement may grant to all or certain identified general partners the right to vote (on a per capita or any other basis), separately or with all or any class of the limited partners, on any matter.

Article 5. Finance

§ 501. Form of Contribution. The contribution of a partner may be in cash, property, or services rendered, or a promissory note or other obligation to contribute cash or property or to perform services.

§ 502. Liability for Contributions.

(a) Except as provided in the certificate of limited partnership, a partner is obligated to the limited partnership to perform any promise to contribute cash or property or to perform services, even if he is unable to perform because of death, disability or any other reason. If a partner does not make the required contribution of property or services, he is obligated at the option of the limited partnership to contribute cash equal to that portion of the value (as stated in the certificate of limited partnership) of the stated contribution that has not been made.

(b) Unless otherwise provided in the partnership agreement, the obligation of a partner to make a contribution or return money or other property paid or distributed in violation of this Act may be compromised only by consent of all the partners. Notwithstanding the compromise, a creditor of a limited partnership who extends credit, or whose claim arises, after the filing of the certificate of limited partnership or an amendment thereto which, in either case, reflects the obligation, and before the amendment or cancellation thereof to reflect the compromise, may enforce the original obligation.

§ 503. Sharing of Profits and Losses. The profits and losses of a limited partnership shall be allocated among the partners, and among classes of partners, in the manner provided in the partnership agreement. If the partnership agreement does not so provide, profits and losses shall be allocated on the basis of the value (as stated in the certificate of limited partnership) of the contributions made by each partner to the extent they have been received by the partnership and have not been returned.

§ 504. Sharing of Distributions. Distributions of cash or other assets of a limited partnership shall be allocated among the partners, and among classes of partners, in the manner provided in the partnership agreement. If the partnership agreement does not so provide, distributions shall be made on the basis of the value (as stated in the certificate of limited partnership) of the contributions made by each partner to the extent they have been received by the partnership and have not been returned.

Article 6. Distributions and Withdrawal

§ 601. Interim Distributions. Except as provided in this Article, a partner is entitled to receive distributions from a limited partnership before his withdrawal from the limited partnership and before the dissolution and winding up thereof:

(1) to the extent and at the times or upon the happening of the events specified in the partnership agreement; and

(2) if any distribution constitutes a return of any part of his contribution under Section 609(c), to the extent and at the times or upon the happening of the events specified in the certificate of limited partnership.

§ 602. Withdrawal of General Partner. A general partner may withdraw from a limited partnership at any time by giving written notice to the other partners, but if the withdrawal violates the partnership agreement, the limited partnership may recover from the withdrawing general partner damages for breach of the partnership agreement and offset the damages against the amount otherwise distributable to him.

§ 603. Withdrawal of Limited Partner. A limited partner may withdraw from a limited partnership at the time or upon the happening of events specified in the certificate of limited partnership and in accordance with the partnership agreement. If the certificate does not specify the time or the events upon the happening of which a limited partner may withdraw or a definite time for the dissolution and winding up of the limited partnership, a limited partner may withdraw upon not less than 6 months' prior written notice to each general partner at his address on the books of the limited partnership at its office in this State.

§ 604. Distribution Upon Withdrawal. Except as provided in this Article, upon withdrawal any withdrawing partner is entitled to receive any distribution to which he is entitled under the partnership agreement and, if not otherwise provided in the agreement, he is entitled to receive, within a reasonable time after withdrawal, the fair value of his interest in the limited partnership as of the date of withdrawal based upon his right to share in distributions from the limited partnership.

§ 605. Distribution in Kind. Except as provided in the certificate of limited partnership, a partner, regardless of the nature of his contribution, has no right to demand and receive any distribution from a limited partnership in any form other than cash. Except as provided in the partnership agreement, a partner may not be compelled to accept a distribution of any asset in kind from a limited partnership to the extent that the percentage of the asset distributed to him exceeds a percentage of that asset which is equal to the percentage in which he shares in distributions from the limited partnership.

§ 606. Right to Distribution. At the time a partner becomes entitled to receive a distribution, he has the status of, and is entitled to all remedies available to, a creditor of the limited partnership with respect to the distribution.

§ 607. Limitations on Distribution. A partner may not receive a distribution from a limited partnership to the extent that, after giving effect to the distribution, all liabilities of the limited partnership, other than liabilities to partners on account of their partnership interests, exceed the fair value of the partnership assets.

§ 608. Liability Upon Return of Contribution.
  (a) If a partner has received the return of any part of his contribution without violation of the partnership agreement or this Act, he is liable to the limited partnership for a period of one year thereafter for the amount of the returned contribution, but only to the extent necessary to discharge the limited partnership's liabilities to creditors who extended credit to the limited partnership during the period the contribution was held by the partnership.
  (b) If a partner has received the return of any part of his contribution in violation of the partnership agreement or this Act, he is liable to the limited partnership for a period of 6 years thereafter for the amount of the contribution wrongfully returned.

  (c) A partner receives a return of his contribution to the extent that a distribution to him reduces his share of the fair value of the net assets of the limited partnership below the value (as set forth in the certificate of limited partnership) of his contribution which has not been distributed to him.

Article 7. Assignment of Partnership Interests

§ 701. Nature of Partnership Interest. A partnership interest is personal property.

§ 702. Assignment of Partnership Interest. Except as provided in the partnership agreement, a partnership interest is assignable in whole or in part. An assignment of a partnership interest does not dissolve a limited partnership or entitle the assignee to become or to exercise any rights of a partner. An assignment entitles the assignee to receive, to the extent assigned, only the distribution to which the assignor would be entitled. Except as provided in the partnership agreement, a partner ceases to be a partner upon assignment of all his partnership interest.

§ 703. Rights of Creditor. On application to a court of competent jurisdiction by any judgment creditor of a partner, the court may charge the partnership interest of the partner with payment of the unsatisfied amount of the judgment with interest. To the extent so charged, the judgment creditor has only the rights of an assignee of the partnership interest. This Act does not deprive any partner of the benefit of any exemption laws applicable to his partnership interest.

§ 704. Right of Assignee to Become Limited Partner.
  (a) An assignee of a partnership interest, including an assignee of a general partner, may become a limited partner if and to the extent that (1) the assignor gives the assignee that right in accordance with authority described in the certificate of limited partnership, or (2) all other partners consent.
  (b) An assignee who has become a limited partner has, to the extent assigned, the rights and powers, and is subject to the restrictions and liabilities, of a limited partner under the partnership agreement and this Act. An assignee who becomes a limited partner also is liable for the obligations of

his assignor to make and return contributions as provided in Article 6. However, the assignee is not obligated for liabilities unknown to the assignee at the time he became a limited partner and which could not be ascertained from the certificate of limited partnership.

(c) If an assignee of a partnership interest becomes a limited partner, the assignor is not released from his liability to the limited partnership under Sections 207 and 502.

§ 705. Power of Estate of Deceased or Incompetent Partner. If a partner who is an individual dies or a court of competent jurisdiction adjudges him to be incompetent to manage his person or his property, the partner's executor, administrator, guardian, conservator, or other legal representative may exercise all of the partner's rights for the purpose of settling his estate or administering his property, including any power the partner had to give an assignee the right to become a limited partner. If a partner is a corporation, trust, or other entity and is dissolved or terminated, the powers of that partner may be exercised by its legal representative or successor.

Article 8. Dissolution

§ 801. Nonjudicial Dissolution. A limited partnership is dissolved and its affairs shall be wound up upon the happening of the first to occur of the following:

(1) at the time or upon the happening of events specified in the certificate of limited partnership;

(2) written consent of all partners;

(3) an event of withdrawal of a general partner unless at the time there is at least one other general partner and the certificate of limited partnership permits the business of the limited partnership to be carried on by the remaining general partner and that partner does so, but the limited partnership is not dissolved and is not required to be wound up by reason of any event of withdrawal if, within 90 days after the withdrawal, all partners agree in writing to continue the business of the limited partnership and to the appointment of one or more additional general partners if necessary or desired; or

(4) entry of a decree of judicial dissolution under Section 802.

§ 802. Judicial Dissolution. On application by or for a partner the [here designate the proper court] court may decree dissolution of a limited partner-

ship whenever it is not reasonably practicable to carry on the business in conformity with the partnership agreement.

§ 803. Winding Up. Except as provided in the partnership agreement, the general partners who have not wrongfully dissolved a limited partnership or, if none, the limited partners, may wind up the limited partnership's affairs: but the [here designate the proper court] court may wind up the limited partnership's affairs upon application of any partner, his legal representative, or assignee.

§ 804. Distribution of Assets. Upon the winding up of a limited partnership, the assets shall be distributed as follows:

(1) to creditors, including partners who are creditors, to the extent otherwise permitted by law, in satisfaction of liabilities of the limited partnership other than liabilities for distributions to partners under Section 601 or 604;

(2) except as provided in the partnership agreement, to partners and former partners in satisfaction of liabilities for distributions under Section 601 or 604; and

(3) except as provided in the partnership agreement, to partners *first* for the return of their contributions and *secondly* respecting their partnership interests, in the proportions in which the partners share in distributions.

Article 9. Foreign Limited Partnerships

§ 901. Law Governing. Subject to the Constitution of this State, (1) the laws of the state under which a foreign limited partnership is organized govern its organization and internal affairs and the liability of its limited partners, and (2) a foreign limited partnership may not be denied registration by reason of any difference between those laws and the laws of this State.

§ 902. Registration. Before transacting business in this State, a foreign limited partnership shall register with the Secretary of State. In order to register, a foreign limited partnership shall submit to the Secretary of State, in duplicate, an application for registration as a foreign limited partnership, signed and sworn to by a general partner and setting forth:

(1) the name of the foreign limited partnership and, if different, the name under which it proposes to register and transact business in this State;

(2) the state and date of its formation;

(3) the general character of the business it proposes to transact in this State;

(4) the name and address of any agent for service of process on the foreign limited partnership whom the foreign limited partnership elects to appoint; the agent must be an individual resident of this State, a domestic corporation, or a foreign corporation having a place of business in, and authorized to do business in this State;

(5) a statement that the Secretary of State is appointed the agent of the foreign limited partnership for service of process if no agent has been appointed under paragraph (4) or, if appointed, the agent's authority has been revoked or if the agent cannot be found or served with the exercise of reasonable diligence;

(6) the address of the office required to be maintained in the State of its organization by the laws of that State or, if not so required, of the principal office of the foreign limited partnership; and

(7) if the certificate or limited partnership filed in the foreign limited partnership's state of organization is not required to include the names and business addresses of the partners, a list of the names and addresses.

§ 903. Issuance of Registration.

(a) If the Secretary of State finds that an application for registration conforms to law and all requisite fees have been paid, he shall:

(1) endorse on the application the word "Filed," and the month, day, and year of the filing thereof;

(2) file in his office a duplicate original of the application; and

(3) issue a certificate of registration to transact business in this State.

(b) The certificate of registration, together with a duplicate original of the application, shall be returned to the person who filed the application or his representative.

§ 904. Name.

A foreign limited partnership may register with the Secretary of State under any name (whether or not it is the name under which it is registered in its state of organization) that includes without abbreviation the words "limited partnership" and that could be registered by a domestic limited partnership.

§ 905. Changes and Amendments.

If any statement in the application for registration of a foreign limited partnership was false when made or any

arrangements or other facts described have changed, making the application inaccurate in any respect, the foreign limited partnership shall promptly file in the office of the Secretary of State a certificate, signed and sworn to by a general partner, correcting such statement.

§ 906. Cancellation or Registration.

A foreign limited partnership may cancel its registration by filing with the Secretary of State a certificate of cancellation signed and sworn to by a general partner. A cancellation does not terminate the authority of the Secretary of State to accept service of process on the foreign limited partnership with respect to [claims for relief] [causes of action] arising out of the transactions of business in this State.

§ 907. Transaction of Business Without Registration.

(a) A foreign limited partnership transacting business in this State may not maintain any action, suit, or proceeding in any court of this State until it has registered in this State.

(b) The failure of a foreign limited partnership to register in this State does not impair the validity of any contract or act of the foreign limited partnership or prevent the foreign limited partnership from defending any action, suit, or proceeding in any court of this State.

(c) A limited partner of a foreign limited partnership is not liable as a general partner of the foreign limited partnership solely by reason of having transacted business in this State without registration.

(d) A foreign limited partnership, by transacting business in this State without registration, appoints the Secretary of State as its agent for service of process with respect to [claims for relief] [causes of action] arising out of the transaction of business in this State.

§ 908. Action by Appropriate Official.

The [appropriate official] may bring an action to restrain a foreign limited partnership from transacting business in this State in violation of this Article.

Article 10. Derivative Actions

§ 1001. Right of Action.

A limited partner may bring an action in the right of a limited partnership to recover a judgment in its favor if general partners with authority to do so have refused to bring the action or if an effort to cause those general partners to bring the action is not likely to succeed.

§ 1002. Proper Plaintiff.   In a derivative action, the plaintiff must be a partner at the time of bringing the action and (1) at the time of the transaction of which he complains or (2) his status as a partner had devolved upon him by operation of law or pursuant to the terms of the partnership agreement from a person who was a partner at the time of the transaction.

§ 1003. Pleading.   In a derivative action, the complaint shall set forth with particularity the effort of the plaintiff to secure initation of the action by a general partner or the reasons for not making the effort.

§ 1004. Expenses.   If a derivative action is successful, in whole or in part, or if anything is received by the plaintiff as a result of a judgment, compromise, or settlement of an action or claim, the court may award the plaintiff reasonable expenses, including reasonable attorney's fees, and shall direct him to remit to the limited partnership the remainder of those proceeds received by him.

Article 11. Miscellaneous

§ 1101. Construction and Application.   This Act shall be so applied and construed to effectuate its general purpose to make uniform the law with respect to the subject of this Act among states enacting it.

§ 1102. Short Title.   This Act may be cited as the Uniform Limited Partnership Act.

§ 1103. Severability.   If any provision of this Act or its application to any person or circumstance is held invalid, the invalidity does not affect other provisions or applications of the Act which can be given effect without the invalid provision or application, and to this end the provisions of this Act are serverable.

§ 1104. Effective Date, Extended Effective Date and Repeal.   Except as set forth below, the effective date of this Act is _____ and the following Acts [list prior limited partnership acts] are hereby repealed:

(1) The existing provisions for execution and filing of certificates of limited partnerships and amendments thereunder and cancellations thereof continue in effect until [specify time required to create central filing system], the extended effective date, and Sections 102, 103, 104, 105, 201, 202, 203, 204 and 206 are not effective until the extended effective date.

(2) Section 402, specifying the conditions under which a general partner ceases to be a member of a limited partnership, is not effective until the extended effective date, and the applicable provisions of existing law continue to govern until the extended effective date.

(3) Sections 501, 502 and 608 apply only to contributions and distributions made after the effective date of this Act.

(4) Section 704 applies only to assignments made after the effective date of this Act.

(5) Article 9, dealing with registration of foreign limited partnerships, is not effective until the extended effective date.

§ 1105. Rules for Cases Not Provided For in This Act.   In any case not provided for in this Act the provisions of the Uniform Partnership Act govern.

Glossary

Abstract of Title A summary of the condition of the title to property based on an examination of public records.

Abuse of Process A tort, the basis of which is a person's intentional use of a proper legal procedure for an improper purpose.

Acceleration Clause A clause, usually in a promissory note or installment contract, providing that if the debtor fails to make a payment when it is due or breaches any other covenant in the instrument, the balance of the obligation can be declared immediately due and payable.

Acceptance The offeree's assent to an offer as made by an offeror, as a result of which an agreement is made and the parties become bound as contracting parties.

Accommodation Party One who signs an instrument in any capacity, without receiving value, for the purpose of lending his or her name to another party to the instrument.

Accord and Satisfaction A method of discharging a contract. An accord is an agreement by the parties to the contract to give and accept some performance different than that originally promised; a satisfaction is the actual performance of the substituted obligation.

Account A statement of the debts and credits between parties, based on contracts or other legal duties; not evidenced by an instrument or chattel paper.

Accounting The act or system of recording, auditing, and balancing a business' financial transactions and verifying and reporting the results; a legal proceeding to settle the accounts of parties to a business transaction under court supervision.

Adhesion Contract A contract drafted unilaterally, then presented on a take-it-or-leave-it basis to a weaker party who has no true opportunity to bargain about its terms.

Adjudication The process of reaching a judgment in a case; also the giving or pronouncement of the judgment, and the judgment itself.

Administrative Law The branch of law dealing with the operation and actions of administrative agencies.

Administrator The person granted authority by the probate court to administer the estate of a deceased person.

Adverse Possession A method of acquiring real property based on an adverse or hostile, continued use of another person's property for a statutorily prescribed period of time.

Affirmative Action A policy, often adopted by or imposed on an employer, that is designed to overcome the effects of past or present discrimination against one or more classes of persons.

Agency A fiduciary relationship that arises when one person (the principal) entrusts to another person (the agent) the management of some business to be transacted in the principal's name or on his account and under his control, and by which the agent assumes to do the business and render an account of it.

Agency by Necessity An agency that arises when an emergency makes it necessary or proper for one person to act as another's agent even though he lacks express authority to do so.

Agent A party to the agency relationship; the person who acts on behalf of and represents the other party (the principal).

A207

Alter Ego Doctrine A doctrine under which a corporate entity is disregarded, the corporation and its primary or sole shareholder being treated as one and the same.

Annual Percentage Rate (APR) Essentially, the cost of consumer credit for one year, expressed as a percentage.

Anticipatory Breach Breach of contract committed before the time for performance of the contract has arrived.

Antitrust A term used to describe the area of the law that is concerned with preserving competition in the marketplace by breaking up trusts or otherwise limiting the power of their members.

Apparent Authority An agent's authority that, although not expressly granted by the principal, the principal either allows the agent to have or holds the agent out to third persons as having.

Appeal Request made by a party to a superior court to correct the error of an inferior court or an administrative agency.

Appraisal An estimate of the real or market value of real estate or other property.

Appraisal Right The right of dissident or minority shareholders who object to a corporate merger or other fundamental change to have their shares appraised and to receive the appraised value in cash.

Appurtenance Anything incidental or belonging to land that is considered part of the real property, such as an improvement or easement.

Arbitration A method of resolving a dispute by which the dispute is brought before a private person (the arbitrator) chosen by both parties to hear the case. An arbitrator's award is enforceable by a court.

Articles of Incorporation The publicly filed document of a corporation giving it power to transact business.

Assignment A transfer of a right or interest.

Assignment for Creditors A debtor relief device by which a debtor transfers property to a third person who liquidates the property and pays off creditors to the extent possible; also known as an assignment for the benefit of creditors.

Assumption of Mortgage A buyer's acceptance of responsibility for an outstanding indebtedness secured by real property, in connection with his taking title to that property.

Assumption of Risk A defense to a negligence action. Its basis is that the plaintiff voluntarily encountered a known danger and, by his conduct, expressly or impliedly consented to accept the risk.

Attachment A prejudgment remedy by which a person suing on a debt has property of the debtor seized so that it may later be used to satisfy a judgment.

Attachment of Security Interest Under UCC Article 9, the process by which a security interest is created.

Attractive Nuisance Doctrine The doctrine that a landowner who creates or maintains a condition that attracts children but is dangerous to them owes a duty to protect children coming on the land, even if they are trespassers.

At-Will Contract A contract, frequently of employment, having no specified term and terminable at the will of either party at any time on notice to the other.

Audit In the accounting sense, an examination of a business' financial records and preparation of a report on its financial condition; in tax law, the process by which a taxpayer's tax return is examined by the taxing authority and the taxpayer is required to substantiate disputed items.

Bailee's Lien The lien that a bailee has on bailed property for the reasonable value of his services with respect to the property.

Bailment The relationship arising when an owner of personal property temporarily transfers possession of the property to another, usually for a particular purpose. A bailment can be for the sole benefit of either party or for the mutual benefit of both parties.

Bankruptcy A federal statutory scheme by which a financially troubled debtor places his property under a court's control, after which either the property is liquidated and creditors are paid to the extent possible, or a plan for the debtor's financial rehabilitation is prepared and executed.

Beneficiary A person entitled to receive a benefit under a contract, trust, or will; in insurance law, the person entitled to the insurance proceeds on occurrence of the event insured against.

Bequest A gift by will of personal property.

Bill of Lading A document of title or receipt issued by a land or marine shipper evidencing the receipt of goods for shipment.

Binder A temporary contract of insurance intended to operate for a short time and couched in brief and general terms to be supplanted later by an insurance policy in which all of the contractual terms are set forth in detail.

Blank Indorsement An indorsement that specifies no particular indorsee.

Blue-Sky Laws State statutes regulating the sale of securities.

Board of Directors The group of persons elected by shareholders of a corporation who are entrusted with the responsibility for managing the corporation.

Bona Fide Purchaser One who gives a valuable consideration for property and is unaware of any defect in the seller's title.

Bond A corporate promise to pay a fixed amount of indebtedness secured by the assets of the corporation; any undertaking in writing binding one party to pay a fixed sum on the happening of a specified event.

Bonus Stock Stock issued by a corporation without valid consideration.

Breach of Warranty The breaking of or failure to live up to the terms of an express or implied warranty.

Bribery A crime that consists of making a gift to a public official for the purpose of influencing the official in his official actions; also, the official's acceptance of such a gift.

Brief A concise statement of legal issues and authorities prepared by a lawyer, usually for submission to an appellate court.

Bulk Transfer Under UCC Article 6, the transfer, in a single transaction that is not in the ordinary course of the transferor's business, of a major part of the goods of a transferor whose principal business is the sale of merchandise from stock.

Business Judgment Rule A judicial doctrine of noninterference in management of corporate affairs on questions of policy, contracts, dividends, executive compensation, and other internal corporate matters.

Bylaws A document consisting of the internal regulations of a corporation and that, unlike the articles of incorporation, need not be filed with the state.

Capital The net worth of a corporation. It consists of the sums subscribed and paid in by shareholders, together with all gains or profits arising from corporate operations, minus any losses that have been sustained.

Capital Stock The declared money value of the outstanding stock of a corporation. It is the amount of money, property, or other assets authorized by the articles of incorporation and contributed, or agreed to be contributed, by the shareholders, and it forms the financial basis of corporate operations. As commonly used, the term refers to a corporation's issued and outstanding stock.

Carmack Amendment A portion of the Interstate Commerce Act that codifies the common-law rule that a common carrier, although not an absolute insurer of goods transported, is liable for damage or loss to such goods unless the carrier can show that damage was caused by an act of God, the public enemy, an act of the shipper, an act by public authorities, or the inherent nature of the goods themselves.

Case Law A rule of law expressed in a judicial decision, rather than in a constitution, statute, ordinance, or regulation.

Cease and Desist Order An order issued by an administrative agency requiring that practices specified in the order be stopped.

Chain of Title The chronological list of recorded instruments affecting title to land, beginning with the earliest evidence of ownership and concluding with the latest.

Chapter 11 Plan A debtor rehabilitation plan prepared in a proceeding under Chapter 11 of the Bankruptcy Code.

Chapter 13 Plan A debtor rehabilitation plan prepared in a proceeding under Chapter 13 of the Bankruptcy Code.

Charge-Back Under UCC Article 4, the process by which a collecting bank reverses a provisional credit given earlier on a deposited check that has been dishonored.

Charter As commonly used, a corporation's articles of incorporation, although the term also includes the statutes and other laws giving the corporation power to act.

Chattel Mortgage A mortgage on personal property.

Chattels Personal property that is visible, tangible, and capable of being moved.

Check Under the UCC, a draft drawn on a bank and payable on demand.

Civil Action An action brought to enforce a private right, as distinguished from a criminal action.

Civil Liability Liability to be sued in a civil action, as distinguished from criminal liability.

Civil Rights Broadly, all rights the law will enforce; in the more restricted sense, rights created by state and federal constitutional and statutory provisions designed to prevent discrimination by reason of a person's age, race, color, sex, religion, or national origin.

Class Action A lawsuit brought by one or more persons on behalf of a larger group of persons, all having a common interest in the subject of the lawsuit.

Clifford Trust An irrevocable living trust having a term of more than 10 years. It is primarily a tax-planning tool.

Close Corporation A corporation owned by a small number of shareholders and the shares of which are not offered for sale to the public.

Close-End Credit Consumer credit extended in a single transaction rather than on a continuing basis.

Closing The completion of a real estate transaction as evidenced by the escrow agent's delivery of a deed to the buyer and his contemporaneous transfer to the seller of the balance of the purchase price remaining after payment of all charges assessed against the seller.

Cloud on Title A claim, or some semblance of title, that appears to be in legal form but is in fact invalid.

Code of Federal Regulations (CFR) An official federal publication setting forth the rules and regulations of the federal administrative agencies.

Codicil A document executed with the same formalities as a will and used to change the terms of a will.

Collateral Under UCC Article 9, the property in which a security interest exists; in a broader sense, any property used as security for an extension of credit.

Collecting Bank Under UCC Article 4, any bank in the collection chain other than the payor bank.

Collective Bargaining Agreement An agreement reached by bargaining as to wages and working conditions, entered into between a union and an employer.

Commerce Clause The provision of the United States Constitution (Art. I, § 8, cl. 3) that grants to Congress the power to regulate commerce with foreign nations and among the states.

Commercial Block Policy A comprehensive insurance policy that insures against several basic, but different, types of risk with respect to commercial property.

Commercial Paper Various types of paper that represent cash value in commercial transactions. Commercial paper includes orders to pay money (drafts and checks) and promises to pay money (notes and certificates of deposit), and it can be negotiable or nonnegotiable.

Common Carrier A bailee who engages in the business of transporting persons or property from place to place for compensation.

Common Law Legal principles, rules, and usages based on court decisions rather than on statutes or a constitution; in a broader sense, the general Anglo-American system of legal concepts forming the basis of the law of most states.

Common Stock The most common type of equity security. The issuance of common stock is a basic corporate financing device. The owner of one or more shares has the right to participate in the control of the corporation, in surplus and profits, and in the distribution of corporate assets on dissolution.

Community Property A system of property rights, adopted in eight western states, under which the earnings of a spouse belong to the "community," which is the entity of husband and wife.

Comparative Negligence The apportionment of damages between negligent parties in proportion to their respective fault.

Composition with Creditors A contractual debtor relief arrangement under which creditors agree to accept in full satisfaction of the debts owed to them less than is actually due.

Concealment The failure to disclose a fact that a person knows and, under the circumstances, should communicate to another. In insurance law, the intentional withholding of any fact material to the risk that the insured in honesty and good faith ought to communicate to the insurer.

Condemnation The taking of private property for public use through exercise of the power of eminent domain.

Condition A provision in a contract that makes a party's duty to perform contingent on the occurrence or nonoccurrence of some event. A condition precedent is one that must occur as a prerequisite to a party's duty to perform. A condition subsequent is one that relieves a party of an obligation to perform, while a condition concurrent requires simultaneous performance by the parties.

Conditional Sale A sale on credit according to the terms of which the seller retains title to the goods sold until the entire purchase price is paid.

Conflict of Laws The body of law that reconciles differences between the law of one state or nation and the law of another; used most frequently where the applicable law of the case is not the law of the jurisdiction in which the case is tried.

Consent Decree A court judgment or decree that is based on a stipulation by the parties to a lawsuit, usually criminal in nature, commenced by a government entity. The stipulation sets forth the remedy or relief that the court should order, but without an acknowledgment of guilt by the defendant.

Conservator A person appointed by a court to manage the affairs of an incompetent.

Consideration The promises or performances that the parties to a contract exchange with each other and on which the contract is based.

Consignment A bailment by which goods are delivered to another with the understanding that the recipient will either sell the goods for the owner or return the goods if they are not sold. The person delivering the goods is the consignor, while the person receiving them is the consignee.

Consolidation The formation of a new corporation by the combination of two or more existing corporations.

Constitution Generally, a system of fundamental laws or principles for governing a nation, state, or society. See also *United States Constitution.*

Constructive Eviction A substantial interference with a tenant's possession by a landlord that either renders premises unfit for the purposes for which they were leased or deprives the tenant of the enjoyment of the premises.

Constructive Notice Circumstances deemed by the law to be the equivalent of actual notice.

Consumer In a broad sense, any individual or business buying or leasing goods or services for consumption or use. In the sense used in consumer credit protection legislation, the term refers to an individual who uses goods or services for personal, family, or household purposes, rather than for business purposes.

Consumer Goods or Services Goods or services bought primarily for personal, family, or household purposes.

Consumer Report Under the federal Fair Credit Reporting Act, a report about a consumer's credit standing and related matters, and which is used in determining the consumer's eligibility for credit, insurance, or employment.

Consumer-Reporting Agency Under the federal Fair Credit Reporting Act, a credit agency that prepares consumer reports.

Contract An agreement, based on consideration, to do or refrain from doing a particular lawful thing.

Contributory Negligence A plaintiff's conduct that contributes to his own harm and falls below the required standard of care.

Conversion The intentional and wrongful acquisition, damage, use, or withholding of the property of another. The interest protected is that of possession or control of property.

Convertible Security Any equity or debt security that can be changed into another type of security.

Conveyance In common usage, a deed transferring title to land; in its broadest sense, any transfer of real or personal property or an interest in it.

Copyright A person's basic right in the tangible expression of his creative works against anyone who deprives him of such works by copying or wrongfully reproducing or using them. See also *Statutory Copyright.*

Corporate Opportunity Doctrine A common-law legal doctrine imposing on corporate officers and directors a duty of loyalty to the corporation they serve to refrain from appropriating for personal benefit a business opportunity that properly belongs to the corporation.

Corporation An association of persons, created under a statute as a legal entity, vested with authority to act separately from its members.

Corporation by Estoppel A business organization that, although not having complied with state incorporation law, holds itself out as a corporation and therefore is prevented from denying its corporate status.

Course and Scope of Employment A term that describes any activity of an employee that is a required or authorized part of the employee's job. The question whether a given activity was within the course and scope of employment usually arises in cases involving an employee's right to workers' compensation benefits or an employer's liability under the respondeat superior doctrine.

Covenant A promise, usually that the person making it will do or refrain from doing something.

Covenant Not to Compete A provision in an employment contract by which the employee agrees, within prescribed limits, not to compete with the employer after leaving the employer's business. Also, a similar provision in a contract for the sale of a business, limiting the seller's activities after the sale.

Covenant of Quiet Enjoyment A covenant or promise that the grantee of land or an interest in it shall have legal and peaceful possession.

Covenant Running with the Land A covenant in a deed, the legal effect of which is binding on subsequent purchasers, although they have not contractually assumed any responsibility or obligation for its performance.

Credit Life Insurance Term insurance carried by a debtor in connection with a credit transaction and of which the creditor is the beneficiary.

Crime An offense against society for which the government can seek redress by instituting a criminal prosecution against the accused.

Criminal Law That branch of law concerned with prosecuting and defending persons accused of having committed crimes.

Cumulative Voting The method of voting for corporate directors whereby each shareholder can cast a number of votes equal to the number of his shares multiplied by the number of directors to be elected, with the option of giving all his votes to a single candidate or of distributing them among two or more candidates.

Cure Under the UCC the right of a seller, after tender of nonconforming goods, to make proper tender of conforming goods within the time allowed by the contract.

Customer List A list of names of customers of a particular business or of persons who have demonstrated their preference for a particular product or service. Such a list is usually entitled to protection against use or disclosure as a trade secret.

Damages Money that the law awards as pecuniary compensation for an injury done or other loss sustained as a result of another's wrongful conduct.

Debenture An unsecured corporate promise to pay a fixed amount of money back only by the general credit of the corporation.

Debt A sum of money due by agreement.

Declaratory Judgment A type of equitable legal procedure in which a person can petition a court to resolve a question before he sustains actual injury.

Dedication Donation of land by the owner for public use.

Deductible In insurance law, the initial amount of a loss that must be paid by the insured, the insurer then paying for the balance of the loss, up to the limit specified in the policy.

Deed A written instrument used to pass legal title of real property from one person to another. It is ordinarily recorded to provide public notice of the transaction.

Deed of Trust Essentially, a three-party mortgage. The owner (trustor) conveys property to a trustee to hold for the benefit of the lender (beneficiary) to secure payment of a debt or obligation owned to the beneficiary.

De Facto Corporation A corporation that has not complied with all the mandatory requirements to obtain de jure status. It is an apparent corporation, asserted to be a corporation by its members, and actually acting as such, but lacking legal sanction.

Defamation Injury to a person's reputation by the publication of false statements, usually tending to expose the person to hatred, ridicule, or contempt.

Default The nonperformance of a duty arising under a note, mortgage, deed of trust, security agreement, or contract.

Defendant   The party against whom a civil lawsuit or criminal action is brought.

Deficiency Judgment   A judgment for the portion of a secured debt that remains outstanding after the collateral has been sold and any available proceeds have been applied to the debt.

De Jure Corporation   A corporation that has been regularly created in strict compliance with all the mandatory legal conditions for incorporation.

Delegation of Duties   A transfer of contractual duties to another party called the delegatee.

Demurrer   An allegation in a pleading that the other party to the suit has not alleged facts sufficient to sustain an action; a claim that even if all facts are true, there is no legal basis for a suit.

Depositary Bank   Under UCC Article 4, the bank in which a check or other item is deposited.

Deposition   An oral, out-of-court, pretrial examination of a party or witness under oath, that is recorded by an official court reporter.

Deposit Receipt   A form of contract employed by real estate brokers in initiating the purchase and sale of real estate; so called because it takes the form of a firm offer made by a prospective buyer to the owner for the purchase of his property, accompanied by a money deposit.

Derivative Action   An action initiated on behalf of a corporation by one or more shareholders. The derivative action is one that the corporation itself could bring, but for some reason does not do so.

Descent   Acquisition of ownership of property by inheritance, or other act of law, as distinguished from "purchase."

Discharge of Debtor   Under the Bankruptcy Code, the freeing of a debtor from liability on certain debts, whether paid or not.

Disclosed Principal   In agency law, a principal whose existence and identity are known by a party who is dealing with the agent.

Discovery   Under the Federal Rules of Civil Procedure, the means by which the party acquires information regarding the facts of the case from other parties or witnesses.

Dishonor   Under UCC Article 4, a payor bank's refusal to pay a check or other item.

Dissolution   Any change in the partnership relation that ultimately culminates in its termination; an event that necessarily leads to the termination of a corporation's existence.

Dividend   A division of profits among shareholders set apart by the board of directors from a corporation's net earnings or surplus funds to be paid to the shareholders in money, stock, or other property.

Dominant Tenement   Land obtaining the benefit of an easement appurtenant.

Down Payment   The cash that a buyer must pay initially in making a purchase, the balance of the price being covered by a loan or other credit arrangement.

Draft   A negotiable instrument that is a written direction that a designated party pay a stated amount of money. An example of a draft is a check.

Dual Purpose Doctrine   A doctrine under which a travelling employee's injury is considered to have occurred in the course and scope of employment even though, at the time of the injury, the employee was serving some purpose of his own. The only requirement is that the employee's work have created the need for the trip.

Due Care   Care that a reasonably prudent individual would exercise under the particular circumstances.

Due-on-Sale Clause   A clause in a mortgage or deed of trust providing that if the mortgagor or trustor sells or transfers the property, the balance of the secured obligation can be declared immediately due.

Due Process   Those principles implicit in the concept of ordered liberty and so rooted in the traditions and conscience of the American people as to be considered fundamental. Every person's right to due process of law is guaranteed by the United States Constitution as to both the federal government (Fifth Amendment) and the states (Fourteenth Amendment).

Easement   A limited, nonpossessory right or interest in land of another entitling the holder to some use, privilege, or benefit from the land.

Easement Appurtenant   An easement created for the benefit of a parcel of land.

Easement in Gross   An easement created for the benefit of an individual apart from ownership of land. An example is a public utility easement.

Electronic Funds Transfer (EFT)   A cashless transfer of money made by use of an electronic terminal, a telephone, a computer, or magnetic tape.

Eminent Domain   The governmental power to take private property for public use, limited only by the Fifth Amendment to the United States Constitution, which requires that compensation be given for property so taken.

Encumbrance   A right to or interest in real property that reduces the interest of the property owner. A common example is a mortgage.

Environmental Impact Statement   A report, prepared in compliance with the National Environmental Policy Act, that analyzes the effect that federal legislation and other major federal actions will have on the environment.

Equal Employment Opportunity Commission (EEOC)   A federal administrative agency established by Congress under Title VII of the Civil Rights Act of 1964. Its function is to enforce Title VII, which forbids employment discrimination.

Equitable Mortgage   An instrument that, although technically invalid as a mortgage because it fails to meet some legal requirement, is nonetheless treated as a mortgage by the courts.

Equity of Redemption   The right of a mortgagor to redeem his property after some covenant of the mortgage has been breached, usually by failing to make a payment when due, and the mortgagee has elected to exercise its rights under an acceleration clause.

Equity Security   A security that represents a shareholder's interest in a corporation rather than a creditor's interest.

Escrow   The conditional delivery of a written instrument or deed to a third party who delivers it unconditionally to a grantee or transferee on the happening of a specified condition or event. The third party who holds the instrument for delivery is the escrow holder or escrow agent.

Estate   The degree, quantity, nature, and extent of a person's interest in real property; in a broader sense, all the property a person owns at a given time.

Estate at Sufferance   A type of tenancy by which a person goes into possession of property lawfully, but later occupies it without right or title.

Estate at Will   A tenancy for an indefinite period of time at the pleasure of both the lessor and lessee.

Estate by Entireties   A term referring to the estate held by a husband and wife as co-owners with the right of survivorship (surviving spouse takes entire estate).

Estate Planning   An activity intended to identify and increase a person's estate, minimize loss through taxation, and allow disposition of the estate in the manner desired by the person.

Estoppel   A bar precluding a person from denying or asserting anything, even if true, to the contrary of what has been represented. Its essential elements are the misleading of a party entitled to rely on the acts or statements in question, and that party's consequent change of position to his detriment.

Eviction   A landlord's act that deprives a tenant of possession, expels him from the premises, or deprives him of enjoyment of the premises.

Evidence   The proof admissible in court to sustain factual allegations.

Excess Insurance   Insurance that covers only loss or damage in excess of the coverage provided by one or more other insurance policies.

Exclusive Agency   A term that embraces several different relationships between a principal and an agent. For example, in a sales agency, the principal might be permitted to make direct sales yet be deprived of the right to appoint other agents; or the agent might be the only person with any right to sell; or the agent might have the right to commissions on all sales, whether made through the agent or not.

Ex-Dividend   Without dividend. The term is used to describe corporate stock that is sold or transferred soon after a dividend was declared and does not carry with it the right to receive the dividend.

Execute   To sign a deed or other document; to perform a contract.

Executed Contract   A contract completely performed by both parties.

Execution   A statutory method by which payment of a money judgment can be enforced, the judgment debtor's property being seized and sold, and the sale proceeds applied to the judgment debt; in a broader sense, the act of signing a document or having performed a contract.

Executive Agreement An agreement made by the President of the United States, acting within his exclusive powers as the Chief Executive, with the authorized representative of a foreign government.

Executory Contract A contract that has not yet been performed.

Exemplary Damages Damages awarded to a victim as a civil penalty against the wrongdoer rather than to compensate the victim for his loss; also known as punitive damages.

Exempt Property A debtor's property that is not subject to the claims of his creditors.

Exhaustion of Administrative Remedies With respect to a person's obtaining judicial review of an administrative order, that person's having first used all available administrative appeal procedures without success.

Express Agency An agency created as the result of an express oral or written agreement between a principal and an agent.

Express Warranty In sales law, a warranty that is written or orally stated rather than being implied; in insurance law, an agreement set forth in an insurance policy by which the insured stipulates that certain facts relating to the risk are or will be true or that certain acts relating to the risk have been or will be done.

Factor A person who is in the business of selling goods on consignment; also called a commission merchant.

Fair Use Doctrine The doctrine that permits a person to use a reasonable portion of a copyrighted work, even without the author's permission, when necessary for a legitimate purpose that is not competitive with the copyright owner's market for his work, such as to parody, review, or criticize the copyrighted work.

False Advertising The making of fraudulent misrepresentations about a product, resulting in injury to competitors or customers.

False Arrest The unlawful restraint by one person of the physical liberty of another under an asserted legal authority to enforce processes of law.

False Imprisonment The detention of a person for a given period, the person being aware of the detention, and the detaining person's intent being to obstruct or detain the other person without privilege or the other person's consent.

Federal Register A daily official federal publication of proposed and approved executive, legislative, and administrative regulations and actions.

Federal Trade Commission (FTC) A federal administrative agency empowered to prevent the use of methods or practices declared unlawful by the Federal Trade Commission Act. The FTC is also partly responsible for enforcing federal antitrust laws.

Fee Simple The estate in real property that gives the owner the greatest possible right to and control over the property.

Fellow Servant Doctrine The common-law rule that absolves an employer from liability to one engaged in his employment for injuries incurred solely as the result of the negligence of others who are in the service of the employer and engaged in the same general employment.

Felony A criminal offense punishable by state or federal imprisonment for more than one year.

Fiduciary A person, such as a trustee, who holds a position of trust and confidence in a relationship with one or more other persons.

Finance Charge Essentially, the total cost of credit; a term that must be used in credit transactions governed by the federal Truth in Lending Act.

Financing Statement Under UCC Article 9, the document filed to perfect a security interest.

Firm Offer Under the UCC, an enforceable promise made by a merchant not to revoke an offer for a period of time.

First Mortgage A first lien on property pledged as security, the holder of which has rights superior to the rights of any other mortgagee.

Fixture Personal property that has been attached to real property and become a part of it.

Floating Lien A lien on inventory or other property that is changing or apt to change.

Foreclosure The legal process by which a mortgagor or other debtor is deprived of his interest in property covered by a mortgage or other security arrangement. It usually occurs because of a default in paying the secured debt.

Foreign Corporation A corporation created by or organized under the laws of another state or country.

Forfeiture An action by a state to terminate a corporation's existence because of a violation of law, the failure to observe a provision or condition contained in its articles of incorporation, or the commission of other illegal acts.

Franchise A system of marketing by which the developer of a product or service (the franchisor) grants to another person (the franchisee) an exclusive right to market the product or service under the franchisor's trademark or trade name through a marketing plan in a given area for a specified period of time.

Fraud Deceit, deception, or trickery operating prejudicially on the rights of another and inducing him to part with property or surrender some legal right.

Fraudulent Conveyance A transaction by which an owner transfers property or a property right to another to hinder, delay, or defraud the transferor's creditors.

Freedom of Information Act Federal legislation allowing access to most public records, and setting forth the procedure for obtaining that access.

Freeze Out The process by which the influence of minority shareholders is eliminated by other shareholders through the latter's use of inside information, powers of control, or strategic position in the corporation.

Freight Forwarder A person in the business of arranging for the transportation of one or more consignors' goods.

Fungible Goods Goods of such nature that one unit is identical to and replaceable by another unit. The classic example is grain.

Future Interest A property interest that, although presently in existence, will not come into the possession of or be enjoyed by the holder until some time in the future.

Garnishment A prejudgment remedy by which a person suing on a debt can have withheld from the debtor property that, although owned by or owed to the debtor, is in someone else's possession.

Gift A transfer of real or personal property to another without consideration.

Going Public The process by which a close corporation offers its stock for sale to the public. It requires either compliance with the registration and prospectus provisions of the Securities Act of 1933 or the availability of one of the act's exemptions.

Good Faith Fairness and equity; acting with a sincere belief that the accomplishment intended is neither unlawful nor harmful to another.

Goods Under UCC Article 9, all tangible personal property; in a broader sense, merchandise held for sale.

Good Samaritan Legislation Legislation to the effect that a doctor or nurse who aids a stranger in an emergency will not be held liable for negligence.

Gratuitous Bailment A bailment for which neither the bailee nor the bailor receives compensation.

Gross Negligence The equivalent of a conscious and deliberate disregard of a high probability that someone will be injured; a state of mind between negligence and intention.

Group Insurance Insurance that covers a number of individuals by means of a single or blanket insurance policy.

Guaranty A promise, usually gratuitous to answer for the debt or duty of another party.

Guest Statute Legislation making a driver liable to a guest passenger (one not paying a fare) only for injuries that are the result of the driver's gross negligence.

Heir A person who succeeds to property, under the rules of law, by the death of a relative, usually an ancestor.

Highest and Best Use The use of property that is capable of producing the greatest net investment return to the owner.

Holder Any person in possession of a bill or note payable, issued, or indorsed to him.

Holder in Due Course (HDC) Under the UCC, a person who takes a negotiable instrument, document of title, or investment security (1) for value, (2) in good faith, and (3) without notice that there is any defense against it.

Holding Company A corporation that holds a controlling interest in one or more other corporations.

Holding Over A tenant who remains in possession of leased premises after the termination of a lease without the landlord's consent.

Home-Solicitation Sale A credit sale to a consumer made at other than the creditor's place of business.

Homestead Exemption The statutory exemption of all or part of the value of a person's dwelling from the claims of creditors (other than a creditor holding a security interest in the dwelling).

Implied Agency An agency, the existence of which is proven by inferences from facts and circumstances of the case as, for example, by a prior course of dealing between the parties.

Implied Contract A contract inferred from conduct of the parties rather than expressed in words.

Implied Warranty In sales law, a seller's warranty that is imposed by operation of law rather than being based on express language. Implied warranties cover the quality and condition of goods sold.

Imputed Negligence Negligence that is charged to a person by reason of his relationship with the person who was actually negligent.

Incidental Beneficiary A person to whom the benefits of a contract accrue simply as an incident to performance of the contract.

Incontestability Clause A clause in a life insurance contract fixing a limited time within which the insurer must discover and assert any grounds it may have to justify rescission of the contract.

Incorporators Persons who organize a corporation and who sign its articles of incorporation.

Indemnification In the corporate context, a corporation's payment of an obligation or liability imposed on an officer or director; in a broader sense, any right a person has to be saved by another from the legal consequences of his or someone else's conduct.

Indenture A written agreement between a corporation seeking to borrow money and a trustee who represents a group of lenders. The indenture defines the borrower's obligations, the lenders' rights and remedies, and the trustee's role.

Independent Contractor A person who is hired to perform work or render a service according to his own methods and using his own employees and equipment.

Independent Covenant A portion of a lease, contract, or deed, the performance of which does not depend on performance of any other covenant by the same or other party.

Indorsement A signature written on an instrument that is already negotiable, or on a paper so firmly attached to the instrument as to become a part thereof, to negotiate the instrument.

Infraction A minor offense or violation, such as illegal parking or littering, that is distinguishable from a misdemeanor or felony and is usually punishable by a small fine.

Infringement Wrongful use or copying of a copyrighted work, patent, trademark, or trade name.

Inherently Dangerous A term used to describe an activity that is dangerous no matter how skillfully or carefully it is performed.

Injunction An order by a court that a party do or refrain from doing a certain act.

In Personam Jurisdiction over a person established by the person's presence in the state.

In Re In the matter of; often used in the name of a case where the nature of the case is to establish rights in particular subject matter.

In Rem Jurisdiction over a thing established by the presence of the thing in the state.

Insider A person who has special access to information concerning a corporation because of his financial interests or role in management.

Insolvent Unable to pay debts as they become due; in bankruptcy, having a lesser amount of assets than liabilities.

Inspection Right The power conferred on shareholders to inspect books and records of the corporation in which they own stock.

Insurance An agreement by which one party (the insurer), for a consideration (the premium), promises to pay money to another (the insured or beneficiary) on the occurrence of a specified type of loss caused by one or more specified events.

Insurance Agent A person expressly or impliedly authorized to represent an insurer in dealing with third persons in matters relating to insurance.

Insurance Broker One who acts as a middleman between an insured and insurer, solicits insurance from the public, and is not generally employed by a particular company.

Insured The person in whose favor a contract of insurance operates and who is indemnified, or is to receive a certain sum on the happening of a specified contingency or event.

Intent A person's fixed and determined purpose. Tortious or criminal intent means the intent to affect a legally protected interest in a way not permitted by law.

Intentional Infliction of Mental Distress A tort in which the plaintiff's severe mental suffering results from emotional disturbance, without physical impact, caused by the defendant's highly aggravated or outrageous words or acts with intent to cause the plaintiff's mental suffering.

Interference A tort consisting of a person's violating the right of another to be secure in his business and contractual relationships or in his relationship with another as an employer or employee.

Interlocking Directors Directors holding seats on the boards of two or more corporations.

Interrogatories Written questions propounded by one party in litigation to the other party, which must be answered under oath prior to trial.

Intestate Succession The distribution of a decedent's property to the persons prescribed by state law, rather than as provided in a will.

Inventory Goods held for sale or lease, or to be furnished under service contracts.

Inverse Condemnation Property taken for public use or damaged by governmental action without a formal taking or eminent domain proceeding.

Invitee A person who directly or impliedly is invited by a landowner to enter land for some purpose of interest or advantage to the owner.

Joint Tenancy Title held by two or more natural persons in equal shares, with right of survivorship (surviving joint tenant or tenants take share of deceased joint tenant).

Joint Tortfeasors Two or more persons who unite in committing a tort or whose acts concur in producing an injury to a third person.

Joint Venture The relationship created when two or more persons combine in a joint business enterprise for their mutual benefit with the understanding that they are to share in the profits or losses and each is to have voice in the management.

Judgment A court's final determination of the rights of the parties on matters submitted to the court in an action or proceeding.

Judgment Debt The debt arising from a judgment ordering the payment of money. The person against whom the judgment is issued is the judgment debtor.

Judgment Lien A lien on the property (usually only real property) of a judgment debtor.

Junior Mortgage A mortgage held by a mortgagee whose rights in the property covered are inferior to the rights of one or more other mortgagees.

Jurisdiction The power of a court to adjudicate a case; the geographical territory within which the court has such power.

Key Employee Insurance Insurance obtained and paid for by a business on the life of one or more of the business' key or most important officers or employees.

Labor Law That body of law, comprised of constitutional provisions, statutes, ordinances, administrative regulations, and court decisions, that regulates such labor relations matters as hours of labor, wages, and working conditions.

Landlord The lessor under a lease of real property.

Land Sales Contract A contract used in connection with the sale of real property under which the seller retains legal title until the buyer pays all or a prescribed part of the purchase price.

Last Clear Chance A doctrine under which the plaintiff's negligence does not bar recovery for the defendant's negligence if, by having exercised reasonable care after noticing the plaintiff's peril, the defendant could have avoided injuring the plaintiff.

Latent Defect A hidden defect that cannot be discovered by ordinary observation or inspection.

Lawsuit An action or proceeding in a civil court, as contrasted with a criminal prosecution.

Lease An agreement giving rise to the relationship of lessor and lessee.

Leasehold A lessee's estate or interest in property under a lease.

Legacy A disposition of personal property by will.

Lessee A person who receives possession of and has the right to use real or personal property under a lease.

Lessor The owner of real or personal property who transfers possession of it to a lessee under a lease.

Letter of Credit A promise made by a bank or other person to honor the drafts or other demands for payment made by the person requesting the letter of credit; conditions to payment may be made.

Liability Insurance Insurance protecting the insured against loss due to his killing or injuring another person or damaging or destroying another's property.

Libel Defamatory material published in the form of printing, writing, or pictures.

License A privilege to do something; in real property law, a privilege to go on another's land and do something, such as hunting or fishing, that otherwise would constitute a trespass.

Licensee In property law, a person who is invited or permitted by a landowner to enter the property for his own convenience, pleasure, or benefit, or for personal reasons not connected with the landowner's interests; in a more general sense, anyone to whom a license has been issued.

Lien A charge on property for the payment or discharge of a debt or duty.

Lien Theory In the law of real property security arrangements, the view that the mortgagee acquires only a lien on the mortgaged property rather than title to it.

Life Estate An estate measured in duration by the life of a natural person.

Life Insurance A contract to pay a specified sum, in a lump sum or installments, to a named beneficiary or to the estate of the insured, on the insured's death.

Limited Partner A partner in a limited partnership who (1) makes a contribution of cash or other property to the partnership and obtains an interest in the partnership in return, but (2) takes no active part in managing the partnership. A limited partner has limited liability for partnership debts.

Liquidation The process of converting property and other assets to cash; in a narrower sense, the process of settling the affairs of a partnership after its dissolution.

Listing Agreement A contract of employment between a seller of real property and a real estate broker for the broker's services in selling or offering to sell the property.

Listing of Securities Placing a corporation's securities with a stock exchange so that the securities can be traded publicly.

Litigant A person engaged in litigation as a party.

"Little FTC Laws" State legislation, patterned after the Federal Trade Commission Act, authorizing the attorney general or a local prosecutor to sue for damages or an injunction on behalf of a defrauded buyer.

Living Trust A trust created by a living trustor rather than by the terms of a decedent's will; also known as an inter vivos trust.

Lloyd's of London The oldest existing insurance organization. It does not offer insurance itself. Instead, insurance for a given risk is offered by a syndicate formed for that purpose, each syndicate being comprised of individual members of Lloyd's.

Long Arm Legislation Legislation that gives a state jurisdiction over a nonresident, even though the nonresident is not personally served with process within the state.

Mail Fraud Use of the mail for any scheme to defraud other persons. It is illegal under federal law.

Malice A state of mind of ill will, hatred, or hostility entertained by one person toward another; the state of mind that prompts the intentional doing of a wrongful act without legal justification or excuse.

Malicious Prosecution A tort, the basis of which is one person's having wrongfully commenced a legal proceeding against another.

Marketable Title A title good as a matter of law, its validity not depending on the determination of any question of fact; title that a person of reasonable intelligence and prudence would be willing to take and pay for according to its fair value; with respect to real property, title that is free of encumbrances and of anything else to which a reasonable buyer would object.

Market Share In antitrust law, the share of a given market that an alleged monopolist holds.

Married Women's Acts Statutes or constitutional provisions adopted in most states to benefit married women by abolishing common-law restrictions on the right to contract, to sue and be sued, and to acquire, hold, and convey property in their own right free from interference by their husbands.

Master Policy An insurance policy, commonly used in group insurance, containing certain general terms that are incorporated by reference into a certificate of insurance issued later.

Mechanic's Lien A lien created by statute in favor of persons who have performed work in or furnished materials for the erection or repair of a building.

Mediation and Conciliation A process by which the parties to a dispute are encouraged by a neutral third person to reach agreement on their own initiative.

Merchantable Of good quality and sellable, but not necessarily the best; reasonably suitable for the ordinary uses of the item.

Merger One corporation's acquisition of the stock or assets of another in such manner that the acquired corporation becomes part of the acquiring one.

Merger Doctrine The doctrine that, after a purchaser accepts a deed, the contract of sale is superseded by the deed, and only the rights and remedies contained in the deed are available to the purchaser.

Metes and Bounds Measurements and boundaries, as used in describing real property.

Minor A person under the age of majority; often referred to as an infant in legal writing.

Misdemeanor A criminal offense less serious than a felony and punishable by a fine or up to one year's imprisonment in jail.

Misrepresentation An all-embracing term characterized as one person's false representation of a material fact on which another person justifiably relies to his detriment; in insurance law, a statement of fact that is false, made with intent to deceive, and material to the risk.

Mitigation of Damages The reduction of damages from what they otherwise would be.

Model Business Corporation Act (MBCA) A uniform law governing the incorporation and operation of corporations. It was drafted by the American Bar Association (ABA) and has been adopted in whole or in part by approximately 35 states. See Appendix C.

Monopoly The power to exclude competitors from a market or to control prices within a relevant market.

Mortgage A contract by which specific property is designated or conveyed as security for the performance of an act or, most often, payment of a debt.

Mortgagee The lending party in a mortgage transaction.

Mortgagor The borrowing party in a mortgage transaction.

Motion An application to a court, frequently made orally, to obtain an order or ruling.

Multinational Corporation A corporation characterized by the melding of foreign affiliates or subsidiaries with domestic operations of the parent corporation.

Multiple Listing Agency Contract A device used by groups of real estate brokers to obtain a wider market for the sale of property. It entails the common listing among them of all property they are offering for sale.

Mutual Insurance Company A cooperative enterprise in which members contribute to the creation of a fund by a system of premiums or assessments from which members' losses and liabilities are paid. Any profits are divided among the members in proportion to their interests.

Mutuality of Obligation A phrase expressing the requirement that a contract impose binding obligations on both parties to be deemed valid and enforceable as to either one.

National Labor Relations Board (NLRB) The federal administrative agency created to administer the National Labor Relations Act, certify unions as proper bargaining representatives of employees, and handle unfair labor practice proceedings.

Necessaries In contract law, such things as are essential to the life or health of a person, such as medical services, food, clothing, and education.

Negative Injunction An injunction that prohibits certain conduct.

Negligence The failure of a person who owes a duty to another to do what a reasonably prudent person would have done under the same or similar circumstances.

Negotiable Instrument Commercial paper that meets the requirements of UCC Article 3 for negotiability (transferability). Examples include drafts, checks, certificates of deposit, and notes.

No-Fault Insurance A system of self-insurance under which compensation for losses is made independently of a fault determination. No-fault automobile insurance typically provides that an insured will receive compensation for losses from his own insurer, and tort liability is abolished, at least to the extent of the benefits received.

Nonconforming Use A use of property that violates a zoning ordinance but is nevertheless permitted to continue because it was in existence when the ordinance was enacted.

Nonfreehold Estate At common law, an estate that conveyed possession and use of real property, but not title to it; the modern equivalent is a leasehold.

Nonnegotiable Instrument Commercial paper not meeting the requirements for negotiability (transferability) specified in UCC Article 3.

Nonprofit Corporation A corporation, ordinarily without shareholders, created for purposes that are often charitable and that do not involve making a profit.

No-Strike Clause A provision in some labor contracts by which a union agrees not to strike or cause work stoppages or slowdowns because of labor disputes or grievances; frequently given in exchange for the employer's agreement to arbitrate grievances.

Note A written promise to pay another a certain sum of money at a certain time; a kind of commercial paper.

Notice of Dishonor A notice that a bill, note, or draft has been dishonored by nonacceptance or nonpayment.

Notice to Creditors Under UCC Article 6, the advance notice of a bulk transfer required to be given to the transferor's creditors.

Notice to Quit A notice to a tenant to perform a lease covenant or condition (most commonly that to pay rent due) or else leave the premises. It is preliminary to the eviction of the tenant.

Novation A contract that immediately discharges a previous contractual duty and creates a new contractual duty, including as a party one who neither owed the previous duty nor was entitled to its performance.

Nuisance An invasion of another person's interest in the use or enjoyment of property. A private nuisance interferes with the private use or enjoyment of property, while a public nuisance interferes with a right common to the general public.

Obstruction of Justice A crime that consists of an interference with the orderly administration of justice.

Offer A proposal of terms made with the purpose of securing their acceptance by another, thereby completing a contract.

Offeree One to whom an offer is made.

Offeror One who makes an offer.

Offset A creditor practice by which a debtor's money already in the creditor's possession is applied directly to the debt.

Open-End Credit A continuing consumer credit arrangement, such as a charge account with a retail store. To be distinguished from closed and credit.

Open-End Mortgage A mortgage or deed of trust that permits and secures additional, future advances on the original loan.

Option A continuing offer, usually limited in time and supported by consideration, to do or perform a certain thing on certain terms and conditions, and that the party to whom it is given can accept within the time allowed.

Ordinance A city or county's local law of a general and permanent nature, covering such matters of local rather than statewide concern as safety, parking, and elections.

Ordinary Care Care that a reasonably prudent individual would exercise under the particular circumstances.

Ordinary Life Insurance Life insurance for which premiums at a fixed rate are paid throughout the insured's life; also known as straight life insurance.

Output Contract A contract in which the buyer promises to purchase the seller's entire production in exchange for the seller's promise to sell the entire production to the buyer.

Outside Director A corporate director who is not an officer or employee of the corporation and is otherwise unaffiliated with it.

Overdraft The situation that arises when a payor bank pays a check drawn for more than is in the drawer's account at the time of payment.

Par The standardized value attributed by law to a share of stock.

Parent Corporation A corporation that owns a controlling interest in another corporation.

Parol Evidence Rule The rule excluding evidence of prior or contemporaneous oral agreements that would vary a written contract.

Partition Action A court action by which co-owners of property can sever their joint ownership, either by a division of land into separate parcels or by a sale of the property and a division of the proceeds according to the respective interests of each owner.

Partnership An association of two or more persons to carry on a business for profit as co-owners.

Patent The exclusive right of manufacture, sale, or use secured by the Federal Patent Act to a person who invents or discovers a new, non-obvious, and useful device or process.

Patent and Trademark Office The federal bureau that processes patent applications and where all records, drawings, models, specifications, and other papers pertaining to patents are required by law to be kept and preserved.

Payor Bank Under UCC Article 4, the bank that is ultimately responsible for paying (or refusing to pay) a check or other item.

Perfection Under UCC Article 9, the process by which a secured party maximizes his rights with respect to the collateral.

Performance The doing of the acts required by a contract at the time and place specified and in the manner stipulated.

Periodic Tenancy A tenancy that continues for fixed periods of time, such as from year to year, until terminated by notice at the end of one of the periods.

Perjury The willful giving of a false statement under oath.

Per Se Doctrine In antitrust law, the doctrine that certain business conduct is considered to be an unreasonable restraint of trade, and hence illegal, without proof that it has caused actual loss or injury.

Personal Property All property other than real property and fixtures.

Personal Representative The person who administers the estate of a deceased person.

Picketing Walking or patrolling in the vicinity of a place of business involved in a labor dispute and, by mouth, banner, or placard, undertaking to inform the public about the dispute.

Plaintiff The party who begins a lawsuit by filing a complaint against the other party (the defendant).

Pleadings The formal written documents filed in court. An example is the complaint by which a civil lawsuit is ordinarily initiated.

Pledge A type of secured transaction in which possession of the collateral is temporarily given to the secured party.

Police Power The power inherent in a state to regulate its affairs and ensure the welfare and best interests of its citizens.

Polygraph An electrical instrument that, by measuring and recording certain physiological data concerning a person being tested, can indicate when the person is telling the truth and when he is not; commonly known as a lie detector.

Posting Process Under UCC Article 4, the usual procedure by which a payor bank decides to pay a check and then records the payment.

Power of Attorney A written instrument that serves as tangible evidence that the agent is acting for and on behalf of the principal; also known as a letter of attorney or warrant of attorney.

Power of Sale A provision in a mortgage (or deed of trust) that empowers the mortgagee (or trustee), without resort to any judicial procedures, to sell the property in the event of default and to apply the sale proceeds to satisfy the secured debt.

Precedent A court decision that serves as the basis of and authority for a subsequent decision by the same court or another court in the same jurisdiction.

Preemptive Right The preferential right of shareholders to purchase newly issued stock in proportion to the number of shares each shareholder already owns.

Preferential Transfer In bankruptcy law, a transfer that involves the debtor's property and can be avoided by the trustee because it gives the transferee creditor an advantage over other creditors.

Preferred Dividend A dividend paid on preferred stock and usually payable only out of the corporation's net earnings.

Preferred Stock An equity security that has priority over the common stock as to the payment of dividends. It also has priority as to the repayment of the sum originally paid in to the corporation (usually termed the liquidation preference).

Prejudgment Remedy A statutory means by which, before a creditor suing on a debt is awarded a judgment, the creditor can obtain an interest in property owned by the debtor.

Premises Liability The area of tort law that concerns the duties of a landowner, land occupier, or person exercising direct control over land to persons entering the land or injured by activities occurring on the land.

Premium The agreed price for assuming and carrying an insurable risk; the consideration paid an insurer for undertaking to indemnify the insured against a specified peril.

Prepayment Penalty A penalty exacted from the borrower for the right to repay a debt before it actually becomes due.

Prescriptive Easement An easement acquired by adverse possession.

Presentment Proper tender of a negotiable instrument to a drawee for acceptance or to a maker or drawee for payment.

Pretrial Conference A conference conducted by a judge prior to trial at which the judge and attorneys isolate the issues for trial and sometimes settle the case.

Price Discrimination The practice by which a seller offers goods of like quality to different buyers at different prices. Certain price discrimination is illegal under the federal Robinson–Patman Act.

Price Fixing An unlawful agreement among manufacturers or dealers to maintain specified prices.

Prima Facie On the face of it; a fact presumed to be true unless disproved.

Principal As used in agency, the person for whom another acts and from whom he derives authority to act; as used with respect to a loan transaction, the unpaid balance of the amount borrowed, as opposed to interest or monetary penalties.

Priority The superiority of one person's rights over the rights of other persons. The term is often used with respect to one creditor's right to be paid before other creditors can be.

Privilege A legal right to engage in particular conduct.

Privileged Communication In defamation law, a statement that, although apparently defamatory, does not constitute actionable defamation because of its character or the occasion on which it was made; in a broader sense, any communication that, because of the relationship between the parties, the recipient should not disclose and cannot be required to disclose.

Privity An elusive term, used to indicate a relationship by which one person is sufficiently related to another that certain legal consequences follow. In law, privity means that there is an identity of interest between persons such that the interest of one person is measured by the same legal right as that of the other.

Probate The procedure by which a court finds that a document is the valid will of a decedent.

Process The means of compelling a defendant to appear in a civil or criminal case; a writ, warrant of arrest, or other means of subjecting a person or property to a court's jurisdiction.

Product Liability The liability of a manufacturer, processor, or seller of a product for injury caused by the condition of or a defect in the product.

Product Liability Insurance Insurance designed to protect a producer or manufacturer against loss by reason of injury to persons or property caused by use of its products.

Profit In a broad sense, gains, such as the excess of receipts over expenses. In real property law, a profit (or profit *a prendre*) is a right to take off or from another's land something that is part of the land, such as timber.

Promise A pledge to perform; a declaration giving the person to whom it is made a right to expect or claim the performance of some particular thing; in commercial paper, a person's undertaking to pay an instrument.

Promissory Estoppel The doctrine that an estoppel may arise from the making of a promise, even though without consideration, if it was intended that the promise be relied on and, in fact, it was relied on, and if a refusal to enforce it would result in an injustice.

Promoter A person who initiates the formation of a corporation.

Property Insurance Insurance that protects against the loss of, damage to, or destruction of personal property, fixtures, or improvements to real property.

Pro Rata Clause An insurance policy clause limiting the insurer's liability for a loss covered by the policy to only a fraction of the total loss, the fraction being determined by dividing the face amount of the policy by the total amount of insurance covering the risk in question.

Prospectus A document required to be furnished to a prospective purchaser of securities and giving all relevant financial information needed for making a decision whether to purchase those securities.

Provisional Settlement Under UCC Article 4, a conditional (as opposed to final) payment, charge, or credit of a check or other item.

Proximate Cause As an element of tort liability, that cause which, in a natural and continuous sequence, unbroken by any intervening cause, produced the injury, and without which the injury would not have occurred.

Proxy The authority given by a shareholder to another person to vote his shares of stock at a stockholder meeting; the person so authorized to vote.

Public Corporation A corporation created for public purposes connected with the administration of government.

Publicly Held Corporation A large corporation whose securities are owned by a large number of people and traded over a national or regional stock exchange.

Public Offering The offer or sale of securities to a number of persons in such a way that the exemption offered to private placements by the Securities Act of 1933 is not available.

Public Use Use of property by or for the public at large rather than by or for a private owner.

Punitive Damages See *Exemplary Damages.*

Purchase in Good Faith See *Bona Fide Purchaser.*

Purchase Money Security Interest An interest taken or retained in collateral to secure payment of the purchase price of that collateral. If the interest is a mortgage, it is called a purchase money mortgage.

Qualified Indorsement An indorsement of a negotiable instrument to which "without recourse" or words of similar meaning are added to the signature of the indorser.

Quantum Meruit Literally, "as much as it is worth." It is the basis on which a party can try to recover for a breach of contract by suing for the reasonable value of the work actually done or services actually rendered.

Quasi-Contract A fiction of the law, adopted to achieve justice and enforce legal duties by means of implying that a contract exists even though there is no true contract.

Quiet Title Suit A suit to cause removal of a cloud on title to real property.

Quitclaim Deed A deed that conveys only whatever present right, title, or interest the grantor has in the property.

Quorum The number of a corporation's directors or shares required to be present or represented at a meeting in order to conduct business.

Ratification Treating as authorized or valid an earlier act, often done by somebody else that otherwise could have been disavowed.

Reaffirmation of Debt Debtor agrees to pay all or part of a debt that would otherwise be discharged, or was discharged, in a bankruptcy case.

Real Property Land and things that are permanent, fixed, and immovable, such as vegetation, buildings, and other permanent structures.

Reasonable Care Care required by the circumstances of the case; due care under the circumstances.

Receiver A person appointed by a court to take temporary custody of the property of another.

Reciprocal Insurance A system by which individuals or business entities, none of which is an insurance company, agree to indemnify each other against certain kinds of risks.

Recordation The filing of a conveyance of encumbrance in a county office to give constructive notice of a title or other interest affecting real property.

Redemption A corporation's purchase of its own securities; under UCC Article 9, the debtor's reacquisition of property that has been repossessed.

Refinancing The process of obtaining a new loan in place of an old one, the proceeds from the new loan being used in part to pay off the old loan.

Reformation An equitable remedy by which parties rectify or reform a written instrument when they failed, through accident, mistake, or fraud, to express their real agreement or intention in the instrument.

Regulation Z The administrative regulations issued by the Board of Governors of the Federal Reserve System to clarify and interpret the federal Truth in Lending Act.

Regulatory Agencies Administrative agencies that have authority to regulate economic activities of individuals and business by making rules, deciding disputes, and imposing fines.

Rehabilitation Plan A plan for restoring a debtor's failing business or personal finances to a sound financial position, prepared under Chapter 11 or 13 of the Federal Bankruptcy Code.

Reinsurance Insurance obtained by an insurer to protect itself against large potential losses under policies issued by it. Reinsurance has the effect of apportioning risks of loss among several insurers.

Rejection Words or acts of an offeree indicating that he declines the offer.

Release A document by which, for a consideration, a person gives up to another person any claim or further claim he might have against that person.

Relevant Market A term used in antitrust law to describe both the geographic market and the product market of a business that is alleged to hold a monopoly.

Remainder A property interest that will give the holder the right to possession of the property only after the expiration of a prior estate.

Rent The consideration paid by a lessee to a lessor for the use of property under a lease.

Reorganization A term often loosely used to cover various rearrangements of corporate financial structures. Included within its scope are mergers, consolidations, sales or exchanges of stock, insolvency proceedings, and even amendments to the articles of incorporation.

Replevin A legal action by which the owner of specific property, or one having rights in it, seeks to recover that property from whoever has possession of it.

Repossession The act by which a secured party takes possession of the collateral after the debtor's default.

Representation A statement of fact that is intended to be relied on by the person to whom the statement is made; in insurance law, a statement by an insured to the insurer, made before the completion of an insurance contract, giving information about a fact that is relevant to the insurance and that is intended to enable the insurer to determine whether it will accept the risk and at what premium.

Repudiation of Contract Renunciation of liability under a contract; either a refusal to recognize the existence of a contract or the doing of an act that is inconsistent with its existence.

Requirements Contract A contract in which the seller agrees to supply all of a certain material required for the operation of the buyer's business over a specified time, in exchange for the buyer's promise to purchase all of that material from the seller.

Rescission Termination of a contract by a court, by mutual consent of the parties, or pursuant to a condition contained in the contract.

Res Ipsa Loquitur Literally, the thing speaks for itself. The term refers to a doctrine sometimes used in negligence cases. It permits an inference that the defendant was negligent without specific proof of any negligent conduct.

Res Judicata The doctrine that a final court judgment rendered on the merits of a case is conclusive of all causes of action and all issues litigated in that case as to the parties.

Respondeat Superior The doctrine under which the employer is liable to injured third persons for the acts of his employees committed during the course and scope of their employment.

Restatements of the Law A series of publications, published by the American Law Institute, that sets forth scholarly comments as to rules of law. While the Restatements do not constitute actual law, they are given weight in many judicial decisions.

Restitution Returning to a person something of which he was wrongfully deprived.

Restraint of Trade Business combinations and practices interfering unreasonably with the normal production and supply of commodities by the suppression of competition.

Restrictive Covenant A private restriction set forth in a deed, limiting the property owner's use of the property.

Restrictive Indorsement An indorsement that in some way limits the effect of the indorsement.

Retail Installment Contract A contract for the credit sale of goods or services to a consumer and requiring payment of the purchase price in periodic installment.

Retaliatory Eviction The eviction of a tenant by a landlord because the tenant complained to a governmental agency about the condition of rented property, its habitability, or other defects. It is unlawful in most states.

Retraction A statement of such nature and published in such manner as to manifest an honest intention to repair the harm done to an injured reputation by a defamatory statement.

Reverse Discrimination A policy or practice that, by favoring minorities over majority groups, operates to discriminate against members of the majority.

Reversion The interest in property remaining after the grant of a particular estate or leasehold less than a fee simple.

Revocation The act of canceling a document by, in effect, withdrawing it; in contract law, an offeror's withdrawal of an offer before it has been accepted.

Rider An attachment to an insurance policy, made a part of the entire policy to modify or change it.

Right of Survivorship The right to automatically acquire the interest of a deceased joint owner. It is the distinguishing feature of a joint tenancy.

Right-of-Way A right to cross or pass over a parcel of land. It can be a right to use a road or driveway, to construct power lines through or over land, or to place pipes underground.

Riparian Rights The right of a landowner to water bordering on his land, such as a stream or lake.

Rule Against Perpetuities A restriction on future gifts; no interest in property is good unless it must vest, if at all, not later than 21 years, plus period of gestation, after some life or lives in being at the time of creation of the interest.

Rule 10b-5 A regulation adopted by the SEC implementing the antifraud provisions of § 10(b) of the Securities Act of 1934 and proscribing the use of fraud, materially untrue statements, or other deceitful business practices in connection with the purchase and sale of securities in interstate commerce.

Sale Transfer of property for a consideration.

Scienter Knowledge.

Secondary Meaning A term used to describe a trade dress, the total image of which has become associated in the public mind with the manufacturer of the goods rather than with the goods themselves. A common example is the distinctively shaped Coca Cola bottle.

Second Mortgage A junior mortgage covering property that is also encumbered by a first mortgage.

Secured Party One holding a security interest in property.

Secured Transaction Any transaction in which an interest in personal property or fixtures is given to secure payment of a debt or performance of some other obligation.

Securities and Exchange Commission (SEC) The federal regulatory agency that administers the federal securities acts.

Security A broad term signifying corporate financing devices, including stocks and bonds.

Security Deposit A sum of money (or other property) given by a lessee before the commencement of a lease to protect the lessor if the lessee fails to perform any of his obligations under the lease.

Security Interest An interest in property intended to secure or guarantee payment of a debt or performance of some other obligation.

Self-Insurance The absence of conventional insurance covering any or, more often, part of a given risk. For example, the owner of a car is self-insured to the extent of any "deductible" stated in his collision coverage.

Servient Tenement An estate burdened by an easement.

Settlement Under UCC Article 4, a general term that includes within its scope payment, giving a credit, or imposing a charge with respect to a check or other item. Such a settlement can be either provisional or final. With respect to a lawsuit, the term refers to an out-of-court agreement between the parties by which all or some of the disputed issues are resolved.

Sexual Harassment   Unwelcome sexual overtures, whether verbal or physical, that the Equal Employment Opportunity Commission has held constitutes a violation of Title VII of the Civil Rights Act of 1964 prohibiting employment discrimination.

Short-Form Merger   A merger without notice to or consent of the minority shareholders, permitted by statute if approved by a high percentage of the shares.

Short Sale   Sale of a security that the seller does not own. The seller delivers to the buyer a security borrowed from another party, gambling that the price of the security will go down and that it will be possible to "cover," that is, to buy the security at a lower price and restore it to the lender.

Short Swing   A term used to describe securities transactions in which a purchase and sale by the same person occurs within a six-month period. Such transactions are subject to regulation under § 16 of the Securities Exchange Act of 1934.

Silent Partner   A member of a partnership who is not publicly associated with it and whose connection with partnership business is ordinarily concealed.

Sinking Fund   A special fund accumulated by a debtor, usually a corporation, and used as security for the payment of a debt at maturity.

Slander   Defamatory material communicated orally or by acts or gestures.

Slander of Title   False and malicious statements, oral or written, that disparage a person's title to real or personal property, causing him damage.

Small Claims Court   A court, sometimes existing independently and at other times constituting a separate division of a trial court, that is available for litigation of small claims not exceeding a specified amount. Small claims court proceedings are often informal, and the parties cannot be represented by attorneys.

Special Agent   An agent authorized to do one or more specific acts under particular instructions.

Special Indorsement   An indorsement that specifies the person to whom or to whose order it makes the instrument payable.

Special Power   Power or authority granted to an agent under a power of attorney and allowing the agent to perform only specified tasks. In contrast, a general power allows the agent to act in any manner consistent with the principal's business or purposes.

Specific Performance   The equitable remedy of compelling performance of a contract according to its precise terms, as distinguished from the legal remedy of awarding damages for breach of contract.

Squeeze Out   Elimination of certain shareholders in a corporation or other business enterprise by one or more of the other shareholders·or owners.

Standing to Sue   The capacity to maintain a lawsuit as a plaintiff. A person has standing to sue when he has an actual interest in the lawsuit.

Stare Decisis   The doctrine that judicial decisions should stand as precedents or guidance for similar cases arising in the future.

Statute of Frauds   A statute requiring certain classes of contracts to be in writing.

Statute of Limitations   A statute limiting the period, after an event, during which a lawsuit relating to that event can be commenced.

Statutory Copyright   Copyright protection under the Federal Copyright Act. It gives the copyright owner the exclusive right to reproduce, perform, or display the copyrighted work.

Statutory Law   Law based on legislative enactments of a state or the federal government.

Statutory Lien   A lien arising under a statute.

Stay of Agency Action   A court order placing an administrative order or decision in abeyance until the court has reviewed that order or decision.

Stock Bonus   Shares of stock given by an issuing corporation to one of its executives or officers as a reward, often measured in terms of corporate earnings.

Stock Dividend   A corporation's issuance of stock to existing shareholders without consideration and usually as a symbolic substitute for a cash dividend.

Stock Split   A division of the par or stated value of a corporation's shares. It adds nothing to the capital fund of a corporation, merely increasing (or decreasing in the case of a reverse stock split) the total number of shares outstanding, and reducing (or increasing) the unit value of each share.

Stop-Payment Order   An order directed to a payor bank by its customer and instructing the bank not to pay a specified check drawn on the bank.

Street Certificate   A stock certificate that is endorsed in blank and does not name the owner or transferee when sold.

Strict Liability   Liability without fault, based on the public policy that some activities are so dangerous that a person who performs them should be liable for injuries, even in the absence of negligence.

Strike   A cessation of work by employees to obtain more favorable employment terms from their employer.

Subagent   A person to whom an agent delegates authority to act on behalf of the principal; in effect, an agent's agent.

Subchapter S Corporation   An ordinary corporation that has elected to be treated as a sole proprietorship or partnership for income tax purposes under the Internal Revenue Code.

Sublease   A landlord–tenant relationship created by a lessee (the sublessor) who leases the property to another (the sublessee) for a period not longer than that of the original lease.

Subordinate   Inferior or of lower priority. For example, a debt security is referred to as being subordinate or subordinated if its principal, interest, or both will not be repaid until some other class of indebtedness has been repaid.

Subpoena   A court order compelling the attendance of a person in court at a stated time and place, and the violation of which may constitute grounds for arrest or contempt of court.

Subscription Agreement   An agreement by a potential future shareholder to contribute money or other assets for stock issued, or to be issued, by a corporation.

Subsidiary   A corporation controlled by another corporation.

Substantial Performance   Performance of a contract which, while not a full performance, is performance in good faith and in compliance with the contract except perhaps for minor and relatively unimportant deviations.

Supremacy Clause   The provision of the United States Constitution (Art. VI, cl.2) that the Constitution, laws, and treaties of the United States shall be the supreme law of the land, anything in the Constitution or laws of any state to the contrary notwithstanding.

Surplus   In corporate accounting terms, what is left over after liabilities and capital have been subtracted from assets. It does not necessarily mean that a corporation has cash to pay a dividend, although no dividend can be paid if there is no surplus.

Survivorship   In a broad sense, the fact of outliving one or more other persons; in the context of property law, the right of a surviving joint tenant under which the deceased tenant's interest in the property passes automatically to the survivor.

Tax Return   The form showing required information about a taxpayer's tax liability and on which the tax due is computed. It is submitted to the Internal Revenue Service or other taxing authority.

Tenancy   As commonly used, a tenant's right to the possession of real property; in a broader sense, any right to possession of real property.

Tenancy of Sufferance   The tenancy of one who continues in possession of premises after his original, lawful right to possession has terminated.

Tenancy at Will   A tenancy that continues for as long as desired by both parties. Either party can terminate it at any time.

Tenancy by the Entireties   A modification of a joint tenancy that can exist between husband and wife. It has the quality of survivorship, but neither spouse can convey his or her interest to break the joint tenancy.

Tenancy for Years   A tenancy in which the beginning and end are fixed in advance. The term is misleading because, although the tenancy can be for a number of years, it can also be for a number of days, weeks, or months.

Tenancy in Common   Ownership of property by any two or more persons in undivided interests (not necessarily equal) without the right of survivorship.

Tenant   The lessee under a lease of real property.

Term Insurance   Life insurance for a specified period of time, and the premium for which is paid during the specified term only and increases with each renewal period.

Testamentary Capacity The legal ability to make a valid will, the relevant factors being the testator's age and mental competence.

Testamentary Trust A trust created by a decedent's will rather than by a living person.

Test Audit An audit in which a business' financial condition is merely sampled on a selective basis rather than being fully examined.

Thin Incorporation A term used to describe a corporation whose capitalization is so inadequate in relation to its obligations and risks as to be vulnerable to a challenge by its creditors or the Internal Revenue Service.

Third-Party Beneficiary The beneficiary of a contract made between two other persons.

Time of the Essence A term used to describe a contract provision that requires one party's performance at or within the time specified in the contract as a prerequisite to the other party's performance.

Title Insurance An agreement under which, for a consideration, the insurer agrees to indemnify the insured in a specified amount against loss through a defective title to real estate in which the insured has an interest.

Title VII The popular name for that part of the Civil Rights Act of 1964 that forbids discrimination on the basis of race, color, religion, sex, or national origin.

Title Theory In the law of real property security arrangements, the view that the mortgagee acquires title to the mortgaged property rather than simply a lien on it.

Tort A civil wrong other than a breach of contract.

Tortfeasor A person guilty of a tort.

Trade Acceptance A draft drawn by a seller on the purchaser of the goods sold and accepted by such purchaser.

Trade Dress The format in which goods are presented to the public; an element of package design, consisting of the peculiar visual appearance produced by a particular arrangement or combination of colors, symbols, words, and designs impressed on a label, package, or product, distinct from any technical copyright or trademark.

Trade Dress Simulation An unfair trade practice by which one business intentionally packages its goods in a manner deceptively similar to that used by a competitor.

Trade Fixtures Personal property affixed to land and used for carrying on a trade or business.

Trade Libel A business tort arising when a person communicates false disparaging statements as to the quality of another's property, goods, or services, resulting in the other person's actual loss of business; also known as disparagement.

Trademark A sign, device, or mark by which articles produced by a particular person or organization are distinguished from those produced by others.

Trade Name A name, word, or phrase employed by one engaged in business, as a means of identifying his products, business, or services, and of establishing goodwill.

Trade Secret Information respecting the business or process of production of a dealer or producer and that would be of special value to competitors.

Trade Usage A uniform course of conduct followed in a particular trade, occupation, or business.

Treble Damages Three times the actual damages.

Trust As usually used, an arrangement by which one party holds property for the benefit of one or more others; in antitrust law, a combination of producers or sellers of a product whose intent is to control prices and suppress competition.

Trustee In trust law, the party having legal title to, but not the beneficial ownership of, the trust property; under a deed of trust, the party holding legal title to the property to secure payment of the debt.

Trustor The person who creates a trust; in a real property security transaction, the borrower under a deed of trust.

Trust Receipt A security device by which a lender retains title to inventory items until they are sold.

Tying Agreement An agreement under which a party agrees to sell a product (the tying product) only on condition that the buyer also purchases a different product (the tied product).

Ultra Vires A term used to describe a corporate act that is beyond the scope of the corporation's powers; also used to describe a similar unauthorized act by an administrative agency.

Unauthorized Practice of Law The giving of legal advice or performance of legal services by a person, such as an accountant, who is not a licensed attorney.

Unconscionable Contract A contract, usually made when one of the parties was in a position of disadvantage, that is oppressive, and especially one unreasonably restricting a party's liberty to earn a living or imposing an extortionate rate of interest.

Underwriter One who purchases securities from an issuer with a view to their resale or distribution. In general, the term refers to those persons who make a regular business of distributing securities.

Undisclosed Agency A situation in which a person dealing with another neither knows nor has reason to know that he is dealing with an agent or that an agency relationship exists.

Undivided Interest The interest of each co-owner in property owned in common.

Undue Influence A type of fraud by which a person's free will is destroyed and the will of another person is substituted in its place.

Unfair Competition Wrongful acts that injure or destroy the business of a competitor.

Unfair Labor Practice Any of a number of specific employer or employee acts that are so labeled in federal labor legislation and the commission of which can lead to sanctions.

Unfair Trade Practice A commercial policy or practice that is illegal because it is used to gain an unfair advantage over business competitors.

Uniform Commercial Code (UCC) A uniform code created through the joint efforts of the National Conference of Commissioners on Uniform State Laws and the American Law Institute. The UCC deals with most aspects of modern business transactions and concerns such matters as sale of goods, commercial paper, bank deposits and collections, documents of title, and secured transactions. The UCC has been adopted by all states except Louisiana, which has adopted only portions of the UCC. See Appendix B.

Uniform Laws A series of proposed types of legislation, created by the National Conference of Commissioners on Uniform State Laws, and proposed for adoption by the state legislatures. Many uniform laws have been widely adopted, most notably the Uniform Commercial Code.

Unilateral Contract A contract in which there is a promise on one side only, the consideration being an act or something other than another promise.

Unilateral Mistake A mistake on the part of only one of the parties to a transaction.

Union An association of workers existing for the purpose of securing, through united action and collective bargaining, more favorable wages, hours of labor, and working conditions for its members.

United States Constitution The fundamental document of the American system of government, constituting the supreme law of the land, as adopted by the people of the United States through their representatives in the Convention of 1787 and since amended. See Appendix A.

United States Supreme Court The highest court in the federal court system, established by the United States Constitution. It occupies a unique position within the dual system of federal and state government in view of its power to review and set aside certain decisions of the highest state courts.

Unlawful Detainer A summary eviction procedure, provided for by statute, by which a landlord is supposed to be able to recover possession of leased property quickly and at low cost.

Unliquidated Debt A debt, the amount of which is disputed.

Unsecured Creditor A creditor who has only the debtor's promise to pay, as distinguished from a secured creditor.

Variance The relief granted to an affected property owner from a general zoning ordinance in cases of undue hardship unique or peculiar to particular real property.

Vendor's Lien The implied lien of a real estate seller who has conveyed legal title, as security for the unpaid purchase money; the common-law lien of a seller of goods for the unpaid portion of the purchase price of the goods, where he has parted with title but not possession.

Vested Right A right, usually relating to property, that presently exists, as distinguished from a contingent right, which may or may not exist in the future.

Vicarious Liability Liability imposed by law on one person because of the act or omission of another, such as his employee.

Voidable Contract   A contract that, although defective so that it *can* be avoided by one of the parties, is valid and binding until it *is* avoided.

Void Contract   A contract having no legal effect whatsoever.

Voluntary Bankruptcy   The term used to describe a bankruptcy proceeding in which the debtor, rather than one or more of his creditors, filed the bankruptcy petition.

Voluntary Conveyance   A conveyance for which no valuable consideration was received.

Voting Trust   An agreement among a group of shareholders by which shares are transferred to a trustee to vote in a certain specified manner under a legally enforceable voting trust agreement.

Wagering Contract   An insurance contract that is void because of the insured's lack of an insurable interest in the subject matter of the insurance.

Waiver   The abandonment or relinquishment of a right or privilege.

Warehouser   A person who stores bailed goods for compensation; traditionally referred to as a warehouseman.

Warehouse Receipt   A receipt issued by a person engaged in the business of storing goods for hire.

Warrant   A negotiable document issued by a corporation and giving the owner an option to purchase the corporation's stock at a specified price.

Warranty   A guaranty, either express or implied, that information is correct, that standards will apply, or that particular activities will take place. In insurance law, a description or undertaking on the part of the insured, appearing in the insurance policy or in another instrument, relating to the risk insured against.

Warranty Deed   A deed containing express warranties of title and quiet possession.

Warranty of Fitness   An implied warranty by the seller of goods sold for a particular use that the goods are fit for that purpose, provided the buyer is relying on the skill, judgment, or experience of the seller.

Warranty of Habitability   An express or implied warranty, given by a landlord at the commencement of a lease, that there are no defects in the rented facilities vital to the use of the premises for residential purposes.

Waste   Damage to property by willful neglect, abuse, or misuse.

Watered Stock   Stock issued in exchange for property or services at an over valuation or at a discount. The term originated in reference to the practice in agricultural communities of causing cattle to ingest large quantities of water so that their weight—and hence their value—when sold would be greater.

White-Collar Crime   An illegal act, or a series of illegal acts, committed by nonphysical means to (1) obtain money or property, (2) avoid paying or losing money or property, or (3) obtain a business or personal advantage.

Will   The document by which a person indicates the desired disposition of his property after his death.

Winding Up   The process of settling partnership affairs after dissolution.

Workers' Compensation   State legislation providing for compensation for loss resulting from the injury, disability, or death of workers by industrial accident, casualty, or disease. These laws have the common feature of providing compensation in accordance with a fixed schedule rather than on the basis of tort liability.

Working Capital   The difference between a corporation's current assets and its current liabilities. It is frequently used as a measure of a company's liquidity and capacity to meet its obligations as they fall due.

Wraparound Mortgage   A second mortgage securing a promissory note, the face amount of which is the sum of the unpaid principal secured by the first mortgage plus the amount advanced by the second mortgage.

Writ   A court's direction authorizing a person's arrest or the seizure of property, or compelling a person to take certain actions.

Zoning   The division of a municipality into districts (zones) according to specific uses or permissible activities. Most zoning ordinances separate commercial or industrial districts from residential districts and prohibit the establishment of places of business or industry in those districts designated as residential.

Table of Statutes

Table of Cases

Index